The Oxford Handbook of Obsessive-Compulsive and Related Disorders

OXFORD LIBRARY OF PSYCHOLOGY
AREA EDITORS:

Clinical Psychology
David H. Barlow

Cognitive Neuroscience
Kevin N. Ochsner and Stephen M. Kosslyn

Cognitive Psychology
Daniel Reisberg

Counseling Psychology
Elizabeth M. Altmaier and Jo-Ida C. Hansen

Developmental Psychology
Philip David Zelazo

Health Psychology
Howard S. Friedman

History of Psychology
David B. Baker

Methods and Measurement
Todd D. Little

Neuropsychology
Kenneth M. Adams

Organizational Psychology
Steve W.J. Kozlowski

Personality and Social Psychology
Kay Deaux and Mark Snyder

OXFORD LIBRARY OF PSYCHOLOGY

The Oxford Handbook of Obsessive-Compulsive and Related Disorders

SECOND EDITION

Edited by
David F. Tolin

OXFORD
UNIVERSITY PRESS

Oxford University Press is a department of the University of Oxford. It furthers the University's objective of excellence in research, scholarship, and education by publishing worldwide. Oxford is a registered trade mark of Oxford University Press in the UK and certain other countries.

Published in the United States of America by Oxford University Press
198 Madison Avenue, New York, NY 10016, United States of America.

© Oxford University Press 2023

All rights reserved. No part of this publication may be reproduced, stored in a retrieval system, or transmitted, in any form or by any means, without the prior permission in writing of Oxford University Press, or as expressly permitted by law, by license, or under terms agreed with the appropriate reproduction rights organization. Inquiries concerning reproduction outside the scope of the above should be sent to the Rights Department, Oxford University Press, at the address above.

You must not circulate this work in any other form
and you must impose this same condition on any acquirer.

Library of Congress Control Number: 2023007360

ISBN 978–0–19–006875–2

DOI: 10.1093/oxfordhb/9780190068752.001.0001

Printed by Integrated Books International, United States of America

CONTENTS

List of Contributors *ix*

1. Introduction 1
   David F. Tolin

Part I · Phenomenology and Epidemiology

2. Phenomenology and Epidemiology of Obsessive-Compulsive Disorder 11
   John E. Calamari and Gregory M. Dams
3. Phenomenology and Epidemiology of Body Dysmorphic Disorder 40
   Megan M. Kelly and Katharine A. Phillips
4. Phenomenology and Epidemiology of Hoarding Disorder 73
   Randy O. Frost and Mercedes Woolley
5. Phenomenology and Epidemiology of Trichotillomania and Skin-Picking Disorder 99
   Emily J. Ricketts, Jordan T. Stiede, Douglas W. Woods, Diana Antinoro, and Martin E. Franklin

Part II · Approaches to Understanding Obsessive-Compulsive and Related Disorders

6. Genetic Understanding of Obsessive-Compulsive Disorder and Related Disorders 127
   Jack Samuels
7. Neuroanatomy of Obsessive-Compulsive and Related Disorders 143
   Anders Lillevik Thorsen and Odile A. van den Heuvel
8. Information Processing in Obsessive-Compulsive and Related Disorders 174
   Gillian M. Alcolado, Martha Giraldo-O'Meara, Sandra C. Krause, Mark W. Leonhart, and Adam S. Radomsky

9. Personality Features of Obsessive-Compulsive and Related Disorders   214
    Anthony Pinto and Ezra Cowan
10. Behavioral Conceptualizations of Obsessive-Compulsive and Related Disorders   248
    Stephanie E. Cassin, Rotem Regev, Sandra Fournier, and Neil A. Rector
11. Cognitive Approaches to Understanding Obsessive-Compulsive and Related Disorders   279
    Steven Taylor, Jonathan S. Abramowitz, Dean McKay, and Charlene Minaya

Part III • Assessment of Obsessive-Compulsive and Related Disorders
12. Assessing OCD Symptoms and Severity   307
    Maria Bleier and Sheila R. Woody
13. Assessing Body Dysmorphic Disorder   334
    Oliver Sündermann and David Veale
14. Assessing Hoarding Disorder   355
    Jordana Muroff
15. Assessing Trichotillomania and Skin-Picking Disorder   392
    Sydney Biscarri Clark, Ashley Lahoud, and Christopher A. Flessner
16. Assessing Comorbidity, Insight, Family, and Functioning   420
    Olivia A. Merritt and Christine Purdon

Part IV • Treatment of Obsessive-Compulsive and Related Disorders
17. Pharmacological Treatments for Obsessive-Compulsive Disorder   451
    Brian P. Brennan, Darin D. Dougherty, Scott L. Rauch, and Michael A. Jenike
18. Biological Approaches to Obsessive-Compulsive Disorder: Psychiatric Neurosurgery and Neuromodulation   473
    Adriel Barrios-Anderson, Nicole C. R. McLaughlin, and Benjamin D. Greenberg
19. Exposure-Based Treatment for Obsessive-Compulsive Disorder   498
    Jonathan S. Abramowitz, Steven Taylor, and Dean McKay
20. Cognitive Treatment for Obsessive-Compulsive Disorder   527
    Morag A. Yule, Maureen L. Whittal, and Melisa Robichaud
21. Combining Pharmacotherapy and Psychological Treatments for Obsessive-Compulsive Disorder   557
    David F. Tolin and Kimberly S. Sain
22. Treatment of Body Dysmorphic Disorder   584
    Berta J. Summers, Zoë E. Laky, Jennifer L. Greenberg, Anne Chosak, Angela Fang, and Sabine Wilhelm
23. Treatment of Hoarding Disorder   615
    Jessica R. Grisham, Melissa M. Norberg, and Keong Yap

24. Treatment of Trichotillomania and Skin-Picking Disorder   647
    Martin E. Franklin, Diana Antinoro, Emily J. Ricketts, and Douglas W. Woods

Part V • Obsessive-Compulsive and Related Disorders in Special Populations

25. Obsessive-Compulsive and Related Disorders in Older Adults   667
    John E. Calamari, Cheryl N. Carmin, Amanda Messerlie, and Sibel Sarac
26. Obsessive-Compulsive and Related Disorders in Children and Adolescents   690
    Scott M. Lee, Gary Liu, Allison Meinert, Jamie Manis, Andrew G. Guzick, Sophie C. Schneider, Wayne K. Goodman, and Eric A. Storch
27. Obsessive-Compulsive Disorder and Cultural Issues   717
    Yoon Hee Yang, Richard Moulding, Maja Nedeljkovic, Elham Foroughi, Guy Doron, and Michael Kyrios

    Index   749

CONTRIBUTORS

Jonathan S. Abramowitz, Ph.D.,
University of North Carolina at Chapel Hill

Gillian M. Alcolado, Ph.D.,
University of Manitoba

Diana Antinoro, Psy.D.,
University of Pennsylvania School of Medicine

Adriel Barrios-Anderson,
Brown University

Maria Bleier, BSc, BA,
University of British Columbia

Brian P. Brennan, MD,
McLean Hospital and Harvard Medical School

John E. Calamari, Ph.D.,
Rosalind Franklin University of Medicine and Science

Cheryl N. Carmin, Ph.D.,
The Ohio State University Wexner Medical Center

Stephanie E. Cassin, Ph.D.,
Ryerson University

Anne Chosak, Ph.D.,
Massachusetts General Hospital and Harvard Medical School

Sydney Biscarri Clark, MA,
Kent State University

Ezra Cowan, Psy.D.,
Center for Cognitive Behavioral Psychotherapy

Gregory M. Dams, Ph.D.,
Rosalind Franklin University of Medicine and Science

Guy Doron, Ph.D.,
Interdisciplinary Centre (IDC) Herzilya

Darin D. Dougherty, MD,
McLean Hospital, Massachusetts General Hospital, and Harvard Medical School

Angela Fang, Ph.D.,
Massachusetts General Hospital, Harvard Medical School, and University of Washington

Christopher A. Flessner, Ph.D.,
Kent State University

Elham Foroughi, Ph.D.,
The Anxiety & OCD Clinic Melbourne

Sandra Fournier, BA,
Sunnybrook Health Sciences Centre

Martin E. Franklin, Ph.D.,
Rogers Behavioral Health

Randy O. Frost, Ph.D.,
Smith College

Martha Giraldo-O'Meara, Ph.D.,
Concordia University

Wayne K. Goodman, MD,
Baylor College of Medicine

Benjamin D. Greenberg, MD,
Brown University

Jennifer L. Greenberg, Psy.D.,
Massachusetts General Hospital and Harvard Medical School

Jessica R. Grisham, Ph.D.,
The University of New South Wales

Andrew G. Guzick, Ph.D.,
  Baylor College of Medicine
Michael A. Jenike, MD,
  McLean Hospital, Massachusetts General Hospital, and Harvard Medical School
Megan M. Kelly, Ph.D.,
  University of Massachusetts Medical School and VA Bedford Healthcare System
Sandra C. Krause, MA,
  Concordia University
Michael Kyrios, Ph.D.,
  Flinders University
Ashley Lahoud, MA,
  Kent State University
Zoë E. Laky, BA,
  Massachusetts General Hospital and Harvard Medical School
Scott M. Lee, MD,
  Baylor College of Medicine
Mark W. Leonhart, MA,
  Concordia University
Gary Liu, MD,
  Baylor College of Medicine
Jamie Manis, Ph.D.,
  Baylor College of Medicine
Dean McKay, Ph.D.,
  Fordham University
Nicole C. R. McLaughlin,
  Brown University
Allison Meinert, Ph.D.,
  Baylor College of Medicine
Olivia A. Merritt, MA,
  University of Waterloo
Amanda Messerlie, MS,
  Rosalind Franklin University of Medicine and Science
Charlene Minaya, MA,
  Fordham University
Richard Moulding, Ph.D.,
  The Cairnmillar Institute

Jordana Muroff, Ph.D.,
  Boston University School of Social Work
Maja Nedeljkovic, Ph.D.,
  Swinburne University of Technology
Melissa M. Norberg, Ph.D.,
  Macquarie University
Katharine A. Phillips, MD,
  Weill Cornell Medicine
Anthony Pinto, Ph.D.,
  Zucker Hillside Hospital
Christine Purdon, Ph.D.,
  University of Waterloo
Adam S. Radomsky, Ph.D.,
  Concordia University
Scott L. Rauch, MD,
  McLean Hospital and Harvard Medical School
Neil A. Rector, Ph.D.,
  University of Toronto
Rotem Regev, MA,
  Sunnybrook Health Sciences Centre
Emily J. Ricketts, Ph.D.,
  UCLA Semel Institute for Neuroscience and Human Behavior
Melisa Robichaud, Ph.D.,
  University of British Columbia and Vancouver CBT Centre
Kimberly S. Sain, Ph.D.,
  The Institute of Living
Jack Samuels, Ph.D.,
  The Johns Hopkins University School of Medicine
Sibel Sarac, MS,
  Rosalind Franklin University of Medicine and Science
Sophie C. Schneider, Ph.D.,
  Baylor College of Medicine
Jordan T. Stiede, Ph.D.,
  Marquette University
Eric A. Storch, Ph.D.,
  Baylor College of Medicine

Berta J. Summers, Ph.D.,
  University of North Carolina Wilmington, Massachusetts General Hospital, and Harvard Medical School
Oliver Sündermann, Ph.D.,
  National University of Singapore
Steven Taylor, Ph.D.,
  University of British Columbia
Anders Lillevik Thorsen, Ph.D.,
  Haukeland University Hospital, University of Bergen, and Vrije Universiteit Amsterdam
David F. Tolin, Ph.D.,
  The Institute of Living and Yale University School of Medicine
Odile A. van den Heuvel, MD, Ph.D.,
  Haukeland University Hospital and Vrije Universiteit Amsterdam
David Veale, MD,
  King's College London

Maureen L. Whittal, Ph.D.,
  University of British Columbia and Vancouver CBT Centre
Sabine Wilhelm, Ph.D.,
  Massachusetts General Hospital and Harvard Medical School
Douglas W. Woods, Ph.D.,
  Marquette University and University of Wisconsin-Milwaukee
Sheila R. Woody, Ph.D.,
  University of British Columbia
Mercedes Woolley, BA,
  Smith College
Yoon Hee Yang, Ph.D.,
  Deakin University
Keong Yap, D.Psych.,
  The University of New South Wales and Australia Catholic University
Morag A. Yule, Ph.D.,
  Ontario Sex Therapy

Introduction

David F. Tolin

Abstract

The second edition of *The Oxford Handbook of Obsessive-Compulsive and Related Disorders* focuses on the obsessive-compulsive and related disorders (OCRDs), newly described in the fifth edition of the *Diagnostic and Statistical Manual of Mental Disorders* (*DSM*). The OCRDs include obsessive-compulsive disorder (OCD), body dysmorphic disorder, hoarding disorder, trichotillomania (hair-pulling disorder), and excoriation (skin-picking) disorder. In the handbook, leading experts review current evidence on the phenomenology, epidemiology, assessment, and treatment of the OCRDs, as well as the presentation of the conditions in special populations. The introductory chapter provides a brief history of OCD, an account of its role in the *DSM*, and an overview of the chapters to follow.

Key Words: obsessive-compulsive disorder, body dysmorphic disorder, hoarding disorder, trichotillomania, skin-picking disorder, epidemiology, assessment, treatment

Conceptual Models of Obsessive-Compulsive Disorder throughout History

Obsessive-compulsive disorder (OCD) has a long history in both the psychiatric and spiritual literature. Saint Ignatius of Loyola (1491–1556) wrote:

> After I have trodden a cross formed by two straws, or after I have thought, said, or done some other thing, there comes to me from "without" a thought that I have sinned, and on the other hand it seems to me that I have not sinned; nevertheless I feel some uneasiness on the subject, inasmuch as I doubt and do not doubt. That is a real scruple and temptation which the enemy sets. (Cited in van Megen et al., 2010)

This writing provides an early account of what we would now call scrupulosity. Later, Bishop John Moore (1646–1714) described a "religious melancholy," in which individuals experienced a fear that what they do is so defective and unfit to be presented unto God, that he will not accept it. Naughty, and sometimes blasphemous, thoughts start in their minds, while they are exercised in the worship of God, despite all their endeavors to stifle and suppress them; the more they struggle with them, the more they increase. (Cited in Mora, 1969)

In addition to describing scrupulous obsessions, Moore's writing also alludes to the presence of compulsions, as well as the well-documented paradoxical effects of efforts to suppress unwanted thoughts (Wegner, 1994).

The psychiatrist Esquirol (1772–1840) is credited with the first description of OCD in the psychiatric literature: he characterized the condition as a form of monomania, or partial insanity. By this, Equirol conveyed that OCD sufferers often have good insight into the irrational nature of their obsessions. In his case study of a 34-year-old female patient, he wrote,

She is never irrational; is aware of her condition; perceives the ridiculous nature of her apprehensions, and the absurdity of her precautions; and laughs at and makes sport of them. She also laments, and sometimes weeps in view of them. (1845/1965)

The OCD construct was further examined by the psychologist Pierre Janet (1859–1947). In his work *Les Obsessions et la Psychasthénie* (Obsessions and Psychasthenia; 1903/1976), Janet proposed that obsessions and compulsions are a form of psychasthenic illness, or weakness of the nerves. Sigmund Freud (1856–1939) coined the term *Zwangsneurose*, or "compulsive neurosis," in which obsessions were defined as "transformed self-reproaches that have re-emerged from repression and that always relate to some sexual act that was performed with pleasure in childhood." Freud further postulated that compulsive behaviors were performed to neutralize obsessive ideas and impulses, and that they stemmed from the defense mechanism of reaction formation (adopting traits that are the opposite of the feared impulses). In his case study colloquially referred to as the "Rat Man," Freud (1909/1955) described the psychoanalysis of a 29-year-old male patient who experienced frightening aggressive and sexual obsessions, which Freud interpreted as reflecting the patient's unconscious ambivalence about his father and his doubts concerning sexual orientation.

Early spiritual and psychoanalytic models of OCD have given way to more modern conceptualizations. Biological models were facilitated by the development of neuroimaging techniques, first positron emission tomography (PET) and later functional magnetic resonance imaging (fMRI). Imaging studies of patients demonstrated that OCD is associated with hyperactivity in cortico-striatal-thalamo-cortical circuitry (Saxena & Rauch, 2000). Behavioral models, building on conceptualizations from learning theory (Mowrer, 1960), posit that obsessive fears are maintained by avoidant behavior (including compulsions). Cognitive models of OCD (Frost & Steketee, 2002) suggest that OCD is characterized by predictable and correctable patterns of faulty thinking, including responsibility and threat overestimation, perfectionism, and intolerance of uncertainty, as well as the importance of thoughts and the need to control them.

The Diagnosis of OCD

The first edition of the *Diagnostic and Statistical Manual of Mental Disorders* (*DSM*; American Psychiatric Association, 1952) listed a diagnosis of "obsessive-compulsive reaction," defined as the "persistence of unwanted ideas and of repetitive impulses to perform acts which may be considered morbid by the patient. The patient himself may regard his ideas and behavior as unreasonable, but nevertheless is compelled to carry out his rituals." The disorder was termed a "reaction" because it was thought that the symptoms arose not from organic abnormalities but in response to life history and the social environment. The *DSM* definition, sparse as it was, outlined the presence of both obsessions and compulsions, as well as the good insight first noted by Esquirol.

DSM-II (American Psychiatric Association, 1968) changed the disorder's label to "obsessive compulsive neurosis," describing it as

> characterized by the persistent intrusion of unwanted thoughts, urges, or actions that the patient is unable to stop. The thoughts may consist of single words or ideas, ruminations, or trains of thought often perceived by the patient as nonsensical. The actions vary from simple movements to complex rituals, such as repeated handwashing. Anxiety and distress are often present either if the patient is prevented from completing his compulsive ritual or if he is concerned about being unable to control it himself.

Here, the insight description from the original *DSM* was dropped, although specific examples of obsessions and compulsions were added. Furthermore, the *DSM-II* definition added an emotional dimension, that of "anxiety and distress."

DSM-III (American Psychiatric Association, 1980) first adopted the label "obsessive-compulsive disorder." The diagnostic criteria were greatly expanded from the prior editions of the *DSM*. OCD, according to *DSM-III*, was characterized by either obsessions or compulsions, suggesting that individuals could have one without the other. Obsessions were described as "recurrent, persistent ideas, thoughts, images, or impulses that are ego-dystonic, i.e., they are not experienced as voluntarily produced, but rather as thoughts that invade consciousness and are experienced as senseless or repugnant. Attempts are made to ignore or suppress them." This definition expanded on the *DSM-II* characterization of obsessions as "unwanted" or "perceived by the patient as nonsensical." Compulsions were described as

> repetitive and seemingly purposeful behaviors that are performed according to certain rules or in a stereotyped fashion. The behavior is not an end in itself, but is designed to produce

or prevent some future event or situation. However, either the activity is not connected in a realistic way with what it is designed to produce or prevent, or may be clearly excessive. The act is performed with a sense of subjective compulsion coupled with a desire to resist the compulsion (at least initially). The individual generally recognizes the senselessness of the behavior (this may not be true for young children) and does not derive pleasure from carrying out the activity, although it provides a release of tension.

Here again, the *DSM-III* indicates that individuals with OCD commonly acknowledge that their behaviors do not make sense. The *DSM-III* also links the obsessions and compulsions, by indicating that the compulsive behaviors are "designed to produce or prevent some future event or situation." In this sense, *DSM-III* marked the first description of the function of compulsive behaviors. Finally, *DSM-III* specified that the symptoms cause significant distress or functional impairment.

In *DSM-IV* (American Psychiatric Association, 1994), OCD was again characterized by the presence of obsessions or compulsions. Obsessions were defined as "recurrent and persistent thoughts, impulses, or images that are experienced, at some time during the disturbance, as intrusive and inappropriate and that cause marked anxiety or distress," and which "are not simply excessive worries about real-life problems." Furthermore, "the person attempts to ignore or suppress such thoughts, impulses, or images, or to neutralize them with some other thought or action," and "the person recognizes that the obsessional thoughts, impulses, or images are a product of his or her own mind (not imposed from without as in thought insertion)." Here we see efforts to differentiate OCD from other disorders, such as generalized anxiety disorder or schizophrenia. The inclusion of compulsions in the definition of obsessions (i.e., attempting to neutralize the thoughts) muddies the conceptual waters but further links obsessive thoughts to compulsive behaviors. Compulsions were defined as "repetitive behaviors (e.g., hand washing, ordering, checking) or mental acts (e.g., praying, counting, repeating words silently) that the person feels driven to perform in response to an obsession, or according to rules that must be applied rigidly," which are "aimed at preventing or reducing distress or preventing some dreaded event or situation; however, these behaviors or mental acts either are not connected in a realistic way with what they are designed to neutralize or prevent or are clearly excessive." Again, the compulsion is identified as a behavioral response to an obsessive thought. *DSM-IV* further expanded on the *DSM-III* concept of insight by specifying that "at some point during the course of the disorder, the person has recognized that the obsessions or compulsions are excessive or unreasonable" (though this did not apply to children). The "at some point during the course of the disorder" language suggests that sufferers may lack insight at the time of evaluation, but have a history of good insight. *DSM-IV* further clarified this issue with a "poor insight" specifier.

DSM-5 (American Psychiatric Association, 2013) retained the definition of obsessions and compulsions from *DSM-IV* and reiterated that individuals with OCD may experience obsessions or compulsions. However, the criteria no longer require that the individual recognizes, or has recognized, that the symptoms are irrational. Instead, *DSM-5* expanded the insight specifier to include designations of "good or fair insight," "poor insight," or "absent insight/delusional beliefs." In addition, *DSM-5* added a new tic-related specifier, when the individual has a current tic disorder or history of one.

The OCD Spectrum and Obsessive-Compulsive and Related Disorders

Between the publication of *DSM-IV* and *DSM-5*, Hollander and colleagues (2005) proposed an "obsessive-compulsive spectrum" of disorders that included neurologic disorders (Tourette's syndrome, Sydenham's chorea, torticollis, and autism), preoccupations with bodily sensations or appearance (body dysmorphic disorder, depersonalization, anorexia nervosa, and hypochondriasis), and impulsive disorders (sexual compulsions, trichotillomania, pathologic gambling, kleptomania, and self-injurious behavior). The argument for including all of these disorders in an obsessive-compulsive spectrum was based on several factors. First, the conditions showed high rates of comorbidity (i.e., individuals with OCD were at increased risk of having one of the spectrum conditions). Second, spectrum conditions were common in relatives of individuals with OCD. Third, at least some of the spectrum conditions exhibited abnormalities of neurocircuitry (particularly in the basal ganglia) that were comparable to abnormalities seen in OCD. Fourth, OCD and the spectrum conditions were associated with serotonergic dysfunction. Fifth, following from the serotonin hypothesis, OCD and the spectrum conditions were responsive to serotonin reuptake inhibitors (SRIs).

Conversely, Abramowitz and Deacon (2005) argued that the proposed obsessive-compulsive spectrum conditions were not as similar as they might seem. They suggested that many of the spectrum conditions had been included because they shared topographical similarities with OCD (i.e., perseverative thinking and repetitive behaviors), but that they did not share the same functional properties. Specifically, in OCD, obsessions were unwanted and resisted, and compulsions were performed to relieve obsessional fear and/or to prevent disaster. Although some of the proposed spectrum conditions (e.g., body dysmorphic disorder) shared this function, others did not: for example, trichotillomania and other impulse control disorders consisted of behaviors that elicited positive or pleasurable sensations and were not performed in response to obsessional fears. The authors further noted that most individuals with OCD did not meet criteria for the proposed spectrum conditions, and that anxiety disorders were more common in relatives of OCD patients than were the spectrum disorders. They further noted that evidence for shared neurocircuitry is sparse. Finally, they noted that response to SRIs was not universal across the spectrum conditions and could not be interpreted to indicate a shared neurotransmitter dysfunction.

With the publication of *DSM-5*, OCD was removed from the category of anxiety disorders and was placed in the new category of obsessive-compulsive and related disorders

(OCRDs). Most of the spectrum conditions proposed by Hollander et al. (2005) were not included in the OCRDs. In addition to OCD, the OCRD category included:

- Body dysmorphic disorder (BDD), in which sufferers are preoccupied with a perceived physical flaw that is either not observable or would appear slight to others. Individuals with BDD also engage in repetitive behaviors (e.g., mirror-checking, excessive grooming, skin-picking, reassurance-seeking) or mental acts (e.g., comparing their appearance with that of others) in response to the appearance concerns. BDD was moved from the somatoform disorders in *DSM-IV* to the OCRDs in *DSM-5*.
- Hoarding disorder (HD), which is characterized by persistent difficulty in parting with possessions, regardless of their actual value, due to a perceived need to save the items as well as distress associated with discarding them. This inability to discard possessions results in the accumulation of clutter in the person's living spaces that compromises their intended use. HD is a new diagnosis in *DSM-5*.
- Trichotillomania (TTM), which consists of recurrent pulling out of one's hair, resulting in hair loss, accompanied by repeated attempts to decrease or stop hair pulling. TTM was moved from the impulse control disorders in *DSM-IV* to the OCRDs in *DSM-5*.
- Skin-picking disorder (SPD; also called excoriation), which is characterized by recurrent picking of one's skin, resulting in skin lesions, accompanied by repeated attempts to decrease or stop picking. SPD is a new diagnosis in *DSM-5*, although it was one of several examples of stereotypic movement disorder in *DSM-IV*.

Overview of This Handbook

This book covers the OCRDs as described in *DSM-5*. Because of the similarity between TTM and SPD (both topographically and functionally), the two conditions are covered in the same chapters. Part I of the book addresses the phenomenology and epidemiology of the OCRDs. The chapters aim to familiarize the reader with the OCRD diagnoses and their symptoms, as well as to examine the prevalence and features of the OCRDs in epidemiologic research. In Chapter 2, Calamari and Dams describe the phenomenology and epidemiology of OCD. Chapter 3, by Kelly and Phillips, reviews the phenomenology and epidemiology of BDD. In Chapter 4, Frost and Woolley discuss the phenomenology and epidemiology of HD. Ricketts et al., in Chapter 5, review the phenomenology and epidemiology of TTM and SPD.

Part II addresses contemporary approaches to understanding the OCRDs. It begins with biological models in Chapter 6, in which Samuels describes the genetic bases of the disorders, and Chapter 7, in which Thorsen and van den Heuvel review the neuroanatomy of OCRDs. The focus then shifts to psychological models of the OCRDs: in Chapter 8, Alcolado and colleagues discuss how to understand OCRDs from an information-processing perspective, and in Chapter 9, Pinto and Cowan describe personality features associated with OCRDs. The behavioral model of OCRDs is reviewed in Chapter 10 by Cassin et al., and cognitive (belief-based) approaches are discussed by Taylor and colleagues in Chapter 11.

Part III reviews current assessment strategies for the OCRDs. Chapter 12, by Bleier and Woody, describes the assessment of OCD. Sündermann and Veale discuss the assessment of BDD in Chapter 13. Muroff, in Chapter 14, reviews assessment strategies for HD; and in Chapter 15, Clark and colleagues describe how to assess TTM and SPD. Finally, in Chapter 16, Merritt and Purdon discuss the assessment of features associated with the OCRDs, including comorbidity, insight, and family functioning.

The book then moves on to describe treatment strategies for the OCRDs. To begin, Part IV specifically focuses on the treatment of OCD, because it has been the target of the most controlled research. In Chapter 17, Brennan and colleagues discuss pharmacological treatment of OCD. Chapter 18, by Barrios-Anderson and colleagues, continues the review of somatic treatments by describing other biological approaches (e.g., deep brain stimulation, neurosurgery) for the treatment of OCD. The focus then shifts to psychotherapeutic approaches: Abramowitz and colleagues, in Chapter 19, discuss exposure-based treatment for OCD, and in Chapter 20, Yule et al. review cognitive treatment strategies. Finally, in Chapter 21, Tolin and Stevens present a meta-analytic review of combining pharmacotherapy and psychological treatments for OCD.

The discussion in Part IV then turns to the treatment (both pharmacological and psychological) of the remaining OCRDs. Chapter 22, by Summers and colleagues, reviews the treatment of BDD. Grisham et al. discuss the treatment of HD in Chapter 23. In Chapter 24, Franklin et al. describe the treatment of TTM and SPD.

To conclude the book, Part V discusses OCRDs in special populations. Chapter 25, by Calamari and colleagues, reviews issues related to OCRDs in older adults, and in Chapter 26, Lee et al. describe the presentation of OCRDs in children and adolescents. Finally, Yang et al. discuss cultural issues and the OCRDs in Chapter 27.

I would like to take the opportunity to acknowledge and thank Dr. Gail Steketee, who edited the first edition of this volume (Steketee, 2012). This second (and re-titled) edition follows the basic layout that Dr. Steketee envisioned, and I am deeply grateful for her efforts.

References

Abramowitz, J. S., & Deacon, B. J. (2005). Reply to Hollander et al.: The OC spectrum: A closer look at the arguments and the data. In J. S. Abramowitz & A. C. Houts (Eds.), *Concepts and controversies in obsessive-compulsive disorder* (pp. 141–149). Springer.

American Psychiatric Association (APA). (1952). *Diagnostic and statistical manual of mental disorders*.

American Psychiatric Association (APA). (1968). *Diagnostic and statistical manual of mental disorders* (2nd ed.).

American Psychiatric Association (APA). (1980). *Diagnostic and statistical manual of mental disorders* (3rd ed.).

American Psychiatric Association (APA). (1994). *Diagnostic and statistical manual of mental disorders* (4th ed.).

American Psychiatric Association (APA). (2013). *Diagnostic and statistical manual of mental disorders* (5th ed.).

Esquirol, J. E. D. (1965). *Mental maladies*. Hafner. (Original work published 1845)

Freud, S. (1955). Notes upon a case of obsessional neurosis. *The standard edition of the complete psychological works of Sigmund Freud* (Vol. 10, pp. 151–318). Hogarth. (Original work published 1909)

Frost, R. O., & Steketee, G. (Eds.). (2002). *Cognitive approaches to obsessions and compulsions: Theory, assessment, and treatment*. Pergamon.

Hollander, E., Friedberg, J. P., Wasserman, S., Yeh, C.-C., & Iyengar, R. (2005). The case for the OCD spectrum. In J. S. Abramowitz & A. C. Houts (Eds.), *Concepts and controversies in obsessive-compulsive disorder* (pp. 95–118). Springer.

Janet, P. (1976). *Les obsessions et la psychasthénie* [Obsessions and psychasthenia] (Vol. 1). Arno. (Original work published 1903)

Mora, G. (1969). The scrupulosity syndrome. *International Psychiatry Clinics, 5*(4), 163–174.

Mowrer, O. H. (1960). *Learning theory and behavior*. Wiley.

Saxena, S., & Rauch, S. L. (2000). Functional neuroimaging and the neuroanatomy of obsessive-compulsive disorder. *Psychiatric Clinics of North America, 23*(3), 563–586.

Steketee, G. (Ed.). (2012). *The Oxford handbook of obsessive compulsive and spectrum disorders*. Oxford University Press.

van Megen, H. J. G. M., den Boer-Wolters, D., & Verhagen, P. J. (2010). Obsessive compulsive disorder and religion: A reconnaissance. In P. Verhagen, H. M. Van Praag, J. J. López-Ibor, J. Cox, & D. Moussaoui (Eds.), *Religion and psychiatry: Beyond boundaries* (pp. 271–282). Wiley.

Wegner, D. M. (1994). Ironic processes of mental control. *Psychological Review, 101*(1), 34–52.

PART I

Phenomenology and Epidemiology

CHAPTER 2

Phenomenology and Epidemiology of Obsessive-Compulsive Disorder

John E. Calamari *and* Gregory M. Dams

Abstract

The phenomenology and epidemiology of obsessive-compulsive disorder (OCD) are reviewed. Early observers of human behavior identified core OCD phenomenology, the experience of intrusive negative thoughts, and the related repetitive and compulsive behaviors. The evolution of the understanding of OCD is reflected in the psychiatric disorder taxonomy. Both the evolution and how the changes led to the condition's current conceptualization and definition are evaluated, along with the new obsessive-compulsive and related disorders category. Comorbidity is the rule, not the exception, with OCD. We summarize which conditions co-occur with OCD and how often comorbidity happens. OCD epidemiology is reviewed including the condition's prevalence, age at onset, and the significant associated disability and high levels of suicidality. OCD heterogeneity is seen in the many types of obsessions and compulsion symptoms observed, the variability in the age of onset, and the different comorbid conditions and the frequency of their comorbidity. Significant heterogeneity across multiple domains is a continuing challenge to the clinician attempting to identify or treat OCD, and to researchers working to better understand the disorder. Significant gains have been made in understanding OCD, but many challenges remain.

Key Words: obsessive-compulsive disorder, phenomenology, epidemiology, obsessions, compulsions

Obsessive-compulsive disorder (OCD) is now recognized as both a commonly occurring psychiatric disorder and as a highly disabling condition that broadly diminishes quality of life (for a review, see Tolin & Springer, 2018). The condition is defined in the current psychiatric taxonomy (*Diagnostic and Statistical Manual of Mental Disorders*, 5th edition; *DSM-5*) as the experience of obsessions or compulsions that cause marked distress and impairment (American Psychiatric Association [APA], 2013).

In the *Oxford Handbook of Obsessive-Compulsive and Related Disorders*, both OCD and several conditions understood as importantly related to OCD are reviewed. These related conditions have been described as obsessive-compulsive spectrum disorders (Hollander, 1993; Hollander et al., 2005). Obsessive-compulsive spectrum disorders are understood as being related to OCD because of several commonalities, including similar phenomenological features, shared etiologic processes, and similar responsiveness to specific interventions (Hollander et al., 2005). Although this chapter focuses only on the phenomenology and epidemiology of OCD, the obsessive-compulsive spectrum construct is reviewed as are the debates about its utility and scientific validity. This provides a context for understanding the significant changes that occurred in the classification of OCD in the *DSM-5*. In the new taxonomy, OCD was separated from the anxiety disorders, and a new grouping of conditions was created, the obsessive-compulsive and related disorders (OCRDs).

This chapter reviews early descriptions of obsessional disorders and ideas about symptom meaning and causes, as was done in the first edition of the handbook (Calamari et al., 2012). Early observers astutely identified the two core components of OCD, obsessions and compulsions, and additionally judged that the two phenomena were interrelated. Two early theorists who significantly contributed to efforts to understand and treat obsessional conditions, Sigmund Freud and Pierre Janet, are reviewed. While Janet's ideas may be less well known than Freud's, his work on feelings of incompleteness continues to have a significant influence on contemporary understandings of OCD.

As part of the review of how the conceptualization of OCD has evolved, the significant changes in the APA's taxonomy of psychiatric disorders, the *Diagnostic and Statistical Manual of Mental Disorders* (*DSM*; APA, 1952–2013), are reviewed. The changes in the understandings of OCD seen in the *DSM* classification are outlined, noting that the changes occurred in the context of evolving conceptualizations of mental disorders, their interrelationships, and their appropriate classification. After review of the first four *DSM* taxonomies, the concept of the OCD spectrum is introduced. The OCD spectrum is discussed as an important to understand the significant changes in the classification of OCD seen in the *DSM-5*. The *DSM-5* description of OCD and the OCRDs is summarized.

The discussion then turns to the important issues of how cultural differences and individual diversity influence OCD. Although research on these issues remains limited, the existing evidence on whether these differences affect the experience of obsessions and compulsions is reviewed. Next the chapter turns to a review of research on OCD comorbidity. As has been recognized for some time, comorbidity is the rule, not the exception, with OCD, and the discussion summarizes which conditions co-occur with OCD and how often they are comorbid.

The epidemiology section of the chapter reviews the current understandings of the prevalence of OCD and how demographic factors like gender and age are related to prevalence. This section also examines the life course of OCD, which has often been characterized as involving a waxing and waning of symptom severity (Eisen & Steketee, 1998). The section also summarizes the substantial disability and diminished quality of life experienced by people with OCD.

Overall, the greatest challenge to understanding OCD is the condition's heterogeneity. The significant symptom heterogeneity of OCD (McKay et al., 2004) and the related challenges to assessment and treatment (Antony et al., 2007) have been recognized for some time. As new aspects of OCD heterogeneity continue to emerge, they advance understanding of this complex condition.

Phenomenology and Nosology of OCD

Early Conceptualizations of Obsessional Disorders

As reviewed in the first edition of this handbook (Calamari et al., 2012), obsessional disorder symptoms have been observed and described throughout history. Often, early descriptions of the condition captured important aspects of the phenomenology of OCD as it is understood today: intrusive unwanted thoughts and related repetitive behaviors. Although some aspects of the early descriptions of OCD were congruent with the diagnostic conceptualizations developed later, ideas about OCD etiology were limited by the pre-scientific thinking of the time. Because religious authorities were often called on to explain the symptoms of psychiatric disorders, including OCD (Nezirogu & Yaryura-Tobias, 1997; Simpson & Reddy, 2014), OCD symptoms were often understood as indicators of an individual's morality or spiritual well-being. As a result of this understanding, at the time the treatments for people with obsessions and compulsions would sometimes involve the same methods applied to the correction of blasphemy or used to treat those that were judged possessed. The methods included various forms of torture, which were judged as necessary to restore the person to normal functioning (Neziroglu & Yaryura-Tobias, 1997).

Possibly as a result of viewing the symptoms of OCD as a reflection of spiritual wellbeing, early observers of the condition often focused on what is described today as scrupulosity, understood now as an important OCD symptom variant. Scrupulosity symptoms have been described as repugnant and highly distressing obsessions involving one of several themes: intrusive blasphemous thoughts, intrusive unacceptable sexual thoughts, or intrusive unacceptable thoughts of harming others (Rachman, 2007). In one of the very early descriptions of obsessional symptoms, Burton described "religious melancholy" in *The Anatomy of Melancholy* (1628). He depicted a person who intensely feared he might speak aloud ideas considered indecent or inappropriate. Similarly, O'Flaherty described obsessional disorder symptoms in several individuals characterized as "persistently concerned with incident, thought, word, or deed," whose "thoughts caused uneasiness and distress," and who experienced these symptoms while being otherwise "healthy, normal, and free of other pathological disorders" (O'Flaherty, cited in Rapoport, 1989, p. 312). Saint Alphonsus Liguori (cited in Rapoport, 1989) described a case involving an individual who experienced repetitive groundless fears of sinning.

Possibly as a result of the historic connection of OCD symptoms to scrupulosity, the Roman Catholic Church became an early sponsor of OCD research (reviewed in Rapoport, 1989). Mullen (1927) conducted a study of the pastoral treatment of scrupulosity. Study participants were 400 women in a Catholic high school who were asked to respond to questions about both scrupulosity symptoms as well as contamination concerns and cleaning and washing behaviors they felt compelled to perform. Scrupulosity symptoms were frequently reported, often involving doubts about the moral correctness of one's behavior (Rapoport, 1989).

Beginning in the 1800s, as scientific thinking developed, a movement toward understanding mental disorders as medical conditions began, and this shift influenced thinking about OCD (Krochmalik & Menzies, 2003). The medicalization of mental illness connected the conditions to the rapidly evolving health sciences of the period and led to initial efforts to develop a more systematic conceptualization of psychiatric disorders (Krochmalik & Menzies, 2003). For example, Esquirol, who was a physician of the time, described the case of "Mademoiselle F," characterizing his patient as experiencing monomania (partial insanity; cited in Bynum et al., 2005. Monomania was understood as a physical disease of the brain that occurred without fever and that resulted from partial lesion of the intellect, the emotions, or the will.

Alverenga et al. (2007) reviewed later theories of obsessional disorders developed in the 1800s as alternatives to the monomania conceptualization. In these models, compulsive behaviors were sometimes seen as impulsive in nature, acts that were irresistible and imposed on the mind of the affected person, much like hallucinations as they were understood at the time (Dagonet, 1870, cited in Alverenga et al., 2007). Other theorists of the time saw the condition as a disorder of intellect (i.e., a cognitive impairment). These theorists posited that irrational thoughts (obsessional intrusions) occurred because of physical changes in the brain that affected cognitive functioning (Westphal, 1878, cited in Alverenga et al., 2007). They hypothesized that the cause of obsessional symptoms was difficulty inhibiting negative intrusive thoughts, excessive awareness of one's thoughts, and limited understanding of the excessiveness of the related repetitive compulsive behaviors. Westphal also hypothesized that there might be a genetic predisposition for obsessional disorders, and his work is understood to have led to the description of the condition as obsessive-compulsive (Alverenga et al., 2007).

Later, the term *neurasthenia* was introduced by Beard and was used to encompass a heterogeneous set of symptoms that included obsessional disorder symptoms (Beard, 1869). The symptoms of neurasthenia included intrusive thought experiences and the performance of rituals, but the condition was also understood to be characterized by mental and physical fatigue and muscular weakness (Beard, 1869). Neurasthenia was understood to result from insufficient psychological tension, seen as needed to perform more sophisticated mental activities (van der Hart & Friedman, 1989). The limited nervous energy that obsessional individuals had was directed toward their preoccupation with obsessions and compulsions.

In summary, careful observers of human behavior have long described many of the symptoms we understand today as characteristic of OCD. Very early observations of obsessional disorder symptoms identified several aspects of what are now recognized as core to OCD phenomenology: the frequent experience of unwanted and unpleasant thoughts, and co-occurring repetitive compulsive behaviors. Possibly because the affected individuals often reported that they could exert little control over their obsessions or compulsions, in some early descriptions of OCD, volitional control was often believed to have been lost and the condition was judged like forms of major mental illness (Calamari et al., 2012). The functional relationship between obsessions and compulsions was sometimes recognized, as was the distress-neutralizing function of compulsive behaviors (Liguori, cited in Rapoport, 1989). Also sometimes recognized by the early observers was the often ego-dystonic nature of obsessional intrusions (O'Flaherty, cited in Rapoport, 1989) and the individual's ability to recognize their reactivity to intrusive thoughts as excessive, or to understand that their compulsive behaviors had little utility (Esquirol, cited in Bynum et al., 2005; O'Flaherty, cited in Rapoport, 1989).

Early Theoretical Accounts of Obsessional Disorders
PSYCHOANALYTIC THEORY

Early in his work on psychoanalytic theory, Freud developed several constructs that he used to explain the complex symptoms of obsessional disorders (Calamari et al., 2012). His ideas on anxiety neurosis and his conceptualization of neurasthenia (Freud, 1895/1958) were among the important concepts that he believed explained obsessional disorders. He hypothesized that the anxiety neuroses that involved obsessions and compulsive behaviors were a manifestation of the affected individual's unconscious struggle over drives and feelings that were experienced as highly unacceptable. The obsessional individual struggled to prevent these thoughts and feelings from entering conscious awareness because of the associated distress, and obsessional symptoms were understood as a failure of the psychological defense systems, repression specifically (Freud, 1913/1958). The psychological defense system's breakdown resulted in the individual's experiencing frequent improper or unwanted thoughts. Compulsive behaviors were an attempt to distract the self by focusing energy on repeatedly and exactly performing certain actions. Compulsive behavior was understood to function to avoid, or at least to minimize, conscious awareness of the unacceptable feelings. Simply put, Freud hypothesized that compulsive behaviors were the attempts of individuals with obsessional intrusions to distract themselves from thinking about what they unconsciously felt they should not think or feel (Carr, 1974; Rachman, 1963).

Psychoanalytic theory posited that the root cause of obsessional syndromes was precocity of ego development (Freud, 1913/1958). According to Freud's theory, individuals who progress through the psychosexual developmental stages normally develop their libido first, followed by development of the ego. For people with obsessive-compulsive conditions, the reverse was thought to be true, which predisposed the individual to what was described as an immature way of relating to others. As a result, "obsessional neurotics have to develop a super-morality in order to protect their object-love from the hostility lurking behind it" (Freud, 1913/1958, p. 325). Further, Freud observed that people with OCD often judged that having an unacceptable thought (e.g., harming someone) was highly significant. The experience of these unacceptable thoughts was intensely distressing, a level of distress approximating the feelings that might result if the person had performed the action (Freud, 1909/1958). Freud's observations are congruent with contemporary cognitive theories of OCD emphasizing exaggerated beliefs about the importance and meaning of thought experiences (Rachman, 1997, 1998). Rachman's important construct, thought–action fusion, the sense that thoughts of behaviors believed improper are immoral acts in themselves (Rachman, 1993), describes an important type of dysfunctional belief. In cognitive theories of OCD, dysfunctional beliefs are understood to precipitate the misappraisal of intrusive thought experiences, and this misappraisal process is judged to be the central mechanism in the pathogenesis of OCD (Frost & Steketee, 2002).

One of Freud's best-known descriptions of obsessional conditions is often referred to as the case of the "Rat Man" (Freud, 1909/1958). The case description that Freud provided has been carefully reviewed in the psychiatric disorders' literature because of its importance to an understanding of Freud's psychoanalytic theory and his related treatment intervention, psychoanalysis (Thapaliya, 2017). Thapaliya summarized several details of Freud's Rat Man case that were discovered after Freud's publication of the case (Freud, 1909/1958). The patient was a 29-year-old university-educated man who reported experiencing obsessional symptoms since his childhood. The individual experienced intrusive thoughts focused on harm coming to loved ones, and these obsessions included thoughts and gruesome images of torture with wild rats, a practice the patient had heard about during his military service. Freud (1909/1958) described his psychoanalysis of the patient, which occurred over approximately six months. His intervention involved having his patient review events from early childhood that focused on his abusive father. The patient also described his thoughts and feelings about more recent life events, typically focusing on emotional interactions with the major people in the patient's life. As is characteristic of psychoanalysis, the patient reported the thoughts entering his mind during treatment sessions, in what Freud characterized as the free association technique. The process was intended to provide opportunities for the clinician to gain insight into repressed feelings and underlying psychological meanings for the patient. With these insights, the clinician could then guide the patient through a process of better understanding and integrating the life experiences. Freud reported that his intervention cured his patient's problem, although this claim has been questioned in later literature (Thapaliya, 2017).

JANET'S CONTRIBUTION TO UNDERSTANDING OCD

Although his work is not as well known as Freud's, Pierre Janet made important and long-lasting contributions to the understanding of OCD. His work arguably has greater continuing impact on OCD research and treatment than psychoanalytic theory. Janet's work around the incompleteness construct is arguably his most significant and enduring contribution to OCD, and his work is credited with helping elucidate the heterogeneous motivational processes underlying obsessional disorders (Davine et al., 2019; Summerfeldt et al., 2014).

Janet began his career before Freud and was an outspoken critic of Freud's psychoanalytic theory (for reviews, see Bühler & Heim, 2001; Pitman, 1987). Janet's work broadly focused on trauma and dissociation and centered on his conceptualization of what he came to call fixed ideas, the formation of cognitive-emotional complexes that impaired the cognitive processing of stressful life experiences. He saw traumatic life events (broadly understood) as important precipitants of mental illness (Bühler & Heim, 2001).

In Janet's seminal work *Les Obsessions et la Psychasthénie* (Obsessions and Psychasthenia), he described the experience of feelings of incompleteness, which he posited was a core component of what he labeled *psychasthenia* (see Pitman, 1987, for a review). Janet described incompleteness as the experience of an inner sense of imperfection, a sense that actions had not been performed correctly: "They feel that actions they perform are incompletely achieved, or they do not produce the sought-for satisfaction, though to observe these actions they may appear to have been performed perfectly well" (quoted in Pitman, 1987, p. 226). Janet believed that a sense of imperfection (feeling of incompletely achieving an objective) was an important process in the development of obsessive-compulsive syndromes. Janet considered anxiety to be a secondary characteristic of OCD (Swinson et al., 1998), seeing anxiety or fear as a sometimes-seen reaction to obsessional symptoms rather than their cause. He contended that fear or anxiety is no more often observed in OCD than is indifference or a lack of motivation (Pitman, 1987).

Following a period where psychology and psychiatry largely ignored Janet's ideas, Rasmussen and Eisen (1992) are credited with reintroducing Janet to the field (Davine et al., 2019). Rasmussen and Eisen (1992) carefully detailed Janet's ideas about incompleteness and psychasthenia and suggested that these concepts found support from several contemporary lines of OCD-related research. Rasmussen and Eisen suggested that the distinctions between harm avoidance and incompleteness could be a framework for understanding the many symptom variants of OCD. Renewed interest in the incompleteness construct has led to important new OCD research.

In a review, Summerfeldt (2004) noted several lines of OCD research evaluating constructs similar to Janet's incompleteness: deficits in the feeling of knowing (Rapoport, 1991), "just right" experiences (Coles et al., 2003; Leckman et al., 1994), sensory phenomena (Miguel et al., 2000), and sensitivity of perception (Veale et al., 1996). While these constructs differ to a degree in how they are conceptualized, OCD researchers have largely settled on the use of two terms to describe feelings of incompleteness and closely related phenomena. These terms connect to the most widely used measures of the construct: "not just right" experiences ("Not Just Right" Questionnaire-Revised; Coles et al., 2003) and "incompleteness" (The Obsessive-Compulsive Trait Core Dimensions Questionnaire; Summerfeldt et al., 2014), with the latter measure assessing both harm avoidance and incompleteness. Summerfeldt and colleagues posit that harm avoidance and incompleteness are the two core motivational processes that drive the symptoms of OCD. Harm avoidance is considered a motivation shared with anxiety disorders, while incompleteness is specific to obsessional disorders.

OCD in the Psychiatric Disorder Taxonomy

Changes in understandings of OCD are reflected in the revisions made to the psychiatric disorder classification system, the *DSM*. Changes to this nosology were precipitated by advances in the conceptualization and classification of psychopathology broadly, and as a result of the accelerating scientific study of OCD. This section first reviews the early conceptualizations of OCD in the *DSM*, and then reviews the important OCD spectrum construct. This construct is central to the current conceptualization of OCD, its move from the anxiety disorders, and the creation of a new category of conditions, referred to as OCD and related disorders (OCRDs), for *DSM-5*.

OBSESSIONAL DISORDERS IN THE EARLY DSM

As reviewed in the first edition of this handbook (Calamari et al., 2012), the first edition of the *Diagnostic and Statistical Manual of Mental Disorders* (*DSM-I*; APA, 1952) was a major development in the field. The *DSM* brought together for the first time in the United States a relatively comprehensive listing of mental disorders in a single classification framework. At the time of the publication of *DSM-I*, psychoanalytic theory dominated psychiatry, and not surprisingly, it greatly influenced the initial attempt to classify mental disorders. In *DSM-I*, an "obsessive-compulsive reaction" was described within a broader category of psychoneurotic disorders, with the commonality across the conditions being the experience of anxiety. An obsessive-compulsive reaction was diagnosed if the patient experienced ideas that were unwanted, or if the patient felt compelled to perform rituals (APA, 1952). A revision of the *DSM* occurred in the late 1960s (*DSM-II*; APA, 1968). *DSM-II* drew heavily from the mental disorders section of the then recently published eighth revision of the *International Classification of Diseases* (*ICD-8*; World Health Organization, 1965). *DSM-II* shared significant similarities with the *ICD-8* classification structure and its descriptions of specific psychiatric disorders. Because of psychoanalytic theory's continued influence in psychiatry, a group of conditions called neurotic disorders was described. Again, the commonality across the conditions was the experience of anxiety symptoms, which were understood to result from underlying intrapsychic conflicts. The *DSM-II* description of a neurosis with an obsessive-compulsive reaction was very similar to the description that appeared in *DSM-I*. An addition to the description of OCD in *DSM-II* was a clarification on disorder-related distress, "often present either if the patient is prevented from completing his compulsive ritual or if he is concerned about being unable to control it himself" (APA, 1968, p. 40).

DSM III AND IV

A significantly different approach was taken to the classification of psychopathology in *DSM-III*, the third edition of *DSM* (APA, 1980). The changes were precipitated by several significant limitations of the earlier classification systems (Calamari et al., 2012), including diagnostic reliability, which was thought to result from the vague descriptions of disorders in *DSM-I* and *DSM-II* (Beck et al., 1962; Nathan et al., 1969). In the development of *DSM-III*, two fundamental changes were made to address the limitations of the earlier classification approaches (Bayer & Spitzer, 1985; Millon, 1983). An attempt was made to significantly better detail the core characteristics of each specific disorder. This strategy included the use of more descriptive, behavioral criteria in disorder descriptions. Further, the developers of the *DSM-III* attempted to make disorder descriptions and the broader classification system independent of specific psychopathology theories. As a result, in the atheoretical *DSM-III*, disorders were defined by sets of more specific and often observable symptoms thought to reflect the condition's core characteristics (Millon, 1983; Spitzer et al., 1980). Seemingly a side effect of this new approach was the creation of a substantially greater number of diagnostic categories in *DSM-III*.

In *DSM-III*, OCD was placed in the new group of conditions called anxiety disorders. In that group, OCD was designated a member of the subcategory anxiety states, which included panic disorder and generalized anxiety disorder. OCD was characterized by the experience of obsessions or compulsions that cause significant distress or that "interfere with social or role functioning" (APA, 1980, p. 235). Obsessions were defined as "recurrent, persistent ideas, thoughts, images, or impulses that are ego-dystonic . . . and are experienced as senseless or repugnant" (p. 235). Compulsions were defined as "repetitive and seemingly purposeful behaviors that are performed according to certain rules or in a stereotyped fashion, that were designed to produce or prevent some future event or situation" (p. 235). Further, in *DSM-III*, people with OCD were understood to recognize most often "the senselessness of the behavior" (p. 235), although insight was acknowledged as being absent in young children with OCD. Distinguished from the repetitive behaviors seen in other disorders, compulsions were understood to be performed in order to reduce distress or to release the tension that was precipitated by obsessions.

A detailed description of OCD and its core symptoms was provided in *DSM-III* for the first time. This definition captured several core aspects of the condition's phenomenology that remain central to OCD's more recent definitions (Calamari et al., 2012), including its characterization in *DSM-5*. They include the basic definitions of obsessions and compulsions, recognition of the interrelationship between obsessions and compulsions, and noting the distress-reducing function of compulsions.

In the 1987 revision of *DSM-III* (*DSM-III-R*; APA, 1987), several changes were made to the anxiety disorders category, including elimination of the distinction previously made between phobic disorders and anxiety states. Further refinements to the definitions of obsessions and compulsions were made, and condition-related life interference was better detailed, including the time-consuming nature of OCD, which took "more than an hour a day" (APA, 1987, p. 247).

Prior to the planned fourth edition of *DSM* (*DSM-IV*; APA, 1994), field trials were conducted to obtain empirical data on specific disorders or groups of disorders. As a result of the field trials evaluating OCD, recommendations were made for improving the description of disorder-related insight. In the field trials, people with OCD showed greater variability in their insight than had been previously understood (Foa & Kozak, 1995; Foa et al., 1995). A substantial percentage of the clinical population with OCD was at least uncertain that their obsessional concerns or compulsive behaviors were unreasonable or excessive. As a result of these findings, variability in patient insight was explicitly recognized in *DSM-IV* and a diagnostic specifier of "with poor insight" was added. Patients' levels of insight have been recognized as important for several reasons, including the association between low insight and a diminished OCD treatment response (Foa et al., 1999).

The field trials for *DSM-IV* also clarified that the experience of mental compulsions was common in OCD (Foa & Kozak, 1995; Foa et al., 1995). Mental compulsions came to be defined as "mental acts (e.g., praying, counting, repeating words silently) the goal of which is to prevent anxiety or distress, not to provide pleasure or gratification" (*DSM-IV-TR*; APA, 2000, p. 457). Covert mental compulsions are now well recognized as characteristic of obsessional disorders, occurring in people with OCD in many different forms and requiring skillful adaptations of cognitive-behavioral therapy (CBT; Rowa et al., 2007).

Additionally, the *DSM-IV* clarifications were made to help distinguish obsessional disorders from conditions with similar phenomenology. For example, the distinction between intrusive obsessional thoughts, which are often ego-dystonic, and the excessive worries about real-life problems characteristic of generalized anxiety disorder was clarified. Finally, a greater number of obsession and compulsion symptom examples were provided in *DSM-IV* that better captured the symptom heterogeneity of OCD (cf. McKay et al., 2004). These examples included feelings of being contaminated, doubting obsessions, symmetry concerns precipitating ordering compulsions, aggressive impulses, intrusive sexual imagery, and checking behaviors, among others.

The OCD Spectrum

Theorists who endorsed the idea of the OCD spectrum posited that certain forms of psychopathology are importantly related to OCD, and that the identification of these conditions will help inform understanding and possibly treatment of both OCD and the related disorders (Hollander, 2005). Theories range from the position of Hollander and colleagues, who advocated for a very broad conceptualization of the OCD spectrum (Hollander, 1993; Hollander et al., 2005), to the positions of other OCD experts who contend that empirical support for a very broad OCD spectrum is limited or absent and further assert that only a much smaller number of disorders have important commonalities with OCD (Abramowitz, 2018; Abramowitz & Mahaffey, 2011). The different positions are discussed here, including the dimensions held to be most important in determining which disorders are on the OCD spectrum.

Development of a sound disorder spectrum model requires careful consideration of what dimensions are core to the conceptualization of the reference condition (e.g., aspects of phenomenology, disorder-related risk factors, neurobiology). Additionally, the scientific study of each of the purported important disorder dimensions and the specific variables that operationalize them must have progressed far enough that the dimension's relationship to the reference condition is well established. Further, research findings should exist indicating that the dimension has an important role in the development of the reference disorder. It should be noted that while work addressing the many research questions important to the OCD spectrum has progressed, it is still a work in progress.

Prior to the release of *DSM-5*, Hollander and colleagues advocated for both a broad OCD spectrum and for removing OCD from the anxiety disorders, as well as for the development of a separate grouping of OCD and OCD-related disorders (Hollander et al., 2008). Hollander and colleagues argued that development of a classification for OCRDs would improve diagnostic accuracy, as well as bring the *DSM* taxonomy better in line with the World Health Organization's classifications of mental disorders. In the *International Classification of Diseases* 10th revision (*ICD-10*; World Health Organization, 2016), OCD was classified in a category separate from the anxiety disorders.

In Hollander et al.'s (2008) broad OCD spectrum model, the authors hypothesized that the spectrum consisted of disorders that lie along a compulsivity–impulsivity continuum. They posited that the compulsivity–impulsivity continuum was an important framework for understanding the OCD spectrum. At the compulsivity end of the continuum were disorders characterized by risk aversion and harm avoidance. At the opposite, impulsive, end were disorders typified by impulsive behavior, risk-taking or gratification-seeking (e.g., pathological gambling; Hollander et al., 2005). For compulsive disorders, repetitive behaviors were understood to function to reduce perceived threat or anxiety, and OCD, body dysmorphic disorder (BDD), anorexia nervosa, and hypochondriasis were considered disorders lying toward the compulsive end of the continuum. Impulsive disorders also included sexual compulsions and forms of self-injurious behavior (Hollander, 1993; Hollander et al., 2005). In the model, conditions positioned toward the middle of the compulsive–impulsive continuum included Tourette disorder, autism, and binge eating. Further, the OCD spectrum conditions were grouped into three clusters: disorders involving bodily sensations or appearance concerns (e.g., BDD, anorexia nervosa, hypochondriasis); impulsive disorders (e.g., trichotillomania, pathological gambling); and neurologic disorders (Tourette disorder, autism, Sydenham's chorea; Hollander et al., 2005). Hollander and colleagues argued that empirical support for their broad OCD spectrum came from multiple lines of study that provided evidence for the following: important overlapping phenomenology, similar patterns of comorbidity, commonalities in heritability, and similarities in the brain circuitry and neurotransmitter systems affected (for a review, see Hollander et al., 2008). Critiques of the broad OCD spectrum model questioned the strength of the phenomenological similarities and indicated that the comorbidity findings did not support the model, concluding that phenomenology and comorbidity better connected OCD to the anxiety disorders (Abramowitz, 2018).

Abramowitz and Mahaffey (2011) reviewed the evidence for the broad OCD spectrum and concluded there were several significant limitations to Hollander and colleagues' model, a conclusion congruent with earlier reviews (Storch et al., 2008). They argued that the phenomenology similarities between OCD and many purported spectrum disorders are superficial. A critical component of OCD phenomenology was more often missing in spectrum disorders: the functional relationship seen in OCD between distress-increasing intrusive thoughts and the neutralizing function of compulsive behaviors (Abramowitz & Mahaffey, 2011). Additionally, Abramowitz and Mahaffey noted that the repetitive behaviors seen in several of the disorders considered OCD-related in the broad-spectrum model are driven by efforts to experience pleasure (e.g., pathological gambling), rather than attempts to reduce distress or anxiety, and are therefore motivationally distinct from the compulsions seen in OCD. Further, the purported relationship between obsessional disorders and impulse control problems that is central to Hollander and colleagues' broad OCD spectrum model has not been supported in several investigations (Bienvenu et al., 2000; Summerfeldt et al., 2004). Finally, neither compulsivity or impulsivity is clearly defined in the model, nor was a compulsivity–impulsivity cutoff point established (Storch et al., 2008). Abramowitz and Jacoby (2014) argued that the compulsivity–impulsivity continuum rests on the repetitive-behavior similarities observed across the purported spectrum conditions, which again are superficial.

An additional prediction of the broad OCD spectrum model is that there are high levels of comorbidity between OCD and the conditions on the spectrum (Hollander et al., 2005). The results of several studies indicated that while many purported spectrum conditions co-occur with OCD more often than other conditions, the comorbidity rates are generally low compared to the comorbidities reported between OCD, anxiety disorders, or major depression. For example, Bienvenu et al. (2000) found low comorbidity rates between OCD and several spectrum conditions: anorexia nervosa (9%), bulimia (4%), trichotillomania (4%), and pathological gambling (0%). OCD's comorbidity with BDD was relatively high (15%). A consistent finding across OCD comorbidity studies is that the highest rates occur with the anxiety disorders (Abramowitz, 2018); the comorbidity seen with specific anxiety disorders is often reported to range between 10% and 20% (Calamari et al., 2012).

Abramowitz (2018) pointed out that the consistently high levels of comorbidity between anxiety disorders and OCD, and the substantially lower comorbidity seen with many conditions hypothesized to be OCD spectrum disorders, was inconsistent with the move of OCD from the anxiety disorders category that occurred in the *DSM-5*.

Nonetheless, there have been long-standing debates about how central the experience of anxiety is to OCD. As discussed earlier, Janet saw anxiety as being of secondary importance to OCD, a reaction to obsessional symptoms rather than their precipitant (Swinson et al., 1998). Empirical support for anxiety's secondary role in OCD is found in studies where anxiety symptom severity scores failed to be strongly related to OCD symptom severity (Storch et al., 2009) or OCD-related disability (Storch et al., 2010). Additional evidence of OCD's possible distinctiveness from anxiety disorders comes from new research on the motivational processes in OCD.

Summerfeldt and colleagues' motivational theory of OCD, the obsessive-compulsive core dimensions model, posits that OCD is often driven by a motivational process not seen in the anxiety disorders, feelings of incompleteness (Summerfeldt et al., 2014). While OCD symptoms can often be driven by the harm avoidance characteristic of anxiety disorders (e.g., compulsive washing to avoid getting sick), feelings of incompleteness or the need to achieve a "just right" feeling is also important to OCD (e.g., repetitive washing until it feels done correctly). In their review, Summerfeldt et al. (2014) noted that in evaluations of clinical samples of OCD patients, approximately half reported that incompleteness was associated with their need to perform compulsions. Further, incompleteness is understood to play a greater role in some OCD symptom subtypes (e.g., symmetry obsessions; Summerfeldt, 2004). As investigations of incompleteness or "not just right" experiences and related phenomena (e.g., sensory phenomena; Miguel et al., 2000) continue to progress, the importance of these experiences in OCD will become clearer and possibly support its distinctiveness from the anxiety disorders.

Finally, as previously mentioned, an additional factor in changing the classification of OCD was the structure of the *ICD* taxonomy. OCD was not categorized as an anxiety disorder in *ICD-10* (the contemporary of the *DSM-IV*), and OCD's grouping as an anxiety condition had been challenged as early as 1968 in the *ICD-8* taxonomy. At that time, OCD's similarities with the anxiety disorders were questioned based on judgments that the condition's phenomenology was importantly different (Montgomery, 1993).

As the work on the development of *DSM-5* progressed and the systematic reviews of the related scientific evidence were completed, the expert consensus was that the disorders importantly related to OCD were much fewer than what had been proposed in broad OCD spectrum models. Although the OCD work group supported moving OCD from the anxiety disorders and the creation of a new classification, the consensus was for a narrower OCD spectrum (Hollander et. al., 2009). Addictive disorders and several impulse control disorders, including pathological gambling and binge eating, were excluded from the OCRD category. The work group supported the inclusion of BDD and the body-focused repetitive disorders (trichotillomania and excoriation disorder). The work group concluded that if hoarding was added to the *DSM-5* as a new disorder, it would be reasonable to include it among OCRDs (Phillips et al., 2010).

OCD and OCRDs

The OCRDs are a group of disorders that first appeared in *DSM-5* (APA, 2013), and in the final formulation of the *DSM-5* nosology, OCD was separated from the anxiety disorders, where it had been grouped since the anxiety disorders category was first developed in 1980. The basis for the new category was summarized as evidence of the disorders' "relatedness to one another in terms of a range of diagnostic validators as well as the clinical utility of grouping these disorders in the same chapter" (p. 235). Although OCD was removed from the anxiety disorders, the similarities between OCD and the anxiety disorders were acknowledged in the *DSM-5*: "Moreover, there are close relationships between the anxiety disorders and some of the obsessive-compulsive related disorders (e.g., OCD), which is reflected in the sequence of the *DSM-5* chapters, with obsessive-compulsive and related disorders following the anxiety disorders" (p. 235). A summary of the description of OCD in the *DSM-5* follows here, but because the other conditions now in the OCRD category are the focus of other chapters in the present volume, these conditions are only briefly described in this chapter's overview of the OCRD category.

The definition of OCD was not substantially altered in *DSM-5* (Abramowitz & Jacoby, 2014; Guzick et al., 2017). Minor phrasing changes were made in the descriptions of obsessions and compulsions; the word *impulse* replaced the word *urge* in the description of obsessions. The word *inappropriate*, which had been used to describe the content of obsessional thoughts, was replaced with *unwanted* (Abramowitz & Jacoby, 2014). Additionally, disorder-associated insight variability was better detailed with ordinal categories: *With good or fair insight*; *With poor insight*; *With absent insight/delusional beliefs*. Last, a tic-related specifier was added (i.e., to indicate the presence of a current or past tic disorder). The tic-related specifier was added because research has associated tic-related OCD with specific symptoms or "not just right" experiences (Guzick et al., 2017).

Five disorders are defined in the OCRD section: OCD, BDD, hoarding disorder (HD), trichotillomania, and excoriation disorder. Two of the disorders (BDD and trichotillomania) had been classified in the *DSM-IV* in other diagnostic groupings, and two disorders (HD and excoriation disorder) were new to the *DSM* nosology.

In *DSM-5*, BDD is described as a preoccupation with one or more perceived defects or flaws in physical appearance, which are not observable or appear slight or insignificant to other people (p. 242). Further, the physical appearance concerns are associated with repetitive behaviors, which can include actions like checking one's appearance in the mirror or reassurance-seeking from others about the severity of the perceived appearance defect. BDD had been classified in *DSM-IV* as a somatoform disorder. The diagnostic criteria defining BDD in *DSM-5* were not substantially changed from the previous description (for a detailed review of the OCRD category, see Abramowitz & Jacoby, 2014). In the *DSM-5* characterization of BDD, the interrelationship between disorder-related obsession like preoccupations with appearance and related repetitive behaviors was noted. Further, in *DSM-5*, two BDD specifiers were added, an insight specifier like the one provided for OCD, and a specifier indicating whether muscle dysmorphia (a concern focused on muscle development) was present (Abramowitz & Jacoby, 2014).

HD was previously considered a symptom of OCD. As a result of several decades of research on compulsive hoarding that detailed its unique phenomenology, the condition is now recognized as importantly different from OCD (for a review, see Pertusa et al., 2010). HD appeared for the first time as a psychiatric disorder in *DSM-5*. In earlier versions of *DSM*, several symptoms of HD were attributed to obsessive-compulsive personality disorder. The description of obsessive-compulsive personality disorder in *DSM-5* continued to include characteristics that have been associated with HD (e.g., perfectionism, inflexibility) as well an "an inability to discard worn-out or worthless objects even when they have no sentimental value" (APA, 2013, p. 679). The absence of possession-associated sentimentality may distinguish this personality disorder from HD.

The characterization of HD in *DSM-5* is highly congruent with Frost and colleagues' formulations of the condition's core phenomenology (Frost & Hartl, 1996; Steketee & Frost, 2003). In their model, HD was described as being associated with several core cognitive-processing difficulties that lead to the disorder's symptoms. The difficulties include deficits in attention, some aspects of memory, and organizational skills (Steketee & Frost, 2003).

In *DSM-5*, three symptom clusters define HD: persistent difficulty discarding possessions, regardless of their actual value, that results from a perceived need to save the items, and because of distress associated with discarding them; the excessive accumulation of possessions that congest and clutter living areas and substantially compromise the living areas' intended use (e.g., cannot cook in the kitchen); and clinically significant distress and impairment (p. 247; APA, 2013).

The two other disorders included in the OCRD category are both described as body-focused repetitive behaviors. Trichotillomania has three core symptoms: "recurrent pulling out of one's hair, resulting in hair loss"; "repeated attempts to decrease or stop hair pulling"; and "the hair pulling causes significant distress or impairment in social, occupational, or other areas of functioning" (p. 251). Excoriation disorder appeared for the first time in *DSM-5*. The diagnostic criteria for the excessive skin-picking seen for the disorder are very similar to those for trichotillomania (p. 254).

The OCRD category of the *DSM-5* includes several additional diagnostic categories, a structure like other sections of the *DSM*. Substance- or medication-induced OCRD is diagnosed when evidence indicates that symptom development occurred during, or soon after, substance or medication use or withdrawal. Any of the primary OCRD symptoms might predominate in the clinical presentation. For example, Gahr et al. (2020) reported a case where OCD symptoms developed following the abrupt discontinuation of venlafaxine in an individual with no history of obsessional disorders. Diagnosis of OCRD due to another medical condition is applied when direct evidence is present that the OCRD condition symptoms resulted from "the direct pathophysiological consequence of another medical condition" (p. 236). Brain injury involving the striatal system is provided as an example. The diagnostic category "other specified OCRD" applies to presentations where OCRD symptoms predominate, full diagnostic criteria for any specific OCRD disorder are not met, but the specific clinical presentation symptoms can be detailed. An example provided in *DSM-5* is obsessional jealousy, which is described as a nondelusional preoccupation with a partner's perceived infidelity that may lead to related repetitive behaviors or mental acts (p. 264; for a review, see Doron & Derby, 2017). Additionally, three culture-related syndromes are also described as relevant to the diagnostic category (p. 264). For example, shubo-kyofu and jikoshu-kyofu are characterized as variants of taijin kyofusho, a fear that one's behavior will cause offense or embarrassment to others. Taijin kyofusho is recognized as a common anxiety-related disorder in Japanese culture (McNally et al., 1990). "Unspecified OCRD" is a second residual category intended to capture situations where symptoms fail to meet diagnostic criteria for any of the specific OCRD disorders, and the clinician does not provide detailed information about the symptom presentation (e.g., limited information available).

Comorbidity

OCD most often co-occurs with another psychiatric disorder (Bogotto et al., 1999; Hofmeijer-Sevink et al., 2013; Huang et al., 2014; Rasmussen & Eisen, 1992; Ruscio et al., 2010; Subramaniam et al., 2012; Torres, Prince, et al., 2006). OCD presenting without another co-occurring condition is the exception (see Lieb et al., 2019; Torres et al., 2017), and evaluations of adults with OCD have reported comorbidity rates of 90% or higher (Pigott et al., 1994; Pinto et al., 2006; Rusio et al., 2010; Torres et al., 2013). In addition to the high overall comorbidity rates, there are substantial differences in which disorders are most often comorbid.

FREQUENT COMORBID DISORDERS

Investigations of OCD comorbidity indicate that OCD most frequently co-occurs with an anxiety disorder, with some variability seen across specific anxiety disorders. Ruscio et al. (2010) reported a lifetime comorbidity with any anxiety disorder of 75.8%; for social anxiety disorder, 43.5%; specific phobia, 42.7%; separation anxiety disorder, 37.1%; panic disorder, 20.0%; and generalized anxiety disorder, 8.3%.

Mood disorders are also commonly comorbid with OCD. Possibly because of some of the methodological differences across studies, there has been variability in the estimates of major depression comorbidity, although estimates are consistently high (40.7%–51%; Osland et al., 2018; Ruscio et al., 2010; Subramaniam et al., 2020). More often, findings indicate that major depression occurs following the development of OCD (for a review, see Torres et al., 2017). When major depression is comorbid with OCD, OCD symptoms may become more severe over time (Rickelt et al., 2016), and recovery from the disorder is less likely (Marcks et al., 2011). Bipolar disorder and dysthymia have lower lifetime comorbidity rates by comparison, but rates are also high, 10.9% to 23.4% and 6% to 13.1%, respectively (Ferentinos et al., 2020; Osland et al., 2018; Ruscio et al., 2010; Subramaniam et al., 2020).

Although the co-occurrence of OCD and substance use disorders (SUDs) has been relatively understudied, the available information indicates OCD and SUDs have frequent comorbidity. In Calamari et al.'s (2012) earlier review, lifetime comorbidity rates between OCD and SUDs were high, and several studies reported a comorbidity rate of OCD with an alcohol use disorder of over 20%. Ruscio et al. (2010) estimated OCD and SUD comorbidity using United States epidemiologic data. Lifetime comorbidity with any SUD was 38.6%, and an identical estimate was found for comorbidity with alcohol abuse or dependence. Lifetime comorbidity with drug abuse or dependence was 21.7%.

High OCD and SUD comorbidity was found in an evaluation of a large health incidence database from the Netherlands. Lifetime OCD and SUD comorbidity was 28% for men and 7.2% for women (Blom et al., 2011). The SUD comorbidity rate for men with OCD was greater than the SUD comorbidity rate found in a psychiatric disorder comparison group of men with disorders other than OCD (Blom et al., 2011). Last, in a recent study of United States military veterans, Ecker et al. (2019) evaluated a large medical record database. Estimates of SUD comorbidity with OCD were again high for alcohol (36.7%), but lower for opioids (3.60%).

LESS FREQUENTLY COMORBID DISORDERS

OCD can co-occur with psychotic disorders, and comorbidity with OCD has been investigated both for psychotic disorders and for subclinical levels of the disorders' symptoms (for a review, see Mawn et al., 2020). Several reviews of the lifetime comorbidity of OCD with schizophrenia or schizophrenia spectrum disorders found above-chance co-occurrence (12% and 12.3%, respectively; Mawn et al., 2020; Swets et al., 2014). Although the causal mechanisms responsible for the comorbidity remain unclear, an initial diagnosis of either schizophrenia or OCD increases the risk for developing the other disorder. Compared to base rates of these disorders in the general population, individuals already diagnosed with schizophrenia have approximately seven times the risk of developing OCD, whereas individuals already diagnosed with OCD have 12 to 13 times greater risk of developing schizophrenia (Cederlöf et al., 2015). For individuals with OCD, the highest risk for developing schizophrenia appears to be within the first five years of initial diagnosis (Huang et al., 2014).

Estimates of personality disorders and OCD comorbidity vary considerably. In one large longitudinal study of 293 adults with OCD, Pinto and colleagues (2006) found that 38% of participants met diagnostic criteria for a personality disorder. In the British National Psychiatric Morbidity Survey of 2000, Torres, Moran, et al. (2006) reported that among the subsample of respondents with OCD (n = 108), 74% screened positive for a personality disorder. To provide needed clarification, Friborg and colleagues (2013) conducted a meta-analysis of studies that evaluated OCD comorbidity with personality pathology. Evaluations of clinical samples from both the United States and Europe were included in the meta-analysis. Friborg et al. (2013) found that OCD co-occurred with at least one personality disorder in over half the cases (52%). The most frequent personality disorder comorbidities were with obsessive-compulsive (20%), avoidant (17%), and dependent (10%) personality disorders.

Comorbidity rates among OCD and the other OCRD disorders have often been reported to be relatively low, although further study is warranted. Brakoulias and colleagues (2017) conducted a review of OCD and other OCRDs comorbidity that included studies conducted in seven different countries. The combined studies sample was large (*N* = 3,711) and all participants were adults with a primary OCD diagnosis. At the time of assessment, estimates of OCD comorbidity with other OCRD disorders were variable. Hoarding symptoms were often comorbid with OCD (23.4%). Comorbidity with the other OCRDs was much lower: excoriation disorder, 7.9%; trichotillomania, 6.2%; and BDD, 5.4%. As Brakoulias and colleagues noted, the diagnostic criteria for hoarding disorder that now appear in the *DSM-5* were not available at the time of the study, and the criteria used for the hoarding symptoms designation used in the review were not clear. For comparison, Brakoulias and colleagues found an at-time-of-assessment comorbidity between OCD and major depression of 28.4%, between OCD and obsessive-compulsive personality disorder of 24.5%, and between OCD and generalized anxiety disorder of 19.3%.

Culture or Individual Differences and OCD Phenomenology
The effects of culture or individual differences on OCD phenomenology has been understudied. This may result from the often-reported commonalities seen in OCD cross-nationally. This understanding is reflected in the brief description of OCD and culture that appears in the *DSM-5* (p. 240), which notes that the cross-national similarities seen with OCD include the gender distribution of the disorder, the age at which OCD begins, and the patterns of comorbidity. The possible cultural influences on symptom expression or content are acknowledged.

Several cross-national studies have evaluated the frequency of OCD symptom types. Contamination or doubting obsessions have been among the most frequently reported symptoms in clinical samples in Egypt (Okasha et al., 1994), Iran (Ghassemzadeh et al., 2002), Turkey (Tezcan & Millet, 1997), Mexico (Nicolini et al., 1992, 1997), and Taiwan (Juang & Liu, 2001), as well as in the United States (Rasmussen & Eisen, 1992; for reviews, see Fontenelle et al., 2004; McKay et al., 2004). When OCD symptom content is examined more closely, the effects of cultural differences are observed. Nedeljkovic et al. (2012) suggested in their review that the more frequent current concerns within a culture will influence obsessional symptom content. For example, when societal concerns have focused on asbestos pollution or on HIV infection, contamination obsessions are often observed to have related content. Similarly, Williams et al. (2017) concluded in their review that cultural taboos will influence the themes of intrusive thought. They suggested that in societies where, for example, homosexual orientation is considered controversial or undesirable, intrusive thoughts with related themes are more frequent.

Williams et al. (2012) noted that African Americans with OCD have reported higher levels of contamination obsessions than do Caucasian clinical samples. These concerns, according to Williams and colleagues, may reflect an internalization of European-Americans' fear of sharing surfaces with African Americans. Additional exploration of core OCD phenomenology found that African Americans were reported to be more likely to experience elevated disgust sensitivity (Olatunji et al., 2014), which may also help explain the more frequent contamination symptoms.

The Epidemiology of OCD

Prevalence

Although once believed to be an extremely rare disorder (Rasmussen & Eisen, 1992), OCD is now recognized as both a frequently occurring and often debilitating psychiatric condition (Mathers et al., 2006). In the United States, OCD has been estimated to have a lifetime prevalence rate of 2.3%, and a 12-month prevalence of 1.2% (Ruscio et al., 2010). Studies of other developed Western nations reported similar estimates. In the United Kingdom, lifetime prevalence was between 2% and 2.5% (Torres, Prince, et al., 2006). When broader cross-national comparisons are undertaken or non-Western countries are studied, prevalence estimates are more variable (Baxter et al., 2013; Fawcett et al., 2020).

Huang et al. (2014) evaluated OCD prevalence in Taiwan. The lifetime prevalence estimate was very low, 0.9%, which has been a consistent finding in evaluations of Asian cultures (Baxter et al., 2013 ; Fawcett et al., 2020). The reasons for this difference are unclear, although prevalence estimates for anxiety disorders are also reported to be low in studies of Eastern cultures (Baxter et al., 2013; Remes et al., 2016; Somers et al., 2006). Fontenelle et al. (2006) suggested that methodological differences may be responsible for the variability in estimated prevalence. In Fawcett and colleagues' (2020) quantitative review of OCD prevalence, the authors found lifetime prevalence rates by region that were relatively consistent and not significantly different: North America (2.1%), Asia/Pacific (1.2%), Europe (1.4%), and the Middle East (1.4%).

Recent investigations have examined several individual-difference factors' relationship to OCD prevalence (for a review, see Williams et al., 2017). Millet et al. (2017) conducted the only meta-analysis that evaluated OCD and anxiety disorder prevalence in transgender people. The Millet group found that lifetime prevalence rate estimates were approximately the same in the transgender population (1.9%–2.8%) as the rates in the cisgender population. Using data from the National Survey of American Life, a study of mental health disorders in African Americans (Jackson et al., 2004), Himle and colleagues

(2008) evaluated the prevalence of OCD, and their study is the only epidemiologic evaluation of OCD prevalence conducted with African American and Caribbean American populations to date. The lifetime prevalence rate of OCD was 1.63%, and the 12-month rate was 1.49%. Gender differences were not found, although rates of comorbidity were very high (95%).

Age at Onset
OCD had been understood to have a relatively uniform onset in early adulthood. Today, the age of onset of OCD is known to be more variable, although study results have consistently shown that the disorder begins most often early in life (Ruscio et al., 2010). Onset after age 40 occurs infrequently, although there is some evidence that there may be a small subgroup of individuals who experience OCD onset as older adults (for a review, see Chapter 25).

In an evaluation of epidemiologic data from the United States, Ruscio et al. (2010) reported a mean age at onset for OCD of 19.5 years, although a significant gender difference was identified. Males had an earlier onset and were more likely to report childhood onset. Approximately a quarter of the male sample reported onset before age 10. In a meta-analysis of studies of the age of onset of OCD, Taylor (2011) found support for two patterns using latent profile analysis. The early-onset group had a mean onset at approximately age 11, while the late-onset group's mean onset was at age 23. Most cases were classified as early-onset (76%), and most early-onset cases were in males, had greater OCD symptom severity, and had a greater likelihood that their OCD would be comorbid with tic disorders. An early-onset subtype was also recognized in a recent review of OCD epidemiology by Sharma and Math (2019).

Mathes et al. (2019) noted in their review of gender differences in the age of onset of OCD that the results of studies have been inconsistent. While differences were found in multiple studies that suggested earlier onset for men (Fineberg et al., 2013; Lieb et al., 2019; Mathes et al., 2019; Ruscio et al., 2010; Torres et al., 2020), no gender differences were identified in several other studies (Kenyon & Eaton, 2015; Torresan et al., 2013; Vivian et al., 2014). Dell'Osso et al. (2017) evaluated a large multinational clinical sample (N = 416) of individuals with OCD presenting for treatment. Participants had a primary OCD diagnosis and the sample's mean age was 42 years (SD = 12.6). The investigators evaluated the relationship between the participants' current age and their age at onset of OCD. The mean age at onset was approximately 19. Although only 6% of the large, treatment-seeking clinical sample were 65 years old or older, older people reported a significantly later age at onset compared to younger patients (approximately age 29).

Life Course and Associated Impairment
OCD is commonly understood as a chronic disorder with waxing and waning symptom severity (Sharma & Math, 2019). Although the life course of untreated OCD has been

understudied, Calamari et al. (2012) concluded in their review that OCD symptoms are most likely to continue at clinical levels of severity and to follow a chronic course. Rasmussen and Tsuang (1986) reported that only 2% of people with OCD experienced what they called an episodic course (i.e., periods of full remission). In a long-term follow-up study of treated OCD patients, Skoog and Skoog (1999) followed participants over approximately 40 years. Although 83% of their sample was judged to have experienced a meaningful reduction in symptoms, only 20% were considered recovered.

Several more recent investigations of the life course of OCD have reported different patterns. Fineberg et al. (2013) followed a population sample in Switzerland over 30 years. OCD was present in 5% of the sample. The investigators used stringent criteria for remission, which was the absence of OCD symptoms for three consecutive years. Over 60% of the sample were judged to have experienced a complete remission of OCD symptoms, although only a third of the sample were treated. Predictors of remission were a shorter duration of OCD and not receiving treatment, although analyses revealed that individuals with more severe symptoms more often sought treatment.

The majority of contemporary studies suggest that individuals who have received treatment for their OCD have fewer continuing symptoms, which is not surprising. In a recent meta-analysis of the resilience of treatment effects, at five-year follow-up, the average remission rate was 53% (Sharma et al., 2014). Treatment outcomes are negatively affected by comorbidity (Sharma et al., 2014), and comorbidity with depression has been identified as particularly problematic (Marcks et al., 2011; Rickelt et al., 2016). A more resilient treatment effect is associated with being married (Marcks et al., 2011), shorter duration of illness, and lower symptom severity upon treatment initiation (Sharma et al., 2014). Sharma and Math (2019) concluded in their review of the long-term course of OCD that the current prognosis is positive. More than half of the people with OCD experience disorder remission. Sharma and Math concluded that remission was importantly related to early intensive intervention. Additionally, Sharma and Math noted the importance of evaluating treatment effectiveness by examining both symptom reduction and change in quality of life (QoL), because symptom reduction does not guarantee improvements in QoL (Noberg et al., 2008). In the growing number of studies that have evaluated QoL effects, treatment-related improvements are found, which may often be mediated by decreased depression symptoms (Sharma & Math, 2019).

OCD has been consistently identified as one of the most disabling forms of mental illness (Torres et al., 2006). OCD negatively impacts functioning across life domains, diminishing QoL (for reviews, see Lieb et al., 2019; Torres et al., 2017). OCD may have its greatest negative effects on relationships and social functioning. For example, OCD has been associated with not marrying or marrying later in life (Steketee, 1997). Even individuals with subclinical OCD symptoms report a reduced ability to fulfill occupational and social responsibilities (Lieb et al., 2019). Furthermore, OCD is often comorbid with other conditions. When comorbidity is present (especially major depression), a lower level of QoL results (Subramaniam et al., 2013) and risk of suicide increases (Angelakis et al., 2015; Pellegrini et al., 2020).

A marker of OCD's impact on an affected individual's life is the condition's association with suicide. In two recent meta-analyses, OCD has been strongly associated with suicidality. Angelakis et al. (2015) found that the relationship between OCD and suicide was associated with large effects, both for suicidal ideation and for suicide attempts. Across the studies reviewed, the median rate of suicidal ideation was 27.9%, and the median rate of suicide attempts was 10.3%. Pellegrini and colleagues (2020) reported similar findings in their review. Approximately 13% of patients with OCD had attempted suicide in their lifetime.

Summary and Future Directions

Early in history, careful observers of human behavior identified the distinct characteristics of OCD. The characteristics included the frequent experience of unwanted thoughts and co-occurring repetitive compulsive behaviors, and this basic description remains central to the contemporary conceptualization and definition of OCD. Descriptions of OCD evolved as the *DSM* was revised. The initial vague description of OCD found in *DSM-I* in 1952 was replaced by the first clear description and definition of the condition in *DSM-III*, which classified OCD as an anxiety disorder. Refinements in the descriptions of obsessions and compulsions followed, as did more detailed descriptions of the many forms that obsessions or compulsions might take. In more recent versions of the *DSM* taxonomy, the frequent occurrence of mental rituals was recognized, as was their functional equivalence to overt compulsive behaviors. The functional relationship between the distress-increasing nature of obsessions and distress-reducing role of compulsions was more clearly acknowledged in the most recent *DSM* revisions.

Several decades of research and theory development relating to the OCD spectrum concept precipitated the significant changes in the classification of OCD that took place in *DSM-5*. The OCD spectrum is predicated on ideas that other disorders are importantly related to OCD, with commonalities in phenomenology, overlapping etiologic processes, and a similar response to specific treatments. Further, OCD is hypothesized to be frequently comorbid with disorders judged to be on its spectrum. Criticisms of the broad OCD spectrum model include contentions that the phenomenological similarities between OCD and many of the purported spectrum conditions are superficial, and that comorbidity data better connect OCD to the anxiety disorders.

Other information reviewed in the chapter is relevant to considerations of whether OCD is an anxiety disorder or not. The *ICD* taxonomy has long judged OCD's phenomenology as sufficiently distinct to group it separately from anxiety disorders. Summerfeldt and colleagues' (2004, 2014) work suggests that incompleteness and harm avoidance are two fundamental motivations in OCD, only one of which is shared with the anxiety disorders.

OCD comorbidity is a fundamental aspect of the disorder's phenomenology as well as another dimension of its heterogeneity. Both conditions highly comorbid with OCD as well as conditions that co-occur less frequently have very high comorbidity rates reported in most investigations. Although studies of the age at onset of OCD have consistently shown that OCD most often begins early in life, here, too, more recent investigations reveal more variability than was previously understood. Most studies suggest that the early-onset subtype of OCD may occur more often, is more likely to occur in males, and often has more severe symptoms. Last, OCD has long been associated with substantial disability.

The significant heterogeneity of OCD across multiple domains is a fundamental and continuing challenge. This heterogeneity confronts the clinician attempting to identify or treat the condition, as well as researchers working to better understand the disorder. Significant gains have been made in understanding OCD, but many challenges remain.

References

Abramowitz, J. S. (2018). Presidential address: Are the obsessive-compulsive related disorders related to obsessive-compulsive disorder? A critical look at DSM-5's new category. *Behavior Therapy, 49*(1), 1–11.

Abramowitz, J. S., & Jacoby, R. J. (2014). Obsessive-compulsive disorder in the DSM-5. *Clinical Psychology: Science and Practice, 21*(3), 221–235.

Abramowitz, J. S., & Mahaffey, B. L. (2011). The obsessive-compulsive disorder spectrum. In D. H. Barlow (Ed.), *The Oxford handbook of clinical psychology* (pp. 311–333). Oxford University Press.

Alvarenga, P. G., Hounie, A. G., Mercadante, M. T., Miguel, E. C., & Conceicao, M. (2007). Obsessive-compulsive disorder: A historical overview. In E. A. Storch, G. R. Geffken, & T. K. Murphy (Eds.), *Handbook of child and adolescent obsessive-compulsive disorder* (pp. 1–15). Lawrewnce Erlbaum.

American Psychiatric Association (APA). (1952). *Diagnostic and statistical manual of mental disorders*.

American Psychiatric Association (APA). (1968). *Diagnostic and statistical manual of mental disorders* (2nd ed.).

American Psychiatric Association (APA). (1980). *Diagnostic and Statistical Manual of Mental Disorders* (3rd ed.).

American Psychiatric Association (APA). (1987). *Diagnostic and statistical manual of mental disorders* (3rd ed., revised).

American Psychiatric Association (APA). (1994). *Diagnostic and statistical manual of mental disorders* (4th ed.).

American Psychiatric Association (APA). (2000). *Diagnostic and statistical manual of mental disorders* (4th ed., text revision).

American Psychiatric Association (APA). (2013). *Diagnostic and statistical manual of mental disorders* (5th ed.).

Angelakis, I., Gooding, P., Tarrier, N., & Panagioti, M. (2015). Suicidality in obsessive compulsive disorder (OCD): A systematic review and meta-analysis. *Clinical Psychology Review, 39*, 1–15.

Antony, M. M., Purdon, C., & Summerfeldt, L. J. (Eds.). (2007). *Psychological treatment of obsessive-compulsive disorder: Fundamentals and beyond. American Psychological Association*. https://doi.org/10.1037/11543-000

Baxter, A. J., Scott, K. M., Vos, T., & Whiteford, H. A. (2013). Global prevalence of anxiety disorders: A systematic review and meta-regression. *Psychological Medicine, 43*(5), 897–910. https://doi.org/10.1017/S003329171200147X

Bayer, R., & Spitzer, R. L. (1985). Neurosis, psychodynamics, and DSM-III: A history of the controversy. *Archives of General Psychiatry, 42*(2), 187–196.

Beard, G. (1869). Neurasthenia, or nervous exhaustion. *The Boston Medical and Surgical Journal, 80*(13), 217–221.

Beck, A. T., Ward, C. H., Mendelson, M., Mock, J. E., & Erbaugh, J. K. (1962). Reliability of psychiatric diagnoses: 2. A study of consistency of clinical judgments and ratings. *The American Journal of Psychiatry, 119*(4), 351–357.

Bienvenu, O. J., Samuels, J. F., Riddle, M. A., Hoehn-Saric, R., Liang, K.-Y., Cullen, B. A. M., Grados, M. A., & Nestadt, G. (2000). The relationship of obsessive-compulsive disorder to possible spectrum disorders: Results from a family study. *Biological Psychiatry, 48*(4), 287–293. https://doi.org/10.1016/S0006-3223(00)00831-3

Blom, R. M., Koeter, M., van den Brink, W., de Graaf, R., Ten Have, M., & Denys, D. (2011). Co-occurrence of obsessive-compulsive disorder and substance use disorder in the general population. *Addiction, 106*(12), 2178–2185.

Bogetto, F., Venturello, S., Albert, U., Maina, G., & Ravizza, L. (1999). Gender-related clinical differences in obsessive-compulsive disorder. *European Psychiatry, 14*(8), 434–441.

Brakoulias, V., Starcevic, V., Belloch, A., Brown, C., Ferrao, Y. A., Fontenelle, L. F., Lochner, C., Marazziti, D., Matsunaga, H., Miguel, E. C., Reddy, Y. C. J., do Rosario, M. C., Shavitt, R. G., Shyam Sundar, A., Stein, D. J., Torres, A. R., & Viswasam, K. (2017). Comorbidity, age of onset and suicidality in obsessive–compulsive disorder (OCD): An international collaboration. *Comprehensive Psychiatry, 76*, 79–86. https://doi.org/10.1016/j.comppsych.2017.04.002

Bühler, K. E., & Heim, G. (2001). Introduction générale à la psychopathologie et à la psychothérapie de Pierre Janet [General introduction to Pierre Janet's psychopathology and psychotherapy]. *Annales Médico-Psychologiques, 159*(4), 261–272. https://doi.org/10.1016/S0003-4487(01)00014-2

Burton, R. (1628. *The anatomy of melancholy* (3rd ed.). Thomas Tegg.

Bynum, W. F., Porter, R., & Shepherd, M. (2005). *The anatomy of madness: Essays in the history of psychiatry*. Taylor & Francis.

Calamari, J. E., Chik, H. M., Ponttarelli, N. K., & DeJong, B. L. (2012). Phenomenology and epidemiology of obsessive-compulsive disorder. In G. Steketee (Ed.), *The Oxford handbook of obsessive compulsive and spectrum disorders* (pp. 11–47). Oxford University Press.

Carr, A. T. (1974). Compulsive neurosis: A review of the literature. *Psychological Bulletin, 81*(5), 311.

Cederlöf, M., Lichtenstein, P., Larsson, H., Boman, M., Rück, C., Landén, M., & Mataix-Cols, D. (2015). Obsessive-compulsive disorder, psychosis, and bipolarity: A longitudinal cohort and multigenerational family study. *Schizophrenia Bulletin, 41*(5), 1076–1083.

Coles, M. E., Frost, R. O., Heimberg, R. G., & Rhéaume, J. (2003). "Not just right experiences": Perfectionism, obsessive-compulsive features and general psychopathology. *Behaviour Research and Therapy, 41*(6), 681–700.

Dagonet, M. (1870). Des impulsions dans la folie et de la folie impulsive. *Annales Médico Psychologiques, 4*, 215.

Davine, T., Snorrason, I., Berlin, G., Harvey, A. M., Lotfi, S., & Lee, H. (2019). Development of a picture-based measure for "not just right" experiences associated with compulsive sorting, ordering, and arranging. *Cognitive Therapy and Research, 43*(2), 481–497.

Dell'Osso, B., Benatti, B., Rodriguez, C. I., Arici, C., Palazzo, C., Altamura, A. C., Hollander, E., Fineberg, N., Stein, D. J., Nicolini, H., Lanzagorta, N., Marazziti, D., Pallanti, S., Van Ameringen, M., Lochner, C., Karamustafalioglu, O., Hranov, L., Figee, M., Drummond, L., . . . Zohar, J. (2017). Obsessive-compulsive disorder in the elderly: A report from the International College of Obsessive-Compulsive Spectrum Disorders (ICOCS). *European Psychiatry, 45*, 36–40. https://doi.org/10.1016/j.eurpsy.2017.06.008

Doron, G., & Derby, D. (2017). Assessment and treatment of relationship-related OCD symptoms (ROCD): A modular approach. In J. S. Abramowitz, D. McKay, & E. A. Storch (Eds.), *The Wiley handbook of obsessive-compulsive disorders* (Vol. 1, pp. 547–564). Wiley.

Ecker, A. H., Stanley, M. A., Smith, T. L., Teng, E. J., Fletcher, T. L., Van Kirk, N., Amspoker, A. B., Walder, A., McIngvale, E., & Lindsay, J. A. (2019). Co-occurrence of obsessive-compulsive disorder and substance use disorders among U.S. veterans: Prevalence and mental health utilization. *Journal of Cognitive Psychotherapy, 33*(1), 23–32. https://doi.org/10.1891/0889-8391.33.1.23

Eisen, J. L., & Steketee, G. (1998). Course of illness in obsessive-compulsive disorder. In L. J. Dickstein, M. B. Riba, & J. M. Oldham (Eds.), *Review of psychiatry* (Vol. 16, pp. III-73–III-95). American Psychiatric Press.

Fawcett, E. J., Power, H., & Fawcett, J. M. (2020). Women are at greater risk of OCD than men: A meta-analytic review of OCD prevalence worldwide. *The Journal of Clinical Psychiatry, 81*(4), 1–13.

Ferentinos, P., Mendlowicz, M., & Versiani, M. (2006). The descriptive epidemiology of obsessive-compulsive disorder. *Progress in Neuro-Psychophmacology & Biological Psychiatry, 30*, 327–337.

Ferentinos, P., Preti, A., Veroniki, A. A., Pitsalidis, K. G., Theofilidis, A. T., Antoniou, A., & Fountoulakis, K. N. (2020). Comorbidity of obsessive-compulsive disorder in bipolar spectrum disorders: Systematic review and meta-analysis of its prevalence. *Journal of Affective Disorders, 263*, 193–208.

Fineberg, N. A., Hengartner, M. P., Bergbaum, C. E., Gale, T. M., Gamma, A., Ajdacic-Gross, V., Rössler, W., & Angst, J. (2013). A prospective population-based cohort study of the prevalence, incidence and impact of obsessive-compulsive symptomatology. *International Journal of Psychiatry in Clinical Practice*, *17*(3), 170–178. https://doi.org/10.3109/13651501.2012.755206

Foa, E. B., Abramowitz, J. S., Franklin, M. E., & Kozak, M. J. (1999). Feared consequences, fixity of belief, and treatment outcome in patients with obsessive-compulsive disorder. *Behavior Therapy*, *30*(4), 717–724.

Foa, E. B., & Kozak, M. J. (1995). DSM-IV field trial: Obsessive-compulsive disorder. *The American Journal of Psychiatry*, *152*(1), 90–96.

Foa, E. B., Kozak, M. J., Goodman, W. K., Hollander, E., Jenike, M. A., & Rasmussen, S. A. (1995). "DSM-IV field trial: Obsessive-compulsive disorder": Correction. *The American Journal of Psychiatry*, *152*(4), 654.

Fontenelle, L. F., Mendlowicz, M. V., Marques, C., & Versiani, M. (2004). Trans-cultural aspects of obsessive-compulsive disorder: A description of a Brazilian sample and a systematic review of international clinical studies. *Journal of Psychiatric Research*, *38*(4), 403–411.

Freud, S. (1909). Notes upon a case of obsessional neurosis (J. Strarchy, Trans.). In J. Strachey (Ed.), *The standard edition of the complete psychological works of Sigmund Freud, Volume 10* (pp. 151–249). Hogarth Press (Original work published 1958).

Freud, S. (1913). The disposition to obsessional neurosis: A contribution to the problem of choice of neurosis (J. Strarchy, Trans.). In J. Strachey (Ed.), *The standard edition of the complete psychological works of Sigmund Freud, Volume 12* (pp. 311–326). Hogarth Press (Original work published 1958).

Freud, S. (1958). Uber die Berechtigung, von der Neurasthenie einen bestimmter Symptomen-komplex als "Angstneurose" abzutrennen. In J. Starchey (Ed.), *The standard edition of the complete works of Sigmund Freud, Vol. 3* (pp. 90–115). Hogarth Press (Original work published 1895).

Friborg, O., Martinussen, M., Kaiser, S., Øvergård, K. T., & Rosenvinge, J. H. (2013). Comorbidity of personality disorders in anxiety disorders: A meta-analysis of 30 years of research. *Journal of Affective Disorders*, *145*(2), 143–155.

Frost, R. O., & Hartl, T. L. (1996). A cognitive-behavioral model of compulsive hoarding. *Behaviour Research and Therapy*, *34*(4), 341–350.

Frost, R. O., & Steketee, G. (2002). *Cognitive approaches to obsessions and compulsions: Theory, assessment, and treatment*. Elsevier.

Gahr, M., Hiemke, C., & Kölle, M. A. (2020). Development of obsessive-compulsive symptoms following abrupt discontinuation of venlafaxine. *Frontiers in Psychiatry*, *11*, 32.

Ghassemzadeh, H., Mojtabai, R., Khamseh, A., Ebrahimkhani, N., Issazadegan, A., & Saif-Nobakht, Z. (2002). Symptoms of obsessive-compulsive disorder in a sample of Iranian patients. *International Journal of Social Psychiatry*, *48*(1), 20–28.

Guzick, A. G., Reid, A. M., Balki, A. M., Flores, C., Hancock-Smith, A. D., Olsen, B., Muller, G., Geffken, G. R., & McNamara, J. P. H. (2017). Diagnostic description and prevalence. In J. S. Abramowitz, D. McKay, & E. A. Storch (Eds.), *The Wiley handbook of obsessive compulsive disorders* (pp. 24–43). Wiley Blackwell. https://doi.org/10.1002/9781118890233.ch2

Himle, J. A., Muroff, J. R., Taylor, R. J., Baser, R. E., Abelson, J. M., Hanna, G. L., Abelson, J. L., & Jackson, J. S. (2008). Obsessive-compulsive disorder among African Americans and blacks of Caribbean descent: Results from the National Survey of American Life. *Depression and Anxiety*, *25*(12), 993–1005. https://doi.org/10.1002/da.20434

Hollander, E. (1993). Obsessive-compulsive spectrum disorders: An overview. *Psychiatric Annals*, *23*(7), 355–358.

Hollander, E. (2005). Obsessive-compulsive disorder and spectrum cross the life span. *International Journal of Psychiatry in Clinical Practice*, *9*(2), 79–86.

Hollander, E., Braun, A., & Simeon, D. (2008). Should OCD leave the anxiety disorders in DSM-V? The case for obsessive compulsive-related disorders. *Depression and Anxiety*, *25*(4), 317–329.

Hollander, E., Friedberg, J. P., Wasserman, S., Yeh, C., & Iyengar, R. (2005). The case for the OCD spectrum. In J. S. Abramowitz & A. C. Houts (Eds.), *Concepts and controversies in obsessive-compulsive disorder* (pp. 95–118). Springer Science + Business Media.

Hollander, E., Kim, S., Braun, A., Simeon, D., & Zohar, J. (2009). Cross-cutting issues and future directions for the OCD spectrum. *Psychiatry Research*, *170*(1), 3–6.

Huang, L., Tsai, K., Wang, H., Sung, P., Wu, M., Hung, K., & Lin, S. (2014). Prevalence, incidence, and comorbidity of clinically diagnosed obsessive-compulsive disorder in Taiwan: A national population-based study. *Psychiatry Research*, *220*(1-2), 335–341.

Jackson, J. S., Torres, M., Caldwell, C. H., Neighbors, H. W., Nesse, R. M., Taylor, R. J., Trierweiler, S. J., & Williams, D. R. (2004). The National Survey of American Life: A study of racial, ethnic and cultural influences on mental disorders and mental health. *International Journal of Methods in Psychiatric Research*, *13*(4), 196–207.

Juang, Y., & Liu, C. (2001). Phenomenology of obsessive-compulsive disorder in Taiwan. *Psychiatry and Clinical Neurosciences*, *55*(6), 623–627.

Kenyon, K. M., & Eaton, W. O. (2015). Age at child obsessive-compulsive disorder onset and its relation to gender, symptom severity, and family functioning. *Archives of Scientific Psychology*, *3*(1), 150.

Krochmalik, A., & Menzies, R. G. (2003). The classification and diagnosis of obsessive-compulsive disorder. *Obsessive-Compulsive Research and Therapy*, *35*, 793–802.

Leckman, J. F., Walker, D. E., Goodman, W. K., Pauls, D. L., & Cohen, D. J. (1994). "Just right" perceptions associated with compulsive behavior in Tourette's syndrome. *The American Journal of Psychiatry*, *151*(5), 675–680.

Lieb, R., Hofer, P. D., & Wahl, K. (2019). Epidemiology of obsessive-compulsive disorder. In L. Fontenelle & M. Yücel (Eds.), *A transdiagnostic approach to obsessions, compulsions and related phenomena* (pp. 113–127). Cambridge University Press.

Marcks, B. A., Weisberg, R. B., Dyck, I., & Keller, M. B. (2011). Longitudinal course of obsessive-compulsive disorder in patients with anxiety disorders: A 15-year prospective follow-up study. *Comprehensive Psychiatry*, *52*(6), 670–677.

Mathers, C. D., & Loncar, D. (2006). Projections of global mortality and burden of disease from 2002 to 2030. *PLOS Medicine*, *3*(11), e442.

Mathes, B. M., Morabito, D. M., & Schmidt, N. B. (2019). Epidemiological and clinical gender differences in OCD. *Current Psychiatry Reports*, *21*(5), 36.

Mawn, L., Campbell, T., Aynsworth, C., Beckwith, H., Luce, A., Barclay, N., Dodgeson, G., & Freeston, M. H. (2020). Comorbidity of obsessive-compulsive and psychotic experiences: A systematic review and meta-analysis. *Journal of Obsessive-Compulsive and Related Disorders*, *26*, 1–18.

McKay, D., Abramowitz, J. S., Calamari, J. E., Kyrios, M., Radomsky, A., Sookman, D., Taylor, S., & Wilhelm, S. (2004). A critical evaluation of obsessive-compulsive disorder subtypes: Symptoms versus mechanisms. *Clinical Psychology Review*, *24*(3), 283–313.

McNally, R. J., Cassiday, K. L., & Calamari, J. E. (1990). Taijin-kyofu-sho in a Black American woman: Behavioral treatment of a "culture-bound" anxiety disorder. *Journal of Anxiety Disorders*, *4*(1), 83–87.

Millet, N., Longworth, J., & Arcelus, J. (2017). Prevalence of anxiety symptoms and disorders in the transgender population: A systematic review of the literature. *International Journal of Transgenderism*, *18*(1), 27–38.

Millon, T. (1983). The DSM-III: An insider's perspective. *American Psychologist*, *38*(7), 804.

Montgomery, S. A. (1993). Obsessive compulsive disorder is not an anxiety disorder. *International Clinical Psychopharmacology*, *8*(Suppl. 1), 57–62.

Mullen, J. J. (1927). *Psychological factors in the pastoral treatment of scruples: Studies in psychology and psychiatry*. Catholic University of America.

Nathan, P. E., Andberg, M. M., Behan, P. O., & Patch, V. D. (1969). Thirty-two observers and one patient: A study of diagnostic reliability. *Journal of Clinical Psychology*, *25*, 9–15.

Nedeljkovic, M., Moulding, R., Foroughi, E., Kyrios, M., & Doron, G. (2012). Cultural issues in understanding and treating obsessive compulsive and spectrum disorders. In G. Steketee (Ed.), *The Oxford handbook of obsessive compulsive and spectrum disorders* (pp. 1–66). Oxford University Press.

Neziroglu, F. A., & Yaryura-Tobias, J. A. (1997). *Over and over again: Understanding obsessive-compulsive disorder*. Jossey-Bass.

Nicolini, H., Mejia, J. M., Merino, J., & Decarmona, M. S. (1992). Study of the obsessive-compulsive patient in a Mexican sample: Experience of the Mexican institute of psychiatry. *Salud Mental*, *15*(4), 1–11.

Nicolini, H., Orozco, B., Giuffra, L., Páez, F., Mejía, J., Sánchez de Carmona, M., Sidenberg, D., & Ramón de la Fuente, J. (1997). Age of onset, gender and severity in obsessive-compulsive disorder: Study of a Mexican population. *Salud Mental*, *20*(2), 1–4.

Norberg, M. M., Calamari, J. E., Cohen, R. J., & Riemann, B. C. (2008). Quality of life in obsessive-compulsive disorder: An evaluation of impairment and a preliminary analysis of the ameliorating effects of treatment. *Depression and Anxiety, 25*(3), 248–259.

O'Flaherty, V. M. (1966). *How to cure scruples*. Bruce Publishing Company.

Okasha, A., Saad, A., Khalil, A. H., El Dawla, A. S., & Yehia, N. (1994). Phenomenology of obsessive-compulsive disorder: A transcultural study. *Comprehensive Psychiatry, 35*(3), 191–197.

Olatunji, B. O., Tomarken, A., & Zhao, M. (2014). Effects of exposure to stereotype cues on contamination aversion and avoidance in African Americans. *Journal of Social and Clinical Psychology, 33*(3), 229–249.

Osland, S., Arnold, P. D., & Pringsheim, T. (2018). The prevalence of diagnosed obsessive compulsive disorder and associated comorbidities: A population-based Canadian study. *Psychiatry Research, 268*, 137–142.

Pellegrini, L., Maietti, E., Rucci, P., Casadei, G., Maina, G., Fineberg, N. A., & Albert, U. (2020). Suicide attempts and suicidal ideation in patients with obsessive-compulsive disorder: A systematic review and meta-analysis. *Journal of Affective Disorders, 276*, 1001–1021.

Pertusa, A., Frost, R. O., Fullana, M. A., Samuels, J., Steketee, G., Tolin, D., Saxena, S., Leckman, J. F., &Mataix-Cols, D. (2010). Refining the diagnostic boundaries of compulsive hoarding: A critical review. *Clinical Psychology Review, 30*(4), 371–386.

Phillips, K. A., Wilhelm, S., Koran, L. M., Didie, E. R., Fallon, B. A., Feusner, J., & Stein, D. J. (2010). Body dysmorphic disorder: Some key issues for DSM-V. *Depression and Anxiety, 27*(6), 573–591.

Pigott, T. A., L'Heureux, F., Dubbert, B., Bernstein, S., & Murphy, D. L. (1994). Obsessive compulsive disorder: Comorbid conditions. *The Journal of Clinical Psychiatry, 55*(Suppl.), 15–32.

Pinto, A., Mancebo, M. C., Eisen, J. L., Pagano, M. E., & Rasmussen, S. A. (2006). The Brown Longitudinal Obsessive-Compulsive Study: Clinical features and symptoms of the sample at intake. *The Journal of Clinical Psychiatry, 67*(5), 703–711.

Pitman, R. K. (1987). Pierre Janet on obsessive-compulsive disorder (1903): Review and commentary. *Archives of General Psychiatry, 44*(3), 226–232.

Rachman, S. (1993). Obsessions, responsibility, and guilt. *Behaviour Research and Therapy, 32*, 149–154.

Rachman, S. (1963). *Critical essays on psychoanalysis*. Pergamon Press.

Rachman, S. (1997). A cognitive theory of obsessions. *Behaviour Research and Therapy, 35*(9), 793–802.

Rachman, S. (1998). A cognitive theory of obsessions: Elaborations. *Behaviour Research and Therapy, 36*(4), 385–401.

Rachman, S. (2007). Treating religious, sexual, and aggressive obsessions. In M. M. Anthony, C. Purdon, & L. J. Summerfeldt (Eds.), *Psychological treatment of obsessive-compulsive disorder: Fundamentals and beyond* (pp. 209–229). American Psychological Association.

Rapoport, J. L. (1989). *Obsessive-compulsive disorder in children and adolescents*. American Psychiatric Press.

Rapoport, J. L. (1991). Recent advances in obsessive-compulsive disorder. *Neuropsychopharmacology, 5*(1), 1–10.

Rasmussen, S. A., & Eisen, J. L. (1992). The epidemiology and clinical features of obsessive-compulsive disorder. *Psychiatric Clinics, 15*(4), 743–758.

Rasmussen, S. A., & Tsuang, M. T. (1986). Clinical characteristics and family history in DSM-III obsessive-compulsive disorder. *The American Journal of Psychiatry, 143*, 317–322.

Remes, O., Brayne, C., Van Der Linde, R., & Lafortune, L. (2016). A systematic review of reviews on the prevalence of anxiety disorders in adult populations. *Brain and Behavior, 6*(7), e00497.

Rickelt, J., Viechtbauer, W., Lieverse, R., Overbeek, T., van Balkom, A. J., van Oppen, P., van den Heuvel, O. A., Marcelis, M., Eikelenboom, M., Tibi, L., & Schruers, K. R. (2016). The relation between depressive and obsessive-compulsive symptoms in obsessive-compulsive disorder: Results from a large, naturalistic follow-up study. *Journal of Affective Disorders, 203*, 241–247. https://doi.org/10.1016/j.jad.2016.06.009

Rowa, K., Antony, M. M., & Swinson, R. P. (2007). Exposure and response prevention. In M. M. Anthony, C. Purdon, & L. J. Summerfeldt (Eds.), *Psychological treatment of obsessive-compulsive disorder: Fundamentals and beyond* (pp. 79–109). American Psychological Association.

Ruscio, A. M., Stein, D. J., Chiu, W. T., & Kessler, R. C. (2010). The epidemiology of obsessive-compulsive disorder in the National Comorbidity Survey Replication. *Molecular Psychiatry, 15*(1), 53–63.

Sharma, E., & Math, S. B. (2019). Course and outcome of obsessive-compulsive disorder. *Indian Journal of Psychiatry, 61*, S43–S50.

Sharma, E., Thennarasu, K., & Reddy, Y. C. (2014). Long-term outcome of obsessive-compulsive disorder in adults: A meta-analysis. *The Journal of Clinical Psychiatry, 75*(9), 1019–1027.

Simpson, H. B., & Reddy, Y. (2014). Obsessive-compulsive disorder for ICD-11: Proposed changes to the diagnostic guidelines and specifiers. *Brazilian Journal of Psychiatry, 36*, 3–13.

Skoog, G., & Skoog, I. (1999). A 40-year follow-up of patients with obsessive-compulsive disorder. *Archives of General Psychiatry, 56*(2), 121–127.

Somers, J. M., Goldner, E. M., Waraich, P., & Hsu, L. (2006). Prevalence and incidence studies of anxiety disorders: A systematic review of the literature. *The Canadian Journal of Psychiatry, 51*(2), 100–113.

Spitzer, R. L., Williams, J. B., & Skodol, A. E. (1980). DSM-III: The major achievements and an overview. *The American Journal of Psychiatry, 137*, 151–164.

Steketee, G. (1997). Disability and family burden in obsessive-compulsive disorder. *The Canadian Journal of Psychiatry, 42*(9), 919–928.

Steketee, G., & Frost, R. (2003). Compulsive hoarding: Current status of the research. *Clinical Psychology Review, 23*(7), 905–927.

Storch, E. A., Abramowitz, J., & Goodman, W. K. (2008). Where does obsessive-compulsive disorder belong in DSM-V? *Depression and Anxiety, 25*(4), 336–347.

Storch, E. A., Abramowitz, J. S., & Keeley, M. (2009). Correlates and mediators of functional disability in obsessive-compulsive disorder. *Depression and Anxiety, 26*(9), 806–813.

Storch, E. A., Larson, M. J., Muroff, J., Caporino, N., Geller, D., Reid, J. M., Morgan, J., Jordan, P., & Murphy, T. K. (2010). Predictors of functional impairment in pediatric obsessive-compulsive disorder. *Journal of Anxiety Disorders, 24*(2), 275–283. https://doi.org/10.1016/j.janxdis.2009.12.004

Subramaniam, M., Abdin, E., Vaingankar, J. A., & Chong, S. A. (2012). Obsessive-compulsive disorder: Prevalence, correlates, help-seeking and quality of life in a multiracial Asian population. *Social Psychiatry and Psychiatric Epidemiology, 47*(12), 2035–2043.

Subramaniam, M., Abdin, E., Vaingankar, J., Shafie, S., Chang, S., Seow, E., Chua, B. Y., Jeyagurunathan, A., Heng, D., Kwok, K. W., & Chong, S. A. (2020). Obsessive-compulsive disorder in Singapore: Prevalence, comorbidity, quality of life and social support. *Annals of the Academy of Medicine, Singapore, 49*(1), 15–25.

Subramaniam, M., Soh, P., Vaingankar, J. A., Picco, L., & Chong, S. A. (2013). Quality of life in obsessive-compulsive disorder: Impact of the disorder and of treatment. *CNS Drugs, 27*(5), 367–383.

Summerfeldt, L. J. (2004). Understanding and treating incompleteness in obsessive-compulsive disorder. *Journal of Clinical Psychology, 60*(11), 1155–1168. https://doi.org/10.1002/jclp.20080

Summerfeldt, L. J., Hood, K., Antony, M. M., Richter, M. A., & Swinson, R. P. (2004). Impulsivity in obsessive-compulsive disorder: Comparisons with other anxiety disorders and within tic-related subgroups. *Personality and Individual Differences, 36*(3), 539–553.

Summerfeldt, L. J., Kloosterman, P. H., Antony, M. M., & Swinson, R. P. (2014). Examining an obsessive-compulsive core dimensions model: Structural validity of harm avoidance and incompleteness. *Journal of Obsessive-Compulsive and Related Disorders, 3*(2), 83–94.

Swets, M., Dekker, J., van Emmerik-van Oortmerssen, K., Smid, G. E., Smit, F., de Haan, L., & Schoevers, R. A. (2014). The obsessive-compulsive spectrum in schizophrenia, a meta-analysis and meta-regression exploring prevalence rates. *Schizophrenia Research, 152*(2–3), 458–468.

Swinson, R. P., Antony, M. M., Rachman, S., & Richter, M. A. (1998). *Obsessive-compulsive disorder: Theory, research, and treatment*. Guilford.

Taylor, S. (2011). Early versus late onset obsessive-compulsive disorder: Evidence for distinct subtypes. *Clinical Psychology Review, 31*(7), 1083–1100.

Tezcan, E., & Millet, B. (1997). Phenomenologie des troubles obsessionnels compulsifs. Formes et contenus des obsessions et des compulsions dans l'Est de la Turquie [Phenomenology of obsessive-compulsive disorders. Forms and characteristics of obsessions and compulsions in East Turkey]. *L'Encephale, 23*(5), 342–350.

Thapaliya, S. (2017). The case of Rat Man: A psychoanalytic understanding of obsessive-compulsive disorder. *Journal of Mental Health and Human Behaviour, 22*(2), 132.

Tolin, D. F., & Springer, K. S. (2018). Obsessive-compulsive and related disorders. In J. N. Butcher & J. M. Hooley (Eds.), *APA handbook of psychopathology, Volume 1: Psychopathology: Understanding, assessing, and treating adult mental disorders* (pp. 455–479). American Psychological Association.

Torres, A. R., Fontenelle, L., Shavitt, R. G., Hoexter, M. Q., Pittenger, C., & Miguel, E. (2017). In C. Pittenger (Ed.), *Obsessive-compulsive disorder: Phenomenology, pathophysiology, and treatment* (pp. 35–45). Oxford University Press.

Torres, A. R., Moran, P., Bebbington, P., Brugha, T., Bhugra, D., Coid, J. W., Farrell, M., Jenkins, R., Lewis, G., Meltzer, H., & Prince, M. (2006). Obsessive–compulsive disorder and personality disorder: Evidence from the British National Survey of Psychiatric Morbidity 2000. *Social Psychiatry and Psychiatric Epidemiology: The International Journal for Research in Social and Genetic Epidemiology and Mental Health Services, 41*(11), 862–867. https://doi.org/10.1007/s00127-006-0118-3

Torres, A. R., Prince, M. J., Bebbington, P. E., Bhugra, D., Brugha, T. S., Farrell, M., Jenkins, R., Lewis, G., Meltzer, H., & Singleton, N. (2006). Obsessive-compulsive disorder: Prevalence, comorbidity, impact, and help-seeking in the British National Psychiatric Morbidity Survey of 2000. *The American Journal of Psychiatry, 163*(11), 1978–1985.

Torres, A. R., Shavitt, R. G., Torresan, R. C., Ferrão, Y. A., Miguel, E. C., & Fontenelle, L. F. (2013). Clinical features of pure obsessive-compulsive disorder. *Comprehensive Psychiatry, 54*(7), 1042–1052.

Torres, A. R., Torresan, R. C., de Mathis, M. A., & Shavitt, R. G. (2020). Obsessive-compulsive disorder in women. In J. Rennó, G. Valadares, A. Cantilino, J. Mendes-Ribeiro, R. Rocha, & A. Geraldo da Silva (Eds.), *Women's mental health* (pp. 125–139). Springer.

Torresan, R. C., Ramos-Cerqueira, A. T. A., Shavitt, R. G., do Rosário, M. C., de Mathis, M. A., Miguel, E. C., & Torres, A. R. (2013). Symptom dimensions, clinical course and comorbidity in men and women with obsessive-compulsive disorder. *Psychiatry Research, 209*(2), 186–195.

Van der Hart, O., & Friedman, B. (1989). A reader's guide to Pierre Janet on dissociation: A neglected intellectual heritage. *Dissociation: Progress in the Dissociative Disorders.*

Veale, D., Gournay, K., Dryden, W., Boocock, A., Shah, F., Willson, R., & Walburn, J. (1996). Body dysmorphic disorder: A cognitive behavioural model and pilot randomised controlled trial. *Behaviour Research and Therapy, 34*(9), 717–729.

Viswasam, K., Eslick, G. D., & Starcevic, V. (2019). Prevalence, onset and course of anxiety disorders during pregnancy: A systematic review and meta-analysis. *Journal of Affective Disorders, 255,* 27–40.

Vivan, A. d. S., Rodrigues, L., Wendt, G., Bicca, M. G., Braga, D. T., & Cordioli, A. V. (2014). Obsessive-compulsive symptoms and obsessive-compulsive disorder in adolescents: A population-based study. *Brazilian Journal of Psychiatry, 36*(2), 111–118.

Westphal, C. (1878). Zwangsvorstellungen. *Arch. Psychiat. Nervenk, 8,* 734–750.

Williams, M., Chapman, L., Simms, J., & Tellawi, G. (2017). Cross-cultural phenomenology of obsessive-compulsive disorder. In J. S. Abramowitz, D. McKay, & E. A. Storch (Eds.), *The Wiley handbook of obsessive-compulsive disorders* (pp. 56–74). Wiley.

Williams, M. T., Elstein, J., Buckner, E., Abelson, J. M., & Himle, J. A. (2012). Symptom dimensions in two samples of African Americans with obsessive-compulsive disorder. *Journal of Obsessive-Compulsive and Related Disorders, 1*(3), 145–152.

Wolpe, J., & Rachman, S. (1963). Psychoanalytic evidence: A critique based on Freud's case of Little Hans. In S. Rachman (Ed.), *Critical essays on psychoanalysis* (pp. 198–220). Pergamon.

World Health Organization (WHO). (1967). *The ICD-8 classification of mental and behavioural disorders: Diagnostic criteria for research.*

World Health Organization. (2016). *International statistical classification of diseases and related health problems* (10th ed.). https://icd.who.int/browse10/2016/en

CHAPTER 3

Phenomenology and Epidemiology of Body Dysmorphic Disorder

Megan M. Kelly *and* Katharine A. Phillips

Abstract

Body dysmorphic disorder (BDD) is an often-severe disorder characterized by distressing or impairing preoccupations with nonexistent or slight defects in one's physical appearance. Individuals with BDD suffer from time-consuming obsessions about their bodily appearance and excessive compulsive behaviors (for example, mirror-checking, excessive grooming, and skin-picking). Functioning and quality of life are typically very poor, and suicidality is markedly elevated. BDD currently affects 0.7% to 2.9% of the population; however, BDD typically goes unrecognized in clinical settings. This chapter discusses BDD's definition and classification, epidemiology, demographics, and clinical features, including several case descriptions of BDD, age at onset, course of illness, comorbidity, morbidity (including suicidality), gender similarities and differences, and healthcare utilization. In addition, BDD's relationships to obsessive-compulsive disorder, psychotic disorders, and social anxiety disorder are discussed.

Key Words: body dysmorphic disorder, clinical features, epidemiology, phenomenology, morbidity, comorbidity

Definition of Body Dysmorphic Disorder

Body dysmorphic disorder (BDD) is an often-severe disorder characterized by distressing or impairing preoccupations with nonexistent or slight defects or flaws in physical appearance in a person who appears normal. If a physical defect is observable, it must be only slight (as opposed to clearly observable by others; American Psychiatric Association [APA], 2013). If a bodily defect is readily apparent and significant (for example, a person who is preoccupied with hair loss is actually bald), the person would not meet the criteria for BDD in the 5th edition of the *Diagnostic and Statistical Manual of Mental Disorders* (*DSM-5*; American Psychiatric Association [APA], 2013). Instead, if the readily apparent appearance concern is preoccupying, is associated with excessive repetitive behaviors, and causes clinically significant distress or impairment in functioning, it would be diagnosed as "other specified obsessive and compulsive-related disorder" ("body dysmorphic-like disorder with actual flaws"; APA, 2013).

In addition, at some point during the course of the illness, the appearance preoccupations must have caused repetitive behaviors (also referred to as rituals or compulsive behaviors). Examples are repeated comparison of one's appearance with that of others, checking of mirrors and other reflective surfaces (e.g., windows), excessive grooming (e.g., hair styling, makeup application), reassurance-seeking, or excessive exercise or weightlifting. The compulsive behaviors are usually distressing, time-consuming (taking up an average of 3 to 8 hours a day), and difficult to resist or control (Phillips et al., 1998). The aim of the behaviors is to examine, improve, hide, or obtain reassurance about the perceived defects. However, the behaviors often do not reduce BDD-triggered distress, even in the short term, and may even increase distress.

For BDD to be diagnosed, the appearance concerns must also cause clinically significant impairment in psychosocial functioning (for example, in social, academic, or occupational functioning) or cause clinically significant distress. This criterion (in addition to the requirement for preoccupation) differentiates BDD from normal appearance concerns, which are quite common in the general population (Cash et al., 1986). Furthermore, to qualify for a diagnosis of BDD, the appearance concerns cannot be better explained by another psychiatric disorder, such as anorexia nervosa.

This chapter focuses on *DSM*-defined BDD rather than the broader and very large literature on body image dissatisfaction. Increasingly, the published literature refers to "BDD symptoms"; in many cases such studies examine broader body image dissatisfaction or concern, which is not necessarily pathological, rather than the specific disorder BDD, which reflects psychopathology.

History and Classification

BDD is included in the obsessive-compulsive and related disorders (OCRDs) category of *DSM-5* and the *International Classification of Diseases*, eleventh revision (*ICD-11*; World Health Organization, 2019). It was first described in 1886 by Morselli, an Italian physician, who called it dysmorphophobia (Morselli, 1891; Phillips, 1991). As Morselli wrote,

> The dysmorphophobic patient is really miserable; in the middle of his daily routines, conversations, while reading, during meals, in fact everywhere and at any time, is overcome by the fear of deformity, which may reach a very painful intensity, even to the point of weeping and desperation. (Morselli, 1891)

Kraepelin and Janet are other prominent psychopathologists who subsequently described this disorder (Janet, 1903; Kraepelin, 1915; Phillips, 1991).

For more than a century after Morselli first described BDD, it was largely neglected by clinicians and researchers alike, perhaps because many patients do not reveal their symptoms—because they are too ashamed, fear being judged negatively (e.g., as vain) for having such concerns, or fear their clinician will not understand them or cannot help them

(Conroy et al., 2008; Grant et al., 2001). In recent years, however, BDD has received far greater attention and systematic research, and much has been learned about its clinical features, epidemiology, and relationship to other disorders.

In 1980, BDD was included in *DSM-III* as an example of an atypical somatoform disorder under the rubric dysmorphophobia. In *DSM-III-R*, its name was changed to body dysmorphic disorder, and it was made a separate diagnostic category in the somatoform disorder section (APA, 1987). In *DSM-IV*, BDD continued to be classified as a somatoform disorder (APA, 2000). The delusional form of BDD was classified in *DSM-IV* in the psychosis section of the manual as a type of delusional disorder (somatic type), although BDD's delusional variant could be double-coded as both BDD and delusional disorder, somatic type, in *DSM-IV*. However, in *DSM-5*, the separate designation of BDD's delusional form as a type of psychotic disorder was removed, and level of BDD-related insight (including absent insight/delusional beliefs) was included as a specifier for BDD (good or fair, poor, or absent insight/delusional beliefs; APA, 2013; Phillips et al., 2014).

Other significant changes were made to the classification of BDD in *DSM-5*, including moving BDD from the somatoform category to the new OCRDs chapter. A new criterion requiring excessive repetitive behaviors was added. In addition to the new insight specifier, *DSM-5* added a specifier for muscle dysmorphia, which is defined as the individual's preoccupation that their body is not muscular or lean enough. Furthermore, panic attacks triggered by BDD may be designated by *DSM-5*'s panic attack specifier, which can be used for any disorder that triggers panic attacks. In BDD, common triggers include feeling scrutinized by others, looking at perceived defects in mirrors, and being under bright lights (Phillips, Menard, & Bjornsson, 2013).

Examples of Patients with BDD

Amy—Preoccupation with the Appearance of Her Eyebrows

Amy, a 45-year-old woman, was obsessed with her eyebrows. She believed she had too few eyebrow hairs, that they were too gray, and that their shape was abnormal. She was also preoccupied with the appearance of her hair, believing that it always looked "messy." Amy spent hours each day thinking about her eyebrows, staring at them in the mirror and examining them with a magnifying mirror, as well as plucking any hairs that were gray or not in the desired shape. As she stated, "My eyebrows are like a map—I know every single hair." Amy had electrolysis done to reshape her eyebrows, but she believed that this process irreparably damaged them. She felt intensely angry over the perceived damage and wanted the electrologist to "feel the despair" that Amy felt about her eyebrows. She was so angry that she stalked her electrologist, who pressed harassment charges and obtained a restraining order against Amy. Amy also tried minoxidil to make her eyebrow hairs grow back, but she believed the drug did not help. Because she thought she looked so bad, Amy had few social contacts, and when she did interact socially, she worried about how others perceived her appearance. She had difficulty holding a job and worked part-time selling beauty products in a mall. She sought this job because she could get a discount on products that would improve how her eyebrows looked. Amy finally sought psychiatric treatment at the suggestion of a surgeon from whom she had sought treatment for further "eyebrow repair." She stated that she recognized that her appearance concerns were severely interfering with her ability to hold jobs and maintain relationships, and that her anger over the "damage" to her eyebrows was still consuming her years after the electrolysis procedure had been done.

John—A Case of Muscle Dysmorphia

John, a 50-year-old man, presented with concerns about his muscles not being "big enough." He was actually quite muscular, because he worked out for several hours a day at the gym. John was frequently worried that he looked "shriveled and puny." He constantly felt anxious about what others thought of how he looked. Despite experiencing significant social anxiety because he thought he looked so bad, John was able to work as a grocery clerk. However, his anxiety prevented him from maintaining friendships and interactions with family members. John's appearance concerns led him to repeatedly check the mirror; to compare himself to other men in body-building magazines, on television, and online; and to seek products on the Internet that he hoped would make him more muscular. He spent about an hour each day in the health food store, searching for nutritional supplements to help him "bulk up." He had considered taking anabolic steroids to make himself bigger, but he was concerned about potential health risks. John sought treatment after seriously considering suicide because he believed his coworkers mocked and rejected him because of how he looked.

Epidemiology

BDD is a common disorder. (Note that this section does not include studies based on the Dysmorphic Concern Questionnaire, because other diagnostic and screening measures more specifically identify BDD.) Five nationwide epidemiologic studies have examined BDD's prevalence, with a reported point (current) prevalence of 0.7% to 2.9% in the general population (Brohede et al., 2014; Buhlmann et al., 2010; Koran et al., 2008; Rief et al., 2006; Schieber et al., 2015). The studies were done in the United States, Germany, and Sweden, with sample sizes ranges ranging from 2,129 to 2,891 (Hartmann & Buhlmann, 2017). Gender ratios have varied across epidemiologic and clinical studies, but overall BDD appears to be slightly more common in women than in men. It is important to recognize that BDD clearly does not occur only in women, as is sometimes assumed.

In a German nationwide survey (N = 2,552), which examined selected demographic and clinical features, individuals with BDD were more likely to report suicidal ideation and suicide attempts due to appearance concerns than individuals without BDD (Rief et al., 2006). Those with BDD also had higher somatization scores, had lower income, were more likely to be divorced, were less likely to be married, and were more likely to be unemployed. Schieber and colleagues (2015) made similar findings, showing that individuals with BDD had fewer committed relationships as well as a lower educational level than the general population.

Epidemiologic studies have great value in their ability to screen large samples and determine the prevalence of mental disorders, like BDD, in the general population. These studies also have some limitations, however, one of which is the inability to do in-depth clinical interviews that can obtain more detailed information about symptoms, clarify ambiguities in participant responses, and use clinical judgment regarding information that is obtained. In some studies (including some of those below), self-report questionnaires have been used without confirmation of the diagnosis via interview. This is a particularly important issue for BDD, because appearance concerns are common in the general population, and clinical judgment is helpful in differentiating normal concerns and eating disorders from BDD.

Studies have also been done in smaller, nonclinical student samples, and many of the studies used self-report measures. The prevalence of BDD in these studies ranged from 2% to 13% (Biby, 1998; Bohne et al., 2002; Cansever et al., 2003; Mayville et al., 1999; Taqui et al., 2008). In a more recent study in a student sample in China, a prevalence of 1.3% was reported, which is lower than that in other studies, perhaps because individuals who reported significant weight concerns on the Body Dysmorphic Disorder Questionnaire (BDDQ; a widely used self-report BDD screening measure; Phillips, 2005) were considered not to have BDD (Liao et al., 2010. However, the BDDQ item that assesses weight concerns is included to ensure that individuals with a primary diagnosis of an eating disorder are not misidentified as having BDD. Indeed, a notable proportion of those with BDD have clinically significant preoccupation with their weight that reflects BDD rather than an eating disorder; percentages were 29% in one BDD sample (Kittler et al., 2007) and 14% in another (Phillips & Diaz, 1997). The complex differential diagnosis between BDD and eating disorders in some cases highlights the importance of obtaining diagnostic information via clinical interviews, if possible, to verify the BDD diagnosis.

A majority of individuals with BDD seek and receive dermatologic treatment, cosmetic surgery, and other types of cosmetic treatments in an attempt to "fix" their perceived appearance flaws (Crerand et al., 2005; Hollander et al., 1993; Phillips, Grant, et al., 2001; Veale et al., 1996). Thus, the prevalence of BDD tends to be higher in these settings than in epidemiologic studies (Crerand et al., 2017). In dermatology settings, a prevalence of 4.2% to 42% has been reported (Crerand et al., 2017). A study that calculated the weighted prevalence across published studies in dermatology settings reported a prevalence of 13.2% (Veale et al., 2016).

Veale et al. (2016) also reported an overall weighted prevalence for BDD in cosmetic surgery settings of 13.2%, with an even higher weighted prevalence in rhinoplasty settings

(20.1%). In orthodontic patients, the prevalence of BDD ranges from 5.5% to 7.5%; in cosmetic dentistry patients, a prevalence of 9.5% has been reported; and among patients presenting for orthognathic surgery, the prevalence ranges from 10% to 13% (Crerand et al., 2017). Methodological limitations, such as small sample sizes, selection bias, and differences in study design (including different methods for diagnosing BDD), may account for varied findings across studies.

The high prevalence of BDD in cosmetic settings is important because the dermatology, surgery, and psychiatry literature emphasize that BDD usually responds poorly to cosmetic treatments and that these patients may be at risk for suicide or violence toward the surgeon because of dissatisfaction with the cosmetic outcome (Cotterill, 1981; Cotterill & Cunliffe, 1997; Crerand et al., 2004, 2017; Dey et al., 2015; Koblenzer, 1985; Phillips, 1991; Phillips et al., 1992; Phillips, Grant, et al., 2001; Tignol et al., 2007; Veale et al., 1996).

Studies similarly suggest that BDD is relatively common in various outpatient mental health settings, including among patients with obsessive-compulsive disorder (OCD), social phobia, trichotillomania, and atypical major depressive disorder (Brawman-Mintzer et al., 1995; Costa et al., 2012; Frías et al., 2015; Hollander et al., 1993; Nierenberg et al., 2002; Perugi et al., 1998; Phillips et al., 1996, 1998; Phillips, Pinto, et al., 2007; Soriano et al., 1996; Wilhelm et al., 1997). In a study of atypical major depressive disorder, the prevalence of BDD (42%) was higher than the prevalence of OCD, social phobia, generalized anxiety disorder, bulimia, and substance use disorders (Perugi et al., 1998).

Several studies have been done in psychiatric inpatient settings in the United States. In a study of 122 general inpatients, 13% (n = 16; 95% CI = 6.9%–19.3%) had BDD, making BDD more common than many other disorders, including schizophrenia, OCD, posttraumatic stress disorder, and eating disorders (Grant et al., 2001). In another study in a general adult inpatient setting, BDD was diagnosed in 16.0% of patients (n = 16; 95% CI = 8.7%–23.3%). In the first study, inpatients with BDD had significantly lower scores on the Global Assessment of Functioning (GAF) and twice the lifetime rate of suicide attempts as patients without BDD (Grant et al., 2001). In the second study, a high proportion of BDD patients reported that their BDD symptoms were a major reason or "somewhat of a reason" for their suicidal thinking (50% of subjects), suicide attempts (33%), or substance use (42%; Conroy et al., 2008). In a study in 432 inpatients in the United Kingdom, a lower prevalence of 5.8% was reported; different referral patterns or other differences between the U.K. and U.S. healthcare systems might at least partially explain these somewhat different findings (Veale et al., 2015). The U.K. study concurred with the U.S. studies in finding that BDD was poorly identified in psychiatric inpatients.

The prevalence of BDD has also been studied in military and veteran populations. In a U.S. Veterans Affairs primary care behavioral health clinic, Kelly and colleagues (2015) found that 11% (95% CI = 6.3%–18.6%) of 100 veterans had current BDD, indicating a relatively high rate of BDD in this setting. In a survey study of 1,150 enlisted U.S. military personnel, Campagna and Bowsher (2016) showed that 13% of men and 22% of women had BDD. These studies suggest that military personnel and veterans might be at particularly high risk of having BDD, but that it often goes unrecognized in military and veteran healthcare settings.

A number of prevalence studies have been done in youth. Among 566 high school students, BDD's current prevalence was 2.2%, based on a self-report questionnaire (Mayville et al., 1999). Among adolescent psychiatric inpatients, using the self-report BDDQ (which has a sensitivity of 100% and a specificity of 89%; Phillips, 2005), 4.8% of 208 patients had definite BDD, and an additional 1.9% had probable BDD (Dyl et al., 2006). In the latter study, youth with BDD had significantly greater anxiety, depression, and suicide risk on standardized measures than those without significant body image concerns. In a community study of 3,149 adolescents in Australia that also used the self-report BDDQ, 5.1% reported probable BDD (Schneider et al., 2019). Finally, in a study of 308 German adolescents and young adults (ages 15 to 21 years) that used a self-report measure of BDD based on *DSM-5* diagnostic criteria, 3.6% of those assessed met criteria for BDD, and individuals with BDD reported more obsessive-compulsive symptoms than did those without BDD (Möllmann et al., 2017).

Despite the above findings, which indicate that BDD is common, BDD usually goes undiagnosed in clinical settings. In five studies that examined this issue, no patient who was identified as having BDD by the investigators had the diagnosis recorded in their clinical record (Conroy et al., 2008; Grant et al., 2001; Phillips et al., 1993, 1996; Zimmerman & Mattia, 1998). In the study by Kelly and colleagues (2015) of veterans, only one of 11 veterans who had BDD had previously received the diagnosis. These findings highlight the importance of screening specifically for BDD in clinical settings.

Demographics

Gender

Studies in adults yield somewhat varying findings on gender ratio. In the four above-noted population-based studies that included both females and males, BDD was slightly more common in women than in men. Studies in clinical samples of adults have had widely varying proportions of males and females. Some have contained more females (Phillips, Menard, & Fay, 2006; Rosen & Reiter, 1996; Veale et al., 1996), whereas others have contained an equal proportion of females and males (Phillips & Diaz, 1997) or more males than females (Hollander et al., 1993; Neziroglu & Yaryura-Tobias, 1993; Perugi et al., 1997). In some cases, these differences may have been attributable to recruitment methods. In the two largest published clinical series of individuals with BDD, 49% of 188 subjects in a clinical setting, and 64% of a largely clinical sample ($N = 200$), were female (Phillips & Diaz, 1997; Phillips, Menard, & Fay, 2006).

Marital Status

In epidemiologic samples, individuals with BDD are less likely to be married than are those without BDD in the United States (36.2% vs. 55.5%) and in Germany (21.4% vs. 52.7%) (Koran et al., 2008; Rief et al., 2006). In the U.S. study, a significantly higher proportion of those with BDD were separated (10.6% vs. 1.5%) or never married (34.0% vs. 17.5%). While the U.S. study did not find a higher divorce rate among those with BDD (10.6% of both groups; Koran et al., 2008), the German study found that a higher proportion of individuals with BDD were divorced (28.6% vs. 9.9%; Rief et al., 2006). Supporting these studies, Schieber and colleagues (2015) found that individuals with BDD had fewer committed relationships compared to the general population. Clinical impressions indicate that BDD symptoms often negatively impact a person's ability to pursue, take part in, or effectively manage relationships (although such a causal relationship cannot be confirmed in cross-sectional studies).

In the largest clinical samples of individuals ascertained for BDD, a majority were not married (81% of 200 subjects in one study, and 80% of 293 subjects in the other; Gunstad & Phillips, 2003; Phillips, Menard, Fay, & Weisberg 2005). Furthermore, in a clinical sample, 55.7% of adults with BDD reported that they did not currently have a primary relationship. Subjects who reported this were significantly more likely to be male, younger, and less educated than were those with a primary relationship (Didie, Tortolani, Walters, et al., 2006).

Socioeconomic Status

In the German epidemiologic sample, those with BDD were significantly more likely to be unemployed than were those without BDD (21.4% vs. 6.8%; Rief et al., 2006). In a largely clinical sample of 200 broadly ascertained adults with BDD, 39.0% of subjects reported that they did not work for at least one consecutive week in the past month due, at least in part, to psychopathology (BDD was the primary diagnosis for most of this sample); 32.6% reported that they wanted to be in school (at least part-time) but were not enrolled in school solely because of psychopathology, or because of psychopathology plus some other reason; and 23% were currently receiving disability payments (Didie et al., 2008). Brohede and colleagues (2014) also found that women with BDD had lower levels of completed education, greater unemployment and sick leave, and a lower household income than women in the general population. Overall, it appears that socioeconomic status can be severely affected by the presence of BDD.

Core Clinical Features

Preoccupation with Perceived Appearance Flaws
Individuals with BDD are preoccupied with perceived appearance defects, thinking that some aspect of their appearance is ugly, unattractive, abnormal, deformed, or defective

(Phillips, 2009; Simmons & Phillips, 2017). Concerns range from looking "not right" or "unattractive" to looking "hideous" or like "a monster" (Phillips, 2009). Appearance concerns can focus on any part of the body. Most commonly, they focus on the skin (e.g., perceived acne, marks, scars, lines, wrinkles, or skin color), hair (e.g., too thin, too thick, balding, excessive body or facial hair), or the size or shape of the nose (Fontenelle et al., 2006; Hollander et al., 1993; Perugi et al., 1997; Phillips & Diaz, 1997; Phillips et al., 1993; Phillips, Menard, Fay, & Weisberg, 2005; Veale et al., 1996). Most patients are preoccupied with several body areas, with the lifetime number of areas in the range of three to four in one sample (N = 188; Phillips & Diaz, 1997) and six in another sample (N = 200; Phillips, Menard, Fay, & Weisberg, 2005). Some patients, however, are concerned with only one body area, whereas others dislike virtually everything about how they look (Phillips, 2005).

The appearance preoccupations are time-consuming, occupying on average three to eight hours a day (Phillips, 2009; Phillips et al., 1998). Clinical studies of BDD typically require that the preoccupations be present for at least one hour a day in order to differentiate BDD from more normal appearance concerns. It is typically difficult for patients with BDD to resist or control their preoccupations (Phillips, 2005; Phillips et al., 1998). Appearance concerns are often associated with significant anxiety and social anxiety (Kelly et al., 2010; Pinto & Phillips, 2005) as well as depression (Conroy et al., 2008; Phillips, 1999; Phillips, Siniscalchi, & McElroy, 2004; Veale et al., 2003), low self-esteem (Buhlmann et al., 2009; Phillips, Pinto, & Jain, 2004), and fear of rejection and embarrassment (Kelly et al., 2014; Veale et al., 1996).

Insight/Delusionality of BDD Beliefs

Prior to effective treatment, most individuals with BDD do not recognize that they actually look normal. Studies (many of which have used the Brown Assessment of Beliefs Scale; Eisen et al., 1998; Phillips, Hart, et al., 2013) have found that insight is typically poor or absent. In other words, a majority of patients believe that their view of their appearance is probably or definitely accurate (Mancuso et al., 2010; Phillips, 2004; Phillips, Menard, Pagano, et al., 2006). However, insight can range from good to fair to poor to absent (i.e., delusional beliefs, or complete conviction that they look abnormal, ugly, unattractive, or deformed; Phillips, 2004; Phillips et al., 2012).

Studies based on the Brown Assessment of Beliefs Scale have found that 32% to 38% of patients have BDD beliefs that are currently delusional (Eisen et al., 2004; Phillips, 2017a; Phillips, Menard, Pagano, et al., 2006). Clinical impressions suggest that poor insight or delusional BDD beliefs can interfere with patients' willingness to engage in, and remain in, psychiatric treatment and can fuel desire for cosmetic treatment (which is usually ineffective), because patients do not recognize that their appearance concerns are attributable to a mental illness (Eisen et al., 2004; Phillips, 2005).

Studies have found more similarities than differences between delusional and nondelusional patients across a range of variables, suggesting that these BDD variants constitute the same disorder (Mancuso et al., 2010; Phillips et al., 1994, 2014; Phillips, Menard, Pagano, et al., 2006). Patients with delusional BDD beliefs tend to have more severe BDD symptoms; lower educational attainment; more impairment in social functioning; decreased quality of life on some (but not all) measures; higher levels of perceived stress, anxiety, depression, and anger-hostility; and higher suicide attempt rates (DeMarco et al., 1998; Mancuso et al., 2010; Phillips, 2000; Phillips et al., 1994, 2004; Phillips, Menard, Fay, & Pagano, 2005; Phillips, Menard, Pagano, et al., 2006 Phillips, Siniscalchi, & McElroy, 2004). However, when controlling for BDD symptom severity, fewer differences are found between the delusional and nondelusional groups (Mancuso et al., 2010; Phillips, 2017a; Phillips, Menard, Pagano, et al., 2006).

Many patients with BDD have ideas or delusions of reference, believing that other people take special notice of them or mock them because of their appearance (Eisen et al., 2004; Phillips, 2004). Clinical experience suggests that such symptoms may contribute to the social morbidity experienced by most individuals with BDD. For example, they may be less willing to leave the house if they believe people will mock them because they are "ugly."

Although it is not known why people with BDD typically have poor or absent insight and referential thinking regarding their perceived appearance flaws, findings that BDD involves aberrations in visual processing (Feusner et al., 2010), as well as a bias for threatening interpretations of neutral or ambiguous stimuli (Buhlmann et al., 2002), may offer at least a partial explanation. In addition, a diffusion tensor imaging study, which examined brain white matter in individuals with BDD and healthy controls, found correlations between fiber disorganization in the inferior longitudinal fasciculus and the forceps major and poorer BDD-related insight on the Brown Assessment of Beliefs Scale (Feusner et al., 2013). Thus, poor BDD-related insight appears to be associated with fiber disorganization in white matter tracts that facilitate communication between visual and emotion/memory systems as well as interhemispheric communication, which might cause difficulty in accurate perception of appearance and in turn lead to poor insight.

Compulsive and Safety Behaviors

According to *DSM*-5, the diagnostic criteria for BDD include repetitive, compulsive behaviors, and all individuals with BDD engage in them at some point during the course of their disorder (Phillips & Diaz, 1997; Phillips, Menard, Fay, & Weisberg, 2005). The intent of these behaviors is to reduce the patient's anxiety about their appearance by fixing it, hiding it, or obtaining reassurance that they look acceptable (Phillips, 2005). Like appearance preoccupations, BDD-related behaviors are typically time-consuming and difficult to stop or control (Phillips, 2005; Phillips et al., 1998). One typical behavior is the patient's comparison of their appearance with that of others, including people in newspapers, in magazines, online, on video platforms, or on television. Other compulsive behaviors include repeated checking of mirrors and other reflective surfaces (e.g., windows), checking the "flawed" body part by looking at it directly (if visible, such as "hairy" arms), excessive grooming (e.g., makeup application, hair styling, shaving, hair combing or plucking), reassurance-seeking, taking excessive selfies, modifying their appearance via online apps, and excessive exercise or weightlifting. Some people with BDD engage in excessive tanning (for example, to minimize the appearance of acne or wrinkles, or to darken "pale" skin), repetitive clothes-changing in an attempt to better camouflage the perceived defects or to find a more flattering outfit, and compulsive shopping (e.g., for beauty products or clothes; Phillips, 2005; Phillips, Conroy, et al., 2006; Phillips & Diaz, 1997; Phillips, Menard, Fay, & Weisberg, 2005). Many patients perform other, often idiosyncratic behaviors, such as repeatedly checking to see if their hair is "breaking."

Compulsive skin-picking that occurs as a symptom of BDD is worth highlighting. Studies have found that 27% to 45% of BDD patients have lifetime skin-picking as a symptom of BDD (Grant et al., 2006; Phillips & Taub, 1995). The intent of this behavior is to improve perceived flaws in the appearance of one's skin by making it smoother or removing tiny blemishes (Phillips & Taub, 1995). However, because this behavior is typically time-consuming and difficult to control, it often causes irritation, scabbing, or scarring, and it can cause skin infections and ruptured blood vessels, which are occasionally life-threatening (Grant et al., 2006; O'Sullivan et al., 1999; Phillips & Taub, 1995). It is important to differentiate skin-picking as a symptom of BDD from excoriation (skin-picking) disorder, because the former requires treatment for BDD, not just for skin-picking.

The compulsive behaviors described above resemble OCD compulsions in several ways. First, the behaviors are performed intentionally, in response to an obsessional preoccupation with appearance, and the acts are not pleasurable. Furthermore, the intent is to reduce anxiety or distress and to prevent an unwanted event (e.g., being rejected by others or looking "ugly"), and most of the behaviors are repetitive, time-consuming, and excessive. Furthermore, they may be rule-bound or done in a rigid manner (Phillips & Kaye, 2007). While compulsions can be conceptualized as a type of avoidance behavior (Kozak & Foa, 1997; Maltby & Tolin, 2003), BDD repetitive behaviors involve an increased focus on perceived flaws, and most of these behaviors may further fuel BDD preoccupations (Phillips, 2009). In addition, a developmental and evolutionary perspective emphasizes the highly conserved nature of compulsive behaviors, such as compulsive grooming (Feusner et al., 2009; Leckman & Mayes, 1998).

One common BDD behavior that may be conceptualized as avoidant in nature is camouflaging. Most people with BDD attempt to camouflage body areas of concern— for example, they may cover disliked areas with makeup, clothing, a hat, hair, a beard, sunglasses, or posture. Some refuse to participate in activities if it requires them to stop camouflaging (e.g., remove a hat for a wedding). Camouflaging can, however, be done repeatedly, resembling a compulsive behavior (for example, reapplying makeup 30 times a day).

Distraction techniques are another common BDD behavior (Phillips, 2009; Phillips, Menard, Fay, & Weisberg, 2005). The purpose of such behaviors is to distract other people from noticing the "defective" body areas. For example, wearing flamboyant makeup, unusual clothing, or a dramatic hairstyle may be an attempt to draw attention to another feature so that the disliked body areas will go unnoticed.

Emotional Features

BDD thoughts can cause a range of disturbing emotions, including anxiety, social anxiety, depression, shame, hostility/anger, guilt, disgust, and grief (Simmons & Phillips, 2017).

ANXIETY AND SOCIAL ANXIETY

Anxiety levels are usually high in individuals with BDD. A nationwide epidemiologic study from Sweden found that twice as many of those with BDD had symptoms of anxiety compared to those without BDD (72.1% vs. 31.8%; Brohede et al., 2014). One study reported a significant association between BDD severity and anxiety severity ($r = .32$, $p < .01$; Phillips, Siniscalchi, & McElroy, 2004).

Social anxiety is also common in persons with BDD. Levels of social anxiety range from 1.3 to 1.7 standard deviations (SD) higher than in normative samples (Kelly et al., 2010; Pinto & Phillips, 2005; Veale et al., 1996). Social anxiety is also significantly correlated with BDD severity (Pinto & Phillips, 2005), including in those without concurrent social phobia (Kelly et al., 2010).

The majority of participants (62%) in a sample of 108 individuals with BDD but without comorbid social phobia had clinically significant social anxiety (Kelly et al., 2010). Only 14% endorsed clinically significant social anxiety that was not related to appearance concerns, suggesting that much of the social anxiety in this sample was secondary to BDD symptoms. Social anxiety was associated with significant functional impairment both cross-sectionally and prospectively, with greater social anxiety predicting subsequent impairment in psychosocial functioning (Kelly et al., 2010).

DEPRESSION

Depressive symptoms are another common emotional feature of BDD. Major depressive disorder is the most common comorbidity for individuals with BDD (see comorbidity section below; Phillips et al., 2007). Levels of depression are more than 2 SD above those for psychiatric controls (Phillips, Siniscalchi, & McElroy, 2004). In a study of major depressive disorder and BDD from a network analysis perspective ($N = 148$ patients with BDD; Summers et al., 2020), the symptoms "interference in functioning due to compulsions," "feelings of worthlessness," and "loss of pleasure" were most strongly associated with other BDD and depressive symptoms. In a prospective longitudinal study, change in the status of BDD and major depression was closely linked in time, with improvement in major depression predicting BDD remission, and, conversely, improvement in BDD predicting depression remission (Phillips & Stout, 2006). However, BDD symptoms persisted in a sizable proportion of subjects who remitted from major depressive disorder, indicating that BDD is not simply a symptom of depression.

ANGER/HOSTILITY

Anger can also be a prominent emotional feature of BDD (Phillips, 2005). Based on clinical observations, individuals with BDD can be angry at themselves or their parents for how they look. Other causes of anger include misperceptions about how others have mistreated them because of their appearance, inability to fix the perceived defects, attempts by other people to interfere with BDD rituals (such as mirror-checking), delusions of reference (e.g., believing that other people are mocking the defect), misperception of neutral faces as angry or contemptuous, feeling thwarted in attempts to obtain cosmetic procedures, believing that a cosmetic procedure worsened the appearance problem, use of anabolic steroids (by individuals with muscle dysmorphia), or feeling rejected by others because of the perceived defects (Kelly et al., 2014; Phillips, 2017b).

Individuals with BDD score more than 2 SD higher than psychiatric controls on anger/hostility (Phillips, Siniscalchi, & McElroy, 2004). Greater anger/hostility is significantly correlated with BDD severity ($r = .41$) and greater delusionality of BDD beliefs ($r = .34$; Phillips, Siniscalchi, & McElroy, 2004). In a study that used the NEO Five-Factor Inventory, 52% of 100 subjects with BDD scored in the low or very low range for agreeableness (vs. antagonism), whereas only 15% scored in the high or very high range for agreeableness (Phillips & McElroy, 2000). High levels of anger and hostility can lead to aggressive behavior toward others.

Forms of BDD

BDD symptoms are generally quite similar across patients; however, BDD can have different forms (Phillips, 2009). Two important forms of BDD require a modified cognitive-behavioral treatment (CBT) approach: muscle dysmorphia and BDD by proxy.

Muscle Dysmorphia

Muscle dysmorphia is a form of BDD that occurs almost exclusively in males (Phillips & Diaz, 1997; Sreshta et al., 2017). Muscle dysmorphia consists of preoccupation with the idea that one's body is insufficiently muscular or lean, or is "too small" (Phillips et al., 1997; Pope et al., 1997, 2000). In reality, these men look normal or may even be very muscular. (The case of John presented above illustrates this form of BDD.) Many men with muscle dysmorphia adhere to a meticulous diet and a time-consuming and excessive workout schedule, which can cause bodily damage (Phillips et al., 1997; Pope et al., 1997, 2000, 2005).

In addition, many people with the muscle dysmorphia form of BDD use potentially dangerous anabolic-androgenic steroids and other substances in an attempt to get bigger (Hitzeroth et al., 2001; Olivardia et al., 2000; Pope et al., 2005); this association has been extensively documented (Sreshta et al., 2017). Treatment that specifically focuses on abuse of anabolic-androgenic steroids and other drugs that can build muscle or enhance leanness (such as stimulants) may be needed in addition to treatment that targets BDD.

A study (N = 63) that compared men with and without muscle dysmorphia (86% of whom had additional non-muscle-related concerns) found similarities in demographic features, BDD severity, delusionality of BDD beliefs, and number of non-muscle-related body parts of concern (Pope et al., 2005). However, men with muscle dysmorphia were significantly more likely to lift weights excessively (71% vs. 12%), diet (71% vs. 27%), and exercise excessively (64% vs. 10%). Those with muscle dysmorphia also had significantly poorer quality of life and higher lifetime rates of suicide attempts (50% vs. 16%) and substance use disorders (86% vs. 51%), including anabolic steroid abuse/dependence (21% vs. 0%). Thus, this form of BDD appears to be associated with severe psychopathology.

BDD by Proxy

Individuals with BDD by proxy are preoccupied with what they perceive to be defects or flaws in the appearance of another person who actually looks normal, such as a family member (Atiullah & Phillips, 2001; Greenberg et al., 2017; Phillips, 2005). BDD by proxy can substantially damage relationships, such as marital relationships. Like more typical forms of BDD, it can also cause suicide. In one case, a man in his fifties was so distressed by his conviction that he had caused his daughter to go bald (she actually looked normal), which he thought made her look ugly, that he committed suicide (Atiullah & Phillips, 2001). There are only limited studies of BDD by proxy, but the disorder is likely more common than is recognized.

Age of Onset and Course of Illness

BDD usually has an early onset, typically during early adolescence. In the largest clinical BDD sample (N = 293) and in a largely clinical sample (N = 200), BDD's mean age at onset was 16.0 ± 6.9 years (range 4–43) and 16.4 ± 7.0 years (range 5–49), respectively (Gunstad & Phillips, 2003; Phillips, Menard, Fay, & Weisberg, 2005). The mode was 13 in both samples, and two thirds of cases in both samples had onset of BDD before age 18. In the latter sample, the mean age of onset of subclinical BDD was 12.9 years (SD = 5.8; Phillips, Menard, Fay, & Weisberg, 2005). In a sample of patients selected for major depressive disorder who had lifetime or current BDD, the mean age of onset of BDD was 17.5 years (SD = 10.0; Nierenberg et al., 2002).

Unless it is appropriately treated, BDD is usually a chronic condition. In the only prospective observational study of BDD's course, the Longitudinal Interval Follow-up Evaluation (LIFE; Keller et al., 1987) obtained data on weekly BDD symptom status and treatment received over up to four years of follow-up for 166 subjects in a broadly selected sample. The probability of full remission from BDD (for at least eight consecutive weeks) was only 0.14 for up to two years of follow-up and only 0.20 for up to four years; the probability of full or partial remission was 0.44 for up to two years of follow-up and 0.55 for up to four years. On average, patients met full *DSM-IV* diagnostic criteria for BDD 69% of the time over the four-year follow-up period. These low remission probabilities occurred despite the fact that the majority of the sample received mental health treatment, although most treatment was not considered minimally adequate for treating BDD. In addition, more severe BDD symptoms at intake and a longer duration of BDD predicted a lower likelihood of partial or full remission from BDD (Phillips, Menard, Quinn, et al., 2013).

In the same study, psychosocial functioning was typically very poor at baseline and was significantly associated with more severe BDD symptoms (Phillips, Menard, Fay, & Pagano, 2005). Psychosocial functioning continued to be stably poor over one to three years of follow-up (Phillips et al, 2008). Only 5.7% of participants attained functional remission on the GAF (score of 70 or higher for at least two consecutive months), and only 10.6% attained functional remission on the Social and Occupational Functioning Assessment Scale (same definition of remission) during the follow-up period. Greater BDD symptom severity predicted poorer psychosocial functioning over time. More delusional BDD symptoms also prospectively predicted poorer functioning, but this finding was no longer significant when controlling for BDD severity.

Comorbidity

BDD is commonly comorbid with a number of disorders. In the largest BDD studies in a clinical sample (N = 293) and a largely clinical sample (N = 200), the most common comorbid disorder was major depressive disorder, with three quarters of both samples having lifetime major depression, and BDD usually had its onset before major depressive disorder (Gunstad & Phillips, 2003; Phillips et al., 2005). In these samples, 37% to 39% had lifetime social anxiety disorder, and 32% to 33% had lifetime OCD.

Substance use disorders were also common, with lifetime rates of 50% and 30% in the two studies. The lifetime prevalence of substance use disorders appears even higher in specific populations with BDD, such as veterans (75%; Kelly et al., 2010). Individuals with BDD who have a comorbid substance use disorder are significantly more likely than those without a substance use disorder to have attempted suicide (Grant et al., 2005). Use and abuse of anabolic-androgenic steroids are particularly common in people with the muscle dysmorphia form of BDD, which poses significant health risks (Kanayama et al., 2020). In addition, of note, in a study of entry-level military personnel, muscle dysmorphia was associated with a 5.4 times greater likelihood of using body-building supplements to get bigger (Campagna & Bowsher, 2016). These supplements can be dangerous and put individuals at risk for serious physical problems (Sreshta et al., 2017).

Regarding motives for substance use in people with BDD, in a study in a BDD sample of convenience that had very few exclusion criteria, nearly 70% of subjects with a substance use disorder said that BDD contributed to their substance use, with 30% of them citing BDD as the main reason, or a major reason, for their substance use (Grant et al., 2005). In another report that used an overlapping sample, among 101 adults with lifetime BDD who completed the Drinking Motives Questionnaire, scores for drinking to cope with negative affect were 1.6 SD higher than published community sample scores, followed by enhancement of positive affect (1.1 SD higher) and social motives (0.5 SD higher). In this study and a study of motives for drug use, coping motives were strongly associated with using substances because body image concerns were upsetting and with attempted suicide (Houchins et al., 2019; Kelly et al., 2017).

When other disorders (e.g., OCD, social phobia, major depression) are comorbid with BDD, individuals tend to have more severe BDD symptoms (Phillips, Didie, & Menard, 2007; Phillips, Pinto, et al., 2007; Ruffolo et al., 2006), more suicidality (Phillips, Didie, & Menard, 2007; Phillips, Pinto, et al., 2007), and greater functional impairment (Coles et al., 2006; Grant et al., 2005; Phillips, Didie, & Menard, 2007). The individuals are also more likely to have sought mental health treatment (Phillips, Didie, & Menard, 2007; Ruffolo et al., 2006) and to have a lifetime history of psychiatric hospitalization (Grant et al., 2005; Ruffolo et al., 2006).

Functional Impairment and Quality of Life

Psychosocial functioning and quality of life in BDD, as in other disorders, range from moderate to very poor, although on average psychosocial functioning and quality of life in BDD are notably poor (Didie et al., 2008; Hollander et al., 1999; Phillips, 2000, 2009; Phillips & Diaz, 1997; Phillips et al., 2008; Phillips, Menard, Fay, & Pagano, 2005). Unless BDD is well treated, functioning is usually substantially impaired in social, academic, occupational, and other important areas (Kelly, Brault, et al., 2017).

Social functioning is notably poor in BDD when assessed with standard measures. Social adjustment scores on the Social Adjustment Scale–Self-Report (SAS-SR) are significantly below community norms (Cohen d ranging from 0.82 to 2.07; Phillips, Menard, Fay, & Pagano, 2005). Similarly, social functioning scores on the SF-36 are 1.7 to 2.2 SD below community norms and 0.4 to 0.7 SD poorer than norms for depression (Phillips, 2000; Phillips, Menard, Fay, & Weisberg, 2005). People with BDD often feel embarrassed and ashamed of their appearance and fear they will be rejected by others because of their "ugliness." Thus, they tend to have high rates of social avoidance (Kelly et al., 2010), which can lead to few friendships and romantic relationships, as well as overall poor functioning (Kelly et al., 2010; Phillips, 2009). Individuals with BDD may also withdraw from others to the point that relationships and interpersonal skills are eroded, which can in turn lead to even more social avoidance and impairment. Supporting this, results from a prospective longitudinal study of individuals with BDD showed that social avoidance, both related and unrelated to body image, is associated with poorer psychosocial functioning over time (Ritzert et al., 2020).

Some individuals with BDD find it difficult to leave their homes because they don't want to be seen or because they become overwhelmed by BDD rituals, such as compulsive grooming, that they believe they must perform before they leave the house. Two studies found that 31% of 188 people with BDD and 27% of 200 people with BDD had been completely housebound for at least one week because of their BDD symptoms (Phillips & Diaz, 1997; Phillips, Menard, Fay, & Weisberg, 2005).

Impairment in academic or occupational functioning is nearly universal (Didie et al., 2008). Impairment may occur due to poor concentration, being late for work or school, or missing work or school days. In a sample of 200 adults, most of whom had a primary diagnosis of BDD, 32% wanted to attend school but were unable to because of psychopathology (Phillips, Menard, Fay, & Pagano, 2005). And, in a sample of 33 youth with BDD, 18% had dropped out of elementary school or high school primarily because of BDD symptoms (Albertini & Phillips, 1999). Furthermore, 39% of the adult sample reported not working in the past month because of psychopathology; fewer than half were working full time, and a significant proportion (23%) were receiving disability benefits (Didie et al., 2008). Those who were not working had more chronic and severe BDD symptoms. They were also more often males and had less education and more severe depressive symptoms (Didie et al., 2008). These individuals were also more likely to have been psychiatrically hospitalized and had a higher lifetime rate of suicidal ideation and attempted suicide.

Suicidality

Suicidal ideation and attempts are very common in persons with BDD (Phillips, 2007). In clinical cross-sectional samples, lifetime rates of suicidal ideation (78%–81%) and suicide attempts (24%–28%) are very high (Perugi et al., 1997; Phillips, 2007; Phillips, Coles, et al., 2005; Phillips & Diaz, 1997; Veale et al., 1996). The lifetime suicide attempt rate in BDD is an estimated 6 to 23 times higher than the rate in the U.S. population (Moscicki, 1997; Moscicki et al., 1989). In a retrospective study in two dermatology practices over 20 years, most patients who committed suicide had acne or BDD (Cotterill & Cunliffe, 1997).

In a German nationwide population survey (N = 2,552), those with current BDD reported notably higher rates of suicidal ideation (19% v. 3%) and suicide attempts due to appearance concerns (7% vs. 1%) than those without BDD (Rief et al. 2006). A subsequent epidemiologic study in Germany from the same group of authors found far higher suicidality rates among those with BDD: suicidal ideation due to appearance concerns occurred in 31% of the BDD group versus 4% of the non-BDD group; suicide attempts due to appearance concerns occurred in 22% of the BDD group versus 2% of the non-BDD group (Buhlmann et al., 2010).

More recent studies confirm these and other earlier reports. In a 2016 systematic review and meta-analysis of 17 studies that compared individuals with BDD to those without BDD (e.g., healthy controls, individuals diagnosed with eating disorders, OCD, or any anxiety disorder), those with BDD were nearly four times more likely to have experienced suicidal ideation (pooled odds ratio [OR] = 3.87) and 2.6 times more likely to have attempted suicide (pooled OR = 2.57). In a subsequent study in a partial hospital setting (N = 498), after adjustment for age, gender, and other psychiatric disorders, BDD had a significant association with suicidal ideation (OR = 6.62) and suicidal behaviors (OR = 2.45); in fact, these odds ratios were higher than for any other psychiatric disorder examined (Snorrason et al., 2019). In a replication study in a larger sample (N = 1,612), BDD was associated with suicide risk and inpatient hospitalization even after adjustment for age, gender, and other psychiatric disorders (Snorrason et al., 2020). And in the largest study of BDD and suicidality in two independent twin samples (N = 6,027 and N = 3,454), BDD was associated with a substantial risk of suicidal ideation and behaviors in late adolescence and early adulthood (Krebs et al., 2020).

In a logistic regression analysis using cross-sectional/retrospective data, more severe lifetime BDD was independently associated with an increased risk of lifetime suicidality (Phillips, Coles, et al. 2005). For each 1-point increase on a 9-point BDD severity scale, the odds of experiencing lifetime suicidal ideation increased by 1.48 (p = .003), and the odds of a suicide attempt increased by 1.59 (p = .005). The above-noted meta-analysis similarly concluded that the severity of BDD strengthens the association of BDD with suicidal thoughts and behaviors (Angelakis et al., 2016). Lifetime suicidal ideation was also independently associated with comorbid major depression, and lifetime suicide attempts were also independently associated with a comorbid substance use disorder or PTSD (Phillips, Coles, et al., 2005).

Taken together, these studies suggest that the relationship between BDD and elevated suicidality is independent of comorbidity, but that certain comorbidities, such as major depressive disorder, may further strengthen this relationship (Angelakis et al., 2016; Krebs et al., 2020; Snorrason et al., 2019, 2020).

The only study of completed suicide, to our knowledge, found that the annual rate of completed suicide appears to be very high (0.3%; Phillips & Menard, 2006) and higher than annual rates of completed suicide for other psychiatric disorders (Harris & Barraclough, 1997). The confidence interval in this study was large, however, and this important topic needs further study.

A number of factors that are characteristic of many individuals with BDD may potentially contribute to suicidality risk, including high rates of suicidal ideation and attempts, poor self-esteem, a history of abuse, high rates of unemployment and being on disability, being single or divorced, and poor social support (Didie, Tortolani, Pope, et al., 2006; Gunstad & Phillips, 2003; Perugi et al., 1997; Phillips, 2005; Phillips, Coles, et al., 2005; Phillips & Diaz, 1997; Phillips & Menard, 2006; Phillips, Menard, Fay, & Pagano, 2005; Phillips, Menard, Fay, & Weisberg, 2005; Phillips, Pinto, & Jain, 2004; Veale et al., 1996). Furthermore, BDD patients' often-delusional beliefs that they look deformed causes severe distress and self-loathing. This distress is further fueled by time-consuming, intrusive obsessions about the perceived "defects" and a belief that others mock and reject them because of how they look (Phillips, 2004), which in turn can fuel suicidal thinking and behavior.

BDD in Children and Adolescents

OCRDs in children and adolescents are discussed in Chapter 26. Thus, just a few key points are briefly noted here:

1. BDD is common among adolescents (Hartmann & Buhlmann, 2017).
2. BDD usually has its onset during early adolescence (Bjornsson et al., 2013).
3. BDD's clinical features are largely similar in adults and youth, although youth have significantly higher rates of suicidality and current substance use disorders (30.6% vs. 12.8%) as well as significantly poorer BDD-related insight (Phillips, Didie, et al., 2006; Scheider et al., 2019).
4. Suicidality is a significant concern in youth with BDD (Albertini & Phillips, 1999; Dyl et al., 2006; Krebs et al., 2020; Phillips, Didie, et al., 2006).
5. Aggression and violent behavior also appear common in youth with BDD (Albertini & Phillips, 1999; Phillips et al., 2017b).

Gender Similarities and Differences

Three studies with sample sizes ranging from 58 to 200 have directly compared females and males with BDD (Perugi et al., 1997; Phillips & Diaz, 1997; Phillips, Menard, & Fay, 2006); the studies contained mostly adults but also some adolescents. The studies found that females and males had more similarities than differences across a number of domains. The two groups were similar in terms of most demographic and clinical characteristics, such as which body areas were disliked, types of compulsive BDD behaviors, BDD severity, suicidality, and comorbidity. Of note, males were as likely as females to seek and receive cosmetic treatment, such as surgery, for their BDD concerns, whereas this is not the case in the general population (American Society for Aesthetic Plastic Surgery, 2008).

However, all three studies found some gender-related differences (Perugi et al., 1997; Phillips & Diaz, 1997; Phillips, Menard, & Fay, 2006). In all three studies, females were more likely to have a comorbid eating disorder, and males were more likely to be preoccupied with their genitals. Two of the three studies found the following differences: females were more likely to be preoccupied with their weight, hips, breasts, legs, and excessive body hair, and were more likely to hide their perceived defects with camouflaging techniques, to check mirrors, and to pick their skin as a symptom of BDD. In contrast, males were more likely to have muscle dysmorphia, to be preoccupied with thinning hair, to be single, and to have a substance-related disorder. Males also had significantly worse scores on one measure of psychosocial functioning, were less likely to be working because of psychopathology (for most, BDD was the primary diagnosis), and were more likely to be receiving disability payments (because of BDD symptoms or for any reason).

A study among 3,149 adolescents with probable BDD in a community setting found that, similar to findings from the above studies, males and females had largely similar clinical presentations (e.g., similar BDD symptom severity, rates of most elevated comorbid symptoms, and mental health service use; Schneider et al., 2019). Again, adolescent males were more concerned than females about their muscularity, and adolescent females were more concerned than adolescent males about their breasts/nipples and thighs. Adolescent male participants were more also likely than adolescent females to report elevated generalized anxiety symptoms.

Social support may also be an important factor that differs somewhat between men and women. In an Internet-based study of 400 participants with symptoms consistent with a diagnosis of BDD, greater perceived social support from friends and significant others was associated with less severe BDD symptoms for men, and greater perceived social support from family and friends was associated with less severe BDD symptoms for women (Marques et al., 2011). Perceived social support from a significant other was significantly negatively associated with BDD symptom severity in men, but not in women (Marques et al., 2011). Therefore, the type of support received and how that is associated with BDD symptom severity appear to differ between men and women.

Muscle dysmorphia is a form of BDD that occurs almost exclusively in males. Muscle dysmorphia appears to be particularly severe and to have some unique features that potentially have health risks, such as use of anabolic steroids (Brower, 2002; Kanayama et al., 2020; Pope et al., 2005). CBT approaches (see Chapter 22 in this volume) need to be modified somewhat to treat this form of BDD.

Sociocultural Factors

Because cultural issues pertaining to OCRDs are discussed in a separate chapter, it is just briefly noted here that there is very little research on racial and ethnic differences or cultural factors in BDD. BDD appears largely similar across cultures, but cultural values and preferences appear to influence BDD symptoms to some degree (Phillips, 2005). There is no evidence to suggest that BDD is more prevalent in some cultures than others, although this important topic has not been well studied.

Healthcare Utilization

BDD is often undertreated. In an early epidemiologic study from Florence, Italy, 40% of those with BDD had sought treatment from a psychiatrist and 20% from a general practitioner, 20% had sought psychotherapy, and 40% had sought no treatment for their BDD symptoms (Faravelli et al., 1997). More recently, literature has addressed healthcare utilization by individuals with BDD, but many of the studies utilized online self-report survey methods, which have the limitation of identifying people with probable BDD based on self-reported symptoms rather than a confirmed diagnosis. An online survey study of 172 individuals with BDD found that that only 18.6% were currently receiving psychopharmacological treatment, and only 19.8% were engaged in psychotherapy (particularly CBT, the first-line psychotherapy for BDD; Buhlmann, 2011). In another online survey study of 401 individuals with BDD, only 34.4% had been prescribed serotonin reuptake inhibitors (SRIs; the first-line medication for BDD), and only 17.4% had received CBT (Marques et al., 2011). Another healthcare utilization study using an online survey of people who met self-reported diagnostic criteria for BDD (N = 429) found that only 15.2% of those with BDD had been diagnosed with BDD (Schulte et al., 2020), and lifetime rates of engagement in mental health treatment were low (39.9%). Several barriers to mental health treatment for people with BDD were identified, including shame, a low perceived need for mental health treatment, and a preference for cosmetic and medical treatments (even though such treatments are rarely helpful and can worsen BDD symptoms).

BDD is commonly comorbid with certain psychiatric disorders and is relatively common in psychiatric samples, but it is unclear how many patients seek treatment for BDD specifically. It appears that individuals with BDD only rarely bring up their BDD symptoms with their healthcare providers. For instance, in two inpatient studies from the United States, 0% to 0.6% of patients mentioned their BDD symptoms to their clinicians (Conroy et al., 2008; Grant et al., 2001). This reticence appeared to be primarily due to embarrassment about BDD symptoms, fear of being negatively judged (e.g., as "vain"), and fear that the clinician would not understand their concerns (Conroy et al., 2008). This was the case even though in the first study, 81% of patients with BDD said that BDD was their major (or biggest) problem (Grant et al., 2001). Our clinical impression is that BDD is often misdiagnosed as another disorder (e.g., OCD, depression, anxiety disorder, and schizophrenia, as well as trichotillomania or excoriation disorder when BDD-related hair pulling or skin-picking are present), which may lead to ineffective treatment (Phillips, 2005).

A majority of those with BDD prefer, seek, and receive cosmetic treatment for their appearance concerns (Crerand et al., 2005; Hollander et al., 1993; Phillips, Grant, et al., 2001; Veale et al., 1996), and, conversely, a substantial proportion of persons seeking dermatologic treatment, cosmetic surgery, and other cosmetic procedures have BDD (see the section "Epidemiology"). In a general population sample in Germany, 7.2% of those with BDD had received cosmetic surgery, compared to only 2.8% of those without BDD (Rief et al., 2006). The psychiatric, surgical, and dermatologic literatures note that some patients with BDD pursue large amounts of cosmetic treatment, including repeat treatments for "failed" procedures (Cotterill, 1996; Crerand et al., 2004; Koblenzer, 1994). This is particularly concerning, given the poor outcomes that can occur. In a survey of plastic surgeons, 40% said a patient with BDD had threatened them legally and/or physically (Sarwer, 2002). Indeed, surgeons have been sued by patients with BDD in high-profile cases (Kaplan, 2000). Occasionally, dissatisfied patients have even murdered the physician who provided cosmetic treatment (Cotterill, 1996; Ladee, 1966; Phillips, 1991; Phillips et al., 1992).

Relationship to Other Disorders

OCD

BDD is a distinct disorder that nonetheless shares some clinical features with, and may be related to, certain other psychiatric disorders, including OCD, social anxiety disorder, and psychotic disorders. The largest number of studies that have directly compared BDD to another disorder have compared it to OCD. Indeed, for more than a century, BDD has been considered to be closely related to OCD (Janet, 1903; Morselli, 1891; Phillips, 1991; Stekel, 1949), and it is currently classified as an OCRD in both *DSM-5* and *ICD-11*.

Several studies have directly compared BDD and OCD across a broad array of clinical and demographic variables (Frare et al., 2004; Phillips et al., 1998; Phillips, Pinto, et al., 2007), and smaller studies have directly compared the disorders on selected variables. Data from various validators—including phenomenology, family history, comorbidity, and treatment response—indicate that BDD and OCD have similarities and may be related disorders. At the same time, the disorders also have some important differences. Some of the findings are briefly summarized here; more detailed reviews can be found elsewhere (e.g., Phillips et al., 2010; Simberlund & Hollander, 2017).

A notable similarity is that both BDD and OCD are characterized by obsessional preoccupation and compulsive behaviors (Phillips & Kaye, 2007). The preoccupations and behaviors focus on perceived appearance flaws in BDD, and on various non-appearance-related themes in OCD. Preoccupations/obsessions and compulsive behaviors in both disorders are equivalently intrusive, time-consuming, and difficult to resist or control (Phillips et al., 1998); they are also unwanted and not pleasurable (Phillips et al., 1994, 1995). One difference, however, is that BDD-related beliefs (e.g., "I am ugly") are more likely than OCD-related beliefs (e.g., "If I don't check the stove 30 times, the house will burn down") to be characterized by poor insight or delusional thinking (Eisen et al., 2004; McKay et al., 1997; Phillips et al., 2012; Phillips, Pinto, et al., 2007). Approximately 2% to 4% of OCD patients have absent insight/delusional disorder-related beliefs, compared to 32% to 38% of BDD patients (Eisen et al., 2004; Phillips, 2017a). Compared to individuals with OCD, those with BDD have significantly higher total scores (indicating poorer insight) on the Brown Assessment of Beliefs Scale and score significantly higher on all seven questions on the scale, which assess various components of insight (Phillips et al., 2012).

In three studies that directly compared BDD to OCD across a broad range of clinical characteristics, the disorders had many similarities—for example, many demographic features, gender ratio, age of disorder onset, disorder severity, course of illness (retrospectively assessed), and most comorbidity (Frare et al., 2004, Phillips et al., 1998; Phillips, Pinto, et al., 2007). However, in two of the three studies, individuals with BDD were significantly younger and less likely to be married than individuals with OCD (Frare et al., 2004; Phillips et al., 1998), and in one study, those with BDD had lower educational attainment (Frare et al., 2004). One study found that patients with BDD were more likely than those with OCD to have an occupation or education in art and design (20% vs. 3%), raising the possibility that an interest in aesthetics may contribute to BDD's development (Veale et al., 2002).

BDD and OCD are both associated with high rates and levels of functional impairment (Didie et al., 2007), although impairment may be somewhat worse in BDD than in OCD in education, employment, and other domains (Didie et al., 2007; Frare et al., 2004; Phillips et al., 1998). Several studies have suggested that individuals with BDD may be more likely to have comorbid major depressive disorder or a substance use disorder. BDD is also associated with higher rates of suicidality than is OCD (Angelakis et al., 2016; Frare et al., 2004; Phillips et al., 1998; Phillips, Pinto, et al., 2007; Snorrason et al., 2019, 2020).

High rates of comorbidity between BDD and OCD suggest that they may be related disorders. Lifetime rates of BDD in patients with OCD range from 3% to 37%, with an average of about 17% across studies (e.g., Brawman-Mintzer et al., 1995; Diniz et al., 2004; Hollander et al., 1993; Jaisoorya et al., 2003; Phillips et al., 1998; Simeon et al., 1995; Wilhelm et al., 1997). Conversely, about one third of individuals with BDD have comorbid OCD (Gunstad & Phillips, 2003; Phillips, Menard, Fay, & Weisberg, 2005). Despite such high rates of comorbidity, prospective comorbidity data suggest that BDD and OCD are not identical disorders. In a prospective study of the course of BDD, among persons with comorbid OCD, an improvement in OCD symptoms predicted subsequent BDD remission, but improvement in BDD symptoms did not predict subsequent OCD remission (Phillips & Stout, 2006). Furthermore, BDD symptoms continued to persist in about half of individuals whose OCD remitted (Phillips & Stout, 2006). If BDD were simply a symptom of OCD, improvement in BDD would be expected to predict OCD remission, and BDD would not be expected to persist after OCD symptoms remitted.

A family study found an elevated rate of BDD in first-degree relatives of probands with OCD compared to first-degree relatives of control probands (Bienvenu et al., 2000). More recent twin studies indicate that BDD and OCD (and other OCRDs) share genetic vulnerability but also have disorder-specific genetic influences (Monzani et al., 2013; for a more detailed discussion, see Chapter 6 in this volume).

While no studies have directly compared treatment outcome in BDD versus OCD, pharmacotherapy approaches have many similarities. BDD, like OCD, appears to preferentially respond to SRIs. Psychotherapeutic approaches for the disorders have notable similarities but also some differences (see Chapter 22 on the treatment of BDD).

Taken together, direct comparison studies of BDD and OCD are still limited, but the growing literature on the topic suggests that BDD and OCD have many similarities as well as some important differences, and that they are probably closely related but distinct disorders.

Psychotic Disorders
Although earlier editions of DSM and ICD classified BDD's delusional form (which applies to patients who are completely convinced that their view of their appearance is accurate) as a psychotic disorder (a type of delusional disorder, somatic type), this is no longer the case. BDD's delusional variant is now diagnosed as BDD with the absent insight/delusional beliefs specifier. Indeed, a number of studies indicate that there are many more similarities than differences between delusional and nondelusional BDD across a broad range of features (Mancuso et al., 2010; Phillips et al., 1994, 2014; Phillips, Menard, Pagano, et al., 2006). Delusional and nondelusional BDD have been shown to not significantly differ in terms of most demographic features, core BDD symptoms (preoccupations and compulsive behaviors), most measures of functional impairment and quality of life, comorbidity, and family history. Two studies found that on a number of measures, delusional subjects evidenced greater morbidity; however, this finding appeared to be accounted for by greater BDD symptom severity (Mancuso et al., 2010; Phillips, Menard, Pagano, et al., 2006).

Of clinical importance, pharmacotherapy studies have consistently found that delusional BDD responds as robustly as nondelusional BDD to SRI monotherapy, which differs from the treatment of delusions in patients with schizophrenia or other psychotic disorders (Hollander et al., 1999; Phillips et al., 2002; Phillips & Hollander, 2008; Phillips, McElroy, et al., 2001). Data on response to antipsychotics as monotherapy are very limited, but it appears that they may not be efficacious as monotherapy for either delusional or nondelusional BDD (Phillips, 2017c).

Our clinical experience indicates that BDD is sometimes misdiagnosed as schizophrenia or another psychotic disorder, because BDD beliefs can be delusional, and patients can have prominent delusions of reference. However, BDD beliefs are usually not bizarre, nor is BDD characterized by other psychotic symptoms or formal thought disorder. Nor does BDD appear to be closely related to schizophrenia when other validators, such as comorbidity, family history, or treatment response, are considered (Phillips, 2005).

Social Anxiety Disorder
BDD and social anxiety disorder (SAD) are distinct mental health disorders that also have several features in common. The most important clinical similarities between SAD and BDD are high levels of social anxiety and social avoidance (Kelly & Kent, 2017). The

two disorders also share fear of shame, embarrassment, and scrutiny by others. Studies of BDD indicate that social anxiety symptoms range from 1.3 to 1.7 SD higher than in normative samples (Kelly et al., 2010; Pinto & Phillips, 2005; Veale et al., 2003). In SAD, the social fear and avoidance are due to fear of negative evaluation, embarrassment, and judgment in social and performance-based situations. In contrast to SAD, the social fear and avoidance often observed in BDD are largely related to perceived appearance concerns and not to a more general fear of negative evaluation (Kelly et al., 2010). Although social anxiety and fear of negative evaluation are also common in BDD, these are not included in the diagnostic criteria for BDD in *DSM-5*, although they are included in the accompanying text. Because social anxiety is a prominent characteristic of both BDD and SAD, BDD has been proposed to be part of a SAD spectrum (Stein et al., 2004), although this recommendation does not consider the prominence of rituals in BDD.

In the general population, the lifetime prevalence of SAD ranges from 7% to 13% (Furmark, 2002), whereas the lifetime prevalence of BDD is approximately 1.7% to 2.9% (Hartmann & Buhlmann, 2017). Point prevalence rates of comorbid BDD in individuals with SAD range from 8% to 12% (Wilhelm et al., 1997; Zimmerman & Mattia, 1998). Conversely, the point prevalence rate and lifetime prevalence rate of comorbid SAD in BDD is much higher (31%–37%; Gunstad & Phillips, 2003, Phillips, Menard, Fay, & Weisberg, 2005). These findings of elevated comorbidity suggest that BDD and SAD may have shared etiology and pathophysiology and thus may be related conditions.

Evidence for the treatment of both BDD and SAD supports the use of SRIs as first-line medications for both disorders (Phillips & Hollander, 2008; Stein & Stein, 2008). However, the pharmacotherapy of SAD differs in some ways from that of BDD (Phillips & McElroy, 2000). When CBT is used as the first-line psychosocial treatment for both BDD and SAD (Stein & Stein, 2008; Wilhelm et al., 2014) the approaches are similar, including cognitive restructuring and exposure exercises for anxiety-provoking stimuli and situations, which involve exposure to distressing and typically avoided social situations (Stein & Stein, 2008; Wilhelm et al., 2014). However, CBT for BDD (see Chapter 22) also includes different treatment components, including response (ritual) prevention for compulsive behaviors and perceptual retraining to help patients with BDD to develop a more global and nonjudgmental view of their body (Wilhelm et al., 2014).

Overall, although BDD is classified as an OCRD in *DSM-5*, there is a significant overlap in clinical features, high comorbidity rates, and similarities in intervention approaches for both BDD and SAD. More research is necessary to understand their relationship and the underlying mechanisms that may connect the disorders.

Conclusion

BDD is common in the general population, and its prevalence is even higher in mental health and cosmetic treatment settings. BDD is distressing and often severely impairing, yet it often goes unrecognized and undiagnosed. BDD is associated with notable morbidity and markedly elevated rates of suicidality. BDD is related to OCD and likely to other disorders as well, but it is also a distinct disorder with unique clinical features.

Future Directions

Knowledge of BDD's phenomenology is greatly advancing; however, BDD is still understudied compared to many other severe mental disorders, and much more research is needed on its clinical features. Further investigation is needed on all aspects of BDD, including its prevalence, clinical features, associated suicidality, other forms of morbidity, and pathogenesis. Such research is expected to improve detection, treatment, and prevention of this often-disabling disorder.

Research on BDD is especially limited and greatly needed in youth, when this disorder usually has it onset, as well as in the elderly. Research related to race, ethnicity, and cultural context is especially limited and needed. Another important research area is understanding of why and how frequently BDD is underrecognized in mental health settings, cosmetic treatment settings, and other settings, and how barriers to its recognition can be overcome.

Little is known about the course of BDD. To date, there has been only one prospective longitudinal observational study of BDD (Phillips, Pagano, Menard, Fay, & Stout, 2005; Phillips, Pagano, Menard, & Stout, 2006; Phillips et al., 2008). More research is necessary to understand the longitudinal course of BDD, particularly with regard to morbidity and mortality.

Finally, another major avenue of future research should focus on the relationship between BDD and other disorders. A number of direct comparison studies have examined BDD's relationship to OCD, but because social anxiety appears to be a prominent feature of BDD, future studies should investigate BDD's relationship to SAD and other anxiety disorders. As continued research elucidates BDD's pathogenesis, this work is expected to shed further light on its relationship to other disorders, such as OCD. In summary, much more research is necessary to further our understanding of this common and severe disorder.

References

Albertini, R. S., & Phillips, K. A. (1999). Thirty-three cases of body dysmorphic disorder in children and adolescents. *Journal of the American Academy of Child and Adolescent Psychiatry, 38*, 453–459.

American Psychiatric Association (APA). (1987). *Diagnostic and statistical manual of mental disorders* (3rd ed., revised).

American Psychiatric Association (APA). (2000). *Diagnostic and statistical manual of mental disorders* (4th ed., text revision).

American Psychiatric Association (APA). (2013). *Diagnostic and statistical manual of mental disorders* (5th ed.).

American Society for Aesthetic Plastic Surgery. (2008). *Cosmetic Surgery National Data Bank statistics*.

Angelakis, I., Gooding, P., & Panagioti, M. (2016). Suicidality in body dysmorphic disorder (BDD): A systematic review with meta-analysis. *Clinical Psychology Review, 49*, 55–66.

Atiullah, N., & Phillips, K. A. (2001). Fatal body dysmorphic disorder by proxy [Letter]. *The Journal of Clinical Psychiatry, 62*, 204–205.

Biby, E. L. (1998). The relationship between body dysmorphic disorder and depression, self-esteem, somatization, and obsessive-compulsive disorder. *Journal of Clinical Psychology, 54*, 489–499.

Bienvenu, O. J., Samuels, J. F., Riddle, M. A., Hoehn-Saric, R., Liang, K. Y., Cullen, B. A., et al. (2000). The relationship of obsessive-compulsive disorder to possible spectrum disorders: Results from a family study. *Biological Psychiatry, 48*, 287–293.

Bjornsson, A. S., Didie, E. R., Grant, J. E., Menard, W., Stalker, E., & Phillips, K. A. (2013). Age at onset and clinical correlates in body dysmorphic disorder. *Comprehensive Psychiatry, 54*, 893–903.

Bohne, A., Wilhelm, S., Keuthen, N. J., Florin, I., Baer, L., & Jenike, M. A. (2002). Prevalence of body dysmorphic disorder in a German college student sample. *Psychiatry Research, 109*, 101–104.

Brohede, S., Wingren, G., Wijma, B., & Wijma, K. (2014). Prevalence of body dysmorphic disorder among Swedish women: A population-based study. *Comprehensive Psychiatry, 58*, 108–115.

Brawman-Mintzer, O., Lydiard, R. B., Phillips, K. A., Morton, A., Czepowicz, V., Emmanuel, N., et al. (1995). Body dysmorphic disorder in patients with anxiety disorders and major depression: A comorbidity survey. *The American Journal of Psychiatry, 152*, 1665–1667.

Brower, K. (2002). Anabolic steroid abuse and dependence. *Current Psychiatry Reports, 4*, 377–383.

Buhlmann, U. (2011). Treatment barriers for individuals with body dysmorphic disorder: An Internet survey. *The Journal of Nervous and Mental Disease, 199*, 268–271.

Buhlmann, U., Glaesmer, H., Mewes, R., Fama, J. M., Wilhelm, S., Brähler, E., & Rief, W. (2010). Updates on the prevalence of body dysmorphic disorder: A population-based survey. *Psychiatry Research, 178*, 171–175.

Buhlmann, U., Teachman, B. A., Naumann, E., Fehlinger, T., & Rief, W. (2009). The meaning of beauty: Implicit and explicit self-esteem and attractiveness beliefs in body dysmorphic disorder. *Journal of Anxiety Disorders, 23*, 694–702.

Buhlmann, U., Wilhelm, S., McNally, R. J., Tuschen-Caffier, B., Baer, L., & Jenike, M. A. (2002). Interpretative biases for ambiguous information in body dysmorphic disorder. *CNS Spectrums, 7*, 441–443.

Campagna, J. D., & Bowsher, B. (2016). Prevalence of body dysmorphic disorder and muscle dysmorphia among entry-level military personnel. *Military Medicine, 181*, 494–501.

Cansever, A., Uzun, O., Donmez, E., & Ozsahin, A. (2003). The prevalence and clinical features of body dysmorphic disorder in college students: A study in a Turkish sample. *Comprehensive Psychiatry, 44*, 60–64.

Cash, T. F., Winstead, B. A., & Janda, L. H. (1986). The great American shape-up: Body image survey report. *Psychology Today, 20*, 30–37.

Coles, M. E., Phillips, K. A., Menard, W., Pagano, M. E., Fay, C., Weisberg, R. B., & Stout, R. L. (2006). Body dysmorphic disorder and social phobia: Cross-sectional and prospective data. *Depression and Anxiety, 23*, 26–33.

Conroy, M., Menard, W., Fleming-Ives, K., Modha, P., Cerullo, H., & Phillips, K. (2008). Prevalence and clinical characteristics of body dysmorphic disorder in an adult inpatient setting. *General Hospital Psychiatry, 30*, 67–72.

Cotterill, J. A. (1981). Dermatological non-disease: A common and potentially fatal disturbance of cutaneous body image. *British Journal of Dermatology, 104*, 611–619.

Cotterill, J. A. (1996). Body dysmorphic disorder. *Dermatology Clinics, 14*, 457–463.

Cotterill, J. A., & Cunliffe, W. J. (1997). Suicide in dermatological patients. *British Journal of Dermatology, 137*, 246–250.

Costa, C., Lucas, D., Chagas Assunção, M., Arzeno Ferrão, Y., Archetti Conrado, L., Hajaj Gonzalez, C., et al. (2012). Body dysmorphic disorder in patients with obsessive-compulsive disorder: Prevalence and clinical correlates. *Depression and Anxiety, 29*, 966–975.

Crerand, C. E., Phillips, K. A., Menard, W., & Fay, C. (2005). Non-psychiatric medical treatment of body dysmorphic disorder. *Psychosomatics, 46*, 549–555.

Crerand, C. E., Sarwer, D. B., Magee, L., Gibbons, C., Lowe, M., Bartlett, S., et al. (2004). Rate of body dysmorphic disorder among patients seeking facial plastic surgery. *Psychiatric Annals, 34*, 958–965.

Crerand, C. E., Sarwer, D. B., & Ryan, M. (2017). Cosmetic medical and surgical treatments and body dysmorphic disorder. In K. A. Phillips (Ed.), *Body dysmorphic disorder: Advances in research and clinical practice*. Oxford University Press.

DeMarco, L. M., Li, L. C., Phillips, K. A., & McElroy, S. L. (1998). Perceived stress in body dysmorphic disorder. *The Journal of Nervous and Mental Disease, 186*, 724–726.

Dey, J. K., Ishii, M., Phillis, M., Byrne, P. J., Boahene, K. D., & Ishii, L. E. (2015). Body dysmorphic disorder in a facial plastic and reconstructive surgery clinic: Measuring prevalence, assessing comorbidities, and validating a feasible screening instrument. *JAMA Facial Plastic Surgery, 17*, 137–143.

Didie, E. R., Menard, W., Stern, A. P., & Phillips, K. A. (2008). Occupational functioning and impairment in adults with body dysmorphic disorder. *Comprehensive Psychiatry, 49*, 561–569.

Didie, E. R., Tortolani, C. C., Pope, C. G., Menard, W., Fay, C., & Phillips, K. A. (2006). Childhood abuse and neglect in body dysmorphic disorder. *Child Abuse and Neglect, 30*, 1105–1115.

Didie, E. R., Tortolani, C. C., Walters, M., Menard, W., Fay, C., & Phillips, K. A. (2006). Social functioning in body dysmorphic disorder: Assessment considerations. *Psychiatric Quarterly, 77*, 223–229.

Didie, E. R., Walters, M. M., Pinto, A., Menard, W., Eisen, J. L., Mancebo, M., et al. (2007). A comparison of quality of life and psychosocial functioning in obsessive-compulsive disorder and body dysmorphic disorder. *Annals of Clinical Psychiatry, 19*, 181–186.

Diniz, J. B., Rosario-Campos, M. C., Shavitt, R. G., Curi, M., Hounie, A. G., Brotto, S. A., et al. (2004). Impact of age at onset and duration of illness on the expression of comorbidities in obsessive-compulsive disorder. *The Journal of Clinical Psychiatry, 65*, 22–27.

Dyl, J., Kittler, J., Phillips, K. A., & Hunt, J. I. (2006). Body dysmorphic disorder and other clinically significant body image concerns in adolescent psychiatric inpatients: Prevalence and clinical characteristics. *Child Psychiatry and Human Development, 36*, 369–382.

Eisen, J. L., Phillips, K. A., Baer, L., Beer, D. A., Atala, K. D., & Rasmussen, S. A. (1998). The Brown Assessment of Beliefs Scale: Reliability and validity. *The American Journal of Psychiatry, 155*, 102–108.

Eisen, J. L., Phillips, K. A., Coles, M. E., & Rasmussen, S. A. (2004). Insight in obsessive compulsive disorder and body dysmorphic disorder. *Comprehensive Psychiatry, 45*, 10–15.

Faravelli, C., Salvatori, S., Galassi, F., Aiazzi, L., Drei, C., & Cabras, P. (1997). Epidemiology of somatoform disorders: A community survey in Florence. *Social Psychiatry and Psychiatric Epidemiology, 32*, 24–29.

Feusner, J. D., Arienzo, D., Li, W., et al. (2013). White matter microstructure in body dysmorphic disorder and its clinical correlates. *Psychiatry Research, 211*, 132–140.

Feusner, J. D., Hembacher, E., & Phillips, K. A. (2009). The mouse who couldn't stop washing: Pathologic grooming in animals and humans. *CNS Spectrums, 14*, 503–513.

Feusner, J. D., Moody, T., Hembacher, E., Townsend, J., McKinley, M., et al. (2010). Abnormalities of visual processing and fronto-striatal systems in body dysmorphic disorder. *Archives of General Psychiatry, 67*, 197–205.

Fontenelle, L. F., Telles, L. L., Nazar, B. P., de Menezes, G. B., do Nascimento, A. L., Mendlowicz, M. V., & Versiani, M. (2006). A sociodemographic, phenomenological, and long-term follow-up study of patients with body dysmorphic disorder in Brazil. *International Journal of Psychiatry Medicine, 36*, 243–259.

Frare, F., Perugi, G., Ruffolo, G., & Toni, C. (2004). Obsessive-compulsive disorder and body dysmorphic disorder: A comparison of clinical features. *European Psychiatry, 19*, 292–298.

Frías, Á., Palma, C., Farriols, N., & González, L. (2015). Comorbidity between obsessive-compulsive disorder and body dysmorphic disorder: Prevalence, explanatory theories, and clinical characterization. *Neuropsychiatric Disease and Treatment, 11*, 2233.

Furmark, T. (2002). Social phobia: Overview of community surveys. *Acta Psychiatrica Scandinavica, 105*, 84–93.

Grant, J. E., Kim, S. W., & Crow, S. J. (2001). Prevalence and clinical features of body dysmorphic disorder in adolescent and adult psychiatric inpatients. *The Journal of Clinical Psychiatry, 62*, 517–522.

Grant, J. E., Menard, W., Pagano, M. E., Fay, C., & Phillips, K. A. (2005). Substance use disorders in individuals with body dysmorphic disorder. *The Journal of Clinical Psychiatry, 66*, 309–311.

Grant, J. E., Menard, W., & Phillips, K. A. (2006). Pathological skin picking in individuals with body dysmorphic disorder. *General Hospital Psychiatry, 28*, 487–493.

Greenberg, J. L., Limoncelli, K. E., & Wilhelm, S. W. (2017). Body dysmorphic disorder by proxy. In K. A. Phillips (Ed.), *Body dysmorphic disorder: Advances in research and clinical practice*. Oxford University Press.

Gunstad, J., & Phillips, K. A. (2003). Axis I comorbidity in body dysmorphic disorder. *Comprehensive Psychiatry, 44*, 270–276.

Harris, E. C., & Barraclough, B. (1997). Suicide as an outcome for mental disorders: A meta-analysis. *The British Journal of Psychiatry, 170*, 205–228.

Hartmann, A. S., & Buhlmann, U. (2017). Prevalence and underrecognition of body dysmorphic disorder. In K. A. Phillips (Ed.), *Body dysmorphic disorder: Advances in research and clinical practice*. Oxford University Press.

Hitzeroth, V., Wessels, C., Zungu-Dirwayi, N., Oosthuizen, P., & Stein, D. J. (2001). Muscle dysmorphia: A South African sample. *Psychiatry and Clinical Neuroscience, 55*, 521–523.

Hollander, E., Allen, A., Kwon, J., Aronowitz, B., Schmeidler, J., Wong, C., et al. (1999). Clomipramine vs desipramine crossover trial in body dysmorphic disorder: Selective efficacy of a serotonin reuptake inhibitor in imagined ugliness. *Archives of General Psychiatry, 56*, 1033–1039.

Hollander, E., Cohen, L. J., & Simeon, D. (1993). Body dysmorphic disorder. *Psychiatric Annals, 23*, 359–364.

Houchins, J. R., Kelly, M. M., & Phillips, K. A. (2019). Motives for illicit drug use among individuals with body dysmorphic disorder. *Journal of Psychiatric Practice, 25*, 427–436.

Jaisoorya, T. S., Reddy, Y. C., & Srinath, S. (2003). The relationship of obsessive-compulsive disorder to putative spectrum disorders: Results from an Indian study. *Comprehensive Psychiatry, 44*, 317–323.

Janet, P. (1903). *Les obsessions et la psychasthénie* [Obsessions and psychasthenia]. Feliz Alcan.

Kanayama, G., Hudson, J. I., & Pope, H. G. (2020). Anabolic-androgenic steroid use and body image in men: A growing concern for clinicians. *Psychotherapy and Psychosomatics, 89*, 65–73.

Kaplan, R. (2000, March 7). What should plastic surgeons do when crazy patients demand work? *The New York Observer*, 1.

Keller, M. B., Lavori, P. W., Friedman, B., Nielsen, E., Endicott, J., McDonald-Scott, P., et al. (1987). The Longitudinal Interval Follow-up Evaluation: A comprehensive method for assessing outcome in prospective longitudinal studies. *Archives of General Psychiatry, 44*, 540–548.

Kelly, M. M., Brault, M., & Didie, E. R. (2017). Quality of life in body dysmorphic disorder. In K. A. Phillips (Ed.), *Oxford handbook of body dysmorphic disorder*. Oxford University Press.

Kelly, M. M., Didie, E. R., & Phillips, K. A. (2014). Personal and appearance-based rejection sensitivity in body dysmorphic disorder. *Body Image, 11*, 260–265.

Kelly, M. M., & Kent, M. (2017). Associations between body dysmorphic disorder and social anxiety disorder. In K. A. Phillips (Ed.), *Body dysmorphic disorder: Advances in research and clinical practice*. Oxford University Press.

Kelly, M. M., Simmons, R., Kraus, S., Wang, S., Donahue, J., & Phillips, K. A. (2017). Motives to drink alcohol in body dysmorphic disorder. *Journal of Obsessive-Compulsive and Related Disorders, 12*, 52–57.

Kelly, M. M., Walters, C., & Phillips, K. A. (2010). Social anxiety and functional impairment in body dysmorphic disorder. *Behavior Therapy, 41*, 143–153.

Kelly, M. M., Zhang, J., & Phillips, K. A. (2015). The prevalence of body dysmorphic disorder in a VA primary care behavioral health clinic. *Psychiatry Research, 228*, 162–165.

Kittler, J. E., Menard, W., & Phillips, K. A. (2007). Weight concerns in individuals with body dysmorphic disorder. *Eating Behaviors, 8*, 115–120.

Koblenzer, C. S. (1985). The dysmorphic syndrome. *Archives of Dermatology, 121*, 780–784.

Koblenzer, C. S. (1994). The broken mirror: Dysmorphic syndrome in the dermatologist's practice. *Fitz Journal of Clinical Dermatology, March/April*, 14–19.

Koran, L. M., Abujaoude, E., Large, M. D., & Serpe, R. T. (2008). The prevalence of body dysmorphic disorder in the United States adult population. *CNS Spectrums, 13*, 316–322.

Kozak, M. J., & Foa, E. B. (1997). *Mastery of obsessive-compulsive disorder: A cognitive behavioral approach*. The Psychological Corporation.

Kraepelin, E. (1915). *Psychiatrie* (8th ed.). JA Barth.

Krebs, G., Fernández de la Cruz, L., Rijsdijk, F. V., Rautio, D., Enander, J., Christian Rück, et al. (2020). The association between body dysmorphic symptoms and suicidality among adolescents and young adults: a genetically informative study. *Psychological Medicine*, 1–9.

Ladee, G. A. (1966). *Hypochondriacal syndromes*. Elsevier.

Leckman, J. L., & Mayes, L. C. (1998). Understanding developmental psychopathology: How useful are evolutionary accounts? *Journal of the American Academy of Child and Adolescent Psychiatry, 37*, 1011–1021.

Liao, Y., Knoesen, N. P., Deng, Y., Tang, J., Castle, D. J., Bookun, R., et al. (2010). Body dysmorphic disorder, social anxiety and depressive symptoms in Chinese medical students. *Social Psychiatry and Epidemiology, 45*, 963–971.

Maltby, N., & Tolin, D. F. (2003). Overview of treatments for obsessive-compulsive disorder and spectrum conditions: Conceptualization, theory, & practice. *Brief Treatment and Crisis Intervention, 3*, 127–144.

Mancuso, S. G., Knoesen, N. P., & Castle, D. J. (2010). Delusional versus nondelusional body dysmorphic disorder. *Comprehensive Psychiatry, 51*, 177–182.

Marques, L., Weingarden, H. M., LeBlanc, N. J., Siev, J., & Wilhelm, S. (2011). The relationship between perceived social support and severity of body dysmorphic disorder symptoms: The role of gender. *Revista Brasileira de Psiquiatria, 33*, 238.

Mayville, S., Katz, R. C., Gipson, M. T., & Cabral, K. (1999). Assessing the prevalence of body dysmorphic disorder in an ethnically diverse group of adolescents. *Journal of Child and Family Studies, 8*, 357–362.

McKay, D., Neziroglu, F., & Yaryura-Tobias, J. A. (1997). Comparison of clinical characteristics in obsessive-compulsive disorder and body dysmorphic disorder. *Journal of Anxiety Disorders*, *11*, 447–454.

Möllmann, A., Dietel, F. A., Hunger, A., & Buhlmann, U. (2017). Prevalence of body dysmorphic disorder and associated features in German adolescents: A self-report survey. *Psychiatry Research*, *254*, 263–267.

Monzani, B., Rijsdijk, F., Harris, J., & Mataix-Cols, D. (2013). The structure of genetic and environmental risk factors for dimensional representations of DSM-5 obsessive-compulsive spectrum disorders. *JAMA Psychiatry*, *71*, 182–189.

Morselli, E. (1891). Sulla dismorfofobia e sulla tafefobia. *Bolletinno Della R Accademia Di Genova*, *6*, 110–119.

Moscicki, E. K. (1997). Identification of suicide risk factors using epidemiologic studies. *Psychiatric Clinics of North America*, *20*, 499–517.

Moscicki, E. K., O'Carroll, P., & Locke, B. Z. (1989). Suicidal ideation and attempts: The Epidemiologic Catchment Area Study. In *Alcohol, drug abuse, and mental health administration: Report of the Secretary's Task Force on Youth Suicide, Volume 4: Strategies for the Prevention of Youth Suicide* (DHHS Publication No [ADM]89–1624). US Government Printing Office.

Neziroglu, F. A., & Yaryura-Tobias, J. A. (1993). Body dysmorphic disorder: Phenomenology and case descriptions. *Behavioural Psychotherapy*, *21*, 27–36.

Nierenberg, A. A., Phillips, K. A., Petersen, T. J., Kelly, K. E., Alpert, J. E., Worthington, J. J., et al. (2002). Body dysmorphic disorder in outpatients with major depression. *Journal of Affective Disorders*, *69*, 141–148.

Olivardia, R., Pope, H. G., & Hudson, J. I. (2000). Muscle dysmorphia in male weightlifters: A case-control study. *American Journal of Psychiatry*, *157*, 1291–1296.

O'Sullivan, R. L., Phillips, K. A., Keuthen, N. J., & Wilhelm, S. (1999). Near fatal skin picking from delusional body dysmorphic disorder responsive to fluvoxamine. *Psychosomatics*, *40*, 79–81.

Perugi, G., Akiskal, H. S., Giannotti, D., Frare, F., Di Vaio, S., & Cassano, G. B. (1997). Gender-related differences in body dysmorphic disorder (dysmorphophobia). *The Journal of Nervous and Mental Disease*, *185*, 578–582.

Perugi, G., Akiskal, H. S., Lattanzi, L., Cecconi, D., Mastrocinque, C., Patronelli, A., et al. (1998). The high prevalence of "soft" bipolar (II) features in atypical depression. *Comprehensive Psychiatry*, *39*, 63–71.

Phillips, K. A. (1991). Body dysmorphic disorder: The distress of imagined ugliness. *The American Journal of Psychiatry*, *148*, 1138–1149.

Phillips, K. A. (1999). Body dysmorphic disorder and depression: Theoretical considerations and treatment strategies. *Psychiatric Quarterly*, *70*, 313–331.

Phillips, K. A. (2000). Quality of life for patients with body dysmorphic disorder. *The Journal of Nervous and Mental Disease*, *188*, 170–175.

Phillips, K. A. (2004). Psychosis in body dysmorphic disorder. *Journal of Psychiatric Research*, *38*, 63–72.

Phillips, K. A. (2005). *The broken mirror: Understanding and treating body dysmorphic disorder* (revised and expanded text). Oxford University Press.

Phillips, K. A. (2007). Suicidality in body dysmorphic disorder. *Primary Psychiatry*, *14*, 58–66.

Phillips, K. A. (2009). *Understanding body dysmorphic disorder: An essential guide*. Oxford University Press.

Phillips, K. A. (2017a). Insight and delusional beliefs in body dysmorphic disorder. In K. A. Phillips (Ed.), *Body dysmorphic disorder: Advances in research and clinical practice*. Oxford University Press.

Phillips, K. A. (2017b). Suicidality and aggressive behavior in body dysmorphic disorder. In K. A. Phillips (Ed.), *Body dysmorphic disorder: Advances in research and clinical practice*. Oxford University Press.

Phillips, K. A. (2017c). Pharmacotherapy and other somatic treatments for body dysmorphic disorder. In K. A. Phillips (Ed.), *Body dysmorphic disorder: Advances in research and clinical practice*. Oxford University Press.

Phillips, K. A., Albertini, R. S., & Rasmussen, S.A. (2002). A randomized placebo-controlled trial of fluoxetine in body dysmorphic disorder. *Archives of General Psychiatry*, *59*, 381–388.

Phillips, K. A., Coles, M. E., Menard, W., Yen, S., Fay, C., & Weisberg, R. B. (2005). Suicidal ideation and suicide attempts in body dysmorphic disorder. *The Journal of Clinical Psychiatry*, *66*, 717–725.

Phillips, K. A., Conroy, M., Dufresne, R. G., Menard, W., Didie, E. R., Hunter-Yates, J., et al. (2006). Tanning in body dysmorphic disorder. *Psychiatric Quarterly*, *77*, 129–138.

Phillips, K. A., & Diaz, S. (1997). Gender differences in body dysmorphic disorder. *The Journal of Nervous and Mental Disease*, *185*, 570–577.

Phillips, K. A., Didie, E. R., & Menard, W. (2007). Clinical features and correlates of major depressive disorder in individuals with body dysmorphic disorder. *Journal of Affective Disorders*, *97*, 129–135.

Phillips, K. A., Didie, E. R., Menard, W., Pagano, M. E., Fay, C., & Weisberg, R. B. (2006). Clinical features of body dysmorphic disorder in adolescents and adults. *Psychiatry Research, 141*, 305–314.

Phillips, K. A., Grant, J. E., Siniscalchi, J., & Albertini, R. S. (2001). Surgical and nonpsychiatric medical treatment of patients with body dysmorphic disorder. *Psychosomatics, 42*, 504–510.

Phillips, K. A., Gunderson, C. G., Mallya, G., McElroy, S. L., & Carter, W. (1998). A comparison study of body dysmorphic disorder and obsessive-compulsive disorder. *The Journal of Clinical Psychiatry, 59*, 568–575.

Phillips, K. A., Hart, A., Menard, W., & Eisen, J. L. (2013). Psychometric evaluation of the Brown Assessment of Beliefs Scale in body dysmorphic disorder. *The Journal of Nervous and Mental Disease, 201*, 640–643.

Phillips, K. A., Hart, A. S., Simpson, H. B., & Stein, D. J. (2014). Delusional versus nondelusional body dysmorphic disorder: Recommendations for DSM-5. *CNS Spectrums, 19*, 10–20.

Phillips, K. A., & Hollander, E. (2008). Treating body dysmorphic disorder with medication: Evidence, misconceptions, and a suggested approach. *Body Image, 5*, 13–27.

Phillips, K. A., & Kaye, W. (2007). The relationship of body dysmorphic disorder and eating disorders to obsessive compulsive disorder. *CNS Spectrums, 12*, 347–358.

Phillips, K. A., & McElroy, S. L. (2000). Personality disorders and traits in patients with body dysmorphic disorder. *Comprehensive Psychiatry, 41*, 229–236.

Phillips, K. A., McElroy, S. L., Dwight, M. M., Eisen, J. L., & Rasmussen, S. A. (2001). Delusionality and response to open-label fluvoxamine in body dysmorphic disorder. *The Journal of Clinical Psychiatry, 62*, 87–91.

Phillips, K. A., McElroy, S. L., Hudson, J. I., & Pope, H. G. (1995). Body dysmorphic disorder: An obsessive-compulsive spectrum disorder, a form of affective spectrum disorder, or both? *The Journal of Clinical Psychiatry, 56*, 41–51.

Phillips, K. A., McElroy, S. L., & Keck, P. E. (1994). Obsessive compulsive spectrum disorder. *The Journal of Clinical Psychiatry, 55*, 33–51.

Phillips, K. A., McElroy, S. L., Keck, P.E., Pope, H. G., & Hudson, J. I. (1993). Body dysmorphic disorder: 30 cases of imagined ugliness. *The American Journal of Psychiatry, 150*, 302–308.

Phillips, K. A., McElroy, S. L., Keck, P. E., Pope, H. G., & Hudson, J. I. (1994). A comparison of delusional and nondelusional body dysmorphic disorder in 100 cases. *Psychopharmacology Bulletin, 30*, 179–186.

Phillips, K. A., McElroy, S. L., & Lion, J. R. (1992). Body dysmorphic disorder in cosmetic surgery patients [Letter]. *Plastic and Reconstructive Surgery, 90*, 333–334.

Phillips, K. A., & Menard, W. (2006). Suicidality in body dysmorphic disorder: A prospective study. *The American Journal of Psychiatry, 163*, 1280–1282.

Phillips, K. A., Menard, W., & Bjornsson, A. S. (2013). Cued panic attacks in body dysmorphic disorder. *Journal of Psychiatric Practice, 19*, 194–203.

Phillips, K. A., Menard, W., & Fay, C. (2006). Gender similarities and differences in 200 individuals with body dysmorphic disorder. *Comprehensive Psychiatry, 47*, 77–78.

Phillips, K. A., Menard, W., Fay, C., & Pagano, M. E. (2005). Psychosocial functioning and quality of life in body dysmorphic disorder. *Comprehensive Psychiatry, 46*, 254–260.

Phillips, K. A., Menard, W., Fay, C., & Weisberg, R. (2005). Demographic characteristics, phenomenology, comorbidity, and family history in 200 individuals with body dysmorphic disorder. *Psychosomatics, 46*, 317–325.

Phillips, K. A., Menard, W., Pagano, M. E., Fay, C., & Stout, R. L. (2006). Delusional versus nondelusional body dysmorphic disorder: Clinical features and course of illness. *Journal of Psychiatric Research, 40*, 95–104.

Phillips, K. A., Menard, W., Quinn, E., Didie, E. R., & Stout, R. L. (2013). A four-year prospective observational follow-up study of course and predictors of course in body dysmorphic disorder. *Psychological Medicine, 43*, 1109–1117.

Phillips, K. A., Nierenberg, A. A., Brendel, G., & Fava, M. (1996). Prevalence and clinical features of body dysmorphic disorder in atypical major depression. *The Journal of Nervous and Mental Disease, 184*, 125–129.

Phillips, K. A., O'Sullivan, R. L., & Pope, H. G. (1997). Muscle dysmorphia [Letter]. *The Journal of Clinical Psychiatry, 58*, 361.

Phillips, K. A., Pagano, M. E., Menard, W., Fay, C., &, Stout, R. L. (2005). Predictors of remission from body dysmorphic disorder: A prospective study. *The Journal of Nervous and Mental Disease, 193*, 564–567.

Phillips, K. A., Pagano, M. E., Menard, W., &, Stout, R. L. (2006). A 12-month follow-up study of the course of body disorder. *The American Journal of Psychiatry*, *163*, 907–912.

Phillips, K. A., Pinto, A., Hart, A. S., Coles, M. E., Eisen, J. L., Menard, W., & Rasmussen, S. A. (2012). A comparison of insight in body dysmorphic disorder and obsessive-compulsive disorder. *Journal of Psychiatric Research*, *46*, 1293–1299.

Phillips, K. A., Pinto, A., & Jain, S. (2004). Self-esteem in body dysmorphic disorder. *Body Image*, *1*, 385–390.

Phillips, K. A., Pinto, A., Menard, W., Eisen, J. L., Mancebo, M., & Rasmussen, S. A. (2007). Obsessive-compulsive disorder versus body dysmorphic disorder: A comparison study of two possibly related disorders. *Depression and Anxiety*, *24*, 399–409.

Phillips, K. A., Quinn, E., & Stout, R. L. (2008). Functional impairment in body dysmorphic disorder: A prospective, follow-up study. *Journal of Psychiatric Research*, *42*, 701–707.

Phillips, K. A., Siniscalchi, J. M., & McElroy, S. L. (2004). Depression, anxiety, anger, and somatic symptoms in patients with body dysmorphic disorder. *Psychiatric Quarterly*, *75*, 309–320.

Phillips, K. A., Stein, D. J., Rauch, S. L., Hollander, E., Fallon, B. A., Barsky, A., et al. (2010). Should an obsessive-compulsive spectrum grouping of disorders be included in DSM-V? *Depression and Anxiety*, *27*, 528–555.

Phillips, K. A., & Stout, R. L. (2006). Associations in the longitudinal course of body dysmorphic disorder with major depression, obsessive-compulsive disorder, and social phobia. *Journal of Psychiatric Research*, *40*, 360–369.

Phillips, K. A., & Taub, S. L. (1995). Skin picking as a symptom of body dysmorphic disorder. *Psychopharmacology Bulletin*, *31*, 279–288.

Pinto, A., & Phillips, K. A. (2005). Social anxiety in body dysmorphic disorder. *Body Image*, *2*, 401–405.

Pope, H. G., Gruber, A. J., Choi, P. Olivardia, R., & Phillips, K. A. (1997). Muscle dysmorphia: An under-recognized form of body dysmorphic disorder. *Psychosomatics*, *38*, 548–557.

Pope, H. G., Phillips, K. A., & Olivardia, R. (2000). *The Adonis complex: The secret crisis of male body obsession*. The Free Press.

Pope, C. G., Pope, H. G., Menard, W., Fay, C., Olivardia, R., & Phillips, K. A. (2005). Clinical features of muscle dysmorphia among males with body dysmorphic disorder. *Body Image*, *2*, 395–400.

Rief, W., Buhlmann, U., Wilhelm, S., Borkenhagen, A., & Brähler, E. (2006). The prevalence of body dysmorphic disorder: A population-based survey. *Psychological Medicine*, *36*, 877–885.

Ritzert, T., Brodt, M., Kelly, M.M., Menard, W., & Phillips, K.A. (2020). Social avoidance as a predictor of psychosocial functioning in body dysmorphic disorder: A prospective longitudinal analysis. *Cognitive Theory & Research*, *44*, 557–566.

Rosen, J. C., & Reiter, J. (1996). Development of the Body Dysmorphic Disorder Examination. *Behaviour Research and Therapy*, *34*, 755–766.

Ruffolo, J. S., Phillips, K. A., Menard, W., Fay, C., & Weisberg, R. B. (2006). Comorbidity of body dysmorphic disorder and eating disorders: Severity of psychopathology and body image disturbance. *International Journal of Eating Disorders*, *39*, 11–19.

Sarwer, D. B. (2002). Awareness and identification of body dysmorphic disorder by aesthetic surgeons: Results of a survey of American Society for Aesthetic Plastic Surgery members. *Aesthetic Surgery Journal*, *22*, 531–535.

Schieber, K., Kollei, I., de Zwaan, M., & Martin, A. (2015). Classification of body dysmorphic disorder—What is the advantage of the new DSM-5 criteria? *Journal of Psychosomatic Research*, *78*, 223–227.

Schneider, S. C., Turner, C. M., Mond, J., & Hudson, J. L. (2019). Sex differences in the presentation of body dysmorphic disorder in a community sample of adolescents. *Journal of Clinical Child & Adolescent Psychology*, *48*, 516–528.

Schulte, J., Schulz, C., Wilhelm, S., & Buhlmann, U. (2020). Treatment utilization and treatment barriers in individuals with body dysmorphic disorder. *BMC Psychiatry*, *20*, 69.

Simberlund, J., & Hollander, E. (2017). The relationship of body dysmorphic disorder to obsessive-compulsive disorder and the concept of the obsessive-compulsive spectrum. In K. A. Phillips (Ed.), *Body dysmorphic disorder: Advances in research and clinical practice*. Oxford University Press.

Simeon, D., Hollander, E., Stein, D. J., Cohen, L., & Aronowitz, B. (1995). Body dysmorphic disorder in the DSM-IV field trial for obsessive-compulsive disorder. *The American Journal of Psychiatry*, *152*, 1207–1209.

Simmons, R., & Phillips, K. A. (2017). Core clinical features of body dysmorphic disorder: Appearance preoccupations, negative emotions, core beliefs, and repetitive and avoidance behaviors. In K. A. Phillips (Ed.), *Body dysmorphic disorder: Advances in research and clinical practice*. Oxford University Press.

Snorrason, I., Beard, C., Christensena, K., Bjornsson, A. S., & Björgvinsson, T. (2019). Body dysmorphic disorder and major depressive episode have comorbidity independent associations with suicidality in an acute psychiatric setting. *Journal of Affective Disorders*, *259*, 266–270.

Snorrason, I., Beard, C., Christensena, K., Bjornsson, A. S., & Björgvinsson, T. (2020). Body dysmorphic disorder is associated with risk for suicidality and inpatient hospitalization: A replication study. *Psychiatry Research*, *293*, 113478.

Soriano, J. L., O'Sullivan, R. L., Baer, L., Phillips, K. A., McNally, R. J., & Jenike, M. A. (1996). Trichotillomania and self-esteem: A survey of 62 female hair pullers. *The Journal of Clinical Psychiatry*, *57*, 77–82.

Sreshta, N., Pope, H. G., Hudson, J. I., & Kanayama, G. (2017). Muscle dysmorphia. In K. A. Phillips (Ed.), *Body dysmorphic disorder: Advances in research and clinical practice*. Oxford University Press.

Stein, D. J., Ono, Y., Tajima, O., & Muller, J. E. (2004). The social anxiety disorder spectrum. *The Journal of Clinical Psychiatry*, *65*(Suppl. 14), 27–33.

Stein, M. B., & Stein, D. J. (2008). Social anxiety disorder. *Lancet*, *371*, 1115–1125.

Stekel, W. (1949). *Compulsion and doubt* (E. A. Gutheil, Trans.). Liveright.

Summers, B. J., Aalbers, G., Jones, P. J., McNally, R. J., Phillips, K. A., & Wilhelm, S. (2020). A network perspective on body dysmorphic disorder and major depressive disorder. *Journal of Affective Disorders*, *262*, 165–173.

Taqui, A. M., Shaikh, M., Gowani, S. A., Shahid, F., Khan, A., Tayyeb, S. M., et al. (2008). Body dysmorphic disorder: Gender differences and prevalence in a Pakistani medical student population. *BMC Psychiatry*, *8*, 20.

Tignol, J., Biraben-Gotzamanis, L., Martin-Guehl, C., Grabot, D., & Aouizerate, B. (2007). Body dysmorphic disorder and cosmetic surgery: Evolution of 24 subjects with a minimal defect in appearance 5 years after their request for cosmetic surgery. *European Psychiatry*, *22*, 520–524.

Veale, D., Akyuz, E. U., & Hodsoll, J. (2015). Prevalence of body dysmorphic disorder on a psychiatric inpatient ward and the value of a screening question. *Psychiatry Research*, *230*, 383–386.

Veale, D., Boocock, A., Gournay, K., Dryden, W., Shah, F., Willson, R., & Walburn, J. (1996). Body dysmorphic disorder: A survey of fifty cases. *The British Journal of Psychiatry*, *169*, 196–201.

Veale, D., Ennis, M., & Lambrou, C. (2002). Possible association of body dysmorphic disorder with an occupation or education in art and design. *The American Journal of Psychiatry*, *159*, 1788–1790.

Veale, D., Gledhill, L. J., Christodoulou, P., & Hodsoll, J. (2016). Body dysmorphic disorder in different settings: A systematic review and estimated weighted prevalence. *Body Image*, *18*, 168–186.

Veale, D., Kinderman, P., Riley, S., & Lambrou, C. (2003). Self-discrepancy in body dysmorphic disorder. *British Journal of Clinical Psychology*, *42*, 157–169.

Wilhelm, S., Otto, M. W., Zucker, B. G., & Pollack, M. H. (1997). Prevalence of body dysmorphic disorder in patients with anxiety disorders. *Journal of Anxiety Disorders*, *11*, 499–502.

Wilhelm, S., Phillips, K. A., Didie, E., Buhlmann, U., Greenberg, J. L., Fama, J. M., et al. (2014). Modular cognitive-behavioral therapy for body dysmorphic disorder: A randomized controlled trial. *Behavior Therapy*, *45*, 314–327.

World Health Organization. (2019). *International classification of diseases*, eleventh revision (*ICD-11*). https://icd.who.int/en

Zimmerman, M., & Mattia, J. I. (1998). Body dysmorphic disorder in psychiatric outpatients: Recognition, prevalence, comorbidity, demographic, and clinical correlates. *Comprehensive Psychiatry*, *39*, 265–270.

CHAPTER 4

Phenomenology and Epidemiology of Hoarding Disorder

Randy O. Frost *and* Mercedes Woolley

Abstract

Although scientific research on it began only in 1993, hoarding became an official mental disorder 20 years later with the publication of the 5th edition of the *Diagnostic and Statistical Manual of Mental Disorders*. In more than 25 years of research, a great deal has been learned about this fascinating disorder. This chapter addresses the phenomenology and epidemiology of hoarding disorder. Diagnostic criteria and specifying features of the disorder are reviewed in detail, with a focus on research related to each, including an overview of the attachments to possessions that define the need to save them. Among the attachments to possessions are opportunity and identity-related, comfort and safety-related, responsibility-related, and aesthetically related attachments. Also covered is the research on prevalence, onset, course, demographics, comorbidities, and associated features, along with an overview of the relatively few cross-cultural studies.

Key Words: hoarding disorder, clutter, attachments, difficulty discarding, excessive acquisition, squalor

Introduction

Hoarding disorder (HD) was introduced as a separate disorder in 2013, in the 5th edition of the *Diagnostic and Statistical Manual of Mental Disorders* (*DSM-5;* American Psychiatric Association [APA], 2013). Before its inclusion, scientific research on hoarding had a very short history, but outside of the scientific world, descriptions of hoarding appeared with some regularity in literature and the popular press. For instance, in the 14th century, hoarding appeared in Dante Aligheri's *Inferno*, where the fourth circle of Hell was reserved for "hoarders" and "wasters." In 1842, the Russian writer Nikolai Gogol described a classic hoarding case in his epic novel *Dead Souls*. In the novel, a widowed Russian aristocrat named Plyushkin

> wandered about the streets of his village every day looking under the bridges, under the planks thrown over puddles, and everything he came across, an old sole, a bit of a peasant woman's rag, an iron nail, a piece of broken earthenware, he carried them all to his room and put them on the heap. (Gogol & Magarshack, 1961, p. 126)

In perhaps the first recognition of hoarding as a psychiatric disorder, Russian psychiatry labeled the behavior Plyushkin syndrome. In the 19th century, similar characters regularly appeared in the novels of Charles Dickens, as well as those of George Eliot and Sir Arthur Conan Doyle.

Perhaps the most well-known hoarding case appeared in newspaper accounts of the Collyer brothers in New York City in the 1940s. The accounts started with a report that there was a dead body in the well-known eccentric brothers' brownstone. The severely cluttered state of the home set off an intense media frenzy that resulted in the brothers' name becoming synonymous with hoarding. Even today, among NYC firefighters, an extremely cluttered home is called a Collyer residence.

In psychiatric circles, some early theorizing about hoarding appeared prior to the 1990s, but with little follow-up. Eric Fromm (1947) described a "hoarding orientation," which he deemed one of four types of nonproductive character in which a sense of security was derived by collecting and saving things. In the 1970s, a Spanish psychiatrist, Juan Antonio Vallejo-Nagera, suggested a disorder that was a "mirror image" of a phobia. Instead of fear of a target stimulus, the person showed an abnormal attachment to it that provided an unjustified feeling of safety, leading to hoarding behaviors. Vallejo-Nagera termed the disorder Soteric neurosis, after the Greek goddess of safety (Fontenelle, 2016).

The first scientific study of hoarding was published in 1993 (Frost & Gross, 1993), and just 20 years later, HD entered the *DSM* as a separate disorder. Early research during this era considered hoarding to be a subtype of obsessive-compulsive disorder (OCD). However, as more research accumulated, it became clear that there were important differences in neurological and phenomenological features of hoarding that set it apart from OCD (Mataix-Cols et al., 2010). Research during this period also indicated that hoarding could be distinguished from normative collecting both in the way objects were collected and stored and with respect to demographic features of collectors versus people with hoarding problems (Nordsletten, Fernandez de la Cruz, et al., 2013).

Diagnosis

Difficulty Discarding Criterion

The *DSM-5* diagnostic criteria for HD contain four inclusion and two exclusion criteria, as well as two diagnostic specifiers (APA, 2013; Table 4.1). The first inclusion criterion is "persistent difficulty discarding or parting with possessions, regardless of their actual value" (p. 247, Criterion A). This is the cardinal feature of HD and refers not just to difficulty throwing possessions in the trash, but to any attempt to relinquish them (e.g., selling, donating, losing). The criterion requires that this difficulty be persistent and not just an acute problem that might, for instance, be experienced by the sudden inheritance of possessions of a deceased loved one. The wording of this criterion is carefully crafted to distinguish it from the *DSM* criterion for obsessive-compulsive personality disorder

Table 4.1 *DSM-5 Diagnostic Criteria for Hoarding Disorder*

A. Persistent difficulty discarding or parting with possessions regardless of their actual value.
B. The difficulty is due to a perceived need to save the items and to distress associated with discarding them.
C. The difficulty discarding possessions results in the accumulation of possessions that congest and clutter active living areas and substantially compromises their intended use. If living areas are uncluttered, it is only because of the interventions of third parties (e.g., family member, cleaners, authorities).
D. The hoarding causes clinically significant distress or impairment in social, occupational, or other important areas of functioning (including maintaining a safe environment for self and others).
E. The hoarding is not attributable to another medical condition (e.g., brain injury, cerebrovascular disease, Prader-Willi syndrome).
F. The hoarding is not better accounted for by the symptoms of another mental disorder (e.g., obsessions in obsessive-compulsive disorder, decreased energy in major depressive disorder, delusions in schizophrenia or another psychotic disorder, cognitive deficits in major neurocognitive disorder, restricted interests in autism spectrum disorder).
Specify if:
• With excessive acquisition: If difficulty discarding possessions is accompanied by excessive acquisition of items that are not needed or for which there is no available space.
Specify if:
• With good or fair insight: The individual recognizes that hoarding-related beliefs and behaviors (pertaining to difficulty discarding items, clutter, or excessive acquisition) are problematic. • With poor insight: The individual is mostly convinced that hoarding-related beliefs and behaviors (pertaining to difficulty discarding items, clutter, or excessive acquisition) are not problematic despite evidence to the contrary. • With absent insight or delusional: The individual is completely convinced that hoarding-related beliefs and behaviors (pertaining to difficulty discarding items, clutter, or excessive acquisition) are not problematic despite evidence to the contrary.

Reprinted with permission from the *Diagnostic and Statistical Manual of Mental Disorders*, Fifth edition, (Copyright 2013). American Psychiatric Association. All Rights Reserved.

(OCPD) that refers to the inability to "discard worn-out or worthless objects even when they have no sentimental value" (APA, 2013, p. 679). Research on problematic hoarding has shown that this description is inaccurate with respect to people with HD. Items collected by people with hoarding problems are not restricted to things that are "worn-out or worthless," and many of them are infused with sentimental meaning (Mataix-Cols et al., 2010).

Perceived Need to Save Criterion
The second criterion—"the difficulty is due to a perceived need to save the items and to distress associated with discarding them" (p. 247, Criterion B)—indicates that the hoarding behaviors are intentional. In other words, the difficulty discarding is not due to simply not caring about messiness or not being sufficiently motivated to get rid of things.

A growing body of literature has examined the nature of the perceived need to save and what makes discarding difficult.

Research on the perceived need to save items has focused on the meaning of possessions for people with HD. By and large, the nature of the items saved by people who hoard, and the reasons why they choose to save them, are strikingly similar to those of people who do not hoard (Frost & Gross, 1993). The reasons are simply experienced more intensely and applied more rigidly. They can be roughly classified into four meanings: opportunity and identity-related, comfort and safety-related, responsibility-related, and aesthetically related. These meaning types are by no means mutually exclusive. People with hoarding disorder usually report that several or all of the meanings are relevant to their saving behavior (Steketee et al., 2003).

Opportunity and identity-related attachments include an assortment of emotional and self-concept-related beliefs. Many of these are captured in the Emotional Attachment subscale of the Saving Cognitions Inventory (SCI; Steketee et al., 2003), which has been shown to be highly correlated with hoarding symptoms (Grisham et al., 2009; Kehoe & Egan, 2019; Phung et al., 2015; Taylor et al., 2018). For instance, one of the items, "I see my belongings as extensions of myself, they are part of who I am," is a common refrain among people with hoarding problems. The use of possessions to define a sense of self is normative (see Belk, 1988). However, for people with HD, the strength and rigidity of the beliefs and the wide variety and number of possessions to which they apply sets them apart from the beliefs of people without HD. Discarding any of the items raises fundamental questions about identity and is therefore threatening. "Throwing away this possession is like throwing away a part of me" is one of the items on the Emotional Attachment subscale of the SCI (Steketee et al., 2003). An intriguing aspect of this fusion of identity with possessions concerns what Markus and Nurius (1986) describe as the "possible self," which has to do with how people think about their future. For many people with HD, items are saved with a plan to do something with them. The plan forms a fantasized future self that never gets realized (Kings et al., 2017). Nevertheless, being in possession of the item provides the opportunity for the realization of that fantasy and discarding it would mean the abandonment of that future identity. Maintaining that opportunity is a frequent theme in hoarding clients. The experience is summed up by a quote from one hoarding client,

> Life is a river of opportunities. If I don't grab everything interesting, I'll lose out. Things will pass me by. The stuff I have is like a river. It flows into my house, and I try to keep it from flowing out. I want to stop it long enough to take advantage of it. (Frost & Steketee, 2010, p. 134)

At the same time, many people with HD save things to immortalize their past self, or at least an idealized version of it. Possessions serve as cues to past experiences that have emotional significance and a way to preserve an association with a specific person, place, or event that is part of one's personal history. People with HD experience this phenomenon in a more intense way than most people (Cherrier & Ponnor, 2010). For people with HD, physical possessions appear to be especially powerful memory cues. The Memory subscale of the SCI contains items pertaining to this phenomenon and reflects research findings that people with HD have poor confidence in their memory (Hartl et al., 2004): "I must remember something about this, and I can't if I throw this away." One hoarding client recounted the experience of trying to discard a memento from her daughter's childhood this way, tying it to her sense of self and her personal history. "If I don't keep it, it gets erased from my memory, as if it never happened."

Views of the self, both past and future, seem to be confused and ambivalent among people who hoard (Claes et al., 2016; Frost et al., 2007). Kings et al. (2017) suggested that saving possessions represents an attempt to resolve this self-ambivalence. The struggle to preserve both a fantasized future and an idealized past appears to reflect problems with the formation of identity and may be related to the attachment insecurities often found in people with HD (David et al., 2020).

The second prominent theme in attachment to possessions has to do with the safety signal value of possessions. Frost and Hartl (1996) suggested that possessions become strong signals of safety among people who hoard. Attempts to let go of them create feelings of vulnerability. A similar idea was developed by Kellett (2007), who proposed a "site-security" model of hoarding. According to this model, possessions are a major source of security, comfort, and safety for people who hoard. These ideas are similar to those of Vallejo-Nagera's Soteric neurosis (Fontenelle, 2016). Support for the association between hoarding behavior and beliefs about comfort, safety, and security have come from several studies (Frost et al., 1995; Hartl et al., 2005; Saxena et al., 2011).

Themes of comfort and safety are consistent with several other characteristics of people with HD. A large number of people with HD have experienced significant trauma (Hartl et al., 2005; Frost et al., 2011a), yet the frequency of posttraumatic stress disorder (PTSD) in them is not any higher than it is in patients with other disorders not characterized by a high frequency of trauma. Frost et al. (2011a) have suggested that hoarding or clutter may form a buffer against the development of PTSD. Frost and Steketee (2010) described a patient in treatment for HD whose PTSD symptoms surfaced only when the clutter near the area of a sexual assault occurred. A second characteristic tying comfort beliefs to hoarding is the tendency among people who have hoarding problems to give possessions humanlike qualities. Several investigations have found associations between hoarding symptoms and anthropomorphism (Burgess et al., 2018; Neave et al., 2015, 2016; Timpano & Shaw, 2013), especially for people who are lonely. There are numerous anecdotes from hoarding clients who ascribe humanlike qualities to objects like silverware or empty yogurt cups (Frost & Steketee, 2010). Kehoe and Egan (2019) suggested that such tendencies develop as an attempt to find comfort that cannot be obtained from other people, especially since interpersonal attachments are insecure.

Like OCD, HD is also associated with an exaggerated sense of responsibility for preventing harm. But in HD, the concern is for harm coming to possessions. The Responsibility subscale of the SCI reflects this belief and has been found to be closely associated with HD symptoms (Steketee et al., 2003). For the most part, the individual does not desire to save certain possessions, but simply does not want them harmed by being discarded. Frost and Steketee (2010) described the case of a woman who was troubled by the suffering of an empty yogurt container when it was discarded. She had no desire to save the container, but simply did not want it harmed. Such concerns overlap heavily with the tendency to anthropomorphize objects.

Frost et al. (2018) described a more intense form of responsibility they referred to as "material scrupulosity." They defined it as "an exaggerated sense of duty or moral/ethical responsibility for the care and disposition of possessions to prevent them from being harmed or wasted" (Frost et al., 2018, p. 20). The hallmark of this motive is the avoidance of waste. Examples include a woman who could not discard a three-quarters-full trash bag because it would be wasting the unused space, or a man who peeled the labels off food cans and used them as stationery so the labels would not be wasted. The basic principle behind this thinking is that things cannot be discarded until they are maximally used up. Violation of this duty results in a sense of guilt and moral failure.

This sense seems to cover a variety of concerns, including feeling responsible for finding a use for all possessions and an ethical obligation not to waste them. Concern about waste is one of the most frequent rationales for saving among people with HD (Bratiotis et al., 2019). It has been found to be the strongest and most consistent predictor of both excessive acquisition and difficulty discarding among HD individuals (Dozier & Ayers, 2014; Frost et al., 2015). Concerns about waste vary across cultures. For instance, Timpano et al. (2015) found concern about waste and usefulness to be the only belief related to hoarding symptoms among Chinese students, but it was one of many concerns among American students. Although material scrupulosity overlaps the Responsibility subscale of the SCI, it explains additional variance in hoarding symptoms (especially difficulty discarding) beyond the Responsibility subscale of the SCI (Frost et al., 2018).

One consequence of exaggerated responsibility and material scrupulosity is the amount of time and effort that must go into the management and letting go of possessions. People with hoarding problems often insist that they don't have a problem with saving too many things, but that they just don't have the time to get rid of them. Their attempts to let go of possessions are characterized by a great deal of time and effort to make sure that possessions are disposed of properly. The attempts are so involved and time-consuming that very few things end up being discarded. An example is the insistence that a good home must be found for any possession deemed to still have a useful life. The home must be one that ensures the item will be used to its full potential and not wasted.

The standards for what makes a good home are so high that finding one is nearly impossible. In such cases, the clinical picture is one in which clients with HD complain that they are working tirelessly to manage their possessions (and often they are), but little progress is evident. Difficulties with discarding appear to lead people with hoarding problems to eventually avoid any kind of "processing" and organizing of possessions. Once possessions come into the home, very little time is spent using, organizing, or doing anything with them (Frost et al., 1995). The limited categorizing and organizing abilities of people with HD exacerbate this tendency (Ayers et al., 2013; Wincze et al., 2007).

Another manifestation of the sense of responsibility is the intense effort to maintain control over possessions exerted by people with HD (Frost et al., 1995; Steketee et al., 2003). They often display intense anxiety and anger if anyone touches, moves, uses, or shares any of their possessions. This can lead to serious family conflicts unless family members "learn" what can and cannot be touched. This pattern of behavior may be responsible for the development of accommodating behaviors by family members, which can exacerbate hoarding severity. Several investigations have found significant accommodation in families in response to the hoarding family member's reactions to attempts to touch, move, or discard items (Drury et al., 2014; Nordsletten et al., 2014).

Finally, people with HD save possessions because they are aesthetically pleasing to a significantly greater extent than do people without HD (Dozier & Ayers, 2014; Frost et al., 2015). A special sensitivity to the aesthetic properties of physical objects, even those that appear dull or uninteresting to most people, seems to be a characteristic of those with hoarding tendencies. Frost and Steketee (2010) described a woman who was so awed by the shapes, colors, and textures or bottle caps that she saved large bags of them, and another case of a woman who saved everything with the color purple on it because of its beauty. Many anecdotal accounts describe people with HD collecting physically pleasing objects, often with plans to create works of art with them. However, little effort goes into actually creating a product. The exceptions to this are well-known artists who have shown clear hoarding tendencies (Frost & Steketee, 2010). The aesthetic sensitivity of people with HD has not been the subject of much research to date.

Clutter Criterion

The third criterion in the *DSM-5* diagnostic scheme for hoarding is: "The difficulty discarding possessions results in the accumulation of possessions that congest and clutter active living areas and substantially compromises their intended use" (APA, 2013, p. 247, Criterion C). This criterion describes the most visible feature of the disorder: clutter. It is a consequence of the behaviors described in the first two criteria. The emphasis here is on the "active living areas" of the home that are substantially affected. Having cluttered basements, attics, or garages is relatively normative in U.S. culture. Clutter in those areas of the home does not cause serious difficulties, while clutter in the living areas is most likely to interfere with normal functioning. There is a caveat in this criterion that if someone other than the individual has prevented the clutter, the diagnosis can still be made. This caveat is especially relevant for children, who have less control over their living environment. Making the determination will require some investigation by the clinician.

Clutter is not only a product of difficulty discarding, but also the result of a serious problem with the ability to organize. Neurocognitive impairments that are common in people with HD interfere with the ability to organize information as well as possessions (Woody et al., 2014). The impairments involve problem-solving, decision-making, categorization/concept formation, sustained attention, memory, cognitive flexibility, and organization (Woody et al., 2014). These features have not yet been fully explored, but they may be important to the etiology of hoarding. These cognitive challenges as well as difficulty discarding may lead people with hoarding problems to avoid the task of organizing possessions once items enter the home. Some findings suggest that once possessions are in the home, they are seldom used or moved (Frost et al., 1995).

In extreme cases, clutter and gross disorganization are accompanied by squalor, which has several health risks. Infestations, rotting food, mold, feces, and odors can all constribute to squalid living conditions. Historically, hoarding and squalor have been researched separately. Only a small number of studies to date have looked at squalor in the context of HD. The frequency of squalor in HD varies based on origin of the sample under study. Among research volunteers, the frequency of squalor in hoarding cases appears to be small (16%), but among cases identified by community agencies, the frequency is above 50% (Kim et al., 2001; Woody et al., 2020). When hoarding and squalor are combined, the health and safety risks of both become exacerbated. Squalor is more likely to be found in homes with increased clutter and animal hoarding (Frost et al., 2000; Kim et al., 2001; Luu, et al., 2018; Woody et al., 2020). In many cases, squalor interferes with the ability of community agencies to provide assistance because of health threats to workers exposed to such environments. Reports from one community agency indicated that as many as 71% of those looking to receive help for squalor were rejected because of health risks (McDermott & Gleeson, 2009, as cited in Luu et al., 2018).

Between one quarter and one half of identified squalor cases are accompanied by hoarding (Norberg & Snowdon, 2014). Lee et al. (2017) found greater impairment in visuospatial reasoning, abstraction, planning, organization, problem-solving, and mental flexibility among people with squalor only compared to the impairments in people with squalor and hoarding. Squalor in the absence of hoarding appears to be distinct from squalor in hoarding and is more likely to result from frontal lobe dysfunction (Norberg & Snowdon, 2014).

Impairment and Interference Criterion
The final *DSM-5* inclusion criterion is that "the hoarding causes clinically significant distress or impairment in social, occupational, or other important areas of functioning (including maintaining a safe environment for self and others)" (p. 247, Criterion

D). Impairment from hoarding ranges from mild to life-threatening. Mild impairments include the inability to find things as well as difficulties completing normal daily activities like cooking, using appliances, and moving about the home. At the more severe end of the spectrum, hoarding increases the risk of death by house fire (Lucini et al., 2009). Other risks include loss of work days due to the problem, being fired from a job, family conflict over the hoarding, financial difficulties, and legal problems, including having children taken away or being judged as committing elder abuse and neglect (Tolin et al, 2008).

Medical Condition Exclusion

The first *DSM-5* exclusion criterion for hoarding is that "the hoarding is not attributable to another medical condition (e.g., brain injury, cerebrovascular disease, Prader-Willi syndrome)" (Criterion E). There have been recorded instances of hoarding behavior developing following certain kinds of brain injury or cerebrovascular disease (Anderson et al., 2005). Several other conditions have been associated with hoarding behavior as well. One of the symptoms of Prader-Willi syndrome is hoarding of objects (Clarke et al., 2002). In addition, frontotemporal dementia may underlie some of the self-neglect and hoarding symptoms seen in conditions described as Diogenes syndrome (Finney & Mendez, 2017).

Mental Disorder Exclusion

The second exclusion criterion is that

> The hoarding is not better accounted for by the symptoms of another mental disorder (e.g., obsessions in obsessive-compulsive disorder, decreased energy in major depressive disorder, delusions in schizophrenia or another psychotic disorder, cognitive deficits in major neurocognitive disorder, restricted interest in autism spectrum disorder). (APA, 2013, p. 247, Criterion E)

Certain obsessive-compulsive symptoms like checking and cleaning can lead to the accumulation of, and failure to discard, large numbers of objects. However, the motivation behind the saving is clearly tied to the OCD symptom (Pertusa et al., 2010). Similarly, the focused interest characteristic of autism spectrum disorder can also lead to similar behaviors, although the disorders are clearly distinct (Pertusa et al., 2012).

Excessive Acquisition Specifier

Research suggests that a large percentage of people with HD engage in excessive acquisition (Frost & Mueller, 2014; Mataix-Cols et al., 2013; Timpano et al., 2011). However, it is not clear that all people who struggle with hoarding problems acquire excessively. For that reason, the *DSM-5* includes excessive acquisition as a specifier rather than a core criterion. Whatever underlies difficulty discarding may also underlie excessive acquisition, meaning that both are closely tied to the endophenotype (Timpano et al., 2011). The newest revision of the *International Classification of Diseases* (*ICD-11*) included excessive acquisition as a core feature of the disorder (Fontenelle & Grant, 2014).

Insight Specifier

The insight specifier in *DSM-5* is standard for the anxiety disorders. The percentage of individuals with HD falling within each insight category is unclear. Family members' ratings of insight in their hoarding loved one suggest a high percentage with poor (36%) or absent (19%) insight, defined as the extent of problem recognition (Tolin, Fitch, et al., 2010). Woody et al. (2020) reported poor insight in between 41% and 65% of clients in four samples drawn from community agencies, but in only 16% of a comparative research-based sample. Further, healthcare and other service professional rated insight among hoarding clients as significantly worse than that of nonhoarding clients. Despite these indications of poor insight, some research has shown "good or fair" insight in larger percentages of clients with HD (86%; Mataix-Cols et al., 2013), and that the vast majority of hoarding individuals report a willingness to seek treatment if it is available (85%; Tolin et al., 2008). Also, ratings of clutter severity done by clients with HD are reasonably accurate compared to assessor ratings of the same spaces (DiMauro et al., 2013; Drury et al., 2015; Frost et al., 2008). Some research suggests that the conflicting findings may relate to family and friends' overestimation of hoarding severity due to long-standing frustration with the individual's hoarding behavior (DiMauro et al., 2013).

Admission of a hoarding problem may be heavily influenced by the context of any interaction related to it. If the individual is feeling pressured or coerced into getting rid of possessions, the likelihood of a defensive denial of a problem increases. Hoarding behaviors are heavily stigmatized (Chasson et al., 2018), and people with HD experience intense self-criticism and shame associated with the behavior (Chou et al., 2018). Some have suggested that many people with HD recognize the hoarding as a problem, but they refuse to admit it to others in an attempt to forestall criticism and scorn (Frost et al., 2010).

Animal Hoarding

While *DSM-5* does not identify animal hoarding as an official subtype of HD, the accompanying text provides a description of the behavior and the suggestion that it may be a special manifestation of HD. The *DSM-5* text describes animal hoarding as

> the accumulation of a large number of animals and a failure to provide minimal standards of nutrition, sanitation, and veterinary care as well as failure to act on the deteriorating condition of the animals (including disease, starvation, or death) and the environment (e.g., severe overcrowding, extremely unsanitary conditions). Animal hoarding may be a special manifestation of hoarding disorder. (APA, 2013, p. 247)

Descriptions of the behavior and experience of people who hoard animals are similar to descriptions of object hoarding. People who hoard animals are extremely reluctant to let them go, even to shelters where proper care can be provided. The emotional attachments formed with the animals are extreme and rigid, with intense urges to "save" the animals, as well as distress when animals are removed by authorities (Steketee et al., 2011). Living areas are extremely cluttered with animals and related paraphernalia, and the resulting living environment and saving behavior interfere with normal living and use of the home. Animal hoarding appears to run a chronic course characterized by an exaggerated sense of responsibility and need for control over animals (Ferreira et al., 2017; Frost, Patronek, et al., 2011). These similarities indicate that the behavior meets the inclusion criteria for HD.

In contrast to object hoarding, where the hoarded objects themselves are not harmed by being hoarded, hoarded animals are neglected, are malnourished, and endure considerable suffering. Despite expressing great emotional attachment to their animals, animal control officials report that people who hoard animals express intense denials of any problems caring for animals even while standing in a room with malnourished, sick, and dying animals (Lockwood, 2018). In addition, many identified cases refuse to cooperate with authorities to ensure proper care for the animals (Frost et al., 2000). Such clear absence of insight has led to the suggestion that animal hoarding may be better considered as a form of delusional disorder (Lockwood, 2018). In addition to lack of proper care of the animals, the vast majority of animal hoarding cases are characterized by extreme squalor (Frost et al., 2000). In severe cases, the house requires demolition due to levels of urine and feces that have built up over the years. High levels of animal waste can generate toxic levels of ammonia and contribute to the spread of zoonotic diseases (Castrodale et al., 2010). While the number of animals contributes to these problems, how animals are cared for defines the problem more accurately than does the number of animals (Lockwood, 2018). Some states have attempted to criminalize animal hoarding (Lockwood, 2018), but at present, there is a pushback against the criminal prosecution of a recognized mental illness.

Although there is a paucity of epidemiologic data, animal hoarding appears to be more prevalent in women than in men (Ferreira et al., 2017; Hoarding of Animals Research Consortium [HARC], 2002). Case reports indicate that the average age of people who hoard animals ranges from mid-50s to 60s (HARC, 2002). Most are single, divorced, or widowed (Ferreira et al., 2017) and frequently are estranged from family and friends (Patronek & Nathanson, 2009). The average duration of identified cases is over 20 years (Ferreira et al., 2017). The resulting long-term isolation undoubtedly contributes to the increasingly distorted beliefs about animals and their care. The age of onset remains unclear in the current literature. In most animal hoarding cases, only one species is saved; this is unlike object hoarding, where variation in the type of objects collected is seemingly infinite (Frost & Gross, 1993). Prevalence of animal hoarding has not been carefully studied; however, based on case reports from humane societies and health and animal control agencies, Lockwood (2018) estimated over 5,000 cases per year in the United States. The most commonly hoarded animals in the United States are cats, followed by dogs, then birds. In addition, as many as 50% of people who hoard animals also hoard objects (Ferreira et al., 2017).

Patronek and colleagues (2006) suggested that there may be three types of animal hoarding, based on the motivations to save animals. "Overwhelmed caregivers" have a history of adequate care of animals, but because of a change in circumstances (e.g., health, loss of partner, job, financial resources) no longer have the resources to deal with large numbers of animals. Social isolation interferes with help-seeking under these circumstances. These cases tend to be the least severe and easiest to resolve. "Rescuers" harbor the belief that it is their mission to save animals. In contrast to overwhelmed caregivers, they actively acquire large numbers of animals. Their beliefs about their animals frequently appear delusional, especially with respect to their "special abilities" to communicate with, understand, and care for animals, yet they fail to clearly see the animals' suffering. "Exploiters" are the most serious cases. Their hoarding is tied to antisocial behavior. They appear to lack empathy for either animals or people. The absence of true attachment to the animals suggests that instead of HD, these cases may be better classified as antisocial personality disorder.

Prevalence

Prevalence rates for hoarding vary considerably based on the method of assessment and the target population. Some have relied on assessment protocols designed for detecting OCD symptom dimensions or OCPD symptoms, while others have used variations of well-validated hoarding measures, but only one has used the *DSM-5* diagnostic criteria. Several large-scale investigations have used the single-item response about clutter or hoarding embedded in the World Health Organization's Composite International Diagnostic Interview (CIDI). Ruscio et al. (2008) examined CIDI data as part of the National Comorbidity Survey Replication (NCS-R; 2001–2003; $N = 9,282$). Hoarding was endorsed by 14.4% of the sample, the second highest frequency among OCD-related symptoms. Subramaniam et al. (2014) used the CIDI hoarding item in a cross-sectional, nationally representative sample of Singapore residents. They reported a lifetime prevalence rate of 2% for clinically significant hoarding problems. Using the same strategy, Fullana et al. (2010) reported a 2.6% lifetime prevalence rate using data from the European Study of the Epidemiology of Mental Disorders.

Rodriguez et al. (2013) relied on responses to a single item from the OCPD diagnostic criteria (difficulty discarding worn-out or worthless items with no sentimental value) to determine the frequency of hoarding among participants in the National Epidemiologic Survey on Alcohol and Related Conditions. Over 20% of respondents endorsed the item. Samuels et al., (2008) also used the OCPD hoarding criterion to determine prevalence among 742 participants in the Hopkins Epidemiological Personality Disorder Study. They reported a lower estimated prevalence rate of 5.3%. The remarkable variability among these studies probably comes from reliance on a single item, which does not accurately capture the complexity of HD symptoms.

Studies using cutoff scores form various self-report inventories have shown moderate rates of clinically significant hoarding. Studies using the Saving Inventory-Revised (SIR; Frost et al., 2004) have reported rates of 4.6% in Germany (Mueller et al., 2009), 3.7% to 6.0% in Italy (Bulli et al., 2014), and 2.5% in New Zealand (Spittlehouse et al., 2016). Similar rates were observed using the Hoarding Rating Scale (HRS; Tolin, Frost, et al., 2010). Iervolino et al. (2009) reported a prevalence rate of 2.3% among participants from the U.K. Twin Registry. Lopez-Sola et al. (2014) reported that between 1.6% and 3.3% of participants in the Australian Twin Registry exceeded cutoff scores. Timpano et al. (2011) reported a slightly higher prevalence among a representative sample of German citizens (5.8%). Ivanov et al. (2017) found much lower prevalence rates using HRS cutoffs with two adult samples from the Swedish Twin Registry. Among 18-year-olds, the point prevalence rate was 0.9%, and for young adults (ages 20 to 28) the rate was 0.8%. Two studies used data from the Netherlands Twin Registry but reported somewhat different findings. Zihao et al. (2016) found a prevalence rate of 5% for clinically significant hoarding using the HRS. In contrast, Cath et al. (2017) used selected items from the HRS that were associated with each *DSM-5* criterion among a sample of 15,000 from the registry. The overall rate for clinically significant hoarding was 2.12% but varied across ages, with the youngest having a rate below 2%, while for those over 70 the rate was 6%.

In the only study using strict *DSM-5* criteria, Nordsletten, Reichenberg, et al. (2013) reported a point prevalence rate of 1.5% in a two-way epidemiological study in London. However, the door-to-door recruitment strategy may have resulted in lower prevalence due to reticence on the part of potential participants to open the door to investigators.

A review and meta-analysis of 11 of the above-mentioned prevalence studies (Postlethwaite et al., 2019; total N > 53,000 cases) concluded the pooled point prevalence estimate to be 2.6% (95% CI = 1.7%–3.7%). For the two studies examining lifetime prevalence, the pooled prevalence rate was 1.7% (95% CI = 0.4%–6.8%). The overall pooled prevalence rate was 2.5% (95% CI = 1.7%–3.6%). The meta-analysis by Postlethwaite et al. (2019) provides the best estimate to date of the true prevalence of significant hoarding symptoms. However, estimates may be influenced by shame, self-criticism, and limited insight, which are frequently associated with hoarding symptoms (Chou et al., 2018; Kim et al., 2000; Tolin, Fitch, et al., 2010) and undoubtedly play a role in people's willingness to admit hoarding problems, especially to strangers conducting surveys.

Onset

Onset of hoarding symptoms occurs relatively early in life, with the average age of onset being 16.9 years (Zaboski et al., 2019). Onset studies necessarily rely on retrospective accounts of hoarding symptoms, which are subject to memory bias and decay. To reduce this source of variance, several studies have used prompts to assist targeting earliest memories of clutter, difficulty discarding, and excessive acquisition (Ayers et al., 2010; Grisham et al., 2006). These studies have generally shown an earlier age of onset than do studies not employing memory-assistance strategies. Onset studies that examine specific hoarding symptoms have reported that excessive acquisition appears to develop somewhat later than difficulty discarding or clutter (Grisham et al., 2006).

Few studies have directly examined hoarding in children. However, several studies of prevalence rates among 15-year-old participants have been conducted. Ivanov et al. (2013) used *DSM-5* criteria derived from the HRS and found clinically significant hoarding in 2% of 15-year-old twins in Sweden. When the clutter criterion was omitted, the rate rose to 3.7%. In a subsequent study, Ivanov et al. (2017) reported a prevalence rate of 1.5% also in a sample of 15-year-olds. These frequencies match existing retrospective prevalence studies. For instance, Cath et al. (2017) also reported a prevalence rate less than 2% in young adults in a retrospective study of adult hoarding participants.

Collecting and saving behavior is developmentally appropriate in young children. However, pathological saving and difficulty discarding have been observed in young children (Plimpton et al., 2009; Storch et al, 2011). Hoarding in children can be distinguished from normative collecting by the intensity of interest in possessions, the level of distress at discarding or restriction of acquisition, and the impact these behaviors have on the family (Park et al., 2014). While clutter is a primary criterion for HD, it may not be as apparent in childhood cases since parents may exert more control over available spaces in the home. Similarly, parents may also exert control over acquisition of possessions. The most prominent feature of hoarding in childhood is the intense emotional reaction to discarding or losing access to possessions (Storch et al., 2007). To control emotional outbursts related to possessions, families often accommodate the hoarding to some degree in order to keep the peace (Park et al., 2014). Children who hoard also display an abnormal level of personification of objects (Plimpton et al., 2011).

In one of the only prospective studies to date on hoarding, Ivanov et al. (2020) enlisted twins who screened positive for clinically significant hoarding (*DSM-5* criteria A and B) at age 15, and retested them at age 18 using measures of hoarding, family accommodation, and psychiatric diagnoses. At the initial screening, no participants screened positive for clutter, and relatively few screened positive for distress/impairment (*DSM-5* criteria C and D). At age 18, compared to a group of twins who did not screen positive for hoarding at age 15, the hoarding group had significantly higher scores on measures of hoarding symptoms and beliefs. As with the testing at age 15, at age 18 none of the participants in the hoarding group had clutter levels high enough to meet the *DSM-5* clutter criterion. Only 40% of those who met *DSM-5* criteria A and B at age 15 did so again at age 18, suggesting that the hoarding symptoms are not stable over time in adolescence.

They also suggest that the *DSM-5* criteria for HD in childhood and adolescence may need to be revised, possibly to de-emphasize clutter.

In the study by Ivanov et al. (2020), the hoarding group were given a higher percentage of other psychiatric diagnoses than the nonhoarding comparison group (79% vs. 17%). This finding is consistent with other studies of hoarding, in which children rarely present with hoarding as a sole problem. A number of comorbid conditions are often present in children who hoard, including OCD (Storch et al., 2007), autism spectrum conditions (Storch et al., 2016), attention-deficit/hyperactivity disorder (ADHD; Hacker et al., 2016), and anxiety disorders (Hamblin et al., 2015).

Course of Hoarding

The course of hoarding is chronic and, without treatment, unremitting. The hoarder's symptoms generally reach moderate severity levels by age 30 or 40 (Tolin, Meunier, et al., 2010). In a self-identified sample of people with hoarding problems, 94% described the course of their hoarding as increasing in severity or chronic. Only 5% described a remitting and relapsing course, and fewer than 1% reported a course of decreasing severity (Tolin, Meunier, et al., 2010). Other studies corroborate the chronicity of hoarding. Ayers et al. (2010) found hoarding severity to increase with each decade of life. Cath et al. (2017) reported that the prevalence of hoarding rose by 20% for every five years of age, and more sharply than that after age 35. The rate among young people was below 2%, while the rate for those over age 70 was 6%. The increase in severity across ages seemed to be driven largely by increases in difficulty discarding.

There is little evidence that the prevalence of hoarding varies by gender. Among the major prevalence studies, a few have found higher prevalence among males, and a few have found a higher prevalence among females. The majority, however, have found no differences in prevalence by gender. Furthermore, in a review and meta-analysis of prevalence findings from the major studies, Postlethwaite et al. (2019) found no gender differences in prevalence. There is some evidence of differences in severity between males and females as they age, however. Cath et al. (2017) found that hoarding severity was similar for males and females at younger ages, but males' hoarding symptoms grew more severe as they aged, although severity increased for both genders.

Despite the absence of clear gender effects on prevalence, participants in most hoarding studies are disproportionately female. In a comparison of research conducted in academic settings versus community agencies, Woody et al. (2020) found the percentage of male cases found in community agency files (40%–54%) was much greater than the percentage found in academic studies (22%–26%). Since academic studies seek volunteers, while community agencies' data largely come from agency files, these findings suggest that males are less likely to volunteer for research and/or that they have more limited insight into the problematic nature of their hoarding behavior.

Culture

The role of possessions varies across cultures. Some place little value on individual possessions, while others react to the loss of a possession with bereavement. The majority of research on hoarding has been conducted in the United States and Europe, but cross-cultural comparisons have so far suggested that the major features of hoarding are consistent across cultures. For instance, Subramaniam and colleagues (2014) found similar prevalence rates in Singapore. Timpano et al. (2015) found that hoarding symptoms and beliefs in China resemble those in other countries, although college students in China endorse greater hoarding severity on the SIR than do American students. Also, Chinese students appear to place greater emphasis on the utility of possessions and avoiding waste in their decisions about saving and discarding. Hoarding symptoms in Japan also appear to be similar to those observed in Western countries (Nordsletten et al., 2018). Studies in other parts of the world, although limited in number, suggest that hoarding is similar in India (Chakraborty et al., 2013), Iran (Asadi et al., 2016), Turkey (Tükel et al., 2005), Spain (Fontenelle, 2016), Costa Rica (Chavira et al., 2008), and Brazil (Nordsletten et al., 2018).

Few studies have examined minority groups in the United States. Dong (2014) reported significant hoarding behavior in elderly Chinese Americans in Chicago. Three studies have examined hoarding symptoms among African Americans (Friedman et al., 2003; Williams et al., 2012, 2017). Each relied on single-item endorsement of hoarding as an OCD symptom on the Yale-Brown Obsessive-Compulsive Scale (Y-BOCS). The frequency of endorsement in these studies ranged from 39% to 54%, which is in line with the frequency with which hoarding items on the Y-BOCS are endorsed in other samples.

Demographics

Although there are no gender differences in the prevalence of hoarding symptoms, people with hoarding disorder differ from the general population on several important demographic features. Most diagnosed cases of HD are among older adults, consistent with the findings of Cath et al. (2017) with respect to increases in prevalence with advancing age. People with HD also differ in regard to social engagement. They are more likely to be single, divorced, widowed, or never married than the general population (Kim et al., 2001; Nordsletten & Mataix-Cols, 2012; Spittlehouse et al., 2016). Several factors may drive this effect. There is growing literature suggesting some deficits in interpersonal attachment among people with HD (Grisham et al., 2018). It could also result from spouses' inability to tolerate cluttered living conditions. The result is that people with HD are more likely to live alone (Archer et al., 2018). When no one else lives in the home, clutter in the home is more severe (Kim et al., 2001). Several studies have suggested that the resulting lack of social support (Medard & Kellett, 2014) and loneliness (Burgess et al., 2018) are associated with higher levels of clutter. Burgess et al. (2018) also found that loneliness interacted with anthropomorphism to predict severity of clutter. Individuals with high levels of anthropomorphism for comfort-related objects and high levels of loneliness had more severe clutter.

Although there are case reports of wealthy people who suffer from HD, existing evidence suggests that people with HD have lower socioeconomic status (Spittlehouse et al., 2016), higher rates of unemployment (Spittlehouse et al., 2016), and greater difficulty managing their finances (Tolin et al., 2008). These difficulties may stem from deficits in organizing and managing financial responsibilities. For instance, Tolin et al. (2008) reported that nearly one quarter of hoarding cases failed to file tax returns in at least one of the last five years. Samuels et al. (2008) found no significant differences in prevalence by education, living arrangement, or race/ethnicity in a sample of adults with OCD with and without the presence of hoarding; however, in this sample, those in the poorest financial group were four times more likely to hoard compared to those in the wealthy group. In a study of 115 participants seeking help for housing problems, including eviction, from the Eviction Intervention Services Housing Research Center (EIS) in New York City, 22% met criteria for HD (Rodriguez et al., 2012).

Comorbidity

High comorbidity rates with other psychiatric disorders have been observed in people with HD. Archer et al. (2019) found psychiatric comorbidity in 61% of HD patients, while Frost, Steketee, et al. (2011) found 75% of patients with HD had comorbid depression and/or anxiety. Archer et al. also found that 34% of patients with HD had two or more other psychiatric diagnoses. The most frequent comorbid diagnoses were mood disorders, with approximately 50% of patients with HD having a diagnosed depression in the two largest studies of HD comorbidity (Archer et al., 2019; Frost, Steketee, et al., 2011). HD comorbidity with depression was significantly greater than OCD comorbidity with depression (Frost, Steketee, et al., 2011). Depression complicates attempts to treat HD, especially in individuals whose motivation for treatment may be weak.

Anxiety disorders are also highly comorbid with HD. Archer et al. (2019) reported that 48% of individuals with HD had at least one anxiety disorder. Frost, Steketee, et al. (2011) reported high rates of generalized anxiety disorder (GAD; 24%) and social anxiety disorder (24%). Others have found high overlap with these disorders as well (Archer et al., 2019; Wheaton et al., 2008). In the study of hoarding by Frost, Steketee, et al. (2011), 18% of the participants met diagnostic criteria for OCD. The rate of comorbidity with OCD varied by gender, with males having a higher rate (28%) than females (15%). Archer et al. (2019) found lower rates of overlap with OCD (6%). Tolin et al. (2011) reported the frequency of hoarding symptoms among clients in an anxiety disorder clinic. Despite none of the patients' mentioning hoarding as a problem, 29% of GAD clients scored above the SIR cutoff for clinically significant hoarding, while 15% of clients with social anxiety did so. Of patients with OCD, 17% exceeded the clinical cutoff for HD.

Similarly, Novara et al. (2016) found significant hoarding in 7% of patients with anxiety disorders, although none reported hoarding problems to their clinician.

A great deal of research has found high rates of ADHD in adults with HD (Frost, Steketee, et al., 2011; Hall et al., 2013; Hartl et al., 2005; Shepard et al., 2010; Tolin & Villavicencio, 2011) as well as a substantial overlap between hoarding symptoms and ADHD in children (Fullana et al., 2013; Hacker et al., 2016). The inattentive symptoms of ADHD are more closely associated with hoarding than are hyperactivity/impulsivity (Fullana et al., 2013; Tolin & Villavicencio, 2011). Fullana et al. (2013) found that childhood ADHD was a significant risk factor for the later development of HD. In contrast to these findings, however, Archer et al. (2019) found that only 3% of their sample with HD had comorbid ADHD.

Several studies have reported elevated levels of experienced trauma among people with HD (Cromer et al., 2007; Frost, Steketee, et al., 2011; Landau et al., 2011; Samuels et al., 2008). However, despite experiencing significantly more trauma than people with OCD, patients with HD do not show higher of PTSD than patients with OCD (Frost, Steketee, et al., 2011; Wheaton et al., 2008). This may suggest that hoarding symptoms play a buffering role in damping down PTSD symptoms.

Several studies have linked hoarding to eating problems (Novara et al., 2016) and obesity (Nicoli de Mattos et al., 2018; Raines et al., 2015; Tolin et al., 2008; Wheaton et al., 2008). Others have found significant health problems among people with hoarding symptoms. People with HD appear to suffer greater frequencies of chronic illnesses, such as arthritis, asthma, tuberculosis, visual impairments, hypertension, diabetes, heart disease, severe kidney and liver disease, lupus, multiple sclerosis, epilepsy, ulcers, cancer, chronic fatigue syndrome, and stroke (Ong et al., 2015; Saxena et al., 2011; Spittlehouse et al., 2016; Tolin et al., 2008, 2019). The meaning of these findings is unclear, but they suggest that there may be some more general systemic issue underlying hoarding.

Associated Features

In addition to comorbidities, people with HD often suffer from a variety of associated features that influence their symptoms and quality of life. Emotional dysregulation appears to be common in HD (Worden et al., 2019), including anxiety sensitivity (Grisham et al., 2018), intolerance of distress (Grisham et al., 2018), experiential avoidance (Phung et al., 2015), and negative urgency or the tendency to engage in rash and regrettable acts when aroused (Wheaton et al., 2013). In addition, there is growing evidence that hoarding is associated with interpersonal attachment problems. Insecure attachment styles seem to characterize people with hoarding problems (Crone et al., 2019; Neave et al., 2016), and some evidence indicates that attachment insecurity may mediate the relationship between childhood trauma and hoarding (Kehoe & Egan, 2019). Attachment insecurity may result from developmental experiences, such as trauma or early deprivation (Landau et al., 2011). Kyrios et al. (2017) found that lack of family warmth in childhood predicted hoarding severity even after controlling for age and mood. Attachment uncertainty has also been found to be associated with hoarding symptoms (Frost et al., 2007).

Observations of clients with HD have led to hypotheses that hoarding is associated with executive function deficits, particularly in the areas of attention, memory, information processing, categorization, organization, and decision-making (Frost & Hartl, 1996; Kyrios et al., 2017; Steketee & Frost, 2003). Research on these deficits in HD has been mixed, with some studies reporting strong correlations with executive function deficits (Ayers et al., 2013), and some studies failing to find deficits in neurocognitive performance among patients with HD (Sumner et al., 2016). However, in a review of this area, Woody and colleagues (2014) concluded that there were replicable deficits in performance-based tasks of cognitive processes, particularly planning and problem-solving decisions, visuospatial learning and memory, attention, working memory, and organization.

Among the most consistent findings related to information-processing deficits in HD is the strong association of self-reported indecisiveness with hoarding symptoms. HD has been linked with self-reported problems with decision-making and indecisiveness in clinical and community samples. Both the avoidance of decision-making (i.e., decisional procrastination) and the inability to decide (i.e., information-processing deficit) have been found in hoarding samples and have been linked to neurological processes (Frost, Tolin, et al., 2011; Tolin et al., 2012). Frost, Tolin, et al. (2011) surveyed large samples of self-identified hoarding adults, adult children of people who hoard, and spouses of people with hoarding problems. People with hoarding problems reported more indecisiveness than did their spouses and the adult children of hoarding parents. Yet, adult children of hoarding parents reported more indecisiveness than the spouses of hoarding adults. Indecisiveness was correlated with all three features of hoarding (excessive acquisition, difficulty discarding, clutter) independent of their relationships with depression, anxiety, and obsessive-compulsive symptoms. Timpano et al. (2011) surveyed a representative sample of German citizens regarding hoarding and related features, including perfectionism, indecision, and procrastination. All three features were significantly and uniquely associated with hoarding severity. Tolin et al. (2012) conducted an experiment in which participants were asked to engage in discarding tasks using personal possessions, and results indicated that while discarding, hoarding participants show increased activity in areas of the brain responsible for impulse control, emotion regulation, and decision-making compared to healthy controls. These findings, along with others, suggest that problems with decision-making play a unique and important role in hoarding behaviors.

Perfectionism, which is characterized by overly critical self-evaluation and fears of making mistakes, has shown consistent correlations with all dimensions of hoarding (Frost & Gross, 1993; Kyrios et al., 2004; Timpano et al., 2011). Muroff et al. (2014) reported that, in addition to its association with hoarding symptoms, high levels of perfectionism interfere with treatment outcome in HD. A cognitive-behavioral model of hoarding suggests that a high level of perfectionism leads to an avoidance or delay in making decisions about discarding because any decision could involve a mistake. In an evaluation of this model, Burgess et al. (2018) found that decisional procrastination mediated the relationship between perfectionism and hoarding, clutter, and excessive acquisition, and that both indecisiveness and decisional procrastination mediated the relationship between perfectionism and difficulty discarding.

Cognitive-Behavioral Model of Hoarding

Frost and Hartl (1996) proposed a cognitive-behavioral model of hoarding, suggesting that hoarding was a multifaceted problem stemming from information-processing difficulties, maladaptive attachments to and beliefs about possessions, behavioral avoidance associated with attempts to avoid distress produced by disposing of cherished possessions, and learning experiences associated with these features. Since 1996, a great deal of research on individual elements of the model have clarified each of the features as well as suggested additions. This has led to refinements of the model (Steketee & Frost, 2003; Kyrios et al., 2017) that have incorporated vulnerability factors, such as genetic predisposition, emotion dysregulation, mood and anxiety problems, and attachment insecurities. The model has been a useful framework for developing and testing hypotheses about HD. The first 30 years of research on the disorder have increased our understanding tremendously. The next decades will see considerably more progress now that the nature and parameters of the problem are better defined.

Summary

HD is one of the new disorders in *DSM-5*, and although it has a short history of empirical research, descriptions of hoarding behaviors are common in literature as far back as the 14th century. The major features of hoarding include difficulty discarding possessions, a perceived need to save them, and substantial clutter. Other specifying features include excessive acquisition of possessions, which occurs in most cases of HD, and problems with insight, which vary considerably from case to case. Prevalence of HD is approximately 2.5% but varies with age. The disorder first appears in childhood or adolescence, and it is typically chronic. Higher prevalence rates are associated with increasing age. Hoarding appears with equal frequency in men and women and is negatively associated with income. People with HD are more often single, divorced, or widowed and tend to live alone. Hoarding of animals appears to be a special manifestation of HD, but it seems to be more complex and difficult to address. High rates of comorbidity are common in people with HD, the most common comorbid problems being anxiety and depression. Obesity and physical health problems are also common in HD. Symptoms of the disorder appear to be consistent across cultures. Although a considerable amount of knowledge has accrued since hoarding was first identified nearly 30 years ago, there is still a great deal to be discovered.

References

American Psychiatric Association (APA). (2013). *Diagnostic and statistical manual of mental disorders* (5th ed.).

Anderson, S. W., Domasio, H., & Damasio, A. R. (2005). A neural basis for collecting behavior in humans. *Brain*, *128*(1), 201–212.

Archer, C. A., Moran, K., Garza, K., Zakrzewski, J. J., Martin, A., Chou, C.-Y., . . . Mathews, C. A. (2019). Relationship between symptom severity, psychiatric comorbidity, social/occupational impairment, and suicidality in hoarding disorder. *Journal of Obsessive-Compulsive and Related Disorders*, *21*, 158–164.

Asadi, S., Daraeian, A., Rahmani, B., Kargari, A., Ahmadiani, A., & Shams, J. (2016). Exploring Yale-Brown Obsessive-Compulsive Scale symptom structure in Iranian OCD patients using item-based factor analysis. *Psychiatry Research*, *245*, 416–422.

Ayers, C. R., Saxena, S., Golshan, S., & Wetherell, J. L. (2010). Age at onset and clinical features of late life compulsive hoarding. *International Journal of Geriatric Psychiatry*, *25*(2), 142–149.

Ayers, C. R., Wetherell, J. L., Schiehser, D., Almklov, E., Golshan, S., & Saxena, S. (2013). Executive functioning in older adults. *International Journal of Geriatric Psychiatry*, *28*(11), 1175–1181.

Belk, R. W. (1988). Possessions and the extended self. *Journal of Consumer Research*, *15*(2), 139–168.

Bratiotis, C., Steketee, G., Dohn, J., Calderon, C. A., Frost, R. O., & Tolin, D. F. (2019). Should I keep it? Thoughts verbalized during a discarding task. *Cognitive Therapy and Research*, *43*(6), 1075–1085.

Bulli, F., Melli, G., Sara, M., Carraresi, C., Stopani, E., Pertusa, A., & Frost, R.O. (2014). Hoarding behaviour in an Italian non-clinical sample. *Behavioural and Cognitive Psychotherapy*, *42*, 297–311.

Burgess, A. M., Graves, L. M., & Frost, R. O. (2018). My possessions need me: Anthropomorphism and hoarding. *Scandinavian Journal of Psychology*, *59*(3), 340–348.

Castrodale, L., Bellay, Y. M., Brown, C. M., Cantor, F. L., Gibbins, J. D., Headrick, M. L., . . . Yu, D. T. (2010). General public health considerations for responding to animal hoarding cases. *Journal of Environmental Health*, *72*(7), 14–32.

Cath, D. C., Nizar, K., Boomsma, D., & Mathews, C. A. (2017). Age-specific prevalence of hoarding and obsessive-compulsive disorder: A population-based study. *American Journal of Geriatric Psychiatry*, *25*(3), 245–255.

Chakraborty, V., Cherian, A. V., Math, S. B., Venkatasubramanian, G., Thennarasu, K., Mataix-Cols, D., & Reddy, Y. C. (2012). Clinically significant hoarding in obsessive-compulsive disorder: Results from an Indian study. *Comprehensive Psychiatry*, *53*(8), 1153–1160.

Chasson, G. S., Guy, A. A., Bates, S., & Corrigan, P. W. (2018). They aren't like me, they are bad, and they are to blame: A theoretically informed study of stigma of hoarding disorder and obsessive-compulsive disorder. *Journal of Obsessive-Compulsive and Related Disorders*, 16, 56–65.

Chavira, D. A., Garrido, H., Bagnarello, M., Azzam, A., Reus, V. I., & Mathews, C. A. (2008). A comparative study of obsessive-compulsive disorder in Costa Rica and the United States. *Depression and Anxiety*, *25*(7), 609–619.

Cherrier, H., & Ponnor, T. (2010). A study of hoarding behavior and attachment to material possessions. *Qualitative Market Research: An International Journal*, *13*(1), 8–23.

Chou, C.-Y., Tsoh, J., Vigil, O., Bain, D., Uhm, S. Y., Howell, G., . . . Mathews, C. A. (2018). Contributions of self-criticism and shame to hoarding. *Psychiatry Research*, *262*, 488–493.

Claes, L., Müller, A., & Luyckx, K. (2016). Compulsive buying and hoarding as identity substitutes: The role of materialistic value endorsement and depression. *Comprehensive Psychiatry*, *68*, 65–71.

Clarke, D. J., Boer, H., Whittington, J., Holland, A., Butler, J., & Web, T. (2002). Prader-Willi syndrome, compulsive and ritualistic behaviours: The first population-based survey. *The British Journal of Psychiatry*, *180*, 358–362.

Cromer, K. R., Schmidt, N. B., & Murphy, D. L. (2007). Do traumatic events influence the clinical expression of compulsive hoarding? *Behaviour Research and Therapy*, *45*(11), 2581–2592.

Crone, C., Kwok, C., Chau, V., & Norberg, M. M. (2019). Applying attachment theory to indecisiveness in hoarding disorder. *Psychiatry Research*, *273*, 318–324.

David, J., Blonner, M., Forbes, M. K., & Norberg, M. M. (2020). Motives for acquiring and saving and their relationship with object attachment. *Current Opinion in Psychology*.

DiMauro, J., Tolin, D. F., Frost, R. O., & Steketee, G. (2013). Do people with hoarding disorder under-report their symptoms? *Journal of Obsessive-Compulsive and Related Disorders*, *2*(2), 130–136.

Dong, X. (2014). Elder self-neglect in a community-dwelling U.S. Chinese population: Findings from the population study of Chinese elderly in Chicago (PINE) Study. *Journal of the American Geriatric Society*, *62*, 2391–2397.

Dozier, M. E., & Ayers, C. R. (2014). The predictive value of different reasons for saving and acquiring on hoarding disorder symptoms. *Journal of Obsessive-Compulsive and Related Disorders*, *3*(3), 220–227.

Drury, H., Nordsletten, A. E., Ajmi, S., Fernandez de la Cruz, L., & Mataix-Cols, D. (2015). Accuracy of self and informant reports of symptom severity and insight in hoarding disorder. *Journal of Obsessive-Compulsive and Related Disorders*, *5*, 37–42.

Ferreira, E. A., Paloski, L. H., Costa, D. B., Fiametti, V. S., Oliveira, C. R., Argimon, I. I., & Irigaray, T. Q. (2017). Animal hoarding disorder: A new psychopathology? *Psychiatry Research*, *258*, 221–225.

Finney, C. M., & Mendez, M. F. (2017). Diogenes syndrome in frontotemporal dementia, *American Journal of Alzheimer's Disease & Other Dementias*, *32*(7), 438–443.

Fontenelle, L. F. (2016). Vallejo-Nágera (1926–1990) and the concept of 'Soteric neurosis': A forgotten sketch of hoarding disorder in the obsessive-compulsive spectrum literature. *Journal of Medical Biography*, *24*(1), 85–89.

Fontenelle, L. F., & Grant, J. E. (2014). Hoarding disorder: A new diagnostic category in ICD-11? *Revista Brasileira De Psiquiatria*, *36*(1), 28–39.

Fromm, E. (1947). *Man against himself: An inquiry into the psychology of ethics*. Rinehart.

Friedman, S., Smith. L. C., Halpern, B., Levine, C., Paradis, C., Viswanathan, R., . . . Ackerman, R. (2003). Obsessive-compulsive disorder in a multi-ethnic urban outpatient clinic: Initial presentation and treatment outcome with exposure and ritual prevention. *Behavior Therapy*, *34*, 397–410.

Frost, R. O., Gabrielson, I., Deady, S., Dernbach, K. B., Guevara, G., Peebles-Dorin, M., . . . Grisham, J. R. (2018). Scrupulosity and hoarding. *Comprehensive Psychiatry*, *86*, 19–24.

Frost, R. O., & Gross, R. C. (1993). The hoarding of possessions. *Behaviour Research and Therapy*, *31*, 367–381.

Frost, R. O., & Hartl, T. L. (1996). A cognitive-behavioral model of compulsive hoarding. *Behaviour Research and Therapy*, *34*, 341–350.

Frost, R. O., Hartl, T. L., Christian, R., & Williams, N. (1995). The value of possessions in compulsive hoarding: Patterns of use and attachment. *Behaviour Research and Therapy*, *33*(8), 897–902.

Frost, R. O., Kyrios, M., Mccarthy, K. D., & Matthews, Y. (2007). Self-ambivalence and attachment to possessions. *Journal of Cognitive Psychotherapy*, *21*(3), 232–242.

Frost, R. O., & Mueller, A. (2014). Acquisition in hoarding disorder. In R.O. Frost & G. Steketee, *Oxford handbook of hoarding and acquiring*. Oxford University Press.

Frost, R. O., Patronek, G., & Rosenfield, E. (2011). Comparison of object and animal hoarding. *Depression and Anxiety*, *28*, 885–891.

Frost, R. O., Rosenfield, E., Steketee, G., & Tolin, D. F. (2013). An examination of excessive acquisition in hoarding disorder. *Journal of Obsessive-Compulsive and Related Disorders*, *2*, 338–345.

Frost, R. O., & Steketee, G. (2010). *Stuff: Compulsive hoarding and the meaning of things*. Houghton Mifflin Harcourt.

Frost, R. O., Steketee, G., & Tolin, D. F. (2011). Comorbidity in hoarding disorder. *Depression and Anxiety*, *28*, 876–884.

Frost, R. O., Steketee, G., Tolin, D. F., & Renaud, S. (2008). Development and validation of the Clutter Image Rating. *Journal of Psychopathology and Behavioral Assessment*, *30*(3), 193–203.

Frost, R. O., Steketee, G., Tolin, D. F., Sinopoli, N., & Ruby, D. (2015). Motives for acquiring and saving in hoarding disorder, OCD, and community controls. *Journal of Obsessive-Compulsive and Related Disorders*, *4*, 54–59.

Frost, R. O., Steketee, G., & Williams, L. (2000). Hoarding: A community health problem. *Health and Social Care in the Community*, *8*, 229–234.

Frost, R. O., Tolin, D. F., & Maltby, N. (2010). Insight-related challenges in the treatment of hoarding. *Cognitive and Behavioral Practice*, *17*, 404–413.

Frost, R. O., Tolin, D. F., Steketee, G., & Oh, M. (2011). Indecisiveness in hoarding. *International Journal of Cognitive Therapy*, *4*, 253–262.

Fullana, M. A., Vilagut, G., Mataix-Cols, D., Adroher, N. D., Bruffaerts, R., Bunting, B., . . . Alonso, J. (2013). Is ADHD in childhood associated with lifetime hoarding symptoms? An epidemiological study. *Depression and Anxiety*, *30*(8), 741–748.

Fullana, M. A., Vailagut, G., Rojas-Farreras, S., Mataix-Cols, D., de Graff, R., Demyttenaere, K., . . . Alonso, J. (2010). Obsessive compulsive symptom dimensions in the general population: Results from an epidemiological study in six European countries. *Journal of Affective Disorders, 124*, 291–299.

Gogol, N. V., & Magarshack, D. (1961). *Dead souls*. Penguin Books.

Grisham, J., Frost, R. O., Steketee, G., Kim, H., & Hood, S. (2006). Age of onset in compulsive hoarding. *Journal of Anxiety Disorders, 20*, 675–786.

Grisham, J. R., Frost, R. O., Steketee, G., Kim, H., Tarkoff, A., & Hood, S. (2009). Formation of attachment to possessions in compulsive hoarding. *Journal of Anxiety Disorders, 23*(3), 357–361.

Grisham, J. R., Roberts, L., Cerea, S., Isemann, S., Svehla, J., & Norberg, M. M. (2018). The role of distress tolerance, anxiety sensitivity, and intolerance of uncertainty in predicting hoarding symptoms in a clinical sample. *Psychiatry Research, 267*, 94–101.

Hacker, L. E., Park, J. M., Timpano, K. R., Cavitt, M. A., Alvaro, J. L., Lewin, A. B., . . . Storch, E. A. (2012). Hoarding in children with ADHD. *Journal of Attention Disorders, 20*(7), 617–626.

Hall, B. J., Tolin, D. F., Frost, R. O., & Steketee, G. (2013). An exploration of comorbid symptoms and clinical correlates in clinically significant hoarding symptoms. *Depression and Anxiety, 30*, 67–76.

Hamblin, R. J., Lewin, A. B., Salloum, A., Crawford, E. A., Mcbride, N. M., & Storch, E. A. (2015). Clinical characteristics and predictors of hoarding in children with anxiety disorders. *Journal of Anxiety Disorders, 36*, 9–14.

Hartl, T. L., Duffany, S. R., Allen, G. J., Steketee, G., & Frost, R. O. (2005). Relationships among compulsive hoarding, trauma, and attention-deficit/hyperactivity disorder. *Behaviour Research and Therapy, 43*(2), 269–276.

Hartl, T. L., Frost, R. O., Allen, G. J., Deckersbach, T., Steketee, G., Duffany, S. R., & Savage, C. R. (2004). Actual and perceived memory deficits in individuals with compulsive hoarding. *Depression and Anxiety, 20*(2), 59–69.

Hoarding of Animals Research Consortium (HARC). (2002). Health implications of animal hoarding. *Health & Social Work, 27*, 125–13.

Iervolino, A. C., Perroud, N., Fullana, M. A., Guipponi, M., Cherkas, L., Collier, D. A., & Mataix-Cols, D. (2009). Prevalence and heritability of compulsive hoarding: A twin study. *The American Journal of Psychiatry, 166*(10), 1156–1161.

Ivanov, V. Z., Mataix-Cols, D., Serlachius, E., Brander, G., Elmquist, A., Enander, J., & Rück, C. (2020). The developmental origins of hoarding disorder in adolescence: A longitudinal clinical interview study following an epidemiological survey. *European Child & Adolescent Psychiatry*.

Ivanov, V. Z., Mataix-Cols, D., Serlachius, E., Lichtenstein, P., Anckarsäter, H., Chang, Z., . . . Rück, C. (2013). Prevalence, comorbidity and heritability of hoarding symptoms in adolescence: A population-based twin study in 15-year-olds. *PLOS ONE, 8*(7), e69140.

Ivanov, V. Z., Nordsletten, A., Mataix-Cols, D., Serlachius, E., Lichtenstein, P., Lundström, S., . . . Rück, C. (2017). Heritability of hoarding symptoms across adolescence and young adulthood: A longitudinal twin study. *PLOS ONE, 12*(6). e0179541.

Kehoe, E., & Egan, J. (2019). Interpersonal attachment insecurity and emotional attachment to possessions partly mediate the relationship between childhood trauma and hoarding symptoms in a non-clinical sample. *Journal of Obsessive-Compulsive and Related Disorders, 21*, 37–45.

Kellett, S. (2007). Compulsive hoarding: A site-security model and associated psychological treatment strategies. *Clinical Psychology & Psychotherapy, 14*(6), 413–427.

Kim, H-J., Steketee, G., & Frost, R. O. (2001). Hoarding by elderly people. *Health & Social Work. 26*, 176–184.

Kings, C. A., Moulding, R., & Knight, T. (2017). You are what you own: Reviewing the link between possessions, emotional attachment, and the self-concept in hoarding disorder. *Journal of Obsessive-Compulsive and Related Disorders, 14*, 51–58.

Kyrios, M., Frost, R. O., & Steketee, G. (2004). Cognitions in compulsive buying and acquisition. *Cognitive Therapy and Research, 28*, 241–258.

Kyrios, M., Mogan, C., Moulding, R., Frost, R. O., Yap, K., & Fassnacht, D. B. (2017). The cognitive-behavioural model of hoarding disorder: Evidence from clinical and non-clinical cohorts. *Clinical Psychology & Psychotherapy, 25*(2), 311–321.

Landau, D., Iervolino, A. C., Pertusa, A., Santo, S., Singh, S., & Mataix-Cols, D. (2011). Stressful life events and material deprivation in hoarding disorder. *Journal of Anxiety Disorders, 25*(2), 192–202.

Lee, S. M., Lewis, M., Leighton, D., Harris, B., Long, B., & Macfarlane, S. (2017). A comparison of the neuropsychological profiles of people living in squalor without hoarding to those living in squalor associated with hoarding. *International Journal of Geriatric Psychiatry, 32*(12), 1433–1439.

Lockwood, R. (2018). Animal hoarding: The challenge for mental health, law enforcement, and animal welfare professionals. *Behavioral Sciences & the Law, 36*(6), 698–716.

López-Solà, C., Fontenelle, L. F., Alonso, P., Cuadras, D., Foley, D. L., Pantelis, C., . . . Harrison, B. J. (2014). Prevalence and heritability of obsessive-compulsive spectrum and anxiety disorder symptoms: A survey of the Australian Twin Registry. *American Journal of Medical Genetics Part B: Neuropsychiatric Genetics, 165*(4), 314–325.

Lucini, G., Monk, I., & Szlatenyi, C. (2009). *An analysis of fire incidents involving hoarding households* [Thesis]. Worcester Polytechnic Institute, Worcester, MA.

Luu, M., Lauster, N., Bratiotis, C., Edsell-Vetter, J., & Woody, S. R. (2018). Squalor in community-referred hoarded homes. *Journal of Obsessive-Compulsive and Related Disorders, 19*, 66–71.

Markus, H., & Nurius, P. (1986). Possible selves. *American Psychologist, 41*(9), 954–969.

Mataix-Cols, D., Billotti, D., Fernandez de la Cruz, L., & Nordsletten, A. E. (2013). The London field trial for hoarding disorder. *Psychological Medicine, 43*, 837–847.

Mataix-Cols, D., Frost, R. O., Pertusa, A., Clark, L. A., Saxena, S., Leckman, J. F., . . . Wilhelm, S. (2010). Hoarding disorder: A new diagnosis for DSM-V? *Depression and Anxiety, 27*(6), 556–572.

Medard, E., & Kellett, S. (2014). The role of adult attachment and social support in hoarding disorder. *Behavioural and Cognitive Psychotherapy, 42*(5), 629–633.

Mueller, A., Mitchell, J. E., Crosby, R. D., Glaesmer, H., & de Zwaan, M. (2009). The prevalence of compulsive hoarding and its association with compulsive buying in a German population-based sample. *Behaviour Research and Therapy, 47*, 705–709.

Muroff, J. M., Steketee, G., Frost, R. O., & Tolin, D. F. (2014). CBT for hoarding disorder: Follow-up findings and predictors of outcome. *Depression and Anxiety, 31*(12), 964–971.

Neave, N., Jackson, R., Saton, T., & Honekopp, J. (2015). The influence of anthropomorphic tendencies on human hoarding behaviours. *Personality and Individual Differences, 72*, 214–219.

Neave, N., Tyson, H., McInnes, L., & Hamilton, C. (2016). The role of attachment style and anthropomorphism in predicting hoarding behaviours in a non-clinical sample. *Personality and Individual Differences, 99*, 33–37.

Nicoli de Mattos, C., Kim, H. S., Lacroix, E., Requiao, M., Zambrano, F. T., Hodgins, D. C., & Tavares, H. (2018). The need to consume: Hoarding as a shared psychological feature of compulsive buying and binge eating. *Comprehensive Psychiatry, 85*, 67–71.

Norberg, M. M., & Snowdon, J. (2014). Severe domestic squalor. In R. O. Frost & G. Steketee (Eds.). *The Oxford handbook of hoarding and acquiring* (pp. 147–156). Oxford University Press.

Nordsletten, A. E., Fernández de la Cruz, L., Aluco, E., Alonso, P., López-Solà, C., Menchón, J. . . . Mataix-Cols, D. (2018). A transcultural study of hoarding disorder: Insights from the United Kingdom, Spain, Japan, and Brazil. *Transcultural Psychiatry, 55*(2), 261–285.

Nordsletten, A. E., Fernandez de la Cruz, L. F., Billotti, D., & Mataix-Cols, D. (2013). Finders keepers: The features differentiating hoarding disorder from normative collecting. *Comprehensive Psychiatry, 54*(3), 229–237.

Nordsletten, A. E., Fernandez de la Cruz, L. F., Drury, H., Ajmi, S, Saleem, S., & Mataix-Cols, D. (2014). The Family Impact Scale for Hoarding (FISH): Measure development and initial validation. *Journal of Obsessive-Compulsive and Related Disorders, 3*, 29–34.

Nordsletten, A. E., & Mataix-Cols, D. (2012). Hoarding versus collecting: Where does pathology diverge from play? *Clinical Psychology Review, 32*(3), 165–176.

Nordsletten, A. E., Reichenberg, A., Hatch, S. L., Cruz, L. F. D. L., Pertusa, A., Hotopf, M., & Mataix-Cols, D. (2013). Epidemiology of hoarding disorder. *The British Journal of Psychiatry, 203*(6), 445–452.

Novara, C., Bottesi, G., Dorz, S., & Sanavio, E. (2016). Hoarding symptoms are not exclusive to hoarders. *Frontiers in Psychology, 7*, 1742.

Ong, C., Pang, S., Sagayadevan, V., Chong, S. A., & Subramaniam, M. (2015). Functioning and quality of life in hoarding: A systematic review. *Journal of Anxiety Disorders, 32*, 17–30.

Park, J. M., McGuire, J. F., & Storch, E. A. (2014). Compulsive hoarding in children. In R. O. Frost & G. Steketee (Eds). *The Oxford handbook of hoarding and acquiring*. Oxford University Press.

Patronek, G. J., Loar, L., & Nathanson, J. N. (Eds.). (2006). *Animal hoarding: Structuring interdisciplinary responses to people, animals, and communities at risk.* http://www.tufts.edu/vet/hoarding/pubs/AneellReport.pdf

Patronek, G. J., & Nathanson, J. N. (2009). A theoretical perspective to inform assessment and treatment strategies for animal hoarders. *Clinical Psychology Review, 29*(3), 274–281.

Pertusa, A., Bejerot, S., Eriksson, J., Fernandez de la Cruz, L., Bonde, S., Russell, A., & Mataix-Cols, D. (2012). Do patients with hoarding disorder have autistic traits? *Depression and Anxiety, 29,* 210–218.

Pertusa, A., Frost, R. O., & Mataix-Cols, D. (2010). When hoarding is a symptom of OCD: A case series and implications for DSM-V. *Behaviour Research and Therapy, 48,* 1012–1020.

Phung, P. J., Moulding, R., Taylor, J. K., & Nedeljkovic, M. (2015). Emotion regulation, attachment to possessions and hoarding symptoms. *Scandinavian Journal of Psychology, 56*(5), 573–581.

Plimpton, E. H., Frost, R. O., Abbey, B. C., & Dorer, W. (2009). Compulsive hoarding in children: 6 case studies. *International Journal of Cognitive Therapy, 2,* 88–104.

Postlethwaite, A., Kellett, S., & Mataix-Cols, D. (2019). Prevalence of hoarding disorder: A systematic review and meta-analysis. *Journal of Affective Disorders, 256,* 309–316.

Raines, A. M., Bossa, J. W., Allan, N. P., Short, N. A., & Schmidt, N. B. (2015). Hoarding and eating pathology: The mediating role of emotion regulation. *Comprehensive Psychiatry, 57,* 29–35.

Rodriguez, C. I., Herman, D., Alcon, J., Chen, S., Tannen, A, Essock, S., & Simpson, H. B. (2012). Prevalence of hoarding disorder in individuals at potential risk of eviction in New York City: A pilot study. *The Journal of Nervous and Mental Disease, 200,* 91–94.

Rodriguez, C. I., Simpson, H. B., Liu, S.-M., Levinson, A., & Blanco, C. (2013). Prevalence and correlates of difficulty discarding results from a national sample of the US population. *The Journal of Nervous and Mental Disease, 201*(9), 795–801.

Ruscio, A. M., Stein, D. J., Chiu, W. T., & Kessler, R. C. (2008). The epidemiology of obsessive-compulsive disorder in the National Comorbidity Survey Replication. *Molecular Psychiatry, 15*(1), 53–63.

Samuels, J. F., Bienvenu, O. J., Grados, M. A., Cullen, B., Riddle, M. A., Liang, K.-Y., . . . Nestadt, G. (2008). Prevalence and correlates of hoarding behavior in a community-based sample. *Behaviour Research and Therapy, 46*(7), 836–844.

Saxena, S., Ayers, C. R., Maidment, K. M., Vapnik, T., Wetherell, J. L., & Bystritsky, A. (2011). Quality of life and functional impairment in compulsive hoarding. *Journal of Psychiatric Research, 45*(4), 475–480.

Sheppard, B., Chavira, D., Azzam, A., Grados, M. A., Umana, P., Garrido, H., & Mathews, C. A. (2010). ADHD prevalence and association with hoarding behaviors in childhood-onset OCD. *Depression and Anxiety, 27*(7), 667–674.

Spittlehouse, J. K., Vierck, E., Pearson, J. F., & Joyce, P. R. (2016). Personality, mental health and demographic correlates of hoarding behaviours in a midlife sample. *PeerJ, 4.*

Steketee, G., Frost, R. O., & Kyrios, M. (2003). Cognitive aspects of compulsive hoarding. *Cognitive Therapy and Research, 27,* 463–479.

Steketee, G., Gibson, A., Frost, R., Alabiso, J., Arluke, A., & Patronek, G. (2011). Characteristics and antecedents of people who hoard animals: An exploratory comparative interview study. *Review of General Psychology, 15,* 114–124.

Storch, E. A., Lack, C. W., Merlo, L. J., Geffken, G. R., Jacob, M. L., Murphy, T. K., & Goodman, W. K. (2007). Clinical features of children and adolescents with obsessive-compulsive disorder and hoarding symptoms. *Comprehensive Psychiatry, 48*(4), 313–318.

Storch, E. A., Nadeau, J. M., Johnco, C., Timpano, K., Mcbride, N., Mutch, P. J., . . . Murphy, T. K. (2016). Hoarding in youth with autism spectrum disorders and anxiety: Incidence, clinical correlates, and behavioral treatment response. *Journal of Autism and Developmental Disorders, 46*(5), 1602–1612.

Storch, E. A., Rahman, O., Park, J. M., Reid, J., Murphy, T. K., & Lewin, A. B. (2011). Compulsive hoarding in children. *Journal of Clinical Psychology, 67,* 507–516.

Subramaniam, M., Abdin, E., Vaingankar, J. A., Picco, L., & Chong, S. A. (2014). Hoarding in an Asian population: Prevalence, correlates, disability and quality of life. *Annals Academy of Medicine Singapore, 43*(11), 535–543.

Sumner, J. M., Noack, C. G., Filotea, J. V., Maddox, W. T., & Saxena, S. (2016). Neurocognitive performance in unmedicated patients with hoarding disorder. *Neuropsychology, 30*(2), 157–168.

Taylor, J. K., Moulding, R., & Nedeljkovic, M. (2018). Emotion regulation and hoarding symptoms. *Journal of Obsessive-Compulsive and Related Disorders, 18,* 86–97.

Timpano, K. R., Çek, D., Fu, Z., Tang, T., Wang, J., & Chasson, G. S. (2015). A consideration of hoarding disorder symptoms in China. *Comprehensive Psychiatry, 57*, 36–45.

Timpano, K. R., Exner, C., Glaesmer, H., Rief, W., Keshaviah, A., Brähler, E., & Wilhelm, S. (2011). The epidemiology of the proposed DSM-5 hoarding disorder. *The Journal of Clinical Psychiatry, 72*(06), 780–786.

Timpano, K. R., & Shaw, A. M. (2013). Conferring humanness: The role of anthropomorphism in hoarding. *Personality and Individual Differences, 54*(3), 383–388.

Tolin, D. F., Das, A., Hallion, L. S., Levy, H. C., Wootton, B. M., & Stevens, M. C. (2019). Quality of life in patients with hoarding disorder. *Journal of Obsessive-Compulsive and Related Disorders, 21*, 55–59.

Tolin, D. F., Fitch, K. E., Frost, R. O., & Steketee, G. (2010). Family informants' perceptions of insight in compulsive hoarding. *Cognitive Therapy and Research, 34*, 69–81.

Tolin, D. F., Frost, R. O., & Steketee, G. (2010). A brief interview for assessing compulsive hoarding: The Hoarding Rating Scale. *Psychiatry Research, 178*, 147–152.

Tolin, D. F., Frost, R. O., Steketee, G., Gray, K. D., & Fitch, K. E. (2008). The economic and social burden of compulsive hoarding. *Psychiatry Research, 160*(2), 200–211.

Tolin, D. F., Meunier, S. A., Frost, R. O., & Steketee, G. (2010). The course of compulsive hoarding and its relationship to life events. *Depression & Anxiety, 27*, 829–838.

Tolin, D. F., Meunier, S. A., Frost, R. O., & Steketee, G. (2011). Compulsive hoarding among patients seeking treatment for anxiety disorders. *Journal of Anxiety Disorders, 25*, 43–48.

Tolin, D. F., Stevens, M. C., Villavicencio, A. L., Norberg, M. M., Calhoun, V. D., Frost, R. O., . . . Pearlson, G. D. (2012). Neural mechanisms of decision making in hoarding disorder. *Archives of General Psychiatry, 69*(8), 832.

Tolin, D. F., & Villavicencio, A. (2011). Inattention, but not OCD, predicts the core features of hoarding disorder. *Behaviour Research and Therapy, 49*(2), 120–125.

Tükel, R., Ertekin, E., Batmaz, S., Alyanak, F., Sözen, A., Aslantaş, B., . . . Ozyildirim, I. (2005). Influence of age of onset on clinical features in obsessive-compulsive disorder. *Depression and Anxiety, 21*(3), 112–117.

Wheaton, M. G., Fabricant, L. E., Berman, N. C., & Abramowitz, J. S. (2013). Experiential avoidance in individuals with hoarding disorder. *Cognitive Therapy and Research, 37*(4), 779–785.

Wheaton, M., Timpano, K. R., LaSalle-Ricci, V. H., & Murphy, D. (2008). Characterizing the hoarding phenotype in individuals with OCD: Associations with comorbidity, severity and gender. *Journal of Anxiety Disorders, 22*(2), 243–252.

Williams, M. T., Brown, T. L., & Sawyer, B. (2017). Psychiatric comorbidity and hoarding symptoms in African Americans with obsessive-compulsive disorder. *Journal of Black Psychology, 43*, 259–279.

Williams, M. T., Elstein, J., Buckner, E., Abelson, J., & Himle, J. (2012). Symptom dimensions in two samples of African Americans with obsessive-compulsive disorder. *Journal of Obsessive-Compulsive and Related Disorders, 1*, 145–152.

Wincze, J. P., Steketee, G., & Frost, R. O. (2007). Categorization in compulsive hoarding. *Behaviour Research and Therapy, 45*(1), 63–72.

Woody, S. R., Kellman-McFarlane, K., & Welsted, A. (2014). Review of cognitive performance in hoarding disorder. *Clinical Psychology Review, 34*(4), 324–336.

Woody, S. R., Lenkic, P., Bratiotis, C., Kysow, K., Luu, M., Edsell-Vetter, J., Frost, R. O., Lauster, N., Steketee, G., & Tolin, D. F. (2020). How well do hoarding research samples represent cases that rise to community attention? *Behaviour Research and Therapy, 126*, 103555.

Worden, B., Levy, H. C., Das, A., Katz, B. W., Stevens, M., & Tolin, D. F. (2019). Perceived emotion regulation and emotional distress tolerance in patients with hoarding disorder. *Journal of Obsessive-Compulsive and Related Disorders, 22*, 100441.

Zaboski, B. A., Merritt, O. A., Schrack, A. P., Gayle, C., Gonzalez, M., Guerrero, L. A., . . . Mathews, C. A. (2019). Hoarding: A meta-analysis of age of onset. *Depression and Anxiety, 36*(6), 552–564.

Zihao, N. R., Smit, D. J., Boomsma, D. I., & Cath, D. C. (2016). Cross-disorder genetic analysis of tic disorders, obsessive-compulsive, and hoarding symptoms. *Frontiers in Psychiatry, 7*, 120.

CHAPTER 5

Phenomenology and Epidemiology of Trichotillomania and Skin-Picking Disorder

Emily J. Ricketts, Jordan T. Stiede, Douglas W. Woods, Diana Antinoro, and Martin E. Franklin

> **Abstract**
>
> This chapter highlights the diagnostic features and clinical characteristics of trichotillomania, skin-picking, and nail-biting and their diagnostic distinction from obsessive-compulsive disorder (OCD) and other conditions. Nonclinical forms of these disorders are described. Information on the prevalence and limitations of epidemiologic research is discussed. The gender ratio, age of onset, longitudinal course, functional impairment, and healthcare utilization are described for each disorder. The cross-cultural features of the disorders are highlighted, and patterns of psychiatric comorbidity are discussed. Additionally, the chapter briefly discusses the relationship between the disorders and psychotic conditions.
>
> **Key Words:** trichotillomania, skin-picking, nail-biting, psychosis, differential diagnosis, prevalence, impairment, culture, comorbidity

Trichotillomania

Description and Diagnostic Features

Trichotillomania (TTM) has been defined as the recurrent pulling out of one's hair, resulting in hair loss, with repeated attempts to decrease or stop pulling (American Psychiatric Association [APA], 2013). Individuals must also report clinically significant distress or impairment in important areas of functioning because of hair-pulling, and the behavior cannot be attributed to the physiological effects of a substance or other medical condition. Some individuals with TTM report an increasing sense of tension before pulling, followed by a feeling of gratification or relief after the pulling episode, but not all patients who experience pulling-related hair loss report both tension and relief. (Christenson, Mackenzie, & Mitchell, 1991). Children, in particular, may not report such experiences (Hanna, 1997; King, Scahill, et al., 1995; Reeve et al., 1992; Wright & Holmes, 2003).

Pulling sites vary and include, from most to least common, the scalp, eyelashes, eyebrows, pubic region, face, and body (Cohen et al., 1995; Santhanam et al., 2008; Schlosser et al., 1994). Individuals with TTM generally prefer to pull hairs that feel "coarse," "wiry," or "kinky," and it has been noted that sufferers usually pull out their hairs with their dominant hand. Use of a cosmetic aid, such as tweezers, is also common (Christenson, Mackenzie, & Mitchell, 1991; Greenberg & Sarner, 1965; Schlosser et al., 1994).

Many individuals with TTM engage in prepulling behaviors, including hair touching, twirling, or stroking (Casati et al., 2000; du Toit et al., 2001) and postpulling rituals, such as rubbing hair strands across their lips; examining, biting, or chewing the root of the hair; and occasionally ingesting the hair (i.e., trichophagy; Christenson, Mackenzie, & Mitchell, 1991; Schlosser et al., 1994). In some cases, repeated ingestion of hair strands may lead to trichobezoars, which are large masses of hair found in the stomach and digestive tract that can cause several complications, including constipation, diarrhea, poor appetite, and impairment in the functioning of the liver and pancreas (O'Sullivan et al., 1996; Sharma et al., 2000), and can require surgical intervention (Bouwer & Stein, 1998; Frey et al., 2005).

Patients with TTM may experience a variety of affective states before, during, and following a pulling episode. In a nonclinical sample of 66 college students who engaged in hair-pulling, the behavior was associated with decreases in tension, boredom, and sadness over the course of a pulling episode (Stanley et al., 1995). In another study of adults with TTM, participants reported significant decreases in boredom, tension, and anxiety, and significant increases in guilt, relief, sadness, and anger across a pulling episode (Diefenbach et al., 2002). Although some episodes of pulling are related to emotional variables, this does not appear to be true for all pulling episodes.

Studies have suggested that there may be multiple styles or functions of pulling. At least two distinct styles have been noted, including focused and automatic hair-pulling. Focused pulling usually involves a conscious effort to pull and includes using pulling to regulate emotion. In contrast, automatic pulling involves a lack of awareness of the pulling, and generally occurs during sedentary activities, such as watching television, reading, or driving (Christenson & Crow, 1996; Christenson, Mackenzie, & Mitchell, 1991). Although there are discrepancies across studies, predominantly automatic pulling is believed to be the most common, followed by mixed and predominantly focused pulling (Duke et al., 2010; Lochner et al., 2010; du Toit et al., 2001). Further, Flessner et al. (2008) indicated that automatic pulling rarely fluctuates from adolescence to adulthood, whereas changes in focused pulling are typical and are associated with psychological distress and biological changes (e.g., pubertal onset). Other studies have suggested different dimensions of pulling. For instance, Alexander et al. (2016) conducted an exploratory factor analysis of the Milwaukee Inventory of Subtypes of TTM–Adult Version (MIST-A) and found evidence for two different factors: internal-regulated pulling and awareness of pulling (Alexander et al., 2016). Similarly, Keuthen et al. (2015) suggested that "emotion" and "intention" pulling may be two different subtypes. Clearly, future research should continue to explore TTM subtypes.

Research on the phenomenological differences between the different pulling styles is limited. In a study examining styles of hair-pulling in 47 outpatient chronic hair-pullers, findings indicated that participants who were predominantly focused pullers reported pulling from the pubic region at higher rates than automatic pullers (du Toit et al., 2001). Findings on phenomenological differences in pulling styles among adults indicated that participants who were high in focused pulling and low in automatic pulling were less likely to pull from the scalp and more likely to pull from the eyebrows, eyelashes, and pubic area, in comparison to those who were low in both focused and automatic pulling. Participants who were high in both focused and automatic pulling were more likely to pull from the eyebrows than those who were low in both focused and automatic hair-pulling (Flessner et al., 2008). Likewise, although Duke et al. (2010) found few phenomenological differences in pulling sites, results did show that focused pullers were more likely to pull from the eyelashes when compared to automatic pullers.

Skin-Picking Disorder

Description and Diagnostic Features

Skin-picking disorder (SPD), also known as excoriation disorder, has been defined as recurrent skin-picking, resulting in skin lesions, despite repeated attempts to decrease or stop picking (APA, 2013). To receive an SPD diagnosis, the behavior needs to cause significant distress or impairment in important areas of functioning and cannot be attributed to the physiological effects of a substance or other medical condition. The clinical features of SPD overlap with those seen in TTM, as both are obsessive-compulsive related disorders (OCRDs) with nearly identical *DSM-5* diagnostic criteria (Lochner et al., 2012).

Research suggests that most individuals with SPD pick from multiple sites, with the face, scalp, arms, and legs being the most common (Arnold et al., 1998; Tucker et al., 2011). Antecedents of skin-picking include blemishes of the skin, an unpleasant urge, and negative emotional states, such as anxiety, tension, or boredom (Keuthen et al., 2010; Tucker et al., 2011). The behavior is also negatively reinforced, because the urge and negative emotional states are usually reduced after picking (Selles et al., 2016; Tucker et al., 2011). Skin-picking severity is positively correlated with distress and damage to skin (Neziroglu et al., 2008) as well as impulsivity and anxiety (Grant & Chamberlain, 2017). In addition, studies have shown that skin-picking leads to both physical and psychosocial impairment (Flessner & Woods, 2006).

Similar to TTM, SPD appears to have distinct styles. Automatic picking occurs outside one's awareness, and focused picking is more intentional and ritualistic (Pozza et al., 2016; Schienle et al., 2018; Walther et al., 2009). Several studies have examined the association between automatic and focused picking, emotion-regulation capacities, and personality traits (Pozza et al., 2016, 2020; Schienle et al., 2018). Pozza et al. (2016) found that while difficulty engaging in goal-directed behavior was evident in both subtypes, a lack of strategies for regulating negative emotions was specifically related to focused picking. In contrast, Schienle et al. (2018) found that impulse control difficulties predicted focused skin-picking, but a lack of emotional clarity predicted automatic skin-picking. Additionally, Schienle et al. (2018) found that focused picking was related to disgust proneness (e.g., disgust toward stimuli related to contamination and disease transmission) and behavioral self-disgust (e.g., belief that one's own behavior is repulsive). None of the disgust-related personality traits predicted automatic skin-picking.

Body-Focused Repetitive Behavior Disorders

Recurrent body-focused repetitive behaviors (BFRBs; other than TTM, SPD, stereotypic movement disorder, or non-suicidal-self injury), such as nail-biting, lip-biting, and cheek-biting, are known as body-focused repetitive behavior disorders (BFRBDs; APA, 2013) if they occur despite repeated attempts to decrease or stop, and symptoms cause significant distress or impairment in important areas of functioning.

Nail-biting, also known as onychophagia, is the most common type of BFRBD and involves repetitive contact between the nails (finger or toe) and the mouth or teeth, in the form of biting and chewing (Leung & Robson, 1990). Individuals engaging in this behavior usually bite the nails of all ten fingers with no selective preference (Malone & Massler, 1952). Nail-biting severity can range from mild, in which nails come into contact with the teeth, to severe, in which nails are bitten down to the nail bed and may bleed (Leonard et al., 1991; Pacan et al., 2009, 2014; Wells et al., 1998).

Research has suggested a link between various mood states and nail-biting. In a study of 139 men and women, those who regarded their nail-biting as a serious problem had higher manifest anxiety and obsessive-compulsive scores than those who regarded their behavior as mild, suggesting that nail-biting is anxiety related (Joubert, 1993). This link between tension and nail-biting is consistent with the tension-reduction model, which posits that individuals bite their nails to reduce tension during times of situational stress (DeFrancesco et al., 1989; Wells et al., 1998; Williams et al., 2007). Contrary to findings suggesting a link between tension/anxiety and nail-biting, a study of 14 individuals with severe onychophagia found that none met current criteria for an affective or anxiety disorder. Instead, many subjects thought the nail-biting itself was a cause, rather than a symptom, of their distress, leading the authors to conclude that nail-biting does not stem from underlying anxiety (Leonard et al., 1991).

A few studies have examined the link between other affective states and nail-biting. In an examination of repetitive behaviors in preschool children, findings indicated that increases in habits, including nail-biting, were associated with structured times in the day and negative mood states (Foster, 1998). Pacan et al. (2014) found that 92.2% of participants described nail-biting as an automatic behavior, with it mostly occurring during activities like watching television, using a computer, and reading. In another study, activities that were perceived as "inactive" were associated with greater rates of nail-biting

(O'Connor et al., 2003). Using a more experimental approach, Williams et al. (2007) compared the frequency of nail-biting among 40 undergraduate college students in four conditions: boredom, in which the participant was left alone; frustration, in which the participant solved math problems; contingent attention, in which the participant was reprimanded for nail-biting; and noncontingent attention, in which the participant engaged in continuous conversation. Findings indicated that nail-biting occurred most often in the boredom and frustration conditions. Nail-biting occurred least often when people were engaged in social interaction or were reprimanded for the behavior (Williams et al., 2007). Although there appears to be a link between negative emotional states and nail-biting, the direction of the relationship is unclear. Nevertheless, one study suggested that nail-biting may function to manage tension as measured via psychophysiological recording (Wells et al., 1999).

Cheek-biting, also known as morsicatio buccarum, is another BFRB. It is characterized by repetitive chewing, biting, or nibbling that results in irritation of the buccal mucosa (Fatima et al., 2019; Sarkhel et al., 2011). Cheek-biting has been associated with physical and psychological stressors, with some studies demonstrating a significant link between cheek-biting and depression (Bhatia, 2015; Sarkhel et al., 2011).

Nonclinical Forms of the Conditions

Trichotillomania

Hair manipulation in the form of hair twirling, stroking, and pulling is quite common, and in several instances, it has been associated with habits such as thumb-sucking and nail-biting (Byrd et al., 2002; Deaver et al., 2001; Knell & Moore, 1988; Santhanam et al., 2008; Watson & Allen, 1993). In children, transient hair-pulling episodes are common and often go unreported. Some have suggested that early-onset (i.e., at age 2 or 3 years) hair-pulling may be better characterized as a benign habit with a shorter course, as opposed to TTM, which usually has a later age of onset (Byrd et al., 2002; Santhanam et al., 2008; Wright & Holmes, 2003). However, research has not empirically confirmed the differences, either in function or prognosis, between early- and later-onset hair-pulling.

Nonclinical forms of hair-pulling have been studied in college student samples, with results showing that pulling does not always result in noticeable hair loss, impairment, and distress. Nevertheless, Duke et al. (2010) indicated that nonclinical hair-pulling could be a risk factor for symptoms of depression and anxiety. Findings from other studies suggest that nonclinical hair-pulling might be distinct from TTM (Stanley et al., 1994, 1995). For example, a study comparing emotion regulation in clinical and nonclinical hair-pullers found that during and after a pulling episode, nonclinical hair-pullers reported larger increases than the TTM group in happiness, calmness, and relief throughout the pulling episode, whereas the TTM group reported larger increases in sadness and guilt, and larger decreases in boredom (Diefenbach et al., 2008). Similarly, in a nonclinical sample of hair-pullers, Ghisi et al. (2013) found no differences in anger, sadness, or guilt across the pulling cycle, suggesting that these emotions may play a more significant role for clinical pullers. Further, Alexander et al. (2018) showed that participants with BFRBDs demonstrated greater deficits in emotional reactivity, experiential avoidance, and ineffectual response inhibition than did those with subclinical BFRBs. This suggests that if BFRBs occur in individuals with emotion-regulation deficits, it is more likely that they will develop BFRBDs, such as TTM. Other studies have also shown emotion-regulation deficits in individuals with BFRBDs (Arabatzoudis et al., 2017; Snorrason et al., 2010; Wetterneck et al., 2016).

Skin-Picking
Nonclinical skin-picking is common in the general population, because many individuals pick their skin as a part of standard grooming practices (Bohne et al., 2002; Hayes et al., 2009; Prochwicz et al., 2016; Yeo & Lee, 2017). Yeo and Lee (2017) examined skin-picking in 452 elementary and middle school students from South Korea and found that 66.8% of the sample reported past skin-picking. Similarly, Hayes et al. (2009) indicated that 62.7% of a nonclinical community sample of 354 adults endorsed some form of skin-picking, but clinical levels were found in only 5.4%. Additionally, Bohne et al. (2002) found that 92% of German college students endorsed engaging in skin-picking, but only 4.6% felt significantly impaired by the behavior. In contrast, Prochwicz et al. (2016) reported lower rates of nonclinical skin-picking: 46% of Polish young adults endorsed some form of picking, with nearly 8% of participants meeting SPD diagnostic criteria. Overall, these studies demonstrated that nonclinical skin-picking is a common behavior among adolescents and adults. Similar to the findings on TTM, studies have suggested that emotion-regulation deficits may differentiate clinical from nonclinical skin pickers (Alexander et al., 2018; Wetterneck et al., 2016).

BFRBs
Nonclinical nail-biting is quite common in children and adults, occurring in up to 51% of the population (Birch, 1955; Deardorff et al., 1974; Foster, 1998; Odenrick & Brattström, 1985; Teng et al., 2002). Individuals with nonclinical nail-biting have lower frequency, intensity, and duration of the behavior compared to those with pathological nail-biting (Ghanizadeh & Shekoohi, 2011). Due to the transient nature of nonclinical nail-biting, it is less likely to result in bleeding or severe damage to the nail bed than more severe forms of the behavior (Ghanizadeh & Shekoohi, 2011; Tanaka et al., 2008; Wells et al., 1998). For most individuals, nonclinical nail-biting is not a concern (Tanaka et al., 2008). Similarly, nonclinical cheek-biting is common in children; Vanderas and Papagiannoulis (2002) found the behavior in 60.51% of children at a dental checkup.

Diagnostic Distinction from OCD and Other Conditions

TTM and SPD

TTM and SPD are similar OCRDs, although Odlaug and Grant (2008) found some differences in clinical characteristics between the two disorders. For instance, in Odlaug and Grant's study of 77 participants with TTM, SPD, or TTM + SPD, those with SPD spent significantly more time picking than those with TTM spent pulling, and there were some differences in triggers of the behaviors. Further, those with SPD were more likely to have a first-degree relative with the disorder. Additionally, on a stop-signal task, Grant et al. (2011) found significantly more inhibitory deficits in participants with SPD compared to those with TTM.

TTM and SPD are also phenomenologically similar to OCD because patients with any of the three conditions experience aversive states that are relieved by engaging in repetitive behaviors (Stein et al., 1995). However, while OCD patients tend to have multiple symptoms that can change in focus over time (Besiroglu et al., 2007; Rufer et al., 2005), patients with TTM and SPD usually present with only the symptoms of hair-pulling and skin-picking, respectively, which do not progress into non-self-injurious rituals (Lochner et al., 2005). Additionally, intrusive thoughts are a central feature of OCD, while relatively few patients with TTM and SPD experience obsessive thoughts as a precursor to their behaviors (Chamberlain et al., 2007; Grant et al., 2010; Stein et al., 1995; Swedo & Leonard, 1992). Furthermore, while both the performance of rituals in OCD and hair-pulling/skin-picking in TTM and SPD may function to reduce an aversive state, TTM and SPD also include a positively reinforcing component. Further evidence of the distinction between TTM and OCD can be found in results from an analysis of 60 adult chronic hair-pullers, in which only 15% of the sample reported being fully aware of their behavior. The majority lacked full awareness of their hair-pulling, in contrast to those with OCD, who engage in compulsions that are purposeful in nature (Christenson, Mackenzie, & Mitchell, 1991). Likewise, Arnold et al. (1998) indicated that of 34 adult skin-pickers, 76% reported picking sometimes occurring outside awareness.

TTM and SPD can also be difficult to differentiate from body dysmorphic disorder (BDD). Similar to individuals with TTM and SPD, some patients with BDD will remove body hair and pick skin in an attempt to improve imagined defects in their appearance. Although patients with BDD may engage in hair-pulling and skin-picking, individuals with TTM and SPD do not typically pull hair or pick skin in response to imagined defects in their appearance (APA, 2013).

Similar differentiation is needed between SPD and nonsuicidal self-injurious behavior, in which individuals directly and deliberately cause harm to themselves (Klonsky, 2011; Selles et al., 2016). For instance, the behavioral function of self-injurious skin-picking may involve self-punishment, whereas those with SPD usually pick to relieve an unpleasant urge or negative emotional state, such as anxiety, tension, or boredom

(Klonsky, 2011; Selles et al., 2016). Therefore, those with self-injurious skin-picking usually would not be diagnosed with SPD.

TTM may also be misdiagnosed as alopecia areata, a medical condition in which hair is lost from areas of the body like the scalp (Madani & Shapiro, 2000). In contrast to those with TTM, patients with alopecia areata can have changes in the appearance of their nails, including nail thinning, nail pitting, onychomadesis, and severe nail-plate surface irregularities (Tosti et al., 1994). TTM may also be confused with tinea capitis, a disease caused by fungal infection of the scalp, skin, and eyebrows. Distinguishing features of this disease are a scaly scalp and infected hairs that can be easily extracted from the scalp (Gupta & Summerbell, 2000).

BFRBDs

In certain cases, nail-biting may be a symptom of OCD; however, as a BFRB, nail-biting is distinct from OCD. Patients with OCD experience a range of symptoms, but those who engage in nail-biting suffer from only the one symptom and generally do not experience associated intrusive thoughts (APA, 2013). Additionally, in diagnosing an individual with onychophagia, it is important to distinguish associated nail damage from that of childhood nail diseases, including 20-nail dystrophy, lichen planus, onychomycosis, and leukonychia (de Berker, 2006).

Prevalence and Limitations of Epidemiologic Research

TTM

In the first large-scale epidemiologic survey of TTM in the United States, Grant et al. (2020) found that 1.7% of participants met *DSM-5* criteria for TTM. Results also showed consistent prevalence rates across ethnic groups and income and education level among the 10,169 adult participants. Similarly, in a community sample of 520 Italian adults, 2.1% met criteria for TTM (Ghisi et al., 2013). Most other research on the prevalence of TTM has been performed with college students. A study examining the prevalence of TTM in college students yielded a rate of 0.6% among the 2,534 participants, although 4.9% reported hair-pulling that did not meet *DSM-III-R* (APA, 1987) criteria for TTM (Christenson, Pyle, & Mitchell, 1991). Similar results in clinical and nonclinical pulling were found by other researchers (Rothbaum et al., 1993; Woods et al., 1996). Further, a survey of 339 medical students in Poland found that 2.4% met criteria for TTM according to the 10th revision of the *International Classification of Diseases* (*ICD-10*; Grzesiak et al., 2017).

Few studies have assessed the prevalence of hair-pulling in children. However, one such study found a prevalence rate of 9.25% among 108 clinically referred infants and toddlers (Wright & Holmes, 2003). TTM prevalence appears similar in populations with disabilities. Researchers surveyed 259 parents/direct care staff and found that 5% of the persons with intellectual disabilities had TTM (Long et al., 1998), and an examination of 457 children and adolescents with intellectual disabilities found a TTM prevalence rate of 3.06% (Dimoski & Duricić, 1991).

SPD

Several studies have examined the prevalence of SPD across cultures (Calikusu et al., 2012; Hayes et al., 2009; Keuthen et al., 2010; Machado et al., 2018; Monzani et al., 2012; Prochwicz et al., 2016). In various community samples, the prevalence varied from 1.4% in the United States (Keuthen et al., 2010) to 1.2% in the United Kingdom (Monzani et al., 2012) to 2.04% in Turkey (Calikusu et al., 2012) and 3.45% in a Brazilian sample (Machado et al., 2018). Other studies found slightly higher rates of clinically significant skin-picking. For instance, in a sample of 354 adults from the United States, Hayes et al. (2009) indicated that 5.4% met criteria for clinical levels of skin-picking. Further, Prochwicz et al. (2016) showed that 7.7% of Polish adults reported symptoms of SPD, while Siddiqui et al. (2012) found a prevalence rate of 9% in a university sample from Pakistan. Overall, most studies reported a prevalence rate of 1.4% to 5.4%. Future research should focus on the prevalence of SPD in children.

BFRBDs

The epidemiologic literature on nail-biting has several limitations. First, there are no large-scale prevalence studies, which may be due to the fact that disordered nail-biting has only recently been included in the psychiatric taxonomy. Second, findings on gender ratio and prevalence rates are inconsistent across studies, and the lack of an official operational definition has contributed to these inconsistencies. Likewise, much of the literature on nail-biting is older, and various study designs were employed. Existing studies that have been conducted suggest that nail-biting is common, with prevalence rates ranging from 6% to 51% (Birch, 1955; Ballinger, 1970; Deardorff et al., 1974; Foster, 1998; Ghanizadeh & Shekoohi, 2011; Leung & Robson, 1990; Odenrick & Brattström, 1985; Pennington, 1945; Shetty & Munshi, 1998; Teng et al., 2002). When more severe and problematic nail-biting in children is considered, the reported prevalence rate has been up to 14% (Ghanizadeh, 2008; Odenrick & Brattström,1985).

Few studies have examined the prevalence of cheek-biting. In adolescents and young adults, the prevalence of the condition ranges from 1% to 7% (Kovac-Kavcic & Skaleric, 2000; van Wyk et al., 1977), while Reichert (2000) indicated that 10.1% of adults met criteria for the disorder. Vanderas and Papagiannoulis (2002) found nonclinical cheek-biting in 60.51% of children at a dental checkup.

Demographics

TTM

AGE OF ONSET AND GENDER RATIO

The onset of TTM commonly occurs between the ages of 10 and 13 (Christenson, Mackenzie, & Mitchell, 1991; Christenson et al., 1994; Cohen et al., 1995; Ricketts et al., 2019), but ranges from the first year of life (Altman et al., 1982; Christenson,

Mackenzie, & Mitchell, 1991) to the beginning of the seventies (Greenberg & Sarner, 1965). A latent profile analysis of 1,604 adults with TTM showed a two-class solution, consisting of a large group ($n = 1,539$) with an average age of onset of 12.4 years and a small group ($n = 65$) with an average age of onset of 35.6 years (Ricketts et al., 2019). In adult samples, TTM predominantly affects women, with sex ratios ranging from 7.3 to 9.3:1 (Christenson, Mackenzie, & Mitchell, 1991; Cohen et al., 1995; Muller, 1987; Woods et al., 2006). However, Grant et al. (2020) called these findings into question: they found that rates of TTM did not differ between men and women in a sample of approximately 10,000 adults. In children, the female to male ratio is unclear. In 52 preschool children with TTM, almost half (46.2%) were male (Muller, 1987), and among 28 children with TTM age 12 and under, 50% were male (Chang et al., 1991). Nevertheless, some studies have continued to suggest that the female to male ratio is heavily skewed toward females, even in young populations. In studies of 133 children 10 to 17 years old and 110 children 1 to 10 years old with hair-pulling problems, 72% and 83%, respectively, were girls (Franklin et al., 2008; Walther et al., 2014). Reasons for the female to male ratio are unclear, but one possible explanation is that for men with TTM, hair loss may be attributed to male-pattern baldness and therefore may be perceived as more socially acceptable. Also, men who pull hair from their beard or mustache can prevent the behavior by shaving the areas (Christenson, Mackenzie, & Mitchell, 1991).

LONGITUDINAL COURSE

Research on the longitudinal course of TTM is limited. However, studies suggest that with an early childhood onset, the duration of the disorder is brief, usually resolving on its own and requiring minimal treatment (Santhanam et al., 2008; Swedo & Leonard, 1992; Winchel, 1992; Wright & Holmes, 2003). One study suggested that if the duration of TTM was less than 6 months, patients were able to easily resolve the behavior. However, if the duration of TTM was more than 6 months, patients experienced a chronic and more treatment-resistant course (Chang et al., 1991).

FUNCTIONAL IMPAIRMENT

Individuals suffering from TTM can experience impairments in several aspects of their lives. Studies indicate that people with TTM often experience impairments in social functioning, such as social distress, teasing, social rejection, feelings of isolation, and reluctance to form friendships (du Toit et al., 2001; King, Scahill, et al., 1995; Marcks et al., 2005), with many avoiding public and social/leisure activities that may cause embarrassment due to visible hair loss (King, Scahill, et al., 1995; Stemberger et al., 2000; Wetterneck et al., 2006; Woods & Houghton, 2014). Individuals with TTM also report difficulty in situations involving intimacy (Stemberger et al., 2000) and family functioning (King, Scahill, et al., 1995; Stemberger et al., 2000). Further, TTM is associated with impairment in occupational functioning (such as work duties, job advancement, and attending job interviews; Diefenbach et al., 2005; Franklin et al., 2008; Keuthen et al., 2004; Stemberger et al., 2000; Wetterneck et al., 2006; Woods et al., 2006). Patients with TTM also experience psychological and emotional distress. Individuals commonly report lowered body image, feelings of low self-esteem and unattractiveness, and negative self-evaluations (Diefenbach et al., 2005; du Toit et al., 2001; Soriano et al., 1996; Stemberger et al., 2000). Patients may also exhibit negative affect or feelings of depression related to their TTM (Diefenbach et al., 2005; Stemberger et al., 2000). Other emotions commonly reported include guilt, shame, frustration, fear, anger, irritability, and embarrassment (; Stemberger et al., 2000). Additionally, patients may be distracted or experience interference due to the time spent pulling hair (King, Scahill, et al., 1995; Wetterneck et al., 2006).

Several studies have specifically examined functional impairment in children and adolescents with TTM. In a survey of 133 youth (10 to 17 years old) with TTM and their parents, Franklin et al. (2008) indicated that 55.6% of parents reported that their child avoided social events due to pulling. Further, TTM was associated with impairment in academic functioning (e.g., school attendance, studying, and performing schoolwork), with 54.9% of children reporting that TTM made it more difficult to study and 36.1% indicating that their ability to do well in school was impacted by pulling. Parents and children also reported mild to moderate interference in occupational functioning. Walther et al. (2014) indicated that level of functional impairment appeared lower in younger children (1 to 10 years old) than in adolescents, which may be due to the younger children's decreased awareness of social consequences of pulling.

HEALTHCARE UTILIZATION

Surveys of healthcare utilization have been completed with children, adolescents, and adults with TTM (Franklin et al., 2008; Walther et al., 2014; Woods et al., 2006). Among 1,697 adults with TTM, pharmacotherapy was the most commonly sought treatment, followed by behavior therapy, although neither was perceived to be effective (Woods et al., 2006). Among youth (those 10 to 17 years old) with TTM, Franklin et al. (2008) demonstrated that 49% received some form of pharmacotherapy and 45% received behavior therapy. Echoing the finding of Woods et al. (2006), only ~18% of participants perceived treatment to be effective. Finally, Walther et al. (2014) surveyed 110 parents/caregivers of young children with TTM (1 to 10 years old) and found that more children received behavior therapy (76.2%) than pharmacotherapy (41.8%). However, only 9% indicated that their child's TTM improved after treatment. In another study, researchers found that participants with TTM often sought help from multiple healthcare professionals, most commonly psychologists (Wetterneck et al., 2006).

SPD

AGE OF ONSET, GENDER RATIO, AND LONGITUDINAL COURSE

SPD commonly begins in adolescence (at age ~12 years), but studies have shown that the disorder can begin at any age (Flessner & Woods, 2006; Odlaug & Grant, 2007; Ricketts et al., 2018). Using a best-fit latent profile analysis model with 700 SPD participants, Ricketts et al. (2018) found two distinct groups for age of onset of SPD. The first group (N = 650) had an average age of onset of 13.6 years, while the second group (N = 50) had an average age of onset of 42.8 years. In a sample of 40 individuals with SPD, Odlaug and Grant (2007) indicated that 48% had SPD onset before 10 years of age. Like TTM, SPD predominately affects women (Hayes et al., 2009; Machado et al., 2018; Tucker et al., 2011). In a community sample of 7,639 participants, Machado et al. (2018) found that 82% of the 259 individuals who met criteria for SPD were female. Similarly, Hayes et al. (2009) demonstrated that in a community sample of 354 individuals, 15% of women reported clinically significant skin-picking, compared to only 6% of men. Further, in a sample of 760 adults with SPD, Tucker et al. (2011) indicated that 94% were female. There are limited data on the longitudinal course of SPD. Cross-sectional studies suggest that SPD is chronic when not treated, with variability in severity (Monzani et al., 2012; Snorrason et al., 2012).

FUNCTIONAL IMPAIRMENT

Individuals with SPD experience impairment in social, school, and occupational domains (Anderson & Clarke, 2019; Flessner & Woods, 2006; Grant et al., 2016; Tucker et al., 2011). In a sample of 125 adults with SPD, Grant et al. (2016) indicated that 56% reported moderate or severe impairment, with greater impairment being associated with worse symptom severity. Studies have also found that shame related to SPD is associated with social avoidance and efforts to conceal body parts damaged by the behavior, with participants reporting high levels of disgust with themselves and their skin after picking (Anderson & Clarke, 2019). Further, Tucker et al. (2011) indicated that most individuals experience psychosocial impairment at a moderate level, with social impairment being more severe than academic or occupational impairment. They also found that approximately 60% of participants reported avoiding social or entertainment events due to skin-picking, while Flessner and Woods (2006) demonstrated that participants refrained from engaging in intimate relationships due to SPD.

With respect to academic/occupational interference, Tucker et al. (2011) showed that 27% of participants reported having missed school and 37% reported difficulties in managing responsibilities at school due to picking. Additionally, in the study by Flessner and Woods (2006), approximately 50% of participants who currently attended school noted difficulties with school responsibilities, such as taking notes and giving speeches. In the occupational domain, Flessner and Woods (2006) found that 33% of participants reported interference at their job on a weekly basis, while Tucker et al. (2011) noted that

42% of participants indicated that skin-picking led to interference at work in the past month. Finally, those with SPD sometimes experience infections, bleeding, and scarring due to picking (Neziroglu et al., 2008; Wilhelm et al., 1999), which can lead to social avoidance and problems at work (Anderson & Clarke, 2019; Flessner & Woods, 2006; Tucker et al., 2011).

HEALTHCARE UTILIZATION

Although research on healthcare utilization for SPD is limited, some studies have used self-report surveys to examine the treatments provided to those with the disorder. Gallinat et al. (2019) examined healthcare experiences of 133 individuals with SPD and found that 44% sought help, with psychologists and dermatologists being the most common providers approached. Most participants rated appointments with psychotherapists and psychologists as helpful, while few participants were satisfied with their visits with dermatologists. Those who did not seek treatment cited their low perceived need for treatment, insecurity related to treatment providers, and feelings of shame. Tucker et al. (2011) examined treatment utilization in 760 adults with SPD, and results showed that approximately half of the participants had sought treatment for the disorder, with medication and behavior therapy being the most common treatments utilized. Most participants reported that treatment providers had little knowledge about SPD, and approximately 85% of participants showed no improvement after treatment. Overall, these studies suggest that most individuals with SPD do not receive adequate treatment for the disorder.

BFRBDs

AGE OF ONSET, GENDER RATIO, AND LONGITUDINAL COURSE

The literature on gender and nail-biting is limited and mixed, with some studies showing a greater preponderance of the behavior in females than in males (Bakwin, 1971; Foster, 1988; Shetty & Munshi, 1998), some showing a greater preponderance in males (Ghanizadeh, 2008; Joubert, 1993), and some showing no gender differences (Coleman & McCalley, 1948; Ghanizadeh & Shekoohi, 2011; Odenrick & Brattström, 1985). Few studies report an age of onset for nail-biting. However, in a study of 63 children and adolescents who engaged in nail-biting, the reported mean age of onset was 9.4 years (Ghanizadeh, 2008). Further, studies have indicated that the condition usually develops in children 3 to 4 years old and older (Tanaka et al., 2008). Research on the longitudinal course of nail-biting is also limited, but a study of preschool children found that habits like nail-biting decreased as age increased (Foster, 1998).

FUNCTIONAL IMPAIRMENT

Nail-biting can lead to both social and physical impairment. Nail-biting is considered to be a socially undesirable and repulsive behavior (Silber & Haynes, 1992), which has implications for how individuals with a nail-biting problem view themselves. In two separate surveys of those with habits, those who bit their nails reported lower self-esteem (Joubert, 1993) and had more negative perceptions of their appearance and health than those who did not (Hansen et al., 1990). Singal and Daulatabad (2017) also indicated that children who bite their nails are teased by peers, and the teasing may be linked to negative self-perception. Further, Ghanizadeh and Shekoohi (2011) suggested that social and family pressure to stop nail-biting may lead to emotional problems.

Nail-biting can also play a role in several health problems. There is some evidence that nai-biters are at greater risk for infections. For example, one study found that the saliva of children who bit their nails contained higher levels of Enterobacteriaceae and *Escherichia coli* than the saliva of those who did not (Baydaş et al., 2007). Nail-biting may also result in paronychia (i.e., a bacterial or fungal infection occurring at the boundaries of the skin and nails where the cuticle is damaged; Leung & Robson, 1990) and longitudinal melanonychia (i.e., a pigmented stripe of melanin along the length of the nail; Baran, 1990). Additionally, nail-biting may play a role in atypical root resorption, excoriations, and hangnails (Odenrick & Brattström, 1985; Singal & Daulatabad, 2017), and in rare cases, it can lead to epidermoid cysts, malocclusion, and gum injuries (Krejci, 2000; Oliveira et al., 2008; Van Tongel et al., 2012).

Cross-cultural Features

TTM

Some research has examined TTM in minority populations and people of different cultures. Neal-Barnett et al. (2010) examined differences in phenomenology, interference, and impairment related to TTM among 1,393 affected minority and Caucasian participants. Fewer minority individuals reported pulling from their eyebrows and eyelashes, and minorities were less likely to report increased tension before pulling. Further, minority participants indicated that TTM had high levels of interference with home management but not work or academics, while Caucasian participants endorsed greater interference with academics.

A few studies have examined the clinical characteristics of TTM in samples of African Americans. In a sample of over 200 African Americans, results indicated that while no one in the sample met criteria for TTM, 6.3% engaged in hair-pulling (Mansueto et al., 2007), a finding consistent with rates of 10% found in college samples (Rothbaum et al., 1993; Woods et al., 1996). In a study examining the ethnic differences in hair-pulling behavior in 177 African American students and 422 students of other ethnicities, the prevalence of hair-pulling resulting in noticeable hair loss in the total sample was 10.2%. However, the rate was higher in African American women (15.7%) than in all other respondents. An interesting finding was that African Americans, especially African American women, were more likely to report hair-pulling due to skin irritation (McCarley et al., 2002).

Consistent with research on affective correlates conducted in primarily Caucasian samples, studies have shown that African Americans experience a variety of affective states prior to, during, and following the hair-pulling episode, including boredom, happiness, anxiety, guilt, and relief (Diefenbach et al., 2002; Mansueto et al., 2007; Neal-Barnett & Stadulis, 2006; Stanley et al., 1995). However, in a study examining the ethnic differences in hair-pulling in African Americans and people of other ethnicities, African American women reported higher rates of pleasure or relief associated with hair-pulling (McCarley et al., 2002). Further, Neal-Barnett et al. (2011) found that in African American women, higher levels of anxiety and obsessive-compulsive symptoms were related to more severe TTM symptoms.

Findings on functional impairment due to TTM in African Americans are limited. In one study, secondary reports from hair-care professionals with clients who met criteria for TTM revealed that hair-pulling caused their customers much embarrassment, leading them to avoid social events (Neal-Barnett et al., 2000). The avoidance of social situations or potentially embarrassing situations has been observed in several multi-ethnic samples (Casati et al., 2000; King, Scahill, et al., 1995; Stemberger et al., 2000; Wetterneck et al., 2006). Neal-Barnett et al. (2011) also found that functional impairment due to TTM was related to higher general anxiety scores. Studies have indicated that African American individuals' hair presentation is often linked to their identity and self-esteem, which could impact functional impairment (Johnson & Bankhead, 2014). However, in another study of African Americans, Mansueto et al. (2007) found no functional impairment associated with hair-pulling, but positive and significant correlations between hair-pulling and anxiety were reported.

Research on TTM has also been conducted in Eastern cultures, with results similar to those found in Western cultures. Prevalence rates for subjects in India, Israel, and Singapore were 1.24% (Malhotra et al., 2008), 1% (King, Zohar, et al., 1995), and 1% (Fung & Chen, 1999), respectively, consistent with Western prevalence rates (Christenson, Pyle, & Mitchell, 1991; Rothbaum et al., 1993). Studies in Eastern cultures report slightly lower age of onset—10.1 years in India (Malhotra et al., 2008) and 9.3 years in Singapore (Fung & Chen, 1999)— compared to the typical age of onset of 12 or 13 years found among Western samples (Christenson, Mackenzie, & Mitchell, 1991; Christenson et al., 1994). Findings on the gender ratio in East Indian children (Malhotra et al., 2008) were similar to those for Western cultures, with the majority (85%) of the sample being female. However, an Israeli sample (King, Zohar, et al., 1995) consisted of slightly more boys than girls, and a Singaporean sample (Fung & Chen, 1999) had a lower female to male ratio than is typical in Western cultures (Cohen et al., 1995; Woods et al., 2006). Some differences in hair-pulling topography can be noted in the Eastern samples, including the use of only hands to pluck hair in the East Indian children (Malhotra et al., 2008), and pulling out hair solely in tufts observed in the Singaporean sample (Fung & Chen, 1999). In studies performed in Western cultures, individuals often use tweezers to pull hair in addition to using their hands, and the majority of individuals pull their hair out in single strands as opposed to tufts (Christenson, Mackenzie, & Mitchell, 1991; Schlosser et al., 1994).

Findings on psychiatric comorbidity and habits associated with TTM are similar cross-culturally. Consistent with findings from Western cultures (Santhanam et al., 2008), OCD or obsessive-compulsive symptoms, generalized anxiety disorder, and major depressive disorder were commonly found to be comorbid with TTM in Israeli (King, Zohar, et al., 1995), East Indian (Malhotra et al., 2008), and Singaporean (Fung & Chen, 1999) samples. Other disorders and habits found to be comorbid with TTM were enuresis, eating disorder, tics, short temper, thumb-sucking, and nail-biting (Santhanam et al., 2008; Swedo & Leonard, 1992).

SPD

Several studies have examined SPD cross-culturally. Similar prevalence rates have been reported, with most studies indicating a prevalence rate between 1.4% and 5.4% (Calikusu et al., 2012; Leibovici et al., 2015; Monzani et al., 2012). Triggers, characteristics, and consequences of skin-picking also seem similar across cultures. Studies in Germany, Turkey, and Poland indicated that the face was the most common picking site, with many participants experiencing a decrease in negative emotions after picking (Bohne et al., 2002; Calikusu et al., 2012; Prochwicz et al., 2016). Significant social, academic, and occupational impairment related to picking also has been reported across cultures. Despite past studies demonstrating that skin-picking occurs more often in females than in males, studies in South Korea, Israel, Turkey, and Poland found no gender differences (Calikusu et al., 2012; Leibovici et al., 2015; Prochwicz et al., 2016; Yeo & Lee, 2017). This may be due to the studies' use of community samples. Research showing that skin-picking predominantly affects women has often relied on clinical samples, in which males may be underrepresented because they are less likely to seek treatment for picking. Overall, characteristics of SPD seem universal across cultures; however, future research should emphasize large-scale studies in different cultures.

BFRBDs

The general literature on nail-biting is quite limited, and few studies have examined nail-biting cross-culturally. One study assessed the prevalence of oral habits among 4,590 children in Mangalore. Findings indicated that nail-biting, with a prevalence rate of 12.7%, was more common among girls and in children ages 13 to 16 years (Shetty, & Munshi, 1998). The first study to examine psychiatric comorbidity in nail-biting was performed in Iran on a sample of children and adolescents. Nail-biting was comorbid with a range of disorders, most commonly ADHD, but no children had comorbid generalized anxiety disorder (Ghanizadeh, 2008). These findings differ from results of studies performed in Western regions that report that nail-biting is a symptom of anxiety (Joubert, 1993; McClanahan, 1995). Further, in a different sample of children from Iran, Ghanizadeh and Shekoohi (2011) found that 22.3% endorsed nail-biting in the past three months, with no gender differences reported. Of those with nail-biting, 36.8% reported at least one family member who also had the disorder.

Patterns of Mental Health Comorbidity

TTM

TTM is commonly comorbid with other psychiatric disorders; however, inconsistent rates of specific conditions have been reported across studies (Anwar & Jafferany, 2019). Of adults with TTM, 55% to 79% have been diagnosed with a comorbid condition (Anwar & Jafferany, 2019; Christenson et al., 1992; Diefenbach et al., 2002; Houghton et al., 2016; Swedo & Leonard, 1992). Of specific comorbidities, depression seems to be the most common (13% to 65%), followed by anxiety (14% to 32%), OCD (5% to 30%), stress disorder (3% to 29%), SPD (13% to 24%), substance use disorder (5% to 22%), and alcohol use disorder (5% to 20%; Christenson, 1995; Christenson et al., 1992; Christenson, Mackenzie, & Mitchell, 1991; Cohen et al., 1995; Grant et al., 2020; Houghton et al., 2016; Schlosser et al., 1994; Swedo & Leonard, 1992; Tung et al., 2015). There is limited research on psychiatric comorbidity in children with TTM. Studies have shown that 23% to 70% of children with TTM have been diagnosed with a comorbid condition (Franklin et al., 2008; Reeves et al., 1992; Santhanam et al., 2008; Walther et al., 2014). Of specific comorbidities, anxiety disorders seem to be the most common (20% to 60%), followed by mood disorders (3% to 20%), ADHD (10% to 17%), and tic disorders (3% to 13%; Franklin et al., 2008; King, Scahill, et al., 1995; Reeves et al., 1992; Santhanam et al., 2008; Walther et al., 2014).

SPD

SPD is commonly comorbid with several other disorders. Of adults with SPD, 57% to 100% have been diagnosed with a comorbid condition (Arnold et al., 1998; Odlaug & Grant, 2008; Wilhelm et al., 1999). Of specific comorbidities, depression seems to be the most common (32% to 79%), followed by anxiety (19% to 56%), OCD (6% to 52%), TTM (30% to 38%), borderline personality disorder (26% to 33%), BDD (9% to 32%), and nail-biting (32%; Arnold et al., 1998; Christenson & Mansueto, 1999; Lochner et al., 2002; Odlaug & Grant, 2008; Snorrason et al., 2012; Wilhelm et al., 1999). Future research should examine comorbidities in children and adolescents with SPD.

In a study of 60 adults with SPD, 38% had TTM, 32% had compulsive nail-biting, 32% had a depressive disorder, and 17% had OCD (Odlaug & Grant, 2008). In a sample of 21 adults with SPD, major depressive disorder (48%), borderline personality disorder (33%), OCD (19%), and generalized anxiety disorder (19%) were the most common lifetime comorbidities (Lochner et al., 2002). Arnold et al. (1998) found that of the 34 patients at an outpatient clinic with SPD, 79% had a co-occurring mood disorder, 56% had a co-occurring anxiety disorder, and 9% had co-occurring BDD. In addition, Wilhelm et al. (1999) indicated that in 31 individuals with SPD, the most common comorbid diagnoses were OCD (52%), alcohol abuse/dependence (39%), and BDD (32%).

BFRBDs
Few studies have examined the relationship between nail-biting and psychiatric comorbidities. Pacan et al. (2014) found that of those with nail-biting, 22.5% met criteria for an anxiety disorder, while 3.1% met criteria for OCD. The first known study to analyze psychiatric comorbidity among children and adolescents who engaged in nail-biting assessed 63 participants who were referred to a mental healthcare clinic (Ghanizadeh, 2008). Nail-biting was found to be comorbid with ADHD (74.6%), oppositional defiant disorder (ODD; 36%), social phobia (20.6%), enuresis (15.6%), tic disorder (12.7%), OCD (11.1%), major depressive disorder (6.7%), intellectual disabilities (9.5%), and PDD (3.2%). The rate of general psychiatric comorbidity was higher in boys than in girls. Additionally, the severity and frequency of nail-biting were not associated with any comorbid psychiatric disorder (Ghanizadeh, 2008). Ghanizadeh and Shekoohi (2011) also found that emotional and behavioral problems were more common in children with nail-biting than in those without the condition.

Relationship to Psychotic Conditions

Although research on the relation and prevalence of BFRBs in psychotic conditions is limited, hair-pulling has been observed in those with psychotic conditions. Findings indicate that hair-pulling may be caused by delusions or hallucinations involving hair and may be associated with mania or schizophrenia (Slagle & Martin, 1991). Nevertheless, pulling resulting from such variables is unlikely to be classified as TTM. Substances such as methamphetamine and cocaine are associated with tactile hallucinations in which users have a feeling of something traveling under their skin (Chen et al., 2003; Zweben et al., 2004). In a case study, a female with a history of substance abuse had excoriations in both her hand and leg flexor areas (Tas et al., 2018). Tas et al. (2018) indicated that her skin felt irritated after the use of methamphetamines, which led to the picking. Future research should be conducted to establish other possible links between skin-picking, nail-biting, and psychotic conditions.

Conclusion

Overall, this chapter examines the diagnostic features and clinical characteristics of TTM, SPD, and other BFRBs. Nonclinical forms of the disorders are described, as well as their diagnostic distinction from OCD and other conditions. For each condition, the prevalence and limitations of epidemiological research are analyzed, and gender ratio, age of onset, longitudinal course, functional impairment, and healthcare utilization are described. Finally, cross-cultural factors and comorbidities are examined, and the relationship between the disorders and psychotic conditions is briefly discussed.

References

Alexander, J. R., Houghton, D. C., Bauer, C. C., Lench, H. C., & Woods, D. W. (2018). Emotion regulation deficits in persons with body-focused repetitive behavior disorders. *Journal of Affective Disorders, 227*, 463–470.

Alexander, J. R., Houghton, D. C., Twohig, M. P., Franklin, M. E., Saunders, S. M., Neal-Barnett, A. M., Compton, S. N., & Woods, D. W. (2016). Factor analysis of the Milwaukee Inventory for Subtypes of Trichotillomania–Adult Version. *Journal of Obsessive-Compulsive and Related Disorders, 11*, 31–38.

Altman, K., Grahs, C., & Friman, P. (1982). Treatment of unobserved trichotillomania by attention-reflection and punishment of an apparent covariant. *Journal of Behavior Therapy and Experimental Psychiatry, 13*, 337–340.

American Psychiatric Association (APA). (1987). *Diagnostic and statistical manual of mental disorders* (3rd ed., revised).

American Psychiatric Association (APA). (2013). *Diagnostic and statistical manual of mental disorders* (5th ed.).

Anderson, S., & Clarke, V. (2019). Disgust, shame and the psychosocial impact of skin picking: Evidence from an online support forum. *Journal of Health Psychology, 24*, 1773–1784.

Anwar, S., & Jafferany, M. (2019). Trichotillomania: A psychopathological perspective and the psychiatric comorbidity of hair pulling. *Acta Dermatovenerologica, 28*, 33–36.

Arabatzoudis, T., Rehm, I. C., Nedeljkovic, M., & Moulding, R. (2017). Emotion regulation in individuals with and without trichotillomania. *Journal of Obsessive-Compulsive Related Disorders, 12*, 87–94.

Arnold, L. M., McElroy, S. L., Mutasim, D. F., Dwight, M. M., Lamerson, C. L., & Morris, E. M. (1998). Characteristics of 34 adults with psychogenic excoriation. *The Journal of Clinical Psychiatry 59*, 509–514.

Bakwin, H. (1971). Nail-biting in twins. *Developmental Medicine & Child Neurology, 13*, 277–418. https://doi.org/10.1111/j.1469-8749.1971.tb03265.x

Ballinger, B. R. (1970). The prevalence of nail-biting in normal and abnormal populations. *The British Journal of Psychiatry, 117*, 445–446.

Baran, R. (1990). Nail biting and picking as a possible cause of longitudinal melanonychia: A study of 6 cases. *Dermatologica, 181*, 126–128.

Baydaş, B., Uslu, H., Yavuz, I., Ceylan, I., & Dağsuyu, M. (2007). Effect of a chronic nail-biting habit on the oral carriage of Enterobacteriaceae. *Oral Microbiology and Immunology, 22*, 1–4.

Besiroglu, L., Uguz, F., Ozbebit, O., Guler, O., Cilli, A. S., & Askin, R. (2007). Longitudinal assessment of symptom and subtype categories in obsessive-compulsive disorder. *Depression and Anxiety, 24*, 461–466.

Bhatia, N. K. (2015). Morsicatio buccarum and labiorum with depression. *International Journal of Dental and Health Sciences, 2*, 1639–1642.

Birch, L. B. (1955). The incidence of nail biting among school children. *British Journal of Educational Psychology, 25*, 123–128.

Bohne, A., Wilhelm, S., Keuthen, N. J., Baker, L., & Jenike, M. A. (2002). Skin picking in German students: Prevalence, phenomenology, and associated characteristics. *Behavior Modification, 26*, 320–339.

Bouwer, C., & Stein, D. J. (1998). Trichobezoars in trichotillomania: Case report and literature overview. *Psychosomatic Medicine, 60*, 658–660.

Byrd, M. R., Richards, D. F., Hove, G., & Friman, P. C. (2002). Treatment of early onset hair pulling as a simple habit. *Behavior Modification, 26*, 400–411.

Casati, J., Toner, B. B., & Yu, B. (2000). Psychosocial issues for women with trichotillomania. *Comprehensive Psychiatry, 41*, 344–351.

Calikusu, C., Kucukgoncu, S., Tecer, Ö., & Bestepe, E. (2012). Skin picking in Turkish students. *Behavior Modification, 36*, 49–66.

Chamberlain, S. R., Fineberg, N. A., Blackwell, A. D., Clark, L., Robbins, T. W., & Sahakian, B. J. (2007). A neuropsychological comparison of obsessive-compulsive disorder and trichotillomania. *Neuropsychologia, 45*, 654–662.

Chang, C. H., Lee, M. B., Chiang, Y. C., & Lü, Y. C. (1991). Trichotillomania: A clinical study of 36 patients. *Journal of the Formosan Medical Association, 90*, 176–180.

Chen, C., Lin, S., Sham, P. C., Ball, D., Loh, E., Hsiao, C., Chiang, Y., Ree, S., Lee, C., & Murray, R. M. (2003). Pre-morbid characteristics and co-morbidity of methamphetamine users with and without psychosis. *Psychological Medicine, 33*, 1407–1414. doi:10.1017/s0033291703008353

Christenson, G. A. (1995). Trichotillomania: From prevalence to comorbidity. *Psychiatric Times, 12*, 44–48.

Christenson, G. A., Chernoff-Clementz, E., & Clementz, B. (1992). Personality and clinical characteristics in patients with trichotillomania. *The Journal of Clinical Psychiatry, 53*, 407–413.

Christenson, G. A., & Crow, S. J. (1996). The characterization and treatment of trichotillomania. *The Journal of Clinical Psychiatry, 57*, 42–47.

Christenson, G. A., Mackenzie, T. B., & Mitchell, J. E. (1991). Characteristics of 60 adult chronic hair pullers. *The American Journal of Psychiatry, 148*, 365–370.

Christenson, G. A., Mackenzie, T. B., & Mitchell, J. E. (1994). Adult men and women with trichotillomania: A comparison of male and female characteristics. *Psychosomatics, 35*, 142–149.

Christenson, G. A., Pyle, R. L., & Mitchell, J. E. (1991). Estimated lifetime prevalence of trichotillomania in college students. *The Journal of Clinical Psychiatry, 52*, 415–417.

Christenson, G. A., & Mansueto, C. S. (1999): Trichotillomania: Descriptive characteristics and phenomenology. In D. J. Stein, G. Christianson, & E. Hollander (Eds.), *Trichotillomania* (pp. 1–41). American Psychiatric Press.

Cohen, L. J., Stein, D. J., Simeon, D., Spadaccini, E., Rosen, J., Aronowitz, B., & Hollander, E. (1995). Clinical profile, comorbidity, and treatment history in 123 hair pullers: A survey study. *The Journal of Clinical Psychiatry, 56*, 319–326.

Coleman, J. C., & McCalley, J. E. (1948). Nail-biting among college students. *Journal of Abnormal and Social Psychology, 43*, 517–525.

de Berker, D. (2006). Childhood nail diseases. *Dermatologic Clinics, 24*, 355–363.

Deardorff, P. A., Finch, A. J., & Royall, L. R. (1974). Manifest anxiety and nail-biting. *Journal of Clinical Psychology, 30*, 378.

Deaver, C. M., Miltenberger, R. G., & Stricker, J. M. (2001). Functional analysis of hair twirling in a young child. *Journal of Applied Behavior Analysis, 34*, 535–538.

DeFrancesco, J. J., Zahner, G. E. P., & Pawelkiewicz, W. (1989). Childhood nailbiting. *Journal of Social Behaviour and Personality, 4*, 157–161.

Diefenbach, G. J., Mouton-Odom, S., & Stanley, M. A. (2002). Affective correlates of trichotillomania. *Behaviour Research and Therapy, 40*, 1305–1315.

Diefenbach, G. J., Tolin, D. F., Hannan, S., Crocetto, J., & Worhunsky, P. (2005). Trichotillomania: Impact on psychosocial functioning and quality of life. *Behaviour Research and Therapy, 43*, 869–884.

Diefenbach, G. J., Tolin, D. F., Meunier, S., & Worhunsky, P. (2008). Emotion regulation and trichotillomania: A comparison of clinical and nonclinical hair pulling. *Journal of Behavior Therapy and Experimental Psychiatry, 39*, 32–41.

Dimoski, A., & Duricić, S. (1991). Dermatitis artefacta, onychophagia and trichotillomania in mentally retarded children and adolescents. *Medicinski Pregled, 44*, 471–472.

du Toit, P. L., van Kradenburg, J., Niehaus, D. J. H., & Stein, D. J. (2001). Characteristics and phenomenology of hair pulling: An exploration of subtypes. *Comprehensive Psychiatry, 42*, 247–256.

Duke, D. C., Keeley, M. L., Ricketts, E. J., Geffken, G. R., & Storch, E. A. (2010). The phenomenology of hairpulling in college students. *Journal of Psychopathology and Behavioral Assessment, 32*, 281–292.

Fatima, R., Abid, K., Baig, N. N., & Ahsan, S. B. (2019). Association of cheek-biting and depression. *Journal of the Pakistan Medical Association, 69*, 49.

Flessner, C. A., Conelea, C. A., Woods, D. W., Franklin, M. E., Keuthen, N. J., & Cashin, S. E. (2008). Styles of pulling in trichotillomania: Exploring differences in symptom severity, phenomenology, and functional impact. *Behaviour Research and Therapy, 46*, 345–347.

Flessner, C. A., & Woods, D. W. (2006). Phenomenological characteristics, social problems, and the economic impact associated with chronic skin picking. *Behavior Modification, 30*, 944–963.

Foster, L. G. (1998). Nervous habits and stereotyped behaviors in preschool children. *Journal of the American Academy of Child and Adolescent Psychiatry, 37*, 711–717.

Franklin, M. E., Flessner, C. A., Woods, D. W., Keuthen, N. J., Piacentini, J. C., Moore, P., Stein, D. J., Cohen, S. B., Wilson, M. A., & Trichotillomania Learning Center Scientific Advisory Board. (2008). The Child and Adolescent Trichotillomania Impact Project: Descriptive psychopathology, comorbidity, functional impairment, and treatment utilization. *Journal of Developmental & Behavioral Pediatrics, 29*, 493–500.

Frey, A. S., McKee, M., King, R. A., & Martin, A. (2005). Hair apparent: Rapunzel syndrome. *The American Journal of Psychiatry, 162*, 242–248.

Fung, D. S., & Chen, Y. (1999). A clinical study of seven cases of trichotillomania in Singapore. *Annals of the Academy of Medicine, 28*, 519–524.

Gallinat, C., Moessner, M., Haenssle, H. A., Winkler, J. K., Backenstrass, M., & Bauer, S. (2019). Help-seeking attitudes and experiences in individuals affected by skin picking. *Journal of Obsessive-Compulsive and Related Disorders, 23*, 1–5.

Ghanizadeh, A. (2008). Association of nail biting and psychiatric disorders in children and their parents in a psychiatrically referred sample of children. *Child and Adolescent Psychiatry and Mental Health, 2*, 1–7.

Ghanizadeh, A., & Shekoohi, H. (2011). Prevalence of nail biting and its association with mental health in a community sample of children. *BMC Research Notes, 4*, 116.

Ghisi, M., Bottesi, G., Sica, C., Ouimet, A. J., & Sanavio, E. (2013). Prevalence, phenomenology and diagnostic criteria of hair-pulling in an Italian non-clinical sample: A preliminary study. *Journal of Obsessive-Compulsive and Related Disorders, 2*, 22–29.

Grant, J. E., & Chamberlain, S. R. (2017). Clinical correlates of symptom severity in skin picking disorder. *Comprehensive Psychiatry, 78*, 25–30.

Grant, J. E., Dougherty, D. D., & Chamberlain, S. R. (2020). Prevalence, gender correlates, and co-morbidity of trichotillomania. *Psychiatry Research, 288*, 1–6, 112948.

Grant, J. E., Odlaug, B. L., & Chamberlain, S. R. (2011). A cognitive comparison of pathological skin picking and trichotillomania. *Journal of Psychiatric Research, 45*, 1634–1638.

Grant, J. E., Odlaug, B. L., & Kim, S. W. (2010). A clinical comparison of pathologic skin picking and obsessive-compulsive disorder. *Comprehensive Psychiatry, 51*, 347–352.

Grant, J. E., Redden, S. A., Leppink, E. W., Odlaug, B. L., & Chamberlain, S. R. (2016). Psychosocial dysfunction associated with skin picking disorder and trichotillomania. *Psychiatry Research, 239*, 68–71.

Greenberg, H. R., & Sarner, C. A. (1965). Trichotillomania: Symptom and syndrome. *Archives of General Psychiatry, 12*, 482–489.

Grzesiak, M., Reich, A., Szepietowski, J., Hadryś, T., & Pacan, P. (2017). Trichotillomania among young adults: Prevalence and comorbidity. *Acta Dermato Venereologica, 97*, 509–512.

Gupta, A. K., & Summerbell, R. C. (2000). Tinea capitis. *Medical Mycology, 38*, 255–287.

Hanna, G. L. (1997). Trichotillomania and related disorders in children and adolescents. *Psychiatry and Human Development, 27*, 255–268.

Hansen, D. J., Tishelman, A. C., Hawkins, R. P., & Doepke, K. J. (1990). Habits with potential as disorders: Prevalence, severity, and other characteristics among college students. *Behavior Modification, 14*, 66–80.

Hayes, S. L., Storch, E. A., & Berlanga, L. (2009). Skin picking behaviors: An examination of the prevalence and severity in a community sample. *Journal of Anxiety Disorders, 23*, 314–319.

Houghton, D. C., Maas, J., Twohig, M. P., Saunders, S. M., Compton, S. N., Neal-Barnett, A. M., Franklin, M. E., & Woods, D. W. (2016). Comorbidity and quality of life in adults with hair pulling disorder. *Psychiatry Research, 239*, 12–19.

Johnson, T. A., & Bankhead, T. (2014). Hair it is: Examining the experiences of Black women with natural hair. *Open Journal of Social Sciences, 2*, 86–100.

Joubert, C. E. (1993). Relationship of self-esteem, manifest anxiety, and obsessive-compulsiveness to personal habits. *Psychological Reports, 73*, 579–583.

Keuthen, N. J., Dougherty, D. D., Franklin, M. E., Bohne, A., Loh, R., Levy, J., Beals, A., Matthews, M., & Deckersbach, T. (2004). Quality of life and functional impairment in individuals with trichotillomania. *Journal of Applied Research, 4*, 186–197.

Keuthen, N. J., Koran, L. M., Aboujaoude, E., Large, M. D., & Serpe, R. T. (2010). The prevalence of pathologic skin picking in United States adults. *Comprehensive Psychiatry, 51*, 183–186.

Keuthen, N., Tung, E., Woods, D., Franklin, M., Altenburger, E., Pauls, D., & Flessner, C. (2015). Replication study of the Milwaukee Inventory for Subtypes of Trichotillomania–Adult Version in a clinically characterized sample. *Behavior Modification, 39*, 580–599.

King, R. A., Scahill, L., Vitulano, L. A., Schwab-Stone, M., Tercyak, K., & Riddle, M. (1995). Childhood trichotillomania: Clinical phenomenology, comorbidity, and family genetics. *Journal of the American Academy of Child and Adolescent Psychiatry, 34*, 1451–1459.

King, R. A., Zohar, A. H., Ratzoni, G., Binder, M., Kron, S., Dycian, A., Cohen, D. J., Pauls, D. L., & Apter, A. (1995). An epidemiological study of trichotillomania in Israeli adolescents. *Journal of the American Academy of Child and Adolescent Psychiatry, 34*, 1212–1215.

Klonsky, E. D. (2011). Non-suicidal self-injury in United States adults: Prevalence, sociodemographics, topography and functions. *Psychological Medicine, 41*, 1981–1986.

Knell, S. M., & Moore, D. J. (1988). Childhood trichotillomania treated indirectly by punishing thumb sucking. *Journal of Behavior Therapy and Experimental Psychiatry, 19*, 305–310.

Kovac-Kavcic, M., & Skaleric, U. (2000). The prevalence of oral mucosal lesions in a population in Ljubljana, Slovenia. *Journal of Oral Pathology and Medicine, 29*, 331–335.

Krejci, C. B. (2000). Self-inflicted gingival injury due to habitual fingernail biting. *Journal of Periodontology, 71*, 29–31.

Leibovici, V., Koran, L. M., Murad, S., Siam, I., Odlaug, B. L., Mandelkorn, U., Feldman-Weisz, V., & Keuthen, N. J. (2015). Excoriation (skin-picking) disorder in adults: A cross-cultural survey of Israeli Jewish and Arab samples. *Comprehensive Psychiatry, 58*, 102–107.

Leonard, H. L., Lenane, M. C., Swedo, S. E., Rettew, D. C., & Rapoport, J. L. (1991). A double-blind comparison of clomipramine and desipramine treatment of severe onychophagia (nailbiting). *Archives of General Psychiatry, 48*, 821–827.

Leung, A. K., & Robson, W. L. (1990). Nailbiting. *Clinical Pediatrics, 29*, 690–692.

Lochner, C., Grant, J. E., Odlaug, B. L., Woods, D. W., Keuthen, N. J., & Stein, D. J. (2012). DSM-5 field survey: Hair-pulling disorder (Trichotillomania). *Depression and Anxiety, 29*, 1025–1031. https://doi.org/10.1002/da.22011

Lochner, C., Seedat, S., du Toit, P. L., Nel, D. G., Niehaus, D. J., Sandler, R., & Stein, D. J. (2005). Obsessive-compulsive disorder and trichotillomania: A phenomenological comparison. *BMC Psychiatry, 5*, 2.

Lochner, C., Seedat, S., & Stein, D. J. (2010). Chronic hair-pulling: Phenomenology-based subtypes. *Journal of Anxiety Disorders, 24*, 196–202.

Lochner, C., Simeon, D., Niehaus, D. J., & Stein, D. J. (2002). Trichotillomania and skin-picking: A phenomenological comparison. *Depression and Anxiety, 15*, 83–86.

Long, E. S., Miltenberger, R. G., & Rapp, J. T. (1998). A survey of habit behaviors exhibited by individuals with mental retardation. *Behavioral Interventions, 13*, 79–89.

Machado, M. O., Köhler, C. A., Stubbs, B., Nunes-Neto, P. R., Koyanagi, A., Quevedo, J., Soares, J. C., Hyphantis, T. N., Marazziti, D., Maes, M., Stein, D. J., & Carvalho, A. F. (2018). Skin picking disorder: Prevalence, correlates, and associations with quality of life in a large sample. *CNS Spectrums, 23*, 311–320.

Madani, S., & Shapiro, J. (2000). Alopecia areata update. *Journal of the American Academy of Dermatology, 42*, 549–566.

Malhotra, S., Grover, S., Baweja, R., & Bhateja, G. (2008). Trichotillomania in children. *Indian Pediatrics, 45*, 403–405.

Malone, A. J., & Massler, M. (1952). Index of nail biting in children. *Journal of Abnormal Psychology, 47*, 193–202.

Mansueto, C. S., Thomas, A. M., & Brice, L. (2007). Hair pulling and its affective correlates in an African-American university sample. *Journal of Anxiety Disorders, 21*, 590–599.

Marcks, B. A., Woods, D. W., & Ridosko, J. L. (2005). The effects of trichotillomania disclosure on peer perceptions and social acceptability. *Body Image, 2*, 299–306.

McCarley, N. G., Spirrison, C. L., & Ceminsky, J. L. (2002). Hair pulling behavior reported by African American and non-African college students. *Journal of Psychopathology and Behavioral Assessment, 24*, 139–144.

McClanahan, T. M. (1995). Operant learning (R-S) principles applied to nail biting. *Psychological Reports, 77*, 507–514.

Monzani, B., Rijsdijk, F., Cherkas, L., Harris, J., Keuthen, N., & Mataix-Cols, D. (2012). Prevalence and heritability of skin picking in an adult community sample: A twin study. *American Journal of Medical Genetics Part B: Neuropsychiatric Genetics, 159*, 605–610.

Muller, S. A. (1987). Trichotillomania. *Dermatologic Clinics, 5*, 595–601.

Neal-Barnett, A., Flessner, C., Franklin, M. E., Woods, D. W., Keuthen, N. J., & Stein, D. J. (2010). Ethnic differences in trichotillomania: Phenomenology, interference, impairment, and treatment efficacy. *Journal of Anxiety Disorders, 24*, 553–558.

Neal-Barnett, A., Statom, D., & Stadulis, R. (2011). Trichotillomania symptoms in African American women: Are they related to anxiety and culture? *CNS Neuroscience & Therapeutics, 17*, 207–213.

Neal-Barnett, A., & Stadulis, R. (2006). Affective states and racial identity among African-American women with trichotillomania. *Journal of the National Medical Association, 98*, 753–757.

Neal-Barnett, A. M., Ward-Brown, B. J., Mitchell, M., & Krownapple, M. (2000). Hair pulling African American women—Only your hairdresser knows for sure: An exploratory study. *Cultural Diversity & Ethnic Minority Psychology, 6*, 352–362.

Neziroglu, F., Rabinowitz, D., Breytman, A., & Jacofsky, M. (2008). Skin picking phenomenology and severity comparison. *The Journal of Clinical Psychiatry, 10*, 306–312.

O'Connor, K., Brisebois, H., Brault, M., Robillard, S., & Loiselle, J. (2003). Behavioral activity associated with onset in chronic tic and habit disorder. *Behaviour Research and Therapy, 41*, 241–249.

Odenrick, L., & Brattström, V. (1985). Nailbiting: Frequency and association with root resorption during orthodontic treatment. *British Journal of Orthodontics, 12*, 78–81.

Odlaug, B. L., & Grant, J. E. (2007). Childhood-onset pathologic skin picking: Clinical characteristics and psychiatric comorbidity. *Comprehensive Psychiatry, 48*, 388–393.

Odlaug, B. L., & Grant, J. E. (2008). Trichotillomania and pathologic skin picking: Clinical comparison with an examination of comorbidity. *Annals of Clinical Psychiatry, 20*, 57–63.

Oliveira, A. C., Paiva, S. M., Campos, M. R., & Czeresnia, D. (2008). Factors associated with malocclusions in children and adolescents with Down syndrome. *American Journal Orthodontics and Dentofacial Orthopedics, 133*, 489.

O'Sullivan, M. J., McGreal, G., Walsh, J. G., & Redmond, H. P. (1996). Trichobezoar. *Journal of the Royal Society of Medicine, 94*, 68–70.

Pacan, P., Grzesiak, M., Reich, A., Kantorska-Janiec, M., & Szepietowski, J. (2014). Onychophagia and onychotillomania: Prevalence, clinical picture, and comorbidities. *Acta Dermato Venereologica, 94*, 67–71.

Pacan, P., Grzesiak, M., Reich, A., & Szepietowski, C. J. (2009). Onychophagia as a spectrum of obsessive-compulsive disorder. *Acta Dermato Venereologica, 89*, 278–280.

Pennington, L. A. (1945). The incidence of nail-biting among adults. *The American Journal of Psychiatry, 102*, 241–244.

Pozza, A., Albert, U., & Dèttore, D. (2020). Early maladaptive schemas as common and specific predictors of skin picking subtypes. *BMC Psychology, 8*, 1–11

Pozza, A., Giaquinta, N., & Dèttore, D. (2016). Borderline, avoidant, sadistic personality traits and emotion dysregulation predict different pathological skin picking subtypes in a community sample. *Neuropsychiatric Disease and Treatment, 12*, 1861–1867.

Prochwicz, K., Kałużna-Wielobób, A., & Kłosowska, J. (2016). Skin picking in a non-clinical sample of young Polish adults. Prevalence and characteristics. *ComprehensivePsychiatry, 71*, 77–85.

Reeve, E. A., Bernstein, G. A., & Christenson, G. A. (1992). Clinical characteristics and psychiatric comorbidity in children with trichotillomania. *Journal of the American Academy of Child and Adolescent Psychiatry, 31*, 132–138.

Reichert, P. (2000). Oral mucosal lesions in a representative cross-sectional study of aging Germans. *Community Dentistry and Oral Epidemiology, 28*, 390–398.

Ricketts, E. J., Snorrason, Í., Kircanski, K., Alexander, J. R., Thamrin, H., Flessner, C. A., Franklin, M. E., Piacentini, J., & Woods, D. W. (2018). A latent profile analysis of age of onset in pathological skin picking. *Comprehensive Psychiatry, 87*, 46–52.

Ricketts, E. J., Snorrason, I., Kircanski, K., Stiede, J., Thamrin, H., Flessner, C. A., Franklin, M. E., Keuthen, N. J., Walther, M. R., Piacentini, J., Stein, D. J., & Woods, D. W. (2019). A latent profile analysis of age of onset in trichotillomania. *Annals of Clinical Psychology, 31*, 169–178.

Rothbaum, B. O., Shaw, L., Morris, R., & Ninan, P. T. (1993). Prevalence of trichotillomania in a college freshman population. *The Journal of Clinical Psychiatry, 54*, 72.

Rufer, M., Grothusen, A., Maszlig, R., Peter, H., & Hand, I. (2005). Temporal stability of symptom dimensions in adult patients with obsessive-compulsive disorder. *Journal of Affective Disorders, 88*, 99–102.

Santhanam, R., Fairley, M., & Rogers, M. (2008). Is it trichotillomania? Hair pulling in childhood: A developmental perspective. *Clinical Child Psychology and Psychiatry, 13*, 409–418.

Sarkhel, S., Praharaj, S. K., & Akhtar, S. (2011). Cheek-biting disorder: Another stereotypic movement disorder? *Journal of Anxiety Disorders, 25*, 1085–1086.

Schienle, A., Zorjan, S., Übel, S., & Wabnegger, A. (2018). Prediction of automatic and focused skin picking based on trait disgust and emotion dysregulation. *Journal of Obsessive-Compulsive and Related Disorders, 16*, 1–5.

Schlosser, S., Black, D. W., Blum, N., & Goldstein, R. B. (1994). The demography, phenomenology, and family history of 22 persons with compulsive hair pulling. *Annals of Clinical Psychiatry, 6*, 147–152.

Selles, R. R., McGuire, J. F., Small, B. J., & Storch, E. A. (2016). A systematic review and meta-analysis of psychiatric treatments for excoriation (skin-picking) disorder. *General Hospital Psychiatry*, *41*, 29–37.

Sharma, N. L., Sharma, R. C., Mahajan, V. K., Sharma, R. C., Chauhan, D., & Sharma, A. K. (2000). Trichotillomania and trichophagia leading to trichobezoar. *Journal of Dermatology*, *27*, 24–26.

Shetty, S. R., & Munshi, A. K. (1998). Oral habits in children—A prevalence study. *Journal of the Indian Society of Pedodontics and Preventive Dentistry*, *16*, 61–66.

Siddiqui, E. U., Naeem, S. S., Naqvi, H., & Ahmed, B. (2012). Prevalence of body-focused repetitive behaviors in three large medical colleges of Karachi: A cross-sectional study. *BMC Research Notes*, *5*, 614.

Silber, K. P., & Haynes, C. E. (1992). Treating nail biting: A comparative analysis of mild aversion and competing response therapies. *Behaviour Research and Therapy*, *30*, 15–22.

Singal, A., & Daulatabad, D. (2017). Nail tic disorders: Manifestations, pathogenesis and management. *Indian Journal of Dermatology, Venereology, and Leprology*, *83*, 19.

Slagle, D. A., & Martin, T. A. (1991). Trichotillomania. *American Family Physician*, *43*, 2019–2024.

Snorrason, I., Ólafsson, R. P., Flessner, C. A., Keuthen, N. J., Franklin, M. E., & Woods, D. W. (2012). The Skin Picking Scale–Revised: Factor structure and psychometric properties. *Journal of Obsessive-Compulsive and Related Disorders*, *1*, 133–137.

Snorrason, I., Smari, J., & Olafsson, R. P. (2010). Emotion regulation in pathological skin picking: Findings from a non-treatment-seeking sample. *Journal of Behavior Therapy and Experimental Psychiatry*, *41*, 238–245.

Soriano, J. L., O'Sullivan, R. L., Baer, L., Philips, K. A., McNally, R. J., & Jenike, M. A. (1996). Trichotillomania and self-esteem: A survey of 62 hair pullers. *The Journal of Clinical Psychiatry*, *57*, 77–82.

Stanley, M. A., Borden, J. W., Bell, G. E., & Wagner, A. L. (1994). Nonclinical hair pulling: Phenomenology and related psychopathology. *Journal of Anxiety Disorders*, *8*, 119–130.

Stanley, M. A., Borden, J. W., Mouton, S. G., & Breckenridge, J. K. (1995). Nonclinical hair pulling: Affective correlates and comparison with clinical samples. *Behaviour Research and Therapy*, *33*, 179–186.

Stein, D. J., Simeon, D., Cohen, L. J., & Hollander, E. (1995). Trichotillomania and obsessive-compulsive disorder. *The Journal of Clinical Psychiatry*, *56*, 28–34.

Stemberger, R. M., Thomas, A. M., Mansueto, C. S., & Carter, J. G. (2000). Personal toll of trichotillomania: Behavioral and interpersonal sequelae. *Journal of Anxiety Disorders*, *14*, 97–104.

Swedo, S. E., & Leonard, H. L. (1992). Trichotillomania. An obsessive-compulsive spectrum disorder? *Psychiatric Clinics of North America*, *15*, 777–790.

Tanaka, O. M., Vitral, R. W., Tanaka, G. Y., Guerrero, A. P., & Camargo, E. S. (2008). Nailbiting, or onychophagia: A special habit. *American Journal of Orthodontics and Dentofacial Orthopedics*, *134*, 305–308.

Tas, I., Yasar, S. A., Inanli, I., Eren, I., & Yildiz, M. C. (2018). Drug-induced skin picking associated with tactile hallucination due to methamphetamine. *Klinik Psikofarmakoloji Bulteni*, *28*, 141–142.

Teng, E. J., Woods, D. W., Twohig, M. P., & Marcks, B. A. (2002). Body-focused repetitive behavior problems: Prevalence in a non-referred population and differences in perceived somatic activity. *Behavior Modification*, *26*, 340–360.

Tosti, A., Morelli, R., Bardazzi, F., & Peluso, A. M. (1994). Prevalence of nail abnormalities in children with alopecia areata. *Pediatric Dermatology*, *11*, 112–115.

Tucker, B. T., Woods, D. W., Flessner, C. A., Franklin, S. A., & Franklin, M. E. (2011). The Skin Picking Impact Project: Phenomenology, interference, and treatment utilization of pathological skin picking in a population-based sample. *Journal of Anxiety Disorders*, *25*, 88–95.

Tung, E. S., Flessner, C. A., Grant, J. E., & Keuthen, N. J. (2015). Predictors of life disability in trichotillomania. *Comprehensive Psychiatry*, *56*, 239–244. https://doi.org/10.1016/j.comppsych.2014.09.018

Van Tongel, A., De Paepe, P., & Berghs, B. (2012). Epidermoid cyst of the phalanx of the finger caused by nail biting. *Journal of Plastic Surgery and Hand Surgery*, *46*, 450–451.

van Wyk, C. W., Staz, J., & Farman, A. G. (1977). The chewing lesion of the cheeks and lips: Its features and prevalence among a selected group of adolescents. *Journal of Dentistry*, *5*, 193–199.

Vanderas, A. P., & Papagiannoulis, L. (2002). Multifactorial analysis of the etiology of craniomandibular dysfunction in children. *International Journal of Paediatric Dentistry*, *12*, 336–346.

Walther, M. R., Flessner, C. A., Conelea, C. A., & Woods, D. W. (2009). The Milwaukee Inventory for the Dimensions of Adult Skin Picking (MIDAS): Initial development and psychometric properties. *Journal of Behavior Therapy and Experimental Psychiatry*, *40*, 127–135.

Walther, M. R., Snorrason, I., Flessner, C. A., Franklin, M. E., Burkel, R., & Woods, D. W. (2014). The Trichotillomania Impact Project in Young Children (TIP-YC): Clinical characteristics, comorbidity, functional impairment, and treatment utilization. *Child Psychiatry & Human Development, 45*, 24–31.

Watson, T. S., & Allen, D. K. (1993). Elimination of thumb-sucking as a treatment for severe trichotillomania. *Journal of the American Academy of Child and Adolescent Psychiatry, 32*, 830–834.

Wells, J. H., Haines, J., & Williams, C. L. (1998). Severe morbid onychophagia: The classification of self-mutilation and a proposed model of maintenance. *The Australian and New Zealand Journal of Psychiatry, 32*, 534–545.

Wells, J. H., Haines, J., Williams, C. L., & Brain, K. L. (1999). The self-mutilative nature of severe onychophagia: A comparison with self-cutting. *The Canadian Journal of Psychiatry, 44*, 40–47.

Wetterneck, C. T., Lee, E. B., Flessner, C. A., Leonard, R. C., & Woods, D. W. (2016). Personality characteristics and experiential avoidance in trichotillomania: Results from an age and gender matched sample. *Journal of Obsessive-Compulsive Related Disorders, 8*, 64–69.

Wetterneck, C. T., Woods, D. W., Norberg, M. N., & Begotka, A. M. (2006). The social and economic impact of trichotillomania: Results from two non-referred samples. *Behavioral Interventions, 21*, 97–109.

Wilhelm, S., Keuthen, N. J., Deckersbach, T., Engelhard, I. M., Forker, A. E., Baer, L., O'Sullivan, R. L., & Jenike, M. A. (1999) Self-injurious skin picking: Clinical characteristics and comorbidity. *The Journal of Clinical Psychiatry, 60*, 454–459.

Williams, T. I., Rose, R., & Chisholm, S. (2007). What is the function of nail biting: An analog assessment study. *Behaviour Research and Therapy, 45*, 989–995.

Winchel, R. M. (1992). Trichotillomania: Presentation and treatment. *Psychiatric Annals, 22*, 84–89.

Woods, D. W., Flessner, C. A., Franklin, M. E., Keuthen, N. J., Goodwin, R. D., Stein, D. J., & Walther, M. R. (2006). The Trichotillomania Impact Project (TIP): Exploring phenomenology, functional impairment, and treatment utilization. *The Journal of Clinical Psychiatry, 2006*, 1877–1888.

Woods, D. W., & Houghton, D. C. (2014). Diagnosis, evaluation, and management of trichotillomania. *Psychiatric Clinics of North America, 37*, 301–317.

Wright, H. H., & Holmes, G. R. (2003). Trichotillomania (hair pulling) in toddlers. *Psychological Reports, 92*, 228–230.

Yeo, S. K., & Lee, W. K. (2017). The relationship between adolescents' academic stress, impulsivity, anxiety, and skin picking behavior. *Asian Journal of Psychiatry, 28*, 111–114. doi:10.1016/j.ajp.2017.03.039

Zweben, J. E., Cohen, J. B., Christian, D., Galloway, G. P., Salinardi, M., Parent, D., & Iguchi, M. (2004). Psychiatric symptoms in methamphetamine users. *American Journal on Addiction, 13*, 181–190.

PART II

Approaches to Understanding Obsessive-Compulsive and Related Disorders

CHAPTER 6

Genetic Understanding of Obsessive-Compulsive Disorder and Related Disorders

Jack Samuels

Abstract

This chapter reviews current understanding of the genetic basis of obsessive-compulsive disorder (OCD), focusing on recent findings from genome-wide association studies and other molecular genetic research. Several genetic variants have been found to be associated with OCD, including genes implicated in glutamate signaling in brain circuits relevant to OCD. However, OCD is probably genetically complex, with interactions between multiple genetic and environmental factors contributing to the risk, course, and severity of the disorder, as well as response to treatment. Large studies to identify common and rare genetic variants are underway, and new methods are being developed to integrate the findings from multiple interaction networks and to elucidate the genetic basis of OCD.

Key Words: obsessive-compulsive disorder, genetics, family study, twin studies, genetic linkage, genetic association, candidate genes, genome-wide association studies, rare variants

Introduction

Clinicians have long been aware that patients with obsessive-compulsive disorder (OCD) often have relatives with the disorder, and they have suspected that this familial aggregation may be due, at least in part, to genetic transmission (Lewis, 1936; Slater, 1964). Moreover, early clinical reports of substantially greater concordance of obsessive-compulsive symptoms in monozygotic (identical) twins than in dizygotic (fraternal) twins supported a familial basis of the disorder (Carey & Gottesman, 1981). However, methodically rigorous investigations into the genetic basis of OCD and related disorders have been conducted only since the early 1990s. These investigations may be grouped into four major overlapping phases, and results from them have been described in recent reviews (Pauls et al., 2014; Fernandez et al., 2018), including the author's own review, which has been adapted and updated for this chapter (Nestadt & Samuels, 2020).

In the first, or genetic epidemiology, phase of research, family studies showed that the lifetime prevalence of OCD is much greater in the first-degree relatives of OCD-affected probands (index cases) than in the relatives of OCD-unaffected probands (10% to 12%

vs. 1% to 2%, respectively; Grabe et al., 2006; Nestadt et al., 2000b; Pauls et al., 1995). This difference in the prevalence of OCD between the first-degree relatives of OCD-affected vs. OCD-unaffected probands is even greater if the OCD-affected proband has onset of OCD before 18 years of age (23% vs. 3%; Hanna et al., 2005). Complex segregation analyses suggest that dominant Mendelian models of inheritance best fit the pattern of familial aggregation of OCD in families with multiple affected individuals (Hanna et al., 2005; Nestadt et al., 2000a). In addition to OCD, other psychiatric disorders also are more prevalent in first-degree relatives of OCD-affected probands, including generalized anxiety disorder, obsessive-compulsive personality disorder, tic disorders, and putative OCD-related disorders, such as body dysmorphic disorder, trichotillomania, and pathological skin-picking, suggesting that these may comprise a spectrum of conditions etiologically related to OCD in these families (Bienvenu et al., 2000; Nestadt et al., 2001). In this research phase, twin studies provided further support for a substantial genetic contribution to OCD, with the finding that the concordance of obsessive-compulsive symptoms is substantially greater in monozygotic (identical) twins than in dizygotic (fraternal) twins, and that heritability (the proportion of variation in dimensional obsessive-compulsive symptom scores explained by genetic factors) is 45% to 65%, with most of the remaining variation explained by nonshared environmental influences (Grootheest et al., 2005).

In the second research phase, genetic linkage studies analyzed the co-segregation of genetic markers with OCD in families, in order to locate possible chromosomal regions containing OCD-related genes. Two studies found a suggestive linkage peak on chromosome 9 (chromosomal region 9p24), in a region that includes a gene involved in neurotransmission, the glutamate transporter gene (*SLC1A1*), although the identified region is wide and might contain dozens of candidate genes for OCD (Hanna et al., 2002; Willour et al., 2004). Another genome-wide linkage study found a suggestive linkage signal on chromosome 3 (chromosomal region 3q27-28), and additional linkage signals on regions in chromosomes 1, 6, 7, and 15 (Shugart et al., 2006). In subsequent studies, a suggestive linkage signal was found in the 11p15 region in families with a male proband (Wang et al., 2009), and significant linkage in the chromosome 14q23-32 region in families with two or more relatives with compulsive hoarding behavior (Samuels et al., 2007), suggesting that there may be more genetically homogeneous subtypes of the disorder.

In the third research phase, candidate gene studies selected potential candidate genes for further study, based on their location within linkage peaks, as well as knowledge of the pathophysiology of OCD and its response to specific pharmacological treatments. Some studies found evidence of association of OCD with one or more genes involved in serotonergic or dopaminergic neurotransmission, including *SLC6A4*, *DRD4*, *COMT*, and *MAO-A* genes, although the results have been inconsistent (Hemmings & Stein, 2006; Taylor, 2013). To date, the strongest evidence of an association with OCD is for the neuronal glutamate transporter gene, *SLC1A1*. As already noted, this gene is located in the 9p24 linkage region found in two prior linkage studies. The gene encodes a neuronal glutamate transporter that is highly expressed in brain regions that are connected in functional circuits implicated in OCD (the cerebral cortex, striatum, and thalamus). Several studies have found association between OCD and single nucleotide polymorphisms (SNPs) in the *SLC1A1* gene, or upstream or downstream of the gene, specifically in families with male probands or in OCD-affected male relatives (Arnold et al., 2006; Dickel et al., 2006; Samuels et al., 2011; Shugart et al., 2009; Stewart et al., 2007).

These first three phases of OCD genetics research were based on the hypothesis that relatively few genes have a "major effect" on the genetic risk of OCD. However, findings from linkage and candidate gene studies have not been consistently replicated, nor has a gene strongly associated with OCD been definitively identified, although the findings for the *SLC1A1* gene are intriguing. Subsequently, the "common gene–common disorder" hypothesis has become predominant in psychiatric genetics, positing that relatively frequent genetic variants in multiple genes, each with a "small effect," and diffusely distributed across the genome, incrementally contribute to the overall risk of disorders (Duncan et al., 2019). This idea, along with rapid development of genotyping technology and computational genetics, has ushered in the era of genome-wide association studies (GWASs) and whole exome sequencing (WES) studies of neuropsychiatric disorders, and has led to the fourth and current phase of OCD genetics research.

This chapter focuses on the current phase of OCD genetics research, primarily studies conducted in the last decade or so. The major findings from GWASs that have searched for genetic variants (polymorphisms) associated with OCD are presented, and the discussion covers how the findings have provided estimates of the heritability of, and polygenic risk for, the disorder. Also covered is research from recent GWASs and other genetic analyses on alternate phenotypes for genetic investigation of OCD, the pharmacogenetics of OCD, and genetic research in OCD-like behaviors in animal models.

GWASs

GWASs of OCD involve scanning hundreds of thousands, or even millions, of SNPs across the genome to detect relatively common genetic variants associated with the disorder. The studies have compared the variants between OCD-affected and unaffected individuals (case-control analysis) or have focused the analysis on "trios": OCD-affected individuals and their parents, whether affected or unaffected.

Results of several GWASs have been reported. The International OCD Foundation Genetics Collaborative (IOCDF-GC) study included almost 1,500 OCD cases, 5,600 non-OCD controls, and 400 trios and genotyped nearly 500,000 SNPs. In case-control analyses, the two most significantly associated SNPs were in the *DLGAP1* gene, although neither association had "genome-wide significance" after correcting for the large number of comparisons. In the analysis limited to trios, a SNP near the *BTBD3* gene was found to be significantly associated with OCD. However, no SNPs were associated with OCD with genome-wide significance in the analyses combining the case-control and trio samples. Interestingly, *BTBD3* is expressed in the frontal cortex, a region implicated in OCD, and *DLGAP1* influences glutamate signaling (Stewart et al., 2013).

The OCD Collaborative Genetic Association Study (OCGAS) included over 1,000 families with OCD, including 460 trios, and analyzed more than 500,000 SNPs. Although no association had genome-wide significance, the most significant finding was for a SNP on chromosome 9, near the protein tyrosine phosphate receptor D (*PTPRD*) gene. Several additional candidate genes emerged, including Fas apoptotic inhibitory molecule 2 (*FAIM2*), glutamate ionotropic receptor NMDA type subunit 2B (*GRIN2B*), and cadherin genes *CDH9* and *CDH10*. Several of these genes appear to be involved in glutamatergic neurotransmission. *PTPRD* is known to be involved in the differentiation of glutamatergic synapses and to interact with *SLITRK3* to regulate the development of inhibitory GABAergic synapses. The gene with the next strongest association, *CDH9*, has been found associated with OCD (Mattheisen et al., 2015).

Meta-analysis of the two studies included nearly 2,700 OCD-affected individuals of European ancestry and 7,000 genomically matched controls. Although no SNP reached genome-wide significance, the p values were more significant than in the two individual GWASs. Among the top signals were for variants identified in linkage peaks found in the original GWASs, including *PTPRD*, *DLGAP1*, and *GRID2*. Several of these genes are involved in glutamate transmission. About 65% of the SNP-based heritability in the OCGAS sample was accounted for by SNPs with minor allele frequencies ≥ 40% (IOCDF-GC & OCGAS, 2018).

Another GWAS, based on the Netherlands Twin Registry (NTR), included almost 7,000 individuals and analyzed almost 31 million SNPs, using a quantitative measure of obsessive-compulsive symptoms. A genome-wide significant association was found for a SNP in the myocyte enhance factor 2B neighbor (*MEF2BNB*) gene on chromosome 19 (region 19p13). Additional gene-based testing found that there were three significantly associated genes in the same region—*MEF2BNB*, *MEF2B*, and *RFXANK* (den Braber et al., 2016).

Several analytic approaches have been used to estimate heritability of OCD, based on SNP genotypes in GWASs. Using genome-wide complex trait analysis (GCTA), the estimated heritability of quantitative obsessive-compulsive symptoms in the NTR sample was 34%. The estimated heritability of OCD in the OCGAS sample was 37%; further, it was found that common alleles contribute more to OCD than do rarer alleles, and that certain chromosomes contribute more to OCD risk than do others (Davis et al., 2013).

Alternate Phenotypes

A remarkable feature of OCD is extensive clinical heterogeneity, with a large number of specific obsessions and compulsions and wide variation among affected individuals in the specific constellations of symptoms they exhibit. These clinical differences may reflect different underlying genetic or environmental etiologies. In addition, OCD may share genetic variants with other disorders that co-occur with OCD, or OCD cases with a history of other specific disorders may be genetically distinct from cases without these disorders. Moreover, there may be underlying biological dimensions (endophenotypes) that are more proximal than the OCD diagnosis to the ultimate genetic causes of the disorder. The challenge is to identify more genetically homogeneous clinical subtypes, genetically related disorders, and genetically relevant subclinical dimensions that help elucidate the underlying genetic etiology.

Clinical Subtypes and Dimensions

As already noted, several family studies have found a much greater proportion of OCD-affected relatives in families in which the proband has OCD onset in childhood or adolescence, suggesting that early-onset OCD may indicate a more genetic subtype of the disorder (Hanna et al., 2005; Nestadt et al., 2000b; Pauls et al., 1995). In addition, several linkage and candidate gene studies have found stronger associations for one gender than the other; for example, some association studies have found stronger evidence of association of OCD with the *SLC1A1* gene in men than in women (Samuels et al., 2011).

More recently, a GWAS study was conducted to identify sex differences in genetic associations in OCD. The sample included over 4,000 men and 5,800 women in the Psychiatric Genetics Consortium OCD sample, which included participants in the IOCDF-GC and OCGAS. Two genome-wide significant gene-based associations (*GRID2* and *GRP135*) were found in women but not in men. The *GRID2* gene is involved in glutamatergic signaling and is expressed in brain regions implicated in OCD, including the caudate, putamen, and anterior cingulate cortex, and *GPR135* also is expressed in the brain. Moreover, SNPs with the greatest heterogeneity in effect size between men and women were enriched for gene regulatory function in the brain (Khramtsova et al., 2019).

Recent GWASs also have investigated genetic association with specific OCD symptom dimensions. For example, a GWAS analysis was conducted on about 8,300 participants in the NTR, separately evaluating obsession and compulsion subscale scores. The SNP-based heritability was greater for the compulsions than obsessions subscale. In gene-based meta-analysis of the NTR and PGC-OCGAS GWAS samples, four genes reached genome-wide significant association with the compulsion subscale: *GRID2*, *KIT*, *WDR7*, and *ADCK1* (Smit et al., 2020). Another GWAS analyzed separate obsessive-compulsive symptom dimensions as measured by the Dimensional Yale-Brown Obsessive Compulsive Scale (DY-BOCS). Although no SNP association reached genome-wide significance for any OC dimension, suggestive associations with different SNPs were found for aggressive, contamination, order, and hoarding dimensions. Six of the eight variants associated with the order dimension were within a region of chromosome 12 containing the importin 8 (*IPO8*) and caprin family member2 (*CAPRIN2*) genes. In addition, in gene-based analyses, the SET domain containing 3 actin histidine methyltransferase (*SETD3*) gene was associated with the hoarding dimension, and the carboxypeptidase E (*CPE*) gene with the aggressive dimension, at genome-wide levels of significance (Alemany-Navarro et al., 2020). These findings suggest that clinical heterogeneity reflects genetic heterogeneity, and that different genes may contribute to the expression of different OCD dimensions.

Cross-Disorder Relationships

Many individuals with OCD have a lifetime history of other disorders, and there is great interest in elucidating shared and distinct genetic underpinnings explaining this co-occurrence. As noted above, several psychiatric disorders have been found to aggregate in OCD families, including generalized anxiety disorder, obsessive-compulsive personality disorder, and *DSM-5* OCD-related disorders, such as body dysmorphic disorder, trichotillomania, and pathologic skin-picking (Bienvenu et al., 2000).

There has been much interest in the genetic relationship between OCD and tic disorders, especially Tourette syndrome (TS). Family studies have found that the prevalence of OCD is significantly higher in relatives of OCD probands with a tic disorder than in relatives of probands without a tic disorder, and that the prevalence of OCD is significantly higher in relatives of TS-affected probands than control probands, whether or not the TS-affected proband has OCD, supporting the hypothesis that the disorders share genetic risk factors (Brander et al., 2019). More recent analyses of SNPs genotyped in GWASs found a genetic correlation between OCD and TS of 0.41, comparable to heritability estimates based on twin and family studies (Davis et al., 2013). Other studies have found that, although genetically related, the two disorders have distinct genetic components, and that OCD with co-occurring tic disorders may be genetically different from OCD alone (Yu et al., 2015).

Genetic relationships between OCD and other co-occurring disorders have also been investigated. For example, a recent GWAS meta-analysis investigated the shared genetic background of nearly 3,500 anorexia nervosa (AN) cases and 2,700 OCD cases. The study found a high genetic correlation (0.49) between the two disorders and substantial SNP heritability (0.21) for the cross-disorder phenotype (Yilmaz et al., 2018). Similar GWAS analyses recently have been conducted on the genetic overlap between OCD and autism spectrum disorders (Guo et al., 2017), schizophrenia (Costa et al., 2016), and attention-deficit/hyperactivity disorder (ADHD; Ritter et al., 2017). In addition, as part of the Brainstorm Consortium, genetic correlations between OCD and several other psychiatric disorders were estimated in analyses that included 3,000 OCD cases and 7,200 non-OCD cases. It was found that OCD, AN, and schizophrenia had significant genetic sharing among themselves, as did OCD, major depressive disorder, and TS. OCD also was significantly genetically correlated with neuroticism (Brainstorm Consortium, 2018). In a further analysis, exploratory factor analysis and genomic structural equation modeling identified three groups of disorders based on shared genomics; OCD, AN, and TS comprised one of the groups (Cross-Disorder Group of the Psychiatric Genetics Consortium,

2019). Findings from these and other cross-disorder GWAS analyses suggest that the lifetime co-occurrence of OCD and several other psychiatric disorders may reflect partially shared genetic background.

Endophenotypes

An endophenotype, or "intermediate phenotype," is a biological marker of a process (biochemical, neuroanatomical, neurophysiological, neuropsychological, or behavioral) that may be intermediate in the etiologic pathway between genes and the clinical phenotype. A candidate endophenotype to investigate in genetic studies should be associated with the disorder, should be heritable, should co-segregate with the disorder within families, and should occur in nonaffected as well as affected family members with greater frequency than in controls (Gottesman & Gould, 2003).

A large number of studies have found differences between OCD cases and non-cases in a variety of neurocognitive domains, including response inhibition, planning, decision-making, working memory, and visuospatial abilities (Chamberlain et al., 2005). Several of these domains involve functioning of orbitofrontal-striatal-thalamic networks in the brain, which imaging studies have implicated in OCD. For example, several studies have found that patients with OCD and their first-degree relatives are less able than controls to inhibit responses on a stop-signal task; moreover, this impairment was associated with gray matter volume in the orbitofrontal cortex and in cingulate, parietal, and striatal brain regions, and there were significant familial effects for response inhibition and brain volumes in these regions (Menzies et al., 2007). Other studies, using a variety of neurocognitive paradigms, as well as structural and functional imaging approaches, have supported deficits in inhibitory control, as well as structure, function, and connectivity in cortico-striatal-thalamo-cortical (CSTC) circuits, as candidate endophenotypes for OCD (Chamberlain & Menzies, 2009).

Another neurocognitive domain of interest is performance monitoring. Many studies have found that individuals with OCD show a negative deflection of the event-related potential following making an error on a flanker task. Error-related hyperactivity of the anterior cingulate cortex has been found in patients with OCD and their relatives compared to controls (Riesel et al., 2011). Higher-level executive functions have also been investigated as candidate endophenotypes for OCD; for example, a recent study found that individuals with OCD and their unaffected first-degree relatives had deficits in decision-making under ambiguous conditions, as well as in planning (Zhang et al., 2015).

Given numerous studies showing brain structural and functional abnormalities in many individuals with OCD, there has been great interest in investigating potential neuroimaging endophenotypes for genetic studies of OCD. The Enhancing Neuro Imaging Genetics through Meta-Analysis (ENIGMA) Consortium OCD Working Group, which has collected neuroimaging data on thousands of OCD cases and controls, is an important potential resource for genetic studies (van den Heuvel et al., 2020). For example,

Hibar et al. (2018) found significant SNP concordance between OCD and volume of the nucleus accumbens and putamen. Sinopoli et al. (2020) investigated the association between genetic variants in several serotonin candidate genes for OCD and regional brain volume within CSTC circuits in pediatric OCD patients, and the researchers found a significant association between two SNPs in the *HTR2C* gene and increased volume of the anterior cingulate cortex in females with OCD.

Pharmacogenetics

A substantial proportion of patients with OCD show poor response to serotonin reuptake inhibitors (SRIs) and/or significant adverse side effects that make treatment intolerable. Genetic variation appears to be an important contributor to antidepressant response in major depression, but less is known about the genetic contribution to response to SRIs in OCD. Some studies have reported associations between treatment response and SNPs in genes known to be involved in serotonergic, dopaminergic, or glutamatergic neurotransmission (e.g., *HTR1B*, *5-HT2A*, *HTR2A*, *BDNF*, *SLC1A1*, *SLC6A4*, *COMT*; Brandl et al., 2012; Zai et al., 2014). However, findings have mostly been based on small samples, have small effect sizes, and have not been replicated, so further studies are needed. More recently, results from a GWAS of SRI treatment response in nearly 1,600 individuals with OCD in over 1,000 families were reported. The most strongly associated SNP is located near the *DISP1* gene, and two other moderately associated SNPs are near the *PCDH10* gene; both genes are known to be involved in cell–cell adhesion. An additional 35 SNPs with signals of potential significance were in several genes expressed in the brain and implicated in neuronal development, psychiatric disorders, or drug effects, including *GRIN2B*, *GPC6*, *NTM*, *PARK2*, *PLCB1*, and *PKC*. Results from enrichment analysis indicated that variants in genes involved in glutamatergic neurotransmission were most enriched, followed by variants in genes involved in serotonergic transmission (Qin et al., 2016).

Rare Variants

Although GWASs search for more common genetic variants, the search continues for less common variants associated with OCD that may have a major effect and provide additional insight into the pathophysiology of the disorder. Three types of variants have been reported in OCD: chromosomal rearrangements, copy number variants (CNVs), and rare variants identified by "deep sequencing" of the genome. Variants may be inherited or they may be de novo variants (DNVs), which are new mutations that occur for the first time in a family member, arising from a germ cell mutation in one of the parents or in the fertilized egg during embryogenesis.

There are a few reports of chromosomal rearrangements in OCD cases. One report described a 21-year-old male with TS, OCD, and ADHD who inherited a translocation of a piece of chromosome 3 to chromosome 9 from his mother, who had a complex motor tic. Sequencing indicated that the translocation breakpoints truncated the olfactomedin 1 (*OLFM1*) gene, which influences neuronal development and is a candidate gene for other neuropsychiatric disorders (Bertelsen et al., 2015). Another report described a balanced chromosomal translocation in siblings multiply affected with TS, OCD, complex motor tics, and ADHD (Devor & Magee, 1999).

Several studies have investigated rare CNVs of various sizes in OCD. McGrath and colleagues reported on a GWAS study of large (> 500 kilobases) CNVs in OCD. They found that the proportion of individuals with deletions in known pathogenic neurodevelopmental loci was four times greater in the patients with OCD than in controls. Deletions in the 16p13.11 region, which contributed disproportionately in the OCD cases, have been implicated in other neuropsychiatric conditions (McGrath et al., 2014). In another study, Gazzellone and colleagues genotyped approximately 300 pediatric patients with OCD and 3,800 population controls to identify rare CNVs of at least 15 kilobases that might be associated with the disorder. They found de novo CNVs in four (2.3%) of the probands who were part of complete parent–child trios. Moreover, they identified deletions or duplications of exomes in specific genes involved in neuronal migration (*ASTN2*), synapse formation (*NLGN1* and *PTPRD*), and postsynaptic scaffolding (*DLGAP1* and *DLGAP2*; Gazzellone et al., 2016). As already mentioned, SNPs near *DLGAP1* and *PTPRD* are among the strongest signals in previous GWAS studies of OCD (Stewart et al., 2013; Mattheisen et al., 2015).

WES studies, which sequence protein-coding regions, have also been conducted in OCD. The most recent compared 184 OCD parent–child trios to 777 unaffected trios. The study found that de novo gene-disrupting and damaging missense variants are enriched in OCD probands. Moreover, the study identified damaging DNVs in each of two risk genes, *SBUBE1* and *CDH8*. Interestingly, one of the participants with a *CDH8* mutation was diagnosed with trichotillomania, and another with TS and ADHD, as well as OCD (Cappi et al., 2020).

Deep sequencing involves sequencing a genomic region multiple times, allowing detection of rare variants, including DNVs. Cappi and colleagues sequenced all genome coding regions in 20 sporadic OCD cases and their unaffected parents in order to identify rare de novo single-nucleotide variants. They study found a higher-than-expected rate of DNVs that alter the amino acid sequence of a protein in OCD cases. Analysis of the protein–protein interaction network suggested an enrichment of genes involved in immunological and central nervous system functioning and development (Cappi et al., 2016).

Genetic Studies in Animals

Canine Compulsive Behaviors

Ethologists have described stereotypical behaviors in nonhuman mammals that appear to be excessive, maladaptive variants of normal behaviors involved in grooming, predation, eating, suckling, or locomotion. Among the best studied are canine compulsive behaviors, including acral lick dermatitis, tail-chasing, flank-sucking, and pacing and circling. A GWAS of 92 Doberman pinschers with compulsive flank- and/or blanket-sucking behaviors and 68 control dogs found a significant genome-wide association with a SNP in the *CDH2* gene, which codes for cadherin, a neuronal adhesion protein. Dogs having both flank- and blanket-sucking behaviors had the greatest frequency of the risk allele (60%), compared to 43% of dogs with only one behavior, and 22% of unaffected dogs (Dodman et al., 2010).

Using a more powerful genotype-calling algorithm, 13 new regions were found to be associated with OCD-like behaviors in dogs, in addition to the *CDH2* locus; these regions included genes involved in catenin binding and regulation of dendrite morphogenesis. Sequencing of these regions found variants specific to dogs with OCD and that were significantly more common in dog breeds at high risk for OCD; four genes in these regions are involved in synaptic function: neuronal cadherin (*CDH2*), catenin alpha-2 (*CTNNA2*), ataxin-1 (*ATXN1*), and plasma glutamate carboxypeptidase (*PGPC*). Several of these genes appear to be functionally connected to several of the SNPs most strongly associated with OCD in genome-wide OCD studies in humans (Stewart et al., 2013) and are involved in glutamatergic signaling pathways (Tang et al., 2014). Recently, variants in the *CDH2* gene have been reported to be associated with OCD in humans (McGregor et al., 2016).

Knockout Mice Models

A mouse model of compulsive grooming behavior has been developed by genetic deletion of the *Sapap3* gene, which codes for a scaffolding protein at excitatory synapses and is highly expressed in the striatum. Knockout mice express increased anxiety and compulsive grooming behavior leading to facial skins lesions and hair loss, and they have reduced activity in corticostriatal synapses, which comprise the majority of glutamatergic synapses in the striatum. When viruses containing the gene were injected into the striatum of these mice, the grooming behavior, lesion severity, and anxious behavior were reduced, and corticostriatal synaptic transmission increased (Welch et al., 2007). In humans, a strong association between SNPs in the *SAPAP33* gene and grooming behaviors in OCD families has subsequently been reported (Bienvenu et al., 2009), and mutations in SNPs in the *SAPAP3* gene have been found to be more frequent in individuals with OCD/trichotillomania than in controls (Zuchner et al., 2009). Mice with deletions of other genes involved in corticostriatal functioning, including *Slitrk5*, *Hox-B8*, *Slc1a1*, and *Btbd3*, have been studied as possible models of compulsive grooming behaviors and OCD (Thompson et al., 2019; Ting & Feng, 2011).

Conclusions and Future Directions

Evidence from genetic epidemiologic studies provides strong presumptive evidence for genetic susceptibility to OCD. OCD often aggregates in families, and findings from twin studies suggest substantial heritability of the disorder. Family studies also suggest that other disorders, including the *DSM-5* OCD-related disorders, may be alternate expressions of an underlying genetic vulnerability.

Molecular genetic studies have identified multiple genetic variants associated with OCD, although only rarely have the associations been found to reach stringent levels of statistical significance. The most replicated findings, from genetic association, GWAS, and animal studies, identify variants in genes involved in glutamate signaling in CSTC circuits in the brain, including *SLC1A1, DLGAP1, GRIN2B, GRID2, PTPRD, SAPAP3,* and *SLITRK3* genes.

Like other neuropsychiatric disorders, OCD appears to be etiologically complex, with contribution from many common genetic variants, each of which has a relatively small overall effect on disease risk, as well as rarer genetic variants, each with potentially greater impact on disease risk. It is probable that multiple genes interact in complex ways to produce multiple etiologic subtypes of OCD, and there are likely complex interactions between genes and environmental risk factors for OCD.

The ongoing investigation of the genetic basis of OCD will involve multiple approaches in the near and more distant future. International research collaborations are continuing the ongoing efforts to recruit, diagnose, and genotype the tens of thousands of participants that may be required by GWASs and WES studies to detect statistically significant genetic variants associated with OCD (Mahjani et al., 2020; Mataix-Cols et al., 2020; Sullivan et al., 2018). Moreover, methods are being further developed for integrating the genetic findings from multiple domains, including gene sequence, gene expression, gene regulation, and gene–gene and protein–protein interaction networks, as well as cognitive and neuroimaging endophenotypes (Wang et al., 2018). Ultimately, elucidating how these networks influence the risk of developing OCD, as well as how they affect disease severity, course, and treatment response, will lead to a better understanding of the pathogenesis of OCD at the truly "personalized" level (Rees & Owen, 2020).

References

Alemany-Navarro, M., Cruz, R., Real, E., Segalàs, C., Bertolín, S., Baenas, I., Domènech, L., Rabionet, R., Carracedo, Á., Menchón, J. M., & Alonso, P. (2020). Exploring genetic variants in obsessive-compulsive disorder severity: A GWAS approach. *Journal of Affective Disorders, 267,* 23–32.

Arnold, P. D., Sicard, T., Burroughs, E., Richter, M. A., & Kennedy, J. L.. (2006). Glutamate transporter gene *SLC1A1* associated with obsessive-compulsive disorder. *Archives of General Psychiatry, 63,* 769–776.

Bertelsen, B., Melchior, L., Jensen, L. R., Groth, C., Nazaryan, L., Debes, N. M., Skov, L., Xie, G., Sun, W., Brøndum-Nielsen, K., Kuss, A. W., Chen, W., & Tümer, Z. (2015). A t(3;9)(q25.1;q34.3) translocation leading to OLFM1 fusion transcripts in Gilles de la Tourette syndrome, OCD, and ADHD. *Psychiatry Research, 225,* 268–275.

Bienvenu, O. J., Samuels, J. F., Riddle, M. A., Hoehn-Saric, R., Liang, K. Y., Cullen, B. A., Grados, M. A., & Nestadt, G. (2000). The relationship of obsessive-compulsive disorder to possible spectrum disorders: Results from a family study. *Biological Psychiatry, 48,* 287–293.

Bienvenu, O. J., Wang, Y., Shugart, Y. Y., Welch, J. M., Grados, M. A., Fyer, A. J., Rauch, S. L., McCracken, J. .T, Rasmussen, S. A., Murphy, D. L., Cullen, B., Valle, D., Hoehn-Saric, R,, Greenberg, B. D., Pinto, A.,

Knowles, J. A., Piacentini, J., Pauls, D. L., Liang, K. Y., . . . , Nestadt G. (2009). Sapap3 and pathological grooming in humans. *American Journal of Medical Genetics Part B: Neuropsychiatric Genetics, 50B*, 710–720.

Brainstorm Consortium. (2018). Analysis of shared heritability in common disorders of the brain. *Science, 360*, eaap8757.

Brander, G., Kuja-Halkola, R., Rosenqvist, M. A., Rück, C., Serlachius, E., Fernández de la Cruz, L., Lichtenstein, P., Crowley, J. J., Larsson, H., & Mataix-Cols D. (2019). A population-based family clustering study of tic-related obsessive-compulsive disorder. *Molecular Psychiatry, 26*, 1224–1233.

Brandl, E. J., Müller, D. J., & Richter, M. A. (2012). Pharmacogenetics of obsessive-compulsive disorder. *Pharmacogenomics, 13*, 71–81.

Cappi, C., Brentani, H., Lima, L., Sanders, S. J., Zai, G., Diniz, B. J., Reis, V. N., Hounie, A. G., Conceição do Rosário, M., Mariani, D., Requena, G. L., Puga, R., Souza-Duran, F. L., Shavitt, R. G., Pauls, D. L., Miguel, E. C., & Fernandez, T.V. (2016). Whole-exome sequencing in obsessive-compulsive disorder identifies rare mutations in immunological and neurodevelopmental pathways. *Translational Psychiatry, 6*, e764.

Cappi, C., Oliphant, M. E., Péter, Z., Zai, G., Conceição do Rosário, M., Sullivan, C. A. W., Gupta, A. R., Hoffman, E. J., Virdee, M., Olfson, E., Abdallah, S. B., Willsey, A. J., Shavitt, R. G., Miguel, E. C., Kennedy, J. L., Richter, M. A., & Fernandez, T. V. (2020). De novo damaging DNA coding mutations are associated with obsessive-compulsive disorder and overlap with Tourette's disorder and autism. *Biological Psychiatry, 87*, 1034–1044.

Carey, G., & Gottesman, I. I. (1981). Twin and family studies of anxiety, phobias, and obsessive disorders. In D. F. Klein & J. Rabkin (Eds.), *Anxiety: New research and changing concepts* (pp. 117–136). Raven.

Chamberlain, S. R., Blackwell, A. D., Fineberg, N. A., Robbins, T. W., & Sahakian, B. J. (2005). The neuropsychology of obsessive-compulsive disorder: The importance of failures in cognitive and behavioural inhibition as candidate endophenotypic markers. *Neuroscience & Biobehavioral Reviews, 23*, 399–419.

Chamberlain, S. R., & Menzies, L. (2009). Endophenotypes of obsessive-compulsive disorder: Rationale, evidence and future potential. *Expert Review of Neurotherapeutics, 9*, 1133–1146.

Costas, J., Carrera, N., Alonso, P., Gurriarán, X., Segalàs, C., Real, E., López-Solà, C., Mas, S., Gassó, P., Domènech, L., Morell, M., Quintela, I., Lázaro, L., Menchón, J. M., Estivill, X., & Carracedo, Á. (2016). Exon-focused genome-wide association study of obsessive-compulsive disorder and shared polygenic risk with schizophrenia. *Translational Psychiatry, 6*, e768.

Cross-Disorder Group of the Psychiatric Genetics Consortium. (2019). Genomic relationships, novel loci, and pleiotropic mechanisms across eight psychiatric disorders. *Cell, 179*, 1469–1482.

Davis LK, Yu D, Keenan CL, Gamazon ER, Konkashbaev AI, Derks EM, Neale BM, Yang J, Lee SH, Evans P, Barr CL, Bellodi L, Benarroch F, Berrio GB, Bienvenu OJ, Bloch MH, Blom RM, Bruun RD, Budman CL, . . . , Scharf, J. M. (2013). Partitioning the heritability of Tourette syndrome and obsessive-compulsive disorder reveals differences in genetic architecture. *PLOS Genetics, 9*, e1003864.

den Braber, A., Zilhão, N. R., Fedko, I. O., Hottenga, J. J., Pool, R., Smit, D. J., Cath, D. C., & Boomsma, D. L. (2016). Obsessive-compulsive symptoms in a large population-based twin-family sample are predicted by clinically based polygenic scores and by genome-wide SNPs. *Translational Psychiatry, 6*, e731.

Devor, E. J., & Magee, H. J. (1999). Multiple childhood behavioral disorder (Tourette syndrome, multiple tics, ADD and OCD) presenting in a family with a balanced chromosomal translocation (t1;8)(q21.1;q22.1). *Psychiatric Genetics, 9*, 149–151.

Dickel, D. E., Veenstra-VanderWeele, J., Cox, N. J., Wu, X., Fischer, D. J., Van Etten-Lee, M., Himle, J. A., Leventhal, B. L., Cook, E. H., Jr, & Hanna, G. L. (2006). Association testing of the positional and functional candidate gene *SLC1A1/EAAC1* in early-onset obsessive-compulsive disorder. *Archives of General Psychiatry, 63*, 778–785.

Dodman, N. H., Karlsson, E. K., Moon-Fanelli, A., Galdzicka, M., Perloski, M., Shuster, L., Lindblad-Toh, K., & Ginns, E. I. (2010). A canine chromosome 7 locus confers OCD susceptibility. *Molecular Psychiatry, 15*, 8–10.

Duncan, L. E., Ostacher, M., & Ballon, J. (2019). How genome-wide association studies (GWAS) made traditional candidate gene studies obsolete. *Neuropsychopharmacology, 44*, 1518–1523.

Fernandez, T. V., Leckman, J. F., & Pittinger, C. (2018). Genetic susceptibility in obsessive-compulsive disorder. In D. H. Geschwind, H. L. Paulson, & C. Klein (Eds.), *Handbook of clinical neurology*, Vol. 148 (3rd series), *Neurogenetics* (Part II, pp. 767–781).

Gazzellone, M. J., Zarrei, M., Burton, C. L., Walker, S., Uddin, M., Shaheen, S. M., Coste, J., Rajendram, R., Schachter, R. J., Colasanto, M., Hanna, G. L., Rosenberg, D. R., Soreni, N., Fitzgerald, K. D., Marshall, C. R., Buchanan, J. A., Merico, D., Arnold, P. D., & Scherer, S. W. (2016). Uncovering obsessive-compulsive disorder risk genes in a pediatric cohort by high-resolution analysis of copy number variation. *Journal of Neurodevelopmental Disorders, 8*, 1–10.

Gottesman, I. I., & Gould, T. D. (2003). The endophenotype concept in psychiatry: Etymology and strategic intentions. *The American Journal of Psychiatry, 160*, 636–645.

Grabe, H. J., Ruhrmann, S., Ettelt, S., Buhtz, F., Hochrein, A., Schulze-Rauschenbach, S., Meyer, K., Kraft, S., Reck, C., Pukrop, R., Freyberger, H. J., Klosterkötter, J., Falkai, P., John, U., Maier, W., & Wagner, M. (2006). Familiality of obsessive-compulsive disorder in nonclinical and clinical subjects. *The American Journal of Psychiatry, 163*, 1986–1992.

Grootheest, D. S., Cath, D. C., Beekman, A. T., & Boomsma, D. I. (2005). Twin studies on obsessive-compulsive disorder: A review. *Twin Research and Human Genetics, 8*, 450–458

Guo W, Samuels JF, Wang Y, Cao H, Ritter M, Nestadt PS, Krasnow J, Greenberg BD, Fyer AJ, McCracken JT, Geller DA, Murphy DL, Knowles JA, Grados MA, Riddle MA, Rasmussen SA, McLaughlin NC, Nurmi EL, Askland KD, & Shugart, Y. Y. (2017). Polygenic risk score and heritability estimates reveals a genetic relationship between ASD and OCD. *European Neuropsychopharmacology, 27*, 657–666.

Hanna, G. L., Fingerlin, T. E., Himle, J. A., & Boehnke, M. (2005). Complex segregation analysis of obsessive-compulsive disorder in families with pediatric probands. *Human Heredity, 60*, 1–9.

Hanna, G. L., Himle, J. A., Curtis, G. C., & Gillespie, B. W. (2005). A family study of obsessive-compulsive disorder with pediatric probands. *American Journal of Medical Genetics Part B: Neuropsychiatric Genetics, 134B*, 13–19.

Hanna, G. L., Veenstra-VanderWeele, J., Cox, N. J., Boehnke, M., Himle, J. A., Curtis, G. C., Leventhal, B. L., &Cook, E. H. Jr. (2002). Genome-wide linkage analysis of families with obsessive-compulsive disorder ascertained through pediatric probands. *American Journal of Medical Genetics Part B: Neuropsychiatric Genetics, 114*, 541–552.

Hemmings, S. M. J., & Stein, D. J. (2006). The current status of association studies in obsessive-compulsive disorder. *Psychiatric Clinics of North America, 29*, 411–444.

Hibar, D. P., Cheung, J. W., Medland, S. E., Mufford, M. S., Jahanshad, N., Dalvie, S., Ramesar, R., Stewart, E., van den Heuvel, O. A., Pauls, D. L., Knowles, J. A., Stein, D. J., Thompson, P. M.; Enhancing Neuro Imaging Genetics through Meta Analysis (ENIGMA) Consortium and International Obsessive Compulsive Disorder Foundation Genetics Collaborative (IOCDF-GC). (2018). Significant concordance of genetic variation that increases both the risk for obsessive-compulsive disorder and the volumes of the nucleus accumbens and putamen. *British Journal of Psychiatry, 213*, 430–436.

International Obsessive Compulsive Disorder Foundation Genetics Collaborative (IOCDF-GC) and OCD Collaborative Genetics Association Studies (OCGAS). (2018). Revealing the complex genetic architecture of obsessive-compulsive disorder using meta-analysis. *Molecular Psychiatry, 23*, 1181–1188.

Khramtsova, E. A., Heldman , R., Derks, E. M., Yu, D.; Tourette Syndrome/Obsessive-Compulsive Disorder Working Group of the Psychiatric Genomics Consortium; Davis, L. K., & Stranger, B. E. (2019). Sex differences in the genetic architecture of obsessive-compulsive disorder. *American Journal of Medical Genetics, 180B*, 351–364.

Lewis, A. (1936). Problems of obsessional illness. *Proceedings of the Royal Society of Medicine, 29*, 325–336.

Mahjani B., Kellenvall, K., Säll Grahnaat, A-C., Karlsson, G., Tuuliainen, A., Reichert, J., Mahjani, C. G., Klei, L., De Rubeis, S., Reichenberg, A., Devlin, B., Hultman, C. M., Buxbaum, J. D., Sandin, S., & Grice, D. E. (2020). Cohort profile: Epidemiology and genetics of obsessive-compulsive disorder and chronic tic disorders in Sweden (EGOS). *Social Psychiatry and Psychiatric Epidemiology, 55*, 1383–1393.

Mattheisen, M., Samuels, J. F., Wang, Y., Greenberg, B. D., Fyer, A. J., McCracken, J. T., Geller, D. A., Murphy, D. L., Knowles, J. A., Grados, M. A., Riddle, M. A. Rasmussen, S. A., McLaughlin, N. C., Nurmi, E. L., Askland, K. D., Qin, H. D., Cullen, B. A., Piacentini, J., Pauls, D. L., . . . , Nestadt G. (2015). Genome-wide association study in obsessive-compulsive disorder: Results from the OCGAS. *Molecular Psychiatry, 20*, 337–344.

Mataix-Cols, D., Hansen, B., Mattheisen, M., Karlsson, E. K., Addington, A. M., Boberg, J., Djurfeldt, D. R., Halvorsen, M., Lichtenstein, P., Solem, S., Lindblad-Toh, K.; Nordic OCD and Related Disorders Consortium (NORDiC); Haavik, J., Kvale, G., Rück, C., & Crowley, J. J. (2020). Nordic OCD & Related Disorders Consortium: Rationale, design, and methods. *American Journal of Medical Genetics, 183B*, 38–50.

McGrath, L. M., Yu, D., Marshall, C., Davis, L. K., Thiruvahindrapuram, B., Li, B., Cappi, C., Gerber, G., Wolf, A., Schroeder, F. A., Osiecki, L., O'Dushlaine, C., Kirby, A., Illmann, C., Haddad, S., Gallagher, P., Fagerness, J. A., Barr, C. L., Bellodi, L., & Scharf, J. M. (2014). Copy number variation in obsessive-compulsive disorder and Tourette syndrome: A cross-disorder study. *Journal of the American Academy of Child and Adolescent Psychiatry*, *53*, 910–919.

McGregor, N. W., Lochner, C., Stein, D. J., & Hemmings, S. M. (2016). Polymorphisms within the neuronal cadherin gene (*CDH2*) are associated with obsessive-compulsive disorder (OCD) in a South African cohort. *Metabolic Brain Disease*, *31*, 191–196.

Menzies, L., Achard, S., Chamberlain, S. R., Fineberg, N., Chen, C. H., del Campo, N., Sahakian, B. J., Robbins, T. W., & Bullmore, E. (2007). Neurocognitive endophenotypes of obsessive-compulsive disorder. *Brain*, *130*, 3223–3236.

Nestadt, G., Lan, T., Samuels, J., Riddle, M., Bienvenu, O. J. 3rd, Liang, K. Y., Hoehn-Saric, R., Cullen, B., Grados, M., Beaty, T. H., & Shugart Y. Y. (2000a). Complex segregation analysis provides compelling evidence for a major gene underlying obsessive-compulsive disorder and for heterogeneity by sex. *American Journal of Human Genetics*, *67*, 1611–1616.

Nestadt, G., & Samuels, J. (2020). Genetics of obsessive-compulsive disorder. In J. R. Geddes, N. C. Andreasen, & G. M. Goodwin (Eds.), *New Oxford textbook of psychiatry* (3rd ed., pp. 995–1002). Oxford University Press.

Nestadt, G., Samuels, J., Riddle, M., Bienvenu, O. J. 3rd, Liang, K. Y., LaBuda, M., Walkup, J,. Grados, M., Hoehn-Saric, R. (2000b). A family study of obsessive-compulsive disorder. *Archives of General Psychiatry*, *57*, 358–363.

Nestadt, G., Samuels, J., Riddle, M. A., Liang, K. Y., Bienvenu, O. J., Hoehn-Saric, R., Grados, M., & Cullen, B. (2001). The relationship between obsessive-compulsive disorder and anxiety and affective disorders: Results from the Johns Hopkins OCD Family Study. *Psychological Medicine*, *31*, 481–487.

Pauls, D. L., Abramovitch, A., Rauch, S. L., & Geller, D. A. (2014). Obsessive-compulsive disorder: An integrative genetic and neurobiological perspective. *Nature Reviews Neuroscience*, *15*, 410–424.

Pauls, D. L., Alsobrook, J. P., Goodman, W. K., Rasmussen, S. A., & Leckman, J. F. (1995). A family study of obsessive-compulsive disorder. *American Journal of Psychiatry*, *152*, 76–84.

Qin, H., Samuels, J. F., Wang, Y., Zhu, Y., Grados, M. A., Riddle, M. A., Greenberg, B. D., Knowles, J. A., Fyer, A. J., McCracken, J. T., Murphy, D. L., Rasmussen, S. A., Cullen, B. A., Piacentini, J., Geller, D., Stewart, S. E., Pauls, D., Bienvenu, O. J., Goes, F. S, & Shugart, Y. Y. (2016). Whole genome association analysis of treatment response in obsessive-compulsive disorder. *Molecular Psychiatry*, *21*, 270–276.

Rees, E., & Owen, M. J. (2020). Translating insights from neuropsychiatric genetics and genomics for precision psychiatry. *Genome Medicine*, *12*(43), 1–16.

Riesel, A., Endures, T., Kaufmann, C., & Kathmann, N. (2011). Overactive error-related brain activity as a candidate endophenotype for obsessive-compulsive disorder: Evidence from unaffected first-degree relatives. *The American Journal of Psychiatry*, *168*, 317–324.

Ritter, M. L., Guo, W., Samuels, J. F., Wang, Y., Nestadt, P. S., Krasnow, J., Greenberg, B. D., Fyer, A. J., McCracken, J. T., Geller, D. A., Murphy, D. L., Knowles, J. A., Grados, M. A., Riddle, M. A., Rasmussen, S. A., McLaughlin, N. C., Nurmi, E. L., Askland, K. D., Cullen, B., , & Shugart Y. Y. (2017). Genome wide association study (GWAS) between attention deficit hyperactivity disorders (ADHD) and obsessive-compulsive disorder (OCD). *Frontiers in Molecular Neuroscience*, *10*(83), 1–9.

Samuels, J., Shugart, Y. Y., Grados, M. A., Willour, V. L., Bienvenu, O. J., Greenberg, B. D., Knowles, J. A., McCracken, J. T., Rauch, S. L., Murphy, D. L., Wang, Y., Pinto, A., Fyer, A. J., Piacentini, J., Pauls, D. L., Cullen, B., Rasmussen, S. A., Hoehn-Saric, R., Valle, D., & Nestadt G. (2007). Significant linkage to compulsive hoarding on chromosome 14 in families with obsessive-compulsive disorder: Results from the OCD Collaborative Genetics Study. *American Journal of Psychiatry*, *164*, 493–499.

Samuels, J., Wang, Y., Riddle, M. A., Greenberg, B. D., Fyer, A. J,. McCracken, J. T., Rauch, S. L., Murphy, D. L., Grados, M. A., Knowles, J. A., Piacentini, J., Cullen, B., Bienvenu, O. J. 3rd, Rasmussen, S. A., Geller, D., Pauls, D. L., Liang, K. Y., Shugart, Y. Y., & Nestadt G. (2011). Comprehensive family-based association study of the glutamate transporter gene *SLC1A1* in obsessive-compulsive disorder. *American Journal of Medical Genetics Part B: Neuropsychiatric Genetics*, *156*, 472–477.

Shugart, Y. Y., Samuels, J., Willour, V. L., Grados, M. A., Greenberg, B. D., Knowles, J. A., McCracken, J. T., Rauch, S. L., Murphy, D. L., Wang, Y., Pinto, A., Fyer, A. J., Piacentini, J., Pauls, D. L., Cullen, B., Page, J., Rasmussen, S. A., Bienvenu, O. J., Hoehn-Saric, R., & Nestadt G. (2006). Genome-wide linkage scan for obsessive-compulsive disorder: Evidence for susceptibility loci on chromosomes 3q, 7p, 1q, 15q, and 6q. *Molecular Psychiatry, 11*, 763–770.

Shugart, Y. Y., Wang, Y., Samuels, J. F., Grados, M. A., Greenberg, B. D., Knowles, J. A., McCracken, J. T., Rauch, S. L., Murphy, D. L., Rasmussen, S. A., Cullen, B., Hoehn-Saric, R., Pinto, A., Fyer, A. J., Piacentini, J., Pauls, D. L., Bienvenu, O. J., Riddle, M. A., Liang, K. Y., & Nestadt, G. (2009). A family-based association study of the glutamate transporter gene *SLC1A1* in obsessive-compulsive disorder in 378 families. *American Journal of Medical Genetics, 150B*, 886–892.

Sinopoli, V. M., Erdman, L., Burton, C. L., Easter, P., Rajendram, R., Baldwin, G., Peterman, K., Coste, J., Shaheen, S. M., Hanna, G. L., Rosenberg, D. R., & Arnold, P. D. (2020). Serotonin system gene variants and regional brain volume differences in pediatric OCD. *Brain Imaging and Behavior, 14*, 1612–1625.

Slater, E. (1964). Genetical factors in neurosis. *British Journal of Psychology, 55*, 265–269.

Smit, D. J. A., Cath, D., Zilhão, N. R., Ip, H. F., Denys, D., den Braber, A., de Geus, E. J. C., Verweij, K. J. H., Hottenga, J. J., & Boomsma, D. I. (2020). Genetic meta-analysis of obsessive-compulsive disorder and self-report compulsive symptoms. *American Journal of Medical Genetics, 183B*, 208–216.

Stewart, S. E., Fagerness, J. A., Platko, J., Smoller, J. W., Scharf, J. M., Illmann, C., Jenike, E., Chabane, N., Leboyer, M., Delorme, R., Jenike, M. A., & Pauls, D. L. (2007). Association of the *SLC1A1* glutamate transporter gene and obsessive-compulsive disorder. *American Journal of Medical Genetics, 144B*, 1027–1033.

Stewart, S. E., Yu, D., Scharf, J. M., Neale, B. M., Fagerness, J. A., Mathews, C. A., Arnold, P. D., Evans, P. D., Gamazon, E. R., Davis, L. K., Osiecki, L., McGrath, L., Haddad, S., Crane, J., Hezel, D., Illman, C., Mayerfeld, C., Konkashbaev, A., Liu, C., . . . , Pauls, D. L. (2013). Genome-wide association study of obsessive-compulsive disorder. *Molecular Psychiatry, 18*, 788–798.

Sullivan, P. F., Agrawal, A., Bulik, C. M., Andreassen, O. A., Børglum, A. D., Breen, G., Cichon, S., Edenberg, H. J., Faraone, S. V., Gelernter, J., Mathews, C. A., Nievergelt, C. M., Smoller, J. W., O'Donovan, M. C.; & Psychiatric Genomics Consortium. (2018). Psychiatric genomics: An update and an agenda. *American Journal of Psychiatry, 175*, 15–27.

Tang, R., Noh, H. J., Wang, D., Sigurdsson, S., Swofford, R., Perloski, M., Duxbury, M., Patterson, E. E., Albright, J., Castelhano, M., Auton, A., Boyko, A. R., Feng, G., Lindblad-Toh, K., & Karlsson EK. (2014). Candidate genes and functional noncoding variants identified in a canine model of obsessive-compulsive disorder. *Genome Biology, 15*, R25.

Taylor, S. (2013). Molecular genetics of obsessive-compulsive disorder: A comprehensive meta-analysis of genetic association studies. *Molecular Psychiatry, 18*, 799–805.

Thompson, S. L., Welch, A. C., Ho, E. V., Bessa, J. M., Portugal-Nunes, C., Morais, M., Young, J. W., Knowles, J. A., & Dulawa, S. C. (2019). BTBD3 expression regulates compulsive-like and exploratory behaviors in mice. *Translational Psychiatry, 9*, 222, 1–14.

Ting, J. T., & Feng, G. (2011). Neurobiology of obsessive-compulsive disorder: Insights into neural circuitry dysfunction through mouse genetics. *Current Opinion in Neurobiology, 21*, 842–848.

van den Heuvel, O. A., Boedhoe, P. S. W., Bertolin, S., Bruin, W. B., Francks, C., Ivanov, I., Jahanshad, N., Kong, X. Z., Kwon, J. S., O'Neill, J., Paus, T., Patel, Y., Piras, F., Schmaal, L., Soriano-Mas, C., Spalletta, G., van Wingen, G. A., Yun, J. Y., Vriend, C., Stein, D. J., & ENIGMA-OCD working group. (2020). An overview of the first 5 years of the ENIGMA obsessive-compulsive disorder working group: The power of worldwide collaboration. *Human Brain Mapping, 43*(1), 1–14.

Wang, D., Liu, S., Warrell, J., Won, H., Shi, X., Navarro, F. C. P., Clarke, D., Gu, M., Emani, P., Yang, Y. T., Xu, M., Gandal, M. J., Lou, S., Zhang, J., Park, J. J., Yan, C., Rhie, S. K., Manakongtreecheep, K., Zhou, H., & Gerstein, M. B. (2018). Comprehensive functional genomic resource and integrative model for the human brain. *Science, 362*, 1–13.

Wang, Y., Samuels, J. F., Chang, Y. C., Grados, M. A., Greenberg, B. D., Knowles, J. A., McCracken, J. T., Rauch, S. L., Murphy, D. L., Rasmussen, S. A., Cullen, B., Hoehn-Saric, R., Pinto, A., Fyer, A. J., Piacentini, J., Pauls, D. L., Bienvenu, O. J., Riddle, M., Shugart, Y. Y., Liang, K. Y., & Nestadt G. (2009). Gender differences in genetic linkage and association on 11p15 in obsessive-compulsive disorder families. *American Journal of Medical Genetics Part B: Neuropsychiatric Genetics, 150B*, 33–40.

Welch, J. M., Lu, J., Rodriguiz, R. M., Trotta, N. C., Peca, J., Ding, J. D., Feliciano, C., Chen, M., Adams, J. P., Luo, J., Dudek, S. M., Weinberg, R. J., Calakos, N., Wetsel, W. C., & Feng, G. (2007). Cortico-striatal synaptic defects and OCD-like behaviors in *Sapap3*-mutant mice. *Nature, 448*, 894–900.

Willour, V. L., Shugart, Y. Y., Samuels, J., Grados, M., Cullen, B., Bienvenu, O. J. 3rd, Wang, Y., Liang, K. Y., Valle, D., Hoehn-Saric, R., Riddle, M., & Nestadt G. (2004). Replication study supports evidence for linkage to 9p24 in obsessive-compulsive disorder. *American Journal of Human Genetics*, 75, 508–513.

Yilmaz, Z., Halvorsen, M., Bryois, J., Yu, D., Thornton, L. M., Zerwas, S., Micali, N., Moessner, R., Burton, C. L., Zai, G., Erdman, L., Kas, M. J., Arnold, P. D., Davis, L. K., Knowles, J. A., Breen, G., Scharf, J. M., Nestadt, G., Mathews, C. A., . . . Tourette Syndrome/Obsessive–Compulsive Disorder Working Group of the Psychiatric Genomics Consortium. (2018). Examination of the shared genetic basis of anorexia nervosa and obsessive-compulsive disorder. *Molecular Psychiatry*, 25(9), 2036–2046.

Yu, D., Mathews, C. A., Scharf, J. M., Neale, B. M., Davis, L. K., Gamazon, E. R., Derks, E. M., Evans, P., Edlund, C. K., Crane, J., Fagerness, J. A., Osiecki, L., Gallagher, P., Gerber, G., Haddad, S., Illmann, C., McGrath, L. M., Mayerfeld, C., Arepalli, S., & Pauls, D. L. (2015). Cross-disorder genome-wide analyses suggest a complex genetic relationship between Tourette syndrome and obsessive-compulsive disorder. *American Journal of Psychiatry*, 172, 82–93.

Zai, G., Brandl, E. J., Müller, D. J., Richter, M. A., & Kennedy, J. L. (2014). Pharmacogenetics of antidepressant treatment in obsessive-compulsive disorder: An update and implications for clinicians. *Pharmacogenomics*, 15, 1147–1157.

Zhang, L., Dong, Y., Ji, Y., Zhu, C., Yu, F., Ma, H., Chen, X., & Wang, K. (2015). Dissociation of decision making under ambiguity and decision making under risk: A neurocognitive endophenotype candidate for obsessive-compulsive disorder. *Progress in Neuro-Psychopharmacology & Biological Psychiatry*, 57, 60–68.

Zuchner, S., Wendland, J. R., Ashley-Koch, A. E., Collins, A. L., Tran-Viet, K. N., Quinn, K., Timpano, K. C., Cuccaro, M. L., Pericak-Vance, M. A., Steffens, D. C., Krishnan, K. R., Feng, G., & Murphy, D. L. (2009). Multiple rare *SAPAP3* missense variants in trichotillomania and OCD. *Molecular Psychiatry*, 14, 6–9.

CHAPTER 7

Neuroanatomy of Obsessive-Compulsive and Related Disorders

Anders Lillevik Thorsen *and* Odile A. van den Heuvel

Abstract

The structure, function, and chemistry of the brain in obsessive-compulsive and related disorders (OCRDs), and obsessive-compulsive disorder in particular, have long been the topic of scientific inquiry. Current findings suggest that OCRDs share alterations in frontolimbic, frontostriatal, and frontoparietal circuits related to emotional, cognitive, and sensorimotor processing. Ongoing research is focused on combining imaging modalities to better understand the complexity of the brain, as well as how to translate neurobiological findings into treatment innovations. New research is also employing increased rigor and attempts to increase replicability through larger sample sizes and forming a consensus on how to image and analyze the brain.

Key Words: brain circuits, neuroimaging, obsessive-compulsive disorder, skin-picking disorder, hair-pulling, body dysmorphic disorder

Author Note

Odile A. van den Heuvel has received a speaker's honorarium from Benecke. Anders Lillevik Thorsen reports no financial relationships with commercial interests.

Introduction

Have you ever experienced a thought or impulse that really grabbed your attention, even when you tried to ignore it? Perhaps you even spent some time and energy getting rid of this thought or impulse, although you were somewhat sure that it was exaggerated or even irrational. This is a common struggle for people with obsessive-compulsive and related disorders (OCRDs) and shows how the brain can handle the opposing forces of trying not to give something attention while at the same time responding to it as potentially dangerous or unneglectable. Understanding the biological processes underlying OCRDs will yield not only better understanding of how to treat the disorders, but also increase our knowledge of the immense complexity of parallel and interacting emotional, cognitive, and behavioral processes that are relevant for other disorders as well.

The fifth edition of the *Diagnostic and Statistical Manual of Mental Disorders* (*DSM-5*; American Psychiatric Association, 2013) grouped obsessive-compulsive disorder (OCD), body dysmorphic disorder (BDD), hoarding disorder, excoriation (skin-picking disorder [SPD]), and trichotillomania (hair-pulling) into one common chapter for OCRDs. The *International Classification of Diseases*, 11th revision (*ICD-11*; Stein et al., 2016) additionally added hypochondriasis (health anxiety disorder) and olfactory reference disorder to a similar chapter. Neurobiological findings have been used as arguments both for and against the current groupings. Some argue that neurobiological findings point to shared deficits in cognitive control underlying compulsivity, while others argue that fear and anxiety drive OCRDs (Abramowitz & Jacoby, 2014; Stein et al., 2010, 2016). Understanding the key neurobiological findings in these disorders, and how they are measured, is therefore important to understand how ORCRDs are both related and distinct from each other.

Aims of This Chapter
This chapter provides a contemporary overview of neuroimaging studies of OCRDs, focusing on how different brain circuits can be related to the core symptoms of each disorder. The chapter builds on current meta-analyses and reviews, while also discussing novel studies from recent years. The aim is not to provide a complete overview of all neuroimaging studies of OCRDs, but instead to show the most important or discussed findings. The chapter also describes how different methods and study designs enable the disorders to be understood from different perspectives. Furthermore, the chapter discusses shortcomings in the current literature and suggests future directions in the field. The goal is to increase readers' understanding of, and curiosity about, how brain circuits are involved in complex phenomena like OCRDs, and what they tell us about potential targets for treatment. Ultimately, the goal is that practitioners can use this knowledge to educate patients and make shared decisions on how to treat the disorder.

The Neuroanatomy of OCRDs
The most important things to know about the neurobiology of OCRDs are that:

1. Differences between people with an OCRD and people without mental disorders are likely only small to moderate in magnitude (Isobe et al., 2018; van den Heuvel et al., 2020).
2. The neurobiology of OCRDs can vary with symptom presentation, comorbidity, age of onset, course and stage of illness, age, gender, and medication use (Boedhoe, Schmaal, et al., 2018; Fineberg et al., 2018; Schienle & Wabnegger, 2020; Thorsen, Hagland, et al., 2018; Thorsen, Kvale, et al., 2018). The lack of clear-cut disease markers makes it impossible to reliably separate the patients and healthy controls solely based on neuroimaging data (Bruin et al., 2020; Takagi et al., 2017; Zhou et al., 2018).

3. Some abnormalities in patients seem to represent vulnerability to development of OCRDs and are also present in unaffected family members (Shaw et al., 2015; Vaghi et al., 2017). Other abnormalities appear only after individuals have the disorder for many years or after long-term medication usage (van den Heuvel et al., 2020).
4. Differences between patients and controls are not limited to a few regions, but involve multiple brain regions as well as connections within and between different brain circuits (Grace, Labuschagne, et al., 2017; Gursel et al., 2018; Stein et al., 2019). The pathophysiology of OCRDs also cuts across many biological levels, including (epi)genetics (Yue et al., 2016), immunology (Marazziti et al., 2018), and the autonomic nervous system (Beauchaine & Thayer, 2015).

Contemporary Neuroanatomical Models of OCRDs

Neuroanatomical models of OCRDs attempt to tie together findings from imaging studies in clinical populations along with recent discoveries about normal brain organization and development (Thompson et al., 2020). The models have evolved and become more differentiated over time, although it is important to remember that no model can account for all findings nor fully grasp the complexity of the brain and how it interacts with the environment. Earlier models mostly focused on imbalances between direct and indirect cortico-striatal-thalamo-cortical (CSTC) circuits, focused on the orbitofrontal cortex (OFC), anterior cingulate cortex (ACC), and caudate nucleus through the thalamus (Graybiel & Rauch, 2000; Phillips et al., 2010). Recently, models shifted toward a multicircuit perspective encompassing cognitive control, emotional processing, fear conditioning, motivational processes, and habit formation (Fineberg et al., 2018; Mataix-Cols & van den Heuvel, 2006; Milad & Rauch, 2012).

A recent model by van den Heuvel and colleagues (shown in Figure 7.1; Stein et al., 2019; van den Heuvel et al., 2016) integrates previous models and proposes how OCRDs can be related to the function and structure of sensorimotor, dorsal cognitive, ventral cognitive, frontoparietal, ventral motivational, and frontolimbic brain circuits. The sensorimotor circuit includes the supplementary motor area (SMA) and posterior putamen and is related to behaviors that do not require explicit motivation, such as automated actions and habit formation (Fineberg et al., 2018; Gillan et al., 2015). The ventral motivational circuit includes the OFC, nucleus accumbens/ventral striatum, and ventromedial prefrontal cortex (PFC) and is related to tasks that require explicit motivation to pursue a goal, such as seeking reward or avoiding aversive consequences (Alves-Pinto et al., 2019; Thorsen, Hagland, et al., 2018; White et al., 2013). The dorsal cognitive circuit includes the dorsomedial and dorsolateral PFC, SMA, and dorsal caudate nucleus. It is related to demanding and complex cognitive tasks, such as working memory, planning, and emotion regulation (Odlaug et al., 2016; Picó-Pérez et al., 2020). The ventral cognitive circuit includes the

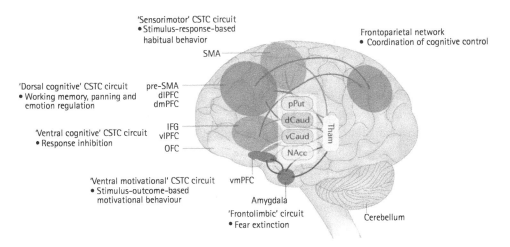

Figure 7.1. Model of brain circuits involved in OCRDs (Stein et al., 2019). CSTC, cortico-striato-thalamo-cortical; dlPFC, dorsolateral prefrontal cortex; dmPFC, dorsomedial prefrontal cortex; IFG, inferior frontal gyrus; OFC, orbitofrontal cortex; SMA, supplementary motor area; vlPFC, ventrolateral prefrontal cortex; vmPFC, ventromedial prefrontal cortex.

inferior frontal gyrus, ventrolateral PFC, and ventral caudate nucleus and is related to tasks like response inhibition, which require fast and accurate responses (Norman et al., 2019). The frontoparietal network contributes during most cognitive tasks and coordinates other networks (Allen et al., 2019; Gursel et al., 2018). The frontolimbic circuit is related to the processing of aversive stimuli, including conditioning and extinction of emotional learning. It includes the amygdala and ventromedial PFC (Apergis-Schoute et al., 2017; Thorsen, Hagland, et al., 2018). In addition, OCRDs and other mental disorders are often related to abnormalities in the default mode network, which is typically deactivated during tasks but active during mind-wandering and self-referential processing (Allen et al., 2019; Grace, Labuschagne, et al., 2017; Gursel et al., 2018).

Approaches and Methods in Neuroimaging

Neuroimaging of OCRDs has been done using a variety of methods, including T1-weighted magnetic resonance imaging (MRI), which is used to investigate gray matter structures, either through whole-brain statistical maps comparing regional volumes or through vertex-based segmentation of individual structures. White matter microstructure is often assessed using diffusion-weighted imaging or magnetization transfer imaging. Fractional anisotropy is a common measure of white matter integrity; it measures the degree to which the flow of water molecules is restricted to one direction, such as within an axon. Functional neuroimaging, such as functional MRI (fMRI), positron emission tomography (PET), or single-photon emission computed tomography (SPECT), allows measurement of blood flow or metabolism in vivo and can been used to probe the correlates of emotional and cognitive processes. A variety of experimental tasks have been developed and validated for functional neuroimaging. They include classical neuropsychological tasks and emotional provocation and regulation, as well as tasks probing the interaction between cognition and emotion. Electroencephalography (EEG) and magnetoencephalography (MEG) can also be used to measure changes in electrical activity, and they have the benefit of a high temporal resolution compared to other methods of functional neuroimaging. Task-free resting-state imaging is also used to investigate the connectivity between different circuits and regions.

PET and SPECT can also be used with radioactive ligands to study receptor availability and binding of neurotransmitters. Finally, magnetic resonance spectroscopy (MRS) can be used to study the concentration of different neurochemicals and neurotransmitter metabolites.

Understanding OCRDs Using the Right Study Design

Most brain imaging research on OCRDs has been performed to test hypotheses about differences between patient and control groups. Cross-sectional case-control comparisons are therefore the most common, comparing for example brain structure or activation between the two groups. However, this design makes it impossible to infer causality and does not reveal how disorders develop over time. Endophenotype (or family) studies extend the case-control design by adding a group of family members who are related to the patient group but who are not affected by the disorder. The risk of developing an OCRD is influenced by genetic and environmental factors (Stein et al., 2019); therefore, the endophenotype design makes it possible to infer that abnormalities found in affected patients and unaffected family members, but not in unrelated healthy controls, are likely related to some of these risk factors (vulnerability markers) and not just to the disorder itself. It may also be possible to identify distinct findings in the unaffected family members that are not present in patients or healthy controls. Such findings may indicate a marker of resilience or a protective factor against developing the disorder. On the other hand, abnormalities found only in affected patients but not unaffected family members or healthy controls are more likely a result of having the disorder (Gottesman & Gould, 2003; Miller & Rockstroh, 2013).

Both case-control and endophenotype studies are needed to uncover potential biomarkers but are often cross-sectional, meaning that they only provide a snapshot of the brain from a single point in time. Longitudinal studies, where participants are scanned multiple times, are therefore needed to see how the brain develops over time. These studies can be especially useful if combined with treatments aimed to improve symptoms or target specific biological processes (Thorsen et al., 2015). For example, patients can be scanned before and after treatment or a wait-list period. Normalization that occurs in patients who received treatment but not those who just waited may then reflect how the brain normalizes in parallel to the decrease in symptoms. Changes in the brain after treatment may potentially even reveal why the treatment was effective.

Longitudinal designs are also needed to determine if a difference in patients compared to healthy controls is a trait or a state, because traits should not be affected by even very effective treatments.

Regardless of the type of hypothesis and design of a study, it is vital that the study have enough statistical power to answer the research question with some certainty. However, many studies are underpowered due to the considerable cost of brain imaging and the logistic complexity of running a study. It can also be difficult to know how large of an effect is to be expected, especially if a novel method is used for the first time. Most studies are able to detect only very large differences between groups or time points. When combined with lenient statistical thresholds and many statistical tests, this may lead to high risks for both false-positive and false-negative findings. Low power and lack of consensus on how to process and analyze data have also contributed to limited replicability in imaging studies of OCRDs. Meta-analysis of published results is therefore an important tool to determine the strongest findings in the field and to filter out nonreplicable or weak findings (Müller et al., 2018). There is also a recent push for mega-analysis, which improves upon meta-analysis by pooling individual participant data across studies and not just summary information from each study. This means that mega-analysis can be more powerful and representative, since it does not depend on how the data were presented in any prior publication (Boedhoe, Heymans, et al., 2018).

Key Findings in OCD

Structural Studies

The Enhancing Neuro Imaging Genetics through Meta-Analysis (ENIGMA) OCD Working Group has recently published large-scale studies investigating the gray and white matter correlates of OCD in pediatric, adolescent, and adult patients (Boedhoe, Schmaal, et al., 2018; Boedhoe et al., 2017, 2020; Bruin et al., 2020; Piras et al., 2019; van den Heuvel et al., 2020; Yun et al., 2020). The studies have included 1,600 to 2,300 patients with OCD and 1,400 to 5,800 healthy controls from different sites worldwide, where data processing, quality control, and analysis are harmonized through standardized pipelines to reduce unwanted variability. The studies suggested that the differences in brain structure between OCD patients and healthy controls are very small, and that age, illness duration, and medication use likely moderate how large the difference is. Unmedicated pediatric patients appear to show a slightly larger thalamus than controls (Boedhoe et al., 2017), a finding that was recently replicated in school-age children with obsessive-compulsive symptoms in a population-based study (Weeland et al., 2020). Adult patients with OCD show smaller amygdala and hippocampus volumes compared to healthy controls, and this finding is particulary strong in patients with comorbid depression. Adult OCD patients show larger pallidum volumes compared to healthy controls, particulary in patients on medication and with childhood onset of OCD (Boedhoe, Schmaal, et al., 2018; Boedhoe et al., 2020). Both pediatric/adolescent and adult OCD patients show slightly thinner parietal cortices (Abramowitz & Jacoby, 2014; Boedhoe et al., 2020). It appears that adult medicated patients (mostly patients taking selective serotonin reuptake inhibitors) have considerably thinner cortices, while medicated pediatric patients show a smaller surface area than controls in frontal and temporal regions (Boedhoe, Schmaal, et al., 2018). Norman et al. (2016) performed a meta-analysis of 30 published studies comparing 928 patients with OCD and 942 healthy controls using voxel-based morphometry to measure regional volumes of gray matter. Patients with OCD showed less gray matter volume in the ACC, dorsolateral PFC, ventromedial PFC, parietal cortex and temporal cortex compared to healthy controls. OCD patients also showed larger volumes in subcortical regions, such as the putamen, pallidum, and amygdala. Furthermore, medication did not appear to moderate the findings in this meta-analysis (Norman et al., 2016). The results matched the lower parietal cortex thickness found by the ENIGMA OCD Working Group (Boedhoe et al., 2017), but they diverged for many other regions. However, differences in image processing, statistical analysis, and using published studies versus raw data make it difficult to compare the studies directly.

Piras et al. (2019) investigated white matter microstructure in individuals with OCD and found that adult patients have slightly lower fractional anisotropy in the sagittal stratum, posterior thalamic radiation, and, to a weaker degree, the corpus callosum. These findings were stronger in sites with more medicated patients and longer illness duration (Piras et al., 2019). Some studies have also found that patients with OCD show lower fractional anisotropy in the cingulum bundle, a finding relevant for frontolimbic connectivity (de Salles Andrade et al., 2019; Fan et al., 2015; Hu et al., 2020; Versace et al., 2019).

There are few studies on changes in brain structure after treatment, with one small study finding increased left putamen volume after fluoxetine or cognitive-behavioral therapy (CBT; Hoexter et al., 2012). Recently, Zhong et al. (2019) found increased fractional anisotropy in several brain regions after CBT, as well as decreased anisotropy in the internal capsule. Family studies have further shown that patients with OCD and unaffected relatives may share abnormal regional cortical thickness and lower fractional anisotropy (Fan et al., 2015; Peng et al., 2014; Shaw et al., 2015). The few available studies make it difficult to establish if abnormal brain structure reliably changes when patients recover, or if it is a potential trait or vulnerability marker signifying elevated risk of developing OCD.

Functional Studies
COGNITIVE PARADIGMS

During cognitive tasks, patients with OCD tend to show hyper- or hypoactivation in the dorsal ventral cognitive circuit, as well as the frontoparietal circuit, depending on the type and difficulty of the task (Norman et al., 2019; Picó-Pérez et al., 2020). Response inhibition is one of the most commonly used tasks in OCD, as it may be a relevant way to study the difficulties patients experience when resisting giving attention to obsessions or performing compulsions. Norman et al. (2019) performed a meta-analysis of unthresholded statistical parametric maps from nine studies comparing patients with OCD and healthy controls during various response inhibition tasks. Norman and colleagues found that patients with OCD showed more activation than controls in the premotor cortex, inferior temporal, and superior parietal areas. Recently, Picó-Pérez et al. (2020) performed a meta-analysis of executive function in general, including tasks like the N-back, Tower of London, and response inhibition. They found that patients with OCD showed less activation than healthy controls in the ACC, caudate nucleus, and postcentral and inferior occipital gyri. Patients also showed more activation in the insula, putamen, dorsolateral PFC, precentral gyrus, and cuneus. Hyperactivation in OCD also overlapped with more gray matter volume in the left putamen in patients with OCD compared to healthy controls (Picó-Pérez et al., 2020). The results of this meta-analysis suggest that patients with OCD show both hyper- and hypoactivation in several circuits that can also be related to altered brain structure. However, the authors did not run analyses to establish differentiation by task type or to relate altered activation patterns to better or worse task performance.

In contrast to hyperactivation in the dorsolateral PFC in OCD when summarizing across different tasks (Picó-Pérez et al., 2020), hypoactivation in the dorsolateral PFC has been found in studies using the Tower of London task (a measure of planning) in both adult and pediatric OCD (den Braber et al., 2010; Huyser et al., 2010; Vaghi et al., 2017; van den Heuvel et al., 2005). Meanwhile, hyperactivation in the pre-SMA and premotor cortex has been found during response inhibition (de Wit et al., 2012; Norman et al., 2019). This suggests that relative hypo- or hyperactivation depends on the type and difficulty of the task. Prefrontal hyperactivation has been reported during the performance of an N-back and response inhibition in OCD and prefrontal hyperactivation has been related to better task performance, which indicates that hyperactivation in the dorsal cognitive circuit may be compensatory (de Vries et al., 2014; Heinzel et al., 2018). Finally, a recent study in pediatric OCD found that patients (compared to controls) showed medial frontal cortex hyperactivation in response to errors during response inhibition. Age of patients with OCD was related to stronger medial frontal cortex activation.

Many studies have used EEG to study electrophysiological markers during rest, different tasks, and sleep, but few replicable differences have emerged between patients with OCD and healthy controls (reviewed in Perera et al., 2019). The strongest and most replicable finding is greater error-related negativity (ERN) after erroneous responses during response inhibition, which may be a marker of overactive error processing in OCD (Perera et al., 2019; Riesel, 2019). Greater ERN also appears to be an endophenotype of OCD because it persists after treatment, both in adults and adolescents (Hajcak et al., 2008; Riesel et al., 2015) and it is present in unaffected family members (Riesel et al., 2011). However, greater ERN may not be specific to OCD, because it has also been observed in unaffected relatives of patients with anxiety or substance abuse disorders (Riesel et al., 2019). Simultaneous EEG and fMRI have been used to gain both high temporal and spatial resolution during response inhibition, since key regions of the cognitive circuits are close to the scalp. For example, Grutzmann et al. (2016) found that a greater ERN is detectable without a significant increase in pre-SMA activation in OCD, and that the relation between the ERN and pre-SMA activation was stronger in patients with OCD than in healthy controls. This provides multimodal evidence for the contribution of the pre-SMA and the dorsal cognitive circuit to error monitoring in OCD (Grutzmann et al., 2016). Error-related activation in the posterior medial frontal cortex was found to be positively related to age in pediatric OCD, and this further suggested that medial frontal hyperactivation in OCD may be a progressive compensatory response because it was also related to better task performance (Fitzgerald et al., 2018), corroborating that hyperactivation in the dorsal cognitive circuit may be compensatory (de Vries et al., 2014; Heinzel et al., 2018).

EMOTIONAL PARADIGMS

If and how patients with OCD activate the frontolimbic circuit during emotional processing has been a topic of much debate in the literature. Some authors have argued that OCD differs from anxiety disorders by showing hypoactivation or no abnormalities in amygdala activation during symptom provocation, which could suggest that OCD is more related to OCRDs (Shin & Liberzon, 2010; Stein et al., 2010). However, a recent meta-analysis by Thorsen, Hagland, et al. (2018) found that patients with OCD (compared to controls) show more activation in the frontolimbic and ventral motivational circuit. This included the bilateral amygdala, right putamen, OFC, ACC, ventromedial PFC, and middle temporal and left inferior occipital cortices (see Figure 7.2). The results also showed that studies with more medicated patients also found less limbic hyperactivation, which suggests that medication may be an important confounding variable (Thorsen, Hagland, et al., 2018). It also suggests that patients with OCD indeed activate the frontolimbic and ventral motivational circuit when experiencing fearful, disgusting, or aversive situations. A key issue for further research in functional imaging is to better understand the processes behind more or less activation in patients with OCD than in healthy controls. Banca et al. (2015) used a live video feed to investigate the neural dynamics in patients when researchers provoked symptoms in the patients' home, where the patients could stop the provocation at any time while in the scanner. The authors found that provocation itself activated many of the same regions found in previous studies. More importantly, they were also able to show that activation in the putamen increased right up to when the patients aborted the provocation, followed by a decrease in activation (Banca et al., 2015). This study provides one of the clearer examples of how to investigate the role of brain circuits during specific phases of emotional and behavioral states, and not just their activation relative to a control group or control condition.

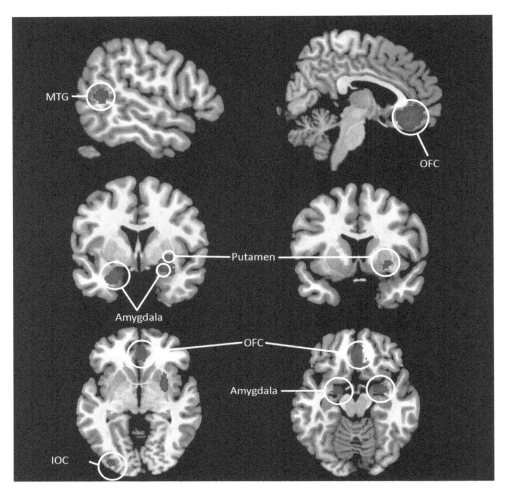

Figure 7.2. Increased regional activation during emotion processing in OCD versus healthy controls (Thorsen, Hagland, et al., 2018). IOC, lateral occipital cortex; MTG, medial temporal gyrus; OFC, orbitofrontal gyrus

Fear conditioning has been used to study if OCD is related to the process of conditioning and updating learned associations between stimuli and threats, such as a mild electric shock (Apergis-Schoute et al., 2017; Milad et al., 2013). Individuals with OCD do not seem to differ from healthy controls in the rate of learning an association between a stimulus and threat, based on elevated skin conductance (Apergis-Schoute et al., 2017; Milad et al., 2013). However, one study found that patients with OCD failed to learn when the shock was shifted to another image (Apergis-Schoute et al., 2017), while another study found that patients continued to show elevated skin conductance even when the stimulus was no longer linked with shocks (Milad et al., 2013). Both ventromedial PFC hyperactivation and hypoactivation have been reported in OCD during acquiring and remembering whether a stimulus is safe or not.

HABIT FORMATION

One of the most discussed hypotheses in recent years is that OCD may be a result of maladaptive habit formation, where compulsions lead to obsessions as a post hoc rationalization of behavior rather than serving as goal-directed ways of reducing anxiety (Robbins et al., 2019). Evidence for excessive habit formation is supported by findings that individuals with OCD do not differ from controls in learning new behaviors, such as which button to press to gain a reward or to avoid a shock. However, patients with OCD fail to stop these behaviors when they are no longer needed, which is similar to the conditioned fear responses to electric shocks (Gillan et al., 2011, 2014). At first it was suspected that the behavior was related to abnormal involvement of the putamen and sensorimotor circuit, which is often implicated in habit-driven behaviors. However, neuroimaging studies suggest that excessive habit formation in OCD is related to hyperactivation in the caudate nucleus, which is thought to underlie goal-directed, not habitual, behavior (Gillan et al., 2015; Robbins et al., 2019). It is therefore unclear if the mechanism behind the tendency to repeat maladaptive compulsions is excessive habit formation or a shift in goals toward minimizing risk, even when compulsions likely do not protect from harm (Robbins et al., 2019).

EMOTIONAL INTERFERENCE

Recent studies have explored if worse performance during cognitive tasks in OCD may be a result of emotional interference, rather than a neuropsychological deficit (Abramovitch et al., 2019). In a recent study of response inhibition, patients with OCD showed less inferior frontal gyrus activation (a direct replication of the findings of de Wit et al., 2012) and stronger connectivity between the right amygdala and right inferior frontal gyrus than healthy controls, and stronger connectivity also predicted worse task performance (Thorsen, de Wit, et al., 2020). Worse performance during working memory has also been seen for patients with altered connectivity between the right amygdala and pre-SMA (de Vries et al., 2014). This provides some evidence that frontolimbic interference negatively affects cognitive performance, but it is also possible that greater anxiety is evoked in patients who suspect that they perform poorly (Moritz et al., 2018).

RESTING STATE

The use of resting-state fMRI to study connectivity between and within brain circuits is currently one of the most vibrant areas of research in neuroscience, with many recent methodological advances (Avena-Koenigsberger et al., 2017). In a recent meta-analysis of seed-based connectivity studies in OCD, Gursel et al. (2018) found evidence for abnormal connectivity both between and within specific circuits, especially for the frontoparietal circuit, which bridges limbic, frontostriatal, default mode, and salience circuits. This fits the proposed role for the frontoparietal network in most cognitive tasks and in coordinating other circuits (Allen et al., 2019; Stein et al., 2019). Other studies have found the limbic circuit to be more strongly connected to the frontoparietal and default mode circuits (de Vries et al., 2017; Fan et al., 2017; Thorsen, Vriend, et al., 2020). Graph theoretical models have been used to unravel the network structure of functional connectivity and to allow measurement of how effective and closely connected the brain is at the global, circuit, and regional level. Such studies suggest that people with OCD likely do not show very disorganized brain networks at the global level (Jung et al., 2017; Shin et al., 2014), but instead show subtle abnormalities in the organization and interaction at the circuit level (Fan et al., 2017; Gottlich et al., 2014; Thorsen, Vriend, et al., 2020). Recent advances in dynamic connectivity may allow studying how information flows between different circuits (Bassett & Sporns, 2017). The results of the first study of dynamic connectivty in OCD suggest that subgenual ACC flexibility, which measures how often this region switches the functional modules it belongs to, reduces after concentrated exposure-based therapy. However, the authors did not find a significant difference between patients and healthy controls before treatment. Future studies are therefore warranted to better understand if the dynamic communication between circuits is related to OCRDs (Thorsen, Vriend, et al., 2020).

TREATMENT STUDIES

Alterations in both task-related activation and resting-state connectivity have been found to change after psychological or pharmacological treatment of OCD (Thorsen et al., 2015). For example, Morgieve et al. (2014) found reduced OFC and ACC activation during symptom provocation after CBT, which has also been partially found in previous studies (Baioui et al., 2013; Schiepek et al., 2013). More recent studies have focused on changes in resting-state connectivity. One study reported widespread greater connectivity between cerebellar, striatal, prefrontal, and parietal regions after treatment (Moody et al., 2017), while another study reported more specific reductions in connectivity between frontoparietal and limbic networks (Thorsen, Vriend, et al., 2020). The studies showed inconsistent findings on whether whole-brain graph theoretical metrics, such as small worldness, modularity, or mean clustering coefficient, change after treatment (Feusner et al., 2015; D. J. Shin et al., 2014; Thorsen, Vriend, et al., 2020). There is some evidence that activation in the frontoparietal network may change after CBT, as observed during response inhibition and reversal learning (Freyer et al., 2011; Nabeyama et al., 2008). In a recent study, Thorsen, de Wit, et al. (2020) found no changes in right inferior frontal gyrus activation or amygdala-inferior frontal gyrus connectivity after effective CBT. However, these studies often have small sample sizes and lenient statistical thresholds, making it unclear if, and how, treatment affects brain function during cognitive tasks.

Neurochemical Studies

The concentration and binding of central neurotransmitters, including serotonin and dopamine, have received interest in neuroimaging because of the efficacy of serotonin reuptake inhibitors and adjuvant antipsychotic drugs in OCD (Dougherty et al., 2018), as well as the frequency of single nucleotide polymorphisms relevant for the serotonergic and glutamatergic systems (International Obsessive Compulsive Disorder Foundation Genetics Collaborative [IOCDF-GC] and OCD Collaborative Genetics Association Studies [OCGAS], 2018). PET and SPECT studies using ligands have used different tracers (reviewed in Fineberg et al., 2018). For example, some have reported reduced serotonin receptor availability in cortical areas (Matsumoto et al., 2010; Perani et al., 2008) or reduced serotonin transporter binding in the thalamus/hypothalamus (Zitterl et al., 2007). Meanwhile, others have reported no significant differences in serotonin transporter binding (Simpson et al., 2003; van der Wee et al., 2004). Greater dopamine receptor availability or binding has been found in caudate, putamen, and nucleus accumbens (Perani et al., 2008; van der Wee et al., 2004), while others have found less dopamine receptor availability in the putamen, especially in patients with comorbid OCD and Tourette syndrome (Denys et al., 2013). In contrast to imaging using ligands, MRS can be done quickly and without the need for expensive radioactive tracers. Current MRS studies have mostly focused on regional concentrations of neurometabolites, such as glutamate/glutamine and gamma-aminobutyric acid (GABA), as well as choline and *N*-acetyl aspartate (NAA; Vester et al., 2020). Although the findings are not very consistent, there is some evidence that adults with OCD (compared to controls) show lower GABA concentrations in the ACC and higher choline concentrations in the thalamus (Vester et al., 2020). There is also some evidence that glutamate/glutamine concentrations in subregions of the ACC may decrease after CBT in adult and pediatric patients (O'Neill et al., 2013, 2017). Overall, ligand and MRS studies have not provided conclusive evidence for the involvement of different neurotransmitter systems in OCD (Fineberg et al., 2018; Vester et al., 2020). Different imaging approaches make it difficult to directly compare individual studies, which has so far hindered meta-analysis.

Conclusion for OCD
Large studies and meta-analyses have found that OCD is related to altered brain structure and function across the major circuits in the brain. However, heterogeneous findings are partly explained by factors like medication, developmental age, disease stage, and symptom profile (including comorbidity), which suggest that there may not be a unitary "brain signature" of the disorder. Therefore, larger studies with longitudinal and lifespan data are needed to better understand how OCD is related to the brain. Nevertheless, OCD has still received far more interest from neuroscientists than have other OCRDs.

Key Findings in Hoarding Disorder

Structural Studies
In the first study of hoarding disorder using *DSM-5* criteria, Yamada et al. (2018) found that patients with hoarding disorder had larger gray matter volume in the OFC than both patients with OCD and healthy controls. Before hoarding disorder became a separate

diagnosis, previous studies mostly relied on correlating brain structure with hoarding severity in patients with OCD. However, findings were mixed, with some studies finding lower volume in the cerebellum (de Wit et al., 2014), precentral gyrus (Gilbert et al., 2008), and caudate nucleus (Valente et al., 2005) in patients with more hoarding symptoms.

Functional Studies
COGNITIVE PARADIGMS

Suñol et al. (2020) found hypoactivation in the dorsomedial PFC, OFC, and dorsolateral PFC during error-processing in patients performing a response inhibition and task-switching paradigm. In contrast, Hough et al. (2016) reported hyperactivation in the OFC and middle cingulate among other regions during errors on a Go/No-Go task. Both studies found hyperactivation in the OFC when comparing patients with hoarding disorder to patients with OCD (Hough et al., 2016; Suñol et al., 2020).

EMOTIONAL PARADIGMS

Stevens et al. (2020) recently showed that patients with hoarding disorder showed abnormal activation in the frontoparietal circuit, particularly in the insula and ACC, during imaginary discarding, while hypoactivation in these areas was found when patients were deciding to discard others' objects. Meanwhile, a previous study found hyperactivation when patients were deciding to discard their own objects (Tolin et al., 2012). Previous studies also reported that patients with OCD with prominent hoarding symptoms show more activation in the ventromedial PFC and cerebellum when imagining throwing away objects (An et al., 2009).

RESTING STATE

The first resting-state connectivity study of patients with hoarding disorder (compared to both healthy controls and patients with depression) reported less connectivity in the cingulo-opercular network and more connectivity in the default mode network (Levy et al., 2019). A study of mixed-type patients with OCD found that greater hoarding severity was related to stronger connections between the ventral caudate and the OFC, and between the dorsal caudate and the superior frontal gyrus (Harrison et al., 2013).

Conclusion for Hoarding Disorder

Current studies, although sparse, suggest that patients with hoarding disorder likely show abnormal structure and activation in the OFC. Altered activation in the frontoparietal circuit has also been found when patients are deciding to discard objects or not. The lack of longitudinal or multimodal studies is a clear limitation for the understanding of hoarding disorder. The separation of hoarding disorder from OCD ideally will motivate researchers to study these patients in larger studies and with approaches that are tailored to the disorder.

Key Findings in BDD

Structural Studies

There are mostly mixed findings regarding brain structure in BDD, where the largest study (comparing only 49 patients and 44 healthy controls) found no significant differences in regional volume or thickness (Madsen et al., 2015). However, even smaller studies have reported thinner cortices in the parietal temporal cortex (Grace, Buchanan, et al., 2017) and smaller OFC and ACC (Atmaca et al., 2010; Buchanan et al., 2014). A small diffusion tensor imaging study (comparing 20 patients and 20 healthy controls) reported lower fractional anisotropy in most white matter tracts (Buchanan et al., 2013). Another study found no significant difference in white matter brain modularity between patients with BDD and healthy controls (Zhang et al., 2016).

Functional Studies

EMOTIONAL PARADIGMS

A line of studies suggests that patients with BDD have difficulties in the balance between the dorsal and ventral visual stream associated with detailed and holistic information processing (reviewed in Grace, Labuschagne, et al., 2017). Patients with BDD (versus controls) viewing pictures of faces showed lower activation in the dorsal visual stream and more activation in the ventral motivational circuit, frontolimbic areas, and ventral visual stream (Feusner et al., 2010; Grace, Labuschagne, et al., 2017; Moody et al., 2020). Using combined EEG and fMRI, Li et al. (2015) reported hypoactivation in the dorsal visual stream in patients with BDD when viewing faces (Li et al., 2015). To our knowledge, no neuroimaging studies have been published that used cognitive or cognitive-emotional tasks, leaving it unclear if and how such processes are affected in BDD.

RESTING-STATE AND TREATMENT STUDIES

The first resting-state fMRI study of BDD found significantly stronger connectivity between the left amygdala and the left middle temporal gyrus, middle inferior temporal gyrus, and superior frontal gyrus in patients compared to healthy controls. These alterations reversed after oxytocin administration, although the study did not assess whether oxytocin had an effect on symptom severity (Grace et al., 2019). To our knowledge, there are no other treatment studies using neuroimaging in BDD.

Neurochemical Studies

In the only ligand study of BDD, Vulink et al. (2016) found that patients with BDD (versus controls) have less dopamine availability in the putamen and caudate nucleus. There is, to our knowledge, no published MRS study of BDD.

Conclusion for BDD

Studies on visual processing suggest that BDD is linked to difficulties balancing detailed and holistic visual processing, particularly with one's own face. Due to inconsistent findings from small-sample studies, it's unclear if the difficulties are also linked to underlying brain structure. It is also unclear if the findings change after treatment, but a single study found that oxytocin might affect limbic functional connectivity in patients with BDD.

Key Findings in SPD and Trichotillomania

Structural Studies

By pooling multisite data, Chamberlain et al. (2018) found higher cortical thickness in the right inferior frontal gyrus in patients with trichotillomania compared to healthy controls (see Figure 7.3). This has also been partially found for first-degree relatives without the disorder (Odlaug et al., 2014). Patients with trichotillomania also had a smaller right amygdala and left putamen, as well as altered shape of the nucleus accumbens, amygdala, caudate and putamen (Isobe et al., 2018). Longer illness duration was related to a thinner superior frontal cortex and middle frontal cortex (Grant et al., 2020).

In a study of 35 patients with SPD and 35 healthy controls, patients showed smaller OFC, insula, and cerebellum (Schienle et al., 2018; Wabnegger & Schienle, 2019). Patients who experience that their picking behavior elicits negative emotions showed smaller insula and larger operculum volumes than did healthy controls, while patients who found picking to elicit positive emotions showed larger insula volume than patients with negative emotions after picking (Schienle & Wabnegger, 2020). However, a smaller

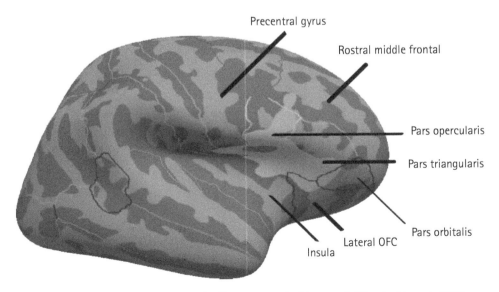

Figure 7.3. Increased cortical thickness in trichotillomania versus healthy controls (Chamberlain et al., 2018).

study found no significant group difference but a positive correlation between symptom severity and left insula thickness (Harries et al., 2017).

Two small studies have found lower fractional anisotropy in white matter in both SPD and trichotillomania, mainly in the dorsal cingulate, temporal, and parietal regions (Chamberlain et al., 2010; Grant et al., 2013). There are few studies directly comparing the disorders, with one finding that SPD was related to larger nucleus accumbens and smaller frontal cortical thickness than trichotillomania, whereas patients with trichotillomania showed a thicker parahippocampal gyrus (Roos et al., 2015). Large-scale replication is needed to uncover any structural abnormalities related to SPD and trichotillomania.

Functional Studies

COGNITIVE PARADIGMS

Using a planning task, Odlaug et al. (2016) found that patients with SPD (compared to healthy controls) hypoactivate the bilateral caudate nucleus, without a difference in task performance. Grant et al. (2018) found that trichotillomania patients showed more activation in the middle frontal gyrus and less activation in the occipital cortex than healthy controls during set shifting and reversal learning, but the results did not survive whole-brain comparisons. An earlier study also found that trichotillomania was related to abnormal activation during reward processing and stronger functional connectivity between reward-related structures and the amygdala (White et al., 2013).

EMOTIONAL PARADIGMS

Studies using visual symptom provocation in patients with SPD reported more activation in the amygdala, insula, and OFC than in healthy controls, implicating the ventral motivational and frontolimbic circuit (Schienle et al., 2018b; Wabnegger et al., 2018). Patients showed no significant difference from controls when skin scratching and caressing were compared, although female patients (compared to female controls) showed hypoactivation in the middle frontal gyrus and somatosensory cortex during caressing (Schienle et al., 2018a).

RESTING STATE

One study investigated the relation between symptom severity of skin-picking and resting-state connectivity using the pre-SMA and inferior frontal gyrus as seed regions. The study found that higher symptom severity was related to weaker resting-state connectivity between the pre-SMA and the OFC and angular gyrus (Huggins et al., 2020).

Neurochemical Studies

One study found that patients with comorbid OCD and SPD showed lower levels of glutamate/glutamine in the pregenual ACC than did both healthy controls and patients with OCD without SPD (Zheng et al., 2020). A study of pediatric patients with trichotillomania (compared to healthy controls) found no baseline differences in glutamate or GABA across the pregenual ACC, caudate, putamen, globus pallidus, thalamus, and white matter. However, levels of GABA in the putamen increased after behavioral therapy (Peris et al., 2020).

Conclusions for SPD and Trichotillomania
SPD and trichotillomania have both been related to altered structure and function of the ventral motivational and frontolimbic circuits. The insula has also been implicated, which is not surprising given its role in interoception and emotional processing. There are fewer studies of trichotillomania and SPD than other OCRDs (Slikboer et al., 2018), so larger studies and international collaboration across smaller samples are required to improve our understanding of the disorders' neurobiology.

OCRDs and Anxiety Disorders

Structural Studies
An early meta-analysis compared the results of voxel-based morphometry studies of patients with OCD and patients with other anxiety disorders (e.g., panic disorder, social anxiety disorder, generalized anxiety disorder [GAD], and posttraumatic stress disorder), finding that both patient groups showed lower volume of the dorsomedial PFC and ACC compared to healthy controls, but that patients with OCD had larger basal ganglia than patients with anxiety disorders (Radua et al., 2010). Smaller ACC and OFC volumes have also been found in direct comparisons of patients with OCD and GAD versus healthy controls, while only patients with GAD also showed lower medial PFC gray matter volume (Kim et al., 2018). Meanwhile, other studies have not replicated these findings (Cheng et al., 2015). Future cross-disorder comparisons using harmonized data processing are underway in the ENIGMA Anxiety Working Group (Bas-Hoogendam et al., 2020).

Functional Studies
Both anxiety disorders and OCD seem to share less ventromedial PFC activation during fear conditioning, suggesting common alterations in fear and extinction learning (Marin et al., 2017; Milad et al., 2013). Both patients with OCD and patients with social anxiety disorder also show elevated amygdala, caudate nucleus, and OFC activation when anticipating emotional stimuli with unknown valence (Weidt et al., 2016). Common patterns of frontal, striatal, and amygdala hyperactivation have also been found during disorder-specific emotional interference processing in patients with OCD, panic disorder, and health anxiety (van den Heuvel et al., 2005, 2011).

Conclusion for OCRDs and Anxiety Disorders
Patients with OCD and anxiety disorders show overlapping abnormalities in structure and function of the frontolimbic and ventral motivation circuits, together with reduced

volume of the dorsal ACC/dorsomedial PFC. This suggests that brain alterations in both anxiety disorders and OCD seem to reflect shared dysfunctional emotional, cognitive, and sensorimotor processing.

Future Directions

Improving How and What We Measure

So far, researchers have used different ways of acquiring, processing, and analyzing neuroimaging data. The brain has also been investigated from many different perspectives, including brain morphology, activation during cognitive and emotional tasks, and connectivity between circuits. However, it is still far from clear which method is better or worse than the other. Also, little is known about the mechanisms underlying effective treatments for OCRDs and how they can be measured using neuroimaging.

Recent work has highlighted the utility of multimodal analyses to identify common and unique contributions from each type of imaging, as well as symptom scores, genetics, and other potentially useful markers (Picó-Pérez et al., 2020; Vaughn et al., 2019). Machine learning methods can be valuable for combining many variables and identifying combinations that reveal which facets separate healthy controls from different OCRDs. However, such studies will likely need very large data sets for testing and validating algorithms in independent samples (Dinga et al., 2019). Large data sets and machine learning are also needed to understand how the neurobiology of OCRDs is affected by age, illness duration/chronicity, medication, symptom profile, and comorbidity, where current studies have mostly used univariate analyses to investigate the contribution of these factors (Boedhoe et al., 2020; Fitzgerald et al., 2018; van den Heuvel et al., 2020).

Cross-disorder meta-analyses suggest that many disorders share abnormalities in brain structure and function (Goodkind et al., 2015; Jenkins et al., 2016; McTeague et al., 2017, 2020). It is therefore unclear to what degree the findings reviewed above reflect disorder-specific alterations or a general psychopathology factor (Caspi et al., 2014). Recent research has revealed shared genetic markers of risk for many mental disorders (Anttila et al., 2018), suggesting that heritable risk for one disorder likely confers risk for other disorders as well. Combining genetics and neuroimaging might be an important way to form better models of OCRDs (Stein et al., 2019). For example, Hibar et al. (2018) found that genetic markers of risk for OCD were also related to variance in the volume of the putamen, amygdala, and thalamus, which suggested that subcortical abnormalities may be a correlate of heritable vulnerability for the disorder.

A current issue in the field is how to compare findings from meta-analyses of published studies, because their results do not always overlap (de Wit et al., 2014; Hu et al., 2020; Norman et al., 2016, 2019; Piras et al., 2019). Meta-analyses rely on summary data from published (or unpublished) studies, which may introduce bias if nonsignificant or unexpected findings are suppressed. Mega-analysis relies on data from individual participant data from each site, which may provide greater power and the opportunity to investigate variation between individuals. It is important to consider how choices in image acquisition, processing, and analysis could affect meta- and mega-analyses (Clarkson et al., 2011), although tools have recently been developed for adjusting unwanted variation between different sites (Radua et al., 2020).

Improving Transparency and Replicability in Neuroscience

There are now many neuroimaging studies of OCRDs in the literature, particularly of OCD, but most are underpowered and cannot detect the subtle differences that likely distinguish patients from healthy controls. It is clear that different choices in data acquisition, processing, and statistical analysis can hinder the replicability and comparability of current findings (Botvinik-Nezer et al., 2020; Elliott et al., 2020), making the neurobiological correlates of OCRDs even harder to detect. There are several ways to tackle these crucial issues. First, making hypotheses, data, and analysis pipelines publicly available could lead to greater transparence and replicability (Nichols et al., 2017). Second, groups and institutions should collaborate on harmonized multicenter studies rather than running separate studies with nearly identical aims but very different methods and small samples (Casey et al., 2018; Simpson et al., 2020). That does not mean that smaller, single-site studies should be discontinued entirely. Indeed, smaller studies have the potential to contribute to innovation in experimental paradigms. For example, many studies are currently unable to explain which processes underlie altered activation during a task or what altered activation really means. There is an unmet need for paradigms where the participants can flexibly choose how to react, allowing the study of the processes involved in the starting and stopping of compulsions and avoidance (Banca et al., 2015; Schienle et al., 2018a). Similarly, recent work in habit formation shows that new tasks can also bring about new perspectives on OCRDs and other disorders (Fineberg et al., 2018; Gillan et al., 2017). However, the next crucial step is to test the replicability of such methods in new samples and patient groups.

Improving Treatments Through Neuroscience

Current research increasingly tries to use neuroscience to personalize and improve treatment through targeting specific brain circuits (Stein et al., 2019). Neuroimaging can be used to individually guide repetitive transcranial magnetic stimulation (Carmi et al., 2018) or deep brain stimulation (Liebrand et al., 2019). There are currently no robust neurobiological variables that predict if a patient will improve after an established treatment for an OCRD, and most studies have relied on testing a limited number of concurrent predictors using small sample sizes (Fullana & Simpson, 2016; Greenberg et al., 2019). Future studies should combine imaging markers with comprehensive clinical, physiological, neuropsychological, and genetic testing to better evaluate the predictive value of multiple biological and psychological levels.

Conclusions

OCRDs are related to biological processes at several levels, ranging from genetic and cellular factors to brain structure, function, and neurochemistry. The strongest findings in current studies suggest that OCRDs share altered activation and structure across frontolimbic, frontostriatal, and frontoparietal circuits related to emotional, cognitive, and sensorimotor processing. However, small studies with high chances of false-positive and false-negative results, suboptimal collaboration and harmonization on data acquisition and processing, and methodological limitations of techniques have made it difficult to bridge these levels and find reliable biomarkers. The problem is compounded by the heterogeneity of symptom profiles across individuals and changes in the involvement of the biological processes during the various stages of development and disease, as well medication. The scarcity of well-sampled treatment studies also limits our understanding of whether the abnormalities in brain structure and function normalize when patients recover or if they remain as trait vulnerabilities that contribute to relapse. Ideally, the recent shift toward large, international, and multimodal studies with longitudinal designs will pave the way for a more robust understanding of OCRDs and will facilitate the translation from neuroscience to clinical practice in the future.

References

Abramovitch, A., McCormack, B., Brunner, D., Johnson, M., & Wofford, N. (2019). The impact of symptom severity on cognitive function in obsessive-compulsive disorder: A meta-analysis. *Clinical Psychology Review*, *67*, 36–44.

Abramowitz, J. S., & Jacoby, R. J. (2014). Obsessive-compulsive disorder in the DSM-5. *Clinical Psychology: Science and Practice*, *21*(3), 221–235.

Allen, P., Sommer, I. E., Jardri, R., Eysenck, M. W., & Hugdahl, K. (2019). Extrinsic and default mode networks in psychiatric conditions: Relationship to excitatory-inhibitory transmitter balance and early trauma. *Neuroscience Biobehavioral Reviews*, *99*, 90–100.

Alves-Pinto, A., Rus, O. G., Reess, T. J., Wohlschläger, A., Wagner, G., Berberich, G., & Koch, K. (2019). Altered reward-related effective connectivity in obsessive-compulsive disorder: An fMRI study. *Journal of Psychiatry & Neuroscience*, *44*(6), 395–406.

American Psychiatric Association (APA). (2013). *Diagnostic and statistical manual of mental disorders* (5th ed.).

An, S. K., Mataix-Cols, D., Lawrence, N. S., Wooderson, S., Giampietro, V., Speckens, A., Brammer, M. J., & Phillips, M. L. (2009). To discard or not to discard: the neural basis of hoarding symptoms in obsessive-compulsive disorder. *Molecular Psychiatry*, *14*(3), 318–331.

Anttila, V., Bulik-Sullivan, B., Finucane, H. K., Walters, R. K., Bras, J., Duncan, L., Escott-Price, V., Falcone, G. J., Gormley, P., Malik, R., Patsopoulos, N. A., Ripke, S., Wei, Z., Yu, D., Lee, P. H., Turley, P., Grenier-Boley, B., Chouraki, V., Kamatani, Y., . . . Murray, R. (2018). Analysis of shared heritability in common disorders of the brain. *Science*, *360*(6395), eaap8757.

Apergis-Schoute, A. M., Gillan, C. M., Fineberg, N. A., Fernandez-Egea, E., Sahakian, B. J., & Robbins, T. W. (2017). Neural basis of impaired safety signaling in obsessive compulsive disorder. *Proceedings of the National Academy of Sciences of the United States of America*, *114*(12), 3216–3221.

Atmaca, M., Bingol, I., Aydin, A., Yildirim, H., Okur, I., Yildirim, M. A., Mermi, O., &, Gurok, M. G. (2010). Brain morphology of patients with body dysmorphic disorder. *Journal of Affective Disorders*, *123*(1–3), 258–263.

Avena-Koenigsberger, A., Misic, B., & Sporns, O. (2017). Communication dynamics in complex brain networks. *Nature Reviews Neuroscience*, *19*(1), 17–33.

Baioui, A., Pilgramm, J., Kagerer, S., Walter, B., Vaitl, D., & Stark, R. (2013). Neural correlates of symptom reduction after CBT in obsessive-compulsive washers—An fMRI symptom provocation study. *Journal of Obsessive-Compulsive and Related Disorders, 2*(3), 322–330.

Banca, P., Voon, V., Vestergaard, M. D., Philipiak, G., Almeida, I., Pocinho, F., Relvas, J., & Castelo-Branco, M. (2015). Imbalance in habitual versus goal directed neural systems during symptom provocation in obsessive-compulsive disorder. *Brain, 138*(3), 798–811.

Bas-Hoogendam, J. M., Groenewold, N. A., Aghajani, M., Freitag, G. F., Harrewijn, A., Hilbert, K., Jahanshad, N., Thomopoulos, S. I., Thompson, P. M., Veltman, D. J., Winkler, A. M., Lueken, U., Pine, D. S., van der Wee, N. J. A., & Stein, D. J. (2020). ENIGMA-Anxiety Working Group: Rationale for and organization of large-scale neuroimaging studies of anxiety disorders. *Hum Brain Mapp*, 83–112.

Bassett, D. S., & Sporns, O. (2017). Network neuroscience. *Nature Neuroscience, 20*(3), 353–364.

Beauchaine, T. P., & Thayer, J. F. (2015). Heart rate variability as a transdiagnostic biomarker of psychopathology. *Int J Psychophysiol, 98*(2 Pt. 2), 338–350.

Boedhoe, P. S. W., Heymans, M. W., Schmaal, L., Abe, Y., Alonso, P., Ameis, S. H., Anticevic, A., Arnold, P. D., Batistuzzo, M. C., Benedetti, F., Beucke, J. C., Bollettini, I., Bose, A., Brem, S., Calvo, A., Calvo, R., Cheng, Y., Cho, K. I. K., Ciullo, V., . . . Twisk, J. W. R. (2018). An empirical comparison of meta- and mega-analysis with data from the ENIGMA Obsessive-Compulsive Disorder Working Group. *Front Neuroinform, 12*, 102.

Boedhoe, P. S. W., Schmaal, L., Abe, Y., Alonso, P., Ameis, S. H., Anticevic, A., Arnold, P. D., Batistuzzo, M. C., Benedetti, F., Beucke, J. C., Bollettini, I., Bose, A., Brem, S., Calvo, A., Calvo, R., Cheng, Y., Cho, K. I. K., Ciullo, V., Dallaspezia, S., . . . van den Heuvel, O. A. (2018). Cortical abnormalities associated with pediatric and adult obsessive-compulsive disorder: Findings from the ENIGMA Obsessive-Compulsive Disorder Working Group. *The American Journal of Psychiatry, 175*(5), 453–462.

Boedhoe, P. S. W., Schmaal, L., Abe, Y., Ameis, S. H., Arnold, P. D., Batistuzzo, M. C., Benedetti, F., Beucke, J. C., Bollettini, I., Bose, A., Brem, S., Calvo, A., Cheng, Y., Cho, K. I., Dallaspezia, S., Denys, D., Fitzgerald, K. D., Fouche, J. P., Giménez, M., . . . van den Heuvel, O. A. (2017). Distinct subcortical volume alterations in pediatric and adult OCD: A worldwide meta-and mega-analysis. *The American Journal of Psychiatry, 174*(1), 60–69.

Boedhoe, P. S. W., van Rooij, D., Hoogman, M., Twisk, J. W. R., Schmaal, L., Abe, Y., Alonso, P., Ameis, S. H., Anikin, A., Anticevic, A., Arango, C., Arnold, P. D., Asherson, P., Assogna, F., Auzias, G., Banaschewski, T., Baranov, A., Batistuzzo, M. C., Baumeister, S., . . . van den Heuvel, O. A. (2020). Subcortical brain volume, regional cortical thickness, and cortical surface area across disorders: Findings From the ENIGMA ADHD, ASD, and OCD Working Groups. *The American Journal of Psychiatry, 177*(9), 834–843, appiajp202019030331.

Botvinik-Nezer, R., Holzmeister, F., Camerer, C. F., Dreber, A., Huber, J., Johannesson, M., Kirchler, M., Iwanir, R., Mumford, J. A., Adcock, R. A., Avesani, P., Baczkowski, B. M., Bajracharya, A., Bakst, L., Ball, S., Barilari, M., Bault, N., Beaton, D., Beitner, J., . . . Schonberg, T. (2020). Variability in the analysis of a single neuroimaging dataset by many teams. *Nature, 582*(7810), 84–88.

Bruin, W. B., Taylor, L., Thomas, R. M., Shock, J. P., Zhutovsky, P., Abe, Y., Alonso, P., Ameis, S. H., Anticevic, A., Arnold, P. D., Assogna, F., Benedetti, F., Beucke, J. C., Boedhoe, P. S. W., Bollettini, I., Bose, A., Brem, S., Brennan, B. P., Buitelaar, J. K., . . . van Wingen, G. A. (2020). Structural neuroimaging biomarkers for obsessive-compulsive disorder in the ENIGMA-OCD Consortium: Medication matters. *Translational Psychiatry, 10*(1), 342.

Buchanan, B. G., Rossell, S. L., Maller, J. J., Toh, W. L., Brennan, S., & Castle, D. J. (2013). Brain connectivity in body dysmorphic disorder compared with controls: A diffusion tensor imaging study. *Psychological Medicine, 43*(12), 2513–2521.

Buchanan, B. G., Rossell, S., Maller, J. J., Toh, W. L., Brennan, S., & Castle, D. (2014). Regional brain volumes in body dysmorphic disorder compared to controls. *Australian New Zealand Journal of Psychiatry, 48*(7), 654–662.

Carmi, L., Alyagon, U., Barnea-Ygael, N., Zohar, J., Dar, R., & Zangen, A. (2018). Clinical and electrophysiological outcomes of deep TMS over the medial prefrontal and anterior cingulate cortices in OCD patients. *Brain Stimulation, 11*(1), 158–165.

Casey, B. J., Cannonier, T., Conley, M. I., Cohen, A. O., Barch, D. M., Heitzeg, M. M., Soules, M. E., Teslovich, T., Dellarco, D. V., Garavan, H., Orr, C. A., Wager, T. D., Banich, M. T., Speer, N. K., Sutherland, M. T., Riedel, M. C., Dick, A. S., Bjork, J. M., Thomas, K. M., . . . Dale, A. M. (2018). The Adolescent

Brain Cognitive Development (ABCD) study: Imaging acquisition across 21 sites. *Developmental Cognitive Neuroscience, 32*, 43–54.

Caspi, A., Houts, R. M., Belsky, D. W., Goldman-Mellor, S. J., Harrington, H., Israel, S., Meier, M. H., Ramrakha, S., Shalev, I., Poulton, R., & Moffitt, T. E. (2014). The p factor: One general psychopathology factor in the structure of psychiatric disorders? *Clinical Psychological Science, 2*(2), 119–137.

Chamberlain, S. R., Hampshire, A., Menzies, L. A., Garyfallidis, E., Grant, J. E., Odlaug, B. L., Craig, K., Fineberg, N., & Sahakian, B. J. (2010). Reduced brain white matter integrity in trichotillomania: A diffusion tensor imaging study. *Archives of General Psychiatry, 67*(9), 965–971.

Chamberlain, S. R., Harries, M., Redden, S. A., Keuthen, N. J., Stein, D. J., Lochner, C., & Grant, J. E. (2018). Cortical thickness abnormalities in trichotillomania: International multi-site analysis. *Brain Imaging and Behavior, 12*(3), 823–828.

Cheng, B., Huang, X., Li, S., Hu, X., Luo, Y., Wang, X., Yang, X., Qiu, C., Yang, Y., Zhang, W., Bi, F., Roberts, N., & Gong, Q. (2015). Gray matter alterations in post-traumatic stress disorder, obsessive-compulsive disorder, and social anxiety disorder. *Frontiers in Behavioral Neuroscience, 9*, 219.

Clarkson, M. J., Cardoso, M. J., Ridgway, G. R., Modat, M., Leung, K. K., Rohrer, J. D., Fox, N. C., & Ourselin, S. (2011). A comparison of voxel and surface based cortical thickness estimation methods. *Neuroimage, 57*(3), 856–865.

de Salles Andrade, J. B., Ferreira, F. M., Suo, C., Yücel, M., Frydman, I., Monteiro, M., Vigne, P., Fontenelle, L. F., & Tovar-Moll, F. (2019). An MRI study of the metabolic and structural abnormalities in obsessive-compulsive disorder. *Frontiers in Human Neuroscience, 13*, 186.

de Vries, F. E., de Wit, S. J., Cath, D. C., van der Werf, Y. D., van der Borden, V., van Rossum, T. B., van Balkom, A. J., van der Wee, N. J., Veltman, D. J., & van den Heuvel, O. A. (2014). Compensatory frontoparietal activity during working memory: An endophenotype of obsessive-compulsive disorder. *Biological Psychiatry, 76*(11), 878–887.

de Vries, F. E., de Wit, S. J., van den Heuvel, O. A., Veltman, D. J., Cath, D. C., van Balkom, A., & van der Werf, Y. D. (2017). Cognitive control networks in OCD: A resting-state connectivity study in unmedicated patients with obsessive-compulsive disorder and their unaffected relatives. *World Journal of Biological Psychiatry, 20*(3), 230–242.

de Wit, S. J., Alonso, P., Schweren, L., Mataix-Cols, D., Lochner, C., Menchon, J. M., Stein, D. J., Fouche, J. P., Soriano-Mas, C., Sato, J. R., Hoexter, M. Q., Denys, D., Nakamae, T., Nishida, S., Kwon, J. S., Jang, J. H., Busatto, G. F., Cardoner, N., Cath, D. C., . . . van den Heuvel, O. A. (2014). Multicenter voxel-based morphometry mega-analysis of structural brain scans in obsessive-compulsive disorder. *The American Journal of Psychiatry, 171*(3), 340–349.

de Wit, S. J., de Vries, F. E., van der Werf, Y. D., Cath, D. C., Heslenfeld, D. J., Veltman, E. M., van Balkom, A. J., Veltman, D. J., & van den Heuvel, O. A. (2012). Presupplementary motor area hyperactivity during response inhibition: A candidate endophenotype of obsessive-compulsive disorder. *The American Journal of Psychiatry, 169*(10), 1100–1108.

den Braber, A., van't Ent, D., Cath, D. C., Wagner, J., Boomsma, D. I., & de Geus, E. J. (2010). Brain activation during cognitive planning in twins discordant or concordant for obsessive-compulsive symptoms. *Brain, 133*(10), 3123–3140.

Denys, D., de Vries, F., Cath, D., Figee, M., Vulink, N., Veltman, D. J., van der Doef, T. F., Boellaard, R., Westenberg, H., van Balkom, A., Lammertsma, A. A., & van Berckel, B. N. (2013). Dopaminergic activity in Tourette syndrome and obsessive-compulsive disorder. *European Neuropsychopharmacology, 23*(11), 1423–1431.

Dinga, R., Penninx, B. W. J. H., Veltman, D. J., Schmaal, L., & Marquand, A. F. (2019). Beyond accuracy: Measures for assessing machine learning models, pitfalls and guidelines. *bioRxiv*, 743138.

Dougherty, D. D., Brennan, B. P., Stewart, S. E., Wilhelm, S., Widge, A. S., & Rauch, S. L. (2018). Neuroscientifically informed formulation and treatment planning for patients with obsessive-compulsive disorder: A review. *JAMA Psychiatry, 75*(10), 1081–1087.

Elliott, M. L., Knodt, A. R., Ireland, D., Morris, M. L., Poulton, R., Ramrakha, S., Sison, M. L., Moffitt, T. E., Caspi, A., & Hariri, A. R. (2020). What is the test-retest reliability of common task-functional MRI measures? New empirical evidence and a meta-analysis. *Psychological Science, 31*(7), 792–806.

Fan, J., Zhong, M., Gan, J., Liu, W., Niu, C., Liao, H., Zhang, H., Yi, J., Chan, R. C. K., Tan, C., & Zhu, X. (2017). Altered connectivity within and between the default mode, central executive, and salience networks in obsessive-compulsive disorder. *Journal of Affective Disorders, 223*, 106–114.

Fan, S., van den Heuvel, O. A., Cath, D. C., van der Werf, Y. D., de Wit, S. J., de Vries, F. E., Veltman, D. J., & Pouwels, P. J. (2015). Mild white matter changes in un-medicated obsessive-compulsive disorder patients and their unaffected siblings. *Frontiers in Neuroscience*, *9*, 495.

Feusner, J. D., Moody, T., Hembacher, E., Townsend, J., McKinley, M., Moller, H., & Bookheimer, S. (2010). Abnormalities of visual processing and frontostriatal systems in body dysmorphic disorder. *Archives of General Psychiatry*, *67*(2), 197–205.

Feusner, J. D., Moody, T., Lai, T. M., Sheen, C., Khalsa, S., Brown, J., Levitt, J., Alger, J., & O'Neill, J. (2015). Brain connectivity and prediction of relapse after cognitive-behavioral therapy in obsessive-compulsive disorder. *Frontiers in Psychiatry*, *6*, 74.

Fineberg, N. A., Apergis-Schoute, A. M., Vaghi, M. M., Banca, P., Gillan, C. M., Voon, V., Chamberlain, S. R., Cinosi, E., Reid, J., Shahper, S., Bullmore, E. T., Sahakian, B. J., & Robbins, T. W. (2018). Mapping compulsivity in the DSM-5 obsessive compulsive and related disorders: Cognitive domains, neural circuitry, and treatment. *International Journal of Neuropsychopharmacology*, *21*(1), 42–58.

Fitzgerald, K. D., Liu, Y., Johnson, T. D., Moser, J. S., Marsh, R., Hanna, G. L., & Taylor, S. F. (2018). Development of posterior medial frontal cortex function in pediatric obsessive-compulsive disorder. *Journal of the American Academy of Child and Adolescent Psychiatry*, *57*(6), 397–406.

Freyer, T., Kloppel, S., Tuscher, O., Kordon, A., Zurowski, B., Kuelz, A. K., Speck, O., Glauche, V., & Voderholzer, U. (2011). Frontostriatal activation in patients with obsessive-compulsive disorder before and after cognitive behavioral therapy. *Psychological Medicine*, *41*(1), 207–216.

Fullana, M. A., & Simpson, H. B. (2016). The potential use of neuroimaging biomarkers in the treatment of obsessive-compulsive disorder. *Current Treatment Options in Psychiatry*, *3*(3), 246–252.

Gilbert, A. R., Mataix-Cols, D., Almeida, J. R., Lawrence, N., Nutche, J., Diwadkar, V., Keshavan, M. S., & Phillips, M. L. (2008). Brain structure and symptom dimension relationships in obsessive-compulsive disorder: A voxel-based morphometry study. *Journal of Affective Disorders*, *109*(1–2), 117–126.

Gillan, C. M., Apergis-Schoute, A. M., Morein-Zamir, S., Urcelay, G. P., Sule, A., Fineberg, N. A., Sahakian, B. J., & Robbins, T. W. (2015). Functional neuroimaging of avoidance habits in obsessive-compulsive disorder. *The American Journal of Psychiatry*, *172*(3), 284–293.

Gillan, C. M., Fineberg, N. A., & Robbins, T. W. (2017). A trans-diagnostic perspective on obsessive-compulsive disorder. *Psychological Medicine*, *47*(9), 1528–1548.

Gillan, C. M., Morein-Zamir, S., Urcelay, G. P., Sule, A., Voon, V., Apergis-Schoute, A. M., Fineberg, N. A., Sahakian, B. J., & Robbins, T. W. (2014). Enhanced avoidance habits in obsessive-compulsive disorder. *Biological Psychiatry*, *75*(8), 631–638.

Gillan, C. M., Papmeyer, M., Morein-Zamir, S., Sahakian, B. J., Fineberg, N. A., Robbins, T. W., & de Wit, S. (2011). Disruption in the balance between goal-directed behavior and habit learning in obsessive-compulsive disorder. *The American Journal of Psychiatry*, *168*(7), 718–726.

Goodkind, M., Eickhoff, S. B., Oathes, D. J., Jiang, Y., Chang, A., Jones-Hagata, L. B., Ortega, B. N., Zaiko, Y. V., Roach, E. L., Korgaonkar, M. S., Grieve, S. M., Galatzer-Levy, I., Fox, P. T., & Etkin, A. (2015). Identification of a common neurobiological substrate for mental illness. *JAMA Psychiatry*, *72*(4), 305–315.

Gottesman, II, & Gould, T. D. (2003). The endophenotype concept in psychiatry: Etymology and strategic intentions. *The American Journal of Psychiatry*, *160*(4), 636–645.

Gottlich, M., Kramer, U. M., Kordon, A., Hohagen, F., & Zurowski, B. (2014). Decreased limbic and increased fronto-parietal connectivity in unmedicated patients with obsessive-compulsive disorder. *Human Brain Mapping*, *35*(11), 5617–5632.

Grace, S. A., Buchanan, B. G., Maller, J. J., Toh, W. L., Castle, D. J., & Rossell, S. L. (2017). Reduced cortical thickness in body dysmorphic disorder. *Psychiatry Research: Neuroimaging*, *259*, 25–28.

Grace, S. A., Labuschagne, I., Castle, D. J., & Rossell, S. L. (2019). Intranasal oxytocin alters amygdala-temporal resting-state functional connectivity in body dysmorphic disorder: A double-blind placebo-controlled randomized trial. *Psychoneuroendocrinology*, *107*, 179–186.

Grace, S. A., Labuschagne, I., Kaplan, R. A., & Rossell, S. L. (2017). The neurobiology of body dysmorphic disorder: A systematic review and theoretical model. *Neuroscience and Biobehavioral Reviews*, *83*, 83–96.

Grant, J. E., Daws, R., Hampshire, A., & Chamberlain, S. R. (2018). An fMRI pilot study of cognitive flexibility in trichotillomania. *The Journal of Neuropsychiatry and Clinical Neurosciences*, *30*(4), 318–324.

Grant, J. E., Keuthen, N. J., Stein, D. J., Lochner, C., & Chamberlain, S. R. (2020). Duration of illness and cortical thickness in trichotillomania: Preliminary evidence for illness change over time. *European Neuropsychopharmacology*, *32*, 88–93.

Grant, J. E., Odlaug, B. L., Hampshire, A., Schreiber, L. R., & Chamberlain, S. R. (2013). White matter abnormalities in skin picking disorder: A diffusion tensor imaging study. *Neuropsychopharmacology, 38*(5), 763–769.

Graybiel, A. M., & Rauch, S. L. (2000). Toward a neurobiology of obsessive-compulsive disorder. *Neuron, 28*(2), 343–347.

Greenberg, J. L., Phillips, K. A., Steketee, G., Hoeppner, S. S., & Wilhelm, S. (2019). Predictors of response to cognitive-behavioral therapy for body dysmorphic disorder. *Behavioral Therapy, 50*(4), 839–849.

Grutzmann, R., Endrass, T., Kaufmann, C., Allen, E., Eichele, T., & Kathmann, N. (2016). Presupplementary motor area contributes to altered error monitoring in obsessive-compulsive disorder. *Biological Psychiatry, 80*(7), 562–571.

Gursel, D. A., Avram, M., Sorg, C., Brandl, F., & Koch, K. (2018). Frontoparietal areas link impairments of large-scale intrinsic brain networks with aberrant fronto-striatal interactions in OCD: A meta-analysis of resting-state functional connectivity. *Neuroscience and Biobehavioral Reviews, 87*, 151–160.

Hajcak, G., Franklin, M. E., Foa, E. B., & Simons, R. F. (2008). Increased error-related brain activity in pediatric obsessive-compulsive disorder before and after treatment. *The American Journal of Psychiatry, 165*(1), 116–123.

Harries, M. D., Chamberlain, S. R., Redden, S. A., Odlaug, B. L., Blum, A. W., & Grant, J. E. (2017). A structural MRI study of excoriation (skin-picking) disorder and its relationship to clinical severity. *Psychiatry Research: Neuroimaging, 269*, 26–30.

Harrison, B. J., Pujol, J., Cardoner, N., Deus, J., Alonso, P., Lopez-Sola, M., Contreras-Rodriguez, O., Real, E., Segalas, C., Blanco-Hinojo, L., Menchon, J. M., & Soriano-Mas, C. (2013). Brain corticostriatal systems and the major clinical symptom dimensions of obsessive-compulsive disorder. *Biological Psychiatry, 73*(4), 321–328.

Heinzel, S., Kaufmann, C., Grutzmann, R., Hummel, R., Klawohn, J., Riesel, A., Bey, K., Lennertz, L., Wagner, M., & Kathmann, N. (2018). Neural correlates of working memory deficits and associations to response inhibition in obsessive compulsive disorder. *Neuroimage: Clinical, 17*, 426–434.

Hibar, D. P., Cheung, J. W., Medland, S. E., Mufford, M. S., Jahanshad, N., Dalvie, S., Ramesar, R., Stewart, E., van den Heuvel, O. A., Pauls, D. L., Knowles, J. A., Stein, D. J., & Thompson, P. M. (2018). Significant concordance of genetic variation that increases both the risk for obsessive-compulsive disorder and the volumes of the nucleus accumbens and putamen. *The British Journal of Psychiatry, 213*(1), 430–436.

Hoexter, M. Q., de Souza Duran, F. L., D'Alcante, C. C., Dougherty, D. D., Shavitt, R. G., Lopes, A. C., Lopes, A. C., Diniz, J. B., Deckersbach, T., Batistuzzo, M. C., Bressan, R. A., Miguel, E. C., & Busatto, G. F. (2012). Gray matter volumes in obsessive-compulsive disorder before and after fluoxetine or cognitive-behavior therapy: A randomized clinical trial. *Neuropsychopharmacology, 37*(3), 734–745.

Hough, C. M., Luks, T. L., Lai, K., Vigil, O., Guillory, S., Nongpiur, A., Fekri, S. M., Kupferman, E., Mathalon, D. H., & Mathews, C. A. (2016). Comparison of brain activation patterns during executive function tasks in hoarding disorder and non-hoarding OCD. *Psychiatry Research: Neuroimaging, 255*, 50–59.

Hu, X., Zhang, L., Bu, X., Li, H., Gao, Y., Lu, L., Tang, S., Wang, Y., Huang, X., & Gong, Q. (2020). White matter disruption in obsessive-compulsive disorder revealed by meta-analysis of tract-based spatial statistics. *Depression and Anxiety, 37*(7), 620–631.

Huggins, A. A., Harvey, A. M., Miskovich, T. A., Lee, H.-J., & Larson, C. L. (2020). Resting-state functional connectivity of supplementary motor area associated with skin-picking symptom severity. *Journal of Obsessive-Compulsive and Related Disorders, 26*, 100551.

Huyser, C., Veltman, D. J., Wolters, L. H., de Haan, E., & Boer, F. (2010). Functional magnetic resonance imaging during planning before and after cognitive-behavioral therapy in pediatric obsessive-compulsive disorder. *Journal of the American Academy of Child and Adolescent Psychiatry, 49*(12), 1238–1248.

International Obsessive Compulsive Disorder Foundation Genetics Collaborative (IOCDF-GC) and OCD Collaborative Genetics Association Studies (OCGAS). (2018). Revealing the complex genetic architecture of obsessive-compulsive disorder using meta-analysis. *Molecular Psychiatry, 23*(5), 1181–1188.

Isobe, M., Redden, S. A., Keuthen, N. J., Stein, D. J., Lochner, C., Grant, J. E., & Chamberlain, S. R. (2018). Striatal abnormalities in trichotillomania: A multi-site MRI analysis. *Neuroimage: Clinical, 17*, 893–898.

Jenkins, L. M., Barba, A., Campbell, M., Lamar, M., Shankman, S. A., Leow, A. D., Ajilore, O., & Langenecker, S. A. (2016). Shared white matter alterations across emotional disorders: A voxel-based meta-analysis of fractional anisotropy. . *Neuroimage: Clinical, 12*, 1022–1034.

Jung, W. H., Yucel, M., Yun, J. Y., Yoon, Y. B., Cho, K. I., Parkes, L., Kim, S. N., & Kwon, J. S. (2017). Altered functional network architecture in orbitofronto-striato-thalamic circuit of unmedicated patients with obsessive-compulsive disorder. *Human Brain Mapping*, *38*(1), 109–119.

Kim, G. W., Yoon, W., & Jeong, G. W. (2018). Whole-brain volume alteration and its correlation with anxiety severity in patients with obsessive-compulsive disorder and generalized anxiety disorder. *Clinical Imaging*, *50*, 164–170.

Levy, H. C., Stevens, M. C., Glahn, D. C., Pancholi, K., & Tolin, D. F. (2019). Distinct resting state functional connectivity abnormalities in hoarding disorder and major depressive disorder. *Journal of Psychiatric Research*, *113*, 108–116.

Li, W., Lai, T. M., Bohon, C., Loo, S. K., McCurdy, D., Strober, M., Bookheimer, S., & Feusner, J. (2015). Anorexia nervosa and body dysmorphic disorder are associated with abnormalities in processing visual information. *Psychological Medicine*, *45*(10), 2111–2122.

Liebrand, L. C., Caan, M. W. A., Schuurman, P. R., van den Munckhof, P., Figee, M., Denys, D., & van Wingen, G. A. (2019). Individual white matter bundle trajectories are associated with deep brain stimulation response in obsessive-compulsive disorder. *Brain Stimulation*, *12*(2), 353–360.

Madsen, S. K., Zai, A., Pirnia, T., Arienzo, D., Zhan, L., Moody, T. D., Thompson, P. M., & Feusner, J. D. (2015). Cortical thickness and brain volumetric analysis in body dysmorphic disorder. *Psychiatry Research*, *232*(1), 115–122.

Marazziti, D., Mucci, F., & Fontenelle, L. F. (2018). Immune system and obsessive-compulsive disorder. *Psychoneuroendocrinology*, *93*, 39–44.

Marin, M. F., Zsido, R. G., Song, H., Lasko, N. B., Killgore, W. D. S., Rauch, S. L., Simon, N. M., & Milad, M. R. (2017). Skin conductance responses and neural activations during fear conditioning and extinction recall across anxiety disorders. *JAMA Psychiatry*, *74*(6), 622–631.

Mataix-Cols, D., & van den Heuvel, O. A. (2006). Common and distinct neural correlates of obsessive-compulsive and related disorders. *Psychiatric Clinics Of North America*, *29*(2), 391–410, viii.

Matsumoto, R., Ichise, M., Ito, H., Ando, T., Takahashi, H., Ikoma, Y., Kosaka, J., Arakawa, R., Fujimura, Y., Ota, M., Takano, A., Fukui, K., Nakayama, K., & Suhara, T. (2010). Reduced serotonin transporter binding in the insular cortex in patients with obsessive-compulsive disorder: A [^{11}C]DASB PET study. *Neuroimage*, *49*(1), 121–126.

McTeague, L. M., Huemer, J., Carreon, D. M., Jiang, Y., Eickhoff, S. B., & Etkin, A. (2017). Identification of common neural circuit disruptions in cognitive control across psychiatric disorders. *The American Journal of Psychiatry*, *174*(7), 676–685.

McTeague, L. M., Rosenberg, B. M., Lopez, J. W., Carreon, D. M., Huemer, J., Jiang, Y., Chick, C. F., Eickhoff, S. B., & Etkin, A. (2020). Identification of common neural circuit disruptions in emotional processing across psychiatric disorders. *The American Journal of Psychiatry*, *177*(5), 411–421.

Milad, M. R., Furtak, S. C., Greenberg, J. L., Keshaviah, A., Im, J. J., Falkenstein, M. J., Jenike, M., Rauch, S. L., & Wilhelm, S. (2013). Deficits in conditioned fear extinction in obsessive-compulsive disorder and neurobiological changes in the fear circuit. *JAMA Psychiatry*, *70*(6), 608–618.

Milad, M. R., & Rauch, S. L. (2012). Obsessive-compulsive disorder: Beyond segregated cortico-striatal pathways. *Trends in Cognitive Sciences*, *16*(1), 43–51.

Miller, G. A., & Rockstroh, B. (2013). Endophenotypes in psychopathology research: Where do we stand? *Annual Review of Clinical Psychology*, *9*, 177–213.

Moody, T. D., Morfini, F., Cheng, G., Sheen, C. L., Kerr, W., Strober, M., & Feusner, J. D. (2020). Brain activation and connectivity in anorexia nervosa and body dysmorphic disorder when viewing bodies: Relationships to clinical symptoms and perception of appearance. *bioRxiv*, 2020.2002.2012.934083.

Moody, T. D., Morfini, F., Cheng, G., Sheen, C., Tadayonnejad, R., Reggente, N., O'Neill, J., & Feusner, J. D. (2017). Mechanisms of cognitive-behavioral therapy for obsessive-compulsive disorder involve robust and extensive increases in brain network connectivity. *Translational Psychiatry*, *7*(9), e1230.

Morgieve, M., N'Diaye, K., Haynes, W. I., Granger, B., Clair, A. H., Pelissolo, A., & Mallet, L. (2014). Dynamics of psychotherapy-related cerebral haemodynamic changes in obsessive compulsive disorder using a personalized exposure task in functional magnetic resonance imaging. *Psychological Medicine*, *44*(7), 1461–1473.

Moritz, S., Spirandelli, K., Happach, I., Lion, D., & Berna, F. (2018). Dysfunction by disclosure? Stereotype threat as a source of secondary neurocognitive malperformance in obsessive-compulsive disorder. *Journal of the International Neuropsychological Society*, *24*(6), 584–592.

Müller, V. I., Cieslik, E. C., Laird, A. R., Fox, P. T., Radua, J., Mataix-Cols, D., Tench, C. R., Yarkoni, T., Nichols, T. E., Turkeltaub, P. E., Wager, T. D., & Eickhoff, S. B. (2018). Ten simple rules for neuroimaging meta-analysis. *Neuroscience and Biobehavioral Reviews, 84*, 151–161.

Nabeyama, M., Nakagawa, A., Yoshiura, T., Nakao, T., Nakatani, E., Togao, O., Yoshizato, C., Yoshioka, K., Tomita, M., & Kanba, S. (2008). Functional MRI study of brain activation alterations in patients with obsessive-compulsive disorder after symptom improvement. *Psychiatry Research, 163*(3), 236–247.

Nichols, T. E., Das, S., Eickhoff, S. B., Evans, A. C., Glatard, T., Hanke, M., Kriegeskorte, N., Milham, M. P., Poldrack, R. A., Poline, J. B., Proal, E., Thirion, B., Van Essen, D. C., White, T., & Yeo, B. T. (2017). Best practices in data analysis and sharing in neuroimaging using MRI. *Nature Neuroscience, 20*(3), 299–303.

Norman, L. J., Carlisi, C., Lukito, S., Hart, H., Mataix-Cols, D., Radua, J., & Rubia, K. (2016). Structural and functional brain abnormalities in attention-deficit/hyperactivity disorder and obsessive-compulsive disorder: A comparative meta-analysis. *JAMA Psychiatry, 73*(8), 815–825.

Norman, L. J., Taylor, S. F., Liu, Y., Radua, J., Chye, Y., De Wit, S. J., Huyser, C., Karahanoglu, F. I., Luks, T., Manoach, D., Mathews, C., Rubia, K., Suo, C., van den Heuvel, O. A., Yucel, M., & Fitzgerald, K. (2019). Error processing and inhibitory control in obsessive-compulsive disorder: A meta-analysis using statistical parametric maps. *Biological Psychiatry, 85*(9), 713–725.

Odlaug, B. L., Chamberlain, S. R., Derbyshire, K. L., Leppink, E. W., & Grant, J. E. (2014). Impaired response inhibition and excess cortical thickness as candidate endophenotypes for trichotillomania. *Journal of Psychiatric Research, 59*, 167–173.

Odlaug, B. L., Hampshire, A., Chamberlain, S. R., & Grant, J. E. (2016). Abnormal brain activation in excoriation (skin-picking) disorder: Evidence from an executive planning fMRI study. *The British Journal of Psychiatry, 208*(2), 168–174.

O'Neill, J., Gorbis, E., Feusner, J. D., Yip, J. C., Chang, S., Maidment, K. M., Levitt, J. G., Salamon, N., Ringman, J. M., & Saxena, S. (2013). Effects of intensive cognitive-behavioral therapy on cingulate neurochemistry in obsessive-compulsive disorder. *Journal of Psychiatric Research, 47*(4), 494–504.

O'Neill, J., Piacentini, J., Chang, S., Ly, R., Lai, T. M., Armstrong, C. C., Bergman, L., Rozenman, M., Peris, T., Vreeland, A., Mudgway, R., Levitt, J. G., Salamon, N., Posse, S., Hellemann, G. S., Alger, J. R., McCracken, J. T., & Nurmi, E. L. (2017). Glutamate in pediatric obsessive-compulsive disorder and response to cognitive-behavioral therapy: Randomized clinical trial. *Neuropsychopharmacology, 42*(12), 2414–2422.

Peng, Z., Shi, F., Shi, C., Miao, G., Yang, Q., Gao, W., Wolff, J. J., Chan, R. C., & Shen, D. (2014). Structural and diffusion property alterations in unaffected siblings of patients with obsessive-compulsive disorder. *PLOS ONE, 9*(1), e85663.

Perani, D., Garibotto, V., Gorini, A., Moresco, R. M., Henin, M., Panzacchi, A., Matarrese, M., Carpinelli, A., Bellodi, L., & Fazio, F. (2008). In vivo PET study of $5HT_{2A}$ serotonin and D_2 dopamine dysfunction in drug-naive obsessive-compulsive disorder. *Neuroimage, 42*(1), 306–314.

Perera, M. P. N., Bailey, N. W., Herring, S. E., & Fitzgerald, P. B. (2019). Electrophysiology of obsessive compulsive disorder: A systematic review of the electroencephalographic literature. *Journal of Anxiety Disorders, 62*, 1–14.

Peris, T. S., Piacentini, J., Vreeland, A., Salgari, G., Levitt, J. G., Alger, J. R., Posse, S., McCracken, J. T., & O'Neill, J. (2020). Neurochemical correlates of behavioral treatment of pediatric trichotillomania. *Journal of Affective Disorders, 273*, 552–561.

Phillips, K. A., Stein, D. J., Rauch, S. L., Hollander, E., Fallon, B. A., Barsky, A., Fineberg, N., Mataix-Cols, D., Ferrao, Y. A., Saxena, S., Wilhelm, S., Kelly, M. M., Clark, L. A., Pinto, A., Bienvenu, O. J., Farrow, J., & Leckman, J. (2010). Should an obsessive-compulsive spectrum grouping of disorders be included in DSM-V? *Depression and Anxiety, 27*(6), 528–555.

Picó-Pérez, M., Moreira, P. S., de Melo Ferreira, V., Radua, J., Mataix-Cols, D., Sousa, N., Soriano-Mas, C., & Morgado, P. (2020). Modality-specific overlaps in brain structure and function in obsessive-compulsive disorder: Multimodal meta-analysis of case-control MRI studies. *Neuroscience and Biobehavioral Reviews, 112*, 83–94.

Piras, F., Piras, F., Abe, Y., Agarwal, S. M., Anticevic, A., Ameis, S., Arnold, P., Banaj, N., Bargalló, N., Batistuzzo, M. C., Benedetti, F., Beucke, J. C., Boedhoe, P. S. W., Bollettini, I., Brem, S., Calvo, A., Cho, K. I. K., Ciullo, V., Dallaspezia, S., . . . Spalletta, G. (2019). White matter microstructure and its relation to clinical features of obsessive-compulsive disorder: Findings from the ENIGMA OCD Working Group. *Translational Psychiatry, 11*(1), 173.

Radua, J., van den Heuvel, O. A., Surguladze, S., & Mataix-Cols, D. (2010). Meta-analytical comparison of voxel-based morphometry studies in obsessive-compulsive disorder vs other anxiety disorders. *Archives of General Psychiatry, 67*(7), 701–711.

Radua, J., Vieta, E., Shinohara, R., Kochunov, P., Quidé, Y., Green, M. J., Weickert, C. S., Weickert, T., Bruggemann, J., Kircher, T., Nenadić, I., Cairns, M. J., Seal, M., Schall, U., Henskens, F., Fullerton, J. M., Mowry, B., Pantelis, C., Lenroot, R., . . . van Erp, T. (2020). Increased power by harmonizing structural MRI site differences with the ComBat batch adjustment method in ENIGMA. *Neuroimage, 218*, 116956.

Riesel, A. (2019). The erring brain: Error-related negativity as an endophenotype for OCD—A review and meta-analysis. *Psychophysiology, 56*(4), e13348.

Riesel, A., Endrass, T., Auerbach, L. A., & Kathmann, N. (2015). Overactive performance monitoring as an endophenotype for obsessive-compulsive disorder: Evidence from a treatment study. *The American Journal of Psychiatry, 172*(7), 665–673.

Riesel, A., Endrass, T., Kaufmann, C., & Kathmann, N. (2011). Overactive error-related brain activity as a candidate endophenotype for obsessive-compulsive disorder: Evidence from unaffected first-degree relatives. *The American Journal of Psychiatry, 168*(3), 317–324.

Riesel, A., Klawohn, J., Grutzmann, R., Kaufmann, C., Heinzel, S., Bey, K., Lennertz, L., Wagner, M., & Kathmann, N. (2019). Error-related brain activity as a transdiagnostic endophenotype for obsessive-compulsive disorder, anxiety and substance use disorder. *Psychological Medicine, 49*(7), 1207–1217.

Robbins, T. W., Vaghi, M. M., & Banca, P. (2019). Obsessive-compulsive disorder: Puzzles and prospects. *Neuron, 102*(1), 27–47.

Roos, A., Grant, J. E., Fouche, J. P., Stein, D. J., & Lochner, C. (2015). A comparison of brain volume and cortical thickness in excoriation (skin picking) disorder and trichotillomania (hair pulling disorder) in women. *Behavioural Brain Research, 279*, 255–258.

Schienle, A., Potthoff, J., & Wabnegger, A. (2018). Voxel-based morphometry analysis of structural brain scans in skin-picking disorder. *Comprehensive Psychiatry, 84*, 82–86.

Schienle, A., Übel, S., & Wabnegger, A. (2018a). Neuronal responses to the scratching and caressing of one's own skin in patients with skin-picking disorder. *Human Brain Mapping, 39*(3), 1263–1269.

Schienle, A., Übel, S., & Wabnegger, A. (2018b). Visual symptom provocation in skin picking disorder: An fMRI study. *Brain Imaging and Behavior, 12*(5), 1504–1512.

Schienle, A., & Wabnegger, A. (2020). Two subtypes of pathological skin-picking: Evidence from a voxel-based morphometry study. *Journal of Obsessive-Compulsive and Related Disorders, 25*, 100534.

Schiepek, G., Tominschek, I., Heinzel, S., Aigner, M., Dold, M., Unger, A., Lenz, G., Windischberger, C., Moser, E., Ploderl, M., Lutz, J., Meindl, T., Zaudig, M., Pogarell, O., & Karch, S. (2013). Discontinuous patterns of brain activation in the psychotherapy process of obsessive-compulsive disorder: Converging results from repeated fMRI and daily self-reports. *PLOS ONE, 8*(8), e71863.

Shaw, P., Sharp, W., Sudre, G., Wharton, A., Greenstein, D., Raznahan, A., Evans, A., Chakravarty, M. M., Lerch, J. P., & Rapoport, J. (2015). Subcortical and cortical morphological anomalies as an endophenotype in obsessive-compulsive disorder. *Molecular Psychiatry, 20*(2), 224–231.

Shin, D. J., Jung, W. H., He, Y., Wang, J., Shim, G., Byun, M. S., Jang, J. H., Kim, S. N., Lee, T. Y., Park, H. Y., & Kwon, J. S. (2014). The effects of pharmacological treatment on functional brain connectome in obsessive-compulsive disorder. *Biological Psychiatry, 75*(8), 606–614.

Shin, L. M., & Liberzon, I. (2010). The neurocircuitry of fear, stress, and anxiety disorders. *Neuropsychopharmacology, 35*(1), 169–191.

Simpson, H. B., Lombardo, I., Slifstein, M., Huang, H. Y., Hwang, D. R., Abi-Dargham, A., Liebowitz, M. R., & Laruelle, M. (2003). Serotonin transporters in obsessive-compulsive disorder: A positron emission tomography study with [^{11}C]McN 5652. *Biological Psychiatry, 54*(12), 1414–1421.

Simpson, H. B., van den Heuvel, O. A., Miguel, E. C., Reddy, Y. C. J., Stein, D. J., Lewis-Fernández, R., Shavitt, R. G., Lochner, C., Pouwels, P. J. W., Narayanawamy, J. C., Venkatasubramanian, G., Hezel, D. M., Vriend, C., Batistuzzo, M. C., Hoexter, M. Q., de Joode, N. T., Costa, D. L., de Mathis, M. A., Sheshachala, K., . . . Wall, M. (2020). Toward identifying reproducible brain signatures of obsessive-compulsive profiles: Rationale and methods for a new global initiative. *BMC Psychiatry, 20*(1), 68.

Slikboer, R., Reser, M. P., Nedeljkovic, M., Castle, D. J., & Rossell, S. L. (2018). Systematic review of published primary studies of neuropsychology and neuroimaging in trichotillomania. *Journal of the International Neuropsychological Society, 24*(2), 188–205.

Stein, D. J., Costa, D. L. C., Lochner, C., Miguel, E. C., Reddy, Y. C. J., Shavitt, R. G., van den Heuvel, O. A., & Simpson, H. B. (2019). Obsessive-compulsive disorder. *Nature Reviews Disease Primers*, 5(1), 1–21.

Stein, D. J., Fineberg, N. A., Bienvenu, O. J., Denys, D., Lochner, C., Nestadt, G., Leckman, J. F., Rauch, S. L., & Phillips, K. A. (2010). Should OCD be classified as an anxiety disorder in DSM-V? *Depression and Anxiety*, 27(6), 495–506.

Stein, D. J., Kogan, C. S., Atmaca, M., Fineberg, N. A., Fontenelle, L. F., Grant, J. E., Matsunaga, H., Reddy, Y. C. J., Simpson, H. B., Thomsen, P. H., van den Heuvel, O. A., Veale, D., Woods, D. W., & Reed, G. M. (2016). The classification of obsessive-compulsive and related disorders in the ICD-11. *Journal of Affective Disorders*, 190, 663–674.

Stevens, M. C., Levy, H. C., Hallion, L. S., Wootton, B. M., & Tolin, D. F. (2020). Functional neuroimaging test of an emerging neurobiological model of hoarding disorder. *Biological Psychiatry: Cognitive Neuroscience and Neuroimaging*, 5(1), 68–75.

Suñol, M., Martínez-Zalacaín, I., Picó-Pérez, M., López-Solà, C., Real, E., Fullana, M., Pujol, J., Cardoner, N., Menchón, J. M., Alonso, P., & Soriano-Mas, C. (2020). Differential patterns of brain activation between hoarding disorder and obsessive-compulsive disorder during executive performance. *Psychological Medicine*, 50(4), 666–673.

Takagi, Y., Sakai, Y., Lisi, G., Yahata, N., Abe, Y., Nishida, S., Nakamae, T., Morimoto, J., Kawato, M., Narumoto, J., & Tanaka, S. C. (2017). A neural marker of obsessive-compulsive disorder from whole-brain functional connectivity. *Scientific Reports*, 7(1), 7538.

Thompson, P. M., Jahanshad, N., Ching, C. R. K., Salminen, L. E., Thomopoulos, S. I., Bright, J., Baune, B. T., Bertolín, S., Bralten, J., Bruin, W. B., Bülow, R., Chen, J., Chye, Y., Dannlowski, U., de Kovel, C. G. F., Donohoe, G., Eyler, L. T., Faraone, S. V., Favre, P., . . . Zelman, V. (2020). ENIGMA and global neuroscience: A decade of large-scale studies of the brain in health and disease across more than 40 countries. *Translational Psychiatry*, 10(1), 100.

Thorsen, A. L., de Wit, S. J., Hagland, P., Ousdal, O. T., Hansen, B., Kvale, G., & van den Heuvel, O. A. (2020). Stable inhibition-related inferior frontal hypoactivation and fronto-limbic hyperconnectivity in obsessive-compulsive disorder after concentrated exposure therapy. *Neuroimage Clin*.

Thorsen, A. L., Hagland, P., Radua, J., Mataix-Cols, D., Kvale, G., Hansen, B., & van den Heuvel, O. A. (2018). Emotional processing in obsessive-compulsive disorder: A systematic review and meta-analysis of 25 functional neuroimaging studies. *Biol Psychiatry Cogn Neurosci Neuroimaging*, 3(6), 563–571.

Thorsen, A. L., Kvale, G., Hansen, B., & van den Heuvel, O. A. (2018). Symptom dimensions in obsessive-compulsive disorder as predictors of neurobiology and treatment response. *Curr Treat Options Psychiatry*, 5(1), 182–194.

Thorsen, A. L., van den Heuvel, O. A., Hansen, B., & Kvale, G. (2015). Neuroimaging of psychotherapy for obsessive-compulsive disorder: A systematic review. *Psychiatry Res: Neuroimaging*, 233, 306–313.

Thorsen, A. L., Vriend, C., de Wit, S. J., Ousdal, O. T., Hagen, K., Hansen, B., . . . van den Heuvel, O. A. (2020). Effects of Bergen 4-day treatment on resting-state graph features in obsessive-compulsive disorder. *Biological Psychiatry: Cognitive Neuroscience and Neuroimaging*, 6(10), 973–982.

Tolin, D. F., Stevens, M. C., Villavicencio, A. L., Norberg, M. M., Calhoun, V. D., Frost, R. O., Steketee, G., Rauch, S. L., & Pearlson, G. D. (2012). Neural mechanisms of decision making in hoarding disorder. *Archives of General Psychiatry*, 69(8), 832–841.

Vaghi, M. M., Hampshire, A., Fineberg, N. A., Kaser, M., Bruhl, A. B., Sahakian, B. J., Chamberlain, S. R., & Robbins, T. W. (2017). Hypoactivation and dysconnectivity of a frontostriatal circuit during goal-directed planning as an endophenotype for obsessive-compulsive disorder. *Biological Psychiatry: Cognitive Neuroscience and Neuroimaging*, 2(8), 655–663.

Valente, A. A., Jr., Miguel, E. C., Castro, C. C., Amaro, E., Jr., Duran, F. L., Buchpiguel, C. A., Chitnis, X., McGuire, P. K., & Busatto, G. F. (2005). Regional gray matter abnormalities in obsessive-compulsive disorder: A voxel-based morphometry study. *Biological Psychiatry*, 58(6), 479–487.

van den Heuvel, O. A., Boedhoe, P. S. W., Bertolin, S., Bruin, W. B., Francks, C., Ivanov, I., Jahanshad, N., Kong, X. Z., Kwon, J. S., O'Neill, J., Paus, T., Patel, Y., Piras, F., Schmaal, L., Soriano-Mas, C., Spalletta, G., van Wingen, G. A., Yun, J. Y., Vriend, C., . . . Stein, D. J.(2020). An overview of the first 5 years of the ENIGMA obsessive-compulsive disorder working group: The power of worldwide collaboration. *Human Brain Mapping* 43(1), 23–36.

van den Heuvel, O. A., Mataix-Cols, D., Zwitser, G., Cath, D. C., van der Werf, Y. D., Groenewegen, H. J., van Balkom, A. J., & Veltman, D. J.(2011). Common limbic and frontal-striatal disturbances in patients with obsessive compulsive disorder, panic disorder and hypochondriasis. *Psychol Med*, *41*(11), 2399–2410.

van den Heuvel, O. A., van Wingen, G., Soriano-Mas, C., Alonso, P., Chamberlain, S. R., Nakamae, T., Denys, D., Goudriaan, A. E., & Veltman, D. J. (2016). Brain circuitry of compulsivity. *European Neuropsychopharmacology*, *26*(5), 810–827.

van den Heuvel, O. A., Veltman, D. J., Groenewegen, H. J., Cath, D. C., van Balkom, A. J., van Hartskamp, J., Barkhof, F., & van Dyck, R. (2005). Frontal-striatal dysfunction during planning in obsessive-compulsive disorder. *Archives of General Psychiatry*, *62*(3), 301–309.

van der Wee, N. J., Stevens, H., Hardeman, J. A., Mandl, R. C., Denys, D. A., van Megen, H. J., Kahn, R. S., & Westenberg, H. M. (2004). Enhanced dopamine transporter density in psychotropic-naive patients with obsessive-compulsive disorder shown by [^{123}I]{beta}-CIT SPECT. *The American Journal of Psychiatry*, *161*(12), 2201–2206.

Vaughn, D. A., Kerr, W. T., Moody, T. D., Cheng, G. K., Morfini, F., Zhang, A., Leow, A. D., Strober, M. A., Cohen, M. S., & Feusner, J. D. (2019). Differentiating weight-restored anorexia nervosa and body dysmorphic disorder using neuroimaging and psychometric markers. *PLOS ONE*, *14*(5), e0213974.

Versace, A., Graur, S., Greenberg, T., Lima Santos, J. P., Chase, H. W., Bonar, L., Stiffler, R. S., Hudak, R., Kim, T., Yendiki, A., Greenberg, B., Rasmussen, S., Liu, H., Haber, S., & Phillips, M. L. (2019). Reduced focal fiber collinearity in the cingulum bundle in adults with obsessive-compulsive disorder. *Neuropsychopharmacology*, *44*(7), 1182–1188.

Vester, E. L., de Joode, N. T., Vriend, C., Pouwels, P. J. W., & van den Heuvel, O. A. (2020). Little evidence for neurometabolite alterations in obsessive-compulsive disorder—A systematic review of magnetic resonance spectroscopy studies at 3 Tesla. *Journal of Obsessive-Compulsive and Related Disorders*, *25*, 100523.

Vulink, N. C., Planting, R. S., Figee, M., Booij, J., & Denys, D. (2016). Reduced striatal dopamine D$_{2/3}$ receptor availability in body dysmorphic disorder. *European Neuropsychopharmacology*, *26*(2), 350–356.

Wabnegger, A., & Schienle, A. (2019). The role of the cerebellum in skin-picking disorder. *Cerebellum*, *18*(1), 91–98.

Wabnegger, A., Übel, S., Suchar, G., & Schienle, A. (2018). Increased emotional reactivity to affective pictures in patients with skin-picking disorder: Evidence from functional magnetic resonance imaging. *Behavioural Brain Research*, *336*, 151–155.

Weeland, C. J., White, T., Vriend, C., Muetzel, R., Starreveld, J., HIllegers, M., Tiemeier, H., & van den Heuvel, O. A. (2020). Subcortical and cortical brain morphology associated with obsessive-compulsive symptoms in 2551 children from the general population. *Journal of the American Academy of Child and Adolescent Psychiatry*,

Weidt, S., Lutz, J., Rufer, M., Delsignore, A., Jakob, N. J., Herwig, U., & Bruehl, A. B. (2016). Common and differential alterations of general emotion processing in obsessive-compulsive and social anxiety disorder. *Psychological Medicine*, *46*(7), 1427–1436.

White, M. P., Shirer, W. R., Molfino, M. J., Tenison, C., Damoiseaux, J. S., & Greicius, M. D. (2013). Disordered reward processing and functional connectivity in trichotillomania: a pilot study. *Journal of Psychiatric Research*, *47*(9), 1264–1272.

Yamada, S., Nakao, T., Ikari, K., Kuwano, M., Murayama, K., Tomiyama, H., Hasuzawa, S., Togao, O., Hiwatashi, A., & Kanba, S. (2018). A unique increase in prefrontal gray matter volume in hoarding disorder compared to obsessive-compulsive disorder. *PLOS ONE*, *13*(7), e0200814.

Yue, W., Cheng, W., Liu, Z., Tang, Y., Lu, T., Zhang, D., Tang, M., & Huang, Y. (2016). Genome-wide DNA methylation analysis in obsessive-compulsive disorder patients. *Sci Rep*, *6*, 31333.

Yun, J. Y., Boedhoe, P. S. W., Vriend, C., Jahanshad, N., Abe, Y., Ameis, S. H., Anticevic, A., Arnold, P. D., Batistuzzo, M. C., Benedetti, F., Beucke, J. C., Bollettini, I., Bose, A., Brem, S., Calvo, A., Cheng, Y., Cho, K. I. K., Ciullo, V., Dallaspezia, S., . . . Kwon, J. S. (2020). Brain structural covariance networks in obsessive-compulsive disorder: a graph analysis from the ENIGMA Consortium. *Brain*, *143*(2), 684–700.

Zhang, A., Leow, A., Zhan, L., GadElkarim, J., Moody, T., Khalsa, S., Strober, M., & Feusner, J. D. (2016). Brain connectome modularity in weight-restored anorexia nervosa and body dysmorphic disorder. *Psychological Medicine*, *46*(13), 2785–2797.

Zheng, H., Yang, W., Zhang, B., Hua, G., Wang, S., Jia, F., Guo, G., Wang, W., & Quan, D. (2020). Reduced anterior cingulate glutamate of comorbid skin-picking disorder in adults with obsessive-compulsive disorder. *Journal of Affective Disorders*, *265*, 193–199.

Zhong, Z., Yang, X., Cao, R., Li, P., Li, Z., Lv, L., & Zhang, D. (2019). Abnormalities of white matter microstructure in unmedicated patients with obsessive-compulsive disorder: Changes after cognitive behavioral therapy. *Brain and Behavior*, *9*(2), e01201.

Zhou, C., Cheng, Y., Ping, L., Xu, J., Shen, Z., Jiang, L., Shi, L., Yang, S., Lu, Y., & Xu, X. (2018). Support vector machine classification of obsessive-compulsive disorder based on whole-brain volumetry and diffusion tensor imaging. *Frontiers in Psychiatry*, *9*, 524.

Zitterl, W., Aigner, M., Stompe, T., Zitterl-Eglseer, K., Gutierrez-Lobos, K., Schmidl-Mohl, B., Wenzel, T., Demal, U., Zettinig, G., Hornik, K., & Thau, K.(2007). [^{123}I]-beta-CIT SPECT imaging shows reduced thalamus-hypothalamus serotonin transporter availability in 24 drug-free obsessive-compulsive checkers. *Neuropsychopharmacology*, *32*(8), 1661–1668.

CHAPTER 8

Information Processing in Obsessive-Compulsive and Related Disorders

Gillian M. Alcolado, Martha Giraldo-O'Meara, Sandra C. Krause, Mark W. Leonhart, *and* Adam S. Radomsky

Abstract

Information-processing (IP) is increasingly understood to be closely related to the cognitions and behaviors symptomatic of a wide range of disorders. This chapter covers key research on the state of IP differences (whether they be biases and/or deficits) seen in the obsessive-compulsive and related disorders. These disorders include obsessive-compulsive disorder, hoarding disorder, body dysmorphic disorder, trichotillomania (hair-pulling disorder), and excoriation (skin-picking disorder). The chapter elucidates how each IP phenomenon appears to be related to its associated disorder. Conclusions are drawn about the relatedness of the disorders based on IP similarities and differences. Remaining uncertainties and gaps in the literature are identified and recommendations for future research that would clarify such questions are discussed.

Key Words: obsessive-compulsive disorder, body dysmorphic disorder, hoarding disorder, trichotillomania (hair-pulling disorder), excoriation (skin-picking disorder), information processing

Introduction

This chapter covers information processing (IP) phenomena seen in obsessive-compulsive and related disorders (OCRDs). This category of mental disorders was first specified in the 5th edition of the *Diagnostic and Statistical Manual of Mental Disorders* (*DSM-5*) based on the assertion that there was increasing evidence that they may be related and that there was clinical utility in doing so (American Psychiatric Association [APA], 2013). The OCRDs are obsessive-compulsive disorder (OCD), hoarding disorder (HD), body dysmorphic disorder (BDD), trichotillomania (TTM; hair-pulling disorder), and excoriation (skin-picking disorder; SPD). A recent study determined the transdiagnostic commonality among the disorders to be (based on expert consensus) that they all share features of compulsivity, habit formation, performance monitoring, and response selection/inhibition (Fontenelle et al., 2020); however, there are good reasons to view the new categorization as problematic from numerous perspectives (Phillips et al., 2010; Storch et al., 2008). Of course, there are major differences between the disorders, as some appear to be more cognitively based (e.g., OCD, BDD, HD), whereas others are more focused on repetitive behaviors (TTM, SPD; Van Ameringen et al., 2014). Although the OCRD group is clearly not an optimal classification (Stein & Phillips, 2014), it is hoped that, at the very least, the categorization will be the impetus for further research that will help determine to what extent the disorders are associated (Goodman, 2014).

Examination of IP in mental health conditions became relevant because of the increasing recognition of the interplay not just between behaviors and thoughts, but also with the cognitive processes that might influence what is perceived, and how actions are carried out (Beck & Clark, 1988; Hofmann et al., 2013). The OCRDs each have theoretical models comprising psychological processes which contribute to our understanding of them. Some of these disorders do not necessarily have an information processing component overtly included in their theoretical models (e.g., OCD), while others do (e.g., BDD, HD). Regardless, deeper understanding of the mechanisms and symptoms of obsessive-compulsive and related disorders contributes to improved theoretical understanding, and thereby better characterization, prevention, detection, and intervention with these problems. The field of research on information processing biases and deficits in OCRDs can contribute important data towards this goal. Further, examining information processing styles in OCRDs may clarify common and distinct processes among the disorders.

The goals of this chapter are threefold: 1) to better understand the information processing characteristics associated with OCRDs, 2) to elucidate the extent to which the current state of these findings are helpful in conceptualizing the disorders, and 3) to use these phenomena to better understand how there may be differences and similarities among OCRDs.

OCD

OCD is characterized by the presence of obsessions (i.e., intrusive thoughts, images, or impulses that give rise to subjective distress) and/or compulsions (i.e., repetitive or ritualistic behaviors; APA, 2013). Cognitive-affective scientific knowledge on perception, attention, learning, and memory (Mowrer, 1951) has been highly influential in the development of current cognitive-behavioral models of OCD. Over the years, researchers have often sought to explain the repetitive thoughts and behaviors characteristic of this disorder through an information processing lens, examining possible biases and deficits in perception, attention, and memory in those with OCD. The previous edition of this chapter outlined the bulk of the seminal research in this domain. Since its publication, our understanding of some of these existing phenomena has shifted, and some new relevant cognitive processes have come to light. Thus, this section will provide an updated review of literature on the role of information processing in OCD.

Visual Perception Biases

Several theories propose a bias toward threatening stimuli in OCD, but research to support these findings has been mixed in OCD (Armstrong & Olatunji, 2012). Some have proposed that this may be because the emotion of disgust plays a larger role in OCD than fear, particularly for those with contamination-related concerns. In a meta-analysis of studies that examined possible facial expression recognition biases or deficits in individuals with OCD, Daros and colleagues (2014) observed an overall emotion recognition deficit in individuals with OCD as compared to healthy controls. However, they found that this overall deficit was mostly accounted for by deficits in the recognition of emotions of disgust and anger. Further, they found that individuals with OCD were more likely to interpret ambiguous facial expressions as disgust rather than as anger (Jhung et al., 2010; Sprengelmeyer et al., 1997). Taken together, these findings suggest that disgust may be a particularly threatening emotion to individuals with OCD, who seem to demonstrate altered cognitive processing of disgust-related information, and a perceptual bias toward facial expressions of disgust. That said, given the absence of clinical control groups in these studies, the specificity of this bias to OCD compared to other disorders remains unknown.

Individuals with OCD also show some perceptual differences when it comes to integrating complex sensory data, more broadly, which might manifest in OCD-relevant scenarios (Ouimet et al., 2019). For example, those with OCD performed worse than healthy controls on a task that required them to indicate whether two different images of bodies had the same or different postures (Shin et al., 2013). Individuals with OCD had difficulties with accuracy and speed on a task where individuals where asked to monitor various qualities (i.e., type, location, direction) of characters on a screen (Tumkaya et al., 2013). Differences in ability to integrate in both of these studies suggest a lack of a holistic visual processing, instead perhaps one that is focused on specific details of visual stimuli. Lack of clinical control groups in these studies limit the interpretability of these results.

Researchers sought to explore whether this also translated to a perceptual bias of object sizes. To test this, Moritz and colleagues (2011) showed individuals with and without OCD a series of images of different sizes, some OCD-relevant (i.e., contamination- and checking-related), and controls (i.e., neutral, and threatening but not OCD-relevant). After viewing the images, participants were asked to report how large each image was. The researchers found that OCD-relevant images were rated as being significantly larger by those with OCD relative to healthy controls. For neutral items, however, the opposite pattern emerged. Though unclear whether this reflects a perceptual bias (i.e., a bias in the way the images were initially encoded) or a memory bias (i.e., a bias in the way the information about the images was recalled), it indicates that this overestimation of threat extends to the perception of object size. However, due to the lack of a clinical control group, it remains unclear whether this effect is present in other disorders.

As one of the hallmarks of OCD is intrusive and distressing mental imagery, researchers have investigated the role of visual perspective on intrusive imagery in individuals with OCD. Findings on the nature of visual perspective in OCD are mixed. Some research has found that individuals with OCD are more likely than healthy undergraduates and anxious controls to experience mental imagery through their own eyes, known as field perspective (Coughtrey et al., 2013). This perspective is typically associated with greater vividness, affective intensity, and sensory detail than those recalled from an observer perspective. However, other experimental studies have found the opposite—that higher OCD symptomatology was correlated with experiencing mental imagery from an observer perspective, perhaps indicating higher levels of cognitive avoidance (Grisham et al., 2019). Given the limited large-scale, controlled study on visual perspective in this population, definitive conclusions about the nature of visual perspective of mental imagery in OCD cannot be drawn at this time.

Attentional Biases and Priming

It is theorized that individuals with OCD attend more to stimuli in their environment that are associated with their primary fears. There are two main hypotheses that have been proposed to explain possible mechanisms for this attention bias. The vigilance hypothesis suggests that these biases result from a hypervigilance toward OCD symptom-related stimuli (Armstrong & Olatunji, 2012). In other words, people with OCD are more likely to orient their gaze toward threatening stimuli associated with their idiosyncratic obsessions and compulsions (e.g., knives) than toward neutral stimuli in their environment (e.g., a book). By contrast, the maintenance hypothesis suggests that rather than being hypervigilant toward threatening stimuli, individuals with OCD, instead, have difficulties disengaging from threatening stimuli (Georgiou et al., 2005). According to this hypothesis, it is not that people with OCD focus on threatening stimuli (e.g., knives) more quickly, but rather that they overly fixate on these stimuli or have a difficult time turning their attention away toward something else. While the vigilance hypothesis has been associated with a more primary level stimulus-driven shift in attention, the maintenance hypothesis is associated more closely with higher-level goal directed systems in cognition.

In an effort to evaluate these competing hypotheses, researchers have begun to use eye tracking paradigms to compare the speed of individuals' first fixations on threatening stimuli (i.e., evidence for the vigilance hypothesis) with the total amount of time individuals spend looking at threatening stimuli (i.e., evidence for the maintenance hypothesis). In a meta-analysis of eye-tracking studies, Armstrong and Olatunji (2012) found that individuals with anxiety disorders oriented their gaze toward threatening stimuli more than did non-anxious controls. Though this lends support for the vigilance hypothesis, the studies included in this meta-analysis collapsed across all anxiety disorders. Research that has evaluated these hypotheses within purely OCD samples has been more mixed. Some have replicated support for the vigilance hypothesis (Armstrong et al., 2012). Others have found greater support for a maintenance bias (Armstrong et al., 2010; Bradley et al., 2016; Cludius et al., 2019), particularly for those with contamination-related OCD (Rouel & Smith, 2018).

These mixed findings may in part be explained by the heterogeneous and idiosyncratic nature of OCD. Specifically, "threat" can be defined very differently for different individuals depending on the nature of their symptoms, thus making it difficult to design experimental stimuli that capture universal threat. For example, someone with harm-related obsessions may find sharp objects threatening, but see blood stains as neutral, whereas someone with contamination-related OCD might have the opposite view. Given the inconsistent findings and methodological issues from current research, it is difficult to make any definitive conclusions about which hypothesis best explains attentional biases in OCD. Future research should consider different OCD symptom domains and idiosyncratic definitions of threat as well as clarify the relevance of such findings to this specific population through the inclusion of non-OCD clinical control groups.

PRIMING

A phenomenon called the "negative priming effect" is demonstrated by slower responses to items in the environment that individuals were previously told to ignore (May et al., 1995). This effect is normative; however, it was hypothesized that individuals with OCD may not exhibit the negative priming effect due to deficits in cognitive inhibition. Researchers have employed a variety of different experimental paradigms that involve asking participants to focus on certain stimuli and ignore others, and subsequently ask them to focus on the previously ignored stimuli. In doing so, they have found that while anxious controls exhibit the typical negative priming effect, this effect is absent in those with OCD (Kathmann et al., 2013). Moreover, some researchers have found evidence for a positive priming effect in those with OCD (Enright & Beech, 1993a, 1993b). In other words, having previously seen a probe stimulus as a distractor allowed individuals with OCD to respond to it faster, whereas those with anxiety displayed delayed responding to these same stimuli. One explanation for such findings is that individuals with OCD may have a more difficult time ignoring irrelevant information in their environment. However, it is also possible that this might, instead, reflect a tendency to process and retain more information in general or to treat information as more significant or meaningful than those without OCD.

Nevertheless, like research on other attentional biases, further examination of this effect has demonstrated that the nature and intensity of this deficit in negative priming is partially moderated by the content of individuals' OCD symptomatology. For example, researchers have found that this effect is more characteristic of individuals who check compulsively than of those with other forms of OCD (Hoenig et al., 2002). Further, researchers have shown that this effect is particularly pronounced when using personally relevant threating stimuli (Amir et al., 2009). That said, many studies that have taken extra care to address previous methodological issues and inconsistencies have not found any of these deficits in individuals with OCD (Abedininasab et al., 2012; Moritz et al., 2010). Thus, the evidence for the presence of negative priming and/or cognitive inhibition deficits in OCD is far from conclusive.

Encoding Biases

Past research has suggested that the impaired memory performance seen in participants with OCD appeared to be mediated by poor encoding strategies (Savage et al., 1999, 2000). More recently, researchers have identified additional factors including cognitive self-consciousness (i.e., the tendency to be aware of and to monitor one's thoughts and cognitive processes) to explain poorer performance on encoding tasks in those with OCD (Kikul et al., 2012; Lewin et al., 2014). In other words, the issue may not have been in retrieving stored memories, but rather a disruption in the encoding of the information in the first place due to the heightened cognitive resources required for cognitive self-consciousness that may take away from those required for task encoding (Kikul et al., 2012).

Memory

EXPLICIT MEMORY AND METAMEMORY

Many patients with OCD often claim that they "can't remember whether" something was properly checked, cleaned, counted, etc. Though many researchers have investigated the presence of possible deficits in explicit memory, evidence has been mixed (for a review, see Coles & Heimberg, 2002). A meta-analysis conducted in 2013 further concluded that even in studies where relative impairments were found, none were of clinical significance (Abramovitch et al., 2013). Using more ecologically valid methods, researchers have failed to find deficits in verbal memory in those with OCD (Radomsky et al., 2001) and have instead found heightened verbal memory capabilities (Radomsky & Rachman, 1999).

Experimental research seems to suggest that compulsive checking and doubt in OCD may actually be a result of issues with *metamemory* processes, such as memory confidence and thought monitoring, rather than deficits in memory capabilities (van den Hout & Kindt, 2003a). There is now a robust literature suggesting a reciprocal relationship between frequent checking and reduced memory confidence, wherein reduced confidence leads people to check, which, in turn, lessens people's confidence in their memory, reinforcing this cycle (Alcolado & Radomsky, 2011; Boschen & Vuksanovic, 2007; Radomsky & Alcolado, 2010; Radomsky et al., 2006; van den Hout & Kindt 2003a; 2003b). It seems, then, that checking and doubt are best explained by decreased memory confidence in those with OCD rather than by deficits in visual or verbal memory capabilities.

MEMORY BIASES

Many individuals with OCD can recall—often with striking detail—large amounts of information (visual and otherwise) related to past fears, triggers, and threatening situations (Radomsky & Rachman, 1999). When using more ecologically valid paradigms, researchers have found a memory bias in favor of threatening information for those with OCD (Ceschi et al., 2003; Radomsky & Rachman, 1999; Radomsky et al., 2001). This memory bias is particularly pronounced when individuals' perceptions of responsibility are higher (Radomsky et al., 2001), and may be absent when the experimental *task* (as opposed to the stimuli) is not specifically related to participants' concerns. These results suggest that participants must perceive both the information and the context as important and significant in order for memory biases to occur (Radomsky et al., 2001; Radomsky & Rachman, 2004).

Reduced Access to Internal States
There are many different theories that have emerged to explain pervasive doubt in OCD. One such theory is the Seeking Proxies for Internal States hypothesis (SPIS; Lazarov et al., 2010, 2012a, 2012b; Liberman & Dar, 2009). According to this model, people with OCD tend to have greater uncertainty about their internal states, including cognitive (e.g., memory), affective (e.g., emotions), and bodily (e.g., muscle tension) states. The authors also propose that actual reduced access to internal states is further decreased by doubt (Lazarov et al., 2015). In order to compensate for this reduced access to these internal states, people with OCD rely on less ambiguous external proxies instead, such as rules and rituals (Liberman & Dar, 2009). For example, to determine whether a person is dirty or contaminated, a person might try to monitor the number of seconds they spend washing their hands on a given day, rather than their internal sensations of cleanliness.

Most evidence in support of the SPIS has employed experimental paradigms that involve the use of biofeedback as an external proxy for the internal state of muscle tension versus relaxation. In doing so, researchers have found that individuals high in OC symptoms are less accurate than those low in OC symptoms at these relaxation and muscle tension tasks without biofeedback (Lazarov et al., 2010, 2012b). Further, those high in OC symptoms also relied more heavily on false feedback when asked to judge their own internal states compared to both healthy and anxious controls (Lazarov et al., 2012a, 2014), indicating that this difficulty appears to be specific to OCD. Finally, Liberman and Dar (2018) have more recently demonstrated that those with greater OCD symptomatology rely more heavily on external proxies for internal states in everyday life as well, suggesting that these findings occur even outside of the laboratory environment.

Effects of Treatment
If biases in information processing are indeed important factors that contribute to the development and maintenance of OCD (and related problems), then current effective

treatments for OCD (for a review, see Öst et al., 2015) may directly or indirectly correct the bias(es) in information processing. Findings in this area, however, have been relatively mixed, with several studies reporting no change in cognitive function following treatment for OCD and others reporting changes in particular domains of cognitive functioning (Vandborg et al., 2012). As such, this might suggest that these biases may either be not fully relevant to OCD symptomatology, and/or not malleable states, but rather enduring traits.

There is evidence to suggest that attentional biases can be improved following both psychological (Foa & McNally, 1986) and medication treatment (Sanz et al., 2001). More recently, interventions have been developed to directly target attentional biases in various anxiety disorders. Termed attentional bias modification (ABM) programs, these interventions typically involve computer training techniques to reduce attentional biases. In individuals with elevated contamination fears, ABM was effective at reducing attentional biases and avoidance of contamination threats at a 1-month follow-up but did not lead to a reduction in OCD symptomatology (Najmi & Amir, 2010; Rouel & Smith, 2018). Therefore, it seems that treatments targeting OCD symptoms may improve relevant attentional biases. However, correcting attentional biases may not improve OCD symptomatology. This provides possible clues for the direction of the relationship between these factors, suggesting that OCD symptoms may precede the attentional biases seen in the disorder.

Researchers have developed cognitive training programs for patients with OCD, consisting of sessions aimed at improving organizational encoding strategies. Interestingly, not only does this intervention seem to improve memory function in these individuals, it was also found to reduce OCD symptomatology (Buhlmann, Deckersbach, et al., 2006; Park et al., 2006).

Some studies have also investigated the opposite relationship (i.e., the impact of treatment aimed at reducing OCD symptomatology on encoding strategies). In doing so, several studies have found a correlation between reductions in OCD symptomatology and improvements in encoding strategies and cognitive inhibition following CBT intervention (Kuelz et al., 2006; Moritz et al., 1999). Kuelz and colleagues (2006) have explained this correlation by suggesting that one mechanism through which CBT might improve both OCD symptomatology and encoding strategies is via improvements in cognitive flexibility.

In a review paper on the impact of treatment on memory and executive function in individuals with OCD, Vandborg and colleagues (2012) highlight the inconsistency in findings of research on this topic. Namely, small sample sizes and the absence of control groups in many of the studies make it difficult to draw conclusions about the impact of CBT and pharmacotherapy on memory processes in OCD. However, in a more rigorously designed study, researchers found that visuospatial memory difficulties in those with OCD remained unchanged after a course of CBT (Vandborg et al., 2015).

Though the performance of individuals with OCD on memory tasks seems to remain unchanged after psychotherapeutic and pharmacotherapeutic interventions, it begs the question, then, of how to explain the reductions in doubt and checking seen after CBT. It seems that the mechanism of action might in fact be the metamemory processes discussed above, rather than memory capabilities. In one experimental study, participants who were provided with the false feedback that they had excellent memories showed an increase in memory confidence and decrease in subsequent doubt and urges to check (Alcolado & Radomsky, 2011), suggesting a potential treatment target. Researchers have since incorporated cognitive-behavioral strategies aimed directly at enhancing memory confidence in those with OCD into treatment protocols for the disorder (Radomsky et al., 2010), and one such intervention has found improvement on neuropsychological tasks of memory performance after treatment (Alcolado & Radomsky, 2016). Moreover, memory confidence improved after it was targeted in this type of intervention, and these changes were predictive of reductions in checking behavior (Alcolado & Radomsky, 2016; Radomsky et al., 2020). Therefore, it appears that visual memory may not be impacted by existing treatments for OCD. However, it seems that metamemory processes—which appear to be more relevant to OCD symptomatology and functional outcomes—do improve after CBT intervention.

HD

HD is a relatively new diagnosis, first articulated about 25 years ago (for a historical review, see Grisham & Baldwin, 2015). Hoarding was previously considered a symptom of OCD and/or obsessive-compulsive personality disorder (APA, 2000). It was not a separate diagnosis until 2013, with the publication of the *DSM-5* (APA, 2013). HD is characterized by difficulty with discarding possessions due to the distress attempts to do so cause (Mataix-Cols et al., 2010). This leads to excessive clutter that impedes one's movement and prevents proper function of living spaces (e.g., a stovetop or bed rendered unusable due to the accumulation of items on the surface; Mataix-Cols et al., 2010). Additionally, the large majority of individuals with HD (approximately 80%) struggle with "excessive acquisition" i.e., acquiring or purchasing large quantities of items that they might not need and for which they do not have space (Albert et al., 2015).

The cognitive-behavioral model of hoarding is one of only two OCRDs that include IP deficits as part of itsconceptualization (the other being BDD). HD's more typical CBT components include addressing problems with avoidance and unhelpful beliefs about possessions. Sufferers also are thought to have increased emotional attachment to possessions. The hypothesized IP deficits are in categorization/organization, decision-making, and memory (Frost & Hartl, 1996). It is proposed that these information processing patterns underlie preexisting vulnerabilities that lead an individual to be more susceptible to develop hoarding in the context of other genetic and/or environmental factors (for a review, see Dozier & Ayers, 2017). This section primarily focuses on these etiologically relevant domains, along with other relevant research.

Perception and Processing

Visual perception/detection has not been studied much in HD. One study (Mackin et al., 2016) found individuals with HD performed worse than age-matched controls as evidenced by their visual detection scores from the Connors' Continuous Performance Test. Importantly, the authors note this difference was only statistical, as the performance of HD participants was not in the impaired range. This finding suggests that impaired visual detection is not central to the disorder. A visual processing style that is detail-oriented is hypothesized to be linked to increased emotional attachment that individuals with HD exhibit (Chou et al., 2018). Worse scores on the drawing process of the Rey-Osterrieth Complex Figure Task (RCFT) in individuals with HD compared to healthy controls were interestingly not predictive of HD severity. They were, however, predictive of intensity of emotional attachment to objects (Chou et al., 2018). This suggests visual processing style may play a role in the development of the disorder, although the presence of a clinical control group would clarify whether this is specific to HD only.

Slower processing speed was found in older adults with HD and depression, as compared to older adults with only depression (Mackin et al., 2011), when using the Symbol Digit Modalities Test. The use of the older and depressed sample as a control group makes it more likely that this difference is attributable to HD, rather than simply to distress. Perhaps this slowed speed contributes to timely sorting of possessions, although the study authors did not interpret the meaning of this finding, as their study assessed other IP processes (see below).

Attention

As many individuals with HD have high levels of self-reported difficulties with attention, and the comorbidity between ADHD and HD is high, it is reasonable that one would investigate attentional processes in this disorder (for a review, see Timpano et al., 2014). Research, however, has revealed that there is more evidence for perceived attentional difficulties, or low-self confidence in their attentional difficulties, rather than real deficits (for a review, see Woody et al., 2014).

Basic attentional processes appear intact in HD, as found in one study (McMillan & Rees, 2013). Participants with clinical levels of hoarding symptoms scored in the normal range on the digit span subtest of the Weschler Adult Intelligence Scale (WAIS-III) and Spatial Span subtest of the Weschler Memory Scale (WMS-R). Similarly, a neurophysiological study found that individuals with symptoms of hoarding compared to healthy controls did not exhibit any differences in electroencephalography (EEG) during an attentional assessment (Baldwin et al., 2018). In contrast, a different group found evidence of difficulties on the digit span task in clinical hoarders (Ayers et al., 2013). A review of the literature concluded that individuals with HD do not exhibit problems with selective or shifting of attention (Timpano et al., 2014). Indeed, individuals with HD may have some strengths in their attentional processing. In alignment with this assertion, one study has shown that level of hoarding symptoms (in a nonclinical sample) predicted more of an attentional bias towards positive faces as measured by eye-tracking (Arditte et al., 2019).

Memory

Although memory deficits are predicted by the cognitive-behavioral model of HD, the evidence for a deficit remains unclear (see Timpano et al., 2014, for a review). There is, on the other hand, strong evidence of a lack of memory *confidence* (see Grisham & Baldwin, 2015, for a review, and below). An early study (Hartl et al., 2004) found that individuals with hoarding symptoms, as compared to healthy controls (matched on a number of demographic variables including age and sex), exhibited differences in visual and verbal recall (assessed via the RCFT and the California Verbal Learning Test [CVLT], respectively). Interestingly, poorer organizational strategies (which can contribute to difficulties encoding and remembering information) were seen in the hoarding individuals on the RCFT but not the CVLT (Hartl et al., 2004). This finding corroborates other evidence (see above) that visual processing style is different in HD and may explain and/or contribute to poor memory in HD. Twenty percent of participants in the sample had comorbid OCD, however, and the lack of a clinical control limits both the specificity and generalizability of the findings.

A more recent study (Mackin et al., 2016) has also found verbal memory (using the Hopkins Verbal Learning Test–Revised) and visuospatial memory difficulties (using the Brief Visuospatial Memory Test–Revised) in individuals with an HD diagnosis. Although visual memory deficits are consistent with the CBT model of HD, it is less clear why one would expect to see problems with verbal memory. Other research has found some evidence for differences in implicit memory processes (as measured by the Serial Reaction Time Task; Blom et al., 2011). One study looked at working memory, which could be considered an attentional, memory, or executive function process. Using age-matched older controls, older adults with HD still had comparative difficulties in working memory (letter-number sequencing from the WAIS-IV; Ayers et al. 2013). However, as noted above, many other studies have also failed to find memory deficits of any kind in HD (Grisham & Baldwin, 2015; Timpano et al., 2014). It is suggested that more consistent rigorous research by using age-matching, clinical samples of individuals with HD, both clinical and non-clinical control, and consistent use of hoarding-relevant tests across studies, would clarify previous findings (see Grisham & Baldwin, 2015).

Metamemory

The cognitive-behavioral model of hoarding also suggests that individuals have low confidence in their memory and that they place great importance on having a good memory for fear of negative consequences (see Frost & Steketee, 1998). This lack of confidence is thought to contribute to saving objects in a disorganized fashion as they need to be in plain sight. Beliefs about memory and cognitive ability in individuals with HD have been studied via self-report measures. An early study confirmed this theory (Hartl et al., 2004) as individuals with severe hoarding symptoms had less confidence in their memory ability and more catastrophic beliefs about the negative consequences of a poor memory.

Beliefs about poor cognitive abilities, including memory (that did not match actual impairments found in the study) have been found in individuals with subclinical hoarding symptoms (Fitch & Cougle, 2013). The authors posited that these beliefs may have the power to negatively influence performance during hoarding-relevant tasks (e.g., organizing belongings). In another study this type of self-reported belief by individuals with an actual HD diagnosis was also was not associated with neuropsychological performance (Moshier et al., 2016). Interestingly, another study found that low memory confidence moderated the association between self- reported inattention symptoms and self-reported saving behaviors (Hallion et al., 2015), further suggesting this metamemory beliefs are key to the processes of the disorder. Finally, a recent study found that individuals with HD believed they had more cognitive deficits than did a rigorous control group of age- and gender-matched participants (Tolin et al., 2018). Overall, most of the research suggests that confidence in memory is lacking, rather than memory ability, in HD (for a review, see Woody et al., 2014).

Executive Function
CATEGORIZING/ORGANIZATION

Deficits in categorization/organization are central to the cognitive-behavioral model of HD (Frost & Hartl, 1996). This assertion was based on clinical evidence that there is an overcategorization in possessions by these individuals that seems to contribute to difficulty sorting and organizing objects (Frost & Steketee, 1998). This hypothesis is largely supported by the research evidence (see Grisham & Baldwin, 2015).

Categorization difficulties have been found on card sorting task of the Delis-Kaplan Executive Function System (D-KEFS; Mackin et al., 2011). This study compared older adults with comorbid depression and HD to older adults with only depression, to rule out that depression or older age could explain this type of difficulty (Mackin et al., 2011). These authors found the same pattern of results using the same task in a later study using pure older-age HD individuals compared to age matched controls (Mackin et al., 2016). Another study also found that individuals with HD as compared to controls struggled on the Perceptual Categorization Task (Sumner et al., 2016). Interestingly, it seemed that use of explicit rather than implicit learning strategies, seemed to be what caused this difference (Sumner et al., 2016). Similarly, poorer organization/learning strategy on the RCFT were found in individuals with HD compared to controls; however, they did not differ from a third group of individuals with OCD in the study, making it less clear whether this problem would be specific to HD (Tolin et al., 2011).

A study examining categorization ability with objects rather than a neuropsychological task, however, suggested that this style of categorization may not be global (Wincze et al., 2007). In this experiment, individuals with HD only took longer to categorize personally relevant objects (Wincze et al., 2007). Another study using objects rather than a test, however, in of non-clinical undergraduate "packrats" found that participants with HD symptoms took longer and sorted objects into more categories than did control participants, even though none of these objects were personally relevant. Finally, although not a categorization finding, one study (Grisham et al., 2010) found that individuals with hoarding performed worse than non-clinical and clinical controls on a neuropsychological test of planning ability (Stockings of Cambridge). This finding suggests that planning difficulties in this population might contribute to difficulties seen in organizing belongings (Grisham et al., 2010).

DECISION-MAKING

Difficulties with decision-making are hypothesized to be a component of HD based on clinical observations and research on indecisiveness in this population (see Frost & Steketee, 1998). Although difficulties in decision-making have been significantly associated with hoarding symptoms when both constructs are assessed via self-report measures, it has been difficult to find reliable differences on many decision-making tasks, perhaps due to differences in procedures used in the literature and because decision-making is a complex phenomenon (Timpano et al., 2014). A recent review suggested that if decision-making requires more effort, it makes discarding a more stressful process, and therefore more difficult (Dozier & Ayers, 2017).

One early study did find individuals with compulsive hoarding had difficulty with decision-making ability (assessed using the Cambridge Gambling Task as compared to both clinical and nonclinical controls; Grisham et al., 2010). A more recent study on brain activation patterns during the Go/No-Go and the Stroop tasks also supports more intense activation of brain structures involved in decision-making in HD participants as compared to participants with OCD and controls (Hough et al., 2016). Hough et al. suggest this finding indicates that individuals with HD have difficulty determining whether a task or stimulus is valuable and are averse to risk-taking.

In contrast, Tolin and colleagues (2011) failed to find any impairment in decision-making in individuals with HD. They hypothesized it might be more of a *belief* that one has such an impairment, rather than an actual deficit, and/or that it only occurs under specific emotional circumstances (e.g., while attempting to discard beloved possessions; Tolin et al., 2011). It is worth noting, however, that the authors made this null conclusion based not on a specific decision-making task but based on findings that there were no general impairments across several neuropsychological measures of executive function.

Across domains of information processing research, it seems clearer conclusions could be reached through the use of consistent measures and better agreement among research as to what processes each task captures.

INHIBITION/IMPULSIVITY

Several information processing studies have tested inhibition and impulsivity processes. This seems to be because the CBT model proposes difficulty in sustained attention and response inhibition (Grisham & Barlow, 2005) and difficulty with these abilities is seen clinically when patients try to sustain attention to sort and place or discard possessions. Additionally, it is theorized that increased impulsivity is linked to the acquiring symptoms often seen in this disorder (see Dozier & Ayers, 2017).

A clever study aimed to increase ecological validity of this type of assessment by having participants with HD complete attentional tasks in a cluttered versus tidy environment (Raines et al., 2014). Performance was not altered by the environment; however, participants were globally impaired on sustained attention ability (i.e., inhibiting of responses) as measured by the Psychology Experiment Building Language Continuous Performance Test. The authors concluded that any information processing difficulties seen are likely to be primarily internal, rather than influenced by the environment (Raines et al., 2014). This experiment (Raines et al., 2014) supports what previous studies have suggested, i.e., that it is not the external clutter that influences performance, but the internal processing style (Tolin et al., 2011). Further, at least one study has found that the extent of the difficulty with inhibition predicted the severity of the participants' HD symptoms (Ashworth & McCown, 2018). Similarly, in another investigation, participants with HD displayed slower reaction times and increased impulsivity on the Connors' CPT-II as compared to OCD and non-clinical controls (Grisham et al., 2007). Their scores on these tasks were also predictive of hoarding symptoms (Grisham et al., 2007).

The Go/No-Go task is another neuropsychological test of inhibition. One study found that participants with HD showed impulsivity in responding on the Go/No-Go task, compared to both individuals with OCD and healthy controls of a similar age range (Suñol et al., 2020). Further, they showed distinct brain activation patterns during this task consistent with impulsivity as assessed via MRI (Suñol et al., 2020). In contrast, another group of researchers found that when controlling for age differences between the hoarding and control groups, there were no problems with impulsivity found in the hoarding group, as measured by the Sustained Attention to Response Task (a variation on the Go/No-Go task; Rasmussen et al., 2013).

Results have also been mixed across a variety of other inhibition tasks, perhaps not surprisingly, given the different tasks used and populations tested. Degree of hoarding symptoms in a non-clinical sample of older community adults was correlated with poor performance on two different tests of inhibition, the Stroop Color Word Naming test and The Trail Making Test—Part B (Stolcis & McCown, 2018). In contrast, a study of clinical-level hoarders found no impairment on motor inhibition via the Stop Signal Task (Blom et al., 2011). This study employed individuals with OCD as their control group, which speaks to the specificity of this difference, but lacked an additional control group of older adults to control for any confound effects of aging. Finally, on the Wisconsin Card Sorting Task (WCST), inhibition (as measured by an increased number of non-perseverative errors) in older adults with HD was impaired when compared to healthy older adults (Ayers et al., 2013). Although a strength of this study was the use of an elderly population control to limit potential confounds of aging, the lack of an additional clinical control means the unique application of these findings to HD remain unclear.

COGNITIVE FLEXIBILITY/SET-SHIFTING

Cognitive flexibility is an important executive function (EF) that may contribute to other higher-order EFs that could be altered in HD. One study of cognitive flexibility found that (as measured by an eye tracking task) those participants higher in self-reported hoarding symptoms had more difficulty disengaging from visually presented numbers (Carbonella & Timpano, 2016). Further, this difficulty seemed to be global, as performance was not affected by the presence of either hoarding-related or neutral distractor images. The authors suggested that difficulty disengaging from previous (perhaps irrelevant) tasks can contribute to other information processing difficulties seen in hoarding, such as sustained attention and difficulty in decision-making (Carbonella & Timpano). Similarly, a couple of studies have found that individuals with HD experienced more perseveration errors (e.g., difficulty set-shifting to a new set of rules) on the WCST (Ayers et al., 2013; McMillan & Rees, 2013). Furthermore, severity of executive function impairment on the WCST (which requires a great deal of set-shifting) has been found to predict severity of hoarding symptoms (Ayers et al., 2016) in individuals with the diagnosis.

Effects of Treatment

If IP deficits are a central symptom of HD (Frost & Hartl, 1996), we would expect them to be resolvable through treatment. One of the modules in the CBT protocol for HD does involve teaching skills in categorizing, organization, planning, and decision-making, and problems-solving (Steketee & Frost, 2007). These skills are geared towards hoarding-specific situations (e.g., filing paperwork, giving away unused items) rather than more broadly towards life situations. Interestingly, despite the core deficits in IP proposed in the model, few treatment studies of HD have examined changes in IP following treatment.

Tolin and colleagues (2012) used CBT to treat hoarding. They assessed cognitive function related to hoarding via a simulated acquiring/discarding task performed in an fMRI. Intriguingly, brain activation patterns seen in the HD sample differed greatly from those of control participants at pre- but not post-treatment. A medication investigation using atomoxetine (typically prescribed for ADHD) examined self-reported cognitive function pre- and post-treatment (Grassi et al., 2016). They found that both hoarding symptoms and cognitive functioning improved following medication. Interestingly, however, these improvements were found to be independent, rather than related to each other (Grassi et al., 2016). Most recently, a behavioral intervention for HD demonstrated that neuropsychological test scores improved across several domains (Zakrzewskia et al., 2020). These included visual detection, processing speed, attention, working memory, visual memory, and decision-making. Interestingly, pre-treatment levels of cognitive impairment were not predictive of treatment outcome (Zakrzewskia et al., 2020). An important caveat is that some declines in neuropsychological test scores were also seen (in reaction-time and categorization ability).

Cognitive remediation (CR) is typically used to improve such function following a brain injury or early onset of a dementia process. An 8-week course of cognitive remediation (24 computerized testing sessions) improved HD participants' attention, but not memory or EF, as assessed by the NeuroTrax battery (DiMauro et al., 2014). Unfortunately, it did not improve hoarding symptoms (DiMauro et al., 2014). Another treatment study combined CR (6 sessions) with some CBT elements (i.e., exposure to sorting; 18-20 more sessions; Ayers et al., 2019). Participants improved their cognitive flexibility and inhibition ability as assessed by subtests of the D-KEFS, in addition to decreasing their symptoms of hoarding (Ayers et al., 2019).

Future research on IP changes following intervention would benefit from assessing these cognitive functions in the context of medication treatment, classic CBT for hoarding, and perhaps looking at whether the module on cognitive skills building is connected to any changes seen.

BDD

BDD is characterized by an excessive preoccupation with a perceived defect in appearance that is not noticeable or appears slight to others (APA, 2013). Individuals with BDD focus on specific features of their physical appearance, fear negative evaluation, present overvalued ideation, and engage in time-consuming repetitive behaviors, which might be indicative of cognitive biases in this disorder. In fact, cognitive behavioral models of BDD postulate that biases in attention, perception, interpretation, and memory of appearance-related stimuli play a role in the etiology and maintenance of BDD (Buhlmann & Wilhelm, 2004; Veale, 2004; Wilhelm & Neziroglu, 2002, p. 210). In the previous edition of this chapter, only a handful of studies were available on attention and memory, revealing scant evidence for the presence of these biases on information processing in BDD. Since then, research on this disorder, and specifically on these cognitive biases has grown significantly. An updated review of the existing literature of these aspects in BDD will be discussed in this section.

Visuoperceptual Biases
HOLISTIC PROCESSING

Clinical observations and some previous findings suggest that individuals with BDD are more easily able to detect and selectively attend to details, which would underlie the distorted perception of appearance in this disorder. This bias can be framed within a wider construct known as central coherence, a limited ability to understand context (Feusner et al., 2010a). There is some evidence suggesting that individuals with BDD overfocus on minor or perceived flaws in their physical appearance. Using the Rey-Osterrieth Complex Figure Test (RCFT), Deckersbach et al. (2000) found that individuals with BDD exhibited a tendency to overfocus on the details of a complex figure, rather than on global aspects, when asked to reproduce the figure from memory. Using two different cognitive tasks (the embedded figures task (EFT) and a modified version of the Navon task), Kerwin and colleagues (2014) examined global (attention to holistic, organizing features) and local (attention to piecemeal, detailed information) visual processing as well as set-shifting in 18 non-medicated individuals with BDD, and 17 non-clinical controls. Results indicated that individuals with BDD, compared to nonclinical controls, processed both global and local stimuli more slowly and less accurately, and there was a further difference in performance when shifting attention between the different levels of stimuli. These difficulties were significantly greater in individuals with higher severity and poor insight. The lack of a clinical control group undermines the specificity of this finding.

Additional evidence for this bias comes from neuroimaging studies, using functional magnetic resonance imaging (fMRI). Some studies have shown some evidence of a hemispheric imbalance, which has been proposed to be related to the visual biases observed in BDD Feusner et al. (2007) found that 12 unmedicated patients with BDD showed greater left hemisphere activity compared to nonclinical controls, especially in lateral prefrontal cortex and lateral temporal lobe regions for unfamiliar face tasks, suggesting a detailed encoding and analysis rather than holistic processing. Feusner et al. (2010b) examined own-face processing, finding relative hyperactivity in the left orbitofrontal cortex and caudate nucleus, and relative hypoactivity in the left occipital cortex. This unusual brain activity in visual processing areas when viewing their own faces suggests a tendency to perceive details and an impaired ability to contextualize them holistically (Feusner et al., 2010b). The results were replicated with objects, in another study by the same authors, in which patients with BDD were asked to match photographs of houses and shapes under low, normal, and high-spatial-frequency conditions while undergoing fMRI (Feusner et al. 2011). Relative to non-clinical controls, individuals with BDD displayed hypoactivity in secondary visual processing systems for holistic elements. Li and colleagues (2015), using fMRI and event-related potentials found hypoactivity in secondary visual processing regions, and hyperactivity in the fusiform cortex when viewing images of faces and houses, indicating a deficiency in holistic processing in individuals with BDD and anorexia nervosa.

Feusner and colleagues (2010a) and Jefferies and colleagues (2012) both investigated the face inversion effect (FIE) in BDD. The FIE refers to the phenomenon whereby the recognition of inverted faces is normally slower and less accurate compared to upright faces and is considered as a classic "signature" for holistic processing (Monzani et al., 2013). A reduced FIE was observed in the BDD group, relative to healthy controls, during long stimulus presentations in these studies. These findings suggest the possibility of differences in holistic processing in BDD. Reduced FIE was not observed during short stimulus presentations (Feusner et al., 2010a). However, other authors have failed to obtain the same results. Monzani et al. (2013), using the FIE and the composite task, found no differences between individuals with BDD and healthy controls in holistic processing aspects. This finding suggests that the excessive focus on specific aspects of appearance in BDD may not be explained by impairments in the global encoding of visual information. Findings from another study (Buhlmann et al., 2004) using the short form of the Benton Facial Recognition Test (BFRT) comparing individuals with BDD, OCD, and healthy controls, were also inconsistent with findings from Deckersbach and colleagues (2000). It is noteworthy that several of these studies did not include clinical controls, and therefore is difficult to establish the uniqueness of these biases to BDD, rather than a general marker of psychopathology or distress.

SELECTIVE ATTENTION

Selective attention has been postulated as a crucial factor in CBT models of BDD (Neziroglu et al., 2008; Veale, 2004; Wilhelm & Neziroglu, 2002). Veale for example, has suggested that self-focused attention, a form of selective attention, leads to a heightened awareness of self-referent, internally generated information (Veale & Neziroglu, 2010, p. 149), which in turn activates assumptions about the importance of one's appearance.

Previously, cognitive tasks, primarily the Stroop test, have been used to assess the presence of attentional biases in BDD, but with mixed results (Buhlmann et al., 2002; Hanes, 1998; Wilhelm et al., 2003). Recent studies using eye-tracking methodology support attentional biases. Grocholewski et al. (2012) examined selective visual attention of facial stimuli, and found that, in comparison to healthy controls and individuals with social phobia, individuals with BDD showed heightened selective attention to the perceived defect in their own face, as well as to corresponding regions in other faces. In another study (Greenberg et al., 2014), participants were instructed to look at photographs of their own face and of a gender-matched face of average attractiveness. Results showed that individuals with BDD overfocused on their negative features, whereas healthy participants had a more balanced focus on their attributes.

Kollei et al. (2017) also examined visual selective attention to the least and most attractive features in own face, in individuals with BDD, bulimia nervosa, and healthy controls, and found similar results to those to Greenberg and colleagues (2014). Individuals with BDD focused more on their least attractive facial part than healthy controls as indicated by dwell time. For other faces, BDD participants paid more attention to the most attractive parts than to least attractive features, compared to healthy controls. Finally, Toh et al. (2017) employed a card version of the emotional Stroop task integrated with an eye-tracking paradigm and found that BDD participants exhibited significant interference for BDD-negative words relative to healthy participants, and a trend toward significance for Stroop delays to BDD-positive words. Results also revealed that viewing strategies adopted by BDD participants were generally disorganised, with varying number of fixations, extended scan paths as well as avoidance of certain disorder-relevant words and considerable visual attention dedicated to non-salient card regions.

It has been suggested that individuals with BDD show an increased sensitivity and accuracy in the perception of facial stimuli (Veale, 2004), but findings are also mixed. Yaryura-Tobias et al. (2002) instructed 10 individuals with BDD, 10 individuals with OCD, and 10 healthy controls to identify whether a series of own and unfamiliar faces were distorted. Authors found that compared to controls, clinical groups detected non-existing distortions significantly more often in their own faces. In another study, Stangier et al. (2008) found that female participants with BDD were better able to discriminate differences in appearance between neutral faces than were individuals who had either disfiguring or non-disfiguring dermatological conditions. Results showed that participants with BDD were more accurate in discriminating changes in relevant features of the face compared to the other control groups. Further, Lambrou et al. (2011) found that individuals with BDD, and individuals with an education or employment in art and design related fields, displayed a greater awareness of their aesthetic facial proportions, compared to individuals without aesthetic training controls, and this effect was also found for other people's faces and a building. Individuals with BDD also showed an increased accuracy specific to their own faces, compared with controls. Nevertheless, participants with BDD displayed no distortion in their perceptual processing, but rather a disturbance in their negative/evaluative processing of their self-image (Lambrou et al., 2011). This is consistent with the overall notion that misinterpretations and/or beliefs may be at the heart of this problem, and not actual deficits in information processing. In fact, other studies have not been able to show that individuals with BDD have an enhanced sense of aesthetics and ability to detect visual changes. Reese et al. (2010), using a facial as well as an appearance-unrelated dot array symmetry detection paradigm, did not detect any group differences between patients with BDD and OCD, and healthy controls. Buhlmann et al. (2014) found no differences with respect to other people's facial images as well as object discrimination in individuals with BDD, but consistent with Yaryura-Tobias et al.'s (2002) findings, participants with BDD showed a "response bias" where they rated facial (but not object) images significantly more often as being changed when they were actually identical images. Hübner et al. (2016) also failed to detect any differences among individuals with BDD, OCD, social anxiety (SA), and healthy controls in their ability to identify facial aberrations when presented with other people's faces. Finally, using different cognitive tasks, Rossell and colleagues (2014) found that patients with BDD performed like controls on tasks measuring information processing and aesthetics. All these studies used different methodologies to assess these variables, which does not allow for comparisons, and can partially explain the mixed results.

Interpretative Biases

Research suggests that individuals with BDD tend to interpret normal and ambiguous social situations in a negative or threatening manner (Buhlmann & Wilhelm, 2004, Fang & Wilhelm, 2015). However, once more, the results are somewhat mixed concerning the specific emotions underlying these biases. Some studies have found that patients with BDD tend to process neutral emotional expressions erroneously, often misinterpreting them as angry, contemptuous, or disgusted (Buhlmann et al., 2004; 2011; Buhlmann, Etcoff, et al., 2006). In two studies by Buhlmann and colleagues, authors found that individuals with BDD tended to misinterpret facial expressions of disgust as angry more often than healthy controls (Buhlmann et al., 2004; Buhlmann, Etcoff, et al., 2006). Nevertheless, in another study by the same authors, an emotion recognition bias was found for anger, but not for disgust (Buhlmann et al., 2011). Individuals with BDD also showed a negative interpretation bias for body-related and social scenarios, compared with individuals with OCD, and healthy controls. They also displayed a bias for general scenarios only compared to healthy controls, but not to OCD patients (Buhlmann et al., 2002b). These findings are consistent with those from other studies where individuals with BDD and undergraduate students with high BDD symptoms exhibited negative biases for self-referent, but not others-referent, ambiguous situations. They rated negative outcomes as more likely to occur to them than individuals low in symptoms (Buhlmann, Etcoff, et al., 2006; Clerkin & Teachman, 2008). Additionally, when BDD participants were required to identify complex emotional states from images of eyes, there were no significant performance differences compared to healthy controls (Buhlmann et al., 2013). As Fang and Wilhelm (2015) state, it is possible that individuals with BDD do not have an impairment in emotion recognition, but rather a bias in situations when they perceive themselves as being directly involved.

Memory

Unlike in OCD, research on memory biases in BDD is still very limited, and the mechanisms underlying these biases are still unclear (Fang & Wilhelm, 2015). Hanes (1998), found no memory impairments on the RCFT and Rey's Auditory-Verbal Learning Test (RALVT). Deckersbach et al. (2000), found that patients with BDD differed significantly from healthy controls on verbal and nonverbal learning and memory indices, but that these results were likely caused by differences across numerous measures of strategic organization and learning, as they did not show problems in storing information once learned.

Dunai et al. (2010) found that in comparison to age and sex-matched healthy controls, patients with BDD exhibited low performance in spatial working memory, but short-term memory capacity, motor speed, and visual memory were very similar to those of controls. These results were confirmed by Labuschagne et al. (2013), where individuals with BDD and OCD showed difficulties in these same facets with no difference in visual recognition memory, immediate auditory memory, and spatial working memory.

In another study comparing patients with BDD and OCD, using the Repeatable Battery for the Assessment of Neuropsychological Status (RBANS), Toh and colleagues (2015) found that both groups of patients showed difficulties with immediate memory, but delayed memory, visuospatial construction and language remained intact. Overall, patients with BDD performed worse than OCD patients. Recently, Yousefi et al. (2020) compared individuals with BDD and OCD relative to healthy controls to explore similarities and differences in memory function, using the Weschler Memory Scale (WMS) and the RCFT. Authors found that BDD patients exhibited lower performance in spatial working memory consistent with Labuschagne and colleagues' findings (2013). They also found differences on the copy condition on the RCFT, but not on copy organization, which contrasts with Deckersbach and colleagues' (2000) findings. These results suggest difficulties with visual working memory, and poor performance in the visual domain (spatial span and RCFT). Working memory problems are suggested to be related to the inability to simultaneously hold and manipulate verbal and spatial information; this inability might underlie inaccurate perceptions of perceived flaws in physical appearance, and social situations (Yousefi et al., 2020). Memory difficulties are also thought to account for inaccurate coding and recall of face or body stimuli (Johnson et al., 2018).

One study has looked at the characteristics and quality of memory in participants with BDD compared to controls (Osman et al., 2004). Researchers found that individuals with BDD had many more memories that were spontaneous, recurrent, and negative, compared to controls. These images contained more details and incorporated more of the sensory modalities than those of controls. These images were seen from an observer perspective, whereas controls saw them from their own point of view. This difference is very telling, and implies that their memory of what happened is not actually how it occurred, but reflects their inner views of themselves as objects to be criticized (Osman et al., 2004), a "self-aesthetic object" as defined by Veale (2004) in his cognitive behavioral model. Furthermore, the specific appearance-related images were associated with stressful childhood experiences. BDD sufferers' thoughts about their appearance tend to be visual in nature, whereas feedback from others about appearance tends to be verbal in nature. This potentially explains why verbal feedback from others is so ineffective at changing erroneous cognitions in these individuals (Osman et al., 2004).

Effects of Treatment

Evidence of cognitive bias modification treatment for BDD comes from studies using computerized training programs or specific training paradigms addressing specific biases. There are a few studies examining the effects of treatment on interpretative and emotion recognition biases. In one study (Summers & Cougle, 2016), 40 individuals with BDD were enrolled in a randomized, four-session trial comparing interpretation bias modification (IBM), with a placebo control training condition. The authors found that the IBM group showed greater reductions in BDD symptoms, when pre-treatment BDD symptoms were high but not low. They also found lower urges to check, and lower fear in response to an in vivo appearance-related stressor in those individuals with high levels of fear at pre-treatment. Effects were maintained at 1-month follow-up. In an extension of this study, Wilver and Cougle (2019) compared an 8-session internet-based IBM with progressive muscle relaxation (PMR) in 50 participants with BDD. Results indicated that individuals in the IBM condition reported fewer negative interpretation biases and greater positive interpretation biases at post-treatment and 3-month follow-up, but no differences were found on BDD symptoms, depression, or anxiety.

Premo et al. (2016) investigated the effects of two sessions of cognitive bias modification for interpretation (CBM-I) in 86 undergraduate students with high scores on the Dysmorphic Concerns Questionnaire. Negative BDD-relevant interpretations were reduced among participants who completed a positive training condition targeting BDD-relevant beliefs. Relative to the comparison training condition, however, they did not demonstrate a reduction in emotional reactivity related to two BDD stressor tasks (mirror gazing and picture tasks). Dietel and colleagues examined the effects of CBM-I in healthy students (2018), and students with high body dissatisfaction in a double-blind randomized controlled trial (RCT; 2020). Results indicated that participants exhibited a pre-post increase in adaptive bias patterns, and a reduction in body dissatisfaction (Dietel et al., 2018), BDD symptom severity, and depression (Dietel et al., 2020), with small to medium effect sizes. These effects remained at 1- and 4-week follow-up, except for depression (Dietel et al., 2020).

Buhlmann and colleagues (2011) examined the effects of a single-session training paradigm to modify emotion recognition in 32 individuals with BDD, 34 individuals with dermatological conditions, and 34 healthy controls. The authors obtained mixed results, with improvements over time for all groups, but no specific training effect on emotion recognition. Training effects were obtained for neutral expressions in the BDD group, and in scared expressions in the BDD and control training group. These findings are promising as potential specific interventions in cognitive-behavioral therapy (CBT).

Although CBT for BDD usually includes perceptual retraining and cognitive restructuring to modify visuoperceptual and interpretative biases (Veale & Neziroglu, 2010; Wilhelm et al., 2013), there is no direct evidence of information processing changes following CBT (Rosen et al., 1995; Veale et al., 2014; Wilhelm et al., 2011, 2014).

Primary outcome measures of these studies are symptom-related questionnaires, such as the Appearance Anxiety Inventory (AAI), the Body Dysmorphic Disorder Examination (BDDE), or the Yale-Brown Obsessive Compulsive Scale modified for BDD (BDD-YBOCS). In order to better assess the effects of treatment in cognitive biases, it would be necessary to include specific measures of change related to these cognitive functions.

TTM

TTM (or hair-pulling disorder) is currently categorized as an OCRD (APA, 2013). It is characterized by the recurrent, often physically painless pulling of one's own hair resulting in otherwise medically uncaused hair loss, despite attempts to decrease or stop hair-pulling (APA, 2013; França et al., 2019; Sah et al., 2008; Stein et al., 2010; Woods & Houghton, 2014). Models of TTM posit that stressful contexts tax coping resources which results in pulling urges/tensions (Arabatzoudis et al., 2017; Maas et al., 2018; Woods et al., 2006). Automatic, "mindless," "trancelike," dissociative-like pulling occurs, often for hours, until a "just right" feeling is achieved or cognitive resources to stop become available (Christensen et al., 1991; França et al., 2019; Houghton et al., 2016; Maas et al., 2018). Over time, one with TTM may develop maladaptive beliefs about control (e.g., "I'm unable to resist urges to pull"; Keijsers et al., 2016; Rehm et al., 2019). The next sections review the literature on information processing characteristics of TTM.

Perception

With respect to verbal perception, individuals with TTM demonstrate no differences compared to those without psychopathology in their ability to discriminate between similar but different English-related phonemes and to recognize identical phoneme pairs (Slikboer et al., 2018; Stanley et al., 1997). They can follow increasingly complex verbally provided instructions in a task involving interacting with tokens and a game board (Stanley et al., 1997). With respect to visual perception, individuals with TTM can locate a target symbol from an array (Stanley et al., 1997). However, there is evidence that people with TTM have problems with auditory perception. TTM is associated with difficulty on tasks involving responding to auditory stimuli in providing definitions of increasingly rare words, responding to questions which probe a bank of culturally normative knowledge (Stanley et al., 1997), and orally generating lists of words based on a letter of the alphabet (Stanley et al., 1997). However, it has been argued that this finding does not indicate auditory perceptual difficulties but is an artifact of the divided attention required on these tasks (Slikboer et al., 2018). Differences may be related to unique attentional but not perceptual characteristics of TTM (see below).

Processing Speed

There were no problems found when processing speed was measured by the Rapid Visual Information Processing Task (Chamberlain et al., 2010; Slikboer et al., 2018). On this task, digits between 2 and 9 appear mostly randomly, 100 per minute, and people are asked to identify when they perceive a target sequence of one to three digits. Similarly, processing speed associated with fine motor control is normal as measured by the Grooved Pegboard task, which requires participants to place pegs with tabs into corresponding grooves in the correct orientation (Slikboer et al., 2018; Stanley et al., 1997). However, there is also some evidence of processing speed difficulties in TTM. Individuals with TTM scored one standard deviation below people without any Axis I diagnoses on the Trails B Test and Digit Symbol (Stanley et al., 1997; Slikboer et al., 2018). However, TTM-related deficits in divided attention, rather than processing speed impairments, may better explain these results (Slikboer et al., 2018).

Attention

There is mixed evidence regarding attention problems in TTM, depending on whether tasks of focused (vs. divided) attention are used. Undivided attentional processes appear unimpaired as measured by the WAIS-R Digit Span, Delayed Recognition Span Test, Visual Search, and Trail-making Test A (Bohne et al., 2005, 2008; Bohne, Savage, et al., 2005; Keuthen et al., 1996; Stanley et al., 1997). However, TTM is thought to be associated with clear difficulties in divided attention as measured by the PASAT, Trail-making Test B, Stroop (Slikboer et al., 2018; Stanley et al., 1997). In summary, it seems that people with TTM have no simple reaction time deficits but can experience slower reaction time in more cognitively demanding reaction time tasks as compared to both healthy and OCD control groups (Bohne et al., 2005, 2008; Bohne, Savage et al., 2005; Stanley et al., 1997).

Regarding attentional biases, the type of cues used to measure attentional biases may matter in TTM, but how this occurs remains to be determined. It may be that TTM is characterized by attentional biases toward hair pulling-related (vs. unrelated) cues, such that the greater saliency of pulling cues, the greater the urges to pull. Another possibility is that TTM may involve difficulty disengaging attention away from pulling-related (vs. unrelated) cues. It may be that it is difficult to dispel such cues and to focus on something else, which promotes hair-pulling (Lee et al., 2012). Lastly, it has been suggested that TTM involves a bias of attentional avoidance of hair-pulling-related cues (Lee et al., 2012). Hair-pulling may function to avoid potentially emotionally distressing negative information and negative emotions themselves (Lee et al., 2012). This would be consistent with the tendency in TTM to avoid negative thoughts, feelings, memories, experiences, and sensations which are associated with hair-pulling severity (Begotka et al., 2004; Lee et al., 2012). The combination of faster reaction times on the Stroop task and delayed responding to pulling cues on Exogenous Cuing Task and Approach-Avoidance Task may indicate that people with TTM exhibit attentional disengagement from (i.e., intentional attentional avoidance of) pulling-related cues (Lee et al., 2012; Maas et al., 2018), unlike attentional biases toward obsessional threats in OCD (Lee et al., 2012).

Slower reaction times were directly related TTM symptom severity (Grant, 2019; Lee et al., 2012; Slikboer et al., 2018). It may be that visual (vs. verbal) cues may have more power to cause the TTM-related attentional bias and that those with TTM (vs. without) disengage more quickly from pulling-related cues as a form of avoidance of potential cuing and associated negative affect.

Memory
Individuals with TTM show no deficits on measures of verbal memory like the Digit Span and Delayed Recognition Span Tests (Keuthen et al., 1996; Weschler, 1981). However, there may be some biases in nonverbal, specifically spatial, working and long-term memory in patients with TTM (Chamberlain et al., 2007; Slikboer et al., 2018; Stanley et al., 1997; Wilton et al., 2020). Participants with TTM and those without psychopathology outperformed those with OCD on a task where they were required to identify a pattern of previously presented visual stimuli from among distractor figures (Chamberlain et al., 2007). However, people with TTM and OCD experienced similar significant difficulty compared to psychologically healthy peers on a task where they were to locate a token from among an array of boxes after being provided with feedback after each guess (Chamberlain et al., 2007). Interestingly, these problems are not observed in children with TTM (Wilton et al., 2020), suggesting that such difficulties develop over time. Current models of TTM do not account for how memory biases might contribute to the etiology and maintenance of the disorder, nor whether they may be a result of behavioral and thought patterns over time (Diefenbach et al., 2002; Mansueto et al., 1997; Wilton et al., 2020).

Executive Function
People with TTM perform normally on several measures of executive functioning processes. These include verbal reasoning, problem-solving, decision-making, use of strategy, ability to shift rules, organization, verbal and visuospatial problem-solving, understanding abstract social norms, abilities in trial-and-error learning, and an ability to adapt responses based on feedback (Bohne et al., 2005, 2008; Bohne, Savage, et al., 2005; Chamberlain et al., 2006, 2007, 2010; Chamberlain, Blackwell, et al., 2006; Coetzer & Stein, 1999; Grant et al., 2011; Keuthen et al., 1996; Slikboer et al., 2018; Stanley et al., 1997; Stein, Coetzer, et al., 1997; Wilton et al., 2020). The results are less clear in other areas of executive function, detailed below.

COGNITIVE FLEXIBILITY

Relative to people without psychopathology or those with OCD, individuals with TTM demonstrated more behavioral perseveration in the Object Alternation Task (OAT), which measures the ability to learn the rule by which a coin alternates from one cup to another after each correct response (Bohne, Savage, et al., 2005). This suggests those with

TTM have an impaired ability to learn new principles governing an experience, and an impaired ability to enact novel behaviors (e.g., hair-pulling as only behavioral response). Further, children with TTM largely have more intact cognitive flexibility than adults with TTM, but reversal learning is still impacted (Flessner et al., 2016).

On the other hand, some evidence suggests cognitive flexibility in TTM is intact and superior to those with OCD (Chamberlain et al., 2006). People with TTM demonstrated no deficits in adapting to shifting contexts nor perseveration errors on the Intradimensional/Extradimensional Task (IDED) (measuring rule acquisition and rule reversal ability) relative to those with SPD and those without psychopathology (Chamberlain et al., 2006; Grant et al., 2011; Wilton et al., 2020). Further, neither age nor the diagnostic status (i.e., TTM vs. no psychopathology) of children predicted performance on the IDED (Flessner et al., 2016). Based on the OAT, those with TTM, OCD, and without psychopathology had the same proportion of completed trials and percentage of errors (Bohne, Savage, et al., 2005). Performance of those with TTM, OCD, and without psychopathology was equivalent on the WCST in terms of success rates, number of trials, percentage of errors, and percentage of perseverative errors (Bohne et al., 2005; Stanley et al., 1997).

This discrepancy may be resolved by acknowledging that Bohne et al. (2005) utilized a slightly different measure of flexibility, asking people to memorize a list of words, making it more a task of memory inhibition, whereas the Stroop task is (reportedly) a task of attentional inhibition—possibly explaining the difference in results between the two experiments (Stanley et al., 1997). People with TTM seem more able to learn from feedback (vs. those with OCD), but tasks involving response (vs. cognitive) flexibility are difficult for those with TTM. On all other measures of cognitive ability (visuospatial, memory, problem solving, and planning), all participants were found to be equally as good as healthy controls. This observed response (vs. cognitive) inflexibility in TTM is consistent with the long, dissociation-like hair pulling episodes observed in the disorder.

IMPULSIVITY/INHIBITION

TTM seems to be associated with mild problems of impulsivity and motor inhibition. While gross motor function appears unimpaired (Stanley et al., 1997), there is evidence of problems with fine motor speed and careful, thoughtful hand-eye coordination with non-dominant hands (Stanley et al., 1997). Further, individuals with TTM display significant difficulties with impulse control and motor inhibition when cues for control are inconsistent (vs. consistent) are concurrent or shortly delayed (vs. a priori) (Chamberlain et al., 2006; Grant et al., 2011). Children and adults with TTM appear to maintain the ability to adapt to changing criteria (as compared to difficulties in cognitive flexibility in OCD) and to inhibit responses if doing so is according to simple, unchanging rules (Bohne et al., 2008, Chamberlain et al., 2007; Slikboer et al., 2018; Stanley et al., 1997; Wilton et al., 2020). That children with (vs. without) TTM demonstrated superior impulse control/motor inhibition after controlling for age and comorbid

ADHD symptoms may indicate that those with TTM develop impulsivity/response disinhibition with progression of the disorder (Wilton et al., 2020), that it is a problem exclusive to adults with TTM (Wilton et al., 2020), or that it is more characteristic of those with adult onset TTM (Brennan et al., 2016; Odlaug et al., 2014). Though TTM is associated with emotional dysregulation (Arabatzoudis et al., 2017; Chamberlain, Menzies, et al., 2007; Diefenbach et al., 2002; Slikboer et al., 2018), TTM was not associated with impairments in reaction time or basic inhibitory rule-following in emotionally laden contexts of the Affective Go/No-Go Test (Bohne et al., 2008; Grant et al., 2011; Slikboer et al., 2018; Wilton et al., 2020). The varied performance in those with TTM on the Stop-Signal Task suggests a range of impulsivity in TTM and the disorder's own phenomenological heterogeneity. The differential results between pediatric and adult TTM in impulsivity on the Stop-Signal Task performance suggests that those with TTM may develop this unique style motor/response inhibition with progression of the disorder, that it is a problem exclusive to adults with TTM (Wilton et al., 2020), or that it is more characteristic of those with adult onset TTM (Brennan et al., 2016; Odlaug et al., 2014). Perhaps children with (vs. without) TTM have a different developmental trajectory for inhibitory control only evident as they age (Wilton et al., 2020).

Why worse motor impulsivity is present with visual (vs. verbal) cues is presently unknown (Maas et al., 2018; Woods & Houghton, 2014). Knowing this could be important, as motor control impairment is thought to be a causal mechanism in TTM (see above; Woods & Houghton, 2014). The strong negative relationship between reaction time and false positives in those with TTM on the Go/No-Go task indicated unique response styles: one style was characterized as fast and inaccurate (a marker of impulsivity). Yet, some individuals with TTM showed the opposite pattern: they were slow and accurate (demonstrating a cautious response style; Bohne et al., 2008). Poorer Stop-Signal performance indicates motor/response inhibition differences (Chamberlain et al., 2006, 2007; Chamberlain, Menzies, et al., 2007; Grant et al., 2011; Odlaug et al., 2014; Wilton et al., 2020). Those with more severe TTM symptoms demonstrated greater difficulty in inhibitory control (Chamberlain et al., 2006). Those with TTM and those with OCD (vs. those without psychopathology) demonstrated similar simple reaction times and number of omission/commission errors on the Stop-Signal task (Bohne et al., 2005, 2008; Chamberlain et al., 2006). TTM, however, was uniquely characterized by impulsive responding, in that motor responses were less often inhibited following presentations of the stop-signal (requiring participants to inhibit an otherwise appropriate response), whereas OCD was not (Chamberlain et al., 2006). In this way, it may represent a problem of impulse control (Brennan et al., 2016). It has been proposed that TTM may fall onto an impulsivity-compulsivity spectrum, where compulsivity disorders (e.g., OCD) may be characterized by harm avoidance and low sensation-seeking and impulsivity disorders (e.g., TTM) may be typified by sensation-seeking and a lack of behavioral inhibition (Brennan et al., 2016). The unique pattern of performance in those with TTM suggests difficulty with top-down response inhibition (Chamberlain et al., 2006; Odlaug et al., 2014).

Effects of Treatment

Very little research has been conducted to examine the effects of treatment on information processing in TTM. Spatial memory, as measured by the Stylus Maze, improves alongside decreased TTM symptoms following the administration of clomipramine (Rettew et al., 1991). Grant and colleagues (2014) found that with the administration of naltrexone (vs. placebo), cognitive flexibility improved as measured by the IDED Task. However, motor/response inhibition as measured by the Stop-Signal Task did not improve (Grant et al., 2014). One treatment protocol was comprised of CBT with the addition of Approach-Avoidance Task, wherein people were also trained to approach (vs. their typical avoidance of) pull-related stimuli (vs. CBT alone) (Maas et al., 2018). Those who had the addition of the Approach-Avoidance Task (vs. CBT alone) had no different outcomes in their reduced TTM symptoms, urges to pull, frequency and resistance of hair pulling, or severity of hair loss (Maas et al., 2018). Given the mixed results in the few studies conducted to date, it is not clear whether IP improves with treatment.

SPD

SPD (excoriation) is characterized by recurrent skin-picking, despite attempts to decrease or stop the behavior, which results in skin lesions, and clinically significant distress and/or impairment (APA, 2013). SPD was new in the *DSM-5* and its association with other OCRDs was novel (APA, 2013). Not surprisingly therefore, to date few studies have examined SPD and IP. Individuals with SPD often report impulsivity or inability to control urges to pick (Odlaug & Grant, 2010; Schuck et al., 2012), suggesting possible problematic IP in this condition.

Attention

One study (Shuck et al., 2012) found that individuals with SPD (as compared to those with TTM, OCD, and healthy controls) had longer general reaction times to approach neutral stimuli via the Approach-Avoidance Task. Interestingly, they also displayed slower reactions to approach images of skin irregularities. The authors posited this may indicate avoidance of emotionally aversive stimuli or motivation to avoid engaging in skin picking (Shuck et al., 2012).

Impulsivity and/or Motor/Response Inhibition

SPD, like TTM, is thought to be characterized by an inability to suppress inappropriate repetitive behavior (Chamberlain et al., 2006; Lamothe et al., 2020; Odlaug et al., 2014; Walther et al., 2010). Indeed, one study found that SPD appears to be characterized by uniquely poorer inhibitory control and impulsivity, even more so than those with TTM and OCD, as measured by the speed at which individuals could inhibit a normal cued response when signaled to do so on the Stop Signal Task (Grant et al., 2011).

Cognitive Flexibility

Individuals with ED had equivalent performance on the Intra-Dimensional/Extra-Dimensional Set Shift Task as those with TTM, OCD, or without psychopathology (Grant et al., 2011). To the authors' knowledge, no other studies have examined cognitive flexibility in SPD.

Effects of Treatment

Unfortunately, to the best of our knowledge, no extant research reports on the effects of treatment on IP in SPD.

Conclusions

The field of research on IP in OCRDs has advanced greatly since the first edition of this volume. Although some of the investigations have been quite broad in aspects of information processing and cognition assessed, the most conclusive findings are mostly interpretable as relatable to the theoretical models of each disorder.

Beginning with OCD, previous mixed evidence regarding the presence of a memory deficit appears to now indicate that it is memory confidence, not memory ability, that is impaired in this population. Indeed, individuals with OCD may even have superior memory for personal and obsessive-relevant stimuli. Newer awareness of and research on "access to internal states" suggest that individuals with OCD may have less access, and this may contribute to some of the uncertainty obsessions and repetition of compulsions. Biased information processing does improve following CBT, but attention retraining treatments do not improve symptoms of OCD. The idiosyncratic nature of OCD symptoms has been one limitation in interpreting these results to-date, when heterogenous samples are used to examine IP processes.

In HD there is also clear evidence of low memory confidence, suggesting a relationship between HD and OCD at least on some information processing aspects. This also runs in contrary to the proposed memory deficits posited by the CBT model of hoarding. HD also appears to be characterized by a detailed visual processing style, again in concordance with some OCD findings, and which is theoretically logical when imagining what would impair the ability of individuals with the disorder to categorize and sort possessions. Relatedly, there is clear evidence for impaired ability to categorize belongings, as also proposed in the model. However, there is still mixed evidence on whether decision-making is impaired, as hypothesized. Finally, there are mixed findings on attention, inhibition, and impulsivity processes in this disorder. These are not part of the theoretical model, but have also been hypothesized to be related to HD. Similar to OCD, CBT may improve IP difficulties, but CR does not appear to improve symptoms.

In BDD the model posits biases in perception and interpretation of appearance-related and visual stimuli. Indeed, individuals with BDD have perceptual biases to not process information holistically, consistent with what would be expected. This finding is also somewhat consistent with similar findings in OCD and HD, suggesting shared vulnerability or psychopathology. Individuals with BDD are sensitive to facial expressions of disgust and interpret them threateningly as angry. Further, interpretive bias modification treatment has been shown to improve BDD symptoms. This is distinct from HD and OCD where changing processing style has not been shown to improve the symptoms of those disorders.

TTM and SPD are both posited to have increased attentional engagement towards relevant "pickable" stimuli. In fact, research has shown the opposite: that these individuals display increased avoidance of such stimuli, perhaps as a protective mechanism to avoid engaging with them and their associated negative emotions in the first place. TTM and SPD are also both posited to have increased impulsivity and difficulty with motor inhibition, and research has supported this.

In summary, from the extant literature on these disorders, they are each characterized by unique IP styles. These biases or differences appear largely consistent with theorized models of the disorders. Encouragingly, they appear amenable to treatment, suggesting these differences are not fixed and unchangeable. With respect to categorization of the OC and related disorders, there appears to be the most overlap in two distinct categories, between TTM and SPD, and then between OCD, HD, and BDD.

Future Directions

It is encouraging to see that in the decade since the first edition of this chapter research on IP biases and/or deficits on OC and related disorders have become more focused on theoretically relevant cognitive processes instead of simply applying a large neuropsychological battery without a hypothesis, leaving previous (and potentially) mixed and incidental findings difficult to interpret.

At the level of each disorder, there are several improvements in research methods that could help further support these findings, including the use of pure samples and appropriate control groups. For example, in OCD, doing investigations by symptom domain, given the heterogeneity of the disorder; in hoarding, using age-matched controls to remove the confound of natural decline in cognitive function; in TTM or SPD making sure participants do not have comorbid OCRDs. Relatedly, increased use of clinical control groups would help elucidate how specific each bias is to each disorder, rather than a general hallmark of psychopathology or distress. Longitudinal assessment across the lifespan, incorporating treatment investigations, would also help clarify whether these IP abnormalities are a vulnerability factor or correlate of the disorder. Certainly, preliminary research in TTM on the lack of IP abnormalities in childhood presentations suggests this is an important avenue for future exploration.

In order that IP research can best contribute to the ongoing discussion of the classification of OCRDs, researcher should consider using the same tests in unified studies of each of these populations, in order to best determine their similarities and differences. In the meantime, meta-analyses (rather than review articles) may help synthesize some of the contradictory findings in the extant literature and provide a clearer picture of the disorder-specific IP deficits (or lack thereof).

Finally, treatment research (be it medication, cognitive remediation, and/or CBT) on OCRDs should more routinely include pre- and post-assessments of relevant cognitive processes to better understand what types of treatment alter these processes. Further research on cognitive remediation as both a stand-alone and adjunct treatment will also help clarify the etiological and maintaining features of IP abnormalities in these conditions.

References

Abedininasab, Z., Rahimi, C., & Goodarzi, M. A. (2012). A comparison of the negative priming effect between subgroups of obsessive-compulsive disorder, other anxiety disorders and control group. *Advances in Cognitive Science*, *13*(4), 58.

Abramovitch, A., Abramowitz, J. S., & Mittelman, A. (2013). The neuropsychology of adult obsessive-compulsive disorder: A meta-analysis. *Clinical Psychology Review*, *33*, 1163–1171.

Albert, U., De Cori, D., Barbaro, F., Fernandez de la Cruz, L., Nordsletten, A. E., & Mataix-Cols, D. (2015). Hoarding disorder: A new obsessive-compulsive related disorder in DSM-5. *Journal of Psychopathology*, *21*, 354–364.

Alcolado, G. M., & Radomsky, A. S. (2011). Believe in yourself: Manipulating beliefs about memory causes checking. *Behaviour Research and Therapy*, *49*, 42–49.

Alcolado, G. M., & Radomsky, A. S. (2016). A novel cognitive intervention for compulsive checking: Targeting maladaptive beliefs about memory. *Journal of Behavior Therapy and Experimental Psychiatry*, *53*, 75–83.

American Psychiatric Association (APA). (2000). *Diagnostic and statistical manual of mental disorders* (4th ed., text revision).

American Psychiatric Association (APA). (2013). *Diagnostic and statistical manual of mental disorders* (5th ed.).

Amir, N., Najmi, S., & Morrison, A. S. (2009). Attenuation of attention bias in obsessive compulsive disorder. *Behaviour Research and Therapy*, *43*, 153–157.

Arabatzoudis, T., Rehm, I. C., Nedeljkovic, M., & Moulding, R. (2017). Emotion regulation in individuals with and without trichotillomania. *Journal of Obsessive-Compulsive and Related Disorders*, *12*, 87–94.

Arditte Hall, K. A., Stamatis, C. A., Shaw, A. M., & Timpano, K. R. (2019). Are hoarding symptoms associated with interpersonally relevant attentional biases? A preliminary investigation. *Journal of Obsessive-Compulsive and Related Disorders*, *22*, 100449.

Armstrong, T., & Olatunji, B. O. (2012). Eye tracking of attention in the affective disorders: A meta-analytic review and synthesis. *Clinical Psychology Review*, *32*(8), 704–723.

Armstrong, T., Olatunji, B. O., Sarawgi, S., & Simmons, C. (2010). Orienting and maintenance of gaze in contamination fear: Biases for disgust and fear cues. *Behaviour Research and Therapy*, *48*(5), 402–408.

Armstrong, T., Sarawgi, S., & Olatunji, B. O. (2012). Attentional bias toward threat in contamination fear: Overt components and behavioral correlates. *Journal of Abnormal Psychology*, *121*, 232–237.

Ashworth, B., & McCown, W. (2018). Trait procrastination, hoarding, and continuous performance attention scores. *Current Psychology*, *37*, 454–459.

Ayers, C., Davidson, E., Dozier, M., & Twamley, E. (2019). Cognitive rehabilitation and exposure/sorting therapy for late-life hoarding: Effects on neuropsychological performance. *The Journals of Gerontology: Series B*, *75*, 1193–1198.

Ayers, C., Dozier, M., Wetherell, J., Twamley, E., & Schiehser, D. (2016). executive functioning in participants over age of 50 with hoarding disorder. *American Journal of Geriatric Psychiatry*, *24*, 342–349.

Ayers, C., Wetherell, J., Schiehser, D., Almklov, E., Golshan, S., & Saxena, S. (2013). Executive functioning in older adults with hoarding disorder: Executive functioning in geriatric hoarding. *International Journal of Geriatric Psychiatry, 28*, 1175–1181.

Baldwin, P., Whitford, T., & Grisham, J. (2018). Psychological and electrophysiological indices of inattention in hoarding. *Psychiatry Research, 270*, 915–921.

Beck, A. T., & Clark, D. A. (1988). Anxiety and depression, an information processing perspective. *Anxiety Research, 1*, 23–36.

Begotka, A. M., Woods, D. W., & Wetterneck, C. T. (2004). The relationship between experiential avoidance and the severity of trichotillomania in a nonreferred sample. *Journal of Behavior Therapy and Experimental Psychiatry, 35*, 17–24.

Blom, R., Samuels, J., Grados, M., Chen, Y., Bienvenu, O., Riddle, M., Liang, K.-Y., Brandt, J., &Nestadt, G. (2011). Cognitive functioning in compulsive hoarding. *Journal of Anxiety Disorders, 25*, 1139–1144.

Bohne, A., Keuthen, N. J., Tuschen-Caffier, B., & Wilhelm, S. (2005). Cognitive inhibition in trichotillomania and obsessive-compulsive disorder. *Behaviour Research and Therapy, 43*, 923–942.

Bohne, A., Savage, C. R., Deckersbach, T., Keuthen, N. J., Jenike, M. A., Tuschen-Caffier, B., & Wilhelm, S. (2005). Visuospatial abilities, memory, and executive functioning in trichotillomania and obsessive-compulsive disorder. *Journal of Clinical and Experimental Neuropsychology, 27*(4), 385–399.

Bohne, A., Savage, C. R., Deckersbach, T., Keuthen, N. J., & Wilhelm, S. (2008). Motor inhibition in trichotillomania and obsessive-compulsive disorder. *Journal of Psychiatric Research, 42*, 141–150.

Boschen, M. J., & Vuksanovic, D. (2007). Deteriorating memory confidence, responsibility perceptions and repeated checking: Comparisons in OCD and control samples. *Behaviour Research and Therapy, 45*(9), 2098–2109.

Bradley, M. C., Hanna, D., Wilson, P., Scott, G., Quinn, P., & Dyer, K. F. (2016). Obsessive-compulsive symptoms and attentional bias: An eye-tracking methodology. *Journal of Behavior Therapy and Experimental Psychiatry, 50*, 303–308.

Brennan, E., Francazio, S., Gunstad, J., & Flessner, C. A. (2016). Inhibitory control in pediatric trichotillomania (hair pulling disorder): The importance of controlling for age and symptoms of inattention and hyperactivity. *Child Psychiatry and Human Development, 47*, 173–182.

Buhlmann, U., Deckersbach, T., Engelhard, I., Cook, L. M., Rauch, S. L., Kathmann, N., Wilhelm, S., & Savage, C. R. (2006). Cognitive retraining for organizational impairment in obsessive–compulsive disorder. *Psychiatry Research, 144*(2–3), 109–116.

Buhlmann, U., Etcoff, N. L., & Wilhelm, S. (2006). Emotion recognition bias for contempt and anger in body dysmorphic disorder. *Journal of Psychiatric Research, 40*, 105–111.

Buhlmann, U., Gleiß, M. J. L., Rupf, L., Zschenderlein, K., & Kathmann, N. (2011). Modifying emotion recognition deficits in body dysmorphic disorder: An experimental investigation. *Depression and Anxiety, 28*, 924–931.

Buhlmann, U., McNally, R. J., Etcoff, N. L., Tuschen-Caffier, B., & Wilhelm, S. (2004). Emotion recognition deficits in body dysmorphic disorder. *Journal of Psychiatric Research, 38*, 201–206.

Buhlmann, U., McNally, R. J., Wilhelm, S., & Florin, I. (2002). Selective processing of emotional information in body dysmorphic disorder. *Journal of Anxiety Disorders, 16*, 289–98.

Buhlmann, U., Rupf, L., Gleiss, M. J. L., Zschenderlein, K., & Kathmann, N. (2014). Seeing "changes" that aren't there: Facial and object discrimination in body dysmorphic disorder. *Comprehensive Psychiatry, 55*, 468–474.

Buhlmann, U., & Wilhelm, S., (2004). Cognitive factors in body dysmorphic disorder. *Psychiatric Annals, 34*, 922–926.

Buhlmann, U., Wilhelm, S., McNally, R.J., Tuschen-Caffier, B., Baer, L., & Jenike, M. (2002b). Interpretive biases for ambiguous information in body dysmorphic disorder. *CNS Spectrums, 7*, 435–443.

Buhlmann, U., Winter, A., & Kathmann, N. (2013). Emotion recognition in body dysmorphic disorder: Application of the Reading the Mind in the Eyes Task. *Body Image, 10*, 247–250.

Carbonella, J., & Timpano, K. (2016). Examining the link between hoarding symptoms and cognitive flexibility deficits. *Behavior Therapy, 47*, 262–273.

Ceschi, G., der Linden, M. V., Dunker, D., Perroud, A., & Bredart, S. (2003). Further exploration memory bias in compulsive washers. *Behaviour Research and Therapy, 41*, 737–747.

Chamberlain, S. R., Blackwell, A. D., Fineberg, N., Robbins, T. W., & Sakahian, B. J. (2006). Strategy implementation in obsessive-compulsive disorder and trichotillomania. *Psychological Medicine, 36*, 91–97.

Chamberlain, S. R., Fineberg, N. A., Blackwell, A. D., Clark, L., Robbins, T. W., & Sahakian, B. J. (2007). A neuropsychological comparison of obsessive-compulsive disorder and trichotillomania. *Neuropsychologia, 45*, 654–662.

Chamberlain, S. R., Fineberg, N. A., Blackwell, A. D., Robbins, T. W., & Sahakian, B. J. (2006). Motor inhibition and cognitive flexibility in obsessive-compulsive disorder and trichotillomania. *The American Journal of Psychiatry, 163*, 1282–1284.

Chamberlain, S. R., Grant, J. E., Costa, A., Müller, U., & Sahakian, B. J. (2010). Effects of acute modafinil on cognition in trichotillomania. *Psychopharmacology, 212*(4), 597–601.

Chamberlain, S. R., Menzies, L., Sahakian, B. J., & Fineberg, N. A. (2007). Lifting the veil on trichotillomania. *The American Journal of Psychiatry, 164*(4), 568–574.

Chou, C. Y., Mackin, R. S., Delucchi, K. L., & Mathews, C. A. (2018). Detail-oriented visual processing style: Its role in the relationships between early life adversity and hoarding-related dysfunctions. *Psychiatry Research, 267*, 30–36.

Christensen, G. A., Mackenzie, T. B., & Mitchell, J. E. (1991). Characteristics of 60 adult chronic hair pullers. *The American Journal of Psychiatry, 148*(3), 365–370.

Clerkin, E. M., & Teachman, B. A. (2008). Perceptual and cognitive biases in individuals with body dysmorphic disorder symptoms. *Cognition and Emotion, 22*, 1327–1339.

Cludius, B., Wenzlaff, F., Briken, P., & Wittekind, C. E. (2019). Attentional biases of vigilance and maintenance in obsessive-compulsive disorder: an eye-tracking study. *Journal of Obsessive-Compulsive and Related Disorders, 20*, 30–38.

Coles, M. E., & Heimberg, R. G. (2002). Memory biases in the anxiety disorders: Current status. *Clinical Psychology Review, 22*, 587–627.

Coetzer, R., & Stein, D. J. (1999). Neuropsychological measures in women with obsessive-compulsive disorder and trichotillomania. *Psychiatry and Clinical Neurosciences, 53*, 413–415.

Coughtrey, A. E., Shafran, R., & Rachman, S. J. (2013). Imagery in mental contamination: a questionnaire study. *Journal of Obsessive-Compulsive and Related Disorders, 2*(4), 385–390.

Daros, A. R., Zakzanis, K. K., & Rector, N. A. (2014). A quantitative analysis of facial emotion recognition in obsessive–compulsive disorder. *Psychiatry Research, 215*(3), 514–521.

Deckersbach, T., Savage, S. R., Phillips, K. A., Wilhelm, S., Buhlmann, U., Rauch, S. L., Baer, L., & Jenike, M. A. (2000). Characteristics of memory dysfunction in body dysmorphic disorder. *Journal of the International Neuropsychological Society, 6*, 673–681.

Diefenbach, G. J., Mouton-Odum, S., & Stanley, M. A. (2002). Affective correlates of trichotillomania. *Behaviour Research and Therapy, 40*(11), 1305–1315.

Dietel, F. A., Möbius, M., Steinbach, L., Dusend, C., Wilhelm, S., & Buhlmann, U. (2018). Effects of induced appearance-related interpretation bias: A test of the cognitive-behavioral model of body dysmorphic disorder. *Journal of Behavior Therapy and Experimental Psychiatry, 61*, 180–187.

Dietel, F. A., Zache, C., Bürkner, P.-C., Schulte, J., Möbius, M., Bischof, A., Wilhelm, S., & Buhlmann, U. (2020). Internet-based interpretation bias modification for body dissatisfaction: A three-armed randomized controlled trial. *International Journal of Eating Disorders, 53*, 972–986.

DiMauro, J., Genova, M., Tolin, D., & Kurtz, M. (2014). Cognitive remediation for neuropsychological impairment in hoarding disorder: A pilot study. *Journal of Obsessive-Compulsive and Related Disorders, 3*, 132–138

Dozier, M. E., & Ayers, C. R. (2017). The etiology of hoarding disorder: A review. *Psychopathology, 50*, 291–296.

Dunai, J., Labuschagne, I., Castle, D. J., Kyrios, M., & Rossell, S. L. (2010). Executive function in body dysmorphic disorder. *Psychological Medicine, 40*, 1541–1548.

Enright, S. J., & Beech, A. R. (1993a). Reduced cognitive inhibition in obsessive-compulsive disorder. *British Journal of Clinical Psychology, 32*, 67–74.

Enright, S. J., & Beech, A. R. (1993b). Further evidence of reduced cognitive inhibition in obsessive-compulsive disorder. *Personality and Individual Differences, 14*, 387–395.

Fang, A., & Wilhelm, S. (2015). Clinical features, cognitive biases, and treatment of body dysmorphic disorder. *Annual Review of Clinical Psychology, 11*, 187–212.

Flessner, C. A., Brennan, E., Murphy, Y. E., & Francazio, S. (2016). Impaired executive functioning in pediatric trichotillomania (hair pulling disorder): Research article: Executive functioning in pediatric TTM. *Depression and Anxiety, 33*, 219–228.

Feusner, J. D., Hembacher, E., Moller, H., & Moody, T. D. (2011). Abnormalities of object visual processing in body dysmorphic disorder. *Psychological Medicine, 41*, 2385–2397.

Feusner, J. D., Moller, H., Altstein, L., Sugar, C., Bookheimer, S., Yoon, J., & Hembacher, E. (2010a). Inverted face processing in body dysmorphic disorder. *Journal of Psychiatric Research, 44*, 1088–1094.

Feusner, J. D., Moody, T., Hembacher, E., Townsend, J., McKinley, M., Moller, H., & Bookheimer, S. (2010b). Abnormalities of visual processing and frontostriatal systems in body dysmorphic disorder. *Archives of General Psychiatry, 67*, 197–205.

Feusner, J. D., Townsend, J., Bystritsky, A., & Bookheimer, S. (2007). Visual information processing of faces in body dysmorphic disorder. *Archives of General Psychiatry, 64*, 1417–1425.

Fitch, K. Ek., & Cougle, J. R. (2013). Perceived and actual information processing deficits in nonclinical hoarding. *Journal of Obsessive-Compulsive and Related Disorders, 2*, 192–199.

Foa, E. B., & McNally, R. J. (1986). Sensitivity to feared stimuli in obsessive-compulsives: A dichotic listening analysis. *Cognitive Therapy and Research, 10*, 477–485.

Fontenelle, L. F., Oldenhoff, E., & the International OCRDs Neuroscience Consensus Group (2020). A transdiagnostic perspective of constructs underlying obsessive-compulsive and related disorders: An international Delphi consensus study. *Australian and New Zealand Journal of Psychiatry, 54*, 719–731.

França, K., Kumar, A., Castillo, D., Jafferany, M., Hyczy da Costa Neto, M., Damevska, K., Wollina, U., & Lotti, T. (2019). Trichotillomania (hair pulling disorder): Clinical characteristics, psychosocial aspects, treatment approaches, and ethical considerations. *Dermatologic Therapy, 32*, e12622.

Frost, R. O., & Hartl, T. L. (1996). A cognitive-behavioral model of compulsive hoarding. *Behaviour Research and Therapy, 34*, 341–350.

Frost, R. O., & Steketee, G. (1998). Hoarding: Clinical aspects and treatment strategies. In M. A. Jenike, L. Baer, & W. E. Minichiello (Eds.) *Obsessive compulsive disorders: Practical management* (pp. 533–554). Elsevier Canada.

Georgiou, G. A., Bleakley, C., Hayward, J., Russo, R., Dutton, K., Eltiti, S., & Fox, E. (2005). Focusing on fear: attentional disengagement from emotional faces. *Visual Cognition, 12*, 145–158.

Goodman, W. K. (2014). Preface obsessive-compulsive and related disorders. *Psychiatric Clinics of North America, 37*, xi–xii.

Grant, J. E. (2019). Trichotillomania (hair pulling disorder). *Indian Journal of Psychiatry, 61*, 136.

Grant, J. E., Odlaug, B. L., & Chamberlain, S. R. (2011). A cognitive comparison of pathological skin picking and trichotillomania. *Journal of Psychiatric Research, 45*, 1634–1638.

Grant, J. E., Odlaug, B. L., Schreiber, L. R. N., & Kim, S. W. (2014). The opiate antagonist, naltrexone, in the treatment of trichotillomania: Results of a double-blind, placebo-controlled study. *Journal of Clinical Psychopharmacology, 34*, 134–138.

Grassi, G., Michelli, L., Di Cesare Manelli, L., Compagno, E., Righi, L., Ghelardini, C., & Pallanti, C. (2016). Atomoxetine for hoarding disorder: A pre-clinical and clinical investigation. *Journal of Psychiatric Research, 83*, 240–248

Greenberg, J. L., Reuman, L., Hartmann, A. S., Kasarskis, I., & Wilhelm, S. (2014). Visual hot spots: An eye tracking study of attention bias in body dysmorphic disorder. *Journal of Psychiatric Research, 57*, 125–132.

Grisham, J., & Baldwin, P. (2015). Neuropsychological and neurophysiological insights into hoarding disorder. *Neuropsychiatric Disease and Treatment, 11*, 951–962.

Grisham, J., & Barlow, D. (2005). Compulsive hoarding: Current research and theory. *Journal of Psychopathology and Behavioral Assessment, 27*, 45–52.

Grisham, J., Brown, T., Savage, C., Steketee, G., & Barlow, D. (2007). Neuropsychological impairment associated with compulsive hoarding. *Behaviour Research and Therapy, 45*, 1471–1483.

Grisham, J. R., Minihan, S., & Winch, C. J. (2019). Imagining as an observer: Manipulating visual perspective in obsessional imagery. *Cognitive Therapy and Research, 43*, 726–736.

Grisham, J. R., Norberg, M. M., Williams, A. D., Certoma, S. P., & Kadib, R. (2010). Categorization and cognitive deficits in compulsive hoarding. *Behaviour Research and Therapy, 48*, 866–872.

Grocholewski, A., Kliem, S., & Heinrichs, N. (2012). Selective attention to imagined facial ugliness is specific to body dysmorphic disorder. *Body Image, 9*, 261–269.

Hallion, L., Diefenbach, G., & Tolin, D. (2015). Poor memory confidence mediates the association between inattention symptoms and hoarding severity and impairment. *Journal of Obsessive-Compulsive and Related Disorders, 7*, 43–48.

Hanes, K. R. (1998) Neuropsychological performance in body dysmorphic disorder. *Journal of the International Neuropsychological Society, 4*, 167–171.

Hartl, T. L., Frost, R. O., Allen, G. J., Deckersbach, T., Steketee, G., Duffay, S. R., & Savage, C. R. (2004). Actual and perceived memory deficits in individuals with compulsive hoarding. *Depression and Anxiety, 20*, 59–69.

Hoenig, K., Hochrein, A., Müller, D. J., & Wagner, M. (2002). Different negative priming impairments in schizophrenia and subgroups of obsessive-compulsive disorder. *Psychological Medicine, 32*, 459–468.

Hofmann, S. G., Asmundson, G. J. G., & Beck, A. T. (2013). The science of cognitive therapy. *Behavior Therapy, 44*, 199–212.

Hough, C., Luks, T., Lai, K., Vigil, O., Guillory, S., Nongpiur, A., Fekri, S., Kupferman, E., Mathalon, D. H., & Mathews, C. A. (2016). Comparison of brain activation patterns during executive function tasks in hoarding disorder and non-hoarding OCD. *Psychiatry Research: Neuroimaging, 255*, 50–59.

Houghton, D. C., Maas, J., Twohig, M. P., Saunders, S. M., Compton, S. N., Neal-Barnett, A. M., Franklin, M. E., & Woods, D. W. (2016). Comorbidity and quality of life in adults with hair pulling disorder. *Psychiatry Research, 239*, 12–19.

Hübner, C., Wiesendahl, W., Kleinstauber, M., Stangier, U., Kathmann, N., & Buhlmann, U. (2016). Facial discrimination in body dysmorphic, obsessive-compulsive and social anxiety disorders. *Psychiatry Research, 236*, 105–111.

Jefferies, K., Laws, K. R., & Fineberg, N. A. (2012). Superior face recognition in body dysmorphic disorder. *Journal of Obsessive-Compulsive and Related Disorders, 1*, 175–179.

Jhung, K., Namkoong, K., Kang, J. I., Ha, R. Y., An, S. K., Kim, C. H., & Kim, S. J. (2010). Perception bias of disgust in ambiguous facial expressions in obsessive–compulsive disorder. *Psychiatry Research, 178*, 126–131.

Johnson, S., Williamson, P., & Wade, T. D. (2018). A systematic review and meta-analysis of cognitive processing deficits associated with body dysmorphic disorder. *Behaviour Research and Therapy, 107*, 83–94.

Kathmann, N., Bogdahn, B., & Endrass, T. (2013). Negative priming in obsessive-compulsive disorder and schizophrenia: Association with symptom patterns. *Journal of Experimental Psychopathology, 4*, 405–419.

Kuelz, A., Riemann, D., Halsband, U., Vielhaber, K., Unterrainer, J., Kordon, A., & Voderholzer, U. (2006). Neuropsychological impairment in obsessive-compulsive disorder—Improvement over the course of cognitive behavioral treatment. *Journal of Clinical and Experimental Neuropsychology, 28*, 1273–1287.

Keijsers, G. P. J., Maas, J., van Opdorp, A., & van Minnen, A. (2016). Addressing self-control cognitions in the treatment of trichotillomania: A randomized controlled trial comparing cognitive therapy to behaviour therapy. *Cognitive Therapy and Research, 40*, 522–531.

Kerwin, L., Hovav, S., Hellemann, G., & Feusner, J.D. (2014). Impairment in local and global processing and set-shifting in body dysmorphic disorder. *Journal of Psychiatric Research, 57*, 41–50.

Keuthen, N. J., Savage, C. R., O'Sullivan, R. L., Brown, H. D., Shera, D. M., Cyr, P., Jenike, M. A., & Baer, L. (1996). Neuropsychological functioning in trichotillomania. *Biological Psychiatry, 39*, 747–749.

Kikul, J., Van Allen, T. S., & Exner, C. (2012). Underlying mechanisms of verbal memory deficits in obsessive-compulsive disorder and major depression–the role of cognitive self-consciousness. *Journal of Behavior Therapy and Experimental Psychiatry, 43*, 863–870.

Kollei, I., Horndasch, S, Erim, Y., & Martin, A. (2017). Visual selective attention in body dysmorphic disorder, bulimia nervosa and healthy controls. *Journal of Psychosomatic Research, 92*, 26–33.

Labuschagne, I., Rossell, S. L., Dunai, J., Castle, D. J., & Kyrios, M. (2013). A comparison of executive function in body dysmorphic disorder (BDD) and obsessive-compulsive disorder (OCD). *Journal of Obsessive-Compulsive and Related Disorders, 2*, 257–262.

Lambrou, C., Veale, D., & Wilson, G. (2011). The role of aesthetic sensitivity in body dysmorphic disorder. *Journal of Abnormal Psychology, 120*, 443–453.

Lamothe, H., Baleyte, J.-M., Mallet, L., & Pelissolo, A. (2020). Trichotillomania is more related to Tourette disorder than to obsessive-compulsive disorder. *Brazilian Journal of Psychiatry, 42*, 87–104.

Lazarov, A., Cohen, T., Liberman, N., & Dar, R. (2015). Can doubt attenuate access to internal states? Implications for obsessive-compulsive disorder. *Journal of Behavior Therapy and Experimental Psychiatry, 49*, 150–156.

Lazarov, A., Dar, R., Liberman, N., & Oded, Y. (2012a). Obsessive-compulsive tendencies and undermined confidence are related to reliance on proxies for internal states in a false feedback paradigm. *Journal of Behavior Therapy and Experimental Psychiatry, 43*, 556–564.

Lazarov, A., Dar, R., Liberman, N., & Oded, Y. (2012b). Obsessive-compulsive tendencies may be associated with attenuated access to internal states: Evidence from a biofeedback-aided muscle tensing task. *Consciousness and Cognition, 21*, 1401–1409.

Lazarov, A., Dar, R., Oded, Y., & Liberman, N. (2010). Are obsessive-compulsive tendencies related to reliance on external proxies for internal states? Evidence from biofeedback-aided relaxation studies. *Behaviour Research and Therapy, 48*, 516–523.

Lazarov, A., Liberman, N., Hermesh, H., & Dar, R. (2014). Seeking proxies for internal states in obsessive–compulsive disorder. *Journal of Abnormal Psychology, 123*, 695.

Lee, H.-J., Franklin, S. A., Turkel, J. E., Goetz, A. R., & Woods, D. W. (2012). Facilitated attentional disengagement from hair-related cues among individuals diagnosed with trichotillomania: An investigation based on the exogenous cueing paradigm. *Journal of Obsessive-Compulsive and Related Disorders, 1*, 8–15.

Lewin, A. B., Larson, M. J., Park, J. M., McGuire, J. F., Murphy, T. K., & Storch, E. A. (2014). Neuropsychological functioning in youth with obsessive compulsive disorder: An examination of executive function and memory impairment. *Psychiatry Research, 216*, 108–115.

Liberman, N., & Dar, R. (2009). Normal and pathological consequences of encountering difficulties in monitoring progress toward goals. In G. B. Moskowitz & H. Grant (Eds.), *The psychology of goals* (pp. 277–303). Guilford.

Liberman, N., & Dar, R. (2018). Obsessive-compulsive tendencies are related to seeking proxies for internal states in everyday life. *Journal of Behavior Therapy and Experimental Psychiatry, 61*, 164–171.

Maas, J., Keijsers, G. P. J., Rinck, M., & Becker, E. S. (2018). Approach-avoidance, attentional and evaluation biases in hair pulling disorder and their relationship with symptom severity. *Journal of Cognitive Psychology, 30*, 743–753.

Mackin, R. S., Areán, P. A., Delucchi, K. L., & Mathews, C. A. (2011). Cognitive functioning in individuals with severe compulsive hoarding behaviors and late life depression. *International Journal of Geriatric Psychiatry, 26*, 314–321.

Mackin, R. S., Vigil, O., Insel, P., Kivowitz, A., Kupferman, E., Hough, C. M., Fekri, S., Crothers, R., Bickford, D., Delucchi, K. L., & Mathews, C. A. (2016). Patterns of clinically significant cognitive impairment in hoarding disorder. *Depression and Anxiety, 33*, 211–218.

Mansueto, C. S., Stemberger, R. M. T., Thomas, A. M., & Golomb, R. G. (1997). Trichotillomania: A comprehensive behavioral model. *Clinical Psychology Review, 17*, 567–577.

Mataix-Cols, D., Frost, R. O., Pertusa, A., Clark, L. A., Saxena, S., Leckman, J. F., Stein, D. J., Matsunaga, H., & Wilhem, S. (2010). Hoarding disorder: A new diagnosis for DSM-V? *Depression and Anxiety, 27*, 556–572.

May, C. P., Kane, M. J., & Hasher, L. (1995). Determinants of negative priming. *Psychological Bulletin, 118*, 35–54.

McMillan, S. G., & Rees, C. S. (2013). An investigation of executive functioning, attention and working memory in compulsive hoarding. *Behavioural and Cognitive Psychotherapy, 41*, 610–625.

Monzani, B., Krebs, G., Anson, M., Veale, D., & Mataix-Cols, D. (2013). Holistic versus detailed visual processing in body dysmorphic disorder: Testing the inversion, composite and global precedence effects. *Psychiatry Research, 210*, 994–999.

Moritz, S., Alpers, G. W., Schilling, L., Jelinek, L., Brooks, A., Willenborg, B., & Nagel, M. (2011). Larger than life: Overestimation of object size is moderated by personal relevance in obsessive–compulsive disorder. *Journal of Behavior Therapy and Experimental Psychiatry, 42*(4), 481–487.

Moritz, S., Kloss, M., & Jelinek, L. (2010). Negative priming (cognitive inhibition) in obsessive-compulsive disorder (OCD). *Journal of Behavior Therapy and Experimental Psychiatry, 41*, 1–5.

Moritz, S., Kloss, M., Katenkamp, B., Birkner, C., & Hand, I. (1999). Neurocognitive functioning in OCD before and after treatment. *CNS Spectrums, 4*(21), 21–22.

Moshier, S. J., Wootton, B. M., Bragdon, L. B., Tolin, D. F., Davis, E., DiMauro, J., & Diefenbach, G. J. (2016). The relationship between self-reported and objective neuropsychological impairments in patients with hoarding disorder. *Journal of Obsessive-Compulsive and Related Disorders, 9*, 9–15.

Mowrer, O. H. (1951). Two-factor learning theory: Summary and comment. *Psychological Review, 58*, 350–354.

Najmi, S., & Amir, N. (2010). The effect of attention training on a behavioral test of contamination fears in individuals with sub- clinical obsessive-compulsive symptoms. *Journal of Abnormal Psychology, 119*, 136–142.

Neziroglu, F., Khemlani-Patel, S., & Veale, D. (2008). Social learning theory and cognitive behavioral models of body dysmorphic disorder. *Body Image, 5*, 28–38.

Odlaug, B. L., Chamberlain, S. R., Derbyshire, K. L., Leppink, E. W., & Grant, J. E. (2014). Impaired response inhibition and excess cortical thickness as candidate endophenotypes for trichotillomania. *Journal of Psychiatric Research, 59*, 167–173.

Odlaug, B. L., & Grant, J. E. (2010). Impulse-control disorders in a college sample: Results from the self-administered Minnesota Impulse Disorders Interview (MIDI). *The Primary Care Companion to The Journal of Clinical Psychiatry, 12*, e1–e5.

Osman, S., Cooper, M., Hackmann, A., & Veale, D. (2004). Spontaneously occurring images and early memories in people with body dysmorphic disorder. *Memory, 12*, 428–436.

Öst, L-G., Havnen, A., Hansen, B., & Kvale, G. (2015). Cognitive behavioral treatments of obsessive-compulsive disorder: A systematic review and meta-analysis of studies published 1993–2014. *Clinical Psychology Review, 40*, 156–169.

Ouimet, A. J., Ashbaugh, A. R., & Radomsky, A. S. (2019). Hoping for more: How cognitive science has and hasn't been helpful to the OCD clinician. *Clinical Psychology Review, 69*, 14.29.

Park, H. S., Shin, Y. W., Ha, T. H., Shin, M. S., Kim, Y. Y., Lee, Y. H., & Kwon, J. S. (2006). Effect of cognitive training focusing on organizational strategies in patients with obsessive-compulsive disorder. *Psychiatry and Clinical Neurosciences, 60*(6), 718–726.

Phillips, K. A., Stein, D. J., Rauch, S. L., Hollander, E., Fallon, B. A., Barsky, A., Fineberg, N., Mataix-Cols, D., Ferrao, Y. A., Saxena, S., Wilhelm, S., Kelly, M. M., Clark, L. A., Pinto, A., Bienvenu, O. J., Farrow, J., & Leckman, J. (2010). Should an obsessive-compulsive spectrum grouping of disorders be included in DSM-V? *Depression and Anxiety, 27*, 528–555.

Premo, J. E., Sarfan, L. D., & Clerkin, E. M. (2016). Training interpretation biases among individuals with body dysmorphic disorder symptoms. *Body Image, 16*, 54–62.

Radomsky, A. S., & Alcolado, G M. (2010). Don't even think about checking: mental checking causes memory distrust. *Journal of Behavior Therapy and Experimental Psychiatry, 41*, 345–351.

Radomsky, A. S., Gilchrist, P. T., & Dussault, D. D. (2006). Repeated checking really does cause memory distrust. *Behaviour Research and Therapy, 44*, 305–316.

Radomsky, A. S., Shafran, R., Coughtrey, A. E., & Rachman, S. (2010). Cognitive-behavior therapy for compulsive checking in OCD. *Cognitive and Behavioral Practice, 17*, 119–131.

Radomsky, A. S., & Rachman, S. (1999). Memory bias in obsessive-compulsive disorder (OCD). *Behaviour Research & Therapy, 37*, 605–618.

Radomsky, A. S., & Rachman, S. (2004). The importance of importance in OCD memory research. *Journal of Behavior Therapy and Experimental Psychiatry, 35*, 137–151.

Radomsky, A. S., Rachman, S. J., & Hammond, D. (2001). Memory bias, confidence and responsibility in compulsive checking. *Behaviour Research & Therapy, 39*, 813–822.

Radomsky, A. S., Wong, S. F., Giraldo-O'Meara, M., Dugas, M. J., Gelfand, L. A., Myhr, G., Schell, S. E., Senn, J. M., Shafran, R., & Whittal, M. L. (2020). When it's at: An examination of when cognitive change occurs during cognitive therapy for compulsive checking in obsessive-compulsive disorder. *Journal of Behavior Therapy and Experimental Psychiatry, 67*, 101442.

Raines, A., Timpano, K., & Schmidt, N. (2014). Effects of clutter on information processing deficits in individuals with hoarding disorder. *Journal of Affective Disorders, 166*, 30–35.

Rasmussen, J. L., Brown, T. A., Steketee, G. S., & Barlow, D. H. (2013). Impulsivity in hoarding. *Journal of Obsessive-Compulsive and Related Disorders, 2*, 183–191.

Reese, H. E., McNally, R. J., & Wilhelm, S. (2010). Facial asymmetry detection in patients with body dysmorphic disorder. *Behaviour Research Therapy, 48*, 936–940.

Rehm, I. C., Nedeljkovic, M., Moulding, R., & Thomas, A. (2019). The Beliefs in Trichotillomania Scale (BiTS): Factor analyses and preliminary validation. *British Journal of Clinical Psychology, 58*, 384–405.

Rettew, D. C., Cheslow, D. L., Rapoport, J. L., Leonard, H. L., Lenane, M. C., Black, B., & Swedo, S. E. (1991). Neuropsychological test performance in trichotillomania: A further link with obsessive-compulsive disorder. *Journal of Anxiety Disorders, 5*, 225–235.

Rosen, J. C., Reiter, J., & Orosan, P. (1995). Cognitive-behavioral body image therapy for body dysmorphic disorder. *Journal of Consulting and Clinical Psychology, 63*, 263–269.

Rossell, S. L., Labuschagne, I., Dunai, J., Kyrios, M., & Castle, D. J. (2014). Using theories of delusion formation to explain abnormal beliefs in body dysmorphic disorder (BDD). *Psychiatry Research, 215*, 599–605.

Rouel, M., & Smith, E. (2018). Attentional bias and its modification in contamination OCD symptomatology. *Cognitive Therapy and Research, 42*(5), 686–698.

Sah, D. E., Koo, J., & Price, V. H. (2008). Trichotillomania. *Dermatologic Therapy, 21*, 13–21.

Sanz, M., Molina, V., Martin-Loeches, M., Calcedo, A., & Rubia, F. J. (2001). Auditory P300 even related potential and serotonin reuptake inhibitor treatment in obsessive- compulsive disorder patients. *Psychiatry Research, 101*, 75–81.

Savage, C. R., Baer, L., Keuthen, N. J., Brown, H. D., Rauch, S. L., & Jenike, M. A. (1999). Organizational strategies mediate nonverbal memory impairment in obsessive compulsive disorder. *Biological Psychiatry, 45*, 905–916.

Savage, C. R., Deckersbach, T., Wilhelm, S., Rauch, S. L., Baer, L., Reid, T., & Jenike, M. A. (2000). Strategic processing and episodic memory impairment in obsessive compulsive disorder. *Neuropsychology, 14*, 141–151.

Schuck, K., Keijsers, G., & Rinck, M. (2012). Implicit processes in pathological skin picking: Responses to skin irregularities predict symptom severity and treatment susceptibility. *Journal of Behavior Therapy and Experimental Psychiatry, 43*, 685–691.

Shin, N. Y., Jang, J. H., Kim, H. S., Shim, G., Hwang, J. Y., Kim, S. N., & Kwon, J. S. (2013). Impaired body but not face perception in patients with obsessive-compulsive disorder. *Journal of Neuropsychology, 7*(1), 58–71.

Slikboer, R., Reser, M. P., Nedeljkovic, M., Castle, D. J., & Rossell, S. L. (2018). Systematic review of published primary studies of neuropsychology and neuroimaging in trichotillomania. *Journal of the International Neuropsychological Society, 24*, 188–205.

Sprengelmeyer, R., Young, A. W., Pundt, I., Sprengelmeyer, A., Calder, A. J., Berrios, G., Winkel, R., Vollmoeller, W., Kuhn, W., Sartory, G., & Przuntek, H. (1997). Disgust implicated in obsessive–compulsive disorder. *Proceedings, Biological Sciences, 264*, 1767–1773.

Stangier, U., Adam-Schwebe, S., Müller, M., & Wolter, M. (2008). Discrimination of facial appearance stimuli in body dysmorphic disorder. *Journal of Abnormal Psychology, 117*, 435–443.

Stanley, M. A., Hannay, H. J., & Breckenridge, J. K. (1997). The neuropsychology of trichotillomania. *Journal of Anxiety Disorders, 11*, 473–488.

Stein, D. J., Coetzer, R., Lee, M., Davids, B., & Bouwer, C. (1997). Magnetic resonance brain imaging in women with obsessive-compulsive disorder and trichotillomania. *Psychiatry Research: Neuroimaging, 74*, 177–182.

Stein, D. J., Grant, J. E., Franklin, M. E., Keuthen, N., Lochner, C., Singer, H. S., & Woods, D. W. (2010). Trichotillomania (hair pulling disorder), skin picking disorder, and stereotypic movement disorder: Toward DSM-V. *Depression and Anxiety, 27*, 611–626.

Stein, D. J., & Phillips, K. A. (2014). Pros and cons of the new DSM-5 chapter of obsessive-compulsive and related disorders. *Current Psychiatry Reviews, 10*, 325–329.

Steketee, G., & Frost, R. O. (2007). *Compulsive hoarding and acquiring: Therapist guide*. Oxford University Press.

Stolcis, G., & McCown, W. (2018). Procrastination, hoarding, and attention beyond age 65: A community-based study. *Current Psychology, 37*, 460–465

Storch, E. A., Abramowitz, J., & Goodman, W. K. (2008). Where does obsessive-compulsive disorder belong in DSM-V? *Depression and Anxiety, 25*, 336–347.

Summers, B. J., & Cougle, J. R. (2016). Modifying interpretation biases in body dysmorphic disorder: Evaluation of a brief computerized treatment. *Behaviour Research and Therapy, 87*, 117–127.

Sumner, J. M., Noack, C. G., Filoteo, J. V., Maddox, W. T., & Saxena, S. (2016). Neurocognitive performance in unmedicated patients with hoarding disorder. *Neuropsychology, 30*, 157.

Suñol, M., Martínez-Zalacaín, I., Picó-Pérez, M., López-Solà, C., Real, E., Fullana, M. A., Pujol, J., Cardoner, N., Menchón, J. M., Alonso, P., & Soriano-Mas, C. (2020). Differential patterns of brain activation between hoarding disorder and obsessive-compulsive disorder during executive performance. *Psychological Medicine 50*, 666–673.

Timpano, K. R., Smith, A. M., Yang, J. C., & Çek, D. (2014). Information processing. In R. O. Frost & G. Steketee (Eds.). *The Oxford handbook of hoarding and acquiring* (pp. 100–119). Oxford University Press.

Toh, W. L., Castle, D. J., & Rossell, S. L. (2015). Examining neurocognition in body dysmorphic disorder using the Repeatable Battery for The Assessment of Neuropsychological Status (RBANS): A comparison with obsessive-compulsive disorder. *Psychiatry Research, 228*, 318–324.

Toh, W. L., Castle, D. J., & Rossell, S. L. (2017). Attentional biases in body dysmorphic disorder (BDD): Eye-tracking using the emotional Stroop task. *Comprehensive Psychiatry, 74*, 151–161.

Tolin, D., Hallion, L. S., Wootton, B. M., Levy, H. C., Billingsley, A. L., Das, A., Katz, B. J., & Stevens, M. C. (2018). Subjective cognitive function in hoarding disorder. *Psychiatry Research, 265*, 215–220.

Tolin, D., Stevens, M., Nave, A., Villavicencio, A., & Morrison, S. (2012). Neural mechanisms of cognitive behavioral therapy response in hoarding disorder: A pilot study. *Journal of Obsessive-Compulsive and Related Disorders, 1*, 180–188.

Tolin, D., Villavicencio, A., Umbach, A., & Kurtz, M. (2011). Neuropsychological functioning in hoarding disorder. *Psychiatry Research, 189*, 413–418.

Tumkaya, S., Karadag, F., Mueller, S. T., Ugurlu, T. T., Oguzhanoglu, N. K., Ozdel, O., Atesci, F. C., & Bayraktutan, M. (2013). Situation awareness in obsessive-compulsive disorder. *Psychiatry Research, 209*(3), 579–588.

Van Ameringen, M., Patterson, B., & Simpson, W. (2014). DSM-5 obsessive-compulsive and related disorders: Clinical implications of new criteria. *Depression and Anxiety, 31*, 487–493.

van den Hout, M., & Kindt, M. (2003a). Repeated checking causes memory distrust. *Behaviour Research and Therapy, 41*, 301–316.

van den Hout, M., & Kindt, M. (2003b). Phenomenological validity of an OCD-memory model and the remember/ know distinction. *Behaviour Research and Therapy, 41*, 369–378.

Vandborg, S. K., Hartmann, T. B., Bennedsen, B. E., Pedersen, A. D., Eskildsen, A., Videbech, P. B. H., & Thomsen, P. H. (2012). Do cognitive functions in obsessive–compulsive disorder change after treatment? A systematic review and a double case report. *Nordic Journal of Psychiatry, 66*(1), 60–67.

Vandborg, S. K., Hartmann, T. B., Bennedsen, B. E., Pedersen, A. D., & Thomsen, P. H. (2015). Are there reliable changes in memory and executive functions after cognitive behavioural therapy in patients with obsessive-compulsive disorder? *Cognitive Neuropsychiatry, 20*, 128–143.

Veale, D. (2004). Advances in a cognitive behavioural model of body dysmorphic disorder. *Body Image, 1*, 113–125.

Veale, D., Anson, M., Miles, S., Pieta, M., Costa, A., & Ellison, N. (2014). Efficacy of cognitive behaviour therapy versus anxiety management for body dysmorphic disorder: A randomised controlled trial. *Psychotherapy and Psychosomatics, 83*, 341–353.

Veale, D., & Neziroglu, F. (2010). *Body dysmorphic disorder—A treatment manual*. Wiley.

Walther, M. R., Ricketts, E. J., Conelea, C. A., & Woods, D. W. (2010). Recent advances in the understanding and treatment of trichotillomania. *Journal of Cognitive Psychotherapy, 24*, 46–64.

Wechsler, D. (1981) *Wechsler adult intelligence scale-revised*. Psychological Corporation.

Wilhelm, S., Buhlmann, U., & McNally, R. J. (2003). Negative priming for threatening vs. non-threatening information in body dysmorphic disorder. *Acta Neuropsychiatrica, 15*, 180–183.

Wilhelm, S., & Neziroglu, F. (2002). Cognitive theory of body dysmorphic disorder. In R. O. Frost & G. Steketee (Eds.), *Cognitive approaches to obsessions and compulsions* (pp. 203–214). Pergamon/Elsevier Science.

Wilhelm, S., Phillips, K. A., Didie, E., Buhlmann, U., Greenberg, J. L., Fama, J. M., Keshaviah, A., & Steketee, G. (2014). Modular cognitive-behavioral therapy for body dysmorphic disorder: a randomized controlled trial. *Behavior Therapy, 45*, 314–327.

Wilhelm, S., Phillips, K. A., Fama, J. M., Greenberg, J. L., & Steketee, G. (2011). Modular cognitive–behavioral therapy for body dysmorphic disorder. *Behavior Therapy, 42*, 624–633.

Wilhelm, S., Phillips, K. A., & Steketee, G. (2013). *A cognitive behavioral treatment manual for body dysmorphic disorder*. Guilford Press.

Wilton, E. P., Flessner, C. A., Brennan, E., Murphy, Y., Walther, M., Garcia, A., Conelea, C., Dickstein, D. P., Stewart, E., Benito, K., & Freeman, J. B. (2020). A neurocognitive comparison of pediatric obsessive-compulsive disorder and trichotillomania (hair pulling disorder). *Journal of Abnormal Child Psychology, 48*, 733–744.

Wilver, N. L., & Cougle, J. R. (2019). An internet-based controlled trial of interpretation bias modification versus progressive muscle relaxation for body dysmorphic disorder. *Journal of Consulting and Clinical Psychology, 87*, 257–269.

Wincze, J., Steketee, G., & Frost, R. (2007). Categorization in compulsive hoarding. *Behaviour Research and Therapy, 45*, 63–72.

Woods, D. W., Flessner, C. A., Franklin, M. E., Keuthen, N. J. K., Goodwin, R. D., Stein, D. J., Walther, M. R., & The Trichotillomania Learning Center-Scientific Advisory Board. (2006). The Trichotillomania

Impact Project (TIP): Exploring phenomenology, functional impairment, and treatment utilization. *The Journal of Clinical Psychiatry, 67*, 1877–1888.

Woods, D. W., & Houghton, D. C. (2014). Diagnosis, evaluation, and management of trichotillomania. *Psychiatric Clinics of North America, 37*, 301–317.

Woody, S. R., Kellman-McFarlane, K., & Welsted, A. (2014). Review of cognitive performance in hoarding disorder. *Clinical Psychology Review, 34*, 324–336.

Yaryura-Tobias, J. A., Neziroglu, F., Chang, R., Lee, S., Pinto, A., & Donohue, L. (2002). Computerized perceptual analysis of patients with body dysmorphic disorder: A pilot study. *CNS Spectrums, 7*, 444–446.

Yousefi, A., Rossell, S. L., Fakour, Y., Ashayeri, H., Naimijoo, P., Fathi, H., Toh, W. L., & Asgharnejad-Farid, A. (2020). Examining memory performance in body dysmorphic disorder (BDD): a comparison study with obsessive compulsive disorder (OCD). *Asian Journal of Psychiatry, 53*, 102110.

Zakrzewski, J. J., Gillet, D. A., Vigil, O. R., Smith, L. C., Komaiko, K., Chou, C., Uhm, S. Y., Bain, L. D., Stark, S. J., Gause, M., Howell, G., Vega, E., Chan, J., Eckfield, M. B., Tsoh, J. Y., Delucchi, K., Mackin, R. S., & Mathews, C. A. (2020). Visually mediated functioning improves following treatment of hoarding disorder. *Journal of Affective Disorders, 264*, 310–317.

CHAPTER 9

Personality Features of Obsessive-Compulsive and Related Disorders

Anthony Pinto *and* Ezra Cowan

Abstract

This chapter reviews personality features (comorbid personality disorders, trait dimensions, and related constructs) in obsessive-compulsive disorder (OCD) and the *DSM-5* obsessive-compulsive and related disorders [body dysmorphic disorder, hoarding disorder, trichotillomania, and excoriation (skin-picking disorder)]. For each disorder, there is a discussion of the impact of personality features on clinical course, including the development and maintenance of symptoms and treatment outcome. The chapter also includes a review of the long-standing, yet often misunderstood, relationship between OCD and obsessive-compulsive personality disorder. Understanding the role of personality variables in the psychopathology of OCD and related conditions has important implications for the study and treatment of the disorders.

Key Words: obsessive-compulsive disorder, personality disorder, trait dimensions, obsessive-compulsive personality disorder, body dysmorphic disorder, hoarding disorder, trichotillomania, excoriation disorder

Obsessive-Compulsive Disorder

Obsessive-compulsive disorder (OCD) is characterized by recurrent, intrusive, and distressing thoughts, images, or impulses (obsessions) and repetitive mental or behavioral acts that the individual feels driven to perform (compulsions) to prevent or reduce distress (*Diagnostic and Statistical Manual of Mental Disorders*, 5th ed. [*DSM-5*], APA, 2013). The disorder produces substantial impairment in social, family, and work functioning (Koran, 2000). This section covers comorbid personality disorder (PD) diagnoses, core trait dimensions, and other personality features associated with OCD, and includes a review of the long-standing, yet often misunderstood, relationship between OCD and obsessive-compulsive PD (OCPD).

Personality Disorder Categories

PDs frequently co-occur in adult patients with OCD, although there is considerable inconsistency in the literature about comorbidity rates of specific PD categories. It can be difficult to compare samples from studies of PDs in OCD due to variability in sample selection and ascertainment, methods of PD assessment (standardized interview versus self-report), unreliability of PD categories, and version of *DSM* applied, given the substantial changes in diagnostic criteria for many PDs across *DSM* editions. This subsection reviews rates of PD categories in OCD, focusing on studies with large clinical samples that apply standardized interviews to assess PD criteria. A sampling of the literature on PD comorbidity in OCD reveals heterogeneity in the personality pathology associated with OCD.

In studies that predate *DSM-IV*, estimates of the prevalence of comorbid Axis II disorders in OCD ranged from 36% (Baer et al., 1990) to 71% (Horesh et al., 1997). In a study of 96 patients with OCD in which the Structured Interview for the DSM-III Personality Disorders (SIDP) was used, 36% met criteria for one or more *DSM-III* PDs, with dependent PD (12%), histrionic PD (9%), and OCPD (6%) diagnosed most frequently (Baer et al., 1990). In a study of 75 outpatients with OCD using the Structured Clinical Interview for DSM-III-R Axis II Personality Disorders (SCID-II), 37% met criteria for one or more Axis II diagnoses, with the most common being the Cluster C disorders, OCPD (12%), avoidant PD (11%), and dependent PD (8%; Mataix-Cols et al., 2000). Horesh et al. (1997) reported that 71% of their OCD patient sample ($n = 51$) had a SCID-II diagnosed PD, including OCPD (18%), schizotypal PD (14%), histrionic PD (14%), dependent PD (10%), and paranoid PD (10%). Summerfeldt et al. (1998) observed that half of participants with OCD diagnosed with any PD are diagnosed with more than one, typically two to four. While all types of PDs have been reported in OCD samples, the most prevalent are those in Cluster C, the "anxious cluster." Other comorbid PDs that have emerged with some consistency include histrionic PD and schizotypal PD. In contrast, several PDs are rarely diagnosed in OCD (less than 5% of cases), including narcissistic PD, schizoid PD, and antisocial PD (Summerfeldt et al., 1998).

Samuels et al. (2000) compared rates of *DSM-IV* PDs, assessed with the Revised SIDP for DSM-IV (SIDP-R), in 72 probands with OCD and 72 community controls. Nearly 45% of case probands had any PD, a prevalence that was more than four times greater than the 10% prevalence in controls. The most common diagnoses in case probands were OCPD (32%) and avoidant PD (15%), both of which were significantly more prevalent in cases than in controls. Similar results were reported in a large clinical sample of primary OCD ($N = 293$), in which 38% of patients met criteria on the SCID-II for at least one *DSM-IV* PD, with OCPD (25%) and avoidant PD (15%) again the most common diagnoses (Pinto et al., 2006). In contrast, Bulli et al. (2016) reported much lower rates of PD in a clinical sample of 159 patients with primary OCD: 20.8% of the participants met criteria on the SCID-II for at least one comorbid *DSM-IV* PD. The most common comorbid disorder was OCPD (9.4%), followed by narcissistic PD (6.3%). In the first comprehensive meta-analysis to identify rates of comorbid PDs across the anxiety disorders, 125 empirical papers from 1980 to 2010 were included (Friborg et al., 2013). The rate of any comorbid PD was high across all anxiety disorders, ranging from 35% for posttraumatic stress disorder to 52% for OCD. The rates of PD clusters within the OCD samples were 34% for Cluster C, 15% for Cluster B, and 13% for Cluster A. The most commonly diagnosed PDs within the OCD samples were all from Cluster C: OCPD (20%), avoidant PD (17%), and dependent PD (10%).

Relationship between OCPD and OCD

OCPD is one of the most common PDs in the general population, with an estimated prevalence ranging from 2.1% to 7.9% (APA, 2013). OCPD is characterized as an enduring pattern that leads to clinically significant distress or functional impairment due to four or more of the following: preoccupation with details and order, self-limiting perfectionism, excessive devotion to work and productivity, inflexibility about morality and ethics, inability to discard worn-out or worthless items, reluctance to delegate tasks, miserliness toward self and others, and rigidity and stubbornness (APA, 2013). Cognitive and behavioral features associated with OCPD include indecision (fear of making a wrong choice), difficulty with change, being excessively bound to rules or routines, having difficulty relating to and sharing emotions, having outbursts of anger or hostility when one's sense of control is threatened, and procrastination (Pinto, 2020). Other features of OCPD include the need to overexplain or qualify statements with excessive detail, a tendency to approach everyday tasks with methodical intensity resulting in delayed progress or avoidance altogether, and a detail-oriented way of processing information that can slow down cognitively demanding tasks like reading (Pinto, 2020). Individuals with this disorder are often characterized as rigid and overly controlling, leading to relationship difficulties. They may find it difficult to relax, feel obligated to plan their activities to the minute, and find unstructured time intolerable (Pinto et al., 2008).

DSM-5 retained the *DSM-IV* criteria for OCPD, categorizing the condition in Cluster C, along with avoidant and dependent PDs, based on the overarching view that these diagnoses represent enduring and pervasive patterns of behavior characterized by excessive anxiety and fear. The diagnostic criteria for OCPD have undergone substantial changes during *DSM* revisions, posing obstacles to studying the disorder (Baer & Jenike, 1998). For example, *DSM-IV* dropped two criteria present in *DSM-III-R*, restricted expression of affection and indecisiveness, because of their poor specificity (i.e., these traits are commonly found in a variety of PDs besides OCPD; Pfohl, 1996).

Interest in the relationship between OCD and OCPD dates back over 100 years. Janet (1904) described the development of frank obsessions and compulsions as being preceded by a period he termed the "psychasthenic state," which was characterized by a sense that actions had been performed incompletely (and the associated need to do them perfectly), a strong focus on order and uniformity, indecisiveness, and restricted emotional expression (Pitman, 1987). Following Janet's observations, Freud (1908/1963) proposed the construct of the anal character, typified by obstinancy, orderliness, and parsimony. Aspects of Janet's description of the psychasthenic state and Freud's description of the anal character were later integrated into definitions of OCPD (Mancebo et al., 2005). For many years, analysts used the term *obsessive-compulsive neurosis* to describe features of both OCD and OCPD (Angyal, 1965).

Despite long-standing interest in the psychiatric community, the controversial relationship between OCD and OCPD remains unclear. While the presence of comorbid OCPD has been suggested as a possible OCD subtype (Coles et al., 2008; Garyfallos et al., 2010) or marker of OCD severity (Lochner et al., 2011), others argue that OCPD should be considered a distinct entity within the OCD spectrum (Bartz et al., 2007). Underlying etiological similarities and differences have not been adequately studied to date, and the lack of data on OCPD treatment limits any comparison of treatment response between the two disorders.

The overlap in symptom presentations between OCD and OCPD can lead to difficulty differentiating them in clinical practice. For example, while excessive list-making can be viewed as a compulsion if it is repetitive and time-consuming, it can also be viewed as a preoccupation with details characteristic of OCPD. Similarly, a preoccupation with order in one's environment can be considered an OCPD criterion but can be a symptom of OCD when associated with arranging rituals. The presence of incompleteness, an inner sense of imperfection, or the uncomfortable subjective state that one's actions or experiences are "just not right" (Janet, 1904), is another area of potential overlap (Summerfeldt, 2004) and is discussed later in this section.

Despite similarities between the criteria for the conditions, OCD and OCPD are distinct diagnostic entities based on particular qualitative differences. First, although both OCD and OCPD often involve time-consuming, methodical behaviors (e.g., writing and rewriting an assignment, organizing and arranging belongings, and making lists), the conditions can be differentiated by the presence of intrusive or unwanted thoughts in OCD and not in OCPD (Pinto et al., 2014). Second, the symptoms of OCD and OCPD appear to spring from distinct motivations when analyzed on a functional level (i.e., what drives/motivates the individual to do them; Pinto et al., 2018; Wheaton & Pinto, 2017). In OCD, obsessions are intrusive, distressing, and generally ego-dystonic. In addition, the majority of OCD patients have sufficient insight to recognize that their symptoms are excessive and irrational (APA, 2013). In contrast, OCPD traits and symptomatic behaviors are considered ego-syntonic and are viewed by affected individuals as appropriate and correct. Although distress is experienced in both conditions, in OCD the distress is typically experienced as a result of the symptoms themselves (i.e., presence of upsetting thoughts, images, or urges), whereas in OCPD distress often comes secondary to the conflict and discrepancy between the OCPD traits and the external world. For example, distress can result from the discrepancy between ideals of perfection and actual performance that does not live up to those standards (Wheaton & Pinto, 2020). Similarly, interpersonal conflict and thus distress can result from attempting to impose rigid rules for conduct on other people. A third difference between OCD and OCPD may be in reward processing. In a study by Pinto et al. (2014), patients with OCPD either with or without comorbid OCD displayed a greater capacity to delay monetary rewards while performing an intertemporal choice task, as compared to participants with OCD (without OCPD) and healthy controls. These findings suggest differences between OCD and OCPD may be related to how the individuals process rewards and point to OCPD as a potential model of excessive self-control.

Although they are best conceptualized as distinct diagnostic entities, there is compelling evidence for a relationship between OCD and OCPD based on comorbidity and familiality. Comorbidity between OCPD and OCD has been reported in numerous studies, most of which have assessed the frequency of OCPD in clinical samples of OCD. (Table 9.1 lists rates of OCPD in OCD clinical samples from studies that used

Table 9.1. Co-Occurrence of OCPD in OCD Clinical Samples

Criteria	Measure	OCD Sample size (N)	OCPD (%)
DSM-III (Baer et al., 1990)	SIDP	96	6
DSM-III (Black et al., 1993)	SIDP	32	28
DSM-III (Eisen & Rasmussen, 1991)	SIDP	114	19
DSM-III-R (Baer & Jenike, 1992)	SIDP-R	55	16
DSM-III-R (Cavedini et al., 1997)	SIDP-R	29	31
DSM-III-R (Crino et al., 1996)	PDE	80	8
DSM-III-R (Diaferia et al., 1997)	SIDP-R	88	31
DSM-III-R (Horesh et al., 1997)	SCID-II	51	18
DSM-III-R (Mataix-Cols et al., 2000)	SCID-II	75	12
DSM-III-R (Matsunaga et al., 1999)	SCID-II	16	11
DSM-III-R (Matsunaga et al., 2000)	SCID-II	94	16
DSM-III-R (Sanderson et al., 1994)	SCID-II	21	5
DSM-III-R (Sciuto et al., 1991)	SIDP-R	30	3
DSM-III-R (Stanley et al., 1990)	SCID-II	25	28
DSM-III-R (Torres & Del Porto, 1995)	SIDP-R	40	18
DSM-IV (Albert et al., 2004)	SCID-II	109	23
DSM-IV (Samuels et al., 2000)	SIDP-R	72	32
DSM-IV (Pinto et al., 2006)	SCID-II	293	25
DSM-IV (Garyfallos et al., 2010)	IPDE	146	31
DSM-IV (Lochner et al., 2011)	SCID-II	403	34
DSM-IV (Starcevic et al., 2013)	MINI	148	47
DSM-IV (Gordon et al., 2016)	SCID-II	92	51

Only studies using standardized, semi-structured diagnostic interviews are listed. Abbreviations:
SIDP = Structured Interview for DSM Personality Disorders; PDE = Personality Disorder Examination;
SCID-II = Structured Clinical Interview for (DSM-III-R or DSM-IV) Axis II Personality Disorders;
IPDE = International Personality Disorder Examination; MINI = Mini International Neuropsychiatric Interview.

standardized, semi-structured diagnostic interviews). Although studies using *DSM-III* and *DSM-III-R* criteria for OCPD showed marked variability in prevalence rates of the disorder in subjects with OCD, recent studies using *DSM-IV/DSM-5* criteria have consistently found elevated rates of OCPD, with estimates ranging from 23% (Albert et al., 2004) to 51% (Gordon et al., 2016) in comparison to rates of OCPD of 2.1% to 7.9% in community samples (APA, 2013). Data from *DSM-IV/DSM-5* OCD studies suggest that the comorbidity rate of OCPD may be higher in treatment trials (e.g., 51%; Gordon et al., 2016) versus naturalistic studies (e.g., 25%; Pinto et al., 2006).

OCPD is the most frequently diagnosed PD in OCD (Garyfallos et al., 2010; Pinto et al., 2006; Samuels et al., 2000). It occurs more frequently in individuals with OCD than in healthy controls (Albert et al., 2004; Samuels et al., 2000) and individuals with other anxiety disorders (panic disorder, social phobia; Crino & Andrews, 1996; Diaferia et al., 1997; Skodol et al., 1995) or major depressive disorder (Diaferia et al., 1997). However, it is important to note that OCPD is not found in most OCD cases.

Although there is evidence of a familial association between OCD and OCPD, the search for a common genetic vulnerability factor has not yet yielded conclusive results. Studies have reported increased frequencies of OCPD traits in the parents of children with OCD (Lenane et al., 1990; Swedo et al., 1989), and a significantly greater frequency of OCPD in first-degree relatives of OCD probands compared to relatives of control probands (11.5% vs. 5.8%, respectively; Samuels et al., 2000). In fact, OCPD was the only PD to occur more often in the relatives of OCD probands. Calvo et al. (2009) reported a higher incidence of *DSM-IV* OCPD in parents of pediatric OCD probands versus the parents of healthy children, even after parents with OCD were excluded. Preoccupation with details, perfectionism, and hoarding were significantly more frequent in parents of children with OCD. Counting, ordering, and cleaning compulsions in OCD children predicted elevated odds of perfectionism and rigidity in their parents. However, as stated, to date the specific genes that may confer a shared vulnerability to both OCPD and OCD have yet to be identified. It remains unknown whether a third variable, such as neuroticism, may explain the familial association between OCPD and OCD.

Individuals with both OCD and OCPD present with distinct clinical characteristics, patterns of functioning, and course of OCD. Data from 629 individuals with PDs indicated that three of the eight *DSM-IV* OCPD criteria (preoccupation with details, perfectionism, and hoarding) were significantly more frequent in patients with comorbid OCD than in those without OCD (Eisen et al., 2006). The relationship between OCD and these three criteria remained significant after controlling for the presence of other anxiety disorders and major depressive disorder, with odds ratios ranging from 2.71 to 2.99. Coles et al. (2008) were the first to systematically examine a range of clinical characteristics in individuals with comorbid OCPD versus individuals without comorbid OCPD in a primary OCD sample, to evaluate the viability of comorbid OCPD as a potential OCD subtype. As compared to subjects without OCPD, the subjects with OCD plus OCPD had a significantly younger age at onset of first OCD symptoms, as well as poorer psychosocial functioning, even though the groups did not differ in overall severity of OCD symptoms. Individuals with OCD plus OCPD also had higher rates of comorbid anxiety disorders and avoidant PD. They reported higher rates of hoarding and incompleteness-related symptoms (including symmetry obsessions and cleaning, ordering, repeating compulsions) than the rates in subjects with OCD without OCPD. As compared to those without comorbid OCPD, those with comorbid OCPD in this naturalistic follow-up sample were only half as likely to remit from OCD after two years (Eisen et al., 2006) and were more than twice as likely to relapse after five years (Eisen et al., 2013), further evidence of a distinct clinical presentation for the putative comorbid OCPD subtype. The findings of Coles et al. (2008) were replicated by Garyfallos et al. (2010). The finding of greater functional impairment in the group with OCD plus OCPD was also supported by Lochner et al. (2011). Subjects with OCD and comorbid OCPD have also been shown to have more severe cognitive inflexibility (Fineberg et al., 2007).

The relationship between OCD and OCPD may be particularly strong for a subgroup of individuals with OCD who have symmetry-related symptoms. In a clinical OCD sample, Baer (1994) found that an OCD symptom factor characterized by symmetry, ordering, repeating, counting, and hoarding was most strongly correlated with the preoccupation with details, perfectionism, and hoarding criteria of OCPD. Similarly, Wellen et al. (2007) reported that the ordering and arranging factor of the Leyton Obsessional Inventory was the only factor associated with OCPD. Finally, high scores on incompleteness in OCD predict meeting criteria for OCPD, and OCD symptoms motivated by feelings of incompleteness (e.g., symmetry/ordering, checking, repeating, counting, slowness) are more strongly related to OCPD than OCD symptoms motivated by harm avoidance (Summerfeldt et al., 2000). Along these lines, Ecker et al. (2014) found positive correlations between obsessive-compulsive personality traits and the OCD symptom dimensions of ordering and checking, which are associated with incompleteness or "not just right experiences" (NJREs). Interestingly, this positive relationship was eliminated when NJREs were statistically controlled. The authors concluded that the dysfunctional behaviors in OCPD may be motivated by efforts to avoid or reduce subjectively intolerable NJREs. More research is needed to better understand the role of incompleteness in OCD and OCPD (Pinto et al., 2017).

There has been speculation about whether OCPD traits are precursors to a later diagnosis of OCD. Pinto et al. (2015) found that childhood OCPD traits were linked to adult diagnosis of OCD. In this study, adults with OCD (without OCPD; $n = 28$), OCPD (without OCD; $n = 27$), both OCD and OCPD ($n = 28$), and healthy controls ($n = 28$) were administered the Childhood Retrospective Perfectionism Questionnaire (CHIRP; Southgate et al., 2008), a retrospective measure of childhood perfectionism, inflexibility, and drive for order. Results indicated that adults with OCD (but without OCPD) reported higher rates of childhood inflexibility and drive for order compared to healthy controls, suggesting that these traits may presage the development of OCD, independent of later OCPD. Furthermore, childhood obsessive-compulsive personality traits were associated with specific OCD symptoms (contamination/washing, doubting/checking, and symmetry/ordering symptoms), controlling for OCPD diagnosis (Pinto et al., 2015). Similarly, in a follow-up study in children with OCD, Park et al. (2016) found that obsessive-compulsive personality traits in youth (using the CHIRP) were associated with concurrent symmetry, contamination, and checking OCD symptoms. Data from this study suggest that childhood OCPD traits may be associated with concurrent or subsequent OCD (at least in some forms), although further longitudinal research is needed.

Relationship between Schizotypal PD and OCD

Schizotypal PD is a pervasive pattern of social and interpersonal deficits, accompanied by discomfort with, and reduced capacity for, close relationships, as well as by cognitive or perceptual aberrations and eccentricities of behavior (APA, 2013). Attademo and Bernardini (2020) reviewed studies on the comorbidity of schizotypal PD and OCD and found a pooled mean prevalence rate of 10.1% of schizotypal PD in OCD, a much higher rate than that found in the general population (1.3%). Their review also pointed to greater impairment in patients with OCD and comorbid schizotypal PD, in that they were more likely to be unemployed, were less educated, were less likely to marry, and had lower general functioning and greater general psychopathology. Perris et al. (2019) reported that compared to patients without schizotypal PD, those with schizotypal PD had a younger age of OCD onset, more severe OCD symptoms, poorer insight, and a higher rate of schizophrenia spectrum disorders in their first-degree relatives.

Personality Dimensions

Considering the variability in results from studies applying PD categories, a dimensional approach to personality, reflecting a comprehensive explanatory model, may be more informative. Determining the nature of the relationship between normal personality traits and OCD may prove helpful in clarifying the disorder's etiology, based on the theoretical view that certain personality traits make individuals vulnerable to the onset of the disorder. Since personality traits are also considered pathoplastic factors that may influence the course and symptom expression of disorders, relating personality dimensions to OCD symptoms may provide a means of identifying more homogeneous phenotypes of the disorder. The psychobiological model of personality and the Five-Factor Model (FFM) are two major conceptualizations of personality that have been studied in OCD.

The psychobiological model of personality (also referred to as the unified biosocial model of personality) proposed by Cloninger and colleagues (1986, 1993) reflects a biogenetic understanding of how temperament and character underlie patterns of human behavior. The model has been applied to a range of psychiatric disorders (Cloninger & Svrakic, 1997). According to the theory, there are four temperament dimensions (novelty-seeking, harm avoidance, reward dependence, persistence) and three character dimensions (self-directedness, cooperativeness, self-transcendence). Temperament dimensions are defined by individual differences in automatic responses to emotional stimuli (e.g., novelty, danger, reward). They are independently heritable, manifest early in life, and are hypothesized to be related to specific neurotransmitter systems. Character dimensions, on the other hand, refer to response biases that are related to concepts of the self, as well as individual differences in goals and values. They are moderately influenced by sociocultural learning and mature progressively throughout life.

The components of Cloninger's model are assessed using the Temperament and Character Inventory (TCI; Cloninger et al., 1994). The TCI is the successor to the Tridimensional Personality Questionnaire (TPQ; Cloninger et al., 1991). Whereas the TPQ assessed only three of the temperament dimensions (novelty-seeking, harm avoidance, and reward dependence), the TCI includes the temperament dimension of persistence in addition to the three character dimensions.

Using the TPQ to evaluate temperament in OCD, Pfohl et al. (1990) found that, compared to healthy controls, subjects with OCD had significantly higher scores on harm avoidance and reward dependence, and lower scores on novelty-seeking. Despite a theoretical link between harm avoidance and serotonin-mediated neuropathways, the elevation in harm avoidance was not associated with a reduction in platelet imipramine binding, a hypothesized indicator of increased serotonergic activity. Richter et al. (1996) also reported that higher scores on the harm-avoidance dimension of the TPQ distinguished patients with OCD from healthy controls. Within that dimension, the authors noted particular elevations on the lower-order trait of fear of uncertainty, consistent with clinical accounts of obsessional doubt and inability to tolerate ambiguity in OCD (Cloninger, 1986). Bejerot et al. (1998) studied the role of temperament and acquired character in OCD using the TCI. They noted significantly higher scores on harm avoidance (temperament) and lower scores on self-directedness and cooperativeness (character) in subjects with OCD versus healthy volunteers. Kusonoki et al. (2000) reported the same profile in a sample of patients with primary OCD compared to healthy controls, as well as in a separate sample with major depression. Lower scores on novelty-seeking distinguished the OCD group from the depression group, leading the authors to conclude that low novelty-seeking may have a specific role in the etiology of OCD. In an OCD patient sample, Lyoo et al. (2001) noted that high harm-avoidance scores and low self-directedness scores predicted greater OCD severity, controlling for age, gender, and level of depression and anxiety. Alonso et al. (2008) reported significantly higher scores on harm avoidance and lower scores on novelty-seeking, self-directedness, and cooperativeness in subjects with OCD than in healthy comparison subjects. These results remained even when subjects with OCD and comorbid disorders were excluded.

The consistent finding of high harm-avoidance and low novelty-seeking temperament dimensions in OCD is congruent with cognitive theories that point to certain belief domains—such as an inflated sense of responsibility and the overestimation of threat—as having a role in the onset of the disorder (Obsessive Compulsive Cognitions Working Group, 1997). These belief domains explain why individuals with OCD tend to view situations as dangerous unless proven safe and tend to become vigilant in novel situations. With regard to character dimensions, Bejerot et al. (1998) hypothesized that the low scores on self-directedness and cooperativeness observed in subjects with OCD across several of the above studies reflect the high frequency of PDs in OCD, since low scores on these dimensions are key elements of personality pathology.

The FFM has emerged as a robust and comprehensive conceptualization of personality. The FFM proposes that personality is composed of five broad personality trait domains (neuroticism, extraversion, openness to experience, agreeableness, and conscientiousness) that are normally distributed in the general population. As described by Costa and McCrae (1992), neuroticism refers to a tendency toward emotional instability, and the predisposition to experience negative affectivity, such as anxiety, depression, anger, guilt, and disgust. Extraversion, a preference for interpersonal interaction and activity, includes sociability, cheerfulness, and liveliness. High levels of neuroticism and low levels of extraversion have been linked to the presence of psychological disorders (Widiger & Trull, 1992). Openness to experience consists of aesthetic sensitivity, intellectual curiosity, and need for variety. Agreeableness incorporates trust, altruism, and sympathy, while conscientiousness includes a strict adherence to principles and a desire to achieve goals. The Revised NEO Personality Inventory (NEO-PI-R) is a widely used, extensive measure of the five trait dimensions (Costa et al., 1992). Each of the five FFM domains contains six separate scales that measure more narrow, lower-order facets of the domains (30 facets in total). Although the domain and facet traits of the FFM were derived from normal, nonclinical samples, the same five domains have been validated in psychiatric patients (Bagby et al., 1997).

The FFM, as assessed by the NEO-PI-R, has been examined in OCD in both community and clinical samples. In an epidemiological study, Samuels et al. (2000) reported that participants with a lifetime diagnosis of OCD scored significantly higher on the neuroticism domain and all its facets, in comparison to healthy subjects. Samuels et al. also reported that individuals with OCD had higher scores on two openness facets (openness to fantasy and openness to feelings) and lower scores on two conscientiousness facets (competence and self-discipline). According to the authors, this profile suggests a description of some individuals with OCD as "highly neurotic, tender-minded people who have difficulty completing tasks" (p. 460). High scores on impulsiveness (a facet of neuroticism) and openness to fantasy may reflect difficulty in resisting intrusive thoughts.

Bienvenu et al. (2004) described normal personality domains and facets in a broad community sample examined by psychiatrists for lifetime anxiety and depressive disorders. High mean neuroticism was associated with all the anxiety disorders studied (including OCD) except for specific phobia. In addition, subjects with lifetime OCD reported high openness to experience, consistent with the finding of high openness to fantasy by Samuels et al. (2000). In a clinical sample, Rector et al. (2002) reported that patients with a primary diagnosis of OCD were very high on neuroticism, very low on extraversion, and low on conscientiousness in comparison to normative means. When compared to patients who were presently in a major depressive episode, the subjects with OCD scored higher on extraversion and agreeableness and lower on neuroticism, controlling for depression severity. In a subset of the patients with OCD, Rector et al. (2005) examined whether specific FFM facets predict the severity of OCD symptoms. After accounting for depression severity, lower scores on openness to ideas were uniquely associated with greater obsession severity, whereas lower openness to actions was uniquely associated with greater compulsion severity. The authors speculated that while neuroticism may confer a nonspecific vulnerability to the development of OCD, facets of openness may impact the particular expression and severity of OCD symptoms. In the largest study to date of personality dimensions in OCD-affected individuals (N = 705), Samuels et al. (2020) found that the odds of examiner-rated severe or extreme impairment increased with neuroticism score and decreased with extraversion score.

Little is known about personality dimensions in relatives of patients with OCD. Samuels et al. (2000) compared scores on FFM domains between the first-degree relatives of OCD cases and controls, in order to determine whether specific personality characteristics are part of a familial spectrum of OCD. Case relatives scored significantly higher on neuroticism, but not other domains. At the facet level, case relatives scored significantly lower on excitement-seeking and openness to actions, and significantly higher on order. The authors noted that this constellation of traits is consistent with a description of obsessionality by Kringlen (1965). Furthermore, Samuels et al. (2000) noted that neuroticism was associated with the presence of OCPD in case relatives, but not in control relatives. That is, the prevalence of OCPD in case relatives increased at higher levels of neuroticism. This relationship remained even after controlling for the presence of OCD in case relatives. The authors concluded that neuroticism and OCPD may share a common familial etiology with OCD.

Perfectionism

Perfectionism has played a major role in theories and clinical descriptions of OCD and has also been linked to OCD symptoms (Raines et al., 2019). The Obsessive Compulsive Cognitions Working Group (1997) considered perfectionism to be a risk factor for the development of the disorder, while others considered it to be a necessary but insufficient predisposing trait for OCD (Rheaume et al., 1995). The trait has been defined as the tendency to set high standards and to employ overly critical self-evaluations (Frost & Marten, 1990). Rasmussen and Eisen (1992) described patients with OCD as being tormented by an inner drive for certainty and perfection, which leads to overwhelming doubt about whether they have performed actions correctly. Patients with OCD show significantly higher levels of perfectionism than do nonclinical controls (Antony et al., 1998; Frost & Steketee, 1997). Measures of perfectionism, especially with regard to excessive concern over mistakes and doubts about actions, are positively correlated with measures of obsessive-compulsive symptoms in both nonclinical (Frost et al., 1994; Rheaume et al., 1995) and clinical (Ferrari, 1995) samples. In addition, perfectionism has been linked to specific types of OCD symptoms, including ordering (Tolin et al., 2003), checking (Gershunny & Sher, 1995), cleaning (Tallis, 1996), and hoarding (Frost & Gross, 1993). In a student sample, Wu and Cortesi (2009) found that perfectionism predicted checking, washing, and ordering symptoms, even after accounting for depression and the cognitive domain of responsibility/threat estimation. In a large sample of patients with eating disorders, perfectionism scores, assessed by the Multidimensional Perfectionism Scale, were highest in individuals with OCPD, whether alone or in combination with OCD (Halmi et al., 2005), suggesting that this trait may be more closely associated with OCPD than OCD.

Maladaptive perfectionism, the tendency to feel that any less-than-perfect performance is unacceptable, is one of the most stable and prevalent OCPD features. It has been studied as a transdiagnostic process (Egan et al., 2011) that can lead to distress and functional impairment both on its own and through various psychiatric disorders. Perfectionism may be a significant vulnerability factor for later depression (Rice & Aldea, 2006). The presence of perfectionism has been shown to impede the treatment of depression, possibly due to its relationship with rigidity, which may interfere in the therapeutic alliance or make it more difficult to modify core beliefs (Blatt et al., 1995, 1998). Socially prescribed perfectionism, the belief that others hold unrealistic expectations for one's behaviors, has been uniquely associated with greater likelihood of suicidal ideation (Hewitt et al., 1994, 1997) and poorer marital adjustment for both the individual and the partner (Haring et al., 2003). Further research is needed to explore the potential maladaptive effects of perfectionism and rigidity, as well as their interaction, on both psychosocial functioning and course of OCD and OCPD.

Role of Personality/PDs in Course and Treatment

PDs and personality dimensions have not been systematically examined as predictors of OCD course in prospective longitudinal studies. However, two studies have investigated longitudinal associations between OCD and OCPD, with conflicting results. In a longitudinal study of PDs, including OCPD, Shea et al. (2004) found that improvement in OCPD generally did not significantly predict remission from OCD. On the other hand, in a longitudinal study of patients with primary OCD, the presence of OCPD was associated with a poorer course of OCD; those with comorbid OCPD at intake were half as likely to remit from OCD after two years (Eisen et al., 2006) and were more than twice as likely to relapse after five years (Eisen et al., 2013), as compared to those without comorbid OCPD at intake. Clearly, the association between OCD and OCPD over time is an understudied area, and further research would shed light on the relationship between the two disorders.

How do comorbid PDs impact the outcome of the gold-standard OCD treatments, serotonin reuptake inhibitors (SRIs) and cognitive-behavioral therapy (CBT)? A review of the literature provided evidence for a negative impact, but there are exceptions. Baer et al. (1992) reported an adverse effect of *DSM-III* PDs on clomipramine treatment for patients with OCD. Specifically, the presence of schizotypal PD, borderline PD, and avoidant PD, along with the total number of PDs, predicted significantly poorer pharmacotherapy outcome. When examined at the cluster level, results showed that only Cluster A disorders predicted poorer outcome. Thiel et al. (2013) systematically reviewed 23 studies on the effect of comorbid PDs on therapy outcomes in adults with OCD. Cluster A disorders (particularly schizotypal PD), narcissistic PD, and the presence of two or more comorbid PDs were associated with poorer treatment outcomes. These findings correspond to reports of greater overall treatment resistance (Jenike et al., 1986) and poorer behavior therapy outcome (Minichiello et al., 1987) among patients with OCD and comorbid schizotypal PD. Over a three-year follow-up period, Perris et al. (2019) reported a poorer response rate to standard pharmacological treatment strategies in patients with OCD and comorbid schizotypal PD. As compared to patients with OCD without a comorbid *DSM-III-R* PD, patients with OCD and comorbid PD had less symptomatic relief after comprehensive behavior therapy, were rated by therapists as more difficult to treat, required more psychiatric hospitalizations during treatment, and were more likely to terminate treatment prematurely (AuBuchon & Malatesta, 1994).

In contrast, a few studies report no negative effect of PDs on OCD treatment outcome, or even improvement in personality pathology as a result of such treatment. For example, Steketee (1990) reported that the presence of PDs, assessed by the revised Personality Diagnostic Questionnaire (PDQ-R) for *DSM-III-R* (a self-report measure), at baseline was not associated with outcome of intensive behavior therapy for OCD. Only the presence of passive-aggressive traits predicted treatment failure in this study. Fricke et al. (2006) noted that, after six months of prospective follow-up, most patients with OCD in their sample had benefited from individually tailored multimodal CBT, regardless of the presence of a comorbid PD. Furthermore, two studies indicated that abnormal personality traits can improve along with successful OCD response to CBT (McKay et al., 1996; Ricciardi et al., 1992). Solem et al. (2015) reported that the presence of schizotypal symptoms did not affect response to exposure with response prevention (E/RP) in nonpsychotic patients with OCD and reductions in the schizotypal symptoms were observed after E/RP.

In a long-term follow-up study of 16 patients with severe and refractory OCD who had undergone ventromedial frontal leucotomy in the 1970s, it was noted that three patients with comorbid OCPD improved significantly less than the rest, a finding implying that OCPD may be associated with a more refractory form of OCD that might involve different neural pathways (Irle et al., 1998). Given this observation, as well as data reviewed earlier indicating poorer course and functioning for subjects with OCD and comorbid OCPD (Coles et al., 2008; Garyfallos et al., 2010), does comorbid OCPD interfere in the clinical efficacy of OCD treatments? The impact of comorbid OCPD on SRI treatment for OCD has been examined in two studies, and results are equivocal. As mentioned previously, in a 12-week study of clomipramine treatment for OCD, only the presence of schizotypal PD, borderline PD, and avoidant PD predicted poorer treatment outcome; there was no effect for *DSM-III* OCPD (Baer et al., 1992). However, Cavedini et al. (1997) reported a worse outcome for patients with comorbid *DSM-III-R* OCPD, as compared to those with uncomplicated OCD, after 10 weeks of SRI treatment (either clomipramine or fluvoxamine). The authors concluded that comorbid OCPD may identify a subtype of OCD with a different pattern of SRI response.

Studies of the impact of comorbid OCPD on CBT response in OCD are also equivocal. Among outpatients with primary OCD, OCPD diagnosis and greater OCPD severity (defined as the number of clinically significant *DSM-IV* OCPD criteria present at baseline) predicted worse ERP outcome (Pinto et al., 2011). Of all the OCPD criteria, the presence of perfectionism was most strongly associated with poor E/RP outcome. In contrast, in a study of patients with OCD receiving more cognitively based CBT (utilizing cognitive restructuring and behavioral experiments to change underlying beliefs), Gordon et al. (2016) reported better outcomes for those with comorbid OCPD, when compared to patients without comorbid OCPD. In light of the discrepancy between these studies, OCPD may have a more negative impact on a behaviorally based treatment (E/RP) than on cognitively based CBT. Therefore, the effect of OCPD on CBT outcome may depend on the specific variant of CBT used to treat OCD.

The relationship between PDs and treatment response is complex and is affected by much more than just interaction between the patient and treatment provider. For instance, higher rates of personality pathology in family members of patients with OCD (versus control relatives), as mentioned previously (Calvo et al., 2009; Samuels et al., 2000), may compromise their ability to support and/or participate in the patient's treatment. It is important for clinicians to recognize that pathological personality features in the close relatives of their patients may influence the course of treatment.

Few studies have investigated the impact of general personality dimensions on the clinical course or treatment response of individuals with OCD. In one study by Sartory and Grey (1982), patients with OCD and high extraversion on the Eysenck Personality Inventory had a better response to clomipramine and/or behavior therapy than patients with low extraversion. An explanation for this finding is that those with high extraversion may have been more engaged with their treatment providers, leading to greater adherence to the intervention. In a prospective study of 296 patients with OCD, neuroticism was a strong predictor of remission during the follow-up period (Askland et al., 2015).

According to Samuels et al. (2020), self-reported response to pharmacotherapy or CBT increased with extraversion scores in 705 individuals with OCD.

Perfectionism has also been shown to be a treatment predictor in patients with OCD. As mentioned, Pinto et al. (2011) found that perfectionism stood out among the individual OCPD symptoms as the only one linked to poorer E/RP outcome in a study of outpatients with OCD. In line with this finding, Kyrios et al. (2015) reported that greater perfectionism or intolerance of uncertainty at baseline was associated with poorer response to CBT for OCD, accounting for baseline severity. These authors further noted that reductions in perfectionism/need for certainty scores over the course of the CBT significantly accounted for improvement in OCD symptoms. Similarly, Wheaton et al. (2020) found that reductions in maladaptive perfectionism over the course of intensive residential treatment for OCD predicted better OCD symptom outcomes. Collectively, these findings suggest that perfectionism may be an important mediator of OCD improvement and could therefore be specifically targeted in OCD treatment.

Body Dysmorphic Disorder

Body dysmorphic disorder (BDD) is characterized by preoccupation with one or more perceived defects or flaws in physical appearance that are not observable or appear slight to others and repetitive behaviors (e.g., mirror-checking, excessive grooming, skin-picking, reassurance-seeking) or mental acts (e.g., comparing one's appearance with that of others) that are performed in response to the appearance concerns (APA, 2013). The symptoms cause clinically significant distress or impairment of functioning.

PD Categories

PD comorbidity has been consistently reported in BDD. In a sample of well-characterized patients with BDD, 57% of the subjects interviewed with the SCID-II reported at least one *DSM-III-R* PD, with avoidant PD (43%) being most common, followed by dependent PD (15%), OCPD (14%), and paranoid PD (14%; Phillips & McElroy, 2000). In a study of patients with primary BDD evaluated with the SCID-II, 72% met criteria for at least one *DSM-III-R* PD, with avoidant PD and paranoid PD most common (each present in 38%), followed by OCPD (28%; Veale et al., 1996). In a study of patients with BDD entering a psychopharmacology trial, 87% met criteria for at least one *DSM-III-R* PD diagnosis, and 53% had more than one PD (Cohen et al., 2000). In a separate report of patients with BDD entering CBT, all had a *DSM-III-R* PD, and 77% had four or more (Neziroglu et al., 1996). In one of the largest clinical samples of BDD ($N = 200$) to date, Phillips, Menard, et al. (2005) described a somewhat lower rate of PDs than found the studies above. They reported that close to 45% of their sample met criteria for at least one *DSM-IV* PD on the SCID-II, with the most prevalent being avoidant PD (25%) and OCPD (13%). As compared to participants with late-onset BDD, participants with early-onset BDD (age 17 or younger) in this sample had a greater number of lifetime comorbid disorders on both *DSM-IV* Axis I and Axis II, including a higher rate of borderline PD (Bjornsson et al., 2013). In the first study to directly compare samples of primary OCD, primary BDD, and a sample with comorbid OCD and BDD in a comprehensive and systematic way (Phillips et al., 2007), a higher proportion of subjects with BDD than subjects with OCD had paranoid PD. Contrary to the authors' hypothesis, subjects with BDD were not significantly more likely than subjects with OCD to have avoidant PD, although the comorbid group was more likely to have the diagnosis than the OCD group. Both the OCD and comorbid groups were more likely than the BDD group to have OCPD, but this finding was at a trend level.

Personality Dimensions

Few studies have systematically examined personality and temperament dimensions in BDD. Cohen et al. (2000) applied the Dimensional Assessment of Personality Impairment (DAPI), a semi-structured interview that measures personality using a dimensional rather than categorical approach. The DAPI instrument is based on the notion that personality impairment arises from dysregulation of affective, conceptual, and interpersonal functioning. Patients with BDD scored in the range of moderate impairment on most DAPI scales, with the greatest impairment in the regulation of depression, anxiety, cognitive filtering of distressing information, self-esteem, and self-inhibition. Phillips and McElroy (2000) reported personality dimension scores of patients with BDD using the NEO-Five-Factor Inventory (NEO-FFI), a shorter version of the NEO-PI-R that assesses the domains of the FFM without the lower-order facets. Scores were in the very high range for neuroticism and the low range for extraversion and conscientiousness, similar to findings from a clinical sample of patients with OCD (Rector et al., 2002). Consistent with the low extraversion score and high rates of avoidant PD in these patients, scores on the Rathus Assertiveness Scale, completed by a subset of the sample, indicated a tendency to be unassertive, with women scoring below the 15th percentile and men scoring below the 10th percentile. In a more recent study of specific personality traits in BDD, perfectionism and behavioral inhibition system (BIS) reactivity (a measure of sensitivity to punishment and proneness to anxiety) were more pronounced in individuals with BDD than in a population-based control sample (Schieber et al., 2013), pointing to these traits as possible vulnerability factors for BDD.

Role of Personality/PDs in Course and Treatment

Based on clinical descriptions and case reports, researchers have hypothesized that particular personality traits, such as perfectionism, self-criticism, insecurity, and sensitivity, may predispose to BDD (Phillips, 1991). On the other hand, to what degree is personality impairment a result of BDD, or of the neurobiological vulnerabilities associated with it? Longitudinal and prospective studies are needed to shed light on these questions.

The presence of comorbid PDs appears to increase the morbidity of BDD. In the first naturalistic, prospective study of the course of BDD, having a PD significantly predicted a lower likelihood of remitting from BDD after one year of follow-up (Phillips, Pagano, et al., 2005). Although personality pathology is expected to play a role in the social impairment noted in BDD, the presence of a PD did not predict psychosocial functioning in this longitudinal study (Phillips et al., 2008). Cohen et al. (2000) reported that the total number of comorbid SCID-II diagnoses in a BDD sample was correlated with depression severity. Compared to subjects with BDD without major depressive disorder, subjects with BDD and current depression were more likely to have avoidant PD, OCPD, borderline PD, or depressive PD (Phillips et al., 2007). In a sample of outpatients with depression, subjects with depression and BDD had higher rates of avoidant PD, histrionic PD, and dependent PD than did subjects with depression without BDD (Nierenberg et al., 2002). Finally, in a BDD sample, both suicidal ideation and suicide attempts were associated with the presence of any PD, particularly borderline PD (Phillips, Menard, et al., 2005).

There are suggestions in the literature that personality impairment may play a role in BDD treatment response, although the findings are equivocal. Cohen et al. (2000) reported that responders to pharmacotherapy demonstrated less personality impairment, as measured by total DAPI score and number of SCID-II diagnoses, than nonresponders. Likewise, Fang et al. (2019) found that higher baseline neuroticism was a significant predictor of nonresponse to escitalopram treatment in a BDD sample, even when controlling for baseline depression severity. Phillips and McElroy (2000) found that the number of PDs assigned to fluvoxamine responders decreased from study baseline to endpoint. However, in a randomized placebo-controlled trial of fluoxetine in BDD, Phillips et al. (2002) reported that treatment response was independent of the presence of a PD. Furthermore, Neziroglu et al. (1996) found no relationship between PD diagnoses and response to intensive CBT in BDD. Studies are needed to investigate whether pharmacotherapy or psychosocial treatments alter personality dimensions associated with BDD, and whether such changes mediate treatment outcome.

Hoarding Disorder

Hoarding disorder (HD) is characterized by persistent difficulty discarding or parting with possessions, regardless of their actual value; perceived need to save the items and distress associated with discarding them; accumulation of significant clutter that impairs function of living space; and clinically significant distress or impairment in social, occupational, or other functioning (including a safe living environment; APA, 2013). HD can lead to legal citations and evictions from home by public health authorities (Frost et al., 2000; Tolin et al., 2008) and represents a profound public health burden (Tolin et al., 2008). HD diagnostic criteria were first established in *DSM-5*, which estimates a lifetime prevalence for HD of 2% to 6% in the United States (APA, 2013).

PD Categories

PDs commonly co-occur with hoarding. In an epidemiological study, Samuels et al. (2008) studied correlates of hoarding behavior in the community. They found that the odds of hoarding in community participants increased with the number of *DSM-IV* symptoms of specific PDs, including paranoid PD, schizotypal PD, avoidant PD, and OCPD. In a study comparing individuals with compulsive hoarding with nonhoarding anxious or depressed patients, as well as with nonclinical community participants, Grisham et al. (2008) reported that the hoarding group endorsed more *DSM-IV* schizotypal PD symptoms than participants in both comparison groups.

With respect to OCD, Mataix-Cols et al. (2000) reported that, independent of OCD symptom severity, hoarding symptoms predict a higher probability of having a PD diagnosis, especially OCPD and avoidant PD. Frost et al. (2000) compared subjects with OCD and hoarding, subjects with OCD without hoarding, subjects with anxiety disorders, and community controls, and found that subjects with OCD and hoarding had more *DSM-IV* symptoms of dependent and schizotypal PD than any of the other groups. The fact that the three clinical groups did not differ on the number of nonhoarding OCPD symptoms endorsed argues against a specific association between hoarding and OCPD. Samuels et al. (2002) reported that OCPD and several Cluster B disorders (borderline, histrionic, and narcissistic PD) are more prevalent in hoarding OCD versus nonhoarding OCD. The magnitude of these relationships did not change appreciably after controlling for OCD severity. Among the symptoms of OCPD, perfectionism and preoccupation with details, in addition to the overlapping hoarding symptom, were much more frequent in individuals with HD. Lochner, Kinnear, et al. (2005) noted a higher prevalence of *DSM-IV* OCPD in hoarding OCD versus nonhoarding OCD. Samuels et al. (2007) found a higher rate of *DSM-IV* OCPD and dependent PD in hoarding OCD versus nonhoarding OCD. Results from multivariate analyses indicate that five PD criteria (miserliness and preoccupation with details from OCPD; difficulty making decisions from dependent PD; odd behavior/appearance and magical thinking from schizotypal PD) were strongly and independently related to hoarding in these individuals. Finally, Pertusa et al. (2008) reported that subjects with hoarding OCD endorsed significantly more *DSM-IV* personality symptoms than did subjects with nonhoarding OCD. In this study, the association between hoarding and OCPD was primarily due to overlapping item content. When the hoarding criterion of OCPD was removed, the number of endorsed OCPD criteria was comparable across four patient groups (patients with OCD and HD, patients with HD without OCPD, patents with OCD without HD, patients with anxiety disorder), evidence that individuals with compulsive hoarding may not be more likely than those with other psychiatric disorders to endorse OCPD. However, these findings conflict with previously mentioned results by Samuels et al. (2002, 2007), which found that several OCPD criteria (besides the hoarding criterion) were strongly associated with hoarding behavior.

Large-scale epidemiological studies (e.g., Grant et al., 2012) and longitudinal studies (e.g., McGlashan et al., 2005) have not yet reported on rates of comorbid HD in OCPD since the formal diagnostic criteria for HD were only codified with the publication of *DSM-5* (APA, 2013). However, research on individuals with HD has generally found that a substantial minority meet criteria for comorbid OCPD. In a study of 217 individuals with primary HD as well as 96 individuals with OCD, Frost et al. (2011) found that comorbid OCPD was observed in 29.5% of the participants with HD, a rate significantly higher than that among the participants with OCD (16.7% of whom had comorbid OCPD). Given that difficulty discarding is one of the eight criteria for OCPD and is also a diagnostic criterion for HD, the authors were concerned that the overlap in criteria could inflate the comorbidity rate of OCPD in an HD sample. Therefore, they tested this by applying a more conservative definition of OCPD and determining how many participants in the HD sample met criteria for OCPD when the difficulty discarding criterion was excluded (i.e., how many participants met four out of the remaining seven OCPD criteria). With this "stricter" definition of OCPD, the two groups did not significantly differ, as 18.8% of the group with HD and 14.6% of the group with OCD met the reduced OCPD criteria. Results from this study suggest that some of the comorbidity between OCPD and HD is driven by overlap in the saving criterion, although this symptom did not account for the relationship between the two disorders: even when hoarding was removed as a criterion, OCPD was the most common PD in HD. Landau et al. (2011) found results similar to those of Frost et al. (2011), although with a smaller sample size. In their study, 50% of 24 individuals with HD had comorbid OCPD, and the rate was 33.3% even when excluding hoarding as an OCPD criterion. Future research is still needed to better understand the comorbidity between OCPD and HD.

Despite the overlap in their diagnostic criteria, several features differentiate HD and OCPD. First, whereas people with OCPD are usually neat and orderly, typically the homes of people with HD are cluttered and disorganized, and possessions are often put away without any organization system. Individuals with HD frequently and excessively acquire unnecessary items (excessive acquisition is included as a *DSM-5* specifier for HD). Excessive acquisition may be less common in people with OCPD, who are typically reserved about spending money (i.e., miserliness). As mentioned previously, recent research suggests that people with OCPD may exhibit an abnormally strong ability to delay monetary rewards (as compared to both individuals with OCD and healthy controls) in an incentive reward task (Pinto et al., 2014). These findings would seem to differentiate OCPD from an inability to deny immediate gratification, which is seen in the excessive acquisition in HD. Second, people with OCPD and HD may differ in their reasons for saving possessions. Some of these reasons include feeling sentimentally attached to possessions, which has been termed hypersentimentality (e.g., feeling that throwing away a possession causes it "emotional" harm), as well as concerns that items are needed due to concerns about memory (e.g., believing that parting with a possession will result in a loss of an ability to remember an important experience). Although there has not been substantial research investigating reasons for saving items in OCPD, the difficulty discarding old or worn-out items may arise from an aim to "maximize" their use (i.e., manifestation of perfectionism). For example, an individual with OCPD may keep a pile of newspapers, books, or magazines because he or she has not read them entirely and therefore has not derived full benefit from them (Wheaton & Pinto, 2020). Last, the number of possessions and the extent of the clutter may help to differentiate HD and OCPD. In HD, the clutter is substantial enough to interfere with the usability of the living space (e.g., a bedroom in which the bed is so covered in material that the bed cannot be slept in) and impacts the ability to perform basic, daily activities. In uncomplicated OCPD, saving possessions would not be expected to result in such extreme levels of clutter. However, it should be noted that the inability to throw out old or worn-out items in OCPD is considered to be one of the least central diagnostic criteria in OCPD. For example, a factor analysis of OCPD symptoms conducted by Fossati et al. (2006) found that the discarding worthless/worn-out items symptom did not load on the OCPD factor and did not discriminate between OCPD and other Cluster C PDs. Therefore, it has been suggested that this symptom should be dropped as an OCPD criterion (Diedrich & Voderholzer, 2015). However, even without this diagnostic symptom overlap, research suggests there is still a substantial association between OCPD and HD.

Personality Dimensions

Little is known about whether personality dimensions are uniquely associated with hoarding behavior, and most studies to date on this topic have been limited to examining hoarding in groups of people with OCD. Fullana et al. (2004) found that, in a sample of OCD, scores on the hoarding dimension positively correlated with sensitivity to punishment (using the Sensitivity to Punishment and Sensitivity to Reward Questionnaire), and inversely correlated with impulsivity/novelty-seeking (as measured by the psychoticism scale of the Eysenck Personality Questionnaire). High sensitivity to punishment and low novelty-seeking in patients with OCD plus HD may be an indicator of poor adherence and response to CBT, but further research in a prospective treatment study is required. Alonso et al. (2008) reported a relationship between the hoarding dimension and harm avoidance in an OCD sample. LaSalle-Ricci et al. (2006) used the NEO-PI-R to measure personality in 204 outpatients with OCD and found that the hoarding dimension was positively related to neuroticism and four of its facets (anxiety, self-consciousness, impulsiveness, and vulnerability) and was inversely related to conscientiousness and one of its facets, order. In a study of veterans diagnosed with HD, the majority of participants had an elevated score on at least one of the Millon Clinical Multiaxial Inventory-III (MCMI-III) Personality scales. The most frequently elevated scores were for the Avoidant, Dependent, Depressive, and Schizoid scales (Dozier et al., 2020). Hoarding severity was a significant predictor of personality traits in 10 out of 14 MCMI-III scales.

Role of Personality/PDs in Course and Treatment
There is a need for research on personality predictors of course and treatment outcome in HD. For example, what role does personality pathology play in the consistent finding of poor response to CBT in patients with hoarding (Abramowitz et al., 2003; Mataix-Cols et al., 2002)? Although it is expected that the presence of PD symptoms—particularly those of schizotypal PD and OCPD—and high scores on dimensions like neuroticism and harm avoidance may complicate the treatment and clinical course of HD, these assumptions have not yet been empirically tested. One exception is the work of Muroff et al. (2014), who tested specific predictors of individual CBT outcome in HD. In this study, only perfectionism (as measured by the Obsessive Beliefs Questionnaire) and male sex predicted worse outcome after controlling for initial hoarding severity. Based on this finding, further study in larger samples is needed to determine whether incorporating a specialized intervention for perfectionism would improve CBT outcome for HD.

Trichotillomania

Trichotillomania (TTM) is characterized by recurrent hair-pulling that results in hair loss and is associated with significant clinical distress and functional impairment (APA, 2013).

PD Categories
PDs are relatively common in individuals with TTM. In a study that compared patients with TTM to patients with OCD, 20% of the TTM sample ($N = 15$) interviewed with the SCID-P reported at least one *DSM-III-R* PD, with narcissistic PD and histrionic PD being the most common (13.3%), followed by borderline PD and passive-aggressive PD (6.7%; Tukel et al., 2001). These rates were significantly lower than rates in the OCD sample, of which 64% reported at least one PD. In a larger sample of patients with TTM ($N = 49$) and OCD ($N = 130$), interviewed with the SCID-II, OCPD (13.3%) and borderline PD (8%) were the most commonly reported PDs in TTM; only OCPD was found to be significantly more prevalent in the OCD sample (Lochner, Seedat, et al., 2005). In a study that compared patients with TTM ($N = 48$) and outpatient psychiatric controls ($N = 48$) on a variety of clinical characteristics, the two groups were found to have equal rates of PDs (each 42%; Christenson et al., 1992). In a smaller clinical sample of patients with TTM ($N = 22$), over 50% of the sample reported at least one PD (Schlosser et al., 1994). While the research is limited, it appears personality pathology is common in TTM.

Personality Dimensions
Several studies have looked at the personality and temperament dimensions in TTM. Lochner et al. (2002) reported personality dimensions, also assessed by the TPQ, in samples of patients with TTM and patients with skin-picking. No differences were found between the two groups, with both scoring high on harm avoidance and reward dependence. According to clinical observations by Summerfeldt (2004), incompleteness may be

a motivating factor underlying some TTM and skin-picking symptoms, but this assertion has not been empirically tested. In a study that explored the predictive value of personality dimensions for TTM, a comparison of patients with TTM (N = 54) and healthy controls (N = 25) found that TTM was significantly predicted by trait neuroticism on the NEO-FFI (Keuthen et al., 2015). Similar results were found in an Iranian sample that utilized the NEO-PI-R (Hagh-Shenas et al., 2015). In a larger sample of patients with TTM (N = 164), higher neuroticism, higher openness, and lower agreeableness were found to be associated with greater hair-pulling severity (Keuthen et al., 2015). In a matched sample of patients with TTM (N = 28) and healthy controls (N = 28), the former were found to have reported significantly greater levels (albeit not in the clinical range) of affective instability (borderline features) and aggression as measured by the PAI relative to healthy controls (Wetterneck et al., 2016). In a community sample, individuals with elevated levels of TTM symptoms reported higher interpersonal sensitivity, neuroticism, and anxiety (Stanley et al., 1994). In a study that compared the presence of multidimensional perfectionism and shame between a clinical sample with TTM (N = 125) and a healthy sample (N = 284), individuals with TTM reported significantly greater levels of both maladaptive perfectionism as well as shame (Noble et al., 2017). In examining three subtypes of shame (characterological, bodily, and behavioral), the authors found that shame about behaviors mediated the relationship between maladaptive perfectionism and TTM in the clinical sample. In a college sample that consisted of hair-pullers (N = 16) and non-hair-pullers (N = 35), the former group reported greater interpersonal problems (Schut et al., 1997). Specifically, the hair-pullers described themselves as more vindictive, domineering, cold, and socially avoidant than the non-hair-pullers. Last, in a study that explored the daily difficulties experienced by patients with TTM, poor body image, low self-esteem, and secretiveness were reported by the majority of patients (Stemberger et al., 2000).

Role of Personality/PDs in Course and Treatment

There is limited research on the role of personality in the course and treatment of TTM. In a naturalistic longitudinal study of patients who were in treatment for TTM, those who were still in treatment 3.5 years after the first follow-up were found to have significantly lower self-esteem scores (Keuthen et al., 2001). Whether lower self-esteem led to prolonged treatment or vice versa was unclear, although the authors suggested that frustration regarding an unsuccessful response to treatment may result in lowered self-esteem. In a study that was the first to examine the efficacy of dialectical behavior therapy (DBT)-enhanced reversal training for TTM, changes in capacity for emotion regulation were positively correlated with improvement in symptoms from baseline to three and six-month follow-ups (Keuthen et al., 2011). Last, in a study that conducted TTM post-treatment follow-ups after three months and two years, neuroticism was theorized to be a potential predictor of relapse but was not found to contribute to variance explained within those who relapsed (Keijsers et al., 2006).

Excoriation (Skin-Picking Disorder)

Excoriation (skin-picking disorder; SPD) is defined as repetitive and compulsive picking of the skin that leads to damage of the tissues and results in clinical distress and impairment (APA, 2013).

PD Categories

The limited data on this condition suggest that PDs are common in SPD. In a small clinical sample of patients with SPD ($N = 31$) interviewed with the SCID for *DSM-IV*, over 50% of patients were found to have at least one PD, with OCPD being most common (48%), followed by borderline PD (26%; Wilhelm et al., 1999). In a study that compared patients with TTM and patients with SPD, the latter group reported several PDs, including borderline PD (33%), OCPD (19%), avoidant PD (4%), and schizotypal PD (9%; Lochner et al., 2002). Grant et al. (2006) looked at clinical characteristics of BDD comorbid with SPD, and their results suggested that the presence of SPD significantly increased the level of associated PDs (57.1%) relative to BDD alone (38.8%). Last, in a study that examined the phenomenology of SPD in a clinical sample ($N = 40$), 8% of patients self-reported a diagnostic history of borderline PD (Neziroglu et al., 2008). Taken together, the available evidence suggests that PDs, especially borderline PD and OCPD, commonly co-occur with SPD.

Personality Dimensions

In a study of a large nonclinical sample ($N = 252$) that explored the characteristics associated with SPD, novelty-seeking and self-directedness were found to predict SPD severity, and self-directedness and cooperativeness were found to predict functional impairment associated with SPD (Prochwicz et al., 2018). In addition, the authors found that use of cognitive reappraisal as a means of emotion regulation was found to predict lower severity of SPD. In a nonclinical sample, an "impulsive" personality profile was associated with greater levels of SPD (Kłosowska et al., 2019). This profile was characterized by elevated novelty-seeking, harm avoidance, and self-transcendence; average reward dependence; and reduced persistence, self-directedness, and cooperativeness. Snorrason at al. (2010) compared clinical and nonclinical subjects to explore the influence of emotion regulation in SPD. They found that difficulties in emotion regulation, as well as emotional reactivity, predicted greater SPD.

Some research has focused on three subtypes of SPD and their relation to personality variables. The subtypes consisted of "automatic" picking occurring outside of one's awareness; "focused" picking, which occurs in a more aware and intentional manner; and "mixed" picking, which is a confluence of the two former subtypes (Pozza et al., 2016). Utilizing the MCMI-III in a community sample, Pozza et al. found that higher scores on the borderline scales predicted both greater automatic and focused skin-picking, while greater scores on avoidant scales predicted automatic skin-picking. Further, focused and automatic skin-picking were predicted by sadistic personality traits. In a related study that examined the relationship of early maladaptive schemas (EMSs) to SPD subtypes, the focused subtype was predicted by Lower Social Isolation/Alienation, Enmeshment/Undeveloped Self, and Mistrust/Abuse, whereas the automatic subtype was predicted by Higher Approval/Recognition Seeking (Pozza et al., 2020). In addition, Failure to Achieve predicted the mixed subtype, and Higher Dependence/Incompetence predicted both focused and automatic subtypes, and lower Emotional Deprivation predicted all three subtypes.

Role of Personality/PDs in Course and Treatment

There is a dearth of research on the role of personality in the course of, and treatment for, SPD. There is some preliminary evidence from case studies that individuals who use SPD as a means of reducing negative affect fare worse in habit reversal training (HRT) than do those whose SPD occurs in a habitual manner (Deckersbach et al., 2002). This suggests that borderline personality traits that may be associated with the use of skin-picking to reduce negative affect (i.e., focused type; Pozza et al., 2016) can interfere with HRT. However further research will be needed to explore this association.

Conclusion

Personality pathology is common in OCD and related disorders (OCRDs). Much of the research on personality pathology in OCD has focused on categorical PDs. Although some consistent patterns have emerged with respect to elevated rates of OCPD and other Cluster C PDs in OCRDs, results from studies using categorical PD diagnoses have been varied and have had limited impact on advancing the understanding of personality in OCD. In recent years, researchers have increasingly moved away from the notion that PDs are distinct, non-overlapping entities toward a view of the disorders as a constellation of traits on a continuum. In addition, there are many problems with the current categorical classification system, including diagnostic unreliability when criteria are applied in clinical practice; inadequate coverage of maladaptive personality functioning seen in clinical practice, with overreliance on the diagnosis PD not otherwise specified (PD NOS) as a "wastebasket diagnosis"; heterogeneity in diagnostic categories; arbitrary diagnostic boundaries without a scientific basis; and excessive diagnostic co-occurrence (Skodol et al., 2011). Section III of *DSM-5*, which consists of measures and models for further study, presents a dimensional conceptualization of personality pathology to address some of these concerns. For example, in this alternative model of PDs, rigid perfectionism is identified as the core pathological personality trait required for a diagnosis of OCPD (APA, 2013).

As documented in this chapter, there has already been substantial progress in research on core personality dimensions in OCD, less so with the related disorders, but there is much work to be done to relate these dimensions to OCD symptom dimensions, as well as to the course, treatment, and etiology of OCD and each of the related conditions. A dimensional view has also been helpful in deconstructing the complex relationship between OCD and OCPD, in that there is now greater appreciation for examining how specific traits of OCPD associate with OCD symptoms (e.g., links between maladaptive perfectionism and incompleteness), and how OCPD traits like maladaptive perfectionism impact the course and treatment of OCD (e.g., findings suggesting that perfectionism may be a mediator of OCD improvement, so that it may be beneficial to specifically target it in treatment). Research on personality dimensions in the related disorders is much more limited, but it is hoped that this trend will change with the field's increased attention to dimensional perspectives.

Future Directions

Future research directions are proposed first for the study of PDs/personality dimensions in OCRDs, and then more specifically for the study of OCPD in OCD. Given the limitations of PD categories, future research should emphasize dimensional constructs of personality. Longitudinal studies will be needed to determine whether dimensional personality traits prospectively predict onset and course of OCRDs. Prospective studies with clinical samples can also help determine whether personality traits are pathoplastic factors that affect remission from OCRDs, and whether there are lasting changes in personality related to having had these disorders. Future studies are needed to examine whether there are specific personality vulnerabilities for the development and/or maintenance of specific obsessions and/or compulsions. Along these lines, researchers should consider extending the definitions of personality dimensions to include biological markers. Since previous conflicting findings on the role of personality domains in OCD may at least be partially due to the phenotypic heterogeneity of the disorder, it is recommended that studies look for differential associations between the personality dimensions and the more homogeneous symptom dimensions of OCD. With regard to treatment approaches for patients with OCD and PDs, adjunct interventions should be considered as a means of addressing problematic interpersonal functioning and potential ambivalence toward behavior change, both of which can interfere in the patient's engagement in and adherence to E/RP. As mentioned, a dimensional view of personality also supports developing specific interventions and tailoring treatment to target particular traits. For example, CBT for maladaptive perfectionism (Egan et al., 2011) can be tested in OCD based on the findings reported earlier that this trait impacts treatment response. Given the prevalence of perfectionism in BDD, this work can be extended to BDD.

To improve understanding of the relationship between OCPD and OCD, several approaches are recommended. First, given recent research linking particular OCPD and OCD symptoms, future studies of OCD course and treatment response should consider the presence of OCPD traits in patients with OCD, rather than just considering the presence of the OCPD category. For instance, it will be important for studies with large samples to examine whether changes in particular OCPD features will predict changes in OCD symptoms over time, and vice versa. Similarly, future studies should further investigate the role of specific OCPD features, such as perfectionism, as mediators of OCD treatment response. Second, longitudinal studies would provide information on the temporal relationship between neuroticism, OCPD, and OCD. Investigation of the relationship between neuroticism and OCPD in OCD families is necessary to further understanding of OCD pathogenesis. Third, there is no definitive, empirically validated treatment for OCPD, nor have there been any controlled treatment trials for uncomplicated OCPD. Advances in OCPD treatment would allow for comparisons in treatment response with possibly related disorders and would inform the treatment of comorbid cases. Fourth, research endeavors in the area of endophenotypes, unobservable characteristics (e.g., neurophysiological, biochemical, neuropsychological, and cognitive) that mediate the relationship between genes and a given behavioral phenotype (Gottesman & Gould, 2003), may provide insights into the underlying mechanisms and genetic underpinnings of OCD and OCPD, and perhaps more broadly for the OCRDs.

Acknowledgments

Thanks to Jonathan Teller for his help in updating the literature review for this second edition.

References

Abramowitz, J. S., Franklin, M. E., Schwartz, S. A., & Furr, J. M. (2003). Symptom presentation and outcome of cognitive-behavioral therapy for obsessive-compulsive disorder. *Journal of Consulting and Clinical Psychology*, *71*(6), 1049–1057.

Albert, U., Maina, G., Forner, F., & Bogetto, F. (2004). DSM-IV obsessive-compulsive personality disorder: Prevalence in patients with anxiety disorders and in healthy comparison subjects. *Comprehensive Psychiatry*, *45*(5), 325–332.

Alonso, P., Menchon, J. M., Jimenez, S., Segalas, J., Mataix-Cols, D., Jaurrieta, N., Labad, J., Vallejo, J., Cardoner, N., & Pujol, J. (2008). Personality dimensions in obsessive-compulsive disorder: Relation to clinical variables. *Psychiatry Research*, *157*(1–3), 159–168.

American Psychiatric Association (APA). (2013). *Diagnostic and statistical manual of mental disorders* (5th ed.).

Angyal, A. (1965). *Neurosis and treatment: A holistic theory*. John Wiley and Sons.

Antony, M. M., Purdon, C. L., Huta, V., & Swinson, R. P. (1998). Dimensions of perfectionism across the anxiety disorders. *Behaviour Research and Therapy*, *36*(12), 1143–1154.

Askland, K. D., Garnaat, S., Sibrava, N. J., Boisseau, C. L., Strong, D., Mancebo, M., Greenberg, B., Rasmussen, S., & Eisen, J. (2015). Prediction of remission in obsessive compulsive disorder using a novel machine learning strategy. *International Journal of Methods in Psychiatric Research*, *24*(2), 156–169.

Attademo, L., & Bernardini, F. (2020). Schizotypal personality disorder in clinical obsessive-compulsive disorder samples: A brief overview. *CNS Spectrums*, *26*(5), 468–480.

AuBuchon, P. G., & Malatesta, V. J. (1994). Obsessive compulsive patients with comorbid personality disorder: Associated problems and response to a comprehensive behavior therapy. *The Journal of Clinical Psychiatry*, *55*(10), 448–453.

Baer, L. (1994). Factor analysis of symptom subtypes of obsessive-compulsive disorder and their relation to personality and tic disorders. *The Journal of Clinical Psychiatry*, *55*(Suppl.), 18–23.

Baer, L., & Jenike, M. A. (1992). Personality disorders in obsessive-compulsive disorder. *Psychiatric Clinics of North America*, *15*(4), 803–812.

Baer, L., & Jenike, M. A. (1998). Personality disorders in obsessive-compulsive disorder. In M. A. Jenike, L. Baer, & W. E. Minichiello. (Eds.), *Obsessive compulsive disorders: Practical management* (3rd ed., pp. 65–83). Mosby.

Baer, L., Jenike, M. A., Black, D. W., Treece, C., Rosenfeld, R., & Greist, J. (1992). Effect of Axis II diagnoses on treatment outcome with clomipramine in 55 patients with obsessive-compulsive disorder. *Archives of General Psychiatry, 49*(11), 862–866.

Baer, L., Jenike, M. A., Ricciardi, J. N. II, Holland, A. D., Seymour, R. J., Minichiello, W. E., & Buttolph, M. L. (1990). Standardized assessment of personality disorders in obsessive-compulsive disorder. *Archives of General Psychiatry, 47*(9), 826–830.

Bagby, R. M., Bindseil, K. D., Schuller, D. R., Rector, N. A., Young, L. T., Cooke, R. G., Seeman, M. V., McCay, E. A., & Joffe, R. T. (1997). Relationship between the Five-Factor Model of personality and unipolar, bipolar and schizophrenic patients. *Psychiatry Research, 70*(2), 83–94.

Bartz, J., Kaplan, A., & Hollander, E. (2007). Obsessive-compulsive personality disorder. In W. T. O'Donohue, K. A. Fowler, & S. O. Lilienfeld. (Eds.), *Personality disorders: Toward the DSM-V* (pp. 325–351). SAGE.

Bejerot, S., Schlette, P., Ekselius, L., Adolfsson, R., & von Knorring, L. (1998). Personality disorders and relationship to personality dimensions measured by the Temperament and Character Inventory in patients with obsessive-compulsive disorder. *Acta Psychiatrica Scandinavica, 98*(3), 243–249.

Bienvenu, O. J., Samuels, J. F., Costa, P. T., Reti, I. M., Eaton, W. W., & Nestadt, G. (2004). Anxiety and depressive disorders and the Five-Factor Model of personality: A higher- and lower-order personality trait investigation in a community sample. *Depression and Anxiety, 20*(2), 92–97.

Bjornsson, A. S., Didie, E. R., Grant, J. E., Menard, W., Stalker, E., & Phillips, K. A. (2013). Age at onset and clinical correlates in body dysmorphic disorder. *Comprehensive Psychiatry, 54*(7), 893–903.

Black, D. W., Noyes, R., Jr., Pfohl, B., Goldstein, R. B., & Blum, N. (1993). Personality disorder in obsessive-compulsive volunteers, well comparison subjects, and their first-degree relatives. *The American Journal of Psychiatry, 150*(8), 1226–1232.

Blatt, S. J., Quinlan, D. M., Pilkonis, P. A., & Shea, M. T. (1995). Impact of perfectionism and need for approval on the brief treatment of depression: The National Institute of Mental Health Treatment of Depression Collaborative Research Program revisited. *Journal of Consulting and Clinical Psychology, 63*(1), 125–132.

Blatt, S. J., Zuroff, D. C., Bondi, C. M., Sanislow, C. A. III, & Pilkonis, P. A. (1998). When and how perfectionism impedes the brief treatment of depression: Further analyses of the National Institute of Mental Health Treatment of Depression Collaborative Research Program. *Journal of Consulting and Clinical Psychology, 66*(2), 423–428.

Bulli, F., Melli, G., Cavalletti, V., Stopani, E., & Carraresi, C. (2016). Comorbid personality disorders in obsessive-compulsive disorder and its symptom dimensions. *Psychiatric Quarterly, 87*, 365–376.

Calvo, R., Lazaro, L., Castro-Fornieles, J., Font, E., Moreno, E., & Toro, J. (2009). Obsessive-compulsive personality disorder traits and personality dimensions in parents of children with obsessive-compulsive disorder. *European Psychiatry, 24*(3), 201–206.

Cavedini, P., Erzegovesi, S., Ronchi, P., & Bellodi, L. (1997). Predictive value of obsessive-compulsive personality disorder in anti-obsessional pharmacological treatment. *European Neuropsychopharmacology, 7*(1), 45–49.

Christenson, G. A., Chernoff-Clementz, E., & Clementz, B. A. (1992). Personality and clinical characteristics in patients with trichotillomania. *The Journal of Clinical Psychiatry, 53*(11), 407–413.

Cloninger, C. R. (1986). A unified biosocial theory of personality and its role in the development of anxiety states. *Psychiatric Developments, 4*(3), 167–226.

Cloninger, C. R., Przybeck, T. R., & Svrakic, D. M. (1991). The Tridimensional Personality Questionnaire: U.S. normative data. *Psychological Reports, 69*(3 Pt. 1), 1047–1057.

Cloninger, C. R., Przybeck, T. R., Svrakic, D. M., & Wetzel, R. D. (1994). *The Temperament and Character Inventory (TCI): A guide to its development and use*. Center for Psychobiology of Personality.

Cloninger, C. R., & Svrakic, D. M. (1997). Integrative psychobiological approach to psychiatric assessment and treatment. *Psychiatry, 60*(2), 120–141.

Cloninger, C. R., Svrakic, D. M., & Przybeck, T. R. (1993). A psychobiological model of temperament and character. *Archives of General Psychiatry, 50*(12), 975–990.

Cohen, L., Kingston, P., Bell, A., Kwon, J., Aronowitz, B., & Hollander, E. (2000). Comorbid personality impairment in body dysmorphic disorder. *Comprehensive Psychiatry, 41*, 4–12.

Coles, M. E., Pinto, A., Mancebo, M. C., Rasmussen, S. A., & Eisen, J. L. (2008). OCD with comorbid OCPD: A subtype of OCD? *Journal of Psychiatric Research, 42*, 289–296.

Costa, P. T., Jr., & McCrae, R. R. (1992). *Revised NEO Personality Inventory (NEO-PI-R) and NEO Five-Factor Inventory (NEO-FFI) professional manual.* Psychological Assessment Resources.

Crino, R. D., & Andrews, G. (1996). Personality disorder in obsessive compulsive disorder: A controlled study. *Journal of Psychiatric Research, 30*(1), 29–38.

Deckersbach, T., Wilhelm, S., Keuthen, N. J., Baer, L., & Jenike, M. A. (2002). Cognitive-behavior therapy for self-injurious skin picking: A case series. *Behavior Modification, 26*(3), 361–377.

Diaferia, G., Bianchi, I., Bianchi, M. L., Cavedini, P., Erzegovesi, S., & Bellodi, L. (1997). Relationship between obsessive-compulsive personality disorder and obsessive-compulsive disorder. *Comprehensive Psychiatry, 38*(1), 38–42.

Diedrich, A., & Voderholzer, U. (2015). Obsessive-compulsive personality disorder: A current review. *Current Psychiatric Reports, 17*(2), 2.

Dozier, M. E., Davidson, E. J., Pittman, J., & Ayers, C. R. (2020). Personality traits in adults with hoarding disorder. *Journal of Affective Disorders, 276*, 191–196.

Ecker, W., Kupfer, J., & Gönner, S. (2014). Incompleteness as a link between obsessive-compulsive personality traits and specific symptom dimensions of obsessive-compulsive disorder. *Clinical Psychology & Psychotherapy, 21*(5), 394–402.

Egan, S. J., Wade, T. D., & Shafran, R. (2011). Perfectionism as a transdiagnostic process: A clinical review. *Clinical Psychology Review, 31*(2), 203–212.

Eisen, J. L., Coles, M. E., Shea, M. T., Pagano, M. E., Stout, R. L., Yen, S., Grilo, C. M., & Rasmussen, S. A. (2006). Clarifying the convergence between obsessive-compulsive personality disorder criteria and obsessive-compulsive disorder. *Journal of Personality Disorders, 20*(3), 294–305.

Eisen, J. L., & Rasmussen, S. A. (1991, May). *OCD and compulsive traits: Phenomenology and outcome* [Paper presentation]. American Psychiatric Association 144th Annual Meeting, New Orleans, LA.

Eisen, J. L., Sibrava, N. J., Boisseau, C. L., Mancebo, M. C., Stout, R. L., Pinto, A., & Rasmussen, S. A. (2013). Five-year course of obsessive-compulsive disorder: Predictors of remission and relapse. *The Journal of Clinical Psychiatry, 74*(3), 233–239.

Fang, A., Porth, R., Phillips, K. A., & Wilhelm, S. (2019). Personality as a predictor of treatment response to escitalopram in adults with body dysmorphic disorder. *Journal of Psychiatric Practice, 25*(5), 347–357.

Ferrari, J. R. (1995). Perfectionism cognitions with nonclinical and clinical samples. *Journal of Social Behavior and Personality, 10*, 143–156.

Fineberg, N. A., Sharma, P., Sivakumaran, T., Sahakian, B., & Chamberlain, S. R. (2007). Does obsessive-compulsive personality disorder belong within the obsessive-compulsive spectrum? *CNS Spectrums, 12*(6), 467–482.

Fossati, A., Beauchaine, T. P., Grazioli, F., Borroni, S., Carretta, I., De Vecchi, C., Cortinovis, F., Danelli, E., & Maffei, C. (2006). Confirmatory factor analyses of DSM-IV Cluster C personality disorder criteria. *Journal of Personality Disorders, 20*(2), 186–203.

Freud, S. (1963). Character and anal eroticism. In P. Rieff. (Ed.), *Collected papers of Sigmund Freud* (Vol. 10, pp. 45–50). Collier. (Original work published 1908)

Friborg, O., Martinussen, M., Kaiser, S., Overgård, K. T., & Rosenvinge, J. H. (2013). Comorbidity of personality disorders in anxiety disorders: A meta-analysis of 30 years of research. *Journal of Affective Disorders, 145*(2), 143–155.

Fricke, S., Moritz, S., Andresen, B., Jacobsen, D., Kloss, M., Rufer, M., & Hand, I. (2006). Do personality disorders predict negative treatment outcome in obsessive-compulsive disorders? A prospective 6-month follow-up study. *European Psychiatry, 21*(5), 319–324.

Frost, R. O., & Gross, R. C. (1993). The hoarding of possessions. *Behaviour Research and Therapy, 31*(4), 367–381.

Frost, R., & Marten, P. A. (1990). Perfectionism and evaluative threat. *Cognitive Therapy and Research, 14*, 559–572.

Frost, R. O., & Steketee, G. (1997). Perfectionism in obsessive-compulsive disorder patients. *Behaviour Research and Therapy, 35*(4), 291–296.

Frost, R. O., Steketee, G., Cohn, L., & Griess, K. (1994). Personality traits in subclinical and non-obsessive-compulsive volunteers and their parents. *Behaviour Research and Therapy, 32*(1), 47–56.

Frost, R. O., Steketee, G., & Tolin, D. F. (2011). Comorbidity in hoarding disorder. *Depression and Anxiety, 28*(10), 876–884.

Frost, R. O., Steketee, G., Williams, L. F., & Warren, R. (2000). Mood, personality disorder symptoms and disability in obsessive compulsive hoarders: A comparison with clinical and nonclinical controls. *Behaviour Research and Therapy, 38*(11), 1071–1081.

Fullana, M. A., Mataix-Cols, D., Trujillo, J. L., Caseras, X., Serrano, F., Alonso, P., Menchon, J. M., Vallejo, J., & Torrubia, R. (2004). Personality characteristics in obsessive-compulsive disorder and individuals with subclinical obsessive-compulsive problems. *British Journal of Clinical Psychology, 43*(Pt. 4), 387–398.

Garyfallos, G., Katsigiannopoulos, K., Adamopoulou, A., Papazisis, G., Karastergiou, A., & Bozikas, V. P. (2010). Comorbidity of obsessive-compulsive disorder with obsessive-compulsive personality disorder: Does it imply a specific subtype of obsessive-compulsive disorder? *Psychiatry Research, 177*(1–2), 156–160.

Gershuny, B., & Sher, K. (1995). Compulsive checking and anxiety in a nonclinical sample: Differences in cognition, behavior, personality, and affect. *Journal of Psychopathology and Behavioral Assessment, 17*, 19–38.

Gordon, O. M., Salkovskis, P. M., & Bream, V. (2016). The impact of obsessive-compulsive personality disorder on cognitive behaviour therapy for obsessive-compulsive disorder. *Behavioural and Cognitive Psychotherapy, 44*(4), 444–459.

Gottesman, I. I., & Gould, T. D. (2003). The endophenotype concept in psychiatry: Etymology and strategic intentions. *The American Journal of Psychiatry, 160*(4), 636–645.

Grant, J. E., Menard, W., & Phillips, K. A. (2006). Pathological skin picking in individuals with body dysmorphic disorder. *General Hospital Psychiatry, 28*(6), 487–493.

Grant, J. E., Mooney, M. E., & Kushner, M. G. (2012). Prevalence, correlates, and comorbidity of DSM-IV obsessive-compulsive personality disorder: Results from the National Epidemiological Survey on Alcohol and Related Conditions. *Journal of Psychiatric Research, 46*(4), 469–475.

Grisham, J. R., Steketee, G., & Frost, R. O. (2008). Interpersonal problems and emotional intelligence in compulsive hoarding. *Depression and Anxiety, 25*(9), E63–71.

Hagh-Shenas, H., Moradi, A., Dehbozorgi, G., Farashbandi, B., & Alishahian, F. (2015). Trichotillomania-associated personality characteristics. *Iranian Journal of Medical Sciences, 29*(3), 105–108.

Halmi, K. A., Tozzi, F., Thornton, L. M., Crow, S., Fichter, M. M., Kaplan, A. S., Keel, P., Klump, K. L., Lilenfeld, L. R., Mitchell, J. E., Plotnicov, K. H., Pollice, C., Rotondo, A., Strober, M., Woodside, D. B., Berrettini, W. H., Kaye, W. H., & Bulik, C. M. (2005). The relation among perfectionism, obsessive-compulsive personality disorder and obsessive-compulsive disorder in individuals with eating disorders. *International Journal of Eating Disorders, 38*(4), 371–374.

Haring, M., Hewitt, P. L., & Flett, G. L. (2003). Perfectionism, coping, and quality of intimate relationships. *Journal of Marriage and Family, 65*, 143–158.

Hewitt, P. L., Flett, G. L., & Weber, C. (1994). Dimensions of perfectionism and suicide ideation. *Cognitive Therapy and Research, 18*, 439–460.

Hewitt, P. L., Newton, J., Flett, G. L., & Callander, L. (1997). Perfectionism and suicide ideation in adolescent psychiatric patients. *Journal of Abnormal Child Psychology, 25*(2), 95–101.

Horesh, N., Dolberg, O. T., Kirschenbaum-Aviner, N., & Kotler, M. (1997). Personality differences between obsessive-compulsive disorder subtypes: Washers versus checkers. *Psychiatry Research, 71*(3), 197–200.

Irle, E., Exner, C., Thielen, K., Weniger, G., & Ruther, E. (1998). Obsessive-compulsive disorder and ventromedial frontal lesions: Clinical and neuropsychological findings. *The American Journal of Psychiatry, 155*(2), 255–263.

Janet, P. (1904). *Les obsessions et la psychasthénie* [Obsessions and psychasthenia] (2nd ed.). Bailliere.

Jenike, M. A., Baer, L., Minichiello, W. E., Schwartz, C. E., & Carey, R. J. (1986). Concomitant obsessive-compulsive disorder and schizotypal personality disorder. *The American Journal of Psychiatry, 143*, 530–532.

Keijsers, G. P., van Minnen, A., Hoogduin, C. A., Klaassen, B. N., Hendriks, M. J., & Tanis-Jacobs, J. (2006). Behavioural treatment of trichotillomania: Two-year follow-up results. *Behaviour Research and Therapy, 44*(3), 359–370.

Keuthen, N. J., Fraim, C., Deckersbach, T., Dougherty, D. D., Baer, L., & Jenike, M. A. (2001). Longitudinal follow-up of naturalistic treatment outcome in patients with trichotillomania. *The Journal of Clinical Psychiatry, 62*(2), 101–107.

Keuthen, N. J., Rothbaum, B. O., Falkenstein, M. J., Meunier, S., Timpano, K. R., Jenike, M. A., & Welch, S. S. (2011). DBT-enhanced habit reversal treatment for trichotillomania: 3-and 6-month follow-up results. *Depression and Anxiety, 28*(4), 310–313.

Keuthen, N. J., Tung, E. S., Altenburger, E. M., Blais, M. A., Pauls, D. L., & Flessner, C. A. (2015). Trichotillomania and personality traits from the Five-Factor Model. *Brazilian Journal of Psychiatry, 37*(4), 317–324.

Kłosowska, J., Prochwicz, K., & Kałużna-Wielobób, A. (2019). The relationship between cognitive reappraisal strategy and skin picking behaviours in a non-clinical sample depends on personality profile. *Journal of Obsessive-Compulsive and Related Disorders, 21*, 129–137.

Koran, L. M. (2000). Quality of life in obsessive-compulsive disorder. *Psychiatric Clinics of North America, 23*(3), 509–517.

Kringlin, E. (1965). Obsessional neurotics: A long-term follow-up. *The British Journal of Psychiatry, 111*, 709–722.

Kusunoki, K., Sato, T., Taga, C., Yoshida, T., Komori, K., Narita, T., Hirano, S., Iwata, N., & Ozaki, N. (2000). Low novelty-seeking differentiates obsessive-compulsive disorder from major depression. *Acta Psychiatrica Scandinavica, 101*(5), 403–405.

Kyrios, M., Hordern, C., & Fassnacht, D. B. (2015). Predictors of response to cognitive behaviour therapy for obsessive-compulsive disorder. *International Journal of Clinical and Health Psychology, 15*(3) 181–190.

Landau, D., Iervolino, A. C., Pertusa, A., Santo, S., Singh, S., & Mataix-Cols, D. (2011). Stressful life events and material deprivation in hoarding disorder. *Journal of Anxiety Disorders, 25*(2), 192–202.

LaSalle-Ricci, V. H., Arnkoff, D. B., Glass, C. R., Crawley, S. A., Ronquillo, J. G., & Murphy, D. L. (2006). The hoarding dimension of OCD: Psychological comorbidity and the five-factor personality model. *Behaviour Research and Therapy, 44*(10), 1503–1512.

Lenane, M., Swedo, S. E., Leonard, H. L., Pauls, D. L., Sceery, W., & Rapoport, J. L. (1990). Psychiatric disorders in first degree relatives of children and adolescents with obsessive-compulsive disorder. *Journal of the American Academy of Child and Adolescent Psychiatry, 29*, 407–412.

Lochner, C., Kinnear, C. J., Hemmings, S. M., Seller, C., Niehaus, D. J., Knowles, J. A., Daniels, W., Moolman-Smook, J. C., Seedat, S., & Stein, D. J. (2005). Hoarding in obsessive-compulsive disorder: Clinical and genetic correlates. *Journal of Clinical Psychiatry, 66*(9), 1155–1160.

Lochner, C., Seedat, S., Du Toit, P. L., Nel, D. G., Niehaus, D. J., Sandler, R., & Stein, D. J. (2005). Obsessive-compulsive disorder and trichotillomania: A phenomenological comparison. *BMC Psychiatry, 5*(1), 2.

Lochner, C., Serebro, P., van der Merwe, L., Hemmings, S., Kinnear, C., Seedat, S., & Stein, D. J. (2011). Comorbid obsessive-compulsive personality disorder in obsessive-compulsive disorder (OCD): A marker of severity. *Progress in Neuro-Psychopharmacology & Biological Psychiatry, 35*(4), 1087–1092.

Lochner, C., Simeon, D., Niehaus, D. J., & Stein, D. J. (2002). Trichotillomania and skin-picking: A phenomenological comparison. *Depression and Anxiety, 15*(2), 83–86.

Lyoo, I. K., Lee, D. W., Kim, Y. S., Kong, S. W., & Kwon, J. S. (2001). Patterns of temperament and character in subjects with obsessive-compulsive disorder. *The Journal of Clinical Psychiatry, 62*(8), 637–641.

Mancebo, M. C., Eisen, J. L., Grant, J. E., & Rasmussen, S. A. (2005). Obsessive-compulsive personality disorder and obsessive-compulsive disorder: Clinical characteristics, diagnostic difficulties, and treatment. *Annals of Clinical Psychiatry, 17*(4), 197–204.

Mataix-Cols, D., Baer, L., Rauch, S. L., & Jenike, M. A. (2000). Relation of factor-analyzed symptom dimensions of obsessive-compulsive disorder to personality disorders. *Acta Psychiatrica Scandinavica, 102*(3), 199–202.

Mataix-Cols, D., Marks, I. M., Greist, J. H., Kobak, K. A., & Baer, L. (2002). Obsessive-compulsive symptom dimensions as predictors of compliance with and response to behaviour therapy: Results from a controlled trial. *Psychotherapy and Psychosomatics, 71*(5), 255–262.

Matsunaga, H., Kiriike, N., Matsui, T., Miyata, A., Iwasaki, Y., Fujimoto, K., Kasai, S., & Kojima, M. (2000). Gender differences in social and interpersonal features and personality disorders among Japanese patients with obsessive-compulsive disorder. *Comprehensive Psychiatry, 41*(4), 266–272.

Matsunaga, H., Miyata, A., Iwasaki, Y., Matsui, T., Fujimoto, K., & Kiriike, N. (1999). A comparison of clinical features among Japanese eating-disordered women with obsessive-compulsive disorder. *Comprehensive Psychiatry, 40*(5), 337–342.

McGlashan, T. H., Grilo, C. M., Sanislow, C. A., Ralevski, E., Morey, L. C., Gunderson, J. G., Skodol, A. E., Shea, M. T., Zanarini, M. C., Bender, D., Stout, R. L., Yen, S., & Pagano, M. (2005). Two-year prevalence and stability of individual DSM-IV criteria for schizotypal, borderline, avoidant, and obsessive-compulsive personality disorders: Toward a hybrid model of Axis II disorders. *The American Journal of Psychiatry, 162*(5), 883–889.

McKay, D., Neziroglu, F., Todaro, J., & Yaryura-Tobias, J. A. (1996). Changes in personality disorders following behavior therapy for obsessive-compulsive disorder. *Journal of Anxiety Disorders, 10*(1), 47–57.

Minichiello, W. E., Baer, L., & Jenike, M. A. (1987). Schizotypal personality disorder: A poor prognostic indicator for behavior therapy in the treatment of obsessive-compulsive disorder. *Journal of Anxiety Disorders, 1*, 273–276.

Muroff, J., Steketee, G., Frost, R. O., & Tolin, D. F. (2014). Cognitive behavior therapy for hoarding disorder: Follow-up findings and predictors of outcome. *Depression and Anxiety, 31*(12), 964–971.

Neziroglu, F., McKay, D., Todaro, J., & Yaryura-Tobias, J. A. (1996). Effect of cognitive behavior therapy on persons with body dysmorphic disorder and comorbid Axis II diagnoses. *Behavior Therapy, 27*, 67–77.

Neziroglu, F., Rabinowitz, D., Breytman, A., & Jacofsky, M. (2008). Skin picking phenomenology and severity comparison. *Primary Care Companion to the Journal of Clinical Psychiatry, 10*(4), 306.

Nierenberg, A. A., Phillips, K. A., Petersen, T. J., Kelly, K. E., Alpert, J. E., Worthington, J. J., Tedlow, J. R., Rosenbaum, J. R., & Fava, M. (2002). Body dysmorphic disorder in outpatients with major depression. *Journal of Affective Disorders, 69*, 141–148.

Noble, C. M., Gnilka, P. B., Ashby, J. S., & McLaulin, S. E. (2017). Perfectionism, shame, and trichotillomania symptoms in clinical and nonclinical samples. *Journal of Mental Health Counseling, 39*(4), 335–350.

Obsessive Compulsive Cognitions Working Group. (1997). Cognitive assessment of obsessive-compulsive disorder. *Behaviour Research and Therapy, 35*(7), 667–681.

Park J. M., Storch E. A., Pinto A, & Lewin, A. B. (2016). Obsessive-compulsive personality traits in youth with obsessive-compulsive disorder. *Child Psychiatry and Human Development, 47*(2), 281–290.

Perris, F., Fabrazzo, M., De Santis, V., Luciano, M., Sampogna, G., Fiorillo, A., & Catapano, F. (2019). Comorbidity of obsessive-compulsive disorder and schizotypal personality disorder: Clinical response and treatment resistance to pharmacotherapy in a 3-year follow-up naturalistic study. *Frontiers in Psychiatry, 10*, 386.

Pertusa, A., Fullana, M. A., Singh, S., Alonso, P., Menchon, J. M., & Mataix-Cols, D. (2008). Compulsive hoarding: OCD symptom, distinct clinical syndrome, or both? *The American Journal of Psychiatry, 165*(10), 1289–1298.

Pfohl, B. (1996). Obsessive-compulsive personality disorder. In T. A. Widiger, H. A. Pincus, R. Ross, M. First, & W. Wakefield. (Eds.), *DSM-IV sourcebook* (Vol. 2, pp. 777–789). American Psychiatric Association.

Pfohl, B., Black, D., Noyes, R., Jr., Kelley, M., & Blum, N. (1990). A test of the tridimensional personality theory: Association with diagnosis and platelet imipramine binding in obsessive-compulsive disorder. *Biological Psychiatry, 28*(1), 41–46.

Phillips, K. A. (1991). Body dysmorphic disorder: The distress of imagined ugliness. *The American Journal of Psychiatry, 148*, 1138–1149.

Phillips, K. A., Albertini, R. S., & Rasmussen, S. A. (2002). A randomized placebo-controlled trial of fluoxetine in body dysmorphic disorder. *Archives of General Psychiatry, 59*, 381–388.

Phillips, K. A., Coles, M. E., Menard, W., Yen, S., Fay, C., & Weisberg, R. B. (2005). Suicidal ideation and suicide attempts in body dysmorphic disorder. *The Journal of Clinical Psychiatry, 66*(6), 717–725.

Phillips, K. A., Didie, E. R., & Menard, W. (2007). Clinical features and correlates of major depressive disorder in individuals with body dysmorphic disorder. *Journal of Affective Disorders, 97*(1–3), 129–135.

Phillips, K. A., & McElroy, S. L. (2000). Personality disorders and traits in patients with body dysmorphic disorder. *Comprehensive Psychiatry, 41*, 229–236.

Phillips, K. A., Menard, W., Fay, C., & Weisberg, R. (2005). Demographic characteristics, phenomenology, comorbidity, and family history in 200 individuals with body dysmorphic disorder. *Psychosomatics, 46*(4), 317–325.

Phillips, K. A., Pagano, M. E., Menard, W., Fay, C., & Stout, R. L. (2005). Predictors of remission from body dysmorphic disorder: A prospective study. *The Journal of Nervous and Mental Disease, 193*(8), 564–567.

Phillips, K. A., Pinto, A., Menard, W., Eisen, J. L., Mancebo, M. C., & Rasmussen, S. A. (2007). Obsessive-compulsive disorder versus body dysmorphic disorder: A comparison study of two possibly related disorders. *Depression and Anxiety, 24*, 399–409.

Phillips, K. A., Quinn, G., & Stout, R. L. (2008). Functional impairment in body dysmorphic disorder: A prospective, follow-up study. *Journal of Psychiatric Research, 42*(9), 701–707.

Pinto, A. (2020). Psychotherapy for obsessive compulsive personality disorder. In J. E. Grant, A. Pinto, & S. R. Chamberlain (Eds.), *Obsessive compulsive personality disorder* (pp. 143–77). American Psychiatric Association Publishing.

Pinto, A., Ansell, E., Wheaton, M. G., Krueger, R. F., Morey, L., Skodol, A. E., & Clark, L. A. (2018). Obsessive compulsive personality disorder and component personality traits. In W. J. Livesley & R. Larstone (Eds.), *Handbook of personality disorders: Theory, research, and treatment* (2nd ed.) (pp. 459–479). Guilford.

Pinto, A., Dargani, N., Wheaton, M. G., Cervoni, C., Rees, C. S., & Egan, S. J. (2017). Perfectionism in obsessive-compulsive disorder and related disorders: What should treating clinicians know? *Journal of Obsessive-Compulsive and Related Disorders, 12*, 102–108.

Pinto, A., Eisen, J. L., Mancebo, M. C., & Rasmussen, S. A. (2008). Obsessive compulsive personality disorder. In J. S. Abramowitz, D. McKay, & S. Taylor (Eds.), *Obsessive-compulsive disorder: Subtypes and spectrum conditions* (pp. 246–270). Elsevier.

Pinto, A., Greene, A. L., Storch, E., & Simpson, H. B. (2015). Prevalence of childhood obsessive-compulsive personality traits in adults with obsessive compulsive disorder versus obsessive compulsive personality disorder. *Journal of Obsessive-Compulsive and Related Disorders, 4*, 25–29.

Pinto, A., Liebowitz, M. R., Foa, E. B., & Simpson, H. B. (2011). Obsessive compulsive personality disorder as a predictor of exposure and ritual prevention outcome for obsessive compulsive disorder. *Behaviour Research and Therapy, 49*, 453–458.

Pinto, A., Mancebo, M. C., Eisen, J. L., Pagano, M. E., & Rasmussen, S. A. (2006). The Brown Longitudinal Obsessive-Compulsive Study: Clinical features and symptoms of the sample at intake. *The Journal of Clinical Psychiatry, 67*, 703–711.

Pinto, A., Steinglass, J. E., Greene, A. L., Weber, E. U., & Simpson, H. B. (2014). Capacity to delay reward differentiates obsessive-compulsive disorder and obsessive-compulsive personality disorder. *Biological Psychiatry, 75*(8), 653–659.

Pitman, R. K. (1987). Pierre Janet on obsessive-compulsive disorder (1903): Review and commentary. *Archives of General Psychiatry, 44*, 226–232.

Pozza, A., Albert, U., & Dèttore, D. (2020). Early maladaptive schemas as common and specific predictors of skin picking subtypes. *BMC Psychology, 8*(1), 1–11.

Pozza, A., Giaquinta, N., & Dèttore, D. (2016). Borderline, avoidant, sadistic personality traits and emotion dysregulation predict different pathological skin picking subtypes in a community sample. *Neuropsychiatric Disease and Treatment, 12*, 1861.

Prochwicz, K., Kłosowska, J., & Kałużna-Wielobób, A. (2018). The relationship between emotion regulation strategies, personality traits and skin picking behaviours in a non-clinical sample of Polish adults. *Psychiatry Research, 264*, 67–75.

Raines, A. M., Carroll, M., Mathes, B. M., Franklin, C. L., Allan, N. P., & Constans, J. I. (2019). Examining the relationships between perfectionism and obsessive-compulsive symptom dimensions among rural veterans. *Journal of Cognitive Psychotherapy, 33*(1), 58–70.

Rasmussen, S. A., & Eisen, J. (1992). The epidemiology and clinical features of obsessive compulsive disorder. *Psychiatric Clinics of North America, 15*(4), 743–758.

Rector, N. A., Hood, K., Richter, M. A., & Bagby, R. M. (2002). Obsessive-compulsive disorder and the Five-Factor Model of personality: Distinction and overlap with major depressive disorder. *Behaviour Research and Therapy, 40*(10), 1205–1219.

Rector, N. A., Richter, M. A., & Bagby, R. M. (2005). The impact of personality on symptom expression in obsessive-compulsive disorder. *The Journal of Nervous and Mental Disease, 193*(4), 231–236.

Rheaume, J., Freeston, M. H., Dugas, M. J., Letarte, H., & Ladouceur, R. (1995). Perfectionism, responsibility and obsessive-compulsive symptoms. *Behaviour Research and Therapy, 33*(7), 785–794.

Ricciardi, J. N., Baer, L., Jenike, M. A., Fischer, S. C., Sholtz, D., & Buttolph, M. L. (1992). Changes in DSM-III-R axis II diagnoses following treatment of obsessive-compulsive disorder. *The American Journal of Psychiatry, 149*(6), 829–831.

Rice, K. G., & Aldea, M. A. (2006). State dependence and trait stability of perfectionism: A short-term longitudinal study. *Journal of Counseling Psychology, 53*, 205–212.

Richter, M. A., Summerfeldt, L. J., Joffe, R. T., & Swinson, R. P. (1996). The Tridimensional Personality Questionnaire in obsessive-compulsive disorder. *Psychiatry Research, 65*(3), 185–188.

Samuels, J., Bienvenu, O. J., Krasnow, J., Wang, Y., Grados, M. A., Cullen, B., Goes, F. S., Maher, B., Greenberg, B. D., Mclaughlin, N. C., Rasmussen, S. A., Fyer, A. J., Knowles, J. A., McCracken, J. T., Piacentini, J., Geller, D., Stewart, S. E., Murphy, D. L., Shugart, Y. Y., . . . Nestadt, G. (2020). General personality dimensions, impairment and treatment response in obsessive-compulsive disorder. *Personality and Mental Health, 14*(2), 186–198.

Samuels, J., Bienvenu, O. J. III, Riddle, M. A., Cullen, B. A., Grados, M. A., Liang, K. Y., Hoehn-Saric, R., & Nestadt, G. (2002). Hoarding in obsessive compulsive disorder: Results from a case-control study. *Behaviour Research and Therapy, 40*(5), 517–528.

Samuels, J., Nestadt, G., Bienvenu, O. J., Costa, P. T., Jr., Riddle, M. A., Liang, K. Y., Hoehn-Saric, R., Grados, M. A., & Cullen, B. A. (2000). Personality disorders and normal personality dimensions in obsessive-compulsive disorder. *The British Journal of Psychiatry, 177*, 457–462.

Samuels, J. F., Bienvenu, O. J., Grados, M. A., Cullen, B., Riddle, M. A., Liang, K. Y., Eaton, W. W., & Nestadt, G. (2008). Prevalence and correlates of hoarding behavior in a community-based sample. *Behaviour Research and Therapy, 46*(7), 836–844.

Samuels, J. F., Bienvenu, O. J., Pinto, A., Fyer, A. J., McCracken, J. T., Rauch, S. L., Murphy, D. L., Grados, M. A., Greenberg, B. D., Knowles, J. A., Piacentini, J., Cannistraro, P. A., Cullen, B., Riddle, M. A., Rasmussen, S. A., Pauls, D. L., Willour, V. L., Shugart, Y. Y., Liang, K., . . . Nestadt, G. (2007). Hoarding in obsessive compulsive disorder: Results from the OCD Collaborative Genetics Study. *Behaviour Research and Therapy, 45*, 673–686.

Sanderson, W. C., Wetzler, S., Beck, A. T., & Betz, F. (1994). Prevalence of personality disorders among patients with anxiety disorders. *Psychiatry Research, 51*(2), 167–174.

Sartory, G., & Grey, S. J. (1982). Personality and treatment outcome in obsessional-compulsive patients. *Behavioural Psychotherapy, 9*, 34–45.

Schieber, K., Kollei, I., de Zwaan, M., Müller, A., & Martin, A. (2013). Personality traits as vulnerability factors in body dysmorphic disorder. *Psychiatry Research, 210*(1), 242–246.

Schlosser, S., Black, D. W., Blum, N., & Goldstein, R. B. (1994). The demography, phenomenology, and family history of 22 persons with compulsive hair pulling. *Annals of Clinical Psychiatry, 6*(3), 147–152.

Schut, A. J., Pincus, A. L., Castonguay, L. G., Bedics, J., Walling, F., Yanni, G., & Truckor, D. (1997). Attachment and interpersonal problems in non-clinical hair pulling. In 31st Annual Convention of the Association for the Advancement of Behavior Therapy, Miami Beach, FL.

Sciuto, G., Diaferia, G., Battaglia, M., Perna, G., Gabriele, A., & Bellodi, L. (1991). DSM-III-R personality disorders in panic and obsessive-compulsive disorder: A comparison study. *Comprehensive Psychiatry, 32*(5), 450–457.

Shea, M. T., Stout, R. L., Yen, S., Pagano, M. E., Skodol, A. E., Morey, L. C., Gunderson, J. G., McGlashan, T. H., Grilo, C. M., Sanislow, C. A., Bender, D. S., & Zanarini, M. C. (2004). Associations in the course of personality disorders and Axis I disorders over time. *Journal of Abnormal Psychology, 113*(4), 499–508.

Skodol, A. E., Clark, L. A., Bender, D. S., Krueger, R. F., Morey, L. C., Verheul, R., Alarcon, R. D., Bell, C. C., Siever, L. J., & Oldham, J. M. (2011). Proposed changes in personality and personality disorder assessment and diagnosis for DSM-5 Part I: Description and rationale. *Personality Disorders: Theory, Research, and Treatment, 2*(1), 4–22.

Skodol, A. E., Oldham, J. M., Hyler, S. E., Stein, D. J., Hollander, E., Gallaher, P. E., & Lopez, A. E. (1995). Patterns of anxiety and personality disorder comorbidity. *Journal of Psychiatric Research, 5*, 361–374.

Snorrason, Í., Smari, J., & Olafsson, R. P. (2010). Emotion regulation in pathological skin picking: Findings from a non-treatment seeking sample. *Journal of Behavior Therapy and Experimental Psychiatry, 41*(3), 238–245.

Solem, S., Hagen, K., Wenaas, C., Håland, Å. T., Launes, G., Vogel, P. A., Hansen, B., & Himle, J. A. (2015). Psychotic and schizotypal symptoms in non-psychotic patients with obsessive-compulsive disorder. *BMC Psychiatry, 15*, 121.

Southgate, L., Tchanturia, K., Collier, D., & Treasure, J. (2008). The development of the Childhood Retrospective Perfectionism Questionnaire (CHIRP) in an eating disorder sample. *European Eating Disorders Review, 16*(6), 451–462.

Stanley, M. A., Borden, J. W., Bell, G. E., & Wagner, A. L. (1994). Nonclinical hair pulling: Phenomenology and related psychopathology. *Journal of Anxiety Disorders, 8*(2), 119–130.

Stanley, M. A., Turner, S. M., & Borden, J. W. (1990). Schizotypal features in obsessive-compulsive disorder. *Comprehensive Psychiatry, 31*(6), 511–518.

Starcevic, V., Berle, D., Brakoulias, V., Sammut P., Moses, K., Milicevic, D., & Hannan A. (2013). Obsessive-compulsive personality disorder co-occurring with obsessive-compulsive disorder: Conceptual and clinical implications. *Australia and New Zealand Journal of Psychiatry, 47*(1), 65–73.

Steketee, G. (1990). Personality traits and disorders in obsessive-compulsives. *Journal of Anxiety Disorders, 4*, 351–364.

Stemberger, R. M. T., Thomas, A. M., Mansueto, C. S., & Carter, J. G. (2000). Personal toll of trichotillomania: Behavioral and interpersonal sequelae. *Journal of Anxiety Disorders, 14*(1), 97–104.

Summerfeldt, L. J. (2004). Understanding and treating incompleteness in obsessive-compulsive disorder. *Journal of Clinical Psychology, 60*(11), 1155–1168.

Summerfeldt, L. J., Antony, M. M., & Swinson, R. P. (2000, November). *Incompleteness: A link between perfectionistic traits and OCD* [Paper presentation]. Association for the Advancement of Behavior Therapy, New Orleans, LA.

Summerfeldt, L. J., Huta, V., & Swinson, R. P. (1998). Personality and obsessive-compulsive disorder. In R. P. Swinson, M. M. Antony, S. Rachman, & M. A. Richter. (Eds.), *Obsessive-compulsive disorder: Theory, research, and treatment* (pp. 79–119). Guilford.

Swedo, S. E., Rapoport, J. L., Leonard, H. L., Lenane, M. C., & Cheslow, D. (1989). Obsessive compulsive disorder in children and adolescents: Clinical and phenomenology of 70 consecutive cases. *Archives of General Psychiatry, 46*, 335–341.

Tallis, F. (1996). Compulsive washing in the absence of phobic and illness anxiety. *Behaviour Research and Therapy, 34*(4), 361–362.

Thiel, N., Hertenstein, E., Nissen, C., Herbst, N., Külz, A. K., & Voderholzer, U. (2013). The effect of personality disorders on treatment outcomes in patients with obsessive-compulsive disorders. *Journal of Personality Disorders, 27*(6), 697–715.

Tolin, D. F., Frost, R. O., Steketee, G., & Fitch, K. E. (2008). Family burden of compulsive hoarding: Results of an Internet survey. *Behaviour Research and Therapy, 46*(3), 334–344.

Tolin, D. F., Frost, R. O., Steketee, G., Gray, K. D., & Fitch, K. E. (2008). The economic and social burden of compulsive hoarding. *Psychiatry Research, 160*(2), 200–211.

Tolin, D. F., Woods, C. M., & Abramowitz, J. S. (2003). Relationship between obsessive beliefs and obsessive-compulsive symptoms. *Cognitive Therapy and Research, 27*(6), 657–669.

Torgersen, S., Kringlen, E., & Cramer, V. (2001). The prevalence of personality disorders in a community sample. *Archives of General Psychiatry, 58*, 590–596.

Torres, A. R., & Del Porto, J. A. (1995). Comorbidity of obsessive-compulsive disorder and personality disorders. *Psychopathology, 28*, 322–329.

Tükel, R., Keser, V., Karalı, N. T., Olgun, T. Ö., & Çalıkuşu, C. (2001). Comparison of clinical characteristics in trichotillomania and obsessive-compulsive disorder. *Journal of Anxiety Disorders, 15*(5), 433–441.

Veale, D., Boocock, A., Gournay, K., Dryden, W., Shah, F., Willson, R., & Walburn, J. (1996). Body dysmorphic disorder: A survey of fifty cases. *The British Journal of Psychiatry, 169*(2), 196–201.

Wellen, D., Samuels, J., Bienvenu, O. J., Grados, M., Cullen, B., Riddle, M., Liang, K. Y., & Nestadt, G. (2007). Utility of the Leyton Obsessional Inventory to distinguish OCD and OCPD. *Depression and Anxiety, 24*(5), 301–306.

Wetterneck, C. T., Lee, E. B., Flessner, C. A., Leonard, R. C., & Woods, D. W. (2016). Personality characteristics and experiential avoidance in trichotillomania: Results from an age and gender matched sample. *Journal of Obsessive-Compulsive and Related Disorders, 8*, 64–69.

Wheaton, M. G., & Pinto, A. (2017). Obsessive-compulsive personality disorder. In D. McKay, E. A. Storch, & J. S. Abramowitz (Eds.), *The Wiley handbook of obsessive-compulsive disorders* (pp. 726–742). Wiley-Blackwell.

Wheaton, M. G., & Pinto, A. (2020). OCPD and its relationship to obsessive-compulsive and hoarding disorders. In J. E. Grant, A. Pinto, & S. R. Chamberlain (Eds.), *Obsessive compulsive personality disorder* (pp. 49–69). American Psychiatric Association Publishing.

Wheaton, M. G., Pinto, A. M., Cervoni, C., Crosby, J., Tifft, E., Mathes, B., Garner, L., Van Kirk, N., Elias, J., & Pinto, A. (2020). Perfectionism in intensive residential treatment of obsessive-compulsive disorder. *Cognitive Therapy and Research, 44*, 136–144.

Widiger, T. A., & Trull, T. J. (1992). Personality and psychopathology: An application of the five-factor model. *Journal of Personality, 60*(2), 363–393.

Wilhelm, S., Keuthen, N. J., Deckersbach, T., Engelhard, I. M., Forker, A. E., Baer, L., O'Sullivan, R. L., & Jenike, M. A. (1999). Self-injurious skin picking: Clinical characteristics and comorbidity. *The Journal of Clinical Psychiatry, 60*(7), 454–459.

Wu, K. D., & Cortesi, G. T. (2009). Relations between perfectionism and obsessive-compulsive symptoms: Examination of specificity among the dimensions. *Journal of Anxiety Disorders, 23*(3), 393–400.

CHAPTER 10

Behavioral Conceptualizations of Obsessive-Compulsive and Related Disorders

Stephanie E. Cassin, Rotem Regev, Sandra Fournier, *and* Neil A. Rector

Abstract

The current chapter provides a selective overview of behavioral theories of obsessive-compulsive and related disorders (OCRDs) and reviews the empirical support for these theories. Behavioral theories revolutionized the psychological conceptualization and treatment of the OCRDs, and there is strong evidence accumulated over the past 50 years demonstrating the seminal role of learning processes in the maintenance of the conditions. The evidence supporting the role of learning factors in the development of the OCRDs is somewhat less clear. In the past decade, there has been renewed interest in modeling the full range of learning factors related to fear extinction in the context of exposure-based therapy, and the principles and empirical evidence for the role of inhibitory learning are addressed in the chapter.

Key Words: obsessive-compulsive and related disorders (OCRDs), OCD, hoarding disorder, body dysmorphic disorder, trichotillomania, skin-picking disorder, behavioral theory, conditioning, inhibitory learning, vulnerability

Introduction

Comprehensive psychological models of obsessive-compulsive and related disorders (OCRDs) have been proposed over the past century and have ranged from the early psychoanalytic formulations to the behavioral models derived from learning theory, to cognitive models, and in recent past, a return to multifactorial learning approaches that introduce new learning concepts for empirical examination. Important theoretical and empirical advancements, not to mention treatment refinements, over the past 20 years have emerged largely from cognitive and information-processing perspectives, making psychoanalytic theory of historical interest and allowing behavioral aspects to be co-opted within broader cognitive-behavioral frameworks. Newly expanded learning models, however, have returned to focus on the mechanisms of action in exposure therapy and to provide fresh and promising new avenues for understanding the development and maintenance of OCRDs and improving treatment outcomes. As detailed, there remains uncertainty about whether behavioral models can contribute theoretically to the understanding of how normal intrusions reach the threshold for conversion into distressing clinical obsessions in the absence of genetic, neurobiological, and cognitive risk factors, although past and present research highlights the central role of learning processes in the maintenance of obsessive-compulsive disorder (OCD) and the OCRDs once initiated and in their successful reduction in treatment.

Diagnostic Features of OCD and the OCRDs

OCD is characterized by the presence of recurrent obsessions and compulsions that are time-consuming and cause marked distress and/or impairment. Obsessions are persistent thoughts, ideas, or images that are regarded by the person as intrusive or inappropriate, whereas compulsions are ritualistic behaviors or mental acts that are performed to neutralize the anxiety caused by obsessions or to prevent a feared event (American Psychiatric Association [APA], 2013). An important change to the fifth edition of the *Diagnostic and Statistical Manual of Mental Disorders* (*DSM-5*; APA, 2013) from its predecessor was the movement of OCD out of the anxiety disorders and into the newly formed OCRDs, a cluster of disorders that includes OCD; body dysmorphic disorder, which is characterized by preoccupation with perceived defects or flaws in physical appearance; hoarding disorder, with marked persistent difficulties discarding or parting with possessions and often with excessive acquisition; trichotillomania, which is defined by recurrent pulling out of one's hair, leading to hair loss and clinical impairment; and skin-picking disorder, or recurrent picking at one's skin that leads to lesions and significant distress, despite repeated attempts to stop (APA, 2013). The shared phenomenology, rates of comorbidity, genetic and neurobiological risk factors, and treatment response provided the ostensible rationale for the OCRD grouping (for review, see Phillips et al., 2010), although the empirical basis of the categorization has been questioned (Abramowitz & Jacoby, 2015). Further, the overlap and distinction in behavioral processes have not been examined in clinically diagnosed OCRD populations to determine the extent of shared versus unique vulnerabilities to the onset and maintenance of the conditions or their treatment. While the etiology of OCRDs is likely multifactorial, with genetic, personality, social, and cognitive factors interacting to constitute risk, aspects of fear conditioning and extinction are hypothesized to play a seminal role in the onset and persistence of the conditions.

OCD

SYMPTOM DEVELOPMENT

The origins of behavioral models of OCD derive largely from Mowrer's two-stage model of fear and avoidance behavior (Mowrer, 1939, 1960), integrated to account for the development and persistence of obsessions and compulsions (Rachman & Hodgson, 1980). Mowrer suggested that fear of stimuli, such as thoughts, images, or objects, is acquired through a classical conditioning process. In the first stage of Mowrer's model, neutral stimuli, such as thoughts and images, become conditioned stimuli (CS) through pairing with an unconditioned stimulus (US) that naturally provokes fear. As theorized, a traumatic event should represent the catalyst for the activation of obsessive-compulsive symptoms. For example, an individual might develop contamination obsessions after a serious illness or doubting obsessions following a house fire.

SYMPTOM MAINTENANCE

According to the second stage of Mowrer's (1960) model, fear is maintained though operant conditioning processes, notably escape and avoidance behaviors. Learning theory frameworks were extended to account for the range of compulsive rituals observed in OCD. Compulsions were conceptualized as active avoidance strategies that are negatively reinforced and become habitual given their success in reducing the fear caused by the arrival of the obsession and the prevention of extinction (Dollard & Miller, 1950). For example, an individual with contamination obsessions might engage in excessive handwashing compulsions, avoid using public restrooms, and exit a room if another person is observed coughing or sneezing in order to reduce the chance of contamination. An individual with doubting obsessions might check the door locks, stove, and other appliances several times before leaving the house to ensure safety. This hypothesized functional relationship between obsessions causing distress and compulsive, escape, and avoidance behaviors reducing obsessional distress is so widely accepted that it is built into the modern nosologic description of the disorder (APA, 2013): as stated, "compulsions are behaviors that individuals feel 'driven to perform in response to an obsession'" (APA, 2013, p. 237). A recent direct test of the longitudinal association between obsessions and compulsions over time examined competing models of change in OCD symptoms (Laposa et al., 2019). Path analyses found four possible coupling relationships between obsessions and compulsions during longitudinal change over time: (a) obsessions and compulsions are not related ("no coupling" model), (b) obsessions lead to changes in compulsions ("goal-directed" model), (c) compulsions lead to changes in obsessions ("habit-driven" model), and (d) a reciprocal model in which (b) and (c) co-occur. Support was found for only the goal-directed model, suggesting that obsessions lead to subsequent changes in compulsions over time but not vice versa, a finding consistent with the purported functional relationship between obsessions and compulsions outlined in original behavioral theories.

Beyond classical overt compulsions (such as washing and checking), a broader range of factors have been implicated in the maintenance of OCD. For instance, "safety behaviors," a term referring to a variety of overt or covert strategies that are typically more subtle than compulsions, are often used to avoid or escape a feared outcome (Deacon & Maack, 2008; Salkovskis, 1991). Using a sleeve to open a restroom door or carrying antibacterial hand sanitizer are two examples of safety behaviors that might be used by an individual with contamination fears. Similar to compulsions, safety behaviors are negatively reinforced by effectively reducing anxiety in the short-term and have been implicated in the maintenance, and perhaps even exacerbation, of OCD symptoms because they focus attention on feared stimuli and may be used to justify the non-occurrence of a catastrophe (Deacon & Maack, 2008; Salkovskis, 1991).

Furthermore, in contemporary cognitive-behavioral approaches, excessive reassurance-seeking (ERS) has been hypothesized to be a key safety behavior related to the maintenance of obsessive-compulsive symptoms (Salkovskis, 1996). Higher levels of ERS are associated with increased symptom severity in OCD (Orr et al., 2018; Rector et al., 2019; Starcevic et al., 2012). In addition, the nature and strength of the relationship between OCD and ERS may differ from that of ERS and other disorders (Rector et al., 2019). Studies have found that individuals with OCD report greater levels of ERS than healthy controls (Orr et al., 2018), seek reassurance more persistently and repeatedly than those with panic disorder (Kobori & Salkovskis, 2013; Rector et al., 2019), and exhibit a greater urge to seek reassurance when it is not provided compared to those with depression (Kobori et al., 2015). Further, the triggers for reassurance may differ between individuals with OCD, who may seek reassurance in response to general threats, and individuals with depression, who may seek reassurance in response to social threat (Parrish & Radomsky, 2010; Katz et al., 2020). Reasons for seeking reassurance among those with OCD include dispelling potential threats, decreasing uncertainty, and sharing responsibility with others (Halldorsson & Salkovskis, 2017). Given the function reassurance serves for individuals with OCD, some researchers have suggested that reassurance sought by individuals with OCD may be best characterized as a form of compulsive checking behavior (Parrish & Radomsky, 2010; Rachman, 2002; Salkovskis & Kobori, 2015) or "checking by proxy" (Rachman, 2002) in response to elevated levels of anxiety or perceived threat (Parrish & Radomsky, 2010).

Furthermore, compulsions and safety behaviors are often performed to prevent a perceived feared outcome, but for more than half of individuals with OCD (particularly those with primary symmetry, ordering, repeating, and counting compulsions), these behaviors may be motivated by a sense of incompleteness (Ecker & Gonner, 2008; Summerfeldt, 2004, 2007). Also known as "not just right experiences" (NJREs; Coles et al., 2003), incompleteness refers to an inner sense of imperfection, connected with the perception that actions or intentions have not been fully achieved or have not produced the sought-after satisfaction. Viewed as a form of "sensation-based perfection" (Coles et al., 2003, p. 683), NJREs drive the performance of rituals until the action (e.g., locking the door) or perception (e.g., arranging books on a shelf) conforms to "absolute, yet often inarticulable subjective criteria" (Summerfeldt et al., 2004, p. 1462). In contrast to harm-avoidant compulsions, which are maintained through negative reinforcement, the rituals performed in response to NJREs may be maintained through both negative and positive reinforcement. That is, the distress associated with imperfection is reduced and the satisfying "just right" feeling is achieved.

Coles and Ravid (2016) examined the clinical presentation of NJREs in patients with OCD (in comparison to controls) and found that those with OCD reported more NJREs and were more distressed by these experiences. Moreover, they reported observations of changes in NJREs after cognitive-behavioral therapy (CBT), finding that the individuals with OCD witness a reduction of these experiences and are less distressed by them after CBT.

In an experimental paradigm using nonclinical undergraduate students, Irwin and Jones (2017) reported strong relationships between task ratings that elicit NJREs and incompleteness, OCD symptoms, perfectionism, and anxiety sensitivity, suggesting a strong link between NJREs, incompleteness motivations, and sensory-affective disturbances in OCD.

EMPIRICAL EVIDENCE

Although the two-factor model hypothesizes a traumatic trigger for anxiety, early empirical research led to the conclusion that there is little evidence to support the direct role of traumatic conditioning in OCD (Emmelkamp, 1982; Mineka & Zinbarg, 2006). However, some research has demonstrated an association between traumatic incidents, such as sexual abuse or combat, and the subsequent onset of OCD (de Silva & Marks, 2001; Freeman & Leonard, 2000). Further, epidemiological studies have demonstrated the risk for OCD to be tenfold in persons with posttraumatic stress disorder (PTSD), while the National Vietnam Veterans Readjustment Study found OCD prevalence rates of 5.3% in veterans exposed to high war-zone stress, compared to a 0.3% prevalence in veterans in low to moderate war-zone stress (Jordan et al., 1991; Sasson et al., 2005). A large-scale study examining the role of traumatic and stressful life events in the onset of OCD found that 54% of the sample reported a lifetime traumatic event, and that the range and severity of traumatic events were associated with a more severe expression of OCD, even when depression and other comorbidities were controlled. Subsidiary analyses found specific and robust associations between a history of traumatic life events and harming obsessions/checking compulsions and symmetry/ordering symptom clusters (Cromer et al., 2007a). A more recent study found that exposure to trauma was associated with more obsessive-compulsive symptoms and the development of "bad thoughts" specifically (Barzilay et al., 2019). There is also recent research that suggests a history of childhood trauma may predict the course of OCD: in a recent naturalistic cohort study conducted in the Netherlands, early age of onset and childhood trauma were found to predict a worse four-year course in patients with OCD (Tibi et al., 2020).

Beyond the role of distinct traumatic events in the development of OCD, a broader literature indicates that more general negative life events and life stress are associated with the onset of OCD (Jones & Menzies, 1998). For instance, early research suggested that patients with OCD report experiencing a greater number of negative life events than do nonpsychiatric controls (McKeon et al., 1984). Another study comparing stressful life events in children and adolescents with OCD to stressful events in those with non-OCD anxiety disorders and healthy controls found that negative life events were significantly more common in youth with OCD in the year prior to the onset of OCD than they were in healthy controls, but they were not significantly different from events experienced by children and adolescents with non-OCD anxiety disorders (Gothelf et al., 2004). Other research has attempted to demonstrate a direct temporal relationship between negative life events and the onset of OCD symptoms. Horowitz (1975) showed that after exposure to stressful events, people tend to experience intrusive and repetitive thoughts. Similarly, Parkinson and Rachman (1980) found that mothers whose children were to undergo surgery experienced a steep rise in anxiety and a range of unwanted thoughts.

Research suggests that particular and paradigmatic life events, such as the perinatal period, represent risk for increased anxiety/distress and the onset of obsessions and compulsions (Brandes et al., 2004; Forray et al., 2010; Russell et al., 2013; Speisman et al., 2011; Uguz et al., 2007). While a growing body of research has indicated that unwanted and intrusive thoughts of harm are a common experience for postpartum women (Fairbrother et al., 2015; Fairbrother & Woody, 2008), the onset of clinically impairing OCD also appears to increase over the perinatal period: based on postpartum assessment, as many as 4% of women without a previous diagnosis of OCD developed the disorder during the postpartum period (Uguz et al., 2007). Less research exists on OCD onset or increased vulnerability during the antenatal period, although a meta-analysis found that pregnancy increased the risk of OCD by approximately 1.5% (Russell et al., 2013). In addition, a study based on retrospective recall found that 5.1% of women with OCD recalled onset during pregnancy (Guglielmi et al., 2014), while another study found that when the sample was restricted to women who had been pregnant in the past, 15.4% recalled developing OCD during the antenatal period (Forray et al., 2010). For women who already have a history of OCD, the antenatal period can also lead to an exacerbation of existing symptoms (Forray et al., 2010). While perhaps not as frequently studied as the postpartum period, pregnancy appears to be a period of high risk and vulnerability for obsessive-compulsive symptoms, and a meta-analysis supports the perinatal period as a time of increased risk of onset of clinically diagnosable OCD (Russell et al., 2013).

In summary, research supports the potential role of trauma and adverse life events in the development of OCD. However, there remain a number of critical challenges to the role of conditioning in the development of OCD. First, the majority of studies examine the role of past traumatic events, so it remains very difficult to draw any conclusions about trauma and the actual temporal onset of OCD. This mirrors the clinical context, where most patients do not report traumatic events as the precipitating factor in the onset of their obsessive-compulsive symptoms. Second, there is very little evidence to support the idea that the particular nature of traumatic or negative life events shapes the particular content of the obsessions. Third, and relatedly, while general life stress may be said to potentiate the onset of OCD within a diathesis-stress framework, general life stress (or historical traumatic events) does not represent discrete unconditioned stimuli in a classical conditioning framework. Fourth, while conditioning of obsessions may also occur via observation and information transmission, little research has examined this question. Fifth, it would appear that a more fulsome neurocognitive model of OCD incorporating genes, neurobiological processes, personality vulnerability, stress reactivity, and more proximal cognitive risk factors may need to be taken into account with learning approaches to model OCD onset risk.

Notwithstanding the uncertainty of the factors that lead to the development of obsessions, there is very strong empirical support showing that once obsessions have developed, their continued occurrence leads to an attendant rise in fear and anxiety, and the compulsive rituals lead to the attenuation of the obsessional anxiety. In a series of early experiments, Rachman and colleagues (for review, see Rachman and Hodgson, 1980), demonstrated that: exposure to obsessional cues was associated with increased anxiety and discomfort and corresponding urges to perform rituals, based on subjective reports but also on pulse rate variability in some of the studies; the engagement in compulsive rituals led to the reduction of anxiety and distress; delaying the compulsive rituals led to a "spontaneous decay" of anxiety and urges to engage in the rituals within 30 minutes; and prevention of the compulsive rituals led to an extinction of anxiety and distress in subsequent exposure to the obsessional cues.

These findings have been replicated in a series of studies examining the effect of covert neutralization on anxiety and distress. Mentally neutralizing obsessive thoughts resulted in short-term reduction in distress, but increased discomfort and stronger urges to neutralize over time (de Silva et al., 2003; Rachman et al., 1996; Salkovskis et al., 1997, 2003). In a finding similar to that of studies noting spontaneous decay of anxiety after compulsive ritual prevention (Rachman & Hodgson, 1980), anxiety reduced to comparable levels without mental neutralizing after 20 minutes (Rachman et al., 1996).

Although safety behaviors may be used judiciously in the early stages of treatment (see Rachman et al., 2008), empirical research suggests that they are negatively reinforced and maintain anxiety over time. The mere availability of safety behaviors has been found to reduce anxiety, regardless of whether they are actually used (Powers et al., 2004). An experimental study found that undergraduates who were instructed to engage in safety behaviors for one week reported significant increases in threat overestimation, contamination fear symptoms, and emotional and avoidant responses on behavioral avoidance tasks, regardless of baseline level of contamination fears (Deacon & Maack, 2008). Furthermore, contamination fears remained elevated above baseline levels even after safety behaviors were decreased, suggesting that heightened awareness of contaminants persisted. Overall, and consistent with the hypothesized pernicious role of safety behaviors in OCD, recent experimental studies demonstrate that greater obsessive-compulsive symptom severity is associated with higher rates of safety behavior use (Angelakis & Austin, 2018), and reduction of safety behavior use in OCD treatment results in reduced obsessive-compulsive symptoms and improved clinical outcomes (Rector et al., 2019).

Early experimental findings provided the rationale for the development of a behavioral-based treatment, exposure and response prevention (E/RP; see Chapter 19), which has provided additional quasi-experimental support for learning processes (i.e., fear extinction) in OCD. Exposure therapy is based on the principles of fear extinction, where classically conditioned stimuli lose their fear-evoking potential through repeated exposure to the stimuli in the absence of the feared negative consequences. E/RP entails prolonged exposure to obsessional cues that induce discomfort and strict abstinence from ritualizing behavior until the discomfort abates. Numerous uncontrolled and controlled studies (e.g., Eddy et al., 2004; Olatunji et al., 2012) have demonstrated the efficacy of E/RP, making it the most efficacious psychological treatment for OCD (e.g., NICE, 2007). Notwithstanding the success of exposure therapy, the long presumed mechanism of action, habituation (Rachman, 1980; Foa & Kozak, 1986), has received only mixed support, with some studies demonstrating successful treatment response to exposure therapy in the absence of within-session and between-session habituation (for detailed reviews, see Craske et al., 2008; Jacoby & Abramowitz, 2016; Knowles & Olatunji, 2019). This has led to the conclusion that habituation is not likely the key learning process in fear reduction and extinction (Craske et al., 2008). The inhibitory learning model has been proposed as an alternative explanation for the mechanism of action in exposure, with an explicit shift away from habituation (Craske et al., 2008, 2014). Given the absence of habituation processes predicting successful exposure treatment, as well as numerous studies showing that feared associations remain intact over time even after exposure therapy, the inhibitory learning model proposes that new nonthreat, or inhibitory, associations are learned in exposures that compete with feared associations to produce fear extinction (Craske et al., 2008). In other words, inhibitory learning suggests the original CS–US association learned during fear conditioning is not erased during extinction but rather is left intact as a new, secondary learning about how the CS–US develops (e.g., CS—no US; Bouton, 1993; for a review, see Craske et al., 2008). Through repeated exposure, these new associations are strengthened enough to inhibit the older fearful associations. Therefore, the inhibitory model asserts that habituation is not necessary, nor is the unlearning (i.e., eradication) of fearful associations, but rather the strengthening and ascension of new competing nonthreat (i.e., safety) associations (Craske et al., 2008). Within this framework, the goal of exposure therapy is to maximize inhibitory associations to exceed the originally classically conditioned fear association, so that future exposure to the feared stimuli results in superior recall of the inhibitory associations rather than the original excitatory fear associations.

The inhibitory learning model (Craske et al., 2008, 2014) outlines a number of mechanisms derived from basic science and extinction learning and includes strategies to enhance exposure therapy through the development of nonthreat associations and strategies to enhance retrievability of nonthreat associations in the future. They are:

Development of nonthreat associations:

1. Create a mismatch with expectancies
2. Employ multiple conditioned excitors
3. Reduce safety signals and safety behaviors
4. Consider biologically based cognitive enhancements
5. Enhance inhibitory regulation (targeting extinction-relevant brain regions prior to extinction training).

Enhancement of accessibility and retrievability of inhibitory associations:

1. Enhance variability throughout exposure
2. Space out exposure trials
3. Employ strategies to prevent return of feared association

Research examining support for the hypothesized variables of inhibitory learning in fear extinction has focused mostly on anxiety and phobic disorders, although there have been recent reviews supporting theoretical and clinical applications to exposures in OCD (for reviews, see Blakey & Abramowitz, 2019; Jacoby & Abramowitz, 2016), taking into consideration each of the exposure-enhancement recommendations above as well as published case material demonstrating the application of inhibitory learning for patients with OCD (Krompinger et al., 2019; McGuire & Storch, 2019). The exciting clinical and research developments in this area are covered in greater depth in Chapter 19. While it is premature to examine the empirical status of the principles of inhibitory learning in OCD, the emphasis on reducing safety aids and safety behaviors is consistent with the substantial empirical literature on their role in OCD, and the pivot from fear reduction to fear tolerance in fear extinction is consistent with recent experimental findings on the importance of distress tolerance in OCD. Laposa and colleagues (2015) demonstrated that distress tolerance was correlated with OCD symptoms in a sample of participants with OCD, and research with nonclinical samples has shown low distress tolerance to be associated with elevated obsessive-compulsive symptoms (Cougle et al., 2012) and to be predictive of the development of intrusions in experimental tasks (Cougle et al., 2011). Hence, research demonstrates that a low tolerance for distress in OCD may hinder the ability to overcome avoidance and reduce compulsive rituals and safety behaviors, and that exposure-based treatments that focus on improving distress tolerance may enhance clinical efficacy. Finally, there is some confusion about how certain aspects of inhibitory learning can be integrated with other empirically supported treatments for OCD, such as cognitive therapy, which have been shown recently to compliment exposure-based treatments (Hawley et al., 2020; Rector et al., 2019) rather than detract from them, which inhibitory learning models would not necessarily predict (see Jacoby & Abramowitz, 2015).

Hoarding Disorder

Hoarding disorder (HD) is defined as a persistent difficulty discarding or parting with possessions regardless of their actual value, resulting in the accumulation of clutter. The difficulty is due to a perceived need to save the items and to distress associated with discarding them (APA, 2013). Hoarding refers to the acquisition of, and failure to discard, a large number of possessions that appear to be useless or of limited value, to the point that living spaces are sufficiently cluttered so as to preclude activities for which those spaces were designed (Frost & Hartl, 1996, p. 341; see also Chapter 4). Individuals with HD feel compelled to acquire and save possessions (Frost & Gross, 1993), and the excessive doubting, checking, and reassurance-seeking that occur when individuals with HD attempt to discard their possessions appear related to compulsive rituals (Steketee & Frost, 2003). Individuals with HD engage in acquiring and saving behaviors to prevent future harm, such as losing important information or being unprepared for a future need (Frost & Gross, 1993). In contrast to the obsessions that occur in OCD, hoarding obsessions are thought to be less ego-dystonic and intrusive (Steketee & Frost, 2003). Indeed, some individuals with HD describe their behavior in positive ways by emphasizing frugality and environmental consciousness (Frost & Gross, 1993).

A study comparing individuals with compulsive hoarding, with and without OCD, on a number of sociodemographic and psychopathological variables found that 100% of individuals with HD but without OCD reported hoarding for practical reasons (i.e., needing the item in the future) or sentimental reasons (i.e., strong emotional attachment to possessions), and none (0%) experienced obsessional ideas related to hoarding (Pertusa et al., 2008). In contrast, 28% of individuals with HD plus OCD reported obsessional ideas related to hoarding, such as fear of catastrophic consequences, fear of accidentally discarding important items (such as letters or receipts), or need for symmetry/order, and 48% reported excessive checking rituals in relation to hoarding.

SYMPTOM DEVELOPMENT

Compared to many of the other OCRDs, HD has received relatively little attention regarding its etiology within a behavioral framework (Grisham & Barlow, 2005; Steketee & Frost, 2003). Most behavioral theories of hoarding are actually cognitive-behavioral theories (Frost & Hartl, 1996; Frost & Steketee, 1998) that propose a variety of vulnerability factors, including impaired executive functioning, information-processing deficits, maladaptive beliefs about possessions, and family/individual history. With respect to this latter factor, it has been proposed that modeling of hoarding behavior or experiencing a significant loss or traumatic event might contribute to the development of hoarding symptoms. Traumatic experiences are hypothesized to leave the individual feeling unsafe, which in turn could make them rely more on their personal belongings for comfort and security (Cromer et al., 2007b; Frost & Hartl, 1996; Hartl et al., 2005).

SYMPTOM MAINTENANCE

The behavioral models of hoarding explicitly integrate cognitive aspects in the maintenance of the condition to arrive at a comprehensive cognitive-behavioral formulation. Hoarding has been conceptualized as an avoidance behavior associated with indecisiveness and perfectionism, which is maintained through both positive and negative reinforcement (Frost & Gross, 1993). Cognitive-behavioral models of HD propose that individuals with the disorder are overly concerned with making mistakes and save things in order to avoid the mistake of throwing away a needed possession or important information (Frost & Gross, 1993; Frost & Hartl, 1996). When coupled with indecisiveness, the concern about making mistakes may result in saving possessions that have a low probability of being used in the future (Frost & Gross, 1993). Saving is negatively reinforced by allowing individuals with hoarding to avoid the worry associated with making the mistake of prematurely discarding a possession that might be needed in the future. Delaying the decision about whether to discard a possession is seen as the "safe" decision. Saving is also negatively reinforced by allowing individuals with hoarding to avoid the feelings of loss associated with discarding a cherished possession (Frost & Gross, 1993; Frost & Hartl, 1996; Frost & Steketee, 1998). Indeed, cognitive accounts of HD highlight how some individuals with the disorder describe their possessions as being part of the self, and discarding their possessions is comparable to losing a close friend (Frost & Hartl, 1996). Some possessions come to signal a safe environment through their acquired association with comfort and safety (Frost & Hartl, 1996). Buying or acquiring new possessions is thought to be positively reinforced by providing a sense of comfort and safety (Grisham & Barlow, 2005), whereas the thought of discarding possessions violates this feeling of safety and is generally avoided (Frost & Hartl, 1996).

EMPIRICAL EVIDENCE

Traumatic events are reported more frequently among individuals with hoarding disorder than among community members without the disorder (Hartl et al., 2005; Samuels et al., 2008). Moreover, individuals with HD have been found to report greater frequency of past traumatic events than individuals with OCD, with no significant difference in the frequency of comorbid PTSD (Frost et al., 2011). Interpersonal violence has also been linked to increased hoarding behaviors in patients with self-reported hoarding (Tolin et al., 2010).

Childhood adversity, including sexual abuse, physical abuse, home break-ins, and having had something taken by force, have all been associated with hoarding behavior (Hartl et al., 2005; Samuels et al., 2008). There is some evidence that individuals with HD who experienced a traumatic or stressful life event have significantly greater hoarding severity (specifically with respect to clutter), even when controlling for nonspecific psychological distress, such as anxiety, depression, and even broadly based obsessive-compulsive symptomatology, suggesting that traumatic events might influence the clinical expression of hoarding (Cromer et al., 2007b). Individuals with a later age of onset are more likely to report a stressful life event directly prior to the onset of hoarding compared to individuals with an early age of onset (Grisham et al., 2005, 2006). This finding has led some to suggest that hoarding behavior develops in response to traumatic or stressful life events for some individuals, whereas it might be a lifelong characterological phenomenon for others (Grisham & Barlow, 2005; Grisham et al., 2006). Research examining the traumatic and stressful life events reported by individuals with HD is limited by the retrospective collection of data, which could potentially be influenced by current functioning.

In support of the cognitive-behavioral conceptualizations of hoarding, a positive correlation has been demonstrated between hoarding and both indecisiveness and perfectionism (specifically concern over mistakes and doubts about actions; Frost & Gross, 1993), and between hoarding and both indecisiveness and procrastination (Frost & Shows, 1993). Individuals with hoarding have been found to report more decision-making problems than community controls and these problems are correlated with excessive acquisition, difficulty discarding and clutter/disorganization independent of depression, anxiety, and obsessive-compulsive symptoms (Frost et al., 2011). Given the indecisiveness and concern over making mistakes seen in individuals with HD, the task of deciding what to save and what to discard becomes very difficult. The majority of individuals with HD reported that they purchase extra food, household supplies, and toiletries to ensure they are prepared for future need, and carry "just in case items" in their purses and cars, including pens, paper, books, utensils, makeup, medication, blankets, and footwear (Frost & Gross, 1993). Moreover, fear of decision-making and lack of confidence in memory have been found to interact with general emotional reactivity to predict hoarding symptoms, and emotional reactivity is hypothesized as a possible vulnerability factor for HD (Shaw et al., 2015).

Qualitative research has also implicated a relationship between emotion regulation and hoarding by demonstrating that individuals with HD have difficulties identifying and describing feelings, hold unhelpful attitudes about emotional experiences, believe they lack effective strategies to manage these experiences, and use avoidance-based strategies (Taylor et al., 2019). Additional research demonstrates an association between hoarding and decreased tolerance for negative emotions (Timpano et al., 2014). Emotion regulation may therefore be a factor in the development and maintenance of hoarding symptoms. Taylor et al. (2018) found associations between emotional regulation difficulties as well as impulsivity and hoarding symptoms that were partially mediated by beliefs about emotional attachment to possessions, and that emotional regulation difficulties predicted difficulties in discarding, acquisition, and hoarding symptoms.

Hoarding has also been associated with intolerance of uncertainty (Castriotta et al., 2019; Oglesby et al., 2013; Wheaton et al., 2016) and distress intolerance (Grisham et al., 2018; Mathes et al., 2017). Individuals with HD reported elevated levels of intolerance of uncertainty in comparison with controls and comparable levels in comparison to those with generalized anxiety disorder and OCD (Wheaton et al., 2016). Recently, Norberg et al. (2020) found that distress intolerance was associated with hoarding severity and that individuals with hoarding reported more trait emotional reactivity and distress intolerance than a control group. Further empirical evidence suggests that emotional distress tolerance and emotion regulation, and in particular intolerance of uncertainty, trouble sticking to goal behaviors when distressed, and low emotional awareness, may elucidate variance in HD symptoms (Worden et al., 2019).

In line with the cognitive-behavioral conceptualization of hoarding, individuals with HD engage in behavioral avoidance of distressing situations that are further strengthened over time. Associations have been reported between hoarding symptom severity and avoidance, after controlling for anxiety and depression (Ayers et al., 2014). Saving possessions and excessive acquisition of items may be a behavioral avoidance tool that helps individuals with hoarding to avoid distress. Individuals with HD also report higher levels of emotional attachment to their possessions and derive more comfort from possessing the items (Frost & Gross, 1993; Frost et al., 1995). Research reports associations between hoarding symptom severity and an increased inclination to anthropomorphize objects (Burgess et al., 2018; Timpano & Shaw, 2013) and that increased instrumental and sentimental values mediate the relationship between anthropomorphism and attachment to objects (Kwok et al., 2018).

Numerous case studies (Damecour & Charron, 1998; Greenberg, 1987; Greenberg et al., 1990; Shafran & Tallis, 1996) have detailed the anxiety-reducing role of compulsive acquisition and saving, indicating that hoarding compulsions function as operant conditioning processes similar to compulsive rituals in OCD. However, numerous randomized controlled trials testing the efficacy of E/RP for treatment of compulsive hoarding show reduced efficacy (Abramowitz et al., 2003), suggesting potential differences in the factors that interfere with extinction (see Chapter 11 for an explication of the important cognitive factors that contribute to the persistence of compulsive hoarding).

Body Dysmorphic Disorder

Body dysmorphic disorder (BDD) is defined as a preoccupation with one or more perceived defects in physical appearance that are slight or not observable to others, coupled with the performance of repetitive behaviors in response to these concerns (APA, 2013). Given the functional parallels between BDD and OCD, it is perhaps not surprising that many of the behavioral models that have been proposed to account for the etiology of OCD have also been applied to BDD (Veale, 2004; see also Chapter 3). Although BDD symptoms are experienced as more ego-syntonic than OCD symptoms (Eisen et al., 2004; McKay et al., 2008; Phillips, 1991; Simeon et al., 1995), both disorders are characterized by distressing and unwanted thoughts coupled with irresistible urges to engage in compulsive behaviors aimed at reducing the distress (McKay et al., 2008; Neziroglu et al., 2004).

SYMPTOM DEVELOPMENT

A comprehensive behavioral model that has been put forth to account for the development and maintenance of BDD (Neziroglu et al., 2004) is based on the two-factor conditioning model of Mowrer (1960). Most people who experience negative body-focused events (e.g., teasing related to appearance) do not develop BDD, and so this diathesis-stress model begins with the assumption that some individuals are at increased risk of developing BDD due to a biological predisposition in conjunction with early operant conditioning whereby physical appearance is positively reinforced by others. According to Neziroglu and colleagues (2004), classical conditioning accounts for the development of BDD symptoms. Individuals with a biological predisposition, who are then exposed to early operant conditioning experiences that reinforce attractiveness, develop a strong belief that physical appearance is of ultimate importance and is intimately connected with personal identity and self-worth. One's own learning experiences can then be further strengthened through social or vicarious learning (Bandura, 1977), whereby an individual observes another person being either positively reinforced for their attractiveness or teased for falling short of the societal ideal.

Aversive experiences, such as being teased, bullied, or abused, and many common changes in appearance, such as pubertal changes, the development of acne, or thinning hair, can serve as unconditioned stimuli that trigger unconditioned negative emotional responses, such as shame, disgust, depression, and anxiety (Neziroglu et al., 2006). The unconditioned responses may become conditioned to certain body parts and continue to trigger the same emotional states even in the absence of the unconditioned stimuli (Neziroglu et al., 2004; Neziroglu et al., 2008; Veale, 2004). For example, a young woman who is sexually assaulted feels anxious, disgusted, and embarrassed and is then conditioned to re-experience these emotional states when observing her body. An adolescent boy who is teased about having acne feels ashamed and disgusted, and then continues to feel ashamed and disgusted when observing his face in the mirror even after his acne has improved and the teasing has stopped. An adolescent boy feels weak and scrawny while being physically bullied by a group of boys at school, and then continues to feel weak and scrawny in the presence of males even after becoming a body-builder.

SYMPTOM MAINTENANCE

Consistent with Mowrer's (1960) two-factor theory of anxiety, Neziroglu and colleagues (2004) proposed that BDD is maintained through operant conditioning processes. When individuals with BDD observe or think about their perceived flaw, their distress level increases. Similar to individuals with OCD, those with BDD develop strategies to reduce distress or avoid it altogether. For example, individuals with BDD are typically considered either "mirror avoiders" or "mirror checkers," and they may alternate from one behavior to the other over time (Gleaves & Ambwani, 2008; Neziroglu et al., 2004; Phillips, 1991; Veale & Riley, 2001). Mirror avoiders are fearful of observing their perceived "grotesque" image, and so cover all mirrors and reflective surfaces, or alternatively, restrict looking in mirrors that are considered to be "bad" mirrors that highlight their disavowed features (Veale & Riley, 2001). They may also avoid social and public situations in an attempt to prevent their appearance concerns and associated negative emotions from being triggered. Mirror checkers, on the other hand, can spend an inordinate amount of time scrutinizing their perceived physical flaws. Moreover, individuals with BDD engage in a host of creative safety behaviors, including camouflaging with makeup or clothing, using excessive skin or hair products, having dermatological and cosmetic procedures, exercising excessively, seeking reassurance, posturing (i.e., positioning themselves to make the defect less apparent), and hiding the perceived defect.

Behavioral models of BDD propose that avoidant, compulsive, and safety behaviors are maintained by negative reinforcement because they serve to temporarily reduce distress regarding appearance. Safety behaviors are often considered as natural and part of a consistent daily routine, therefore providing a perception of control over feelings of distress (Oakes et al., 2016). However, as noted in the OCD section, safety behaviors prevent the natural extinction of the conditioned negative emotional response and are often counterproductive. Mirror-checking is reinforced because individuals with BDD occasionally find their appearance acceptable in a "good" mirror or particular lighting (Veale, 2004), and the variable ratio schedule of reinforcement makes mirror-checking highly resistant to extinction (Neziroglu et al., 2004; Veale & Riley, 2001). As the individual spends more time looking in the mirror, he or she becomes more self-conscious about the perceived defect, which reinforces the belief that the body part is hideous (Veale, 2004). Consequently, the distress experienced prior to mirror-checking can actually be exacerbated (Veale & Riley, 2001), leading to compulsive attempts to correct appearance in order to make the flaw less noticeable. However, these attempts can become counterproductive, because compulsive and safety behaviors often increase self-consciousness and monitoring (e.g., wondering and checking if the camouflage is effective or muscles appear large enough), draw attention to the perceived flaw, and in some cases, make it objectively worse (e.g., skin-picking). This conclusion is supported by the finding that increasing frequency and duration of BDD-focused safety behaviors, such as appearance-checking, over time lead to increased BDD symptoms, as well as an urgent need to seek reassurance regarding appearance, whereas a decrease in safety behaviors led to a similar decrease in BDD symptoms (Summers & Cougle, 2018). This positive correlation between frequency, duration, and severity of safety behaviors may be worsened by a low distress tolerance, as greater BDD symptoms are associated with greater levels of inability to tolerate distressing emotions (Matheny et al., 2017). Therefore, engagement in safety behaviors may play a direct role in exacerbating BDD-related symptoms. Thus, compulsive and safety behaviors maintain BDD by paradoxically sustaining the individual's preoccupation and distress (Neziroglu et al., 2008; Veale, 2004), and, alternatively, reducing safety behaviors is associated with decreased BDD symptoms, particularly in individuals with high BDD symptom severity (Wilver et al., 2020).

Individuals with BDD are often concerned with several body parts, either simultaneously or over time (Phillips, 1991), and higher-order conditioning is the mechanism thought to account for this finding (Neziroglu et al., 2008; Rabinowitz et al., 2007). Through higher-order conditioning, a new conditioned stimulus is paired with the original conditioned stimulus, in the absence of the unconditioned stimulus, until the new conditioned stimulus produces the original conditioned response. For example, an adolescent boy who feels ashamed and disgusted when perceiving acne on his face shifts his attention to his nose, and then continues to feel ashamed and disgusted by the shape and size of his nose from this point forward. The finding that individuals with BDD typically have one primary concern and multiple secondary concerns can be explained by higher-order conditioning, because higher-order conditioned stimuli (e.g., nose) produce a less intense conditioned response than the original conditioned stimulus (e.g., skin).

EMPIRICAL EVIDENCE

There is some evidence that, in childhood, individuals who later developed BDD received more positive reinforcement for their physical appearance than for their behavior, intellect, or personality traits (Neziroglu et al., 2004). However, individuals with BDD also report more appearance-based teasing in childhood, and the frequency of childhood teasing has been found to correlate with BDD severity (Buhlmann et al., 2007). Similarly, bullying victimization has been found to correlate with muscle dysmorphia later in life (Wolke & Sapouna, 2008). Bullying and teasing about appearance have also been found to be triggering events for the onset of symptoms in many individuals with BDD (Weingarden et al., 2017). Other research has found that children with BDD are often both victim and perpetrator of bullying, which is evidence of a unique relationship between victimization and bullying in cases of BDD (Neziroglu et al., 2018). Studies of childhood teasing, bullying, and positive reinforcement of appearance are based on retrospective reports, however, and an individual's perception of past events might be influenced by current body concerns. Physical, sexual, and emotional abuse are prevalent among individuals with BDD (Didie et al., 2006; Neziroglu et al., 2006); however, abuse is thought to be a nonspecific risk factor for psychopathology, and research has not examined whether early abuse leads to later disturbance in adulthood in the perception of particular body parts, as predicted from the model (Fallon & Ackard, 2002).

With respect to operant conditioning processes, it has been demonstrated that individuals with BDD report high levels of distress prior to mirror-gazing and expect that their distress will increase if they resist the urge to look in the mirror. However, in contrast to OCD compulsions, their distress actually increases to a greater extent after checking their appearance in the mirror than after resisting the urge to do so, despite engaging in a series of complex safety behaviors while mirror-gazing (Veale & Riley, 2001). Distress was not assessed during mirror-gazing in the study by Veale and Riley, so it is unclear whether mirror-gazing was negatively reinforced. It is possible that distress reduces at the initial glance, but then increases as mirror-gazing duration increases. This finding is supported by evidence that prolonged mirror-gazing leads to increased levels of dissociation and decreased feelings of attractiveness (Möllmann et al., 2019). Even short-duration mirror-gazing can trigger those with BDD to experience distress and a strong urge to check again, and this does not appear to differ significantly from those with BDD who engage in long-duration gazing (Windheim et al., 2011). The negative reinforcement experienced during mirror-gazing, if any, appears to be very short-lived. Yet research has demonstrated that individuals with BDD continue to feel compelled to look in the mirror in the hopes of looking different, verifying how they appear in public, and camouflaging themselves (Veale & Riley, 2001). Finally, E/RP, a behavioral treatment that aims to reduce mirror-gazing and safety behaviors associated with BDD, has been found to be effective in the treatment of BDD, providing further indirect support for the role of learning principles in its maintenance and improvement in treatment (McKay et al., 1997).

Trichotillomania and Skin-Picking Disorder

Trichotillomania (TTM; hair-pulling disorder) is defined by recurrent pulling out of one's hair, resulting in significant hair loss (APA, 2013). The individual with TTM makes repeated attempts to decrease or stop the hair-pulling, and the behavior causes clinically significant distress or impairment (APA, 2013). Skin-picking disorder (SPD; excoriation) is defined by recurrent skin-picking leading to skin lesions (APA, 2013). The individual makes repeated attempts to decrease or stop the skin-picking, and the behavior causes clinically significant distress or impairment (APA, 2013). While the two disorders are categorized separately in *DSM-5*, there is wide agreement that some of the fundamental etiological mechanisms shared by TTM and SPD are similar, and it is therefore fitting to group the two disorders together. Snorrason et al. (2012) examined evidence for comorbidity of TTM and SPD. They reviewed shared risk factors and similarities in clinical characteristics and concluded that the two disorders co-occur more often than chance and have considerable resemblances as well as risk factors that warrant their being categorized together. Therefore, the two disorders are presented together in this chapter, but empirical evidence is given by relevant disorder.

Despite apparent similarities in their repetitiveness, hair-pulling in TTM and skin-picking in SPD are functionally dissimilar to compulsive rituals in OCD (Franklin et al., 2008; see also Chapter 5). Although both individuals with OCD and those with TTM/SPD experience irresistible urges to engage in repetitive behaviors and perceive the behaviors as unreasonable (Swedo, 1993), they differ in the extent to which they are aware of their repetitive behaviors (Franklin et al., 2008). In addition, OCD and TTM/SPD differ with respect to antecedent events that prompt the repetitive behaviors, as well as the emotions experienced before, during, and after the repetitive behaviors (Franklin et al.,

2008; Stanley et al., 1992). Compulsive rituals are performed in response to obsessions to reduce anxiety, whereas hair-pulling is often performed in response to boredom or tension and initially results in feelings of pleasure and gratification (Franklin et al., 2008; Stanley et al., 1992; Woods et al., 2008). Notwithstanding these functional differences, behavioral models have been proposed to account for the development and maintenance of both disorders.

SYMPTOM DEVELOPMENT

Most behavioral models of TTM/SPD place greater emphasis on the antecedent and consequent variables that perpetuate hair-pulling or skin-picking than on the variables that originally contributed to the development of TTM/SPD (Mansueto et al., 1997, 1999; Woods et al., 2008). It has been suggested that hair-pulling/skin-picking begins as a response to stress or boredom (Azrin & Nunn, 1973) or as a grooming behavior that is eventually shaped into pulling or picking (Wetterneck & Woods, 2007). According to the behavioral model of TTM proposed by Mansueto and colleagues (1997), an association develops between the original hair-pulling cue (conditioned stimulus) and the urge to pull through classical conditioning. For example, an individual may have started hair-pulling when working on a boring task while alone in the office. Over time, an association develops between each of these aspects of hair-pulling (e.g., being alone, bored, and/or in the office) and the urge to pull (Mansueto et al., 1997; Wetterneck & Woods, 2007).

Hair-pulling becomes a conditioned response to a variety of internal or external cues (Franklin et al., 2006; Mansueto et al., 1997, 1999). Internal cues can include positive or negative affective states (e.g., boredom, fatigue, loneliness, indecision, excitement) or sensations (e.g., visual or tactile sensations, such as hair color, appearance, or texture; physical sensations, such as tingling, pressure, or irritation). These sensations can both result from previous pulling episodes and trigger subsequent episodes, thus creating a vicious cycle. External cues can include settings that trigger the urge to pull (e.g., office, bedroom, bathroom), as well as pulling implements (e.g., mirrors, tweezers). The implements may have initially been used to facilitate pulling, but through classical conditioning, the mere observation of the implements may trigger the urge to pull. Hair-pulling cues are thought to differ depending on whether pulling is focused or nonfocused (automatic). Focused pulling is cued by tension and involves a concerted effort to reduce an aversive internal state, whereas nonfocused pulling is cued by low arousal and occurs with little awareness (Woods et al., 2008).

In addition to cues that trigger the urge to pull, other factors (called discriminative stimuli) either facilitate or inhibit the act of pulling (Mansueto et al., 1997). Similar to cues, discriminative stimuli can be internal or external to the individual. Internal facilitators include certain postural stances (e.g., hand resting near scalp) and urges to pull. External facilitators include the presence of pulling implements and the absence of other people.

SYMPTOM MAINTENANCE

Behavioral models propose that TTM functions to modulate emotions and is maintained through operant conditioning (Franklin et al., 2006, 2008; Mansueto et al., 1997). Both negative and positive reinforcement are thought to perpetuate hair-pulling, and urges that are reinforced by pulling will create stronger pulling urges over time (Azrin & Nunn, 1973; Franklin et al., 2008; Mansueto et al., 1997; Wetterneck & Woods, 2007). Hair-pulling frequently produces an immediate feeling of pleasure, invigoration, or desired pain. In addition, the sensations derived from self-stimulatory behaviors (e.g., chewing, rubbing, or manipulating the hairs or hair roots) can be experienced as pleasurable, and through repetition, may create cravings for these sensations, which then serve as cues for subsequent pulling urges (Mansueto et al., 1997). The behavioral model of TTM suggests that pulling urges result from being deprived of a powerful reinforcer for a period of time in the presence of cues that have previously been associated with hair-pulling, and that some individuals have a biological predisposition that makes them more susceptible to specific tactile reinforcers (Wetterneck & Woods, 2007).

The Comprehensive Behavioral (ComB) model that was developed by Mansueto et al. (1997) suggests that there is a wide range of variability with respect to each individual's pulling/picking behavior and evaluates the contribution of each of five factors—the environment, motor response, sensation, affect, and cognition—in terms of their influence on the behavior. This allows for a better understanding of each individual's case of hair-pulling and/or skin-picking and the application of corresponding strategies based on that. Techniques like awareness training serve to decrease automatic pulling/picking by increasing awareness of the behaviors, and stimulus control serves to change the behaviors by modifying the context or environment that has become associated with the behavior, thereby reducing triggers for the behavior. Similarly, competing response training is used to replace the pulling/picking behavior with a healthier incompatible behavior, and relaxation techniques are implemented when individuals are faced with affect-based triggers for pulling/picking in an effort to alleviate stress and/or anxiety that may precipitate the behavior. According to the emotion regulation hypothesis, the distracting effect of hair-pulling can also provide relief from negative affective states (e.g., tension, anxiety, stress, boredom) and sensory discomfort (e.g., pressure or irritation at the pulling site). Contemporary behavioral models of TTM propose that focused hair-pulling represents an attempt to avoid or escape from unpleasant private experiences, a concept referred to as experiential avoidance (Woods et al., 2008). Finally, the successful removal of particular hairs (e.g., coarse gray hairs) can provide both relief and satisfaction. Hair-pulling is typically reinforced on an intermittent schedule (Mansueto et al., 1997), making it highly resistant to extinction. Hair-pulling often continues until the episode is interrupted, the goal has been achieved, or the aversive consequences (e.g., negative affective states, such as guilt and shame) outweigh the reinforcing effects. However, the negative affective states might serve as internal cues that prompt subsequent pulling episodes, creating a vicious cycle (Diefenbach et al., 2002; Franklin et al., 2008; Mansueto et al., 1997). Findings support hair-pulling and skin-picking as a maladaptive emotion regulation approach that individuals use to avoid or alleviate negative emotions (Roberts et al., 2013).

EMPIRICAL EVIDENCE

Recent research implicates the role of trauma in the development of TTM and SPD. In a clinical sample, self-reported traumatic experiences were assessed as part of a structured clinical interview and findings indicated that those individuals with TTM had more depressive symptoms, increased experiential avoidance, and greater global TTM severity (Houghton et al., 2016). While trauma history was not related to the severity of hair-pulling symptoms, depressive symptoms seem to have mediated the association between traumatic experiences and global hair-pulling severity, suggesting that hair-pulling is not necessarily directly linked to trauma, but that trauma leads to negative emotion that people manage through hair-pulling. Another study comparing patients with TTM and SPD with controls found both clinical groups reporting significantly higher numbers of traumatic and negative events in childhood compared to healthy controls, yet increased duration of TTM and SPD was associated with reduced posttraumatic stress symptoms, suggesting that the disorders help patients cope with intrusive thoughts associated with the trauma (Özten et al., 2015).

Although behavioral models of TTM focus little on symptom development, there is considerable empirical support for the purported precipitants of pulling episodes. States of hyperarousal (e.g., feeling rushed, or negative affective states, such as anger, anxiety, or frustration) and hypoarousal (e.g., boredom or fatigue, or sedentary activities, such as reading and studying) often precipitate hair-pulling episodes in individuals with TTM (Christenson et al., 1993; Mackenzie et al., 1995; O'Connor et al., 2003), and there is some preliminary evidence that experiential avoidance might mediate the relationship between antecedent private events and pulling (Begotka et al., 2004). Individuals who frequently engage in focused pulling report more stress, anxiety, and depression than individuals with TTM who rarely engage in focused pulling, suggesting that focused pulling might function to reduce the negative affective states (Flessner et al., 2008).

Individuals with focused pulling also have be found to report more intense negative emotions, and a greater number of emotions regulated by pulling (Siwiec & McBride, 2016). Positive emotions, such as happiness, relief, and calm, were found to play a significant role in reinforcing hair-pulling. In a comparison of the roles of positive and negative affect, it was found that negative emotions before and after pulling were associated with greater symptom severity (Siwiec & McBride, 2016). Supporting the role of operant conditioning in the maintenance of TTM, empirical research has demonstrated that the vast majority of individuals with TTM experience tension before, and gratification or relief after, pulling (Christenson et al., 1991), and a strong positive correlation exists between the two variables (du Toit et al., 2001). A study examining the affective correlates of

TTM found that hair-pulling decreases boredom, anxiety, and tension across the pulling episode and increases guilt, sadness, anger, and relief, suggesting that anxiety and tension may serve as both internal stimulus cues and reinforcers, whereas relief may serve as a reinforcer only (Diefenbach et al., 2002). Compared to a nonclinical sample, individuals with TTM reported larger decreases in boredom, sadness, anger, and tension, and larger increases in relief from before to during an experimental hair-pulling task (Diefenbach et al., 2008). However, they also reported larger increases in guilt, sadness, and anger, which could potentially serve as internal cues that prompt subsequent pulling episodes. The authors interpreted their study findings as supporting a tension-reduction-tension hypothesis (Diefenbach et al., 2002) or an emotion-regulation hypothesis (Diefenbach et al., 2008) of TTM, but the mechanism by which pulling improves negative affective states is unclear (Wetterneck & Woods, 2007). Individuals with TTM spend as much time manipulating the pulled hair as they do pulling it (Rapp et al., 1999), and many have oral self-stimulatory habits associated with pulling (e.g., rubbing hair along lips), suggesting that hair manipulation is positively reinforcing or may be used to self-soothe.

High experiential avoidance has been noted in those with TTM (Wetterneck et al., 2016) and has been found to mediate the relationship between fear of negative evaluation, feelings of shame, and dysfunctional beliefs about appearance and hair-pulling severity (Norberg et al., 2007). Further, a recent exploratory factor analysis identified five areas of avoidance in hair-pullers, including "avoidance of nonsocial goals," "self-concealment," "behavioral social avoidance," "avoidance of relationship problem solving," and "avoidance of thinking about the future" (Slikboer et al., 2018).

In addition, a recent experimental study by Dieringer and colleagues (2019) investigated the role of premonitory urges in skin-picking behavior. Participants were instructed to either pick freely or to suppress their skin-picking behavior. Individuals with skin-picking reported physical urge sensations, "just right" feelings, and urge-only sensations. Results showed a strong temporal relationship between the intensity of premonitory urges and the development of skin-picking behavior that was lessened when skin-picking was suppressed. They suggest that skin-picking behavior is maintained by premonitory urges and that the cycle of negative reinforcement can be broken by suppressing skin-picking behavior. The emotion-regulation model suggests that hair-pulling and skin-picking are instigated by negative emotions and negatively reinforced by the relief from the negative affective states (Roberts et al., 2013). As noted previously, individuals with TTM have been found to use pulling to regulate negative affective states like boredom, fatigue, anxiety, and stress (Diefenbach et al., 2002, 2008; Duke et al., 2010), and individuals with TTM have more difficulty regulating emotions than do controls (Shusterman et al., 2009).

Both hair-pulling and skin-picking, therefore, may work to modulate affective states in addition to providing pleasure, and these affective experiences maintain these disorders (Shusterman et al., 2009; Snorrason et al., 2010). It is therefore hypothesized that the fundamental etiological processes shared by both disorders reflect a tendency for strong affective experiences in relation to body-grooming behaviors (Snorrason et al., 2012). This may further be linked to recent evidence implicating the role of sensory sensitivity in TTM and SPD. Specifically, findings point to abnormal sensory experiences in those with hair-pulling or skin-picking (Houghton et al., 2019) that likely contribute to heightened distress.

Overall, research points to a heightened negative affectivity coupled with lowered tolerance of the negative affectivity and corresponding hair-pulling or skin-picking behaviors aimed at managing the perceived intolerance. Behavioral treatments may in fact bolster an individual's perceived ability to tolerate the negative affective states through the implementation of strategies that indirectly expose the person to the affective states and directly alter their learning by interrupting the association between context and behavior and modifying the behavior following specific triggers that have previously maintained the maladaptive behavior.

Conclusion

Behavioral models have advanced the understanding of the OCRDs over the past 50 years. The role of fear conditioning and fear extinction has been demonstrated through empirical research. As reviewed, it is now widely accepted that compulsive behaviors, avoidance, safety behaviors, and excessive reassurance-seeking temporarily reduce the distress triggered by obsessive fears but inadvertently function to sustain distress over time. Exposure-based therapies, which were developed in response to these empirical findings, aim to weaken the conditioned fear response by exposing individuals to their feared stimuli and preventing the engagement of the maintenance behaviors. As reviewed, while exposure-based treatments are the gold standard for the OCRDs, the exact mechanisms of how these treatments facilitate fear extinction require further empirical exploration.

In contrast to the strong evidence supporting the role of operant conditioning in symptom maintenance, the evidence supporting the role of classical conditioning in symptom development is more equivocal. Indeed, nearly all models of the OCRDs focus exclusively on learning principles that contribute to symptom maintenance and reduction, rather than on symptom development, and this is also reflected in the substantially greater emphasis placed on maintaining factors in exposure treatment approaches. Most behavioral models downplay the role of classical conditioning in symptom development and either attribute onset to operant conditioning (being rewarded/praised for certain behaviors early on) and/or vicarious learning (watching others model the behavior and/or being rewarded). The models that do discuss the role of classical conditioning and that implicate traumatic or stressful life events in the onset of OCRDs have primarily been supported through retrospective research, and even then, for only a subset of individuals with OCRDs. Moreover, the risk factors are not specific to OCD or the OCRDs and do not appear to be contiguous with the onset of conditions in the majority of cases.

How, then, do normal intrusions develop into clinical obsessions? The behavioral model has long been known to be unable to offer a comprehensive account of OCD (Rachman & Hodgson, 1980). This critique would appear even more evident based on our current understanding of the broad-based heterogeneity of the disorder. Given that some individuals develop psychopathology in the absence of learning factors, and many others experience negative events without developing psychopathology, it appears that diathesis-stress models are essential to understanding the onset and maintenance of OCRDs. Biological and/or cognitive factors, when combined with relevant life events, might place some individuals at greater risk of developing OCRDs. As is discussed further in the next chapter, cognitive-behavioral theories have been put forth to better understand vulnerability to developing OCRDs. For example, cognitive-behavioral models of OCD discuss the role of inflated responsibility, threat overestimation, perfectionism, intolerance of uncertainty, and the importance of, and need to control, one's thoughts (Obsessive Compulsive Cognitions Working Group, 1997, 2001, 2003, 2005). Similarly, cognitive-behavioral models of hoarding emphasize the role of beliefs about responsibility, perfectionism, and the importance of possessions (Frost & Hartl, 1996; Frost & Steketee, 1998; Steketee & Frost, 2003). Cognitive-behavioral models of BDD highlight the negative appraisal of body image (Neziroglu et al., 2008). Behavioral accounts are now incomplete without integration with these biological and cognitive factors. Moreover, cognitive models may also account for apparently behavioral phenomena, such as fear extinction, that will need to be addressed in future research on the role of inhibitory learning in the OCRDs. Another important question that emerges is whether the behavioral model can help contribute to a better understanding of the phenomenology, clinical course, and outcome of the OCRDs. As reviewed, from a behavioral perspective, individuals with these disorders engage in a variety of compulsive, safety, avoidant, and reassurance-seeking behaviors to prevent obsessive fears and reduce the associated anxiety, albeit temporarily. In contrast, hair-pulling frequently occurs outside of awareness and may be performed to reduce sensory or physical discomfort or to achieve a sense of pleasure or gratification. Further, hair-pulling disorder does not appear to be associated with prominent reassurance-seeking or avoidance behaviors. Based on similarities in the operant conditioning processes implicated in the maintenance of the disorders, OCD, hoarding, and BDD appear to overlap to the greatest extent.

There also remains a need to examine a greater breadth of behavioral-based constructs, including the role of NJREs that frequently prompt rituals and repetitive behaviors in the OCRDs and the role of distress tolerance in symptom onset, maintenance, and treatment response in the OCRDs. Finally, future programmatic research is required that aims to integrate contemporary behavioral accounts of OCRDs with the findings emerging from clinical neurosciences, including the vast literature on genetic vulnerability to the onset of the OCRDs, neurocognitive research focusing on the amygdala and prefrontal cortex in fear conditioning and fear extinction, and role of cognitive appraisals and beliefs that contribute to the shaping of meaning of OCRD triggers and responses.

References

Abramowitz, J. S., Franklin, M. E., Schwartz, S. A., & Furr, J. M. (2003). Symptom presentation and outcome of cognitive-behavioral therapy for obsessive-compulsive disorder. *Journal of Consulting and Clinical Psychology, 71*, 1049–1057.

Abramowitz, J. S., & Jacoby, R. J. (2015). Obsessive-compulsive and related disorders: A critical review of the diagnostic class. *Annual Review of Clinical Psychology, 11*(1), 165–186.

American Psychiatric Association (APA). (2013). *Diagnostic and statistical manual of mental disorders* (4th ed., text revision).

Angelakis, I., & Austin, J. L. (2018). The effects of the non-contingent presentation of safety signals on the elimination of safety behaviors: An experimental comparison between individuals with low and high obsessive-compulsive profiles. *Journal of Behavior Therapy and Experimental Psychiatry, 59*, 100–106.

Ayers, C. R., Castriotta, N., Dozier, M. E., Espejo, E. P., & Porter, B. (2014). Behavioral and experiential avoidance in patients with hoarding disorder. *Journal of Behavior Therapy and Experimental Psychiatry, 45*(3), 408–414.

Azrin, N. H., & Nunn, R. G. (1973). Habit-reversal: A method of eliminating nervous habits and tics. *Behaviour Research and Therapy, 11*, 619–628.

Bandura, A. (1977). *Social learning theory*. Prentice-Hall.

Barzilay, R., Patrick, A., Calkins, M. E., Moore, T. M., Gur, R. C., & Gur, R. E. (2019). Association between early-life trauma and obsessive-compulsive symptoms in community youth. *Depression and Anxiety, 36*(7), 586–595.

Begotka, A. M., Woods, D. W., & Wetterneck, C. T. (2004). The relationship between experiential avoidance and the severity of trichotillomania in a non-referred sample. *Journal of Behavior Therapy and Experimental Psychiatry, 35*, 17–24.

Blakey, S. M., & Abramowitz, J. S. (2019). Dropping safety aids and maximizing retrieval cues: Two keys to optimizing inhibitory learning during exposure therapy. *Cognitive and Behavioral Practice, 26*(1), 166–175.

Bouton, M.E. (1993). Context, time and memory retrieval in the interference paradigms of Pavlovian learning. *Psychological Bulletin, 114*, 90–99.

Brandes, M., Soares, C. N., & Cohen, L. S. (2004). Postpartum onset obsessive-compulsive disorder: Diagnosis and management. *Archives of Women's Mental Health, 7*(2), 99–110.

Buhlmann, U., Cook, L. M., Fama, J. M., & Wilhelm, S. (2007). Perceived teasing experiences in body dysmorphic disorder. *Body Image, 4*, 381–385.

Burgess, A. M., Graves, L. M., & Frost, R. O. (2018). My possessions need me: Anthropomorphism and hoarding. *Scandinavian Journal of Psychology, 59*(3), 340–348.

Castriotta, N., Dozier, M. E., Taylor, C. T., Mayes, T., & Ayers, C. R. (2019). Intolerance of uncertainty in hoarding disorder. *Journal of Obsessive-Compulsive and Related Disorders, 21*, 97–101.

Christenson, G. A., MacKenzie, T. B., & Mitchell, J. E. (1991). Characteristics of 60 adult chronic hair pullers. *American Journal of Psychiatry, 148*, 365–370.

Christenson, G. A., Ristvedt, S. L., & MacKenzie, T. B. (1993). Identification of trichotillomania cue profiles. *Behaviour Research and Therapy, 31*, 315–320.

Coles, M. E., Frost, R. O., Heimberg, R. G., & Rheaume, J. (2003). "Not just right experiences": Perfectionism, obsessive-compulsive features and general psychopathology. *Behaviour Research and Therapy, 41*, 681–700.

Coles, M. E., & Ravid, A. (2016). Clinical presentation of not-just right experiences (NJREs) in individuals with OCD: Characteristics and response to treatment. *Behaviour Research and Therapy, 87*, 182–187.

Cougle, J. R., Timpano, K. R., Fitch, K. E., & Hawkins, K. A. (2011). Distress tolerance and obsessions: An integrative analysis. *Depression and Anxiety, 28*(10), 906–914.

Cougle, J. R., Timpano, K. R., & Goetz, A. R. (2012). Exploring the unique and interactive roles of distress tolerance and negative urgency in obsessions. *Personality and Individual Differences, 52*(4), 515–520.

Craske, M. G., Kircanski, K., Zelikowsky, M., Mystkowski, J., Chowdhury, N., & Baker, A. (2008). Optimizing inhibitory learning during exposure therapy. *Behaviour Research and Therapy, 46*(1), 5–27.

Craske, M. G., Treanor, M., Conway, C. C., Zbozinek, T., & Vervliet, B. (2014). Maximizing exposure therapy: An inhibitory learning approach. *Behaviour Research and Therapy, 58*, 10–23.

Cromer, K. R., Schmidt, N. B., & Murphy, D. L. (2007a). An investigation of traumatic life events and obsessive-compulsive disorder. *Behaviour Research and Therapy, 45*, 1683–1691.

Cromer, K. R., Schmidt, N. B., & Murphy, D. L. (2007b). Do traumatic events influence the clinical expression of compulsive hoarding? *Behaviour Research and Therapy, 45*, 2581–2592.

Damecour, C. L., & Charron, M. (1998). Hoarding: A symptom, not a syndrome. *Journal of Clinical Psychiatry, 59*, 267–272.

Deacon, B., & Maack, D. J. (2008). The effects of safety behaviors on the fear of contamination: An experimental investigation. *Behaviour Research and Therapy, 46*, 537–547.

de Silva, P., & Marks, M. (2001). Traumatic experiences, post-traumatic stress disorder and obsessive-compulsive disorder. *International Review of Psychiatry, 13*, 172–180.

de Silva, P., Menzies, R. G., & Shafran, R. (2003). Spontaneous decay of compulsive urges: The case of covert compulsions. *Behaviour Research and Therapy, 41*, 129–137.

Didie, E. R., Tortolani, C. C., Pope, C. G., Menard, W., Fay, C., & Philips, K. A. (2006). Childhood abuse and neglect in body dysmorphic disorder. *Child Abuse and Neglect, 30*, 1105–1115.

Diefenbach, G. J., Mouton-Odum, S., & Stanley, M. A. (2002). Affective correlates of trichotillomania. *Behaviour Research and Therapy, 40*, 1305–1315.

Diefenbach, G. J., Tolin, D. F., Meunier, S., & Worhunsky, P. (2008). Emotion regulation and trichotillomania: A comparison of clinical and non-clinical hair pulling. *Journal of Behavior Therapy and Experimental Psychiatry, 39*, 32–41.

Dieringer, M., Beck, C., Verrel, J., Münchau, A., Zurowski, B., & Brandt, V. (2019). Quality and temporal properties of premonitory urges in patients with skin picking disorder. *Cortex, 121*, 125–134.

Dollard, J., & Miller, N. E. (1950). *Personality and psychotherapy: Analysis in terms of learning, thinking and culture*. McGraw-Hill.

Duke, D. C., Keeley, M. L., Ricketts, E. J., Geffken, G. R., & Storch, E. A. (2010). The phenomenology of hairpulling in college students. *Journal of Psychopathology and Behavioral Assessment, 32*(2), 281–292.

du Toit, P. L., van Kradenburg, J., Niehaus, D. J. H., & Stein, D. J. (2001). Characteristics and phenomenology of hair-pulling: An exploration of subtypes. *Comprehensive Psychiatry, 42*, 247–256.

Ecker, W., & Gonner, S. (2008). Incompleteness and harm avoidance in OCD symptom dimensions. *Behaviour Research and Therapy, 46*, 895–904.

Eddy, K. T., Dutra, L., Bradley, R., & Westen, D. (2004) A multidimensional meta-analysis of psychotherapy and pharmacotherapy for obsessive-compulsive disorder. *Clinical Psychology Review, 24*, 1011–1030.

Eisen, J. L., Phillips, K. A., Coles, M. E., & Rasmussen, S. (2004). Insight in obsessive compulsive disorder and body dysmorphic disorder. *Comprehensive Psychiatry, 45*, 10–15.

Emmelkamp, P. M. G. (1982). *Phobic and obsessive-compulsive disorders: Theory, research, and practice*. Plenum.

Fairbrother, N., Barr, R., Pauwels, J., Brant, R., & Green, J. (2015). Maternal thoughts of harm in response to infant crying: An experimental analysis. *Archives of Women's Mental Health, 18*(3), 447–455.

Fairbrother, N., & Woody, S. R. (2008). New mothers' thoughts of harm related to the newborn. *Archives of Women's Mental Health, 11*(3), 221–229.

Fallon, P., & Ackard, D. M. (2002). Sexual abuse and body image. In T. F. Cash & T. Pruzinsky (Eds.), *Body image: A handbook of theory, research, and clinical practice* (pp. 117–124). Guilford.

Flessner, C. A., Conelea, C. A., Woods, D. W., Franklin, M. E., Keuthen, N. J., & Cashin, S. E. (2008). Styles of pulling in trichotillomania: Exploring differences in symptom severity, phenomenology, and functional impact. *Behaviour Research and Therapy, 46*, 345–357.

Foa, E. B., & Kozak, M. J. (1986). Emotional processing of fear: Exposure to corrective information. *Psychological Bulletin, 99*(1), 20–35.

Forray, A., Focseneanu, M., Pittman, B., McDougle, C. J., & Epperson, C. N. (2010). Onset and exacerbation of obsessive-compulsive disorder in pregnancy and the postpartum period. *Journal of Clinical Psychiatry, 71*(8), 1061–1068.

Franklin, M. E., Tolin, D. F., & Diefenbach, D. (2006). Trichotillomania. In E. Hollander & D. J. Stein (Eds.), *Handbook of impulse control disorders* (pp. 149–173). American Psychiatric Publishing.

Franklin, M. E., Tolin, D. F., & Diefenbach, D. (2008). Trichotillomania. In J. S. Abramowitz, D. McKay, & S. Taylor (Eds.), *Obsessive-compulsive disorder: Subtypes and spectrum conditions* (pp. 139–159). Elsevier.

Freeman, J. B., & Leonard, H. L. (2000). Sexual obsessions in obsessive-compulsive disorder. *Journal of the American Academy of Child and Adolescent Psychiatry, 39,* 141–142.

Frost, R. O., & Gross, R. C. (1993). The hoarding of possessions. *Behaviour Research and Therapy, 31,* 367–381.

Frost, R. O., & Hartl, T. L. (1996). A cognitive-behavioral model of compulsive hoarding. *Behaviour Research and Therapy, 34,* 341–350.

Frost, R., & Shows, D. (1993). The nature and measurement of compulsive indecisiveness. *Behaviour Research and Therapy, 31,* 683–692.

Frost, R. O., & Steketee, G. (1998). Hoarding: Clinical aspects and treatment strategies. In M. A. Jenike, L. Baer, & W. E. Minichiello (Eds.), *Obsessive-compulsive disorder: Practical management* (3rd ed., pp. 533–554). Mosby Yearbook Medical.

Frost, R. O., Hartl, T. L., Christian, R., & Williams, N. (1995). The value of possessions in compulsive hoarding: Patterns of use and attachment. *Behaviour Research and Therapy, 33,* 897–902.

Frost, R. O., Steketee, G., & Tolin, D. F. (2011). Comorbidity in hoarding disorder. *Depression and Anxiety, 28,* 876–884.

Frost, R. O., Tolin, D. F., Steketee, G., Fitch, K. E., & Oh, M. (2011). Indecisiveness and hoarding. *International Journal of Cognitive Therapy, 4*(3), 253–262.

Gleaves, D. H., & Ambwani, S. (2008). Body dysmorphic disorder. In J. S. Abramowitz, D. McKay, & S. Taylor (Eds.), *Clinical handbook of obsessive-compulsive disorder and related problems* (pp. 288–303). Johns Hopkins University Press.

Gothelf, D., Aharonovsky, O., Horesh, N., Carty, T., & Apter, A. (2004). Life events and personality factors in children and adolescents with obsessive-compulsive disorder and other anxiety disorders. *Comprehensive Psychiatry, 45,* 192–198.

Greenberg, D. (1987). Compulsive hoarding. *American Journal of Psychotherapy, 41,* 409–416.

Greenberg, D., Witzum, E., & Levy, A. (1990). Hoarding as a psychiatric symptom. *Journal of Clinical Psychiatry, 51,* 417–421.

Grisham, J. R., & Barlow, D. H. (2005). Compulsive hoarding: Current research and theory. *Journal of Psychopathology and Behavioral Assessment, 27,* 45–52.

Grisham, J. R., Brown, T. A., Liverant, G. I., & Campbell-Sills, L. (2005). The distinctiveness of compulsive hoarding from obsessive-compulsive disorder. *Journal of Anxiety Disorders, 19,* 767–779.

Grisham, J. R., Frost, R. O., Steketee, G., Kim, H. J., & Hood, S. (2006). Age of onset of compulsive hoarding. *Journal of Anxiety Disorders, 20,* 675–686.

Grisham, J. R., Roberts, L., Cerea, S., Isemann, S., Svehla, J., & Norberg, M. M. (2018). The role of distress tolerance, anxiety sensitivity, and intolerance of uncertainty in predicting hoarding symptoms in a clinical sample. *Psychiatry Research, 267,* 94–101.

Guglielmi, V., Vulink, N. C. C., Denys, D., Wang, Y., Samuels, J. F., & Nestadt, G. (2014). Obsessive-compulsive disorder and female reproductive cycle events: Results from the OCD and Reproduction Collaborative Study. *Depression and Anxiety, 31*(12), 979–987.

Halldorsson, B., & Salkovskis, P. M. (2017). Why do people with OCD and health anxiety seek reassurance excessively? An investigation of differences and similarities in function. *Cognitive Therapy and Research, 41*(4), 619–631.

Hartl, T. L., Duffany, S. R., Allen, G. J., Steketee, G., & Frost, R. O. (2005). Relationships among compulsive hoarding, trauma, and attention-deficit/hyperactivity disorder. *Behaviour Research and Therapy, 43,* 269–276.

Hawley, L. L., Rector, N. A., & Segal, Z. V. (2020). The relative impact of cognitive and behavioral skill comprehension and skill use during CBT for obsessive compulsive disorder. *Cognitive Therapy and Research,* 1–11.

Horowitz, M. J. (1975). Intrusive and repetitive thoughts after experimental stress. *Archives of General Psychiatry, 32,* 1457–1463.

Houghton, D. C., Mathew, A. S., Twohig, M. P., Saunders, S. M., Franklin, M. E., Compton, S. N., . . . Woods, D. W. (2016). Trauma and trichotillomania: A tenuous relationship. *Journal of Obsessive-Compulsive and Related Disorders, 11,* 91–95.

Houghton, D. C., Tommerdahl, M., & Woods, D. W. (2019). Increased tactile sensitivity and deficient feed-forward inhibition in pathological hair pulling and skin picking. *Behaviour Research and Therapy, 120,* 9.

Irwin, L. D., & Jones, M. K. (2017). The relationship between obsessive-compulsive symptoms, perfectionism, and anxiety sensitivity for not just right experiences. *Behaviour Change, 34*(3), 135–155.

Jacoby, R. J., & Abramowitz, J. S. (2016). Inhibitory learning approaches to exposure therapy: A critical review and translation to obsessive-compulsive disorder. *Clinical Psychology Review, 49*, 28–40.

Jones, M. K., & Menzies, R. G. (1998). Role of perceived danger in the mediation of obsessive-compulsive washing. *Depression and Anxiety, 8*, 121–125.

Jordan, B. K., Schlenger, W. E., Hough, R., Kulka, R. A., Weiss, D., Fairbank, J. A., et al. (1991). Lifetime and current prevalence of specific psychiatric disorders among Vietnam veterans and controls. *Archives of General Psychiatry, 48*, 207–215.

Katz, D. E., Laposa, J. M., & Rector, N. A. (2020). Excessive reassurance seeking in depression versus obsessive-compulsive disorder: Cross-sectional and cognitive behavioural therapy treatment comparisons. *Journal of Anxiety Disorders, 75*, 1–8.

Knowles, K. A., & Olatunji, B. O. (2019). Enhancing inhibitory learning: The utility of variability in exposure. *Cognitive and Behavioral Practice, 26*(1), 186–200.

Kobori, O., & Salkovskis, P. M. (2013). Patterns of reassurance seeking and reassurance-related behaviours in OCD and anxiety disorders. *Behavioural and Cognitive Psychotherapy, 41*, 1–23.

Kobori, O., Sawamiya, Y., Iyo, M., & Shimizu, E. (2015). A comparison of manifestations and impact of reassurance seeking among Japanese individuals with OCD and depression. *Behavioural and Cognitive Psychotherapy, 43*, 623–634.

Krompinger, J. W., Van Kirk, N. P., Garner, L. E., Potluri, S. I., & Elias, J. A. (2019). Hope for the worst: Occasional reinforced extinction and expectancy violation in the treatment of OCD. *Cognitive and Behavioral Practice, 26*(1), 143–153.

Kwok, C., Grisham, J. R., & Norberg, M. M. (2018). Object attachment: Humanness increases sentimental and instrumental values. *Journal of Behavioral Addictions, 7*(4), 1132–1142.

Laposa, J. M., Collimore, K. C., Hawley L. L., & Rector, N. A. (2015). Distress tolerance in OCD and anxiety disorders, and its relationship with anxiety sensitivity and intolerance of uncertainty. *Journal of Anxiety Disorders, 33*, 8–14.

Laposa, J. M., Hawley, L. L., Grimm, K. J., Katz, D., & Rector, N. A. (2019). What drives OCD symptom change during CBT treatment? Temporal relationships among obsessions and compulsions. *Behaviour Therapy, 50*, 87–100.

Mackenzie, T. B., Ristvedt, S. L., Christenson, G. A., Lebow, A. S., & Mitchell, J. E. (1995). Identification of cues associated with compulsive, bulimic, & hair-pulling symptoms. *Journal of Behavior Therapy and Experimental Psychiatry, 26*, 9–16.

Mansueto, C. S. Golumb, R. G., Thomas, A. M., & Stemberger, R. M. T. (1999). A comprehensive model for behavioral treatment of trichotillomania. *Cognitive and Behavioral Practice, 6*, 23–43.

Mansueto, C. S., Stemberger, R. M. T., Thomas, A. M., & Golomb, R. G. (1997). Trichotillomania: A comprehensive behavioral model. *Clinical Psychology Review, 17*, 567–577.

Matheny, N. L., Summers, B. J., Macatee, R. J., Harvey, A. M., Okey, S. A., & Cougle, J. R. (2017). A multimethod analysis of distress tolerance in body dysmorphic disorder. *Body Image, 23*, 50–60.

Mathes, B. M., Oglesby, M. E., Short, N. A., Portero, A. K., Raines, A. M., & Schmidt, N. B. (2017). An examination of the role of intolerance of distress and uncertainty in hoarding symptoms. *Comprehensive Psychiatry, 72*, 121–129.

McGuire, J. F., & Storch, E. A. (2019). An inhibitory learning approach to cognitive-behavioral therapy for children and adolescents. *Cognitive and Behavioral Practice, 26*(1), 214–224.

McKay, D., Abramowitz, J. S., & Taylor, S. (2008). Discussion: The obsessive-compulsive spectrum. In J. S. Abramowitz, D. McKay, & S. Taylor (Eds.), *Obsessive-compulsive disorder: Subtypes and spectrum conditions* (pp. 287–300). Elsevier.

McKay, D., Gosselin, J. T., & Gupta, S. (2008). Body dysmorphic disorder. In J. S. Abramowitz, D. McKay, & S. Taylor (Eds.), *Obsessive-compulsive disorder: Subtypes and spectrum conditions* (pp. 177–193). Elsevier.

McKay, D., Todaro, J., Neziroglu, F., Campisi, T., Moritz, E. K., & Yaryura-Tobias, J. A. (1997). Body dysmorphic disorder: A preliminary evaluation of treatment and maintenance using exposure with response prevention. *Behaviour Research and Therapy, 35*, 67–70.

McKeon, J., Roa, B., & Mann, A. (1984). Life events and personality traits in obsessive-compulsive neurosis. *The British Journal of Psychiatry, 144*, 185–189.

Mineka, S., & Zinbarg, R. E. (2006). A contemporary learning theory perspective on the etiology of anxiety disorder: It's not what you thought it was. *American Psychologist, 61*, 10–26

Möllmann, A., Hunger, A., Dusend, C., van den Hout, M., & Buhlmann, U. (2019). Gazing at facial features increases dissociation and decreases attractiveness ratings in non-clinical females—A potential explanation for a common ritual in body dysmorphic disorder. *PLOS One, 14*(7), 1.

Mowrer, O. H. (1939). A stimulus-response analysis of anxiety and its role as a reinforcing agent. *Psychological Review, 46*, 553–565.

Mowrer, O. H. (1960). *Learning theory and the symbolic processes*. Wiley.

National Institute for Health and Clinical Excellence (NICE). (2007). *Obsessive-compulsive disorder: Core interventions in the treatment of obsessive-compulsive disorder and body dysmorphic disorder* (Clinical Guideline 31). https://www.ocduk.org/overcoming-ocd/nice-guidelines-for-the-treatment-of-ocd/

Norberg, M. M., Beath, A. P., Kerin, F. J., Martyn, C., Baldwin, P., & Grisham, J. R. (2020). Trait versus task-induced emotional reactivity and distress intolerance in hoarding disorder: Transdiagnostic implications. *Behavior Therapy, 51*(1), 123–134.

Norberg, M. M., Wetterneck, C. T., Woods, D. W., & Conelea, C. A. (2007). Experiential avoidance as a mediator of relationships between cognitions and hair-pulling severity. *Behavior Modification, 31*(4), 367–381.

Neziroglu, F., Borda, T., Khemlani-Patel, S., & Bonasera, B. (2018). Prevalence of bullying in a pediatric sample of body dysmorphic disorder. *Comprehensive Psychiatry, 87*, 12–16.

Neziroglu, F., Khemlani-Patel, S., & Veale, D. (2008). Social learning theory and cognitive behavioral models of body dysmorphic disorder. *Body Image, 5*, 28–38.

Neziroglu, F., Khemlani-Patel, S., & Yaryura-Tobias, J. A. (2006). Rates of abuse in body dysmorphic disorder and obsessive-compulsive disorder. *Body Image, 3*, 189–193.

Neziroglu, F., Roberts, M., & Yaryura-Tobias, J. A. (2004). A behavioral model for body dysmorphic disorder. *Psychiatric Annals, 34*, 915–920.

Norberg, M. M., Beath, A. P., Kerin, F. J., Martyn, C., Baldwin, P., & Grisham, J. R. (2020). Trait versus task-induced emotional reactivity and distress intolerance in hoarding disorder: Transdiagnostic implications. *Behavior Therapy, 51*(1), 123–134.

Norberg, M. M., Wetterneck, C. T., Woods, D. W., & Conelea, C. A. (2007). Experiential avoidance as a mediator of relationships between cognitions and hair-pulling severity. *Behavior Modification, 31*(4), 367–381.

Oakes, A., Collison, J., & Milne-Home, J. (2016). Repetitive, safe, and automatic: The experience of appearance-related behaviours in body dysmorphic disorder. *Australian Psychologist, 52*(6), 433–441.

Obsessive Compulsive Cognitions Working Group. (1997). Cognitive assessment of obsessive-compulsive disorder. *Behavior Research and Therapy, 35*, 667–681.

Obsessive Compulsive Cognitions Working Group. (2001). Development and initial validation of the Obsessive Beliefs Questionnaire and the Interpretations of Intrusions Inventory. *Behavior Research and Therapy, 39*, 987–1006.

Obsessive Compulsive Cognitions Working Group. (2003). Psychometric validation of the Obsessional Beliefs Questionnaire and the Interpretations of Intrusions Inventory. *Behavior Research and Therapy, 41*, 863–878.

Obsessive Compulsive Cognitions Working Group. (2005). Psychometric validation of the Obsessive Beliefs Questionnaire and Interpretation of Intrusions Inventory—Part 2: Factor analyses and testing of a brief version. *Behavior Research and Therapy, 43*, 1527–1542.

O'Connor, K., Brisebois, H., Brault, M., Robillard, S., & Loiselle, J. (2003). Behavioral activity associated with onset in chronic tic and habit disorder. *Behavior Research and Therapy, 41*, 241–249.

Oglesby, M. E., Medley, A. N., Norr, A. M., Capron, D. W., Korte, K. J., & Schmidt, N. B. (2013). Intolerance of uncertainty as a vulnerability factor for hoarding behaviors. *Journal of Affective Disorders, 145*(2), 227–231.

Olatunji, B., Davis, M., Powers, M., & Smits, J. (2012). Cognitive-behavioral therapy for obsessive compulsive disorder: A meta-analysis of treatment outcome and moderators. *Journal of Psychiatric Research, 47*, 33–41.

Orr, E., McCabe, R. E., McKinnon, M. C., Rector, N. A., & Ornstein, T. J. (2018). Excessive reassurance seeking and cognitive confidence in obsessive-compulsive disorder. *International Journal of Cognitive Therapy, 11*(1), 17–30.

Özten, E., Sayar, G., Eryılmaz, G., Kağan, G., Işık, S., & Karamustafalıoğlu, O. (2015). The relationship of psychological trauma with trichotillomania and skin picking. *Neuropsychiatric Disease and Treatment, 11*, 1203–1210.

Parkinson, L., & Rachman, S. (1980). Speed of recovery from an uncontrived stress. In S. Rachman (Ed.), *Unwanted intrusive cognitions*. Pergamon.

Parrish, C. L., & Radomsky, A. S. (2010). Why do people seek reassurance and check repeatedly? An investigation of factors involved in compulsive behavior in OCD and depression. *Journal of Anxiety Disorders, 24*, 211–222.

Pertusa, A., Fullana, M. A., Singh, S., Alonso, P., Menchon, J. M., & Mataix-Cols, D. (2008). Compulsive hoarding: OCD symptom, distinct clinical syndrome, or both? *American Journal of Psychiatry, 165*, 1289–1298.

Phillips, K. A. (1991). Body dysmorphic disorder: The distress of imagined ugliness. *American Journal of Psychiatry, 148*, 1138–1149.

Phillips, K. A., Stein, D. J., Rauch, S. L., Hollander, E., Fallon, B. A., Barsky, A., . . . Leckman, J. (2010). Should an obsessive-compulsive spectrum grouping of disorders be included in DSM-V? *Depression and Anxiety, 27*(6), 528–555.

Powers, M. B., Smits, J. A. J., & Telch, M. J. (2004). Disentangling the effects of safety-behavior utilization and safety-behavior availability during exposure-based treatment: A placebo-controlled trial. *Journal of Consulting and Clinical Psychology, 72*, 448–454.

Rabinowitz, D., Neziroglu, F., & Roberts, M. (2007). Clinical application of a behavioral model for the treatment of body dysmorphic disorder. *Cognitive and Behavioral Practice, 14*, 231–237.

Rachman, S. (1980). Emotional processing. *Behaviour Research and Therapy, 18*(1), 51–60. Rachman, S. (2002). A cognitive theory of compulsive checking. *Behaviour Research and Therapy, 40*, 625–639.

Rachman S. J., & Hodgson, R. J. (1980). *Obsessions and compulsions*. Prentice-Hall.

Rachman, S., Radomsky, A. S., & Shafran, R. (2008). Safety behavior: A reconsideration. *Behaviour Research and Therapy, 46*, 163–173.

Rachman, S., Shafran, R., Mitchell, D., Trant, J., & Teachman, B. (1996). How to remain neutral: An experimental analysis of neutralization. *Behaviour Research and Therapy, 34*, 889–898.

Rapp, J. T., Miltenberger, R. G., Galensky, T. L., Ellingson, S. A., & Long, E. S. (1999). A functional analysis of hair pulling. *Journal of Applied Behavior Analysis, 32*, 329–337.

Rector, N. A., Katz, D. E., Quilty, L. C., Laposa, J. M., Collimore, K., & Kay, T. (2019). Reassurance seeking in the anxiety disorders and OCD: Construct validation, clinical correlates, and CBT treatment response. *Journal of Anxiety Disorders, 67*, 1–9.

Roberts, S., O'Connor, K., & Bélanger, C. (2013). Emotion regulation and other psychological models for body-focused repetitive behaviors. *Clinical Psychology Review, 33*, 745–762.

Russell, E. J., Fawcett, J. M., & Mazmanian, D. (2013). Risk of obsessive-compulsive disorder in pregnant and postpartum women: A meta-analysis. *The Journal of Clinical Psychiatry, 74*(4), 377–385.

Salkovskis, P. M. (1991). The importance of behavior in the maintenance of anxiety and panic: A cognitive account. *Behavioral Psychotherapy, 19*, 6–19.

Salkovskis, P. M. (1996). The cognitive approach to anxiety: Threat beliefs, safety-seeking behavior, and the special case of health anxiety and obsessions. In P. M. Salkovskis (Ed.), *Frontiers of cognitive therapy* (pp. 48–74). Guilford.

Salkovskis, P. M., & Kobori, O. (2015). Reassuringly calm? Self-reported patterns of responses to reassurance seeking in obsessive compulsive disorder. *Journal of Behavior Therapy and Experimental Psychiatry, 49*, 203–208.

Salkovskis, P. M., Thorpe, S. J., Wahl, K., Wroe, A. L., & Forrester, E. (2003). Neutralizing increases discomfort associated with obsessional thoughts: An experimental study with obsessional patients. *Journal of Abnormal Psychology, 112*, 709–715.

Salkovskis, P. M., Westbrook, D., Davis, J., Jeavons, A., & Gledhill, A. (1997). Effects of neutralizing on intrusive thoughts: An experiment investigating the etiology of obsessive-compulsive disorder. *Behaviour Research and Therapy, 35*, 211–219.

Samuels, J. F., Bienvenu, O. J., Grados, M. A., Cullen, B., Riddle, M. A. Liang, K. Y., et al. (2008). Prevalence and correlates of hoarding behavior in a community-based sample. *Behaviour Research and Therapy, 46*, 836–844.

Sasson, Y., Dekel, S., Nacasch, N., Chopra, M., Zinger, Y., Amital, D., et al. (2005). Posttraumatic obsessive-compulsive disorder: A case series. *Psychiatry Research, 135*, 145–152.

Shafran, R., & Tallis, F. (1996). Obsessive-compulsive hoarding: A cognitive-behavioral approach. *Behavioural and Cognitive Psychotherapy, 24*, 209–221.

Shaw, A. M., Timpano, K. R., Steketee, G., Tolin, D. F., & Frost, R. O. (2015). Hoarding and emotional reactivity: The link between negative emotional reactions and hoarding symptomatology. *Journal of Psychiatric Research, 63*, 84–90.

Shusterman, A., Feld, L., Baer, L., & Keuthen, N. (2009). Affective regulation in trichotillomania: Evidence from a large-scale internet survey. *Behaviour Research and Therapy, 47*(8), 637–644.

Simeon, D., Hollander, E., Stein, D. J., Cohen, L., & Aronowitz, B. (1995). Body dysmorphic disorder in the DSM-IV field study of obsessive-compulsive disorder. *American Journal of Psychiatry, 152*, 1207–1209.

Siwiec, S., & McBride, D. L. (2016). Emotional regulation cycles in trichotillomania (hair-pulling disorder) across subtypes. *Journal of Obsessive-Compulsive and Related Disorders, 10*, 84–90.

Slikboer, R., Castle, D. J., Nedeljkovic, M., & Rossell, S. L. (2018). Types of avoidance in hair-pulling disorder (trichotillomania): An exploratory and confirmatory analysis. *Psychiatry Research, 261*, 154–160.

Snorrason, I., Belleau, E. L., & Woods, D. W. (2012). How related are hair pulling disorder (trichotillomania) and skin picking disorder? A review of evidence for comorbidity, similarities and shared etiology. *Clinical Psychology Review, 32*(7), 618–629.

Snorrason, Í., Smári, J., & Ólafsson, R. P. (2010). Emotion regulation in pathological skin picking: Findings from a non-treatment seeking sample. *Journal of Behavior Therapy and Experimental Psychiatry, 41*(3), 238–245.

Speisman, B. B., Storch, E. A., & Abramowitz, J. S. (2011). Postpartum obsessive-compulsive disorder. *Journal of Obstetric, Gynecologic, & Neonatal Nursing, 40*(6), 680–690.

Stanley, M., Swann, A., Bowers, T., & Davis, M. (1992). A comparison of clinical features in trichotillomania and obsessive-compulsive disorder. *Behaviour Research and Therapy, 30*, 39–44.

Starcevic, V., Berle, D., Brakoulias, V., Sammut, P., Moses, K., Milicevic, D., ... Hannan, A. (2012). Interpersonal reassurance seeking in obsessive-compulsive disorder and its relationship with checking compulsions. *Psychiatry Research, 200*(2–3), 560–567.

Steketee, G., & Frost, R. (2003). Compulsive hoarding: Current status of the research. *Clinical Psychology Review, 23*, 905–927.

Summerfeldt, L. J. (2004). Understanding and treating incompleteness in obsessive-compulsive disorder. *Journal of Clinical Psychology, 40*, 1–14.

Summerfeldt, L. J. (2007). Treating incompleteness, ordering, and arranging concerns. In M. M. Antony, C. Purdon, & L. J. Summerfeldt (Eds.), *Psychological treatment of obsessive- compulsive disorder: Fundamentals and beyond*. American Psychological Association.

Summerfeldt, L. J., Kloosterman, P. H., Antony, M. M., Richter, M. A., & Swinson, R. M. (2004). The relationship between miscellaneous symptoms and major symptom factors in obsessive-compulsive disorder. *Behaviour Research and Therapy, 42*, 1453–1467.

Summers, B. J., & Cougle, J. R. (2018). An experimental test of the role of appearance-related safety behaviors in body dysmorphic disorder, social anxiety, and body dissatisfaction. *Journal of Abnormal Psychology, 127*(8), 770–780.

Swedo, S. E. (1993). Trichotillomania. *Psychiatric Annals, 23*, 402–407.

Taylor, J. K., Moulding, R., & Nedeljkovic, M. (2018). Emotion regulation and hoarding symptoms. *Journal of Obsessive-Compulsive and Related Disorders, 18*, 86–97.

Taylor, J. K., Theiler, S., Nedeljkovic, M., & Moulding, R. (2019). A qualitative analysis of emotion and emotion regulation in hoarding disorder. *Journal of Clinical Psychology, 75*(3), 520–545.

Tibi, L., van Oppen, P., van Balkom, A. J. L. M., Eikelenboom, M., Hendriks, G., & Anholt, G. E. (2020). Childhood trauma and attachment style predict the four-year course of obsessive-compulsive disorder: Findings from the Netherlands Obsessive Compulsive Disorder study. *Journal of Affective Disorders, 264*, 206–214.

Timpano, K. R., & Shaw, A. M. (2013). Conferring humanness: The role of anthropomorphism in hoarding. *Personality and Individual Differences, 54*(3), 383–388.

Timpano, K. R., Shaw, A. M., Cougle, J. R., & Fitch, K. E. (2014). A multifaceted assessment of emotional tolerance and intensity in hoarding. *Behavior Therapy, 45*(5), 690–699.

Tolin, D. F., Meunier, S. A., Frost, R. O., & Steketee, G. (2010). Course of compulsive hoarding and its relationship to life events. *Depression and Anxiety, 27*(9), 829–838.

Uguz, F., Akman, C., Kaya, N., & Cilli, A. S. (2007). Postpartum-onset obsessive-compulsive disorder: Incidence, clinical features, and related factors. *Journal of Clinical Psychiatry, 68*(1), 132–138.

Veale, D. (2004). Advances in a cognitive behavioral model of body dysmorphic disorder. *Body Image, 1*, 113–125.

Veale, D., & Riley, S. (2001). Mirror, mirror on the wall, who is the ugliest of them all? The psychopathology of mirror gazing in body dysmorphic disorder. *Behavior Research and Therapy, 39*, 1381–1393.

Weingarden, H., Curley, E. E., Renshaw, K. D., & Wilhelm, S. (2017). Patient-identified events implicated in the development of body dysmorphic disorder. *Body Image, 21*, 19–25.

Wetterneck, C. T., & Woods, D. W. (2007). A contemporary behavior analytic model of trichotillomania. In D. W. Woods & J. W. Kanter (Eds.), *Understanding behavior disorders* (pp. 157–180). Context Press.

Wetterneck, C. T., Lee, E. B., Flessner, C. A., Leonard, R. C., & Woods, D. W. (2016). Personality characteristics and experiential avoidance in trichotillomania: Results from an age and gender matched sample. *Journal of Obsessive-Compulsive and Related Disorders, 8*, 64–69.

Wheaton, M. G., Abramowitz, J. S., Jacoby, R. J., Zwerling, J., & Rodriguez, C. I. (2016). An investigation of the role of intolerance of uncertainty in hoarding symptoms. *Journal of Affective Disorders, 193*, 208–214.

Wilver, N. L., Summers, B. J., & Cougle, J. R. (2020). Effects of safety behavior fading on appearance concerns and related symptoms. *Journal of Consulting and Clinical Psychology, 88*(1), 65–74.

Windheim, K., Veale, D., & Anson, M. (2011). Mirror gazing in body dysmorphic disorder and healthy controls: Effects of duration of gazing. *Behaviour Research and Therapy, 49*(9), 555–564.

Wolke, D., & Sapouna, M. (2008). Big men feeling small: Childhood bullying experience, muscle dysmorphia, and other mental health problems in bodybuilders. *Psychology of Sport and Exercise, 9*, 595–604.

Woods, D. W., Adcock, A. C., & Conelea, C. A. (2008). Trichotillomania. In J. S. Abramowitz, D. McKay, & S. Taylor (Eds.), *Clinical handbook of obsessive-compulsive disorder and related problems* (pp. 205–221). Johns Hopkins University Press.

Worden, B., Levy, H. C., Das, A., Katz, B. W., Stevens, M., & Tolin, D. F. (2019). Perceived emotion regulation and emotional distress tolerance in patients with hoarding disorder. *Journal of Obsessive-Compulsive and Related Disorders, 22*, 1–8.

CHAPTER 11

Cognitive Approaches to Understanding Obsessive-Compulsive and Related Disorders

Steven Taylor, Jonathan S. Abramowitz, Dean McKay, *and* Charlene Minaya

Abstract

This chapter focuses on cognitive models (also known as cognitive-behavioral models) of obsessive-compulsive disorder (OCD) and related disorders. The models posit that appraisals, dysfunctional beliefs, and maladaptive behaviors play important roles in the etiology and maintenance of obsessive-compulsive and related disorders (OCRDs). The chapter begins with an historical perspective in which the antecedents of the models are described. Contemporary cognitive models of OCD are described, and their empirical support is reviewed. This is followed by a review of cognitive models of four OCRDs: hoarding disorder, skin-picking disorder (excoriation), body dysmorphic disorder, and hair-pulling disorder (trichotillomania). Conceptual strengths and weaknesses of OCD and OCD-related cognitive models are identified, areas for improvement are identified, and potentially fruitful directions for future research are proposed.

Key Words: obsessive-compulsive disorder, obsessive-compulsive and related disorders, inflated responsibility, overestimation of threat, perfectionism, intolerance of uncertainty

Introduction

Epidemiological and factor analytic research has shown that obsessive-compulsive disorder (OCD) is symptomatically heterogeneous (do Rosario et al., 2017). The major groups of symptoms identified by factor analyses are: (a) aggressive, sexual, religious, or somatic obsessions and associated checking compulsions; (b) symmetry obsessions and ordering, counting, or repeating compulsions; (c) contamination obsessions and cleaning compulsions; and (d) hoarding-related obsessions and compulsions (Bloch et al., 2008). Hoarding-related symptoms were later reconceptualized as an obsessive-compulsive related disorder (OCRD), rather than as central features of OCD (American Psychiatric Association [APA], 2013). The present chapter evaluates the evidence for contemporary cognitive models (also known as cognitive-behavioral models) of OCD and four OCRDs: hoarding disorder, skin-picking disorder (excoriation), body dysmorphic disorder, and trichotillomania (hair-pulling disorder).

The chapter begins with a brief historical perspective on the early behavioral models of OCD and some of the problems with these models. Contemporary cognitive models of OCD, which were developed to address these problems, are then described, and their empirical support is examined. This is followed by a review of cognitive models of the four OCRDs. The chapter ends with a discussion of important future directions, including important conceptual problems that remain to be solved, ways in which the models might be improved, and potentially fruitful directions for further research.

Brief Historical Perspective

In the 1970s and early 1980s, conditioning models were the dominant psychological explanations of OCD and related phenomena. Based on Mowrer's (1960) two-factor model of fear, conditioning models of OCD (Rachman & Hodgson, 1980) proposed that obsessional fears were acquired by classical conditioning and maintained by operant conditioning. To illustrate, the obsessional fear of acquiring a serious disease from a public washroom could arise from an aversive learning experience in which the person became severely ill (the unconditioned stimulus) after visiting an unsanitary public convenience (the conditioned stimulus). This purportedly led to classically conditioned obsessional fears (e.g., fear of public washrooms). Such fears were said to be maintained by negative reinforcement—that is, by the reinforcing, distress-reducing effects of avoiding public washrooms or engaging in compulsive washing after visiting one.

In terms of treatment implications, the conditioning models were highly fruitful; they led to the development of exposure and response prevention (E/RP), which remains one of the most effective treatments for OCD. This treatment involves exposure to harmless but fear-evoking stimuli while delaying or refraining from performing the compulsive rituals (see Chapter 17). Tests of the mechanisms suggested by conditioning models, however, were not so encouraging (for a detailed review of the research, see Clark, 2004). The most important conceptual problems with the conditioning models were:

1. Many, if not most, patients with OCD do not appear to have histories of aversive conditioning experiences that might lead to obsessional fears. In such cases, the conditioning models do not appear to adequately explain the emergence, persistence, and content of obsessions. To illustrate, why would a person suffer from recurrent, repugnant intrusive images of sodomizing a neighbor's pet rabbit even though he had never had any experiences related to such an activity?
2. The models fail to account for the shifts in OCD symptoms that can occur over time (e.g., the patient who had carnal obsessions about a rabbit previously obsessed about inhaling air that had been exhaled by other people, especially by unsavory individuals). Many individuals with OCD

show such symptom shifts in the apparent absence of relevant conditioning experiences.

3. Conditioning models fail to explain why people with OCD display a broad range of insight into the reasonableness of their obsessions and compulsions, as well as why the person's level of insight can fluctuate across time and circumstance. These and other limitations led clinical researchers to consider cognitive explanations of OCD. However, conditioning models were not abandoned in their entirety; elements of these models, particularly mechanisms of operant conditioning, were incorporated into cognitive models.

Contemporary Cognitive Models of OCD

Cognitive Content Specificity Hypothesis

Since the 1980s there has been an increasing emphasis on the role of cognitive factors in OCD. Several cognitive models have been developed as general models of OCD; that is, the models are intended to account for all varieties of OCD symptoms. The models fall into two broad classes. The first are the deficit models, which propose that OCD is due to a dysfunction in cognitive processing, which may have its origins in neurobiological dysfunction. These models are discussed in Chapters 6 and 7. The focus of this chapter is on the second class of models, which propose that OCD symptoms arise from particular types of dysfunctional beliefs and appraisals. Such models are based on Beck's (1976) cognitive content specificity hypothesis concerning emotional disorders in general. The hypothesis proposes that each type of psychopathology is associated with a distinct type or pattern of dysfunctional beliefs. Major depression, for example, is said to arise from beliefs about loss, failure, and self-denigration (e.g., "I'm a defective person"). Social anxiety disorder is thought to be associated with beliefs about the likelihood or importance of rejection or ridicule by others (e.g., "People think I'm a loser because I'm no good at small talk"). With regard to OCD, particular dysfunctional beliefs have been theoretically linked to particular types of symptoms. Beliefs about inflated personal responsibility, for example, have been conceptually linked to checking symptoms (Salkovskis, 1985). Beliefs about the overimportance of one's thoughts (e.g., "Bad thoughts inevitably lead to bad deeds") have been theoretically linked to obsessions about performing dangerous or inappropriate behaviors (e.g., harming others, committing blasphemy, or engaging in personally repugnant sexual acts; Frost & Steketee, 2002).

Salkovskis's Cognitive Model

Based on the cognitive content specificity hypothesis, several models have been developed that propose that obsessions and compulsions arise from specific sorts of dysfunctional beliefs. According to these models, the content of the beliefs and appraisals influences the types of OCD symptoms that the person develops, and the strength of beliefs influences the person's insight into his or her OCD. Among the most sophisticated of these models is Salkovskis's cognitive approach (Salkovskis, 1996; Salkovskis & Millar, 2016) and the elaborations of this model (Frost & Steketee, 2002).

Salkovskis's model begins with the well-established finding that unwanted intrusions (i.e., unwanted thoughts, images, and impulses) are experienced by most people (Gibbs, 1996). These "nonclinical" obsessions, compared to obsessive symptoms in OCD, tend to be less frequent, shorter in duration, associated with less distress, and more readily removed from consciousness. However, clinical and nonclinical obsessive-compulsive symptoms have similar themes, such as violence, contamination, and doubt (Gibbs, 1996). An important task for any model is to explain why almost everyone experiences unwanted intrusions (at least at some point in their lives), yet only a minority of people experience intrusions in the form of clinical obsessions.

Salkovskis argued that intrusions—whether wanted or unwanted—reflect the person's current concerns, which arise from an "idea generator" in the brain. Intrusions are automatically triggered by internal or external reminders of those concerns. For example, intrusive thoughts of being contaminated may be triggered by seeing dirty objects (e.g., trash cans). Salkovskis proposed that intrusions develop into obsessions only when intrusions are evaluated or appraised as posing a threat for which the individual is personally responsible. To illustrate, consider the intrusive image of swerving one's car into oncoming traffic. Most people experiencing such an intrusion would regard it as a meaningless cognitive event, with no harm-related implications (i.e., "mental flotsam"). If, however, the person appraises the intrusion as having serious consequences for which he or she is personally responsible, the intrusion can develop into a clinical obsession. For example the following appraisal could lead to clinical obsessions: "Having thoughts about swerving into traffic means that I'm a dangerous person who must take extra care to ensure that I don't lose control." Such appraisals evoke distress and motivate the person to try to suppress or remove the unwanted intrusion, and to attempt to prevent any harmful events associated with the intrusion (e.g., by avoiding driving). Here, compulsions are framed as efforts to remove intrusions and to prevent any perceived harmful consequences.

Why do only some people make harm- and responsibility-related appraisals of their intrusive thoughts? Life experiences shape the basic assumptions we hold about ourselves and the world (Beck, 1976), including beliefs about personal responsibility and beliefs about the significance of unwanted thoughts (e.g., beliefs that thoughts are important and that it is essential to control one's thoughts). Such beliefs may be acquired from a strict moral or religious upbringing or from other experiences that teach the person to adhere to extreme or rigid codes of conduct and responsibility (Salkovskis et al., 1999).

With regard to compulsions, Salkovskis advanced two main reasons why compulsions become persistent and excessive. First, they are reinforced by short-term distress reduction and by temporary removal of the unwanted thought (i.e., negative reinforcement, as in the aforementioned conditioning models). Second, they prevent the person from learning that their appraisals are unrealistic (e.g., the person fails to learn that unwanted harm-related thoughts do not lead to acts of harm). Attempts at distracting oneself from unwanted intrusions may paradoxically increase the frequency of intrusions, possibly because the distracters become reminders of the intrusions. Compulsions can also strengthen one's perceived responsibility. That is, the absence of the feared consequence after performing the compulsion reinforces the belief that the person is responsible for removing the threat.

To summarize, according to Salkovskis's cognitive model, when a person appraises intrusions as posing a threat for which he or she is personally responsible, the person becomes distressed and attempts to remove the intrusions and prevent their perceived consequences. This increases the frequency of intrusions. Thus, intrusions become persistent and distressing and thereby escalate into clinical obsessions. Compulsions prevent the person from evaluating the accuracy of his or her appraisals.

Extending the Cognitive Model of OCD

Contemporary cognitive models of OCD have extended the work of Salkovskis by expanding the list of dysfunctional beliefs that purportedly contribute to OCD. Although contemporary cognitive models of OCD differ from one another in some ways, their similarities generally outweigh the differences. They differ primarily in the relative emphasis that they attach to various dysfunctional beliefs. For example, Salkovskis emphasized responsibility, whereas Rachman (1998) emphasized beliefs concerning the personal significance of intrusive thoughts (e.g., "Having this thought means that I'm morally corrupt"). According to Rachman, obsessions arise when the person misinterprets the intrusive thought as implying that he or she is bad, mad, or dangerous. This involves beliefs concerning thought–action fusion (Shafran et al., 1996)—that is, beliefs that one's unwanted thoughts will inevitably be translated into actions (e.g., "I can cause an accident simply by thinking about one"), or beliefs that thoughts are the moral equivalent of bad actions (e.g., "Thinking about harming my infant is just as bad as actually doing so").

Building on the work of Salkovskis and others, the most comprehensive contemporary cognitive model of OCD was developed by the Obsessive Compulsive Cognitions Working Group (OCCWG; 1997). The OCCWG was an international group of over 40 investigators who shared a common interest in understanding the role of cognitive factors in OCD. The group began by developing a consensus regarding the most important beliefs (and associated appraisals) in OCD (OCCWG, 1997). They then identified six belief domains, described in Table 11.1, which were said to give rise to dysfunctional appraisals of intrusions. The table contains acronyms for the six belief domains that are used throughout this chapter. Like the cognitive content specificity hypothesis, contemporary cognitive models of OCD account for OCD symptom heterogeneity by proposing that particular beliefs or patterns of beliefs give rise to specific types of OCD symptoms.

Table 11.1. Rationally Derived Domains of Dysfunctional Beliefs Associated with OCD

Belief Domain	Acronym	Description
Inflated responsibility	R	Belief that one has the special power to cause, and/or the duty to prevent, negative outcomes.
Overimportance of thoughts	I	Belief that the mere presence of a thought indicates that the thought is significant. For example, the belief that the thought has ethical or moral ramifications, or that thinking the thought increases the probability of the corresponding behavior or event.
Need to control thoughts	C	Belief that complete control over one's thoughts is possible and necessary.
Overestimation of threat	T	Belief that negative events are especially likely and would be especially awful.
Perfectionism	P	Belief that mistakes and imperfection are intolerable.
Intolerance for uncertainty	U	Belief that it is possible and necessary to be completely certain that negative outcomes will not occur.

Contemporary cognitive models of OCD have led to a promising new cognitive-behavioral therapy. The exposure exercises in this treatment differ from E/RP in that they are framed as experiments to test appraisals and beliefs. To illustrate, consider a patient who has recurrent images of terrorist hijackings, and compulsive rituals in which he repeatedly warns airport officials. His belief was that, "Thinking about terrorist hijackings will make them happen." To challenge this belief, the patient and therapist could devise a test that pits this belief against a more realistic belief, such as, "My thoughts have no impact on the occurrence of hijackings." A behavioral experiment might involve deliberately bringing on thoughts of a hijacking and evaluating the consequences (or lack thereof). Cognitive restructuring methods can also be used to challenge OCD-related beliefs and appraisals (see Chapter 20).

Cognitive Models of OCD: Empirical Status

A positive feature of the cognitive models is that they are readily falsifiable. Accordingly, they have generated a wealth of research. A list of predictions (albeit a non-exhaustive list) derived from these models is given here (see also Table 11.2), along with a discussion of each prediction's degree of empirical support.

Prediction 1

By postulating the various kinds of dysfunctional beliefs listed in Table 11.1, cognitive models of OCD assume that these beliefs are empirically distinguishable from one another. For example, if beliefs about inflated responsibility (R) play a specific role in OCD, then it should be possible to demonstrate that the effects of R are distinct from the effects of

Table 11.2. Predictions Derived from the Cognitive Models of OCD

	Prediction	Empirical Support
1.	The belief domains listed in Table 11.1 are distinct from one another, as indicated by factor analysis.	–
2.	OCD patients, as a group, score higher than clinical and nonclinical controls on measures of putatively OC-related beliefs and appraisals.	+/–
3.	Relative to controls, the majority of people with OCD have elevated scores on measures of OCD-related dysfunctional beliefs.	–
4.	In cross-sectional studies, the beliefs statistically predict, or are correlated, with OC symptoms.	+
5.	The beliefs show patterning, such that specific beliefs or combinations of beliefs predict specific types of OC symptoms. In other words, specific types of OC symptoms (e.g., checking) are characterized by clearly distinct profiles of dysfunctional beliefs.	+/–
6.	The beliefs interact with one another to statistically predict OC symptoms.	–
7.	Experimental manipulations of appraisals (e.g., manipulations that increase or decrease responsibility appraisals) lead to corresponding changes in OC symptoms.	+
8.	Efforts to suppress unwanted cognitive phenomena (e.g., intrusive thoughts or unwanted doubts) leads to an increase in the frequency of these phenomena.	+/–
9.	Naturally occurring events that increase the strength of beliefs or occurrence of appraisals (e.g., events increasing perceived responsibility such as becoming a new parent) lead to increases in OC symptoms.	+
10.	Patients with OCD report learning histories that would logically give rise to OC-related beliefs.	?
11.	Treatment-related reductions in OC symptoms are correlated with reductions in the strength of beliefs and frequency of appraisals.	+
12.	Treatments that directly target beliefs and appraisals should be more tolerable for patients with OCD (i.e., there should be fewer treatment dropouts).	+
13.	Treatments that directly target beliefs and appraisals (e.g., therapies involving cognitive restructuring) should be more effective than treatments that do not directly target these factors (e.g., exposure and response prevention).	–

Note: "Beliefs" and "appraisals" refer to OC-related beliefs and appraisals, such as those listed in Table 11.1.
Key: + = Generally supported by available evidence; +/– = Inconclusive or equivocal support; – = Mostly not supported; ? = Not yet adequately tested.

beliefs concerning the overimportance of thoughts (I), the need to control thoughts (C), the overestimation of threat (T), perfectionism (P), and intolerance of uncertainty (U).

This prediction has been tested in several factor analytic studies of the 44- and 87-item versions of the Obsessive Beliefs Questionnaire (OBQ; OCCWG, 2001, 2003, 2005) as well as related questionnaires. The research uniformly fails to support the prediction, with results suggesting that the OBQ is composed of three or four factors (Julien et al., 2008; OCCWG, 2005; Woods et al., 2004). For example, OCCWG (2005) and Julien et al. (2008) obtained three correlated factors: R and T (hereby designated RT), P and U (PU), and I and C (IC). Hierarchical factor analyses indicated that these factors load on a single higher-order factor, which accounted for 22% of the variance in OBQ scores (Taylor, McKay, & Abramowitz, 2005). The three lower-order factors each accounted for an additional 6% to 7% of variance. Woods et al. (2004) obtained a four-factor solution consisting of a general factor and three smaller factors corresponding to those described above. Although the most stable (replicable) factor structure of the OBQ remains to be identified, the results consistently show that the six types of dysfunctional beliefs listed in Table 11.1 are not distinct from one another. Thus, prediction 1 is not supported.

Prediction 2
Research provides mixed support for the prediction that patients with OCD would tend to score higher than clinical and nonclinical controls on measures of OCD-related beliefs and appraisals. Some studies found support for the prediction (Julien et al., 2008; OCCWG, 2005; Tolin et al., 2006). Other studies provided either mixed support or failed altogether to support the prediction. For example, Julien et al. (2007) found that patients with OCD and controls with anxiety disorders did not differ in OBQ scores once general distress was controlled for. Anholt et al. (2004) found no differences in scores on OCD-related beliefs between patients with OCD and those suffering from pathological gambling. Moritz and Pohl (2006) assessed appraisals concerning T, for events that were either washing-related, checking-related, negative, or neutral (e.g., "What percentage of men's toilet seats are contaminated with fecal or gangrene agents?"). People with OCD and nonclinical controls did not differ in their threat estimates. In summary, there is mixed support for the prediction that, as a group, patients with OCD score higher than do clinical and nonclinical controls on measures of OCD-related beliefs and appraisals.

Prediction 3
Given the importance that cognitive models place on OCD-related dysfunctional beliefs, it is predicted that the majority of people with OCD should have elevated scores on measures of such beliefs, compared to control groups. Using cluster analyses of scores on the OBQ, two studies have independently identified clusters of patients with OCD who do not have elevated scores on the OBQ relative to controls (Calamari et al., 2006; Taylor, Abramowitz, McKay, Calamari, et al., 2005). In these studies, over 50% of OCD patients were found to have normal scores on the OBQ; thus, prediction 3 was not supported.

Prediction 4

Several studies, using clinical or nonclinical samples, have examined the correlations between the OBQ subscales—using either the six belief domains identified in Table 11.1 or subscales derived from factor analysis—and particular types of OCD symptoms. Such research has usually involved regression analyses in which beliefs are used to statistically predict (in a cross-sectional design) particular types of symptoms. Some studies have controlled for general distress, typically measured by general anxiety or depression, in an effort to determine whether the beliefs are specific to OCD symptoms or whether they are simply correlates of general distress. There are pros and cons to this approach. On the one hand, it provides a stringent test of the specificity of the belief–symptom relationship. But on the other hand, such analyses would be inappropriate if the symptoms cause general distress. That is, if beliefs cause the OCD symptoms, which in turn cause general distress, then the statistical relationship between beliefs and symptoms will be artifactually attenuated if distress is controlled for.

Several studies have shown that beliefs assessed by the OBQ or similar measures are correlated with, or predict (in cross-sectional regression analyses), OCD symptoms (Julien et al., 2008; OCCWG, 2005; Taylor et al., 2010). Thus, prediction 4 is supported.

Prediction 5

Based on the cognitive content specificity hypothesis, cognitive models of OCD propose that particular dysfunctional beliefs are linked to particular types of symptoms. In other words, the major types of OCD symptoms (e.g., washing, checking) should be distinguished from one another by their patterns or profiles of OCD-related beliefs. For example, checking should be most strongly predicted by beliefs about inflated responsibility, whereas obsessing should be most predicted by beliefs about the overimportance of, and need to control, thoughts (Frost & Steketee, 2002).

This issue has been investigated in a number of studies (e.g., Taylor et al., 2010; Taylor & Jang, 2011; Tolin et al., 2008). Findings from structural equation modeling of the links between beliefs and symptoms (Taylor et al., 2010), which were largely replicated in a subsequent study (Taylor & Jang, 2011), found mixed evidence of patterning. PU was linked to ordering, whereas IC was linked to neutralizing, obsessing, and washing. RT was broader in its associations, being linked to all OCD-related symptoms. Other studies, using different data analytic procedures, also offered mixed and inconsistent evidence of specificity in the links between beliefs and OCD symptoms (Abramowitz et al., 2007; Mitchell et al., 2020). Those studies found that PU was related to ordering, but they did not replicate the finding that the strongest predictor of obsessing is IC. Finally, research suggests that thought–action fusion (a component of IC) is not specific to OCD but is also prevalent in other anxiety disorders, mood disorders, and eating disorders (Berle & Starcevic, 2005).

In summary, there is mixed support for prediction 5 PU has been consistently linked to ordering, although research specifically on U indicates that it is related to a range of disorders other than OCD, including generalized anxiety disorder and panic disorder (McEvoy et al., 2019). Similarly, perfectionism is not just associated with OCD symptoms; rather, perfectionism is associated with a range of disorders, including anxiety and mood disorders (Pinto et al., 2017). RT also tends to be relatively nonspecific in its links to OCD symptoms. Although the finding concerning RT is consistent with Salkovskis's cognitive model, which emphasized the role of inflated responsibility (Salkovskis & Millar, 2016), the findings fail to explain why beliefs like inflated responsibility would lead, for example, to checking in one person, and washing in another person. The most common OCD symptoms—checking and washing—have not been consistently distinguished from one another or from other OCD symptoms in terms of their profiles of dysfunctional beliefs. This is an important problem for cognitive models of OCD, because these models are based on the core assumption of cognitive content specificity.

Prediction 6

The cognitive models predict that beliefs (and possibly appraisals) should interact with one another to give rise to obsessions and compulsions. To illustrate the potential interactions, one's sense of personal responsibility could influence the perceived importance of controlling one's thoughts so that harm does not occur. Conversely, beliefs about the importance of one's thoughts could inflate responsibility beliefs (Thordarson & Shafran, 2002). Perfectionism could also interact with other beliefs and appraisals; "Perfectionism is usually defined in terms which suggest more enduring personality-type characteristics, which might be expected to interact with the appraisal of intrusions, particularly when such intrusions concern the completion (or non-completion) of particular actions" (Salkovskis et al., 2000, p. 364). Responsibility might also inflate perfectionism (Salkovskis & Forrester, 2002). To examine these conjectures, a series of regression analyses were conducted in which the main effects for each belief domain (IC, PU, RT) and their two- and three-way interactions were entered as predictors of OCD symptom scores. Main effects were significant predictors, but the interactions were not (Taylor, Abramowitz, & McKay, 2005). The findings therefore fail to support the predicted interaction effects.

Prediction 7

A small number of studies have experimentally manipulated OCD-related appraisals, particularly responsibility appraisals, in order to test the prediction that changes in appraisals lead to changes in OCD-like symptoms, such as the frequency of checking while performing an experimental task (Bouchard et al., 1999; Rachman et al., 1996). Research suggests that checking is more frequent when high responsibility is induced (e.g., by making the participant responsible for ensuring that a stove is turned off), compared to when low responsibility is induced (Arntz et al., 2007; Boschen & Vuksanovic, 2007). Thus, the limited available evidence supports prediction 7.

Prediction 8

Cognitive models propose that OCD is maintained, in part, by trying too hard to control one's unwanted thoughts, or by trying too hard to allay one's doubts. Consistent with this, experimental evidence suggests that repetitive checking actually increases doubt and uncertainty (van den Hout & Kindt, 2003a, 2003b). Research on attempts to control unwanted thoughts has yielded inconsistent results. Experimental studies of student samples suggest that deliberate attempts to suppress unwanted thoughts often (but not invariably) lead to a paradoxical increase in the frequency of these thoughts (Marcks & Woods, 2007; Wenzlaff & Wegner, 2000). There is inconsistent evidence for this occurring in OCD. Although research indicates that people with OCD are more likely to try to suppress their unwanted thoughts, there is not necessarily a paradoxical increase in the frequency of these thoughts as a result of attempts at thought suppression (Purdon, 2004). Thus, there is mixed support for prediction 8.

Prediction 9

Cognitive models suggest that OCD-related beliefs may interact with particular types of stressors to influence the onset or exacerbation of OCD symptoms. Childbirth, for example, should increase the sense of personal responsibility in both parents, and therefore should lead to an increase in OCD symptoms. Two longitudinal studies of new parents support this prediction. The studies found that childbirth-related increases in responsibility are followed by an increase in OCD-like symptoms (Abramowitz et al., 2006, 2007). Most new parents experienced unwanted, intrusive infant-related thoughts, such as thoughts of losing the baby or committing deliberate harm. Compulsive behaviors included repetitive checking on the well-being of the infant and reassurance-seeking. These OCD-like symptoms were most prevalent in parents with elevated scores on the OBQ (Abramowitz et al., 2006). Thus, prediction 9 has received encouraging support.

Prediction 10

Cognitive models emphasize the role of learning experiences that purportedly give rise to OCD-related beliefs. This suggests that it should be possible to identify such learning experiences in people with OCD. Case reports have described such learning experiences (e.g., de Silva & Marks, 2001; Salkovskis et al., 1999). Examples include growing up in an environment that encouraged the development of rigid or extreme codes of conduct, and instances in which one's thoughts were followed by serious misfortune (e.g., wishing someone dead and then learning, a short time later, that the person did indeed die from some mishap). Other studies, based on retrospective reports, provided evidence to support the view that learning experiences play a role in the formation of responsibility beliefs (Hezel & McNally, 2016). However, such studies were correlational and subjected to recall bias. Accordingly, such studies did not provide strong evidence about the role of learning experiences in the formation of OCD-related beliefs. Thus, prediction 10 has yet to be adequately tested.

Predictions 11 to 13

The last set of predictions concern the treatment implications of the cognitive models of OCD. The models underscore the importance of OCD-related beliefs in maintaining OCD symptoms, and as such predict that interventions that reduce the strength of the beliefs should lead to reductions in OCD symptoms. Reducing the strength of the beliefs should also lead patients to be more willing to engage in exposure exercises during treatment, such as exposure to "contaminants" for people with washing-related symptoms. Consistent with the cognitive models, studies have shown that treatments that reduce OCD symptoms also reduce the strength of OCD-related beliefs (Bouvard, 2002; Emmelkamp, et al., 2002; McLean et al., 2001). Thus, prediction 11 is supported.

Treatments that directly target OCD-related beliefs (i.e., those using cognitive restructuring and behavioral experiments) are associated with a lower proportion of dropouts than treatments that do not directly target the beliefs (e.g., E/RP; Abramowitz et al., 2005). Accordingly, there is support for prediction 12. However, cognitive or cognitive-behavior therapy for OCD is no more effective than is E/RP (Abramowitz et al., 2005), so prediction 13 is not supported.

Summary

Table 11.2 shows that there is mixed empirical support for contemporary cognitive models of OCD. Of the 13 predictions that were examined, five were generally supported, four were generally not supported, three had equivocal findings, and one has not been adequately tested. The degree of support for the models suggests that they may have some value in accounting for OCD. Accordingly, it may be fruitful to modify the models rather than abandon them. The models may need to be expanded to include other etiologically relevant variables.

Cognitive Models of OCRDs

Hoarding Disorder

CHARACTERISTIC FEATURES

According to *DSM-5* (American Psychiatric Association, 2013), the central features of hoarding disorder (HD) include problems with discarding items due to a perceived need to save them or distress when discarding, and interference with the use of living space due to the accumulation of clutter. Many individuals also demonstrate compulsive acquisition of items (Nicoli de Mattos et al., 2018; Vogel et al., 2019), which appears to be associated with greater hoarding severity (Turna et al., 2018). HD may be associated with severe functional impairment and cost to society.

COGNITIVE MODELS

Cognitive models of HD emphasize exaggerated beliefs related to overattachment to material possessions and exaggerated consequences of not having these possessions (Steketee et al., 2003). Collectively called saving cognitions, these beliefs include unrealistic ideas about the value of saved items (e.g., "I'll probably need that empty soup can in the future"), intense sentimental or aesthetic attachment (e.g., "It represents my grandfather"), fears of being without the item (e.g., "I might need this in the future for something important"), anthropomorphizing (e.g., "This item will be hurt if I throw it away"), and excessive guilt about discarding (e.g., "I would be a bad parent if I discarded my child's old art projects from school"; Frost, et al., 2015).

Individuals with HD most frequently save objects for either anticipated practical use or an aversion to waste (e.g., "This can be used in the future"), or excessive sentimental attachment (e.g., souvenirs, photos, children's art projects; Frost et al., 2015). Frequently, the reason for keeping the object is fear of a negative emotional experience, such as guilt or anxiety in parting with the object, rather than the object's eliciting a positive emotion when it is retained. Whereas individuals with HD may report that they are willing to part with their hoarded possessions, the process of making decisions about what to discard becomes time-consuming and overwhelming. For items that reflect personal attachment and are unlikely to hold practical value to others (i.e., sentimental items, such as photos, inherited mementos), beliefs about memory and excessive guilt in discarding the item are often cited as a primary reason for saving (e.g., "I feel that discarding this item is like throwing away the memory of my mother," or "I will forget my son's graduation day unless I save this reminder").

Some neuropsychological research indicates that individuals with HD have specific executive functioning deficits (Woody et al., 2014). However, patients with HD tend to overestimate any cognitive deficits they might have. Few studies have directly compared perceived cognitive ability with actual cognitive ability, but in general, individuals with HD tend to self-report difficulty with memory and attention (Tolin et al., 2018), while existing neuropsychological test batteries do not consistently report deficits in these areas (Moshier et al., 2016; Woody et al., 2014). In addition, one study used a behavioral paradigm of a computerized task examining reaction time and error detection (a stop-change task) and found that individuals with HD were less accurate in their estimation of their own error rates, despite making similar amounts of errors as healthy controls (Zakrzewski et al., 2018). Negative self-perception about cognitive ability is likely to contribute to HD symptoms as well, because individuals with HD often report engaging in hoarding behaviors to compensate for the perceived lack of confidence in their memory (e.g., "I have to save this information so I don't forget it," or "I have to leave things lying out or I will forget them"; Hartl et al., 2004).

EMPIRICAL SUPPORT

A growing body of literature supports the prediction that hoarding behavior is correlated with beliefs about the value of possessions and with beliefs concerning one's responsibility for taking care of them (Frost et al., 2015). There is also evidence that hoarding is associated with difficulties performing tasks in which the person is required to categorize items, such as organizing items into categories like "keep this item", "keep it for now, but possibly discard later," and "discard this item." To illustrate, in one study, individuals with hoarding (compared to nonclinical controls) found it more stressful to organize items and organized the items into more categories, thereby leading to greater disorganization (Luchian et al., 2007). These results are even more pronounced when individuals with hoarding are asked to categorize personally relevant items (Wincze et al., 2007).

Whereas there is strong support for the cognitive model of hoarding, OCD and HD appear to share maladaptive belief patterns, including an excessive sense of responsibility for prevention of feared outcomes. In OCD, the inflated responsibility is generally characterized by a need to protect others, while in HD it is a pronounced aversion to wastefulness. Some authors have noted overlaps between the aversion to waste and a strong sense of guilt, similar to scrupulosity beliefs in OCD. However, the moral prescription in HD appears largely limited to the disposition of material items, and therefore has been termed "material scrupulosity" by Frost et al. (2018).

Another overlapping belief domain in HD and OCD is the tendency to overestimate the likelihood and severity of feared consequences. Individuals with HD and OCD often perceive feared outcomes (e.g., illness from contamination in OCD, not having needed information in HD) as highly likely, although the outcomes are objectively unlikely. Both groups also report an intolerance of uncertainty. That is, individuals with HD often recognize that they do not need their saved items, are unlikely to use them in the future, and that most people would not need to keep the items. However, they still feel they must keep such things just in case of an unlikely outcome. This is similar to individuals with OCD, who often recognize their feared outcomes as unlikely, but have difficulty with even the slightest possibility of the feared negative outcome. However, in both HD and OCD, insight varies within and between individuals.

Body Dysmorphic Disorder
CHARACTERISTIC FEATURES

Body dysmorphic disorder (BDD) is characterized by imagined or exaggerated concerns about one's physical defects (e.g., obsessions about facial asymmetry). Ethnocultural differences in phenomenology or prevalence of BDD are largely unknown, although there is limited support around lower rates in non-Western cultures (Liao et al., 2010) and with differing standards of appearance (Marques et al., 2011). Appearance-related preoccupations in BDD are similar to obsessions in OCD because both trigger anxiety or distress. Similarly, avoidance and excessive behaviors to conceal, correct, check, or seek reassurance about the imagined defects among people with BDD serve the same purpose as compulsive rituals in OCD—namely, to reduce distress. For instance, some individuals with BDD check their appearance for prolonged periods of time, looking in mirrors, windows, and so forth. Others focus their energies on avoiding all reflective surfaces. Additional compulsive behaviors include comparing oneself to others, defect-related skin-picking, reading all relevant information on the body part(s) of concern, measuring the "flawed" body part(s), and seeking cures (e.g., cosmetic procedures) for perceived defects (Fang & Wilhelm, 2015). These similarities have prompted *DSM-5* reclassification of BDD from a somatoform disorder to the OCRDs.

COGNITIVE MODEL

Veale's (2004) model remains the best articulated cognitive model of BDD and continues to inform BDD treatment (Neziroglu & Lippman, 2015). The model begins with the proposition that episodes of heightened concern with body image in BDD are often precipitated by "external representations" of the individual's appearance (e.g., seeing one's reflection), which trigger a defective mental image. Through selective attention toward appearance-related details, the individual experiences heightened awareness of specific characteristics within the image, and thereby assumes that the perceived defect is clearly apparent to other people. This imagery is associated with heightened self-focused attention, to the extent that in more severe cases of BDD, all of the individual's attention may be focused on the distorted image and on the negative evaluation of the image.

According to Veale's model, the afflicted person also negatively appraises his or her appearance in the context of dysfunctional beliefs about the importance of physical appearance. The individual may hold beliefs like, "If I'm unattractive, life isn't worth living." Beliefs regarding inadequacy, worthlessness, abnormality, and rejection are implicated in Veale's model. The individual also compares his or her "defective" features with the ideal, which leads to self-loathing, fear of embarrassment and rejection, depression, and anger at oneself. These emotional responses lead to defensive behaviors, such as avoidance or active escape and concealment of the imagined defect, to prevent the feared outcomes and to reduce distress. Although these defensive behaviors may temporarily alleviate distress, in the long run, they maintain the self-conscious preoccupation with the imagined defect and negative appraisal of oneself.

EMPIRICAL SUPPORT

A number of research findings support Veale's model (for a review, see Fang & Wilhelm, 2015). For example, studies show that people with BDD deploy selective attention toward minute details and features, which might explain the focus on specific appearance-related details while ignoring more global features (Feusner et al., 2007). In a relatively recent study by Grocholewski and colleagues (2012), individuals with BDD demonstrated greater selective attention to imagined defects in their faces and corresponding areas on unfamiliar faces than did healthy controls or individuals with social phobia. These findings are consistent with the attentional biases and image-related preoccupations proposed in Veale's model.

Trichotillomania (Hair-Pulling Disorder)
CHARACTERISTIC FEATURES

DSM-5 classifies trichotillomania (TTM) as an OCRD. TTM involves recurrent hair-pulling resulting in hair loss and repeated attempts to reduce or cease pulling. Hair-pulling in TTM may be automatic (outside of conscious awareness) or focused (in response to an urge, impulse, or negative affectivity). TTM appears to share some characteristics with OCD, namely, repetitive compulsive behaviors and associated rituals (Duke et al., 2010). There are, however, some important functional differences between the disorders. First, the intrusive anxiety-evoking obsessional thoughts that occur in OCD are typically not present in TTM. Second, the compulsive rituals demonstrated by people with OCD are performed in response to obsessions, and often result in decreased anxiety, whereas hair-pulling in TTM is precipitated by feelings of general tension, depression, anger, boredom, frustration, indecision, or fatigue (Christenson et al., 1993; Stanley & Mouton, 1996). Finally, hair-pulling in TTM, unlike compulsive rituals in OCD, is often associated with pleasurable feelings (Diefenbach et al., 2008). Limited research on TTM in ethnic or racial minorities has yielded mixed findings about phenomenological differences from TTM in Caucasians, suggesting that few differences may exist, but further research is required (Houghton & Woods, 2017).

COGNITIVE MODEL

Most psychological models emphasize the role of learning in TTM. For instance, Azrin and Nun (1973) argued that urges to pull hair become conditioned responses to one or more situations (e.g., being alone), internal sensations (e.g., tension), or activities (e.g., reading). Pulling is followed by feelings of sensory stimulation or gratification that serve as an escape from negative feeling states, thereby reinforcing (both positively and negatively) the pulling behavior (Woods et al., 2008).

The role of cognition has been incorporated into models of TTM relatively recently. Franklin and Tolin (2007) argued that dysfunctional beliefs can increase negative emotion in people with TTM, thereby increasing urges to pull. These beliefs include perfectionistic beliefs, beliefs about the persistence and controllability of urges to pull (e.g., "The urge will last forever unless I pull"), beliefs about the hair-pulling habit itself ("This is an appalling behavior"), and beliefs about negative evaluation from others ("Other people will notice my hair loss and won't want to associate with me"). Episodes of hair-pulling may also be exacerbated by beliefs about the positive effects of hair-pulling (e.g., "Hair-pulling will make me feel better") and facilitative thoughts (e.g., "I'll just pull one more"; Gluhoski, 1995).

EMPIRICAL SUPPORT

Few studies have investigated the role of cognition in TTM. Norberg and colleagues (2007) assessed, in a self-described sample of people with hair-pulling problems, beliefs pertaining to appearance and shame or social rejection in regard to hair-pulling. These beliefs were correlated with the severity of the person's hair-pulling. Similarly, Rehm and colleagues (2019) found that negative self-beliefs, perfectionism, and low coping efficacy were significantly related to hair-pulling severity in a study of individuals with self-reported TTM symptoms. Although these findings are consistent with the cognitive model of TTM, directionality remains unclear (whether they are a cause or consequence of hair-pulling). Further research is needed to test and refine cognitive models of TTM.

Skin-Picking Disorder
CHARACTERISTIC FEATURES

Skin-picking disorder (SPD; also called excoriation), like TTM, is another body-focused OCRD. According to the *DSM-5* classification, central features of the disorder include recurrent picking of one's skin, leading to skin lesions, and repeated attempts to reduce or cease the behavior. Limited support exists for similarities of SPD across cultures (Grant et al., 2012). SPD frequently co-occurs with TTM, and the two disorders share some characteristics, such as automatic and focused styles and a similar range of negative emotional states as triggers (Snorrason et al., 2017). Like OCD, SPD involves repetitive, compulsive behaviors, albeit specifically related to skin-picking, which are often done in a ritualistic manner (Phillips & Stein, 2015). However, functional differences may exist between OCD and SPD. Furthermore, obsessions are not included as a central feature of SPD, although picking-related preoccupations may be common, but further research is required.

COGNITIVE MODEL AND EMPIRICAL SUPPORT

SPD models typically focus on reinforcement and emotion regulation (Lang et al., 2010). As in TTM, in SPD there may be emotional or sensory antecedents gratified by skin-picking, which is then reinforced. The role of cognition in SPD remains largely uninvestigated, except as part of clinical treatment studies exploring the use of cognitive, cognitive-behavioral, or other therapies for SPD (Snorrason et al., 2017). Commonly encountered dysfunctional cognitions in SPD may include those related to low self-efficacy and impaired control (Schuck et al., 2011). Given that dysfunctional thoughts may trigger or exacerbate OCD symptoms, identification of maladaptive cognitions in SPD requires additional exploration.

Future Directions for Cognitive Models of OCRDs

There are several important challenges and research issues for contemporary cognitive models of OCRDs. The failures to find empirical support for several of the predictions derived from contemporary cognitive models of OCD (Table 11.2) suggest that the six domains of OCD-related beliefs (as described in Table 11.1) are insufficient for explaining OCD. This situation has arisen despite the fact that the belief domains were identified on the basis of research reviews and the clinical experience of over 40 OCD experts (OCCWG, 1997). It may be necessary to identify and include other types of dysfunctional beliefs in cognitive models of OCD in order to improve the predictive power of the models (e.g., beliefs about the acquisition of possessions, as discussed earlier). OCD models also may need to be expanded to account for other important features. The phenomena of "not just right" experiences and the emotion of disgust are two features that have received renewed attention in recent years.

Not Just Right Experiences

Not just right experiences (NJREs) entail problems terminating activities due to a feeling that the activities have not been properly completed or executed satisfactorily. Satisfactory completion can involve arranging objects, walking a precise number of steps, or washing a particular number of times until a "just right" experience is attained. Here, the motivation for performing compulsions appears to be the attainment of tension reduction rather than averting some feared outcome (Summerfeldt et al., 2014). For example, a person might engage in compulsive handwashing until he or she no longer feels distressed, rather than washing with the aim of removing contaminants. NJREs are correlated with all of the major types of OCD symptoms (Taylor et al., 2013). Contemporary cognitive models have little to say about the causes of NJREs. Perfectionism has been implicated (Moretz & McKay, 2009) and demonstrates strong associations (Boisseau et al., 2018), although the role that perfectionism plays in NJREs is poorly understood. Perfectionism is multidimensional (Flett & Hewitt, 2002) and it is possible that some aspects of perfectionism are more important than others in NJREs. For example, self-directed perfectionism (high personal standards and need for perfection) may have stronger ties to incompleteness than harm avoidance (Pietrefesa & Coles, 2008), compared to socially prescribed perfectionism (high standards or need for perfection imposed by others). Additional investigations are needed into the role of NJREs and their relevant components in cognitive models of OCD.

Disgust

Over the past 20 years, there has been a growing emphasis on the importance of disgust in various forms of psychopathology, particularly anxiety disorders (Olatunji & McKay, 2007). In OCD, disgust has been particularly useful in describing contamination fears (McKay & Moretz, 2009). Disgust is a learned, culturally specific emotional state designed to prevent the ingestion of toxins. A cognitive component of disgust that is relevant to contamination fear concerns "sympathetic magic" (Rozin & Fallon, 1987). This entails a mechanism whereby otherwise neutral stimuli accrue properties associated with disgust. To illustrate, a pen that comes in momentary contact with feces would become an object of disgust, even if it was cleaned after contact with the contaminant. Sympathetic magic confers the component of disgust when, once a stimulus comes in contact with a disgust-evoking object, it takes on the disgusting properties (called the law of contagion). Another feature of sympathetic magic involves the degree that an object resembles stimuli associated with disgust (called the law of similarity). For example, reshaping a candy bar to resemble feces would be associated with disgust by virtue of the similar appearance, even without any direct contact with a disgust-evoking stimulus.

Several studies have examined the role of disgust in contamination fear. For instance, a study using structural equation modeling showed that contamination fears were associated with disgust, and that this relationship fit the data best when trait anxiety was eliminated from the model as a moderator (Moretz & McKay, 2009). That is, contamination fears appeared to be directly influenced by disgust, independent of trait anxiety, and other studies have also revealed associations between disgust and contamination independent of negative affectivity or depression (Olatunji, 2010). Tolin et al. (2003) conducted an experiment with individuals diagnosed with OCD, compared to anxious and non-anxious control participants, to examine the degree of sympathetic magic transfer of contaminants. Participants were asked to identify a "contaminated" object, which was then touched with a pencil. Participants then rated the extent that the pencil became contaminated. Following this, a clean pencil was brought into contact with the "contaminated" pencil, and participants again rated the contamination level of the second pencil. This was repeated for a total of 12 pencils. Individuals with OCD, compared to controls, made higher ratings of the degree of contamination of all the pencils.

Such studies suggest that a deeper understanding of the causes of OCD may be attained by investigating how the cognitive mechanisms associated with sympathetic magic distinguish individuals with OCD from controls. Contemporary cognitive models of OCD have placed little if any emphasis on disgust. Such models may provide a more comprehensive account of OCD-related phenomena if the models encompass disgust-related cognitive mechanisms.

Testing and Integrating Cognitive Models of OCRDs
Cognitive models of OCRDs have not been tested as extensively as models of OCD. Given that the cognitive models of the related disorders have been derived from, or are conceptually similar to, the cognitive models of OCD, it is possible that models of OCRDs will encounter problems similar to those of OCD models. The models of OCRDs also need to be better integrated with one another, in order to better explain why a person develops one disorder (e.g., OCD) instead of another (e.g., BDD), why OCD and OCRDs

commonly co-occur at the same time (i.e., current comorbidity, such as the concurrent onset of OCD and TTM), and why a person with one of these disorders is at heightened risk for developing, at some time in the future, a related disorder (i.e., lifetime comorbidity; such as OCD in childhood followed by TTM in adulthood; American Psychiatric Association, 2013).

Developmental and Cultural Considerations
Developmental aspects of the cognitive models also require further investigation and elaboration, particularly considering age-related changes in cognitive functioning. There is preliminary evidence that the beliefs listed in Table 11.1 can be identified in children as young as 6 years old, in adolescents, and in the elderly, and that these beliefs are correlated with OCD symptoms in these age groups (Farrell & Barrett, 2006; Teachman, 2007). However, the cognitive models need to be modified to account for developmental differences across the life span (see Chapters 25 and 26 for additional discussion). Beliefs about one's thoughts, for example, play less of a role in OCD in young children, particularly in children who have not yet fully developed the capacity to appraise their own thinking (i.e., the child requires a "formal operations" level of cognitive development; Farrell & Barrett, 2006). There is also evidence that responsibility beliefs are less important in childhood OCD than they are in OCD in adolescence and adulthood (Farrell & Barrett, 2006). However, exploring cognitive biases or maladaptive cognitions in very young children can be challenging, because young children may have difficulty communicating their thoughts depending on their developmental stage (linguistic roadblocks, lack of metacognitive awareness, etc.; Garnaat et al., 2019). In the elderly, the models may need to be revised to give greater emphasis to beliefs that are more specific to the elderly, such as beliefs relating to cognitive decline (e.g., "I need to keep checking things because my memory isn't what it used to be"; Teachman, 2007).

Underrepresentation of diverse cultural groups, particularly ethnic or racial minorities, is a significant issue in OCD research (Williams et al., 2010) and psychological research more broadly (see Chapter 27 for additional discussion). This lack of representation can be problematic because research outcomes tend to impact future investigations, funding, diagnosis, treatment, and educational, health-related, or other social policies. Given that cultural beliefs and values influence cognitive development, this exclusion may obscure important information about ethnocultural differences in OCD-related beliefs. Contemporary cognitive models have little to say about cross-cultural differences in OCD-related beliefs. Some support exists for cultural differences in OCD-related beliefs and symptoms; Wheaton and colleagues (2013) found that group membership moderated the relationship between OCD-related beliefs and OCD symptoms (e.g., contamination, unacceptable thoughts). Nonetheless, there is preliminary evidence that the cognitive models can be applied to people from different cultures (Sica et al. 2006;

Yorulmaz et al. 2008), although more research is needed to account for cultural factors in the development of beliefs associated with OCD symptoms.

Information Processing and Neuroscience

The cognitive models draw, to some degree, on information-processing models (Chapter 7) but could be more tightly integrated with those models and findings. For example, information-processing research suggests that implicit (nonconscious) factors play a role in OCD (Chapter 7), and yet the contemporary cognitive models focus almost entirely on conscious factors. A more comprehensive approach would encompass both types of factors in models of OCRDs.

The cognitive models of OCRDs need to be better integrated with research implicating the roles of genetic and neurobiological factors (see Chapters 5 and 6). This may be important not only for understanding mind–brain relationships, but also for identifying possible boundary constraints on cognitive models. That is, the models may be able to account for only a subset of cases. As noted earlier, many patients with OCD have essentially normal scores on measures of dysfunctional beliefs, thereby suggesting that such beliefs do not play an etiologic role in all forms of OCD. Some models of OCD do not regard dysfunctional beliefs as playing an important role (see Chapters 5 and 6). Contemporary cognitive models of OCD may be applicable for explaining OCD symptoms that arise in the context of particular learning experiences or life stressors but may be unable to account for OCD symptoms that arise as a consequence of biological assaults, such as traumatic brain injury or streptococcal infection (see Chapter 6).

Summary and Conclusions

Contemporary models of OCD have many of the properties that a good model ought to possess: the models are falsifiable, make clear predictions, are parsimonious, and have treatment relevance. Moreover, the models have led to a rich program of research. Although there is some empirical support for the models, there are many ways in which the models can be improved. The models are "works in progress" and will no doubt be refined in the coming years. Cognitive models of OCRDs, such as hoarding disorder, are also promising, but more work needs to be done, especially in the area of integrating the models of OCD with models of OCRDs.

Perhaps a more important concern is that the cognitive models have been developed in a way that has largely ignored the mounting body of research on the importance of neurobiological factors. A more complete understanding of OCRDs is likely to arise if theorists and researchers are willing to tackle the challenging task of integrating mind and brain—that is, finding a rapprochement between cognitive models and neuroscience. Such efforts may eventually lead to a comprehensive model of OCRDs.

Another potentially important avenue of research is to extend the conceptual and empirical work on OCD subtypes. It is possible that different theoretical models apply to different subtypes of OCD. Models emphasizing the role of dysfunctional beliefs and appraisals might apply only to a subgroup of cases of OCD or to particular symptom presentations. Further research is needed to explore this intriguing possibility.

References

Abramowitz, J. S., Khandker, M., Nelson, C. A., Deacon, B. J., & Rygwall, R. (2006). The role of cognitive factors in the pathogenesis of obsessive-compulsive symptoms: A prospective study. *Behaviour Research and Therapy, 44,* 1361–1374.

Abramowitz. J. S., Nelson, C. A., Rygwall, R., & Khandker, M. (2007). The cognitive mediation of obsessive-compulsive symptoms: A longitudinal study. *Journal of Anxiety Disorders, 21,* 91–104.

Abramowitz, J. S., Taylor, S., & McKay, D. (2005). Potentials and limitations of cognitive therapy for obsessive-compulsive disorder. *Cognitive Behaviour Therapy, 34,* 140–147.

American Psychiatric Association (APA). (2013). *Diagnostic and statistical manual of mental disorders* (5th ed.).

Anholt, G. E., Emmelkamp, P. M. G., Cath, D. C., van Oppen, P., Nelissen, H., & Smit, J. H. (2004). Do patients with OCD and pathological gambling have similar dysfunctional cognitions? *Behaviour Research and Therapy, 42,* 529–537.

Arntz, A., Voncken, M., & Goosen, A. C .A. (2007). Responsibility and obsessive-compulsive disorder: An experimental test. *Behaviour Research and Therapy, 45,* 425–435.

Azrin, N. H., & Nunn, R. G. (1973). Habit reversal: A method of eliminating nervous habits and tics. *Behaviour Research and Therapy, 11,* 619–628.

Beck, A. T. (1976). *Cognitive therapy and the emotional disorders.* International Universities Press.

Berle, D., & Starcevic, V. (2005). Thought–action fusion: Review of the literature and future directions. *Clinical Psychology Review, 25,* 263–284.

Bloch, M. H., Landeros-Weisenberger, A., Rosario, M. C., Pittenger, C., & Leckman, J. F. (2008). Meta-analysis of the symptom structure of obsessive-compulsive disorder. *The American Journal of Psychiatry, 165,* 1532–1542.

Boisseau, C. L., Sibrava, N. J., Garnaat, S. L., Mancebo, M. C., Eisen, J. L., & Rasmussen, S. A. (2018). The Brown Incompleteness Scale (BINCS): Measure development and initial evaluation. *Journal of Obsessive-Compulsive and Related Disorders, 16,* 66–71.

Boschen, M. J., & Vuksanovic, D. (2007). Deteriorating memory confidence, responsibility perceptions, and repeated checking: Comparisons in OCD and control samples. *Behaviour Research and Therapy, 45,* 2098–2109.

Bouchard, C., Rheaume, J., & Ladouceur, R. (1999). Responsibility and perfectionism in OCD: An experimental study. *Behaviour Research and Therapy, 37,* 239–248.

Bouvard, M. (2002). Cognitive effects of cognitive-behavior therapy for obsessive compulsive disorder. In R. O. Frost & G. S. Steketee (Eds.), *Cognitive approaches to obsessions and compulsions: Theory, assessment, and treatment* (pp. 403–416). Elsevier.

Calamari, J. E., Cohen, R. J., Rector, N. A., Szacun-Shimizu, K., Riemann, B. C., & Norberg, M. M. (2006). Dysfunctional belief-based obsessive-compulsive disorder subgroups. *Behaviour Research and Therapy, 44,* 1347–1360.

Christenson, G., Ristvedt, S., & Mackenzie, T. (1993). Identification of trichotillomania cue profiles. *Behaviour Research and Therapy, 31,* 315–320.

Clark, D. A. (2004). *Cognitive-behavioral therapy for OCD.* Guilford.

de Silva, P., & Marks, M. (2001). Traumatic experiences, post-traumatic stress disorder and obsessive-compulsive disorder. *International Review of Psychiatry, 13,* 172–180.

Diefenbach, G. J., Tolin, D. F., Meunier, S., & Worhunsky, P. (2008). Emotion regulation and trichotillomania: A comparison of clinical and nonclinical hair pulling. *Journal of Behavior Therapy and Experimental Psychiatry, 39,* 32–41.

do Rosario, M. C., Batistuzzo, M. C., & Ferrao, V. (2017). Symptom heterogeneity in OCD: A dimensional approach. In C. Pittenger (Ed.), *Obsessive-compulsive disorder: Phenomenology, pathophysiology, and treatment* (pp. 75–92). Oxford University Press.

Duke, D. C., Keeley, M. L., Geffken, G. R., & Storch, E. A. (2010). Trichotillomania: A current review. *Clinical Psychology Review, 30,* 181–193.

Emmelkamp, P. M. G., van Oppen, P., & van Balkom, A. J. (2002). Cognitive changes in patients with obsessive compulsive rituals treated with exposure in vivo and response prevention. In R. O. Frost & G. S. Steketee (Eds.), *Cognitive approaches to obsessions and compulsions: Theory, assessment, and treatment* (pp. 391–401). Elsevier.

Fang, A., & Wilhelm, S. (2015). Clinical features, cognitive biases, and treatment of body dysmorphic disorder. *Annual Review of Clinical Psychology, 11*, 187–212.

Farrell, L., & Barrett, P. (2006). Obsessive-compulsive disorder across developmental trajectory: Cognitive processing of threat in children, adolescents and adults. *British Journal of Psychology, 97*, 95–114.

Feusner, J. D., Townsend, J., Bystritsky, A., & Bookheimer, S. (2007). Visual information processing of faces in body dysmorphic disorder. *Archives of General Psychiatry, 64*, 1417–1425.

Flett, G. L., & Hewitt, P. L. (2002). *Perfectionism: Theory, research, and treatment.* American Psychological Association Press.

Franklin, M. E., & Tolin, D. F. (2007). *Treating trichotillomania: Cognitive-behavioral therapy of hairpulling and related problems.* Springer Science.

Frost, R. O., Gabrielson, I., Deady, S., Dernbach, K. B., Guevara, G., Peebles-Dorin, M., . . . Grisham, J. R. (2018). Scrupulosity and hoarding. *Comprehensive Psychiatry, 86*, 19–24.

Frost, R.O., & Steketee, G. (2002). *Cognitive approaches to obsessions and compulsions: Theory, assessment and treatment.* Elsevier.

Frost, R. O., Steketee, G., Tolin, D. F., Sinopoli, N., & Ruby, D. (2015). Motives for acquiring and saving in hoarding disorder, OCD, and community controls. *Journal of Obsessive-Compulsive and Related Disorders, 4*, 54–59.

Garnaat, S. L., Conelea, C. A., McLaughlin, N. C. R., & Benito, K. (2019). Pediatric OCD in the era of RDoC. *Journal of Obsessive-Compulsive and Related Disorders, 23.*

Gibbs, N. (1996). Nonclinical populations in research on obsessive-compulsive disorder. *Clinical Psychology Review, 16*, 729–773.

Gluhoski, V. L. (1995). A cognitive approach for treating trichotillomania. *Journal of Psychotherapy Practice and Research, 4*, 277–285.

Grant, J. E., Odlaug, B. L., Chamberlain, S. R., Keuthen, N. J., Lochner, C., & Stein, D. J. (2012). Skin picking disorder. *The American Journal of Psychiatry, 169*, 1143–1149.

Grocholewski, A., Kliem, S., & Heinrichs, N. (2012). Selective attention to imagined facial ugliness is specific to body dysmorphic disorder. *Body Image, 9*, 261–269.

Hartl, T. L., Frost, R. O., Allen, G. J., Deckersbach, T., Steketee, G., Duffany, S. R., . . . Savage, C. R. (2004). Actual and perceived memory deficits in individuals with compulsive hoarding. *Depression and Anxiety, 20*, 59–69.

Hezel, D. M., & McNally, R. J. (2016). A theoretical review of cognitive biases and deficits in obsessive-compulsive disorder. *Biological Psychology, 121*, 221–232.

Houghton, D. C., & Woods, D. W. (2017). Phenomenology of trichotillomania. In J. S. Abramowitz, D. McKay, & E. A. Storch (Eds.), *The Wiley handbook of obsessive-compulsive disorders* (pp. 817–831). Wiley.

Julien, D., Careau, Y., O'Connor, K. P., Bouvard, M., Rheaume, J., Langlois, F., . . . Cottraux, J. (2008). Specificity of belief domains in OCD: Validation of the French version of the Obsessive Beliefs Questionnaire and a comparison across samples. *Journal of Anxiety Disorders, 22*, 1029–1041.

Julien, D., O'Connor, K. P., & Aardema, F. (2007). Intrusive thoughts, obsessions, and appraisals in obsessive-compulsive disorder: A critical review. *Clinical Psychology Review, 27*, 366–383.

Lang, R., Didden, R., Machalicek, W., Rispoli, M., Sigafoos, J., Lancioni, G., . . . Kang, S. (2010). Behavioral treatment of chronic skin-picking in individuals with developmental disabilities: A systematic review. *Research on Developmental Disabilities, 31*, 304–315.

Liao, Y., Knoesen, N. P., Deng, Y., Tang, J., Castle, D. J., Bookun, R., . . . Liu, T. (2010). Body dysmorphic disorder, social anxiety and depressive symptoms in Chinese medical students. *Social Psychiatry and Psychiatric Epidemiology, 45*, 963–971.

Luchian, S. A., McNally, R. J., & Hooley, J. M. (2007). Cognitive aspects of nonclinical obsessive-compulsive hoarding. *Behaviour Research and Therapy, 45*, 1657–1662.

Marcks, B. A., & Woods, D. W. (2007). Role of thought-related beliefs and coping strategies in the escalation of intrusive thoughts: An analog to obsessive-compulsive disorder. *Behaviour Research and Therapy, 45*, 2640–2651.

Marques, L., LeBlanc, N., Weingarden, H., Greenberg, J. L., Traeger, L. N., Keshaviah, A., & Wilhelm, S. (2011). Body dysmorphic symptoms: Phenomenology and ethnicity. *Body Image, 8*(2), 163–167.

McEvoy, P. M., Hyett, M. P., Shihata, S., Price, J. E., & Strachan, L. (2019). The impact of methodological and measurement factors on transdiagnostic associations with intolerance of uncertainty: A meta-analysis. *Clinical Psychology Review, 73*, 101778.

McKay, D., & Moretz, M. W. (2009). The intersection of disgust and contamination fear. In B. O. Olatunji & D. McKay (Eds.), *Disgust and its disorders: Theory, assessment, and treatment implications* (pp. 211–227). American Psychological Association.

McLean, P. D., Whittal, M. L., Thordarson, D., Taylor, S., Söchting, I., Koch, W. J., . . . Anderson, K. W. (2001). Cognitive versus behavior therapy in the group treatment of obsessive-compulsive disorder. *Journal of Consulting and Clinical Psychology, 69*, 205–214.

Mitchell, R., Donncha, H., & Dyer, K. F. W. (2020). Modelling OCD: A test of the inflated responsibility model. *Behavioural and Cognitive Psychotherapy, 48*, 327–340.

Moretz, M. W., & McKay, D. (2009). The role of perfectionism in obsessive-compulsive symptoms: "Not just right" experiences and checking compulsions. *Journal of Anxiety Disorders, 23*, 640–644.

Moritz, S., & Pohl, R. F. (2006). False beliefs maintenance for fear-related information in obsessive-compulsive disorder: An investigation with the hindsight paradigm. *Neuropsychology, 20*, 737–742.

Moshier, S. J., Wootton, B., Bragdon, L., Tolin, D. F., Davis, E., DiMauro, J., ... Diefenbach, G. J. (2016). The relationship between self-reported and objective neuropsychological impairments in patients with hoarding disorder. *Journal of Obsessive-Compulsive and Related Disorders, 9*, 9–15.

Mowrer, O. H. (1960). *Learning theory and behavior*. Wiley.

Neziroglu, F., & Lippman, N., (2015). A review of body dysmorphic disorder after 20 years of research. *Australian Clinical Psychologist, 1*, 23–28.

Nicoli de Mattos, C., Kim, H. S., Lacroix, E., Requiao, M., Zambrano Filomensky, T., Hodgins, D. C., . . . Tavares, H. (2018). The need to consume: Hoarding as a shared psychological feature of compulsive buying and binge eating. *Comprehensive Psychiatry, 85*, 67–71.

Norberg, M. M., Wetterneck, C. T., Woods, D. W., & Conelea, C. A. (2007). Experiential avoidance as a mediator of relationships between cognitions and hair-pulling severity. *Behavior Modification, 31*, 367–381.

Obsessive Compulsive Cognitions Working Group (OCCWG). (1997). Cognitive assessment of obsessive-compulsive disorder. *Behaviour Research and Therapy, 35*, 667–681.

Obsessive Compulsive Cognitions Working Group (OCCWG). (2001). Development and initial validation of the Obsessive Beliefs Questionnaire and the Interpretation of Intrusions Inventory. *Behaviour Research and Therapy, 39*, 987–1005.

Obsessive Compulsive Cognitions Working Group (OCCWG). (2003). Psychometric validation of the Obsessive Beliefs Questionnaire and the Interpretation of Intrusions Inventory: Part 1. *Behaviour Research and Therapy, 41*, 863–878.

Obsessive Compulsive Cognitions Working Group (OCCWG). (2005). Psychometric validation of the obsessive belief questionnaire and interpretation of intrusions inventory—Part 2: Factor analyses and testing of a brief version. *Behaviour Research and Therapy, 43*, 1527–1542.

Olatunji, B. O. (2010). Changes in disgust correspond with changes in symptoms of contamination-based OCD: A prospective examination of specificity. *Journal of Anxiety Disorders, 24*, 313–317.

Olatunji, B. O., & McKay, D. (2007). Disgust and psychiatric illness: Have we remembered? *The British Journal of Psychiatry, 190*, 457–459.

Phillips, K. A., & Stein, D. J. (2015). Obsessive-compulsive and related disorders: Body dysmorphic disorder, trichotillomania (hair-pulling disorder), and excoriation (skin-picking) disorder. In A. Tasman, J. Kay, J. A. Lieberman, M. B. First, & M. B. Riba (Eds.), *Psychiatry* (4th ed., Vol. 1, pp. 1129–1141). Wiley.

Pietrefesa, A. S., & Coles, M. E. (2008). Moving beyond an exclusive focus on harm avoidance in obsessive compulsive disorder: Considering the role of incompleteness. *Behavior Therapy, 39*, 224–231.

Pinto, A., Dargani, N., Wheaton, M. G., Cervoni, C., Rees, C. S., & Egan, S. J. (2017). Perfectionism in obsessive-compulsive disorder and related disorders: What should treating clinicians know? *Journal of Obsessive-Compulsive and Related Disorders, 12*, 102–108.

Purdon, C. (2004). Empirical investigations of thought suppression in OCD. *Journal of Behavior Therapy and Experimental Psychiatry, 35*, 121–136.

Rachman, S. (1998). A cognitive theory of obsessions: Elaborations. *Behaviour Research and Therapy, 36*, 385–401.

Rachman, S., & Hodgson, R. J. (1980). *Obsessions and compulsions*. Prentice-Hall.

Rachman, S., Shafran, R., Mitchell, D., Trant, J., & Teachman, B. (1996). How to remain neutral: An experimental analysis of neutralization. *Behaviour Research and Therapy, 34*, 889–898.

Rehm, I. C., Nedeljkovic, M., Moulding, R., & Thomas, A. (2019). The Beliefs in Trichotillomania Scale (BiTS): Factor analyses and preliminary validation. *British Journal of Clinical Psychology, 58*, 384–405.

Rozin, P., & Fallon, A. E. (1987). A perspective on disgust. *Psychological Review, 94*, 23–41.

Salkovskis, P.M. (1985). Obsessional-compulsive problems: A cognitive-behavioural analysis. *Behaviour Research and Therapy, 23*, 571-583.

Salkovskis, P. M. (1996). Cognitive-behavioral approaches to the understanding of obsessional problems. In R. M. Rapee (Ed.), *Current controversies in the anxiety disorders* (pp. 103–134). Guilford.

Salkovskis, P. M., & Forrester, E. (2002). Responsibility. In R. O. Frost & G. S. Steketee (Eds.), *Cognitive approaches to obsessions and compulsions: Theory, assessment and treatment* (pp. 45–61). Elsevier.

Salkovskis, P. M., & Millar, J. F. (2016). Still cognitive after all these years? Perspectives for a cognitive behavioural theory of obsessions and where we are 30 years later. *Australian Psychologist, 51*, 3–13.

Salkovskis, P. M., Shafran, R., Rachman, S., & Freeston, M. H. (1999). Multiple pathways to inflated responsibility in obsessional problems: Possible origins and implications for therapy and research. *Behaviour Research and Therapy, 37*, 1055–1072.

Salkovskis, P. M., Wroe, A. L., Gledhill, A., Morrison, N., Forrester, E., Richards, C., . . . Thorpe, S. (2000). Responsibility attitudes and interpretations are characteristic of obsessive-compulsive disorder. *Behaviour Research and Therapy, 38*, 347–372.

Schuck, K., Keijsers, G. P., & Rinck, M. (2011). The effects of brief cognitive-behaviour therapy for pathological skin picking: A randomized comparison to wait-list control. *Behaviour Research and Therapy, 49*, 11–17.

Shafran, R., Thordarson, D. S., & Rachman, S. (1996). Thought–action fusion in obsessive-compulsive disorder. *Journal of Anxiety Disorders, 10*, 379–391.

Sica, C., Taylor, S., Arrindell, W. A., & Sanavio, E. (2006). A cross-cultural test of the cognitive theory of obsessions and compulsions: A comparison of Greek, Italian, and American individuals—A preliminary study. *Cognitive Therapy and Research, 30*, 585–597.

Snorrason, I., Goetz, A. R., & Lee, H. J. (2017). Psychological treatment of excoriation disorder. In J. S. Abramowitz, D. McKay, & E. A. Storch (Eds.), *The Wiley handbook of obsessive-compulsive disorders* (pp. 990–1008). Wiley.

Stanley, M., & Mouton, S. (1996). Trichotillomania treatment manual. In V. van Hasselt & M. Hersen (Eds.), *Sourcebook of psychological treatment manuals for adult disorders* (pp. 657–687). Plenum.

Steketee, G., Frost, R. O., & Kyrios, M. (2003). Cognitive aspects of compulsive hoarding. *Cognitive Therapy and Research, 27*, 463–479.

Summerfeldt, L. J., Kloosterman, P. H., Antony, M. M., & Swinson, R. P. (2014). Examining an obsessive-compulsive core dimensions model: Structural validity of harm avoidance and incompleteness. *Journal of Obsessive-Compulsive and Related Disorders, 3*, 83–94.

Taylor, S., Abramowitz, J. S., & McKay, D. (2005). Are there interactions among dysfunctional beliefs in obsessive compulsive disorder? *Cognitive Behaviour Therapy, 34*, 89–98.

Taylor, S., Abramowitz, J. S., McKay, D., Calamari, J. E., Sookman, D., Kyrios, M., . . . Carmin, C. (2005). Do dysfunctional beliefs play a role in all types of obsessive-compulsive disorder? *Journal of Anxiety Disorders, 20*, 85–97.

Taylor, S., Coles, M. E., Abramowitz, J. S., Wu, K. D., Olatunji, B. O., Timpano, K. R., McKay, D., Kim, S.-K., Carmin, C., & Tolin, D. F. (2010). How are dysfunctional beliefs related to obsessive-compulsive symptoms? *Journal of Cognitive Psychotherapy, 24*, 165–176.

Taylor, S., & Jang, K. L. (2011). Biopsychosocial etiology of obsessions and compulsions: An integrated behavioral-genetic and cognitive-behavioral analysis. *Journal of Abnormal Psychology, 120*, 174–186.

Taylor, S., McKay, D., & Abramowitz, J. S. (2005). Hierarchical structure of dysfunctional beliefs in obsessive-compulsive disorder. *Cognitive Behaviour Therapy, 34*, 216–228.

Taylor, S., McKay, D., Crowe, K. B., Abramowitz, J. S., Conelea, C. A., Calamari, J. E., . . . Sica, C. (2013). The sense of incompleteness as a motivator of obsessive-compulsive symptoms: An empirical analysis of concepts and correlates. *Behavior Therapy, 45*, 254–262.

Teachman, B. A. (2007). Linking obsessional beliefs to OCD symptoms in older and younger adults. *Behaviour Research and Therapy, 45*, 1671–1681.

Thordarson, D. S., & Shafran, R. (2002). Importance of thoughts. In R. O. Frost & G. S. Steketee (Eds.), *Cognitive approaches to obsessions and compulsions: Theory, assessment and treatment* (pp. 15–28). Elsevier.

Tolin, D.F., Brady, R.E., & Hannan, S. (2008). Obsessional beliefs and symptoms of obsessive-compulsive disorder in a clinical sample. *Journal of Psychopathology and Behavioral Assessment, 30*, 31-42.

Tolin, D. F., Hallion, L. S., Wootton, B. M., Levy, H. C., Billingsley, A. L., Das, A., . . . Stevens, M. C. (2018). Subjective cognitive function in hoarding disorder. *Psychiatry Research, 265*, 215–220.

Tolin, D. F., Woods, C. M., & Abramowitz, J. S. (2003). Relationship between obsessive beliefs and obsessive-compulsive symptoms. *Cognitive Therapy and Research, 27*, 657–669.

Tolin, D.F., Worhunsky, P., & Maltby, N. (2006). Are "obsessive" beliefs specific to OCD? A comparison across anxiety disorders. *Behaviour Research and Therapy, 44*, 469-480.

Turna, J., Patterson, B., Simpson, W., Pullia, K., Khalesi, Z., Grosman Kaplan, K., . . . Van Ameringen, M. (2018). Prevalence of hoarding behaviours and excessive acquisition in users of online classified advertisements. *Psychiatry Research, 270*, 194–197.

van den Hout, M., & Kindt, M. (2003a). Phenomenological validity of an OCD-memory model and the remember/know distinction. *Behaviour Research and Therapy, 41*, 369–378.

van den Hout, M., & Kindt, M. (2003b). Repeated checking causes memory distrust. *Behaviour Research and Therapy, 41*, 301–316.

Veale, D. (2004). Advances in a cognitive behavioral model of body dysmorphic disorder. *Body Image, 1*, 113–125.

Vogel, B., Trotzke, P., Steins-Loeber, S., Schafer, G., Stenger, J., de Zwaan, M., . . . Muller, A. (2019). An experimental examination of cognitive processes and response inhibition in patients seeking treatment for buying-shopping disorder. *PLOS ONE, 14*, e0212415.

Wenzlaff, R. M., & Wegner, D. M. (2000). Thought suppression. *Annual Review of Psychology, 51*, 59–91.

Wheaton, M. G., Berman, N. C., Fabricant, L. E., & Abramowitz, J. S. (2013). Differences in obsessive-compulsive symptoms and obsessive beliefs: A comparison between African Americans, Asian Americans, Latino Americans, and European Americans. *Cognitive Behaviour Therapy, 42*, 9–20.

Williams, M., Powers, M., Yun, Y. G., & Foa, E. (2010). Minority participation in randomized controlled trials for obsessive-compulsive disorder. *Journal of Anxiety Disorders, 24*, 171–177.

Wincze, J. P., Steketee, G., & Frost, R. O. (2007). Categorization in compulsive hoarding. *Behaviour Research and Therapy, 45*, 63–72.

Woods, C. M., Tolin, D. F., & Abramowitz, J. S. (2004). Dimensionality of the Obsessive Beliefs Questionnaire (OBQ). *Journal of Psychopathology and Behavioral Assessment, 26*, 113–125.

Woods, D., Adcock, A., & Conelea, C. (2008). Trichotillomania. In J. S. Abramowitz, D. McKay, & S. Taylor (Eds.), *Clinical handbook of obsessive-compulsive disorder and related problems* (pp. 205–221). Johns Hopkins University Press.

Woody, S. R., Kellman-McFarlane, K., & Welsted, A. (2014). Review of cognitive performance in hoarding disorder. *Clinical Psychology Review, 34*, 324–336.

Yorulmaz, O., Karanci, A. N., Bastug, B., Kisa, C., & Goka, E. (2008). Responsibility, thought-action fusion, and thought suppression in Turkish patients with obsessive-compulsive disorder. *Journal of Clinical Psychology, 64*, 308–317.

Zakrzewski, J. J., Datta, S., Scherling, C., Nizar, K., Vigil, O., Rosen, H., . . . Mathews, C. A. (2018). Deficits in physiological and self-conscious emotional response to errors in hoarding disorder. *Psychiatry Research, 268*, 157–164.

PART III

Assessment of Obsessive-Compulsive and Related Disorders

CHAPTER 12

Assessing OCD Symptoms and Severity

Maria Bleier *and* Sheila R. Woody

Abstract

This chapter describes the methods and tools for evidence-based assessment of obsessive-compulsive disorder (OCD). Using case material to highlight some of the major tasks of assessment, the chapter outlines the purposes of assessment and discusses special challenges presented by OCD, such as the shame associated with socially unacceptable obsessional content. Several types of assessment tools are discussed, including structured diagnostic interviews, semi-structured interviews to assess the profile and severity of OCD symptoms, self-report instruments, behavioral assessment and self-monitoring, and assessment of OCD-relevant appraisals, beliefs, and functional impairment. The importance of linking assessment findings to an evidence-based treatment plan is discussed.

Key Words: OCD, obsessive-compulsive disorder, assessment, Y-BOCS, diagnosis, self-report, cognition, symptoms

Introduction

This chapter illustrates the general process of assessment of obsessive-compulsive disorder (OCD) using case material to highlight major areas of assessment. The first case shows how a client with OCD may present throughout the course of therapy, outlining the role of assessment in obtaining critical information about the client's history and symptoms.

Anne, a 32-year-old woman who worked in an assisted-living facility for older adults, sought treatment for obsessions, compulsions, and depression. During the initial interview, Anne reported that she engaged in rituals during almost all her waking hours (e.g., checking the stove and appliances), with less frequent rituals when she was at work. She described obsessions about causing harm (e.g., her carelessness resulting in a fire that would cause property damage and injury to her neighbors) as well as checking compulsions. Anne also revealed a history of trauma (assault and traumatic loss of pregnancy), several past episodes of major depression, and a family history of OCD. The initial assessment was obviously the first interaction between Anne and her clinician, and they began developing the therapeutic relationship at this time. The clinician (a psychologist) took a collaborative approach to exploring Anne's presenting symptoms, background, current stressors, cultural context, and goals for treatment. The clinician also ascertained that Anne met diagnostic criteria for both OCD and major depressive disorder.

Over the first few sessions, Anne's working alliance with her psychologist became stronger, and she gradually revealed more details about her symptoms that were relevant for case conceptualization and treatment planning. In addition to the prototypical fear that failing to check the stove might result in a fire, she also had some obsessions that were functionally, but not logically, connected with rituals. For example, she had persistent thoughts that failing to follow an urge to ritualize (e.g., align her sweaters perfectly, turn off the radio before switching off the car) would cause something bad to happen to someone she loved. Anne's list of compulsions came to include rewriting e-mails to ensure that she had caused no offense, counting squares of toilet paper, repeatedly entering and exiting rooms, turning taps on and off, and applying butter or jam to her toast in a ritualized way. Her main criteria for stopping a ritual were a "just right" feeling or having repeated the rituals a "good" number of times. At the time of initial evaluation, Anne's good numbers were 7 and 12.

Because of the breadth of Anne's symptoms, understanding them was greatly facilitated by use of a structured symptom checklist, which is described in the Yale-Brown Obsessive-Compulsive Scale section of this chapter. Anne's obsessions included doubt about whether things were as they should be in her home, office, car, and relationships. Any stimulus associated with an implicit rule about how it should be (e.g., door locked, parking brake set, butter to edge of bread, cutlery lined up) would evoke doubt about whether she had followed the rule properly and even whether she could trust her senses (e.g., whether she correctly perceived the stove knob to be in the "off" position). The symptom checklist prompted Anne's psychologist to ask about a wide variety of obsessions and compulsions, which seemed to make it easier for Anne to disclose symptoms about which she felt shame. Anne was surprised by some of the items on the checklist; before her evaluation, she had thought she was alone in experiencing these symptoms and took them as a sign that she was "crazy."

Compulsions are most typically associated with observable behaviors. In Anne's case, the behaviors included checking, rewriting, and repeating behaviors a certain number of times, ordering and arranging her belongings, and reassurance-seeking. She frequently stored appliances, such as the iron or electric kettle, in the trunk of her car, which helped her to feel more confident that they were indeed unplugged, although she sometimes checked the trunk during the day to be sure the appliances were actually there. Covert compulsions can be more challenging to assess; these are mental rituals that are used to "undo" an obsessive thought or prevent a dreaded outcome. Anne's covert compulsions included mentally repeating things 7 or 12 times and using repetitive stereotyped prayers that her loved ones would be all right.

Assessment of OCD also includes inquiry into avoidance behaviors and accommodations made by family members, as well as functional impairment in areas like work, school, and social life. Anne's life, for example, was extremely restricted, because she used avoidance to help manage the anxiety associated with obsessions and compulsions. Anne found it easier to stay at home on the weekends and evenings rather than endure the anxiety and effort associated with leaving the house. At work, she had been able to adapt her compulsions to function well enough to keep her job, but she often spent her lunch hour driving back home to check appliances and door locks. Anne's restricted life also caused other problems, including difficulties in managing her weight (due to a lack of regular exercise) and depression.

As is normally the case with an initial assessment, it is important to understand the presenting symptoms within the broader context of the client's current life circumstances and historical experiences. These contextual factors include the conditions under which symptoms of OCD first developed, as well as factors that have aggravated or alleviated symptoms in the past. Anne's symptoms had developed gradually during childhood and were initially diagnosed by a psychiatrist when she was in her late teens. Although the co-occurrence of depression typically exacerbates OCD symptoms, Anne's apathy during times of low mood caused her to care less about everything, including her obsessions and compulsions. Trauma triggers, on the other hand, exacerbated her OCD dramatically. Anne had tried numerous medications in the past. At the time of the initial assessment, she was taking a relatively high dose of fluoxetine, but it was not sufficiently managing her symptoms. Anne had seen numerous counselors to help her recover from the traumatic incidents she had experienced, but she had never received psychotherapy for her OCD symptoms.

For the initial evaluation, Anne's psychologist used a fairly typical set of instruments, including a diagnostic interview and a comprehensive symptom assessment, which in this case were the Yale-Brown Obsessive-Compulsive Scale (Y-BOCS) and the Y-BOCS Symptom Checklist (Goodman, Price, Rasmussen, Mazure, Fleischmann, et al., 1989). Anne also engaged in self-monitoring of her symptoms, and her psychologist used direct observation to assess subtle avoidance and compulsions as well as to understand the functional relationship between Anne's obsessions and compulsions. In addition, Anne completed several self-report measures of OCD to elicit further information on the severity of her behavioral and cognitive symptoms. Finally, Anne's husband provided collateral information on the extent of her avoidance behavior at home. These varied forms of assessment are discussed further in the sections that follow.

After completing the initial assessment, the clinician integrated the multiple sources of information into a case formulation that succinctly explained what was known about Anne's presenting problems at that point, including how symptoms and problems in OCD fit together functionally, as well as hypothesized vulnerability factors, triggering situations, and maintaining factors. A case formulation of this kind should consider idiosyncratic features of the client's symptoms and problems, the client's level of insight into the excessiveness of the OCD behaviors, and the client's apparent degree of motivation for change. Anne was highly motivated for treatment, but she showed fluctuating insight, depending on which symptom she was experiencing and how anxious she felt in a given moment.

A case conceptualization should lead to an evidence-based treatment plan for the client. As detailed in Chapters 17, 19, and 20, clinicians currently have several choices for evidence-based treatment of OCD, including exposure and response prevention (E/RP), meta-cognitive approaches, and medications. The assessment accordingly should elicit factors that will guide the choice and pacing of treatment, including the client's view of the acceptability of different treatment options, the feasibility of successfully implementing these options, and the client's motivation for change, psychological mindedness, and tolerance for anxiety. Likewise, the treatment plan selected will influence the level of assessment detail. For example, E/RP requires a thorough understanding of the degree to which various stimuli evoke anxiety and the feared consequences associated with these situations, whereas pharmacotherapy does not require these details. On the other hand, E/RP does not require a detailed analysis of beliefs about intrusive thoughts (e.g., importance of controlling them), which is needed to implement meta-cognitive approaches. Following the initial evaluation, ongoing assessment during the course of treatment can guide the clinical decisions over time, including when to change intervention strategies and when to terminate treatment.

Initial Evaluation

The therapist's objective during the initial assessment is to gather information from the client on their types of obsessions and the internal or external cues that trigger them, to understand the beliefs and behaviors around these obsessions, and to establish a rapport and trust with the client. Trust is a basic and critical element in all clinical interview processes, but it can be particularly important for clients with OCD, as there is often a great deal of shame and fear associated with the content of obsessions.

For example, Joe, a devout Catholic, was mortified by intrusive thoughts that he might be gay, even though he was happily married to a woman with whom he had a mutually satisfying sexual relationship. When he was feeling calm, Joe felt confident that he did not desire sexual relations with other men, but when he became anxious in response to a trigger, he doubted himself. The doubt involved a troubling sense that he could not be 100% sure of his true self. Triggers could include having warm feelings toward one of his longtime male friends or appraising another man as good-looking (e.g., model in a magazine, television actor). Joe had never spoken to anyone about his thoughts and fears, because he was sure he would be excommunicated and lose his wife if others knew. During the interview, he could not say the word "gay," and simply discussing the concept that other men are attractive was very difficult for him because of his shame and fear of social and spiritual consequences.

Unlike many prototypical OCD symptoms, such as washing or checking, some obsessions involve content that is personally abhorrent or socially unacceptable and thus evokes intense shame and secrecy. At times, the content of obsessions may be repugnant or even alien to the clinician; using a warm and accepting tone accompanied by a straightforward manner of asking questions will help the client to disclose the content of such obsessions. The clinician may need to focus special attention on establishing trust prior to asking detailed questions about some types of OCD symptoms. For most clients, initial discussion of safer topics, such as demographics, social and developmental history, recent life stressors, current living situation, and social support network, will allow them to feel more comfortable before discussing difficult content. Some clients may need more reassurance about confidentiality or advance agreements about the details that will appear in the clinician's written notes and reports. Even with these efforts, some clients will withhold their most disturbing obsessions or compulsions until many sessions into the therapy process. When such content is eventually revealed, the clinician will need to briefly return to assessment mode to gain the necessary understanding of the additional symptoms in order to add them to the case conceptualization and treatment plan.

Decisions about how to respond to a client's reluctance to disclose information need to be based on the evolving case conceptualization. For example, Joe's therapist did not press him to use the word "gay" during the evaluation, prioritizing instead the development of rapport and trust. She accepted his euphemisms, frequently checking her understanding of meaning, but she did not shy away from using the word "gay" herself. She agreed not to detail the content of his most disturbing image in her notes. Later in treatment, however, the therapist encouraged Joe to say the word "gay" as part of his exposure hierarchy. Similar situations may arise in the context of assessing and treating obsessions involving topics like religious beliefs or parenting styles.

Clinicians can learn a great deal about their client's OCD symptoms through careful observation during a session. Some clients may be reluctant to shake hands, open a door, or touch furniture in the office with their bare hands—things that would be routine for most office visitors. Other clients may appear distracted and, upon questioning, will describe mental rituals (such as counting) that have preoccupied them during the conversation. Depending on how the alliance is developing, the clinician may inquire about these observations right away or make a mental note to ask about them after developing a good relationship.

Differential Diagnosis

In some cases, a diagnosis of OCD will have been well established in past psychiatric evaluations, and the clinician will be more concerned with assessing current symptoms and triggers, recent exacerbations, current stressors, and other details that directly affect specific treatment planning. If the client is presenting to a mental health professional for the first time, ruling out differential diagnoses and assessing comorbid conditions are still necessary to arrive at an accurate diagnostic picture and to develop an appropriate treatment plan.

Structured diagnostic interviews, such as the Anxiety Disorders Interview Schedule for DSM-5 (ADIS-5; Brown & Barlow, 2014) and the Structured Clinical Interview for DSM-5 (SCID-5; First et al., 2016), can enhance the reliability of *DSM* diagnoses. Commonly used in clinical research, both the ADIS-5 and SCID-5 were designed for use by trained professional interviewers. The interviews guide clinicians through diagnostic criteria for a range of anxiety and mood disorders as well as other disorders, and they provide screening questions for psychotic symptoms. Both diagnostic interviews also query for psychiatric and medical history, prior treatment, age of onset, and other contextual information.

Although no study of the psychometric properties of the ADIS-5 has yet been published, the *DSM-IV* version had acceptable interrater reliability (Brown et al., 2001). The ADIS-5 interview is designed to facilitate differential diagnosis of current anxiety, mood, obsessive-compulsive, and trauma-related disorders and includes modules for other disorders that commonly co-occur with anxiety disorders. An advantage of the ADIS-5 is its use of dimensional ratings of the symptoms of each disorder, including interference and distress associated with OCD symptoms. The ADIS-5 is most useful for differential diagnosis of anxiety and related disorders.

The SCID-5, which is probably the most widely used structured interview, provides a guide for differential diagnosis of a wider range of disorders, with more detailed questioning than the ADIS-5 provides for disorders beyond anxiety and related disorders (First et al., 2016). On the other hand, the SCID-5 provides only screening questions for some anxiety-based disorders, and evidence for the reliability of anxiety disorders diagnoses using the SCID-5 is not consistently strong (Shankman et al., 2018).

A newer interview, the Diagnostic Interview for Anxiety, Mood and OCD and Related Neuropsychiatric Disorders (DIAMOND), is an alternative to the ADIS-5 and SCID-5 (Tolin et al., 2018). The DIAMOND, which is based on the *DSM-5* diagnostic criteria, has good interrater and test–retest reliability for OCD, anxiety, and mood disorders (Tolin et al., 2018). Like the ADIS-5, the DIAMOND provides a detailed guide for anxiety-based and mood disorders, and it includes both categorical diagnostic decisions as well as dimensional severity ratings. The interview includes less detailed modules for other disorders.

All these structured diagnostic interviews require a significant time investment to administer (well over an hour even for a skilled interviewer). More time is needed for clients with a complicated symptom picture and those who are poor historians. Some clients with OCD may require more time to interview, because they feel the need to provide excessive amounts of information or overly precise details for each question. Clinicians can sometimes manage this problem by explaining the structured nature of the interview and the need to interrupt from time to time in order to get through all of the material as well as by providing reassurance that important topics will be revisited numerous times in subsequent sessions. Alternatively, some clinicians may choose to administer only specific modules of interest from one of the interviews. Another option for clinical practice settings is to begin with a brief structured screening interview, such as the MINI International Neuropsychiatric Interview (Sheehan et al., 1998), which takes less than half an hour if used as a screener, followed by more detailed questioning about symptom profiles and severity for the disorders that are most relevant for the client.

Dale's case highlights some of the challenges in differential diagnosis. Dale was a 30-year-old war veteran who presented with frequent obsessions about contamination and germs. He spent many hours washing his hands each day, required two hours for his morning showering ritual, and pressured his wife and children to change out of their "dirty" clothing when arriving home from work or school. When asked about the onset of these symptoms, he described the moment when he was sickened by touching the wound of another soldier who was bleeding to death in his arms. Ever since, the feeling of dirtiness on his skin triggered traumatic memories, stimulus-bound panic attacks, and strong urges to wash for extended periods of time.

Dale's case presents a diagnostic challenge that requires careful assessment and thought. Should his treatment be approached from the perspective of OCD or a trauma-related disorder? Alternatively, should the clinician find some way to incorporate both perspectives in the treatment plan, and if so, on what basis? Although Dale presents a case where one set of symptoms may be considered in the context of different diagnostic formulations, comorbid diagnoses are also common. Depression often presents along with OCD, as do other anxiety disorders and obsessive-compulsive related disorders (OCRDs), such as body dysmorphic disorder or trichotillomania.

Obtaining an accurate diagnosis is just the first step in assessment for OCD. Compared with other anxiety disorders, OCD is extremely heterogeneous. Simply knowing that a client meets diagnosis for OCD provides no information regarding the content of the client's concerns. This heterogeneity, coupled with some clients' reluctance to report their more shameful or bizarre symptoms, makes the use of structured tools especially important in assessing the content of obsessions and compulsions. For behavioral or cognitive therapy, the clinician needs a detailed understanding of obsessions and compulsions in order to develop the case conceptualization that will drive the specifics of the intervention plan. For all treatment approaches, it is important to monitor symptoms over time to ascertain the degree of progress being made, as well as the generalization of symptom reductions across domains. The next few sections of this chapter describe interview, direct observation, and self-report methods for gathering specific information about symptoms in various domains, including obsessions and compulsions, avoidance, family accommodation of the symptoms, functional impairment, and readiness for change.

Yale-Brown Obsessive-Compulsive Scale

The most widely used measure of OCD symptoms in clinical and research settings is the Yale-Brown Obsessive-Compulsive Scale (Y-BOCS; Goodman, Price, Rasmussen, Mazure, Delgado, et al., 1989; Goodman, Price, Rasmussen, Mazure, Fleischmann, et al., 1989). The Y-BOCS is a reliable and valid semi-structured interview that is typically administered after inquiring about the presence of a range of obsessions and compulsions using a checklist. A revised edition is also available (Y-BOCS-II; Storch et al., 2010), and it has good evidence of reliability and validity (Wu, McGuire, et al., 2016). The Y-BOCS Symptom Checklist contains items on current/recent and past obsessions as well as compulsions and, on the revised Y-BOCS-II Symptom Checklist, active avoidance behavior. Together with the Symptom Checklist, the Y-BOCS takes approximately 45 minutes to administer initially, and 5 to 15 minutes on subsequent administrations without the checklist.

The Y-BOCS severity scale consists of 10 items, each rated on a 5-point scale. (The Y-BOCS-II uses a 6-point scale.) The severity ratings are distinct from the Symptom Checklist, so that symptom severity assessment is not influenced by the number of different types of obsessions or compulsions present. Severity ratings include items for time spent on obsessions/compulsions, perceived control over obsessions/compulsions, level of distress from the obsessions/compulsions, interference from obsessions/compulsions, and resistance against compulsions.

The basic assessment of presence of symptoms (using the Symptom Checklist) can be enhanced with detailed probing of symptoms during the interview, to gain a richer understanding and facilitate case conceptualization. To illustrate, reconsider Anne's case: in conducting the Y-BOCS during the initial evaluation, Anne's clinician did not simply name the symptoms on the Y-BOCS Symptom Checklist and check off those that Anne endorsed. Instead, she asked questions about each symptom that Anne described. In relation to checking the stove and other electrical appliances in the home, Anne was prompted to describe her compulsions in detail (e.g., how many episodes per day and how many checks per episode) and sometimes to even act them out for the clinician in the office. Anne's clinician also used this opportunity to elicit feared consequences—Anne's thoughts about what might happen if she did not engage in the rituals. During this more detailed questioning, the clinician learned that Anne believed that if she concentrated hard enough while checking an appliance, then she would feel a satisfying certainty that the appliance was indeed safe.

Note that the Y-BOCS Symptom Checklist simply provides prompts; it does not assess exactly what the client is checking, washing, or ordering. It is up to the clinician to discover the details. Anne's clinician listened carefully for themes and began to ask questions that fit the theme. For example, the threat of fire was a concern Anne mentioned frequently, so her clinician asked about other appliances that she had not mentioned, revealing that Anne had obsessions and compulsions about all heat-producing appliances, including the iron, hair dryer, lamps, clothes dryer, heater, fireplace, dishwasher, and water heater. On bad days, Anne would also be concerned about any dormant electrical appliance over which she did not have perfect oversight, such as the outdoor floodlights, the home security system, and the garage door opener.

Anne's case presents a good example of the importance of such detailed questioning. Some of Anne's symptoms, like those just detailed, had a logical connection to a feared outcome. Most people take precautions to avoid fire; many people without OCD unplug electric kettles or curling irons when they are not in use. In part, Anne's obsessions represented an exaggeration of normal precautions, but with careful questioning, her clinician learned that Anne had many obsessions that did not have a logical connection to a feared outcome—"magical thinking" with no "normal" version. Anne had persistent thoughts that failing to perform rituals would cause harm to someone she loved (e.g., traffic accident, job loss). Even when Anne was able to convince herself that a particular appliance was not a fire hazard, she had difficulty resisting the urge to ritualize because of obsessions about loved ones. Understanding these features of Anne's symptoms was essential for her psychologist to proceed with a clear treatment plan.

The full clinician interview version of the Y-BOCS is extremely informative, but it may be too time-consuming for some purposes. An alternative shorter self-report version of the original Y-BOCS Symptom Checklist and severity scale was developed by Baer et al. (1993). The 10 severity-scale items are each rated on a 0 to 4 scale, consistent with the original Y-BOCS. The self-report scale has shown good internal consistency and test–retest reliability for both total and subscale scores in a sample of patients with OCD (Federici et al., 2010; Steketee, Frost, & Bogart, 1996). Federici et al. (2010) also reported moderately good agreement between ratings on the self-report and interview versions of the Y-BOCS. There is some suggestion that clinicians rate compulsive symptoms, and therefore overall OCD severity, as more severe than do patients (Federici et al., 2010; Steketee, Frost, & Bogart, 1996), possibly because overt compulsions are more straightforward to notice and report. To conclude, the self-report Y-BOCS can be used in the clinical context, especially when assessment efficiency must be maximized, but it may be better to use the clinical interview version for the initial evaluation, reserving the self-report for progress monitoring.

Another clinician-rated measure for OCD that may be useful is the Dimensional Yale-Brown Obsessive-Compulsive Scale (DY-BOCS; Rosario-Campos et al., 2006). Using the DY-BOCS, the client first rates the presence and severity of 88 obsessions and compulsions across the following domains: harm/aggression, sexual/religious, symmetry/just right, contamination, hoarding, and miscellaneous beliefs, such as somatic concerns or superstitions (Rosario-Campos et al., 2006). The clinician reviews these ratings and then discusses them with the client to inform clinician ratings of severity of symptoms in each of the dimensions. The time commitment is comparable to using the interview and self-report versions of the Y-BOCS combined. The DY-BOCS has been shown to have good internal consistency and interrater reliability as well as good correspondence with the original Y-BOCS and self-report assessments of the specific dimensions (Pertusa et al., 2012; Rosario-Campos et al., 2006). On the other hand, the measure shows poor discriminant validity for depression and measures of functional impairment (Pertusa et al., 2012).

Self-Report Measures of Symptom Profile and Severity

Several self-report measures are available for assessing symptom profile and severity of OCD symptoms. These measures can be especially useful for screening purposes and clinical research, but they may be less useful for ongoing targeted assessment of client outcomes because they do not adjust to the client's particular symptom profile the way the ADIS-5 and Y-BOCS do. The measures discussed here represent psychometrically sound instruments that are frequently reported in the literature. Measures focused on beliefs and appraisals associated with OCD are discussed in the Beliefs and Appraisals section of this chapter. Most of the self-report measures assess severity based on symptom content rather than using the Y-BOCS model of assessing symptom severity independent of the specific symptom content (Baraby et al., 2018). An exception is the Florida Obsessive-Compulsive Inventory, which is discussed last in this section.

The Obsessive-Compulsive Inventory–Revised (OCI-R; Foa et al., 2002) is a shortened version of the original OCI (Foa et al., 1998). The OCI-R consists of 18 items rated on a 5-point distress scale, with the measure divided into six subscales (washing, checking, ordering, obsessing, hoarding, and neutralizing). As the subscale names suggest, the OCI-R focuses more on compulsions than on obsessions. Psychometric properties are strong for the total score and subscales in clinical samples, including good internal consistency and test–retest reliability, good convergent validity as assessed by correlations with clinician-rated measures of OCD severity, and sensitivity to treatment change (Abramowitz & Deacon, 2006; Abramowitz et al., 2005, 2010; Foa et al., 2002; Huppert et al., 2007). Discriminant validity is not strong, with moderate to large correlations with measures of depression and anxiety (Abramowitz et al., 2005, 2010; Huppert et al., 2007). The OCI-R is available as an appendix in the publication by Foa et al. (2002).

Several versions of the Padua Inventory have been developed and revised, including the original (Sanavio, 1988), the Padua Inventory–Revised (van Oppen et al., 1995), and the Washington State University Revision (PI-WSUR; Burns et al., 1996). The PI-WSUR includes 39 items scored on a 5-point scale, with five subscales (obsessional thoughts about harm to oneself or others, obsessional impulses to harm oneself or others, contamination obsessions and washing compulsions, checking compulsions, and dressing/grooming compulsions), and it has a stronger focus on obsessions than many other OCD self-report instruments. The revised versions of the Padua Inventory generally have good reliability and convergent validity (Burns et al., 1996; van Oppen et al., 1995), although they are less sensitive to treatment change than is the Y-BOCS (Baraby et al., 2018). In part due to poor replicability of the factor structure of earlier versions of the Padua, a briefer Palatine Revision has recently been developed that shows good psychometric properties (Gönner et al., 2010).

The Vancouver Obsessional Compulsive Inventory (VOCI; Thordarson et al., 2004) is based on a revision of the earlier widely used Maudsley Obsessional Compulsive Inventory (MOCI; Hodgson & Rachman, 1977). The VOCI consists of 55 items rated on a 5-point scale over six subscales (contamination, checking, obsessions, hoarding, just right, and indecisiveness). Psychometric properties of the VOCI total score and subscales are good for clinical samples, including strong internal consistency, excellent test–retest reliability, good correlations with other self-report measures of OCD, and weaker (discriminant) correlations with measures of depression, anxiety and worry, as well as ability to discriminate between individuals with OCD and anxious controls (Thordarson et al., 2004). The VOCI scale items are included in the publication by Thordarson et al. (2004).

The Dimensional Obsessive-Compulsive Scale (DOCS; Abramowitz et al., 2010) is a 20-item measure that assesses four dimensions of OCD (contamination obsessions and cleaning compulsions; responsibility for harm and related compulsions; unacceptable obsessions and related neutralizing; symmetry, order, and "just right" obsessions and compulsions). Each symptom area is rated on a five-item severity scale (time occupied by obsessions and compulsions, avoidance behavior, distress, functional interference, and difficulty disregarding the obsessions or refraining from the compulsions). Psychometric properties are strong for the total score and subscales in clinical and nonclinical samples, including good internal consistency, convergent validity, and discriminant validity. The DOCS and its subscales differentiate patients with OCD from those with other anxiety disorders (Abramowitz et al., 2010) and show a replicable factor structure (Thibodeau et al., 2015). The measure is also sensitive to changes in symptom severity after treatment (Abramowitz et al., 2010; Thibodeau et al., 2015). The DOCS is printed as an appendix in the publication by Abramowitz et al. (2010).

The Florida Obsessive-Compulsive Inventory (FOCI) was derived from the Y-BOCS and mirrors its structure (Storch et al., 2007). The FOCI is a 20-item checklist of common obsessions and compulsions and a 5-item severity scale capturing symptom severity and impairment over the past month, including time occupied with symptoms, distress, control, avoidance, and interference. The severity scale shows good evidence of internal consistency, good convergent validity with self- and clinician-rated measures of OCD symptom severity, and sensitivity to treatment change, but only fair to poor discrimination for measures of depression and anxiety (Aldea et al., 2009; Storch et al., 2007). The scale items for the FOCI are included in the publication by Storch et al. (2007).

Cross-Cultural Validity

Some of the self-report measures mentioned in this chapter have been tested cross-culturally for reliability and validity. The OCI-R has been translated into German, Chinese, Italian, and Korean, with all versions showing good evidence of internal consistency and criterion validity of the subscales as well as adequate discrimination between nonclinical and clinical OCD samples (Gönner et al., 2008; Peng et al., 2011; Sica et al., 2009; Woo et al., 2010). A Chinese version of the FOCI has been studied in a sample of individuals seeking online information about treatment; the translated version demonstrated excellent internal consistency and short-term test–retest reliability (Zhang et al., 2017). The Thai version of the FOCI demonstrated psychometric properties similar to those of the original, with good internal consistency, test–retest reliability, and fair convergent validity with other OCD measures (Saipanish et al., 2015). The DOCS has been tested in Italian, Mexican, and Iranian (Persian) versions, with studies reporting good internal consistency, factorial support, and confirmation of convergent validity with other measures of OCD (Khosravani et al., 2020; Melli et al., 2015; Treviño-de la Garza et al., 2019). In addition, the Italian version of the DOCS showed adequate discrimination among nonclinical, clinically anxious, and OCD samples (Melli et al., 2015).

Avoidance

Avoidance is a critical area to assess, regardless of the client's specific symptom profile. Avoidance comes in many varieties, from obvious overt avoidance to more subtle or covert avoidance. More active forms include avoidance of particular people, places, activities, or situations, such as not using public transit due to a fear of contamination or avoiding young children due to fears that one is dangerous. More passive forms of avoidance include declining to seek opportunities for socializing, schooling, or work advancement due to concerns surrounding OCD symptoms. Cognitive avoidance strategies are also common and include efforts to avoid, suppress, or distract oneself from obsessive thoughts. Clinicians should watch for subtle forms of avoidance during the assessment and subsequent therapy sessions. Some clients may report little distress because they are successfully avoiding OCD triggers, but their lives may be very limited as a result. In severe cases, avoidance is so pervasive that individuals become confined to smaller and smaller areas, eventually not being able to leave the portion of their home that they consider to be safe. Avoidance can also play an important functional role in the symptoms, because clients feel convinced that catastrophe has been averted, and this feeling increases the probability that the client will avoid again when faced with a similar situation in the future.

Functional Impairment

Avoidance is one of the main ways that functioning can become impaired in OCD. For example, Rachel, a 40-year-old stay-at-home mother, reported constant obsessions regarding accidental harm. Each time she left her home, she worried that she had not locked the doors or closed the windows properly, so she engaged in lengthy checking rituals. While driving, she feared that she may have run over a pedestrian or a cyclist and often felt compelled to loop around the block to check for potential victims. She avoided leaving the house during the day and preferred to walk to get groceries rather than to drive and risk harming someone. While cooking dinner in the evening, Rachel feared she would leave the stove on and cause a fire that would gravely harm her young children. As Rachel's obsessions intensified and her rituals became more time-consuming, mentally exhausting, and embarrassing, she began to avoid all triggering situations.

As Rachel's case illustrates, compulsions and avoidance can restrict daily life activities and interfere with functioning. Functional impairment in relation to any identified disorder or problem can be assessed with the Work and Social Adjustment Scale (Mundt et al., 2002). This is a 5-item measure rated on a 9-point scale, which can be completed as self-report or by clinical interview. Items include impairment in relation to work, home management, and social and individual leisure activities, as well as ability to form and maintain close relationships with others. Mundt et al. (2002) reported evidence of good internal consistency and test–retest reliability. The Work and Social Adjustment Scale correlates moderately well with clinician-rated severity of depression as well as the Y-BOCS and shows evidence of sensitivity to treatment change.

Family Accommodation

In addition to Rachel's rituals and her own avoidance, she asked her husband to thoroughly check the windows and door locks before he left for work and then again before going to bed. Her husband took over the cooking duties so that she would not have to use the stove; Rachel would only reheat meals in the microwave when necessary. As she became more and more confined in her daily activities and social life, her relationship with her husband and other social supports became strained. As Rachel's case illustrates, family members are often keenly aware of the client's distress and avoidance, and they often play an active role in the client's OCD symptoms in an effort to support or soothe the person. Almost 90% of family members report some type of accommodation to OCD symptoms (Wu, Pinto, et al., 2016). For example, family members may provide the client with things she needs to complete rituals (e.g., purchase a special type of cleaning product), or they may actually assist with the compulsions. Those suffering with OCD might request that family members observe the rituals to make sure they are done properly (e.g., that the stove was indeed turned off), and family members may accommodate unusual requests for their own behavior in the home. For example, Antonin required his family to keep all knives in the basement and to return them to the basement immediately after use (so that he could feel more assured that he would not harm someone with a knife). Obviously, family members can be a useful source of collateral information regarding the presence, frequency, and duration of problematic behaviors, especially those that a client is unaware of or is reluctant to discuss fully.

The Family Accommodation Scale for Obsessive-Compulsive Disorder (Calvocoressi et al., 1999) can be used to elicit information from family members. This measure includes a detailed symptom checklist adapted from the Y-BOCS and a 12-item scale assessing the frequency and severity of accommodating behaviors that the family member has engaged in: reassurance, avoiding triggering the client, facilitating client avoidance, facilitating or participating in rituals, assisting the client with tasks or decisions, modifying responsibilities or family routine, assuming the client's responsibilities, watching the client complete rituals, waiting for the client, and tolerating aberrant behaviors or conditions in the home. Although interviewing family members is highly informative, often this is not possible. The patient-report version of this instrument shows very good psychometric properties and can be a helpful tool in assessment (Pinto et al., 2013; Wu, Pinto, et al., 2016).

Readiness for Change

An important aspect of the assessment process is determining the client's level of readiness to make important life changes. Most clients with OCD understandably have some ambivalence about beginning a treatment that will bring them into contact with their feared material. In addition to the resistance that fear engenders, some clients with OCD have developed an entire lifestyle around their symptoms. In this context, making behavioral changes can dramatically alter a client's self-concept, daily rhythms, and habitual ways of relating to family members. For example, some clients with more severe symptoms have been spending many hours, sometimes for years, on daily rituals. What will the client do with all this free time if rituals are eliminated? Will they return to work? Take up other responsibilities at home? Assessing the client's readiness for change is important for setting the pace and scope of the intervention. Preparing the client for the potential benefits and consequences of behavior change is important.

Pollard (2007) recommended that clinicians explore several questions during the assessment phase:

- How well does the client understand OCD and the treatment model?
- How realistic are the client's expectations of the anticipated treatment process and likely outcomes?
- What is the client's level of motivation to change? For example, to what degree is the client conscious of, and bothered by, the functional interference that OCD is causing?
- What other treatment obstacles need to be addressed? For example, does the clinician observe possible secondary gain or factors in the client's life context that may motivate resistance to behavioral change?

Assessing readiness should also include ascertaining whether the client can articulate goals (Pollard, 2007), including short-term treatment-oriented goals (e.g., beginning to cook using the stove at home), as well as long-term life goals (e.g., resuming normal social functioning). Denial or dismissal of the severity of symptoms may be a strong sign that the client is not ready for OCD-specific treatment and instead needs some preliminary motivational work. Furthermore, behaviors like missing appointments or failure to return assessment questionnaires may indicate a lack of readiness to engage in treatment. This may be especially evident when a client has entered treatment due to external pressures, such as a frustrated family member.

In addition to collecting information on motivation via interview, clinicians and researchers can use the University of Rhode Island Change Assessment Questionnaire to assess ambivalence (McConnaughy et al., 1983, 1989). This 32-item measure has four subscales (precontemplation, contemplation, action, and maintenance) in addition to an overall readiness-for-change index. While internal reliability of the subscales has generally been good (McConnaughy et al., 1983, 1989; Pinto et al., 2007), predictive validity of the scale for treatment outcome of OCD has been mixed (Pinto et al., 2007). However, the scale has been used as a predictor of symptom severity change in a study that investigated predictors of treatment outcome for modular OCD cognitive therapy (Steketee et al., 2011). Scale items are included as an appendix in the publication by McConnaughy et al. (1989).

Behavioral Assessment

Self-Monitoring

Self-monitoring often provides a helpful bridge between formal in-session assessment and therapy. Using a diary or column format, clients are asked to monitor their symptoms daily, typically over the course of one or two weeks. Information gathered can include triggers and frequency or duration of specific obsessions and compulsions, as well as avoidance behavior. Monitoring helps the client to become more aware of symptoms as they occur and to see the links between triggers, obsessions, and resulting behaviors. Monitoring is also one of the best ways to identify internal triggers, such as physiological symptoms or worries. The client's diary provides the clinician with a snapshot of the client's day and the level of interference with normal functioning. Monitoring forms also help focus the start of the subsequent therapy session, letting the clinician and client review the most critical events that occurred during the week.

While there is no limit to what one can monitor, it is best to keep the forms brief and manageable to facilitate adherence. It may be necessary to limit the self-monitoring if it becomes obsessional in quality—which is sometimes a risk with more perfectionistic clients. Depending on the frequency of symptoms, recording for a designated portion of the day or simply providing estimated ratings each evening will suffice. Table 12.1 shows the self-monitoring form used by Dale, the war veteran described earlier. The form was used early in the assessment process to help him to observe how much time he spent in various cleaning rituals and to notice triggers.

Table 12.1. Example Self-Monitoring Form for Dale's Cleaning Compulsions

Date/Time	Trigger	Anxiety (0–100)	Obsessions	Compulsions
10/14 10:15 am	Wife arrives home from errands	40	Her clothes are dirty—she'll bring germs into the house.	Asked wife to remove clothes and do laundry. Wiped door handle five times.
10/14 3:30 pm	Driving family car	70	The steering wheel is making my hands feel sticky and grimy.	Used hand sanitizer three times. Washed with hot water and soap at home.
10/14 6:00 pm	Watched TV—news of ongoing war	95	Traumatic memories of touching a bloody soldier.	Showered for 2 hours. Used full bottle of liquid soap scrubbing hands and body.

Direct Observation

In addition to noting compulsions that occur spontaneously during a clinical interview or therapy session, it is also useful to create conditions in or near the clinic that trigger a client's most troubling symptoms, so that the client can be assessed in vivo. Although a home visit or "field trip" to a challenging location requires an undeniable time investment, in vivo observations can be invaluable. Most OCD symptoms can be observed in and around the clinic with a little creativity or planning (e.g., requesting that the client bring relevant objects from home to the clinic). If it is not practical for the clinician to do this personally, an assistant, such as a student, can be trained to conduct behavioral assessments and report in detail to the treating clinician.

A behavioral assessment involves some creativity, because it must be tailored to the client's idiosyncratic presenting symptoms. The main idea is to set up a relatively standard situation, preferably one that involves behavior that would be part of the client's normal functioning. Part of Anne's behavioral assessment involved her going to her car together with the therapist, starting the car, using the headlights, radio, and windshield wipers, and then leaving the car to return to the office. Anne described the rituals she felt compelled to engage in as she left the car. The therapist made notes about these rituals and about Anne's degree of anxiety and feared consequences if she did not engage in them. The therapist also conducted a home visit to observe specific eliciting stimuli in Anne's home.

Behavioral assessments of this kind are often referred to as behavioral avoidance tests (BATs). During BATs, the clinician or researcher asks for verbal reports of anxiety on a 0 to 100 or 0 to 10 scale at critical points in the task. This procedure differs from exposure therapy in that the clinician is observing and learning about the client's symptoms at a given point in time, rather than encouraging the client to go further than she or he feels is acceptable. Outcomes of interest include the degree of approach (e.g., proportion of the task that can be completed without ritualizing), distress level, and degree of correspondence between anticipated distress (when discussing the task in advance) and actual distress once in the situation. Accordingly, the therapist should try to reduce the level of demand characteristics communicated by the instructions in a BAT, in order to parallel the natural settings of the client as much as possible. For example, the test should be set up so that responsibility remains with the client (e.g., for correctly checking that a light is off). Prior to the BAT, the therapist should instruct the client to do as much as they feel they can do (e.g., use the opportunity to "test" themselves), but the therapist should not push the client during the actual test.

By using BATs, the therapist learns critical information regarding subtle and more overt avoidance behaviors, and about the quality and intensity of the client's emotional response. In vivo assessments also allow the clinician to identify "hot cognitions" regarding feared consequences of resisting the urge to perform compulsions. This type of assessment can help determine an appropriate starting point for exposure therapy and homework assignments and can permit the clinician to gauge the client's motivation despite their anxiety. For example, some clients may try to "bargain" with the therapist during a behavioral assessment (e.g., I'll touch the doorknob, but only if I can then wash for as long as I want), providing a preview of things the therapist will need to consider when planning exposure therapy sessions.

Designing BATs for clients with contamination fears is relatively straightforward. For instance, Foa's group (1980) asked clients to gradually approach their most feared contaminant in discrete steps, the most challenging of which was touching the object with bare hands. Other researchers have used standardized stimuli for all participants, such as a trash can holding a mixture of potting soil, animal hair, raw meat, and food scraps (Jones & Menzies, 1997), or exposure to a used comb, a cookie that had been on the floor, and a bedpan filled with toilet water (Deacon & Olatunji, 2007). However, restricting BATs to exposures that can be completed in the laboratory or clinic may not accurately reflect a client's level of avoidance or distress in natural settings. For clinical purposes, it is probably most informative to construct an idiosyncratic assessment that involves the client's specific feared situations in the real world.

Given the heterogeneity of presenting symptoms across clients with OCD, as well as the variety of symptoms any one client may present with, multiple tasks may be necessary to gain sufficient understanding of avoidance behaviors. This approach has been used by several researchers; clients are asked to engage in several tasks involving exposure to feared situations without ritualizing (Rachman et al., 1971; Woody et al., 1995a, 1995b). For example, one client with fears of contamination and HIV was asked to sort through household mail (fully touching each envelope) and then to touch her own clothes, hair, and face without washing her hands first. Another BAT task for this client (a medical professional who was unable to work due to OCD) involved a walk to the nearby hospital with the therapist and using doors, elevator buttons, and house phones in the hospital without rituals. Finally, the client, with the assistance of her spouse, brought a bag of her household garbage to the clinic. Steps in the BAT involved touching the outside of the bag and gradually immersing her hand in the garbage as though searching for an item she needed to retrieve.

BATs can be used for initial evaluation of symptoms and to gather important information the client is unable to report. They can also be repeated over time as a highly clinically relevant assessment of progress. If used for ongoing monitoring of progress, BATs can be scored most simply as either completed or avoided (Rachman et al., 1979) or with more fine-grained scoring systems that take into account partial avoidance and ritualizing (Barrett et al., 2003; Steketee, Chambless, et al., 1996; Woody et al., 1995a). Several BAT indices for OCD have demonstrated convergent and divergent validity as well as sensitivity to change over the course of treatment for a variety of OCD concerns (Steketee, Chambless, et al., 1996). However, some OCD symptoms are less conducive to BAT assessments, especially for clients with no overt rituals or avoidance behaviors. For instance, Joe (described earlier with his primary obsessions), engaged in a BAT that involved writing the word "gay" on a piece of paper, looking at magazine ads and commenting aloud on attractive features of men in the ads (e.g., nice hair, good-looking clothing, great teeth), and reading men-seeking-men personal ads in a local newspaper.

Assessment of Beliefs and Appraisals

Understanding the core fears and appraisals that motivate compulsions is a key aspect of assessment that influences the case conceptualization. Excessive handwashing, for example, can arise from fear of disease, an inflated sense of responsibility for transferring germs to others, an intolerance of feeling soiled, a need to wash until feeling "just right," or a sense of contempt, disgust, or moral offense. Therefore, it is critical to understand the thinking behind the handwashing, especially if cognitive interventions will be used as the primary basis of treatment.

Several facets of cognition feature in cognitive theories of OCD and are relevant to case conceptualization and treatment planning.

1. What beliefs does the client have about tangible stimuli that provoke anxiety? Magali, a woman with contamination obsessions and washing compulsions, believed germs could jump, crawl, or otherwise move, so they could be transferred without physical contact. This belief was accompanied by visual images of germs traveling from a hospital to contaminate sidewalks or other remote objects.
2. How does the client appraise the occurrence of intrusive thoughts? Appraisals of thoughts are referred to as metacognition (or thoughts about thoughts). Joe, who was described earlier in this chapter, appraised the occurrence of unwanted sexual ideation as being revelatory about his character and his

sexuality. He judged the repeated occurrences of the thoughts as indications that, deep down, he wanted the thoughts to come true. Finally, he appraised his lack of control over the thoughts (e.g., they kept occurring despite his efforts not to have them) as an indication that he was personally out of control and could not be trusted.
3. What beliefs does the client have about the value of compulsions? Anne, who is described at the outset of this chapter, believed that if she simply persisted in checking an appliance, she would eventually feel certain that it was switched off and she would feel relaxed. Conversely, she believed that she must feel completely certain of a memory of having done something (e.g., stove was turned off) before she could rely on that memory. When anxious, she fully accepted her magical thoughts about catastrophes that would occur if she neglected to perform compulsions correctly, although when calm, she acknowledged the absurdity of these thoughts.

An international group of OCD researchers, the Obsessive Compulsive Cognitions Working Group (OCCWG), collaboratively identified beliefs and appraisals important to OCD and developed two self-report measures to assist in the assessment of those beliefs and appraisals. Their research demonstrated the relevance of beliefs about the personal significance (importance) of thoughts, inflated perceptions of responsibility, overestimation of threat, thought–action fusion, intolerance of uncertainty, and the importance of maintaining perfect thought control, among others (OCCWG, 1997). However, not all clients with OCD endorse maladaptive levels of cognitions compared to healthy and anxious control groups (Calamari et al., 2006). Accordingly, because these cognitions show the same heterogeneity as other OCD symptoms, assessing beliefs and appraisals of thoughts is an important step in preparing a treatment plan that draws from cognitive theories of OCD. (Those theories, and the treatment approaches based on them, are described in other chapters of this book.) The following sections describe self-report scales of cognition relevant to OCD, clinical interviewing strategies used to discover and understand beliefs and appraisals that serve to maintain anxiety in OCD, and thought records that can be useful for between-session homework.

Self-Report Scales

The self-report measures described below can be administered repeatedly for a low-cost standardized assessment of beliefs and appraisals relevant to OCD. The initial versions of the OCCWG's scales were rationally derived (Steketee et al., 2003), but subsequent investigations of their psychometric properties resulted in the development of empirically based scales that have stable factor structures, strong internal consistency, good criterion (i.e., known groups) validity, and good convergent validity (OCCWG, 2005). Discriminant validity, however, is weaker. Although other scales are available that can be (and have been) used to assess cognitive constructs relevant to OCD, the Obsessional Beliefs Questionnaire and Interpretation of Intrusions scale are presented in detail here because they have been extensively tested by an international group of researchers and include most of the pertinent content covered by other scales.

The revised 44-item version of the Obsessional Beliefs Questionnaire (OBQ-44) has three empirically derived subscales (OCCWG, 2005). The 16-item Responsibility/Threat Estimation subscale assesses ideation about preventing harm to oneself or others and responsibility for the occurrence of negative events, including through inaction. Examples of high loading items include "For me, not preventing harm is as bad as causing harm" and "Harmful events will happen unless I am very careful." The Perfectionism/Certainty subscale (also 16 items) reflects perfectionism, rigidity, concern over mistakes, and intolerance of uncertainty, with items like "For me, things are not right if they are not perfect" and "I must be certain of my decisions." Finally, the Importance/Control of Thoughts subscale has 12 items assessing the consequences of having unwanted intrusive thoughts and the need to eliminate such thoughts. High-loading items reflect thought–action fusion and personal significance of unwanted thoughts with content like "Having a bad thought is morally no different than doing a bad deed," "Having bad thoughts means I am weird or abnormal," and "Having intrusive thoughts means I am out of control." All items are rated on a 7-point Likert scale. The scale is in the public domain and is available as an appendix to the OCCWG (2005) article.

Unlike the OBQ-44, the Interpretation of Intrusions (III) scale provides a definition of unwanted intrusive thoughts and space for respondents to write down two intrusions they have recently experienced. The III items are appraisals of these idiographic intrusive thoughts, with strength of belief rated on a scale of 0 ("I did not believe this idea at all") to 100 ("I was completely convinced this idea was true"). The original III had three subscales: Control of Thoughts, Importance of Thoughts, and Responsibility (Steketee et al., 2003), but subsequent investigation showed the scale to have a unifactorial structure (OCCWG, 2005). Therefore, a single total score of the 31 items (divided by 10 to facilitate interpretation) is recommended. Items include, "Having this unwanted thought means I will act on it," "Because I've had this thought, I must want it to happen," and "I would be irresponsible if I ignored this intrusive thought." The III is published as an appendix in the book by Frost and Steketee (2002).

Clinical Interviewing

Because of the heterogeneity of OCD, clinical interviewing remains a very important tool for assessing relevant cognition. A good starting point is to follow up on any items from the self-report scales that the client strongly endorsed. Even when conducting the Symptom Checklist portion of the Y-BOCS, the clinician can begin initial discussions of the client's feared consequences of encountering stimuli without performing rituals. Similarly, if the clinician is using direct observation to assess obsessions and compulsions, the emotional intensity of this procedure can often allow better access to cognitions that are tightly connected to emotional responses. Another important clue is stimulus generalization, a term that describes fear that has generalized from an original anxiety-evoking stimulus (e.g., blood—could carry HIV) to other stimuli (e.g., anything red—could hide blood). Inquiring about what makes the generalized stimulus frightening reveals how the client is thinking about it.

Note that sometimes the rationale for compulsions is not logically connected to the stimulus. It is easy to understand washing as a compulsion to remove perceived dirtiness or germs, but sometimes the compulsion serves as an effort to achieve a sense of completeness (e.g., ordering, arranging, checking) or to alleviate a feeling that things are not "just right." The downward-arrow technique is often useful in understanding feared consequences, appraisals, or beliefs that maintain anxiety. The following exchange between Anne and her clinician illustrates this technique.

> Dr. M: You said you get stuck for hours checking certain things in your apartment, such as the stove, fireplace, or clothes dryer. What about those things makes you the most anxious?
> Anne: I am afraid they might start a fire.
> Dr. M: What about a fire would be the most upsetting to you?
> Anne: Someone could get hurt, or the fire could spread to one of my neighbors' houses. If it happened at the right time of year, when it is hot and dry, then the forest near my house might even go up, and all the animals that live there would be hurt or scared or homeless.
> Dr. M: That doesn't sound good. This might seem obvious to you, but what part of that would be the worst part for you?
> Anne: That it would be my fault. I would be responsible for someone else being inconvenienced or hurt, and I could have prevented it if I had been more careful.
> Dr. M: What would that mean about you if you were responsible for something like that?
> Anne: It would mean I was thoughtless, insensitive—just an awful person. I don't think I could live with myself if I didn't take care to prevent something like that.

The questioning continues until the client is unable to generate any other responses, refuses to continue, or has repeated the same general content several times. After listing all the feared consequences, it is useful to ask clients to rate (perhaps on a 0 to 100 scale) how bad each consequence would be, its likelihood of occurrence, and the degree of influence (control, responsibility) the client feels over the outcome.

Once the feared consequences are established, the clinician needs to understand the degree to which the client recognizes the ideas as realistic or reasonable. Awareness of the irrationality of obsessional beliefs ranges on a continuum from good insight to delusional.

Research has suggested that 15% to 36% of OCD patients show poor insight (Alonso et al., 2008), although whether overvalued ideation predicts poorer treatment outcome is controversial (Eisen et al., 2001; Neziroglu et al., 2001, 2004). Two clinical interview measures are available to assess the strength of obsessional beliefs.

The Brown Assessment of Beliefs Scale (BABS) is a semi-structured interview that is sensitive to changes during treatment (Eisen et al., 1998; Phillips et al., 2013) and has good discriminant validity for symptom severity, depression, and general psychopathology (Eisen et al., 1998; Niu et al., 2016; Phillips et al., 2013). Seven items address the client's conviction of the accuracy of beliefs, perception of other's views of the beliefs, openness to counterfactual information, efforts to challenge the beliefs, and insight (or ideas about the source of the beliefs). Each item is rated from 0 to 4; poor insight is indicated by a total score of ≥ 12 and a score of 3 or 4 on the conviction item (Eisen et al., 2001). The scale has also been applied to OCRDs, such as body dysmorphic disorder (Phillips et al., 2013).

The Overvalued Ideation Scale is another tool that provides structure for assessing the degree to which beliefs are rigid, strongly held, or emotionally overvalued (Neziroglu et al., 1999). Questions on the Overvalued Ideation Scale include:

- How strongly do you believe that _____ is true? Can your belief be "shaken" if it is challenged by you or someone else?
- How reasonable is your belief? Is the belief logical, justified, rational?
- How accurate or correct is your belief?
- How likely is it that others (in the general population) have the same belief? To what extent do others share your belief?
- To what extent are other people as knowledgeable as you are (have as much information as you do) about the belief?
- How effective are your compulsions in preventing negative outcomes other than anxiety? Do they stop the feared outcome?

Thought Records

Some clients are able to report their feared consequences, appraisals, and beliefs with relatively little effort. However, many clients have never considered these questions or are less psychologically minded. In this case, self-monitoring of thoughts can be useful. Thought records are idiographic forms created by the therapist to help answer an assessment question. David, for example, had experienced contamination concerns for several decades, which he "successfully" managed with extensive avoidance strategies. He sought treatment only when he began to coach soccer for youngsters, because he was unable to avoid contaminants—the children often asked for help tying their shoes or adjusting their clothing after using the toilet. The children were also young enough to seek spontaneous hugs from David when they were happy or excited. Because he had avoided triggers for so long, he was unable to spontaneously report what he feared would happen if he did not avoid children or engage in washing rituals. He simply knew he did not want to be exposed to possible contamination. His therapist provided him with a thought record with columns to record anxiety-evoking situations, his anxiety rating for each situation, and what he predicted would be the outcome if he did not avoid or ritualize in each situation.

Conclusion

This chapter outlines tools and methods to assess symptom domains of OCD, including clinician interviews, self-reports, and behavioral observations. As is true with all assessments, the desire for comprehensive multimethod approaches must be balanced with time and financial constraints. Therefore, the selection of assessment tools and the scope of assessment should be driven by the clinical or research goals. In most settings, the Y-BOCS and its Symptom Checklist are recommended for optimal assessment of symptom profile and severity ratings. In contexts where reliable differential diagnosis is important, use of a structured diagnostic interview, such as ADIS-5 or SCID-5, is recommended.

For treatment with medication, it may be sufficient to determine an appropriate diagnosis, obtain a general understanding of the presenting obsessions and compulsions, and quantify the severity of the patient's symptoms in a way that can be repeated in assessing changes over time. For cognitive or behavioral treatment strategies, however, much more detailed information is required to construct a case formulation that will drive the details of the intervention. In particular, the feared consequences, connections between obsessions and compulsions, and beliefs and avoidance behavior that maintain OCD are important areas to assess. A client who expresses an unwillingness to directly confront feared stimuli or who has very low tolerance for anxiety may be better served (at least initially) by cognitive approaches to treatment. In this case, the clinician would need to commit greater time to assess the client's core beliefs and appraisals regarding the meaning of their intrusive thoughts, using structured questionnaires, the downward-arrow technique, and thought records. On the other hand, a client with very concrete thinking or language limitations may do better with an exposure-based intervention, which is less reliant on subtle language. Here, further assessment time can be devoted to developing a hierarchy of feared situations that can be used to guide treatment, and behavioral assessments may be especially valuable to indicate a starting point for therapeutic exposures.

Evidence-based practice relies on accurate initial diagnosis, ongoing assessment of progress, and measurement of treatment outcome. While this chapter is not intended to provide an exhaustive list of OCD measures, the instruments described represent psychometrically sound tools that can capture a variety of features of OCD important for treatment planning and evaluation.

References

Abramowitz, J. S., & Deacon, B. J. (2006). Psychometric properties and construct validity of the Obsessive-Compulsive Inventory–Revised: Replication and extension with a clinical sample. *Journal of Anxiety Disorders, 20*, 1016–1035.

Abramowitz, J. S., Deacon, B. J., Olatunji, B. O., Wheaton, M. G., Berman, N. C., Losardo, D., Timpano, K. R., McGrath, P. B., Riemann, B. C., Adams, T., Bjorgvinsson, T., Storch, E. A., & Hale, L. R. (2010). Assessment of obsessive-compulsive symptom dimensions: Development and evaluation of the Dimensional Obsessive-Compulsive Scale. *Psychological Assessment, 22*, 180–198.

Abramowitz, J. S., Tolin, D. F., & Diefenbach, G. J. (2005). Measuring change in OCD: Sensitivity of the Obsessive-Compulsive Inventory–Revised. *Journal of Psychopathology and Behavioral Assessment, 27*, 317–324.

Aldea, M. A., Geffken, G. R., Jacob, M. L., Goodman, W. K., & Storch, E. A. (2009). Further psychometric analysis of the Florida Obsessive-Compulsive Inventory. *Journal of Anxiety Disorders, 23*, 124–129.

Alonso, P., Menchón, J., Segalàs, C., Juarrieta, N., Jiménez-Murcia, S., Cardoner, N., Labad, J., Pertusa, A., & Vallejo, J. (2008). Clinical implications of insight assessment in obsessive-compulsive disorder. *Comprehensive Psychiatry, 49*, 305–312.

Baer, L., Brown-Beasley, M. W., Sorce, J. F., & Henriques, A. I. (1993). Computer-assisted telephone administration of a structured interview for obsessive-compulsive disorder. *The American Journal of Psychiatry, 150*, 1737–1738.

Baraby, L. P., Audet, J.-S., & Aardema, F. (2018). The sensitivity of three versions of the Padua Inventory to measuring treatment outcome and their relationship to the Yale-Brown Obsessive-Compulsive Scale. *Behavior Change, 35*, 39–53.

Barrett, P., Healy, L., & March, J. S. (2003). Behavioral avoidance test for childhood obsessive-compulsive disorder: A home-based observation. *American Journal of Psychotherapy, 57*, 80–100.

Brown, T. A., & Barlow, D. H. (2014). *Anxiety and Related Disorders Interview Schedule for DSM-5 (ADIS-5)–Adult and Lifetime Version*. Oxford University Press.

Brown, T. A., Di Nardo, P. A., Lehman, C. L., & Campbell, L. A. (2001). Reliability of DSM-IV anxiety and mood disorders: Implications for the classification of emotional disorders. *Journal of Abnormal Psychology, 110*, 49–58.

Burns, G. L., Keortge, S. G., Formea, G. M., & Sternberger, L. G. (1996). Revision of the Padua Inventory of Obsessive-Compulsive Disorder Symptoms: Distinctions between worry, obsessions, and compulsions. *Behaviour Research and Therapy, 34*, 163–173.

Calamari, J. E., Cohen, R. J., Rector, N. A., Szacun-Shimizu, K., Reimann, B. C., & Norberg, M. M. (2006). Dysfunctional belief-based obsessive-compulsive disorder subgroups. *Behaviour Research and Therapy, 44*, 1347–1360.

Calvocoressi, L., Mazure, C., Kasl, S. V., Skolnick, J., Fisk, D., Vegso, S. J., Van Noppen, B. L., & Price, L. H. (1999). Family accommodation of obsessive-compulsive symptoms: Instrument development and assessment of family behavior. *The Journal of Nervous and Mental Disease, 187*, 636–642.

Deacon, B. J., & Olatunji, B. O. (2007). Specificity of disgust sensitivity in the prediction of behavioral avoidance in contamination fear. *Behaviour Research and Therapy, 45*, 2110–2120.

Eisen, J. L., Phillips, K. A., Baer, L., Beer, D. A., Atala, K. D., & Rasmussen, S. A. (1998). The Brown Assessment of Beliefs Scale: Reliability and validity. *The American Journal of Psychiatry, 155*, 102–108.

Eisen, J. L., Rasmussen, S. A., Phillips, K. A., Price, L. H., Davidson, J., Lydiard, R. B., Ninan, P., & Piggott, T. (2001). Insight and treatment outcome in obsessive-compulsive disorder. *Comprehensive Psychiatry, 42*, 494–497.

Federici, A., Summerfeldt, L. J., Harrington, J. L., McCabe, R. E., Purdon, C. L., Rowa, K., & Antony, M. M. (2010). Consistency between self-report and clinician-administered versions of the Yale-Brown Obsessive-Compulsive Scale. *Journal of Anxiety Disorders, 24*, 729–733.

First, M. B., Williams, J. B., Karg, R. S., & Spitzer, R. L. (2016). *Structured Clinical Interview for DSM-5 Disorders, Clinician Version*. American Psychiatric Association.

Foa, E. B., Huppert, J. D., Leiberg, S., Langner, R., Kichic, R., Hajcak, G., & Salkovskis, P. M. (2002). The Obsessive-Compulsive Inventory: Development and validation of a short version. *Psychological Assessment, 2002*(14), 485–496.

Foa, E. B., Kozak, M. J., Salkovskis, P. M., Coles, M. E., & Amir, N. (1998). The validation of a new obsessive-compulsive disorder scale: The Obsessive-Compulsive Inventory. *Psychological Assessment, 10,* 206–214.

Foa, E. B., Steketee, G. S., & Milby, J. B. (1980). Differential effects of exposure and response prevention in obsessive-compulsive washers. *Journal of Consulting and Clinical Psychology, 48,* 71–79.

Frost, R. O., & Steketee, G. (Eds.). (2002). *Cognitive approaches to obsessions and compulsions: Theory, assessment, and treatment.* Pergamon/Elsevier Science.

Gönner, S., Ecker, W., & Leonhart, R. (2010). The Padua Inventory: Do revisions need revision? *Assessment, 17,* 89–106.

Gönner, S., Leonhart, R., & Ecker, W. (2008). The Obsessive-Compulsive Inventory–Revised (OCI-R): Validation of the German version in a sample of patients with OCD, anxiety disorders, and depressive disorders. *Journal of Anxiety Disorders, 22,* 734–749.

Goodman, W. K., Price, L. H., Rasmussen, S. A., Mazure, C., Delgado, P., Heninger, G. R., & Charney, D. S. (1989). Yale-Brown Obsessive-Compulsive Scale: II. Validity. *Archives of General Psychiatry, 46,* 1012–1016.

Goodman, W. K., Price, L. H., Rasmussen, S. A., Mazure, C., Fleischmann, R. L., Hill, C. L., Heninger, G. R., & Charney, D. S. (1989). Yale-Brown Obsessive-Compulsive Scale: I. Development, use, and reliability. *Archives of General Psychiatry, 46,* 1006–1011.

Hodgson, R. J., & Rachman, S. (1977). Obsessional-compulsive complaints. *Behaviour Research and Therapy, 15,* 389–395.

Huppert, J. D., Walther, M. R., Hajak, G., Yadin, E., Foa, E. B., Simpson, H. B., & Liebowitz, M. R. (2007). The OCI-R: Validation of the subscales in a clinical sample. *Journal of Anxiety Disorders, 21,* 394–406.

Jones, M. K., & Menzies, R. G. (1997). The cognitive mediation of obsessive-compulsive handwashing. *Behaviour Research and Therapy, 35,* 843–850.

Khosravani, V., Abramowitz, J. S., Samimi Ardestani, S. M., Sharifi Bastan, F., & Kamali, Z. (2020). The Persian version of the Dimensional Obsessive-Compulsive Scale (P-DOCS): A psychometric evaluation. *Journal of Obsessive-Compulsive and Related Disorders, 25.* doi: 10.1016/j.jocrd.2020.100522

McConnaughy, E. A., DiClemente, C. C., Prochaska, J. O., & Velicer, W. F. (1989). Stages of change in psychotherapy: A follow-up report. *Psychotherapy, 26,* 494–503.

McConnaughy, E. A., Prochaska, J. O., & Velicer, W. F. (1983). Stages of change in psychotherapy: Measurement and sample profiles. *Psychotherapy: Theory, Research and Practice, 20,* 368–375.

Melli, G., Chiorri, C., Bulli, F., Carraresi, C., Stopani, E., & Abramowitz, J. S. (2015). Factor congruence and psychometric properties of the Italian version of the Dimensional Obsessive-Compulsive Scale (DOCS) across non-clinical and clinical samples. *Journal of Psychopathology and Behavioral Assessment, 37,* 329–339.

Mundt, J. C., Marks, I. M., Shear, M. K., & Greist, J. M. (2002). The Work and Social Adjustment Scale: A simple measure of impairment in functioning. *The British Journal of Psychiatry, 180,* 461–464.

Neziroglu, F., McKay, D., Yaryura-Tobias, J. A., Stevens, K. P., & Todaro, J. (1999). The overvalued ideas scale: Development, reliability and validity in obsessive-compulsive disorder. *Behaviour Research and Therapy, 37,* 881–902.

Neziroglu, F., Pinto, A., Yaryura-Tobias, J. A., & McKay, D. (2004). Overvalued ideation as a predictor of fluvoxamine response in patients with obsessive-compulsive disorder. *Psychiatry Research, 125,* 53–60.

Neziroglu, F., Stevens, K. P., McKay, D., & Yaryura-Tobias, J. A. (2001). Predictive validity of the Overvalued Ideas Scale: Outcome in obsessive-compulsive and body dysmorphic disorders. *Behaviour Research and Therapy, 39,* 745–756.

Niu, C., Liu, W., Lei, H., Gan, J., Fan, J., Wang, X., & Zhu, X. (2016). The Chinese version of the Brown Assessment of Beliefs Scale: Psychometric properties and utility in obsessive compulsive disorder. *Journal of Obsessive-Compulsive and Related Disorders, 11,* 39–42.

Obsessive Compulsive Cognitions Working Group (OCCWG). (1997). Cognitive assessment of obsessive-compulsive disorder. *Behaviour Research and Therapy, 35,* 667–681.

Obsessive Compulsive Cognitions Working Group (OCCWG). (2005). Psychometric validation of the Obsessive Belief Questionnaire and Interpretation of Intrusions Inventory–Part 2: Factor analyses and testing of a brief version. *Behaviour Research and Therapy, 43,* 1527–1542.

Peng, Z., Yang, W., Miao, G., Jing, J., & Chan, R. C. (2011). The Chinese version of the Obsessive-Compulsive Inventory–Revised scale: Replication and extension to non-clinical and clinical individuals with OCD symptoms. *BMC Psychiatry, 11,* 129.

Pertusa, A., Fernandez de la Cruz, L., Alonso, P., Menchon, J. M., & Mataix-Cols, D. (2012). Independent validation of the Dimensional Yale-Brown Obsessive-Compulsive Scale (DY-BOCS). *European Psychiatry*, *27*(598–604).

Phillips, K. A., Hart, A. S., Menard, W., & Eisen, J. L. (2013). Psychometric evaluation of the Brown Assessment of Beliefs Scale in body dysmorphic disorder. *The Journal of Nervous and Mental Disease*, *201*, 640–643.

Pinto, A., Pinto, A. M., Neziroglu, F., & Yaryura-Tobias, J. A. (2007). Motivation to change as a predictor of treatment response in obsessive-compulsive disorder. *Annals of Clinical Psychiatry*, *19*, 83–87.

Pinto, A., Van Noppen, B. L., & Calvocoressi, L. (2013). Development and preliminary psychometric evaluation of a self-rated version of the Family Accommodation Scale for Obsessive-Compulsive Disorder. *Journal of Obsessive-Compulsive and Related Disorders*, *2*, 457–465.

Pollard, C. A. (2007). Treatment readiness, ambivalence, and resistance. In M. M. Antony & L. J. Summerfeldt (Eds.), *Psychological treatment of obsessive-compulsive disorder: Fundamentals and beyond* (pp. 61–77). American Psychological Association.

Rachman, S., Cobb, J., Grey, S., McDonald, B., & Mawson, D. (1979). The behavioral treatment of obsessive-compulsive disorders, with and without clomipramine. *Behaviour Research and Therapy*, *17*, 467–478.

Rachman, S., Hodgson, R. J., & Marks, I. M. (1971). The treatment of chronic obsessive-compulsive neurosis. *Behaviour Research and Therapy*, *9*, 237–247.

Rosario-Campos, M. C., Miguel, E. C., Quatrano, S., Chacon, P., Ferrao, Y., Findley, D., Katsovich, L., Scahill, L., King, R. A., Woody, S. R., Tolin, D., Hollander, E., Kano, Y., & Leckman, J. (2006). The Dimensional Yale-Brown Obsessive-Compulsive Scale (DY-BOCS): An instrument for assessing obsessive-compulsive symptom dimensions. *Molecular Psychiatry*, *11*, 495–504.

Saipanish, R., Hiranyatheb, T., Jullagate, S., & Lotrakul, M. (2015). A study of diagnostic accuracy of the Florida Obsessive-Compulsive Inventory—Thai Version (FOCI-T). *BMC Psychiatry*, *15*, 251–258.

Sanavio, E. (1988). Obsessions and compulsions: The Padua Inventory. *Behaviour Research and Therapy*, *26*, 169–177.

Shankman, S. A., Funkhouser, C. J., Klein, D. N., Davila, J., Lerner, D., & Hee, D. (2018). Reliability and validity of severity dimensions of psychopathology assessed using the Structured Clinical Interview for DSM-5 (SCID). *International Journal of Methods in Psychiatric Research*, *27*, 1–12.

Sheehan, D. V., Lecrubier, Y., Harnett Sheehan, K., Amorim, P., Janavs, J., Weiller, E., Hergueta, T., Baker, R., & Dunbar, G. C. (1998). The Mini-International Neuropsychiatric Interview (M.I.N.I.): The development and validation of a structured diagnostic psychiatric interview for DSM-IV and ICD-10. *The Journal of Clinical Psychiatry*, *59*(Suppl. 20), 22–33.

Sica, C., Ghisi, M., Altoè, G., Chiri, L. R., Franceschini, S., Coradeschi, D., & Melli, G. (2009). The Italian version of the Obsessive-Compulsive Inventory: Its psychometric properties on community and clinical samples. *Journal of Anxiety Disorders*, *23*, 204–211.

Steketee, G., Chambless, D. L., Tran, G. Q., Worden, H., & Gillis, M. M. (1996). Behavioral avoidance test for obsessive-compulsive disorder. *Behaviour Research and Therapy*, *34*, 73–83.

Steketee, G., Frost, R., & Bogart, K. (1996). The Yale-Brown Obsessive-Compulsive Scale: Interview versus self-report. *Behaviour Research and Therapy*, *34*, 675–684.

Steketee, G., Frost, R., Sunil, B., Bouvard, M., Calamari, J. E., Carmin, C. N., Clark, D. A., Cottraux, J., Emmelkamp, P. M. G., Forrester, E., Freeston, M. H., Hordern, C., Janeck, A. S., Kyrios, M., McKay, D., Neziroglu, F., Novara, C., Pinard, G., Pollard, C. A., . . . Yaryura-Tobias, J. A. (2003). Psychometric validation of the Obsessive Beliefs Questionnaire and the Interpretation of Intrusions Inventory: Part I. *Behaviour Research and Therapy*, *41*, 863–878.

Steketee, G., Siev, J., Fama, J. M., Keshaviah, A., Chosak, A., & Wilhelm, S. (2011). Predictors of treatment outcome in modular cognitive therapy for obsessive-compulsive disorder. *Depression and Anxiety*, *28*, 333–341.

Storch, E. A., Bagner, D., Merlo, L. J., Shapira, N. A., Geffken, G. R., Murphy, T. K., & Goodman, W. K. (2007). Florida Obsessive-Compulsive Inventory: Development, reliability, and validity. *Journal of Clinical Psychology*, *63*, 851–859.

Storch, E. A., Rasmussen, S. A., Price, L. H., Larson, M. J., Murphy, T. K., & Goodman, W. K. (2010). Development and psychometric evaluation of the Yale-Brown Obsessive-Compulsive Scale–Second edition. *Psychological Assessment*, *22*, 223–232.

Thibodeau, M. A., Leonard, R. C., Abramowitz, J. S., & Riemann, B. C. (2015). Secondary psychometric examination of the Dimensional Obsessive-Compulsive Scale: Classical testing, item response theory, and differential item functioning. *Assessment, 22*, 681–689.

Thordarson, D. S., Radomsky, A. S., Rachman, S., Shafran, R., Sawchuk, C. N., & Hakstian, A. R. (2004). The Vancouver Obsessional Compulsive Inventory (VOCI). *Behaviour Research and Therapy, 42*, 1289–1314.

Tolin, D. F., Gilliam, C., Wootton, B. M., Bowe, W., Bragdon, L. B., Davis, E., Hannan, S. E., Steinman, S. A., Worden, B., & Hallion, L. S. (2018). Psychometric properties of a structured diagnostic interview for DSM-5 anxiety, mood, and obsessive-compulsive and related disorders. *Assessment, 25*, 3–13.

Treviño-de la Garza, B., Berman, N., Fisak, B., Ruvalcaba-Romero, N., & Gallegos-Guajardo, J. (2019). Validation of the Dimensional Obsessive-Compulsive Scale for Mexican population. *Journal of Obsessive-Compulsive and Related Disorders, 21*, 13–17.

van Oppen, P., Hoekstra, R. J., & Emmelkamp, P. M. G. (1995). The structure of obsessive-compulsive symptoms. *Behaviour Research and Therapy, 33*, 15–23.

Woo, C. W., Kwon, S. M., Lim, Y. J., & Shin, M. S. (2010). The Obsessive-Compulsive Inventory–Revised (OCI-R): Psychometric properties of the Korean version and the order, gender, and cultural effects. *Journal of Behavior Therapy and Experimental Psychiatry, 41*, 220–227.

Woody, S. R., Steketee, G., & Chambless, D. L. (1995a). Reliability and validity of the Yale-Brown Obsessive-Compulsive Scale. *Behaviour Research and Therapy, 33*, 597–605.

Woody, S. R., Steketee, G., & Chambless, D. L. (1995b). The usefulness of the Obsessive-Compulsive Scale of the Symptom Checklist-90–Revised. *Behaviour Research and Therapy, 33*, 607–611.

Wu, M. S., McGuire, J. F., Horng, B., & Storch, E. A. (2016). Further psychometric properties of the Yale-Brown Obsessive Compulsive Scale–Second Edition. *Comprehensive Psychiatry, 66*, 96–103.

Wu, M. S., Pinto, A., Horng, B., Phares, V., McGuire, J. F., Dedrick, R. F., Van Noppen, B. L., Calvocoressi, L., & Storch, E. A. (2016). Psychometric properties of the Family Accommodation Scale for Obsessive-Compulsive Disorder–Patient Version. *Psychological Assessment, 28*, 251–262.

Zhang, C. C., McGuire, J. F., Qiu, X., Jin, H., Li, Z., Cepeda, S., Goodman, W. K., & Storch, E. A. (2017). Florida Obsessive-Compulsive Inventory: Psychometric properties in a Chinese psychotherapy-seeking sample. *Journal of Obsessive-Compulsive and Related Disorders, 12*, 41–45.

CHAPTER 13

Assessing Body Dysmorphic Disorder

Oliver Sündermann *and* David Veale

Abstract

Body dysmorphic disorder (BDD) is common but is often overlooked in clinical settings. This chapter first outlines how to screen for BDD in routine clinical practice, how to diagnose it accurately, and how to differentiate it from other mental health problems and normal appearance concerns. Next, the text describes how to assess outcome, severity, body image quality of life, and processes that are thought to maintain BDD. Last, the chapter addresses a cognitive-behavioral framework for assessment that elicits the core information used to build the client's psychological formulation. The cognitive-behavioral assessment is based on an updated CBT model that evolves around the notion that people with BDD experience distressing mental imagery of their disliked features, maintained by self-focused attention and safety-seeking behaviors.

Key Words: body dysmorphic disorder, BDD, body image, appearance anxiety, cognitive-behavioral therapy, CBT, assessment, formulation

Introduction

Body dysmorphic disorder (BDD) is a disabling and common, but largely "hidden" disorder, because health professionals often overlook BDD, while at the same time clients are reluctant to share the true extent of their appearance concerns. BDD is associated with a high risk of suicide, poor quality of life, and significant functional impairments in all areas of the person's life (Angelakis et al., 2016; Bjornsson et al., 2013; Didie et al., 2012). It is therefore important to identify BDD in clinical settings, to diagnose it correctly, and to thoroughly assess the cognitive processes and behaviors that maintain it.

This chapter outlines first how to identify BDD through accurate screening, how to diagnose BDD correctly, how distinguish it from normal appearance concerns and other mental disorders, and how to assess severity and outcome in BDD. The chapter also describes how to conduct an assessment of the person with BDD using a cognitive-behavioral framework, which forms the basis of a psychological formulation and treatment.

Screening for BDD

Unless asked directly, people with BDD are unlikely to share their preoccupation with their disliked feature(s) with the interviewer. This is because clients usually experience great amounts of shame about their appearance: they fear that they will be judged negatively, or they doubt that their clinician would understand their concerns or would be able to help them (Conroy et al., 2008). Often, clients have had a previous unhelpful experience with a health professional who has minimized their concerns ("You look fine") without validating the degree of distress and preoccupation; thus clients are understandably reluctant to reveal the details of their concerns to health professionals. Clients are often unlikely to be able to show their perceived defect(s), which may be camouflaged by makeup or completely hidden by clothing.

BDD prevalence rates vary strongly across different settings (Veale et al., 2016), and screening is especially recommended in settings with elevated BDD rates, such as adult psychiatric wards (7.4%); outpatient clinics with a focus on rhinoplasty surgery (20.1%), general cosmetic surgery (13.2%), or orthognathic surgery (11.2%); and dermatology and acne clinics (9.2% to 11.3%). Because BDD often goes unnoticed in these settings, clinicians should routinely screen for BDD.

Screening Questions for BDD

To identify appearance concerns, adults can be asked, do you worry a lot about your appearance and wish you could do so less? If the client answers affirmatively, the clinician should continue with a structured clinical interview to confirm the diagnosis (see the section "Diagnosing BDD"). For adolescents, the screening question from the Development and Well-Being Assessment (DAWBA)—an online diagnostic tool for people 2 to 17 years old (Goodman et al., 2000)—is helpful:

> Most people are concerned about how they look. This typically varies from time to time, such as being worse if they develop a bad spot or are about to star in the school play. Some people have worries about their appearance that go beyond this, filling their thoughts, taking up a lot of their time and really upsetting them. Does this happen to you?

The utility of the DAWBA screening question in identifying adolescent BDD in routine clinical practice has recently been confirmed (Buckley et al., 2018). If the client gives an affirmative response, the clinician should continue with diagnostic assessment.

Screening Self-Report Measures for Adults

Self-report screening measures can help to identify BDD, and if they indicate of BDD, should prompt further assessment of the client for BDD. Note that screening measures can only suggest the presence of BDD but cannot confirm the diagnosis. The clinician needs to establish whether the person's appearance distress or impairment is significant, whether the person's perceived flaw is not (or is only minimally) noticeable, or whether the person's concern is better explained by another disorder (e.g., an eating disorder). Despite these limitations, screening measures are time-efficient, practical to deliver, and an important first step in identifying individuals with BDD. Table 13.1 gives an overview of BDD screening measures.

Research supports the psychometric properties of the BDD screening measures, but sensitivity and specificity for *Diagnostic and Statistical Manual of Mental Disorders* (5th edition, *DSM-5*) or *International Classification of Diseases* (11th revision, *ICD-11*) diagnostic criteria[1] require further examination (Veale & Matsunaga, 2014). The Body Dysmorphic Disorder Questionnaire (BDDQ) was developed as a self-test, and it is available to the public.[2] The Cosmetic Procedures Screening (COPS; Veale et al., 2012) is recommended for use in cosmetic settings and contains additional information on frequency of repetitive behaviors, extent of interference, and how much the disliked feature dominates the person's life.

Screening Self-Report Measure for Adolescents

The majority of BDD screening measures are for adults, and there is a general lack of up-to-date screening measures for young people. This is problematic because for two thirds of BDD onset occurs during adolescence (Bjornsson et al., 2013). The Body Dysmorphic Disorder Scale for Youth (BDDSY; Hanley et al., 2020) was developed to address this gap. The BDDSY consists of a screening tool (5 items) and a severity scale (15 items). Preliminary data found the BDDSY screener had excellent psychometric properties in a sample of 321 participants age 12 to 25 years (M = 20.42; SD = 3.41; 64% female), correctly identifying those who likely met BDD criteria.

Diagnosing BDD

To diagnose BDD, the clinical interview should establish whether the person meets the diagnostic criteria for BDD in *ICD-11* or *DSM-5*. The interview guide in Box 13.1 provides a structure and suggested questions for assessing the *DSM-5* BDD criteria and specifiers. Various semi-structured and clinician-rated diagnostic tools to diagnose BDD are also available, such as the Structured Clinical Interview for DSM-5 (SCID) BDD module (First et al., 2002), or the Diagnostic Interview for Anxiety, Mood, and OCD and Related Neuropsychiatric Disorders (DIAMOND; Tolin et al., 2018; see Table 13.1). To make a diagnosis of BDD, the clients' perceived flaw(s) should not be noticeable, or only slightly noticeable, by others. In some cases, this may require clinical judgment from the interviewer, but in most cases the client's concern would not be

---

[1] https://icd.who.int/browse11/l-m/en#/http%3a%2f%2fid.who.int%2ficd%2fentity%2f731724655
[2] https://bdd.iocdf.org/about-bdd/do-i-have-bdd/#self-test

Table 13.1. Screening, Diagnostic, and Insight Measures for Body Dysmorphic Disorder

	Name of Measure	Type of Measure	Target Population	Description	Reference
Screening	Body Dysmorphic Disorder Questionnaire (BDDQ)	Self-report	Same version for adults and adolescents	One to four items of yes/no questions mapping DSM criteria for BDD; maximum score of 4 suggests likely diagnosis of BDD.	Phillips (2005)
	Body Image Disturbance Questionnaire (BIDQ)	Self-report	Same version for adults and adolescents	Seven items derived from BDDQ; 5-point Likert scale, with higher scores indicating greater body image disturbance.	Cash et al. (2004)
	Cosmetic Procedure Screening (COPS)	Self-report	Adult version	Nine items scored from 0 to 8, with high scores indicating severity of BDD. Scores above 40 reflect a likely diagnosis of BDD.	Veale et al. (2012)
	Dysmorphic Concern Questionnaire (DCQ)	Self-report	Adult version	Seven items assessing cognitive and behavioral symptoms of BDD. Sum scores ranging from 0 to 21, with scores above 9 indicating possible BDD.	Mancuso et al. (2010)
	Body Dysmorphic Disorder Scale for Youth (BDDSY)	Self-report	Same version for adolescents and young adults	Five items assessing the presence of BDD in young people, including checklist to indicate the disliked feature.	Hanley et al. (2020)
Diagnostic	Structured Clinical Interview for DSM-5 (SCID), BDD module	Semi-structured clinician-rated	Same version for adults and adolescents	Maps onto the DSM-5 criteria for BDD; also allows diagnosis of muscle dysmorphia.	First et al. (2015)
	Diagnostic Interview for Anxiety, Mood, and OCD and Related Neuropsychiatric Disorders (DIAMOND)	Semi-structured clinician-rated	Adult version	New semi-structured interview, assessing the diagnostic criteria for a range of DSM-5 disorders, including BDD. Feasible for research, clinical, and training settings.	Tolin et al. (2018)
	Body Dysmorphic Disorder Diagnostic Module	Semi-structured clinician-rated	Adult version Adolescent version	Five-item measure, also allows for diagnosis of muscle Dysmorphia.	Phillips (2005)
Insight	Brown Assessment of Beliefs Scale (BABS)	Semi-structured clinician-rated	Adult version Adolescent version	Seven-item scale measuring the strength of conviction in a belief. Items are rated from 0 to 4, with scores of 18 or above indicating delusional BDD.	Eisen et al. (1998)
	Overvalued Ideas Scale (OVIS)	Semi-structured clinician-rated	Adult version	Eleven-item scale measuring the severity of overvalued ideas on several continua, including strengths, reasonableness, accuracy, variability, and resistance to the belief.	Neziroglu et al. (1999)

> **Box 13.1 Clinical Questions to Clarify Diagnosis of BDD**
>
> If screening questions were answered affirmatively, or self-reports are indicative of BDD, the following questions help to establish the BDD diagnosis. First, ask the client if they can share more about their appearance concerns. Ask which part of their appearance they dislike the most. *Can you describe what you dislike the most about this feature? Do you feel your feature(s) are defective or ugly?*
>
> 1. [Criterion A]: Preoccupation with non-existent or slight appearance flaw
>   - Do you currently think a lot about the features you dislike? If yes:
>   - On a typical day, how many hour(s) do you spend thinking about your feature(s)?
>   - Could you add up all the time that your feature is on your mind (including on the back of your mind) and make the best estimate?
> 2. [Criterion B]: Repetitive behaviors in response to the appearance concerns
>   - Do you have to repeat yourself a lot, for example checking your appearance in mirrors or taking a photograph of yourself? (Did you use to have to check a lot?)
> 3. [Criterion C]: Clinical distress or impairment in functioning stemming from appearance concerns
>   - Does thinking about your feature(s) cause you a lot of distress?
>   - If no partner: Has disliking your feature(s) had an effect on dating or interfered with your ability to form a close relationship? If regular partner: Has disliking your feature(s) had an effect in the relationship with your partner?
>   - Has disliking your feature(s) interfered with your ability to work, to study, or with your role as a homemaker? How much time off work, school, or college have you had because of this problem? Have you been late for work or college?
>   - Does your dislike of your feature(s) interfere in other relationships with your family or the people you live with? Or your social life?
>   - Have the lives of your family been affected by your preoccupation?
> 4. [Criterion D]: Appearance concerns are not better explained by concerns about body fat or weight
>
> Specifiers:
>
> *Muscle Dysmorphia*
>   - Are you preoccupied with the idea that you are not muscular enough or that your build is too small? Do you worry about body fat?
>
> *Insight*
>   - Elicit a global belief about how convinced the client is that their perceived flaw(s) are true: How convinced are you that [areas of concern] look ugly/hideous/deformed [use client's description]?

noticeable, and most clients look perfectly normal and often are quite attractive. Some clients present with small skin or hair imperfections that are usually unnoticeable from a conversational distance. When the area of concern is slightly visible (e.g., mild acne, a few pimples, or a receding hairline), it can be helpful to acknowledge that the individual's concern is minimally noticeable at close distance. Clear visible differences in appearance (e.g., severe dermatological problems, excessive baldness, or a missing limb) would rule out a BDD diagnosis.

Differential Diagnosis

BDD often remains undetected in clinical settings or is misdiagnosed as another mental disorder. Hence, differential diagnosis is important to accurately rule out other plausible disorders that may superficially match the patients' symptomatic profile. For example, patients often feel too ashamed or embarrassed to share their appearance concerns, and clinicians may only recognize more observable BDD behaviors (e.g., withdrawal or social avoidance) and thus misdiagnose the condition as something else, such as depression or social anxiety. Even when BDD symptoms are recognized, they may be wrongly assigned to another disorder, such as obsessive-compulsive disorder (e.g., when the patient presents with symmetry concerns about their face) or skin-picking disorder (such as when facial scars are noticeable). To clarify whether appearance concerns warrant a diagnosis of BDD or are better explained by another disorder, it is helpful to consider the function of the behavior: does the behavior aim to improve or hide a disliked appearance feature?

Eating Disorders

Differentiating BDD from an eating disorder is the most difficult differential diagnosis. Both disorders are characterized by an altered body image, and they share many features, including low self-esteem and perfectionism. The *DSM-5* criteria for BDD specify that the appearance concerns cannot be better explained by concerns with body fat and/or weight. However, BDD and eating disorders often co-occur (Grant et al., 2002; Phillips et al., 2010; Ruffolo et al., 2006) and when both are present, they should both be diagnosed. Note, some patients with BDD engage in excessive weight-loss activities (dieting, taking laxatives, or exercising) to target their specific disliked features (e.g. jaws, shape of their face or symmetry concerns of their body).

Obsessive-Compulsive Disorder

BDD is often misdiagnosed as obsessive-compulsive disorder (OCD) because repetitive behaviors (e.g., mirror-checking) are falsely assessed as OCD compulsions. Equally, some preoccupations, especially those centering on symmetry (e.g., of the face or hairline), are classified as OCD obsessions. Again, if the function of the repetitive behaviors is on appearance improvement or concealment, the correct diagnosis is BDD.

Social Anxiety Disorder

People with BDD are often afraid of social situations, and appearance-related social evaluative concerns are common in BDD (Anson et al., 2012). BDD and social anxiety disorder (SAD) frequently co-occur, and thus BDD is often missed. The interviewer should clarify if the preoccupation is predominantly with appearance or with a concern of being judged on one's social performance. Both disorders are truly comorbid if additional social anxiety is unrelated to appearance concerns.

Last, BDD should not be diagnosed if either the person has normal appearance concerns or the person suffers from visible defects in appearance. Other differential diagnoses include trichotillomania, skin-picking disorder, illness anxiety disorder, or depression. For a detailed description of a differential diagnostic assessment, see Phillips (2017, Chapter 18).

Outcome and Process Measures

Clinician-Administered Measures

Various measures are available to assess severity of BDD symptoms and treatment outcome (see Table 13.2). The gold standard for assessing outcome and severity of BDD is the Yale-Brown Obsessive-Compulsive Scale Modified for BDD (BDD-YBOCS; Phillips et al., 1997). The BDD-YBOCS, a semi-structured and clinician-administered interview, has good psychometric properties (Phillips et al., 2014), and is sensitive to change. A score of 20 or above best corresponds to a BDD diagnosis, but the BDD-YBOCS is not a diagnostic tool and should only be administered to clients who have already been diagnosed with BDD. Changes on the BDD-YBOCS of ≥ 30% reflect a positive treatment response (de la Cruz et al., 2019; Phillips et al., 2014, 1997), which is defined as a meaningful improvement of symptoms after therapy. A BDD-YBOCS score of less than 16 at the end of treatment is indicative of full or partial remission (de la Cruz et al., 2019).

Self-report versions of the BDD-YBOCS exist, but they have not been psychometrically assessed and are therefore not recommended. Clinician judgment is required to determine accurately which behaviors constitute BDD rituals, to determine to what extent interference and distress are due to appearance preoccupation, and to clarify the level of insight.

Another common clinician-administered severity measure is the Psychiatric Status Rating Scale for BDD (BDD-PSR), which maps onto the *DSM-IV* criteria and can be used to provide a global rating of BDD severity once the diagnosis is confirmed. The Body Dysmorphic Disorder Symptom Scale (BDD-SS; Wilhelm et al., 2016), a 54-item measure, assesses the presence and severity of a wide variety of symptoms associated with BDD. The BDD-SS obtains information on seven symptom categories: checking rituals, grooming rituals, shape/weight-related rituals, hair-pulling/skin-picking rituals, surgery/dermatology-seeking rituals, avoidance, and BDD-related cognitions. The BDD-SS elicits great detail on the person's symptom profile and thus is useful for research and clinical purposes, especially when quick and more in-depth symptom monitoring is required than global severity measures can provide.

It is important to separate outcome measures, which assess improvement in symptoms and quality of life, from BDD process measures. Outcome measures tend to measure the severity and extent of the preoccupation, appearance-related distress, and impairment, but not the processes and behaviors that are thought to maintain the BDD.

Table 13.2. Outcome and Process Measures for Body Dysmorphic Disorder

	Name of Measure	Type of Measure	Target Population	Description	Reference
Outcome / Severity	Yale-Brown Obsessive-Compulsive Scale Modified for BDD (BDD-YBOCS)	Semi-structured clinician-rated	Adult version Adolescent version	12-item scale, ranging from 0 to 48, with higher scores indicating increased severity of BDD; widely seen as the gold standard outcome measure for BDD.	Phillips et al. (2014)
	Body Dysmorphic Disorder Symptom Scale (BDD-SS)	Self-report	Adult version	54-item scale that assesses presence and severity of symptoms from seven categories: checking rituals, grooming rituals, shape/weight-related rituals, hair-pulling/skin-picking rituals, surgery/dermatology-seeking rituals, avoidance, and BDD-related cognitions.	Wilhelm et al. (2016)
	Body Image Quality of Life Inventory (BIQLI)	Self-report	Same version for adults and adolescents	19-item scale, measures impact of body image concerns on various life domains, using a 7-point scale (-3 to +3) ranging from negative to positive, with lower scores reflecting a more negative impact.	Cash & Fleming (2002)
	Body Dysmorphic Disorder Scale for Youth (BDDSY) Severity Scale	Self-report	Same version for adolescents and young adults	15 items assessing the severity of BDD on a 5-point Likert scale by asking how often clients engaged in common BDD behaviors and processes over the past week.	Hanley et al. (2020)
Process	Appearance Anxiety Inventory (AAI)	Self-report	Same version for adults and adolescents	10-item questionnaire ranging from 0 to 4, measures frequency of avoidance behavior and threat-monitoring that are characteristic of a response to a distorted body image; ideal for tracking progress.	Veale et al. (2014)

BDD Process Measures

Veale and colleagues (2014) developed the Appearance Anxiety Inventory (AAI), a 10-item self-report questionnaire that assesses the most common BDD avoidance and threat-monitoring cognitions and the safety-seeking behaviors that are characteristic of a response to a distorted body image. Items from the avoidance scale refer to avoiding cues that might trigger negative judgment from self or others, camouflaging, or avoidance of any reminders of appearance. Items on the threat-monitoring scale refer to attempting to verify how one looks exactly, rumination about one's perceived flaw, questioning others, and comparing. The AAI has excellent psychometric properties and is sensitive to change, and therefore it is optimal for tracking treatment progress. The AAI has recently been evaluated as a tool for measuring treatment response and remission in BDD, and a reduction of $\geq 40\%$ best corresponded to a treatment response, with total score of ≤ 13 of reflecting full or partial remission (Flygare et al., 2020, 2021).

Insight and Overvalued Ideas in BDD

A thorough assessment should clarify the person's insight into their BDD and overvalued ideas (OVI) about the importance of appearance. Insight is also one of the *DSM-5* specifiers. Two insight measures are available. The Brown Assessment of Beliefs Scale (BABS; Eisen et al., 1998), a widely used six-item clinician-rated measure, assesses the degree of conviction in a belief (e.g., "My face is deformed"), perception of others' views of beliefs, explanation of differing views, fixity of ideas, attempts to disprove ideas, and insight (i.e., whether a psychological explanation is considered). The BABS provides a dimensional score along a continuum of current insight to delusionality, with higher scores representing higher conviction in a belief.

Closely related to the concept of insight are OVI, which are unreasonable beliefs that are maintained with less than delusional intensity (i.e., the person can acknowledge the possibility that the belief may or may not be true). OVI are often understood as "poor insight" along a continuum of obsessional doubt to delusional certainty. The Overvalued Ideas Scale (OVIS) (Neziroglu et al., 1999), an 11-item clinician-administered scale, measures the severity of OVI on several continua, including how strong and reasonable a belief is, how accurate, how much it has fluctuated, extent to which others share the belief, and the level of resistance to the belief. The OVIS is predictive of treatment outcome in both OCD and BDD (Neziroglu et al., 2001).

Veale (2002) argued that OVI are derived from idealized values that have developed into such an overriding importance that they totally define the "self" or identity of the individual. Idealized values are also characterized by the rigidity with which they are held. Such patients are unable to adapt to different circumstances and ignore the consequences of acting on their value. Thus, in BDD, there may be a belief (e.g., "My nose is too crooked and red"), an evaluation ("I am ugly"), and an idealized value about the importance of appearance and the way that the person's nose defines their identity. Besides an idealized value about appearance, some people with BDD also hold idealized values about perfectionism, symmetry, youthfulness, or being socially accepted. There is no validated measure for an idealized value, but it can be a helpful clinical concept and allows therapy to focus on key cognitive processes.

Body Image Quality of Life

Body image can profoundly affect one's quality of life. The Body Image Quality of Life (BIQLI) is a 19-item self-report measure that quantifies both the positive and negative effects of body image on one's psychosocial quality of life, including sense of self, social functioning, emotional well-being, sexuality, and exercise. The BIQLI has consistently shown that patients with BDD report significantly poorer body image quality of life than controls and patients with anorexia nervosa (Hrabosky et al., 2009), indicating that patients with BDD suffer from greater psychosocial impairment as a result of their body image than do clients with eating disorders.

Cognitive-Behavioral Assessment of BDD

General Assessment Points

In BDD, the main purpose of cognitive-behavioral assessment, as with any cognitive-behavioral assessment, is to gain a thorough and shared understanding of how the person's BDD developed and which behaviors and processes maintain it. This includes the person's avoidance and safety-seeking behaviors (e.g., mirror-checking, grooming, mental surgery), cognitive processes (e.g., rumination, comparing, imagery, and self-focused attention), and a functional understanding of the behaviors (e.g., threat monitoring, avoidance), including their unintended consequences (e.g., preventing disconfirmation of appearance beliefs, increasing preoccupation).

Since the assessment is usually the person's first point of contact with the healthcare professional, it is important to spend ample time (at least two sessions) on understanding the client's difficulties without rushing the client along. Depending on the chronicity and complexity of the client's presentation, the level of insight and motivation for change, the assessment can take longer. Compared to mental health assessments of other disorders, it is pivotal to spend extra time on rapport-building and motivational interviewing to address ambivalence about the diagnosis and treatment, as otherwise the client may not return. This time is well invested, and the interviewer should remain flexible with regard to the pace of the session and the location of the session (e.g., via tele-health or at the client's home). Key significant others (partners, parents) should be involved where appropriate, and relevant collateral information should be obtained from other health professionals, including dermatologists and surgeons if available. Clients should also be allowed to camouflage their perceived flaws during the assessment interview (e.g., concealing their face with a scarf, or facing away from the interviewer). Importantly, the interviewer should demonstrate genuine curiosity about the client's difficulties and adopt an "inquiring stance" rather than challenging the client's disliked feature(s) or their idealized values about the importance of appearance, because a challenge would most certainly make the client feel misunderstood. It goes without saying that throughout the interview the therapist should express empathy for the client's suffering and normalize and validate their appearance distress, because the client may have had their BDD minimized or dismissed by a health professional in the past. The interviewer should appear knowledgeable about the BDD and provide hope that BDD is treatable. Most clients feel extremely hopeless about their condition and many have had therapy before, but in most cases the therapy was probably not evidence-based cognitive-behavioral therapy (CBT) for BDD.

Assessment scales are helpful for obtaining baseline levels of BDD symptoms, but they should be skipped in the first session, when the client has poor insight and/or has been forced by someone else to attend, because administering the scales can feel mechanistic and is not conducive to rapport-building.

Once the diagnosis of BDD has been established as the client's main problem and comorbidity has been clarified, the assessment can address more detail.

General Observations during Assessment

In observing the patient, notice their social skills (eye contact, verbal fluency, demeanour, dress, posture, safety-seeking behaviors). Clothing and makeup are clues to the person's level of investment in their appearance. Hairstyles, excessive makeup, hats (particularly with a brim to limit eye contact), long hair, scarves, and dark glasses may be used to disguise features. Posture (sitting at an angle to present the best profile), avoiding eye contact, looking to another to answer questions, mood, and emotional reactions suggest social anxiety and fear of negative evaluation. There may also be damage on the skin from skin-picking.

Motivation for the Assessment

Begin by clarifying the referral. Was the client sent by someone (e.g., a surgeon, dermatologist, family member), or did the client initiate the referral and make the appointment? How does the client feel about seeing you? What are they hoping to achieve from the assessment? Often clients come to see the therapist under immense pressure from a loved one, or they may have seen a plastic surgeon first and thus want you to "confirm" that they have a physical appearance problem in order to proceed with surgery.

Developing the Cognitive-Behavioral Formulation

The information elicited during the assessment forms the basis of the cognitive-behavioral formulation. The cognitive-behavioral model of BDD was developed by Veale and colleagues and centers on the concept of the self as an aesthetic object, which refers to the experience of extreme self-consciousness and self-focused attention on distorted images of the person's disliked features, which are negatively appraised and associated with shame, disgust, and anxiety (for a detailed description, see Baldock & Veale, 2017; Veale, 2004). Figure 13.1 shows the vicious flower that maps onto the model, with each petal featuring a key BDD-perpetuating behavior or process and the unintended consequences. How to assess the key processes (the flower petals) of a cognitive-behavioral model of BDD is described here.

ASSESSING THE DISLIKED FEATURE(S)

A good starting point is to ask the client to describe the part of their body they dislike or would like to improve. Ask specifically whether the client has sought or is motivated to seek a medical procedure like dermatological treatment or cosmetic/plastic surgery. For example, if the client's concern is about the size or shape of the nose, ask whether the client is motivated to have rhinoplasty, or whether the client has undergone cosmetic surgery in the past.

Clients who dislike several features can draw a pie chart illustrating the percentages of their concern for each perceived flaw and estimate how much time they typically spend thinking about each feature during the day, how much distress their preoccupation causes them, and how much they are impaired in the various domains of functioning (such as relationships, friendships, and work). If the client is not in a romantic relationship, assess the extent their condition affects potential future relationships, such as whether their perceived flaw(s) would have an effect on meeting someone new because of their appearance-related distress or whether they could enjoy sexual activity. Keep in mind that some clients with BDD have nonspecific appearance complaints (e.g., "I feel ugly" or "My appearance is not right"), and others feel that their features are OK but "don't fit properly together." Also, some male patients feel they look too feminine, while some females with BDD feel they look too masculine.

IMAGERY AND SELF-PORTRAIT OF PERCEIVED DEFECT(S)

Imagery is a core part of the person's BDD experience and thus should be carefully assessed. Images of perceived flaws ("felt impression") are commonly experienced from an observer perspective (Baldock & Veale, 2017; Osman et al., 2004), are appraised very negatively ("My wrinkled skin looks disgusting"), and are associated with strong negative emotions, most notably shame. People with BDD are extremely self-conscious and excessively focus selectively on their felt impression.

A helpful way to capture the client's felt impression/images is to ask them to draw a portrait from the image they hold in mind about how their perceived defect(s) appear to others. The emphasis is explicitly not on artistic skills, and the client can choose any medium they prefer (e.g., draw on tablet or use crayons). Pre- and posttreatment self-portraits, especially when successful, can impressively capture the change in the person's experience of their body image. Imagery of perceived flaws is often linked with past

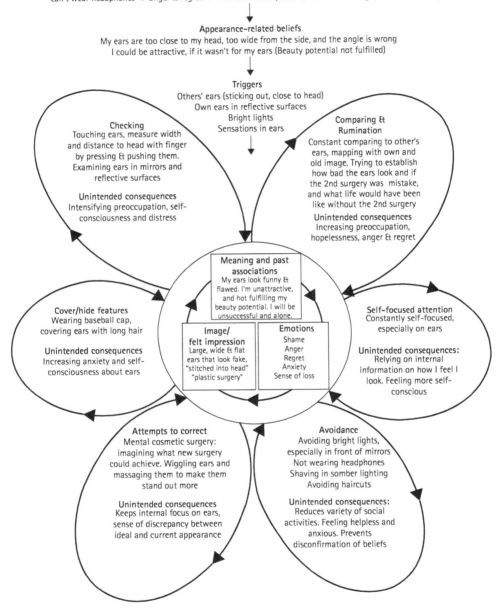

Figure 13.1. John's case formulation, demonstrating how his BDD, characterized by a preoccupation with perceived flaws in his ears, developed from early experiences of being teased and having dissatisfactory cosmetic surgery, and how it was maintained by BDD processes and behaviors that served the function of reducing or averting social threat but came with numerous unintended consequences.

relevant adverse experiences (e.g., when the client was abused, bullied, or teased about their appearance), and the past–present links are an important part of the developmental formulation.

DEVELOPMENTAL HISTORY OF BDD

The developmental history is key to understanding the client's BDD, and it often helps the client to feel understood. The goal is to understand the onset of the appearance concerns and to make clear links between possible past aversive memories, their appraisals, and the BDD. Drawing out a timeline is helpful when going through the client's early childhood, adolescence, and adulthood while focusing on key risk factors for the development of BDD. The risk factors include any traumatic experiences, sexual abuse, and experiences of bullying, teasing, discrimination, or feeling different. Aestheticality is a less often recognized risk factor for BDD. People with BDD are more aesthetically sensitive than people without BDD (Veale et al., 2002), and compared to other psychiatric patients are more likely to pursue education and an occupation in art or design (Veale et al. 2002). The therapist should try to elicit whether there was a particular trigger that marked the onset of the BDD (e.g., a critical comment about appearance by a bully or abuser). How was appearance valued at home? Determine whether the self-focused current imagery of the client's felt impression is associated with past events or periods. It is often helpful to ask the client how old they feel during moments of peak appearance distress; this information often provides an "emotional" bridge to relevant past triggers. Provide a rationale why it is important to have a good grasp of the past. The metaphor of "Ghosts from the Past" is helpful in explaining how unprocessed events, especially those associated with body shame, can "haunt" the person by shaping their experiences and interpretations of events.

APPEARANCE BELIEFS AND ASSUMPTIONS

Cognitive-behavioral models of BDD propose that the felt impression of the perceived flaw activates appearance-related beliefs and idealized values about the importance of appearance in defining the self (Cash, 2012; Veale, 2004; Wilhelm & Neziroglu, 2002). The therapist should elicit the client's assumptions and beliefs about appearance from the person's imagery. Consider the following assessment questions:

- *What's the most distressing aspect about the image/felt impression?*
- *If this was true, what would be so bad about it?*
- *What does this say about you?*
- *To what extent does this feature define you as a person?*

The most common global assumption about being ugly is that the person will be alone or unloved. Dysfunctional assumptions in BDD include "If I am ugly then . . . I am a failure as a human being . . . I will be alone forever . . . Life is not worth living." Some clients may be more invested in the idea that their perceived imperfection prevents them from fulfilling their beauty potential (e.g., "I could be quite attractive if it weren't for my wrinkled skin").

The interviewer should also clarify how much of the appearance distress stems from internal shame and perfectionism. Many patients with BDD are more concerned about not meeting their own perfectionistic aesthetic standards than they are worried about other people judging their feature negatively (external shame). To assess the client's fear of being judged about their feature, ask:

> If you were alone on a desert island and had a guarantee there was no one else on the island and no prospect of being rescued, do you think your preoccupation and distress about your appearance would a) remain the same, b) be slightly better, or c) be much better? (Veale & Neziroglu, 2010, p. 197)

Many patients suffer from comorbid social anxiety, and thus it is helpful to distinguish how much of the anxiety is related to social performance: "If you knew for certain that others would not judge your appearance, would you still be anxious about others rating you negatively?" (Veale & Neziroglu, 2010, p. 197).

Besides global and dysfunctional assumptions, patients with patients often engage in a wide range of unhelpful thinking styles, which include "all or nothing" thinking ("I always look completely deformed"), emotional reasoning ("I feel grotesque, hence I must be"), mind-reading ("I know these people are thinking my ears are too close to my head"), or discounting the positives ("All that matters is my small penis"). Clarify with your client whether their beliefs, assumptions, and thinking styles existed prior to their developing BDD.

COMPARING AND RUMINATION

Comparing is a key cognitive process in BDD that can take several forms. It is usually driven by doubting one's felt impression and by an urge to review and establish how bad the perceived flaw is. Clients often spend significant amounts of time comparing their disliked feature(s) with other people's features, or they may compare their image with a memory of how they think their feature looked in the past, or they may compare it with a photograph or video of their past self. A closely related and common process, especially in depressed clients, is rumination, which is characterized by endless past-focused "why" questions (e.g., Why was I born with these ears?, Why did I go ahead with the surgery?, etc.), which of course are unhelpful because they increase preoccupation and appearance distress. The assessment should clarify the function of both comparing and rumination (e.g., trying to verify or establish how one looks). Rumination may also serve the function of avoiding difficult emotions, such as sadness about being lonely or anger toward a surgeon. Meta-beliefs about comparing and ruminations should be assessed, as clients often hold beliefs that they are helpful (e.g., preparing them for a social event or making them feel safe), while in fact they backfire because they keep the person focused on "solving" the wrong problem. Self-attacking thoughts triggered by comparing and rumination are common and should be elicited. For example, ask if the client criticizes herself when preoccupied with appearance, or whether they experience an inner bully ("You look ugly and revolting").

SAFETY-SEEKING BEHAVIORS IN BDD

Most BDD safety-seeking behaviors serve the function of threat monitoring, including trying to obtain certainty about how bad the feature looks and how others might see it (e.g., mirror-checking or checking by touch). Threat reduction is done by altering or camouflaging the disliked feature (e.g., covering up with a scarf, using excessive makeup). The motivation may also be to "undo" the defect and to reduce threat (such as via cosmetic surgery). Box 13.2 lists common safety-seeking behaviors. The interviewer should clarify the frequency and handicap of each safety-seeking behavior and conduct a functional analysis (i.e., elicit the context in which the behaviors occur), elicit the associated thoughts and behaviors in chronological order (e.g. "What is going through your mind when examining your skin in the mirror?" "What do you do next?"), and determine the behaviors' intended, immediate, and unintended consequences for the person's preoccupation, mood, and functioning. Self-report measures and observer-rated scales are recommended to augment the assessment (see Tables 13.1 and 13.2).

Assess mirror-gazing, which is usually motivated by the hope that the feature does not look as bad as feared and a belief that the person would feel worse if they did not look. Clients also attempt to establish exactly how they look and whether they the need to camouflage the defect. Patients also try to get a "good image" and to compare the reflection with their ideal or how they looked in the past (Windheim et al., 2011). They also fantasize about how they could look if they had a successful cosmetic treatment.

Box 13.2 Common Safety-Seeking Behaviors in People with BDD

- Mirror-gazing or avoiding mirrors
- Checking perceived defect—inspecting, touching, or measuring it
- Comparing self with others or with old photographs
- Grooming behaviors (e.g., combing, smoothing, straightening, plucking, or cutting hair)
- Camouflaging rituals (e.g., makeup, scarves, hats, oversized clothes)
- Skin-cleaning, skin-picking, face-peeling, scrubbing, or bleaching
- Trying to convince others that the defect exists
- Facial exercises (e.g., practicing showing the "best face")
- Monitoring other people's reactions and eye movement
- Controlling body posture to avoid showing "defect"

AVOIDANCE BEHAVIORS

The interviewer should elicit a detailed list of activities and situations the client avoids because of their preoccupation and their motivation for the avoidance, and the client should be asked to rate the anxiety they would experience in those situations or when engaging in the activities, in hierarchical order. The fear hierarchy forms the basis for exposure tasks and behavioral experiments. Some of the avoidance behavior may appear to overlap with depression when the person loses motivation to go out or do anything. The clinician should prompt for plausible avoidance behaviors based on the client's specific concerns if they are not volunteered and should normalize the behaviors as an understandable response to the client's appearance distress. For example, a client might avoid going to the theatre because they can't take off their hat or scarf.

Box 13.3 presents a comprehensive overview of a cognitive-behavioral assessment conducted for a client experiencing body dysmorphic disorder (BDD).

Conclusion

BDD often goes unnoticed for many years and is often not accurately identified and assessed by clinicians. This chapter describes how to screen for BDD and how to diagnose it accurately, as well as how to assess various body-image-related outcomes. The chapter outlines a cognitive-behavioral assessment protocol that focuses on eliciting the relevant clinical information for the client's psychological formulation. The cognitive-behavioral assessment places key emphasis on engaging the client in understanding their appearance anxiety, in making sense of how their BDD developed, and in understanding how BDD is maintained through processes like mental imagery of the disliked features, self-focused attention, comparing, rumination, avoidance, and safety-seeking behaviors.

Box 13.3 Case Vignette: John—Cognitive-Behavioral Assessment and Vicious Flower

John was a 29-year-old man who presented with long-standing BDD characterized by a severe preoccupation with his ears being too close to his head and appearing too wide from the side. He was also, to a lesser degree, concerned about his brow ridge, facial wrinkles, and dark rings under his eyes, which he thought made him look old. John self-referred to a specialist national outpatient clinic for an assessment of his appearance concerns after 11 years of suffering. He attended two 90-minute intake assessments before embarking on a course of CBT for BDD.

Ahead of his first session, John filled out a battery of BDD self-report questionnaires, including the COPS, AAI, and BIQ, which suggested that he suffered from BDD with poor body image quality of life. John was motivated to seek specialized psychological help for his BDD. Over the years he had various courses of counseling and CBT for concerns about his ears and low mood, but the treatments were not specific for BDD. From the outset, John explained that as a young adult he underwent two plastic surgeries (at ages 16 and 17) that pinned his ears back (pinnaplasty). He was not satisfied with the outcome of the first operation, and thus underwent a second operation that was more invasive and changed the anatomy of his ears by removing cartilage adjacent to his head to pin his ears back. He immediately felt that the second operation was a big mistake, and he now thought his ears were too close to his head and appeared too wide from the side, also leaving him with permanent tactile sensations of tightness. The BDD diagnosis was confirmed through a structured clinical interview. The BDD-YBOCS found his BDD to be in the severe range, with most of his waking hours taken up by preoccupation with his ears and BDD behaviors, causing him significant distress and impairment. John was highly intelligent and had managed to complete higher degrees in science, but he lost several top management jobs over the years due to his appearance distress. He experienced a great sense of loss for not having been able to fulfill his potential at work and in relationships due to his BDD. He showed fair to good insight into his BDD, recognizing that his beliefs ("My ears look disgusting"), were probably not completely accurate.

It was very important to John that his therapist understood the minuscule detail of his ear concerns, including in-depth discussion of how his ear anatomy had changed as a result of his second pinnaplasty, and its anatomical consequences (e.g., he was unable to wear earbud headphones), because all his life he felt not understood and had his concerns minimized by his parents, friends, and partners. John's ear preoccupation was pervasive and oscillated between only two modes: he either was intensely triggered and all-consumed by "ear anxiety" or was less anxious but somewhat "consciously aware" and self-conscious about his ears. The few exceptions occurred when he travelled abroad and was intensely involved in sports. John experienced intrusive mental imagery of how he felt his ears looked from an observer perspective. John drew a portrait of his disliked feature to illustrate his distorted mental imagery of his ears, which also helped him to explain the details of his concerns. He described his ears as flat ears, being too close to his head, too stretched and too wide from the side, therefore looking unnatural, fake, stitched to his head, and very "plastic-surgery." The image was fused with tactile sensations of feeling too tight and was accompanied by a sense of hopelessness, regret about the operation, and deeply seated anger toward the surgeon and his parents for not protecting him from the surgery and its consequences. To obtain the relevant past detail, the therapist drew a timeline with John to discuss his childhood experience that led to him having pinnaplasty. As a teenager John had been very athletic (top rugby player), and very popular with girls. Despite his popularity, he was teased and bullied about his ears being too large and "sticking out" and also was mocked for swimming well (e.g., he recalled one bully flapping his ears when John came out of the water, indicating John swam with his ears). Nevertheless, John considered himself generally attractive, "if it wasn't for the ears," which is why he requested to have them pinned back. John found the metaphor of being haunted by ghosts from the past helpful in understanding how his torment about the dissatisfactory surgery outcome and fused difficult feelings (anger, shame) and ear imagery have stayed with him over the years. The therapist normalized John's experience that led to the development of BDD and validated the BDD as a very understandable but unhelpful attempt to cope with the shame and anger stemming from his perceived threat of having "messed up" his ears.

The second assessment session focused on organizing and eliciting the information that formed the basis of John's cognitive-behavioral formulation ("vicious flower," see Figure 13.1). The therapist first discussed common internal and external triggers that exacerbated John's preoccupation with his ears, and how the triggers would usually bring on observer-perspective imagery of John's perceived flaws ("flat and wide ears"), which he appraised very negatively and overall as unattractive and not desirable. John and his therapist drew the formulation jointly on a whiteboard to highlight how the various BDD processes and behaviors maintained the disorder. They also discussed the function of the processes and behaviors and their unintended consequences. The main functions were threat detection (e.g., determining how bad his ears looked), threat avoidance (e.g., reducing the chance of humiliation by wearing a cap or adopting longer hair to cover the ears), or threat mitigation (e.g., mental cosmetic surgery).

Self-focused attention: John was highly self-conscious about his ears, focusing on internal information on how he thought he appeared to others ("felt impression"), which to him was automatic and out of his control.

Checking: John checked his ears by touch during the day, measuring the width and distance to his head with his fingers to establish how bad his ears looked. He also had a "tricky relationship" with mirrors, and would spend hours in front of the mirror, hoping to get a good image of his ears and working out "if he really had a problem and if yes, how bad it was."

Comparing and ruminating: John relentlessly compared current and past images of his ears to other people's ears. He would ruminate and dwell on what life would have been like without the second surgery. John also tried to establish whether the physical sensations in his ears—the tightness, heat, and pressure—were natural or not, or were caused by the surgery.

Attempts to correct: John engaged in mental surgery (i.e., imagining what his ears would look like if he had them operated on again). He also wiggled his ears, massaged them, and spent hours pressing and pushing the ears out to make them look like what he thought they would have looked like without surgery. John also planned for a third operation in case therapy failed. This gave him short-lived relief in the thought that his ears could be improved, but the thought would quickly fuel his preoccupation and worsen his mood.

Avoidance: John avoided bright lights, shaved in somber lighting, generally avoided the barber (had his hair cut infrequently), and was nervous about photographs being taken of him.

Covering disliked features: John wore a baseball hat and kept his hair longer than it would have been otherwise to offer partial camouflage so it would fall over his ears. These safety behaviors aimed to reduce the threat of humiliation but unfortunately intensified his preoccupation and self-consciousness about his ears.

References

Angelakis, I., Gooding, P. A., & Panagioti, M. (2016). Suicidality in body dysmorphic disorder (BDD): A systematic review with meta-analysis. *Clinical Psychology Review*, *49*, 55–66.

Anson, M., Veale, D., & de Silva, P. (2012). Social-evaluative versus self-evaluative appearance concerns in Body Dysmorphic Disorder. *Behaviour Research and Therapy*, *50*(12), 753–760.

Baldock, E., & Veale, D. (2017). The self as an aesthetic object: Body image, beliefs about the self, and shame in a cognitive-behavioural model of body dysmorphic disorder. In *Body dysmorphic disorder: Advances in research and clinical practice* (1st ed.) (pp. 299–312). Oxford University Press.

Bjornsson, A. S., Didie, E. R., Grant, J. E., Menard, W., Stalker, E., & Phillips, K. A. (2013). Age at onset and clinical correlates in body dysmorphic disorder. *Comprehensive Psychiatry*, *54*(7), 893–903.

Buckley, V., Krebs, G., Bowyer, L., Jassi, A., Goodman, R., Clark, B., & Stringaris, A. (2018). Innovations in practice: Body dysmorphic disorder in youth—Using the Development and Well-Being Assessment as a tool to improve detection in routine clinical practice. *Child and Adolescent Mental Health*, *23*(3), 291–294.

Cash, T. F. (2012). Cognitive-behavioral perspectives on body image. In T. F. Cash (Ed.), *Encyclopedia of body image and human appearance* (Vol. 1, pp. 334–342). Elsevier Academic Press.

Cash, T. F., & Fleming, E. C. (2002). The impact of body-image experiences: Development of the body image quality of life inventory. *International Journal of Eating Disorders*, *31*, 455–460.

Cash, T. F., Phillips, K. A., Santos, M. T., & Hrabosky, J. I. (2004). Measuring "negative body image": Validation of the Body Image Disturbance Questionnaire in a nonclinical population. *Body Image*, *1*(4), 363–372.

Conroy, M., Menard, W., Fleming-Ives, K., Modha, P., Cerullo, H., & Phillips, K. A. (2008). Prevalence and clinical characteristics of body dysmorphic disorder in an adult inpatient setting. *General Hospital Psychiatry*, *30*(1), 67–72.

de la Cruz, L. F., Enander, J., Rück, C., Wilhelm, S., Phillips, K. A., Steketee, G., Mothi, S. S., Krebs, G., Bowyer, L., Monzani, B., Veale, D., & Mataix-Cols, D. (2021). Empirically defining treatment response and remission in body dysmorphic disorder. *Psychological Medicine*, *51*(1), 83–89.

Didie, E. R., Loerke, E. H., Howes, S. E., & Phillips, K. A. (2012). Severity of interpersonal problems in individuals with body dysmorphic disorder. *Journal of Personality Disorders*, *26*(3), 345-356.

Eisen, J. L., Phillips, K. A., Baer, L., Beer, D. A., Atala, K. D., & Rasmussen, S. A. (1998). The Brown Assessment of Beliefs Scale: Reliability and validity. *The American Journal of Psychiatry*, *155*(1), 102–108.

First, M. B., Williams, J. B. W., Karg, R. S., & Spitzer, R. L. (2016). *Structured clinical interview for DSM-5 Disorders, Clinician Version (SCID-5-CV)*. American Psychiatric Association.

Flygare, O., Enander, J., Andersson, E., Ljótsson, B., Ivanov, V. Z., Mataix-Cols, D., & Rück, C. (2020). Predictors of remission from body dysmorphic disorder after internet-delivered cognitive behavior therapy: A machine learning approach. *BMC Psychiatry*, *20*(1), 1–9.

Flygare, O., Chen, L.-L., de la Cruz, L. F., Enander, J., Mataix-Cols, D., Rück, C., & Andersson, E. (2021). Empirically defining treatment response and remission in body dysmorphic disorder using a short self-report instrument. *Behavior Therapy*, *52*(4), 821–829.

Goodman, R., Ford, T., Richards, H., Gatward, R., & Meltzer, H. (2000). The Development and Well-Being Assessment: Description and initial validation of an integrated assessment of child and adolescent psychopathology. *Journal of Child Psychology and Psychiatry*, *41*(5), 645–655.

Grant, J. E., Kim, S. W., & Eckert, E. D. (2002). Body dysmorphic disorder in patients with anorexia nervosa: Prevalence, clinical features, and delusionality of body image. *International Journal of Eating Disorders*, *32*(3), 291–300.

Hanley, S. M., Bhullar, N., & Wootton, B. M. (2020). Development and initial validation of the Body Dysmorphic Disorder Scale for Youth. *Clinical Psychologist*, 24, 254–266.

Hrabosky, J. I., Cash, T. F., Veale, D., Neziroglu, F., Soll, E. A., Garner, D. M., Strachan-Kinser, M., Bakke, B., Clauss, L. J., & Phillips, K. A. (2009). Multidimensional body image comparisons among patients with eating disorders, body dysmorphic disorder, and clinical controls: A multisite study. *Body Image*, *6*(3), 155–163.

Mancuso, S. G., Knoesen, N. P., Castle, D. J. (2010). The Dysmorphic Concern Questionnaire: A screening measure for body dysmorphic disorder. *Australian and New Zealand Journal of Psychiatry*, *44*(6), 535–542.

Neziroglu, F., McKay, D., Yaryura-Tobias, J. A., Stevens, K. P., & Todaro, J. (1999). The Overvalued Ideas Scale: Development, reliability and validity in obsessive-compulsive disorder. *Behaviour Research and Therapy*, *37*(9), 881–902.

Neziroglu, F., Stevens, K. P., McKay, D., & Yaryura-Tobias, J. A. (2001). Predictive validity of the Overvalued Ideas Scale: Outcome in obsessive-compulsive and body dysmorphic disorders. *Behaviour Research and Therapy*, *39*(6), 745–756.

Osman, S., Cooper, M., Hackmann, A., & Veale, D. (2004). Spontaneously occurring images and early memories in people with body dysmorphic disorder. *Memory*, *12*(4), 428–436.

Phillips, K. A. (2005). *The broken mirror: Understanding and treating body dysmorphic disorder*. Oxford University Press.

Phillips, K. (2017). *Body dysmorphic disorder: Advances in research and clinical practice*. Oxford University Press.

Phillips, K. A., Hart, A. S., & Menard, W. (2014). Psychometric evaluation of the Yale-Brown Obsessive-Compulsive Scale Modified for Body Dysmorphic Disorder (BDD-YBOCS). *Journal of Obsessive-Compulsive and Related Disorders*, *3*(3), 205–208.

Phillips, K. A., Hollander, E., Rasmussen, S. A., Aronowitz, B. R., DeCaria, R., & Goodman, W. K. (1997). A severity rating scale for body dysmorphic disorder: Development, reliability, and validity of a modified version of the Yale-Brown Obsessive-Compulsive Scale. *Psychopharmacology Bulletin*, *33*(1), 17.

Phillips, K. A., Wilhelm, S., Koran, L. M., Didie, E. R., Fallon, B. A., Feusner, J., & Stein, D. J. (2010). Body dysmorphic disorder: Some key issues for DSM-V. *Depression and Anxiety*, *27*(6), 573–591.

Ruffolo, J. S., Phillips, K. A., Menard, W., Fay, C., & Weisberg, R. B. (2006). Comorbidity of body dysmorphic disorder and eating disorders: Severity of psychopathology and body image disturbance. *International Journal of Eating Disorders*, *39*(1), 11–19.

Tolin, D. F., Gilliam, C., Wootton, B. M., Bowe, W., Bragdon, L. B., Davis, E., Hannan, S. E., Steinman, S. A., Worden, B., & Hallion, L. S. (2018). Psychometric properties of a structured diagnostic interview for DSM-5 anxiety, mood, and obsessive-compulsive and related disorders. *Assessment*, *25*(1), 3–13.

Veale, D. (2002). Over-valued ideas: A conceptual analysis. *Behaviour Research and Therapy*, *40*(4), 383–400.

Veale, D. (2004). Advances in a cognitive behavioural model of body dysmorphic disorder. *Body Image, 1*(1), 113–125. doi:10.1016/S1740-1445(03)00009-3

Veale, D., Ellison, N., Werner, T. G., Dodhia, R., Serfaty, M. A., & Clarke, A. (2012). Development of a cosmetic procedure screening questionnaire (COPS) for body dysmorphic disorder. *Journal of Plastic, Reconstructive & Aesthetic Surgery, 65*(4), 530–532.

Veale, D., Ennis, M., & Lambrou, C. (2002). Possible association of body dysmorphic disorder with an occupation or education in art and design. *American Journal of Psychiatry, 159*(10), 1788–1790.

Veale, D., Eshkevari, E., Kanakam, N., Ellison, N., Costa, A., & Werner, T. (2014). The Appearance Anxiety Inventory: Validation of a process measure in the treatment of body dysmorphic disorder. *Behavioural and Cognitive Psychotherapy, 42*(5), 605–616. doi:10.1017/S1352465813000556

Veale, D., Gledhill, L. J., Christodoulou, P., & Hodsoll, J. (2016). Body dysmorphic disorder in different settings: A systematic review and estimated weighted prevalence. *Body Image, 18*, 168–186.

Veale, D., & Matsunaga, H. (2014). Body dysmorphic disorder and olfactory reference disorder: Proposals for ICD-11. *Revista Brasileira de Psiquiatria, 36*, 14–20.

Veale, D., & Neziroglu, F. (2010). *Body dysmorphic disorder: A treatment manual*. John Wiley & Sons.

Wilhelm, S., Greenberg, J. L., Rosenfield, E., Kasarskis, I., & Blashill, A. J. (2016). The Body Dysmorphic Disorder Symptom Scale: Development and preliminary validation of a self-report scale of symptom specific dysfunction. *Body Image, 17*, 82–87.

Wilhelm, S., & Neziroglu, F. (2002). Cognitive theory of body dysmorphic disorder. In R. O. Frost & G. Steketee (Eds.), *Cognitive approaches to obsessions and compulsions* (pp. 203–214). Elsevier.

Windheim, K., Veale, D., & Anson, M. (2011). Mirror gazing in body dysmorphic disorder and healthy controls: Effects of duration of gazing. *Behaviour Research and Therapy, 49*(9), 555–564.

CHAPTER 14

Assessing Hoarding Disorder

Jordana Muroff

Abstract

Over the past 25 years, assessments of hoarding have evolved substantially. This chapter provides a comprehensive review of hoarding-specific measures of core diagnostic features (e.g., difficulty discarding, clutter, distress), associated cognitive and behavioral symptoms (e.g., beliefs about saving, attachment, acquisition), the living environment (e.g., clutter, risks, presence of squalor), and the impact on individual and family functioning (e.g., activities of daily living, family accommodation). Hoarding-specific assessments are multimodal and include clinician interviews, self-reports from clinical and nonclinical populations, family reports, practitioner reports, and behavioral tasks (e.g., discarding, categorization). This chapter examines the characteristics and psychometric properties of hoarding-specific assessments. It concludes with a discussion of considerations and directions for future research on the assessment of hoarding, including technology-based innovations.

Key Words: hoarding, assessment, measure, clutter, saving, acquisition, distress, home, Saving Inventory–Revised, Hoarding Rating Scale

Introduction

The assessment of hoarding disorder (HD) has evolved greatly since the late 1990s as the understanding of this complex and multifaceted disorder has advanced. Initially, hoarding was conceptualized as a subtype of obsessive-compulsive disorder (OCD; Frost et al., 2012), so earlier research on hoarding focused on patients with OCD, and accordingly individual items and subscales for assessing hoarding were embedded in OCD measures. Several concerns were raised regarding the reliance on hoarding items in OCD measures (for example, the Yale-Brown Obsessive-Compulsive Scale [Y-BOCS]), such as not adequately differentiating those with hoarding from nonhoarding community members (Frost et al., 1996). Now, though, HD has been identified as a distinct disorder in the fifth edition of the *Diagnostic and Statistical Manual of Mental Disorders* (*DSM-5*; American Psychiatric Association, 2013). Hoarding-specific assessments have been developed and the number and types of measures have expanded to include diagnostic and clinical tools, community assessments, and behavioral measures. The measures are administered in varying formats (e.g., semi-structured interview, self-report) and in distinct domains (e.g., clinic, home), and they are completed by various respondents (e.g., individuals with HD, family members, observers, practitioners). This chapter reviews a breadth of hoarding-specific assessments, including those that focus on the diagnostic criteria, specific features (e.g., acquisition, attachment), manifestations of hoarding, and the home environment, as well as behavioral measures. The strengths and limitations of the current hoarding assessments are discussed, and innovations in hoarding assessments as well as future directions are considered. Table 14.1 provides a summary of hoarding-specific assessments as well as supplemental information.

Review of Hoarding-Specific Assessments

Diagnostic and Interview-Based Assessments

Given the complexity of HD, its diagnostic assessment necessitates a comprehensive interview focused on core criteria, to be conducted in the person's living environment if possible. A detailed evaluation of a person's hoarding behavior is crucial to determine if it is due to HD or another psychological or neurological condition.

The Structured Interview for Hoarding Disorder (SIHD; Nordsletten et al., 2013) is a semi-structured diagnostic interview for HD conducted by a clinician or trained interviewer. The SIHD questions address the specific *DSM-5* criteria for HD, assessing each diagnostic criterion as well as the specifiers. It also includes a risk assessment as well as an appendix to assist clinicians with differential diagnosis (e.g., OCD, autism spectrum disorder; SIHD 2.0). It is recommended that the interview be conducted in the client's home environment for a more accurate examination of hoarding features as well as a risk assessment. SIHD has been utilized in the London Field Trial for HD (Mataix-Cols et al., 2013) as well as the South East London Community Health (SELCoH) study (Nordsletten et al., 2013), which included 99 individuals with HD. SIHD has demonstrated high sensitivity (.98) and specificity (1), discriminating between clinical levels of HD and other related behavior such as subthreshold HD, collecting, and OCD-specific hoarding (Mataix-Cols et al., 2013). Interrater reliability was "near perfect" (κ = .87) for the "core HD criteria and specifiers" (range 93.94%–100%). Excellent convergent and discriminant validity (major depression, rate of agreement 64%–67%) also has been demonstrated. The SIHD is recommended for application in research and clinical settings.

While not exclusive to HD, the Diagnostic Interview for Anxiety, Mood, and Obsessive-Compulsive and Related Neuropsychiatric Disorders (DIAMOND; Tolin, Gilliam, Wootton, et al., 2018) is a semi-structured interview that assesses *DSM-5* diagnostic criteria for many psychiatric disorders, including HD. The DIAMOND HD diagnosis has been shown to have very good psychometric properties. The interrater reliability for HD was excellent, with a κ coefficient of .86, 95% CI [0.75–0.98] (with *SE* ≤ 0.1 and 95% CI ≤ 0.5), t = 9.53, p < .001. The test–retest reliability (presence vs. absence) was

Table 14.1. Summary of Hoarding-Specific Assessments

Measure	Number of items; subscales	Item Ratings	Score Range	Cutoffs	(Clinical) Means (M) and Standard Deviation (SD)	Location and Participants
Structured Interview for Hoarding Disorder (SIHD; Nordsletten et al., 2013)	Six HD diagnostic criteria, two specifiers, risk assessment, appendix: differential diagnosis assistant			For an HD diagnosis, all six criteria need to be endorsed		England: 99 individuals with self-reported hoarding behavior.
DIAMOND (Tolin Gilliam, Wootton et al., 2018)	Semi-structured diagnostic interview for *DSM-5* psychiatric disorders including hoarding disorder					United States: 362 outpatients; 121 provided data for interreliability and 115 for test–retest reliability.
UCLA Hoarding Severity Scale (UHSS; Saxena et al., 2015)	Ten items	0 (None or Not at all) to 4 (All or Extreme)	0–40		$M = 25.47$ ($SD = 4.77$)	United States: Adult participants in four separate studies were pooled for analysis— 62 patients with HD and 65 nonclinical controls.
Hoarding Rating Scale-Interview (HRS-I; Tolin, Frost, & Steketee, 2010)	Five items	0 (None/not at all) to 8 (Extreme)	0–40	Total = 14 Item 1 (clutter) = 3 Item 2 (difficulty discarding) = 4 Item 3 (acquiring) = 2 Item 4 (distress) = 3 Item 5 (impairment) = 3	$M = 24.22$ ($SD = 5.67$)	United States: Clinic and newspaper advertisement— 136 adults (age 18+), 73 with compulsive hoarding, 19 with OCD and no hoarding, and 44 nonclinical controls.

(continued)

Table 14.1. Continued

Measure	Number of items; subscales	Item Ratings	Score Range	Cutoffs	(Clinical) Means (M) and Standard Deviation (SD)	Location and Participants
HRS-I Self-report version (HRS-SR; Tolin et al., 2008)	Five items	0 (None) to 8 (Extreme)	0–40	Moderate (4) or greater clutter and difficulty discarding, as well as either moderate (4) or greater distress or impairment caused by hoarding	Self-identified hoarding, M = 6.32 (SD = 1.00) Hoarding family member, M = 6.72 (SD = 0.95)	United States: 864 adults who self-identified with hoarding, 65% met research criteria for clinically relevant compulsive hoarding; 665 adults age 18+ who identified themselves as nonhoarding friends or family members of individuals with hoarding problems (they rated their hoarding family members' behaviors).
Hoarding Scale (HS; Frost & Gross, 1993)	21 items	1 (Strongly disagree) to 5 (Strongly agree)	21–105		M = 78.1 (SD = 10.9)	United States: 32 adults (age 17+) with hoarding.
Hoarding Scale (HS; Frost et al., 1998)	24 items	1 (Strongly disagree) to 5 (Strongly agree)			Those with hoarding, M = 87.6 (SD = 14.2) Those without hoarding, M = 8.1 (SD = 13.0)	Study 1: 161 female college students. Study 2: 14 self-identified with hoarding from a self-help group for people with clutter problems; 13 nonhoarding, nonfaculty employee participants.
Saving Inventory–Revised (SI-R; Frost et al., 2004)	23 items with three subscales: Acquisition, Difficulty discarding, Clutter	0 (No problem) to 4 (Very severe, extreme)	Total: 0–92, Clutter: 0–36 Difficulty discarding: 0–28 Acquisition: 0–28	Total: 41 Clutter: 17 Difficulty discarding: 14 Acquisition: 9	Study 2: SI-R Total, M = 53.7 (SD = 14.9) Difficulty discarding, M = 18.5 (SD = 4.9); Clutter, M = 20.9 (SD = 7.3); Acquisition, M = 14.3 (SD = 5.6) Study 3: Hoarding participants, M = 62.0 (SD = 12.7); Community controls, M = 23.7 (SD = 13.2) Study 4: Hoarding elders, M = 44.6 (SD = 10.1); Nonhoarding elders, M = 13.3 (SD = 7.2)	United States Four studies: Study 1 had 139 participants who suffer from compulsive hoarding. Study 2 had 32 self-identified hoarding participants and 26 with OCD but no hoarding. Study 3 had 70 people with hoarding problems and 23 community controls. Study 4 had 25 elderly participants (12 with no hoarding; 13 with serious clutter).

Saving Inventory–Revised (SI-R; Kellman-McFarlane et al., 2019)			Optimal cutoff score of 39, but data suggested that significantly lower cutoffs (SI-R ≥ 33) be used when assessing adults over the age of 60, while higher cutoffs (SI-R ≥ 43) be used when assessing adults younger than 40.	Hoarding sample Total, $M = 59.17$ ($SD = 13.56$) Nonhoarding sample Total, $M = 21.57$ ($SD = 18.22$)	Archival data from 1,116 participants diagnosed with a clinical interview in 14 studies; 541 diagnosed with HD; 127 diagnosed with primary OCD; 43 diagnosed with another Axis I disorder; 86 subclinical hoarding; 319 healthy community controls.
Hoarding Assessment Scale (HAS; Shytle & Sheehan, 2004; Schneider et al., 2008)	Four items	0 (Not at all), 1, 2, 3 (A little), 4, 5, 6 (Moderately) 7, 8, 9 (Markedly), 10 (Extremely)	0–40, higher scores reflecting more severity		$M = 13.8$ ($SD = 8.3$)	United States: 268 college students.
Hoarding Disorder-Dimensional Scale (HD-D; LeBeau et al., 2013)	Five items	0 (None) to 4 (Extreme)	0–20, higher scores indicating greater hoarding severity		$M = 2.0$ ($SD = 2.4$)	United States: 296 undergraduate students age 18+, nonclinical sample.
Obsessive-Compulsive Inventory–Revised (OCI-R; Foa et al., 2002; Wootton et al., 2015)	OCI-HD: three items	0 (Not at all) to 4 (Extremely)	0–12	Cutoff score of 12	HD, $M = 9.29$ ($SD = 2.45$); OCD, $M = 1.89$ ($SD = 2.59$); Community controls, $M = 1.32$ ($SD = 2.16$)	United States: 474 individuals (118 with OCD, 201 with HD, 155 community controls with no current or past psychiatric disorders).

(continued)

Table 14.1. Continued

Measure	Number of items; subscales	Item Ratings	Score Range	Cutoffs	(Clinical) Means (*M*) and Standard Deviation (*SD*)	Location and Participants
Children's Saving Inventory (CSI; Storch et al., 2011)	20 items with four subscales: Discarding, Clutter, Acquisition, Distress/impairment	0–4	0–80, higher scores indicate more severity		CSI Total Score: Those with hoarding compulsions: *M* = 44.7 (*SD* = 17.7) Those without hoarding compulsions: *M* = 17.9 (*SD* = 12.1) Those with hoarding obsessions: *M* = 37.1 (*SD* = 19.5) Those without hoarding obsessions: *M* = 19.4 (*SD* = 14.5)	United States: 123 youth (age 8–17 years) diagnosed with OCD and their parents at one of two OCD specialty clinical research centers.
Children's Saving Inventory, 15-item version (CSI-15; Soreni et al., 2018)	15 items with three subscales: Difficulty discarding, Clutter, Distress/impairment	0–4	0–60		The mean CSI-15 score: Those endorsing hoarding obsessions, *M* = 19.12 (*SD* = 13.81); Those without hoarding obsessions, *M* = 9.80 (*SD* = 8.28); Those with hoarding compulsions, *M* = 20.97 (*SD* = 13.00); Those without hoarding compulsions, *M* = 10.31 (*SD* = 9.34)	Canada: 191 youth with a principal OCD diagnosis (*DSM-IV-TR*) at a specialty anxiety clinic.
Compulsive Acquisition Scale (CAS; Frost et al., 2002)	18 items with two subscales: CAS-Buy (12 items); CAS-Free (6 items)	1 (Not at all or rarely) to 7 (Very much or very often)	18–126	CAS cutoff, 47.8; CAS-Buy cutoff, 41; CAS-Free cutoff, 23	Compulsive buyers: CAS-Buy, *M* = 61.4 (*SD* = 12.3); CAS-Free, *M* = 24.2 (*SD* = 9.1)	United States: 160 adults, 75 with compulsive buying and 85 controls.

Clutter Image Rating (CIR; Frost et al., 2008)	Three rooms: a living room, bedroom, and kitchen	1 (No clutter) to 9 (Severe clutter)	1–9 Mean composite score for three rooms	Rating of 4 or greater indicates a clinically significant level of clutter	Study 1: Bedroom, $M = 3.49$ ($SD = 1.7$); Living room, $M = 3.21$ ($SD = 1.7$); Kitchen, $M = 2.89$ ($SD = 1.2$) Study 2: Bedroom, $M = 4.34$ ($SD = 2.16$); Living room, $M = 3.87$ ($SD = 2.24$); Kitchen, $M = 3.79$ ($SD = 2.01$) Composite: $M = 4.01$ ($SD = 1.80$)	United States Study 1: 46 people attending a workshop on hoarding and clutter. Study 2: 75 adults with a rating of a 4 or more on HRS clutter or difficulty discarding.
Clutter Hoarding Scale (NSGCD, 2003)	Five levels and four problem areas (i.e., structure and zoning, pets and rodents, household functions, sanitation and cleanliness)		Level I (Low) to Level V (High)	Homes determined to be Level III and higher necessitate assistance to address the hoarding		
HOMES Multidisciplinary Risk Assessment (Bratiotis, 2009, Bratiotis et al., 2011)	Health, obstacles, mental health, endangerment, structure & safety		A specific scoring procedure has not been published			
Environmental Cleanliness and Clutter Scale (ECCS; Halliday & Snowdon, 2009)	Ten items	0–3 with specific anchor points and higher scores indicating more severe conditions	0–30	Scores that exceed 12 typically indicate moderate or severe squalor	NA	Australia: 45 homes, 55 people (some lived together) who were referred to the authors' old age psychiatry team, and whose homes had been reported by referrers to be unclean and/or cluttered to some degree.
Home Environment Index (HEI; Rasmussen et al., 2014)	15 items	0 (No presence of squalor) to 3 (Severe symptoms)	0–45	Cutoff scores have not been determined	$M = 12.96$ ($SD = 6.86$)	United States: 793 adults who self-identified as having hoarding problems (HRS mean 28.30; 7.87).

(*continued*)

Table 14.1. Continued

Measure	Number of items; subscales	Item Ratings	Score Range	Cutoffs	(Clinical) Means (M) and Standard Deviation (SD)	Location and Participants
Activities of Daily Living–Hoarding (ADL-H; Frost et al., 2013)	15 items	1 (None— Can do it easily), 2 (Can do it with little difficulty), 3 (Can do it with moderate difficulty), 4 (Can do it with great difficulty), 5 (Severe— Unable to do), or Not applicable (NA) option			Hoarding no OCD, $M = 2.20$ ($SD = .74$) Hoarding + OCD, $M = 1.95$ ($SD = .75$) OCD, $M = 1.19$ ($SD = .37$) Community controls, $M = 1.15$ ($SD = .75$)	United States: Study 1: 363 adults (18+ years) with "serious hoarding" according to *DSM-5* criteria. Study 2: 165 with clinical levels of hoarding but not OCD, 37 with clinical levels of hoarding and comorbid OCD, 94 with OCD but not hoarding, and 130 community controls.
Family Response to Hoarding Scale (FRHS; Steketee & Frost, 2013; Steketee et al., 2013)	16 items with two subscales: Behavior change and Personal consequences	1-4 (Four indicated greater family accommodation)			Total, $M = 15$ ($SD = 10.4$) Behavior change, $M = 6$ ($SD = 5.9$) Consequences, $M = 6.9$ ($SD = 4.2$)	
Family Impact Scale for Hoarding (FISH; Nordsletten et al., 2014)	17 closed-response items, two subscales: Accommodation and Burden; plus two open-response questions regarding the impact of family member's hoarding	17 closed responses ranging from 0 (Strongly disagree) to 3 (Strongly agree)	0–45		Relatives of those with hoarding: $M = 20.78$; 95% CI [19.16–22] Accommodation: $M = 8.41$; 95% CI [7.62 9.21] Burden: $M = 12.37$; 95% CI [11.16–13.59]	England: 134 self-identified family members of those with hoarding behaviors ($n = 102$) and collectors ($n = 32$)

Family Accommodation Interview for Hoarding (FAI-H; Vorstenbosch et al., 2015)	11 items with two subscales: Frequency and Distress/interference	0 (not at all) to 4 (extreme)	Total: 0–80 Frequency subscale: 0–40 Distress/interference subscale: 0–40	Total, $M = 22.58$ ($SD = 15.98$) Frequency subscale, $M = 11.60$ ($SD = 7.34$) Distress/interference subscale, $M = 10.98$ ($SD = 9.13$)	Canada: 52 dyads, each with one participant with self-reported hoarding behaviors (HRS-SR > 14) and a close significant other (CSO) without clinical hoarding, 18 to 75 years old.
Saving Cognitions Inventory (SCI; Steketee et al., 2003)	24 items with four subscales: Attachment, Responsibility, Need for control, Memory	1 (Not at all) to 7 (Very much)	24–168	Hoarding Group SCI Total, $M = 103.98$ ($SD = 26.64$); Attachment, $M = 39.97$ ($SD = 14.63$); Memory, $M = 23.50$ ($SD = 6.16$); Control, $M = 16.27$ ($SD = 4.29$); Responsibility, $M = 24.70$ ($SD = 7.95$)	United States: 95 individuals with compulsive hoarding, 21 with symptoms of OCD but not hoarding, and 40 community controls.
Beliefs about Hoarding Questionnaire (BAH; Gordon et al., 2013)	28 items with three subscales: Hoarding motivated by harm avoidance/responsibility for harm; Hoarding motivated by previous experience of material deprivation; Hoarding related to attachment disturbance	0 (I did not believe this at all) to 100 (I was completely convinced this item was true)		Hoarding with no OCD: Harm avoidance, $M = 20.8$ ($SD = 13.5$) Material deprivation, $M = 47.1$ ($SD = 19.6$) Attachment disturbance, $M = 39.4$ ($SD = 17.1$) Hoarding with OCD: Harm avoidance, $M = 31.2$ ($SD = 20.1$) Material deprivation, $M = 55.6$ ($SD = 25.6$) Attachment disturbance, $M = 39.4$ ($SD = 24.0$)	$N = 88$. Four subgroups: hoarding with OCD ($n = 21$), hoarding without OCD (pure hoarding; $n = 24$), OCD without hoarding ($n = 22$), and a non-clinical control group ($n = 21$); recruited from nonclinical settings including support groups.

(continued)

Table 14.1. Continued

Measure	Number of items; subscales	Item Ratings	Score Range	Cutoffs	(Clinical) Means (M) and Standard Deviation (SD)	Location and Participants
Object Attachment Questionnaire (OAQ; Grisham et al., 2009)	13 items	1 (Not at all/strongly disagree) to 7 (Very much/strongly agree)			$M = 30.68$ ($SD = 15.56$)	62 OCD conference attendees, 54 with diagnosed OCD, four with self-diagnosed OCD behaviors but were not self-diagnosed. Thirty-five participants (57%) reported that hoarding was one of their symptoms, 26 did not endorse any hoarding symptoms, and one was unsure whether had hoarding symptoms.
Relationship between Self and Items (RSI) Scale (Dozier et al., 2017)	One item	Seven-step interval-level pictorial scale based on the Venn diagrams	1–7		Participants with HD, $M = 4.68$ ($SD = 1.91$) Community controls, $M = 2.9$ ($SD = 1.2$)	United States: 84 adults who met *DSM-5* criteria for HD, 30 community controls.
Acceptance and Action Questionnaire for Hoarding (AAQH; Krafft et al. 2019)	14 items with two subscales: Saving and Acquisition	1 (Never true) to 7 (Always true)	14–98		AAQH total score, $M = 45.17$ ($SD = 13.49$) AAQH-Saving, $M = 26.60$ ($SD = 8.31$) AAQH-Acquisition, $M = 18.56$ ($SD = 6.96$)	United States: Nonclinical sample of 201 undergraduate students with levels of hoarding above SI-R mean score.

also excellent for HD, with a κ coefficient of .94 (95% CI [0.87–1.02], $t = 10.12$, $p < .001$). Effect size estimates were very large. The DIAMOND HD diagnosis has also been shown to have very good convergent validity. Self-report scores on the Saving Inventory–Revised (SI-R; Frost et al., 2004), were 58.76 ($SD = 15.38$) for those diagnosed with HD and 12.85 (SD=12.37) for those without an HD diagnosis; between-group differences were statistically significant ($t = 14.64$, $p < .001$). The effect sizes for HD were very large ($d = 3.29$).

In addition to these diagnostic interviews, several other interview-based measures exist that are similar but distinct from each other. The UCLA Hoarding Severity Scale (UHSS; Saxena et al., 2015) is a clinician-administered semi-structured interview that includes ten items assessing the following symptoms over the week before the interview: clutter severity, clutter-related embarrassment, urges to save items, excessive acquisition, difficulty discarding, social and occupational impairment, slowing, perfectionism, indecisiveness, and procrastination. Each item is scored 0 (None or Not at all) to 4 (All or Extreme), with a maximum score of 40. The UHSS has demonstrated good internal consistency, with a Cronbach's $\alpha = .70$; construct validity, with inter-item correlations ranging from 0.66 to 0.76 ($p < .05$); and known groups discriminant validity between those with HD and a control group ($F = 1141.34$, $p < .001$). The UHSS showed convergent validity, with significant correlations with the SI-R self-report scale ($r = .585$, $p < .001$), as well. It is sensitive to clinical changes in hoarding symptom severity due to pharmacotherapy (Saxena et al., 2007; Saxena & Sumner, 2014) and cognitive-behavioral treatment (Ayers et al., 2014). Home-based assessments to determine clutter were not conducted and therefore were not included in analyses to examine the UHSS. A revised version (UHSS-II) includes updated HD diagnostic criteria, as well as "objective, quantifiable anchor points for ratings" (Saxena et al., 2015, p. 489).

The Hoarding Rating Scale–Interview (HRS-I; Tolin, Frost, & Steketee, 2010) is a brief semi-structured interview that assesses the presence and severity of the main diagnostic dimensions of HD, including difficulty discarding possessions, excessive acquisition of items, difficulty using space in the home environment due to clutter, and emotional distress as well as functional impairment because of hoarding behavior. Follow-up probes are permitted. The five HRS-I items are each rated from 0 (None/not at all) to 8 (Extreme). Scores are calculated by summing the five items and range from 0 to 40. The HRS-I has demonstrated high internal consistency and inter-item correlations in the clinic ($\alpha = 0.97$, $r = 0.77$–0.91) and home ($\alpha = 0.96$, $r_s = 0.76$–0.96). The test–retest reliability across time (1–12 weeks) and context (clinic versus home) were high (total score: 0.96; corresponding items: 0.85–0.94). Results from a receiver operating characteristic (ROC) analysis demonstrated that HRS-I differentiated participants with hoarding from those with OCD (Tolin, Fitch, et al., 2010). The researchers also found that the optimal cutoff was 14 (sensitivity = 0.97 and specificity = 0.97) for the HRS-I sum total, the cutoff was 3 for item 1 (clutter; sensitivity = 0.97, specificity = 0.97), item 4 (distress; sensitivity = 0.93

and specificity = 0.97), and item 5 (impairment; sensitivity = 0.96 and specificity = 0.95), the cutoff was 4 (sensitivity = 0.92 and specificity = 0.93) for item 2 (difficulty discarding), and the cutoff was 2 (sensitivity = 0.93 and specificity = 0.80) for item 3 (acquiring). The HRS-I was highly correlated with other hoarding measures in the home and clinic (e.g., SI-R: r = .91 [clinic], r = .94 [home]; Clutter Image Rating [CIR] (participant): r = .72 [clinic], r = .78 [home]). HRS-I items (e.g., clutter) and corresponding SI-R subscales (SI-R clutter) showed strong correlations, while HRS-I items had low correlations with the other (noncorresponding) SI-R subscales as well as OCD checking, neutralizing, obsessing, and washing subscales, demonstrating discriminant validity. The HRS-I has also been shown to detect cognitive-behavioral therapy (CBT) effects (Steketee et al. 2010). Additionally, within a sample of youth diagnosed with OCD, HRS-I has been demonstrated to have excellent internal consistency and to differentiate between those with and without hoarding (Park et al., 2016).

In a more recent validation study of the HRS-I (Tolin, Gilliam, Davis, et al., 2018), a couple of modifications were made to address some limitations regarding reliability from the initial validation study. Additional detail was added to the scale anchor descriptions, and follow-up questions were added to the five core HRS-I questions. To address group validity concerns from the initial validation study due to the reliance on the HRS-I to identify those with hoarding, the DIAMOND was utilized to assess participants and to determine if they met *DSM-5* diagnostic criteria for HD. Participants were treatment-seeking individuals. The HRS-I demonstrated excellent internal consistency (α = 0.87). Interrater reliability was adequate for each HRS-I item (intraclass coefficient [ICC] = 0.71–0.91) and was good for HRS-I total (ICC = 0.81). Test–retest reliability was adequate for each HRS-I item (ICC = 0.72–0.94) and was good for HRS-I total (ICC = 0.85). HRS-I scores were significantly higher for participants with HD than for healthy controls; the effect sizes were large (d = 1.28–6.58). Regarding convergent validity, the HRS-I and self-report SI-R correlated strongly with each other (range = 0.74–0.94). Partial correlations also demonstrated that the HRS-I items were at least moderately and significantly correlated with the matching SI-R subscale (e.g., HRS-I clutter item with the SI-R clutter subscale), even when controlling for other SI-R subscales (ICC = 0.81 to 0.94). Significant associations were found between the HRS-I distress item and negative affect assessed by the Depression, Anxiety, Stress Scale as well as between the HRS-I impairment item and impairment in emotional role functioning (on the Short Form Health Survey [SF-36]). The sensitivity (1.0) and specificity (1.0) for differentiating those with HD from healthy controls was excellent, as shown by ROC analysis. When the 2018 study was compared to the initial validation 2010 study, in the 2018 study participants with HD showed significantly higher scores and healthy controls reported significantly lower scores, which contributed to the lower optimal cutoff score of 11 (versus 14 in the 2010 study).

These studies examining the psychometric properties of the HRS-I confirm its utility for use both clinically and for research. The HRS-I was also adapted into a self-report version (HRS-SR; Tolin et al., 2008). The HRS-SR has demonstrated very good internal consistency (Cronbach's α = 0.83). The HRS-I and HRS-SR also have been shown to be strongly correlated (r_s = .74–.92), with "73% agreement of diagnostic status between self- and interviewer-report" (p. 337). A number of studies have adapted and tested the HRS in languages other than English, including Chinese (Liu et al., 2020), Italian (Faraci et al., 2019), and Japanese (Tsuchiyagaito et al., 2017), showing good psychometric properties.

Self-Report Hoarding Measures

The following self-report measures do not serve as formal diagnostic measures; however, they serve as practical, reliable, and valid assessments that indicate the likelihood that an individual has clinically significant hoarding challenges (Norsdletten et al., 2013).

The Hoarding Scale (HS) was an initial self-report measure of hoarding based on the Frost and Gross (1993) definition of hoarding as "the acquisition of, and failure to discard, possessions that appear to be useless or of limited value" (p. 367). One version included 21 items (Frost & Gross, 1993) and another included 24 items (Frost et al., 1998) rated on a scale of 1 (Strongly disagree) to 5 (Strongly agree) to assess difficulty discarding, emotional reactions to discarding, challenges with discarding decisions, concerns about future need of discarded items, future use of saved items, and sentimental attachment to possessions. The HS was shown to have excellent internal reliability and validity (Frost & Gross, 1993; Frost et al., 1998, 2000, 2002). For example, the HS correlated with other hoarding manifestations (r = .31–.43, $p < .01$) and clutter (r = .68, $p < .01$) and differentiated between those with self-identified hoarding and those who do not hoard ($t(68)$ = 6.90, $p < 0.001$; Frost & Gross, 1993). However, the HS had a number of limitations because it did not adequately assess acquisition, distress, or impairment (Frost et al., 2004; Steketee & Frost, 2003). To address this, the HS evolved into the Saving Inventory–Revised, which includes acquisition as a construct.

The Saving Inventory–Revised (SI-R; Frost et al., 2004) is a self-report questionnaire that includes 23 items constituting three subscales: Acquisition, Difficulty discarding, and Clutter. Each item is rated on a scale of 0 (No problem) to 4 (Very severe, Extreme), with scores ranging from 0 to 92, higher scores indicating more severe symptoms. The SI-R total score and subscales have been shown to have good test–retest reliability (e.g., SI-R total: 0.86; subscales: 0.78–0.90), internal consistency (SI-R total: 0.94; subscales: 0.80–0.93), construct validity (SI-R total: r = 0.54, $p < 0.001$; Discarding: r = 0.36, $p < .05$; Clutter r = 0.5, $p < .001$; Acquisition: r = .023, NS), and discriminant validity (e.g., low correlations with positive affect). The SI-R is able to differentiate those with hoarding, those with OCD without hoarding, and community controls (Frost et al., 2004). The SI-R is also able to detect symptom changes associated with individual and group CBT (Muroff et al., 2012; Steketee et al., 2010) and peer-based bibliotherapy support groups (Frost et al., 2011, 2012). Ayers and colleagues demonstrated that the SI-R is a clinically valid and reliable assessment for hoarding among older adults, although they cautioned about the use of the SI-R subscales due to the poor fit of the three-factor model (Ayers et al., 2017).

Earlier studies established the cutoff score for the SI-R total score as 41, with subscale cutoff scores of 17 for Clutter, 14 for Difficulty discarding, and 9 for Acquisition (Tolin et al., 2011). A more recent study examined clinical, subclinical, and control participants ($N = 1,116$) across 14 studies to examine the SI-R's psychometrics across the life span (Kellman-McFarlane et al., 2019). Internal consistency was high ($\alpha = 0.93$). The SI-R demonstrated strong convergent validity with other hoarding symptom measures (HRS: $r = 0.90$, CIR: $r = .74$; Saving Cognitions Inventory [SCI]: $r = 0.78$) and discriminant validity with symptoms of anxiety ($r = 0.29$) and depression ($r = 0.33$). The sample was also stratified by age groups (e.g., younger than 40, 40 to 60 years old, over 60). Using ROC analyses, an optimal cutoff score of 39 was found, identifying 93% of those who received an HD diagnosis, although there were also 19% false positives. Data suggested that significantly lower cutoffs (SI-R ≥ 33) should be used when assessing adults over the age of 60, while higher cutoffs (SI-R ≥ 43) should be utilized when assessing adults younger than 40. This study suggests the need to consider changes in hoarding symptoms over the life span and to consider age with the use of clinical cutoffs.

The SI-R has been translated and validated in multiple non-English languages, including Spanish (Tortella-Feliu et al., 2006), Portuguese (Fontenelle et al., 2010), Italian (Melli et al., 2013), German (Mueller et al., 2009), and Farsi (Mohammadzadeh, 2009). Additionally, a 21-item SI-R was shown to have good convergent and discriminant validity among a large sample of Chinese participants from a psychiatric outpatient hospital in Singapore; over 70% were Chinese and all completed the study in English. Some studies suggest that the factor structure of the SI-R may be different among non-U.S. populations, such as the Chinese population (Lee et al., 2016; Tang et al. 2012, Timpano et al. 2015). Constructs related to self-control and difficulty discarding may differ between Asian and U.S. populations and cultures (Lee et al., 2016). More research is needed to examine the SI-R hoarding-related constructs and assessments across varying cultures and languages.

The Hoarding Assessment Scale (HAS; Shytle & Sheehan, 2004) assesses hoarding severity over the past week through four self-rated hoarding symptom items: Difficulty throwing away, Clutter, Urges of acquisition, and Interference/distress. Each is rated using a scale 0 (Not at all), 1, 2, 3 (A little), 4, 5, 6 (Moderately), 7, 8, 9 (Markedly), 10 (Extremely). Total scores are calculated by summing all items, with higher scores reflecting more severity. In a study examining the HAS psychometrics in a college student sample (Schneider et al., 2008), the scale demonstrated an acceptable internal consistency ($\alpha = .725$). The HAS total score and SI-R total score were significantly correlated ($r = .628$, $p < .001$), although the correlations were smaller than those found between the Hoarding Rating Scale (HRS) and SI-R (Frost & Hristova, 2011).

The *DSM-5* Obsessive-Compulsive Spectrum Disorders Subgroup developed the Hoarding Disorder-Dimensional Scale (HD-D; LeBeau et al., 2013), a newer measure of hoarding severity. The five items include the *DSM-5* dimensions of HD, including difficulty discarding, clutter, avoidance, distress, and interference. The HD-D does not include an item for excessive acquisition. Each item is self-rated on a scale of 0 (None) to 4 (Extreme), with total scores ranging from 0 to 20 and higher scores indicating greater hoarding severity. An initial study examining the psychometrics of the HD-D among college students found a single-factor structure with 60% of the variance accounted for, high internal consistency ($\alpha = 0.82$), excellent convergent validity with the HRS ($r_s = 0.75$), and good divergent validity ($r = 0.23$) with the Yale-Brown Obsessive-Compulsive Scale for Body Dysmorphic Disorder (BDD-YBOCS; LeBeau et al., 2013; Phillips et al., 1997). A study with a small sample of participants with self-identified hoarding challenges also reported a single-factor structure (accounting for 82% of the variance), high internal consistency ($\alpha = 0.95$), and excellent convergent validity ($r = 0.89$) with the HRS self-report scale (HRS-SR; Mataix-Cols et al., 2013). A recent community study (Carey et al., 2019) also found a single-factor structure (accounting for 66% of the variance), high internal consistency ($\alpha = 0.87$–0.88) as well as strong test–retest reliability over two weeks ($r = 0.84$, $p < .001$). The HD-D showed good convergent validity, with strong correlations with HRS-SR ($r = 0.85$, $p < .01$) and good discriminant validity with low correlations with depression (PHQ-9: $r = 0.44$, $p < .01$) and anxiety (GAD-7: $r = 0.40$, $p < .01$). The HD-D also demonstrated good convergent validity between the Internet and paper-pencil versions ($r = 0.88$). Future studies may examine the psychometric properties of the HD-D with large clinical samples.

This chapter mainly focuses on the psychometrics of hoarding-specific measures, given the limitations of OCD measures with hoarding items to adequately assess hoarding and HD's becoming a distinct *DSM-5* disorder; however, more recent work examining the self-report OCD measure—Obsessive-Compulsive Inventory–Revised (OCI-R; Foa et al., 2002)—with a hoarding subscale shows promising results. The OCI-R is a commonly used self-report scale that assesses OCD and hoarding symptoms. The 18 items, rated on a 4-point scale (scores range 0 to 72), are divided into six subscales—three items comprise the hoarding subscale. While the OCI hoarding subscale has been criticized regarding the strength of its validity, such studies did not include large samples of individuals with clinical levels of hoarding. Given the *DSM-5* distinction between OCD and HD, Wootton and colleagues conducted a larger study ($N = 474$; 201 participants with primary HD, 118 with primary OCD, and 155 community controls) to examine the psychometrics of the OCI-R. They divided the measures into two subscales, the OCI-OCD (including five OCI subscales) and the OCI-HD, separating the OCD and hoarding dimensions (Wootton et al., 2015). The OCI-OCD includes 15 items, with scores ranging from 0 to 60, while the OCI-HD includes three items with scores ranging from 0 to 12. The OCI-HD demonstrated excellent convergent validity with other hoarding severity measures, including the SI-R ($r = .94$) and HRS ($r = .89$). The OCI-HD showed moderate correlations with anxiety ($r = .36$) showing discriminant validity, while the OCI-OCD was strongly correlated with anxiety ($r = .61$). The OCI-HD ($α = .94$) and OCI-OCD ($α = .92$) both showed excellent reliability across the HD, OCD, and community control groups and within each group, as well. In terms of diagnostic sensitivity, ROC analyses demonstrated good sensitivity and specificity of the OCI-OCD (cutoff score of 6) and OCI-HD (cutoff score of 12) subscales. The subscales were also shown to adequately differentiate the *DSM-5* diagnostic groups (such as HD and OCD) and community controls).

PARENT REPORT OF CHILD HOARDING

Although approximately 80% of individuals with hoarding experience the onset of symptoms before reaching 18 years of age (Grisham et al., 2006), there is limited research that focuses on youth with hoarding behavior. Research examining hoarding behavior among children and adolescents has mainly focused on clinical samples of youth with OCD who may also hoard. Consistent with hoarding assessments for adults, initial assessment of hoarding among youth was conducted by utilizing OCD measures that included a limited number of hoarding-related items or questions, such as the Children's Yale-Brown Obsessive-Compulsive Scale Symptom Checklist (Scahill et al., 1997), Children's Obsessional Compulsive Inventory (Shafran et al., 2003), and the Obsessive Compulsive Inventory (Foa et al., 2010). To address this, the Children's Saving Inventory (CSI; Storch et al., 2011) was developed based on the SI-R, as a parent/caregiver report of the child's hoarding behavior, including difficulty discarding, acquisition, and clutter subscales. The CSI's initial 23 items were reduced to 20 items rated from 0 to 4, with totals ranging from 0 to 80, with higher scores indicating more severe symptoms, similar to the SI-R.

The initial evaluation of the CSI's psychometric properties in youth with a primary diagnosis of OCD demonstrated validity and a factor structure that paralleled the SI-R. The CSI demonstrated strong internal consistency, with the total score $α = .96$ and subscales ranging from $α = .84$ to .95. Test–retest reliability was strong for the CSI total score ($r = .92$) and subscales ($r = .86–.96$) with $p < 0.001$. The CSI showed good convergent validity with the Obsessive-Compulsive Inventory-Child Version (OCI-CV) Hoarding factor ($r = .69, p < .001$) and CY-BOCS hoarding obsessions and compulsions ($r = .53, p < .001$). The CSI total score also showed good divergent validity, with low correlations between the CSI total score and the OCD-CV Checking subscale ($r = .23, p > .24$) as well as the OCI-CV Washing subscale ($r = .23, p < .02$).

A study of the CSI in Canada (Soreni et al., 2018) examined the psychometric properties of a 15-item version of the CSI (CSI-15), which removed acquisition items because acquisition is no longer included in the *DSM-5* diagnostic criteria for HD. The CSI-15 showed a three-factor solution (difficulty discarding, clutter, and distress/impairment) and excellent internal consistency ($α = 0.94$). It also demonstrated good convergent validity, with strong correlations with the CY-BOCS obsessions/compulsions checklist symptoms (Spearman's ρ = 0.43, *p* < .01) and good divergent validity, with nonsignificant correlations with the CY-BOCS Obsessions score (ρ = − 0.10, *p* = .17), the CY-BOCS Compulsions score (ρ = − 0.12, *p* = .10), and anxiety symptoms (Multidimensional Anxiety Scale for Children [MASC] total score: ρ = 0.06, *p* = .44). This study also focused on a sample of youth with a principal *DSM-IV-TR* diagnosis of OCD. Future research is needed to study the psychometric properties of the CSI in youth with primary hoarding challenges. Given that almost all existing hoarding assessments focus on adult hoarding, future measurement development is needed to examine hoarding among youth.

ACQUISITION

While excessive acquisition is not featured as a core diagnostic criterion for HD in the *DSM-5*, it has been repeatedly identified as a key feature of hoarding. Frost and colleagues (2009) found that among those with hoarding challenges, 80% to 95% excessively acquire by purchasing items or acquiring free items. Reducing acquiring behavior is essential component of hoarding treatment.

The Compulsive Acquisition Scale (CAS; Frost et al., 2002) assesses excessive acquisition by addressing both compulsive buying and the acquisition of free items. The scale includes 18 items that are rated on a scale from 1 (Not at all or Rarely) to 7 (Very much or Very often). These items comprise two subscales: CAS-Buy (12 items) assesses reasons for buying and consequences; and CAS-Free assesses compulsive acquisition of free things (6 items). Both subscales have been shown to have good reliability (CAS-Buy α = .94; CAS-Free α = .87; Frost et al., 2002; CAS-Buy α = .90; CAS-Free α = .73; Frost et al., 2009) and both have been correlated with buying cognitions, OCD symptoms, perfectionism, and indecisiveness (see Frost et al., 2002). The subscales have also been significantly correlated (*r* = .50; Frost et al., 2009). The CAS was also shown to have good discriminant validity (Kyrios et al., 2004). The CAS-Buy subscale and CAS-Free subscale were shown to distinguish those with compulsive buying from control participants (Kyrios et al., 2004). The CAS cutoff score, derived from ROC curves including those with and without compulsive buying (AUC = .922, *p* < .001), was established at 47.8 with maximal sensitivity (.85) and specificity (.84; Frost et al., 2002, 2009). Data also suggested that scores higher than one standard deviation above the mean for the subscales were considered "excessive," with cutoffs of 41 for CAS-Buy and 23 for CAS-Free (Frost et al., 2002, 2009). Frost and colleagues' (2009) study showed that among a larger sample of participants with self-identified clinically significant hoarding, 85% had excessive acquisition, 61% met criteria for compulsive buying, and 57% reported compulsive acquisition of free things.

Hoarding-Related Impairment and Home Conditions

As a home-based problem, hoarding behavior manifests as substantial clutter in the home. Several assessment measures exist that are completed by individuals with hoarding and/

or observers (e.g., practitioners, family members) to assess clutter and other aspects of the home environment as well as potential related risks and impairment.

The Clutter Image Rating scale (CIR; Frost et al., 2008) is a pictorial measure developed to assess the amount of clutter in rooms of the home. The scale includes nine "clutter-equidistant" photos depicting increasing levels of clutter for each of three rooms (e.g., bedroom, living room, and kitchen). Each of the set of photos includes a rating of 1 (No clutter) to 9 (Severe clutter). The rater selects one of the nine photos that corresponds to the level of clutter in that specific room of the home. The CIR can be applied by a person with hoarding symptoms, family members, or practitioners to rate levels of room clutter (Frost et al., 2012). The CIR score is determined by calculating a "mean composite score" across the three rooms. A score of 4 or greater indicates a clinically significant level of clutter. The CIR has been shown to demonstrate good psychometric properties, including good internal consistency as well as convergent and discriminant validity (Frost et al., 2008). The CIR correlates strongly with the SI-R clutter subscale ($r = 0.72$) and HRS clutter item ($r = 0.82$) when rated in the home as well as in the clinic (Frost et al., 2008). The CIR had lower correlations with difficulty discarding and acquiring. Test–retest reliability and predictive validity were strong, with an average correlation of $r = .73$ for corresponding rooms, a high clinic/home correlation ($r = 0.82$), and a high self-rater retest (2-month) correlation ($r = .85$) among those attending a workshop and informally screened. Similar results were found among those who completed a diagnostic interview with at least "definitely disturbing/disabling" levels of hoarding, with an average correlation of $r = 0.75$ for corresponding rooms and high participant/experimenter composite correlations ($r = 0.78$). Convergent validity was also strong, with $r = 0.73–0.94$ for corresponding rooms and $r = 0.94$ for the composite score. The CIR may be helpful to confirm self-reported clutter. It also has been shown to be sensitive to changes in clutter during treatment (Frost & Hristova, 2011 Tolin et al., 2007). It is commonly used by clinicians and community providers in domains of public health and housing, as well as first responders, to directly observe and rate clutter severity. Additionally, the CIR has been shown to be a reliable and valid clutter assessment tool for older adults with HD (Dozier & Ayers, 2015). The CIR also showed fair to good psychometric properties in a study with psychiatric outpatient participants in Singapore (Sagayadevan et al., 2016).

The Clutter-Hoarding Scale was developed by the National Study Group on Chronic Disorganization (NSGCD, 2003), to guide professional organizers in their assessment of clutter severity. The Clutter-Hoarding Scale includes five levels and four problem areas (i.e., structure and zoning, pets and rodents, household functions, sanitation, and cleanliness). Those homes determined to be level 3 and higher necessitate assistance to address their hoarding. No psychometric studies exist. The Clutter-Hoarding Scale has been translated into Spanish, Italian, Dutch, Portuguese, French, and German.

The HOMES Multidisciplinary Risk Assessment (Bratiotis, 2009; Bratiotis et al., 2011) is a brief structured tool that assesses the level of risk associated with a hoarded environment. A visual observation of the environment and discussion with the resident(s) inform how clutter and hoarding are associated with **h**ealth-related challenges (e.g., "garbage/trash overflow"), **o**bstacles related to movement (e.g., "egresses, exits, or vents blocked or unusable"), **m**ental health difficulties (e.g., "does not seem to understand seriousness of problem"), **e**ndangerment of others (e.g., "threat to health or safety of child/minor"), as well as **s**tructure and safety concerns (e.g., "blocked/unsafe electric heater or vents"). Additional HOMES questions and items focus on the family/household composition, imminent risk, strengths, and capacity to address the hoarding, as well as the plan for after assessment and any referral information. It can be completed by practitioners, service providers, family, friends, and/or others who have been inside the home. A specific scoring procedure and psychometrics have not been published.

While hoarding and squalor are distinct, some people with hoarding challenges live in unsanitary environments. The Environmental Cleanliness and Clutter Scale (ECCS; Halliday & Snowdon, 2009) assesses the degree of uncleanliness and clutter in a person's living environment. The ECCS consists of 10 items rated from 0 to 3, with specific anchor points and higher scores indicating more severe conditions. In a study of 45 homes in Australia rated by two psychogeriatricians, the ECCS was shown to have high internal consistency (α = 0.94) and satisfactory interreliability ($\varkappa$ = 0.48, varying from 0.31 to 0.58; Halliday & Snowdon, 2009). ECCS scores that exceed 12 typically indicate moderate or severe squalor (Halliday & Snowdon, 2009). In another study, Snowdon and colleagues (2013) conducted a factor analysis for the ECCS based on 203 cases and found a two-factor solution consisting of seven squalor items (accounting for 33.7% of the variance) and accessibility and accumulation of items of limited value (accounting for 17.6% of the variance). The average ECCS score was 18.5. About 30% of cases showed elevated accumulation and hoarding, 38% had high squalor scores, and 15% had high scores for squalor and accumulation.

The Home Environment Index (HEI; Rasmussen et al. 2014) assesses challenges with squalor, including domestic and personal hygiene, among people who hoard and the challenges' impact on performing daily activities and tasks. While the original version of the HEI had 26 items, the revised HEI includes 15 items rated from 0 (No presence of squalor') to 3 (Severe symptoms). The total score is calculated by summing the ratings, and it ranges from 0 to 45. Items include rotten food, dirty surfaces, piles of dirty items, home odor, fire hazards, and sitting water. The HEI was demonstrated to have good concurrent validity and discriminant validity, showing stronger correlations with hoarding severity measures (e.g., HRS-SR: r = .50) than with OCD-related checking (r = .11); (z = 6.67, p < .01). Limitations of this study include reliance on an Internet sample with self-report ratings (without diagnostic interview), no in-home assessor ratings, no control group, and a sample that included mainly White females. Cutoff scores have not been determined.

With regard to daily activities, the Activities of Daily Living–Hoarding (ADL-H; Frost et al., 2013) assesses how much hoarding-related behaviors and clutter interfere with, or cause difficulty with, ordinary daily activities like bathing, dressing, using areas of the home (e.g., sleeping in bed, using the shower), entering/exiting the home, and preparing meals. The ADL-H consists of 15 items that are rated as 1 (None—Can do it easily), 2 (Can do it with little difficulty), 3 (Can do it with moderate difficulty), 4 (Can do it with great difficulty), 5 (Severe— Unable to do), or Not applicable (NA). The score is based on the mean across rated items (NA items are not included). The ADL-H has been shown to be a reliable and valid measure, with strong correlations with hoarding severity measures in samples of those with self-identified hoarding as well as those who have received clinical HD diagnoses. ADL-H scores have been compared among those with hoarding, those with hoarding and OCD, those with OCD without hoarding, and community controls. The test–retest reliability (1 to 12 weeks) was strong, ranging from .79 to .96 even with varying lengths of time between assessments as well as varying contexts, including assessor home-based assessments and participant self-assessments. The ADL-H has demonstrated good convergent validity with SI-R Clutter ($r = .57, p < .001$) and home environment assessments (e.g., Home Environment Index, $r = .61, p < .001$) as well as good discriminant validity with OCD, inattention ($r = .06$, NS), hyperactivity ($r = .24, p < .001$), anxiety, stress, and depression ($r = .13–.23, p < .001$), and perfectionism ($r = .21, p < .001$). Limitations included missing data.

Impact of Hoarding on Family

While family members may serve as respondents for a number of hoarding assessments, additional assessments have been developed and validated to specifically examine the impact of hoarding behavior on the family. The Family Response to Hoarding Scale (FRHS; Steketee et al., 2013) assesses family accommodation, including changing behavior and/or routines for a loved one (e.g., family member, close friend, spouse) with hoarding behaviors. This self-report scale includes 16 items that are each rated from 1 to 4 (4 indicates greater family accommodation). The FRHS includes two subscales: (a) Behavior change, which includes specific accommodating behavior, such as making decisions regarding items and assuming daily responsibilities for the individual with hoarding; and (b) Personal consequences, which includes how the family member's life is negatively affected by the loved one's hoarding behavior (e.g., health, relationships). Initial examination of the FRHS's reliability and validity has shown them to be adequate (Steketee et al., 2013; Steketee & Frost, 2013).

The Family Impact Scale for Hoarding (FISH; Nordsletten et al., 2014) assesses the broader family-level impact of an individual's hoarding behavior. The FISH is comprised of 20 items making up two subscales that measure accommodation and burden. Accommodation was defined as "the act of modifying one's behavior for the purposes of preventing distress or conflict with the person that hoards" while burden was defined as "the extent to which someone's life has been generally (e.g., functionally) impacted by a relative's hoarding problem" (p. 30). The 20 items include 18 closed-response questions, rated from "Strongly disagree" to "Strongly agree" on a 4-point scale, as well as two open-response questions regarding the impact of a family member's hoarding. An initial study examined the validity of the FISH with self-identified family members of those with hoarding behaviors (n = 102) and collectors (n = 32). The FISH's internal consistency was high (α = 0.86) and its subscales (accommodation: α = 0.73; burden: α = 0.87) were acceptable. The FISH overall scale and subscales differentiated relatives of those with hoarding behavior, who scored significantly higher than relatives of collectors. The FISH showed good convergent validity, with strong correlations with family members' hoarding severity measures. For example, the family members' HRS total was strongly correlated with the FISH total (r = 0.71), FISH-Accommodation (r = 0.46, $p < .001$), and FISH-Burden (r = 0.70, $p < .001$). The FISH-Total and family members' CIR were also strongly correlated (r = 0.63, $p < .001$). The FISH also strongly correlated with caregiver burden (Caregiver Burden Inventory: r = 0.74) and functional impairment (Work and Social Adjustment Scale: r = 0.67) and more moderately with quality of life (SF-36: r = -0.46). Future studies need to further examine the psychometric properties of the FISH with a larger sample and its capacity to measure outcomes associated with interventions focused on family members.

The Family Accommodation Interview for Hoarding (FAI-H; Vorstenbosch et al., 2015) assesses the frequency of family accommodation behaviors and the level of distress/interference due to the accommodating behavior. The FAI-H was modified from the Family Accommodation Scale for OCD (FAS for OCD; Calvocoressi, Mazure, Kasl, et al., 1999; Calvocoressi, Mazure, Van Noppen, et al., 1999). The FAI-H is administered by a clinician interviewer and includes 10 items, rated from 0 (Not at all) to 4 (Extreme), that comprise the frequency and distress/interference subscales. Scores are calculating by summing the total items (range 0 to 80) as well as each of the subscale items (0 to 40). In a study by Vorstenbosch et al. (2015) that examined the psychometric properties of the FAI-H in a sample of participants with self-reported hoarding behaviors (HRS-SR > 14) and a close significant other (CSO) without clinical hoarding, the internal consistency was excellent for the total score (α = .91), acceptable for the frequency subscale (α = .78), and good for the distress/interference subscale (α = .86). Excellent convergent validity was shown between the FAI-H total scores and subscales with the FRHS self-report measure (r = .58–.77, $p < .001$). Divergent validity was shown with lower correlations between the FAI-H and self-reported anxiety sensitivity (ASI; r = .26–.29, p = .04–.07; $t \geq 2.05$, $p < .05$). The FAI-H total score was significantly positively correlated with the clinician-rated HRS-I scores (r = .51, $p < .001$), hoarding participant-rated SI-R Difficulty discarding subscale (r = .29, $p < .05$), CSO-rated SI-R total scores (r = .37, $p < .01$), SI-R Difficulty discarding (r = .41, $p < .01$), SI-R Clutter (r = .36, $p < .05$), and CSO-rated CIR (r = .34, $p < .05$). Future studies may examine if specific types of family relationships are associated with greater family accommodation. Additionally, hoarding behavior among CSOs may affect their own accommodation behaviors. Future studies may help unpack whether more severe HD challenges elicit higher rates of family accommodation and/or whether family accommodation increases hoarding severity.

Beliefs, Attachment, and Other Cognitive Features
Beyond measures assessing core aspects of HD, impairment, and the living environment, other tools examine additional features associated with hoarding. The Saving Cognitions Inventory (SCI; Steketee et al., 2003) is a self-report measure that assesses beliefs associated with hoarding behavior and influencing the decision not to discard or to save items. The SCI consists of 24 items rated 1 (Not at all) to 7 (Very much), with scores ranging from 24 to 168 and with higher scores indicating more hoarding-related beliefs when attempting to discard. The four subscales focus on intense emotional attachment to possessions (Attachment subscale), strong sense of responsibility for items and not wasting them (Responsibility), the need for control over possessions and fears that others will touch and/or move possessions (Need for control), and concerns about needing items to aid one's memory (Memory). The SCI total and subscales have high internal consistency (total: α = .96; subscales ranging from α = 0.86 to 0.95). The SCI demonstrates convergent validity with strong correlations with hoarding severity on the SI-R (r = 0.60–0.80) as well as discriminant validity with lower correlations (r = .39–.55) with anxiety (Beck Anxiety Inventory) and depression (Beck Depression Inventory; Steketee et al., 2003). The strong relationship between hoarding beliefs and hoarding behavior was independent of mood and OCD symptoms. Each SCI subscale can differentiate clients with hoarding from those with OCD as well as community controls (Steketee et al., 2003).

The Beliefs about Hoarding Questionnaire (BAH; Gordon et al., 2013) assesses beliefs and experiences characteristic of hoarding. It is comprised of three subscales focused on "hoarding motivated by harm avoidance/responsibility for harm" (six items), "hoarding motivated by previous experience of material deprivation" (nine items), and "hoarding related to attachment disturbance" (12 items; p. 330). An additional item measures the level of positive emotion due to acquiring. The BAH is a self-report measure that consists of a total of 28 items rated from 0 (I did not believe this at all) to 100 (I was completely convinced this item was true); scores are summed and averaged based on the number of items, for an overall score and well as subscale scores. The BAH scale has shown good internal consistency for the overall measure (α = .96) as well as subscales (harm avoidance: α = .79, material deprivation: α = .93, and attachment disturbance: α = .93).

Test–retest reliability among a small subsample of persons with hoarding was good for the BAH total (r = .83) as well as the subscales (harm avoidance: r = .85, material deprivation: r = .89, and attachment disturbance: r = .69). Gordon and colleagues (2013) examined the BAH total and subscales among a sample of four subgroups (N = 88): those with hoarding plus OCD (n = 21), hoarding without OCD (pure hoarding; n = 24), OCD without hoarding (n = 22), and a nonclinical control group (n = 21). The hoarding subgroups were recruited from nonclinical settings, including support groups. Results showed that those with hoarding plus OCD compared to the pure hoarding group (hoarding without OCD) had significantly greater harm avoidance beliefs about possessions, but no significant differences were found between the two hoarding groups on beliefs about material deprivation or attachment disturbance. The hoarding plus OCD subgroup scored significantly higher than did the pure hoarding group on harm avoidance ratings ($t(26) = -2.8$, $p < .05$) and material deprivation ratings ($t(32) = -3.0$, $p < .05$), but not attachment disturbance ratings ($t(30) = -.08$, $p > .5$). This study may indicate that beliefs associated with harm avoidance that are frequent among those with OCD may also generalize to the possessions of those with hoarding and OCD. Future studies may also examine the definition of harm avoidance in the context of hoarding.

The Object Attachment Questionnaire (OAQ; Grisham et al., 2009) was developed to assess a person's level of attachment to an object, including emotional responses and attitudes toward items. This self-report measure includes 13 items rated from 1 (Not at all/strongly disagree) to 7 (Very much/strongly agree) and measures attachment, comfort, anthropomorphizing, identity attachment, and inflated responsibility for possessions. The OAQ was developed as part of a study in which participants were given a keychain at a conference and were asked to rate their level of attachment upon receiving the keychain as well as one week later. The OAQ was shown to have good internal consistency in this sample of people, who were mainly individuals with OCD and some with hoarding symptoms ($\alpha = .94$) as well as undergraduate students ($\alpha = .92$). OAQ average scores have been found to differ for clinical samples ($M = 30.68$) and an undergraduate sample ($M = 24.32$), suggesting discriminant validity. The OAQ showed convergent validity with hoarding symptoms and beliefs (including the total and subscales of the SI-R and SCI) being significantly positively correlated with the OAQ (r ranging from .27 to .50) when receiving the keychain. Thus, those with greater hoarding symptoms initially became more emotionally attached to the keychain. After a week, the OAQ was only significantly positively correlated with the SI-R Acquisition subscale ($r = .40$, $p < .01$), and SCI emotional attachment ($r = .49$, $p < .01$) and control over possessions ($r = .34$, $p < .01$) subscales. Thus, those who often acquire items and experience emotional comfort and control from their possessions had greater emotional attachment to the keychain after having it for a week. Results also showed that changes in attachment OAQ ratings from the time participants received the keychain to a week later were not associated with hoarding severity. The level of attachment evidenced by the OAQ rating at the time the keychain was received was the best predictor of attachment (OAQ) rating a week later. This suggests that initial attachment may occur "upon first sight," with no experience with the object, and that it predicts later attachment, regardless of severity of hoarding symptoms. However, greater initial attachment was reported by participants with beliefs about the emotional value of possessions and participants with acquiring behaviors. Thus, future studies may examine the role of beliefs about the emotional value of possessions and acquisition behaviors to inform understanding of attachment formation and how each may contribute to immediate object attachment.

The Relationship between Self and Items (RSI) Scale (Dozier et al., 2017) adapted from the Inclusion of Other in Self Scale (IOS; Aron et al., 1992) assesses the relationship between one's self and one's items, using seven Venn diagrams with overlapping circles, one labeled "self" and one labeled "items," that constitute an interval-level scale. The RSI is a self-report single-item pictorial measure that assesses object attachment; each respondent selects one picture that illustrates their relationship with their items (1–7). An initial study examining the psychometric properties of the RSI among those with HD compared to community controls found that the mean of the RSI for participants with HD was significantly greater than the RSI mean for the community controls (t (83.88) = –5.84, $p < .0001$). The RSI was also sensitive to treatment change, with significant decreases in scores from before to after treatment (t (29) = 4.7, $p < .0001$). The RSI was significantly positively correlated with hoarding symptoms (e.g., SI-R total: $r = 0.25$, $p = .02$; SI-R Difficulty discarding: $r = 0.37$, $p = .016$), but not clutter (SI-R Clutter: $r = 0.11$, $p = .321$, CIR: $r = -0.01$, $p = .916$), acquisition (SI-R Acquisition: ($r = 0.17$, $p = .118$), anxiety ($r = 0.05$, $p = .734$), or depression ($r = 0.25$, $p = .103$). The RSI was not significantly correlated with the SCI Total ($r = .28$, $p = .226$) or subscales, although it was strongly correlated with one item from the SCI emotional attachment subscale: "I see my belongings as extensions of myself; they are part of who I am" ($r = .62$, $p = .004$). The demographics of participants, who were older, female, and White, limit generalizability. The RSI may serve as a brief screen or as an adjunct to other measures for assessing interconnectedness or level of closeness that someone feels with their possessions. Future studies may examine whether respondents are consistent in their understanding of "interconnectedness" as meaning their emotional closeness with their possessions versus the "physical overlap of their life with their objects" (e.g., clutter level).

The Acceptance and Action Questionnaire for Hoarding (AAQH; Krafft et al. 2019), assesses how psychological inflexibility (i.e., challenges in responding to internal experiences like cognitions and distress) specifically contributes to hoarding. The AAQH includes 14 self-report items rated 1 (Never true) to 7 (Always true); scores are calculated by summing the items and range from 14 to 98. Higher scores indicate greater hoarding-related psychological inflexibility. The psychometric properties of the AAQH were studied among a nonclinical sample of undergraduate students with higher levels of hoarding (above SI-R mean score). The AAQH was shown to have excellent reliability for the total questionnaire ($\alpha = .90$) as well as the two subscales (AAQH Saving $\alpha = 0.89$; AAQH Acquisition $\alpha = 0.84$), which were highly correlated with each other and the total score. The AAQH was highly correlated with the hoarding symptoms on the SI-R total and subscales ($r = 0.31–0.64$). The AAQH showed divergent validity with depression and anxiety. Future studies may examine the psychometric properties of the AAQH among clinical samples with HD and examine whether the AAQH is sensitive to intervention effects.

Hoarding-Related Behavioral Assessment Measures/Tasks

Several behavioral assessment tasks exist to assess for hoarding-related challenges, such as acquiring, difficulty discarding, and categorization. The behavioral measures may extend understanding of hoarding symptoms and severity beyond self-report, which depends on the respondent's level of insight. The combination of behavioral tasks with self-report and clinician interviews can present a more comprehensive understanding of hoarding severity as well as how decision-making, acquiring, etc., contribute to hoarding behavior (Levy et al., 2019).

Preston and colleagues (2009) developed a computerized task assessing acquisition and discarding of everyday objects. Participants viewed photos of many objects that ranged in value and were asked to indicate which they would want to take home for free (this was a hypothetical scenario). Next, the participants engaged in discarding tasks with increasing pressure to discard the objects. Convergent validity was demonstrated, in that those participants who acquired more items (as compared to fewer items) reported greater hoarding symptoms on self-report measures (e.g., SI-R total: $F(2, 82) = 3.241$, $p = 0.044$; OCI-R Hoarding: $F(2, 82) = 2.828$, $p = .065$). This behavioral assessment was feasible and generally simple to apply. Initial study findings were limited in that participants were undergraduate students, restricting its generalizability. The application of this computerized task was extended to a small sample of participants with HD and healthy controls (Tolin et al., 2012). Participants with HD engaged with the behavioral task before and after CBT treatment and showed some improvement from before treatment to after treatment. While those with HD saved more items during the discarding task than the healthy controls, no significant differences were found between those with and without HD with regard to the number of items acquired, reaction time for acquiring tasks, or reaction time for decisions regarding discarding. Given the small sample size, a larger study was conducted to further test the validity of this behavioral task (Levy et al., 2019).

Levy and colleagues (2019) modified Preston and team's computerized task. During the acquiring task, pressure was increased by limiting the participants to acquiring only enough items that could fit into a standard shopping cart. To decrease fatigue, distinct stimuli were presented during the acquiring and discarding phases. A new control task was added whereby respondents identified objects as "once alive" or "never alive." The discarding and acquiring behavioral tasks were conducted during functional magnetic resonance imaging (fMRI), as part of a larger study. Findings demonstrated that participants with a primary diagnosis of at least moderately severe HD acquired and saved more items and showed longer response times (Discarding: group, $F(1, 106) = 10.39$, $p = .002$, $\eta^2_p = .09$; task, $F(1, 106) = 42.50$, $p < .001$, $\eta^2_p = .29$; Acquiring: group, $F(1, 106) = 11.28$, $p = .001$, $\eta^2_p = .10$; task, $F(1, 106) = 57.46$, $p < .001$, $\eta^2_p = .35$) than did healthy controls matched by age and sex. Results suggest that the behavioral task was sensitive to CBT treatment effects, because participants with HD showed decreases in the average number of items saved—participants with HD decreased from 13 items to nine items ($t(40) = 5.08$; $p <$

.001; $d = 0.84$), while healthy controls kept 10 items—and improved average reaction times from before to after treatment—participants with HD decreased discarding time from 2.21 to 1.86 s ($t(40) = 5.08$; $p < .001$; $d = 0.79$) while healthy controls' average time was 1.16 s). Findings showed that for participants with HD, posttreatment acquiring was similar to behaviors of healthy controls—Acquiring: seven items (HD posttreatment and healthy controls); with reaction time of 1.94 s (HD posttreatment) versus 1.96 s (controls). Additionally, the item decisions and reaction times were correlated with HD symptoms, as reported using standardized measures (e.g., SI-R difficulty discarding and acquiring as well as clinician-administered HRS-I). It's important to also note that while the discarding task decisions were highly correlated with the HRS-I, this was not the case for the acquiring items, perhaps suggesting that the discarding task has better validity and reliability as a hoarding measure than the acquiring task and that there are possibly differences in the core features of hoarding. Thus, while such studies support the validation of the behavioral task for clinical and nonclinical samples, future studies using behavioral tasks may further examine potential differences between acquiring and discarding as well as relevance to real-world decision-making about personal possessions in daily living (Levy et al., 2019).

CATEGORIZATION

Behavioral tasks also include categorization tasks to examine executive functioning and categorization difficulties among those with hoarding. Categorization tasks for hoarding include asking participants to categorize varying types of personal and nonpersonal items and tracking time, number of categories, and discomfort ratings before and after the task. A study with an earlier version of this task (Wincze et al., 2007) included the use of index cards with the words for typical household (nonpersonal) items written on the cards as well as words for specific objects that participants had in their homes (personal items). The study included people with hoarding, people with nonhoarding OCD, and nonclinical control participants. Another study with a nonclinical sample examined categorization of actual personal and nonpersonal items (Luchian et al., 2007). A later study (Grisham et al., 2010) examined categorization of personal and nonpersonal objects using index cards and actual items among three participant groups (those with primary hoarding symptoms, those with primary Axis I mood or anxiety disorders who did not have HD [clinical controls], and nonclinical controls). Participants also completed self-report assessments (e.g., hoarding symptoms, cognitive difficulties) as well as neuropsychological tests examining executive functioning and decision-making. Findings indicated that those with hoarding exhibited more challenges with sorting personal items than with nonpersonal items, creating a few more categories (for personal objects [$F(2,46) = 5.09$, $p = .01$] and index cards [$F(2,46) = 3.73$, $p < .05$]) and reporting more anxiety when sorting personal (vs. nonpersonal) items. Those with hoarding spent much more time sorting personal index cards. Participants with hoarding reported more difficulties with inattention and decision-making than nonclinical controls. Such categorization tasks in combination with neuropsychological testing and self-reported symptoms may enhance understanding of hoarding-related executive functioning difficulties, including challenges with categorizing and organizing possessions, as well as attentional and decision-making problems.

INTERPRETIVE BIAS TASKS

David and colleagues (2019) utilized cognitive bias modification of interpretation (CBM-I) training to examine the connection between hoarding-related beliefs and saving behavior. For the CBM-I training, hoarding-related scenarios were developed to activate and modify biases related to the SCI measure (Steketee et al., 2003), including emotional comfort, control, responsibility, and memory. Numerous trials of "ambiguous hoarding-related scenarios" were presented, followed by varying interpretations. A word-fragment task was then administered as well as a comprehension question (yes/no) regarding the scenario ending; after answering it, the participant received feedback about whether they were (in)correct. The researchers also utilized an interpretive bias measure based on the CBM-I to assess changes in hoarding-related beliefs. For the interpretive bias measure, prior to CBM-I training, participants were presented with "novel ambiguous scenarios relating to hoarding beliefs" and then did a neutral image task, rating neutral images for pleasantness and vividness. Next they were presented with "disambiguated versions" of the scenarios (adaptive and related to hoarding beliefs; maladaptive and related to hoarding beliefs; positive and unrelated; negative and unrelated) and were asked to rate the level of similarity between the new scenarios and the original scenarios. The purpose was to assess any changes in hoarding-relevant or general interpretation. To calculate interpretive bias scores, negative (related) scores were subtracted from positive (related scores) to get Target scores, while negative (unrelated) scores were subtracted from positive (unrelated) scores to obtain Foil scores.

In a study with undergraduate students with high levels of hoarding, participants were randomized to a positive CBM-I training condition aimed to decrease bias related to hoarding or to a neutral CBM-I training. Participants engaged in behavioral measures of discarding before and after the CBM-I training and also completed self-report measures about hoarding and related beliefs. Results did not show differences between conditions on behavioral tasks after the CBM-I training (SCI: $F(1, 92) = 3.86$, $p = .053$, $\eta^2_p = 0.04$); however, the positive condition (compared to the neutral condition) showed decreased hoarding symptoms and hoarding beliefs one week after the CBM-I training (SCI: $F(1, 72) = 6.77$, $p = .01$, $\eta^2_p = 0.09$; David et al., 2019). This study demonstrated the strong relationship between interpretive bias and maladaptive hoarding beliefs. Future studies may examine the relationship in clinical samples.

EXAMPLES OF ADDITIONAL BEHAVIORAL TASKS

Additional behavioral tasks have been applied in hoarding research, including the standardized sorting task, in vivo discarding task, attachment and monetary value ratings, and estimate tasks. An initial standardized exposure task for hoarding was developed and tested to examine sorting and discarding behavior (Dozier, 2018). Participants worked with an assessor, who came to the home, and together they placed possessions from cluttered areas of the home into a box to bring to a follow-up office session. During the office session, the participants were asked to take each item out of the box and decide whether to "keep" or "discard" the item, while discarding as many items as possible during a 15-minute interval. Emotions and distress levels were assessed before and after the exposure task and an electrocardiography (ECG) chest band recorded the participant's heart rate. Participants were asked to rate the level of similarity between their experiences with the office-based sorting task and with sorting at home. Initial findings showed that the exposure task was feasible and has "incremental validity in the assessment of hoarding symptomology" (p. xvii) that is "tapping into part of hoarding symptomology" (p. 32). The distress ratings were lower than anticipated, and participants discarded a greater percentage of items than expected (although perhaps this was true because they brought in too few items or the items that were brought in were not distressing to sort; p. 29). Further study of validity and sensitivity to treatment is needed.

In the in vivo discarding task (David et al., 2019), study participants brought 10 "low-value" possessions from home that they were ambivalent about discarding. The participants were told they had 5 minutes to decide to discard as many items as they could (or to keep items) while the experimenter was out of the room. Following this, the experimenter returned and asked the participant to rate their anxiety from 0 (No distress) to 100 (Extreme distress) during the task (Subjective Units of Distress Scale [SUDS]; Thyer et al., 1984).

Attachment and monetary value of items may be assessed by participants using a visual analog scale for rating attachment to items as well as estimating (in dollars) the item's value (David et al., 2019). Estimate tasks include presenting items to participants and asking them to provide a monetary estimate of the object's value (in dollars), to estimate the usefulness of the object in the future, and to estimate their level of anxiety if they did not have the item in the future when they needed it (David et al., 2019).

Another behavioral task, the Titrating Mirror Tracing Task (TMTT; Lejuez & Calvin, 2009), a computer task that includes tracing line drawings of a star using a computer mouse, was used to examine distress tolerance among a sample diagnosed with HD compared to clinical controls.

Behavioral tasks in combination with other hoarding assessments (e.g., clinical interviews, clinician-rated, self-report) can assist with the identification and understanding of underlying factors and processes (e.g., decision-making) in HD. Studies including behavioral tasks can compare clinical and nonclinical samples and can include multiple time points (Levy et al., 2019). Findings can inform the development and enhancement of hoarding assessments and treatments.

Discussion

This chapter presents a comprehensive review of existing hoarding assessments and behavioral tasks, developed and tested since the late 1990s. The hoarding-specific assessments and behavioral tasks examine core hoarding features as well as other hoarding-related cognitive and behavioral symptoms, the impact of hoarding on individuals and families, and the condition of the home environment. Existing hoarding assessments have both strengths and limitations. The development and testing of hoarding assessments have varied in the processes of assessment item development; the size, scope, and characteristics of the samples used (e.g., clinical samples, undergraduate students, age); recruitment procedures (e.g., prescreening, diagnosis); and methodology used to examine psychometric properties. Research on the development and testing of hoarding assessments has mainly used university students and those who are treatment seekers (e.g., clients voluntarily engaged in services; Tolin, Gilliam, Davis, et al., 2018). In addition, samples have included predominantly White, middle-aged females, which limits the examination of the validity and reliability of hoarding measures with more diverse populations as well as the generalizability of the findings. Epidemiological studies suggest that hoarding is at least as common among men as among women (Samuels et al., 2008). Race and ethnic differences in rates of HD are unknown. Furthermore, hoarding behavior may change over the lifetime, and the reasons why older adults save and acquire may differ from the reasons in other adult age groups (Dozier & Ayers, 2014). Levels of clutter may increase among older adults even if other hoarding symptoms, such as difficulty discarding and acquisition, level off (Dozier et al., 2015). Additionally, little information exists about the validity, reliability, and relevance of existing hoarding assessments among the substantial proportion of people with hoarding who do not seek services voluntarily (Frost et al., 2010), and who also may have greater challenges with insight and elevated hoarding severity.

To enhance validity and generalizability, future research on hoarding assessments should be more inclusive in processes for conceptualizing constructs, recruitment efforts (e.g., gender, race, ethnicity, age, treatment seekers and those not seeking treatment), developing and implementing pilot tests (followed by larger studies), as well as increasing adaptations and translations into various languages. While a growing number of hoarding assessments have been translated and their psychometric properties have been tested, most hoarding assessments exist in English exclusively and have been examined mainly with the U.S. population. Cultural differences may exist in the experience, manifestation, comprehension, and interpretation of saving, discarding, and acquiring symptoms (Lee et al., 2016). Specific constructs may vary between populations and cultures. The factor structure of hoarding assessments may also differ between U.S. and other populations (Lee et al., 2016). As examples, the framing and understanding of discarding as distinct from acquiring (versus integrated with it) as well as the role of self-control in hoarding may differ across cultures (Lee et al., 2016). Qualitative studies, including methods like cognitive interviewing, could enhance understanding of such constructs (Patton, 2002; Willis, 2005). Thus, future studies should examine, adapt, and test hoarding assessments as well as behavioral tasks to ensure cultural, linguistic, and phenomenological relevance.

Methods have also varied widely between studies, affecting the robustness of the developing hoarding assessments. Some studies (e.g., Tolin, Gilliam, Wootton, et al., 2018) have implemented valid screening or diagnostic procedures to define comparison groups for testing the validity and reliability of hoarding assessments. Meanwhile, other studies have combined samples of those with self-identified hoarding behaviors and/or subclinical hoarding, including participants at hoarding workshops/conferences and patients with OCD and hoarding behaviors (Frost et al., 2004, 2008, 2013). Another limitation is that some studies were conducted before there was a validated diagnostic measure for hoarding as well as before the establishment of *DSM-5* diagnostic criteria. Another study of hoarding assessments was limited by utilizing the same rater for both the clinic and home-based assessments, which could confound ratings (Tolin, Fitch, et al., 2010). A number of studies require further analysis of interrater and test–retest reliability of hoarding-specific measures in samples of those with HD. Finally, it is notable that only one hoarding-specific assessment focused on children with hoarding—the parent-report CSI—a situation illustrating the need for specific hoarding measures to assess hoarding among children.

Subjectivity of Assessment
The subjectivity of hoarding assessments has been raised as a concern. For example, self-reports of clutter are often not confirmed by an in-home assessment, photographs of the home environment, and/or the use of multiple raters (e.g., family member, providers). Concerns regarding the accuracy of self-reported symptoms from people with hoarding relate to problems with insight, confusion, minimization/exaggeration of symptoms, possible embarrassment, or legal pressure and concerns (eviction, forced cleanouts; Drury et al., 2015; Saxena et al., 2015). Insight is a diagnostic specifier for HD that includes the individual's recognition of the hoarding behavior as problematic and/or the existence of delusional beliefs associated with hoarding, despite evidence. In HD trials, about 10% to 14% of participants are described as having poor or absent insight about their hoarding behavior (Mataix-Cols et al., 2013), while other studies based on responses from family members have found that 50% or more of those with hoarding behavior have poor insight (Tolin, Fitch, et al., 2010). There has also been concern regarding the accuracy of family informant reports (Drury et al., 2015).

A number of studies have examined the correspondence between, and the reliability of, client self-rated hoarding assessments and informant-rated (e.g., family, provider) assessments. A couple of studies (Frost et al., 2008; Mataix-Cols et al., 2013) demonstrated good correspondence between clients' and clinicians' reports regarding level of hoarding-related clutter on the CIR (Frost et al., 2008). Studies examining full HD criteria suggest that individuals with hoarding report significantly more insight and significantly less difficulty with clutter, acquisition, and squalor compared to their family members' ratings regarding these aspects of the individuals' hoarding behavior (DiMauro et al., 2013). These studies found that family informant reports may correspond less with client self-reports than with clinician reports; however, variability in study methods, such as recruitment and hoarding assessments, limit conclusions about consistency between sources of ratings (DiMauro et al., 2013). A study utilizing the SIHD diagnostic interview to confirm HD diagnosis found general correspondence between client-rated and informant-rated hoarding assessments for most key elements, with informants rating clutter minimally higher (but not at a statistically significant level) and squalor levels as significantly greater than client self-ratings (Drury et al., 2015). Additionally, persons who are less likely to self-identify their hoarding challenges and participate in research were rated to have poorer insight and greater hoarding severity than those with HD who do participate in research (Drury et al., 2015). These findings also highlight that most hoarding research includes clients who have self-selected into the studies and are likely to have higher levels of insight; thus, those with hoarding who have less insight are less likely to be included in hoarding assessment and intervention research. This is an important limitation in the generalization of hoarding research to the broader population of those with hoarding behaviors and identifies gaps that should inform future research on hoarding assessment.

Clinical Cutoffs
Building upon existing work (Kellman-McFarlane et al., 2019), future research on hoarding assessments should also extend research on development of cutoff scores that are optimal for the sensitivity and specificity of a particular study versus the use of universal cutoffs. As noted earlier, age-related data may inform the cutoffs, but research also suggests changes in hoarding symptoms across the life span. Some have suggested that attitudes and behaviors related to acquiring, saving, and clutter vary with age. Future studies should also examine other personal factors (e.g., socioeconomic status) in addition to age that may be related to hoarding symptoms. Existing and future data may be utilized as evidence to support the application of specific cutoff scores for various hoarding assessments.

Use of Images/Photos
Given that hoarding behavior typically manifests as clutter, photographs serve as visual assessment data of the living and/or working environment and may enhance assessment processes and outcomes. Photos have been utilized in hoarding assessment processes in combination with, and in place of, regular home visits, to enhance understanding of the types of items saved, use of space in the home, and severity of clutter in varying areas of the home. The use of photographs has been recommended for assessment purposes in

manualized individual (Steketee & Frost, 2013) and group (Muroff et al., 2014) CBT for hoarding and has been incorporated into online interventions as well (Fitzpatrick et al., 2018; Ivanov et al., 2018). Photos of the home environment may also confirm or detect differences (under- or overreporting) in self-reported or informant-rated assessments of hoarding symptoms (Drury et al., 2015).

Digital photos for assessment purposes may be captured and shared more easily and privately. Digital photos can be uploaded to a secure portal or protected and encrypted for additional sharing (Eonta et al., 2011). Digital technology also facilitates and streamlines more frequent photo-based assessment (e.g., in contrast to necessitating frequent home visits for photo capture and sharing of paper-based photos). The images can serve as cross-sectional as well as longitudinal data to inform prevention and intervention efforts (e.g., earlier detection of increasing levels of clutter, hazards, etc.).

Additional Innovations in Hoarding Assessment

Technological advancement and dissemination efforts are enabling development of technology-supported assessment tools for hoarding that are grounded in research (Muroff & Otte, 2019). As technology-based tools and hardware increase in availability and affordability, new opportunities for assessment and broad adoption will arise.

As noted, the use of home visits and photos to assess hoarding and clutter relies on client, practitioner, family, or another observer's ratings; thus, subjectivity remains. Current innovations include developments for automating the assessment of hoarding and clutter by utilizing deep learning and applying convolutional neural networks (CNN). Recent research includes the automatic assessment of clutter using the pictorial Clutter Image Rating (CIR; Frost et al., 2008)—the CIR tool includes nine photos for each of three rooms in the home(living room, kitchen, and bedroom; see CIR description above in the Hoarding-Related Impairment and Home Conditions section). Findings demonstrate that automatic assignment of a CIR rating to an image within ± 1 level can be achieved at 82% accuracy (Tezcan et al., 2018). Automated ratings have the added benefits of enhancing accuracy, decreasing the time and costs associated with home-based assessments, and simplifying and expediting momentary hoarding assessment and feedback. Current research aims to validate automated assessment tools and improve their rating accuracy.

Future innovations in hoarding assessment may also include virtual reality (VR). VR could be used to assess "subjective and physiological experiences" and relationship to personal and nonpersonal items among those with HD and those without it. For example, one study utilized a VR environment with varying levels of clutter and found that adults with and without HD had similar subjective and physiological experiences of varying clutter levels, although those with HD preferred more cluttered rooms and had greater claustrophobia fears (McCabe Bennett et al., 2020). Another study included a VR environment with either embedded images of participants' personal possessions or nonpersonal items (St-Pierre-Delorme & O'Connor, 2016); a similar VR environment could be applied to behavioral tasks to assess hoarding features and other factors (e.g., cognitive processes).

Hoarding-specific assessments and behavioral tasks promise to be an area of substantial growth and innovation. This chapter suggests the need for multimethod assessment approaches; greater consideration of sample inclusion and representativeness; expanding cultural, linguistic, and phenomenological relevance; enhancing research methods; and more rigorous testing of the measures' psychometric properties.

References

American Psychiatric Association (APA). (2013). *Diagnostic and statistical manual of mental disorders* (5th ed.).

Aron, A., Aron, E. N., & Smollan, D. (1992). Inclusion of Other in the Self Scale and the structure of interpersonal closeness. *Journal of Personality and Social Psychology, 63*(4), 596–612.

Ayers, C. R., Dozier, M. E., & Mayes, T. L. (2017). Psychometric evaluation of the Saving Inventory–Revised in older adults. *Clinical Gerontology, 40*(3), 191–196.

Ayers, C. R., Saxena, S., Espejo, E., Twamley, E. W., Granholm, E., & Wetherell, J. L. (2014). Novel treatment for geriatric hoarding disorder: An open trial of cognitive rehabilitation paired with behavior therapy. *The American Journal of Geriatric Psychiatry, 22*(3), 248–252.

Bratiotis, C. (2009). HOMES® Multi-disciplinary Hoarding Risk Assessment.

Bratiotis, C., Sorrentino Schmalisch, C., & Steketee, G. (2011). *The hoarding handbook: A guide for human service professionals.* Oxford University Press.

Calvocoressi, L., Mazure, C. M., Kasl, S. V., Stanislav, K., Skolnick, J., Fisk, D., Vegso, S. J., Van Noppen, B. L., & Price, L. H. (1999). Family accommodation of obsessive-compulsive symptoms: Instrument development and assessment of family behavior. *The Journal of Nervous and Mental Disease, 187,* 636–642.

Calvocoressi, L., Mazure, C. M., Van Noppen, B., & Price, L. H. (1999). The Family Accommodation Scale for obsessive-compulsive disorder. In G. Steketee (Ed.), *Overcoming obsessive-compulsive disorder: A behavioral and cognitive protocol for the treatment of OCD* (pp. 185–200). New Harbinger Publications.

Carey, E. A., del Pozo de Bolger, A., & Wootton, B. M. (2019). Psychometric properties of the Hoarding Disorder–Dimensional Scale. *Journal of Obsessive-Compulsive and Related Disorders, 21,* 91–96.

David, J., Baldwin, P. A., & Grisham, J. R. (2019). To save or not to save: The use of cognitive bias modification in a high-hoarding sample. *Journal of Obsessive-Compulsive and Related Disorders, 23,* 100457.

DiMauro, J., Tolin, D. F., Frost, R. O., & Steketee, G. (2013). Do people with hoarding disorder under-report their symptoms? *Journal of Obsessive-Compulsive and Related Disorders, 2*(2), 130–136.

Dozier, M. E. (2018). *Exploratory investigation of a standardized exposure task for hoarding disorder* (ProQuest ID: Dozier_ucsd_0033D_17276). [Doctoral Dissertation, UC San Diego]. ProQuest Dissertations and Theses Global.

Dozier, M. E., & Ayers, C. R. (2014). The predictive value of different reasons for saving and acquiring on hoarding disorder symptoms. *Journal of Obsessive-Compulsive and Related Disorders, 3,* 220–227.

Dozier, M. E., & Ayers, C. R. (2015). Validation of the Clutter Image Rating in older adults with hoarding disorder. *International Psychogeriatrics, 27,* 769–776.

Dozier, M. E., Porter, B., & Ayers, C. R. (2015). Age of onset and progression of hoarding symptoms in older adults with hoarding disorder. *Aging and Mental Health, 20,* 736–742.

Dozier, M. E., Taylor, C. T., Castriotta, N., Mayes, T. L., & Ayers, C. R. (2017). A preliminary investigation of the measurement of object interconnectedness in hoarding disorder. *Cognitive Theory and Research, 41,* 799–805.

Drury, H., Nordsletten, A. E., Ajmi, S., Fernández de la Cruz, L., & Mataix-Cols, D. (2015). Accuracy of self and informant reports of symptom severity and insight in hoarding disorder. *Journal of Obsessive-Compulsive and Related Disorders, 5,* 37–42.

Eonta, A. M., Christon, L. M., Hourigan, S. E., Ravindran, N., Vrana, S. R., & Southam-Gerow, M. A. (2011). Using everyday technology to enhance evidence-based treatments. *Professional Psychology: Research and Practice, 42*(6), 513–520.

Faraci, P., Perdighe, C., Del Monte, C., & Saliani, A. M. (2019). Hoarding Rating Scale–Interview: Reliability and construct validity in a nonclinical sample. *International Journal of Psychology & Psychological Therapy*, *19*(3), 345–352.

Fitzpatrick, M., Nedeljkovic, M., Abbott, J., Kyrios, M., & Moulding, R. (2018). "Blended" therapy: The development and pilot evaluation of an Internet-facilitated cognitive behavioral intervention to supplement face-to-face therapy for hoarding disorder. *Internet Interventions*, *12*, 16–25.

Foa, E. B., Coles, M., Huppert, J. D., Pasupuleti, R. V., Franklin, M. E., & March, J. (2010). Development and validation of a child version of the Obsessive Compulsive Inventory. *Behavior Therapy*, *41*(1), 121–132.

Foa, E. B., Huppert, J. D., Leiberg, S., Langner, R., Kichic, R., Hajcak, G., & Salkovskis, P. M. (2002). The Obsessive-Compulsive Inventory: Development and validation of a short version. *Psychological Assessment*, *14*(4), 485–496.

Fontenelle, I. S., Prazeres, A. M., Borges, M. C., Rangé, B. P., Versiani, M., & Fontenelle, L. F. (2010). The Brazilian Portuguese version of the Saving Inventory–Revised: Internal consistency, test-retest reliability, and validity of a questionnaire to assess hoarding. *Psychological Reports*, *106*(1), 279–96.

Frost, R. O., & Gross, R. C. (1993). The hoarding of possessions. *Behaviour Research and Therapy*, *31*, 367–381..

Frost, R. O., & Hristova, V. (2011). Assessment of hoarding. *Journal of Clinical Psychology*, *67*(5), 456–466.

Frost, R. O., Hristova, V., Steketee, G., & Tolin, D. F. (2013). Activities of Daily Living Scale in hoarding disorder. *Journal of Obsessive-Compulsive and Related Disorders*, *2*(2), 85–90.

Frost, R. O., Kim, H. J., Morris, C., Bloss, C., Murray-Close, M., & Steketee, G. (1998). Hoarding, compulsive buying and reasons for saving. *Behaviour Research and Therapy*, *36*, 657–664.

Frost, R. O., Krause, M. S., & Steketee, G. (1996). Hoarding and obsessive-compulsive symptoms. *Behavior Modification*, *20*(1), 116–132.

Frost, R. O., Steketee, G., & Grisham, J. R. (2004). Measurement of compulsive hoarding: Saving Inventory–Revised. *Behaviour Research and Therapy*, *42*(10), 1163–1182.

Frost, R. O., Steketee, G., & Tolin, D. F. (2012). Diagnosis and assessment of hoarding disorder. *Annual Review of Clinical Psychology*, *8*, 219–242.

Frost, R. O., Steketee, G., Tolin, D. F., & Renaud, S. (2008). Development and validation of the Clutter Image Rating. *Journal of Psychopathology and Behavioral Assessment*, *30*, 193–203.

Frost, R. O., Steketee, G., & Williams, L. (2002). Compulsive buying, compulsive hoarding, and obsessive-compulsive disorder. *Behavior Therapy*, *33*, 201–214.

Frost, R. O., Steketee, G., Williams, L. F., & Warren, R. (2000). Mood, personality disorder symptoms and disability in obsessive compulsive hoarders: A comparison with clinical and nonclinical controls. *Behaviour Research and Therapy*, *38*(11), 1071–1081.

Frost, R. O., Tolin, D. F., & Maltby, N. (2010). Insight-related challenges in the treatment of hoarding. *Cognitive and Behavioral Practice*, *17*(4), 404–413.

Frost, R., Tolin, D., Steketee, G., Fitch, K., & Selbo-Bruns, A. (2009). Excessive acquisition in hoarding. *Journal of Anxiety Disorders*, *23*(5), 632–639.

Gordon, O. M., Salkovskis, P. M., & Oldenfield, V. B. (2013). Beliefs and experiences in hoarding. *Journal of Anxiety Disorders*, *27*, 328–339.

Grisham, J. R., Frost, R. O., Steketee, G., Kim, H. J., Tarkoff, A., & Hood, S. (2006). Age of onset in compulsive hoarding. *Journal of Anxiety Disorders*, *20*, 675–686.

Grisham, J. R., Frost, R. O., Steketee, G., Kim, H. J., Tarkoff, A., & Hood, S. (2009). Formation of attachment to possessions in compulsive hoarding. *Journal of Anxiety Disorders*, *23*, 357–361.

Grisham, J. R., Norberg, M. M., Williams, A. D., Certoma, S. P., & Kadib, R. (2010). Categorization and cognitive deficits in compulsive hoarding. *Behaviour Research and Therapy*, *48*, 866–872.

Halliday, G., & Snowdon, J. (2009). The Environmental Cleanliness and Clutter Scale (ECCS). *International Psychogeriatrics*, *21*, 1041–1050.

Ivanov, V. Z., Enander, J., Mataix-Cols, D., Serlachius, E., Månsson, K. N. T., Andersson, G., Flygare, O., Tolin, D., & Rück, C. (2018). Enhancing group cognitive-behavioral therapy for hoarding disorder with between-session Internet-based clinician support: A feasibility study. *Journal of Clinical Psychology*, *74*, 1092–1105.

Kellman-McFarlane, K., Stewart, B., Woody, S., Ayers, C., Dozier, M., Frost, R. O., Grisham, J., Isemann, S., Steketee, G., Tolin, D. F., & Welsted, A. (2019). Saving Inventory–Revised: Psychometric performance across the lifespan. *Journal of Affective Disorders*, *252*, 358–364.

Krafft, J., Ong, C. W., Twohig, M. P., & Levin, M. E. (2019). Assessing psychological inflexibility in hoarding: The Acceptance and Action Questionnaire for Hoarding (AAQH). *Journal of Contextual Behavioral Science*, *12*, 234–242.

Kyrios, M., Frost, R. O., & Steketee, G. (2004). Cognitions in compulsive buying and acquisition. *Cognitive Therapy and Research*, *28*, 241–258.

LeBeau, R. T., Mischel, E. R., Simpson, H. B., Mataix-Cols, D., Phillips, K. A., Stein, D. J., & Craske, M. G. (2013). Preliminary assessment of obsessive-compulsive spectrum disorder scales for DSM-5. *Journal of Obsessive-Compulsive and Related Disorders*, *2*(2), 114–118.

Lee, S. P., Ong, C., Sagayadevan, V., Ong, R., Abdin, E., Lim, S., Vaingankar, J., Picco, L., Verma, S., Chong, S. A., & Subramaniam, M. (2016). Hoarding symptoms among psychiatric outpatients: Confirmatory factor analysis and psychometric properties of the Saving Inventory–Revised (SI-R). *BMC Psychiatry*, *16*(1), 364.

Lejuez, C. W., & Calvin, N. T. (2009). *Titrating Mirror Tracing Task manual, Version 1.0*. University of Maryland.

Levy, H. C., Stevens, M. C., & Tolin, D. F. (2019). Validation of a behavioral measure of acquiring and discarding in hoarding disorder. *Journal of Psychopathology and Behavioral Assessment*, *41*(1), 135–143.

Liu, T. W., Lam, S. C., Chung, M. H., & Ho, K. H. M. (2020). Adaptation and psychometric testing of the Hoarding Rating Scale (HRS): A self-administered screening scale for epidemiological study in Chinese population. *BMC Psychiatry*, *20*, 159.

Luchian, S. A., McNally, R. J., & Hooley, J. M. (2007). Cognitive aspects of nonclinical obsessive-compulsive hoarding. *Behaviour Research and Therapy*, *45*, 1657–1662.

Mataix-Cols, D., Billotti, D., Fernández de la Cruz, D., & Nordsletten, A. E. (2013). The London field trial for hoarding disorder. *Psychological Medicine*, *43*(4), 837–848.

McCabe-Bennett, H., Lachman, R., Girard, T. A., & Antony, M. M. (2020). A virtual reality study of the relationships between hoarding, clutter, and claustrophobia. *Cyberpsychology, Behavior, and Social Networking*, *23*(2), 83–89.

Melli, G., Chiorri, C., Smurra, R., & Frost, R. O. (2013). Psychometric properties of the paper-and-pencil and online versions of the Italian Saving Inventory–Revised in nonclinical samples. *International Journal of Cognitive Therapy*, *6*(1), 40–56.

Mohammadzadeh, A. (2009). Validation of Saving Inventory–Revised (SI-R): Compulsive hoarding measure. *Iranian Journal of Psychiatry and Clinical Psychology*, *15*(1), 33–41.

Mueller, A., Mitchell, J. E., Crosby, R. D., Glaesmer, H., & de Zwaan, M. (2009). The prevalence of compulsive hoarding and its association with compulsive buying in a German population-based sample. *Behaviour Research and Therapy*, *47*(8), 705–709.

Muroff, J., & Otte, S. (2019). Innovations in CBT treatment for hoarding: Transcending office walls. *Journal of Obsessive-Compulsive and Related Disorders*, *23*, 100471.

Muroff, J., Steketee, G., Bratiotis, C., & Ross, A. (2012). Group cognitive and behavioral therapy and bibliotherapy for hoarding: A pilot trial. *Depression and Anxiety*, *29*, 597–604.

Muroff, J., Underwood, P., & Steketee, G. (2014). *Group treatment for hoarding disorder: Therapist guide*. Oxford University Press.

National Study Group on Chronic Disorganization (NSGCD). (2003). *The NSGCD Clutter Hoarding Scale*.

Nordsletten, A. E., Fernández de la Cruz, L., Drury, H., Ajmi, S., Saleem, S., & Mataix-Cols, D. (2014). The Family Impact Scale for Hoarding (FISH): Measure intervention through family members. *Journal of Consulting and Clinical Psychology*, *67*, 688–697.

Nordsletten, A. E., Fernández de la Cruz, L., Pertusa, A., Reichenberg, A., Hotopf, M., Hatch, S. L., & Mataix-Cols, D. (2013). The Structured Interview for Hoarding Disorder (SIHD): Development, further validation, and pragmatic usage. *Journal of Obsessive-Compulsive and Related Disorders*, *2*(3), 346–350.

Park, J. M., Samuels, J. F., Grados, M. A., Riddle, M. A., Bienvenu, O. J., Goes, F. S., & Geller, D. A. (2016). ADHD and executive functioning deficits in OCD youths who hoard. *Journal of Psychiatric Research*, *82*, 141–148.

Patton, M. (2002). *Qualitative research & evaluation methods* (Vol. 3). SAGE.

Phillips, K. A., Hollander, E., Rasmussen, S. A., & Aronowitz, B. R. (1997). A severity rating scale for body dysmorphic disorder: Development, reliability, and validity of a modified version of the Yale–Brown Obsessive Compulsive Scale. *Psychopharmacology Bulletin*, *33*(1), 17–22.

Preston, S. D., Muroff, J. R., & Wengrovitz, S. M. (2009). Investigating the mechanisms of hoarding from an experimental perspective. *Depression and Anxiety*, *26*(5), 425–437.

Rasmussen, J. L., Steketee, G., Frost, R. O., Tolin, D. F., & Brown, T. A. (2014). Assessing squalor in hoarding: The Home Environment Index. *Community Mental Health Journal, 50*(5), 591–596.

Sagayadevan, V., Lau, Y. W., Ong, C., Lee, S. P., Chong, S. A., & Subramaniam, M. (2016). Validation of the Clutter Image Rating (CIR) scale among psychiatric outpatients in Singapore. *BMC Psychiatry, 16*(1), 407.

Samuels, J. F., Bienvenu, O. J., Grados, M. A., Cullen, B., Riddle, M. A., Liang, K., Eaton, W. W., & Nestadt, G. (2008). Prevalence and correlates of hoarding behavior in a community-based sample. *Behaviour Research and Therapy, 46,* 836–844.

Saxena, S., Ayers, C. R., Dozier, M. E., & Maidment, K. M. (2015). The UCLA Hoarding Severity Scale: Development and validation. *Journal of Affective Disorders, 175,* 488–493.

Saxena, S., Brody, A. L., Maidment, K. M., & Baxter, L. R., Jr. (2007). Paroxetine treatment of compulsive hoarding. *Journal of Psychiatric Research, 41*(6), 481–487.

Saxena, S., & Sumner, J. (2014). Venlafaxine extended-release treatment of hoarding disorder. *International Clinical Psychopharmacology, 29*(5), 266–273.

Scahill, L., Riddle, M. A., McSwiggin-Hardin, M., Ort, S. I., King, R. A., Goodman, W. K., Cicchetti, D., & Leckman, J. F. (1997). Children's Yale-Brown Obsessive Compulsive Scale: Reliability and validity. *Journal of the American Academy of Child and Adolescent Psychiatry, 36*(6), 844–852.

Schneider, A. F., Storch, E. A., Geffken, G. R., Lack, C. W., & Shytle, R. D. (2008). Psychometric properties of the Hoarding Assessment Scale in college students. *Illness Crisis and Loss, 16*(3), 227–236.

Shafran, R., Frampton, I., Heyman, I., Reynolds, M., Teachman, B., & Rachman, S. (2003). The preliminary development of a new self-report measure for OCD in young people. *Journal of Adolescence, 26*(1), 137–142.

Shytle, R. D., & Sheehan, D. (2004). *Hoarding Assessment Scale* [Unpublished manuscript].

Snowdon, J., Halliday, G., & Hunt, G. E. (2013). Two types of squalor: Findings from a factor analysis of the Environmental Cleanliness and Clutter Scale (ECCS). *International Psychogeriatrics, 25*(7), 1191–1198.

Soreni, N., Cameron, D., Vorstenbosch, V., Duku, E., Rowa, K., Swinson, R., Bullard, C., & McCabe, R. (2018). Psychometric evaluation of a revised scoring approach for the Children's Saving Inventory in a Canadian sample of youth with obsessive-compulsive disorder. *Child Psychiatry & Human Development, 49*(6), 966–973.

Steketee, G., Ayers, C., Umbach, A., Tolin, D., & Frost, R. O. (2013). *Family response to hoarding: Assessment and features in an Internet sample* [Unpublished manuscript].

Steketee, G., & Frost, R. (2003). Compulsive hoarding: Current status of the research. *Clinical Psychology Review, 23*(7), 905–927.

Steketee, G., & Frost, R. O. (2013). *Treatment for hoarding disorder: Therapist guide* (2nd ed.). Oxford University Press.

Steketee, G., Frost, R. O., & Kyrios, M. (2003). Cognitive aspects of compulsive hoarding. *Cognitive Therapy and Research, 27*(4), 463–479.

Steketee, G., Frost, R. O., Tolin, D. F., Rasmussen, J., & Brown, T. A. (2010). Waitlist controlled trial of cognitive behavior therapy for hoarding disorder. *Depression and Anxiety, 27*(5), 476–484.

St-Pierre-Delorme, M. E., & O'Connor, K. (2016). Using virtual reality in the inference-based treatment of compulsive hoarding. *Frontiers in Public Health, 4,* 149.

Storch, E. A., Muroff, J., Lewin, A. B., Geller, D., Ross, A., McCarthy, K., Morgan, J., Murphy, T. K., Frost, R., & Steketee, G. (2011). Development and preliminary psychometric evaluation of the Children's Saving Inventory. *Child Psychiatry & Human Development, 42,* 166–182.

Tang, T., Wang, J., Tang, S., & Zhao, L. (2012). Psychometric properties of the Saving Inventory–Revised in Chinese University students sample. *Chinese Journal of Clinical Psychology, 20,* 21–24.

Tezcan, M. O., Konrad, J., & Muroff, J. (2018, April 8-10). Automatic assessment of hoarding clutter from images using convolutional neural networks [Paper]. *2018 IEEE Southwest Symposium on Image Analysis and Interpretation (SSIAI)*, Las Vegas, NV, pp. 1–4. doi: 10.1109/SSIAI.2018.8470375.

Thyer, B. A., Papsdorf, J. D., Davis, R., & Vallecorsa, S. (1984). Autonomic correlates of the Subjective Anxiety Scale. *Journal of Behavior Therapy and Experimental Psychiatry, 15*(1), 3–7.

Timpano, K. R., Çek, D., Fu, Z. F., Tang, T., Wang, J. P., & Chasson, G. S. (2015). A consideration of hoarding disorder symptoms in China. *Comprehensive Psychiatry, 57,* 36–45.

Tolin, D. F., Fitch, K. E., Frost, R. O., & Steketee, G. (2010). Family informants' perceptions of insight in compulsive hoarding. *Cognitive Therapy and Research, 34*(1), 69–81.

Tolin, D. F., Frost, R. O., & Steketee, G. (2010). A brief interview for assessing compulsive hoarding: The Hoarding Rating Scale-Interview. *Psychiatry Research, 178,* 147–152.

Tolin D. F., Frost, R. O., Steketee, G., & Fitch, K. E. (2008). Family burden of compulsive hoarding: Results of an Internet survey. *Behaviour Research and Therapy, 46*(3), 334–344.

Tolin, D. F., Gilliam, C. M., Davis, E., Springer, K., Levy, H. C., Frost, R. O., Steketee, G., & Stevens, M. C. (2018). Psychometric properties of the Hoarding Rating Scale-Interview. *Journal of Obsessive-Compulsive and Related Disorders, 16,* 76–80.

Tolin, D. F., Gilliam, C., Wootton, B. M., Bowe, W., Bragdon, L. B., Davis, E., Hannan, S. E., Steinman, S. A., Worden, B., & Hallion, L. S. (2018). Psychometric properties of a structured diagnostic interview for DSM-5 anxiety, mood, and obsessive-compulsive and related disorders. *Assessment, 25*(1), 3–13.

Tolin, D. F., Hannan, S., Maltby, N., Diefenbach, G. J., Worhunsky, P., & Brady, R. E. (2007). A randomized controlled trial of self-directed versus therapist-directed cognitive-behavioral therapy for obsessive-compulsive disorder patients with prior medication trials. *Behavior Therapy, 38,* 179–191.

Tolin, D. F., Meunier, S. A., Frost, R. O., & Steketee, G. (2011). Hoarding among patients seeking treatment for anxiety disorders. *Journal of Anxiety Disorders, 25,* 43–48.

Tolin, D. F., Stevens, M. C., Nave, A. M., Villavicencio, A., & Morrison, S. (2012). Neural mechanisms of cognitive behavioral therapy response in hoarding disorder: A pilot study. *Journal of Obsessive-Compulsive and Related Disorders, 1,* 180–188.

Tortella-Feliu, M., Fullana, M. A., Caseras, X., Andión, O., Torrubia, R., & Mataix-Cols, D. (2006). Spanish version of the Savings Inventory–Revised: Adaptation, psychometric properties, and relationship to personality variables. *Behavior Modification, 30*(5), 693–712.

Tsuchiyagaito, A., Horiuchi, S., Igarashi, T., Kawanori, Y., Hirano, Y., Yabe, H., & Nakagawa, A. (2017). Factor structure, reliability, and validity of the Japanese version of the Hoarding Rating Scale–Self-Report (HRS-SR-J). *Neuropsychiatric Disease and Treatment, 13,* 1235–1243.

Vorstenbosch, V., Antony, M. M., Monson, C. M., & Rowa, K. (2015). Family accommodation in problem hoarding. *Journal of Obsessive-Compulsive and Related Disorders, 7,* 7–15.

Willis, G. B. (2005). *Cognitive interviewing: A tool for improving questionnaire design.* SAGE.

Wincze, J. P., Steketee, G., & Frost, R. O. (2007). Categorization in compulsive hoarding. *Behaviour Research and Therapy, 45,* 63–72.

Wootton, B. M., Diefenbach, G. J., Bragdon, L. B., Steketee, G., Frost, R. O., & Tolin, D. F. (2015). A contemporary psychometric evaluation of the Obsessive Compulsive Inventory–Revised (OCI-R). *Psychological Assessment, 27*(3), 874–882.

CHAPTER 15

Assessing Trichotillomania and Skin-Picking Disorder

Sydney Biscarri Clark, Ashley Lahoud, *and* Christopher A. Flessner

Abstract

Pathological hair-pulling (trichotillomania, TTM) and skin-picking disorder (SPD) are body-focused repetitive behaviors (BFRBs) that can cause significant distress and impairment for those affected with the disorders. The literature related to BFRBs is in its infancy compared to literature on other disorders, which can make assessing the conditions particularly difficult for clinicians and clinical researchers. This chapter provides an overview of the available measurement tools for TTM and SPD, along with information related to the psychometric properties of each tool. Many of the measures described require further psychometric testing in larger clinical samples. Furthermore, TTM and SPD should be assessed using multiple modalities, including clinician interview, self-report, and other objective measures. While assessment of TTM and SPD requires further development overall, the development of measures for assessing these disorders in youth is in most need of attention, especially given that the age of onset for the disorders is often during adolescence.

Key Words: hair-pulling, skin-picking, trichotillomania, body-focused repetitive behaviors, assessment, children, adults

Trichotillomania (TTM), also known as hair-pulling disorder, and skin-picking disorder (SPD), also known as excoriation, are body-focused repetitive behaviors (BFRBs) that are categorized under obsessive-compulsive and related disorders (OCRDs) in the fifth edition of the *Diagnostic and Statistical Manual of Mental Disorders* (*DSM-5*; American Psychiatric Association [APA], 2013). TTM and SPD share many of the same phenomenological characteristics, have risk factors in common (e.g., genetic vulnerabilities), and frequently co-occur (Snorrason et al., 2012). In addition, the age of onset for both disorders is most commonly during adolescence (Flessner & Woods, 2006; Grant et al., 2010; Snorrason et al., 2012). Although phenomenologically there is considerable overlap between the disorders, this chapter provides an overview of TTM and SPD assessment separately, with an emphasis on evidence-based assessment (EBA). EBA encompasses scales and surveys that have shown empirical support for measuring a construct within a certain population (McGuire et al., 2012). Psychology has focused less on EBA than on evidence-based treatments (EBTs; McGuire et al., 2012); however, EBTs depend on the use of reliable and valid scales and assessments. For this reason, this chapter emphasizes the degree to which individual scales have been validated, so that researchers and clinicians can make the most informed decisions about scale use (see Tables 15.1 and 15.2). Both TTM and SPD require a multidimensional assessment that includes establishing a diagnosis, evaluating the severity of the behavior, pinpointing precipitating and maintenance factors, and inquiring about distress and impairment.

Assessing TTM

Physician Evaluation

Evaluation by a physician is not always necessary, but it can be beneficial in situations when the existence or presentation of hair-pulling is not straightforward. For example, a physician consultation may be an important first step when a person with TTM lacks awareness of their hair-pulling, when an adult or child denies or is unable to report pulling out hair, or when a person frequently swallows pulled hairs. It is also useful to rule out medical conditions that may result in similar symptoms (e.g. alopecia areata, tinea capitis, traction alopecia, androgenetic alopecia; Kuhn et al. 2017). A dermatologist can conduct a comprehensive evaluation of hair loss using fungal screens, hair pull and tug test, and trichoscopy to assess hair quality and patterns of alopecia (Pinto et al., 2017; Xu et al., 2017). With this information, a physician can differentiate between potential diagnoses. For example, the primary differential diagnosis of TTM, an autoimmune disease called alopecia areata, is characterized by exclamation point hairs and smooth, shiny patches of hair loss (Xu et al., 2017). By contrast, the clinical presentation of TTM is often associated with focal patches of hair loss with irregular borders, broken hairs, and hairs of varying lengths (Pinto et al., 2017; Xu et al., 2017). Evaluation by a physician is also important in the case of trichophagia (ingestion of pulled hairs), which is estimated to occur in 5% to 18% of those with TTM and is more common in males (Carr et al., 2006; Grant & Odlaug, 2008). In some cases, trichophagia may cause a trichobezoar (mass of hair in the gastrointestinal system) that requires surgical removal. If left unattended, a trichobezoar can result in serious health complications, such as gut perforation, acute pancreatic necrosis, and, in extreme cases, death (Carr et al., 2006).

Diagnosing TTM

The Trichotillomania Diagnostic Interview (TDI; Rothbaum & Ninan, 1994) is a standardized clinician-administered interview for use in diagnosing TTM; however, the TDI was created with *DSM-IV* criteria in mind. In the transition from *DSM-IV* to *DSM-5*, two criteria for TTM diagnosis (i.e., increasing tension immediately before pulling out hair or when attempting to resist the behavior, and please gratification, which is relief when pulling out the hair) were removed. Neither of these criteria has been shown to be a universal

Table 15.1. Measures Developed for the Assessment of Trichotillomania

Measure	Reliability	Validity
The Psychiatric Institute Trichotillomania Scale (PITS)	Internal consistency: questionable (α = 0.59–0.60) Test–retest reliability: not tested Interrater agreement: good for most items (ρ = 0.81–1.00)	Convergent validity • Correlated with MGH-HPS (r = 0.55–0.63) • Interference, distress, severity, and total score correlated with MTAI (r = 0.63–0.75) • Did not correlate with number of hairs pulled (r = 0.10) Divergent validity • Not significantly correlated with BDI-II (r = 0.30) • Correlated with STAIT-T (r = 0.54)
NIMH-Trichotillomania Severity Scale (NIMH-TSS)	Internal consistency: questionable (α = 0.63–0.65) Test–retest reliability: not tested Interrater agreement: adequate for the time-spent-pulling items (ρ = 0.81–1.00)	Convergent validity • Highly correlated with PITS (r = 0.75) and CGI (r = 0.63) • Duration items correlated highly with number of hairs pulled and time spent pulling (r = 0.63–0.78) • No items of the NIMH-TSS correlated with the MTAI Divergent validity • Not significantly correlated with BDI-II (r = 0.39) • Correlated with STAIT-T (r = 0.59)
NIMH-Trichotillomania Impairment Scale (NIMH-TIS)	Test–retest reliability: not rated Interrater agreement: adequate (ρ = 0.71)	Convergent validity • Correlates highly with the MTAI (r = 0.87), the CGI (r = 0.69), the PITS (r = 0.64), and alopecia ratings (r = 0.77) Divergent validity • Not significantly correlated with the BDI-II (r = 0.35) • Correlated with the STAI-T (r = 0.59)
Massachusetts General Hospital Hairpulling Scale (MGH-HPS)	Internal consistency: excellent (α = 0.89) Test–retest reliability: excellent (r = 0.97)	Convergent validity • Correlates highly with the PITS (r = 0.63) and CGS (r = 0.75) Divergent validity • Not significantly correlated with the BDI (r = 0.30) • Not significantly correlated with the BAI (r = 0.10)
The Trichotillomania Dimensional Scale (TTM-D)	Internal consistency: excellent (α = 0.89) Test–retest reliability: excellent (r = 0.91)	Convergent validity • Correlates highly with the MGH-HPS (rs = 0.74–0.90) Divergent validity • Weakly correlated with the BDD-YBOCS (rs = 0.19), the HRS (rs = 0.22), and the SPS (rs = 0.15) • Moderately correlated with the DASS-21 (rs = 0.45)

Table 15.1. *Continued*

Measure	Reliability	Validity
The Hair Pulling Reward Scale (HPRS)	Internal consistency • Wanting Scale: acceptable (α = 0.74) • Liking Scale: excellent (α = 0.89) Total score: excellent (α = 0.86) Test–retest reliability: not rated	Convergent validity • Wanting Scale was associated with TTM severity (r = 0.30), impulsiveness (r = 0.20), emotion dysregulation (r = 0.33), psychiatric symptoms (r = 0.12–0.33), and sleep dysfunction (r = 0.16) Divergent validity • Liking Scale had weaker associations with these same measures
The Milwaukee Inventory for Subtypes of Trichotillomania– Adult Version (MIST-A)	Original Version Internal consistency • Focused Scale: good (α = 0.77) • Automatic Scale acceptable (α = 0.73) Test–retest reliability: not rated Revised Version Internal consistency • Awareness of Pulling scale: good (α = 0.80) • Internal-regulated Pulling scale: acceptable (α = 0.74) Test–retest reliability: not tested	Original Version Convergent validity • Automatic Scale was moderately correlated with the proportion of time participants reported they were aware of pulling (r = −0.46) • Focused Scale was moderately correlated with the depression, anxiety, and stress scales of the DASS-21 (r = 0.32–0.36) Divergent validity: good Revised Version Construct validity • Internal-regulated pulling scores were associated with anxiety (r = 0.42), depression (r = 0.32), and experiential avoidance (r = −0.44) Divergent validity: not tested
The Trichotillomania Scale for Children (TSC)	Child-Report Internal consistency: good (α = 0.82–0.83) Test–retest reliability: good (r = 0.89) Parent-Report Internal consistency: acceptable/good (α = 0.70–0.84) Test–retest reliability: good (r = 0.90)	Child-Report Convergent validity • Correlated with self-reported interference with social functioning (r = 0.585) and making friends (r = 0.584) on the MASC • Correlated with CGI-S (r = 0.486) and the NIMH-TSS (r = 0.398) Divergent validity: unclear • Correlated more highly with the CDI (r = 0.605–0.607) than it did with other measures of TTM Parent-Report Convergent validity • Highly correlated with parent-reported child's ability to work (r = 0.516), moderately correlated with interference with social life (r = 0.414), and moderately correlated with missed events (r = 0.466) on the PROCAS • Severity score was moderately correlated with the PITS Severity score (r = 0.325) Divergent validity: not tested

(continued)

Table 15.1. *Continued*

Measure	Reliability	Validity
The Milwaukee Inventory for Styles of Trichotillomania–Child Version (MIST-C)	Internal consistency • Focused Scale: excellent (α = 0.90) • Automatic Scale: good (α = 0.80) Test–retest reliability: not tested	Convergent validity • Focused Scale was moderately correlated with the CDI (r = 0.41) and the MASC (r = 0.36) • Automatic Scale was highly correlated with Item 1 of the Trichotillomania Impact Survey (r = -0.61) Divergent validity • Automatic and Focused Scales did not correlate with each other

experience for those with TTM (Woods & Houghton, 2014). Lochner et al. found success in employing a modified version of the Structured Clinical Interview for DSM-IV Axis I Disorders–Patient Edition (SCID-I/P; First et al., 1998) to assess TTM as part of a *DSM-5* field study (Woods & Houghton, 2014). Currently, only one structured interview aligns with *DSM-5* criteria for TTM. The Diagnostic Interview for Anxiety, Mood, and Obsessive-Compulsive and Related Neuropsychiatric Disorders (DIAMOND; Tolin et al., 2018) is a semi-structured, broad clinical interview that assesses many disorders, including TTM. The full interview takes approximately 30 to 90 minutes to complete. For TTM, it has demonstrated excellent interrater reliability (κ = 1.00) and excellent test–retest reliability (κ = 1.00; Tolin et al., 2018). Convergent validity was assessed by comparing those diagnosed (vs. not diagnosed) with TTM according to the DIAMOND (N = 14) using self-reported hair-pulling severity scores. Findings, as predicted, demonstrated a very large and statistically significant effect between group severity ratings (p < 0.001; d = 4.80; Tolin et al., 2018). Although the DIAMOND is promising for assessing TTM, future studies should examine its psychometric properties in a larger TTM sample. The DIAMOND is recommended for use by clinical researchers and clinicians who prefer a broader assessment of psychological disorders in addition to the diagnosis of TTM. For clinical research wherein ascertaining a prompt TTM diagnosis is the main objective, the TDI is recommended (with items pertaining to tension/relief omitted).

Whether a structured or unstructured clinical interview is conducted, it is important for clinicians to adequately define the behavioral presentation of hair-pulling. TTM is a heterogeneous disorder. Hair-pulling can occur on any region of the body where hair grows; however, the most commonly reported pulling sites are the scalp, eyelashes, and eyebrows (Jones et al., 2018). Clients may pull from one site or multiple sites, and they may use their hands or other implements, such as tweezers, to remove hairs. Specific triggers may set the occasion for pulling to occur, such as the texture of the hair (e.g., kinky, coarse, rough, or curly), the person's location (i.e., in front of a mirror in a bathroom), or anxiety or stress (Grant et al., 2010). Generally speaking, reliable and valid assessment

Table 15.2. *Measures Developed for the Assessment of Skin Picking Disorder*

Measure	Reliability	Validity
Skin Picking Scale (SPS)	**Original** Internal consistency: good ($\alpha = 0.8$) Test-retest reliability: not rated Interrater agreement: not rated **Revised Version** Internal consistency Symptom Severity Subscale: good ($\alpha = 0.81$) Impairment Subscale: good ($\alpha = 0.79$) Total Score: good ($\alpha = 0.83$)	**Original** Convergent validity • In clinically severe skin pickers, SPS total score correlated with self-reported average duration of skin picking ($r = 0.49$) • Significantly correlated with BDI ($r = 0.60$) and BAI ($r = 0.64$) • Significant correlations with self-reported intensity of emotions before, during, and after picking ($r = 0.38$–0.65) Divergent validity: Not tested **Revised Version** Convergent/ Discriminant validity • The Impairment Subscale correlated more highly with the SDS and the DASS ($r = 0.37$–0.64) • The Severity Subscale correlated more highly with urge/ arousal prior to picking and time spent picking in the past week ($r = 0.34$–0.58)
Skin Picking Disorder–Dimensional Scale (SPD-D)	Internal consistency: excellent ($\alpha = 0.86$–0.92 across time points) Test-retest reliability: good ($r = 0.86$) Online/pen-and-paper equivalence • Total scale: excellent ($r = 0.93$) • Individual items: good/excellent ($r = 0.78$–0.92)	Convergent validity • SPD-D correlated with SPS ($r = 0.92$) • SPD-D correlated with SPS-R ($r = 0.90$) Discriminant validity • SPD-D correlated with Yale-Brown Obsessive-Compulsive Scale for Body Dysmorphic Disorder, Hoarding Rating Scale, and Massachusetts General Hospital hair pulling scale ($r = 0.14$–0.21) • SPD-D correlated with Generalized Anxiety Disorder Scale ($r = 0.40$)
Skin Picking Impact Scale (SPIS)	**Original** Internal consistency • Self-injurious skin pickers: excellent ($\alpha = 0.93$) • Non-self-injurious skin pickers: excellent ($\alpha = 0.88$) **Short Version** Internal consistency: excellent ($\alpha = 0.87$)	**Original** Convergent validity • Scores of self-injurious skin pickers correlate with picking duration, satisfaction, shame after picking, BDI scores, and BAI scores ($r = 0.36$–0.52) Discriminant validity • Nonclinical sample showed no correlation between SPIS Total scores and shame after picking, BDI score, or BAI score ($r = -0.02$–0.18) **Short Version** Convergent validity • SPIS-S correlated with the SDS, particularly the social disability subscale ($r = 0.31$–0.61) Discriminant validity • SPIS-S correlated weakly with the DASS ($r = 0.24$–0.31)

(continued)

Table 15.2. *Continued*

Measure	Reliability	Validity
Skin Picking Reward Scale (SPRS)	Internal consistency • Wanting Scale: excellent (α = 0.85–0.93) • Liking Scale: excellent (α = 0.92) • Total Score: excellent (α = 0.93–0.95 across time points) Test–retest reliability • Total and Subscales: good/excellent (r = 0.78–0.87)	Convergent validity • Liking Scale and Wanting Scale correlated with measure of positive affect during picking at multiple time points (r = 0.38–0.67 and 0.65, respectively) • The Wanting Scale at both time points and the Liking Scale at T2 positively correlated with picking-related positive affect (r = 0.65 and 0.67, respectively) • Scores on both the Wanting and the Liking Scale at T1 had positive correlations with SPS-R severity at T1 and T2 (r = 0.49–0.52) Discriminant validity • Picking related negative self-reflections had a significant positive correlation with the change in the Liking Scale from T1 to T2 (r = 0.48) but not the Wanting Scale • The Wanting scale significantly positively correlated with frequency of picking-related habits/routines (r = 0.45) but the Liking scale did not
Milwaukee Inventory for Dimensions of Adult Skin Picking (MIDAS)	Internal consistency • Focused Scale: good (α = 0.81) • Automatic Scale: good (α = 0.77)	Convergent validity • Focused Scale correlated with the SPS (r = 0.51) • Focused Scale correlated with the Acceptance and Action Questionnaire (AAQ), the Beck Anxiety Index (BAI), and the Beck Depression Index (BDI; r = 0.34–0.49) Discriminant validity • Automatic Scale did not correlate with the SPS (r = 0.09) • Automatic Scale did not correlate with the AAQ, BAI, and BDI (r = -0.06–0.02)

tools do not exist to procure much of the information described above. Clinicians and researchers are advised to develop their own line of questioning to assess for these important phenomenological characteristics, with the understanding that no "gold standard" measurement tool exists.

The vast majority of available EBA tools for TTM focus upon the reliable and valid measurement of TTM severity and impairment. Diefenbach et al. (2005) were among the first authors to formally assess the psychometric properties of TTM severity/impairment measures. The measures available at the time of their assessment included the Massachusetts General Hospital Hairpulling Scale (MGH-HPS), NIMH-Trichotillomania Severity Scale (NIMH-TSS), NIMH-Trichotillomania Impairment Scale (NIMH-TIS), and the Psychiatric Institute Trichotillomania Scale (PITS). Mixed results were demonstrated. For example, Diefenbach and colleagues found that reliability was strong for self-report, but not clinician-report, measures. The authors argued that two separate dimensions of TTM exist that do not consistently correlate with each other (i.e., current hair-pulling behaviors and the impact of hair-pulling behaviors). Poor reliability estimates may be due to the fact that the two dimensions are often combined into one overall score. It is probably more informative and accurate to assess and track TTM symptoms using item or subscale scores, rather than a summary score. Consequently, the authors concluded that TTM requires a comprehensive assessment approach. What follows are brief descriptions of currently available assessment tools for TTM.

Clinician Measures
THE PITS

The PITS (Winchel et al., 1992) is a semi-structured clinician-report measure with six items designed to assess hair-pulling history, number of hair-pulling sites, time spent hair-pulling per day, ability to resist urges to pull, interference with functioning, associated distress, and severity of hair loss. Each item is rated on an 8-point Likert scale ranging from 0 to 7. Items are summed to produce an overall symptom severity score ranging from 0 to 42, with higher scores indicating greater TTM severity. There are mixed findings regarding the psychometric properties of the PITS. For example, Stanley et al. (1999) found high interrater agreement ($\rho = 0.92–1.00$) for all items except number of hair-pulling sites ($\rho = 0.55$) and overall symptom severity score ($\rho = 0.60$), while Diefenbach et al. (2005) demonstrated good interrater agreement ($\rho = 0.81–0.96$) for all items with the exception of associated distress ($\rho = 0.45$). The PITS has consistently exhibited poor internal consistency ($\alpha = 0.59–0.60$), although it is unclear whether the low internal consistency is due to error in measurement or variability in the way TTM presents itself (Diefenbach et al., 2005; Stanley et al., 1999). Diefenbach and colleagues also found that the internal consistency of the scale was increased when interference with functioning, associated distress, and severity of hair loss items were combined ($\alpha = 0.72$). The scale's poor internal consistency, in turn, makes the PITS less sensitive to detecting symptom change than self-report measures, such as the MGH-HPS (Nelson et al., 2014).

With respect to convergent validity, the PITS correlates strongly with the MGH-HPS (r = 0.55–0.63; Diefenbach et al., 2005; O'Sullivan et al., 1995). Further, interference, distress, severity, and PITS total score have been shown to correlate strongly (r = 0.63–0.75) with the Minnesota Trichotillomania Assessment Interview (MTAI; Christenson et al., 1991); however, number of pulling sites, time spent hair-pulling per day, and ability to resist urges to pull were not correlated. The PITS total score has also failed to correlate with self-reported number of hairs pulled (r = 0.10; Stanley et al., 1999). Evidence for divergent validity is also mixed. While the PITS has been shown to correlate only moderately with the Beck Depression Inventory-II (BDI-II; Beck et al., 1996; r = 0.30), the PITS correlates strongly with the State-Trait Anxiety Inventory (STAI-T; Spielberger et al., 1983; r = 0.54). Synthesis of the empirical evidence suggests that the PITS, although providing potentially useful ancillary information (i.e., percent of hair missing), is best avoided for purposes of developing a TTM assessment battery designed to measure treatment severity or outcome.

THE NIMH-TSS

The NIMH-TSS (Swedo et al., 1989) is a six-item clinician-report interview that assesses average time spent pulling hair per day in the past week, time spent pulling hair the previous day, thoughts and feeling preceding hair-pulling, attempts to resist the urge to pull, associated distress, and degree of interference with daily life. Items 1, 2, 5, and 6 are rated on a six-point Likert scale ranging from 0 to 5. Item 4 is a multiple-choice question asking whether the patient attempted to resist the urge to pull and if they were successful. The five items rated using a Likert scale are summed to produce an overall symptom severity score ranging from 0 to 25. Higher scores indicate greater pulling severity. Similar to the PITS, the NIMH-TSS has demonstrated mixed psychometric properties (Diefenbach et al., 2005; Stanley et al., 1999). The scale has consistently demonstrated adequate inter-rater agreement with respect to the time-spent-pulling items (ρ = 0.81–1.00); however, only one of two studies that examined the NIMH-TSS demonstrated adequate inter-rater agreement on resistance and interference items and the NIMH-TSS total score (Diefenbach et al., 2005; Stanley et al., 1999). Further, the NIMH-TSS has demonstrated consistently poor internal consistency (total score α = 0.63–0.65; Diefenbach et al., 2005; Stanley et al., 1999). These mixed to poor reliability findings have, perhaps not surprisingly, led to similarly mixed findings with respect to the scale's construct validity.

In one of the first studies to examine the psychometric properties of the NIMH-TSS, Stanley et al. (1999) examined the convergent validity (with MTAI total score) and concurrent validity (i.e., self-reported number of hairs pulled, time spent pulling) of the scale. No items from the NIMH-TSS correlated with the MTAI, whereas NIMH-TSS duration items correlated highly with self-reported number of hairs pulled and time spent pulling (r = 0.63–0.78). Despite this, the NIMH-TSS total score correlated only with number of hairs pulled (r = 0.58)—not time spent pulling (Stanley et al., 1999). Several years later, Diefenbach et al. (2005) demonstrated that the NIMH-TSS total score correlated strongly with both the PITS total score ($r = 0.75$) and the Clinical Global Impression (CGI) Severity Scale total score ($r = 0.63$; Guy, 1976); however, the former relationship should be considered tenuous given the information pertaining to both the reliability and the validity of the PITS. Similar to the PITS, the NIMH-TSS has been shown to correlate only modestly with the BDI-II ($r = 0.39$), but strongly with the STAI-T ($r = 0.59$). More recently, a 30% to 40% reduction or a 6-point raw score change in NIMH-TSS total score has been suggested as the best indicator of clinically significant treatment response, while a 65% reduction represents the best indicator of TTM remission (Houghton et al., 2015). Collectively, empirical evidence suggests that the NIMH-TSS likely has only modestly superior psychometric properties to the PITS and is far below findings specific to the MGH-HPS.

THE NIMH-TIS

The NIMH-TIS is a clinician-report global severity scale. The scale allows for evaluators to categorize patients with TTM into one of four categories: "no impairment," "minimal impairment," "mild impairment," or "moderate/severe impairment," based on an overall summary of their distress, time spent pulling, attempts to stop pulling, hair loss, and money spent concealing disfigurement. Each category corresponds to a range of scores (0, 1–3, 4–6, and 7–10, respectively). The NIMH-TIS has demonstrated adequate interrater agreement ($\rho = 0.71$; Stanley et al., 1999). Evidence for convergent validity has also been supported. The NIMH-TIS correlates highly with the MTAI total score ($r = 0.87$), CGI ($r = 0.69$), PITS ($r = 0.64$), and alopecia ratings (i.e., amount of hair loss; $r = 0.77$; Diefenbach et al., 2005; Stanley et al., 1999). Evidence for divergent validity is mixed and akin to findings demonstrated with respect to both the PITS and NIMH-TSS. That is, the NIMH-TIS does not correlate significantly with the BDI-II ($r = 0.35$) but correlates strongly with the STAI-T ($r = 0.59$; Diefenbach et al., 2005). Although not providing as consistent findings as the MGH-HPS, the NIMH-TIS exhibits the strongest psychometric properties among available clinician-rated measures of TTM severity/impairment and, therefore, represents the first choice among clinician-rated measures of TTM severity in a comprehensive assessment battery.

Self-Report Measures
THE MGH-HPS

The MGH-HPS (Keuthen et al., 1995) was developed to assess TTM severity and is modeled after the Yale-Brown Obsessive-Compulsive Scale (Y-BOCS; Goodman et al., 1989). The scale consists of seven self-report items designed to assess behaviors and feelings associated with TTM over the past week (i.e., the frequency of urges, the intensity of urges, the ability to control urges, the frequency of hair-pulling, attempts to resist hair-pulling, control over hair-pulling, and associated distress). Each item is rated from 0 (no symptoms) to 4 (extreme symptoms). Item ratings are then summed to produce an overall symptom severity score ranging from 0 to 28, with higher scores indicating greater pulling severity.

The MGH-HPS has demonstrated adequate psychometric properties. For example, the scale has demonstrated excellent test–retest reliability ($r = 0.97$) and excellent internal consistency ($\alpha = 0.89$; Keuthen et al., 1995; O'Sullivan et al., 1995). Further, the MGH-HPS has shown strong convergent validity with both the PITS ($r = 0.63$) and Clinical Global Severity (CGS) scores ($r = 0.75$; O'Sullivan et al., 1995). Divergent validity has been demonstrated by way of comparatively lower correlations with both the Beck Depression Inventory (BDI; $r = 0.30$; Beck et al., 1961) and the Beck Anxiety Inventory (BAI; $r = 0.10$; Beck et al., 1988; O'Sullivan et al., 1995). Finally, the MGH-HPS also correlates strongly with changes on the PITS ($r = 0.83$), CGS ($r = 0.74$), and CGI scores ($r = -0.50$; O'Sullivan et al., 1995), suggesting sensitivity to change.

More recently, Keuthen and colleagues (2007) re-examined the factor structure of the MGH-HPS and revealed a two-factor structure. The first factor (Severity) consisted of four items: frequency of urges, intensity of urges, ability to control urges, and associated distress, while the second factor (Resistance and Control) consisted of the remaining three items: frequency of hair-pulling, attempts to resist hair-pulling, and control over hair-pulling (Keuthen et al., 2007). Both subscales demonstrated adequate internal consistency ($\alpha = 0.83$ and $\alpha = 0.81$, respectively; Keuthen et al., 2007). Preliminary evidence from a randomized controlled trial (RCT) suggested a 45% reduction or a 7-point raw score change on the MGH-HPS was the best indicator of clinically significant treatment response and a 55% to 60% reduction or a 7-point raw score change was the best indicator of TTM remission (Houghton et al., 2015).

Although additional research is warranted, these recommended change criteria as well as generally consistent and strong psychometric properties suggest that the MGH-HPS is a useful tool for clinicians and clinical researchers in evaluating pulling severity as well as treatment success or failure. The simplicity and brevity of the measure are inherent strengths. In addition, self-report measures like the MGH-HPS may also be particularly useful when assessing TTM severity, given that hair-pulling behaviors often occur in private. Moreover, Keuthen et al. (2007) theorized that the two-factor structure of the MGH-HPS may be useful for patient characterization, treatment selection, and treatment mechanism identification. One limitation to the measure, however, is the absence of items aimed at assessing severity of hair loss.

THE TRICHOTILLOMANIA DIMENSIONAL SCALE

The Trichotillomania Dimensional Scale (TTM-D; LeBeau et al., 2013) is a five-item self-report scale that uses a 5-point Likert scale to measure hair-pulling symptomatology via items inquiring about frequency, distress, control, avoidance, and life interference of hair-pulling within the past week. Utilizing a large college sample ($N = 296$), LeBeau et al.

(2013) found that the scale consisted of a single factor accounting for 72% of the variance. Internal consistency of the scale was high (α = 0.89). LeBeau et al. (2013) also found that the TTM-D demonstrated good convergent validity, because it was highly correlated with the MGH-HPS (r_s = 0.74), and good divergent validity, because it was more weakly correlated with the Yale-Brown Obsessive-Compulsive Scale for Body Dysmorphic Disorder (BDD-YBOCS; r_s = 0.19; Phillips et al., 1997), the Hoarding Rating Scale (HRS; r_s = 0.22; Tolin et al., 2010), and the Skin Picking Scale (SPS; r_s = 0.15; Keuthen et al., 2001). In a second study by Cheyne et al. (2018) using a large community sample (N = 483), internal consistency of the TTM-D was found to be high (α = 0.89) and test–retest reliability was also high (r = 0.91). The scale demonstrated excellent convergent validity with the MGH-HPS (r_s = 0.90) and was less strongly correlated with the DASS-21 (r_s = 0.45), demonstrating divergent validity. An important limitation of the TTM-D is that it has yet to be validated in a clinical sample.

THE HAIR PULLING REWARD SCALE

The Hair Pulling Reward Scale (HPRS; Snorrason et al., 2019) is a 16-item self-report instrument meant to assess reward-processing in the context of TTM. Confirmatory factor analysis supported a two-factor model: Liking (i.e., pleasure when reward is received) and Wanting (i.e., motivation to seek the reward). The Liking subscale and the HPRS total score demonstrated excellent internal consistency (α = 0.89 and α = 0.86, respectively). The internal consistency of the Wanting subscale was acceptable (α = 0.89). To assess the scale's convergent and divergent validity, the HPRS subscales were examined in relation to theoretically derived validity criteria: TTM severity, psychiatric symptoms, impulsiveness, emotion dysregulation, sleep dysfunction, sensitivity to rewards, and sensitivity to threats. The Wanting scale was associated with TTM severity (r = 0.30), impulsiveness (r = 0.20), emotion dysregulation (r = 0.33), psychiatric symptoms (r = 0.12–0.33), and sleep dysfunction (r = 0.16) to a greater extent than the Liking scale, as predicted by the researchers. The Liking scale was more weakly associated with TTM severity (r = 0.17), impulsiveness (r = 0.14), emotion dysregulation (r = 0.15), psychiatric symptoms (r = -0.11–0.149), and sleep dysfunction (r = -0.11), and, of these correlations, only TTM severity and one psychiatric symptom (responsiveness to threats) were significant. The authors suggest that the Wanting and Liking constructs have strong theoretical and empirical background for TTM reward-processing. Assessing these underlying mechanisms may inform treatment choice for those with hair-pulling disorder (Snorrason et al., 2019). As was the case for the TTM-D, research is needed to examine the psychometric properties of the HPRS in a clinical sample.

Hair-Pulling Style

Evidence-based assessment tools do exist with respect to pulling style among patients with TTM. Originally, researchers conceptualized two styles of hair-pulling—automatic pulling and focused pulling. Automatic pulling occurs outside of one's awareness, often while one is engaged in sedentary activities (e.g., watching television). Conversely, focused pulling involves a conscious intention to pull out hairs in an effort to regulate negative affect. It is commonplace for both children and adults with TTM to engage in both styles of pulling; however, patients may engage in one style more than others. It has been hypothesized that the disparate pulling styles may respond differentially to certain EBT approaches (Keuthen et al., 2015). As a result, the assessment of pulling styles among both youth and adults with TTM can be very important for developing more robust treatment plans. What follows is a brief description of the existing tool for measuring pulling styles in adults.

THE MILWAUKEE INVENTORY FOR SUBTYPES OF TRICHOTILLOMANIA—ADULT VERSION

The Milwaukee Inventory for Subtypes of Trichotillomania–Adult Version (MIST-A; Flessner et al., 2008) was developed to assess both automatic and focused hair-pulling. A self-report measure, the MIST-A consists of 15 items rated on a 0 to 9 scale, with 0 indicating "not true for any of my hairpulling" and 9 indicating "true for all of my hairpulling." The Automatic and Focused Pulling scales consist of five and ten items and have demonstrated adequate internal consistency (α = 0.73 and 0.77, respectively). As part of its initial validation, the MIST-A exhibited good convergent and discriminant validity. For example, the Automatic scale moderately correlated with the proportion of time participants reported they were aware of pulling (r = -0.46), while the Focused scale moderately correlated with the depression, anxiety, and stress scales of the DASS-21 (r = 0.32–0.36; Flessner et al., 2008; Lovibond & Lovibond, 1995). Subsequent research has suggested the original MIST-A's factor structure may have been too simplistic to capture the variability that exists among pulling styles and may improperly merge characteristics of TTM that are actually independent of each other (i.e., awareness of hair-pulling and capacity to regulate emotions; Alexander et al., 2016). Therefore, two recent studies have sought to further investigate the optimal factor structure and number of items for the MIST-A.

Keuthen et al. (2015) were the first researchers to replicate the work of Flessner et al. (2008). Results revealed a two-factor model, including an eight-item Intention scale and a five-item Emotion scale, as opposed to the original Automatic and Focused scales. The revised, 13-item MIST-A accounted for more variance than the original, 15-item version; however, the model still underexplained total variance, suggesting that the MIST-A may not fully capture TTM pulling styles. The MIST-A was subsequently re-examined by Alexander et al. (2016), who suggested a revised structure consisting of a five-item "awareness of pulling" subscale and an eight-item "internal-regulated pulling" subscale. These new subscales demonstrated adequate internal consistency (α = 0.80 and α = 0.74, respectively). Further analyses provided preliminary support for the scale's construct validity because internal-regulated-pulling scores were associated with anxiety (r = 0.42), depression (r = 0.32), and experiential avoidance (r = -0.44), while awareness-of-pulling scores were not. Similar to Keuthen et al. (2015), Alexander and colleagues (2016) concluded that the MIST-A likely does not comprehensively assess all the ways in which hair-pulling can vary within and across TTM patients. Despite the limitations of the MIST-A, the measure is currently the only psychometrically validated scale designed to assess hair-pulling styles in adults. The MIST-A may not provide comprehensive assessment of all possible pulling presentations that exist, yet the measure helps to provide a better understanding of the degree to which a person is aware of their hair-pulling and the function their hair-pulling serves.

Assessing TTM in Youth

The preponderance of validated measures for use among patients with TTM largely target adult populations. The psychometric properties of assessment measures are sample-specific and may not generalize across age groups. TTM measures validated only in adult populations should not be routinely used with children. Assessment results for children with TTM gleaned from adult-specific measures should be viewed tentatively. The two validated measures for assessing impairment/severity and assessing hair-pulling styles among youths with TTM are the Trichotillomania Scale for Children and the Milwaukee Inventory for Styles of Trichotillomania–Child Version.

THE TRICHOTILLOMANIA SCALE FOR CHILDREN

The Trichotillomania Scale for Children (TSC) was originally a 15-item scale comprised of three subscales (with five items each) designed to assess TTM severity, distress, and impairment, and it included both parent- and child-report versions (TSC-P and TSC-C, respectively; Diefenbach et al., 2003). Principal components analysis in a later study by Tolin et al. (2008) refined the scale further and yielded two subscales (Severity and Distress/Impairment) with five and seven items, respectively. Each of the 12 items on the TSC is scored from 0 to 2 based on the highest rating of endorsed statements. For example, some items contain multiple 0-, 1-, and 2-point responses. The score for each item is based upon the value attributed to whichever statement the child endorses. Severity and Distress/Impairment subscale scores are calculated by averaging individual item scores from each subscale. The TSC total score is calculated by summing the two subscale scores. Both the TSC-C and the TSC-P have demonstrated good internal consistency with an Internet sample (α = 0.83 and α = 0.84, respectively) and good to adequate internal consistency with a clinical sample (α = 0.82 and α = 0.70, respectively). The TSC-C and TSC-P have each demonstrated strong test–retest reliability (r = 0.89 and r = 0.90, respectively) with a small clinical sample of children (N = 9) and parents (N = 5; Tolin et al., 2008). Collectively, results suggest that the TSC-C and TSC-P are reliable measures for use with pediatric TTM populations; however, the construct validity of the measures is less clear.

Convergent validity for the TSC has been somewhat mixed. Tolin and colleagues (2008) found the TSC-C total score to correlate strongly with child-reported interference with social functioning ($r = 0.585$) and making friends ($r = 0.584$) on the Multidimensional Anxiety Scale for Children (MASC; March, 1998) as well as the Clinician's Global Impression-Severity (CGI-S; $r = 0.486$) scale. The TSC-C also correlated moderately with the NIMH-TSS ($r = 0.398$); however, in the same study, the TSC-C was shown to correlate more strongly with the Children's Depression Inventory (CDI; Kovacs, 1992; $r = 0.605–0.607$) than other measures of TTM (such as NIMH-TSS and PITS). With respect to parent report, Tolin et al. (2008) found that the TSC-P correlated strongly with a child's ability to work ($r = 0.516$). The scale also correlated moderately to strongly with interference in social life ($r = 0.414$) and missed events ($r = 0.466$), as measured by the Parent Report on Child's Anxiety Symptoms (PROCAS; March et al., 1997). The TSC-P Severity subscale correlated moderately with the PITS Severity score ($r = 0.325$), while the TSC-P Distress/Impairment subscale correlated moderately with the PITS Distress score ($r = 0.338$). Findings on the divergent validity of the TSC-C were unclear, and the divergent validity of the TSC-P was not examined. What is more, agreement between child and parent reports on the TSC-C and TSC-P, respectively, was adequate to high. Clearly, research is needed to more carefully compare the TSC to other measures of TTM severity, distress, and impairment and to determine if it is sensitive to change (McGuire et al., 2012; Tolin et al., 2008). Further, it is equally important to note that some caution should be exercised in interpreting the findings because, in many cases, assessment of the convergent validity of the TSC was undertaken using measures validated for adults, not children.

THE MILWAUKEE INVENTORY FOR STYLES OF TRICHOTILLOMANIA—CHILD VERSION

The Milwaukee Inventory for Styles of Trichotillomania–Child Version (MIST-C; Flessner et al., 2007) is a youth (age 10 to 17) child-report measure designed to assess automatic and focused pulling and is modeled on the MIST-A. The MIST-C consists of 25 items rated on a scale identical to that used in the MIST-A (i.e., 0 to 9). The Automatic scale consists of four items and has demonstrated good internal consistency ($\alpha = 0.80$), while the Focused scale consists of 21 items and has demonstrated excellent internal consistency ($\alpha = 0.90$). What is more, both scales have demonstrated preliminary support for their individual convergent and discriminant validity. More specifically, the Focused scale has demonstrated a moderate correlation with scores from both the CDI ($r = 0.41$) and the MASC ($r = 0.36$). The Automatic scale, alternatively, exhibited a strong correlation with an individual item, embedded within a larger survey, inquiring "How often do you *know* when you are pulling?" ($r = -0.61$). Neither of the MIST-C subscales correlated with each other. To our knowledge, the MIST-C is the only validated measure for children designed to assess phenomenological characteristics of TTM (i.e., automatic and focused pulling). No replication studies of the above-mentioned results have been conducted. Further, the MIST-C has not been validated for use with children younger than 10 years old. Similar to the MIST-A, the MIST-C has been shown to explain only 33% of the total variance in hair-pulling. It is probable that focused and automatic pulling are best conceptualized as dimensional constructs (i.e., clients present with varying degrees of focused and/or automatic pulling) rather than distinct subtypes (i.e., clients fall into one category; Flessner et al. 2007). Despite this, the MIST-C remains an important component of the assessment battery provided to the families of children with TTM.

Adult Measures That Have Been Utilized with Child Populations

Due to the dearth of child-specific hair-pulling measures, clinical researchers have frequently utilized adult measures to assess pulling-related behavior in youth. For example, the MGH-HPS has never been validated with a pediatric sample. In an early study, however, the MGH-HPS appeared to be sensitive to treatment change in a sample that included adolescents (17 years old or older) as part of an RCT (van Minnen et al., 2003). The MGH-HPS may have clinical utility for more mature youth (i.e., late-stage adolescents), but the language of the MGH-HPS is probably too advanced for younger, school-age children. More research is necessary to examine the psychometric properties of the MGH-HPS in a child sample before it can be used confidently with pediatric populations. The NIMH-TSS also has not been validated in a pediatric sample; however, in an RCT of behavior therapy, the NIMH-TSS exhibited adequate test–retest reliability ($r = 0.70$) and good interrater agreement ($\rho = 0.88$) for children (7 to 17 years old) with TTM (Franklin et al., 2011). McGuire et al. (2020) employed the MIST-A with a sample of youth between the ages of 7 and 17 years ($N = 40$). In this sample, the MIST-A demonstrated acceptable internal consistency for the Automatic ($\alpha = 0.76–0.80$) and Focused ($\alpha = 0.77–0.80$) subscales. There was some evidence for convergent validity for both subscales, although significant methodological limitations to the study preclude any firm conclusions about the validity of the MIST-A for use among children and adolescents. Given the existence of a validated measure for assessing pulling styles in youths already, it is strongly recommended that clinicians and clinical researchers continue to use the MIST-C for assessment of pulling styles in youth. Similarly, use of the TSC is recommended for assessment of pulling severity/impairment in a pediatric population. Available, albeit limited, empirical evidence also appears to support the use of the NIMH-TSS as a clinician-rated measure of pulling severity among youth with TTM.

Complementary Assessment Strategies

Additional approaches exist for collecting potentially useful measurements of hair-pulling severity among both children and adults with TTM. For example, photographic ratings and assessment may be a valuable addition to comprehensive TTM assessment. The use of photographic ratings has been employed in a variety of studies in the TTM field (Friman et al., 1984; Rosenbaum & Ayllon, 1981; Rothbaum & Ninan, 1994), yet few studies have sought to examine the psychometric properties of this measurement approach. Houghton et al. (2016) found that photographic assessment of hair-loss change in adults exhibits adequate psychometric properties and was significantly correlated with change in quality of life ($r = 0.42$). The authors found using photographs to document change was good to excellent; however, reliability was only fair. The researchers found that changes on clinician- and self-report measures predicted treatment outcome; however, photographic assessment significantly added to the prediction of treatment response (Houghton et al., 2016). Photographic assessment is a promising method for use in certain pulling sites (e.g., scalp, eyelashes, eyebrows), but it is inappropriate for other pulling sites (e.g., pubic area). The difficulty in achieving reliability, as noted by Houghton and colleagues, is also important to consider. No gold standard exists for obtaining photographic ratings. Additional factors, such as lighting, individual rate of hair regrowth, and pulling site(s), may all impact the reliability of this method. In lieu of a standardized set of photographic rating procedures, the use of such ratings is best considered in the context of additional measures of pulling severity/impairment (i.e., MGH-HPS, TSC, NIMH-TSS).

Other methods of assessment may include self-monitoring procedures, such as asking the client to keep a detailed record of pulling incidents throughout the day. Components of a daily hair-pulling log may include the time of day, the specific situation in which the pulling occurred, preceding emotions or thoughts, subsequent emotions or thoughts, pulling site, and pulling episode duration (Morris et al., 2013). Not only is this type of assessment informative, in that it can give the clinician a sense of the client's patterns of pulling, but also the act of keeping a log, in itself, can reduce hair-pulling by helping those with TTM gain a greater awareness of their behavior (Morris et al., 2013). It may also be beneficial to have clients collect pulled hairs in a resealable plastic bag immediately after pulling. These hairs can be counted later in order to get a sense of how many hairs are being pulled per day and may also prevent clients from engaging in post-pulling behaviors, such as manipulating or eating the hairs (Morris et al., 2013; Woods & Houghton, 2014). Direct or videotaped observation is another method of assessment that can be used. This type of observation may be appropriate for collecting information about frequency of hair-pulling, but intensity and duration are difficult to assess using observation (Elliott & Fuqua, 2000). Given the shame and embarrassment that are often associated with TTM, it is unlikely that direct observation is the most viable option for assessment. The behaviors are more likely to occur in private, and clients may react to being observed. The feasibility of assessment strategies will vary depending on the client and available resources. Clinicians should attempt to include a variety of outcome measures in order to get a comprehensive picture of the client's TTM.

Assessing SPD

Researchers interested in assessing various aspects of SPD among adults will quickly realize that there are few EBAs for the disorder, and only one EBA has been developed for children and adolescents. The latter is particularly troubling, given that the onset of SPD often occurs in adolescence. Unless otherwise specified, the assessment measures and techniques discussed here have all been validated for use within adult populations. This review focuses on clinician-administered and self-report scales. Also mentioned are non-SPD-specific measures (i.e., measures of BFRBs in general that include skin-picking) and observational scales.

Physician Evaluation

As in TTM, a physical examination may be necessary when assessing SPD in individuals who are unable or unwilling to report their skin-picking. SPD often begins after the onset of dermatological conditions like acne, but it continues even after the condition has resolved (Keuthen et al., 2000). Scratching or picking the skin is associated with multiple dermatological conditions, including scabies, psoriasis, and atopic dermatitis; thus, dermatological consultation may be necessary to rule out medical conditions and to evaluate the degree of skin damage. During the consultation, the physician may perform several tests, including microscope examinations, allergy tests, and fungal infection tests, to eliminate other potential causes of skin irritation (Grant et al., 2012). A psychiatric evaluation is also important for accurately diagnosing SPD. It is common for SPD to be misdiagnosed as obsessive-compulsive disorder (OCD) or body dysmorphic disorder (BDD) due to similar characteristics. Traits like repetitive motor movements can be associated with SPD or OCD. Similarly, fixation with the skin can be a feature of SPD or BDD (Grant et al., 2012). In severe cases, serious health conditions can result from skin-picking, such as permanent tissue damage, septicemia, and even death. Therefore, it is imperative that thorough investigative measures address the origin of any skin concerns (Keuthen et al., 2000).

Diagnosing SPD

A majority of the validated skin-picking scales are self-report measures. However, the DIAMOND, which can be used to diagnose TTM, can also be used to assess SPD. The DIAMOND has shown very good interrater reliability ($\kappa = 0.78$) and excellent test–retest reliability ($\kappa = 0.94$) in a sample of people with SPD ($N = 19$; Tolin et al., 2018). Convergent validity has been established by comparing skin-picking severity scores among those with SPD, based upon DIAMOND diagnosis, to scores among those who did not reach the diagnostic threshold. Findings exhibited, as predicted, a very large and statistically significant between-group effect ($p < 0.001$; $d = 2.18$; Tolin et al., 2018). Future studies should examine the psychometric properties of the DIAMOND in a larger SPD sample. The DIAMOND offers researchers and clinicians the same benefits for SPD as it does for TTM—it is able to assess many other potential comorbid diagnoses in one sitting. For those interested in a briefer interview, a modified version of the SCID-I/P (which was created for diagnosis of skin-picking based on *DSM-IV* criteria) can be used to assess skin-picking (First et al., 1998). The Keuthen Diagnostic Inventory for Skin Picking (K-DISP; Keuthen, unpublished) is a six-item, semi-structured diagnostic tool that is similar to the SCID (Hallion et al., 2017). The K-DISP can be used along with the clinical interview to confirm and monitor an SPD diagnosis. Similarly, the Yale-Brown Obsessive-Compulsive Scale Modified for Neurotic Excoriation (NE-YBOCS) is modeled on the original Y-BOCS (Goodman et al., 1989). The NE-YBOCS is a 10-item semi-structured scale designed to assess skin-picking severity and to aid in the evaluation of treatment efficacy in adults. Participants are asked to report their symptom severity, urges/thoughts about picking, and picking behavior within the last week on a 0 to 4 scale. Finally, the Skin Picking Treatment Scale (SPTS; Simeon et al., 1997) is also modeled on the Y-BOCS and consists of five items that measure the urge, frequency, and duration of picking as well as one's control over the behavior and its interference with functioning. Although the Y-BOCS is considered to be the gold standard for assessing and evaluating OCD symptoms in adults, the validity of the scale when modified for SPD is unclear. Therefore, clinicians and researchers must remain cautious when using the NE-YBOCS or SPTS for diagnosis and treatment evaluation.

Self-Report Measures

Validated self-report measures for assessing SPD include scales of severity, impairment, psychosocial consequences, picking styles, and other characteristics. All these measures, with one exception, have been developed and evaluated for use with adult populations.

SKIN PICKING SCALE AND SKIN PICKING SCALE-REVISED

One of the earliest evaluated skin-picking measures is the Skin Picking Scale (SPS; (Keuthen et al., 2001). The SPS is a six-item paper-and-pencil measure of skin-picking severity. Items are rated on a 5-point Likert scale ranging from 0 (None) to 4 (Extreme) and assess frequency of urges, intensity of urges, time spent picking, interference due to picking, distress, and avoidance, with higher scores indicating increased picking severity. A cutoff score of 7 is used to distinguish clinical from nonclinical skin pickers. The SPS has demonstrated acceptable internal consistency ($\alpha = 0.8$) and construct validity, as evidenced by significant correlations between SPS total score and self-reported average duration of skin-picking episodes per day.

The SPS has been re-examined in an effort to refine the items and the factor structure of the measure. The SPS-Revised (SPS-R) is an eight-item self-report measure (Snorrason et al., 2012) based on the original six-item version created by Keuthen and colleagues (2001). An exploratory factor analysis revealed a two-factor model—Impairment and Severity—with each factor containing four items. Snorrason et al. (2012) found that each subscale demonstrated high internal consistency ($\alpha = 0.79$ and $\alpha = 0.81$, respectively) and exhibited acceptable internal consistency for the SPS-R total scale ($\alpha = 0.83$). Furthermore, the scale exhibited good convergent/concurrent and discriminant validity, as exemplified by significant correlations between the SPS-R Impairment scale score and criterion measures of disability and psychopathology. Conversely, the SPS-R Severity scale correlated more highly with self-reported urge/arousal and time spent picking than the SPS-R Impairment scale did (Snorrason et al., 2012). Advantages of the SPS-R include less ambiguous items—for example, the ambiguous distress item has been replaced with a less ambiguous emotional distress item, "How much emotional distress (anxiety/worry, frustration, depression, hopelessness, or feelings of low self-esteem) do you experience from your skin picking?"—as well as more comprehensive coverage of skin-picking symptom profiles. In addition, the SPS-R has been translated into other languages (e.g., German, Chinese, Swedish, Norwegian, and Spanish). The translated versions of the SPS-R are in the process of being psychometrically validated. The German scale has high internal consistency (α = 0.93) and high construct validity, as indicated by positive associations with measures of psychological impairment and negative associations with measures like general life satisfaction (Gallinat et al., 2016).

The SPS-R is the only scale that has been validated with youth. Gallinat et al. (2017) utilized the German version of the SPS-R with an online sample of adolescents between the ages of 14 and 17. The German version of the SPS-R retained the same two-factor model found in previous studies exploring the psychometric properties of the scale (Gallinat et al., 2016, 2017; Snorrason et al., 2012). The German version of the SPS-R also exhibited high internal consistency (α = 0.89) and strong construct validity. To date, the German version of the SPS-R is the only reliable and valid measure of skin-picking severity available for use with youth. Additional research and development of child-specific skin-picking measures are clearly warranted; however, at this time, clinicians and clinical researchers assessing pediatric populations are likely to be best served by the SPS-R.

SKIN PICKING DISORDER—DIMENSIONAL SCALE

The Skin Picking Disorder–Dimensional Scale (SPD-D; LeBeau et al., 2013) mirrors the TTM-D for hair-pulling. It is a five-item scale that uses a 5-point Likert scale to measure skin-picking symptomatology via items inquiring about frequency, distress, control, avoidance, and interference of skin picking within the past week. Two studies have examined the psychometric properties of the SPD-D, with the most recent also examining the scale's temporal stability, although neither study examined its use in a clinical population (LeBeau et al., 2013; Russell et al., 2020). Similar to LeBeau and colleagues, Russell et al. (2020) found a single-factor model with high internal consistency (α = 0.86–0.92 across time points). The scale also demonstrated excellent test–retest reliability (r_s = 0.86). In addition, the SPD-D exhibited good convergent validity with the SPS-R (r_s = 0.9) and divergent validity with the generalized anxiety disorder scale (r_s = 0.4). The factor structure has yet to be examined in a clinical sample, which warrants future attention.

SKIN PICKING IMPACT SCALE AND SKIN PICKING IMPACT SCALE—SHORT

While most existing measures for SPD are designed to assess symptom severity, the Skin Picking Impact Scale (SPIS) measures the psychosocial impact of skin-picking (Keuthen et al., 2001). The SPIS is a ten-item, paper-and-pencil measure utilizing a 6-point Likert scale, with scores ranging from 0 (None) to 5 (Severe); the SPIS assesses the social, behavioral, and emotional consequences of skin-picking experienced during the past week. The scale has exhibited excellent to good internal consistency in self-injurious and non-self-injurious skin-pickers (α = 0.93 and 0.88, respectively; Keuthen et al., 2001). Similar to the cutoff for the SPS, a cutoff score of 7 differentiates clinical from subclinical skin-picking. Scores of self-injurious skin-pickers correlate with picking duration, satisfaction, shame after picking, BDI scores, and BAI scores, demonstrating convergent validity. The non-linical sample failed to show significant correlations between SPIS total scores and shame after picking, BDI score, or BAI score, suggesting strong discriminant validity.

Snorrason and colleagues (2013) sought to evaluate a shorter, four-item version of the SPIS. The Skin Picking Impact Scale–Short (SPIS-S) retained good internal consistency (α = 0.87). Strong convergent validity was demonstrated via correlations with criterion measures of disorder disability as measured by the Sheehan Disability Scale (SDS; Sheehan, 1983) and negative affect as measured by the Depression Anxiety Stress Scale (DASS). As expected, the measure also correlated strongly with the social desirability subscale of the SDS.

SKIN PICKING REWARD SCALE

The Skin Picking Reward Scale (SPRS; Snorrason et al., 2015) is a 12-item self-report instrument capturing the role of reward-processing in skin-picking. It was developed using the same theoretical conceptualization of behavioral addiction and aberrant reward-processing as the HPRS. Exploratory factor analyses revealed a two-factor model: Liking (i.e., pleasure received while experiencing the reward) and Wanting (i.e., motivation to seek the reward). The Liking and Wanting subscales, as well as the SPRS total scale, exhibited high internal consistency at two time points (α = 0.85–0.95) and acceptable temporal stability (r = 0.78–0.87). To assess the scale's convergent validity, the SPIS subscales were examined in relation to four theoretically derived validity criteria: positive affect during picking, symptom severity, cue reactivity, and frequency. The authors hypothesized that the Liking scale would predict positive affect during picking and the Wanting Scale would be associated with skin-picking severity, enhanced cue reactivity, and picking-related habits/routines. The Wanting scale showed adequate validity when tested against the three aforementioned validity indicators. However, the validity and utility of the Liking scale should be examined further.

MILWAUKEE INVENTORY FOR DIMENSIONS OF ADULT SKIN PICKING

The Milwaukee Inventory for Dimensions of Adult Skin Picking (MIDAS; Walther et al., 2009), similar to the MIST-A for TTM, is a 12-item measure of the varying phenomenological dimensions of skin-picking. Exploratory factor analysis of the measure with an Internet sample revealed two six-item scales—Focused and Automatic skin-picking. Items are rated on a scale ranging from 1("not true of any of my skin picking") to 5 ("true for all of my skin picking"). Both the Focused and Automatic scales demonstrate adequate internal consistency (α = 0.81 and 0.77, respectively; Walther et al., 2009). Convergent validity was determined via correlations of the Focused and Automatic scales with SPS, experiential avoidance, BDI, and BAI scores. The Focused subscale was positively correlated with the skin-picking severity, experiential avoidance, depression, and anxiety symptoms, whereas the Automatic subscale was not. These findings were as expected, based upon a priori theoretical hypotheses. Furthermore, the Automatic and Focused scales failed to demonstrate a significant relationship to one another, thus discriminating between the two styles of pulling.

Measures That Are Not SPD-Specific

Not all scales used to measure SPD are exclusive to skin-picking. Researchers have used scales to assess skin-picking along with other BFRBs. One such instrument is the Habit Questionnaire (Teng et al., 2002). The Habit Questionnaire is a five-item, self-report instrument that assesses frequency and duration of mouth-chewing, nail-biting, skin-biting, skin-picking, and skin-scratching. Individuals indicate Yes or No for each behavior, how frequently they engage in the behavior, how long the behavior has been present, and interference or injuries that have occurred as a result of the behavior. Currently, only the test–retest reliability (Φ = 0.69) of the Habit Questionnaire has been examined. The Habit Questionnaire is most beneficial for those working with patients presenting with multiple BFRBs. For patients presenting with skin-picking in the absence of other impairing BFRBs, alternative measures that assess skin-picking impairment and severity are recommended.

Complementary Assessment Strategies

Various observational methodologies have been proposed to assess the severity and improvement of skin-picking in objectively (i.e., in a manner less susceptible to biases or other factors that may influence a person's responses). Xavier et al. (2019) created the photographic instrument (PI) with the help of two dermatologists. The PI measures four domains pertaining to the severity of skin lesions (active excoriation, crust/bleeding, ulceration, and linear lesions) on a 0 (Lowest severity) to 10 (Highest severity) scale. Photos were taken on an iPhone 7 and were scored by two dermatologists, who achieved high interrater reliability (κ = 0.9). The scale demonstrated good internal consistency (α = 0.87) and there was moderate reliability, as indicated by an intraclass correlation of 0.6. The PI did not correlate with either the SPIS or comorbid symptoms, suggesting that the PI is not a simple proxy for life impact; rather, sites of picking may have a larger role in psychosocial impact (Snorrason et al., 2013; Xavier et al., 2019). Further work is needed, but the results suggest that the PI may be an appropriate instrument for clinicians to use to measure lesions caused by skin-picking.

The work by Xavier and colleagues (2019) was not the first study to utilize photographs for purposes of ascertaining skin-picking severity. For example, Teng et al. (2006) took photos of lesion sites at baseline, one week after treatment, and 3 months subsequent to a behavior therapy intervention for skin-picking. Photographs were ranked by ten psychology graduate students in order of least to most damage (Teng et al., 2006); however, the interrater reliability and psychometric properties of using the photographs were not reported. Potential benefits of using photographs over self-report measures include reduction of reporting bias and improvement in diagnosis. Drawbacks to this methodology include time intensiveness and the inappropriateness of using photographs of some skin-picking sites (e.g., pubic area; McGuire et al., 2012; Xavier et al., 2019). Besides photographs, daily logs have also been used in some instances to track time spent picking per day (Grant et al., 2007). Though examinations of the reliability and validity of this assessment approach for SPD are lacking for the most part, Grant et al. (2007) reported strong test–retest reliability in a study utilizing daily logs to examine the effects of a pharmacological intervention for skin-picking. Collectively, observational methods for assessing the impact and severity of skin-picking have exhibited mild to moderate degrees of success in the field. Clinicians should use these methods as a supplement to, not in place of, more validated measures until additional research and refinement of observational methods occurs.

TTM and SPD Future Work

There is limited research related to the assessment of TTM and SPD. Currently, TTM has been studied more than SPD, which is evident by the existence of more measures for assessing TTM. First, because many of the measures have been validated in only a couple of research studies, future work should evaluate the psychometric properties of the measures in larger clinical samples. Second, it would be beneficial to examine the psychometric properties of the DIAMOND more thoroughly for TTM and SPD populations, because the DIAMOND is the only published structured clinical interview for TTM and SPD that aligns with *DSM-5* criteria. No such interview exists for youth with either disorder, which highlights a gap in BFRB assessment that should be filled in the future. Another goal of the field should be to develop and disseminate a standardized method for taking and rating photographs of TTM-related hair loss. In addition, only two measures have been specifically developed for youth, which is a significant gap in the assessment literature given that the onset of TTM is commonly during adolescence.

Currently, there are a few scales available to assess various aspects of SPD. While a majority of the scales have been validated, many are still in need of psychometric evaluation. Clinician-administered and diagnostic skin-picking assessments are particularly in need of evaluation, as only one measure from either of these categories has been validated (the DIAMOND). Furthermore, the literature is also in need of more diagnostic assessments of SPD, because currently only one SPD-specific measure exists and it has not been published yet (Keuthen, unpublished). Scales specifically measuring the physical impact of skin-picking disorder do not exist. The MIDAS measures two categories of skin-picking phenomenology, but Arnold et al., (1998) mentioned a potential third "mixed" style that combines focused and automatic pulling.

Another significant gap in the literature is related to the absence of scales measuring SPD in children and adolescents. Like TTM, SPD often starts in adolescence, but few scales have been created and validated for use with pediatric populations (Wilhelm et al., 1999). The one scale that has been validated with this population (SPS-R, German version, adolescent) is not in English, limiting its use in the United States. In addition, future studies distinguishing psychometric properties of uniquely adolescent experiences, such as psychosocial functioning in school and among peers, are warranted. Furthermore, multi-informant assessment practices are preferable when working with children and adolescents, because children may have limited awareness of problem behaviors and may not exhibit behaviors equivalently in all settings (McGuire et al., 2012; Storch et al., 2008). It is important to note that currently, no SPD-specific measure is specific to outside informants, such as parents or teachers. Finally, despite the measures' having adequate internal consistency and validity, many SPD measures would be enhanced by use with larger sample sizes, the use of clinical samples, evaluation of test–retest reliability, and validation using various forms of recruitment and administration methodologies. Although some strong measures exist that allow assessment of SPD, there is still ample room for growth and improvement.

References

Alexander, J. R., Houghton, D. C., Twohig, M. P., Franklin, M. E., Saunders, S. M., Neal-Barnett, A. M., Compton, S. N., & Woods, D. W. (2016). Factor analysis of the Milwaukee Inventory for Subtypes of Trichotillomania–Adult Version. *Journal of Obsessive-Compulsive and Related Disorders*, *11*, 31–38.

American Psychiatric Association (APA). (2013). *Diagnostic and statistical manual of mental disorders* (5th ed.).

Arnold, L. M., McElroy, S. L., Mutasim, D. F., Dwight, M. M., Lamerson, C. L., & Morris, E. M. (1998). Characteristics of 34 adults with psychogenic excoriation. *The Journal of Clinical Psychiatry*, *59*(10), 509–514.

Beck, A. T., Epstein, N., Brown, G., & Steer, R. A. (1988). An inventory for measuring clinical anxiety: psychometric properties. *Journal of Consulting and Clinical Psychology*, *56*, 893–897.

Beck, A. T., Steer, R. A., & Brown, G. K. (1996). Manual for the Beck Depression Inventory-II. Psychological Corporation.

Beck, A. T., Ward, C. H., Mendelson, M., Mock, J., & Erbaugh, J. (1961). An inventory for measuring depression. *Archives of General Psychiatry*, *4*, 561–571.

Carr, J. R., Sholevar, E. H., & Baron, D. A. (2006). Trichotillomania and trichobezoar: A clinical practice insight with report of illustrative case. *Journal of the American Osteopathic Association*, *106*(11), 647–652.

Cheyne, J. E., del Pozo de Bolger, A., & Wootton, B. M. (2018). Reliability and validity of the Trichotillomania Dimensional Scale (TTM-D). *Journal of Obsessive-Compulsive and Related Disorders*, 19, 61–65.

Christenson, G. A., MacKenzie, T. B., & Mitchell, J. E. (1991). Characteristics of 60 adult chronic hair pullers. *The American Journal of Psychiatry*, *148*, 365–370.

Diefenbach, G. J., Tolin, D. F., Crocetto, J., Maltby, N., & Hannan, S. (2005). Assessment of trichotillomania: A psychometric evaluation of hair-pulling scales. *Journal of Psychopathology and Behavioral Assessment*, *27*(3), 169–178.

Diefenbach, G. J., Tolin, D. F., Franklin, M. E., & Anderson, E. R. (2003, November). *The Trichotillomania Scale for Children (TSC): A new self-report measure to assess pediatric hair pulling* [Paper presentation]. The Annual Meeting of the Association for Advancement of Behavior Therapy, Boston, MA.

Elliott, A. J., & Fuqua, R. W. (2000). Trichotillomania: Conceptualization, measurement, and treatment. *Behavior Therapy, 31*(3), 529–545.

First, M. B., Spitzer, R. L., Gibbon, M., & Williams, J. B. W. (1998). *Structured Clinical Interview for DSM-IV Axis I Disorders–Patient Edition* (SCID-I/P, Version 2.0, 8/98 revision). Biometrics Research Department.

Flessner, C. A., Franklin, M. E., Keuthen, N. J., Piacentini, J., Cashin, S. E., & Moore, P. S. (2007). The Milwaukee Inventory for Styles of Trichotillomania–Child version (MIST-C): Initial development and psychometric properties. *Behavior Modification, 31*(6), 896–918.

Flessner, C. A., & Woods, D. W. (2006). Phenomenological characteristics, social problems, and the economic impact associated with chronic skin picking. *Behavior Modification, 30*, 944–963.

Flessner, C. A., Woods, D. W., Franklin, M. E., Cashin, S. E., & Keuthen, N. J. (2008). The Milwaukee Inventory for Subtypes of Trichotillomania–Adult Version (MIST-A): Development of an instrument for the assessment of "focused" and "automatic" hair pulling. *Journal of Psychopathology and Behavioral Assessment, 30*(1), 20–30.

Flessner, C., Woods, D., Franklin, M., Keuthen, N., Piacentini, J., Cashin, S., & Moore, P. (2007). The Milwaukee Inventory for Styles of Trichotillomania–Child version (MIST-C): Initial development and psychometric properties. *Behavior Modification, 31*(6), 896–918.

Franklin, M. E., Edson, A. L., Ledley, D. A., & Cahill, S. P. (2011). Behavior therapy for pediatric trichotillomania: A randomized controlled trial. *Journal of the American Academy of Child and Adolescent Psychiatry, 50*(8), 763–771.

Friman, P. C., Finney, J. W., & Christophersen, E. R. (1984). Behavioral treatment of trichotillomania: An evaluative review. *Behavior Therapy, 15*(3), 249–265.

Gallinat, C., Keuthen, N. J., & Backenstrass, M. (2016). [A self-report instrument for the assessment of dermatillomania: Reliability and validity of the German Skin Picking Scale–Revised]. *Psychotherapy and Psychosomatic Medical Psychology, 66*(6), 249–255.

Gallinat, C., Keuthen, N. J., Stefini, A., & Backenstrass, M. (2017). The assessment of skin picking in adolescence: Psychometric properties of the Skin Picking Scale–Revised [German version]. *Nordic Journal of Psychiatry, 71*(2), 145–150.

Goodman, W. K., Price, L. H., Rasmussen, S. A., Mazure, C., Fleischmann, R. L., Hill, C. L., Heninger, G. R., & Charney, D. S. (1989). The Yale-Brown Obsessive Compulsive Scale. I. Development, use, and reliability. *Archives of General Psychiatry, 46*(11), 1006–1011.

Grant J. E., & Odlaug, B. L. (2008). Clinical characteristics of trichotillomania with trichophagia. *Comprehensive Psychiatry, 49*(6), 579–584.

Grant, J. E., Odlaug, B. L., Chamberlain, S. R., Keuthen, N. J., Lochner, C., & Stein, D. J. (2012). Skin picking disorder. *The American Journal of Psychiatry, 169*(11), 1143–1149.

Grant, J. E., Odlaug, B. L., Chamberlain, S. R., & Kim, S. W. (2010). A double-blind, placebo-controlled trial of lamotrigine for pathological skin picking: Treatment efficacy and neurocognitive predictors of response. *Journal of Clinical Psychopharmacology, 30*, 396–403.

Grant, J. E., Odlaug, B. L., & Kim, S. W. (2007). Lamotrigine treatment of pathologic skin picking: An open-label study. *The Journal of Clinical Psychiatry, 68*(9), 1384–1391.

Guy, W. (Ed.). (1976). *Clinical global impressions.* National Institute of Mental Health.

Hallion, L. S., Tung, E. S., & Keuthen, N. J. (2017). Phenomenology of excoriation (skin picking) disorder. In J. A. Abramowitz, D. McKay, & E. A. Storch (Eds.), *The Wiley handbook of obsessive-compulsive disorders* (Vol. 2, pp. 806–816). Wiley-Blackwell.

Houghton, D. C., Capriotti, M. R., De Nadai, A. S., Compton, S. N., Twohig, M. P., Neal-Barnett, A. M., Saunders, S. M., Franklin, M. E., & Woods, D. W. (2015). Defining treatment response in trichotillomania: A signal detection analysis. *Journal of Anxiety Disorders, 36*, 44–51.

Houghton, D., Franklin, M., Twohig, M., Franklin, M., Compton, S., Neal-Barnett, A., Saunders, S., & Woods, D. (2016). Photographic assessment of change in trichotillomania: Psychometric properties and variables influencing interpretation. *Journal of Psychopathology and Behavioral Assessment, 38*(3), 505–513.

Jones, G., Keuthen, N., & Greenberg, E. (2018). Assessment and treatment of trichotillomania (hair pulling disorder) and excoriation (skin picking) disorder. *Clinics in Dermatology*, *36*(6), 728–736.

Keuthen, N. J. *The Keuthen Diagnostic Inventory for Skin Picking for DSM-5 (K-DISP)* [Unpublished inventory].

Keuthen, N. J., Deckersbach, T., Wilhelm, S., Engelhard, I., Forker, A., O'Sullivan, R. L., Jenike, M. A., & Baer, L. (2001). The Skin Picking Impact Scale (SPIS): Scale development and psychometric analyses. *Psychosomatics*, *42*(5), 397–403.

Keuthen, N. J., Deckersbach, T., Wilhelm, S., Hale, E., Fraim, C., Baer, L., O'Sullivan, R. L., & Jenike, M. A. (2000). Repetitive skin-picking in a student population and comparison with a sample of self-injurious skin-pickers. *Psychosomatics*, *41*(3), 210–215.

Keuthen, N. J., Flessner, C. A., Woods, D. W., Franklin, M. E., Stein, D. J., Cashin, S. E., & Trichotillomania Learning Center Scientific Advisory Board. (2007). Factor analysis of the Massachusetts General Hospital Hairpulling Scale. *Journal of Psychosomatic Research*, *62*(6), 707–709.

Keuthen, N. J., O'Sullivan, R. L., Ricciardi, J. N., Shera, D., Savage, C. R., Borgmann, A. S., Jenike, M. A., & Baer, L. (1995). The Massachusetts General Hospital (MGH) Hairpulling Scale: I. Development and factor analyses. *Psychotherapy and Psychosomatics*, *64*(3–4), 141–145.

Keuthen, N. J., Tung, E. S., Pauls, D. L., Woods, D. W., Franklin, M. E., Altenburger, E. M., & Flessner, C. A. (2015). Replication study of the Milwaukee Inventory for Subtypes of Trichotillomania–Adult version in a clinically characterized sample. *Behavior Modification*, *42*(5), 580–599.

Keuthen, N. J., Wilhelm, S., Deckersbach, T., Engelhard, I. M., Forker, A. E., Baer, L., & Jenike, M. A. (2001). The Skin Picking Scale: Scale construction and psychometric analyses. *Journal of Psychosomatic Research*, *50*(6), 337–341.

Kovacs, M. (1992). *Children's Depression Inventory*. Multi-Health Systems.

Kuhn, H., Mennella, C., Magid, M., Stamu-O' Brien, C., & Kroumpouzos, G. (2017). Psychocutaneous disease: Clinical perspectives. *Journal of the American Academy of Dermatology*, *76*(5), 779–791.

LeBeau, R. T., Mischel, E. R., Simpson, H. B., Mataix-Cols, D., Phillips, K. A., Stein, D. J., & Craske, M. G. (2013). Preliminary assessment of obsessive-compulsive spectrum disorder scales for DSM-5. *Journal of Obsessive-Compulsive and Related Disorders*, *2*(2), 114–118.

Lovibond, S. H., & Lovibond, P. F. (1995). *Manual for the depression and anxiety stress scales* (2nd ed.). Psychological Foundation of Australia.

March, J. S. (1998). *Multidimensional Anxiety Scale for Children*. Multi-Health Systems.

March, J. S., Parker, J. D. A., Sullivan, K., Stallings, P., & Conners, C. K. (1997). The Multidimensional Anxiety Scale for Children (MASC): Factor structure, reliability, and validity. *Journal of the American Academy of Child and Adolescent Psychiatry*, *36*(4), 554–565.

McGuire, J. F., Kugler, B. B., Park, J. M., Horng, B., Lewin, A. B., Murphy, T. K., & Storch, E. A. (2012). Evidence-based assessment of compulsive skin picking, chronic tic disorders and trichotillomania in children. *Child Psychiatry & Human Development*, *43*(6), 855–883.

McGuire, J. F., Myers, N. S., Lewin, A. B., Rahman, O., & Storch, E. A. (2020). The influence of hair pulling styles in the treatment of trichotillomania. *Behavior Therapy*. *51*(6), 895–904.

Morris, S. H., Zickgraf, H. F., Dingfelder, H. E., & Franklin, M. E. (2013). Habit reversal training in trichotillomania: Guide for the clinician. *Expert Review of Neurotherapeutics*, *13*(9), 1069–1077.

Nelson, S. O., Rogers, K., Rusch, N., McDonough, L., Malloy, E. J., Falkenstein, M. J., Banis, M., & Haaga, D. A. F. (2014). Validating indicators of treatment response: Application to trichotillomania. *Psychological Assessment*, *26*(3), 857–864.

O'Sullivan, R. L., Keuthen, N. J., Hayday, C. F., Ricciardi, J. N., Buttolph, M. L., Jenike, M. A., & Baer, L. (1995). The Massachusetts General Hospital (MGH) Hairpulling Scale: 2. Reliability and validity. *Psychotherapy and Psychosomatics*, *64*, 146–148.

Phillips, K. A., Hollander, E., Rasmussen, S. A., & Aronowitz, B. R. (1997). A severity rating scale for body dysmorphic disorder: Development, reliability, and validity of a modified version of the Yale-Brown Obsessive-Compulsive Scale. *Psychopharmacology Bulletin*, *33*(1), 17–22.

Pinto, A. C. V. D., de Brito, F. F., Cavalcante, M. L. L. L., de Andrade, T. C. P. C., da Silva, G. V., & Martelli, A. C. C. (2017). Trichotillomania: A case report with clinical and dermatoscopic differential diagnosis with alopecia areata. *Anais Brasileiros de Dermatologia*, *92*(1), 118–120.

Rosenbaum, M. S., & Ayllon, T. (1981). The habit-reversal technique in treating trichotillomania. *Behavior Therapy*, *12*(4), 473–481.

Rothbaum, B. O., & Ninan, P. T. (1994). The assessment of trichotillomania. *Behaviour Research and Therapy, 32*(6), 651–662.

Russell, A., Del Pozo de Bolger, A., Moses, K., Luo, A., & Wootton, B. M. (2020). Psychometric properties of the excoriation (skin-picking disorder) dimensional scale. *Clinical Psychologist, 24*(3), 246–253.

Sheehan, D. V. (1983). *The anxiety disease.* Scribner's.

Simeon, D., Stein, D. J., Gross, S., Islam, N., Schmeidler, J., & Hollander, E. (1997). A double-blind trial of fluoxetine in pathologic skin picking. *The Journal of Clinical Psychiatry, 58*, 341–347.

Snorrason, I., Olafsson, R. P., Flessner, C. A., Keuthen, N. J., Franklin, M. E., & Woods, D. W. (2012). The Skin Picking Scale revised: Factor structure and psychometric properties. *Journal of Obsessive-Compulsive and Related Disorders, 1*, 133–137.

Snorrason, I., Olafsson, R. P., Flessner, C. A., Keuthen, N. J., Franklin, M. E., & Woods, D. W. (2013). The Skin Picking Impact Scale: Factor structure, validity and development of a short version. *Scandinavian Journal of Psychology, 54*(4), 344–348.

Snorrason, I., Olafsson, R. P., Houghton, D. C., Woods, D. W., & Lee, H. J. (2015). 'Wanting' and 'liking' skin picking: A validation of the Skin Picking Reward Scale. *Journal of Behavioral Addictions, 4*(4), 250–262.

Snorrason, I., Ricketts, E. J., Olafsson, R. P., Rozenman, M., Colwell, C. S., & Piacentini, J. (2019). Disentangling reward processing in trichotillomania: 'Wanting' and 'liking' hair pulling have distinct clinical correlates. *Journal of Psychopathology and Behavioral Assessment, 41*(2), 271–279.

Spielberger, C. D., Gorsuch, R. L., Lushene, R., Vagg, P. R., & Jacobs, G. A. (1983). *Manual for the State-Trait Anxiety Inventory.* Consulting Psychologists Press.

Stanley, M. A., Breckenridge, J. K., Snyder, A. G., & Novy, D. M. (1999). Clinician-rated measures of hair pulling: A preliminary psychometric evaluation. *Journal of Psychopathology and Behavioral Assessment, 21*, 157–170.

Storch, E. A., Milsom, V. A., Merlo, L. J., Larson, M., Geffken, G. R., Jacob, M. L., Murphy, T. K., & Goodman, W. K. (2008). Insight in pediatric obsessive-compulsive disorder: Associations with clinical presentation. *Psychiatry Research, 160*(2), 212–220.

Swedo, S. E., Rapoport, J. L., Leonard, H., Lenane, M., & Cheslow, D. (1989). Obsessive-compulsive disorder in children and adolescents. *Archives of General Psychiatry, 46*(4), 335–341.

Teng, E. J., Woods, D. W., & Twohig, M. P. (2006). Habit reversal as a treatment for chronic skin picking: A pilot investigation. *Behavior Modification, 30*(4), 411–422.

Teng, E. J., Woods, D. W., Twohig, M. P., & Marcks, B. A. (2002). Body-focused repetitive behavior problems: Prevalence in a nonreferred population and differences in perceived somatic activity. *Behavior Modification, 26*(3), 340–360.

Tolin, D. F., Diefenbach, G. J., Flessner, C. A., Woods, D. W., Franklin, M. E., Keuthen, N. J., Moore, P., Piacentini, J., & Stein, D. J. (2008). The Trichotillomania Scale for Children: Development and validation. *Child Psychiatry & Human Development, 39*(3), 331–349.

Tolin, D. F., Frost, R. O., & Steketee, G. (2010). A brief interview for assessing compulsive hoarding: The Hoarding Rating Scale–Interview. *Psychiatry Research, 178*(1), 147–152.

Tolin, D. F., Gilliam, C., Wootton, B. M., Bowe, W., Bragdon, L. B., Davis, E., Hannan, S. E., Steinman, S. A., Worden, B., & Hallion, L. S. (2018). Psychometric properties of a structured diagnostic interview for DSM-5 anxiety, mood, and obsessive-compulsive and related disorders. *Assessment, 25*(1), 3–13.

van Minnen, A., Hoogduin, K. A., Keijsers, G. P., Hellenbrand, I., & Hendriks, G. J. (2003). Treatment of trichotillomania with behavioral therapy or fluoxetine: A randomized, waiting-list controlled study. *Archives of General Psychiatry, 60*(5), 517–522.

Walther, M. R., Flessner, C. A., Conelea, C. A., & Woods, D. W. (2009). The Milwaukee Inventory for the Dimensions of Adult Skin Picking (MIDAS): Initial development and psychometric properties. *Journal of Behavior Therapy and Experimental Psychiatry, 40*(1), 127–135.

Wilhelm, S., Keuthen, N. J., Deckersbach, T., Engelhard, I. M., Forker, A. E., & Baer, L., O'Sullivan, R. L., & Jenike, M. A. (1999). Self-injurious skin picking: Clinical characteristics and comorbidity. *The Journal of Clinical Psychiatry, 60*, 454–459.

Winchel, R. M., Jones, J. S., Molcho, A., Parsons, B., Stanley, B., & Stanley, M. (1992). The Psychiatric Institute Trichotillomania Scale (PITS). *Psychopharmacology Bulletin, 28*(4), 463–476.

Woods, D. W., & Houghton, D. C. (2014). Diagnosis, evaluation, and management of trichotillomania. *Psychiatric Clinics of North America, 37*, 301–317.

Xavier, A. C. M., Souza, C. M. B., Flores, L. H. F., Prati, C., Cassal, C., & Dreher, C. B. (2019). Improving skin picking diagnosis among Brazilians: Validation of the Skin Picking Impact Scale and development of a photographic instrument. *Anais Brasileiros de Dermatologia, 94*(5), 553–560.

Xu, L., Liu, K. X., & Senna, M. M. (2017). A practical approach to the diagnosis and management of hair loss in children and adolescents. *Frontiers in Medicine, 4*, 112.

CHAPTER 16

Assessing Comorbidity, Insight, Family, and Functioning

Olivia A. Merritt *and* Christine Purdon

Abstract

Obsessive-compulsive disorder (OCD) is a complex and debilitating disorder that has a high degree of comorbidity with mood and anxiety disorders. Strategies for differential diagnosis of OCD and these disorders, as well as the interactions of the diagnoses in treatment settings, are discussed. The chapter also explores the relationships between OCD and personality disorders, as well as between OCD and the OCD-related disorders. OCD is also characterized by impaired quality of life, family involvement, and varying insight. The presence of OCD is associated with high levels of functional impairment, especially in the social and emotional domains. Relationships with important others can be affected by the disorder. Family members are often involved in OCD symptoms, and family variables like symptom accommodation and hostility are related to poorer treatment outcomes. Treatment outcomes can also be influenced by level of insight held by the individual with OCD; those with poor insight into the irrationality of their symptoms often face challenges with treatment engagement. The chapter aims to provide a brief overview of comorbidity, family, insight, and quality-of-life issues and to review assessment and treatment implications of those issues. Measures for assessing relevant constructs are described.

Key Words: treatment outcomes, insight, family functioning, quality of life, comorbidity

Introduction

Obsessive-compulsive disorder (OCD) is a complex and debilitating disorder that has a high degree of comorbidity: Up to 90% of individuals with OCD have one or more co-occurring diagnoses (Adam et al., 2012; Ruscio et al., 2010). This chapter reviews important comorbidities, provides recommendations for assessing comorbid conditions, and discusses their implications for treatment. In addition to comorbidities, assessment of insight, family functioning, and quality of life is important in OCD. The chapter also provides an overview of these factors and describes assessment and treatment implications. Measures for assessing relevant constructs are described.

Comorbid Mood Disorders

Depression is the most frequent comorbid condition in adults and children with OCD (see Crino & Andrews, 1996; Rasmussen & Tsuang, 1986; Swedo et al., 1989; Tükel et al., 2002). Epidemiologic research shows that about 41% (Ruscio et al., 2010) to 45% (Adam et al., 2012) of persons with OCD have comorbid major depressive disorder. However, one non-Western community sample showed a much lower prevalence rate of 14% (Mohammadi et al., 2007). In clinical samples, the comorbidity rate of OCD with depression ranges from 21% (Denys et al., 2004) to 50% (Hong et al., 2004). The comorbidity rate of OCD with depression is not necessarily different from the comorbidity between anxiety disorders and depression (Adam et al., 2012; Crino & Andrews, 1996).

Angst et al. (2005) asserted that OCD is most comorbid with "minor bipolar disorders" characterized by low levels of hypomanic symptoms, arguing that the association between depression and OCD found in previous studies was due to the presence of bipolar disorder, as opposed to major depressive disorder. Relatedly, Fineberg et al. (2013) sampled a large group of participants from Switzerland and found that bipolar disorder was associated with OCD, whereas unipolar mood disorders were not. Ruscio et al. (2010) found that 23.8% of those with OCD qualified for a diagnosis of bipolar disorder. Similarly, in their sample, Tükel et al. (2006) found that 22% of people with OCD had comorbid bipolar disorder. Those with OCD and bipolar disorder had more symmetry/exactness and ordering/arranging compulsions, a more episodic course of illness, and better insight. Perugi et al. (2002) identified 68 patients with OCD and comorbid major depressive episode, and 56% of those had lifetime comorbid bipolar disorder. Contrary to the finding of Tükel et al. (2006), ordering rituals were less common, as were sexual obsessions, in persons with OCD and mood disorder compared to individuals without comorbid bipolar disorder. Those with OCD and bipolar disorder seem to be more at risk for substance use (Angst et al., 2005; Magalhães et al., 2010; Perugi et al., 2002) and suicidality (Fineberg et al., 2013; Goes et al., 2012; Magalhães et al., 2010; but see Koyuncu et al., 2010).

The variance in rates of mood disorders likely has much to do with diverse sampling and assessment procedures. What is generally consistent across studies is that OCD has its highest or second-highest rate of comorbidity with depression. In terms of clinical presentation, patients with comorbid depression have an earlier age of OCD onset, greater symptom severity (Goes et al., 2012; Hong et al., 2004; Storch et al., 2010; Tükel et al., 2006; but see Denys et al., 2004), and greater functional impairment (Abramowitz et al., 2007).

Cognitive inflexibility characterizes both OCD and depression (Remijnse et al., 2013), and depressive symptoms may be more strongly related to obsessive symptoms than to compulsive symptoms (Ricciardi & McNally, 1995). Obsessions can be differentiated from depressive rumination through an examination of how the thoughts are experienced: in depression, ruminations are typically mood-congruent and are not experienced as unwanted or intrusive (American Psychiatric Association [APA], 2013). Additionally, clinicians should investigate whether compulsions, even covert compulsions like mental rituals, are present, which would indicate OCD.

Although findings are mixed, some research suggests that comorbid depression is a predictor of poorer OCD treatment outcome (Abramowitz & Foa, 2000; Abramowitz et al., 2000; Steketee et al., 2001; but see Farrell et al., 2012; Garcia et al., 2010; Steketee et al., 2000; Storch et al., 2010). Comorbid bipolarity can also complicate OCD treatment. Mood stabilization is typically prioritized, with interventions focusing on OCD undertaken after stability is achieved (Amerio et al., 2014). Research on the onset of comorbid OCD and depression suggests that OCD usually precedes major depressive disorder (Bellodi et al., 1992; Demal et al., 1993), whereas bipolar disorder tends to precede OCD (Ruscio et al., 2010). Depression tends to be alleviated when OCD is successfully treated (Ricciardi & McNally, 1995). There is evidence that a negative mood state increases the individual's fear that having the obsession will lead to harm for which the sufferer will be responsible, which in turn leads to greater perseveration of the compulsive ritual (Davey et al., 2003; MacDonald & Davey, 2005). Furthermore, Abramowitz et al. (2007) found that more severe depression was associated with greater negative appraisal of obsessions.

Taken together, these data suggest that comorbid depression may complicate treatment of OCD in several ways. Depression is characterized by motivational deficits. It is reasonable to propose that these motivational deficits interfere with treatment engagement and compliance (Pallanti et al., 2011). There is also a considerable body of research suggesting that depression is associated with greater recall of negative memories and with greater accessibility of negative appraisal (Abramson et al., 2002). Thus, depression is likely to make negative appraisal of the obsession, and of the consequences of not performing the compulsion, more accessible. Also, as noted by Rachman (1993), the type of negative appraisal one sees in OCD often concerns the implications of the obsession for the person's self-worth, which ties directly into the appraisals and beliefs viewed as central to depression.

Clinicians treating OCD are well advised, then, to ensure that they assess for mood disorders both at the outset and periodically throughout treatment. A good diagnostic interview will establish whether there are depressive symptoms, either at the clinical or subclinical level. Determining whether it is the mood disorder or OCD that is primary requires clinical judgment, as well as a good understanding of how the two clusters of symptoms affect the client's functioning. Assessment of depression severity is straightforward, and there are several well-validated self-report symptom measures, including the Beck Depression Inventory (Beck et al., 1996) and the Depression Anxiety Stress Scales (Lovibond & Lovibond, 1995). The Hamilton Rating Scale for Depression (Hamilton, 1986) is an interviewer-administered measure with good psychometric properties that is widely used in inpatient and outpatient settings (Schwab et al., 1967).

What may be more important than assessing symptom severity, though, is assessing the types of depressogenic thoughts that can interfere with treatment. Obvious thoughts include negative predictions about the success of treatment itself and about the success of treatment exercises, such as exposure with response prevention (E/RP). Depression can also be associated with a self-punitive orientation, such that the person feels they do not deserve to get better, or at least feels ambivalent about treatment. Some OCD sufferers with comorbid depression view their obsessions as a punishment and submit to the compulsion as a form of atonement. They may believe that they do not deserve to feel better, or that if they do not continue to atone, they or their loved ones will be punished. Patients with superstitious fears (e.g., that something bad might happen if an action is not performed in a precise way) or with perfectionism often act upon their compulsions not only to ensure that nothing bad will happen and to reduce distress, but also to protect themselves from later recrimination from self and others for having caused harm or having failed to be perfect. These fears feed directly into the sense of self as a bad, immoral, or deeply flawed person, which is often at the heart of depression. Addressing depressogenic thoughts may be a necessary concomitant to helping individuals view the potential costs of treatment as being less than the potential benefits, as well as developing the sense of self-efficacy required to endure exposure exercises.

Comorbid Anxiety Disorders

After major depressive disorder, anxiety disorders are most commonly comorbid with OCD. In their nationally representative sample, Ruscio et al. (2010) found that 75.8% of those with OCD also met criteria for an anxiety disorder, and that OCD was significantly associated with other anxiety conditions, even when controlling for age, sex, and ethnicity. They reported comorbidity rates that ranged from 7.8% (agoraphobia without panic) to 43.5% (social anxiety disorder; SAD). In treatment-seeking samples, comorbidity rates can be even higher; for example, in their sample of clients with OCD, Tükel et al. (2002) found that comorbidity rates were 26% for specific phobia, 23% for SAD, 18% for generalized anxiety disorder (GAD), and 14% for panic disorder. In their sample of adult outpatients with OCD, Antony et al. (1998) found that 41.4% met criteria for SAD, 20.7% for specific phobia, 11.5% for panic disorder, and 8% for GAD. In their larger sample of outpatients with OCD, Denys et al. (2004) found that 12.8% of those with OCD had a comorbid anxiety disorder, including SAD (3.6%), panic disorder with agoraphobia (2.6%), and anxiety disorder not otherwise specified (1.4%). There are fewer studies of comorbidity in children. In a Brazilian sample of children 6 to 12 years old, 26% of those with OCD met criteria for an anxiety disorder, with separation anxiety (14.3%) and GAD (13%) having the highest comorbidity rates (Alvarenga et al., 2016). Although the actual rates of comorbidity vary considerably across studies, the trends are relatively consistent, with SAD, GAD, and panic disorder being the most frequent comorbid anxiety disorders. High rates of comorbidity have been attributed to shared genetic susceptibility

(Goes et al., 2012) and transdiagnostic factors (e.g., intolerance of uncertainty; Gentes & Ruscio, 2011).

Some studies have explored the phenomenology of anxiety comorbidities. In a longitudinal study, Fineberg et al. (2013) followed 30 individuals with OCD over a 30-year period. They found that those with comorbid panic disorder were more likely to seek professional help and those with comorbid agoraphobia and/or GAD were likely to have more severe OCD. Abramowitz and Foa (1998) found that OCD comorbid with GAD was characterized by more indecisiveness and more extreme responsibility beliefs than was OCD without GAD.

There are several tools available for assessment of comorbid anxiety disorders. The Anxiety Disorders Interview Schedule for DSM-IV (ADIS; Brown et al., 1994) is a thorough and comprehensive means of assessing anxiety disorders. It assesses more subtle manifestations of the disorders than the Structured Clinical Interview for DSM-IV (SCID; First et al., 1995), but it is very long. In addition, the Diagnostic Interview for Anxiety, Mood, and OCD and Related Neuropsychiatric Disorders (DIAMOND) shows good interrater and test–retest reliability, assesses a wide range of disorders in a relatively short amount of time, and can be administered well by trainees (Tolin et al., 2018). There are also numerous self-report measures of anxiety (for a compendium of measures, see Antony et al., 2001).

Differential diagnosis of OCD and GAD can sometimes be difficult, because people with GAD sometimes exhibit excessive reassurance-seeking and checking behaviors (e.g., calling family members to ensure that they are okay; Steketee, 1987), and obsessional preoccupations often take the form, as well as content, of worry (e.g., fears of contracting an illness). However, the checking and reassurance-seeking typical of GAD are less frequent, intense, and ritualized than they are in OCD (Brown et al., 1993; Comer et al., 2004). Differentiating worries from obsessions can also pose a challenge to practitioners. Cases of OCD without overt compulsions (e.g., only mental rituals) may be especially difficult to differentiate from GAD (Freeston et al., 1994). However, the fifth edition of the *Diagnostic and Statistical Manual of Mental Disorders* (*DSM-5*) notes that worries characteristic of GAD are more often future-oriented, and OCD concerns are often "odd, irrational, or of a seemingly magical nature" (APA, 2013, p. 241). Additionally, research shows that obsessions are more likely to be ego-dystonic, centered on personal responsibility, and more visual in nature, as well as being more likely to evoke guilt than worry (Romero-Sanchiz et al., 2017). Studies suggest that beliefs about the importance of thoughts, the need to control thoughts, and thought–action fusion predict the presence of obsessions (Belloch et al., 2007; Calleo et al., 2010), whereas worries are predicted by beliefs about danger and perfectionism, as well as the presence of positive beliefs about worry (Belloch et al., 2007; Calleo et al., 2010; Wells & Papageorgiou, 1998).

Clinicians may also explore the extent of intrusive cognitions. Whereas worries that occur within the context of OCD tend to reflect the theme of the primary obsessions, the worries characteristic of GAD tend to occur across content domains. Additionally, in OCD, the concern is perceived as having a fairly low probability of occurrence (e.g., the thought of deliberately swerving into the next lane while driving, resulting in death), whereas worry is typically a generation of worst-case scenarios that are perceived as being high in probability (e.g., worry that while driving on an unfamiliar narrow country lane, you might hit an animal or get lost, which would make you late for your dinner party, and people will be angry with you and not want to invite you back, etc.; Turner et al., 1992).

Many obsessional thoughts stand in violation of the person's values and personality and/or sense of what is rational. This is certainly the case with repugnant obsessions of causing harm or danger to loved ones, or of engaging in behavior contrary to religious principles. However, obsessions can also be very consistent with values, personality, and sense of what is rational (Purdon et al., 2007; Rasmussen & Eisen, 1992; Tallis, 1996). A father who is concerned about transmitting contamination to his family may view his obsessions as consistent with his values, and his compulsions as important protective actions, even if he acknowledges that the chance of harm is fairly low. The difference between these types of obsessions and worry is in the perceived probability of the event, and in the frequency, intensity, and nature of the action taken to ameliorate the distress the concern causes. For example, a father with GAD may worry that his son has been in an accident if he fails to arrive home on time, whereas a father with OCD may worry that, in the absence of any contact with dangerous substances, he will transmit a fatal illness to his son if he fails to wash his hands according to rigid and excessive rules. Furthermore, if there are multiple concerns crossing many content domains, the problem may be better conceptualized as excessive worry rather than as an obsession.

Comorbid anxiety disorders can complicate assessment. Standard assessment of OCD requires that the sufferer reveal the content of his or her obsessions. We know that this is already a difficult task for sufferers (Newth & Rachman, 2001), but the presence of a comorbid anxiety disorder may complicate disclosure further. For example, social anxiety is characterized by the need to make a good impression on others, as well as fears of failing to do so. Revealing the content of obsessions that have antisocial themes, or describing compulsive rituals that are odd or excessive, may be especially difficult for individuals with comorbid social anxiety. Also, people with repugnant obsessions that involve harm to others, especially children, are often concerned that the therapist will be required to report them to the authorities. Such concerns may be more intense in people with comorbid GAD, who more readily contemplate catastrophic outcomes. It is important to be aware of the ways in which comorbidity may influence disclosure and to provide reasonable assurances (e.g., that the person's disclosure does not require a breach of confidentiality at this time). Given that the occurrence of obsessional thoughts is normal and common, even in those without OCD (Freeston et al., 1991; Purdon & Clark, 1993, 1994; Rachman & de Silva, 1978), it may be helpful to normalize the content of obsessions for the client. Purdon and Clark (2005) provide a list of repugnant thoughts reported by people without OCD that can be helpful in normalizing the content of obsessions.

Does comorbidity with anxiety disorders result in greater difficulties with engaging in treatment? Qualitative data about treatment fears were collected from patients with OCD, SAD, GAD, panic disorder, and anxiety disorder not otherwise specified, and the data were used to develop a 30-item quantitative measure called the Treatment Ambivalence Questionnaire (TAQ; Purdon et al., 2005; Rowa et al., 2014). Administration of the TAQ to 372 outpatients from an anxiety disorders clinic showed that the measure had three reliable subscales: fears of the personal consequences of engaging in treatment (e.g., personality change); fears of negative or adverse reactions to treatment (e.g., not getting better); and concerns about the inconvenience of engaging in treatment (e.g., treatment will be time-consuming; Rowa et al., 2014). The data also showed no differences in TAQ subscale scores between individuals with OCD and those with other diagnoses, nor between those with and without comorbidity, suggesting that the treatment concerns exhibited by individuals with OCD are neither unique nor related to comorbidity. However, correlations between the TAQ and the Interpretation of Intrusions Inventory (III; Obsessive Compulsive Cognitions Working Group, 2005)—which assesses overvalued responsibility, need to control thoughts, and importance of thoughts—revealed correlations between the TAQ adverse reactions subscale and the III control of thoughts scale. Thus, greater perceived need to control obsessions was associated with greater fears of having an adverse reaction to treatment. These findings suggest that identifying and targeting negative predictions about treatment may benefit treatment engagement.

Comorbidity with anxiety disorders may complicate engagement with treatment, particularly exposure, in other ways. Individuals with comorbid panic disorder are likely to find it difficult to engage in activities that put them at risk for a panic attack, such as doing exposure exercises. It may be necessary to conduct interoceptive exercises to reduce reactivity to physical sensations, in advance of OCD treatment or concomitant with it. Individuals with social anxiety may find it difficult to engage in exposure in front of the therapist, or in other social settings. People with GAD may worry more about the impact of exposure on their daily functioning (e.g., "What if the obsession stays with me all day and I can't get my work done and I get in trouble?") and may find it difficult to distinguish between worries and obsessions, and thus refer to them interchangeably (Roth Ledley et al., 2007). A large treatment study suggested that, for youth with OCD, diagnoses of additional internalizing disorders are not predictors of treatment outcome (Garcia et al., 2010). In contrast, Steketee et al. (2000) reported that comorbid GAD was related to more dropout and poorer outcome at posttreatment follow-up. It is important to be aware of this potential, to discuss client apprehensions about exposures, and to work together with the client to establish feasible exercises. The therapist must establish a climate in which the client is free to express and discuss treatment concerns, and in which the client is encouraged to treat negative predictions about treatment as hypotheses that can be tested.

Comorbid Personality Disorders

Many individuals with OCD have a comorbid personality disorder. Samuels et al. (2000) found that 44% of people with OCD had a comorbid personality disorder, compared to a 10% prevalence rate in age-, gender-, and race-matched controls without OCD. Friborg and colleagues found that approximately 52% of those with OCD also had at least one personality disorder, with the avoidant/dependent/compulsive cluster being the most common (Friborg et al., 2013). In their large sample of people with OCD, Denys and colleagues (2004) found that 36% met criteria for a current comorbid personality disorder, the most prevalent being obsessive-compulsive personality disorder (OCPD; 9%), followed by dependent personality disorder (7.6%) and personality disorder not otherwise specified (6.6%). Those with comorbid personality disorders did not differ from those without a personality disorder on measures of severity, anxiety, and depression, although they did have lower global functioning scores. However, several studies have found avoidant personality disorder to be the personality disorder most commonly occurring with OCD (Samuels et al., 2000; Steketee et al., 2000; Wu et al., 2006).

Studies that explore the comorbidity of OCD with OCPD specifically seem to indicate that the presence of OCPD is associated with more severe OCD symptoms (Gordon et al., 2013; Lochner et al., 2011), as well as poorer insight and greater functional impairment (Lochner et al., 2011). In one study, individuals with comorbid OCD and OCPD exhibited some important differences from those without OCPD, including a younger age of onset of first OCD symptoms, more symptoms of hoarding, more symmetry concerns, and more cleaning, ordering, and repeating compulsions (Coles et al., 2008). There is a higher rate of OCPD in persons with OCD than in those with panic disorder (Gordon et al., 2013), and higher rates of OCPD in first-degree relatives of those with OCD than in controls (Bienvenu et al., 2012; Coles et al., 2008; Samuels et al., 2000). Studies with large OCD samples show high rates of OCPD occurrence, from 27% to 34% (Coles et al., 2008, and Bienvenu et al., 2012, respectively). A longitudinal study of the course of anxiety disorders in those with personality disorders found that the presence of OCPD or avoidant personality disorder predicted onset of OCD symptoms (Ansell et al., 2011).

The relationship of OCD to OCPD has always been of special theoretical and diagnostic interest. The psychoanalytic view was that OCPD was a precursor to OCD, although there is little empirical support for this notion (Black & Noyes, 1997). Diaferia et al. (1997) found that the OCPD criteria of hoarding, inability to delegate, and excessive devotion to work reliably distinguished individuals with OCD from those with a mood disorder or panic disorder. Further, those with OCPD are not likely to report obsessions (Pinto et al., 2014). Additionally, Pinto and colleagues (2014) found that individuals with

OCPD had greater ability to delay rewards than those with OCD; the authors argued that excessive self-control may be related to OCPD symptoms like rigidity and perfectionism.

Summerfeldt et al. (1998) observed that there is considerable symptom overlap between OCD and personality disorders. For example, reassurance-seeking is a common symptom of both OCD and avoidant personality disorder, and both OCD and schizotypal personality disorder can be characterized by cognitive distortions and magical thinking. It is also important to note that OCPD is characterized by perfectionism and rigidity in routines, which introduces the possibility of methodological confounds. Summerfeldt et al. noted that OCD symptoms have been distinguished from OCPD traits by the degree to which the symptoms are ego-dystonic. However, as discussed previously, ego-dystonicity may not be universally applicable to OCD symptoms.

With respect to assessing personality comorbidity, then, it is important to be sensitive to symptom overlap and to ensure that symptoms are not better accounted for by one of the disorders before making a diagnosis of both. This is more easily done in the context of an interview. A commonly used diagnostic interview for personality disorders is the Structured Clinical Interview for DSM-5 Personality Disorders (SCID-5-PD; First et al., 2015), but it is lengthy. There are numerous self-report measures of personality disorders, two prominent ones being the Millon Clinical Multiaxial Inventory–4th edition (MCMI-IV; Millon et al., 2015) and the Schedule for Nonadaptive and Adaptive Personality (SNAP; Simms & Clark, 2006). The MCMI-IV yields information about both personality and clinical syndromes (Choca & Grossman, 2015). The SNAP has the advantage of including behavioral indices of the criteria, so it requires less insight on the part of the respondent into personality pathology; additionally, a brief version has recently been developed (Kotelnikova et al., 2015).

What are the implications of personality comorbidity for OCD treatment? Pinto et al. (2011) found that the success of OCD treatment (E/RP) was affected by the presence of an additional OCPD diagnosis; OCPD presence and OCPD severity were predictors of worse treatment outcomes, even when controlling for baseline OCD severity and prior treatment. Fals-Stewart and Lucente (1993) examined personality characteristics and OCD symptoms before treatment, after treatment, and at 6-month follow-up. They found that whereas 35% of patients had no personality elevations, 28% had elevations on the OCPD and dependent personality disorder scales, 21% had elevations on the borderline and histrionic scales, and 15% had elevations on the schizoid, avoidant, dependent, and schizotypal scales. The last group had the highest treatment refusal rate and the poorest treatment response, which is consistent with the report by Jenike et al. (1986), who found that patients with OCD and schizotypal personality disorder had much higher rates of treatment failure than those with OCD and no schizotypal comorbidity. Otherwise, there were no group differences in treatment compliance or in symptom reduction after treatment. However, at 6-month follow-up, patients with elevations on the borderline and histrionic scales showed symptom increases from posttreatment levels. This is consistent with Ansell and colleagues (2011), who found that the presence of borderline personality disorder predicted OCD relapse.

Conversely, Steketee et al. (2000) found that personality traits predicted poorer immediate outcome of OCD treatment, but not longer-term outcome. Some previous studies found no impact of comorbid personality disorders on treatment outcome (e.g., Dreesen et al., 1997; Steketee et al., 2001). However, in their review of 23 studies on the impact of personality disorders on OCD treatment (pharmacological and psychological), Thiel et al. (2013) noted that the most consistent findings were the negative effects of schizotypal personality disorder, narcissistic personality disorder, and multiple personality disorders on treatment outcomes. There is some evidence that treatment of an anxiety disorder results in improvement in the personality disorder symptoms (Brandes & Bienvenu, 2009), but that body of work did not include investigation of treatment of OCD specifically. The mixed results suggest that certain personality disorders may complicate OCD treatment, whereas others may be less interfering.

How might personality disorders affect OCD treatment? Personality disorders are characterized, of course, by traits that are long-standing. Certain traits may interfere with treatment more than others. In general, the presence of a personality disorder may make it more difficult to establish and maintain rapport, and for the patient to accept the therapist's recommendations on trust. AuBuchon and Malatesta (1994) found that OCD patients with comorbid personality disorders more often dropped out of treatment and had more difficulty engaging with treatment. When the personality traits "cross" with the OCD symptoms, they may especially complicate treatment engagement and adherence. For example, people with OCPD may find it very difficult to abandon the pursuit of perfection and may be more self-critical around treatment exercises. In fact, Pinto and colleagues (2011) showed that OCPD-related perfectionism predicts worse treatment outcomes. The authors suggested that, for clients with comorbid OCD and OCPD, addressing OCPD traits, such as perfectionism, may be beneficial. People with dependent personality disorder and obsessions of harming others may find it difficult to risk upsetting others by failing to perform the protective compulsive act. It is important to ensure that the therapeutic climate allows for open discussion of obstacles to executing the treatment plan, and when a personality disorder is present, the therapist may need to devote more time helping the client prepare for change.

Treatment is likely to be most effective if the therapist maximizes the patient's control, choice, and autonomy. Salkovskis summed up the goal of therapy thus: "The patient and therapist . . . work together to construct and test a new, less threatening explanation of the patient's experience, and then . . . explicitly examine the validity of the contrasting accounts" (Salkovskis, 1999, p. S36). That is, the therapist is not committed to a particular explanation of the obsessions and compulsions that the patient must be persuaded to adopt; rather, the therapist helps the patient explore contrasting views of the obsessions and compulsions and facilitates the development of new insights about their meaning. It can be helpful to remind patients that they may always choose their OCD again in the future if they do not like the changes that treatment brings.

Comorbid Obsessive-Compulsive and Related Disorders

Whereas *DSM-IV* classified OCD as an anxiety disorder, *DSM-5* includes a new category of disorders called obsessive-compulsive and related disorders (OCRDs). The OCRDs are characterized by preoccupations and repetitive behaviors, and the category includes OCD, body dysmorphic disorder (BDD), hoarding disorder (HD), trichotillomania (hair-pulling disorder; TTM), and excoriation (skin-picking disorder; SPD). According to Stein and Philips (2014), the OCRDs have important similarities and can be distinguished from the anxiety disorders. However, it is important to note that some disagree with this grouping, arguing that OCD and BDD are more functionally similar to anxiety disorders, and HD, SPD, and TTM are related to OCD on only a superficial level (Abramowitz & Jacoby, 2015). Although Tourette syndrome (TS) shares some similarities with these symptom clusters, it was not included in the OCRDs, because it was thought to have more in common with neurodevelopmental disorders. However, a "tic-related" specifier is available for OCD in recognition that OCD comorbid with TS may have a distinct presentation from OCD without comorbid TS (Stein & Philips, 2014).

Comorbidity among the OCRDs is common. Both BDD and TTM seem to be more common in people with OCD than in people without OCD (Jaisoorya et al., 2003) or in people with anxiety disorders, such as SAD and panic disorder (Lochner & Stein, 2010). Approximately 4% to 5% of those with OCD also have TTM (Bienvenu et al., 2000; Lochner et al., 2014, Lovato et al., 2012), whereas 16% to 24% of those with OCD have comorbid SPD (Bienvenu et al., 2000; Lovato et al., 2012). OCD has a significant overlap with BDD, with estimates that 34% of BDD sufferers also have OCD, and 8% to 37% of those with OCD have BDD (Bienvenu et al., 2000; Lochner et al., 2014; Philips, 2000). Frost et al. (2011) found that, among those with HD, 18% also have OCD. Richter et al. (2003) compared OCRD comorbidity rates in people with OCD, SAD, and panic disorder using diagnostic interviews conducted by interviewers blind to the study hypotheses. The OCD group had a higher rate of comorbid OCRDs than did the other groups. Additionally, more people with OCD had comorbid TTM than did those with SAD, and comorbid SPD was found at a higher rate among people with OCD than among people with panic disorder.

OCRDs are said to be part of the OCD "family" due to similarities in symptomatology and selective response to specific medications (Richter et al., 2003). However, some have suggested subgroupings within the OCRDs. For example, OCD and BDD are more closely related to anxiety disorders, in that repetitive behaviors are used to reduce fear, and these two disorders are best treated by cognitive-behavioral therapy (CBT) with E/RP. On the other hand, TTM and SPD are similar to each other in that they are body-focused repetitive behaviors, which can be treated with habit-reversal paradigms or specific medications (Stein & Phillips, 2014). Some researchers deem OCD, BDD, and HD to be the "cognitive" OCRDs, while TTM and SPD are the "motorically focused" OCRDs (Phillips et al., 2010). A twin study supported this division, finding stronger phenotypic associations between subgroupings of OCD/BDD/HD and TTM/SPD (Monzani et al., 2014). The authors found two latent factors: one representing genetic vulnerability to all OCRDs, but with strongest loadings for OCD, BDD, and HD, and a second loading exclusively on TTM and SPD. A review by Snorrason et al. (2012) found "strong evidence" for the relatedness of TTM and SPD, including phenomenological similarities, risk factors, and treatment response.

Phenomenological comparisons can shed light on differences between OCRDs. One study compared OCD and TTM and found that individuals with OCD had higher levels of impairment across a number of life domains and were more likely to report childhood sexual abuse, but these individuals were also more likely to benefit from selective serotonin reuptake inhibitors (SSRIs) or CBT interventions than were those with TTM (Lochner et al., 2005). Additionally, persons with OCD scored higher on harm avoidance, whereas those with TTM scored higher on novelty seeking (Lochner et al., 2005). Research has shown that persons with SPD are more likely to be female than those with OCD, and those with OCD spend more time on their thoughts and behaviors than do those with SPD (Grant et al., 2010). While compulsive behaviors may be observed in both OCD and TTM/SPD, persons with OCD are significantly more likely to experience obsessions (Ferrão et al., 2006).

Diagnostic distinctions between OCD and OCRDs can be subtle. Radomsky et al. (2007) summarized the primary difference as follows: whereas the compulsions symptomatic of OCD are enacted to reduce fear, anxiety, or the perceived likelihood that something awful will happen, *impulsions* reduce tension or discomfort, and can in fact feel pleasurable. Consider people who need to perform a behavior until they get a "just right" feeling. This could be symptomatic of a body-focused repetitive behavior (i.e., skin-picking or hair-pulling), or of OCD. However, as Radomsky et al. (2007) observed, in the case of OCD, the person is more likely to seek a just right feeling in order to avoid bringing harm to someone else, whereas, in the case of body-focused repetitive behaviors, the feeling itself is the goal. Indeed, individuals with OCD report feeling that harm may come from their not acting out a compulsion, whereas those with TTM/SPD report that it would be beneficial if they were stopped from acting (Ferrão et al., 2006). Although repetitive behaviors occur across the OCRDs, Abramowitz and Jacoby (2015) described a key difference in symptom function: in OCD and BDD, repetitive behavior provides an escape from anxiety, and is thus negatively reinforced. However, in SPD and TTM, the behavior itself is gratifying, and is thus positively reinforcing.

BDD is characterized by repetitive, time-consuming behavior, but again, the functionality of the symptoms is important in distinguishing it from OCD. In BDD the goal is to examine, hide, improve, or seek reassurance about the perceived defect, whereas in

OCD it is to prevent harm. People with BDD tend to have poorer insight into the irrationality of their concerns, and indeed at times they are delusional (Philips, 2000; Phillips et al., 2012).

Whereas hoarding had previously been categorized as a symptom of OCD, it is now classified as its own disorder. However, hoarding behaviors may still occur within the context of OCD. HD involves difficulty discarding, distress associated with discarding, and excessive acquisition of items (APA, 2013). Alternatively, hoarding behaviors in the context of OCD are related to OCD-like concerns, such as accumulation of objects to attain a sense of completeness, not discarding old newspapers because they may contain information that could prevent harm, or the clutter accumulated as a byproduct of avoidance of washing and/or checking rituals (APA, 2013). In their review of the research on hoarding, Mataix-Cols and colleagues (2010) noted that, unlike in OCD, hoarding-related thoughts are not experienced as intrusive, repetitive, and distressing, and they may even be associated with excitement, pleasure, or a sense of self or purpose. People with hoarding symptoms may have an idealized sense of the value and importance of an object, may anthropomorphize objects (e.g., "If I don't buy this stuffed kitten it will be all by itself on the shelf!"), and discarding objects is often met with grief, anxiety, or anger. In contrast, those with OCD are not typically interested in the objects themselves, beyond the purpose they serve for the OCD concerns.

There are a number of interviewer-administered and self-report measures to assess the severity of OCRD symptoms. The Yale-Brown Obsessive-Compulsive Scale (Y-BOCS) has been adapted to assess BDD (Philips et al., 1997), and the Dysmorphic Concerns Questionnaire is a brief self-report measure of BDD symptoms with strong psychometric properties (Oosthuizen et al., 1998). TTM can be assessed with the NIMH Trichotillomania Severity Scale and NIMH Trichotillomania Impairment Scale, both of which are based on the Y-BOCS (Stanley et al., 1999). The Massachusetts General Hospital Hairpulling Scale (Keuthen et al., 1995) is a brief self-report instrument with strong reliability. Similarly, the Skin Picking Scale-Revised (SPS-R; Snorrason et al., 2012) is an eight-item scale assessing severity and impairment of skin-picking symptoms, which correlates with measures of disability and time spent picking. The Saving Inventory-Revised assesses clutter, difficulty discarding, and excessive acquisition, and it shows good reliability (Frost et al., 2004). Some clinicians may also find it useful to assess hoarding severity with a Clutter Image Rating (Frost et al., 2008).

Comorbid OCRDs can complicate treatment. Steketee and Neziroglu (2003) noted that patients with OCD and comorbid BDD tend to have greater overvalued ideation than those without such comorbidity. This is likely to make it more difficult for them to consider alternate views of the meaning of their obsessions and to resist their compulsions, so treatment engagement and compliance may be more challenging. Low insight is also common in HD (Tolin et al., 2010), which can be a challenge for treatment; in this case, Frost et al. (2010) recommended a focus on behavioral experiments rather than on thought reappraisal.

Assessment of Beliefs and Insight

Individuals with OCD are likely to hold particular beliefs about the meaning or importance of their obsessions and/or compulsions. A group of researchers with expertise in theoretical models of OCD and its treatment have identified several types of beliefs that may be especially important to understanding the development and persistence of OCD (see Chapter 11 for additional discussion). Themes include perfectionism, the importance of controlling thoughts, the importance of thoughts, responsibility, intolerance of uncertainty, and overestimation of threat. The research group, known as the Obsessive Compulsive Cognitions Working Group (OCCWG), has developed a measure of general beliefs, as well as a measure of specific appraisals of obsessional thoughts. The first is known as the Obsessive Beliefs Questionnaire (OBQ), which is a self-report measure consisting of 44 items (OCCWG, 2005). The appraisal measure is the Interpretation of Intrusions Inventory (III), a 31-item self-report measure of the importance of thoughts, the need to control thoughts, and responsibility (OCCWG, 2005). The measures have strong psychometric properties, although the subscale scores within each measure tend to be highly correlated.

Individuals who hold very strong beliefs about their obsessions may have poor insight. The term *insight* refers to "the degree to which the sufferer is aware of the irrationality of their symptoms" (Steketee & Neziroglu, 2003, p. 179). Those with poor insight, then, are extremely certain that the feared consequences of their obsessions are reasonable and warrant the time spent on compulsions, avoidance, etc. As Veale (2007) described, at one end of the insight continuum is the recognition that the obsessional idea is irrational (e.g., "My mother probably will not die if I do not arrange my books properly"); at the other end of the continuum, the person holds a delusional belief in which they fully believe (e.g., "I know that my mother will die if I do not arrange my books properly"). According to the *DSM-5*, the former would be categorized as "good or fair insight," whereas the latter would be specified as "absent insight/delusional beliefs." Between the two extremes lies "poor insight" (e.g., "My mother will probably die if I do not arrange my books properly"). Brakoulias and Starcevic (2011) described how overvalued ideas are usually perceived as well justified and tend not to change in response to contrary evidence.

Insight can have important implications for illness onset, course, and response to treatment. Kishore et al. (2004) found that 25% of their sample of patients met criteria for poor insight. Poor insight was associated with earlier age of onset, longer duration of illness, greater symptom severity, higher comorbidity, and poorer response to drug treatment. Several studies have shown that poor insight is associated with more severe OCD (Bipeta et al., 2013; Catapano et al., 2010; Cherian et al., 2012; Fontenelle et al., 2013; Jacob et al., 2014; Jakubovski et al., 2011) and poorer outcome of CBT (for a review, see Veale, 2007). Catapano and colleagues (2010) also found that persons with OCD and poor insight were more likely to need treatment augmented with antipsychotics. It may be that those with poor insight are less motivated to resist and combat their obsessions, less willing to engage in ER/P, and/or more likely to find alternative explanations for the outcomes of exposures (Adelman & Lebowitz, 2012; Jakubovski et al., 2011). Matsunaga et al. (2002) found that persons with OCD and poor insight had the same degree of functional impairment as did persons with OCD and comorbid schizophrenia.

Recent research into OCD with poor insight has elucidated some of the factors that may underlie, or at least be associated with, insight issues. Moritz and colleagues (2014) found that those who experience obsessions as containing sensory qualities (i.e., obsessions having visual, olfactory, somatic, or tactile properties) were more likely to have a lack of insight. The authors concluded that the sensory features may make obsessions feel more "real" and less dismissible as absurd. Several studies have shown a relationship between poor insight and less resistance to OCD symptoms (Jacob et al., 2014; Storch et al., 2014), and Jaafari and colleagues (2011) suggested that those with poor insight are likely to check longer due to higher levels of uncertainty. Other researchers have found evidence for neurologic and neuropsychological abnormalities in those with poor insight (Aigner et al., 2005; Fan et al., 2017; Karadag et al., 2011; Kashyap et al., 2012).

There are several measures of insight. The Y-BOCS includes an item that assesses insight, and this single item (Item 11) has been used in many studies. However, more comprehensive measures have also been developed. The Brown Assessment of Beliefs Scale (BABS; Eisen et al., 1998) is a seven-item clinician-administered scale that addresses conviction, perception of others' view of beliefs, fixity of ideas, stability of beliefs, and attempt to disprove beliefs. It has excellent psychometric properties and is commonly used in research. Neziroglu et al. (1999) developed the Overvalued Ideas Scale, which consists of nine clinician-administered items assessing the reasonableness of obsessions and compulsions, others' perceptions about the necessity of completing compulsions, and whether the symptoms are viewed as unusual. The nine items can be assessed for up to three beliefs associated with the person's OCD. Neziroglu et al. reported that the measure has strong validity and reliability. Veale (2007) noted, though, that the current insight measures do not assess what kinds of core beliefs or values may underlie lack of insight (e.g., "Unless I do this perfectly, I am worthless").

Individuals with poor insight may present a treatment challenge. These individuals may not seek treatment at all (García-Soriano et al., 2014), or they may be resistant to change. For treatment purposes, Veale (2007) conceptualized overvalued ideas as "beliefs that are associated with specific values which have become dominant, idealized and excessively identified with the self" (p. 271). In general, Veale recommended that treatment involve helping the person identify other important values (e.g., being a good mother, being good at one's job) and develop the person's recognition of how pursuing the OCD-relevant value compromises the other values, as well as explore whether the OCD-relevant value is one they would expect or want their children or other loved ones to hold.

Assessing the Family

People with OCD often involve family members in their avoidance or compulsions. For example, they may require family members to be the last to leave the house, to wash their hands in a highly circumscribed way, not to touch certain objects, or to answer questions in a specific way. They may turn to family members for reassurance that something has or has not happened, or they may insist that family members perform certain tasks, such as checking the appliances and locking the doors (conversely, they may insist on doing such things themselves). These are examples of accommodation by family members. Providing reassurance, waiting for compulsions to be completed, and/or participating in rituals are the most common forms of accommodation (Peris et al., 2008; Stewart et al., 2008).

Family involvement in OCD is exceedingly common and can have adverse consequences for the family system. In their sample of OCD sufferers ($N = 419$), Hollander et al. (1996) found that 73% reported that OCD interfered with family relationships. Cooper (1994) found that 85% of family members reported being bothered by their relatives' rituals, and 75% of relatives of child OCD sufferers were drawn into the rituals, as were 58% of relatives of adult sufferers. Shafran et al. (1995) similarly found that only 10% of respondents reported that their relatives' OCD did not interfere in their lives, and 60% of the family members of sufferers reported that they were asked to conduct a ritual, observe a ritual, or avoid a feared stimulus. Of those, 40% reported that they complied with the request of the relative with OCD to conduct a ritual themselves (e.g., washing or checking), and almost half of respondents reported being unsure about how to respond to requests for involvement.

Calvocoressi et al. (1995) found that 88% of family members surveyed reported accommodating rituals, and that degree of family accommodation was associated with degree of family dysfunction and stress. In their review, Renshaw and colleagues (2005) found that rates of accommodation of symptoms among family members range from 62% to 100%, and participation from 39% to 75%. Family members of individuals with OCD have poorer quality of life (QoL) than do those in the general population (Cicek et al., 2013; Stengler-Wenzke et al., 2006). In fact, family members of individuals with OCD show a social burden similar to that of family members of persons with schizophrenia (Thomas et al., 2004). Disrupted family leisure and interaction, as well as practical problems faced by families with OCD, were predictors of poor QoL in caregivers (Grover & Dutt, 2011).

Despite the additional strain on family members, requests for accommodation are often met with compliance. Family members may find it difficult to resist accommodation because they find it hard to tolerate the distress that OCD causes. OCD sufferers can also feel exceptional anger and a sense of being uncared for when family members do not comply with their rules, even if the noncompliance is not intended to be coercive or is not driven by hostility. Storch et al. (2007) found that 16% of the parents of children with OCD reported that their children experienced anger and distress daily in response to parent refusal of accommodation of rituals. Given that the "OCD voice" can be rather convincing, OCD sufferers may experience a noncompliant family member as untrustworthy, uncaring, or cold for failing to perform an action that would relieve distress and reduce the perceived chance of the feared outcome.

On the other hand, compliance with accommodation requests can strain relationships, as relatives may feel that the sufferer is putting their OCD ahead of the best interests of the family. Sometimes, family members can behave antagonistically toward the person with OCD. For example, family members may use compliance or noncompliance coercively (e.g., "I will only recheck the stove for you if you let me go out tonight") and may exploit sufferers' distress ("If you don't let me use the car, I'm going to go into your room and rub my shoes all over your bed"). Family members may also mock the sufferer for having the symptoms, accusing them of being weak, weird, sick, selfish, or the cause of family distress. Amir and colleagues (2000) found that OCD sufferers were more likely to engage in their rituals when their family members made critical comments. The authors reasoned that the ritual is performed as "punishment" for the criticism, or that the criticism increases anxiety, which in turn leads to more frequent rituals.

Neither compliance nor hostile noncompliance is conducive to overcoming OCD symptoms. Family accommodation of symptoms interferes with treatment predicated on exposure and response prevention, because it terminates exposure to the distress associated with the obsession and disallows new learning about the meaning or importance of the obsession. In their meta-analysis, Wu et al. (2016) found that family accommodation was related to OCD severity with a moderate effect size. Family accommodation has also been shown to mediate the relationship between symptom severity and functional impairment (Bipeta et al., 2013; Storch et al., 2007). Furthermore, family accommodation is related to treatment outcome: greater accommodation was associated with higher symptom severity at the end of treatment, controlling for pretreatment severity (Amir et al., 2000). Garcia et al. (2010) also found lower levels of accommodation to be predictive of greater OCD improvement across treatment modalities (CBT + medication, medication only, CBT only, or pill placebo) for those with pediatric OCD. Importantly, Piacentini et al. (2011) found that reduction in family accommodation temporally preceded improvements in OCD symptoms.

In addition to accommodation, other types of family interactions can also affect treatment. Steketee (1993) found that the degree of empathy and positive interactions exhibited by significant others of sufferers were associated with maintenance of treatment gains, whereas criticism, anger, and belief that sufferers could control their symptoms were associated with relapse. Chambless and Steketee (1999) examined the degree of expressed emotion (EE) in the families of OCD sufferers. Expressed emotion refers to the family members' feelings about a patient, including emotional overinvolvement, criticism, and hostility. Chambless and Steketee found that relatives' hostility was a major predictor of treatment dropout, poorer treatment gains, and poorer functioning. However, the degree of familial nonhostile criticism was associated with better treatment outcome; the authors noted that rejection of patients' symptoms, but not rejection of the patients themselves, may motivate patients to improve. In their summation of the relevant literature, Renshaw et al. (2005) concluded that having family who are either overly accommodating of symptoms or overly antagonistic about symptoms is associated with poorer treatment outcome.

There are a number of measures of family accommodation and climate. The Family Accommodation Scale is a 12-item measure that is administered by a clinician to relatives of the OCD sufferer, and it is reported to have excellent psychometric properties (Calvocoressi et al., 1999). Self-report versions of this measure (for parents, relatives, and patients) have since been developed for ease of administration (Flessner et al., 2011; Pinto et al., 2013; Wu et al., 2016). For assessing expressed emotion, The Camberwell Family Interview (Vaughn & Leff, 1976) is an intensive 1- to 2-hour interview that is taped and then scored. The length of the interview itself, and the scoring process, may render it infeasible in many clinical settings; however, there are a number of briefer methods for assessing expressed emotion, such as using a Five Minute Speech Sample or self-report scales (for a review, see Hooley & Parker, 2006). For example, the Perceived Criticism Measure (Hooley & Teasdale, 1989) requires patients to rate the extent of relatives' criticism. Chambless and Steketee (1999) expressed concern about the measure's convergent validity, although its reliability across time is strong. Last, to assess perceived availability of social support, the Interpersonal Support Evaluation List, a 40-item true/false measure, may be used (Cohen et al., 1985).

Family accommodation and climate have several implications for treatment planning. First, it may be important to meet with key family members to educate them about the treatment model and collaboratively brainstorm ways of offering noncritical support without accommodating rituals. Indeed, Grunes et al. (2001) found that patients whose family members were randomly assigned to a psychoeducational group had a greater reduction in OCD symptoms and depressed mood, compared with those whose family members did not participate. In addition, treatments that specifically target accommodation have been developed, such as Positive Family Interaction Therapy (PFIT) and Supportive Parenting for Anxious Childhood Emotions (SPACE); these treatments show preliminary evidence for success in reducing accommodation (Lebowitz et al., 2013; Peris & Piacentini, 2013).

Steketee (1993) made the important point that the OCD sufferer and the family's attitude are nested; just as criticism by the family can evoke more ritualizing by the sufferer, so can ritualizing put pressure on the family. This issue has important implications for research on family–sufferer dyads, in that statistical analyses must assume a nested design and be performed accordingly. The issue also has implications for treatment of family members; as Steketee noted, one cannot simply direct the family to behave differently without taking their feelings and perspective into account. Van Noppen and Steketee (2003) and Renshaw et al. (2005) advocated for a multifamily behavioral treatment, in which family members are trained in exposure to rituals and contract to improve communication in the family and to reduce hostile and antagonistic responses to OCD. Both Van Noppen and Steketee (2003) and Renshaw et al. (2005) provide guidelines for this approach.

Quality of Life (QoL) in OCD

OCD is recognized as a major mental illness in which sufferers experience impaired functioning on par with that in major physical illnesses. For example, Koran and colleagues (1996) found that QoL for those with OCD was substantially poorer than QoL for those with diabetes. Kugler and colleagues (2013) found that participants with OCD had significantly worse social functioning QoL than those with major depressive disorder, panic disorder, or schizophrenia. Eisen et al. (2006) found that one-third of their treatment-seeking sample were unable to work due to their OCD symptoms. Social and family functioning, as well as general well-being and ability to enjoy leisure time, were impaired across the board relative to normative samples. This is consistent with work by Hollander et al. (1996), who found that individuals with OCD reported substantial disruption in their family relationships and with friends, lowered academic achievement, lowered career aspirations, and substantial work interference. In their review of 58 papers on the topic, Macy and colleagues (2013) concluded that those with OCD see the most impairment in QoL in the social and emotional domains. Hauschildt and colleagues (2010) developed an OCD-specific measure of QoL that reflected the different pathways through which OCD could affect QoL. The pathways included family involvement in the disorder, symptoms interfering with career or leisure, and the impact of symptoms on self-concept and coping abilities.

Research has indicated that OCD symptoms have a negative impact on QoL. For example, washing/contamination symptoms have been associated with lower QoL (Albert et al., 2010; Hauschildt et al., 2010; Jacoby et al., 2014). In a number of studies, higher severity of OCD symptoms was associated with poorer QoL (Eisen et al., 2006; Hauschildt et al., 2010; Kulger et al., 2013; Weidle et al., 2014). There is also evidence that comorbid depression symptoms have an impact on QoL for those with OCD (Albert et al., 2010; Fontenelle et al., 2010; Hauschildt et al., 2010; Jacoby et al., 2014; Kugler et al., 2013; Vivan et al., 2013). Despite the mounting evidence of impaired QoL in OCD, there is also evidence that symptom alleviation is associated with an improvement in QoL for people with OCD (Bystritsky et al., 1999, 2001; Cordioloi et al., 2003; Diefenbach et al., 2007; Ooms et al., 2014).

Several QoL measures are commonly used in psychiatric settings. The Range of Impaired Functioning Tool (LIFE-RIFT) is a brief semi-structured interview that assesses functioning across the domains of work, interpersonal relations, recreation, and global satisfaction. It has good validity and reliability (Leon et al., 1999). There are also a number of available self-report measures with strong psychometric properties. The Quality of Life Enjoyment and Satisfaction Questionnaire consists of 91 self-report items that address eight domains (Endicott et al., 1993). The Medical Outcomes Survey 36-item Short-Form Health Survey (McHorney et al., 1993) is widely used to assess functioning problems and limitations due to both mental and physical problems. The World Health Organization Quality of Life Assessment (WHOQOL-100; World Health Organization, 1995) and its short form (WHOQOL-BREF; Skevington et al., 2004) have been used internationally to assess physical health, psychological health, social relationships, and environment (e.g., finances, recreation, safety). The Lancashire Quality of Life Profile is a self-report measure assessing nine domains, including religion, health, and education (van Nieuwenhuizen et al., 2001). The Sheehan Disability Scale (Sheehan, 1986) has also been widely used, particularly for individuals with anxiety disorders (Mendlowicz & Stein, 2000). Respondents rate the degree to which their symptoms are impairing in three domains. In terms of treatment planning, Macy et al. (2013) emphasized QoL as an important indicator of treatment success, and they recommended assessing and monitoring QoL throughout treatment using standardized measures.

Summary

OCD has high comorbidity rates with mood and anxiety disorders. Comorbid depression or bipolar disorder can complicate treatment, and treatment-interfering beliefs should be addressed. GAD, SAD, and panic disorder are also very commonly comorbid with OCD, and it can be especially challenging for clinicians to distinguish between OCD and GAD or between obsessions and worries. Comorbid anxiety disorders can interfere with patients' willingness to disclose OCD concerns. OCD also has associations with personality disorders—in particular the avoidant/dependent/compulsive cluster—and symptom overlap between personality disorders and OCD can make differential diagnosis and research challenging. Clinicians should be sensitive to the unique ways in which personality challenges may interact with OCD and contribute to treatment difficulties. New to the *DSM-5* are OCRDs, including BDD, HD, TTM, and SPD, and clinicians should become familiar with making differentials between these disorders and OCD.

OCD is a problem associated with severe impairment, difficulty functioning, and poorer QoL, both for the sufferer and the sufferer's family. Individuals with OCD vary considerably in their insight into the irrationality of their obsessional concerns, and those with poorer insight can face significant challenges in treatment engagement. The family environment is also important to consider, as symptom accommodation and expressed hostility can both contribute to OCD symptom severity and treatment outcome. However, higher symptom severity may also evoke more accommodation and hostility in relatives. Where possible, involving and educating relatives can be helpful in OCD recovery.

References

Abramowitz, J. S., & Foa, E. B. (1998). Worries and obsession in individuals with obsessive-compulsive disorder with and without comorbid generalize anxiety disorder. *Behaviour Research and Therapy, 36*, 695–700.

Abramowitz, J. S., & Foa, E. B. (2000). Does major depressive disorder influence outcome of exposure and response prevention for OCD? *Behavior Therapy, 31*, 795–800.

Abramowitz, J. S., Franklin, M. E., Street, G. P., Kozak, M. J., & Foa, E. B. (2000). Effects of comorbid depression on response to treatment for obsessive-compulsive disorder. *Behavior Therapy, 31*, 517–528.

Abramowitz, J. S., & Jacoby, R. J. (2015). Obsessive-compulsive and related disorders: A critical review of the new diagnostic class. *Annual Review of Clinical Psychology, 11*, 165–186.

Abramowitz, J. S., Storch, E. A., Keeley, M., & Cordell, E. (2007). Obsessive-compulsive disorder with comorbid depression: What is the role of cognitive factors? *Behaviour Research and Therapy, 45*, 2257–2267.

Abramson, L. Y, Alloy, L. B., Hankin, B. L., Haeffel, G. J., MacCoon, D. G., & Gibb, B. E. (2002). Cognitive vulnerability-stress models of depression in a self-regulatory and psychobiological context. In I. H. Gotlib & C. L. Hammen (Eds.), *Handbook of depression* (pp. 268–294). Guilford.

Adam, Y., Meinlschmidt, G., Gloster, A. T., & Lieb, R. (2012). Obsessive-compulsive disorder in the community: 12-month prevalence, comorbidity and impairment. *Social Psychiatry and Psychiatric Epidemiology, 47*(3), 339–349.

Adelman, C. B., & Lebowitz, E. R. (2012). Poor insight in pediatric obsessive-compulsive disorder: Developmental considerations, treatment implications, and potential strategies for improving insight. *Journal of Obsessive-Compulsive and Related Disorders, 1*(2), 119–124.

Aigner, M., Zitterl, W., Prayer, D., Demal, U., Bach, M., Prayer, L., Stompe, T., & Lenz, G. (2005). Magnetic resonance imaging in patients with obsessive-compulsive disorder with good versus poor insight. *Psychiatry Research: Neuroimaging, 140*(2), 173–179.

Albert, U., Maina, G., Bogetto, F., Chiarle, A., & Mataix-Cols, D. (2010). Clinical predictors of health-related quality of life in obsessive-compulsive disorder. *Comprehensive Psychiatry, 51*(2), 193–200.

Alvarenga, P. G., Do Rosario, M. C., Cesar, R. C., Manfro, G. G., Moriyama, T. S., Bloch, M. H., Shavitt, R. G., Hoexter, M. Q., Coughlin, C. G., Leckman, J. F., & Miguel, E. C. (2016). Obsessive-compulsive symptoms are associated with psychiatric comorbidities, behavioral and clinical problems: A population-based study of Brazilian school children. *European Child & Adolescent Psychiatry, 25*(2), 175–182.

American Psychiatric Association (APA). (2013). *Diagnostic and statistical manual of mental disorders* (5th ed.).

Amerio, A., Odone, A., Marchesi, C., & Ghaemi, S. N. (2014). Treatment of comorbid bipolar disorder and obsessive-compulsive disorder: A systematic review. *Journal of Affective Disorders, 166*, 258–263.

Amir, N., Freshman, M., & Foa, E. B. (2000). Family distress and involvement in relatives of obsessive-compulsive disorder patients. *Journal of Anxiety Disorders, 14*, 209–217.

Angst, J., Gamma, A., Endrass, J., Hantouche, E., Goodwin, R., Ajdacic, V., Eich, D., & Rossler, W. (2005). Obsessive-compulsive syndromes and disorders: Significance of bipolar and anxiety syndromes. *European Archives of Psychiatry and Clinical Neuroscience, 255*, 65–71.

Ansell, E. B., Pinto, A., Edelen, M. O., Markowitz, J. C., Sanislow, Yen, S., Zanarini, M., Skodol, A. E., Shea, M. T., Morey, L. C., Gunderson, J. G., McGlashan, T. H., & Grilo, C. M. (2011). The association of personality disorders with the prospective 7-year course of anxiety disorders. *Psychological Medicine, 41*(5), 1019–1028.

Antony, M. M., Downie, F., & Swinson, R. P. (1998). Diagnostic issues and epidemiology in obsessive-compulsive disorder. *Obsessive-compulsive Disorder: Theory, Research, and Treatment*, 3–32.

Antony, M. M., Orsillo, S. M., & Roemer, L. (2001). *Practitioner's guide to empirically based measures of anxiety.* Kluwer.

AuBuchon, P. G., & Malatesta, V. J. (1994). Obsessive-compulsive patients with co-morbid personality disorders: Associated problems and response to a comprehensive behavior therapy. *The Journal of Clinical Psychiatry, 5*, 448–452.

Beck, A. T. B., Steer, R. A., & Brown, R. K. (1996). *Manual for the Beck Depression Inventory—II*. Psychological Corporation.

Belloch, A., Morillo, C., & García-Soriano, G. (2007). Are the dysfunctional beliefs that predict worry different from those that predict obsessions? *Clinical Psychology & Psychotherapy, 14*(6), 438–448.

Bellodi, L., Scioto, G., Diaferia, G., Ronchi, P., & Smiraldi, E. 106 (1992). Psychiatric disorders in families of patients with obsessive-compulsive disorder. *Psychiatry Research, 42*, 111–120.

Bienvenu, O. J., Samuels, J. F., Riddle, M. A., Hoehn-Saric, R., Liang, K. Y., Cullen, B. A., Grados, M. A., & Nestadt, G. (2000). The relationship of obsessive-compulsive disorder to possible spectrum disorders: Results from a family study. *Biological Psychiatry, 48*(4), 287–293.

Bienvenu, O. J., Samuels, J. F., Wuyek, L. A., Liang, K. Y., Wang, Y., Grados, M. A., ... Fyer, A. J. (2012). Is obsessive-compulsive disorder an anxiety disorder, and what, if any, are spectrum conditions? A family study perspective. *Psychological Medicine, 42*(1), 1–13.

Bipeta, R., Yerramilli, S. S., Pingali, S., Karredla, A. R., & Ali, M. O. (2013). A cross-sectional study of insight and family accommodation in pediatric obsessive-compulsive disorder. *Child and Adolescent Psychiatry and Mental Health, 7*(1), 20.

Black, D. W., & Noyes, R. (1997). Obsessive-compulsive disorder and Axis II. *International Review of Psychiatry, 9*, 111–118.

Brakoulias, V., & Starcevic, V. (2011). The characterization of beliefs in obsessive-compulsive disorder. *Psychiatric Quarterly, 82*(2), 151–161.

Brandes, M., & Bienvenu, O. J. (2009). Anxiety disorders and personality disorders comorbidity. In M. M. Antony & M. B. Stein (Eds.), *Oxford handbook of anxiety and related disorders* (pp. 587–595). Oxford University Press.

Brown, T. A., DiNardo, P. A., & Barlow, D. H. (1994). *Anxiety Disorders Interview Schedule for DSM-IV*. Oxford University Press.

Brown, T. A., Moras, K., Zinbarg, R. E., & Barlow, D. H. (1993). Diagnostic and symptom distinguishability of generalized anxiety disorder and obsessive-compulsive disorder. *Behavior Therapy, 24*, 227–240.

Bystritsky, A., Liberman, R. P., Hwang, S., Wallace, C. J., Vapnik, T., Maindment, K., & Saxena, S. (2001). Social functioning and quality of life comparisons between obsessive-compulsive and schizophrenic disorders. *Depression and Anxiety, 14*(4), 214–218.

Calleo, J. S., Hart, J., Björgvinsson, T., & Stanley, M. A. (2010). Obsessions and worry beliefs in an inpatient OCD population. *Journal of Anxiety Disorders, 24*(8), 903–908.

Calvocoressi, L., Lewis, B., Harris, M., Trufan, S. J., Goodman, W. K., McDougle, C. J., & Price, L. H. (1995). Family accommodation in obsessive-compulsive disorder. *The American Journal of Psychiatry, 152*, 441–443.

Calvocoressi, L., Mazure, C. M., Stanislav, V. K., Skolnick, J., Fisk, D., Vegso, S. J., Van Noppen, B. L., & Price, L. H. (1999). Family accommodation of obsessive-compulsive symptoms: Instrument development and assessment of family behavior. *The Journal of Nervous and Mental Disease, 187*, 636–642.

Catapano, F., Perris, F., Fabrazzo, M., Cioffi, V., Giacco, D., De Santis, V., & Maj, M. (2010). Obsessive-compulsive disorder with poor insight: A three-year prospective study. *Progress in Neuro-Psychopharmacology and Biological Psychiatry, 34*(2), 323–330.

Chambless, D. L., & Steketee, G. (1999). Expressed emotion and behavior therapy outcome: A prospective study with obsessive-compulsive and agoraphobic outpatients. *Journal of Consulting and Clinical Psychology, 67*, 658–665.

Cherian, A. V., Narayanaswamy, J. C., Srinivasaraju, R., Viswanath, B., Math, S. B., Kandavel, T., & Reddy, Y. J. (2012). Does insight have specific correlation with symptom dimensions in OCD? *Journal of Affective Disorders, 138*(3), 352–359.

Choca, J. P., & Grossman, S. D. (2015). Evolution of the Millon Clinical Multiaxial Inventory. *Journal of Personality Assessment, 97*(6), 541–549.

Cicek, E., Cicek, I. E., Kayhan, F., Uguz, F., & Kaya, N. (2013). Quality of life, family burden and associated factors in relatives with obsessive-compulsive disorder. *General Hospital Psychiatry, 35*(3), 253–258.

Cohen, S., Mermelstein, R., Kamarck, T., & Hoberman, H. (1985). Measuring the functional components of social support. In I. G. Sarason & B. R. Sarason (Eds.), *Social support: Theory, research and applications* (pp. 73–94). Martines Ujhoff.

Coles, M. E., Pinto, A., Mancebo, M. C., Rasmussen, S. A., & Eisen, J. L. (2008). OCD with comorbid OCPD: A subtype of OCD? *Journal of Psychiatric Research, 42*, 289–296.

Comer, J. S., Kendall, P. C., Franklin, M. E., Hudson, J. L., & Pimentel, S. S. (2004). Obsessing/worrying about the overlap between obsessive-compulsive disorder and generalized anxiety disorder in youth. *Clinical Psychology Review, 24*(6), 663–683.

Cooper, M. (1994). Report on the findings of a study of OCD family members. *OCD Newsletter, 8*, 1–2.

Cordiolia, A. V., Heldt, E., Bochia, D. B., Margis, R., deSousa, M. B., Tonello, J. F., Manfro, G. G., & Kapczinski, F. (2003). Cognitive-behavioral group therapy in obsessive-compulsive disorder: A randomized clinical trial. *Psychotherapy and Psychosomatics, 72*, 211–216.

Crino, R. D., & Andres, G. (1996). Obsessive-compulsive disorder and Axis I comorbidity. *Journal of Anxiety Disorders, 10*, 37–46.

Davey, G. C., Startup, H. M., Zara, A., MacDonald, C. B., & Field, A. P. (2003). The perseveration of checking thoughts and mood-as-input hypothesis. *Journal of Behavior Therapy and Experimental Psychiatry, 34*(2), 141–160.

Demal, U., Lenz, G., Mayrhofer, A., Zapotoczky, H-G., & Zitterl, W. (1993). Obsessive-compulsive disorder and depression: A retrospective study on course and interaction. *Psychopathology, 26*, 145–150.

Denys, D., Tenney, N., van Megen, H. J. G. M., de Geus, F., & Westenberg, H. G. M. (2004). Axis I and II comorbidity in a large sample of patients with obsessive-compulsive disorder. *Journal of Affective Disorders, 80*, 155–162.

Diaferia, G., Bianchi, I., Bianchi, M. L., Cavedini, P., Erzegovesi, S., & Bellodi, L. (1997). Relationship between obsessive-compulsive personality disorder and obsessive-compulsive disorder. *Comprehensive Psychiatry, 38*, 38–42.

Diefenbach, G. J., Abramowitz, J. S., Norberg, M. M., & Tolin, D. F. (2007). Changes in quality of life following cognitive-behavioral therapy for obsessive-compulsive disorder. *Behaviour Research and Therapy, 45*, 3060–3068.

Dreesen, L., Hoekstra, R., & Arntz, A. (1997). Personality disorders do not influence the results of cognitive and behavior therapy for obsessive-compulsive disorder. *Journal of Anxiety Disorders, 11*, 503–521.

Eisen, J. L., Mancebo, M. A., Pinto, A., Coles, M. E., Pagano, M. E., Stout, R., & Rasmussen, S. A. (2006). Impact of obsessive-compulsive disorder on quality of life. *Comprehensive Psychiatry, 47*, 270–275.

Eisen, J. L., Phillips, K. A., Baer, L., Beer, D. A., Atala, K. D., & Rasmussen, S. A. (1998). The Brown Assessment of Beliefs Scale: Reliability and validity. *The American Journal of Psychiatry, 155*, 102–108.

Endicott, J., Knee, J., Harrison, W., & Blumenthal, R. (1993). Quality of Life Enjoyment and Satisfaction Questionnaire: A new measure. *Psychopharmacology Bulletin, 29*, 321–326.

Fals-Stewart, W., & Lucente, S. (1993). An MCMI cluster typology of obsessive-compulsives: A measure of personality characteristics and its relationship to treatment participation, compliance and outcome in behavior therapy. *Journal of Psychiatric Research, 27*, 139–154.

Fan, J., Zhong, M., Zhu, X., Gan, J., Liu, W., Niu, C., Liao, H., Zhang, H., Yi, J., & Tan, C. (2017). Resting-state functional connectivity between right anterior insula and right orbital frontal cortex correlate with insight level in obsessive-compulsive disorder. *NeuroImage: Clinical, 15*, 1–7.

Farrell, L., Waters, A., Milliner, E., & Ollendick, T. (2012). Comorbidity and treatment response in pediatric obsessive-compulsive disorder: A pilot study of group cognitive-behavioral treatment. *Psychiatry Research, 199*(2), 115–123.

Ferrão, Y. A., Almeida, V. P., Bedin, N. R., Rosa, R., & Busnello, E. D. A. (2006). Impulsivity and compulsivity in patients with trichotillomania or skin picking compared with patients with obsessive-compulsive disorder. *Comprehensive Psychiatry, 47*(4), 282–288.

Fineberg, N. A., Hengartner, M. P., Bergbaum, C., Gale, T., Rössler, W., & Angst, J. (2013). Lifetime comorbidity of obsessive-compulsive disorder and sub-threshold obsessive-compulsive symptomatology in the community: Impact, prevalence, socio-demographic and clinical characteristics. *International Journal of Psychiatry in Clinical Practice, 17*(3), 188–196.

First, M. B., Gibbon, M., Spitzer, R. L., Williams, J. B. W., & Benjam, L. S. (1995). *Structured Clinical Interview for DSM-IV Axis I Disorders (SCID-I/P)*. Biometrics Press.

First, M. B., Williams, J. B. W., Benjamin, L. S., & Spitzer, R. L. (2015). *User's guide for the SCID-5-PD (Structured Clinical Interview for DSM-5 Personality Disorder)*. American Psychiatric Association.

Flessner, C. A., Sapyta, J., Garcia, A., Freeman, J. B., Franklin, M. E., Foa, E., & March, J. (2011). Examining the psychometric properties of the Family Accommodation Scale-Parent-Report (FAS-PR). *Journal of Psychopathology and Behavioral Assessment, 33*(1), 38–46.

Fontenelle, I. S., Fontenelle, L. F., Borges, M. C., Prazeres, A. M., Rangé, B. P., Mendlowicz, M. V., & Versiani, M. (2010). Quality of life and symptom dimensions of patients with obsessive-compulsive disorder. *Psychiatry Research, 179*(2), 198–203.

Fontenelle, J. M., Harrison, B. J., Santana, L., do Rosário Conceição, M., Versiani, M., & Fontenelle, L. F. (2013). Correlates of insight into different symptom dimensions in obsessive-compulsive disorder. *Annals of Clinical Psychiatry, 25*(1), 11–16.

Freeston, M. H., Ladouceur, R., Rhéaume, J., Letarte, H., Gagnon, F., & Thibodeau, N. (1994). Self-report of obsessions and worry. *Behaviour Research and Therapy, 32*(1), 29–36.

Freeston, M. H., Ladouceur, R., Thibodeau, N., & Gagnon, F. (1991). Cognitive intrusions in a nonclinical population. I. Response style, subjective experience and appraisal. *Behaviour Research and Therapy, 29*, 585–597.

Friborg, O., Martinussen, M., Kaiser, S., Øvergård, K. T., & Rosenvinge, J. H. (2013). Comorbidity of personality disorders in anxiety disorders: A meta-analysis of 30 years of research. *Journal of Affective Disorders, 145*(2), 143–155.

Frost, R. O., Steketee, G., & Grisham, J. (2004). Measurement of compulsive hoarding: Saving Inventory-Revised. *Behaviour Research and Therapy, 42*(10), 1163–1182.

Frost, R. O., Steketee, G., & Tolin, D. F. (2011). Comorbidity in hoarding disorder. *Depression and Anxiety, 28*(10), 876–884.

Frost, R. O., Steketee, G., Tolin, D. F., & Renaud, S. (2008). Development and validation of the Clutter Image Rating. *Journal of Psychopathology and Behavioral Assessment, 30*(3), 193–203.

Frost, R. O., Tolin, D. F., & Maltby, N. (2010). Insight-related challenges in the treatment of hoarding. *Cognitive and Behavioral Practice, 17*(4), 404–413.

Garcia, A. M., Sapyta, J. J., Moore, P. S., Freeman, J. B., Franklin, M. E., March, J. S., & Foa, E. B. (2010). Predictors and moderators of treatment outcome in the Pediatric Obsessive Compulsive Treatment Study (POTS I). *Journal of the American Academy of Child and Adolescent Psychiatry, 49*(10), 1024–1033.

García-Soriano, G., Rufer, M., Delsignore, A., & Weidt, S. (2014). Factors associated with non-treatment or delayed treatment seeking in OCD sufferers: A review of the literature. *Psychiatry Research, 220*(1–2), 1–10.

Gentes, E. L., & Ruscio, A. M. (2011). A meta-analysis of the relation of intolerance of uncertainty to symptoms of generalized anxiety disorder, major depressive disorder, and obsessive-compulsive disorder. *Clinical Psychology Review, 31*(6), 923–933.

Goes, F. S., McCusker, M. G., Bienvenu, O. J., Mackinnon, D. F., Mondimore, F. M., Schweizer, B., National Institute of Mental Health Genetics Initiative Bipolar Disorder Consortium, Depaulo, J. R., & Potash, J. B. (2012). Co-morbid anxiety disorders in bipolar disorder and major depression: Familial aggregation and clinical characteristics of co-morbid panic disorder, social phobia, specific phobia and obsessive-compulsive disorder. *Psychological Medicine, 42*(7), 1449.

Gordon, O. M., Salkovskis, P. M., Oldfield, V. B., & Carter, N. (2013). The association between obsessive-compulsive disorder and obsessive-compulsive personality disorder: Prevalence and clinical presentation. *British Journal of Clinical Psychology, 52*(3), 300–315.

Grant, J. E., Odlaug, B. L., & Kim, S. W. (2010). A clinical comparison of pathologic skin picking and obsessive-compulsive disorder. *Comprehensive Psychiatry, 51*(4), 347–352.

Grover, S., & Dutt, A. (2011). Perceived burden and quality of life of caregivers in obsessive-compulsive disorder. *Psychiatry and Clinical Neurosciences, 65*(5), 416–422.

Grunes, M. S., Neziroglu, F., & McKay, D. (2001). Family involvement in the behavioral treatment of obsessive-compulsive disorder: A preliminary investigation. *Behavior Therapy, 32*, 803–820.

Hamilton, M. (1986). The Hamilton Rating Scale for Depression. In *Assessment of depression* (pp. 143–152). Springer.

Hauschildt, M., Jelinek, L., Randjbar, S., Hottenrott, B., & Moritz, S. (2010). Generic and illness-specific quality of life in obsessive-compulsive disorder. *Behavioural and Cognitive Psychotherapy, 38*(4), 417–436.

Hollander, E., Kwon, K., Won, J. H., Stein, D. J., Broatch, J., Rowland, C. T., & Himelein, C. A. (1996). Obsessive-compulsive and spectrum disorders: Overview and quality of life issues. *The Journal of Clinical Psychiatry, 57*(Suppl. 8), 3–6.

Hong, J. P., Samuels, J., Bienvenu III, O. J., Cannistraro, P., Grados, M., Riddle, M. A., Liang, K., Cullen, B., Hoehn-Saric, R., & Nestadt, G. (2004). Clinical correlates of recurrent major depression in obsessive-compulsive disorder. *Depression and Anxiety, 20*, 86–91.

Hooley, J. M., & Parker, H. A. (2006). Measuring expressed emotion: An evaluation of the shortcuts. *Journal of Family Psychology, 20*(3), 386.

Hooley, J. M., & Teasdale, J. D. (1989). Predictors of relapse in unipolar depressives: Expressed emotion, marital distress, and perceived criticism. *Journal of Abnormal Psychology, 98*, 229–235.

Jaafari, N., Aouizerate, B., Tignol, J., El-Hage, W., Wassouf, I., Guehl, D., Bioulac, B., Daniel, M., Lacoste, J., Gil, R., Burbaud, P., Rotge, J., & Insight Study Group. (2011). The relationship between insight and uncertainty in obsessive-compulsive disorder. *Psychopathology, 44*(4), 272–276.

Jacob, M. L., Larson, M. J., & Storch, E. A. (2014). Insight in adults with obsessive-compulsive disorder. *Comprehensive Psychiatry, 55*(4), 896–903.

Jacoby, R. J., Leonard, R. C., Riemann, B. C., & Abramowitz, J. S. (2014). Predictors of quality of life and functional impairment in obsessive-compulsive disorder. *Comprehensive Psychiatry, 55*(5), 1195–1202.

Jaisoorya, T. S., Reddy, Y. J., & Srinath, S. (2003). The relationship of obsessive-compulsive disorder to putative spectrum disorders: Results from an Indian study. *Comprehensive Psychiatry, 44*(4), 317–323.

Jakubovski, E., Pittenger, C., Torres, A. R., Fontenelle, L. F., do Rosario, M. C., Ferrão, Y. A., de Mathis, M. A., Miguel, E. C., & Bloch, M. H. (2011). Dimensional correlates of poor insight in obsessive-compulsive disorder. *Progress in Neuro-Psychopharmacology and Biological Psychiatry, 35*(7), 1677–1681.

Jenike, M. A., Baer, L., Minichiello, W. E., Schwartz, C. E., & Carey, R. J. (1986). Concomitant obsessive-compulsive disorder and schizotypal personality disorders. *The American Journal of Psychiatry, 143*, 530–532.

Karadag, F., Tumkaya, S., Kırtaş, D., Efe, M., Alacam, H., & Oguzhanoglu, N. K. (2011). Neurological soft signs in obsessive-compulsive disorder with good and poor insight. *Progress in Neuro-Psychopharmacology and Biological Psychiatry, 35*(4), 1074–1079.

Kashyap, H., Kumar, J. K., Kandavel, T., & Reddy, Y. J. (2012). Neuropsychological correlates of insight in obsessive-compulsive disorder. *Acta Psychiatrica Scandinavica, 126*(2), 106–114.

Kishore, V. R., Samar, R., Reddy, Y. C. J., Chandrasekhar, C. R., & Thennarasu, K. (2004). Clinical characteristics and treatment response in poor and good insight obsessive-compulsive disorder. *European Psychiatry, 19*, 202–208.

Koran, L. M., Thienemann, M. L., & Davenport, R. (1996). Quality of life for patients with obsessive-compulsive disorder. *The American Journal of Psychiatry, 153*, 783–788.

Kotelnikova, Y., Clark, L. A., Vernon, P. A., & Hayden, E. P. (2015). Development and validation of the Schedule for Nonadaptive and Adaptive Personality Brief Self-description Rating Form (SNAP-BSRF). *Assessment, 22*(1), 3–16.

Koyuncu, A., Tükel, R., Özyıldırım, İ., Meteris, H., & Yazıcı, O. (2010). Impact of obsessive-compulsive disorder comorbidity on the sociodemographic and clinical features of patients with bipolar disorder. *Comprehensive Psychiatry, 51*(3), 293–297.

Kugler, B. B., Lewin, A. B., Phares, V., Geffken, G. R., Murphy, T. K., & Storch, E. A. (2013). Quality of life in obsessive-compulsive disorder: The role of mediating variables. *Psychiatry Research, 206*(1), 43–49.

Lebowitz, E. R. (2013). Parent-based treatment for childhood and adolescent OCD. *Journal of Obsessive-Compulsive and Related Disorders, 2*(4), 425–431.

Leon, A. C., Solomon, D. A., Mueller, T. I., Turvey, C. L., Endicott, J., & Keller, M. B. (1999). The Range of Impaired Functioning Tool (LIFE–RIFT): A brief measure of functional impairment. *Psychological Medicine, 29*(4), 869–878.

Lochner, C., Fineberg, N. A., Zohar, J., Van Ameringen, M., Juven-Wetzler, A., Altamura, A. C., Cuzen, N. L., Hollander, E., Denys, D., Nicolini, H., Dell'Osso, B., Pallanti, S., & Stein, D. J. (2014). Comorbidity in obsessive-compulsive disorder (OCD): A report from the International College of Obsessive-Compulsive Spectrum Disorders (ICOCS). *Comprehensive Psychiatry, 55*(7), 1513–1519.

Lochner, C., Hemmings, S. M. J., Kinnear, C. J., Niehaus, D. J. H., Nel, D. G., Corfield, V. A., Moolman-Smook, J. C., Seedat, S., & Stein, D. J. (2005). Cluster analysis of obsessive-compulsive spectrum disorders in patients with obsessive-compulsive disorder: Clinical and genetic correlates. *Comprehensive Psychiatry, 46*, 14–19.

Lochner, C., Seedat, S., Du Toit, P. L., Nel, D. G., Niehaus, D. J., Sandler, R., & Stein, D. J. (2005). Obsessive-compulsive disorder and trichotillomania: A phenomenological comparison. *BMC Psychiatry, 5*(1), 1–10.

Lochner, C., Serebro, P., van der Merwe, L., Hemmings, S., Kinnear, C., Seedat, S., & Stein, D. J. (2011). Comorbid obsessive-compulsive personality disorder in obsessive-compulsive disorder (OCD): A marker of severity. *Progress in Neuro-Psychopharmacology and Biological Psychiatry, 35*(4), 1087–1092.

Lochner, C., & Stein, D. J. (2010). Obsessive-compulsive spectrum disorders in obsessive-compulsive disorder and other anxiety disorders. *Psychopathology, 43*(6), 389–396.

Lovato, L., Ferrão, Y. A., Stein, D. J., Shavitt, R. G., Fontenelle, L. F., Vivan, A., Miguel, E. C., & Cordioli, A. V. (2012). Skin picking and trichotillomania in adults with obsessive-compulsive disorder. *Comprehensive Psychiatry, 53*(5), 562–568.

Lovibond, S. H., & Lovibond, P. F. (1995). *Manual for the Depression Anxiety Stress Scales* (2nd ed.). Psychology Foundation.

MacDonald, B., & Davey, G. C. L. (2005). Inflated responsibility and perseverative checking: The effect of negative mood. *Journal of Abnormal Psychology, 114*, 176–182.

Macy, A. S., Theo, J. N., Kaufmann, S. C., Ghazzaoui, R. B., Pawlowski, P. A., Fakhry, H. I., Cassmassi, B. J., & IsHak, W. W. (2013). Quality of life in obsessive-compulsive disorder. *CNS Spectrums, 18*(1), 21–33.

Magalhães, P. V., Kapczinski, N. S., & Kapczinski, F. (2010). Correlates and impact of obsessive-compulsive comorbidity in bipolar disorder. *Comprehensive Psychiatry, 51*(4), 353–356.

Mataix-Cols, D., Frost, R. O., Pertusa, A., Clark, L. A., Saxena, S., Leckman, J. F., Stein, D. J., Matsunaga, H., & Wilhelm, S. (2010). Hoarding disorder: A new diagnosis for DSM-V?. *Depression and Anxiety, 27*(6), 556–572.

Matsunaga, H., Kiriike, N., Matsui, T., Oya, K., Iwasaki, I., Koshimune, K., Miyata, A., & Stein, D. J. (2002). Obsessive-compulsive disorder with poor insight. *Comprehensive Psychiatry, 43*, 150–157.

McHorney, C. A., Ware, J. E., & Raczek, A. E. (1993). The MOS 36-Item Short Form Health Survey (SF-36), II: Psychometric and clinical tests of validity in measuring physical and mental health constructs. *Medical Care, 31*, 247–263.

Mendlowicz, M. V., & Stein, M. B. (2000). Quality of life in individuals with anxiety disorder. *The American Journal of Psychiatry, 157*, 669–682.

Millon, T., Grossman, S., & Millon, C. (2015). *Millon Clinical Multiaxial Inventory: MCMI-IV*. Pearson Assessments.

Mohammadi, M-R., Ghanizadeh, A., & Moini, R. (2007). Lifetime comorbidity of obsessive-compulsive disorder with psychiatric disorders in a community sample. *Depression and Anxiety, 24*, 602–607.

Monzani, B., Rijsdijk, F., Harris, J., & Mataix-Cols, D. (2014). The structure of genetic and environmental risk factors for dimensional representations of DSM-5 obsessive-compulsive spectrum disorders. *JAMA Psychiatry, 71*(2), 182–189.

Moritz, S., Claussen, M., Hauschildt, M., & Kellner, M. (2014). Perceptual properties of obsessive thoughts are associated with low insight in obsessive-compulsive disorder. *The Journal of Nervous and Mental Disease, 202*(7), 562–565.

Newth, S., & Rachman, S. (2001). The concealment of obsessions. *Behaviour Research and Therapy, 39*, 457–464.

Neziroglu, F., McKay, D., Yaryura-Tobias, J., Stevens, K. P., & Todaro, J. (1999). The Overvalued Ideas Scale: Development, reliability and validity in obsessive-compulsive disorder. *Behaviour Research and Therapy, 37*, 881–902.

Obsessive Compulsive Cognitions Working Group. (2005). Psychometric validation of the Obsessive Belief Questionnaire and Interpretation of Intrusions Inventory part 2: Factor analyses and testing of a brief version. *Behaviour Research and Therapy, 43*, 1527–1542.

Ooms, P., Mantione, M., Figee, M., Schuurman, P. R., van den Munckhof, P., & Denys, D. (2014). Deep brain stimulation for obsessive-compulsive disorders: Long-term analysis of quality of life. *Journal of Neurology, Neurosurgery, and Psychiatry, 85*(2), 153–158.

Oosthuizen, P., Lambert, T., & Castle, D. J. (1998). Dysmorphic concern: Prevalence and associations with clinical variables. *Australian and New Zealand Journal of Psychiatry, 32*, 129–132.

Pallanti, S., Grassi, G., Cantisani, A., Sarrecchia, E., & Pellegrini, M. (2011). Obsessive-compulsive disorder comorbidity: Clinical assessment and therapeutic implications. *Frontiers in Psychiatry, 2*, 70.

Peris, T. S., & Piacentini, J. (2013). Optimizing treatment for complex cases of childhood obsessive-compulsive disorder: A preliminary trial. *Journal of Clinical Child & Adolescent Psychology, 42*(1), 1–8.

Peris, T. S., Bergman, R. L., Langley, A., Chang, S., Mccracken, J. T., & Piacentini, J. (2008). Correlates of accommodation of pediatric obsessive-compulsive disorder: Parent, child, and family characteristics. *Journal of the American Academy of Child and Adolescent Psychiatry, 47*(10), 1173–1181.

Perugi G., Toni, C., Franco, F., Travierso, M. C., Hantouche, E., & Akiskal, H. S. (2002). Obsessive-compulsive-bipolar comorbidity: A systematic exploration of clinical features and treatment outcome. *The Journal of Clinical Psychiatry, 63*, 1129–1134.

Philips, K. A. (2000). Connection between obsessive-compulsive disorder and body dysmorphic disorder. In W. K. Goodman, M. V. Rudorfer, & J. D. Maser (Eds.), *Obsessive-compulsive disorder: Contemporary issues in treatment* (pp. 23–41). Lawrence Erlbaum.

Philips, K. A., Hollander, E., Rasmussen, S. A., Aronowitz, B. R., DeCaria, C., & Goodman, W. K. (1997). A severity rating scale for body dysmorphic disorder: Development, reliability and validity of a modified version of the Yale-Brown Obsessive-Compulsive Scale. *Psychopharmacology Bulletin, 33*, 17–22.

Phillips, K. A., Pinto, A., Hart, A. S., Coles, M. E., Eisen, J. L., Menard, W., & Rasmussen, S. A. (2012). A comparison of insight in body dysmorphic disorder and obsessive-compulsive disorder. *Journal of Psychiatric Research, 46*(10), 1293–1299.

Phillips, K. A., Stein, D. J., Rauch, S. L., Hollander, E., Fallon, B. A., Barsky, A., Fineber, N., Mataix-Cols, D., Ferrão, Y. A., Saxena, S., Wilhelm, S., Kelly, M. M., Clark, L. A., Pinto, A., Bienvenu, J. O., Farrow,

J., & Leckman, J. (2010). Should an obsessive-compulsive spectrum grouping of disorders be included in DSM-V? *Depression and Anxiety, 27*(6), 528–555.

Piacentini, J., Bergman, R. L., Chang, S., Langley, A., Peris, T., Wood, J. J., & McCracken, J. (2011). Controlled comparison of family cognitive behavioral therapy and psychoeducation/relaxation training for child obsessive-compulsive disorder. *Journal of the American Academy of Child and Adolescent Psychiatry, 50*(11), 1149–1161.

Pinto, A., Liebowitz, M. R., Foa, E. B., & Simpson, H. B. (2011). Obsessive-compulsive personality disorder as a predictor of exposure and ritual prevention outcome for obsessive-compulsive disorder. *Behaviour Research and Therapy, 49*(8), 453–458.

Pinto, A., Steinglass, J. E., Greene, A. L., Weber, E. U., & Simpson, H. B. (2014). Capacity to delay reward differentiates obsessive-compulsive disorder and obsessive-compulsive personality disorder. *Biological Psychiatry, 75*(8), 653–659.

Pinto, A., Van Noppen, B., & Calvocoressi, L. (2013). Development and preliminary psychometric evaluation of a self-rated version of the Family Accommodation Scale for Obsessive-Compulsive Disorder. *Journal of Obsessive-Compulsive and Related Disorders, 2*(4), 457–465.

Purdon, C., & Clark, D. A. (1993). Obsessional intrusive thoughts in nonclinical subjects. Part I: Content and relation with depressive, anxious and obsessional symptoms. *Behaviour Research and Therapy, 31*, 713–720.

Purdon, C., & Clark, D. A. (1994). Perceived control and appraisal of obsessive intrusive thoughts: A replication and extension. *Behavioural and Cognitive Psychotherapy, 22*, 269–286.

Purdon, C., & Clark, D. A. (2005). *Overcoming obsessive thoughts*. New Harbinger.

Purdon, C., Cripps, E., Faull, M., Joseph, S., & Rowa, K. (2007). Development of a measure of ego-dystonicity. *Journal of Cognitive Psychotherapy, 21*, 198–216.

Purdon, C., Gifford, S., Young, L., & Antony, M. M. (2005). *Treatment ambivalence in anxiety disorders* [Poster presentation]. Association for the Advancement of Behavior and Cognitive Therapies Anxiety Disorders Special Interest Group, Washington, DC.

Rachman, S., & de Silva, P. (1978). Abnormal and normal obsessions. *Behaviour Research and Therapy, 16*, 233–248.

Rachman, S. J. (1993). Obsessions, responsibility and guilt. *Behaviour Research and Therapy, 31*, 149–154.

Radomsky, A. S., Bohne, A., & O'Connor, K. (2007). Treating co-morbid presentations: Obsessive-compulsive disorder and disorders of impulse control. In M. M. Antony, C. Purdon, & L. J. Summerfeldt (Eds.), *Psychological treatment of obsessive-compulsive disorder: Fundamentals and beyond* (pp. 295–309). American Psychological Association.

Rasmussen, S. A., & Eisen, J. L. (1992). The epidemiology and clinical features of obsessive-compulsive disorder. *Psychiatric Clinics of North America, 15*, 743–758.

Rasmussen, S. A., & Tsuang, M. T. (1986). Clinical characteristics and family history in DSM-III obsessive-compulsive disorder. *The American Journal of Psychiatry, 143*, 317–322.

Remijnse, P. L., van den Heuvel, O. A., Nielen, M. M., Vriend, C., Hendriks, G. J., Hoogendijk, W. J. G., Uylings, H. B. M., & Veltman, D. J. (2013). Cognitive inflexibility in obsessive-compulsive disorder and major depression is associated with distinct neural correlates. *PLOS ONE, 8*(4), e59600.

Renshaw, K. D., Steketee, G., & Chambless, D. L. (2005). Involving family members in the treatment of OCD. *Cognitive Behaviour Therapy, 34*, 164–175.

Ricciardi, J. N., & McNally, R. J. (1995). Depressed mood is related to obsessions, but not to compulsions, in obsessive-compulsive disorder. *Journal of Anxiety Disorders, 9*, 249–256.

Richter, M. A., Summerfeldt, L. J., Antony, M. M., & Swinson, R. P. (2003). Obsessive-compulsive spectrum conditions in obsessive-compulsive disorder and other anxiety disorders. *Depression and Anxiety, 18*, 118–127.

Romero-Sanchiz, P., Nogueira-Arjona, R., Godoy-Ávila, A., Gavino-Lázaro, A., & Freeston, M. H. (2017). Differences in clinical intrusive thoughts between obsessive-compulsive disorder, generalized anxiety disorder, and hypochondria. *Clinical Psychology & Psychotherapy, 24*(6), O1464-O1473.

Roth Ledley, D., Pai, A., & Franklin, M. E. (2007). Treating comorbid presentations: Obsessive-compulsive disorder, anxiety disorders, and depression. In M. M. Antony, C. Purdon & L. Summerfeldt (Eds.), *Psychological treatment of obsessive-compulsive disorder: Fundamentals and beyond* (pp. 281–294). American Psychological Association.

Rowa, K., Gifford, S., McCabe, R., Milosevic, I., Antony, M. M., & Purdon, C. (2014). Treatment fears in anxiety disorders: Development and validation of the Treatment Ambivalence Questionnaire. *The Journal of Clinical Psychology, 70*(10), 979–993.

Ruscio, A. M., Stein, D. J., Chiu, W. T., & Kessler, R. C. (2010). The epidemiology of obsessive-compulsive disorder in the National Comorbidity Survey Replication. *Molecular Psychiatry, 15*(1), 53–63.

Salkovskis, P. M. (1999). Understanding and treating obsessive-compulsive disorder. *Behaviour Research and Therapy, 37*, S29–S52.

Samuels, J., Nestadt, G., Bienvenu, O. J., Costa, P. T., Riddle, M. A., Jr., Liang, K-Y., Hoehn Saric, R., Grados, M. A., & Cullen, B. A. M. (2000). Personality disorders and normal personality dimensions in obsessive-compulsive disorder. *The British Journal of Psychiatry, 177*, 457–462.

Schwab, J. J., Bialow, M. R., & Clemens, R. S. (1967). Hamilton Rating Scale for Depression with medical inpatients. *The British Journal of Psychiatry, 113*, 83–88.

Shafran, R., Ralph, J., & Tallis, F. (1995). Obsessive-compulsive symptoms and the family. *Bulletin of the Menninger Clinic, 59*, 472–478.

Sheehan, D. V. (1986). *The anxiety disease*. Bantam Books.

Simms, L. J., & Clark, L. A. (2006). The Schedule for Nonadaptive and Adaptive Personality (SNAP): A dimensional measure of traits relevant to personality and personality pathology. In S. Strack (Ed.), *Differentiating normal and abnormal personality* (pp. 431–450). Springer.

Skevington, S. M., Lotfy, M., & O'Connell, K. A. (2004). The World Health Organization's WHOQOL-BREF quality of life assessment: Psychometric properties and results of the international field trial. A report from the WHOQOL group. *Quality of Life Research, 13*(2), 299–310.

Snorrason, I., Olafsson, R. P., Flessner, C. A., Keuthen, N. J., Franklin, M. E., & Woods, D. W. (2012). The Skin Picking Scale-Revised: Factor structure and psychometric properties. *Journal of Obsessive-Compulsive and Related Disorders, 1*(2), 133–137.

Stanley, M. A., Breckenridge, J. K., Snyder, A. G., & Novy, D. M. (1999). Clinician-rated measures of hair pulling: A preliminary psychometric evaluation. *Journal of Psychopathology and Behavioral Assessment, 21*, 157–170.

Stein, D. J., & Phillips, K. A. (2014). Pros and cons of the new DSM-5 chapter of obsessive-compulsive and related disorders. *Current Psychiatry Reviews, 10*(4), 325–329.

Steketee, G. (1987). Behavioral social work with obsessive-compulsive disorder. *Journal of Social Service Research, 10*(2–4), 53–72.

Steketee, G. (1993). Social support and treatment outcome of obsessive-compulsive disorder at 9-month follow-up. *Behavioural and Cognitive Psychotherapy, 21*, 81–95.

Steketee, G., Chambless, D. L., & Tran, G. Q. (2001). Effects of Axis I and II comorbidity on behavior therapy outcome for obsessive-compulsive disorder and agoraphobia. *Comprehensive Psychiatry, 42*, 76–86.

Steketee, G., Henninger, N. J., & Pollard, C. A. (2000). Predicting treatment outcome for obsessive-compulsive disorder: Effects of comorbidity. In W. K. Goodman, M. V. Rudorfer, & J. D. Maser (Eds.), *Obsessive-compulsive disorder: Contemporary issues in treatment* (pp. 257–274). Lawrence Erlbaum.

Steketee, G., & Neziroglu, F. (2003). Assessment of obsessive-compulsive disorder and spectrum disorders. *Brief Treatment and Crisis Intervention, 3*, 169–185.

Stengler-Wenzke, K., Kroll, M., Matschinger, H., & Angermeyer, M. C. (2006). Quality of life of relatives of patients with obsessive-compulsive disorder. *Comprehensive Psychiatry, 47*, 523–527.

Stewart, S. E., Beresin, C., Haddad, S., Egan Stack, D., Fama, J., & Jenike, M. (2008). Predictors of family accommodation in obsessive-compulsive disorder. *Annals of Clinical Psychiatry, 20*(2), 65–70.

Storch, E. A., De Nadai, A. S., Jacob, M. L., Lewin, A. B., Muroff, J., Eisen, J., Abramowitz, J. S., Geller, D. A., & Murphy, T. K. (2014). Phenomenology and correlates of insight in pediatric obsessive-compulsive disorder. *Comprehensive Psychiatry, 55*(3), 613–620.

Storch, E. A., Geffken, G. R., Merlo, L. J., Jacob, M. L., Murphy, T. K., Goodman, W. K., Larson, M. J., Fernandez, M., & Grabill, K. (2007). Family accommodation in pediatric obsessive-compulsive disorder. *Journal of Clinical Child & Adolescent Psychology, 36*, 207–216.

Storch, E. A., Lewin, A. B., Geffken, G. R., Morgan, J. R., & Murphy, T. K. (2010). The role of comorbid disruptive behavior in the clinical expression of pediatric obsessive-compulsive disorder. *Behaviour Research and Therapy, 48*(12), 1204–1210.

Summerfeldt, L. J., Huta, V., & Swinson, R. P. (1998). Personality and obsessive-compulsive disorder. In R. P. Swinson, M. M. Antony, S. Rachman, & M. A. Richter (Eds.), *Obsessive-compulsive disorder: Theory, research and treatment* (pp. 79–119). Guilford.

Swedo, S. E., Rapaport, J. L., Leonard, M., & Cheslow, D. (1989). Obsessive-compulsive disorder in children and adolescents. Clinical phenomenology of 70 consecutive cases. *Archives of General Psychiatry, 46*, 335–341.

Tallis, F. (1996). Compulsive washing in the absence of phobic and illness anxiety. *Behaviour Research and Therapy, 34*, 361–362.

Thiel, N., Hertenstein, E., Nissen, C., Herbst, N., Külz, A. K., & Voderholzer, U. (2013). The effect of personality disorders on treatment outcomes in patients with obsessive-compulsive disorders. *Journal of Personality Disorders, 27*(6), 697–715.

Thomas, J. K., Kumar, P. S., Verma, A. N., Sinha, V. K., & Andrade, C. (2004). Psychosocial dysfunction and family burden in schizophrenia and obsessive-compulsive disorder. *Indian Journal of Psychiatry, 46*(3), 238.

Tolin, D. F., Fitch, K. E., Frost, R. O., & Steketee, G. (2010). Family informants' perceptions of insight in compulsive hoarding. *Cognitive Therapy and Research, 34*(1), 69–81.

Tolin, D. F., Gilliam, C., Wootton, B. M., Bowe, W., Bragdon, L. B., Davis, E., Hannan, S. E., Steinman, S. A., Worden, B., & Hallion, L. S. (2018). Psychometric properties of a structured diagnostic interview for DSM-5 anxiety, mood, and obsessive-compulsive and related disorders. *Assessment, 25*(1), 3–13.

Tükel, R., Meteris, H., Koyuncu, A., Tecer, A., & Yazici, O. (2006). The clinical impact of mood disorder and comorbidity on obsessive-compulsive disorder. *European Archives of Psychiatry and Clinical Neuroscience, 256*, 240–245.

Tükel, R., Polat, A., Özdemir, O., Aksüt, D., & Türksoy, N. (2002). Comorbid conditions in obsessive-compulsive disorder. *Comprehensive Psychiatry, 43*, 204–209.

Turner, S. M., Beidel, D. C., & Stanley, M. A. (1992). Are obsessional thoughts and worry different cognitive phenomena? *Clinical Psychology Review, 12*, 257–270.

Van Nieuwenhuizen, C., Schene, A. H., Koeter, M. W. J., & Huxley, P. J. (2001). The Lancashire Quality of Life Profile: Modification and psychometric evaluation. *Social Psychiatry and Psychiatry Epidemiology, 36*, 36–44.

Van Noppen, B., & Steketee, G. (2003). Family responses and multifamily behavioral treatment for obsessive-compulsive disorder. *Brief Treatment and Crisis Intervention, 3*, 231–247.

Vaughn, C., & Leff, J. (1976). The measurement of expressed emotion in the families of psychiatric patients. *British Journal of Social and Clinical Psychology, 15*, 157–165.

Veale, D. (2007). Treating obsessive-compulsive disorder in people with poor insight and overvalued ideation. In M. M. Antony, C. Purdon, & L. J. Summerfeldt (Eds.), *Psychological treatment of obsessive-compulsive disorder: Fundamentals and beyond* (pp. 267–280). American Psychological Association.

Vivan, A. D. S., Rodrigues, L., Wendt, G., Bicca, M. G., & Cordioli, A. V. (2013). Quality of life in adolescents with obsessive-compulsive disorder. *Brazilian Journal of Psychiatry, 35*(4), 369–374.

Weidle, B., Jozefiak, T., Ivarsson, T., & Thomsen, P. H. (2014). Quality of life in children with OCD with and without comorbidity. *Health and Quality of Life Outcomes, 12*(1), 152.

Wells, A., & Papageorgiou, C. (1998). Relationships between worry, obsessive-compulsive symptoms and meta-cognitive beliefs. *Behaviour Research and Therapy, 36*(9), 899–913.

World Health Organization. (1995). The World Health Organization Quality of Life assessment (WHO/QOL): Position paper from the World Health Organization. *Social Science & Medicine, 41*, 1403–1409.

Wu, K. D., Clark, L. A., & Watson, D. (2006). Relations between obsessive-compulsive disorder and personality: Beyond Axis I–Axis II comorbidity. *Anxiety Disorders, 20*, 695–717.

Wu, M. S., McGuire, J. F., Martino, C., Phares, V., Selles, R. R., & Storch, E. A. (2016). A meta-analysis of family accommodation and OCD symptom severity. *Clinical Psychology Review, 45*, 34–44.

Wu, M. S., Pinto, A., Horng, B., Phares, V., McGuire, J. F., Dedrick, R. F., Van Noppen, B., Calvocoressi, L., & Storch, E. A. (2016). Psychometric properties of the Family Accommodation Scale for Obsessive-Compulsive Disorder–Patient Version. *Psychological Assessment, 28*(3), 251–262.

PART IV

Treatment of Obsessive-Compulsive and Related Disorders

CHAPTER 17

Pharmacological Treatments for Obsessive-Compulsive Disorder

Brian P. Brennan, Darin D. Dougherty, Scott L. Rauch, *and* Michael A. Jenike

> **Abstract**
>
> Progress in treating obsessive-compulsive disorder (OCD) has accelerated in recent years. Effective first-line treatments include behavior therapy and medications, with overwhelming evidence supporting the efficacy of serotonin reuptake inhibitors (SRIs). Second-line medication treatments for OCD include augmentation of SRIs with neuroleptics, glutamate modulators, clonazepam, or buspirone, with limited support for other strategies at present. Alternative monotherapies (e.g., buspirone, clonazepam, phenelzine) have more limited supporting data and require further study. Behavior therapy is as effective as medication and may be superior in risks, costs, and enduring benefits. Future rigorous research is needed to determine which patients respond preferentially to which medications, at what dose, and after what duration. Emerging treatments include new compounds acting via serotonergic, dopaminergic, glutamatergic, and opioid systems.
>
> **Key Words:** serotonin reuptake inhibitors, SRI, SSRI, monotherapy, augmentation, pharmacotherapy

It was not until 1967 that the tricyclic antidepressant clomipramine, the first available serotonin reuptake inhibitor (SRI), emerged as an effective treatment for obsessive-compulsive disorder (OCD; Fernandez & Lopez-Ibor, 1967). Contemporaneously, behavioral therapy for OCD was emerging as a viable treatment modality and the object of formal study (Rachman et al., 1971). The subsequent five decades have seen great development in the assessment and treatment of OCD. Several educational and self-help books written for lay audiences (e.g., Baer, 1991, 2002; Rapoport, 1980), articles appearing in the general medical literature (Heyman et al., 2006; Jenike, 1989, 2004), and the birth of an advocacy group (International OCD Foundation, www.ocfoundation.org) all contributed to a growing awareness of OCD. During this same era, the pharmaceutical industry produced a new class of compounds, known as selective serotonin reuptake inhibitors (SSRIs), that, like clomipramine, acted via blockade of serotonergic reuptake sites. Unlike clomipramine, however, these new SSRIs had much lower affinities for adrenergic and cholinergic receptors, presumably giving the SSRIs a more favorable side-effect profile.

Investigators in psychopharmacology proceeded to systematically study these new agents, as well as other novel compounds, while their psychotherapist counterparts conducted investigations of cognitive and behavioral treatments. During the 1990s alone, there were more than 1,500 reports published in medical sources about drug treatments and OCD. Moreover, neuroscience advances have brought us closer to understanding the etiology and pathophysiology of OCD and related disorders.

Contemporary Treatment for OCD

Numerous reviews have been written in the last few years regarding pharmacotherapy recommendations for OCD (Dougherty et al., 2004; Jenike, 1998; see Table 17.1). There is broad agreement among experts in the field that first-line treatments for OCD include SRIs (clomipramine or SSRIs) and/or behavior therapy. When the first-line interventions fail, second-line pharmacological approaches include augmentation of SRIs with additional medications, or trials of alternative medications as monotherapies in place of SRIs. Third-line treatments include unproven alternative monotherapies and augmentation therapies. Finally, other nonpharmacological treatments, including transcranial magnetic stimulation (TMS) and neurosurgery, are reserved for particular clinical situations or as treatments of last resort. Although the focus in this chapter is on psychopharmacology, the authors wish to explicitly emphasize that most experts view behavior therapy (see Chapter 19) as a critical and effective first-line treatment for OCD, and that behavior therapy is all too often overlooked or unavailable.

First-Line Pharmacotherapy: SRIs

Currently, the SRIs are the first-line treatment for OCD (Dougherty & Rauch, 1997; Dougherty et al., 2004; Soomro et al., 2008). There is overwhelming evidence from multiple randomized, double-blind, placebo-controlled studies supporting the efficacy of SRIs in the treatment of OCD (Table 17.2). Specifically, in adults, well-designed and well-controlled trials have demonstrated the relative efficacy of clomipramine versus placebo, as well as the relative efficacy of SSRIs, including fluoxetine, sertraline, paroxetine, fluvoxamine, citalopram, and escitalopram, versus placebo. Moreover, SRIs have been shown to be significantly more effective than non-SRI tricyclic antidepressants (TCAs) in placebo-controlled (Table 17.2) as well as non-placebo-controlled studies (Table 17.3). In the only randomized, double-blind, placebo-controlled study involving non-SRI TCAs, nortriptyline was not shown to be significantly more effective than placebo (Thoren et al., 1980), supporting the view that non-SRI TCAs are not an effective monotherapy for OCD.

Despite a wide range of observed SRI response rates, large-scale studies have generally yielded approximately 40% to 60% responders, with mean improvement in the active treatment group of approximately 20% to 40% (see Greist, Jefferson, Kobak, Chouinard, et al., 1995). In terms of the relative efficacy among SRIs, a large-scale meta-analysis of

Table 17.1. Sample Treatment Recommendations for OCD

First-Line Treatment		
Behavior Therapy		
Exposure & response prevention		At least 20 hours
Medication: Serial SRI trials (consider at least two SSRI trials and one of clomipramine)		
Clomipramine	150–250 mg/day	12 weeks
Fluoxetine	40–80 mg/day	12 weeks
Sertraline	50–200 mg/day	12 weeks
Fluvoxamine	200–300 mg/day	12 weeks
Paroxetine	40–60 mg/day	12 weeks
Citalopram	40–60 mg/day	12 weeks
Escitalopram	20–30 mg/day	12 weeks
Second-Line Treatment		
Modifications to Behavior Therapy:		
Consider inpatient sessions, home visits or other in situ sessions, or cognitive therapy		
Medication: SRI augmentation (with controlled data)		
Clonazepam	0.5–5 mg/day	4 weeks
Buspirone	15–60 mg/day	8 weeks
Pimozide	1–3 mg/day	4 weeks
Haloperidol	0.5–10 mg/day	4 weeks
Risperidone	0.5–6 mg/day	4 weeks
Olanzapine	2.5–15 mg/day	4 weeks
Quetiapine	200–600 mg/day	4 weeks
Aripiprazole	5–15 mg/day	4 weeks
Memantine	10 mg twice daily	8 weeks
Riluzole	50 mg twice daily	8 weeks
N-Acetylcysteine	1200–1500 mg twice daily	12 weeks
Medication: Alternative monotherapies		
Clonazepam	0.5–5 mg/day	4 weeks
Buspirone	30–60 mg/day	6 weeks
Phenelzine	60–90 mg/day	10 weeks
Venlafaxine	Up to 375 mg/day	12 weeks
Duloxetine	Up to 120 mg/day	12 weeks
Deep transcranial magnetic stimulation (TMS) targeting anterior cingulate cortex/dorsomedial prefrontal cortex		
Third-Line Treatment		
Low-risk experimental or insufficiently studied therapies		
Alternative monotherapies without controlled data		
Alternative augmentation strategies without controlled data		
Fourth-Line Treatment		
Consider neurosurgery (only if OCD is long-standing, severe, debilitating, and unresponsive to an exhaustive array of other treatments)		

Table 17.2. Placebo-Controlled Trials of SRI Therapy for OCD (Adults)

Treatment Conditions	N	Results	Study
Clomipramine vs. placebo	20	Clomipramine significantly superior to placebo	Karabanow (1977)
Clomipramine vs. placebo crossover	14	Clomipramine significantly superior to placebo	Montgomery (1980)
Clomipramine vs. nortriptyline vs. placebo	24	Clomipramine, but not nortriptyline, superior to placebo	Thoren et al. (1980)
Clomipramine vs. placebo	12	Clomipramine significantly superior to placebo	Mavissakalian et al. (1985)
Clomipramine vs. placebo	27	Clomipramine significantly superior to placebo	Jenike et al. (1989)*
Clomipramine vs. placebo	32	Clomipramine significantly superior to placebo	Greist et al. (1990)*
Clomipramine vs. placebo	239	Clomipramine significantly superior to placebo	Clomipramine Collaborative Group (1991)
Clomipramine vs. placebo	281	Clomipramine significantly superior to placebo	Clomipramine Collaborative Group (1991)
Clomipramine vs. placebo	36	Clomipramine significantly superior to placebo	Foa et al. (2005)
Sertraline vs. placebo	87	Sertraline significantly superior to placebo	Chouinard et al. (1990)
Sertraline vs. placebo	19	Sertraline significantly superior to placebo	Jenike et al. (1990a)**
Sertraline vs. placebo	325	Sertraline significantly superior to placebo	Greist, Chouinard, et al. (1995)
Sertraline vs. placebo	167	Sertraline significantly superior to placebo	Kronig et al. (1999)
Fluvoxamine vs. placebo	16	Fluvoxamine significantly superior to placebo	Perse et al. (1987)
Fluvoxamine vs. placebo	42	Fluvoxamine significantly superior to placebo	Goodman et al. (1989)
Fluvoxamine vs. placebo	38	Fluvoxamine significantly superior to placebo	Jenike et al. (1990b)
Fluvoxamine vs. placebo	320	Fluvoxamine significantly superior to placebo	
Fluvoxamine vs. placebo	160	Fluvoxamine significantly superior to placebo	Goodman et al. (1996)
Fluvoxamine vs. behavioral therapy vs. placebo	31	Behavioral therapy > fluvoxamine > placebo	Nakatani et al. (2005)

Table 17.2. *Continued*

Treatment Conditions	N	Results	Study
Fluvoxamine CR vs. placebo	127	Fluvoxamine CR significantly superior to placebo	Hollander et al. (2003)
Fluoxetine vs. placebo	355	Fluoxetine (20, 40, 60 mg) significantly superior to placebo	Tollefson et al. (1994)
Fluoxetine vs. placebo	217	Fluoxetine (40, 60 mg) significantly superior to placebo	Montgomery et al. (1993)
Paroxetine vs. placebo	348	Paroxetine (40, 60 mg) significantly superior to placebo while 20 mg effects equal to placebo	Wheadon et al. (1993)
Citalopram vs. placebo	401	Citalopram (20, 40, 60 mg) significantly superior to placebo	Montgomery et al. (2001)
Escitalopram vs. paroxetine vs. placebo	466	Escitalopram (20 mg, 10 mg) and paroxetine (40 mg) significantly superior to placebo	Stein et al. (2007)

* Included in Clomipramine Collaborative Group (1991).

** Included in Chouinard et al. (1990).

multicenter trials of SRIs was performed by Greist, Jefferson, Kobak, Katzelnick, and colleagues (1995) in which CMI ($N = 520$), fluoxetine ($N = 355$), sertraline ($N = 325$), and fluvoxamine ($N = 320$) were all shown to be significantly superior to placebo. This meta-analysis further indicated that clomipramine might have superior efficacy over SSRIs. Although the meta-analysis of Greist et al. had many strengths, including that all studies used comparable parameters and were conducted at essentially the same centers, the results should be interpreted with caution. Since there was a serial progression in the availability of the agents, and in the performance of the trials, clomipramine was studied in an SRI-naive population, whereas each successive agent was undoubtedly tried in a cohort comprising a larger subpopulation of patients with histories of past SRI unresponsiveness. Consequently, each successive trial might well have been conducted in a more treatment-resistant population, biasing the efficacy in favor of an agent studied in earlier years (i.e., clomipramine). In fact, a growing number of studies (see Table 17.3) and a comprehensive literature review (Pigott & Seay, 1999), as well as a meta-analysis (Soomro et al., 2008), all suggest that the SRIs all have comparable efficacy. However, despite these group data, any single individual may respond very well to one or two of the SRIs and not the others. Thus, serial trials of each agent may be required to determine which drug is best.

Table 17.3. Non-Placebo-Controlled Trials of Drug Therapy for OCD (Adults)

Treatment Conditions	N	Results	Study
Clomipramine vs. amitriptyline	20	Clomipramine superior to amitriptyline	Ananth et al. (1981)
Clomipramine vs. amitriptyline	39	Clomipramine superior to amitriptyline	Zhao (1991)
Clomipramine vs. clorgyline	13	Clomipramine superior to clorgyline	Insel et al. (1983)
Clomipramine vs. clorgyline	12	Clomipramine superior to clorgyline	Zahn et al. (1984)
Clomipramine vs. doxepin	32	Clomipramine superior to doxepin	Cui (1986)
Clomipramine vs. fluvoxamine	6	Comparable efficacy	Den Boer et al. (1987)
Clomipramine vs. fluvoxamine	66	Comparable efficacy	Freeman et al. (1994)
Clomipramine vs. fluvoxamine	79	Comparable efficacy	Koran et al. (1996)
Clomipramine vs. fluvoxamine	26	Comparable efficacy	Milanfranchi et al. (1997)
Clomipramine vs. fluvoxamine	133	Comparable efficacy	Mundo et al. (2000)
Clomipramine vs. fluvoxamine	227	Comparable efficacy	Mundo et al. (2001)
Clomipramine vs. fluoxetine	11	Comparable efficacy	Pigott et al. (1990)
Clomipramine vs. fluoxetine	55	Comparable efficacy	Lopez-Ibor et al. (1996)
Clomipramine vs. imipramine	16	Clomipramine superior to imipramine	Volavka et al. (1985)
Clomipramine vs. imipramine crossover	12	Clomipramine superior to imipramine	Lei (1986)
Clomipramine vs. paroxetine	406	Comparable efficacy	Zohar et al. (1996)
Clomipramine vs. sertraline	168	Comparable efficacy (fewer dropouts with sertraline)	Bisserbe et al. (1995)
Clomipramine vs. venlafaxine	73	Comparable efficacy	Albert et al. (2002)
Fluvoxamine vs. desipramine	40	Fluvoxamine superior to desipramine	Goodman et al. (1990)
Fluvoxamine vs. paroxetine vs. citalopram	30	Comparable efficacy	Mundo et al. (1997)
Paroxetine vs. venlafaxine	150	Comparable efficacy	Denys et al. (2003)
Sertraline vs. fluoxetine	150	Comparable efficacy	Bergeron et al. (2002)
Sertraline vs. desipramine	166	Sertraline superior to desipramine	Hoehn-Saric et al. (2000)
Citalopram	29	76% improved in 24-week open-label trial	Koponen et al. (1997)
Citalopram	18	14 of 18 showed reduced Y-BOCS score in open-label trial	Marazziti et al. (2001)
Venlafaxine	39	69% improved in open-label trial	Hollander et al. (2003)
Duloxetine	20	Significant reduction in Y-BOCS score in open-label trial	Dougherty et al. (2015)

Data regarding duration of treatment, optimal dose, and side effects are also plentiful but are difficult to interpret with confidence because studies often were not designed to specifically answer these questions. The collective wisdom, purportedly supported by the data from the multicenter trials as well as anecdotal clinical experience, has been that response to SRIs is typically delayed, such that an adequate trial of an SRI requires at least 10 weeks. Indeed, a meaningful proportion of responders continue to emerge past the eight-week mark in these studies, as well as in anecdotal clinical experience. Experts also suggest that optimal doses of SRIs for OCD may exceed those typically used for major depression (Montgomery et al., 1993), although the dose-comparison studies of OCD have not always shown significant dose-dependent responses across the OCD study population (Greist, Chouinard, et al., 1995). As for side effects, although meta-analyses (Greist, Jefferson, Kobak, Katzelnick, et al., 1995; Soomro et al., 2008) did not find any significant difference between medication groups regarding drop-out rates due to side effects, this is a relatively insensitive measure of side-effect profile. However, as with other TCAs, the risks and side effects mediated by anticholinergic and antiadrenergic mechanisms (e.g., constipation, cardiac conduction disturbances, orthostatic hypotension) are more commonly associated with clomipramine than with SSRIs. Furthermore, clomipramine is believed to pose a significant risk with regard to lowering seizure threshold. All SRIs can pose risks (e.g., serotonergic syndrome) and produce a variety of side effects (e.g., nausea, sleep disturbances, sexual disturbances) attributable to their primary mechanism of action via serotonergic reuptake blockade. There is no substantive evidence that any SRI is significantly superior or inferior to any other with regard to serotonergically mediated side effects.

Though many clinicians use SRIs as a long-term treatment for OCD, few controlled studies of long-term pharmacotherapy of OCD have been conducted. While most open studies have demonstrated high relapse rates of OCD symptoms within weeks of discontinuation (Pato et al., 1988; Thoren et al., 1980), one open-label study of SRI discontinuation found that only 23% of patients relapsed within one year (Fontaine & Chouinard, 1989). One randomized, double-blind study incorporating substitution of desipramine for clomipramine in a crossover design found that 89% of patients in the substituted group encountered relapse during a two-month period (Leonard et al., 1991). More recently, four placebo-controlled relapse-prevention studies have been conducted. One study assigned fluoxetine responders either to continued treatment with fluoxetine (n = 36) or to placebo (n = 35) and found one-year relapse rates of 17.5% and 38%, respectively (Romano et al., 2001). Another study assigned sertraline responders either to continued treatment with sertraline or to placebo and found relapse rates of 21% versus 59%, respectively (Koran et al., 2002). One study found that paroxetine responders assigned to continued treatment with paroxetine or to placebo exhibited relapse rates of 38% versus 59%, respectively (Hollander, Allen, et al., 2003). Last, one study found that escitalopram responders assigned to continued treatment with escitalopram or to placebo exhibited relapse rates of 23% versus 52%, respectively, at 24 weeks (Fineberg et al., 2007). Some investigators have proposed using lower doses of SRIs for OCD maintenance treatment based on open-label trials (Pato et al., 1990; Ravizza et al., 1996a), and two controlled studies have demonstrated the efficacy of this approach (Mundo, Bareggi, et al., 1997; Tollefson et al., 1994). Thus, the data suggest that discontinuation of SRIs in patients with OCD results in a high relapse rate, although there is still some debate regarding maintenance dosages of SRIs.

Second-Line Pharmacotherapy: SRI Augmentation and Alternative Monotherapies

For patients who do not derive satisfactory reduction of symptoms with SRI therapy, second-line pharmacological treatments include SRI augmentation and alternative monotherapies. It is important to appreciate that only a minority of patients with OCD do not respond favorably to SRIs, and that this relatively treatment-resistant group may be quite heterogeneous, including with respect to underlying pathophysiology. Therefore, specific subsequent treatments may be very effective for some subset of this population, while having only modest mean efficacy for the overall cohort. Consequently, some second-line treatment trials have focused on the number or proportion of patients who meet responder criteria, rather than the mean decrease in symptom severity over the entire study population. Moreover, in some instances, attention has been focused on the clinical characteristics that might distinguish responders from nonresponders.

Augmentation of SRIs

Numerous agents have been tried as augmentors in combination with SRIs for patients who were unresponsive or only partially responsive to SRIs alone. However, few controlled trials of such strategies have been conducted (see Table 17.4). Despite numerous case reports suggesting that lithium might be an effective augmentor in combination with various SRIs, the only two controlled trials of lithium—added to fluvoxamine (McDougle et al., 1991) and clomipramine (Pigott et al., 1991), respectively—speak against the efficacy of these combinations.

Similarly, the encouraging results from case series and uncontrolled trials of buspirone augmentation were followed by only marginal success in controlled trials. In the study by Pigott et al. (1982) of buspirone plus clomipramine, despite a 29% responder rate, there was not significant improvement over the entire cohort with respect to OCD symptoms, and three of 14 patients suffered an exacerbation of more than 25% on measures of depression, for unclear reasons. In Grady and colleagues' (1993) double-blind crossover study of buspirone augmentation of fluoxetine, only one of 14 subjects showed improvement, which may have reflected the brief duration of treatment (only four weeks in each phase). Finally, McDougle, Goodman, Leckman, Holzer, and colleagues (1993)

Table 17.4. SRI Augmentation Therapies for OCD: Controlled Trials

Augmenting agent	SRI	N	Trial	Results	Study
Lithium	Fluvoxamine	30	Two-week or four-week double-blind placebo-controlled	No significant difference between lithium and placebo	McDougle et al. (1991)
Lithium	Clomipramine	9	Double-blind crossover (with T3)	No significant improvement in OCD symptoms	Pigott et al. (1991)
L-Triiodothyronine (T3)	Clomipramine	9	Double-blind crossover (with lithium)	No significant improvement in OCD symptoms	Pigott et al. (1991)
Buspirone	Clomipramine	14	Two weeks of placebo, then 10 weeks of buspirone	Four of 14 (29%) improved, but not statistically significant overall	Pigott et al. (1992)
Buspirone	Fluoxetine	14	Double-blind crossover with placebo; four weeks per treatment condition	No significant difference between buspirone and placebo	Grady et al. (1993)
Haloperidol	Fluvoxamine	34	Double-blind placebo-controlled, with 17 per group; four-week trial; after failing fluvoxamine alone	Eleven of 17 (65%) responded to haloperidol; none of 17 to placebo; eight of eight with tics responded to haloperidol	McDougle et al. (1994)
Clonazepam	Clomipramine or fluoxetine	16	Placebo-controlled, crossover; four-week trial; after 20 weeks stable dose on clomipramine	Significant improvement in OCD on one of three measures for clonazepam vs. placebo	Pigott et al. (1992)
Clonazepam	Sertraline	37	Placebo-controlled, 12-week trial	No significant difference between clonazepam and placebo	Crockett et al. (2004)
Pindolol	Paroxetine	14	Double-blind, placebo-controlled, four-week trial after 17 weeks stable dose on paroxetine	Significant improvement in Y-BOCS vs. placebo	Dannon et al. (2000)
Risperidone	SRI	36	Double-blind, placebo-controlled; six-week trial after 12 weeks on SRI	50% responders; significant reduction in Y-BOCS vs. placebo	McDougle et al. (2000)

(continued)

Table 17.4. Continued

Augmenting agent	SRI	N	Trial	Results	Study
Risperidone	SRI	16	Double-blind, placebo-controlled; eight-week trial after at least 12 weeks on SRI	40% risperidone ($n = 10$) responders vs. no placebo ($n = 6$) responders	Hollander et al. (2003)
Risperidone	SRI	16	Double-blind, placebo-controlled; two-week crossover trial with haloperidol	Both risperidone and haloperidol superior to placebo	Li et al. (2005)
Olanzapine	Fluoxetine	44	Placebo-controlled; six-week trial after eight weeks on fluoxetine	No significant difference between olanzapine and placebo	Shapira et al. (2004)
Olanzapine	SRI	26	Double-blind, placebo-controlled; six-week trial	Significant improvement of Y-BOCS vs. placebo	Bystritsky et al. (2004)
Quetiapine	SRI	40	Double-blind, placebo-controlled; eight-week trial	Quetiapine superior to placebo	Denys et al. (2004)
Quetiapine	SRI	42	Double-blind, placebo-controlled; six-week trial	No significant difference between quetiapine and placebo	Carey et al. (2005)
Quetiapine	SRI	27	Single-blind, placebo-controlled; eight-week trial	Nine of 14 in active group had 60% or greater decrease in Y-BOCS score vs. none in placebo group	Atmaca et al. (2002)
Quetiapine	SRI	76	Double-blind, placebo-controlled; 10-week trial	Quetiapine superior to placebo	Vulink et al. (2009)
Quetiapine	SRI	40	Double-blind, placebo-controlled; 12-week trial	No significant difference between quetiapine and placebo	Kordon et al. (2008)
Aripiprazole	SRI	39	Double-blind, placebo-controlled; 12-week trial	Aripiprazole superior to placebo	Sayyah et al. (2012)
Aripiprazole	SRI	30	Double-blind, placebo-controlled; 16-week trial	Aripiprazole superior to placebo	Muscatello et al. (2011)

Memantine	SRI	40	Double-blind, placebo-controlled; 12-week trial	Memantine superior to placebo	Haghighi et al. (2013)
Memantine	Fluvoxamine	42	Double-blind, placebo-controlled; 12-week trial	Memantine superior to placebo	Ghaleiha et al. (2013)
Memantine	SRI	32	Double-blind, placebo-controlled; 12-week trial	Memantine superior to placebo	Modarresi et al. (2018)
Riluzole	Fluvoxamine	50	Double-blind, placebo-controlled; 10-week trial	Riluzole superior to placebo	Emamzadehfard et al. (2016)
Riluzole	SRI	60	Double-blind, placebo-controlled; 12-week trial; pediatric OCD	No significant difference between riluzole and placebo	Grant et al. (2014)
Riluzole	SRI	38	Double-blind, placebo-controlled; 12-week trial	No significant difference between riluzole and placebo	Pittenger et al. (2015)
N-Acetylcysteine	SRI	40	Double-blind, placebo-controlled; 12-week trial	N-Acetylcysteine superior to placebo	Afshar et al. (2012)
N-Acetylcysteine	Fluvoxamine	44	Double-blind, placebo-controlled; 10-week trial	N-Acetylcysteine superior to placebo	Paydary et al. (2016)
N-Acetylcysteine	Citalopram	34	Double-blind, placebo-controlled; 10-week trial	N-Acetylcysteine superior to placebo	Ghanizadeh et al. (2016)
N-Acetylcysteine	SRI	44	Double-blind, placebo-controlled; 16-week trial	No significant difference between N-acetylcysteine and placebo	Sarris et al. (2015)
N-Acetylcysteine	SRI	40	Double-blind, placebo-controlled; 16-week trial	No significant difference between N-acetylcysteine and placebo	Costa et al. (2017)

found greater improvement with placebo than with buspirone in a double-blind, placebo-controlled study of buspirone augmentation of fluvoxamine for six weeks.

Contrary to a small case series reporting unimpressive results (Jenike, 1998), the use of clonazepam as an augmentor with clomipramine or fluoxetine has been studied in a placebo-controlled fashion, with some studies suggesting significant anti-obsessional efficacy, as well as a nonspecific decrease in anxiety measures (Pigott et al., 1992) and another study finding no significant difference when compared with placebo (Crockett et al., 2004).

The most impressive augmentation data document the benefits of adding low doses of dopamine antagonists (both conventional and atypical neuroleptics) to SRI pharmacotherapy in patients with treatment-refractory OCD (McDougle et al., 1990, 1994, 2000). Some data (McDougle, Goodman, Leckman, Barr, et al., 1993) initially suggested that patients with OCD and comorbid tics may be less responsive to SRI monotherapy than are patients with OCD and without tics. More recent studies have demonstrated the efficacy of SRI augmentation with neuroleptics in patients with OCD with and without comorbid tics (McDougle et al., 2000). Although initial studies demonstrated the efficacy of SRI augmentation with conventional neuroleptics, more recent controlled studies of augmentation with atypical neuroleptics have yielded encouraging results as well. Three controlled trials of risperidone augmentation of an SRI (Hollander, Baldini Rossi, et al., 2003; Li et al., 2005; McDougle et al., 2000) demonstrated efficacy. Of two controlled trials of olanzapine augmentation, one study (Bystritsky et al., 2004) yielded positive results, but the other (Shapira et al., 2004) did not. Three controlled studies (Atmaca et al., 2002; Denys, de Geus, et al., 2004; Vulink et al., 2009) of quetiapine augmentation yielded positive results, while two studies (Carey et al., 2005; Kordon et al., 2008) did not. Finally, two small controlled trials of aripiprazole augmentation (Muscatello et al., 2011; Sayyah et al., 2012) yielded positive results. It is worth mentioning that, although atypical neuroleptics are efficacious as SRI augmentation agents, they are ineffective when used as monotherapy and may even precipitate or worsen OCD symptoms when used as monotherapy (for review, see Lykouras et al., 2003).

More recently, interest in the role of glutamate in the pathophysiology of OCD has spawned research into the use of glutamatergic medications as augmentation agents (Pittenger, 2015). The most studied of these medications is the N-methyl-D-aspartate (NMDA) receptor antagonist memantine. Three randomized controlled trials of memantine augmentation for OCD have demonstrated positive results (Ghaleiha et al., 2013; Haghighi et al., 2013; Modarresi et al., 2018). However, it is worth noting that all of these trials were performed in one geographical location, potentially limiting generalizability, and the effect sizes reported were uncharacteristically large. Therefore, some have questioned the legitimacy of the findings (Andrade, 2019). Riluzole, an inhibitor of presynaptic glutamate release approved for the treatment of amyotrophic lateral sclerosis, is another glutamatergic medication that has been studied. One randomized controlled trial of riluzole augmentation for OCD yielded positive results (Emamzadehfard et al., 2016). However, two other controlled trials found no significant benefit for riluzole over placebo augmentation in both adult (Pittenger et al., 2015) and pediatric (Grant et al., 2014) OCD. The evidence for the over-the-counter supplement *N*-acetylcysteine (NAC) as an augmentation approach is similarly mixed, with three controlled trials yielding positive results (Afshar et al., 2012; Ghanizadeh et al., 2017; Paydary et al., 2016) and two finding no benefit over placebo (Costa et al., 2017; Sarris et al., 2015). Considering the equivocal nature of the existing evidence, the three glutamatergic interventions remain second-tier options for SRI augmentation in those who have either not responded to, or are unable to tolerate, neuroleptic augmentation. Other glutamatergic medications, such as topiramate and lamotrigine, have also been studied as augmentation treatments, but there are few data to support their use at this time.

Finally, two small studies have examined the use of the NMDA antagonist ketamine to treat OCD symptoms, with mixed results. An initial open-label trial of intravenous ketamine in medicated patients with severe, treatment-resistant OCD showed no significant benefit (Bloch et al., 2012). In contrast, a subsequent double-blind, crossover study of unmedicated OCD patients found a significant and rapid reduction in OCD symptoms that persisted for one week after a single administration of intravenous ketamine compared to saline (Rodriguez et al., 2013). Further work is ongoing to gather more definitive data from larger randomized controlled trials using an active placebo (e.g., midazolam) to determine whether ketamine may have future utility as a rapidly acting OCD treatment and, if so, in which patient populations.

Numerous other agents have been tried in combination with SRIs, including ondansetron, gabapentin, clonidine, tryptophan, fenfluramine, pindolol, trazodone, thyroid hormone, and nortriptyline, as well as other antidepressants (for reviews, see Dougherty et al., 2004; Jenike, 1998; McDougle & Goodman, 1997). The small number of subjects, lack of sufficient controls, and mixed results preclude drawing conclusions regarding the potential efficacy of such strategies. If an augmenting agent is indicated for treatment of some comorbid condition (e.g., lithium for bipolar disorder, trazodone for insomnia, or clonidine for Tourette syndrome), and no strong contraindication is present, then a trial of the agent in combination with an SRI is easily rationalized. Anecdotally, these strategies have appeared to be of tremendous benefit in some isolated cases. No studies have sought to establish the optimal dosage or duration of treatment for any of these augmentation strategies. Therefore, current guidelines reflect the parameters used in the reported successful trials, as well as anecdotal experience with OCD and other psychiatric disorders.

Alternative Monotherapies

For patients who fail to derive satisfactory response from trials of SRIs alone, as well as augmentation strategies, the next recommended step is to consider alternative monotherapies in place of SRIs. In addition to uncontrolled data, positive controlled studies

Table 17.5. Alternative Medications as Monotherapies for OCD: Controlled Trials

Treatment Conditions	N	Comments	Study
Clorgyline vs. clomipramine	13	Clorgyline ineffective; clomipramine effective	Insel et al. (1983)
Clorgyline vs. clomipramine	12	Clorgyline inferior to clomipramine	Zahn et al. (1984)
Phenelzine vs. clomipramine	30	Both effective and comparable	Vallejo et al. (1992)
Clonazepam vs. clomipramine vs. clonidine vs. active placebo crossover	25	35% avg. decrease with clonazepam; clonazepam comparable to clomipramine and superior to active placebo	Hewlett et al. (1992)
Clonazepam vs. placebo	27	No significant difference	Hollander et al. (2003)
Buspirone vs. clomipramine crossover	20	Both effective and comparable, > 20% improvement in > 55% in both groups	Pato et al. (1991)
Fluoxetine vs. phenelzine vs. placebo	64	Fluoxetine group improved significantly more than phenelzine or placebo groups	Jenike et al. (1997)
Trazodone vs. placebo	21	No significant difference	Pigott et al. (1992)

lend some support for trials of clonazepam, monoamine oxidase inhibitors (MAOIs), and buspirone (see Table 17.5).

In the case of clonazepam, one placebo-controlled study (Hewlett et al., 1992) supported its efficacy in OCD, while another placebo-controlled study failed to demonstrate efficacy in OCD (Hollander et al., , 2003). If clonazepam is used as a monotherapy for OCD, recommendations regarding dosage (i.e., 0.5 to 5 mg/day) and duration (i.e., 4 weeks or longer) have no controlled empirical basis and are simply extrapolated from clinical experience with benzodiazepines for other anxiety disorders and the few reports of its use for OCD.

Non-placebo-controlled studies involving the MAOI clorgyline speak against its efficacy in OCD, showing no significant decrease in OCD severity (Insel et al., 1983) and inferior efficacy in comparison to SRIs (Insel et al., 1983; Zahn et al., 1984). While one non-placebo-controlled study of phenelzine versus clomipramine suggested significant clinical improvement in both groups, and no significant difference in efficacy between the two agents (Vallejo et al., 1992), a subsequent placebo-controlled trial of phenelzine and fluoxetine demonstrated that patients treated with fluoxetine improved significantly more than did those in the placebo or phenelzine groups (Jenike et al., 1997). This study did note that a subgroup of patients with symmetry obsessions did respond to phenelzine, however. Therefore, the efficacy of phenelzine as a monotherapy for OCD should be regarded as provisional. Specific recommendations regarding dosage (i.e., phenelzine 60 to 90 mg/day) have little empirical basis, reflecting extrapolation from clinical practice with MAOIs for major depression and panic disorder; duration of trials (i.e., 10 weeks or longer) mirrors that of SRIs for OCD. In addition to the usual low-tyramine diet and other precautions typically indicated in the context of an MAOI trial, it is critical to be cautious regarding the transition from serotonergic medications to an MAOI due to the risks of dangerous interactions, including serotonergic crisis. Current guidelines are based primarily on the half-life of the agents involved, rather than direct empirical data related to adverse events per se. Conservative recommendations are washout periods of at least two weeks when transitioning from clomipramine or a short-half-life SSRI to an MAOI, at least five weeks when transitioning from fluoxetine to an MAOI, and at least two weeks when transitioning from phenelzine to an SRI.

Although one open trial of buspirone did not yield significant anti-obsessional benefit (Jenike & Baer, 1988), a controlled trial of buspirone versus clomipramine suggested that they were comparably effective (Pato et al., 1991). The relatively short duration of the trial, the modest power for detecting a difference between treatments, and the absence of a placebo group mitigate against drawing firm conclusions from Pato and colleagues' study. Still, given the excellent tolerability of buspirone, other circumstantial evidence of possible efficacy as an augmenting agent, and its general efficacy as an anxiolytic, the clinical use of buspirone as an alternative monotherapy for cases of treatment-resistant OCD seems justified pending further information. Specific recommendations regarding dosage (i.e., up to 60 mg/day) and duration of trials (i.e., 6 weeks or longer) have little empirical basis, simply reflecting the protocol adopted in the study by Pato and colleagues.

Because the serotonin-norepinephrine reuptake inhibitors (SNRIs), venlafaxine and duloxetine, have serotonin reuptake inhibition properties, one would expect that the SNRIs might be efficacious in the treatment of OCD. Indeed, small open-label studies have found a significant reduction in OCD symptoms after treatment with both venlafaxine (Hollander, Friedberg, et al., 2003) and duloxetine (Dougherty et al., 2015). Additionally, a randomized, double-blind comparison study found venlafaxine to be equally as effective as paroxetine in treating patients with OCD (Denys et al., 2003). However, no placebo-controlled trials of SNRIs for the treatment of OCD have been reported. A review of the literature (Dell'Osso et al., 2006) found that the data that was available suggested that SNRIs seem to be as effective as SSRIs in treating OCD. Nonetheless, additional data from controlled trials are needed.

Agents targeting opioid receptors have shown promise as well, including controlled trials suggesting that both oral morphine (Koran et al., 2005) and buprenorphine (Ahmadpanah et al., 2017) may be effective augmentation treatments for refractory OCD. However, more research in this area is required before this approach can be confidently recommended. Last, controlled trials have failed to demonstrate the efficacy of trazodone (Pigott et al., 1992), clonidine (Hewlett et al., 1992), and diphenhydramine (Hewlett et al., 1992) as monotherapies for OCD.

Summary

In conclusion, the past 40 years have seen tremendous advances in the treatment and understanding of OCD, with a recent acceleration of progress. It is now appreciated that OCD is a common disorder, and effective treatments, including medication and behavior therapy, have emerged. There is overwhelming evidence of the most rigorous type supporting the efficacy of SRIs in the treatment of OCD. Along with SRIs, behavior therapy must be considered a viable first-line therapy. The best available data suggest that behavior therapy is at least as effective as medication in some instances, and it may be superior with respect to risks, costs, and enduring benefits. A variety of second-line medication treatments for OCD have been studied in a controlled or systematic fashion. Augmentation of SRIs with neuroleptics, glutamate modulators, clonazepam, or buspirone are all recommended based on the available data. Other augmentation strategies find very limited support at present. Alternative monotherapies, including buspirone, clonazepam, and phenelzine, have all been the subject of positive controlled or partially controlled studies. However, the limited quality of the data makes recommendations for these strategies tentative as well, pending additional information. Beyond second-line treatments, the current database is inadequate for making difficult treatment decisions. Ideally, the future of OCD treatment will entail rigorous research to more clearly establish the efficacy and safety of preexisting treatment options, as well as a refined sense of which patients might respond preferentially to which interventions, at what dose, and after how long. Furthermore, the future promises novel treatment strategies that may include modified cognitive-behavior therapies and new compounds acting via serotonergic, dopaminergic, glutamatergic, or opioid systems.

Acknowledgment

This chapter is adapted from Dougherty, D. D., Rauch, S. L., & Jenike, M. A. (2007). Treatment of obsessive-compulsive disorder. In P. E. Nathan & J. M. Gorman (Eds.), *A guide to treatments that work* (3rd ed., pp. 447–473). Oxford University Press.

References

Afshar, H., Roohafza, H., Mohammad-Beigi, H., Haghighi, M., Jahangard, L., Shokouh, P., Sadeghi, M., & Hafezian, H. (2012). *N*-Acetylcysteine add-on treatment in refractory obsessive-compulsive disorder: A randomized, double-blind, placebo-controlled trial. *Journal of Clinical Psychopharmacology, 32*, 797–803.

Ahmadpanah, M., Reihani, A., Ghaleiha, A., Soltanian, A., Haghighi, M., Jahangard, L., Bahmani, D. S., Holsboer-Trachsler, E., & Brand, S. (2017). Buprenorphine augmentation improved symptoms of OCD, compared to placebo—Results from a randomized, double-blind and placebo-controlled clinical trial. *Journal of Psychiatric Research, 94*, 23–28.

Albert, U., Aguglia, E., Maina, G., & Bogetto, F. (2002). Venlafaxine versus clomipramine in the treatment of obsessive-compulsive disorder: A preliminary single-blind, 12-week, controlled study. *Journal of Clinical Psychiatry, 63*, 1004–1009.

Ananth, J., Pecknold, J. C., van den Steen, N., & Engelsmann, F. (1981). Double-blind comparative study of clomipramine and amitriptyline in obsessive neurosis. *Progress in Neuropsychopharmacology, 5*, 257–262.

Andrade, C. (2019). Augmentation with memantine in obsessive-compulsive disorder. *The Journal of Clinical Psychiatry, 80*, 19f13163.

Atmaca, M., Kuloglu, M., Tezcan, E., & Gecici, O. (2002). Quetiapine augmentation in patients with treatment resistant obsessive-compulsive disorder: A single-blind, placebo-controlled study. *International Clinical Psychopharmacology, 17*, 115–119.

Baer, L. (1991). *Getting control*. Little, Brown.

Baer, L. (2002). *The imp of the mind: Exploring the silent epidemic of obsessive bad thoughts*. Penguin.

Bergeron, R., Ravindran, A. V., Chaput, Y. Goldner, E., Swinson, R., van Ameringen, M. A., Austin, C., & Hadrava, V. (2002). Sertraline and fluoxetine treatment of obsessive-compulsive disorder: Results of a double-blind, 6-month treatment study. *Journal of Clinical Psychopharmacology, 22*, 148–154.

Bisserbe, J. C., Wiseman, R. L., Goldberg, M. S., & The Franco-Belgian OCD Study Group. (1995). *A double-blind comparison of sertraline and clomipramine in outpatients with obsessive-compulsive disorder* [Research abstract 173]. American Psychiatric Association Annual Meeting.

Bloch, M. H., Wasylink, S., Landeros-Weisenberger, A., Panza, K. E., Billingslea, E., Leckman, J. F., Krystal, J. H., Bhagwagar, Z., Sanacora, G., & Pittenger, C. (2012). Effects of ketamine in treatment-refractory obsessive-compulsive disorder. *Biological Psychiatry, 72*, 964–970.

Bystritsky, A., Ackerman, S. L., Rosen, R. M., Vapnik, T., Borbis, E., Maidment, K. M., & Saxena, S. (2004). Augmentation of serotonin reuptake inhibitors in refractory obsessive-compulsive disorder using adjunctive olanzapine: A placebo-controlled trial. *Journal of Clinical Psychiatry, 65*, 565–568.

Carey, P. D., Vythilingum, B., Seedat, S., Muller, J. E., van Ameringen, M., & Stein, D. J. (2005). Quetiapine augmentation of SRIs in treatment refractory obsessive-compulsive disorder: A double-blind, randomised, placebo-controlled study. *BioMed Central Psychiatry, 5*(1), 5–13.

Chouinard, G., Goodman, W., Greist, J., Jenike, M., Rasmussen, S., White, K., Hackett, E., Gaffney, M., & Bick, P. A. (1990). Results of a double-blind placebo controlled trial using a new serotonin uptake inhibitor, sertraline, in obsessive-compulsive disorder. *Psychopharmacology Bulletin, 26*, 279–284.

Clomipramine Collaborative Group. (1991). Clomipramine in the treatment of patients with obsessive-compulsive disorder. *Archives of General Psychiatry, 48*, 730–738.

Costa, D. L. C., Diniz, J. B., Requena, G., Joaquim, M. A., Pittenger, C., Bloch, M. H., Miguel, E. C., & Shavitt, R. G. (2017). Randomized, double-blind, placebo-controlled trial of *N*-acetylcysteine for treatment-resistant obsessive-compulsive disorder. *The Journal of Clinical Psychiatry, 78*, e766–e773.

Crockett, B. A., Churchill, E., & Davidson, J. R. (2004). A double-blind combination study of clonazepam with sertraline in obsessive-compulsive disorder. *Annals of Clinical Psychiatry, 16*, 127–132.

Cui, Y. E. (1986). A double-blind trial of chlorimipramine and doxepin in obsessive-compulsive disorder. *Chung Hua Shen Ching Shen Ko Tsa Chih, 19*, 279–281.

Dannon, P. N., Sasson, Y., Hirschmann, S., Iancu, I., Grunhaus, L. J., & Zohar, J. (2000). Pindolol augmentation in treatment-resistant obsessive compulsive disorder: A double-blind placebo controlled trial. *European Neuropsychopharmacology, 10*, 165–169.

Dell'Osso, B., Nestadt, G., Allen, A., & Hollander, E. (2006). Serotonin-norepinephrine reuptake inhibitors in the treatment of obsessive-compulsive disorder: A critical review. *The Journal of Clinical Psychiatry, 67*, 600–610.

Den Boer, J. A., Westenberg, H. G. M., Kamerbeek, W. D. J., Verhoeven, W. M., & Kahn, R. S. (1987). Effect of serotonin uptake inhibitors in anxiety disorders: A double-blind comparison of clomipramine and fluvoxamine. *International Clinical Psychopharmacology, 2*, 21–32.

Denys, D., de Geus, F., van Megen, H. J., & Westenberg, H. G. (2004). A double-blind, placebo-controlled trial of quetiapine addition in patients with obsessive-compulsive disorder refractory to serotonin reuptake inhibitors. *The Journal of Clinical Psychiatry, 65*, 1040–1048.

Denys, D., van der Wee, N., van Megen, H. J., & Westenberg, H. G. (2003). A double-blind comparison of venlafaxine and paroxetine in obsessive-compulsive disorder. *Journal of Clinical Psychopharmacology, 23*, 568–575.

Dougherty, D. D., Corse, A. K., Chou, T., Duffy, A., Arulpragassam, A. R., Deckersbach, T., Jenike, M. A., & Keuthen, N. J. (2015). Open-label study of duloxetine for the treatment of obsessive-compulsive disorder. *International Journal of Neuropsychopharmacology, 18*, 1–4.

Dougherty, D. D., & Rauch, S. L. (1997). Serotonin-reuptake inhibitors in the treatment of OCD. In E. Hollander & D. J. Stein (Eds.), *Obsessive-compulsive disorders: Diagnosis, etiology, treatment* (pp. 145–160). Marcel Dekker.

Dougherty, D. D., Rauch, S. L., & Jenike, M. A. (2004). Pharmacotherapy for obsessive-compulsive disorder. *Journal of Clinical Psychology, 60*, 1195–1202.

Emamzadehfard, S., Kamaloo, A., Paydary, K., Ahmadipour, A., Zeinoddini, A., Ghaleiha, A., Mohammedinejad, P., Zeinoddini, A., & Akhondzadeh, S. (2016). Riluzole in augmentation of fluvoxamine for moderate to severe obsessive-compulsive disorder: Randomized, double-blind, placebo-controlled study. *Psychiatry and Clinical Neurosciences, 70*, 332–341.

Fernandez, C. E., & Lopez-Ibor, A. J. (1967). Monochlorimipramine in the treatment of psychiatric patients resistant to other therapies. *Actas Luso Espanolas de Neurologia, Psiquiatria y Ciencias Afines, 26*, 119–147.

Fineberg, N. A., Tonnoir, B., Lemming, O., & Stein, D. J. (2007). Escitalopram prevents relapse of obsessive-compulsive disorder. *European Neuropsychopharmacology, 17*, 430–439.

Foa, E. B., Liebowitz, M. R., Kozak, M. J., Davies, S., Campeas, R., Franklin, M. E., Huppert, J. D., Kjernisted, K., Rowan, V., Schmidt, A. B., Simpson, H. B., & Tu, X. (2005). Randomized, placebo-controlled trial of exposure and ritual prevention, clomipramine, and their combination in the treatment of obsessive-compulsive disorder. *The American Journal of Psychiatry, 162*, 151–161.

Fontaine, R., & Chouinard, G. (1989). Fluoxetine in the long-term maintenance treatment of obsessive-compulsive disorder. *Psychiatric Annals, 19*, 88–91.

Freeman, C. P. L., Trimble, M. R., Deakin, J. F. W., Stokes, T. M., & Ashford, J. J. (1994). Fluvoxamine versus clomipramine in the treatment of obsessive compulsive disorder: A multicenter, randomized, double-blind, parallel group comparison. *The Journal of Clinical Psychiatry, 55*, 301–305.

Ghaleiha, A., Entezari, N., Modabbernia, A., Najand, B., Askari, N., Tabrizi, M., Ashrafi, M., Hajiaghaee, R., & Akhondzadeh, S. (2013). Memantine add-on in moderate to severe obsessive-compulsive disorder: Randomized double-blind placebo-controlled study. *Journal of Psychiatric Research, 47*, 175–180.

Ghanizadeh, A., Mohammadi, M. R., Bahrani, S., Keshavarzi, Z., Firoozabadi, A., & Shostari, A. A. (2017). Efficacy of *N*-acetylcysteine augmentation on obsessive compulsive disorder: A multicenter randomized double-blind placebo controlled trial. *Iranian Journal of Psychiatry, 12*, 134–141.

Goodman, W. K., Kozak, M. J., Liebowitz, M., & White, K. L. (1996). Treatment of obsessive-compulsive disorder with fluvoxamine: A multicentre, double-blind, placebo-controlled trial. *International Clinical Psychopharmacology, 11*, 21–29.

Goodman, W. K., Price, L. H., Delgado, P. L., Palumbo, J., Krystal, J. H., Nagy, L. M., Rasmussen, S. A., Heninger, G. R., & Charney, D. S. (1990). Specificity of serotonin reuptake inhibitors in the treatment of obsessive compulsive disorder. *Archives of General Psychiatry, 47*, 577–585.

Goodman, W. K., Price, L. H., Rasmussen, S. A., Delgado, P. L., Heninger, G. R., & Charney, D. S. (1989). Efficacy of fluvoxamine in obsessive-compulsive disorder: A double-blind comparison with placebo. *Archives of General Psychiatry, 46*, 36–44.

Grady, T. A., Pigott, T. A., L'Heureux, F., Hill, J. L., Bernstein, S. E., & Murphy, D. L. (1993). A double-blind study of adjuvant buspirone hydrochloride in fluoxetine treated patients with obsessive compulsive disorder. *American Journal of Psychiatry, 150*, 819–821.

Grant, P. J., Joseph, L. A., Farmer, C. A., Luckenbaugh, D. A., Lougee, L. C., Zarate, C. A., Jr., & Swedo, S. E. (2014). 12-week, placebo-controlled trial of add-on riluzole in the treatment of childhood-onset obsessive-compulsive disorder. *Neuropsychopharmacology, 39*, 1453–1459.

Greist, J. H., Chouinard, G., DuBoff, E., Halaris, A., Kim, S. W., Koran, L., Liebowitz, M., Lydiard, R. B., Rasmussen, S., & White, K. (1995). Double-blind comparison of three doses of sertraline and placebo in the treatment of outpatients with obsessive compulsive disorder. *Archives of General Psychiatry, 52*, 289–295.

Greist, J. H., Jefferson, J. W., Kobak, K. A., Chouinard, G., Duboff, E., Halaris, A., Kim, S. W., Koran, L., Liebowitz, M. R., & Lydiard, B. (1995). A 1-year double-blind placebo-controlled fixed dose study of sertraline in the treatment of obsessive-compulsive disorder. *International Clinical Psychopharmacology, 10*, 57–65.

Greist, J. H., Jefferson, J. W., Kobak, K. A., Katzelnick, D. J., & Serlin, R. C. (1995). Efficacy and tolerability of serotonin transport inhibitors in obsessive-compulsive disorder: A meta-analysis. *Archives of General Psychiatry, 52*, 53–60.

Greist, J. H., Jefferson, J. W., Rosenfeld, R., Gutzmann, L. D., March, J. S., & Barklage, N. E. (1990). Clomipramine and obsessive-compulsive disorder: A placebo-controlled double-blind study of 32 patients. *The Journal of Clinical Psychiatry, 51*, 292–297.

Haghighi, M., Jahangard, L., Mohammad-Beigi, H., Bajoghli, H., Hafezian, H., Rahimi, A., Afshar, H., Holsboer-Trachsler, E., & Brand, E. (2013). In a double-blind, randomized and placebo-controlled trial, adjuvant memantine improved symptoms in inpatients suffering from refractory obsessive-compulsive disorders (OCD). *Psychopharmacology, 228*, 633–640.

Hewlett, W., Vinogradov, S., & Agras, W. (1992). Clomipramine, clonazepam, and clonidine treatment of obsessive compulsive disorder. *Journal of Clinical Psychopharmacology, 12*, 420–430.

Heyman, I., Mataix-Cols, D., & Fineberg, N. A. (2006). Obsessive-compulsive disorder. *British Medical Journal, 333*, 424–429.

Hoehn-Saric, R., Ninan, P., Black, D. W., Stahl, S., Greist, J. H., Lydiard, B., McElroy, S., Zajecka, J., Chapman, D., Clary, C., & Harrison, W. (2000). Multicenter double-blind comparison of sertraline and desipramine for concurrent obsessive-compulsive disorder and major depressive disorders. *Archives of General Psychiatry, 57*, 76–82.

Hollander, E., Allen, A., Steiner, M., Wheadon, D. E., Oakes, R., Burnham, D. B.; Paroxetine OCD Study Group. (2003). Acute and long-term treatment and prevention of relapse of obsessive-compulsive disorder with paroxetine. *Journal of Clinical Psychiatry, 64*, 1113–1121.

Hollander, E., Baldini Rossi, N., Sood, E., & Pallanti, S. (2003). Risperidone augmentation in treatment-resistant obsessive-compulsive disorder: A double-blind, placebo-controlled study. *International Journal of Neuropsychopharmacology, 6*, 397–401.

Hollander, E., Friedberg, J., Wasserman, S., Allan, A., Birnbaum, M., & Koran, L. M. (2003). Venlafaxine in treatment-resistant obsessive-compulsive disorder. *The Journal of Clinical Psychiatry, 64*, 546–550.

Hollander, E., Kaplan, A., & Stahl, S. M. (2003). A double-blind, placebo-controlled trial of clonazepam in obsessive-compulsive disorder. *The World Journal of Biological Psychiatry, 4*, 30–34.

Insel, T. R., Murphy, D. L., Cohen, R. M., Alterman, I., Kilts, C., & Linnoila, M. (1983). Obsessive-compulsive disorder: A double-blind trial of clomipramine and clorgyline. *Archives of General Psychiatry, 40*, 605–612.

Jenike, M. A. (1989). Obsessive compulsive and related disorders: A hidden epidemic. *The New England Journal of Medicine, 321*, 539–541.

Jenike, M. A. (1998). Drug treatment of obsessive-compulsive disorders. In M. A. Jenike, L. Baer, & W. E. Minichiello (Eds.), *Obsessive-compulsive disorders: Practical management* (3rd ed., pp. 469–532). Mosby–Year Book.

Jenike, M. A. (2004). Clinical practice. Obsessive-compulsive disorder. *The New England Journal of Medicine, 350*(3), 259–265.

Jenike, M. A., & Baer, L. (1988). Buspirone in obsessive-compulsive disorder: An open trial. *The American Journal of Psychiatry, 145*, 1285–1286.

Jenike, M. A., Baer, L., Minichiello, W. E., Rauch, S. L., & Buttolph, M. L. (1997). Placebo-controlled trial of fluoxetine and phenelzine for obsessive-compulsive disorder. *The American Journal of Psychiatry, 154*, 1261–1264.

Jenike, M. A., Baer, L., Summergrad, P., Weilburg, J. B., Holland, A., & Seymour, R. (1989). Obsessive-compulsive disorder: A double-blind, placebo-controlled trial of clomipramine in 27 patients. *The American Journal of Psychiatry, 146*, 1328–1330.

Jenike, M. A., Baer, L., Summergrad, P., Minichiello, W. E., Holland, A., & Seymour, R. (1990a). Sertraline in obsessive-compulsive disorder: A double-blind comparison with placebo. *The American Journal of Psychiatry, 147*, 923–928.

Jenike, M. A., Hyman, S. E., Baer, L., Holland, A., Minichiello, W. E., Buttolph, L., Summergrad, P., Seymour, R., & Riiciardi, J. (1990b). A controlled trial of fluvoxamine for obsessive-compulsive disorder: Implications for a serotonergic theory. *The American Journal of Psychiatry, 147*, 1209–1215.

Karabanow, O. (1977). Double-blind controlled study in phobias and obsessions. *Journal of International Medical Research, 5*(Suppl. 5), 42–48.

Koponen, H., Lepola, U., Leinonen, E., Jokinen, R., Penttinen, J., & Turtonen, J. (1997). Citalopram in the treatment of obsessive-compulsive disorder: An open pilot study. *Acta Psychiatrica Scandinavica, 96*, 343–346.

Koran, L. M., Aboujaoude, E., Bullock, K. D., Franz, B., Gamel, N., & Elliott, M. (2005). Double-blind treatment with oral morphine in treatment-resistant obsessive-compulsive disorder. *The Journal of Clinical Psychiatry, 66*, 353–359.

Koran, L. M., Hackett, E., Rubin, A., Wolkow, R., & Robinson, D. (2002). Efficacy of sertraline in the long-term treatment of obsessive-compulsive disorder. *The American Journal of Psychiatry, 159*, 88–95.

Koran, L. M., McElroy, S. L., Davidson, J. R. T., Rasmussen, S. A., Hollander, E., & Jenike, M. A. (1996). Fluvoxamine versus clomipramine for obsessive-compulsive disorder: A double-blind comparison. *Journal of Clinical Psychopharmacology, 16*, 121–129.

Kordon, A., Wahl, K., Zurowski, B., Anlauf, M., Vielhaber, K., Kahl, K. G., Broocks, A., Voderholzer, U., & Hohagen, F. (2008). Quetiapine addition to serotonin reuptake inhibitors in patients with severe obsessive-compulsive disorder: A double-blind, randomized, placebo-controlled study. *Journal of Clinical Psychopharmacology, 28*, 550–554.

Kronig, M. H., Apter, J., Asnis, G., Bystritsky, A., Curtis, G., Ferguson, J., et al. (1999). Placebo-controlled, multicenter study of sertraline treatment for obsessive-compulsive disorder. *Journal of Clinical Psychopharmacology, 19*, 172–176.

Lei, B. S. (1986). A cross-over treatment of obsessive compulsive neurosis with imipramine and chlorimipramine. *Chung Hua Shen Ching Shen Ko Tsa Chih, 19*, 275–278.

Leonard, H. L., Swedo, S. E., Lenane, M. C., Rettew, D. C., Cheslow, D. L., Hamburger, S. D., & Rapoport, J. L. (1991). A double-blind desipramine substitution during long-term clomipramine treatment in children and adolescents with obsessive compulsive disorder. *Archives of General Psychiatry, 48*, 922–927.

Li, X., May, R. S., Tolbert, L. C., Jackson, W. T., Flournoy, J. M., & Baxter, L. R. (2005). Risperidone and haloperidol augmentation of serotonin reuptake inhibitors in refractory obsessive-compulsive disorder: A crossover study. *The Journal of Clinical Psychiatry, 66*, 736–743.

Lopez-Ibor, J. J., Jr., Saiz, J., Cottraux, J., Vinas, R., Bourgeois, M., Hernandez, M., & Gomez-Perez, J. C (1996). Double-blind comparison of fluoxetine versus clomipramine in the treatment of obsessive compulsive disorder. *European Neuropsychopharmacology, 6*, 111–118.

Lykouras, L., Alevizos, B., Michalopoulo, P., & Rabavilas, A. (2003). Obsessive-compulsive symptoms induced by atypical antipsychotics: A review of reported cases. *Progress in Neuropsychopharmacology and Biological Psychiatry, 27*, 333–346.

Marazziti, D., Dell'Osso, L., Gemignani, A., Ciapparelli, A., Presta, S., Nasso, E. D., Pfanner, C., & Cassano, G. B. (2001). Citalopram in refractory obsessive-compulsive disorder: An open study. *International Clinical Psychopharmacology, 16*, 215–219.

Mavissakalian, M., Turner, S. M., Michelson, L., & Jacob, R. (1985). Tricyclic antidepressants in obsessive-compulsive disorder: Antiobsessional or antidepressant agents? *The American Journal of Psychiatry, 142*, 572–576.

McDougle, C. J., & Goodman, W. K. (1997). Combination pharmacological treatment strategies. In E. Hollander & D. J. Stein (Eds.), *Obsessive-compulsive disorders: Diagnosis, etiology, treatment* (pp. 203–224). Marcel Dekker.

McDougle, C. J., Goodman, W. K., Leckman, J. F., Barr, L. C., Heninger, G. R., & Price, L. H. 1993. The efficacy of fluvoxamine in obsessive-compulsive disorder: Effects of comorbid chronic tic disorder. *Journal of Clinical Psychopharmacology, 13*, 354–358.

McDougle, C. J., Goodman, W. K., Leckman, J. F., Holzer, J. C., Barr, L. C., McCance-Katz, E., Henninger, G. R., & Price, L. H. (1993). Limited therapeutic effect of addition of buspirone in fluvoxamine-refractory obsessive-compulsive disorder. *The American Journal of Psychiatry, 150*, 647–649.

McDougle, C. J., Epperson, C. N., Pelton, G. H., Wasylink, S., & Price, L. H. (2000). A double-blind, placebo-controlled study of risperidone addition in serotonin reuptake inhibitor-refractory obsessive-compulsive disorder. *Archives of General Psychiatry, 57*, 794–801.

McDougle, C. J., Goodman, W. K., Leckman, J. F., Lee, N. C., Heninger, G. R., & Price, L. H. (1994). Haloperidol addition in fluvoxamine-refractory obsessive-compulsive disorder: A double-blind, placebo-controlled study in patients with and without tics. *Archives of General Psychiatry, 51*, 302–308.

McDougle, C. J., Goodman, W. K., Price, L. H., Delgado, P. L., Krystal, J. H., Charney, D. S., & Henninger, G. R. (1990). Neuroleptic addition in fluvoxamine refractory obsessive compulsive disorder. *The American Journal of Psychiatry, 147*, 652–654.

McDougle, C. J., Price, L. H., Goodman, W. K., Charney, D. S., & Heninger, G. R. (1991). A controlled trial of lithium augmentation in fluvoxamine-refractory obsessive compulsive disorder: Lack of efficacy. *Journal of Clinical Psychopharmacology, 11*, 175–184.

Milanfranchi, A., Ravagli, S., Lensi, P., Marazziti, D., & Cassano, G. B. (1997). A double-blind study of fluvoxamine and clomipramine in the treatment of obsessive-compulsive disorder. *International Clinical Psychopharmacology, 12*, 131–136.

Modarresi, A., Sayyah, M., Razooghi, S., Eslami, K., Javadi, M., & Kouti, L. (2018). Memantine augmentation improves symptoms in serotonin reuptake inhibitor-refractory obsessive-compulsive disorder: A randomized controlled trial. *Pharmacopsychiatry, 51*, 263–269.

Montgomery, S. A. (1980). Clomipramine in obsessional neurosis: A placebo-controlled trial. *Pharmaceutical Medicine, 1*, 189–192.

Montgomery, S. A., Kasper, S., Stein, D. J., Bang Hedegaard, K., & Lemming, O. M. (2001). Citalopram 20 mg, 40 mg and 60 mg are all effective and well tolerated compared with placebo in obsessive compulsive disorder. *International Clinical Psychopharmacology, 16*, 75–86.

Montgomery, S. A., McIntyre, A., Osterheider, M., Sarteschi, P., Zitterl, W., Zohar, J., Birkett, M., Wood, A. J. (1993). A double-blind placebo-controlled study of fluoxetine in patients with *DSM-IIIR* obsessive-compulsive disorder. *European Neuropsychopharmacology, 3*, 143–152.

Mundo, E., Bareggi, S. R., Pirola, R., Bellodi, L., & Smeraldi, E. (1997). Long-term pharmacotherapy of obsessive-compulsive disorder: A double-blind controlled study. *Journal of Clinical Psychopharmacology, 17*, 4–10.

Mundo, E., Maina, G., & Uslenghi, C. (2000). Multicentre, double-blind, comparison of fluvoxamine and clomipramine in the treatment of obsessive-compulsive disorder. *International Clinical Psychopharmacology, 15*, 69–76.

Mundo, E., Rouillon, F., Figuera, M. L., & Stigler, M. (2001). Fluvoxamine in obsessive-compulsive disorder: Similar efficacy but superior tolerability in comparison with clomipramine. *Human Psychopharmacology, 16*, 461–468.

Muscatello, A. R. A., Bruno, A., Pandolfo, G., Mico, U., Scimeca, G., Romeo, V. M., Santoro, V., Settineri, S., Spina, E., & Zoccali, R. A. (2011). Effect of aripiprazole augmentation of serotonin reuptake inhibitors or clomipramine in treatment-resistant obsessive-compulsive disorder: A double-blind, placebo-controlled study. *Journal of Clinical Psychopharmacology, 31*, 174–179.

Nakatani, E., Nakagawa, A., Nakao, T., Yoshizato, C., Nabeyama, M., Kudo, A., Issomura, K., Kato, N., Yoshioka, K., & Kawamoto, M. (2005). A randomized controlled trial of Japanese patients with obsessive-compulsive disorder: Effectiveness of behavioral therapy and fluvoxamine. *Psychotherapy and Psychosomatics, 74*, 269–276.

Pato, M. T., Hill, J. L., & Murphy, D. L. (1990). A clomipramine dosage reduction study in the course of long-term treatment of obsessive-compulsive patients. *Psychopharmacology Bulletin, 26*, 211–214.

Pato, M. T., Pigott, T. A., Hill, J. L., Grover, G. N., Bernstein, S., & Murphy, D. L. (1991). Controlled comparison of buspirone and clomipramine in obsessive-compulsive disorder. *The American Journal of Psychiatry, 148*, 127–129.

Pato, M. T., Zohar-Kaduch, R., Zohar, J., & Muphy, D. L. (1988). Return of symptoms after discontinuation of clomipramine in patients with obsessive compulsive disorder. *The American Journal of Psychiatry, 145*, 1521–1525.

Paydary, K., Akamaloo, A., Ahmadipour, A., Pishgar, F., Emamzadehfard, S., & Akhondzadeh, S. (2016). N-Acetylcysteine augmentation therapy for moderate-to-severe obsessive-compulsive disorder: Randomized, double-blind, placebo-controlled trial. *Journal of Clinical Pharmacy and Therapeutics, 41*, 214–219.

Perse, T. L., Greist, J. H., Jefferson, J. W., Rosenfeld, R., & Dar, R. (1987). Fluvoxamine treatment of obsessive-compulsive disorder. *The American Journal of Psychiatry, 144*, 1543–1548.

Pigott, T. A., L'Heureux, F., Hill, J. L., Bihari, K., Bernstien, S. E., & Murphy, D. L. (1982). A double-blind study of adjuvant buspirone hydrochloride in clomipramine-treated patients. *Journal of Clinical Psychopharmacology, 12*, 11–18.

Pigott, T. A., L'Heureux, F., Rubenstein, C. S., Bernstein, S. E., Hill, J. L., & Murphy, D. L. (1992). A double-blind, placebo controlled study of trazodone in patients with obsessive-compulsive disorder. *Journal of Clinical Psychopharmacology, 12*, 156–162.

Pigott, T. A., L'Heureux, F., Rubenstein, C. S., Hill, J. L., & Murphy, D. L. (1992, May). *A controlled trial of clonazepam augmentation in OCD patients treated with clomipramine or fluoxetine*. American Psychiatry Association Annual Meeting, Washington, DC.

Pigott, T. A., Pato, M. T., Bernstein, S. E., Grover, G. N., Hill, J. L., Tolliver, T. J., Murphy, D. L. (1990). Controlled comparisons of clomipramine and fluoxetine in the treatment of obsessive-compulsive disorder. *Archives of General Psychiatry, 47*, 926–932.

Pigott, T. A., Pato, M. T., L'Heureux, F., Hill, J. L., Grover, G. N., Bernstein, S. E., & Murphy, D. L. (1991). A controlled comparison of adjuvant lithium carbonate or thyroid hormone in clomipramine-treated patients with obsessive compulsive disorder. *Journal of Clinical Psychopharmacology, 11*, 242–248.

Pigott, T. A., & Seay, S. M. (1999). A review of the efficacy of selective serotonin reuptake inhibitors in obsessive-compulsive disorders. *The Journal of Clinical Psychiatry, 60*, 101–106.

Pittenger, C. (2015). Glutamatergic agents for OCD and related disorders. *Current Treatment Options in Psychiatry, 2*, 271–283.

Pittenger, C., Bloch, M. H., Wasylink, S., Billingslea, E., Simpson, R., Jakubovski, E., Kelmendi, B., Sanacora, G., & Coric, V. (2015). Riluzole augmentation in treatment-refractory obsessive-compulsive disorder: A pilot randomized placebo-controlled trial. *The Journal of Clinical Psychiatry, 76*, 1075–1084.

Rachman, S., Hodgson, R., & Marks, I. M. (1971). The treatment of chronic obsessive-compulsive neurosis. *Behaviour Research and Therapy, 9*, 237–247.

Rapoport, J. L. (1980). *The boy who couldn't stop washing*. Dutton.

Ravizza, L., Barzega, G., Bellino, S., Bogetto, F., & Maina, G. (1996). Drug treatment of obsessive-compulsive disorder (OCD): Long-term trial with clomipramine and selective serotonin reuptake inhibitors (SSRIs). *Psychopharmacology Bulletin, 32*, 167–173.

Rodriguez, C. I., Kegeles, L. S., Levinson, A., Feng, T., Marcus, S. M., Vermes, D., Flood, P., & Simpson, H. B. (2013). Randomized controlled crossover trial of ketamine in obsessive-compulsive disorder: Proof of concept. *Neuropsychopharmacology, 38*, 2475–2483.

Romano, S., Goodman, W., Tamura, R., & Gonzales, J. (2001). Long-term treatment of obsessive-compulsive disorder after an acute response: A comparison of fluoxetine versus placebo. *Journal of Clinical Psychopharmacology, 21*, 46–52.

Sarris, J., Oliver, G., Camfield, D. A., Dean, O. M., Dowling, N., Smith, D. J., Murphy, J., Menon, R., Berk, M., Blair-West, S., & Ng, C. H. (2015). *N*-Acetylcysteine (NAC) in the treatment of obsessive-compulsive disorder: A 16-week, double-blind, randomized, placebo-controlled study. *CNS Drugs, 29*, 801–809.

Sayyah, M., Sayyah, M., Boostani, H., Ghaffari, S. M., & Hoseini, A. (2012). Effects of aripiprazole augmentation in treatment-resistant obsessive-compulsive disorder (a double blind clinical trial). *Depression and Anxiety, 29*, 850–854.

Shapira, N. A., Ward, H. E., Mandoki, M., Murphy, T. K., Yang, M. C., Blier, P., & Goodman, W. K. (2004). A double-blind, placebo- controlled trial of olanzapine addition in fluoxetine-refractory obsessive-compulsive disorder. *Biological Psychiatry, 55*, 553–555.

Soomro, G. M., Altman, D., Rajaqopal, S., & Oakley-Browne, M. (2008). Selective serotonin reuptake inhibitors (SSRIs) versus placebo for obsessive-compulsive disorder (OCD). *Cochrane Database Systematic Review, 23*, CD001765.

Stein, D. J., Andersen, E. W., Tonnoir, B., & Fineberg, N. (2007). Escitalopram in obsessive-compulsive disorder: A randomized, placebo-controlled, paroxetine-referenced, fixed-dose, 24-week study. *Current Medical Research Opinion, 23*, 701–711.

Thoren, P., Åsberg, M., Cronholm, B., Jornestedt, L., & Traskman, L. (1980). Clomipramine treatment of obsessive compulsive disorder: I. A controlled clinical trial. *Archives of General Psychiatry, 37*, 1281–1285.

Tollefson, G. D., Birkett, M., Koran, L., & Genduso, L. (1994). Continuation treatment of OCD: Double-blind and open-label experience with fluoxetine. *The Journal of Clinical Psychiatry, 55*(10, Suppl.), 69–76.

Vallejo, J., Olivares, J., Marcos, T., Bulbena, A., & Menchon, J. (1992). Clomipramine versus phenelzine in obsessive-compulsive disorder: A controlled trial. *The British Journal of Psychiatry, 161*, 665–670.

Volavka, J., Neziroglu, F., & Yaryura-Tobias, J. A. (1985). Clomipramine and imipramine in obsessive-compulsive disorder. *Psychiatry Research, 14*, 83–91.

Vulink, N. C., Denys, D., Fluitman, S. B., Meinardi, J. C., & Westenberg, H. G. (2009). Quetiapine augments the effect of citalopram in non-refractory obsessive-compulsive disorder: A randomized, double-blind, placebo-controlled study of 76 patients. *The Journal of Clinical Psychiatry, 70*(7), 1001–1008.

Wheadon, D. E., Bushnell, W. D., & Steiner, M. (1993, December). *A fixed dose comparison of 20, 40, or 60 mg of paroxetine to placebo in the treatment of OCD* [Paper presentation]. Annual meeting of the American College of Neuropsychopharmacology, Honolulu, HI.

Zahn, T. P., Insel, T. R., &Murphy, D. L. (1984). Psychophysiological changes during pharmacological treatment of patients with obsessive-compulsive disorder. *The British Journal of Psychiatry, 145*, 39–44.

Zhao, J. P. (1991). A controlled study of clomipramine and amitriptyline for treating obsessive-compulsive disorder. *Chung Hua Shen Ching Shen Ko Tsa Chih, 24*, 68–70.

Zohar, J., & Judge, R. (1996). Paroxetine versus clomipramine in the treatment of obsessive-compulsive disorder. *The British Journal of Psychiatry, 169*, 468–474.

CHAPTER 18

Biological Approaches to Obsessive-Compulsive Disorder: Psychiatric Neurosurgery and Neuromodulation

Adriel Barrios-Anderson, Nicole C. R. McLaughlin, *and* Benjamin D. Greenberg

Abstract

Interest in alternative, nonpharmacological approaches for psychiatric illness, specifically psychiatric neurosurgery and more recent nonsurgical methods of neuromodulation, has grown with the emergence of novel technologies. This chapter briefly reviews the history of the nonpharmacological treatment modalities for obsessive-compulsive disorder (OCD). The chapter covers how patients, who are often resistant to standard pharmacological and behavioral treatment for OCD, are selected for the alternative biological approaches. The other biological approaches to OCD that are reviewed in the chapter include modern psychiatric neurosurgical procedures for OCD, such as lesion procedures, deep brain stimulation, and vagus nerve stimulation, and nonsurgical approaches, such as transcranial magnetic stimulation and electroconvulsive therapy.

Key Words: obsessive-compulsive disorder, deep brain stimulation, cingulotomy, capsulotomy, leucotomy, tractotomy, psychiatric neurosurgery, transcranial magnetic stimulation

Introduction

Obsessive-compulsive disorder (OCD) is a common illness for which the current standard treatment includes a combination of pharmacotherapy and cognitive-behavioral therapy (Stein et al., 2019). It is estimated that approximately 20% of individuals with OCD have refractory disease that is not responsive to first-line medication or behavioral therapies (Hirschtritt et al., 2017; Miguel et al., 2019). Since 2000, several promising methods have evolved or have been developed anew to target a subset of the refractory population (Camprodon et al., 2016; Hirschtritt et al., 2017). Psychiatric neurosurgery, for instance, offers a growing array of neurosurgical approaches to treat a very small number of individuals with severe, "intractable" OCD (Barrios-Anderson & McLaughlin, 2020; Hirschtritt et al., 2017). Although neurosurgery for psychiatric disorders has been conducted for decades, current techniques have evolved past the initial, relatively primitive methods. Surgical interventions using a variety of techniques include neuroablative procedures and neurostimulation, such as deep brain stimulation (DBS; Stein et al., 2019). Although the pathophysiology of OCD is not completely clear, it appears to involve abnormal functioning in the medial and orbital-frontal-basal ganglia-thalamic circuits, and psychiatric neurosurgical interventions have been designed to target this circuitry (Greenberg, Rauch, et al., 2010). Similarly, advances in OCD phenomenology, diagnosis, and conventional management have guided patient selection for the interventions that might be broadly termed neurocircuit-based treatments.

For neuroablation, four procedures are best known: anterior cingulotomy, limbic leucotomy, capsulotomy, and subcaudate tractotomy (Doshi, 2009). These "lesion" procedures make use of well-established technologies applied to other disorders (Doshi, 2009). For example, gamma knife radiosurgery (GKRS) has been used to treat brain tumors, arteriovenous malformations, and trigeminal neuralgia for many years (Harris & Das, 2020; Hasegawa et al., 2019; Tavakol et al., 2020). Novel tools for neuroablation, such as laser interstitial thermal therapy and high-intensity focused ultrasound, have also emerged (Asaad & McLaughlin, 2020; Quadri et al., 2018). Any neurosurgical approach has risks that are higher than the risks of noninvasive procedures; therefore, compared to than the noninvasive methods, neurosurgery requires a higher standard in patient selection in terms of definitively established treatment refractoriness, severity, chronicity, and functional impairment. In addition, psychiatric neurosurgery requires a dedicated multidisciplinary team at all stages of care, including long-term follow-up.

Neuromodulation, or methods designed to selectively and reversibly alter functional neural dynamics, has been an area of fruitful research in psychiatric disorders in the early 2000's (Bais et al., 2014). In OCD, neurosurgical and nonsurgical techniques have been employed with varying degrees of efficacy. DBS, for instance, requires a neurosurgical approach that involves the creation of burr holes to allow electrode implantation, but it is nonablative and allows for modulation of brain function. The FDA granted approval for use of DBS in essential tremor (1997) and Parkinson's disease (2002/2003). Due to increased interest in neurosurgical interventions for refractory psychiatric disorders, the use of DBS has increased. In February 2009, the FDA approved DBS for a Humanitarian Device Exemption (HDE) in the treatment of severely refractory OCD. Other nonsurgical forms of neuromodulation that have been studied in OCD include electroconvulsive therapy (ECT) and transcranial magnetic stimulation (TMS). A form of TMS was FDA approved for OCD in 2018.

This chapter first provides a brief historical overview of psychiatric neurosurgery and neuromodulation, followed by discussion of the current landscape of nonpharmacological approaches, then it highlights the current state of the science of psychiatric neurosurgical procedures for neuroablation and neuromodulation, followed by a brief discussion of nonsurgical neuromodulation techniques.

Brief History of Psychiatric Neurosurgery and Neuromodulation

Neurosurgical interventions for psychiatric disorders have a long history, marked by initial enthusiasm, followed by indiscriminate use and belated attention to severe adverse effects. The first report of more modern neurosurgical treatment for psychiatric disorders was published in 1891 by Gottlieb Burckhardt, considered by some to be the father of modern "psychosurgery," a term that has been superseded by psychiatric neurosurgery. Burckhardt described the first experimental topectomy (selective removal of parts of the cerebral cortex), with bilateral cortical excisions in aggressive and demented patients. Burckhardt presented his preliminary results for a six-patient cohort. The outcomes were varied, including one patient death five days after the operation. Burckhardt described improvement as patients' becoming "quieter" as a result of the surgery, although a couple of individuals demonstrated no changes. Despite Burckhardt's presenting what he believed was some benefit in this population, the responses from his colleagues and the medical community at large were strongly negative, prompting Burckhardt to abandon his efforts (Manjila et al., 2008; Stone, 2001).

In 1910, Lodovicus (or "Ludvig") Puusepp (Estonia) sectioned the cortex between frontal and parietal lobes in manic depressive and epileptic patients; in 1937, he reported that patients who had later undergone a procedure that destroys white matter tracts in the frontal lobe, known as a frontal leucotomy, had decreased aggressive symptoms. As early as 1932, Ducoste, Marotti, and Sciuti, as well as Ferdiere and Coulloudon (France, Italy), had injected blood from malarial patients or from the patients themselves into the frontal lobes of psychiatric patients, and they reported some improvement in their patients' "psychoses" as a result (Feldman et al., 2001; Valenstein & Valenstein, 1974).

In 1935, Fulton and Jacobsen presented their research on primates who had frontal cortical ablation. The primates showed a reduction in "experimental neurosis" and were less fearful, but they were still able to perform complex tasks (El-Hai, 2007). Stimulated by this initial research, Moniz and Lima later extended some of the work to humans, and in 1935 they performed a prefrontal leucotomy. This involved injection of alcohol into the centrum ovale of both frontal lobes, through trephine holes in the lateral surfaces of the skull. Moniz chose the centrum ovale for the initial lesions because of the high density of fibers connecting the anterior frontal cortex with the thalamus and other cortical areas, as well as the relative lack of major vasculature in this area. At the time, it appeared that the greatest benefit occurred in patients with predominantly affective symptoms. After these initial forays into surgical interventions, the pair started making lesions in the white matter of the frontal lobes. By the end of 1937, Moniz had coined the term *psychosurgery*, and in 1949, he won the Nobel Prize for his work (El-Hai, 2007).

The first surgery for psychiatric disorders completed in the United States was carried out by Freeman and Watts in 1936 (El-Hai, 2007). Techniques ranged from a "minimal lobotomy" (minimal and anterior) for patients with "affective psychoneurotic disorders" to a "radical lobotomy" (large and posterior) for patients with schizophrenia or for those requiring reoperations. Freeman and Watts soon began to realize that specific symptoms responded best to localized lesions, and in 1942 they reported on 200 cases. The selection of specific lesion locations was, for many of these early neurosurgeons, influenced by the proposed anatomical basis of emotions suggested by Papez in 1937. The classic Papez circuit involves connections from the cingulate gyrus to the hippocampus, fornix, mammillary body, and anterior thalamic nucleus, then to the orbitofrontal cortex (OFC) and septal nuclei. Current psychiatric neurosurgical methods also target frontolimbic connections (subcaudate tractotomy and capsulotomy), the Papez circuit (anterior cingulotomy), or both areas (limbic leucotomy).

In the 1940s, stereotactic neurosurgery (using internal landmarks) in humans was initiated by Spiegel and Wycis (Gildenberg, 2001). At the time, they reported that dorsomedial thalamotomies decreased obsessive-compulsive symptoms, but the rate of case fatalities for this procedure was high, at 3.4% among 58 individuals with various psychiatric illnesses (Spiegel et al., 1952). The anterior cingulate was suggested as a target in 1947 (Fodstad et al., 1982; Pribram & Fulton, 1954) because stimulation of the anterior cingulum in monkeys produced autonomic responses of a type associated with emotions, and lesions in this area resulted in decreased fear and aggression.

At its peak in the 1940s to early 1950s, lobotomy was being performed on approximately 5,000 patients per year in the United States alone. In 1954, chlorpromazine was launched, and with the introduction of this pharmacological intervention, the use of surgical interventions was substantially reduced. Fierce opposition to psychiatric neurosurgery by subsets of the medical community continued, largely based upon their reactions to the crude operations that had been carried out earlier in the century. In the early 1970s, several states passed legislation as a result of this concern. For example, Oregon required the approval of a Psychosurgery Review Board, and California required a mandatory judicial review before surgery. From 1965 to 1975, two independent scientific teams conducted pilot studies evaluating four different neurosurgical procedures. In the 1970s, the National Commission for the Protection of Human Subjects of Biomedical and Behavioral Research (NCPHS) was convened and was the first national body established for examining bioethics policy. The NCPHS contracted for an evaluation of psychiatric patients who had undergone psychosurgery, led by neuropsychologists Allan Mirsky and Maressa Orzack at Boston University. The NCPHS also contracted to expand a study already started at the Massachusetts Institute of Technology, led by neuropsychologists Hans-Lukas Teuber and Suzanne Corkin, as well as neurologist Thomas Twitchell. Overall, it was concluded that "(1) more than half of the patients improved significantly following psychosurgery, although a few were worse and some unchanged, and (2) none of the patients experience significant neurological or psychological impairment attributable to the surgery." This was the primary reason that a ban on psychosurgery was not instituted (United States Department of Health, Education, and Welfare [DHEW], 1978). The NCPHS report offered guidelines for the ethical use, continued investigation, and regulation of psychiatric neurosurgery. The report also recommended continued research and the establishment of a national registry documenting techniques and outcomes of psychosurgery, to assist the national Psychosurgery Advisory Board in making evaluations of the safety and efficacy of specific procedures (DHEW, 1978). It was recommended that data be collected regarding the presenting symptoms and preoperative diagnosis, past medical and social history of the patients, and outcome, requiring that psychosurgery become a "reportable operation." Summary reports would be sent to Congress every year. The national registry has not yet been established, although there have been recent calls to do so. However, leaders in the field have continually emphasized the need for caution.

In the past two decades, media coverage has generally been favorable and medical professionals generally favor the use of neurosurgical procedures in the small number of appropriate cases. One Canadian national survey of psychiatrists and psychiatry residents found that 53% of practitioners would favor referring a patient with treatment-resistant OCD for DBS (Cormier et al., 2019). Another survey of functional neurosurgeons in the United States found that 71% of respondents agreed that neuroablative surgeries are a valid treatment for OCD (Cabrera et al., 2019). Despite emerging, well-validated literature on psychiatric neurosurgical procedures and broader agreement on the possible efficacy of DBS and neuroablative procedures in medically refractory OCD, many clinicians note that a lack of knowledge about the procedures and concerns about safety still predominate in the broader medical community (Cormier et al., 2019). Emerging noninvasive or less invasive neuromodulation methods, such as TMS, have gained significant attention in recent years as alternative therapies for treatment-resistant OCD. At this time, there are limited data on the comparative efficacy of all the approaches under investigation for treatment-resistant or refractory OCD; therefore, no therapy has emerged as the most popular or favored option.

Current Landscape for Nonpharmacological Approaches

Scientific Context
Over the years, although there had been some theoretical basis for lesion or stimulation location, initially based on the work of Fulton and Moniz among others, surgical treatments were developed largely empirically. Psychiatric neurosurgery and indeed the other biological approaches to OCD discussed in this chapter, including nonsurgical neuromodulation, remain within empirical psychiatry, since the pathophysiological processes involved in major neuropsychiatric disorders have yet to be fully elucidated. Although work has been increasingly informed by neuroimaging and translational work in neuroanatomy, investigations remain primarily concerned with safety and efficacy. But non-pharmocological approaches for OCD are also being utilized to identify and characterize maladaptive neural circuitry and the functional connectivity potentially underlying OCD pathophysiology and responses to treatment with circuit-based interventions.

Procedures and Practices

Despite growing evidence, neurosurgical interventions and nonsurgical neuromodulation (the most common example of the latter being TMS in major depression) are not often used to treat any psychiatric disorder, including OCD. This is mainly due to the success of conventional behavioral and pharmacological treatments, the time demands of weeks-long TMS treatment, the costs (which are commonly not yet reimbursed), and worries about adverse effects of neurosurgical intervention in particular. While neurosurgical safety has dramatically improved compared to safety levels in the mid-twentieth century, serious adverse outcomes do occur, and the issue is discussed in the extensive informed consent process for both prospective candidates and (ideally) family/significant others. The remainder of the discussion here on patient selection focuses on guidelines for psychiatric neurosurgical procedures, since the procedures have explicit, agreed-upon guidelines for their use in patients with severe, intractable OCD (Fins et al., 2006; Garnaat et al., 2014; OCD-DBS Collaborative Group, 2002). On the other hand, nonsurgical neuromodulation with TMS has a lower threshold for entry, as would be expected, both in FDA-approved practice and in research. While patient selection for neurosurgery is more (although not fully) uniform in published research (which typically involves relatively small samples), there is more variability in studies of noninvasive methods regarding patient selection, brain targets, devices used, and stimulation parameters. Still, sample sizes are typically relatively small (Bais et al., 2014; Cocchi et al., 2018).

Patient Selection for Psychiatric Neurosurgery

The majority of psychiatric neurosurgery procedures take place, as they should, in specialized centers or programs around the globe that consist of interdisciplinary teams of psychiatrists, neurosurgeons, neuropsychologists, neurologists, and medical ethicists, among other specialists. The teams rigorously consider individual cases, applying strict and generally consistent criteria for patient selection. A small number of psychiatric neurosurgical cases are estimated to be completed per year in most countries where such procedures are available (Barrett, 2017). Beyond first-line therapies for OCD, an array of pharmacological and behavioral interventions appear efficacious, including non-SSRI/SNRIs for treatment augmentation (Pittenger & Bloch, 2014). Specialized centers prioritize patient safety and screen patients' medical histories, ensuring they have exhausted all established pharmacological interventions and behavioral therapy before the patient may be considered a surgical candidate.

Current recommendations are similar to those developed by the NCPHS, which issued guidelines in its 1977 report for what was then called psychosurgery. The recommendations included rigorous criteria for diagnostic accuracy, illness severity, documentation of an exhaustive array of failed treatments, and a stringent informed consent process. Notably, it is estimated that < 1% of treatment-seeking individuals with OCD will meet screening criteria for neurosurgical intervention, despite estimated rates of treatment-resistant OCD as high as 20% (Garnaat et al., 2014; Hirschtritt et al., 2017; Miguel et al., 2019).

Guidelines for expert centers engaged in neurosurgical interventions for OCD emphasize a cautious and comprehensive approach to the assessment, treatment, and follow-up of patients (OCD-DBS Collaborative Group, 2002). An example is:

- Prospective candidates must have severe and chronic (intractable) OCD despite adequate documented treatment trials. The severity threshold has varied, but patients must be judged to have "severe" or "extreme" illness. The FDA criterion for Humanitarian Use of neurosurgery is a Yale-Brown Obsessive-Compulsive Scale (Y-BOCS) severity score of 30 or more, despite aggressive and ongoing conventional treatments. This degree of illness is functionally debilitating.
- If the context is research, Institutional Review Board (IRB) or ethics committee oversight is required. In the United States, there is also an IRB review for FDA-approved Humanitarian Use of DBS for OCD. In addition to an IRB, ongoing studies typically have an external data safety monitoring board (DSMB) and will be reported to a clinical trials database.
- Previous behavior therapy, primarily exposure and ritual (or response) prevention (E/RP), generally for 20 or more hours with an experienced therapist, is required. In practice, this criterion is exceeded. It should be documented that real E/RP was delivered, and if not completed, that therapy was interrupted due to marked intolerance of the procedures and not simply moderate or less discomfort. Residential treatment in a specialized OCD program is encouraged if available.
- The patient must have undergone extensive prior pharmacotherapy, including treatment with several serotonin reuptake inhibitor antidepressants (SRIs; usually a trial of clomipramine is required, alone or carefully combined with a more selective SRI), at maximally tolerated doses for at least 12 weeks. At least two augmenting agents (usually a second-generation antipsychotic added to a high-dose "OCD range" antidepressant, plus another agent, such as a benzodiazepine) have to be tried for a minimum of two weeks. In practice, the criterion for the number and duration of medication trials is exceeded in most cases.
- While OCD should be the major cause of suffering and functional impairment, neuropsychiatric comorbidities should be assessed. The neurosurgical interventions are typically not carried out on individuals judged to have been recently or imminently suicidal. Bipolar disorder is a relative contraindication, especially to DBS, as there is a potential for neurostimulation to induce manic episodes. Patients must also be free of substance use disorders,

including those judged to be unstably remitted. Patients who are of limited intellectual capability are also typically excluded, because patients need to be able to understand the procedure and consent process and to be able to actively participate in treatment. Preoperative assessment should include an extensive neuropsychological battery, to be used both in ruling out intellectual limitation and as a baseline measure for comparison of future cognitive skills. Patients less than 18 years old are also not optimal candidates.

- Medical conditions that increase neurosurgical risks are contraindications. EEG and MRI, as well as specific laboratory tests (e.g., PT, INR), are typically included in the preoperative assessment.
- The patient must have access to adequate and specialized postoperative care. Continued psychotherapy and psychiatric treatment are essential. In some cases, surgery may enhance a patient's ability to engage in E/RP or other psychotherapies. Continued, and indefinite, follow-up is especially important with patients who have had DBS, due to the ongoing need for expert device programming and coordination of care with clinicians delivering conventional therapies. And, importantly, there needs to be insurance reimbursement for the necessary expert postoperative psychiatric, psychological, and neurosurgical care. This is a critical issue, given treatment costs, that needs to be addressed before an individual is deemed a surgical candidate.
- The comprehensive clinical information obtained during evaluation should be reviewed by an independent multidisciplinary group with appropriate expertise in the relevant disciplines, plus a community representative. In Britain and Belgium, and possibly elsewhere, a similar function is performed by national multidisciplinary boards.
- If the independent review deems a patient is an appropriate surgical candidate, the extensive consent process, which in effect began during evaluation, continues. Prospective candidates should be assessed for their expectations of improvement after surgery and (in the case of DBS) ongoing stimulation. Patients might have unrealistic expectations of great or rapid improvement in many if not all spheres of their lives after such dramatic interventions. These expectations, if not elicited and addressed before surgery, might lead a patient to precipitously discontinue needed medications or behavioral therapies after surgery. Alternatively, even after marked improvement in the severity of the patient's psychiatric illness, the patient may die by suicide if their psychosocial functioning and quality of life do not improve to match the expectations they had before surgery (Rück et al., 2017).

Long-term data collection for all patients undergoing neurosurgery for psychiatric reasons is extremely important but is not yet centralized, at least in the United States. Advances in terms of optimal (and potentially individualized) targets, device designs, and stimulation parameters depend on systematic data collection, as do potential improvements in the criteria for patient selection. The creation of a national registry for reliable data collection of this information remains a very important goal (initially proposed by a national commission in 1977 but never implemented). Specifics of data that should be collected in a registry have been proposed (Goodman & Insel, 2009).

Modern Biological Approaches

Psychiatric Neurosurgery: Lesion (Neuroablative) Procedures

The oldest surgical approaches for psychiatric illness involved ablation. Psychiatric neurosurgery—specifically, more precise procedures targeting much smaller brain areas—still includes neuroablative procedures in its armamentarium. These procedures are thought to be effective by selectively destroying white matter fiber tracts implicated in OCD (Doshi, 2009; Greenberg, Rauch, et al., 2010). Clinicians have made use of a variety of neurosurgical tools, including radiation, thermocoagulation, radiofrequency, and MRI-guided laser technology, for neuroablative procedures (Greenberg, Rauch, et al., 2010). Of the lesion procedures, subcaudate tractotomy and limbic leucotomy are currently less used, while anterior cingulotomy and, for OCD in particular, anterior capsulotomy, especially focused on the ventral part of the anterior limb of the internal capsule (hence the term "ventral capsulotomy"), are more often used.

SUBCAUDATE TRACTOTOMY

Introduced in 1964 by Knight and colleagues as a procedure to make bilateral lesions in the substantia innominata, ventral to the caudate nucleus (Greenberg, Gabriels, et al., 2010; Knight, 1965), subcaudate tractotomy interrupts tracts between the OFC and subcortical structures. This area contains fiber tracts connecting nodes within ventral fronto-basal-thalamic circuitry, as well as neurons with similar connections to those of the ventral portions of the striatum and ventral globus pallidus (Andrei Novac, 2014). More recent studies have used thermocoagulation and stereotactically controlled radiofrequency ablation to form this lesion in select patients with OCD or depression (Barrios-Anderson & McLaughlin, 2020; Kim & Lee, 2008; Woerdeman et al., 2006). Success rates reported in over 650 cases of major depressive disorder, OCD, or non-OCD anxiety were approximately 50% (Knight, 1973), with a similar rate of improvement in OCD specifically (Göktepe et al., 1975; Knight, 1973). In 1994, a large review of 342 patients (not restricted to OCD) concluded that subcaudate tractotomy enables 40% to 60% of patients to live normal or near-normal lives, with a reduction in suicide rate (Bridges et al., 1994). Subcaudate tractotomy has been minimally reported on since 2000 (Sinha et al., 2015). One study assessing retrospective data on past lesions found notable interpatient variation in brain anatomy in the target region (Sinha et al., 2015; Yang et al., 2015).

Adverse Effects. The most common complication reported was transient postoperative disorientation, likely due to edema (Knight, 1973). Long-term complications included seizures in 1.6% to 5% of patients (Knight, 1973). Fatigue and weight gain were also common (6% and 3%, respectively), and one death resulted from a neurosurgical complication (reviewed in Lopes et al., 2004). According to one review, 5% of patients who received subcaudate tractotomy attempted suicide, and 1.3% completed suicide after surgery (Lopes et al., 2004).

ANTERIOR CINGULOTOMY

In 1947, the anterior cingulate cortex (ACC) was first suggested as a target for treating psychiatric illness by Fulton (Sinha et al., 2015). In anterior cingulotomy, lesions are placed in the dorsal anterior cingulate cortex (dACC), typically impinging on the cingulum bundle. This may influence reciprocal connections between the ACC and other structures, including the OFC, amygdala, hippocampus, and posterior cingulate cortex (Shah et al., 2008; Sheth et al., 2013; Sinha et al., 2015). Lesions were initially guided using air ventriculography, allowing for stereotactic ablation through burr holes (Ballantine et al., 1967). Since 1991, this method has been replaced by MRI guidance. Ballantine and colleagues developed a method in which thermistor electrodes lesion the cingulum (thermocoagulation; Sinha et al., 2015). Anterior cingulotomy has been the most widely used neurosurgical treatment of OCD in the United States (Sheth et al., 2013).

A recent retrospective analysis by Sheth et al. demonstrated that five years postcingulotomy, 47% of patients experienced at least a 35% reduction in OCD severity, broadly considered a "full response" (Sheth et al., 2013). A recent systematic review corroborated this, reporting that 38% to 47% of individuals demonstrate a full response in terms of OCD severity after cingulotomy (Brown et al., 2016). In addition, nonresponders to anterior cingulotomy may respond to a repeat cingulotomy procedure (Bourne et al., 2013). In one cohort study, 53% of patients who underwent a repeat cingulotomy experienced a significant reduction in OCD severity, compared to only 17% of patients who had only a single cingulotomy procedure (Bourne et al., 2013). This result is similar to results for gamma ventral capsulotomy and suggests that the placebo response in well-selected patients is likely to be small, since even an actual (single-lesion) procedure was associated with a low response rate. Also of note is that anterior cingulotomy has demonstrated some efficacy as a treatment for refractory depression and appears to improve comorbid depression severity in intractable OCD (Sinha et al., 2015), a result also seen with capsulotomy.

Adverse Effects. Among the most serious complications is medication-responsive seizures, which were reported in 1% to 3% of the largest reported cohort of cingulotomy patients (Brown et al., 2016; Sheth et al., 2013). Suicide after surgery occurred in 2% of patients in this 64-patient cohort (Sheth et al., 2013; Brown et al., 2016). A comprehensive review found transient adverse events, including transient memory difficulty or dysfunction in 5.1% to 17.6% of patients, postcingulotomy abulia (a lack of motivation affecting function) in 1.6%, and urinary retention in 2%.

LIMBIC LEUCOTOMY

Introduced in 1973 by Kelly and colleagues, limbic leucotomy in essence combined bilateral cingulotomy with subcaudate tractotomy, based on the idea that the combined procedure would produce better functional results (Kelly et al., 1972, 1973). Limbic leucotomy usually involves the placement of three 6-mm lesions in the posterior inferior medial quadrant of the frontal lobes, and two lesions in the cingulate gyrus bilaterally (Sinha et al., 2015). A ventromedial frontal lesion is targeted to interrupt frontolimbic connections, and another lesion is targeted to interrupt the Papez circuit. Limbic leucotomy has been performed as either a single or staged procedure, depending on response to the initial lesion (Bourne et al., 2013; Sinha et al., 2015).

Early experience using global scales and clinical impressions found clinical improvement in 87% of patients at 1.5 months, with 69% being judged very much improved or even symptom-free at 17 months (Kelly et al., 1973). A more recent study reported that 68.8% of patients had a marked response, 18.9% had a possible response, and 12.6% did not improve or became worse (Cho et al., 2008).

Adverse Effects. Reported short-term adverse effects include headache, confusion/delirium, temporary hallucinations, extrapyramidal signs, lethargy, perseveration, local scalp infection, and urinary incontinence, as well as short-term memory deficits (Cho et al., 2008; Sinha et al., 2015). Although many of the adverse effects were temporary, due to this pattern of effects, patients often had longer postoperative hospital stays than are typically seen with either cingulotomy or subcaudate tractotomy alone (Sinha et al., 2015). The most significant adverse effects are seizures (in approximately 3% of patients) and enduring lethargy (Lopes et al., 2004). According to a recent review, 3.2% of individuals with OCD completed suicide after limbic leucotomy (Lopes et al., 2004). Transient postoperative abulia, a notable side effect also seen with anterior cingulotomy, occurred in 4.7% of patients in one cohort after limbic leucotomy (Bourne et al., 2013; Sheth et al., 2013; Sinha et al., 2015).

ANTERIOR CAPSULOTOMY

Anterior capsulotomy was first developed by Talairach in France and was further developed by Leksell in Sweden for OCD (Greenberg, Rauch, & Haber, 2010). As currently practiced, the procedure consists of placing a lesion in the ventral region of the anterior limb of the internal capsule; the lesion is intended to interfere with orbitofrontal and anterior cingulate efferent fibers connecting the prefrontal cortex and subcortical nuclei, such as the dorsomedial thalamus (Rasmussen et al., 2018; Sinha et al., 2015). The procedure has been conducted either with thermolesion by radiofrequency or with gamma knife capsulotomy (GKC), which employs stereotactic radiation via gamma knife radiosurgery, a technique developed in Sweden by Leksell and colleagues. Gamma knife radiosurgery focuses multiple beams of gamma radiation, which can pass through the skull without causing harm, to converge on a single point, allowing directed lesioning of intracranial structures without requiring craniotomy or placement of burr holes (Rasmussen et al., 2018). GKC is a procedure that leverages this technology to make small, targeted lesions in the ventral anterior internal capsule (Lopes et al., 2015; Rasmussen et al., 2018). GKC, which is often termed "gamma capsulotomy," has proven efficacious and has been an active area of research and clinical utility in severe, intractable OCD, in part because of its less invasive method of achieving neuroablation in the target region (Lopes et al., 2014; Rasmussen et al., 2018; Sinha et al., 2015).

The largest cohort of GKC to date was recently reported by Rasmussen and colleagues, who demonstrated a significant reduction in OCD symptom severity (Y-BOCS reduction of > 35%) in 56% of a 55-patient cohort dating back to the early 1990s (Rasmussen et al., 2018). In another long-term cohort of 25 patients, Rück et al demonstrated that 48% of patients showed more than 35% reduction in Y-BOCS score at four to 17 years after capsulotomy via both GKC and thermocoagulation (Miguel et al., 2019; Rück et al., 2017). As with cingulotomy, depression also appears significantly improved after capsulotomy, and the same was seen for nonspecific anxiety (Miguel et al., 2019; Rasmussen et al., 2018; Rück et al., 2008; Spatola et al., 2018). In addition to these larger cohort studies, smaller studies appear to corroborate the efficacy of GKC in treating severe, refractory OCD. One recent report on 10 patients with OCD by Spatola et al. demonstrated that 70% of patients were full responders after GKC (Spatola et al., 2018). A preliminary attempt to conduct a randomized, double-blind, placebo-controlled trial by Lopes and colleagues randomized participants to either active or inactive GKC for severe OCD, but, unfortunately, the study was terminated due to gamma knife equipment malfunction. No significant differences between active and inactive arms of the study were observed in the patient sample at the end of the 12-month controlled phase. Analysis of the difference in Y-BOCS outcomes between active and sham groups in the controlled phase yielded $p = 0.054$, which did not meet the conventional statistical threshold of $p < 0.05$ (Lopes et al., 2015; Miguel et al., 2019). This may have been due to the small sample, the relatively short sham-controlled phase, or both.

Adverse Effects. Short-term adverse effects include nausea, vomiting, headache, confusion, and incontinence, varying by the method used (Barrios-Anderson & McLaughlin, 2020; Rasmussen et al., 2018). In some cases, GKC, in particular, has been associated with cerebral cyst formation and radiation necrosis, a risk associated with the use of gamma knife radiosurgery for other indications as well (Camprodon et al., 2016; Lopes et al., 2014; Miguel et al., 2019; Rasmussen et al., 2018). Frontal lobe edema resulting in fatigue, apathy, disinhibition, and loss of initiative was noted in one of the earliest cohorts of GKC (Miguel et al., 2019). Notably, despite the targeting of white fibers involved in the frontal lobe and prefrontal cortex connectivity in gamma knife anterior capsulotomy, clinical studies have shown no changes in personality and improved cognitive functioning postprocedure (Batistuzzo et al., 2015; Miguel et al., 2019; Paiva et al., 2018).

The Future of Surgical Neuroablation

In recent years, innovation in neuroablative procedures has come in the form of utilizing emerging technology to enhance and optimize outcomes while mitigating risks. One such emerging technology is MRI-guided, high-intensity focused ultrasound (HIFU), which utilizes high-power sonication to create targeted thermal lesions in neural tissue (Kim et al., 2018; Quadri et al., 2018). Like GKC, HIFU can be used to make targeted intracranial lesions without the need for burr holes or craniotomies (Kim et al., 2018; Quadri et al., 2018). One group, Kim and colleagues in South Korea, recently demonstrated that 54.5% of patients in a cohort of 11 experienced > 35% reduction in OCD severity, as measured by Y-BOCS, with no significant side effects, after anterior capsulotomy using MRI-guided HIFU (Kim et al., 2018). Another emerging technology utilized in functional neurosurgical procedures for epilepsy and brain tumors is MRI-guided laser interstitial thermal therapy (LITT). This procedure is a minimally invasive ablative approach that utilizes laser thermal energy transmitted via fiberoptic catheters fed through cranial burr holes (Asaad & McLaughlin, 2020). LITT, while more invasive than GKC and HIFU because it involves making burr holes, is of interest because of the ability for surgeons to place lesions with more reliable boundaries than those achieved in radiation therapy and because the lesioning can be observed in real time (Asaad & McLaughlin, 2020). Recently, McLaughlin et al. demonstrated a full responder rate of 77.8% in a preliminary cohort of nine patients with severe OCD (McLaughlin et al., 2021). Research is ongoing on the benefits and efficacy of these novel approaches for neuroablative psychiatric neurosurgery.

In summary, neuroablative psychiatric neurosurgical procedures, despite emerging from the oldest and most preliminary forms of psychosurgery, have remained valuable clinical tools for select patients with severe intractable OCD. This is in part due to the practical benefits that a single-lesion procedure may confer for some patients, in contrast to neuromodulation procedures, such as DBS, which require considerable expert follow-up as well as possible repeat surgical procedures (Cabrera et al., 2019; Kumar et al., 2019). Perhaps more importantly, lesion procedures have demonstrated significantly high efficacy rates that rival those results achieved using neuromodulation methods. One recent comparative meta-analysis uncovered that neuroablative techniques, such as anterior capsulotomy and cingulotomy, demonstrated superior efficacy when compared to DBS as well as lower complication rates overall (Kumar et al., 2019). Neuroablative psychiatric neurosurgery may be a helpful option for some patients, and further study of these approaches to OCD is imperative.

Surgical Neuromodulation

Surgical approaches for neuromodulation, such as DBS and vagus nerve stimulation (VNS), have been researched extensively. Most notably, DBS has garnered significant interest in the past two decades. This section addresses DBS in detail as well as the less frequently studied VNS.

DBS

While DBS was developed much later than ablative procedures, it has been of interest for many decades. In 1948, Pool implanted an electrode in the caudate nucleus to treat depression and anorexia (Pool, 1954). A half-century later, Nuttin and colleagues reported on treatment of OCD with DBS of an anterior capsulotomy target (Nuttin et al., 1999). In their application of DBS for OCD, Nuttin and colleagues placed electrodes (via burr holes in the skull) in the anterior limb of the internal capsule and adjacent ventral striatum and connected the electrodes to a pacemaker-like device. Following the success of this initial report of DBS in the anterior internal capsule, target locations for DBS primarily included the ventral capsule/ventral striatum (VC/VS); however, other target areas have been explored for DBS in OCD, including the nucleus accumbens, inferior thalamic peduncle, globus pallidus interna, subthalamic nucleus, and more recently the bed nucleus of the stria terminalis (Bais et al., 2014; Karas et al., 2019). The electrodes typically deliver high-frequency stimulation to a defined target site. Lead placement is usually bilateral and is guided by imaging and targeting platforms. A neurostimulator is placed subdermally (for example, in the upper chest wall) and is connected to the brain leads through wires under the skin.

Neurostimulation can be independently adjusted in several important ways, including the number of active contacts on a lead, and via stimulation polarity, intensity, and frequency. Patients may opt for DBS over lesion procedures because DBS may be reversible and is potentially modifiable. For example, DBS may be modified to optimize benefit, or the stimulation can be changed or stopped to improve DBS-induced side effects. However, the procedure is not innocuous (potential risks are described under "Adverse Effects/Considerations").

Over the past two decades, several double-blind controlled studies and various case reports have reported on the efficacy of DBS for OCD in several anatomical stimulation targets (Bais et al., 2014). One study by Greenberg and colleagues, and the largest study of DBS for intractable OCD to date, targeted the VC/VS in 26 participants and showed > 35% improvement on the Y-BOCS in 61.5% of the study population after surgery (Greenberg, Gabriels, et al., 2010). Another relatively large ($N = 16$) study by Denys and colleagues demonstrated that by targeting the nucleus accumbens, 56% of the study population of patients with intractable OCD saw a > 35% reduction in Y-BOCS score (Denys et al., 2010). Both anatomical targets, which are in fact closely related, appear to also demonstrate the efficacy of DBS in reducing co-occurring depression and generalized anxiety as well as in improving global functioning and quality of life (Bais et al., 2014; Denys et al., 2010; Greenberg, Gabriels, et al., 2010).

DBS targeting the subthalamic nucleus (STN) in OCD has also been studied; initially uncovered since the STN is a common area for DBS in Parkinson's disease (Bais et al., 2014). In early work treating Parkinson's disease it was uncovered, by chance, that patiens with comorbid OCD had reduction in OC symptoms after DBS (Bais et al., 2014). One randomized, double-blind clinical trial with a patient crossover design demonstrated > 25% reduction in Y-BOCS score in 75% of the 16-patient cohort who received active stimulation of the STN (Bais et al., 2014; Mallet et al., 2008). Stimulation in the inferior thalamic peduncle and globus pallidus interna has also shown some promising results in small cohort studies, reducing Y-BOCS score significantly (Jiménez et al., 2013; Nair et al., 2014). Larger studies of these stimulation regions are merited.

Most recently Luyten and colleagues demonstrated in a crossover study of 24 patients that stimulation along the anterior limb of the internal capsule (ALIC) and bed nucleus of the stria terminalis (BNST), areas that are closely related from a network standpoint to both the VC/VS and nucleus accumbens targets, was effective in highly resistant OCD, with 67% of patients being classified as full responders (Karas et al., 2019; Luyten et al., 2015). Luyten et al. performed a post hoc analysis that examined the anatomical location of the active contacts and found that a significantly higher proportion of patients with active contacts in only the BNST were full responders to DBS when compared to patients with active contacts in only the ALIC (80% vs. 16.7%, respectively; Luyten et al., 2015). The study suggested that optimal targeting of fibers in the VC/VS warrants further study and that the fibers in the BNST, specifically, may be better targets than more anterior white matter fibers (Luyten et al., 2015).

Adverse Effects/Considerations. Despite both the promise of DBS as a reversible (and titratable) treatment for OCD and its demonstrated efficacy, the procedure is not without risk. Reported complications have included intracerebral hemorrhage, seizures, superficial infection, and hypomanic/manic symptoms (Bais et al., 2014; Haq et al., 2010; Luyten et al., 2015). In addition, stimulator battery depletion may lead to worsened depression and OCD (Greenberg et al., 2006). Stimulation may also cause transient sensorimotor effects, such as paresthesias, muscle contraction, dysarthria, and diplopia. Longer-term or more serious adverse effects have included permanent neurological sequelae and seizures (Luyten et al., 2015; Mallet et al., 2008), as well as serious psychiatric consequences, including hypomania and suicide in the context of psychosocial stress (Abelson et al., 2005; Bais et al., 2014; Haq et al., 2010). But, as is also the case for DBS efficacy, only tentative conclusions about DBS safety can be drawn given the limited data available.

Overall, DBS remains an active area of research, because while current studies have demonstrated some efficacy comparable to lesion procedures, significant adverse effects remain. To date, how the therapeutic potential of DBS compares to that of lesion procedures remains an open question. Although DBS is titratable, overall, open studies have found its effectiveness to be similar to, or perhaps slightly less than, the effectiveness of lesion procedures (as highlighted in the section "The Future of Surgical Neuroablation"; Kumar et al., 2019; Provenza et al., 2019). A definitive answer to the question of comparable efficacy, however, requires an adequately large (in fact, very large) controlled trial of DBS versus neuroablation, which is unlikely to ever be carried out. Research on reducing the adverse effects and improving the overall effectiveness of DBS for OCD has been focused on uncovering an electrophysiological biomarker for OCD that could be used to drive adaptive DBS systems that respond to pathological signals (Goodman et al., 2020; Provenza et al., 2019). This approach could reduce the effects of overstimulation while potentially improving efficacy rates; however, much work is still needed to uncover reliable biomarkers for OCD that could drive therapeutic stimulation based upon an individual's degree of distress at any given time (Goodman et al., 2020; Provenza et al., 2019).

VNS

The vagus nerve, the tenth cranial nerve, has reciprocal influences on the limbic system and higher cortical activity. Vagal cell bodies convey information centrally to the nucleus tractus solitarius, which then projects to the brain through three pathways: an autonomic feedback loop, direct projections to the medullary reticular formation, and ascending projections to the forebrain. Ascending projections have connections to the locus ceruleus, parabrachial nucleus, thalamus, hypothalamus, amygdala, and stria terminalis. VNS uses an implanted stimulator that employs a bipolar pulse generator to send electrical impulses to the vagus nerve. VNS is FDA approved for partial-onset epilepsy and depression, but there is minimal information regarding the use of VNS for OCD. However, one study found that at 3 and 6 months after use of VNS, 43% of treated patients met response criteria (score reduction > 25%) for the Y-BOCS (George et al., 2008). Five of the seven treated patients remained in the study for two years and showed some benefit, though not as robust a benefit as shown with DBS for OCD (George et al., 2008). Since then, very few long-term research efforts on VNS therapy for OCD have been published, and to date there have been no sham-controlled studies (Rapinesi et al., 2019).

Adverse Effects. While recent data on VNS are limited given the absence of sham-controlled studies, an early pilot study reported adverse effects, including surgical site infection, transient device-site pain, voice alteration, dysphagia, and cough (George et al., 2008; Rapinesi et al., 2019). In the same pilot study, one out of 11 patients experienced worsening suicidal ideation and another patient had rectal bleeding, neither of which "could be clearly attributed to VNS" (George et al., 2008).

Nonsurgical Neuromodulation

In addition to the neurosurgical forms of neuromodulation discussed above, progress has been made in recent years in studying nonsurgical forms of neuromodulation (e.g., TMS and ECT). In particular, TMS has received significant attention as a noninvasive method of targeting relevant circuitry in OCD (Bais et al., 2014).

TMS

TMS creates a pulsed magnetic field over the scalp, causing electrical current induction in the cortex of the brain that leads either to net stimulation or to disruption of the neurons in the given brain region (Bais et al., 2014; Lusicic et al., 2018). The first study of TMS for OCD was not a treatment trial but used the technique as an anatomical probe of prefrontal regions that could be involved in OCD symptoms. The study used an anatomical control (occipital cortex), and it found there was a decrease in compulsive urges (but not obsessions) after repeated stimulation of the right lateral prefrontal cortex (Greenberg et al., 1997). TMS, in particular repetitive TMS (rTMS), multiple sessions of TMS given over time to a patient, is being studied for its ability to modulate frontal-striatal circuitry, which is thought to underlie OCD pathophysiology (Bais et al., 2014; Lusicic et al., 2018). Some regions that have been studied in clinical research examining the use of TMS in OCD include the dorsolateral prefrontal cortex (DLPFC), OFC, ACC, and supplementary motor area (SMA; Bais et al., 2014). Research on TMS for OCD has received ongoing attention in recent years, and sham control studies persuaded the FDA to expand the list of "approved indications for TMS" to include OCD in 2018 (Voelker, 2018).

Since 1997, approximately 300 patients with OCD have undergone rTMS in randomized controlled trials (RCTs), an estimate based on published reports examined by Bais and colleagues (Bais et al., 2014). Studies in the DLPFC have shown promise, with several studies showing a short-term reduction in Y-BOCS severity after both unilateral and bilateral high-frequency stimulation of this target region (Berlim et al., 2013; Lusicic et al., 2018). Despite this, several meta-analyses and systematic reviews have shown that stimulation of the DLPFC resulted in no significant difference compared to sham in the short term (Berlim et al., 2013; Lusicic et al., 2018). At this point, data are limited and have yet to demonstrate that stimulation of the DLPFC is effective as a treatment for OCD (Bais et al., 2014).

Another region of interest in rTMS is the OFC, a region that has been strongly implicated in OCD by functional neuroimaging studies (Bais et al., 2014; Lusicic et al., 2018). In particular, OFC hyperactivity has been associated with OCD symptoms; therefore, low-frequency inhibitory rTMS to this region is being investigated (Bais et al., 2014; Lusicic et al., 2018). To date, a small number of double-blind RCTs of rTMS in the OFC have shown significant positive results, with inhibitory stimulation of the OFC demonstrating a significant reduction in OCD symptom severity compared to sham stimulation (Lusicic et al., 2018; Ruffini et al., 2009). Thus far, the differences appear to be short-term responses, since the benefits of rTMS in this region on OCD severity appear limited after several weeks (Berlim et al., 2013; Lusicic et al., 2018; Ruffini et al., 2009).

The SMA is another region that may show promise as a site for rTMS "inhibitory" stimulation (Berlim et al., 2013; Lusicic et al., 2018). In particular, the beneficial effects of rTMS in the SMA appear to be significant compared to sham for up to 14 weeks (Lusicic et al., 2018). Gomes and colleagues demonstrated in a sham-controlled trial that rTMS of the SMA reduced Y-BOCS score by at least 35% in seven out of 12 participants with OCD, and this effect was maintained up until 14 weeks after stimulation (Gomes et al., 2012).

Overall, rTMS appears promising, particularly in the SMA and OFC; however, these results and the clinical conclusions that can be drawn from them are limited. While rTMS is an active area of research in OCD, current research suggests that improvement in OCD symptoms that some protocols achieve is transient and in some cases may not be better than sham stimulation. rTMS does appear to have similar efficacy when compared to antipsychotic augmentation strategies in OCD (Berlim et al., 2013; Dold et al., 2013). Given the transient effects of rTMS in OCD and the ongoing investigation of appropriate targets and stimulation parameters, many clinicians and researchers hold that TMS should be paired with additional efficacious treatments for OCD, including E/RP and pharmacotherapy (Cocchi et al., 2018). As is true for surgery, considering TMS as an augmentation strategy may yield the best clinical outcomes. Researchers have also begun to consider the concept of multimodal treatment and have investigated strategies for improving TMS, such as "state-dependent" stimulation, where individuals are exposed to a "symptom-provoking stimulus," as in E/RP, while receiving TMS (Pittenger & Bloch, 2014). The idea behind this strategy is that TMS may be able to intervene when certain maladaptive circuitry involved in OCD symptoms is activated more effectively. This is in fact the idea behind the current FDA-approved use of TMS in OCD (see Carmi et al., 2018). Further investigation is critical for characterizing efficacious target regions, stimulation parameters, and the appropriate treatment population(s) and strategies for this promising tool.

Adverse Effects. Reported adverse effects of rTMS include transient effects, such as headache (the most commonly reported adverse effect), scalp discomfort, weepiness, twitching of the facial muscles, hearing changes, and dizziness (Bais et al., 2014; Voelker, 2018). High-frequency TMS carries the risk of inducing seizures, but a case of seizure caused by rTMS in OCD has not been reported thus far. However, the rare phenomenon of seizure has been observed in TMS treatment of other illnesses (Bais et al., 2014; Rapinesi et al., 2019).

ECT

Although ECT has been used for many years to treat depression, its use in OCD has yielded less promising results (Bais et al., 2014). There are several case reports in the literature, but these studies had very small numbers and showed limited effect (Bais et al., 2014). The current consensus appears to be that ECT for OCD is generally ineffective for primary OCD symptoms, although it may improve symptoms that are secondary to severe comorbid psychiatric illnesses, such as depression, bipolar disorder, psychotic disorders, catatonia, or anorexia nervosa (Bais et al., 2014; Loi & Bonwick, 2010; Makhinson et al., 2012; Raveendranathan et al., 2012).

Models of OCD Brain Neurocircuitry

As techniques become more specific, researchers are beginning to develop more specific hypotheses regarding discrete neuroanatomical regions and their effects on cognition and behavior. Emerging research technology that allows investigators to interrogate functional neurocircuitry, combined with neurosurgery and nonsurgical neuromodulation, has uncovered and confirmed the involvement of brain regions and tracts in OCD pathology that empiric psychiatric neurosurgical studies initially implicated.

Individuals with OCD most likely have dysfunction in frontal-subcortical circuitry, especially between the OFC/cingulate and the thalamus and/or basal ganglia (Ahmari & Dougherty, 2015; Greenberg, Rauch, & Haber, 2010; Rasmussen et al., 2018). The current hypothesis on the neurobiology of OCD that is receiving increasing attention is the cortico-striato-thalamo-cortical (CSTC) loop model. Developed through a study using a collection of tools, including functional MRI (fMRI), structural MRI, positron emission tomography (PET), and diffusion imaging studies, the CSTC loop model describes interconnected loops that include the cortex, basal ganglia, thalamus, and amygdala to form functional circuits, and these circuits can be dysfunctional in OCD (Kopell et al., 2004; McGovern & Sheth, 2017; Wichmann & Delong, 2006). The lateral orbitofrontal loop, anterior cingulate loop, and Papez circuit are circuits in the CSTC model that are understood to be involved in OCD pathology (Kopell et al., 2004).

Numerous studies have shown elevated activity in the OFC and ACC in patients with OCD, and this observation has led to the development of hypotheses that hyperactivity in these regions and the shared neural circuitry gives rise to OCD (Ahmari & Dougherty, 2015; Camprodon et al., 2016; Greenberg, Rauch, et al., 2010; Kopell et al., 2004). It is hypothesized that the two regions work in tandem when an aberrant positive feedback loop develops in the frontothalamic neuronal pathways and leads to inadequate inhibition of the OFC and thalamus. The Papez circuit, long implicated in anxiety and negative valence states, is interconnected with the OFC and the amygdala (Kopell et al., 2004). These regions, and indeed this hypothesis, explain OCD in part because studies have demonstrated the proposed hyperactivity at baseline, during symptom provocation to some extent, and after pharmacological, behavioral, and surgical intervention (Ahmari & Dougherty, 2015; Banks et al., 2015; Hartmann et al., 2015; Nakao et al., 2005; Rauch et al., 1997, 2006).

Studies in neurosurgical patients have been particularly valuable in developing this hypothesis because neurosurgical interventions represent specific, measurable manipulations of the implicated circuitry. For instance, some pilot studies with FDG-PET have found decreased metabolism in the anterior cingulate, OFC, and caudate nucleus after bilateral capsulotomy, bringing metabolism to levels comparable with controls (Liu et al., 2008). Research using FDG-PET has shown decreased metabolism in the frontal cortex after months of ventral capsule DBS (Nuttin et al., 2008). There is also activation of the OFC, ACC, striatum, pallidum, and thalamus on perfusion PET during acute stimulation at the VC/VS site compared to sham and/or low-frequency (5-Hz) DBS (Rauch et al., 2006).

The decades-long search for neural circuits and anatomical loci involved in OCD pathology has been fruitful, aided by modern neuroscience tools, but an understanding of the neural activity in these circuits and how they give rise to OCD phenotypes remains elusive. Indeed, the next frontier in OCD is uncovering electrophysiological biomarker(s) of the disease, and the biological approaches to OCD discussed in this chapter are promising interventions that are being used to develop an improved understanding of the functional circuitry of the disease.

Conclusions and Future Directions

Initial forays into neurosurgery for psychiatric disorders began over a century ago. The mid-twentieth century witnessed the indiscriminate use of a crude freehand procedure, prefrontal lobotomy, in an era of otherwise pervasive therapeutic nihilism. Recently, however, neurosurgery has been the focus of renewed interest and a more rigorous approach to research, yet the state of knowledge remains incomplete. While the safety of the procedures in current use has improved substantially, the potential for adverse effects remains for both lesion procedures and deep brain stimulation. We are still in the early stages of determining the degree of clinical effectiveness of these procedures, their associated burdens, and the mechanisms that may underlie their actions. This is particularly true for the more recently developed modalities, such as TMS, although TMS is amenable to application in a wide range of patients. Fortunately, an understanding of the mechanisms of therapeutic benefit is not a prerequisite for careful clinical use of the safest procedures at expert centers. The key clinical questions are: Do the procedures help some otherwise untreatable people? Are the procedures' adverse-effect profiles acceptable in the context of the probable benefit?

Improving treatment modalities, including neurosurgery, for OCD will depend on a better understanding of the mediating mechanisms at the anatomical, pharmacological, and behavioral levels. In the realm of behavior, it will be important to further explore the strong clinical impression that behavior therapy for OCD is facilitated by neurosurgery in patients who were not helped by rigorous behavioral approaches before surgery. Additional knowledge on all levels, gained by continuing clinical and translational research, should enable us to determine the best candidates for existing biological approaches and other procedures in development.

References

Abelson, J. L., Curtis, G. C., Sagher, O., Albucher, R. C., Harrigan, M., Taylor, S. F., Martis, B., & Giordani, B. (2005). Deep brain stimulation for refractory obsessive-compulsive disorder. *Biological Psychiatry, 57*(5), 510–516.

Ahmari, S. E., & Dougherty, D. D. (2015). Dissecting OCD circuits: From animal models to targeted treatments. *Depression and Anxiety, 32*(8), 550–562.

Andrei Novac, R. G. B. (2014). Transprocessing: A proposed neurobiological mechanism of psychotherapeutic processing. *Mental Illness, 6*(5077), 20–35.

Asaad, W. F., & McLaughlin, N. C. R. (2020). LITT for intractable psychiatric disease. In V. L. Chiang, S. F. Danish, & R. E. Gross (Eds.), *Laser interstitial thermal therapy in neurosurgery* (pp. 119–126). Springer.

Bais, M., Figee, M., & Denys, D. (2014). Neuromodulation in obsessive-compulsive disorder. *The Psychiatric Clinics of North America, 37*(3), 393–413.

Ballantine, H. T., Jr., Cassidy, W. L., Flanagan, N. B., & Marino, R., Jr. (1967). Stereotaxic anterior cingulotomy for neuropsychiatric illness and intractable pain. *Journal of Neurosurgery, 26*(5), 488–495.

Banks, G. P., Mikell, C. B., Youngerman, B. E., Henriques, B., Kelly, K. M., Chan, A. K., Herrera, D., Dougherty, D. D., Eskandar, E. N., & Sheth, S. A. (2015). Neuroanatomical characteristics associated with response to dorsal anterior cingulotomy for obsessive-compulsive disorder. *JAMA Psychiatry, 72*(2), 127–135.

Barrett, K. (2017). Psychiatric neurosurgery in the 21st century: Overview and the growth of deep brain stimulation. *BJPsych Bulletin, 41*(5), 281.

Barrios-Anderson, A., & McLaughlin, N. C. R. (2020). Obsessive-compulsive disorder: Lesions. In N. Pouratain & S. A. Sheth (Eds.), *Stereotactic and functional neurosurgery* (pp. 445–456). Springer.

Batistuzzo, M. C., Hoexter, M. Q., Taub, A., Gentil, A. F., Cesar, R. C. C., Joaquim, M. A., D'Alcante, C. C., McLaughlin, N. C., Canteras, M. M., Shavitt, R. G., Savage, C. R., Greenberg, B. D., Norén, G., Miguel, E. C., & Lopes, A. C. (2015). Visuospatial memory improvement after gamma ventral capsulotomy in treatment refractory obsessive-compulsive disorder patients. *Neuropsychopharmacology, 40*(8), 1837–1845.

Berlim, M. T., Neufeld, N. H., & den Eynde, F. V. (2013). Repetitive transcranial magnetic stimulation (rTMS) for obsessive-compulsive disorder (OCD): An exploratory meta-analysis of randomized and sham-controlled trials. *Journal of Psychiatric Research, 47*(8), 999–1006.

Bourne, S. K., Sheth, S. A., Neal, J., Strong, C., Mian, M. K., Cosgrove, G. R., Eskandar, E. N., & Dougherty, D. D. (2013). Beneficial effect of subsequent lesion procedures after nonresponse to initial cingulotomy for severe, treatment-refractory obsessive-compulsive disorder. *Neurosurgery, 72*(2), 196–202.

Bridges, P. K., Bartlett, J. R., Hale, A. S., Poynton, A. M., Malizia, A. L., & Hodgkiss, A. D. (1994). Psychosurgery: Stereotactic subcaudate tractomy—An indispensable treatment. *The British Journal of Psychiatry, 165*(5), 599–613.

Brown, L. T., Mikell, C. B., Youngerman, B. E., Zhang, Y., McKhann, G. M., & Sheth, S. A. (2016). Dorsal anterior cingulotomy and anterior capsulotomy for severe, refractory obsessive-compulsive disorder: A systematic review of observational studies. *Journal of Neurosurgery, 124*(1), 77–89.

Cabrera, L. Y., Courchesne, C., Kiss, Z. H. T., & Illes, J. (2019). Clinical perspectives on psychiatric neurosurgery. *Stereotactic and Functional Neurosurgery, 97*(5–6), 391–398.

Camprodon, J. A., Rauch, S. L., Greenberg, B. D., & Dougherty, D. D. (2016). *Psychiatric neurotherapeutics: Contemporary surgical and device-based treatments.* Humana Press.

Carmi, L., Alyagon, U., Barnea-Ygael, N., Zohar, J., Dar, R., & Zangen, A. (2018). Clinical and electrophysiological outcomes of deep TMS over the medial prefrontal and anterior cingulate cortices in OCD patients. *Brain Stimulation, 11*(1), 158–165.

Cho, D. Y., Lee, W. Y., & Chen, C. C. (2008). Limbic leukotomy for intractable major affective disorders: A 7-year follow-up study using nine comprehensive psychiatric test evaluations. *Journal of Clinical Neuroscience, 15*(2), 138–142.

Cocchi, L., Zalesky, A., Nott, Z., Whybird, G., Fitzgerald, P. B., & Breakspear, M. (2018). Transcranial magnetic stimulation in obsessive-compulsive disorder: A focus on network mechanisms and state dependence. *NeuroImage: Clinical, 19*, 661.

Cormier, J., Iorio-Morin, C., Mathieu, D., & Ducharme, S. (2019). Psychiatric neurosurgery: A survey on the perceptions of psychiatrists and residents. *The Canadian Journal of Neurological Sciences, 46*(3), 303–310.

Denys, D., Mantione, M., Figee, M., van den Munckhof, P., Koerselman, F., Westenberg, H., Bosch, A., & Schuurman, R. (2010). Deep brain stimulation of the nucleus accumbens for treatment-refractory obsessive-compulsive disorder. *Archives of General Psychiatry, 67*(10), 1061–1068.

Dold, M., Aigner, M., Lanzenberger, R., & Kasper, S. (2013). Antipsychotic augmentation of serotonin reuptake inhibitors in treatment-resistant obsessive-compulsive disorder: A meta-analysis of double-blind, randomized, placebo-controlled trials. *The International Journal of Neuropsychopharmacology, 16*(3), 557–574.

Doshi, P. K. (2009). Surgical treatment of obsessive-compulsive disorders: Current status. *Indian Journal of Psychiatry, 51*(3), 216.

El-Hai, J. (2007). *The lobotomist: A maverick medical genius and his tragic quest to rid the world of mental illness*. John Wiley & Sons.

Feldman, R. P., Alterman, R. L., & Goodrich, J. T. (2001). Contemporary psychosurgery and a look to the future. *Journal of Neurosurgery*, *95*(6), 944–956.

Fins, J. J., Rezai, A. R., & Greenberg, B. D. (2006). Psychosurgery: Avoiding an ethical redux while advancing a therapeutic future. *Neurosurgery*, *59*(4), 713–716.

Fodstad, H., Strandman, E., Karlsson, B., & West, K. A. (1982). Treatment of chronic obsessive-compulsive states with stereotactic anterior capsulotomy or cingulotomy. *Acta Neurochirurgica*, *62*(1–2), 1–23.

Garnaat, S. L., Greenberg, B. D., Sibrava, N. J., Goodman, W. K., Mancebo, M. C., Eisen, J. L., & Rasmussen, S. A. (2014). Who qualifies for deep brain stimulation for OCD? Data from a naturalistic clinical sample. *The Journal of Neuropsychiatry and Clinical Neurosciences*, *26*(1), 81–86.

George, M. S., Ward, H. E., Ninan, P. T., Pollack, M., Nahas, Z., Anderson, B., Kose, S., Howland, R. H., Goodman, W. K., & Ballenger, J. C. (2008). A pilot study of vagus nerve stimulation (VNS) for treatment-resistant anxiety disorders. *Brain Stimulation*, *1*(2), 112–121.

Gildenberg, P. L. (2001). Spiegel and Wycis—The early years. *Stereotactic and Functional Neurosurgery*, *77*(1–4), 11–16.

Göktepe, E. O., Young, L. B., & Bridges, P. K. (1975). A further review of the results of stereotactic subcaudate tractotomy. *The British Journal of Psychiatry*, *126*, 270–280.

Gomes, P. V. O., Brasil-Neto, J. P., Allam, N., & Rodrigues de Souza, E. (2012). A randomized, double-blind trial of repetitive transcranial magnetic stimulation in obsessive-compulsive disorder with three-month follow-up. *The Journal of Neuropsychiatry and Clinical Neurosciences*, *24*(4), 437–443.

Goodman, W. K., & Insel, T. R. (2009). Deep brain stimulation in psychiatry: Concentrating on the road ahead. *Biological Psychiatry*, *65*(4), 263–266.

Goodman, W. K., Storch, E. A., Cohn, J. F., & Sheth, S. A. (2020). Deep brain stimulation for intractable obsessive-compulsive disorder: Progress and opportunities [Review of *Deep brain stimulation for intractable obsessive-compulsive disorder: Progress and opportunities*]. *The American Journal of Psychiatry*, *177*(3), 200–203.

Greenberg, B. D., Gabriels, L. A., Malone, D. A., Jr., Rezai, A. R., Friehs, G. M., Okun, M. S., Shapira, N. A., Foote, K. D., Cosyns, P. R., Kubu, C. S., Malloy, P. F., Salloway, S. P., Giftakis, J. E., Rise, M. T., Machado, A. G., Baker, K. B., Stypulkowski, P. H., Goodman, W. K., Rasmussen, S. A., & Nuttin, B. J. (2010). Deep brain stimulation of the ventral internal capsule/ventral striatum for obsessive-compulsive disorder: Worldwide experience. *Molecular Psychiatry*, *15*(1), 64–79.

Greenberg, B. D., George, M. S., Martin, J. D., Benjamin, J., Schlaepfer, T. E., Altemus, M., Wassermann, E. M., Post, R. M., & Murphy, D. L. (1997). Effect of prefrontal repetitive transcranial magnetic stimulation in obsessive-compulsive disorder: A preliminary study. *The American Journal of Psychiatry*, *154*(6), 867–869.

Greenberg, B. D., Malone, D. A., Friehs, G. M., Rezai, A. R., Kubu, C. S., Malloy, P. F., Salloway, S. P., Okun, M. S., Goodman, W. K., & Rasmussen, S. A. (2006). Three-year outcomes in deep brain stimulation for highly resistant obsessive-compulsive disorder. *Neuropsychopharmacology*, *31*(11), 2384–2393.

Greenberg, B. D., Rauch, S. L., & Haber, S. N. (2010). Invasive circuitry-based neurotherapeutics: Stereotactic ablation and deep brain stimulation for OCD. *Neuropsychopharmacology*, *35*(1), 317–336.

Haq, I. U., Foote, K. D., Goodman, W. K., Ricciuti, N., Ward, H., Sudhyadhom, A., Jacobson, C. E., Siddiqui, M. S., & Okun, M. S. (2010). A case of mania following deep brain stimulation for obsessive compulsive disorder. *Stereotactic and Functional Neurosurgery*, *88*(5), 322–328.

Harris, L., & Das, J. M. (2020). Stereotactic radiosurgery. Treasure Island (FL): StatPearls Publishing. *StatPearls*.

Hartmann, C. J., Lujan, J. L., Chaturvedi, A., Goodman, W. K., Okun, M. S., McIntyre, C. C., & Haq, I. U. (2015). Tractography activation patterns in dorsolateral prefrontal cortex suggest better clinical responses in OCD DBS. *Frontiers in Neuroscience*, *9*, 519.

Hasegawa, H., Yamamoto, M., Shin, M., & Barfod, B. E. (2019). Gamma knife radiosurgery for brain vascular malformations: Current evidence and future tasks. *Therapeutics and Clinical Risk Management*, *15*, 1351.

Hirschtritt, M. E., Bloch, M. H., & Mathews, C. A. (2017). Obsessive-compulsive disorder: Advances in diagnosis and treatment. *JAMA*, *317*(13), 1358–1367.

Jiménez, F., Nicolini, H., Lozano, A. M., Piedimonte, F., Salín, R., & Velasco, F. (2013). Electrical stimulation of the inferior thalamic peduncle in the treatment of major depression and obsessive compulsive disorders. *World Neurosurgery*, *80*(3–4), S30.e17–e25.

Karas, P. J., Lee, S., Jimenez-Shahed, J., Goodman, W. K., Viswanathan, A., & Sheth, S. A. (2019). Deep brain stimulation for obsessive compulsive disorder: Evolution of surgical stimulation target parallels changing model of dysfunctional brain circuits. *Frontiers in Neuroscience, 12*, 998.

Kelly, D., Richardson, A., & Mitchell-Heggs, N. (1973). Stereotactic limbic leucotomy: Neurophysiological aspects and operative technique. *The British Journal of Psychiatry, 123*(573), 133–140.

Kelly, D., Walter, C. J., Mitchell-Heggs, N., & Sargant, W. (1972). Modified leucotomy assessed clinically, physiologically and psychologically at six weeks and eighteen months. *The British Journal of Psychiatry, 120*(554), 19–29.

Kim, M.-C., & Lee, T.-K. (2008). Stereotactic lesioning for mental illness. *Acta Neurochirurgica, 101*(Suppl.), 39–43.

Kim, S. J., Roh, D., Jung, H. H., Chang, W. S., Kim, C.-H., & Chang, J. W. (2018). A study of novel bilateral thermal capsulotomy with focused ultrasound for treatment-refractory obsessive-compulsive disorder: 2-year follow-up. *Journal of Psychiatry & Neuroscience, 43*(5), 327–337.

Knight, G. (1965). Stereotactic tractotomy in the surgical treatment of mental illness. *Journal of Neurology, Neurosurgery, and Psychiatry, 28*, 304–310.

Knight, G. (1973). Further observations from an experience of 660 cases of stereotactic tractotomy. *Postgraduate Medical Journal, 49*(578), 845–854.

Kopell, B. H., Greenberg, B., & Rezai, A. R. (2004). Deep brain stimulation for psychiatric disorders. *Journal of Clinical Neurophysiology, 21*(1), 51–67.

Kumar, K. K., Appelboom, G., Lamsam, L., Caplan, A. L., Williams, N. R., Bhati, M. T., Stein, S. C., & Halpern, C. H. (2019). Comparative effectiveness of neuroablation and deep brain stimulation for treatment-resistant obsessive-compulsive disorder: A meta-analytic study. *Journal of Neurology, Neurosurgery, and Psychiatry, 90*(4), 469–473.

Liu, K., Zhang, H., Liu, C., Guan, Y., Lang, L., Cheng, Y., Sun, B., Wang, H., Zuo, C., Pan, L., Xu, H., Li, S., Shi, L., Qian, J., & Yang, Y. (2008). Stereotactic treatment of refractory obsessive-compulsive disorder by bilateral capsulotomy with 3 years follow-up. *Journal of Clinical Neuroscience, 15*(6), 622–629.

Loi, S., & Bonwick, R. (2010). Electroconvulsive therapy for treatment of late-onset obsessive compulsive disorder. *International Psychogeriatrics, 22*(5), 830–831.

Lopes, A. C., de Mathis, M. E., Canteras, M. M., Salvajoli, J. V., Del Porto, J. A., & Miguel, E. C. (2004). [Update on neurosurgical treatment for obsessive compulsive disorder.] *Revista Brasileira de Psiquiatria, 26*(1), 62–66.

Lopes, A. C., Greenberg, B. D., Canteras, M. M., Batistuzzo, M. C., Hoexter, M. Q., Gentil, A. F., Pereira, C. A. B., Joaquim, M. A., de Mathis, M. E., D'Alcante, C. C., Taub, A., de Castro, D. G., Tokeshi, L., Sampaio, L. A. N. P. C., Leite, C. C., Shavitt, R. G., Diniz, J. B., Busatto, G., Norén, G., ... Miguel, E. C. (2014). Gamma ventral capsulotomy for obsessive-compulsive disorder: A randomized clinical trial. *JAMA Psychiatry, 71*(9), 1066–1076.

Lopes, A. C., Greenberg, B. D., Pereira, C. A. B., Norén, G., & Miguel, E. C. (2015). Notice of retraction and replacement. Lopes et al. Gamma ventral capsulotomy for obsessive-compulsive disorder: A randomized clinical trial. JAMA Psychiatry. 2014;71(9):1066–1076 [Review of *Notice of retraction and replacement. Lopes et al. Gamma ventral capsulotomy for obsessive-compulsive disorder: A randomized clinical trial. JAMA Psychiatry. 2014;71(9):1066–1076*]. *JAMA Psychiatry, 72*(12), 1258.

Lusicic, A., Schruers, K. R. J., Pallanti, S., & Castle, D. J. (2018). Transcranial magnetic stimulation in the treatment of obsessive-compulsive disorder: Current perspectives. *Neuropsychiatric Disease and Treatment, 14*, 1721.

Luyten, L., Hendrickx, S., Raymaekers, S., Gabriëls, L., & Nuttin, B. (2015). Electrical stimulation in the bed nucleus of the stria terminalis alleviates severe obsessive-compulsive disorder. *Molecular Psychiatry, 21*(9), 1272–1280.

Makhinson, M., Furst, B. A., Shuff, M. K., & Kwon, G. E. (2012). Successful treatment of co-occurring catatonia and obsessive-compulsive disorder with concurrent electroconvulsive therapy and benzodiazepine administration. *The Journal of ECT, 28*(3), e35–e36.

Mallet, L., Polosan, M., Jaafari, N., Baup, N., Welter, M. L., Fontaine, D., du Montcel, S. T., Yelnik, J., Chéreau, I., Arbus, C., Raoul, S., Aouizerate, B., Damier, P., Chabardès, S., Czernecki, V., Ardouin, C., Krebs, M. O., Bardinet, E., Chaynes, P., ... Pelissolo, A. (2008). Subthalamic nucleus stimulation in severe obsessive-compulsive disorder. *The New England Journal of Medicine, 359*(20), 2121–2134.

Manjila, S., Rengachary, S., Xavier, A. R., Parker, B., & Guthikonda, M. (2008). Modern psychosurgery before Egas Moniz: A tribute to Gottlieb Burckhardt. *Neurosurgical Focus*, *25*(1), E9.

McGovern, R. A., & Sheth, S. A. (2017). Role of the dorsal anterior cingulate cortex in obsessive-compulsive disorder: Converging evidence from cognitive neuroscience and psychiatric neurosurgery. *Journal of Neurosurgery*, *126*(1), 132–147.

McLaughlin, N. C. R., Lauro, P. M., Patrick, M. T., Pucci, F. G., Barrios-Anderson, A., Greenberg, B. D., Rasmussen, S. A., & Asaad, W. F. (2021). Magnetic resonance imaging-guided laser thermal ventral capsulotomy for intractable obsessive-compulsive disorder. *Neurosurgery*, *88*(6), 1128–1135.

Miguel, E. C., Lopes, A. C., McLaughlin, N. C. R., Norén, G., Gentil, A. F., Hamani, C., Shavitt, R. G., Batistuzzo, M. C., Vattimo, E. F. Q., Canteras, M., De Salles, A., Gorgulho, A., Salvajoli, J. V., Fonoff, E. T., Paddick, I., Hoexter, M. Q., Lindquist, C., Haber, S. N., Greenberg, B. D., & Sheth, S. A. (2019). Evolution of gamma knife capsulotomy for intractable obsessive-compulsive disorder. *Molecular Psychiatry*, *24*(2), 218–240.

Nair, G., Evans, A., Bear, R. E., Velakoulis, D., & Bittar, R. G. (2014). The anteromedial GPi as a new target for deep brain stimulation in obsessive compulsive disorder. *Journal of Clinical Neuroscience*, *21*(5), 815–821.

Nakao, T., Nakagawa, A., Yoshiura, T., Nakatani, E., Nabeyama, M., Yoshizato, C., Kudoh, A., Tada, K., Yoshioka, K., Kawamoto, M., Togao, O., & Kanba, S. (2005). Brain activation of patients with obsessive-compulsive disorder during neuropsychological and symptom provocation tasks before and after symptom improvement: A functional magnetic resonance imaging study. *Biological Psychiatry*, *57*(8), 901–910.

Nuttin, B., Cosyns, P., Demeulemeester, H., Gybels, J., & Meyerson, B. (1999). Electrical stimulation in anterior limbs of internal capsules in patients with obsessive-compulsive disorder. *Lancet*, *354*(9189), 1526.

Nuttin, B. J., Gabriëls, L. A., Cosyns, P. R., Meyerson, B. A., Andréewitch, S., Sunaert, S. G., Maes, A. F., Dupont, P. J., Gybels, J. M., Gielen, F., & Demeulemeester, H. G. (2008). Long-term electrical capsular stimulation in patients with obsessive-compulsive disorder. *Neurosurgery*, *62*(6 Suppl. 3), 966–977.

OCD-DBS Collaborative Group. (2002). Deep brain stimulation for psychiatric disorders. *Neurosurgery*, *51*(2), 519.

Paiva, R. R., Batistuzzo, M. C., McLaughlin, N. C., Canteras, M. M., de Mathis, M. E., Requena, G., Shavitt, R. G., Greenberg, B. D., Norén, G., Rasmussen, S. A., Tavares, H., Miguel, E. C., Lopes, A. C., & Hoexter, M. Q. (2018). Personality measures after gamma ventral capsulotomy in intractable OCD. *Progress in Neuro-Psychopharmacology & Biological Psychiatry*, *81*, 161–168.

Pittenger, C., & Bloch, M. H. (2014). Pharmacological treatment of obsessive-compulsive disorder. *The Psychiatric Clinics of North America*, *37*(3), 375.

Pool, J. L. (1954). Psychosurgery in older people. *Journal of the American Geriatrics Society*, *2*(7), 456–466.

Pribram, K. H., & Fulton, J. F. (1954). An experimental critique of the effects of anterior cingulate ablations in monkey. *Brain*, *77*(1), 34–44.

Provenza, N. R., Matteson, E. R., Allawala, A. B., Barrios-Anderson, A., Sheth, S. A., Viswanathan, A., McIngvale, E., Storch, E. A., Frank, M. J., McLaughlin, N. C. R., Cohn, J. F., Goodman, W. K., & Borton, D. A. (2019). The case for adaptive neuromodulation to treat severe intractable mental disorders. *Frontiers in Neuroscience*, *13*, 152.

Quadri, S. A., Waqas, M., Khan, I., Khan, M. A., Suriya, S. S., Farooqui, M., & Fiani, B. (2018). High-intensity focused ultrasound: Past, present, and future in neurosurgery. *Neurosurgical Focus*, *44*(2), E16.

Rapinesi, C., Kotzalidis, G. D., Ferracuti, S., Sani, G., Girardi, P., & Del Casale, A. (2019). Brain stimulation in obsessive-compulsive disorder (OCD): A systematic review. *Current Neuropharmacology*, *17*(8), 787.

Rasmussen, S. A., Noren, G., Greenberg, B. D., Marsland, R., McLaughlin, N. C., Malloy, P. J., Salloway, S. P., Strong, D. R., Eisen, J. L., Jenike, M. A., Rauch, S. L., Baer, L., & Lindquist, C. (2018). Gamma ventral capsulotomy in intractable obsessive-compulsive disorder. *Biological Psychiatry*, *84*(5), 355–364.

Rauch, S. L., Dougherty, D. D., Malone, D., Rezai, A., Friehs, G., Fischman, A. J., Alpert, N. M., Haber, S. N., Stypulkowski, P. H., Rise, M. T., Rasmussen, S. A., & Greenberg, B. D. (2006). A functional neuroimaging investigation of deep brain stimulation in patients with obsessive-compulsive disorder. *Journal of Neurosurgery*, *104*(4), 558–565.

Rauch, S. L., Savage, C. R., Alpert, N. M., Fischman, A. J., & Jenike, M. A. (1997). The functional neuroanatomy of anxiety: A study of three disorders using positron emission tomography and symptom provocation. *Biological Psychiatry*, *42*(6), 446–452.

Raveendranathan, D., Srinivasaraju, R., Ratheesh, A., Math, S. B., & Reddy, Y. C. J. (2012). Treatment-refractory OCD responding to maintenance electroconvulsive therapy. *The Journal of Neuropsychiatry and Clinical Neurosciences, 24*(2), E16–E17.

Rück, C., Karlsson, A., Steele, J. D., Edman, G., Meyerson, B. A., Ericson, K., Nyman, H., Asberg, M., & Svanborg, P. (2008). Capsulotomy for obsessive-compulsive disorder: Long-term follow-up of 25 patients. *Archives of General Psychiatry, 65*(8), 914–921.

Rück, C., Larsson, J. K., Mataix-Cols, D., & Ljung, R. (2017). A register-based 13-year to 43-year follow-up of 70 patients with obsessive-compulsive disorder treated with capsulotomy. *BMJ Open, 7*(5), E013133.

Ruffini, C., Locatelli, M., Lucca, A., Benedetti, F., Insacco, C., & Smeraldi, E. (2009). Augmentation effect of repetitive transcranial magnetic stimulation over the orbitofrontal cortex in drug-resistant obsessive-compulsive disorder patients: A controlled investigation. *Primary Care Companion to the Journal of Clinical Psychiatry, 11*(5), 226–230.

Shah, D. B., Pesiridou, A., Baltuch, G. H., Malone, D. A., & O'Reardon, J. P. (2008). Functional neurosurgery in the treatment of severe obsessive-compulsive disorder and major depression: Overview of disease circuits and therapeutic targeting for the clinician. *Psychiatry, 5*(9), 24.

Sheth, S. A., Neal, J., Tangherlini, F., Mian, M. K., Gentil, A., Rees Cosgrove, G., Eskandar, E. N., & Dougherty, D. D. (2013). Limbic system surgery for treatment-refractory obsessive-compulsive disorder: A prospective long-term follow-up of 64 patients; Clinical article. *Journal of Neurosurgery, 118*(3), 491–497.

Sinha, S., McGovern, R. A., Mikell, C. B., Banks, G. P., & Sheth, S. A. (2015). Ablative limbic system surgery: Review and future directions. *Current Behavioral Neuroscience Reports, 2*(2), 49–59.

Spatola, G., Martinez-Alvarez, R., Martínez-Moreno, N., Rey, G., Linera, J., Rios-Lago, M., Sanz, M., Gutiérrez, J., Vidal, P., Richieri, R., & Régis, J. (2018). Results of gamma knife anterior capsulotomy for refractory obsessive-compulsive disorder: Results in a series of 10 consecutive patients. *Journal of Neurosurgery, 131*(2), 376–383.

Spiegel, E. A., Wycis, H. T., & Freed, H. (1952). Stereoencephalotomy: Thalamotomy and related procedures. *JAMA, 148*(6), 446–451.

Stein, D. J., Costa, D. L. C., Lochner, C., Miguel, E. C., Janardhan Reddy, Y. C., Shavitt, R. G., van den Heuvel, O. A., & Simpson, H. B. (2019). Obsessive-compulsive disorder. *Nature Reviews Disease Primers, 5*(1), 52.

Stone, J. L. (2001). Dr. Gottlieb Burckhardt—The pioneer of psychosurgery. *Journal of the History of the Neurosciences, 10*(1), 79–92.

Tavakol, S., Jackanich, A., Strickland, B. A., Marietta, M., Ravina, K., Yu, C., Chang, E. L., Giannotta, S., & Zada, G. (2020). Effectiveness of gamma knife radiosurgery in the treatment of refractory trigeminal neuralgia: A case series. *Operative Neurosurgery, 18*(6), 571–576.

United States Department of Health, Education, and Welfare. (1978). Determination of Secretary regarding recommendation on psychosurgery of the National Commission for the Protection of Human Subjects of Biomedical and Behavioral Research. *Federal Register, 43*(221), 53241–53244.

Valenstein, E. S., & Valenstein, E. S. (1974). *Brain control: A critical examination of brain stimulation and psychosurgery*. Wiley-Interscience.

Voelker, R. (2018). Brain stimulation approved for obsessive-compulsive disorder. *JAMA, 320*(11), 1098.

Wichmann, T., & Delong, M. R. (2006). Deep brain stimulation for neurologic and neuropsychiatric disorders. *Neuron, 52*(1), 197–204.

Woerdeman, P. A., Willems, P. W. A., Noordmans, H. J., Berkelbach van der Sprenkel, J. W., & van Rijen, P. C. (2006). Frameless stereotactic subcaudate tractotomy for intractable obsessive-compulsive disorder. *Acta Neurochirurgica, 148*(6), 633–637.

Yang, J. C., Papadimitriou, G., Eckbo, R., Yeterian, E. H., Liang, L., Dougherty, D. D., Bouix, S., Rathi, Y., Shenton, M., Kubicki, M., Eskandar, E. N., & Makris, N. (2015). Multi-tensor investigation of orbitofrontal cortex tracts affected in subcaudate tractotomy. *Brain Imaging and Behavior, 9*(2), 342–352.

CHAPTER 19

Exposure-Based Treatment for Obsessive-Compulsive Disorder

Jonathan S. Abramowitz, Steven Taylor, *and* Dean McKay

Abstract

Exposure and response prevention (E/RP) is one of the oldest and most effective treatments for obsessive-compulsive disorder. The present chapter describes the empirical foundations, development, delivery, and latest research on E/RP. Commonly used methods and procedural variants of E/RP are described, along with the underlying mechanisms of action. The efficacy of E/RP in relation to other treatments is discussed, in addition to research on the long-term effects of E/RP and its effects in non-research settings. Pretreatment predictors of the outcome of using E/RP are also considered. Efforts to improve treatment outcome are discussed, such as research into the benefits of including a spouse or partner in E/RP. The chapter concludes by considering important future research directions for improving the outcome of treatment packages that include E/RP.

Key Words: exposure and response prevention, inhibitory learning, fear extinction, obsessive-compulsive disorder, serotonin reuptake inhibitors

Obsessive-compulsive disorder (OCD) involves excessive fear and anxiety that the person tries to control or to remove by using strategies that paradoxically maintain the fear and anxiety. The anxiety in OCD is triggered by obsessions, which are recurrent, unwanted, and seemingly bizarre thoughts, impulses, or doubts (e.g., the thought that one might have struck a pedestrian with an automobile). The anxiety-reduction strategies are typically repetitive (compulsive) behavioral or mental rituals (e.g., constantly checking the rear-view mirror for injured persons). Obsessional fears tend to focus on uncertainty about personal safety or the safety of others, and they can take various forms and have numerous themes (e.g., contamination, violence, religion). Rituals are deliberately performed to reduce this uncertainty.

Although many OCD sufferers recognize (at least at some point during the course of their disorder) that their obsessional fears and rituals are senseless and excessive, others strongly believe that their rituals serve to prevent the occurrence of disastrous consequences; that is, they have poor insight (Foa et al., 1995). The patient's degree of insight can vary over time as well as across symptom categories. For example, one patient evaluated in our clinic realized that her fears of being contaminated by mercury if she changed a fluorescent light bulb were unrealistic (although she avoided fluorescent bulbs—just to be on the safe side), yet she was strongly convinced that if she didn't wash her hands after handling pieces of mail sent by her father, who had hepatitis, she would develop the disease as well.

The lifetime prevalence rate of OCD in adults is 2% to 3% (American Psychiatric Association, 2013). Although symptoms typically wax and wane as a function of general life stress, a chronic and deteriorating course is the norm if adequate treatment is not received. Fortunately, effective psychological treatments for OCD have been developed from empirical research on the nature of the problem. The best-studied psychotherapy takes a cognitive-behavioral approach involving two procedures: exposure and response prevention (E/RP). The present chapter provides an overview of the development and delivery of this therapy and reviews the latest treatment-related research.

History of Exposure-Based Treatments for OCD

Prior to the 1960s, treatment for OCD consisted largely of supportive therapy or psychodynamic psychotherapy derived from psychoanalytic ideas of unconscious motivation. The general consensus of clinicians of that time was that OCD was an unmanageable condition with a very poor prognosis, with some suggesting no treatment at all, because the interventions of the time only worsened the disorder (Kringlen, 1965). This characterization clearly shows the degree of confidence (or perhaps the lack thereof) clinicians had in psychodynamic treatments for OCD. Indeed, the available anecdotal reports suggest that the effects of the psychodynamic approach were neither robust nor durable. The few reports that included outcome data suggested that psychodynamic approaches worsened the condition (Christensen et al., 1987).

By the last quarter of the twentieth century, however, the prognosis for OCD had improved dramatically. This was due in large part to the work of Victor Meyer (1966) and other behaviorally oriented clinicians and researchers; they adapted animal laboratory research on fear reduction conducted in the first half of the century so that the strategies could be used to treat human anxiety problems. The behaviorists carefully derived behaviorally based therapy for OCD from this early experimental work. This historical event is discussed in detail here because it represents a model for the derivation of a treatment from existing experimental findings.

Early Laboratory Research

The work of Richard Solomon and his colleagues (Solomon et al., 1953) provided an elegant, yet often overlooked animal behavior model of what is now referred to as OCD. This model of compulsive behavior, and its reduction through behavioral methods, is probably the closest theoretical and practical antecedent of contemporary exposure-based therapy for OCD. Solomon et al. worked with dogs in shuttle boxes (which were small rooms divided in two by a hurdle over which the animal could jump). Each half of the shuttle box was separately furnished with an electric floor grating, which could be independently electrified to give the dog an electric shock. In addition, there was a flickering light, which served as a conditioned stimulus. The procedure for producing a compulsive ritual-like behavior was to pair the flickering light with an electric shock (the shock occurred 10 seconds after the light was turned on). The dog soon learned to jump into the other compartment of the shuttle box, which was not electrified, once he had received the shock. After several trials, the dog learned to successfully avoid the shock by jumping to the non-electrified compartment in response to the flickering light (i.e., within 10 seconds). In other words, the experimenter had produced a conditioned response to the light— namely, jumping from one compartment of the box to the other.

Once the conditioned response was established, the electricity was disconnected, and the dog never received another shock. Nevertheless, the animal continued to jump across the hurdle each time the conditioned stimulus (i.e., the light) was turned on, as if shock was imminent. This continued for hundreds (and in some cases, thousands) of trials, despite no actual risk of shock. Apparently, the dog had acquired an obsessive-compulsive habit—jumping across the hurdle—that was maintained by negative reinforcement (i.e., avoidance of pain and emotional distress). This serves as an animal analog to human OCD, wherein compulsive behavior is triggered by fear that is associated with situations or stimuli, such as toilets, floors, and obsessional thoughts (conditioned stimuli), which pose little or no objective risk of harm. The fear is reduced by avoidance and by compulsive rituals (e.g., washing) that serve as an escape from distress and thus are negatively reinforced (i.e., they become habitual).

Solomon's work provided experimental evidence for Mowrer's (1947, 1960) two-factor theory of the acquisition and maintenance of fear and avoidance behavior, which was adapted by Dollard and Miller (1950) to explain OCD from a human learning perspective. The first stage of the model (acquisition) involves classical conditioning: A neutral stimulus or event (e.g., leaving the house) comes to evoke obsessional fear by being paired with another stimulus that, by its nature, provokes discomfort or anxiety (e.g., the idea that a house fire could occur while no one is home). In the second stage (maintenance), active avoidance (e.g., unplugging electrical appliances) or passive avoidance (e.g., not using any appliances) is used to reduce the anxiety or discomfort associated with the conditioned stimulus, in this case, leaving the house. The avoidance behavior is negatively reinforced because it provides an immediate reduction in anxiety (operant conditioning). Thus, the avoidance becomes habitual.

Dollard and Miller (1950) explained the development of compulsive rituals by arguing that many obsessional stimuli, such as using the bathroom, leaving the house, and intrusive obsessional thoughts themselves, cannot be easily avoided because of their ubiquitous nature. Thus, compulsive rituals (e.g., washing, checking, neutralizing unacceptable thoughts) develop as active avoidance strategies to cope with anxiety and to restore a sense of safety. The rituals are therefore also maintained (negatively reinforced) because of their success in reducing obsessional fear. Although rituals provide a temporary respite from obsessional fear, they prevent the natural extinction of obsessional anxiety, thereby perpetuating the fear.

An Animal Model of Exposure-Based Therapy

Solomon and his colleagues also attempted to reduce the compulsive jumping behavior of their "obsessive-compulsive" dogs using various techniques, the most effective of which involved a combination of procedures we would now call E/RP. Specifically, the experimenter turned on the conditioned stimulus (the light; an in vivo exposure technique), and increased the height of the hurdle in the shuttle box so that the dog was unable to jump (response prevention). When this was done, the dog immediately showed signs of a strong fear response: running around the chamber, jumping on the walls, defecating, urinating, and yelping. Gradually, however, this emotional reaction subsided, until finally the dog displayed calmness without the slightest hint of distress. In behavioral terms, this experimental paradigm produced fear extinction. After several "extinction trials," the entire emotional response was extinguished, so that even when the light was turned on and the height of the hurdle was lowered, the dog did not attempt to jump.

Translational Research: From the Lab to the Clinic

During the 1960s and 1970s, behaviorally oriented researchers became interested in adapting similar treatment paradigms to human beings with OCD (for a review, see Rachman & Hodgson, 1980). Of course, no electric shocks were used, but the adaptation was as follows. After providing informed consent, patients with OCD who had handwashing rituals were seated at a table with a container of dirt and miscellaneous garbage. The experimenter, after placing his own hands in the mixture, asked the patient to do the same and explained that he or she would not be permitted to wash his or her hands for some length of time. When the patient began the procedure, increased anxiety, fear, and urges to wash his or her hands were (of course) observed. The increased distress was conceptualized as being akin to the dogs' response once the light was turned on and the hurdle had been increased in height, making jumping impossible. However, like the dogs, the patients eventually evidenced a substantial reduction in fear and urge to wash, thus demonstrating therapeutic extinction. The procedure was repeated on subsequent days; behavioral theory predicted that after some time, extinction would be complete and the OCD symptoms would be reduced.

Meyer was the first to apply this approach in the treatment of OCD, and he articulated the rationale for doing so eloquently from a cognitive-behavioral perspective:

> Learning theories take into account the mediation of responses by goal expectancies, developed from previously reinforcing situations. When these expectations are not fulfilled,

new expectancies may evolve, which, in turn, may mediate new behavior. Thus, if the obsessional is persuaded or forced to remain in feared situations and [is] prevented from carrying out the rituals, he may discover that the feared consequences no longer take place. Such modification of expectations should result in the cessation of ritualistic behavior. (Meyer, 1966, p. 275)

Essentially, Meyer argued that when a patient with OCD confronts his or her obsessional fear without performing rituals, estimates of the probability and costs of feared outcomes can be corrected, leading to the reduction of obsessive fear and ritualistic behavior. These procedures form the backbone of E/RP.

In Meyer's (1966) initial report on the use of E/RP, for two hours each day his patients deliberately confronted obsessional situations and stimuli they usually avoided (e.g., floors, bathrooms), while also refraining from compulsive rituals (e.g., no washing or checking). Most of the patients demonstrated at least partial improvement after treatment, and very few had relapsed at follow-up (Meyer et al., 1974). The interest generated by these initial findings led to additional studies in centers around the world using more advanced methodology in both inpatient and outpatient settings. Research conducted in the United Kingdom (Hodgson et al., 1972), Holland (Emmelkamp & Kraanen, 1977), Greece (Rabavilas et al., 1976), and the United States (Foa & Goldstein, 1978) with hundreds of patients and many therapists affirmed the beneficial effects and generalizability of exposure-based treatment for OCD. By the end of the 1980s, E/RP was widely considered the psychosocial treatment of choice for obsessions and compulsions.

Contemporary Exposure-Based Treatment

Contemporary E/RP entails therapist-guided, systematic, repeated, and prolonged exposure to situations that provoke obsessional fear. During the exposure trials, the patient is encouraged to refrain from performing compulsive behaviors. The exposure might take the form of either repeated actual confrontation with feared low-risk situations (i.e., in vivo exposure) or imaginal confrontation with the feared disastrous consequences of confronting the low-risk situations (imaginal exposure). For example, an individual who fears getting herpes from touching bathroom doors, and that she will die if she encounters the color red, would practice touching bathroom doors and imagining being diagnosed with herpes, as well as wearing red clothing and imagining her own death.

Refraining from performing compulsive rituals (response prevention) is a vital component of treatment because the performance of such rituals to reduce obsessional anxiety would prematurely discontinue exposure and rob the patient of learning that (a) the obsessional situation is not truly dangerous, and (b) the accompanying anxiety/uncertainty is safe, manageable, and will subside on its own even if the ritual is not performed. Thus, successful E/RP requires that the patient remain in the exposure situation, without attempting to reduce the distress, until the optimal conditions for such learning to occur have been achieved. For the individual described above, response prevention would entail refraining from handwashing after touching the bathroom door and refraining from any rituals designed to prevent death from exposure to the color red.

At the start of exposure tasks (situational and imaginal), the patient typically experiences a rapid elevation in subjective anxiety and physiological arousal. In fact, patients are often told that "bringing on" and "leaning into" their fear is an important part of optimizing the effects of E/RP. During the course of an exposure session, the subjective distress (and associated physiological responding) typically subsides (in a natural process known as habituation), even if the individual remains exposed to the feared stimulus. The success of E/RP, however, is not completely dependent on within- or between-session habituation, because some individuals experience habituation and do not improve.

Implementation of E/RP

Contemporary ERP can be delivered in several ways, including in the typical outpatient format (once a week or greater) and in day, partial hospitalization, and residential treatment settings. Typically, treatment involves a few hours of assessment, psychoeducation, and treatment planning, followed by 12 to 20 exposure trials, which can vary in length depending upon the nature of the particular exposure task (Abramowitz et al., 2003). Generally, the therapist supervises the patient by conducting exposure during the therapy sessions and assigns self-exposure practice to be completed by the patient between appointments. Depending on the patient's symptom presentation and the practicality of confronting actual feared situations, treatment sessions might involve varying amounts of situational and imaginal exposure practice. They might also involve leaving the therapist's office to confront stimuli for exposure (e.g., items in a grocery store).

A course of E/RP typically begins with the assessment of (a) obsessional thoughts, ideas, impulses, (b) stimuli that trigger the obsessions, (c) rituals and avoidance behavior, and (d) the anticipated harmful consequences of confronting feared situations without performing rituals. Before actual treatment commences, the therapist uses psychoeducational techniques to socialize the patient to a psychological model of OCD that is based on the principles of learning and emotion (Salkovskis, 1996). The patient is also given a clear rationale for how E/RP is expected to be helpful in reducing OCD. Conveying this information to the patient clearly and effectively is a critical step in therapy because it helps the patient develop the incentive to endure the discomfort that typically accompanies carrying out exposure exercises. A helpful rationale includes information about how E/RP involves learning new information: that feared situations are less dangerous than anticipated, and that anxiety, unwanted thoughts, and uncertainty are safe and manageable as well. Information gathered during the assessment sessions is then used to plan, collaboratively with the patient, the specific exposure exercises that will be practiced.

In addition to developing a list (sometimes called a hierarchy) of exposure exercises, the educational stage of E/RP also acquaints the patient with response prevention.

Importantly, the term "response prevention" does not imply that the therapist actively restrains the patient from performing rituals. Instead, the therapist must convince the patient to make the difficult decision to resist on their own even strong urges to perform rituals. Self-monitoring of rituals is often used in support of this goal.

In Vivo (Situational) Exposure

The exposure exercises themselves typically begin with the patient confronting moderately distressing situations and stimuli. Stimuli that trigger low levels of anxiety are left off the treatment plan since they would not teach the patient how to manage obsessional anxiety. The treatment plan may be arranged so that gradually the patient practices confronting more and more difficult situations, until the most distressing situations are presented, although research indicates that it is not essential to proceed hierarchically (Jacoby et al., 2019). Beginning with less anxiety-evoking exposure tasks, however, may increase confidence in the treatment and help the patient persevere during later, more difficult, exercises. The most feared items must be confronted in treatment to allow the patient to learn that even these stimuli are manageable and not dangerous.

Imaginal Exposure

In contrast to situational fear cues, which are often concrete, obsessional thoughts, ideas, and images are intangible, and therefore can be elusive targets when designing exposure. Although in vivo exposure often evokes obsessional thoughts, imaginal exposure provides a more systematic way of exposing the patient to the key fear-evoking elements of their obsessions. The recommended methods for conducting imaginal exposure include (a) using digital voice recorders or audiocassette tapes (continuous-loop tapes work especially well) or (b) written scripts containing the anxiety-evoking material (Abramowitz et al. , 2019). Both of these media allow for prolonged confrontation with an otherwise covert event and, if necessary, manipulation of the content of the stimulus. The use of a digital voice recorder or audio tape further ensures that unsupervised (homework) exposure will include confrontation with the correct stimuli.

Response Prevention

Response prevention, which is a necessary accessory to exposure in the treatment of OCD, entails resisting the urge to perform compulsive rituals and other safety-seeking or neutralizing behaviors that serve as an escape from obsessive fear (e.g., no handwashing after exposure to touching the floor). This allows prolonged exposure and facilitates safety learning as described previously. If the patient engages in compulsive rituals in an effort to reduce anxiety during exposure, the patient cannot learn that anxiety and feared situations are safe.

At the end of each treatment session, the therapist instructs the patient to continue exposure in different contexts, without the therapist. Any violations of response prevention rules are recorded by the patient on self-monitoring forms and are discussed with the therapist as areas in need of additional work. Exposure to the most anxiety-evoking situations is not left to the end of the treatment program, but instead is practiced about midway through the schedule of treatment sessions. This allows the patient ample opportunity to repeat exposure to the most difficult situations in different contexts, to allow generalization of treatment effects. During the later treatment sessions, the therapist emphasizes the importance of the patient's continuing to apply the E/RP procedures after treatment is complete.

Mechanisms Underlying the Effects of Exposure-Based Therapy

Two primary theoretical accounts have been proposed to explain the mechanism of action of exposure-based therapy for fear-related problems like OCD. While both models propose that exposure-based therapy leads to learning in one form or another, what exactly is learned and how it is learned differ across models.

Emotional-Processing Theory

Foa and Kozak (1986) attempted to explain the mechanisms of exposure therapy by building on the work of Rachman (1980) and Lang (1977), who proposed that fear is represented in memory as a network comprising (a) stimulus propositions that express information about feared cues, (b) response propositions that express information about behavioral and physiologic responses to these cues, and (c) meaning propositions that elaborate on the significance of other elements in the fear structure. Foa and Kozak likened this fear network to a computer program for avoiding threat in which pathological fear amounted to bugs in the program characterized by excessive response elements, resistance to change, and impairments in processing certain types of information about danger and safety. Exposure therapy, they proposed, amounted to reprogramming the computer to diminish fear by providing information incompatible with pathological aspects of the program.

Activating the fear network and incorporating incompatible information is referred to as emotional processing. Foa and Kozak (1986) proposed that emotional processing requires a close match between the feared stimulus and elements in the fear network. That is, the extent to which an exposure situation or image matches elements of the fear structure determines how accessible the fear program is for modification. They also asserted that successful exposure therapy depends on the patient's attending to the feared stimulus. Cognitive avoidance (i.e., distraction), on the other hand, would prevent activation of the fear structure and prevent new, nonfearful information from being incorporated.

Foa and Kozak (1986) also delineated three indicators of emotional processing: (a) activation of the fear network, as evidenced by an increase in fear; (b) decreases in the fear response during an exposure session (i.e., within-session habituation); and (c) a gradual decline in the peak anxiety level across exposure sessions (between-sessions habituation).

Further, they proposed that as emotional processing occurs, habituation of fear weakens associations between feared stimuli and fear responses, and that subjective estimates of the probability and severity of harm arising from the feared stimulus diminish.

The emotional-processing explanation is not without limitations, however. First, as McNally (2007) has pointed out, the propositional network characterization of fear appears to be circular, in that it merely rephrases the phenomenon it is designed to explain. For example, Foa and Kozak propose that response propositions regarding intrusive obsessional images are linked in the fear network with meaning propositions regarding danger. But this simply reiterates what astute clinicians already know: that people with OCD respond fearfully to their own intrusive thoughts and images, often misinterpreting them as threatening and as having implications for causing or preventing harm (Salkovskis, 1996). To assert that individuals with OCD are characterized by fear networks in which propositions about feared stimuli (e.g., intrusive thoughts) are linked to propositions about danger seems merely to restate clinical observations using a different terminology.

Research on learning and memory (LeDoux, 2000) also indicates that rather than "reprogramming," exposure therapy facilitates the generation of new safety-based learning, so that after exposure trials, a feared stimulus is associated with both its original (danger) meaning and its new inhibitory (safety) meaning. This explains the fact that even after seemingly sufficient habituation, obsessional fear may return. Thus, an updated inhibitory learning framework, which draws on experimental animal and human research on basic learning processes, has been proposed for understanding and implementing exposure (Craske et al., 2008).

Inhibitory Learning Theory

In an inhibitory learning framework, the aim of exposure therapy is to help patients generate and strengthen inhibitory associations relative to older, fearful associations. Although not altogether incongruous with emotional-processing theory, the inhibitory learning model is distinct, in that it rejects the emphasis on fear reduction (habituation) during exposure, focusing instead on short-term fear tolerance and the longer-term extinction of fear through the disconfirmation of threat-based expectations (Craske et al., 2008). There are several more or less specific clinical strategies for maximizing E/RP outcomes by optimizing inhibitory learning (discussed in detail in Jacoby & Abramowitz, 2016; but see also Abramowitz & Arch, 2014, and Arch & Abramowitz, 2015), and they converge to facilitate two critical treatment goals: the (a) violation of negative expectancies, and (b) generalization of inhibitory associations across multiple contexts.

VIOLATING NEGATIVE EXPECTANCIES

Violation of negative expectancies refers to the discrepancy between a patient's anticipated consequence of an exposure task (e.g., becoming violent as a result of thinking about committing harm) and the actual consequence (e.g., not harming anyone). Strong inhibitory associations may be generated by maximally violating a patient's fear-based predictions for harm (Rescorla, 1972). To this end, clinicians can maximize the likelihood that patients will be "pleasantly surprised" by the non-occurrence of their feared catastrophe by orchestrating opportunities for feared outcomes that are unlikely or impossible (e.g., causing "bad luck" by writing certain numbers), or at least tolerable (e.g., feeling uncertain). Specifically, clinicians can capitalize on the element of surprise by encouraging patients to conduct exposures at a greater level of intensity, duration, or frequency than the patient believes would be "safe."

A second strategy to generate inhibitory associations involves combining multiple fear cues during exposure to "deepen" extinction learning (Rescorla, 2006). This might involve helping someone who fears murdering a loved one (a) to conduct imaginal exposure to stabbing a loved one, then (b) to engage in in vivo exposure by holding a knife near this person, and finally (c) to engage in exposure to holding a knife near the loved one while imagining stabbing them.

DECONTEXTUALIZING INHIBITORY ASSOCIATIONS

Optimal inhibitory learning also requires the violation of negative expectancies in a variety of contexts. This is because inhibitory associations are context-specific, such that if safety is learned in Context A, it may not necessarily be recalled in Context B (Bouton, 2002). Accordingly, exposure tasks should be deliberately conducted under various conditions, be they stimulus-specific (e.g., a doorknob versus the floor), geographic (e.g., the trash can at home versus a public restroom trash can), interpersonal (e.g., with the therapist versus alone), affective (e.g., when calm versus when already anxious), or physiological (e.g., when relaxed versus caffeinated).

The clinical recommendations described here are based on a large body of experimental research (for a review, see Jacoby & Abramowitz, 2016), yet most of this work has been with animals or nonclinical human samples. Moreover, although some translational research has been conducted in the context of panic disorder and specific phobias, no studies have applied the inhibitory learning model to E/RP for OCD to date. Therefore, although inhibitory learning-based recommendations are derived from an empirically based theoretical model, the translation of inhibitory learning principles to E/RP for OCD awaits empirical testing.

The inhibitory learning perspective is consistent with Clark's (1999) proposal that exposure therapy is effective because it corrects dysfunctional beliefs that underlie fear, such as overestimations of threat, pathologic interpretations of intrusive thoughts, and the intolerance of risk or uncertainty. Belief change is thought to occur because exposure presents the patient with information that disconfirms the anxiogenic dysfunctional beliefs. Exposure therapy might also help patients gain more positive feelings about themselves and their ability to cope with feared situations and stimuli by helping them to master their fears without having to rely on avoidance or compulsive rituals. The importance of this sense of mastery is an oft-overlooked effect of exposure-based treatment.

Summary and Synthesis

Neither model provides completely satisfactory accounts of the mechanisms of exposure-based therapies at this time. A limitation of the emotional-processing model is that it suggests fears are unlearned through E/RP, whereas research indicates that such learning is suppressed by new learning, and learned fears can be reactivated later. The inhibitory learning model is therefore more closely tied to animal research on the neurobiology of fear reduction. It has the added advantage of explaining the conditions under which E/RP will be most effective (e.g., using multiple exposure contexts). On the other hand, the inhibitory learning theory has not yet received consistent empirical support in studies of humans with OCD or other fear-based disorders. It may be that some hybrid of these models ultimately provides the best explanation of fear reduction as it occurs during /ERP.

Efficacy and Effectiveness of E/RP

Dismantling Studies

Dismantling studies, which examine the effects of individual treatment procedures in multicomponent therapy programs, have addressed three questions with respect to E/RP: What are the differential effects of exposure and response prevention? How do these individual treatment components compare to the complete E/RP package? And is adding exposure in imagination to situational (in vivo) exposure superior to situational exposure alone?

DIFFERENTIAL EFFECTS OF EXPOSURE AND RESPONSE PREVENTION

The two studies that have examined the separate effects of exposure and response prevention have found similar results (Foa et al., 1980, 1984). Using a sample of individuals with contamination fear, Foa, Steketee, and Milby (1980) randomly assigned participants to exposure only (E) or to response prevention only (RP). They found that RP reduced rituals to a greater extent than it reduced anxiety, while E produced the opposite effects. Foa et al. (1984) randomly assigned another group of contamination phobic OCD "washers" to one of three treatment groups: exposure (E) only, response prevention (RP) only, or combination treatment (E/RP). After treatment, patients who received only E evidenced greater reductions in contamination fears than did those who received only RP. In contrast, RP was superior to E in reducing washing rituals. These results suggested that exposure and response prevention have differential effects on OCD symptoms: response prevention is superior to exposure in decreasing compulsive rituals, and exposure is superior to response prevention for decreasing obsessional fear.

Foa et al.'s (1984) study also addressed the question of whether there is an additive effect of combining E and RP. As these authors hypothesized, E/RP was indeed more effective than either of its individual components, and the E/RP combination led to the greatest short- and long-term reduction of anxiety (i.e., contamination fear) and urges to ritualize. To explain this finding, Foa et al. (1984) proposed that response prevention helps render information learned during exposure more incompatible with the patient's expectations. For example, without response prevention, a patient who repeatedly practices exposure to touching garbage cans, yet does not become very sick, may attribute his or her good health to compulsive washing. In this case, the maladaptive beliefs that garbage cans are dangerous and washing rituals prevent illness will persist. If, however, response prevention is implemented along with exposure, good health cannot be attributed to washing rituals and thus the patient's overestimations of danger can be corrected.

IMAGINAL AND SITUATIONAL EXPOSURE

Most individuals with OCD experience intrusive anxiety-evoking thoughts, images, ideas, or impulses that elicit excessive anxiety and therefore must also be dealt with in therapy. Whereas confrontation with tangible fear cues like dirt or unlucky numbers can be accomplished through situational exposure, confrontation with imagined disasters—the feared consequences of confronting feared situations without performing rituals—obviously cannot. A woman afraid of causing fires, and therefore constantly checking light switches, can conduct situational exposure by leaving her house lights on and her iron plugged in; yet she cannot be exposed to actually causing a fire as a result of not checking carefully enough. Confrontation with such situations must, therefore, be conducted in imagination. It follows from Foa and Kozak's (1986) proposition regarding the importance of matching the exposure stimulus with the patient's fear that obsessional fears of disastrous consequences should improve when imaginal exposure is added to in vivo exposure.

To examine the additive effect of imaginal exposure, Foa et al. (1980) assigned 15 patients with OCD and checking compulsions to either 10 daily sessions of E/RP with only situational exposure, or to a similar regimen of E/RP that incorporated both situational and imaginal exposure. Imaginal exposure consisted of repeated and prolonged confrontation with thoughts of anxiety-evoking scenes related to particular obsessional fears. For example, a woman who performed rituals in order to protect her family from death purposely imaged that her husband died as a result of her failure to perform her rituals. After treatment, both groups of patients improved substantially, but they did not differ significantly from one another. However, at follow-up (3 months to 2.5 years), the group that received both imaginal and situational exposure better maintained their improvements relative to the group that had received only situational exposure. Thus, imaginal exposure to the consequences of not ritualizing appears to be an important adjunct to situational exposure when stimuli that match patients' obsessional fears cannot be directly reproduced in the context of situational exposure.

SUMMARY OF DISMANTLING STUDIES

In summary, the findings of dismantling studies of E/RP reveal that: (a) exposure techniques are more effective than response prevention when it comes to reducing obsessional fear; (b) response prevention is more effective than exposure in reducing compulsive urges; (c) the combination of exposure and response prevention is more effective than either component by itself for reducing both obsessional fear and compulsive rituals; and (d) imaginal exposure adds to the effectiveness of situational exposure, especially when the patient's obsessional fears focus on imagined disasters that cannot be confronted in situational exposure.

Short- and Long-Term Effects of E/RP

Expert consensus and practice guidelines state that E/RP is the first-line psychosocial intervention for OCD (American Psychiatric Association, 2007; Hirschtritt et al., 2017; March et al., 1997). This section reviews meta-analyses and controlled studies of the short- and long-term outcomes of E/RP.

META-ANALYTIC FINDINGS

Data from a large number of controlled and uncontrolled outcome trials consistently indicate that E/RP is extremely helpful in reducing OCD symptoms. A meta-analysis of this literature (Abramowitz, 1996) that included 24 studies conducted between 1975 and 1995 (and involving over 800 patients) revealed very large within-group treatment effect sizes of 1.16 (on self-report measures) and 1.41 (interview measures) at posttest and 1.10 (for self-report measures) and 1.57 (for interview measures) at follow-up. Using a different meta-analytic approach, Foa and Kozak (1996) calculated the percent of patients in each study who were "responders" (usually defined as achieving a pre- to posttreatment improvement of at least 30%). They found that across 13 E/RP studies, 83% of patients were responders after treatment, and across 16 studies, 76% were responders at follow-up (mean follow-up was 29 months). In concert, these findings suggest that the majority of patients with OCD who undergo treatment with E/RP evidence substantial short- and long-term benefit. More recent meta-analyses have found results consistent with the previous reports (Eddy et al., 2004). Considering the heterogeneity of OCD, it would be anticipated that there would be high variation in treatment outcome with E/RP. Despite this expectation, meta-analytic findings have not supported moderation of outcome. Olatunji et al. (2013) reported that baseline OCD symptom severity and depression did not moderate treatment outcome. There also does not appear to be significant incremental symptom improvement from the addition of antidepressant medication (Öst et al., 2015; see also Chapter 21).

RANDOMIZED CONTROLLED TRIALS

The Yale-Brown Obsessive-Compulsive Scale (Y-BOCS; Goodman et al., 1989a, 1989b), a 10-item semi-structured clinical interview, is considered the gold standard measure of OCD severity. Due to its respectable psychometric properties (Taylor, 1995), the Y-BOCS is widely utilized in OCD treatment outcome research, providing an excellent "measuring stick" by which to compare results across studies. When administering the Y-BOCS, the interviewer rates the following parameters of obsessions (items 1 to 5) and compulsions (items 6 to 10) on a scale from 0 (no symptoms) to 4 (extreme): time, interference with functioning, distress, resistance, and control. The total score is the sum of the 10 items and therefore ranges from 0 to 40. Y-BOCS scores of 0 to 7 tend to indicate subclinical OCD symptoms, scores of 8 to 15 = mild symptoms, 16 to 25 = moderate symptoms, 26 to 35 = severe symptoms, and 36 to 40 = extreme severity. Table 19.1 summarizes the results of the five published randomized controlled trials (RCTs) that examined the efficacy of E/RP using the Y-BOCS as an outcome measure.

Two studies have compared E/RP to credible psychotherapy placebos (Lindsay et al., 1997; Fals-Stewart et al., 1993). In the study by Fals-Stewart et al., patients were randomly assigned patients to receive 24 sessions of individual E/RP, group E/RP, or progressive relaxation treatment, which was not expected to produce OCD symptom reduction. All treatments were delivered over 12 weeks with twice-weekly sessions. Although both E/RP treatments were superior to relaxation, there was no effect of E/RP format (i.e., group and individual treatment produced similar outcomes). The average improvement across the two E/RP groups was 41% on the Y-BOCS, and posttreatment scores fell to within the mild range of severity.

In the study by Lindsay et al. (1997), patients were assigned to receive either E/RP or anxiety management training (AMT), which consisted of breathing retraining,

Table 19.1. Results of Randomized Controlled Trials Examining the Efficacy of Exposure and Response Prevention for OCD

Study	Control Condition	E/RP Group n	E/RP Pre	E/RP Post	Control n	Control Pre	Control Post
Fals-Stewart et al. (1993)[1]	Relaxation	31	20.2	12.1	32	19.9	18.1
Lindsay et al. (1997)	Anxiety management	9	28.7 (4.6)	11.0 (3.8)	9	24.4 (7.0)	25.9 (5.8)
Van Balkom et al. (1998)	Waiting list	19	25.0 (7.9)	17.1 (8.4)	18	26.8 (6.4)	26.4 (6.8)
Foa et al. (2005)	Pill placebo	29	24.6 (4.8)	11.0 (7.9)	26	25.0 (4.0)	22.2 (6.4)
Nakatani et al. (2005)	Pill placebo	10	29.9 (3.1)	12.9 (4.9)	8	30.5 (3.7)	28.4 (5.5)

Note. Y-BOCS = Yale-Brown Obsessive-Compulsive Scale.

[1]Standard deviation not reported.

Table 19.2. Comparisons Between Cognitive Therapy and Exposure and Response Prevention (E/RP)

| | | Y-BOCS Total Score (*SD*) ||||||
| | | Cognitive Therapy Group ||| ERP Group |||
Study	Comments	n	Pre	Post	n	Pre	Post
van Oppen et al. (1995)	No therapist-supervised E/RP	28	24.1 (5.5)	13.3 (8.5)	29	31.4 (5.0)	17.9 (9.0)
Van Balkom et al. (1998)	Sample overlapped with van Oppen et al. (1995)	25	25.3 (6.6)	13.5 (9.7)	22	25.0 (7.9)	17.1 (8.4)
Cottraux et al. (2001)	Both treatments included exposure-like procedures	30	28.6 (5.1)	16.1 (8.2)	30	28.5 (4.9)	16.4 (7.8)
McLean et al. (2001)	All treatment in groups	31	21.9 (5.8)	16.1 (6.7)	32	21.8 (4.6)	13.2 (7.2)

Y-BOCS = Yale-Brown Obsessive-Compulsive Scale.

relaxation, and training in the use of problem-solving skills. Both treatments were intensive: 15 daily sessions conducted over a three-week period. On average, patients receiving E/RP improved almost 62% from before to after treatment on the Y-BOCS, with posttest scores ending up in the mild range. In contrast, there was no improvement with AMT.

The clear superiority of E/RP over credible psychotherapy placebos like relaxation and AMT indicates that improvement in OCD symptoms can be attributed to the E/RP procedures themselves, over and above any nonspecific factors, such as time, attention, or expectancy of positive outcome. Just as importantly, the findings described above clearly show that despite the intuitive appeal of using strategies like relaxation, deep breathing, and problem-solving with individuals suffering from obsessional anxiety and persistent rituals, these techniques do not work in the treatment of OCD.

In their study on the relative efficacy of various combinations of E/RP, cognitive therapy, and fluvoxamine, van Balkom et al. (1998) included a waiting-list control group, affording a somewhat less rigorous test of the efficacy of E/RP as compared to the studies reviewed directly above. E/RP fared somewhat less well in this study than in other RCTs. One explanation for the mere 32% symptom reduction is that the E/RP protocol in van Balkom et al.'s study was less than optimal: First, all exposure was conducted as homework assignments rather than in session under the therapist's supervision. Second, therapists did not discuss expectations of disastrous consequences during the first eight weeks of E/RP because this would have overlapped substantially with cognitive therapy. However, such discussions are a necessary part of E/RP. Still, patients who received this self-directed and disadvantaged version of E/RP fared significantly better than those in the waiting-list condition.

Foa et al. (2005) examined the relative efficacy of (a) intensive (15 daily sessions) E/RP (including in-session exposure), (b) the serotonin and norepinephrine reuptake inhibitor clomipramine, (c) combined treatment (E/RP + clomipramine), and (d) pill placebo. Intensive E/RP produced a 50% Y-BOCS score reduction, which was far superior to the effects of pill placebo, as is shown in Table 19.1. Moreover, endpoint Y-BOCS scores fell within the mild range of OCD severity.

In a study conducted in Japan, Nakatani and colleagues (2005) randomly assigned patients to receive either weekly E/RP sessions, fluvoxamine, or pill placebo. The E/RP group achieved a mean Y-BOCS score reduction of nearly 60%, which was superior to that reported for the placebo group (7%). Moreover, at posttest, the E/RP group's Y-BOCS scores were again within the mild range of symptoms.

More recently, it was found that the crucial determinant of long-term symptom improvement with E/RP was compliance with between-session behavioral activities. Simpson et al. (2012), in a treatment program wherein 15 sessions of E/RP were administered weekly, showed there was a direct relationship between homework compliance and symptom relief. Individuals with the highest compliance showed more than a 6-point improvement on the Y-BOCS at six-month follow-up, whereas those with the lowest compliance showed a 3-point improvement.

Overall, the findings from RCTs suggest that E/RP—even when delivered in a suboptimal fashion—produces substantial and clinically meaningful improvement in OCD symptoms. There is also consistent evidence from these studies that symptom reduction is due to the specific techniques used in E/RP (i.e., exposure to fear-provoking stimuli while refraining from rituals) over and above the nonspecific factors (e.g., expectations, attention) that are common to all psychological treatments.

E/RP for Mental Rituals

Traditionally, it was thought that individuals with OCD who had severe obsessions without overt rituals like washing, checking, ordering, and repeating were resistant to E/RP (Baer, 1994). This belief was predicated on the erroneous (as it turns out) notion that such patients do not have rituals that could be resisted as part of response prevention; thus the maintenance of their obsessional fear was less understood. A clearer recognition of the phenomenology and function of mental rituals (often mistaken for obsessions because they are not visibly apparent behaviors) and other subtle anxiety-reduction strategies that are present among patients without overt rituals (Freeston et al., 1997; Rachman, 1993), however, enabled the adaptation of E/RP for this presentation of OCD.

Specifically, Freeston and colleagues (1997) obtained excellent results with a treatment package that entailed (a) psychoeducation about intrusive thoughts and their development into obsessions; (b) E/RP consisting of in-session and homework exposure in which the patient repeatedly writes out the unwanted obsessional thought, says it aloud, or records it on a continuous-loop audiotape and then plays it back repeatedly on a portable audiocassette player while refraining from covert rituals and mental compulsions; and (c) cognitive therapy targeting exaggerated responsibility, inappropriate interpretations of intrusive thoughts, and inflated estimates of the probability and severity of negative outcomes. Compared to a wait-list control group, treated patients achieved substantial improvement: among all patients (N = 28) Y-BOCS scores improved from 23.9 to 9.8 after an average of 25.7 sessions over 19.2 weeks. Moreover, patients retained their gains at six-month follow-up (mean Y-BOCS score = 10.8). This study demonstrated that E/RP can be successfully adapted for the management of a presentation of OCD that had previously been considered resistant to psychological treatment. In a later study, Abramowitz et al. (2003) found that E/RP was no less effective for such patients than it was for patients with OCD who display primarily overt washing, checking, and arranging/ordering rituals.

Group E/RP
In most of the studies reviewed so far, treatment was delivered on an individual basis. Group OCD treatment programs emphasizing E/RP, however, have been found to be effective in reducing OCD symptoms (Anderson & Rees, 2007; Cordioli et al., 2003; McLean et al., 2001). In one study, 12 weeks of group E/RP was more effective than group therapy emphasizing cognitive techniques, although both programs were more effective than wait-list (McLean et al., 2001). In another investigation, group E/RP resulted in significant improvement relative to waiting list, and patients continued to improve at three-month follow-up (Cordioli et al., 2003). In the only study directly comparing individual and group therapy for OCD, Anderson and Rees (2007) found that 10 weeks of either treatment format was more effective than wait list, but there were no differences between treatments. Therapy included E/RP and cognitive therapy techniques, and the average posttest and follow-up Y-BOCS scores were in the 16 to 18 range (indicating mild symptom severity). Strengths of a group approach to the treatment of OCD include the support and cohesion that are nonspecific effects of group therapy. Potential disadvantages, however, include the relative lack of attention to each individual's particular symptom presentation, particularly given the heterogeneity of OCD.

Research on group-based delivery of treatment has expanded in recent years, and while the limitations noted here remain unchanged, there does appear to be an advantage in lower dropout from intervention (Pozza & Dèttore, 2017). Examination of group-based treatment has focused primarily on efficacy of the overall intervention, and there has been little attention to differential outcome based on symptom subtype or other putative moderators that have been examined in studies of individual treatment, such as baseline severity or comorbid depression.

Home-Based versus Office-Based Treatment
Rowa et al. (2007) examined whether the effects of E/RP differ depending on whether treatment was delivered exclusively in the therapist's office versus in the patient's home

or other natural environments where symptoms tend to occur (e.g., at work, in public places, in the car). The authors randomly assigned 28 individuals with OCD to the aforementioned treatment conditions. Patients received 14 sessions of E/RP (90 minutes each session) with an individual therapist. Results suggested that participants improved significantly, regardless of where treatment occurred. Posttreatment Y-BOCS reductions were 44% for office-based therapy and 48% for home-based treatment. At six-month follow-up, reductions were 39% and 48%, respectively. Although the home-based group appeared to show greater symptom reduction, the differences in improvement rates were not statistically significant—probably due to the relatively small sample size (14 patients per group).

Although Rowa et al. (2007) found that home-based E/RP was no more effective than office-based E/RP, it is possible that home-based E/RP is beneficial and useful for certain individuals with particular symptom presentations. For example, patients whose symptoms cannot be replicated in any meaningful way in an office setting or who are unable to try E/RP on their own may find home-based E/RP especially effective. For example, individuals with fears of disasters in the home (e.g., fires and burglaries) and checking rituals have symptoms that are very difficult to replicate in an office setting due to the decrease in received responsibility. Clinical observations suggest that home-based treatment may also be helpful for patients who have not benefited from previous office-based E/RP.

In summary, research related to E/RP now spans several decades, and the findings broadly support its use for all of the major symptom presentations associated with OCD in adults (McKay et al., 2015) and children (Franklin et al., 2015). The majority of the research that has accumulated demonstrating efficacy is in individual face-to-face treatment. A long-held concern has been that E/RP is a demanding intervention and leads to high drop-out rates, and thus the benefits of E/RP may not be as high as the previous controlled research would suggest. However, recent analyses show that drop-out rates for E?RP are no higher than for other forms of treatment, in both adults (Ong et al., 2016) and children (Johnco et al., 2020).

Relapse Prevention
Hiss and colleagues (1994) reported encouraging results of a relapse prevention program following E/RP treatment of OCD. Eighteen patients were treated with three weeks of intensive E/RP and then were randomly assigned to either a relapse prevention condition (consisting of four 90-minute sessions over one week) or a control condition (consisting of relaxation training and associative therapy). Based on a 50% improvement on the Y-BOCS score as the criterion for treatment response, 75% of the patients assigned to the relapse prevention condition were responders after initial treatment, and 75% were responders at six-month follow-up. In contrast, 70% of the patients assigned to the control condition were responders after initial treatment, but only 33% were responders at

six-month follow-up. Although there were few statistically significant results because of the small sample size, this study suggested that a brief relapse prevention program, including brief telephone contacts, may help prevent relapse, at least in cleaning and checking rituals.

Internet, Telehealth, and Smartphone Application Delivery of E/RP

There has been a proliferation of research into technology-assisted approaches to E/RP for OCD. This shift is significant, in that it accommodates the large proportion of people with OCD who either do not seek intervention or do not receive evidence-based care when they do, because it increases the likelihood individuals with OCD will find relief. One reason many people with OCD do not receive evidence-based treatment is a shortage of well-trained OCD therapists in the healthcare system, which results in long waiting lists and leaves many impaired individuals untreated or inadequately treated (Mataix-Cols & Marks, 2006). Stigma, cost, and a lack of accurate information about OCD treatment are additional barriers to care (Glazier et al., 2015). Furthermore, members of underrepresented groups are less likely to have access to care or to seek treatment when access is available, compared to other groups (Goodwin et al., 2002; Williams et al., 2012). Thus, innovative delivery formats that increase accessibility without compromising efficacy are gaining popularity. Internet, telehealth, and smartphone application (app) platforms show considerable promise for improving treatment dissemination by creating low-cost and efficient alternatives to traditional face-to-face therapy.

RELEVANT RESEARCH EVIDENCE AND CLINICAL APPLICATION

Internet-based cognitive-behavioral therapy (ICBT) with therapist support has demonstrated efficacy for several psychiatric conditions, including depression, social anxiety disorder, and panic disorder (Andersson et al., 2009). However, few studies have empirically examined ICBT for OCD. Andersson and colleagues (2012) conducted an RCT investigating the efficacy of an ICBT program for OCD that gave patients access to self-help modules and an online therapist. They found that ICBT led to larger improvements relative to the attention control group, with a large effect size of 1.12. CBT delivery methods that utilize telephone and web-camera communication have also demonstrated efficacy. In a systematic review, Tumur et al. (2007) found that BT Steps, a self-help book and a touchtone telephone system that provided automated guidance, consistently led to symptom reduction (within-group ES = 0.84) and demonstrated acceptability and feasibility. Storch and colleagues (2011) conducted a wait-list controlled randomized trial of family-based CBT delivered via web-camera (W-CBT) to children and adolescents with OCD. Those receiving W-CBT improved on all OCD-related outcome measures relative to the wait-list control group, with a large between-group ES of 1.36; and 56% of individuals in the W-CBT group met remission criteria. This preliminary study suggested that W-CBT may be useful in reducing OCD symptoms in children and adolescents.

Further, in a case series of six outpatient clients with OCD, Vogel and colleagues (2012) found that 15 sessions of CBT delivered by teleconference and cell phone led to considerable improvement in symptoms at both posttreatment and follow-up assessments. All six patients rated the treatment format as acceptable. Combined ICBT and phone guidance may enhance outcomes, because evidence suggests that brief phone support provided by a clinician improves adherence to computerized OCD treatment and leads to larger symptom reduction (Kenwright et al., 2005).

The rapid growth in smartphone use has led to the development of apps for behavioral health that include symptom assessment, psychoeducation, resource location, and progress tracking (Luxton et al., 2011). One such app is the Mayo Clinic Anxiety Coach, which was designed to deliver CBT for anxiety disorders and OCD through assessment, psychoeducation, and treatment modules. Case examples suggest that Anxiety Coach enhances treatment of pediatric OCD (Whiteside et al., 2014). Additional apps have been developed for OCD assessment and treatment, but they have not yet established empirical support (Van Ameringen et al., 2017). For example, iTunes offers a mobile Y-BOCS assessment app and OCD treatment app based on E/RP principles. Although neither app has been formally validated, the latter is currently being studied at Brown University. The lack of empirical support for the available apps for OCD is not surprising. A recent review showed that while app development has been growing rapidly (McKay, 2018), the overwhelming majority of the apps have not been investigated for their efficacy, although most rely on evidence-based approaches (Van Ameringen et al., 2017).

CBT delivered through Internet-based programs, telehealth, and smartphone apps can reduce barriers to care and improve the efficiency of dissemination. As evidenced by the studies described here, technology can be used in various ways to augment traditional therapy. Some programs have been developed to replace face-to-face therapy entirely, whereas others are used to supplement traditional care (e.g., in a psychiatric clinic). Mataix-Cols and Marks (2006) proposed a stepped-care model for the treatment of OCD, in which individuals with less complex symptoms receive immediate access to self-guided treatment, freeing up time for experienced therapists to work with more complex cases. By reducing the time clinicians spend with each patient, the stepped-care approach allows more people to receive effective treatment without increasing therapist burden or healthcare costs. For example, therapists in the trial conducted by Andersson et al. (2009) spent an average of 129 minutes per participant over the 10-week intervention period, which is substantially lower than time spent in face-to-face CBT. Future research is necessary to determine the optimal amount of therapist contact for patients with OCD. Given that telemedicine, and by extension other technology-assisted approaches to treatment, has been available for several decades, there is enough research to develop recommendations regarding who would most benefit from this level of care. It appears that mobile apps and remotely delivered treatment, as well as other solely technology-delivered approaches, are most suitable for mild to moderate symptom presentations (Aboujaoude, 2017). However, limited controlled research has been conducted.

Additional research is warranted to identify patient characteristics associated with treatment adherence and outcome. Regarding treatment expectations, Wootton et al., (2011) found that only 22% of patients believed that online therapy would improve their symptoms substantially. This suggests that some patients may be unwilling to incorporate technology into treatment, and additional efforts may be necessary to disseminate findings about the effectiveness of innovative OCD interventions. Despite potential challenges and limitations, the integration of technology and behavioral health is an exciting step toward improving access and adherence to evidence-based treatments for OCD.

Involving Family Members in E/RP

OCD affects not only the individual with the disorder, but also family members with whom they live. Indeed, there is a bidirectional association: OCD symptoms often lead to a strain on family relationships, and reciprocally, aspects of family relationships contribute to the maintenance of OCD. For example, a non-affected partner or family member might (albeit inadvertently) maintain a loved one's OCD symptoms by accommodating (i.e., "helping" with) avoidance and rituals (e.g., by checking or providing reassurance; Calvocoressi et al., 1999). Such accommodation occurs among couples and within families, and E/RP has been adapted accordingly, as described in this section.

Couple-Based E/RP

A handful of early studies examined "partner-assisted" E/RP for OCD, reporting somewhat mixed results. Mehta (1990), for example, found that including a partner (or other family member) as a coach during E/RP was more effective than when E/RP did not involve such a coach. In a similarly designed study, however, Emmelkamp et al. (1990) found no between-group differences. Earlier, Emmelkamp and De Lange (1983) had reported that partner-assisted E/RP was more effective at posttest evaluation, but not at one-month follow-up. It is difficult to draw strong conclusions from these older studies because they suffered from various methodological limitations, such as suboptimal implementation of E/RP (e.g., there was no therapist-supervised exposure), often resulting in substandard outcomes. Moreover, involvement of the partner was limited to helping only with exposure tasks, and couples were not helped to reduce accommodation behaviors or improve maladaptive communication patterns.

More recently, Abramowitz et al. (2013a, 2013b) developed a couple-based E/RP program focusing on communication training, partner-assisted exposure, and reducing accommodation. In a trial of 16 couples, Abramowitz et al. found a large within-group effect size on OCD symptoms after treatment (ES = 2.68) that was maintained at the 12-month follow-up (ES = 2.42). Moreover, these changes were notably larger than those of comparable individual E/RP-based treatment: at 12-month follow-up Vogel et al. (2004) reported a within-group effect size of 2.06. Couples E/RT treatment involves an assessment of the patient's OCD symptoms, along with identifying ways the couple has structured their environment to accommodate OCD symptoms. Next, the conceptual model of OCD and rationale for E/RP are presented to both partners, to increase patience and hopefulness and to reduce misunderstanding and criticism. The patient and partner are also taught communication skills to help them complete E/RP as a team, and the process of partner-assisted E/RP is broken into four phases: (a) clarifying the exposure task and identifying obstacles, (b) beginning the task, (c) managing heightened distress, and (d) evaluating the experience and giving praise for working hard. Treatment also focuses on reducing accommodation and addressing significant non-OCD-related relationship stressors.

Family-Based E/RP for Youth

In adaptations for E/RP for youth with OCD, parents are taught skills (e.g., psychoeducation, self-monitoring, and response prevention) for minimizing accommodation of their child's OCD symptoms (Lebowitz et al., 2014), and they are also given a rationale for E/RP and education about the harmlessness of anxiety. Parents are coached on alternative ways of handling requests for accommodation and how to provide more helpful (nonritualistic) answers to reassurance-seeking questions. Additionally, parents are taught to reinforce their child's engagement in (and completion of) E/RP tasks and to use contingency-management skills (instead of engaging in power struggles) to shape their child's behavior regarding interpersonal boundaries. Parents are then involved as (a) consultants who provide information to the therapist; (b) collaborators who provide information to the therapist, aid the child with learning new skills as a "coach" throughout treatment, and assist with exposures; or (c) co-clients who jointly work on skills to manage their own anxiety. Although family-based E/RP is superior to individual and family-based relaxation training (Freeman et al., 2014) among youth with OCD of varying ages, studies have not found "enhanced" effects of family-based E/RP in comparison to individual E/RP. Ultimately, decisions about the extent to which parental involvement is important are left to clinical judgment based on the child's presentation of OCD, the nature of the family involvement, and the characteristics of the caregivers.

Predictors of Response to Exposure-Based Treatment

Given that not all individuals with OCD respond uniformly well to E/RP, investigators have been interested in determining the predictors of success and failure. A number of possible prognostic factors have been investigated, most of which can be grouped into three broad categories: E/RP procedural variations, patient-related characteristics, and supportive factors.

E/RP Procedural Variations

In a meta-analysis of many treatment studies, Abramowitz (1996) examined the relationship between short- and long-term treatment outcome and the manner in which E/RP is delivered. The results from this study can be summarized as follows: First, E/RP programs that involved more in-session, therapist-supervised exposure practice produced greater short- and long-term improvements compared to programs in which all exposure was performed by the patient as homework assignments. Second, combining in vivo and imaginal exposure was superior to in vivo exposure alone in reducing anxiety symptoms. Third, programs in which patients refrained completely from ritualizing during the treatment period (i.e., total response prevention) produced superior immediate and long-term effects compared to those that involved only partial response prevention.

If in-session exposure practice is an important component of E/RP, what is the optimal session frequency? To examine whether the robust effects of intensive (daily) therapy are substantially compromised by reducing the session frequency, Abramowitz et al. (2003) compared 15 sessions of intensive (daily) E/RP to 15 sessions of E/RP delivered on a twice-weekly basis. Whereas intensive therapy was minimally superior to the twice-weekly regimen immediately following treatment (posttreatment Y-BOCS scores were 10 for intensive E/RP and 13 for twice-weekly E/RP), this difference disappeared at three-month follow-up (Y-BOCS = 13 for intensive and 14 for twice-weekly). The results of this study suggest that a twice-weekly therapy schedule provides clinicians with a more pragmatic, yet equally effective, alternative to the highly demanding and often impractical intensive protocol.

Homework adherence also predicts better outcome. In a recent review of the literature, Wheaton and Chen (2020) found that greater patient completion of between-session E/RP exercises predicted better treatment outcome. This finding generalized across delivery methods (individual outpatient vs. intensive residential treatments) for both adult and pediatric patients. Poorer homework completion was associated with OCD features (e.g., strength of avoidance, poorer insight), low patient expectancies for improvement, and a poorer therapeutic alliance.

A related finding is that there is a relationship between adherence to E/RP instructions and treatment outcome (Abramowitz et al., 2002; Lax et al., 1992). For example, Abramowitz et al. (2002) found that better outcomes were associated with understanding the rationale for E/RP techniques and adhering to the therapist's instructions for exposure practice (both in-session and homework assignments). These findings suggest that it is important for clinicians to provide a compelling explanation for using E/RP procedures and to elicit the patient's input when developing an exposure plan.

Patient Characteristics

Several patient characteristics have been identified as predictors of poorer treatment response. These include the presence of extremely poor insight into the senselessness of obsessions and compulsions (Foa, 1979; Foa et al., 1999; Wheaton et al., 2020), severe depression (Abramowitz & Foa, 2000; Abramowitz et al., 2000; Keeley et al., 2008; Steketee et al., 2001), generalized anxiety disorder (Steketee et al., 2001), extreme emotional reactivity during exposure (Foa et al., 1983), and severe borderline personality traits (Steketee et al., 2001). Whereas some studies have reported that more severe OCD symptoms predicted poorer outcome (Franklin et al., 2000), others have not (Foa et al., 1983), and indeed some studies have found that greater pretreatment OCD severity is associated with better outcome (Tibi et al., 2019). Preliminary evidence suggests that better outcome for E/RP occurs in patients with OCD who have higher levels of treatment-related distress tolerance; that is, willingness to experience unpleasant thoughts, emotions, and bodily sensations during E/RP (Nargesi et al., 2019).

Supportive Factors

The majority of studies have found that hostility from intimate partners and relatives toward the individual with OCD is predictive of premature drop-out from E/RP and poor response among patients who complete treatment (Knopp et al., 2013). However, not all studies have replicated this finding (Tibi et al., 2019). Further research is needed to better understand the potential effect of the patient's family environment on treatment outcome for E/RP.

Conclusions

Prior to the advent of E/RP, clinicians were pessimistic about their ability to help people suffering from OCD. Since the pioneering work of the 1960s, E/RP has emerged as one of the most effective treatments for OCD. Several types of empirically supported E/RP protocols have been developed, with some being more effective than others. Despite the initial promise of multicomponent interventions for OCD, the incorporation of cognitive therapy into E/RP programs has not greatly improved treatment outcome. Further research is required to determine how, if at all, treatment outcome can be augmented by combining E/RP with other interventions, such as cognitive interventions and acceptance-based interventions. There also remain significant subgroups of patients for whom E/RP has limited efficacy. Research into how E/RP may be modified to address the needs of specific subgroups (i.e., individuals with higher overvalued ideas) is therefore warranted.

Further research is required to determine whether treatment outcome can be improved by augmenting E/RP with serotonin reuptake inhibitors (SRIs). Treatment outcome is improved when E/RP is added to SRIs. However, the converse has yet to be demonstrated; that is, it has yet to be clearly shown that the effects of E/RP are augmented when SRIs are added. One of the most promising options for augmenting E/RP is D-cycloserine, but even here, the initial findings have been mixed and more research is required (see Chapter 21).

Translational research has long been important in developing exposure-based treatments for OCD, beginning with the application of animal behavioral models to humans (Dollard & Miller, 1950), which led to the development of E/RP. Later translational research on fear extinction has also informed the refinement of E/RP, such as animal research suggesting that E/RP will be most effective when conducted under multiple exposure contexts (Bouton, 2002). If the promise of D-cycloserine is fulfilled, then this will be another translational milestone, in which animal research on an "exposure enhancer" (D-cycloserine) has led to treatment advances in humans.

References

Aboujaoude, E. (2017). Three decades of telemedicine in obsessive-compulsive disorder: A review across platforms. *Journal of Obsessive-Compulsive and Related Disorders, 14*, 65–70.

Abramowitz, J. S. (1996). Variants of exposure and response prevention in the treatment of obsessive-compulsive disorder: A meta-analysis. *Behavior Therapy, 27*, 583–600.

Abramowitz, J. S., & Arch, J. J. (2014). Strategies for improving long-term outcomes in cognitive behavioral therapy for obsessive-compulsive disorder: Insights from learning theory. *Cognitive and Behavioral Practice, 21*, 20–31.

Abramowitz, J. S., Baucom, D. H., Boeding, S., Wheaton, M. G., Pukay-Martin, N. D., Fabricant, L. E., Paprocki, C., & Fischer, M. S. (2013a). Treating obsessive-compulsive disorder in intimate relationships: A pilot study of couple-based cognitive-behavior therapy. *Behavior Therapy, 44*(3), 395–407.

Abramowitz, J. S., Baucom, D. H., Wheaton, M. G., Boeding, S., Fabricant, L. E., Paprocki, C., & Fischer, M. S. (2013b). Enhancing exposure and response prevention for OCD: A couple-based approach. *Behavior Modification, 37*(2), 189–210.

Abramowitz, J. S., Deacon, B. J., & Whiteside, S. P. (2019). *Exposure therapy for anxiety: Principles and practice*. Guilford.

Abramowitz, J. S., & Foa, E. (2000). Does comorbid major depressive disorder influence outcome of exposure and response prevention for OCD? *Behavior Therapy, 31*, 795–800.

Abramowitz, J. S., Foa, E. B., & Franklin, M. E. (2003). Exposure and ritual prevention for obsessive-compulsive disorder: Effects of intensive versus twice-weekly sessions. *Journal of Consulting and Clinical Psychology, 71*, 394–398.

Abramowitz, J. S., Franklin, M. E., Schwartz, S. A., & Furr, J. M. (2003). Symptom presentation and outcome of cognitive-behavioral therapy for obsessive-compulsive disorder. *Journal of Consulting and Clinical Psychology, 71*, 1049–1057.

Abramowitz, J. S., Franklin, M. E., Street, G. P., Kozak, M. J., & Foa, E. B. (2000). Effects of comorbid depression on response to treatment for obsessive-compulsive disorder. *Behavior Therapy, 31*, 517–528.

Abramowitz, J. S., Franklin, M., Zoellner, L., & DiBernardo, C. (2002). Treatment compliance and outcome in obsessive-compulsive disorder. *Behavior Modification, 26*, 447–463.

American Psychiatric Association (APA). (2007). *Practice guidelines: Treatment of patients with obsessive-compulsive disorder*. http://www.psychiatryonline.com/pracGuide/pracGuideTopic_10.aspx

American Psychiatric Association (APA). (2013). *Diagnostic and statistical manual of mental disorders* (5th ed.).

Anderson, R. A., & Rees, C. S. (2007) Group versus individual cognitive-behavioural treatment for obsessive-compulsive disorder: A controlled trial. *Behaviour Research and Therapy, 45*, 123–137

Andersson, E., Enander, J., Andrén, P., Hedman, E., Ljótsson, B., Hursti, T., . . . Rück, C. (2012). Internet-based cognitive behaviour therapy for obsessive–compulsive disorder: A randomized controlled trial. *Psychological Medicine, 42*(10), 2193–2203.

Andersson, G., Carlbring, P., Berger, T., Almlöv, J., & Cuijpers, P. (2009). What makes Internet Therapy work? *Cognitive Behaviour Therapy, 38*, 55–60.

Arch, J. J., & Abramowitz, J. S. (2015). Exposure therapy for obsessive-compulsive disorder: An optimizing inhibitory learning approach. *Journal of Obsessive-Compulsive and Related Disorders, 6*, 174–182.

Baer, L. (1994). Factor analysis of symptom subtypes of obsessive compulsive disorder and their relation to personality and tic disorders. *The Journal of Clinical Psychiatry, 55*, 18–23.

Bouton, M. E. (2002). Context, ambiguity, and unlearning: sources of relapse after behavioral extinction. *Biological Psychiatry, 52*(10), 976–986.

Calvocoressi, L., Mazure, C. M., Kasl, S. V., Skolnick, J., Fisk, D., Vegso, S. J., van Noppen, B., & Price, L. H. (1999). Family accommodation of obsessive-compulsive symptoms: Instrument development and assessment of family behavior. *The Journal of Nervous and Mental Disease, 187*(10), 636–642.

Christensen, H., Hadzi-Pavlovic, D., Andrews, G., & Mattick, R. (1987). Behavior therapy and tricyclic medication in the treatment of obsessive-compulsive disorder: A quantitative review. *Journal of Consulting and Clinical Psychology, 55,* 701–711.

Clark, D. M. (1999). Anxiety disorders: Why they persist and how to treat them. *Behaviour Research & Therapy, 37,* S5–S27.

Cordioli, V., Heldt, A., Braga, E., Bochi, D., Margis, R., Basso de Sousa, M., Fonseca Tonello, J., Gus Manfro, G., & Kapczinski, F. (2003). Cognitive-behavioral group therapy in obsessive-compulsive disorder: A randomized clinical trial. *Psychotherapy and Psychosomatics, 72,* 211–216.

Cottraux, J., Note, I., Yao, S. N., Lafont, S., Note, B., Mollard, E., & Dartigues, J. F. (2001). A randomized controlled trial of cognitive therapy versus intensive behavior therapy in obsessive compulsive disorder. *Psychotherapy and Psychosomatics, 70*(6), 288–297.

Craske, M. G., Kircanski, K., Zelikowsky, M., Mystkowski, J., Chowdhury, N., & Baker, A. (2008). Optimizing inhibitory learning during exposure therapy. *Behaviour Research and Therapy, 46*(1), 5–27.

Dollard, J., & Miller, N. E. (1950). *Personality and psychotherapy: An analysis in terms of learning, thinking, and culture.* McGraw-Hill.

Eddy, K., Dutra, L., Bradley, R., & Weston, D. (2004). A multidimensional meta-analysis of psychotherapy and pharmacotherapy for obsessive-compulsive disorder. *Clinical Psychology Review, 24,* 1011–1030.

Emmelkamp, P. M., de Haan, E., & Hoogduin, C. A. (1990). Marital adjustment and obsessive-compulsive disorder. *The British Journal of Psychiatry, 156,* 55–60.

Emmelkamp, P. M., & de Lange, I. (1983). Spouse involvement in the treatment of obsessive-compulsive patients. *Behaviour Research and Therapy, 21*(4), 341–346.

Emmelkamp, P. M., & Kraanen, J. (1977). Therapist-controlled exposure in vivo versus self-controlled exposure in vivo: A comparison with obsessive-compulsive patients. *Behaviour Research and Therapy, 15*(6), 491–495.

Fals-Stewart, W., Marks, A. P., & Schafer, J. (1993). A comparison of behavioral group therapy and individual behavior therapy in treating obsessive-compulsive disorder. *The Journal of Nervous and Mental Disease, 181*(3), 189–193.

Foa, E. B. (1979). Failure in treating obsessive-compulsives. *Behaviour Research and Therapy, 17,* 169–176.

Foa, E. B., Abramowitz, J. S., Franklin, M. E., & Kozak, M. J. (1999). Feared consequences, fixity of belief, and treatment outcome in patients with obsessive-compulsive disorder. *Behavior Therapy, 30,* 717–724.

Foa, E. B., & Goldstein, A. (1978). Continuous exposure and complete response prevention in the treatment of obsessive-compulsive neurosis. *Behavior Therapy, 9,* 821–829.

Foa, E. B., Grayson, J. B., Steketee, G. S., Doppelt, H. G., Turner, R. M., & Latimer, P. R. (1983). Success and failure in the behavioral treatment of obsessive-compulsives. *Journal of Consulting and Clinical Psychology, 51,* 287–297.

Foa, E. B., & Kozak, M. J. (1986). Emotional processing of fear: Exposure to corrective information. *Psychological Bulletin, 99,* 20–35.

Foa, E. B., & Kozak, M. J. (1996). Psychological treatment for obsessive-compulsive disorder. In M. R. Mavissakalian & R. F. Prien (Eds.), *Long-term treatments of anxiety disorders* (pp. 285–309). American Psychiatric Press.

Foa, E. B., & Kozak, M. J., Goodman, W. K., Hollander, E., Jenike, M. A., & Rasmussen, S. A. (1995). DSM-IV field trial: Obsessive-compulsive disorder. *The American Journal of Psychiatry, 152*(1), 90–96.

Foa, E., Liebowitz, M. R., Kozak, M. J., Davies, S., Campeas, R., Franklin, M. E., Huppert, J., Kjernisted, K., Rowan, V., Schmidt, A., Simpson, H. B., & Tu, X. (2005). Randomized, placebo-controlled trial of exposure and ritual prevention, clomipramine, and their combination in the treatment of obsessive-compulsive disorder. *The American Journal of Psychiatry, 162,* 151–161.

Foa, E. B., Steketee, G, Grayson, J., Turner, R., & Lattimer, P. (1984). Deliberate exposure and blocking of obsessive-compulsive rituals: Immediate and long-term effects. *Behavior Therapy, 15,* 450–472.

Foa, E. B., Steketee, G., & Milby, J. (1980). Differential effects of exposure and response prevention in obsessive-compulsive washers. *Journal of Consulting and Clinical Psychology, 48,* 71–79.

Foa, E. B., Steketee, G., Turner, R. M., & Fischer, S. C. (1980). Effects of imaginal exposure to feared disasters in obsessive-compulsive checkers. *Behaviour Research and Therapy, 18*, 449–455.

Franklin, M. E., Abramowitz, J. S., Kozak, M. J., Levitt, J. T., & Foa, E. B. (2000). Effectiveness of exposure and ritual prevention for obsessive-compulsive disorder: Randomized compared with nonrandomized samples. *Journal of Consulting and Clinical Psychology, 68*(4), 594.

Franklin, M. S., Dingfelder, H. E., Freeman, J. B., Ivarsson, T., Heyman, I., Sookman, D., McKay, D., Storch, E. A., & March, J. (2015). Cognitive behavioral therapy for pediatric obsessive-compulsive disorder: Empirical review and clinical recommendations. *Psychiatry Research, 227*, 78–92.

Freeman, J., Sapyta, J., Garcia, A., Compton, S., Khanna, M., Flessner, C., Fitzgerald, D., Mauro, C., Dingfelder, R., Benito, K., Harrison, J., Curry, J., Foa, E., March, J., Moore, P., & Franklin, M. (2014). Family-based treatment of early childhood obsessive-compulsive disorder: The Pediatric Obsessive-Compulsive Disorder Treatment Study for Young Children (POTS Jr)—A randomized clinical trial. *JAMA Psychiatry, 71*(6), 689–698.

Freeston, M. H., Ladouceur, R., Gagnon, F., Thibodeau, N., Rheaume, J., Letarte, H., & Bujold, A. (1997). Cognitive-behavioral treatment of obsessive thoughts: A controlled study. *Journal of Consulting and Clinical Psychology, 65*(3), 405–413.

Glazier, K., Wetterneck, C., Singh, S., & Williams, M. (2015). Stigma and shame as barriers to treatment for obsessive-compulsive related disorders. *Journal of Depression & Anxiety, 4*, 3.

Goodman, W. K., Price, L. H., Rasmussen, S. A., Mazure, C., Delgado, P., Heninger, G. R., & Charney, D. S. (1989a). The Yale-Brown Obsessive-Compulsive Scale: Validity. *Archives of General Psychiatry, 46*, 1012–1016.

Goodman, W. K., Price, L. H., Rasmussen, S. A., Mazure, C., Fleischmann, R. L., Hill, C. L., Heninger, G. R., & Charney, D. S. (1989b). The Yale-Brown Obsessive-Compulsive Scale: Development, use, and reliability. *Archives of General Psychiatry, 46*, 1006–1011.

Goodwin, R., Koenen, K.C., Hellman, F., Guardino, M., & Struening, E. (2002). Helpseeking and access to mental health treatment for obsessive-compulsive disorder. *Acta Psychiatrica Scandinavica, 106*, 143–149.

Hirschtritt, M. E., Bloch, M. H., & Matthews, C. A. (2017). Obsessive-compulsive disorder: Advances in diagnosis and treatment. *JAMA, 317*, 1358–1367.

Hiss, H., Foa, E. B., & Kozak, M. J. (1994). Relapse prevention program for treatment of obsessive-compulsive disorder. *Journal of Consulting and Clinical Psychology, 62*, 801–808.

Hodgson, R., Rachman, S., & Marks, I. (1972). The treatment of chronic obsessive-compulsive neurosis: Follow-up and further findings. *Behaviour Research and Therapy, 10*, 181–189.

Jacoby, R. J., & Abramowitz, J. S. (2016). Inhibitory learning approaches to exposure therapy: A critical review and translation to obsessive-compulsive disorder. *Clinical Psychology Review, 49*, 28–40.

Jacoby, R. J., Abramowitz, J. S., Blakey, S. M., & Reuman, L. (2019). Is the hierarchy necessary? Gradual versus variable exposure intensity in the treatment of unacceptable obsessional thoughts. *Journal of Behavior Therapy and Experimental Psychiatry, 64*, 54–63.

Johnco, C., McGuire, J. F., Roper, T., & Storch, E. A. (2020). A meta-analysis of dropout rates from exposure with response prevention and pharmacological treatment for youth with obsessive compulsive disorder. *Depression and Anxiety, 37*, 407–417.

Keeley, M. L., Storch, E. A., Merlo, L. J., & Geffken, G. R. (2008). Clinical predictors of response to cognitive-behavioral therapy for obsessive-compulsive disorder. *Clinical Psychology Review, 28*(1), 118–130.

Kenwright, M., Marks, I., Graham, C., Franses, A., & Mataix-Cols, D. (2005). Brief scheduled phone support from a clinician to enhance computer-aided self-help for obsessive-compulsive disorder: Randomized controlled trial. *Journal of Clinical Psychology, 61*(12), 1499–1508.

Knopp, J., Knowles, S., Bee, P., Lovell, K., & Bower, P. (2013). A systematic review of predictors and moderators of response to psychological therapies in OCD: Do we have enough empirical evidence to target treatment? *Clinical Psychology Review, 33*(8), 1067–1081.

Kringlen, E. (1965). Obsessional neurotics: A long-term follow-up. *The British Journal of Psychiatry, 111*, 709–722.

Lang, P. (1977). Imagery in therapy: An information processing analysis of fear. *Behavior Therapy, 8*, 862–886.

Lax, T., Basoglu, M., & Marks, I. M. (1992). Expectancy and compliance as predictors of outcome in obsessive-compulsive disorder. *Behavioural Psychotherapy, 20*, 257–266.

Lebowitz, E. R., Omer, H., Hermes, H., & Scahill, L. (2014). Parent training for childhood anxiety disorders: The SPACE Program. *Cognitive and Behavioral Practice, 21*(4), 456–469.

LeDoux, J. E. (2000). Emotion circuits in the brain. *Annual Review of Neuroscience, 23,* 155–184.

Lindsay, M., Crino, R., & Andrews, G. (1997). Controlled trial of exposure and response prevention in obsessive-compulsive disorder. *The British Journal of Psychiatry, 171,* 135–139.

Luxton, D. D., McCann, R. A., Bush, N. E., Mishkind, M. C., & Reger, G. M. (2011). mHealth for mental health: Integrating smartphone technology in behavioral healthcare. *Professional Psychology: Research and Practice, 42*(6), 505.

March, J. S., Frances, A., Carpenter, D., & Kahn, D. (1997). The expert consensus guidelines series: Treatment of obsessive-compulsive disorder. *The Journal of Clinical Psychiatry, 58*(Suppl. 4), 1–25.

Mataix-Cols, D., & Marks, I. M. (2006). Self-help with minimal therapist contact for obsessive–compulsive disorder: A review. *European Psychiatry, 21*(2), 75–80.

McKay, D. (2018). Introduction to the special issue: Integration of technological advances in cognitive-behavior therapy. *Behavior Therapy, 49,* 851–852.

McKay, D., Sookman, D., Neziroglu, F., Wilhelm, S., Stein, D., Kyrios, M., Mathews, K., & Veale, D. (2015). Efficacy of cognitive-behavior therapy for obsessive-compulsive disorder. *Psychiatry Research, 227,* 104–113.

McLean, P. D., Whittal, M. L., Thordarson, D. S., Taylor, S., Söchting, I., Koch, W. J., . . . Anderson, K. W. (2001). Cognitive versus behavior therapy in the group treatment of obsessive-compulsive disorder. Journal of Consulting and Clinical Psychology, 69(2), 205.

McNally, R. J. (2007). Mechanisms of exposure therapy: How neuroscience can improve psychological treatments for anxiety disorders. *Clinical Psychology Review, 27,* 750–759.

Mehta, M. (1990). A comparative study of family-based and patient-based behavioural management in obsessive-compulsive disorder. *The British Journal of Psychiatry, 157,* 133–135.

Meyer, V. (1966). Modification of expectations in cases with obsessional rituals. *Behaviour Research and Therapy, 4,* 273–280.

Meyer, V., Levy, R., & Schnurer, A. (1974). The behavioral treatment of obsessive-compulsive disorders. In H. R. Beech (Ed.), *Obsessional states* (pp. 233–258). Methuen.

Mowrer, O. H. (1947). On the dual nature of learning—a reinterpretation of "conditioning" and "problem solving." *Harvard Education Review, 17,* 102–148.

Mowrer, O. (1960). *Learning theory and behavior.* Wiley.

Nakatani, E., Nakagawa, A., Nakao, T., Yoshizato, C., Nabeyama, M., Kudo, A., Isomura, K., Kato, N., Yoshioka, K., & Kawamoto, M. (2005). A randomized trial of Japanese patients with obsessive-compulsive disorder: Effectiveness of behavior therapy and fluvoxamine. *Psychotherapy and Psychosomatics, 74,* 269–276.

Nargesi, F., Fathiashtiani, A., Davodi, I., & Ashrafi, E. (2019). The effect of unified transdiagnostic treatment on anxiety sensitivity, distress tolerance and obsessive-compulsive symptoms in individuals with obsessive-compulsive disorder. *Psychological Achievements, 26*(2), 49–66.

Olatunji, B. O., Davis, M. L., Powers, M. B., & Smits, J. A. J. (2013). Cognitive-behavioral therapy for obsessive-compulsive disorder: A meta-analysis of treatment outcome and moderators. *Journal of Psychiatric Research, 47,* 33–41.

Ong, C. W., Clyde, J. W., Bluett, E. J., Levin, M. E., & Twohig, M. P. (2016). Dropout rates in exposure with response prevention for obsessive-compulsive disorder: What do the data really say? *Journal of Anxiety Disorders, 40,* 8–17.

Öst, L. G., Havnen, A., Hansen, B., & Kvale, G. (2015). Cognitive behavioral treatments of obsessive-compulsive disorder: A systematic review and meta-analysis of studies published 1993–2013. *Clinical Psychology Review, 40,* 156–169.

Pozza, A., & Dèttore, D. (2017). Drop-out and efficacy of group versus individual cognitive behavioural therapy: What works best for obsessive-compulsive disorder? A systematic review and meta-analysis of direct comparisons. *Psychiatry Research, 258,* 24–36.

Rabavilas, A., Boulougouris, J., & Stefanis, C. (1976). Duration of flooding sessions in the treatment of obsessive-compulsive patients. *Behaviour Research and Therapy, 14,* 349–355.

Rachman, S. (1980) Emotional processing. *Behaviour Research and Therapy, 18,* 51–60.

Rachman, S. (1993). Obsessions, responsibility and guilt. *Behaviour Research and Therapy, 31,* 149–154.

Rachman, S., & Hodgson, R. J. (1980). *Obsessions and compulsions.* Prentice Hall.

Rescorla, R. A. (1972). A theory of Pavlovian conditioning: Variations in the effectiveness of reinforcement and nonreinforcement. *Classical conditioning, Current research and theory, 2,* 64–69..

Rescorla, R. A. (2006). Deepened extinction from compound stimulus presentation. *Journal of Experimental Psychology: Animal Behavior Processes, 32*(2), 135–144.

Rowa, K., Antony, M. M., Summerfeldt, L. J., Purdon, C., Young, L., & Swinson, R. P. (2007). Office-based vs. home-based behavioral treatment for obsessive compulsive disorder: A preliminary study. *Behaviour Research and Therapy, 45*, 1883–1892.

Salkovskis, P. M. (1996). Cognitive-behavioral approaches to the understanding of obsessional problems. In R. Rapee (Ed.), *Current controversies in the anxiety disorders* (pp. 103–133). Guilford.

Simpson, H. B., Marcus, S. M., Zuckoff, A., Franklin, M., & Foa, E. B. (2012). Patient adherence to cognitive-behavioral therapy predicts long-term outcome in obsessive-compulsive disorder. *The Journal of Clinical Psychiatry, 73*, 1265–1266.

Solomon, R. L., Kamin, L. J., & Wynne, L. C. (1953). Traumatic avoidance learning: The outcomes of several extinction procedures with dogs. *Journal of Abnormal Social Psychology, 48*, 291–302.

Steketee, G. S., Chambless, D. L., & Tran, G. Q. (2001). Effects of Axis I and II comorbidity on behavior therapy outcome for obsessive-compulsive disorder and agoraphobia. *Comprehensive Psychiatry, 42*, 76–86.

Storch, E. A., Caporino, N. E., Morgan, J. R., Lewin, A. B., Rojas, A., Brauer, L., . . . Murphy, T. K. (2011). Preliminary investigation of web-camera delivered cognitive-behavioral therapy for youth with obsessive-compulsive disorder. *Psychiatry Research, 189*(3), 407–412.

Taylor, S. (1995). Assessment of obsessions and compulsions: Reliability, validity, and sensitivity to treatment effects. *Clinical Psychology Review, 15*, 261–296.

Tibi, L., van Oppen, P., van Balkom, A. J. L. M., Eikelenboom, M., Emmelkamp, P. M. G., & Anholt, G. E. (2019). Predictors of treatment outcome in OCD: An interpersonal perspective. *Journal of Anxiety Disorders, 68*, 102153.

Tumur, I., Kaltenthaler, E., Ferriter, M., Beverley, C., & Parry, G. (2007). Computerised cognitive behaviour therapy for obsessive-compulsive disorder: A systematic review. *Psychotherapy and Psychosomatics, 76*(4), 196–202.

Van Ameringen, M., Turna, J., Khalesi, Z., Pullia, K., & Patterson, B. (2017). There is an app for that! The current state of mobile applications (apps) for DSM-5 obsessive-compulsive disorder, posttraumatic stress disorder, anxiety, and mood disorders. *Depression and Anxiety, 34*, 526–539.

van Balkom, A. J., de Haan, E., van Oppen, P., Spinhoven, P., Hoogduin, K. A., & van Dyck, R. (1998). Cognitive and behavioral therapies alone versus in combination with fluvoxamine in the treatment of obsessive compulsive disorder. *The Journal of Nervous and Mental Disease, 186*(8), 492–499.

Vogel, P. A., Launes, G., Moen, E. M., Solem, S., Hansen, B., Håland, Å. T., & Himle, J. A. (2012). Videoconference-and cell phone-based cognitive-behavioral therapy of obsessive-compulsive disorder: A case series. *Journal of Anxiety Disorders, 26*(1), 158–164.

Vogel, P. A., Stiles, T. C., & Gotestam, K. G. (2004). Adding cognitive therapy elements to exposure therapy for obsessive compulsive disorder: A controlled study. *Behavioural and Cognitive Psychotherapy, 32*, 275–290.

Wheaton, M. G., & Chen, S. R. (2020). Homework completion in treating obsessive-compulsive disorder with exposure and ritual prevention: A review of the empirical literature. *Cognitive Therapy and Research, 45*, 236–249. https://doi.org/10.1007/s10608-020-10125-0

Williams, M. T., Domanico, J., Marques, L., Leblanc, N. J., & Turkheimer, E. (2012). Barriers to treatment among African Americans with obsessive-compulsive disorder. *Journal of Anxiety Disorders, 26*, 555–563.

Wootton, B. M., Titov, N., Dear, B. F., Spence, J., & Kemp, A. (2011). The acceptability of Internet-based treatment and characteristics of an adult sample with obsessive compulsive disorder: An Internet survey. *PLoS One, 6*(6), e20548.

CHAPTER 20
Cognitive Treatment for Obsessive-Compulsive Disorder

Morag A. Yule, Maureen L. Whittal, *and* Melisa Robichaud

Abstract

The cornerstone of cognitive therapy (CT) for OCD is based upon the knowledge that unwanted intrusions are essentially a universal experience. Therefore, it is not the presence of the intrusion that is problematic, but rather the associated meaning or interpretation of the intrusion. Treatment is flexible, depending upon the nature of the appraisals and beliefs, but it can include strategies focused on targeting inflated responsibility and overestimation of threat, importance and control of thoughts, and the need for perfectionism and certainty. The role of concealment and the relationship to personal values are important maintaining and etiological factors. Short- and long-term treatment outcomes are reviewed, along with predictors of treatment response and mechanisms of action, and the discussion concludes with future directions for CT for OCD.

Key Words: cognitive treatment, OCD, treatment outcome, mediators, prediction

The treatment of obsessive-compulsive disorder (OCD) has advanced greatly in the past 40 years, shifting from a view of OCD as a highly treatment-resistant disorder to that of a disorder that responds well to empirically supported psychotherapies. A relatively recent treatment that has shown promise is cognitively focused therapy for OCD. This chapter reviews the evolution from behavior therapy to cognitive therapy (CT) for OCD, and it provides a detailed description of the OCD CT protocol using clinical case examples. In addition, the chapter presents a thorough review of research on the short- and long-term efficacy of CT, both in isolation and in combination with exposure and response prevention (E/RP). Finally, mediating variables underlying the effectiveness of the treatment, as well as predictors of treatment outcome, are discussed.

The Evolution of CT for OCD

The introduction of behavioral conceptualizations to the understanding of anxiety disorders led to great strides in the treatment for OCD. Previously OCD was viewed as an intractable disorder when psychoanalytic theories were applied, but the two-stage theory of fear acquisition (Dollard & Miller, 1950; Mowrer, 1939) provided the first behavioral foray into a model for the development and maintenance of OCD (see Chapter 10 for more detail on behavioral theories of OCD). The resulting psychosocial treatment, exposure and response prevention (E/RP), remains the gold standard treatment for OCD. Used alone, E/RP is considered efficacious for mild to moderate forms of the disorder, and in more severe forms of the disorder, a combination of medication and E/RP is the recommendation (March et al., 1997; Katzman et al., 2014). Similarly, Koran et al. (2007) recommended combined treatment in cases where cognitive-behavioral therapy (CBT) monotherapy failed or when patients were deemed too severe to benefit from CBT monotherapy. Moreover, a number of clinical trials conducted throughout the world identified significant treatment gains when E/RP was the assigned treatment: in one meta-analysis, Yale-Brown Obsessive-Compulsive Scale (Y-BOCS) scores showed an average decline of 43.5% after E/RP, and an aggregate effect size (ES) of $d = 1.50$ for E/RP was found (Abramowitz et al., 2002). In a more recent meta-analysis, Öst et al. (2015) reported a similar ES for E/RP and an average Y-BOCS score posttreatment decline of 55% . It is clear that E/RP is a highly efficacious treatment for OCD, and that significant gains result both in the short and long term (see Chapter 19 for more detail on treatment outcome with behavior therapy).

Despite the obvious benefits of E/RP, it also has some limitations that dampen its salutary effects, largely due to the nature of the intervention itself. In brief, E/RP involves repeated exposure to feared situations and the suspension of compulsive responses. For example, an individual with contamination obsessions and associated washing rituals might be asked to touch a bathroom door handle and resist the compulsion to wash their hands. Repeated exposure to a feared situation and blocking of the compulsive response are posited to provide disconfirmatory evidence about the dangerousness of the situation and to allow for habituation (Foa & Kozak, 1986). Although E/RP is typically conducted in a graduated fashion, wherein the patient addresses moderate fears prior to facing more severe fears, individuals are nonetheless required to deliberately and repeatedly approach situations that are perceived as threatening, that cause marked anxiety, and that have typically been avoided. As a result, it is unsurprising that a significant minority of patients with OCD either refuse or drop out of treatment. Up to 25% of patients refuse E/RP treatment, and between 3% and 12% will drop out of treatment early (Foa et al., 1983; Kobak et al., 1998; van Oppen et al., 1995; Öst et al., 2015). Although E/RP remains an efficacious treatment for OCD, Stanley and Turner (1995) found that the benefits were attenuated when a conservative estimate of 30% was used to account for individuals who refuse or drop out of treatment. Of note, only 63% of patients with OCD will display at least a moderate reduction in symptoms after treatment. Moreover, research suggests that between 10% and 33% of patients with OCD fail to show any benefits from E/RP, meet criteria for improvement, or maintain their treatment gains (Foa et al., 1985; Foa & Kozak, 1996; Steketee et al., 2000).

The efficacy of E/RP may also be impacted by the particular symptom presentation of OCD patients. Compulsions are highly varied and idiographic, ranging from behavioral rituals like washing, checking, or ordering/arranging, to mental rituals and neutralizations, such as the mental repetition of prayers or specific words or sentences. In a review of treatment outcome studies, Ball et al. (1996) concluded that although E/RP has established benefits for patients with OCD presenting with washing and checking compulsions, its effectiveness for other OCD subtypes was less clear. In particular, E/RP alone is viewed as inadequate for the treatment of pure or classic obsessionals and ruminators, primary obsessional slowness, and symmetry/ordering rituals (Frost & Steketee, 1998; Rachman, 1985, 2003; Salkovskis & Westbrook, 1989).

Despite the obvious efficacy of E/RP in treating many OCD symptoms, there clearly remain significant limitations, so that alternative treatment options are warranted. Since the seminal article by Salkovskis (1985) elucidating the role of cognitive factors in the maintenance of OCD, researchers have identified a number of dysfunctional beliefs linked to OCD, including overimportance of thoughts, exaggerated responsibility, the need to control thoughts, and overestimation of threat (for a review, see Obsessive Compulsive Cognitions Working Group [OCCWG], 1997, and Frost & Steketee, 2002). To date, a number of cognitive theories of OCD and associated treatments have been developed (Clark & Purdon, 1993; Rachman, 1997, 1998). The underlying principle of the current cognitive conceptualizations of OCD is that unwanted intrusions are a universal and normal experience, and it is the individual's appraisal of the intrusion and resultant response to that appraisal that lead to the development and maintenance of OCD (see Chapter 11 for a discussion of cognitive models of OCD). Inherent in cognitive theory is the development of an idiographic model for OCD, such that treatment is tailored to a patient's particular symptom presentation and dysfunctional beliefs. Given the limitations of E/RP in addressing certain OCD subtypes, as well as many patients' difficulty in tolerating exposure, CT was developed as an alternative to E/RP and a complement to existing behavioral interventions.

Treatment

PSYCHOEDUCATION

Subsequent to assessment, CT begins with presentation of an idiographic cognitive model for the maintenance of OCD. The goals of the educational sessions are to discuss the ubiquity of unwanted intrusions (Rachman & de Silva, 1978; Radomsky et al., 2014) and to identify the importance of the appraisal process. Appraisals are differentiated from feared consequences and are identified as the meaning given to the intrusive thought. Appraisals indicate the individual's belief about what the intrusive thought says about them as a person. For example, upon leaving the house, a typical doubter/checker may have an intrusive thought of the stove being on. An appraisal typically associated with this intrusion may be related to responsibility (e.g., "It will be my fault if there is a fire; I'm careless"). Depending upon the content of the intrusion, some appraisals are more easily accessible than others. Obsessionals with ego-dystonic repugnant intrusions typically have little trouble in identifying appraisals (e.g., "I'm evil, dangerous," etc.), whereas others may have more difficulty. Given that unwanted intrusions are essentially universal, treatment does not directly target obsessions. However, because appraisals tend to differentiate clinical from nonclinical presentations, treatment is focused on identifying, challenging, and testing existing interpretations.

To illustrate the importance of the appraisal process, patients are provided a list of intrusions experienced by people without OCD (Rachman & de Silva, 1978). Using this list, patients are asked to identify infrequent intrusions that are associated with little to no distress. The appraisals of the frequent and infrequent intrusions can be graphically illustrated side by side using a white board. Figure 20.1 illustrates the idiographic cognitive model. The right side of the figure reflects the appraisal process experienced by a doubter/checker, whereas the left side of Figure 20.1 illustrates a typical but relatively nondistressing intrusion. The difference between the appraisals is clear. The OCD appraisals on the right side of Figure 20.1 are characterized by negative, personally relevant meaning. Conversely, the appraisals of the nonclinical individuals who experience infrequent intrusions, on the left side of Figure 20.1, tend to be neutral in meaning and nonthreatening and therefore they are not associated with neutralizing actions or the establishment of a cycle of maintenance.

Because treatment is focused on the appraisals, initial assignments involve increasing familiarity with the cognitive model by identifying appraisals while experiencing an obsession. Patients are provided self-monitoring forms and are asked to track a variety of real-time situations in which intrusions and associated appraisals are experienced, as well as the coping behavior (e.g., compulsion, other neutralization, avoidance) used in the moment.

The universality of unwanted intrusions is the foundation from which treatment is based. Therefore, this information is emphasized throughout treatment. For some patients, the ubiquity of unwanted intrusions comes as a surprise and a relief. Others may question that everyone experiences unwanted intrusions. Regardless of the patient's pre-existing knowledge of intrusive thoughts, they are asked to share the list of intrusions with friends and family members. For those patients who have concealed their OCD, this task is placed later in treatment. Alternatively, clinicians can ask their coworkers to anonymously complete a survey regarding their own experience of unwanted intrusions and the associated appraisals. The goal with these surveys is to normalize the presence of intrusions and for patients to have explicit knowledge that people they know also experience unwanted intrusions that potentially do not differ in content from their own. Part of the exercise is also to enquire about how others appraise their intrusions. The latter is another opportunity for patients to distinguish the threatening appraisals that characterize their OCD from those experienced by people with infrequent intrusions. If therapists

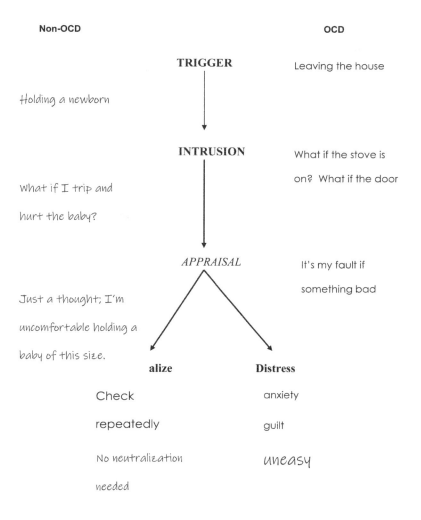

Figure 20.1. Please pick-up Figure 18.1 from 1st ed (ISBN: 9780195376210)

are comfortable sharing their own experiences with infrequent intrusions, it would be appropriate to do so at this stage of treatment, because it aids in the normalization process.

THE COGNITIVE APPROACH TO OCD

Given the heterogeneous presentation of OCD, the direction of treatment depends upon the characteristics of the appraisals. Self-monitoring and self-report questionnaires (e.g., the Obsessional Belief Questionnaire [OBQ] and Interpretations of Intrusions Inventory [III]) are helpful tools to ascertain the relative importance of cognitive domains. The approaches suggested herein are discussed according to cognitive domain, but how they are put together in the course of treatment is idiographic. The existing published treatment manuals (e.g., Rachman, 2003; Wilhelm & Steketee, 2006) reflect this flexible approach to treatment. Despite the varying presentations and treatment strategies, the overarching goal remains the same for each patient; to help them construct a less threatening explanation based upon their own experience that accounts for the development and maintenance of the intrusions. The following cognitive domains are discussed in accordance with the work completed by the OCCWG and the factor analysis of the primary measure of cognitive domains in OCD, the OBQ (OCCWG, 2005).

IMPORTANCE AND CONTROL OF THOUGHTS

This cognitive domain reflects the tendency to view the mere presence of a thought as suggestive of its importance, as well as the belief that one should be able to control one's thoughts. This domain is likely to be a central one for obsessionals and for those with OCD themes that include ego-dystonic, repugnant thoughts, images, and impulses. If a thought is considered important, a common response is to dwell on that thought, which ultimately strengthens the belief in the importance of the thought. In dwelling on thoughts, patients often wonder why such an unusual thought is present, that it must mean something if it occurred. With ex consequentia reasoning (Arntz et al., 1995), the anxiety that typically accompanies these thoughts may also provide evidence that the thought is important (i.e., "If I'm anxious when I have this thought, there must be danger").

Thought–action fusion (TAF; Shafran et al., 1996), as the term suggests, is the belief that thought and outcome or action are linked. Factor analysis of this construct supports a two-factor solution, Likelihood TAF and Moral TAF. Likelihood TAF reflects the belief that merely having a thought (e.g., of a family member's being involved in a motor vehicle accident) increases the probability of occurrence of that event. Moral TAF involves the judgment that thought and actions are morally equivalent (e.g., an unwanted thought of stabbing the family dog is as bad as stabbing the dog).

To the extent that a thought is appraised as foreshadowing the future (i.e., Likelihood TAF) or as morally equivalent to engaging in the action (Moral TAF), it follows that the thought is likely to be considered important. Thought experiments can be used to challenge the power and independence of thought (i.e., a thought does not start a chain reaction resulting in the feared consequence). Patients are asked to think about an untoward event happening to an individual who is a routine part of the patient's life. Often the clinician is the "target" of these initial thought experiments, but it can also include family and friends. The untoward event is meant to be something that is observable to the patient and uncommon but not rare. If a low (e.g., getting typhoid) or high (e.g., stomach flu in January) base rate event is chosen, it provides no information on the power or independence of thought.

The strength of belief in TAF lies on a continuum. For those who hold strong TAF beliefs, Freeston et al. (1996) suggested using inanimate objects (e.g., thinking about a reliable appliance breaking) for initial thought experiments. Interestingly, Likelihood TAF almost always focuses on negative outcomes, and TAF for positive events (e.g., thinking about winning the lottery increases the likelihood) is rare in OCD. However, TAF experiments (e.g., purchasing inexpensive scratch tickets and thinking about winning) can be instituted as a starting point if positively oriented TAF is present. Thought experiments continue throughout treatment, with the severity of the outcome increasing (e.g., mild ankle sprain, broken bone, coma, death). All experiments are debriefed according to what they reveal about the ability of thought to produce outcome and the independence of thought and action.

Using a continuum can be a helpful strategy to challenge Moral TAF. Depending upon the intent of the exercise, the continuum can take several forms. In one version, the continuum is anchored at each extreme with "best person" and "worst person." The people chosen in these extremes are either public figures or individuals personally known to the patient. In the context of the best and worst anchors, the patient places themselves on the continuum. Individuals experiencing ego-dystonic obsessions often place themselves near or at the worst end of the continuum. Situations varying in intentionality are put forward, as well as those that are differentiated by thought and action. Examples include thoughts of cheating on your taxes versus actually doing so, using your vehicle as a weapon to murder another person, accidentally killing someone (manslaughter), and killing an individual who committed suicide by jumping in front of the car. Typically, patients have no trouble rating the relative goodness/badness of the person despite the brief descriptions, perhaps secondary to a tendency to engage in black-and-white thinking. A double standard often becomes apparent: patients are able to separate thought from action for others, but not for themselves. Investigating the origin of the double standard and challenging its utility, as well as exploring the feared consequences associated with eradicating it, can result in patients' reassessment of themselves in a more positive light.

A different type of continuum may be helpful for individuals with a strong moral code or the belief that being a responsible person is a positive personality trait. Anchors similar to the previous continuum are used, and the patient provides names of people they personally know at each of the anchors. Relative "goodness" and "badness" is emphasized during this exercise, because patients often do not personally know people who are "truly bad," just people who are "bad" relative to the other people in their lives. Once these anchors are identified, the patient once again places themself on the continuum. The patient and therapist collaborate on the adjectives that would describe each of the people at the anchors (e.g., kind, caring, responsible, selfish, insensitive) and the percentage of time the person displays this characteristic. The clinician endeavors to ensure that the patient proposes realistic percentages, as opposed to those that may reflect black-and-white thinking. The patient is then asked to rate the percentage of time they display the same behaviors (e.g., "How often do you show others that you care?" "How often are you selfish?"). The goal of this type of continuum is twofold. An initial goal is to have patients recognize that that they do not have access to the same information in judging other people as when judging themselves. In judging themselves, they have access to their thoughts as well as their behaviors, whereas for others, judgments of worth/value/responsibility are based exclusively upon observable behaviors. It is emphasized that we see only what others want to show us, and we cannot know the thoughts of other people. More importantly, how others judge us is based upon our actions and not on our thoughts.

If a thought is appraised as important and it may start a chain reaction of events terminating in catastrophe, it follows that the intrusion should be controlled by either its quick removal or efforts to prevent its initial appearance. Mental control strategies include thought suppression, distraction, and mental rituals (e.g., changing the word "kill" into "kiss"). Mental control strategies paradoxically serve to increase the frequency of intrusions, probably in part because of the heightened focus of attention on the thought process. Attention experiments can illustrate this process. A meaningless target is identified (e.g., "for sale" signs, flags) and patients are asked to recall instances of seeing the target item in the previous week. Patients are then given an assignment to look for and record sightings of the target item. Not surprisingly, attention toward a stimulus increases the frequency with which it is seen and remembered, particularly when it has meaning. Other examples of the latter include buying a new vehicle and seeing it with increasing frequency on the street. Couples who are pregnant also commonly report seeing more pregnant women than they saw in the months prior to starting a family. These examples provide an alternate explanation for the increased frequency of the thoughts—that they are more frequent secondary to the meaning attributed to them and the resulting attention/focus on the person's own thinking.

In an alternating day experiment, being "on duty" or hypervigilant for intrusions is contrasted with being "off duty" regarding thoughts (Rachman, 2002). At the end of each day, patients are asked to record the severity of their OCD, anxiety, and responsibility and the percentage of the day they were able to complete the strategy of the day (i.e., either being off duty/letting thoughts come and go, versus being on duty/hypervigilant for intrusions). Patients may be surprised to find that, when they are able to be off duty, it often results in fewer obsessions and reduced anxiety and sense of personal responsibility. Using the conclusions reached with the alternating day experiment, patients are encouraged to let thoughts in and to decrease their reliance on efforts to block or get rid of thoughts.

INFLATED RESPONSIBILITY AND OVERESTIMATION OF THREAT

Salkovskis (1985) highlighted responsibility interpretations in his cognitive model of OCD, and subsequently suggested that appraisals of responsibility are associated with increased awareness of intrusions and associated triggers and attempts to discharge responsibility that include overt and covert neutralizing (Salkovskis, 1999). Inflated responsibility potentially plays a role in all OCD presentations, but it is particularly evident among individuals with contamination concerns and doubting/checking (e.g., "It will be my fault if something bad happens to my family"). Pie-charting is a central strategy for challenging responsibility. Ratings of subjective probability for either a hypothetical event (e.g., if there was a house fire tomorrow) or actual event (e.g., a child falls and scrapes their knee) can be used to illustrate this strategy. The patient and therapist collaborate on determining the other people or situations that contribute to the event under investigation. The patient is included in this list but is only considered after others are given consideration. Relative proportions of responsibility are graphically assigned, again with the patient's portion assigned at the end. Logical estimates of responsibility, once other factors are considered, are often much lower than subjective responsibility estimates. For some, responsibility is seen as absolute (i.e., they are either responsible or not). The goal with pie-charting is viewing responsibility as a shared phenomenon. Figure 20.2 demonstrates a pie chart for an individual concerned about contaminating a person who broke into their car. The individual initially assumed high amounts of responsibility, but after considering the other people and factors involved, the amount of responsibility the individual assumed was notably lower.

Responsibility transfers can be useful if the patient cannot delegate tasks to others (e.g., a spouse who must retire for the evening prior to the patient's nighttime checking routine). However, the transfers not helpful if patients are purposely avoiding responsibility (e.g., the patient who quickly exits the house, leaving the spouse to lock the door). In the example of a checker, the patient's spouse or family member who lives in the same house is asked to assume physical and psychological responsibility for the safety and security of the household. If it would be helpful, a contract that both parties sign can be written up to reflect the agreement. The spouse then assumes the checking duties if they so wish, as the choice to check now belongs to them. The patient refrains from overseeing the process or seeking reassurance regarding completion of the activities. A slight variation of this exercise includes an alternating day experiment that also addresses overestimation of threat. The spouse or family member is asked to check on some nights but not on others,, and although they keep track of each condition, the patient is deliberately not informed of the schedule. Each morning, the patient is asked to review the safety and security of the household. The goal of this behavioral experiment is twofold: allowing the sharing of

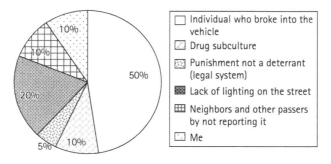

Figure 20.2. Please pick-up Figure 18.2 from 1st ed (ISBN: 9780195376210)

Subjective probability of the feared consequence = 70%

Event	Probability
1. Leaving stove burner on	1/100
2. Something flammable on or near stove	10/100
3. Catches fire	50/100
4. Smoke alarm doesn't go off	1/1000
5. Goes un-noticed by occupants of the house	10/100
6. House engulfed in flames	

Probability of that final step is

$$\frac{1 \times 10 \times 50 \times 1 \times 10}{100 \times 100 \times 100 \times 1000 \times 100} = \frac{5000}{100{,}000{,}000{,}000} = .000005\%$$

Figure 20.3. Subjective probability of the feared consequence = 70% Probability of that final step is 1,000, 000,000

$(1 \times 10 \times 50 \times 1 \times 10)/(100 \times 100 \times 100 \times 1000 \times 100) = 5{,}000/100{,}000{,}000{,}000 = .00000005\%$

responsibility and assessing the lack of catastrophe associated with the patient's not checking. Responsibility transfers are temporary strategies; often, the learning that comes from these methods occurs quickly and there is a natural return to sharing of responsibility. In instances where the natural resumption of shared responsibility does not occur, it can be made explicit, so as to not establish a precedent for family accommodation.

As already mentioned, overestimation of threat is closely related to inflated responsibility. In part, the patient's failure to account for all the steps that would need to occur prior to a final feared consequence leads to threat overestimation. For example, leaving a stove burner on is often seen as a direct line to an uncontrollable fire. Figure 20.3 lists the other necessary steps prior to the final feared consequence. Probabilities associated with each step are estimated. The logical probability of the final feared event is the multiplicative product of the steps before it. For example, if there are three steps, each with a 1 in 10 chance of occurrence, the overall probability is 1 in 1,000.

PERFECTIONISM AND CERTAINTY

The need to have order and to do things in a particular way is a characteristic feature of people with OCD. For some, it is associated with magical thinking and the patient's compulsions involve efforts to keep others safe, which is probably a reflection of appraisals of overimportance of thoughts and inflated responsibility. For others, the need to have things in a particular place or done in a particular way reflects personal preference and avoidance of the tension and anxiety that arise if it the task is not completed to the individual's satisfaction. There is often an ego-syntonic foundation to the behaviors (e.g., the person likes to have things clean). What is distressing is the amount of time it takes to achieve an acceptable standard. Challenging this perfectionism involves identifying the feared consequences, beyond anxiety/tension, associated with not being perfect. Once the function of the perfectionism is identified, designing a behavioral experiment to test these beliefs is the main thrust of treatment. As is typical in other behavioral experiments, it is important to construct experiments with observable and measurable effects (i.e., an increase in anxiety is not sufficient, but testing the consequences of high anxiety may be the focus of the experiment). Outcomes that are concrete and observable allow for maximal disconfirmation. For example, a patient intentionally leaves the towels in the bathroom askew, with the outcome measure being whether a guest responds to this with a judgmental comment.

The need for certainty is closely related to perfectionism. With the exception of the need to know (e.g., people who have difficulty driving secondary to looping back to read billboards), the need for certainty likely plays a role in many OCD presentations (e.g., certainty that the door is locked, or that something is clean, and that danger is removed). If uncertainty exists, then it is possible that a mistake is looming; not knowing for certain is often equated with the possibility that it isn't correct. Normalizing uncertainty is helpful, and it can be done through surveys. A typical example is surveying people without OCD who remember locking their door and contrasting that number with the number of people who are certain that the door is locked. It is quite common for people to not recall locking their door, yet they "know" that it is locked. This finding can be surprising, because it is often not the case for individuals with OCD. The goal with the surveys is to demonstrate that just because something is not recalled, that does not mean that it was not done correctly. Not knowing for sure or not remembering is a normal part of the human experience, because many overlearned activities occur so frequently that they are not encoded as meaningful.

RELATIONSHIP AMONG VALUES, BELIEFS, AND INTRUSIONS

Although the experience of unwanted intrusions is essentially universal, the content of the intrusions is often a reflection of the individual's values. Using a nonclinical sample, Rowa and Purdon (2003) reported that participants who were asked questions regarding their most upsetting thought were more likely to state that the thought contradicted valued aspects of self, in contrast to participants reporting on a least upsetting thought. People tend not to have intrusions about individuals who are confident and strong but instead about those who are perceived as weak and vulnerable (e.g., children or the elderly). Moreover, intrusions tend to also focus on people or groups who are particularly important to the individual (e.g., a new mother who experiences intrusions regarding her infant).

Personal values likely also play an important role in the development of repetitive intrusions. For a thought to be noticed and recalled, it must be memorable in some way, perhaps as running counter to existing values. For something to be appraised as "bad" or inappropriate, there must be a framework to identify it as such, and it must be distinguished from "right" or acceptable. For instance, it is antithetical for an atheist to experience an intrusion perceived as blasphemous. If an individual with a history of violence has a thought about harming another person, the thought would be considered consistent with the existing value system and would not raise internal alarm bells regarding the possibility of losing control. On the other hand, a pacifist who has a violent thought would be more likely to react and to remember that thought due to its inconsistency with the person's value system.

The relationship among values, beliefs, and intrusions is explained to patients, and a tentative reinterpretation is put forward (Whittal et al., 2010). As mentioned, the person often believes that the intrusion is evidence that they are evil and untrustworthy. Alternatively, the therapist suggests that intrusions became repetitive because they are so different from the fundamental nature of the individual, and that the individual reacted with horror because they are especially kind, caring, and sensitive. Although this interchange is typically presented after several sessions, patients may respond with skepticism. If so, they are encouraged not to reject the reinterpretation but to let it remain as a possibility. Patients are then asked to "build their case" that they are indeed a kind, caring, and sensitive person. This exercise is idiographic but can include categorizing everyday behaviors (e.g., giving up a seat on a crowded bus to an elderly person) as reflective of someone who is kind or sensitive.

THE MAINTAINING ROLE OF CONCEALMENT

It is not uncommon for people with OCD to conceal their unwanted thoughts and compulsive behaviors from others. As discussed by Newth and Rachman (2001), there are a variety of reasons for concealment. However, the central fear that promotes concealment is the person's concern that others will think about them the same way they think of themselves (i.e., mad, bad, or dangerous) and ultimately abandon or reject them (e.g., "If my spouse knew about my violent thoughts toward her, she would be scared of me and leave the home"). As treatment progresses, if concealment is an issue, decreasing it becomes a therapeutic target provided there is a safe person in the patient's life to whom they can disclose.

Addressing concealment is typically introduced in the latter third of treatment for two primary reasons. It is often a very difficult task for the patient and is quite anxiety-provoking. The delay also provides the therapist the time to get to know the patient, to establish trust and rapport, and to become informed about the people in the patient's life. It is recommended that only those close to the patient who know the individual well be considered as candidates for receiving revealed information. A close friend or family member who has the benefit of knowing the person in a variety of situations is in a better position to offer an opinion than a casual acquaintance.

Concealment is particularly common among people with ego-dystonic obsessions (e.g., intrusive thoughts about harm to loved ones). The goal of revealing obsessions is a disconfirmation of the belief that the obsessional individual is in fact dangerous or evil and will be rejected or abandoned by others. That this disconfirmatory information is coming from someone who knows the patient well in a variety of settings or has longevity in the relationship strengthens the conclusion. Alternatively, if the patient is surrounded by critical people who seemingly have little to no understanding of psychological disorders, or if they choose to tell a casual acquaintance, this exercise has a high likelihood of failure and is not initiated.

Treatment Outcome/Literature Review
CT ALONE COMPARED TO EITHER WAIT-LISTING OR E/RP

The difficulty in separating CT from behavior therapy is broadly acknowledged. As pointed out by Abramowitz et al. (2005), behavior therapy contains cognitive elements and CT contains exposure. However, the thrust of each type of treatment does differ and is distinguishable. CT focuses on reappraising the meaning of intrusions and testing the veracity of these reappraisals through behavioral experiments. Behavior therapy emphasizes prolonged and repetitive exposure to the intrusions combined with refraining from engaging in the compulsive behavior (see Chapter 19), with the goal of extinguishing the fear response. In the context of exposure, it is common to discuss cognitive concepts, such as threat overestimation and responsibility, although this discussion is not central to the treatment. Although there are definite overlaps between the two types of treatment, the therapeutic techniques are quite different. The subsequent paragraphs describe the outcomes of cognitively focused treatments, followed by outcomes of CT combined with traditional E/RP.

van Oppen et al. (1995) completed the first randomized controlled trial (RCT) with contemporary CT, comparing it to E/RP using 71 participants randomized to either individual CT or E/RP. Session duration was 50 to 60 minutes. In the first six sessions, CT was completed without behavioral experiments, and E/RP was completed without a discussion of feared consequences. The groups were equivalent on all measures at the end of session six. An additional 10 sessions were completed that included behavioral experiments for the CT group and a discussion of feared consequences for the E/RP group. Seven participants from each condition dropped out of treatment. The following results are based upon the 57 participants who completed treatment. Although there were no between-group differences on any dependent measures, significantly more participants treated with CT improved to a clinically significant degree (50%) compared to those treated with E/RP (28%). There is a suggestion that the self-directed E/RP used by van Oppen et al. (1995) was less effective than that used in other studies and that the relatively high posttreatment Y-BOCS score of the exposure group (17.3) made the CT group look relatively strong (Foa et al., 1998; Steketee et al., 1998).

Jones and Menzies (1998) conducted a small RCT with a subgroup of individuals with OCD and contamination obsessions. Participants ($N=23$) were randomized to either a waiting list or active treatment focused on reducing the perception of danger associated with potential contaminants. Danger Ideation Reduction Therapy (DIRT), primarily a cognitive intervention, consisted of restructuring contamination thoughts, normalizing information from people who worked with potential contaminants (e.g., cleaners, bank tellers, and medical personnel), corrective information regarding illness and disease, logical probabilities, attentional focusing, and a discussion of the results of microbiological experiments. (In the microbiological component, the authors "contaminated" one hand using a variety of stimuli, such as petting a cat, shaking multiple hands, or touching the door of a public toilet. The control hand, which did not come into contact with the stimuli, was compared to the "contaminated" hand regarding the number of microorganisms present. In no case did the microbiologist detect differences between the control and experimental hand.) Treatment consisted of eight 60-minute sessions in groups of five to six participants over nine weeks. Assessments were completed before and after treatment and at three-month follow-up. On self-report measures of OCD and depression, the participants who completed DIRT ($n = 11$) reported significantly lower scores than wait-list participants ($n = 10$). Gains were maintained through the three-month follow-up, but there was no further decline in symptoms.

Cottraux et al. (2001) randomized 65 participants to either CT or intensive E/RP. Each group received 20 hours of individual treatment. Treatment in the CT group occurred weekly over 16 weeks. Participants in the E/RP group received 16 hours of treatment in the first four weeks and the remaining four hours of maintenance occurred over 12 weeks. Improvement was defined as a 25% reduction in Y-BOCS total scores from before to after treatment. Nonclinical status was defined as 50% Y-BOCS score reduction and a final posttreatment Y-BOCS score of < 8. The numbers of participants who reported improvement and reached nonclinical status after treatment and through a one-year follow-up did not differ between groups. Cottraux et al. (2001) concluded that the treatments had largely equivalent effects on OCD symptoms, but that CT recipients showed a broader change in other variables, including depression, interpretations of obsessions, and general fear.

McLean et al. (2001) used group treatment to compare CT and E/RP with 63 participants. Sessions were conducted over 12 consecutive weeks. Group treatment lasted 150 minutes and had two therapists and six to eight participants per group. The CT involved challenging appraisals of overimportance of thoughts, inflated responsibility, overestimation of threat, need for certainty, and perfectionism as well as the need to control thoughts. Behavioral experiments were utilized to test reappraisals. Repetitive and prolonged exposure for the purpose of extinction was not used in the CT group. E/RP consisted of in-session and home-based exposure modeled by the therapist and completed according to hierarchies collaboratively developed during assessment. Any discussion of cognitive factors initiated by the patients was redirected by the therapists in favor of an extinction explanation to account for change. After treatment there was a slight advantage for the E/RP group that was retained through the three-month follow-up. Significantly more participants treated with E/RP reached a clinically significant improvement criterion (45%), compared to only 13% in the CT group. The group format was thought to favor exposure-based treatments, whereas the more idiographic CT was hypothesized to be better suited to individual treatment.

Whittal et al. (2005) randomized 59 participants to individual treatment using the same protocol as McLean et al. (2001). Both treatments resulted in significant symptom decreases from before treatment, but Y-BOCS scores after treatment (Y-BOCS total for the CT group was 10.6 and it was 10.4 for the E/RP group) and at three-month follow-up (Y-BOCS total was 9.7 for the CT group and 10.6 for the E/RP group) were equivalent for CT and E/RP. There was also no difference between groups on the percentages of participants who made clinically significant changes. After treatment, 67% of the CT participants were classified as recovered, compared to 58% of those who received E/RP.

Wilson and Chambless (2005) used a multiple baseline design to treat six participants with OCD using a modular treatment protocol that allowed tailoring of treatment to a variety of automatic thoughts and underlying schemas. Behavioral experiments were minimized to allow for a more stringent test of cognitive restructuring. Treatment was delivered in 10 to 18 one-hour sessions. Termination was flexible and according to improvement. Using a reliable change index plus a statistically significant change on the Y-BOCS score and a posttreatment Y-BOCS score of 14 or lower, two of six participants were considered recovered. Although the effect size for OCD symptoms was large, the magnitude of change was notably lower than that in other studies. The average posttreatment Y-BOCS score for the six participants was 14.0. Wilson and Chambless (2005) speculated that perhaps the relatively pure CT that de-emphasized behavioral experiments was associated with the smaller change.

Wilhelm et al. (2005) treated 15 participants using a modular CT protocol based on the Beckian principles of Socratic dialogue and the identification of cognitive errors. Five participants were E/RP treatment failures and the remainder had not received E/RP. Treatment entailed 14 weekly individual sessions (each 50 to 60 minutes). Treatment modules were selected according to participant presentation. Behavioral experiments were used to test and correct a belief, but the exposure was not repetitive or prolonged. Y-BOCS total scores declined significantly (posttreatment YBOCS was 13.5). Although E/RP-refractory patients also demonstrated significant declines, the magnitude of change was smaller than in E/RP-naïve patients. However, caution is needed in interpreting these results, because only four E/RP-refractory patients completed treatment. The follow-up study by Wilhelm et al. (2015) replicated these results, demonstrating that CT has both short- and long-term effects on OCD symptoms.

Whittal et al. (2010) used a CT protocol for patients with OCD who had few to no overt compulsions (i.e., primary obsessionals) and compared it to an active control of stress management training (SMT) as well as a wait-list control. Participants were provided 12 individual 50- to 60-minute sessions. Treatment consisted of reappraising the personally relevant and threatening meaning of intrusions using a variety of strategies focused on overimportance and the need to control thoughts as well as behavioral experiments to test cognitive challenging. When compared to wait-list controls, the CT group had substantially lower Y-BOCS scores as well as lower scores on OCD-related cognitions. With an intent-to-treat sample ($N = 73$), both CT and SMT showed large equivalent effects on Y-BOCS score that persisted through a 12-month follow-up. The strong treatment effect of SMT was surprising but not unwelcome and demonstrates that obsessions without overt compulsions are amenable to treatment.

In sum, the clinical trials conducted to assess the treatment outcome of cognitive protocols for OCD suggest that CT produces significant reductions in OCD symptoms. When compared to the gold standard E/RP, CT is at least as efficacious as behavior therapy. With slight variations across treatment studies, equivalent gains tend to emerge for both treatment modalities, although it appears that CT is less beneficial for patients receiving group treatment, given the idiographic nature of cognitive interventions. Not surprisingly, a number of clinical trials have also been conducted to determine the efficacy of cognitive-behavioral therapy (CBT) for OCD, since CBT combines both cognitive and behavioral interventions. The next section reviews the outcomes of combining behavior therapy and CT.

COMBINED COGNITIVE AND BEHAVIORAL TREATMENT

Freeston et al. (1998) completed a randomized trial using primary obsessionals with no overt compulsions. Treatment consisted of cognitive strategies combined with the use of loop audiotapes to repeatedly expose patients to their obsessions. The cognitive strategies included challenging the overimportance of thoughts and magical thinking, exaggerated responsibility, perfectionistic expectations regarding control and uncertainty, and the overestimations of the threat and severity of consequences associated with feared events. In cases where the participant would have otherwise refused exposure, cognitive restructuring occurred first. In other cases, the cognitive challenging and imaginal exposure occurred in parallel. Sessions were 90 minutes and were held twice a week for the first two-thirds of treatment. Therapy was terminated when the participant felt that they made sufficient clinical improvement or a maximum of 40 sessions was reached. Follow-up sessions were conducted at one, two, three, and six months. Treatment completers attended an average of 26 sessions and three follow-up sessions, for approximately 41 hours of therapy. Compared to wait-list controls, participants in the combined treatment had significantly lower Y-BOCS scores after treatment (mean Y-BOCS posttreatment score for the 22 completers was 7.2 [SD = 5.2]). Among those who completed treatment, 77% showed clinically significant change after treatment, but this percentage declined to 59% at six-month follow-up.

Cordioli et al. (2003) conducted a randomized trial testing whether adding prolonged and repeated exposure to CT improves immediate outcomes compared to outcomes for CT without prolonged exposure. Specifically, the trial used a group treatment format with 12 two-hour weekly sessions, and the 23 completers reported an average posttreatment Y-BOCS score of 15.1 (43.4% decline from before treatment). This result is an improvement over the outcome with the group CT condition used by McLean et al. (26.5% decline from before to after) and is similar to the outcome for the E/RP group (39.4%).

Vogel et al. (2004) randomized 35 participants to a standard E/RP treatment that was either augmented with cognitive or relaxation strategies or to a six-week waiting list. The first phase of treatment entailed twice-weekly two-hour sessions for six weeks. A habituation model was presented, and hierarchies were developed. For those in the cognitive group, the addition of cognitive strategies was framed as an aid to increase motivation for the completion of exposure and to prevent drop-out and relapse by addressing comorbid problems. Relaxation was framed as making stressful exposures easier to tolerate and as being potentially helpful for comorbid anxiety and depressive disorders. Traditional E/RP was carried out for both treatment groups according to predetermined hierarchies over 10 sessions. Participants were offered monthly 15-minute telephone follow-ups to address relapse prevention and to provide support. Additionally, 60-minute supportive follow-up sessions were offered at three, six, nine, and 12 months. Significantly more participants dropped out of the relaxation condition ($n = 7$) compared to the CT condition ($n = 1$). Both groups reported significantly lower posttreatment Y-BOCS scores compared to the wait-list scores, but there were no between-group differences among the active treatments (ERP/CT and ERP/relaxation posttreatment Y-BOCS scores were 16.7 and 16.1, respectively). These results were retained in an intent-to-treat analysis. Likewise, there were no group differences in the number of participants who made clinically significant changes after acute treatment or during follow-up.

O'Connor et al. (2005) randomized 29 obsessionals with no or minimal overt compulsions to either group or individual combined treatment. Refusal to be randomized was high (38%), primarily because of a hesitation to share obsessional content in a group setting. The final sample consisted of nine group treatment completers and seventeen individual treatment completers. Treatment included explaining the role of beliefs in maintaining cognitive biases associated with faulty appraisals of threat. Participants were taught to identify key beliefs, which were then addressed through Socratic challenging. E/RP was introduced approximately one-third into treatment and was conceptualized as a method to disconfirm beliefs by reality testing. E/RP was completed using loop tape or in vivo exposure and was linked to the cognitive biases identified earlier in treatment. Follow-ups were completed at three-week intervals for three months after treatment. Each participant received 20 hours of therapy. Not surprisingly, individual treatment resulted in a significantly lower Y-BOCS total score (mean = 8.0, SD = 2.8) compared to group treatment (mean 10.8, SD = 6.8). Participants in individual treatment reported an average decline of 68% on the Y-BOCS score from before to after treatment compared to 38% in the group treatment. Gains were maintained at six-month follow-up and continued to demonstrate superiority for individual treatment.

Fineberg et al. (2005) allocated 48 patients to either CBT or a relaxation therapy (RT) control. Patients were not randomized to type of treatment but rather were placed in the group that was next to be conducted, alternating between CBT and RT. Treatment sessions were conducted on 12 consecutive weeks for two hours each. The CBT condition consisted of home-based E/RP, challenging of automatic thoughts with the goal of developing less-threatening alternatives, refraining from seeking reassurance, a cost–benefit analysis of OCD, and relapse prevention. Assessments were completed before and after treatment and at three-month follow-up. Fineberg et al. (2005) reported that participants in both groups "tended toward improvement" during acute treatment, but there was no significant difference between the groups on Y-BOCS score or any of the secondary outcome measures after treatment or at three-month follow-up.

Anderson and Rees (2007) randomized 63 participants to a combined cognitive and behavioral treatment completed either individually or in group. Treatment involved 10 two-hour (group) or one-hour (individual) sessions. Cognitive challenging using logical analysis and hypothesis-testing augmented specific cognitive strategies to target overestimations of danger, inflated responsibility, and thought–action fusion. Exposure exercises were introduced as a method of testing beliefs and an opportunity to habituate to anxiety. When compared to wait-listers, participants in group and individual treatment reported significantly lower Y-BOCS scores. There were no significant Y-BOCS differences between the two active treatments among treatment completers or in an intent-to-treat analysis. There were also no between-group differences in clinical improvement or recovery rates. Although the results of this study were initially encouraging from the standpoint of treatment efficacy, it appears that the magnitude of change in the individual treatment was less (30.4%) than the average of 51% reported by Eddy et al. (2004). Therefore, there is still an empirical question whether group and individual treatment are equally effective.

Rector et al. (2019) explored whether the addition of CT to E/RP enhanced treatment outcomes. Participants (N = 127) were randomized to E/RP (n = 62) or ERP + CT (n = 65). Treatment was delivered individually over 16 weekly one-hour sessions. In the E/RP + CT condition, cognitive work began in session 4 and was incorporated with E/RP for 10 sessions. Sessions 15 and 16 were devoted to relapse prevention in both conditions. In both an intent-to-treat and completer analysis, the E/RP + CT group had significantly lower Y-BOCS scores after treatment compared to the E/RP-alone group, and these results were maintained over a six-month follow-up. However, as noted by Rector et al. (2019), the reported effect size for E/RP was lower ($d = 1.27$, posttreatment Y-BOCS total score of 17.3) than in some other E/RP treatment trials. Therefore, the reported difference between the conditions may also be due to E/RP-alone treatment that was not as effective as other studies.

A recent meta-analysis by Öst et al. (2015) examined RCTs of CBT for OCD published between 1993 and 2014. This meta-analysis included 37 RCTs that used clinician-administered Y-BOCS scores as an outcome measure, and it explored methodological stringency and outcome, refusal rates, and attrition among the measures investigated. The findings echoed previous findings that CBT is significantly more effective than both wait-list and placebo conditions, including psychological placebo. Six studies that directly compared CT with E/RP were included, and the two treatments were found to be equivalent in both efficacy and attrition rate. The study also found individual and group treatment to have no significant difference in treatment outcome. Interestingly, the analysis found that studies published in the latter 10 years of the 20-year inclusion period displayed significantly increased methodological stringency. Methodological rigor, however, was not related to effect size. Finally, Öst et al. (2015) commented on the wide range of refusal rates among the studies, concluding that treatment refusal may not necessarily be due to patients' difficulty with tolerating exposure therapy, but instead may be due to a range of factors. Unfortunately, because individual studies did not provide reasons for treatment refusal or drop-out, it is not possible to make any definitive statements regarding attrition.

It appears from the studies summarized in the preceding paragraphs that cognitive and behavioral treatments are equal, at least in the short term. Given the small number of studies that have compared the combination of cognitive and behavioral treatments with the strategies of a singular approach, it is premature to conclude that combined CT and E/RP treatment is superior to either of the singular approaches. Perhaps the commonality between the treatments (i.e., behavioral experiments in CT and discussions of risk and responsibility in E/RP) is one of the reasons for the equivalent effects. Regardless, that practitioners have additional strategies that are equally as effective as the gold standard treatment is positive.

Another strategy to measure the utility of a treatment is to examine the durability of the treatment over a long-term follow-up. Although there are only a few studies that reported and examined in detail follow-ups of one year or longer, they are discussed in the subsequent paragraphs.

Long-term Follow-up
Whereas the long-term follow-up results of E/RP have been extensively evaluated (e.g., Foa & Kozak, 1996), given the more recent development of cognitive approaches for OCD, the literature on long-term follow-up remains scant. A number of the previously described

studies included either no follow-up or only a short-term follow-up (e.g., Anderson & Rees, 2007; McLean et al., 2001; Whittal et al., 2005; Wilhelm et al., 2005; Wilson & Chambless, 2005). Other studies reported a 12-month follow-up (e.g., Vogel et al., 2004; Cottraux et al., 2001; Freeston et al., 1998; Whittal et al., 2010), but results were generally limited to listing the primary and secondary dependent measures as opposed to a detailed examination of treatment durability. Eddy et al. (2004) indicated that there were too few studies with a follow-up of at least 12 months to calculate an aggregate effect size for E/RP or CT studies. Since the publication of the Eddy et al. meta-analysis, three additional long-term follow-up studies have been conducted, and they are described here.

van Oppen and colleagues (1995) reported a five-year follow-up study of two randomized trials comparing CT and E/RP to each other (van Oppen et al., 1995) or in combination with fluvoxamine (van Balkom et al., 1998). Given the focus of the current chapter, the results discussed are limited to the comparison of the CT and E/RP groups and do not include the medication group. Of the 71 participants randomized in the study by van Oppen et al. (1995), follow-up data were available for 62 and included patients who dropped out of the initial study. This 87% retention rate is remarkable, particularly given the length of the follow-up. The Y-BOCS total scores at five years (CT = 12.3 and E/RP = 15.1) were significantly lower than scores before treatment, with most change occurring from before to after treatment. There were no significant Y-BOCS score changes from after treatment to follow-up. A decrease of 7 points on the Y-BOCS score was considered to be a reliable change, and if it was combined with a final Y-BOCS score of 12 or less, the participant was considered clinically recovered. In the CT group, 53% were considered recovered, compared to 40% in the E/RP group, which was not a significant difference. Moreover, only 19% ($n = 6$) of the CT patients and 33% ($n = 10$) of the E/RP patients were using antidepressants at follow-up. Initially, this percentage of patients on medication appears surprisingly low. However, it should be noted that these participants were not on any medication when they were randomized to the original 1995 study (i.e., exclusion criterion was use of antidepressant medication). Higher numbers of patients did receive additional psychotherapy for unstated reasons during the follow-up (53% of the CT sample and 63% of the E/RP sample).

Braga et al. (2005) reported on the one-year follow-up from the study by Cordioli et al. (2003). Results are based on 42 patients (95% retention) who completed group CBT. Improvement was arbitrarily defined as a minimum decline of 35% on the Y-BOCS score. Full remission equated to a Y-BOCS total score of less than 8 plus a clinical global impression (CGI) score of 2 or less (CGI score ranges from 1, minimal symptoms, to 7, very severe). Partial remission was determined when the score declined at least 35% from before treatment but the final Y-BOCS total score was above 8 and CGI was 2. The significant Y-BOCS score decline achieved during acute treatment was maintained through follow-up (Y-BOCS of 13.2 after treatment and 11.6 at 12-month follow-up). At 12-month follow-up, 16 patients (38%) met criteria for full remission and 16 for partial remission. Of the 31 patients who improved during acute treatment, 35.5% relapsed during the 12-month follow-up period.

Whittal et al. (2008) reported on the two-year follow-up from the McLean et al. (2001) group treatment and the Whittal et al. (2005) individual treatment. Among treatment completers (N = 41; 69.5% retention), Y-BOCS total scores for individual CT (10.3) and E/RP (11.2) were not significantly different over the two-year follow-up. However, for those patients treated in groups (N = 45; 71.4% retention), E/RP resulted in lower Y-BOCS scores (12.9) over time compared to group CT (14.2). Less than 10% of treatment completers relapsed in each of the treatment trials, and there was no difference according to type of treatment. Participants who scored 11 or below on the Y-BOCS and experienced a minimum decline of 6 points compared to before treatment were considered recovered. Among patients given individual treatment, 61% met criteria for recovery, with 51.2% maintaining this status from after treatment to follow-up, and 9.7% (four participants) achieving recovery during the follow-up. There was no significant difference in recovery status according to type of treatment at two-year follow-up (68.4% of CT participants and 54.5% of E/RP participants were recovered). At their follow-up assessment, 25 participants (61%) reported taking medication, with approximately 50% maintaining their medications during follow-up. Five participants (12.2%) discontinued medication and four (9.7%) started medication. Fourteen participants (34%) sought out additional psychological treatment for OCD. However, additional treatment did not lead to further improvements in recovery status.

Among participants who received treatment in groups, 40% were recovered at follow-up, with 20% maintaining this status from after treatment and 20% achieving recovery during the follow-up. Recovery status did not differ according to type of treatment received (33.3% of CT patients were recovered and 47.6% of E/RP patients). At two-year follow-up, 25 participants reported being on medication, with 44.5% continuing their medication from after treatment. Three participants (6.7%) discontinued medication and five (11.1%) began medication. During the follow-up, 21 participants (46.7%) sought out additional psychological treatment for OCD. Similar to the individual study, additional treatment did not result in a change in recovery status.

In sum, it appears from the few long-term outcome studies that the long-term efficacy of CT for OCD echoes the short-term efficacy. CT and behavior therapy are equally beneficial in reducing symptoms, although it seems that behavior therapy consistently outperforms CT when treatment is conducted in a group format. Taken together and contrary to initial expectation, the results suggest that CT does not provide any incremental benefits above and beyond that seen with behavior therapy. However, as noted by Clark (2005), there are still too few studies comparing behavioral and cognitive interventions to allow for any definitive conclusions about CT's utility. In addition, it is noteworthy that most clinical trials include OCD participants with varied symptom presentations, and it has been posited that CT may be most suitable for specific OCD subtypes, such as primary obsessionals and ruminators. In fact, treatment studies for pure obsessionals that included either CT (Whittal et al., 2010) or a combined CBT protocol (Freeston et al., 1998) were highly efficacious. Given that pure behavioral interventions for this OCD subtype have shown poor outcomes (for discussion, see Rachman, 2003), these results are encouraging and point to the need for more controlled studies on the efficacy of CT.

Although they are indirect measures and likely are confounded by other factors, medication use and additional psychotherapy sessions in the months and years following treatment offer another indicator of treatment utility. The few studies listing these statistics suggest that the long-term functioning of the participants who complete acute treatment and receive benefit may not be as promising as initially suggested by measures of OCD symptoms, such as the Y-BOCS. Although most people who complete treatment experience on average over a 50% decline in the intensity, severity, and duration of their OCD, long-term follow-ups suggest that over half either stay on medications or seek out additional psychological treatment for OCD or perhaps related conditions.

Moreover, treatment effectiveness has reached a plateau in the past 30 years. As reported by Rachman (2006), it appears that "improvement rates are not improving" (p. 8), a statement based upon a comparison of the results obtained by Rachman et al. (1979) and Foa et al. (2005). The plateau in response rates becomes more evident when the same dependent measure is used to compare studies. In the first reported psychological treatment study using the Y-BOCS, Fals-Stewart et al. (1993) reported posttreatment Y-BOCS scores of 12.0 and 12.1, respectively, for group and individual treatment. The percent decline from pretreatment Y-BOCS scores was 45% for group participants and 40% for individuals, using 48 (group) or 24 (individual) therapist hours. Foa et al. (2005) used an intensive individual treatment protocol with two months of weekly maintenance sessions and approximately 38 hours of therapist time. They reported a posttreatment Y-BOCS score of 11.0, which represents a decline of 55% from pretreatment score. Although the initial treatment gains with the Foa study were greater than those in the study by Fals-Stewart et al., they also used more therapist time when the individual treatment conditions are compared.

Perhaps an in-depth exploration of predictors and mediators of treatment response will provide clues to what is helpful and what is not, which will ultimately allow development of treatments that have a deeper, broader, and more durable impact.

Prediction of Treatment Response

In comparison to behavioral traditions that have a long and rich history of clinical trial outcome data, there are fewer cognitively focused randomized trials, making it potentially more challenging to identify participant variables that may predict treatment outcome and durability of treatment gains. In the literature on prediction of treatment outcome with E/RP, notable obstacles to success include severe depression (Steketee & Shapiro, 1995; Steketee et al., 2000) and, as previously mentioned, symptom presentations that do not include overt behavioral compulsions. It is postulated that CT might address these limitations, as its idiographic nature lends itself to varying symptom subtypes, and cognitive restructuring could be used to reduce depressive mood (Salkovskis & Warwick, 1988).

In a one-year follow-up study of patients receiving CBT for OCD in a group format, predictors of relapse were evaluated (Braga et al., 2005). The presence or absence of comorbidity, pretreatment OCD severity, depression scores, and the intensity of overvalued ideas did not impact relapse rates. Of note, patients who exhibited full remission after treatment, as well as those who displayed more intense improvement (i.e., greater than 54% reduction in Y-BOCS scores), were less likely to relapse at one-year follow-up.

Hansen et al. (2007) researched potential predictors of treatment outcome in the clinical trial by Vogel et al. (2004), where participants received either E/RP + CT or E/RP + REL (relaxation). The authors reported that comorbid diagnoses of panic disorder or generalized anxiety disorder led to poorer treatment outcome for both conditions; however, the comorbid subgroup of participants who received the combined treatment that included CT displayed more treatment gains than those in the E/RP + REL condition (when intent-to-treat criteria were used). Patients with comorbid cluster A or B personality disorders displayed poorer treatment outcomes irrespective of the treatment modality.

Kempe et al. (2007) investigated predictors across five years for participants in the clinical trials led by van Oppen and colleagues (1995, 2005). Results suggested that participants with more severe OCD symptoms, longer duration of symptoms, and comorbid personality or Axis I disorders were less likely to experience remission, although the authors noted that predictors of remission differ according to the time period in which participants are measured (e.g., two months vs. five years). These results should nevertheless be interpreted with caution, because participants in both the CT and behavior therapy trials were combined for the assessment of predictors, and therefore no general conclusions about CT predictors can be made.

Steketee et al. (2011) investigated predictors of a 22-session CT for OCD in 39 participants using the Y-BOCS as an outcome measure. Overall, they found that the presence of comorbid depressive and anxiety disorders predicted greater improvement with treatment, as did the presence of OCD symptoms that included intrusive sexual (but not religious) thoughts, as well as stronger treatment motivation. They also noted that more severe OCD symptoms were associated with less improvement with treatment, suggesting that longer treatment may be required for those with more severe symptoms.

As the results of the above studies demonstrate, it can often be challenging to identify consistent predictors of outcome or factors that account for durability of treatment gains. Perhaps one of the issues is that in analysis of individual studies, the relatively small sample sizes and the idiosyncrasies of the samples may contribute to the problem.

In an effort to address the above issue, Steketee et al. (2019) evaluated treatment outcome and predictors of treatment success with cognitive and behavioral treatments from eight treatment centers around the world. Steketee et al. (2019) compared treatment outcomes and predictors for 359 participants with a primary diagnosis of OCD who were treated individually with either CT (N = 108), behavior therapy (N = 125), or a combination thereof (CBT, N = 126). Participants treated with CT or CBT had significantly lower posttreatment Y-BOCS scores than participants treated with behavior therapy. This result is at odds with previously published meta-analyses that found no difference between outcomes by type of treatment (Öst et al., 2015). The discrepancy may reflect the studies that were included by Steketee et al. (2019). For example, Öst et al. (2015) included studies going back as far as 1993, whereas Steketee et al. (2019) chose studies that had been completed more recently, all of which used manualized treatments that shared similar features.

When all treatment groups were combined, there were no significant predictors of outcome in a residual gain analysis. When treatment groups were separated, higher pretreatment depression scores predicted worse outcome for patients receiving behavior therapy, which is consistent with earlier findings. Depression scores did not impact treatment success or clinically significant improvement for those receiving CBT or CT, but for those participants who received behavior therapy, higher pretreatment depression scores resulted in significantly higher posttreatment Y-BOCS scores. Higher pretreatment Y-BOCS scores resulted in worse treatment outcome in the CT group but not in the behavior therapy or CBT groups. More advanced education had a positive relationship to treatment success, although only for patients receiving CT.

Clearly, more clinical trials of CT and CBT for OCD need to be conducted to better understand both the efficacy of cognitive interventions and the predictors of favorable treatment response. However, some of the preliminary findings suggest that the treatment response with CT and behavior therapy and their combination is more complex than previously believed. For example, it appears that severe comorbid depression has a notably deleterious impact on treatment response for those receiving behavior therapy, and that this negative effect is either dampened or eliminated with CT or CBT.

Mechanisms of Action
Early work into potential mediators of treatment utilized a pre/post focus, and a number of CT and E/RP studies reported largely equivalent amounts of cognitive change (Cottraux et al., 2001; McLean et al., 2001; Whittal et al., 2005), but there was no indication of the direction or timing of change. Rhéaume and Ladouceur (2000) examined individual cognitive change in a group of six checkers treated with a "pure" CT protocol devoid of behavioral experiments or E/RP. Using multivariate time series analysis, the authors reported that for most of the participants treated with either CT or E/RP, some cognitive change precedes change in checking. However, the reverse was also reported, in that for many participants, behavioral changes were noted prior to cognitive changes. Perhaps not surprisingly, the researchers concluded that cognitive change clearly occurs in OCD but that behavioral strategies appeared to be the most efficacious way to produce this change.

Woody et al. (2011) analyzed data from the study by Whittal et al. (2010), an RCT comparing CBT and SMT among 73 people with primary obsessions, using a traditional mediation analysis with pretreatment, posttreatment, and follow-up scores on the Y-BOCS and self-report measures of cognitions related to OCD. The mediation analysis found that changes in maladaptive beliefs accounted for a significant reduction in OCD symptom severity, and rating of the importance of thought predicted Y-BOCS severity at one-year follow-up. However, in traditional mediation analysis, statements about causality and temporal precedence cannot be made. The session-by-session monitoring in the Whittal et al. (2010) study of the personal significance and severity of obsessions allowed for tests of temporal precedence using bivariate dual change score (BDCS) and latent difference scores. This subsequent analysis clearly identified that prior obsession severity was the leading indicator for changes in personal significance (i.e., more severe obsessional symptoms led to a strengthening of appraisals of personal significance, and as symptom severity declined, it led to lower scores of personal significance). This finding was surprising and did not match the hypothesized model.

In a large-scale study, Olatunji and colleagues (2013) examined the potential of obsessive beliefs as a mediator in OCD treatments. They randomized 62 adults with OCD to 20 sessions of CT or behavior therapy in four weeks of intensive treatment (16 hours total) and 12 weeks of maintenance treatment (four hours total). OCD severity was assessed using the Y-BOCS at baseline and up to 52 weeks after treatment. Olatunji and colleagues found that beliefs about responsibility for negative events did account for improvement in OCD symptoms when examined as a single mediator, but that this finding did not hold when controlling for other potential mediators, such as depression and behavioral avoidance. Thus, they concluded that reductions in OCD symptoms were mediated by reductions in depressed mood rather than decreases in OCD belief systems, but this finding was limited by their investigation of only one of several potential OCD beliefs.

Wilhelm et al. (2015) used 36 participants with OCD to investigate whether reductions in obsessive beliefs operate as mechanisms of change in a 24-week trial of CT for OCD, and they explored how underlying maladaptive schemas influence treatment response. They found that a reduction in beliefs about perfectionism/certainty and dependence/incompetence was associated with improved symptoms over time. Longitudinal outcomes revealed that a reduction in perfection and certainty beliefs, but not inflated responsibility or importance of/need to control thoughts, significantly mediated treatment response. The authors hypothesized that, because beliefs about perfectionism are linked to other types of cognitive distortions (Bouchard et al., 1999), a reduction in these beliefs also impacts other unhelpful thought patterns and results in a cascading effect of interrelated cognitive changes that yield behavioral modification. Similarly, a reduction in beliefs about dependency on others and a corresponding increase in autonomy, confidence, and self-reliance accounted for reductions in severity of OCD symptoms. Self-efficacy appears to mitigate fear and to improve treatment response in CT for OCD, and it has also been shown to be a mechanism of change in CBT more generally (Bouchard et al., 2007). Overall, the study provides evidence that cognitive changes precede behavioral changes in OCD treatment.

In summary, the work on CT's mechanism of action thus far is demonstrating that cognitive change is associated with decreases in symptom severity and strength of beliefs/meaning after treatment, and it might be functioning as a predictor that accounts for the durability (or lack thereof) of treatment gains over a follow-up period. Furthermore, in the very few studies where the research design allowed for examination of temporal precedence, it appears that behavioral change may be the driver for cognitive change. However, given the relatively few studies that have been designed to allow for such analyses to be conducted, the latter conclusion should be considered tentative.

Summary and Future Directions

The number of treatment outcome studies in OCD increased notably in the past 25 years, perhaps due to interest in testing cognitive theory and treatment. Based upon the review of recent treatment trials and meta-analyses, it appears that CT is equally as effective as the gold standard E/RP, at least when CT is delivered on an individual basis. For those who complete treatment, the prospect of maintaining gains is promising, although it may be secondary to occasional appointments with mental health providers. There are substantial numbers of people who remain on medication or seek out additional psychological treatments, which suggests that there is additional work to do. Studies examining mediation and the temporal precedence of change indicate that treatment outcome is mediated by cognitive change (particularly overestimation of threat and inflated responsibility), but that behavior change drives cognitive change and not vice versa.

On a positive note, over time treatments have become more targeted, requiring fewer clinician hours while maintaining treatment efficacy. However, there appears to be a plateau regarding further improvements in effect size. This indicates that we must continue to look at complementary types of treatment protocols. Examples include: extended maintenance sessions similar to those used by Hiss et al. (1994); involving family to a greater degree, so that they are not inadvertently supporting OCD behaviors; working with patients longer and aiming for a broader treatment response that includes medication discontinuation (i.e., is it possible that some patients continue on medication out of habit rather than genuine ongoing need because that's what they have always done?); and treating the whole person along with their comorbidities, as opposed to just treating the primary presenting problem.

Fresh conceptualizations like that of mental contamination (Rachman et al., 2014) have ignited much theoretical interest and experimental work. To date, however, the literature contains only a case study (Zysk et al., 2018) and one case series (Coughtrey et al., 2013). We need to further develop treatment for mental contamination and to find ways to make existing treatments more approachable, in order to further reduce refusal and drop-out rates, thereby ideally increasing treatment efficacy for this intriguing clinical presentation.

References

Abramowitz, J. S., Franklin, M. E., & Foa, E. B. (2002). Empirical status of cognitive-behavioral therapy for obsessive-compulsive disorder: A meta-analytic review. *Romanian Journal of Cognitive and Behavioral Psychotherapies*, 2, 89–104.

Abramowitz, J. S., Taylor, S., & McKay, D. (2005). Potentials and limitations of cognitive treatments for obsessive-compulsive disorder. *Cognitive Behaviour Therapy*, 34, 140–147.

Anderson, R. A., & Rees, C. S. (2007). Group versus individual cognitive-behavioural treatment for obsessive-compulsive disorder: A controlled trial. *Behaviour Research and Therapy*, 45, 123–138.

Arntz, A., Rauner, M., & van den Hout, M. (1995). 'If I feel anxious, there must be danger': Ex-consequentia reasoning in inferring danger in anxiety disorders. *Behaviour Research and Therapy*, 33, 917–925.

Ball, S. G., Baer, L., & Otto, M. W. (1996). Symptom subtypes of obsessive-compulsive disorder in behavioral treatment studies: A quantitative review. *Behaviour Research and Therapy*, 34, 47–51.

Bouchard, S., Gauthier, J., Nouwen, A., Ivers, H., Vallieres, A., Simard, S., & Fournier, T. (2007). Temporal relationship between dysfunctional beliefs, self-efficacy and panic apprehension in the treatment of panic disorder with agoraphobia. *Journal of Behavior Therapy and Experimental Psychiatry*, 38, 275–292.

Bouchard, C., Rheaume, J., & Ladouceur, R. (1999). Responsibility and perfectionism in OCD: An experimental study. *Behaviour Research and Therapy*, 37, 239–248.

Braga, D. T., Cordioli, A. V., Niederauer, K., & Manfro, G. G. (2005). Cognitive-behavioral group therapy for obsessive-compulsive disorder: A 1-year follow-up. *Acta Psychiatrica Scandinavica*, 112, 180–186.

Clark, D. A. (2005). *Intrusive thoughts in clinical disorders: Theory, Research and Treatment*. Guildford Press.

Clark, D. A., & Purdon, C. (1993). New perspectives for a cognitive theory of obsessions. *Australian Psychologist*, 28, 161–167.

Cordioli, A. V., Heldt, E., Bochi, D. B., Margis, R., de Sousa, M. B., Tonello, J. F., Manfro, G. G., & Kapczinski, F. (2003). Cognitive-behavioral group therapy in obsessive-compulsive disorder: A randomized clinical trial. *Psychotherapy and Psychosomatics*, 72, 211–216.

Cottraux, J., Note, I., Yao, S. N., Lafont, S., Note, B., Mollard, E., Bouvard, M., Sauteraud, A., Bourgeois, M., & Dartigues, J. F. (2001). A randomized controlled trial of cognitive therapy versus intensive behavior therapy in obsessive compulsive disorder. *Psychotherapy and Psychosomatics*, 70, 288–297.

Coughtrey, A. E., Shafran, R., Lee, M., & Rachman, S. (2013). The treatment of mental contamination: A case series. *Cognitive and Behavioral Practice*, 20, 221–231.

Dollard, J., & Miller, N. L. (1950). *Personality and psychotherapy: An analysis in terms of learning, thinking and culture*. McGraw-Hill.

Eddy, K. T., Dutra, L., Bradley, R., & Westen, D. (2004). A multidimensional meta-analysis of psychotherapy and pharmacotherapy for obsessive-compulsive disorder. *Clinical Psychology Review*, 24, 1011–1030.

Fals-Stewart, W., Marks, A. P., & Schafer, J. (1993). A comparison of behavioral group therapy and individual behavior therapy in treating obsessive-compulsive disorder. *The Journal of Nervous and Mental Disease*, 181, 189–193.

Fineberg, N. A., Hughes, A., Gale, T. M., & Roberts, A. (2005). Group cognitive behaviour therapy in obsessive-compulsive disorder (OCD): A controlled study. *International Journal of Psychiatry in Clinical Practice*, 9, 257–263.

Frost, R. O., & Steketee, G. (2002). *Cognitive approaches to obsessions and compulsions: Theory, assessment and treatment*. Pergamon

Foa, E. B., Franklin, M .E., & Kozak, M. J. (1998). Psychosocial treatment for obsessive-compulsive disorder. In R. P. Swinson, M. M. Antony, S. J. Rachman, & M. A. Richter (Eds.), *Obsessive-compulsive disorder: Theory, research and treatment* (pp. 258–276). Guilford.

Foa, E. B., & Kozak, M. J. (1986). Emotional processing of fear: Exposure to corrective information. *Psychological Bulletin*, 99, 20–35.

Foa, E. B., & Kozak, M. J. (1996). Psychological treatment for obsessive-compulsive disorder. In M. R. Mavissakalian & R. F. Prien (Eds.), *Long-term treatments of anxiety disorders* (pp. 285–309). American Psychiatric Press.

Foa, E. B., Liebowitz, M. R., Kozak, M. J., Davies, S., Campeas, R., Franklin, M. E., Huppert, J. D., Kjernisted, K., Rowan, V., Schmidt, A. B., Simpson, H. B., & Tu, X. (2005). Randomized, placebo-controlled trials of exposure and ritual prevention, clomipramine, and their combination in the treatment of obsessive-compulsive disorder. *The American Journal of Psychiatry, 162*, 151–161.

Foa, E. B., Steketee, G. S., & Ozarow, B. J. (1985). Behavior therapy with obsessive-compulsives: From theory to treatment. In M. Mavissakalian, S. M. Turner, & L. Michelson (Eds.), *Obsessive-compulsive disorder: Psychological and pharmacological treatment* (pp. 49–129). Springer.

Foa, E. B., Steketee, G., Grayson, J. B., & Doppelt, H. G. (1983). Treatment of obsessive-compulsives: When do we fail? In E. B. Foa & P. M. G. Emmelkamp (Eds.), *Failures in behavior therapy* (pp. 10–34). Wiley.

Freeston, M. H., Ladouceur, R., Gagnon, F., Thibodeau, N. Rhéaume, J., Letarte, H., & Bujold, A. (1997). Cognitive-behavioral treatment of obsessive thoughts: A controlled study. *Journal of Consulting and Clinical Psychology, 65*, 405–413.

Freeston, M. H., Rhéume, J., & Ladouceur, R. (1996). Correcting faulty appraisals of obsessional thoughts. *Behaviour Research and Therapy, 34*, 433–446.

Frost, R. O., & Steketee, G. (1998). Hoarding: Clinical aspects and treatment strategies. In M. A. Jenike, L. Baer, & W. E. Minichiello (Eds.), *Obsessive-compulsive disorder: Practical management* (3rd ed.) (pp. 533–554). Elsevier.

Hansen, B., Vogel, P. A., Stiles, T. C., & Götestam, K. G. (2007). Influence of co-morbid generalized anxiety disorder, panic disorder and personality disorders on the outcome of cognitive behavioural treatment of obsessive-compulsive disorder. *Cognitive Behaviour Therapy, 36*, 145–155.

Hiss, H., Foa, E. B., & Kozak, M. J. (1994). Relapse prevention program for treatment of obsessive-compulsive disorder. *Journal of Consulting and Clinical Psychology, 62*, 801–808.

Jones, M. K., & Menzies, R. G. (1998). Danger ideation reduction therapy (DIRT) for obsessive-compulsive washers: A controlled trial. *Behaviour Research and Therapy, 36*, 959–970

Katzman, M. A., Bleau, P., Blier, P., Chokka, P., Kjernisted, K., Van Ameringen, M.; Canadian Anxiety Guidelines Initiative Group. (2014). Canadian clinical practice guidelines for the management of anxiety, posttraumatic stress and obsessive compulsive disorders. *BMC Psychiatry, 14*(Suppl. 1), 1–83.

Kempe, P. T., van Oppen, P., de Haan, E., Twisk, J. W. R., Sluis, A., Smit, J. H., van Dyck, R., & van Balkom, A. J. L. M. (2007). Predictors of course in obsessive-compulsive disorder: Logistic regression versus Cox regression for recurrent events. *Acta Psychiatrica Scandinavica, 116*, 201–210.

Kobak, K. A., Greist, J. H., Jefferson, J. W., Katzelnick, D. J., & Henk, H. J. (1998). Behavioral versus pharmacological treatments of obsessive compulsive disorder: A meta-analysis. *Psychopharmacology, 136*, 205–216.

Koran, L. M., Hanna, G. L., Hollander, E., Nestadt, G., & Simpson, H. B. (2007). Practice guideline for the treatment of patients with obsessive-compulsive disorder. *The American Journal of Psychiatry, 164*(7 Suppl.), 5–53.

March, J., Frances, A., Carpenter, D., & Kahn, D. (1997). The expert consensus guideline series: Treatment of obsessive-compulsive disorder. *The Journal of Clinical Psychiatry, 58*(Suppl. 4), 1–16.

McLean, P. D., Whittal, M. L., Thordarson, D. S., Taylor, S., Sochting, I., Koch, W. J., Paterson, R., & Anderson K. W. (2001). Cognitive versus behavior therapy in the group treatment of obsessive-compulsive disorder. *Journal of Consulting and Clinical Psychology, 69*, 205–214.

Mowrer, O. H. (1939). A stimulus-response analysis of anxiety and its role as a reinforcing agent. *Psychological Review, 46*, 553–565.

Newth, S., & Rachman, S. (2001). The concealment of obsessions. *Behaviour Research and Therapy, 39*, 457–464.

Obsessive Compulsive Cognitions Working Group (OCCWG). (1997). Cognitive assessment of obsessive-compulsive disorder. *Behaviour Research and Therapy, 35*, 667–681.

Obsessive Compulsive Cognitions Working Group (OCCWG). (2005). Psychometric validation of the Obsessional Beliefs Questionnaire and Interpretation of Intrusions Inventory—Part 2: Factor analyses and test of a brief version. *Behaviour Research and Therapy, 43*, 1527–1542.

O'Connor, K., Freeston, M. H., Gareau, D., Careau, Y, Dufour, M. J., Aardema, F., & Todorov, C. (2005). Group versus individual treatment in obsessions without compulsions. *Clinical Psychology and Psychotherapy*, *12*, 87–96.

Olatunji, B. O., Rosenfield, D., Tart, C. D., Cottraux, J., Powers, M. B., & Smits, J. A. J. (2013). Behavioural versus cognitive treatment of obsessive-compulsive disorder: An examination of outcome and mediators of change. *Journal of Clinical & Consulting Psychology*, *81*, 415–428.

Öst, L. G., Havnen, A., Hansen, B., & Kvale, G. (2015). Cognitive behavioral treatments of obsessive-compulsive disorder. A systematic review and meta-analysis of studies published 1993–2014. *Clinical Psychology Review*, *40*, 156–169.

Rachman, S. (1985). An overview of clinical and research issues in obsessional-compulsive disorder. In M. Mavissakalian, S. M. Turner, & L. Michelson (Eds.), *Obsessive-compulsive disorder: Psychological and pharmacological treatment* (pp. 1–47). Springer.

Rachman, S. (1997). A cognitive theory of obsessions. *Behaviour Research and Therapy*, *35*, 793–802.

Rachman, S. (1998). A cognitive theory of obsessions: Elaborations. *Behaviour Research and Therapy*, *36*, 385–401.

Rachman, S. (2002). A cognitive theory of compulsive checking. *Behaviour Research and Therapy*, *40*, 625–639.

Rachman, S. (2003). *The treatment of obsessions*. Oxford University Press.

Rachman, S. (2006). *Fear of contamination: Assessment and treatment* (p. 8). Oxford University Press.

Rachman, S., Cobb, C., Grey, S., McDonald, B., & Sartory, G. (1979). Behavioural treatment of obsessional compulsive disorder, with and without clomipramine. *Behaviour Research and Therapy*, *17*, 467–478.

Rachman, S., Coughtrey, A., Shafran, R., & Radomsky, A (2014). *Oxford Guide to the Treatment of Mental Contamination*. Oxford University Press.

Rachman, S., & de Silva, P. (1978). Abnormal and normal obsessions. *Behaviour Research and Therapy*, *16*, 233–248.

Radomsky, A. S., Alcolado, G. M., Abramowitz, J. S., Alonso, P., Belloch, A., Bouvard, M., Clark, D. A., Coles, M. E., Doron, G., Fernández-Álvarez, Garcia-Soriano, G., Ghisi, M., Gomez, B., Inozu, M., Moulding, R., Shams, G., Sica, C., Simos, G., & Wong, W (2014). Part 1—You can run but you can't hide: Intrusive thoughts on 6 continents. *Journal of Obsessive-Compulsive and Related Disorders*, *3*, 269–279.

Rector, N. A., Richter, M. A., Katz, D., & Laybman, M (2019). Does the addition of cognitive therapy to exposure and response prevention for obsessive compulsive disorder enhance clinical efficacy? A randomized controlled trial in a community setting. *British Journal of Clinical Psychology*, *58*, 1–18. doi:10.1111/bjc.12188

Rhéaume, J., & Ladouceur, R. (2000). Cognitive and behavioural treatments of checking behaviours: An examination of individual cognitive change. *Clinical Psychology and Psychotherapy*, *7*, 118–127.

Rowa, K., & Purdon, C. (2003). Why are certain intrusive thoughts more upsetting than others? *Behavioural and Cognitive Psychotherapy*, *31*, 1–11.

Salkovskis, P. M. (1985). Obsessional-compulsive problems: A cognitive-behavioural analysis. *Behaviour Research and Therapy*, *23*, 571–583.

Salkovskis, P. M. (1999). Understand and treating obsessive-compulsive disorder. *Behaviour Research and Therapy*, *37*, S29–S52.

Salkovskis, P. M., & Warwick, H. M. C. (1988). Cognitive therapy of obsessive-compulsive disorder. In C. Perris, I. M. Blackburn, & H. Perris (Eds.), *Cognitive psychotherapy: Theory and practice* (pp. 376–395). Springer-Verlag.

Salkovskis, P. M., & Westbrook, D. (1989). Behaviour therapy and obsessional ruminations: Can failure be turned into success? *Behaviour Research and Therapy*, *27*, 211–219.

Shafran, R., Thordarson, D. S., & Rachman, S. (1996). Thought–action fusion in obsessive compulsive disorder. *Journal of Anxiety Disorders*, *10*, 379–391.

Steketee, G. S., Frost, R. O., Rheaume, J., & Wilhelm, S. (1998). Cognitive theory and treatment of obsessive-compulsive disorder. In M. A. Jenike, L. Baer, & W. E. Minichiello (Eds.), *Obsessive-compulsive disorder: Practical management* (pp. 368–399). Elsevier

Steketee, G. S., Henninger, N. J., & Pollard, C. A. (2000). Predicting treatment outcome for obsessive-compulsive disorder: Effects of comorbidity. In W. K. Goodman, M. V. Rudorfer, & J. D. Maser (Eds.), *Obsessive-compulsive disorder: Contemporary issues in treatment* (pp. 257–274). Lawrence Erlbaum Associates.

Steketee, G. S., & Shapiro, L. J. (1995). Predicting behavioral treatment outcome for agoraphobia and obsessive-compulsive disorder. *Clinical Psychology Review*, *15*, 317–346.

Steketee, G., Siev J., Fama, J. F., Keshaviah, A., Chosak, A., & Wilhelm, S. (2011). Predictors of treatment outcome in modular cognitive therapy for obsessive-compulsive disorder. *Depression and Anxiety, 28*, 333–341.

Steketee, G., Siev, J., Yovel, I., Lit, K., & Wilhelm, S. (2019). Predictors and moderators of cognitive and behavioral therapy outcomes for OCD: A patient-level mega-analysis of eight sites. *Behavior Therapy, 50*, 165–176.

Stanley, M. A., & Turner, S. M. (1995). Current status of pharmacological and behavioral treatment of obsessive-compulsive disorder. *Behavior Therapy, 26*, 163–186.

van Balkom, A. J., de Haan, E., van Oppen, P., Spinhoven, P., Hoogduin, K. A. L., & van Dyck, R. (1998). Cognitive and behavioral therapies alone versus in combination with fluvoxamine in the treatment of obsessive compulsive disorder. *The Journal of Nervous and Mental Disease, 186*, 492–499.

van Oppen, P., de Haan, E., van Balkom, A. J. L. M., Spinhoven, P., Hoogduin, K., & van Dyck, R. (1995). Cognitive therapy and exposure in vivo in the treatment of obsessive compulsive disorder. *Behaviour Research and Therapy, 33*, 379–390.

van Oppen, P., van Balkom, A. J. L. M., de Haan, E., & van Dyck, R. (2005). Cognitive therapy and exposure in vivo alone and in combination with fluvoxamine in obsessive-compulsive disorder: A 5-year follow-up. *The Journal of Clinical Psychiatry, 66*, 1415–1422.

Vogel, P. A., Stiles, T. C., & Götestam, K. G. (2004). Adding cognitive therapy elements to exposure therapy for obsessive compulsive disorder: A controlled study. *Behavioural and Cognitive Psychotherapy, 32*, 275–290.

Whittal, M. L., Robichaud, M., Thordarson, D. S., & McLean, P. D. (2008). Group and individual treatment of OCD using cognitive therapy and exposure plus response prevention: A two-year follow-up of 2 randomized trials. *Journal of Consulting and Clinical Psychology, 76*, 1003–1014.

Whittal, M. L., Robichaud, M. L., & Woody S. R. (2010). Cognitive therapy of obsessions: Using video components to enhance dissemination. *Cognitive and Behavioral Practice, 17*, 1–8.

Whittal, M. L, Thordarson, D., & McLean, P. (2005). Treatment of obsessive-compulsive disorder: Cognitive behavior therapy vs. exposure and response prevention. *Behaviour Research and Therapy, 43*, 1559–1576.

Whittal, M. L., Woody, S. R., McLean, P. D., Rachman, S. J., & Robichaud, M. (2010). Treatment of obsessions: A randomized controlled trial. *Behaviour Research and Therapy, 48*, 295–303.

Wilhelm, S., Berman, N. C., Keshaviah, A., Schwartz, R. A., & Steketee, G. (2015). Mechanisms of change in cognitive therapy for obsessive compulsive disorder: Role of maladaptive beliefs and schema. *Behaviour Research and Therapy, 65*, 5–10.

Wilhelm, S., & Steketee, G. S. (2006). *Cognitive therapy for obsessive-compulsive disorder: A guide for professionals.* New Harbinger Press.

Wilhelm, S., Steketee, G., Reilly-Harrington, N. A., Deckersbach, T., Buhlmann, U., & Baer, L. (2005). Effectiveness of cognitive therapy for obsessive-compulsive disorder: An open trial. *Journal of Cognitive Psychotherapy, 19*, 173–179.

Wilson, K. A., & Chambless, D. L. (2005). Cognitive therapy for obsessive-compulsive disorder. *Behaviour Research and Therapy, 43*, 1645–1654.

Woody, S., Whittal, M. L., & McLean, P. D. (2011). Mechanisms of symptom reduction in treatment of obsessions. *Journal of Consulting and Clinical Psychology, 79*, 653–654.

Zysk, E., Shafran, R., & Williams, T. I. (2018). A single-subject evaluation of the treatment of morphing. *Cognitive and Behavioral Practice, 25*, 168–151.

CHAPTER 21

Combining Pharmacotherapy and Psychological Treatments for Obsessive-Compulsive Disorder

David F. Tolin *and* Kimberly S. Sain

Abstract

It is well established that pharmacotherapy and cognitive-behavioral therapy (CBT) are effective monotherapies for obsessive-compulsive disorder (OCD). This chapter examines the efficacy of combining the two treatments. First, the chapter covers meta-analytic strategies for studies in which the two treatments were applied simultaneously, compared to monotherapy. Results indicate that combined therapy is superior to medication monotherapy, whereas the superiority of combined therapy over CBT monotherapy is small to negligible. Second, the chapter gives a systematic review of studies in which one treatment was applied after the initiation of the other, often when the first treatment failed. Results show that second-line CBT and medications can be effective when patients do not respond adequately to first-line monotherapy. Finally, meta-analysis is used to examine the efficacy of D-cycloserine (DCS), a compound purported to potentiate a biological mechanism of CBT. Results suggest that DCS, when combined with CBT, is associated with a small but significant advantage over placebo after treatment, and some data suggest that the advantage may be more evident mid-treatment.

Key Words: cognitive-behavioral therapy, pharmacotherapy, serotonin reuptake inhibitors, D-cycloserine, meta-analysis

As discussed in Chapters 19 and 20 of this volume, cognitive-behavioral therapy (CBT) has robust evidence of efficacy in the treatment of obsessive-compulsive disorder (OCD) in adults and children. In addition, as discussed in Chapter 17, pharmacotherapy, particularly with serotonin reuptake inhibitors (SRIs), has also been shown to be effective in adults and children. This chapter examines the efficacy of combining the two treatment modalities.

It should be noted that although CBT and medications are effective as monotherapies, the superiority of the treatments in combination cannot be taken for granted. In a meta-analysis of treatments for anxiety-related disorders, Foa et al. (2002) examined 10 published randomized controlled trials (RCTs) that compared combined treatment to monotherapy with CBT or medication. Within-subject effect sizes for each type of treatment were calculated and compared across treatment type for the different disorders (social phobia, panic disorder, generalized anxiety disorder, and OCD). In general, the effect sizes did not suggest that the results of combined treatment were superior to those of CBT monotherapy. Conversely, there appeared to be an advantage of combined treatment over medication monotherapy, although the number of studies in the analysis was small.

Similarly, Tolin (2017) conducted a meta-analysis of the augmentation of CBT with medications for patients with anxiety-related and depressive disorders. Between-group effect sizes were calculated, allowing for a more direct comparison of combined therapy to CBT monotherapy. The additive effect of medications was small for both anxiety and depressive disorders after treatment, and there was no additive benefit after medications were discontinued. Tolin also examined randomized trials in which pharmacotherapy was initiated after patients had failed to respond to CBT monotherapy. A small number of trials suggested that medications were superior to placebo (medium to large effect) for patients who had previously been unresponsive to CBT.

How might pharmacotherapy and CBT theoretically complement each other? One possibility is that because neither medication nor CBT is a perfect solution, their combination might more thoroughly affect the biological mechanisms of therapeutic change. A seminal positron emission tomography (PET) study by Baxter et al. (1992), in which patients with OCD received either fluoxetine or behavior therapy, showed that patients who responded to either treatment showed comparable decreases in activity in the caudate nucleus, as well as decreased correlations between orbital cortex and thalamus. Thus, if behavior therapy and medications produce similar changes in brain activity, it could be argued that the combination of the two would more thoroughly address these mechanisms.

Furthermore, it could be argued that the anxiety-reducing properties of medications would make CBT more tolerable, particularly when exposure therapy is emphasized. As Foa et al. (2002) suggested, the use of anxiety-reducing medications might permit patients to engage in longer exposures to feared and avoided stimuli, although more recent research on fear extinction raises questions about the necessity of long exposures (see Craske et al., 2008). Medications might also help with the calibration of exposures, so that patients' anxiety remains in the moderate range, rather than becoming overwhelming.

Conversely, it could be argued that certain medications might interfere with the effects of CBT by blocking the activation of fear, which is thought to be necessary for fear reduction during exposure therapy (see Foa & Kozak, 1986). Therefore, the use of medications could serve as a safety behavior, which can impede exposure (Kim, 2005; Morgan & Raffle, 1999; Powers et al., 2004; Salkovskis, 1999; Sloan & Telch, 2002; Wells et al., 1995). To illustrate this principle, in one study, individuals with claustrophobia received exposure therapy along with a placebo pill; some of the patients were told that the pill was a sedating drug that would make exposure easier. Although all patients did comparably well with exposure therapy in the short term, at one-week follow-up, over a third of the group who believed they were taking a drug that would make exposure easier showed a return of their fear, in contrast to no return of fear in the patients who did not think they were taking an exposure-easing drug (Powers et al., 2008).

In addition, although medications can reduce patients' anxiety, this effect might not be particularly useful in the context of CBT, at least when exposure therapy is a component. It is not clear how much anxiety needs to be elicited for exposure therapy to be successful in OCD, although it is noted that in other anxiety-related disorders, activation, rather than deactivation, of fear appears to be critical. As one example, among individuals with claustrophobia, higher heart rate at the beginning of exposures predicted better outcomes of exposure therapy (Alpers & Sell, 2008), although not all studies have replicated this result (Meuret et al., 2012; van Minnen & Hagenaars, 2002). It could further be argued (Otto et al., 2016) that the medications (via anxiety reduction or side effects) create an internal context for state-dependent learning, resulting in increased risk of return of fear once that context (medication) is withdrawn (see Bouton, 2002). In other words, patients might learn that they can tolerate feared stimuli only in the context of the medication, which can obstruct the learning of unconditional safety during exposure therapy.

Over 20 years ago, an expert consensus panel (March et al., 1997) recommended that for more severe cases of adult OCD, CBT should be combined with SRIs. The implication, therefore, was that CBT + SRI should be more efficacious than CBT alone. A later practice guideline issued by the American Psychiatric Association (APA), however, recommended a different course of treatment, with SRIs prescribed only for patients who fail to respond to CBT monotherapy or for patients who are "too depressed, anxious, or severely ill to cooperate with this treatment modality" (Koran et al., 2007, p. 9). Thus, expert opinion appears to have shifted somewhat, with greater emphasis on CBT monotherapy, decreased claims of the superiority of combined treatment, and a suggestion of a sequential administration of pharmacotherapy after CBT has failed.

The aim of this chapter is to review the extant literature on the efficacy of combined pharmacotherapy and CBT for OCD. In most cases, this means that we examined studies in which both treatments were started simultaneously, compared to conditions in which only one treatment was provided. However, in keeping with the more recent expert consensus guidelines, we also examined studies in which CBT and pharmacotherapy were applied sequentially, sometimes after patients failed to respond to one of the monotherapies. Finally, the chapter discusses a recent line of research investigating the *N*-methyl-D-aspartic acid (NMDA) receptor partial agonist D-cycloserine, a compound purported to potentiate the mechanisms of CBT.

Simultaneous Psychological and Pharmacologic Treatments

To identify studies that compared combined therapy to monotherapy, the authors conducted a search on PubMed and PsychInfo (8/11/2020)[1]. The search was limited to

---

[1] The exact search string for the PubMed and PsychInfo search was as follows: ((((CBT) OR (cognitive-behavioral therapy) OR (behavior therapy) OR (cognitive therapy) OR (ERP) OR (exposure therapy))

peer-reviewed journals published in English and listed as clinical trials, empirical studies, longitudinal studies, prospective studies, or treatment outcome studies. Recent empirical and review articles were also searched for additional references. Criteria for inclusion were RCTs in patients with OCD (adults or children) that included a CBT + SRI (SSRI or clomipramine) condition and one of the following: (a) an SRI monotherapy condition or an SRI + inert psychological treatment condition, or (b) a CBT monotherapy or CBT + pill placebo (PBO) condition. This process resulted in 14 studies, listed in Table 21.1.

As Figure 21.1 shows, CBT monotherapy ranged widely in degree of symptom reduction, from a low of 18% (Cottraux et al., 1990) to a high of 76% (Shareh et al., 2010), with a mean 42% reduction. Medication monotherapy showed less variability, with symptom reduction ranging from 22% (Fineberg et al., 2018; Vakili et al., 2015) to 47% (Meng et al., 2019) and a mean of 33%. When combination therapy was provided, symptom reduction ranged from a low of 35% (Fineberg et al., 2018; Storch et al., 2013) to a high of 81% (Ma et al., 2013), with a mean of 53%.

Table 21.1 also shows the percentage of participants who were considered treatment responders. Treatment response was defined in various ways, as shown in the Table 21.1 footnotes. Almost half of the studies (Foa et al., 2005; Ma et al., 2013; Pediatric OCD Treatment Study Team, 2004; Shareh et al., 2010; Storch et al., 2013; Vakili et al., 2015) also considered remission rates, defined as scoring below various thresholds on the Yale-Brown Obsessive-Compulsive Scale (Y-BOCS) or Children's Yale-Brown Obsessive-Compulsive Scale (CY-BOCS). As is shown in Table 21.1, response and remission rates for combination therapy were generally higher than were those for medication monotherapy, whereas the difference in response and remission rates between combination therapy and CBT monotherapy was more variable.

The sampled studies also suggested that CBT monotherapy, medication monotherapy, and combined therapy showed continued symptom reduction through follow-up (31%, 39%, and 54%, respectively, not shown). Cottraux et al. (1990) reported that the advantage of combined treatment over monotherapy was maintained at one-year follow-up. However, examining the treatment responders in Foa et al. (2005) at three-month follow-up, Simpson et al. (2006) found that patients who did not receive exposure and response prevention (E/RP; with or without clomipramine) were significantly more likely to have relapsed than were those whose treatment included E/RP.

As Table 21.1 and Figure 21.1 show, there is a fair amount of discrepancy across studies. To examine trends across these reports, random-effects model meta-analytic strategies (Glass et al., 1981) were employed using Comprehensive Meta-Analysis (Borenstein et al., 2007). One study (Peter et al., 2000) met the inclusion criteria listed above but did

---

AND (OCD) AND ((pharmacotherapy) OR (SRI) OR (SSRI) OR (antidepressant) OR (selective serotonin reuptake inhibitors) OR (sertraline) OR (fluoxetine) OR (escitalopram) OR (fluvoxamine) OR (clomipramine) OR (paroxetine)))

Table 21.1. Randomized Trials of Combined Therapy (CBT + Medication) versus Medication or CBT Monotherapy

Study	N	Age Group	Measure	Conditions	Decrease	Response Rate	Remission Rate
Cottraux et al. (1990)	60	Adult	CAC	E/RP + FLV E/RP + PBO FLV + anti-exposure	44% 18% 34%	69%[a] 40% 54%	
Hohagen et al. (1998)	49	Adult	Y-BOCS	E/RP + FLV E/RP + PBO	56% 44%	88%[b] 60%	
van Balkom et al. (1998)	117	Adult	Y-BOCS	CT E/RP CT + FLV E/RP + FLV	47% 32% 43% 49%		
Peter et al. (2000)	33	Adult	Y-BOCS	BT + FLV BT + PBO	54% 34%		
Pediatric OCD Treatment Study Team (2004)	112	Child	CY-BOCS	E/RP SERT E/RP + SERT	46% 30% 53%		39%[c] 21% 54%
Foa et al. (2005)	149	Adult	Y-BOCS	E/RP CMI E/RP + CMI	55% 31% 59%	86%[d] 48% 79%	57%[e] 19% 47%
Shareh et al. (2010)	21	Adult	Y-BOCS	MCT FLV MCT + FLV	76% 35% 68%	100%[f] 17% 83%	57%[g] 0% 33%
Giasuddin et al. (2013)	30	Adult	DUOCS	FLU FLU + CBT	39% 49%		
Ma et al. (2013)	145	Adult	Y-BOCS	CMI + supportive therapy CMI + CCT	41% 81%	52%[2] 100%	3%[h] 82%
Storch et al. (2013)	47	Child	CY-BOCS	CBT + RegSERT CBT + SloSERT CBT + PBO	35% 36% 38%	57%[i] 65% 62%	43%[j] 24% 19%

(*continued*)

Table 21.1. Continued

Study	N	Age Group	Measure	Conditions	Decrease	Response Rate	Remission Rate
Vakili et al. (2015)	32	Adult	Y-BOCS	ACT SRI ACT + SRI	41% 22% 43%	44%[k] 12% 40%	22%[l] 0% 20%
Fineberg et al. (2018)	49	Adult	Y-BOCS	CBT SERT CBT + SERT	31% 22% 35%	12%[2] 43% 47%	
Samantaray et al. (2018)	32	Adult	Y-BOCS	SRI SRI + ILT	30% 49%		
Meng et al. (2019)	167	Adult	Y-BOCS	SRI CBT + SRI	47% 61%	52%[2] 83%	

Note. ACT = acceptance and commitment therapy; BT = behavior therapy; CAC = Compulsive Activity Checklist; CCT = cognitive coping therapy; CBT = cognitive-behavioral therapy; CGI = Clinical Global Impression; CT = cognitive therapy; CY-BOCS = Children's Yale-Brown Obsessive-Compulsive Scale; DUOCS = Dhaka University Obsessive-Compulsive Scale; E/RP = exposure and response prevention; FLV = fluvoxamine; FLX = fluoxetine; ILT = inhibitory learning theory-based exposure and response prevention; MCT = metacognitive therapy; PBO = placebo; RegSERT = regularly dosed sertraline; SERT = sertraline; SloSERT = slowly titrated sertraline; SRI = serotonin reuptake inhibitor; Y-BOCS = Yale-Brown Obsessive-Compulsive Scale.

[a] ≥ 30% reduction in compulsive behavior.
[b] ≥ 35% CY-BOCS/Y-BOCS score reduction.
[c] Posttreatment CY-BOCS score ≤ 10.
[d] CGI improvement = 2 (much improved).
[e] CGI improvement = 1 (very much improved).
[f] ≥ 10-point Y-BOCS score reduction.
[g] Asymptomatic.
[h] ≥ 80% Y-BOCS score reduction.
[i] ≥ 30% Y-BOCS/CY-BOCS score reduction.
[j] Posttreatment CY-BOCS score < 10.
[k] ≥ 8 point Y-BOCS score reduction.
[l] Posttreatment Y-BOCS score ≤ 8.

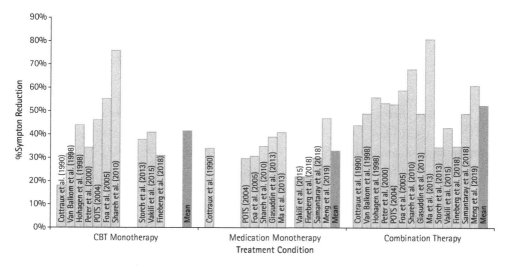

Figure 21.1. Symptom reduction in randomized trials of CBT, serotonergic medications, and their combination for patients with OCD. *Note*: CBT = Cognitive-behavioral therapy. All investigators used the Y-BOCS/CY-BOCS, with the exception of Cottraux et al. (1990) and Giasuddin et al. (2013), who used the CAC and the DUOCS, respectively. The E/RP and E/RP + SRI conditions used by van Balkom et al. (1998) were included in the CBT monotherapy and combination therapy conditions (as opposed to the cognitive therapy and cognitive therapy + E/RP conditions).

not report mean pre- and post-treatment OCD severity; thus, this study was excluded from the meta-analysis. This process resulted in 19 comparisons from 13 studies that met inclusion criteria.

Effect size estimates were calculated using the mean and standard deviation of OCD severity at the pre- and posttreatment time points. For each comparison of combined therapy versus monotherapy, Hedges's g (weighted according to sample size) was calculated. Hedges's g is a small-sample correction of Cohen's d, for which values of 0.2, 0.5, and 0.8 are conventionally accepted to represent small, medium, and large effects, respectively (Cohen, 1988). Calculation of g for pre/post designs requires an estimate of the correlation (r) between the pre- and posttreatment scores; because this was not available in published reports, r was conservatively estimated at 0.7 according to the recommendation of Rosenthal (1991). The I^2 statistic was used to assess the percentage of variation due to true heterogeneity rather than chance and was interpreted as follows: 25% = little heterogeneity, 50% = moderate heterogeneity, and 75% = high heterogeneity (Higgins et al., 2003). Significance of heterogeneity was established using the Q statistic. To test the file-drawer effect (the probability that unpublished null results would eliminate the obtained results), for each result, the fail-safe N (FSN), or the number of null results that would be needed to overturn a significant result, was calculated. Generally, if the FSN is greater than or equal to five times the number of studies in the analysis plus 10, the obtained results are considered robust against the file-drawer effect (Rosenthal, 1991).

Results indicated that CBT + medication combined therapy was associated with lower posttreatment symptom severity than was medication monotherapy [k (number of samples) = 10, g = 1.185 (0.409–1.961), p = .003; see Figure 21.2]. This finding was robust against the file-drawer effect (FSN = 335). Significant heterogeneity was detected across studies, $Q(9)$ = 131.015, $p < .001$, I^2 = 93.131. When adult and child samples were examined separately, adults (k = 9) showed a large and significant effect in favor of combined therapy [g = 1.210 (0.324–2.096), p = 0.007], and this finding was robust against the file-drawer effect (FSN = 274). Significant heterogeneity was still evident across studies, $Q(8)$ = 130.148, $p < .001$, I^2 = 93.853. The lone pediatric sample also showed a large effect in favor of combined therapy [g = 0.960 (0.414–1.507), p = .001]. FSN could not be calculated due to the small number of studies.

Combined therapy was associated with a small but significant effect showing lower posttreatment severity compared to CBT monotherapy [k = 9, g = 0.253 (0.031–0.475), p = 0.026; see Figure 21.3]. This effect was not robust against the file-drawer effect (FSN = 2). There was not significant heterogeneity across studies, $Q(8)$ = 8.548, p = .382, I^2 = 6.413, although we opted to examine adult and child samples separately for exploratory purposes. Adult samples showed a small but significant effect in favor of combined therapy over CBT monotherapy [k = 7, g = 0.361 (-0.106–0.616), p = .005]. This difference was not seen in pediatric samples [k = 2, g = -0.018 (-0.081–0.409) p = .934].

Thus, across studies, combined therapy appears to have a large and significant advantage over medication monotherapy, whereas the advantage of combined therapy over CBT monotherapy is small for adults, and was not found for children. However, these impressions must be considered tentative for several reasons. First, the number of studies is relatively small, although the finding of combined therapy's advantage over medication monotherapy is robust against the file-drawer effect. Second, substantial variability in treatment administration was noted—such as self-administered E/RP in Hohagen et al. (1998) versus the more intensive version of the treatment in Foa et al. (2005). Third, the long-term outcome of these treatments after discontinuation is unclear; only three of the reviewed studies included follow-up data (Cottraux et al., 1990; Fineberg et al., 2018; Samantaray et al., 2018). Fourth, patients in these studies were generally selected for the absence of certain comorbid conditions, such as psychosis, substance abuse, suicidality, or developmental disorders, although other conditions, such as depression and personality disorders, were usually allowed. It could be argued that some comorbid conditions, such as severe depression, might indicate the use of medications, particularly when such comorbidity makes OCD treatment difficult or impossible (for example, a depressed patient who is unable to get out of bed and come to therapy reliably). Further, in children, secondary data analysis of the Pediatric OCD Treatment Study (POTS I; March et al., 2007) found that the presence of tics was associated with better outcomes in CBT monotherapy or in CBT + sertraline (SERT), compared to SERT alone. Finally, studies that randomly assign patients to treatment conditions might fail to account for the potentially large impact of patients' preference for one treatment over the other (TenHave et al., 2003). There are several ways that patient preference may impact treatment outcome,

Study name	Monotherapy	Hedges's g	Standard error	Variance	Lower limit	Upper limit	Z-Value	p-Value
Cottraux et al. (1990)	Med	0.021	0.363	0.132	-0.691	0.732	0.057	0.954
Fineberg et al. (2018)	Med	0.144	0.450	0.202	-0.737	1.025	0.320	0.749
Foa et al. (2005)	Med	1.154	0.318	0.101	0.531	1.777	3.629	0.000
Giasuddin et al. (2013)	Med	0.128	0.380	0.145	-0.617	0.873	0.337	0.736
Ma et al. (2013)	Med	4.179	0.302	0.091	3.587	4.771	13.831	0.000
Meng et al. (2019)	Med	0.712	0.189	0.036	0.341	1.082	3.766	0.000
POTS (2004)	Med	0.960	0.279	0.078	0.414	1.507	3.445	0.001
Samantaray et al. (2018)	Med	1.492	0.418	0.174	0.673	2.310	3.572	0.000
Shareh et al. (2010)	Med	1.384	0.627	0.394	0.154	2.613	2.206	0.027
Vakili et al. (2015)	Med	1.612	0.310	0.096	1.005	2.219	5.203	0.000
		1.185	0.396	0.157	0.409	1.961	2.992	0.003

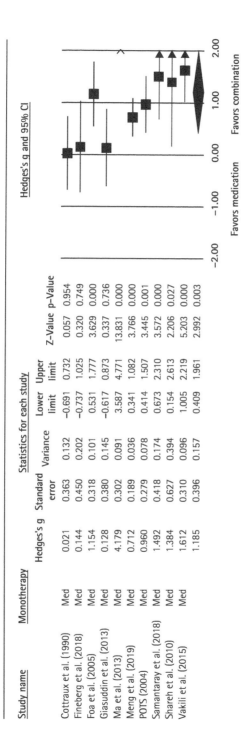

Figure 21.2. Effect sizes (Hedges's *g*) for randomized comparisons of medication monotherapy versus CBT + medication for OCD.

Study name	Monotherapy	Hedges's g	Standard error	Variance	Lower limit	Upper limit	Z-Value	p-Value
Cottraux et al. (1990)	CBT	0.421	0.354	0.125	-0.273	1.115	1.189	0.235
Foa et al. (2005)	CBT	0.219	0.311	0.097	-0.391	0.829	0.703	0.482
Hohagen et al. (1988)	CBT	0.530	0.286	0.082	-0.031	1.091	1.852	0.064
POTS (2004)	CBT	0.085	0.264	0.070	-0.432	0.602	0.323	0.747
Storch et al. (2013)	CBT	-0.206	0.357	0.127	-0.906	0.494	-0.577	0.564
Van Balkom et al. (1998)	CBT	0.728	0.333	0.111	0.075	1.380	2.187	0.029
Fineberg et al. (2018)	CBT	0.570	0.426	0.181	-0.265	1.404	1.338	0.181
Vakili et al. (2015)	CBT	0.139	0.269	0.072	-0.387	0.665	0.517	0.605
Shareh et al. (2010)	CBT	-0.659	0.571	0.326	-1.778	0.461	-1.153	0.249
		0.253	0.113	0.013	0.031	0.475	2.232	0.026

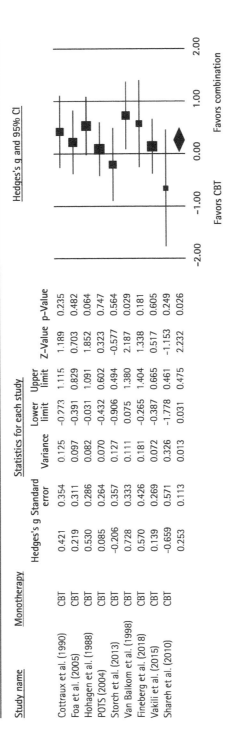

Figure 21.3. Effect sizes (Hedges's g) for randomized comparisons of CBT monotherapy versus CBT + medications for OCD.

including enrollment and attrition, homework and medication compliance, and expectancy for improvement.

Sequential Treatment with CBT and SRIs

Rather than applying two treatments simultaneously, an alternative clinical strategy is to apply one treatment first, reserving the second treatment only for patients who fail to respond adequately to the initial treatment. To date, only two studies have been published in which an adjunctive SRI was administered following a failure to respond adequately to CBT, as was suggested in the APA treatment guidelines (Koran et al., 2007). Conversely, 16 studies tested the addition of CBT after an initial trial of SRI medication. Of these 16 studies, four applied CBT regardless of patients' response to pharmacotherapy, whereas 12 investigated the addition of CBT for patients who failed to respond adequately to the SRI. A summary of the studies is provided in Table 21.2.

In the two studies that applied an adjunctive SRI following a lack of adequate response to CBT, the criteria for inadequate initial CBT response were less than a 33.33% Y-BOCS score decrease (van Balkom et al., 2012) or post-CBT CY-BOCS ≥ 16 (Skarphedinsson, Weidle, Thomsen, et al., 2015). Both studies found greater symptom reduction in the group that added an SRI (26% and 45%), rather than continued psychotherapy (–2% and 36%). The Nordic Long-Term OCD study (NordLOTS) group randomly assigned CBT nonresponders to continued CBT or an SRI. Those who did not respond in the continued CBT group (i.e., failed two consecutive rounds of CBT; $N = 11$) were assigned in a subsequent study to receive SERT treatment (Skarphedinsson, Weidle, & Ivarsson, 2015). After SERT was added, these same participants showed an additional average CY-BOCS reduction of 19%, with 27% achieving clinical response (CY-BOCS ≤ 15). In sum, SRIs may be beneficial not only for patients who do not respond to their first dose of CBT, but also for the smaller number of patients who demonstrate persistent nonresponse to CBT.

Five studies examined the impact of adjunctive E/RP following SRI monotherapy, regardless of initial SRI treatment response. Overall, there appeared to be a positive effect once E/RP was added to SRI, with symptom decreases ranging from 19% to 84%. When included next to a comparison condition, E/RP outperformed relaxation (Marks et al., 1980), SRI monotherapy (Neziroglu et al., 2000; Tenneij et al., 2005), and risperidone (RIS; Foa et al., 2015). Further, two studies with follow-up assessments showed that the benefits of adding E/RP compared to SRI monotherapy or RIS were maintained through six-month and two-year follow-up (Foa et al., 2015; Neziroglu et al., 2000). Thus, evidence suggests that E/RP is an efficacious add-on to SRI therapy.

Twelve studies examined the addition of adjunctive CBT following an inadequate response to one or more SRI trials. Criteria for inadequate initial SRI response varied across studies and included less than a 25% Y-BOCS score reduction (Albert et al., 2012; Kampman et al., 2002), less than 35% Y-BOCS score reduction (Albert et al., 2003; Nakatani & Nakagawa, 2008), CY-BOCS/Y-BOCS of at least 16 (Franklin et al., 2011; Simpson et al.,

Table 21.2. Trials of the Sequential Administration of CBT and Medication for OCD

Study	N	Age Group	Measure	Condition Sequence	Decrease	Response Rate	Remission Rate
van Balkom et al. (2012)	48	Adult	Y-BOCS	E/RP nonresponse →FLV ERP nonresponse →CT	26% -2%	32%[a] 5%	
Skarphedinsson, Weidle, Thomsen, et al. (2015)	55	Child	CY-BOCS	CBT nonresponse →SERT CBT nonresponse →CBT	45% 36%	45%[b] 50%	27%[c] 32%
Marks et al. (1980)	40	Adult	Compulsion Time	CMI →E/RP CMI →Relaxation	80% 46%		
Foa et al. (1992)	38	Adult	CAC	IMI →E/RP	84%	45%[d]	
Neziroglu et al. (2000)	10	Child	CY-BOCS	FLV →E/RP FLV →FLV	41% 16%	60%[e] 20%	
Tenneij et al. (2005)	96	Adult	Y-BOCS	SRI →E/RP SRI →SRI	19% -21%		40%[f] 25%
Foa et al. (2015)	100	Adult	Y-BOCS	SRI →E/RP SRI →RIS	58% 54%	70%[g] 23%	50%[h] 5%
Simpson et al. (1999)	6	Adult	Y-BOCS	SRI nonresponse →E/RP	49%	100%[i or j]	
Kampman et al. (2002)	14	Adult	Y-BOCS	FLU nonresponse →CBT	41%		
Albert et al. (2003)	19	Adult	Y-BOCS	SRI nonresponse →CBT	35%		
Tolin et al. (2004)	20	Adult	Y-BOCS	Multiple SRI nonresponse →E/RP	37%	53%[5,k]	
Storch, Bagner, et al. (2007)	5	Child	CY-BOCS	SRI nonresponse →CBT	65%	100%[9 or 10]	40%[l]
Tundo et al. (2007)	36	Adult	Y-BOCS	SRI nonresponse →CBT	19%	42%[9 or 10]	11%[7]
Simpson et al. (2008)	108	Adult	Y-BOCS	SRI nonresponse →E/RP SRI nonresponse →SMT	44% 14%	74%[7] 22%	33%[8] 4%

Nakatani & Nakagawa (2008)	8	Adult	Y-BOCS	FLV nonresponse →E/RP	47%	88%[10,m]	
Anand et al. (2011)	31	Adult	Y-BOCS	Multiple SRI nonresponse →CBT	45%	74%[2,5]	55%[2]
Franklin et al. (2011)	124	Child	CY-BOCS	SERT nonresponse →SERT	18%	30%[n]	
				SERT nonresponse →CBT	44%	69%	
				SERT nonresponse →I-CBT	27%	34%	
Albert et al. (2012)	119	Adult	Y-BOCS	SRI nonresponse →CBT	29%	58%[7]	31%[2,7]
Simpson et al. (2013)	100	Adult	Y-BOCS	SRI nonresponse →E/RP	52%	80%[7]	43%[8]
				SRI nonresponse →RIS	13%	23%	13%
				SRI nonresponse →PBO	11%	15%	5%

Note. CAC = Compulsive Activity Checklist; CBT = cognitive-behavioral therapy; CGI = Clinical Global Impression; CMI = clomipramine; CT = cognitive therapy; CY-BOCS = Children's Yale-Brown Obsessive-Compulsive Scale; E/RP = exposure and response prevention; FLU = fluoxetine; FLV = fluvoxamine; I-CBT = instructions in CBT; IMI = imipramine; PBO = placebo; RIS = risperidone; SERT = sertraline; SMT = stress management training; SRI = serotonin reuptake inhibitor; Y-BOCS = Yale-Brown Obsessive-Compulsive Scale.

[a] ≥ 33.33% Y-BOCS score reduction.
[b] Posttreatment Y-BOCS/CY-BOCS score ≤ 15.
[c] Posttreatment CY-BOCS score ≤ 10.
[d] 25% Y-BOCS score reduction.
[e] Reliable Change Index ≥ 1.96.
[f] Posttreatment Y-BOCS score ≤ 8.
[g] ≥ 25% Y-BOCS score reduction.
[h] Posttreatment CY-BOCS/Y-BOCS score ≤ 12.
[i] CGI improvement = 2 (much improved).
[j] CGI improvement = 1 (very much improved).
[k] Posttreatment Y-BOCS score ≤ 14.4.
[l] No longer met OCD criteria.
[m] Y-BOCS score ≥ 35% reduction.
[n] CY-BOCS score ≥ 30% reduction.

1999, 2008, 2013; Tolin et al., 2004; Tundo et al., 2007), "limited response" or side effects preventing a complete dose (Storch, Bagner, et al., 2007), or a CGI-Improvement rating greater than 3 ("minimally improved") or worse (Anand et al., 2011). On average, studies showed a 42% reduction in OCD severity, ranging from a low of 19% (Tundo et al., 2007) to a high of 65% (Storch, Bagner, et al., 2007). Three of the studies included a control comparison condition for treatment following SRI nonresponse (continued SRI, PBO, or inert psychological intervention). In all cases, the addition of CBT was more effective than the control comparison treatment (Franklin et al., 2011; Simpson et al., 2008, 2013). Thus, CBT appears efficacious for patients who do not respond to pharmacotherapy alone.

The presence of tics has been evaluated as a potential moderator of treatment outcome, although findings have been mixed. For example, the NordLOTS group found that after an initial CBT nonresponse, the presence of tics was associated with greater symptom reduction in the SERT group than in the continued CBT group (Skarphedinsson, Compton, et al., 2015). This finding is in contrast to secondary POTS II data analysis, which found that the presence of tics was associated with equivalent treatment response across conditions (SRI, SRI + instructions in CBT, or SRI + full CBT) after SRI partial response (Conelea et al., 2014). Further, in treatment-naïve patients (POTS I), the presence of tics was associated with better outcomes in combined SERT and CBT, or CBT alone, compared to SERT monotherapy (March et al., 2007).

From Addition to Interaction: New Medication Possibilities

The CBT + SRI combined treatments described above consist of an additive strategy in which two known monotherapies are applied, either simultaneously or sequentially. The expectation underlying this strategy is that if CBT produces x benefit, and SRIs produce y benefit, then the benefit of CBT + SRI should approximate $x + y$. This is clearly not the case, however. At best (with numerous caveats described previously), combined treatment offers a small to negligible advantage over CBT monotherapy, although the advantage over medication monotherapy is more substantial in both simultaneous and sequential intervention protocols.

The search for new psychotherapy/pharmacotherapy combinations might be aided by a re-examination of the mechanisms underlying the efficacy of psychotherapy. The most well-studied psychotherapy for OCD, E/RP, is based on the principle of extinction, in which repeated presentations of a conditioned stimulus (CS, e.g., dirt), outside the presence of an unconditioned stimulus (US, e.g., illness), eventually leads to reductions in the conditioned response (CR, e.g., fear). Extinction does not imply that the patient forgets the original CS–US association; rather, extinction is thought to represent the learning of new associations (e.g., the CS becomes associated with stimuli other than the US) that eventually inhibit the original association (Bouton, 1993; Craske et al., 2008). Cognitive theorists have modified the model slightly by suggesting that through repeated benign experiences with the feared stimulus, the person learns that the stimulus is not dangerous or harmful (e.g., that touching "dirty" objects does not lead to fatal illness; Beck et al.,

1985; Foa & Kozak, 1986; Williams et al., 1997). In both of these models, however, the therapy process is viewed as a form of new learning.

At the neural level, learning (including extinction learning) reflects a synaptic association between two or more neurons. During extinction, the neural association is not broken (as would be the case in "unlearning"); rather, new neural associations are formed that eventually predominate. Extinction of fear appears to be mediated by the NMDA subtype of glutamate receptor in the basolateral amygdala (Baker & Azorlosa, 1996; Cox & Westbrook, 1994; Davis, 2002; Davis & Myers, 2002; Fanselow & LeDoux, 1999; Goosens & Maren, 2002; Rogan et al., 1997; Royer & Pare, 2002).

NMDA receptor antagonists seem to block the extinction of learned fear associations in rats and in humans (Santini et al., 2001). In contrast, NMDA receptor agonists (drugs that facilitate NMDA activity) may accentuate extinction effects. In one study by Walker et al. (2002), rats were conditioned to exhibit a startle reflex toward a light after the light was repeatedly paired with a foot shock. The rats were then given the NMDA partial agonist D-cycloserine (DCS) and underwent extinction training, in which the light was presented repeatedly without the accompanying shock. Rats receiving DCS in addition to extinction training showed significantly less startle after treatment than did rats receiving extinction alone. Interestingly, rats receiving DCS without extinction training did not benefit, suggesting that the impact of DCS on extinction training is interactive, rather than additive. Although DCS has no apparent value as a monotherapy for fear, when combined with extinction, it appears to potentiate the underlying mechanisms of extinction training.

Could the facilitative effects of DCS + extinction also apply to fearful humans receiving exposure therapy? In the first test of DCS augmentation of exposure therapy in patients with anxiety disorders, Ressler et al. (2004) randomly assigned patients with acrophobia to receive DCS or PBO two to four hours before two sessions of virtual reality-based exposure therapy. Consistent with the animal findings, there was no effect of DCS on baseline fear level, but patients receiving DCS benefited more from exposure therapy than did those receiving PBO. At posttreatment assessment, approximately 60% of patients who received exposure + DCS, versus approximately 20% of those receiving exposure + PBO, rated themselves "much improved" or "very much improved." Meta-analysis of all studies in which DCS was compared to PBO in addition to exposure therapy for a broad range of anxiety-related disorders revealed that DCS enhances exposure therapy outcomes (Mataix-Cols et al., 2017), although the effect across studies was small.

To examine the effect of adding DCS to CBT for OCD, we conducted a search on PubMed and PsychInfo (8/25/2020).[2] We also examined prior review articles for references. This process resulted in 10 studies. Table 21.3 lists the degree of symptom

---

[2] The exact search string for the PubMed and PsychInfo search was as follows: ((((CBT) OR (cognitive-behavioral therapy) OR (behavior therapy) OR (cognitive therapy) OR (ERP) OR (exposure therapy)) AND (OCD) AND (d-cycloserine)))

Table 21.3. Comparison of D-Cycloserine and Placebo Augmentation of Exposure and Response Prevention

Study	N	Age Group	Dose/Timing of DCS	Conditions	Decrease	Response rate	Remission rate
Kushner et al. (2007)	32	Adult	125 mg 2 hr before E/RP	E/RP + DCS E/RP + PBO	60% 60%		
Storch, Merlo, et al. (2007)	24	Adult	250 mg 4 hr before E/RP	E/RP + DCS E/RP + PBO	66% 72%	83%[a,b] 92%	42%[c,d] 58%
Wilhelm et al. (2008)	23	Adult	100 mg 1 hr before E/RP	E/RP + DCS E/RP + PBO	62% 43%		
Storch et al. (2010)	30	Child	25 mg/50 mg 1 hr before E/RP	E/RP + DCS E/RP + PBO	72% 58%		
Farrell et al. (2013)	17	Child E/RP nonresponders	25 mg/50 mg 1 hr before E/RP	E/RP + DCS E/RP + PBO	54% 52%	100%[e] 88%	56%[f,g] 50%
Mataix-Cols et al. (2014)	27	Child	50 mg immediately after E/RP	E/RP + DCS E/RP + PBO	61% 60%	62%[h] 69%	54%[d] 46%
Andersson et al. (2015)	128	Adult	50 mg 1 hr before E/RP	E/RP + DCS E/RP + PBO	41% 48%	61%[g] 69%	47%[i] 61%
Storch et al. (2016)	142	Child	25 mg/50 mg 1 hr before E/RP	E/RP + DCS E/RP + PBO	45% 42%	83%[j] 72%	50%[g] 46%
de Leeuw et al. (2017)	39	Adult	125 mg 1 hr before E/RP	E/RP + DCS E/RP + PBO	25% 17%	37%[k] 15%	
Kvale et al. (2020)	163	Adult E/RP nonresponders	Timing of dosage not reported	E/RP + DCS 100 mg E/RP + DCS 250 mg E/RP + PBO	56% 55% 48%	34%[g] 23% 23%	54%[g,9] 60% 55%

Note. E/RP = exposure and response prevention; DCS = D-Cycloserine; PBO = placebo; RIS = risperidone; SERT = sertraline; SMT = stress management training; SRI = serotonin reuptake inhibitor; CGI = Clinical Global Impression; ADIS = Anxiety Disorders Interview Schedule; CY-BOCS = Children's Yale-Brown Obsessive-Compulsive Scale; Y-BOCS = Yale-Brown Obsessive-Compulsive Scale.

[a] CGI improvement = 2 (much improved).
[b] CGI improvement = 1 (very much improved).
[c] Posttreatment ADIS rating ≤ 3.
[d] Posttreatment CY-BOCS score ≤ 10.
[e] > 25% CY-BOCS score reduction.
[f] > 50% reduction in CY-BOCS score.
[g] Posttreatment CY-BOCS score < 14.
[h] ≥ 35% Y-BOCS/CY-BOCS score reduction.
[i] Posttreatment Y-BOCS/CY-BOCS score ≤ 12.
[j] Posttreatment CY-BOCS score ≤ 14.
[k] ≥ 30% Y-BOCS score reduction.

reduction as well as response and remission rates for each study. Average response rate was 66% in the DCS condition (range 29% to 100%) compared to 59% in PBO (range 15% to 92%). Importantly, the definition for response was variable across studies, as shown in the table's footnotes. Five studies assessed remission (variously defined) and found a similar remission rate between DCS and PBO (an average of 52% and 53%, respectively).

To examine symptom reduction across studies, we used meta-analytic strategies to examine the effect of DCS versus PBO when added to E/RP using pre- and posttreatment Y-BOCS/CY-BOCS scores. Across all samples (k = 11), there was a small effect in favor of DCS that just missed statistical significance: g = 0.212 (−0.012–0.436), p = .063 (see Figure 21.4). Heterogeneity also just missed significance: Q(10) = 17.614, p = .062, I^2 = 43.228. For exploratory purposes, we examined adult and pediatric samples separately. For adults (k = 7), the effect was small—g = 0.223 (−0.131–0.577), p = 0.217—and heterogeneity was significant: Q(6) = 16.700, p = .010, I^2 = 64.072. For children (k = 4), the effect was also small—g = 0.203 (−0.065–0.471), p = 0.137—and heterogeneity was not significant: Q(3) = 0.863, p = .834, I^2 = 0.000. Thus, the available evidence suggests that DCS may augment the effects of CBT, although the effect is small at posttreatment measurement.

Other data suggest that the trajectory of symptom reduction may vary as a function of DCS. An analysis of Wilhelm et al.'s (2008) data suggested that the facilitative effects of DCS are more evident early in treatment, implying that DCS accelerates treatment effects (Chasson et al., 2010). Other studies have also found support for greater midtreatment symptom reduction with DCS compared to PBO (de Leeuw et al., 2017; Kushner et al., 2007; Mataix-Cols et al., 2014; Storch, Merlo, et al., 2007). Among antidepressant-free patients, 60% of those receiving DCS were considered treatment responders, compared to 50% of those receiving PBO, a finding suggesting that the presence of antidepressant medications may inhibit the effects of DCS (Andersson et al., 2015). Further investigation is needed to assess for other potential moderators of DCS outcomes in OCD. Finally, evidence suggests that DCS might be effective only when administered following a "successful" exposure session (e.g., the patient experienced a significant reduction in fear). Among social phobia patients who reported low fear at the end of exposure sessions (successful exposure), those who had received DCS showed more clinical improvement at the next session, compared to those who had received PBO. Conversely, when fear at the end of the exposure was high (unsuccessful exposure), patients receiving DCS showed less clinical improvement at the following session than did those receiving PBO (Smits et al., 2013). Thus, DCS's effect may be to strengthen learning during exposure sessions, for better or for worse.

This line of research is noteworthy for two primary reasons. First, it is likely that a more rapid response would translate to decreased attrition, decreased direct (e.g., therapy, medications) and indirect (e.g., forgone earnings) costs of illness, decreased suffering (e.g., fear and impairment), and increased caseload capacity for clinicians. Second, and perhaps

Study name	Subgroup within study		Statistics for each study						Hedges's g and 95% CI
		Hedges's g	Standard error	Variance	Lower limit	Upper limit	Z-Value	p-Value	
Andersson et al. (2015)	Blank	-0.326	0.177	0.031	-0.673	0.021	-1.842	0.065	
De Leeuw et al. (2017)	Blank	0.517	0.319	0.102	-0.109	1.143	1.620	0.105	
Farrell et al. (2013)	Blank	0.213	0.463	0.214	-0.693	1.120	0.461	0.644	
Kushner et al. (2007)	Blank	-0.189	0.391	0.153	-0.954	0.577	-0.483	0.629	
Kvale et al. (2020) 100 mg	Blank	0.480	0.219	0.048	0.051	0.910	2.191	0.028	
Kvale et al. (2020) 250 mg	Blank	0.292	0.217	0.047	-0.132	0.716	1.348	0.178	
Mataix-Cols et al. (2014)	Blank	0.234	0.375	0.141	-0.501	0.968	0.623	0.533	
Storch et al. (2007)	Blank	-0.061	0.394	0.155	-0.834	0.711	-0.156	0.876	
Storch et al. (2010)	Blank	0.493	0.361	0.130	-0.215	1.200	1.365	0.172	
Storch et al. (2016)	Blank	0.130	0.167	0.028	-0.197	0.458	0.780	0.435	
Wilhelm et al. (2008)	Blank	1.058	0.434	0.189	0.207	1.909	2.436	0.015	
		0.212	0.114	0.013	-0.012	0.436	1.859	0.063	

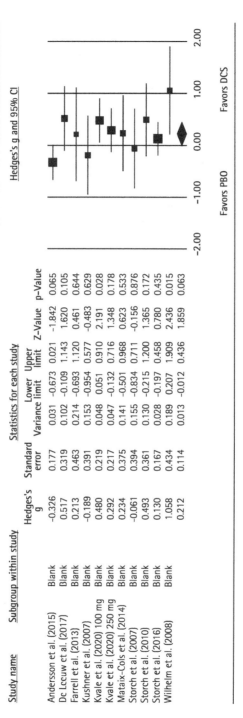

Figure 21.4. Effect sizes (Hedges's *g*) for randomized comparisons of CBT + D-cycloserine (DCS) versus CBT + placebo (PBO) for OCD.

more critical, research on DCS provides proof of concept that pharmacotherapy aimed at enhancing the neural underpinnings of psychotherapy can influence outcomes. This represents an interactive approach, rather than an additive one in which two known monotherapies are applied simultaneously, and a significant success of translational research from basic science to practice. Other novel compounds that might potentiate the mechanisms of exposure therapy/fear extinction, but have yet to be evaluated for OCD within the context of an RCT, include (but are not limited to):

(a) *Yohimbine*, an $α_2$-adrenergic receptor antagonist that enhances fear extinction in animals (Cain et al., 2004; Morris & Bouton, 2007). Yohimbine did not appear to augment the efficacy of virtual reality-based exposure therapy for fear of flying (Meyerbroeker et al. , 2012), although some evidence on self-report measures suggested that, for patients who had successful exposure sessions, yohimbine facilitated a brief exposure-based treatment for social phobia (Smits et al., 2014).

(b) Methylene blue, an autoxidizing agent that potentiates fear extinction in animals (Gonzalez-Lima & Bruchey, 2004; Wrubel et al., 2007). Methlylene blue has been demonstrated to lead to greater response and better quality of life when combined with exposure therapy, for patients with posttraumatic stress disorder (PTSD; Zoellner et al., 2017). Echoing the findings for DCS, among patients with claustrophobia, methylene blue appeared to have beneficial effects for patients who had successful exposure sessions, but it may have had deleterious effects when exposure sessions were not successful (Telch et al., 2014).

(c) Oxytocin, a neuropeptide that disrupts signals from the amygdala to the autonomic nervous system (Huber et al., 2005; Kirsch et al., 2005). Among individuals with social phobia receiving exposure-based therapy, those taking oxytocin showed improved positive evaluations of appearance and speech performance, although these effects did not generalize to improved overall outcome from exposure therapy (Guastella et al., 2009). In a small trial of patients with PTSD receiving exposure therapy, oxytocin produced numerically lower PTSD and depression symptoms, although this did not reach statistical significance (Flanagan et al., 2018).

(d) Estradiol, a sex hormone that regulates menstrual cycles and fluctuates throughout the female reproductive cycle. When estradiol levels are high (either naturally or following estradiol administration), female rats (Graham & Milad, 2013; Zeidan et al., 2011), healthy women (Graham et al., 2017; Graham & Milad, 2013), and women with PTSD (Glover et al., 2012) demonstrate greater recall of extinction to a conditioned fear stimulus. Estradiol has not yet been tested as an augmentation to exposure-based CBT in anxiety-related disorders.

(e) Ketamine, a noncompetitive NMDA receptor antagonist that increases the production of brain-derived neurotrophic factor and facilitates AMPA receptor currents, thereby increasing synaptic plasticity, which has been demonstrated to enhance fear extinction in a subset of rats (Fortress et al., 2018). Ketamine appears to have anti-obsessional properties (Bloch et al., 2012), although its direct effects appear to be short-lived. In a small open trial, patients with OCD receiving ketamine plus exposure-based therapy showed a more durable response to treatment, suggesting a potential additive effect (Rodriguez et al., 2016).

(f) Aripiprazole, an atypical antipsychotic, has been used to augment SRIs in OCD (for a review, see Veale et al., 2014) and may be beneficial as a monotherapy as well (Ercan et al., 2015). Some evidence from animal studies suggests that aripiprazole leads to improved recall of extinction of conditioned fear, accompanied by increased activation of neurons in the medial prefrontal cortex (Ganella et al., 2017). In a case report, a child with OCD who had failed to respond to CBT + SERT showed an improved response when given CBT + aripiprazole (Storch et al., 2008).

(g) Cannabidiol, a nonpsychotomimetic component of *Cannabis sativa*, has anxiolytic effects (Bergamaschi et al., 2011) but also facilitates extinction of contextual fear memory in rats, with persistent effects (Bitencourt et al., 2008). In healthy humans, cannabidiol given after extinction appears to enhance consolidation of extinction learning as assessed by shock expectancy (Das et al., 2013). To date, no studies have been published in which cannabidiol was used to augment exposure-based CBT in humans with anxiety-related disorders, although such work is currently underway (van der Flier et al., 2019).

Conclusion

Both SRIs and CBT have proven effective as monotherapies for OCD, as described in Chapters 17, 19, and 20 in this volume. Intuitively, it might be expected that their combination would be more effective than either treatment alone. However, controlled research affirms this hypothesis only partially. When two treatments are applied simultaneously, combined therapy shows a distinct advantage over pharmacotherapy. However, combined therapy offers a small to negligible advantage over CBT monotherapy (in adults, and no advantage in children), and the potential side effects of medication might tip the cost–benefit ratio to CBT monotherapy as the first-line treatment of choice. Thus, the available data are more consistent with the APA's practice guidelines (Koran et al., 2007), in which CBT monotherapy was recommended as an initial treatment for all patients who could comply with this prescription, than with the previous Expert Consensus Guidelines (March et al., 1997) in which combined treatment was recommended for the more severe OCD cases.

The APA practice guidelines recommend that SRIs be prescribed when patients have failed to respond to an adequate trial of CBT monotherapy. Only three published studies have evaluated the efficacy of CBT + SRI for CBT nonresponders or partial responders (Skarphedinsson, Weidle, & Ivarsson, 2015; Skarphedinsson, Weidle, Thomsen, et al., 2015; van Balkom et al., 2012). Each study noted support for the adjunctive effect of SRI following nonresponse to CBT. Of note, one of the studies was a second-step data analysis from the Nordic Long-Term OCD study, warranting replication in additional samples and treatment groups. Given the greater availability of pharmacotherapy and the likelihood that many patients with OCD will not seek CBT until after at least one failed medication trial, it is encouraging that CBT appears reasonably effective even for these patients. Further, for providers, there are initial data to support referring the patient for adjunctive SRI medication following initial nonresponse to CBT. Recently, research has investigated an entirely different approach to combined treatment: instead of applying two known monotherapies, compounds are being investigated that potentiate the neural mechanisms thought to underline successful CBT. In the first development of this line of research, the NMDA receptor agonist D-cycloserine appears to augment the neural mechanisms of extinction learning, resulting in more rapid response to CBT. Ideally, ongoing basic research in neuroplasticity can lead to increasingly refined methods.

References

Albert, U., Aguglia, A., Bogetto, F., Cieri, L., Daniele, M., Maina, G., Necci, R., Parena, A., Salvati, L., & Tundo, A. (2012). Effectiveness of cognitive-behavioral therapy addition to pharmacotherapy in resistant obsessive-compulsive disorder: A multicenter study. *Psychotherapy and Psychosomatics, 81*(6), 383–385.

Albert, U., Maina, G., Forner, F., & Bogetto, F. (2003). Cognitive-behavioral therapy in obsessive-compulsive disorder patients partially unresponsive to SRIs. *European Neuropsychopharmacology, 13*, S357–S358.

Alpers, G. W., & Sell, R. (2008). And yet they correlate: Psychophysiological activation predicts self-report outcomes of exposure therapy in claustrophobia. *Journal of Anxiety Disorders, 22*(7), 1101–1109.

Anand, N., Sudhir, P. M., Math, S. B., Thennarasu, K., & Janardhan Reddy, Y. C. (2011). Cognitive behavior therapy in medication non-responders with obsessive-compulsive disorder: A prospective 1-year follow-up study. *Journal of Anxiety Disorders, 25*(7), 939–945.

Andersson, E., Hedman, E., Enander, J., Radu Djurfeldt, D., Ljotsson, B., Cervenka, S., Isung, J., Svanborg, C., Mataix-Cols, D., Kaldo, V., Andersson, G., Lindefors, N., & Ruck, C. (2015). D-Cycloserine vs placebo as adjunct to cognitive behavioral therapy for obsessive-compulsive disorder and interaction with antidepressants: A randomized clinical trial. *JAMA Psychiatry, 72*(7), 659–667.

Baker, J. D., & Azorlosa, J. L. (1996). The NMDA antagonist MK-801 blocks the extinction of Pavlovian fear conditioning. *Behavioral Neuroscience, 110*(3), 618–620.

Baxter, L. R., Jr., Schwartz, J. M., Bergman, K. S., Szuba, M. P., Guze, B. H., Mazziotta, J. C., Alazraki, A., Selin, C. E., Ferng, H. K., Munford, P., & Phelps, M. E. (1992). Caudate glucose metabolic rate changes with both drug and behavior therapy for obsessive-compulsive disorder. *Archives of General Psychiatry, 49*(9), 681–689.

Beck, A. T., Emery, G., & Greenberg, R. L. (1985). *Anxiety disorders and phobias: A cognitive perspective.* Basic Books.

Bergamaschi, M. M., Queiroz, R. H., Chagas, M. H., de Oliveira, D. C., De Martinis, B. S., Kapczinski, F., Quevedo, J., Roesler, R., Schröder, N., Nardi, A. E., Martín-Santos, R., Hallak, J. E., Zuardi, A. W., & Crippa, J. A. (2011). Cannabidiol reduces the anxiety induced by simulated public speaking in treatment-naive social phobia patients. *Neuropsychopharmacology*, *36*(6), 1219–1226.

Bitencourt, R. M., Pamplona, F. A., & Takahashi, R. N. (2008). Facilitation of contextual fear memory extinction and anti-anxiogenic effects of AM404 and cannabidiol in conditioned rats. *European Neuropsychopharmacology*, *18*(12), 849–859.

Bloch, M. H., Wasylink, S., Landeros-Weisenberger, A., Panza, K. E., Billingslea, E., Leckman, J. F., Krystal, J. H., Bhagwagar, Z., Sanacora, G., & Pittenger, C. (2012). Effects of ketamine in treatment-refractory obsessive-compulsive disorder. *Biological Psychiatry*, *72*(11), 964–970.

Borenstein, M., Hedges, L., Higgins, J., & Rothstein, H. (2007). *Manual: Comprehensive Meta-Analysis Software (v. 2.0)*. Biostat.

Bouton, M. E. (1993). Context, time, and memory retrieval in the interference paradigms of Pavlovian learning. *Psychological Bulletin*, *114*(1), 80–99.

Bouton, M. E. (2002). Context, ambiguity, and unlearning: Sources of relapse after behavioral extinction. *Biological Psychiatry*, *52*(10), 976–986.

Cain, C. K., Blouin, A. M., & Barad, M. (2004). Adrenergic transmission facilitates extinction of conditional fear in mice. *Learning and Memory*, *11*(2), 179–187.

Chasson, G. S., Buhlmann, U., Tolin, D. F., Rao, S. R., Reese, H. E., Rowley, T., Welsh, K. S., & Wilhelm, S. (2010). Need for speed: Evaluating slopes of OCD recovery in behavior therapy enhanced with D-cycloserine. *Behaviour Research and Therapy*, *48*(7), 675–679.

Cohen, J. (1988). *Statistical power analysis for the behavioral sciences* (2nd ed.). Lawrence Erlbaum Associates.

Conelea, C. A., Walther, M. R., Freeman, J. B., Garcia, A. M., Sapyta, J., Khanna, M., & Franklin, M. (2014). Tic-related obsessive-compulsive disorder (OCD): Phenomenology and treatment outcome in the Pediatric OCD Treatment Study II. *Journal of the American Academy of Child and Adolescent Psychiatry*, *53*(12), 1308–1316.

Cottraux, J., Mollard, E., Bouvard, M., Marks, I., Sluys, M., Nury, A. M., Douge, R., & Cialdella, P. (1990). A controlled study of fluvoxamine and exposure in obsessive-compulsive disorder. *International Clinical Psychopharmacology*, *5*(1), 17–30.

Cox, J., & Westbrook, R. F. (1994). The NMDA receptor antagonist MK-801 blocks acquisition and extinction of conditioned hypoalgesic responses in the rat. *Quarterly Journal of Experimental Psychology B: Comparative and Physiological Psychology*, *47*(2), 187–210.

Craske, M. G., Kircanski, K., Zelikowsky, M., Mystkowski, J., Chowdhury, N., & Baker, A. (2008). Optimizing inhibitory learning during exposure therapy. *Behaviour Research and Therapy*, *46*(1), 5–27.

Das, R. K., Kamboj, S. K., Ramadas, M., Yogan, K., Gupta, V., Redman, E., Curran, H. V., & Morgan, C. J. (2013). Cannabidiol enhances consolidation of explicit fear extinction in humans. *Psychopharmacology*, *226*(4), 781–792.

Davis, M. (2002). Role of NMDA receptors and MAP kinase in the amygdala in extinction of fear: Clinical implications for exposure therapy. *European Journal of Neuroscience*, *16*(3), 395–398.

Davis, M., & Myers, K. M. (2002). The role of glutamate and gamma-aminobutyric acid in fear extinction: Clinical implications for exposure therapy. *Biological Psychiatry*, *52*(10), 998–1007.

de Leeuw, A. S., van Megen, H. J., Kahn, R. S., & Westenberg, H. G. (2017). D-Cycloserine addition to exposure sessions in the treatment of patients with obsessive-compulsive disorder. *European Psychiatry*, *40*, 38–44.

Ercan, E. S., Ardic, U. A., Ercan, E., Yuce, D., & Durak, S. (2015). A promising preliminary study of aripiprazole for treatment-resistant childhood obsessive-compulsive disorder. *Journal of Child and Adolescent Psychopharmacology*, *25*(7), 580–584.

Fanselow, M. S., & LeDoux, J. E. (1999). Why we think plasticity underlying Pavlovian fear conditioning occurs in the basolateral amygdala. *Neuron*, *23*(2), 229–232.

Farrell, L. J., Waters, A. M., Boschen, M. J., Hattingh, L., McConnell, H., Milliner, E. L., Collings, N., Zimmer-Gembeck, M., Shelton, D., Ollendick, T. H., Testa, C., & Storch, E. A. (2013). Difficult-to-treat pediatric obsessive-compulsive disorder: Feasibility and preliminary results of a randomized pilot trial of D-cycloserine-augmented behavior therapy. *Depression and Anxiety*, *30*(8), 723–731.

Fineberg, N. A., Baldwin, D. S., Drummond, L. M., Wyatt, S., Hanson, J., Gopi, S., Kaur, S., Reid, J., Marwah., V., Sachdev, R. A., Pampaloni, I., Shahper, S., Varlakova, Y., Mpavaenda, D., Manson, C.,

O'Leary, C. O., Irvine, K., Monji-Patel, D., Shodunke, A., . . . Wellsted, D. (2018). Optimal treatment for obsessive compulsive disorder: A randomized controlled feasibility study of the clinical-effectiveness and cost-effectiveness of cognitive-behavioural therapy, selective serotonin reuptake inhibitors and their combination in the management of obsessive compulsive disorder. *International Clinical Psychopharmacology, 33*(6), 334–348.

Flanagan, J. C., Sippel, L. M., Wahlquist, A., Moran-Santa Maria, M. M., & Back, S. E. (2018). Augmenting prolonged exposure therapy for PTSD with intranasal oxytocin: A randomized, placebo-controlled pilot trial. *Journal of Psychiatric Research, 98*, 64–69.

Foa, E. B., Franklin, M. E., & Moser, J. (2002). Context in the clinic: How well do cognitive-behavioral therapies and medications work in combination? *Biological Psychiatry, 52*(10), 987–997.

Foa, E. B., & Kozak, M. J. (1986). Emotional processing of fear: Exposure to corrective information. *Psychological Bulletin, 99*(1), 20–35.

Foa, E. B., Kozak, M. J., Steketee, G., & McCarthy, P. R. (1992). Treatment of depressive and obsessive-compulsive symptoms in OCD by imipramine and behaviour therapy. *British Journal of Clinical Psychology, 31*(Pt. 3), 279–292.

Foa, E. B., Liebowitz, M. R., Kozak, M. J., Davies, S., Campeas, R., Franklin, M. E., Huppert, J. D., Kjernisted, K., Rowan, V., Schmidt, A. B., Simpson, H. B., & Tu, X. (2005). Randomized, placebo-controlled trial of exposure and ritual prevention, clomipramine, and their combination in the treatment of obsessive-compulsive disorder. *The American Journal of Psychiatry, 162*(1), 151–161.

Foa, E. B., Simpson, H. B., Rosenfield, D., Liebowitz, M. R., Cahill, S. P., Huppert, J. D., Bender Jr., J., McLean, C. P., Maher, M. J., Campeas, R., Hahn, C., Imms, P., Pinto, A., Powers, M. B., Rodriguez, C. I., Van Meter, P., E., Vermes, D., & Williams, M. T. (2015). Six-month outcomes from a randomized trial augmenting serotonin reuptake inhibitors with exposure and response prevention or risperidone in adults with obsessive-compulsive disorder. *The Journal of Clinical Psychiatry, 76*(4), 440–446.

Fortress, A. M., Smith, I. M., & Pang, K. C. H. (2018). Ketamine facilitates extinction of avoidance behavior and enhances synaptic plasticity in a rat model of anxiety vulnerability: Implications for the pathophysiology and treatment of anxiety disorders. *Neuropharmacology, 137*, 372–381.

Franklin, M. E., Sapyta, J., Freeman, J. B., Khanna, M., Compton, S., Almirall, D., Moore, P., Choate-Summers, M., Garcia, A., Edson, A., Foa, E. B., & March, J. S. (2011). Cognitive behavior therapy augmentation of pharmacotherapy in pediatric obsessive-compulsive disorder: The Pediatric OCD Treatment Study II (POTS II) randomized controlled trial. *JAMA, 306*(11), 1224–1232.

Ganella, D. E., Lee-Kardashyan, L., Luikinga, S. J., Nguyen, D. L. D., Madsen, H. B., Zbukvic, I. C., Coulthard, R., Lawrence, A. J., & Kim, J. H. (2017). Aripiprazole facilitates extinction of conditioned fear in adolescent rats. *Frontiers in Behavioral Neuroscience, 11*, 76.

Giasuddin, N. A., Nahar, J. S., Morshed, N. M., Balhara, Y. P., & Sobhan, M. A. (2013). Efficacy of combination of fluoxetine and cognitive behavioral therapy and fluoxetine alone for the treatment of obsessive compulsive disorder. *Pakistan Journal Pharmaceutical Sciences, 26*(1), 95–98.

Glass, G. V., McGaw, B., & Smith, M. L. (1981). *Meta-analysis in social research*. SAGE.

Glover, E. M., Jovanovic, T., Mercer, K. B., Kerley, K., Bradley, B., Ressler, K. J., & Norrholm, S. D. (2012). Estrogen levels are associated with extinction deficits in women with posttraumatic stress disorder. *Biological Psychiatry, 72*(1), 19–24.

Gonzalez-Lima, F., & Bruchey, A. K. (2004). Extinction memory improvement by the metabolic enhancer methylene blue. *Learning and Memory, 11*(5), 633–640.

Goosens, K. A., & Maren, S. (2002). Long-term potentiation as a substrate for memory: Evidence from studies of amygdaloid plasticity and Pavlovian fear conditioning. *Hippocampus, 12*(5), 592–599.

Graham, B. M., Ash, C., & Den, M. L. (2017). High endogenous estradiol is associated with enhanced cognitive emotion regulation of physiological conditioned fear responses in women. *Psychoneuroendocrinology, 80*, 7–14.

Graham, B. M., & Milad, M. R. (2013). Blockade of estrogen by hormonal contraceptives impairs fear extinction in female rats and women. *Biological Psychiatry, 73*(4), 371–378.

Guastella, A. J., Howard, A. L., Dadds, M. R., Mitchell, P., & Carson, D. S. (2009). A randomized controlled trial of intranasal oxytocin as an adjunct to exposure therapy for social anxiety disorder. *Psychoneuroendocrinology, 34*(6), 917–923.

Higgins, J. P., Thompson, S. G., Deeks, J. J., & Altman, D. G. (2003). Measuring inconsistency in meta-analyses. *British Medical Journal, 327*(7414), 557–560.

Hohagen, F., Winkelmann, G., Rasche-Ruchle, H., Hand, I., Konig, A., Munchau, N., Hiss, H., Geiger-Kabisch, C., Käppler, C., Schramm, P., Rey, E., Aldenhoff, J., & Berger, M. (1998). Combination of behaviour therapy with fluvoxamine in comparison with behaviour therapy and placebo: Results of a multicentre study. *The British Journal of Psychiatry*, *35*, 71–78.

Huber, D., Veinante, P., & Stoop, R. (2005). Vasopressin and oxytocin excite distinct neuronal populations in the central amygdala. *Science*, *308*(5719), 245–248.

Kampman, M., Keijsers, G. P., Hoogduin, C. A., & Verbraak, M. J. (2002). Addition of cognitive-behaviour therapy for obsessive-compulsive disorder patients non-responding to fluoxetine. *Acta Psychiatrica Scandinavica*, *106*(4), 314–319.

Kim, E. J. (2005). The effect of the decreased safety behaviors on anxiety and negative thoughts in social phobics. *Journal of Anxiety Disorders*, *19*(1), 69–86.

Kirsch, P., Esslinger, C., Chen, Q., Mier, D., Lis, S., Siddhanti, S., Gruppe, H., Mattay, V. S., Gallhofer, B., & Meyer-Lindenberg, A. (2005). Oxytocin modulates neural circuitry for social cognition and fear in humans. *Journal of Neuroscience*, *25*(49), 11489–11493.

Koran, L. M., Hanna, G. L., Hollander, E., Nestadt, G., & Simpson, H. B. (2007). Practice guideline for the treatment of patients with obsessive-compulsive disorder. *The American Journal of Psychiatry*, *164*(7 Suppl.), 5–53.

Kushner, M. G., Kim, S. W., Donahue, C., Thuras, P., Adson, D., Kotlyar, M., McCabe, J., Peterson, J., & Foa, E. B. (2007). D-Cycloserine augmented exposure therapy for obsessive-compulsive disorder. *Biological Psychiatry*, *62*(8), 835–838.

Kvale, G., Hansen, B., Hagen, K., Abramowitz, J. S., Bortveit, T., Craske, M. G., Franklin, M. E., Haseth, S., Himle, J. A., Hystad, S., Kristensen, U. B., Launes, G., Lund, A., Solem, S., & Ost, L. G. (2020). Effect of D-cycloserine on the effect of concentrated exposure and response prevention in difficult-to-treat obsessive-compulsive disorder: A randomized clinical trial. *JAMA Netw Open*, *3*(8), e2013249.

Ma, J. D., Wang, C. H., Li, H. F., Zhang, X. L., Zhang, Y. L., Hou, Y. H., Liu, X. H. & Hu, X. Z. (2013). Cognitive-coping therapy for obsessive-compulsive disorder: A randomized controlled trial. *Journal of Psychiatric Research*, *47*(11), 1785–1790.

March, J. S., Frances, A., Carpenter, D., & Kahn, D. A. (1997). The expert consensus guideline series: Treatment of obsessive-compulsive disorder. *The Journal of Clinical Psychiatry*, *58*(Suppl. 4), 1–72.

March, J. S., Franklin, M. E., Leonard, H., Garcia, A., Moore, P., Freeman, J., & Foa, E. (2007). Tics moderate treatment outcome with sertraline but not cognitive-behavior therapy in pediatric obsessive-compulsive disorder. *Biological Psychiatry*, *61*(3), 344–347.

Marks, I. M., Stern, R. S., Mawson, D., Cobb, J., & McDonald, R. (1980). Clomipramine and exposure for obsessive-compulsive rituals: I. *The British Journal of Psychiatry*, *136*, 1–25.

Mataix-Cols, D., Fernandez de la Cruz, L., Monzani, B., Rosenfield, D., Andersson, E., Perez-Vigil, A., Frument, P., de Kleine, R. A., Difede, J., Dunlop, B. W., Farrell, L. J., Geller, D., Gerardi, M., Guastella, A. J., Hofmann, S. G., Hendriks, G. J., Kushner, M. G., Lee, F. S., . . . Thuras, P. (2017). D-Cycloserine augmentation of exposure-based cognitive behavior therapy for anxiety, obsessive-compulsive, and post-traumatic stress disorders: A systematic review and meta-analysis of individual participant data. *JAMA Psychiatry*, *74*(5), 501–510.

Mataix-Cols, D., Turner, C., Monzani, B., Isomura, K., Murphy, C., Krebs, G., & Heyman, I. (2014). Cognitive-behavioural therapy with post-session D-cycloserine augmentation for paediatric obsessive-compulsive disorder: Pilot randomised controlled trial. *The British Journal of Psychiatry*, *204*(1), 77–78.

Meng, F. Q., Han, H. Y., Luo, J., Liu, J., Liu, Z. R., Tang, Y., Yan, Y. P., Huang, Y. Q., Sun, J., & Li, Z. J. (2019). Efficacy of cognitive behavioural therapy with medication for patients with obsessive-compulsive disorder: A multicentre randomised controlled trial in China. *Journal of Affective Disorders*, *253*, 184–192.

Meuret, A. E., Seidel, A., Rosenfield, B., Hofmann, S. G., & Rosenfield, D. (2012). Does fear reactivity during exposure predict panic symptom reduction? *Journal of Consulting and Clinical Psychology*, *80*(5), 773–785.

Meyerbroeker, K., Powers, M. B., van Stegeren, A., & Emmelkamp, P. M. (2012). Does yohimbine hydrochloride facilitate fear extinction in virtual reality treatment of fear of flying? A randomized placebo-controlled trial. *Psychotherapy and Psychosomatics*, *81*(1), 29–37.

Morgan, H., & Raffle, C. (1999). Does reducing safety behaviours improve treatment response in patients with social phobia? *Australian and New Zealand Journal of Psychiatry*, *33*(4), 503–510.

Morris, R. W., & Bouton, M. E. (2007). The effect of yohimbine on the extinction of conditioned fear: A role for context. *Behavioral Neuroscience*, *121*(3), 501–514.

Nakatani, E., & Nakagawa, A. (2008). Outcome of additional behaviour therapy including treatment discontinuation for fluvoxamine non-responders with obsessive-compulsive disorder. *Psychotherapy and Psychosomatics, 77*(6), 393–394.

Neziroglu, F., Yaryura-Tobias, J. A., Walz, J., & McKay, D. (2000). The effect of fluvoxamine and behavior therapy on children and adolescents with obsessive-compulsive disorder. *Journal of Child and Adolescent Psychopharmacology, 10*(4), 295–306.

Otto, M. W., Kredlow, M. A., Smits, J. A. J., Hofmann, S. G., Tolin, D. F., de Kleine, R. A., van Minnen, A., Evins, A. E., & Pollack, M. H. (2016). Enhancement of psychosocial treatment with D-cycloserine: Models, moderators, and future directions. *Biological Psychiatry, 80*(4), 274–283.

Pediatric OCD Treatment Study Team. (2004). Cognitive-behavior therapy, sertraline, and their combination for children and adolescents with obsessive-compulsive disorder: The Pediatric OCD Treatment Study (POTS) randomized controlled trial. *JAMA, 292*(16), 1969–1976.

Peter, H., Tabrizian, S., & Hand, I. (2000). Serum cholesterol in patients with obsessive compulsive disorder during treatment with behavior therapy and SSRI or placebo. *International Journal of Psychiatry in Medicine, 30*(1), 27–39.

Powers, M. B., Smits, J. A., & Telch, M. J. (2004). Disentangling the effects of safety-behavior utilization and safety-behavior availability during exposure-based treatment: A placebo-controlled trial. *Journal of Consulting and Clinical Psychology, 72*(3), 448–454.

Powers, M. B., Smits, J. A., Whitley, D., Bystritsky, A., & Telch, M. J. (2008). The effect of attributional processes concerning medication taking on return of fear. *Journal of Consulting and Clinical Psychology, 76*(3), 478–490.

Ressler, K. J., Rothbaum, B. O., Tannenbaum, L., Anderson, P., Graap, K., Zimand, E., Hodges, L., & Davis, M. (2004). Cognitive enhancers as adjuncts to psychotherapy: Use of D-cycloserine in phobic individuals to facilitate extinction of fear. *Archives of General Psychiatry, 61*(11), 1136–1144.

Rodriguez, C. I., Wheaton, M., Zwerling, J., Steinman, S. A., Sonnenfeld, D., Galfalvy, H., & Simpson, H. B. (2016). Can exposure-based CBT extend the effects of intravenous ketamine in obsessive-compulsive disorder? An open-label trial. *Journal of Clinical Psychiatry, 77*(3), 408–409.

Rogan, M. T., Staubli, U. V., & LeDoux, J. E. (1997). Fear conditioning induces associative long-term potentiation in the amygdala. *Nature, 390*(6660), 604–607.

Rosenthal, R. (1991). *Meta-analytic procedures for social research*. SAGE.

Royer, S., & Pare, D. (2002). Bidirectional synaptic plasticity in intercalated amygdala neurons and the extinction of conditioned fear responses. *Neuroscience, 115*(2), 455–462.

Salkovskis, P. M. (1999). An experimental investigation of the role of safety-seeking behaviours in the maintenance of panic disorder with agoraphobia. *Behaviour Research and Therapy, 37*, 559–574.

Samantaray, N. N., Chaudhury, S., & Singh, P. (2018). Efficacy of inhibitory learning theory-based exposure and response prevention and selective serotonin reuptake inhibitor in obsessive-compulsive disorder management: A treatment comparison. *Industrial Psychiatry Journal, 27*(1), 53–60.

Santini, E., Muller, R. U., & Quirk, G. J. (2001). Consolidation of extinction learning involves transfer from NMDA-independent to NMDA-dependent memory. *Journal of Neuroscience, 21*(22), 9009–9017.

Shareh, H., Gharraee, B., Atef-Vahid, M., & Eftekhar, M. (2010). Metacognitive therapy (MCT), fluvoxamine, and combined treatment in improving obsessive-compulsive, depressive and anxiety symptoms in patients with obsessive-compulsive disorder (OCD). *Iranian Journal of Psychiatry and Behavioral Sciences, 4*, 17–25.

Simpson, H. B., Foa, E. B., Liebowitz, M. R., Huppert, J. D., Cahill, S., Maher, M. J., McLean, C. P., Bender, J. Jr., Marcus, S. M., Williams, M. T., Weaver, J., Vermes, D., Van Meter, P. E., Rodriguez, C. I., Powers, M., Pinto, A., Imms, P., Hahn, C. G., & Campeas, R. (2013). Cognitive-behavioral therapy vs risperidone for augmenting serotonin reuptake inhibitors in obsessive-compulsive disorder: A randomized clinical trial. *JAMA Psychiatry, 70*(11), 1190–1199.

Simpson, H. B., Foa, E. B., Liebowitz, M. R., Ledley, D. R., Huppert, J. D., Cahill, S., Vermes, D., Schmidt, A. B., Hembree, E., Franklin, M., Campeas, R., Hahn, C. G., & Petkova, E. (2008). A randomized, controlled trial of cognitive-behavioral therapy for augmenting pharmacotherapy in obsessive-compulsive disorder. *The American Journal of Psychiatry, 165*(5), 621–630.

Simpson, H. B., Gorfinkle, K. S., & Liebowitz, M. R. (1999). Cognitive-behavioral therapy as an adjunct to serotonin reuptake inhibitors in obsessive-compulsive disorder: An open trial. *The Journal of Clinical Psychiatry, 60*(9), 584–590.

Simpson, H. B., Huppert, J. D., Petkova, E., Foa, E. B., & Liebowitz, M. R. (2006). Response versus remission in obsessive-compulsive disorder. *The Journal of Clinical Psychiatry, 67*(2), 269–276.

Skarphedinsson, G., Compton, S., Thomsen, P. H., Weidle, B., Dahl, K., Nissen, J. B., Torp, N. C., Hybel, K., Melin, K. H., Valderhaug, R., Wentzel-Larson, T., & Ivarsson, T. (2015). Tics moderate sertraline, but not cognitive-behavior therapy response in pediatric obsessive-compulsive disorder patients who do not respond to cognitive-behavior therapy. *Journal of Child and Adolescent Psychopharmacology, 25*(5), 432–439.

Skarphedinsson, G., Weidle, B., & Ivarsson, T. (2015). Sertraline treatment of nonresponders to extended cognitive-behavior therapy in pediatric obsessive-compulsive disorder. *Journal of Child and Adolescent Psychopharmacology, 25*(7), 574–579.

Skarphedinsson, G., Weidle, B., Thomsen, P. H., Dahl, K., Torp, N. C., Nissen, J. B., Melin, K. H., Hybel, K., Valderhaug, R., Wentzel-Larsen, T., Compton, S. N., & Ivarsson, T. (2015). Continued cognitive-behavior therapy versus sertraline for children and adolescents with obsessive-compulsive disorder that were non-responders to cognitive-behavior therapy: A randomized controlled trial. *European Child and Adolescent Psychiatry, 24*(5), 591–602.

Sloan, T., & Telch, M. J. (2002). The effects of safety-seeking behavior and guided threat reappraisal on fear reduction during exposure: An experimental investigation. *Behaviour Research and Therapy, 40*, 235–251.

Smits, J. A., Rosenfield, D., Davis, M. L., Julian, K., Handelsman, P. R., Otto, M. W., Tuerk, P., Shiekh, M., Rosenfield, B., Hofmann, S. G., & Powers, M. B. (2014). Yohimbine enhancement of exposure therapy for social anxiety disorder: A randomized controlled trial. *Biological Psychiatry, 75*(11), 840–846.

Smits, J. A., Rosenfield, D., Otto, M. W., Marques, L., Davis, M. L., Meuret, A. E., Simon, N. M., Pollack, M. H., & Hofmann, S. G. (2013). D-Cycloserine enhancement of exposure therapy for social anxiety disorder depends on the success of exposure sessions. *Journal of Psychiatric Research, 47*(10), 1455–1461.

Storch, E. A., Bagner, D. M., Geffken, G. R., Adkins, J. W., Murphy, T. K., & Goodman, W. K. (2007). Sequential cognitive-behavioral therapy for children with obsessive-compulsive disorder with an inadequate medication response: A case series of five patients. *Depression and Anxiety, 24*(6), 375–381.

Storch, E. A., Bussing, R., Small, B. J., Geffken, G. R., McNamara, J. P., Rahman, O., Lewin, A. B., Garvan, C. S., Goodman, W. K., & Murphy, T. K. (2013). Randomized, placebo-controlled trial of cognitive-behavioral therapy alone or combined with sertraline in the treatment of pediatric obsessive-compulsive disorder. *Behaviour Research and Therapy, 51*(12), 823–829.

Storch, E. A., Lehmkuhl, H., Geffken, G. R., Touchton, A., & Murphy, T. K. (2008). Aripiprazole augmentation of incomplete treatment response in an adolescent male with obsessive-compulsive disorder. *Depression and Anxiety, 25*(2), 172–174.

Storch, E. A., Merlo, L. J., Bengtson, M., Murphy, T. K., Lewis, M. H., Yang, M. C., Jacob, M. L., Larson, M., Hirsh, A., Fernandez, M., Geffken, G. R., & Goodman, W. K. (2007). D-Cycloserine does not enhance exposure-response prevention therapy in obsessive-compulsive disorder. *International Clinical Psychopharmacology, 22*(4), 230–237.

Storch, E. A., Murphy, T. K., Goodman, W. K., Geffken, G. R., Lewin, A. B., Henin, A., Micco, J. A., Sprich, S., Wilhelm, S., Bengtson, M., & Geller, D. A. (2010). A preliminary study of D-cycloserine augmentation of cognitive-behavioral therapy in pediatric obsessive-compulsive disorder. *Biological Psychiatry, 68*(11), 1073–1076.

Storch, E. A., Wilhelm, S., Sprich, S., Henin, A., Micco, J., Small, B. J., McGuire, J., Mutch, P. J., Lewin, A. B., Murphy, T. K., & Geller, D. A. (2016). Efficacy of augmentation of cognitive behavior therapy with weight-adjusted D-cycloserine vs placebo in pediatric obsessive-compulsive disorder: A randomized clinical trial. *JAMA Psychiatry, 73*(8), 779–788.

Telch, M. J., Bruchey, A. K., Rosenfield, D., Cobb, A. R., Smits, J., Pahl, S., & Gonzalez-Lima, F. (2014). Effects of post-session administration of methylene blue on fear extinction and contextual memory in adults with claustrophobia. *The American Journal of Psychiatry, 171*(10), 1091–1098.

TenHave, T. R., Coyne, J., Salzer, M., & Katz, I. (2003). Research to improve the quality of care for depression: Alternatives to the simple randomized clinical trial. *General Hospital Psychiatry, 25*(2), 115–123.

Tenneij, N. H., van Megen, H. J., Denys, D. A., & Westenberg, H. G. (2005). Behavior therapy augments response of patients with obsessive-compulsive disorder responding to drug treatment. *The Journal of Clinical Psychiatry, 66*(9), 1169–1175.

Tolin, D. F. (2017). Can cognitive behavioral therapy for anxiety and depression be improved with pharmacotherapy? A meta-analysis. *Psychiatric Clinics of North America, 40*(4), 715–738.

Tolin, D. F., Maltby, N., Diefenbach, G. J., Hannan, S. E., & Worhunsky, P. (2004). Cognitive-behavioral therapy for medication nonresponders with obsessive-compulsive disorder: A wait-list-controlled open trial. *The Journal of Clinical Psychiatry, 65*(7), 922–931.

Tundo, A., Salvati, L., Busto, G., Di Spigno, D., & Falcini, R. (2007). Addition of cognitive-behavioral therapy for nonresponders to medication for obsessive-compulsive disorder: A naturalistic study. *The Journal of Clinical Psychiatry, 68*(10), 1552–1556.

Vakili, Y., Gharaee, B., & Habibi, M. (2015). Acceptance and commitment therapy, selective serotonin reuptake inhibitors and their combination in the improvement of obsessive-compulsive symptoms and experiential avoidance in patients with obsessive-compulsive disorder. *Iranian Journal of Psychiatry and Behavioral Sciences, 9*(2), e845.

van Balkom, A. J., de Haan, E., van Oppen, P., Spinhoven, P., Hoogduin, K. A., & van Dyck, R. (1998). Cognitive and behavioral therapies alone versus in combination with fluvoxamine in the treatment of obsessive compulsive disorder. *The Journal of Nervous and Mental Disease, 186*(8), 492–499.

van Balkom, A. J., Emmelkamp, P. M., Eikelenboom, M., Hoogendoorn, A. W., Smit, J. H., & van Oppen, P. (2012). Cognitive therapy versus fluvoxamine as a second-step treatment in obsessive-compulsive disorder nonresponsive to first-step behavior therapy. *Psychotherapy and Psychosomatics, 81*(6), 366–374.

van der Flier, F. E., Kwee, C. M. B., Cath, D. C., Batelaan, N. M., Groenink, L., Duits, P., van der Veen, D. C., van Balkom, A. J. L. M., & Baas, J. M. P. (2019). Cannabidiol enhancement of exposure therapy in treatment refractory patients with phobias: Study protocol of a randomized controlled trial. *BMC Psychiatry, 19*(1), 69.

van Minnen, A., & Hagenaars, M. (2002). Fear activation and habituation patterns as early process predictors of response to prolonged exposure treatment in PTSD. *Journal of Traumatic Stress, 15*(5), 359–367.

Veale, D., Miles, S., Smallcombe, N., Ghezai, H., Goldacre, B., & Hodsoll, J. (2014). Atypical antipsychotic augmentation in SSRI treatment refractory obsessive-compulsive disorder: A systematic review and meta-analysis. *BMC Psychiatry, 14*, 317.

Walker, D. L., Ressler, K. J., Lu, K. T., & Davis, M. (2002). Facilitation of conditioned fear extinction by systemic administration or intra-amygdala infusions of D-cycloserine as assessed with fear-potentiated startle in rats. *Journal of Neuroscience, 22*(6), 2343–2351.

Wells, A., Clark, D. M., Salkovskis, P. M., Ludgate, J., Hackmann, A., & Gelder, M. (1995). Social phobia: The role of in-situation safety behaviors in maintaining anxiety and negative beliefs. *Behavior Therapy, 26*, 153–161.

Wilhelm, S., Buhlmann, U., Tolin, D. F., Meunier, S. A., Pearlson, G. D., Reese, H. E., Cannistraro, P., Jenike, M. A., & Rauch, S. L. (2008). Augmentation of behavior therapy with D-cycloserine for obsessive-compulsive disorder. *The American Journal of Psychiatry, 165*(3), 335–341.

Williams, J. M. G., Watts, F. N., MacLeod, C., & Mathews, A. (1997). *Cognitive psychology and emotional disorders* (2nd ed.). John Wiley & Sons.

Wrubel, K. M., Barrett, D., Shumake, J., Johnson, S. E., & Gonzalez-Lima, F. (2007). Methylene blue facilitates the extinction of fear in an animal model of susceptibility to learned helplessness. *Neurobiology of Learning and Memory, 87*(2), 209–217.

Zeidan, M. A., Igoe, S. A., Linnman, C., Vitalo, A., Levine, J. B., Klibanski, A., Goldstein, J. M., & Milad, M. R. (2011). Estradiol modulates medial prefrontal cortex and amygdala activity during fear extinction in women and female rats. *Biological Psychiatry, 70*(10), 920–927.

Zoellner, L. A., Telch, M., Foa, E. B., Farach, F. J., McLean, C. P., Gallop, R., Bluett, E. J., Cobb, A., & Gonzalez-Lima, F. (2017). Enhancing extinction learning in posttraumatic stress disorder with brief daily imaginal exposure and methylene blue: A randomized controlled trial. *The Journal of Clinical Psychiatry, 78*(7), e782–e789.

CHAPTER 22

Treatment of Body Dysmorphic Disorder

Berta J. Summers, Zoë E. Laky, Jennifer L. Greenberg, Anne Chosak, Angela Fang, *and* Sabine Wilhelm

Abstract

Body dysmorphic disorder (BDD) is characterized by an excessive preoccupation with an imagined or slight defect in one's appearance. BDD is a severe and common disorder associated with high levels of functional impairment and high rates of suicidality. Interventions, including cognitive-behavioral therapy and pharmacotherapy, are effective for BDD. This chapter outlines the cognitive-behavioral model and therapy of BDD. The chapter reviews pharmacotherapy of BDD and discusses the role of combination therapy. The chapter also addresses ineffective approaches for the treatment of BDD, including the role of cosmetic procedures. Early recognition and intervention are critical, as they limit the disorder's chronicity and subsequent morbidity.

Key Words: BDD, body dysmorphic disorder, cognitive-behavioral therapy, pharmacotherapy, empirically supported treatment

Introduction

Julia, a 24-year-old Asian American woman, was brought in by her husband for the treatment of body dysmorphic disorder (BDD). Julia reported that as a child she received a lot of positive attention based on her "button nose" and "silky" hair. However, during puberty, around age 13, Julia experienced a growth spurt, her facial features became more pronounced, and her smooth, silky hair developed a coarse, wavy texture. In an effort to smooth out her tresses, Julia combed her hair each morning and night, at first for 10 to 15 minutes, but over time the combing progressed to over one hour. Julia spent hundreds of dollars on styling products intended to improve the texture of her hair. She found it increasingly difficult to be around friends in school or in social situations, because she would become completely caught up in comparing their hair or noses to her own. She frequently touched her hair and checked the mirror to see whether her hair or nose had grown or changed in any way. When she sat in class or interacted with peers, she used her hands or her hair to cover her nose so that nobody would notice the "lumpy mound" in the middle of her face.

Julia frequently referenced social media and magazines, looking for "perfect" noses and for cosmetic surgeons who specialized in rhinoplasty. By the time she was 22, Julia had sought consultations from 12 plastic surgeons and had received two rhinoplasty procedures. She was devastated with the results of the first procedure, after which she described feeling regret for having undergone the surgery ("I looked better before"). Julia had the second procedure to correct the first one, but felt "the surgeon messed up and made [her nose] look even worse." Although Julia's husband and friends told her she looked fine, Julia found it difficult to leave the house for fear that others would judge her based on her "disfigured nose." When Julia did leave the house, it was only after she undertook an extensive two- to three-hour routine involving camouflaging (e.g., with makeup, clothing, sunglasses, hat) and checking. Julia took precautions to attend only situations in which she knew there would be few people and dim lighting. She rarely returned phone calls from friends, because it triggered such intense anxiety about having to leave the house. When Julia's husband brought her in for treatment, she was convinced that a third surgery was her only solution.

Description of the Disorder

It is typical for people to experience some degree of concern or discontent about their appearance. However, some individuals are so distressed about the way they look that it interferes with their daily life. Concerns similar to those experienced by Julia reflect a diagnosis of BDD, a severe disorder of body image characterized by an excessive and time-consuming preoccupation with perceived flaws in appearance (American Psychiatric Association [APA], 2013). BDD is classified in the DSM-5 under the category of "Obsessive-Compulsive and Related Disorders," as a primary feature of the diagnosis is engagement in compulsive, appearance-related rituals and avoidant behavior aimed at hiding, checking, or "fixing" their perceived flaw (e.g., mirror-checking, grooming, camouflaging, reassurance-seeking, and social avoidance). BDD affects an estimated 0.7%–2.9% of the general population, and manifests in men and women at roughly equal rates (Bienvenu et al., 2000; Buhlmann et al., 2010; Koran et al., 2008; Otto et al., 2001; Rief et al., 2006; Schieber et al., 2015); however, recent research suggests that BDD may be slightly more common among women (Phillips, Menard, et al., 2006). Onset typically occurs in early adolescence (mode = 12 years, mean = 16.7 years; Bjornsson et al., 2013). The disorder is associated with significant public health sequelae, thus underscoring the need for the development and dissemination of effective treatments. BDD is associated with functional impairment (i.e., social, academic, and work-related problems), compromised quality of life, and significant morbidity, including hospitalization and suicide (Angelakis et al., 2016; Phillips et al., 2008; Phillips, Menard, Fay, & Pagano, 2005). Individuals with BDD frequently spend several hours per day worrying about their appearance.

Common areas of concern include the skin, hair, nose, eyes, and teeth (Phillips, Didie, et al., 2006; Phillips, Menard, Fay, & Weisberg, 2005); however, any body part may be the focus of concern, including the ears, hips, butt, bone structure, breasts, and genitals (Cansever et al., 2003; Phillips, 2005). In muscle dysmorphia, a subtype of BDD that more commonly affects men, the primary concern focuses on muscle shape and size and the sense that the individual is not muscular enough (Pope et al., 2005; Sreshta et al., 2017). Male patients with muscle dysmorphia more often adhere to traditional masculine norms, such as the use of violence to solve problems and sexual promiscuity, as compared to men with other forms of BDD (Blashill et al., 2020). The number of concerns can progress and shift focus over time (Phillips, 2005; Phillips et al., 1993), with patients averaging a preoccupation with five to seven body areas over the course of their illness (Phillips, Menard, Fay, & Weisberg, 2005). Some researchers have found that men are more likely to be concerned about genitals, body build, and balding, while women are more likely to be concerned with a greater number of total body parts (e.g., skin, stomach, buttocks, legs, hips, toes; Phillips, Menard, et al., 2006). Left untreated, BDD is associated with a chronic course and severe lifetime morbidity. For more information about the phenomenology and epidemiology of BDD, please refer to Chapter 2.

Etiology

Biological, psychological, and socioenvironmental factors play a role in the development and maintenance of BDD and are thus highly relevant to the conceptualization and treatment of this debilitating pathology.

Biological Factors

The current understanding of biological factors in BDD has been largely informed by neuroimaging studies (for review, see Grace, Labuschagne, et al., 2017); these data may be used to predict treatment response and examine neural correlates of treatment response. Additionally, studies have examined the role of specific neurotransmitters and neuromodulators (e.g., serotonin, dopamine, and oxytocin) as well as investigations into the heritability of BDD pathology.

Data from neuroimaging and neuropsychological studies suggest abnormal structure and function of frontolimbic and occipitotemporal regions, with evidence suggesting cortical gray matter thinning in the left temporal and left inferior parietal regions (Grace, Buchanan, et al., 2017). Imaging studies have also demonstrated evidence of greater total white matter volume and asymmetry in caudate volume in BDD (Rauch et al., 2003; Tasios & Michopoulos, 2017). Transfer deficits and hypoactive structural connectivity between the primary and secondary occipital regions have also been observed (Carey et al., 2004; Feusner, Neziroglu, et al., 2010). Emotions and body image are largely processed in the right hemisphere, and new onset of BDD has been described subsequent to inflammatory medical illness (Gabbay et al., 2002; Mathew,

2001; Salib, 1988) and right temporal lobe lesions (Gabbay et al., 2003; Naga et al., 2004). Right amygdala volume has been shown to be positively correlated with BDD symptom severity, which may partially explain heightened fear sensitivity and pathological face-processing observed in this population (Tasios & Michopoulos, 2017). Increased left hemispheric activation (involving the prefrontal and lateral temporal regions) may contribute to early-stage visual processing biases observed in patients with BDD (Feusner et al., 2007).

In studies using fMRI to examine visual processing in individuals with BDD compared with healthy controls, individuals with BDD exhibited aberrant visual processing when viewing high, low, and normal spatial frequency faces of others (Feusner et al., 2007) and of themselves (Feusner, Moody, et al., 2010). High spatial frequencies (HSF) are used for perceiving details (e.g., eyes and lips), whereas low spatial frequencies (LSF) convey configural aspects of faces (e.g., general shape of face); normal spatial frequency images are unaltered. When viewing faces of others, individuals with BDD demonstrated overactivation of the left hemisphere, which suggests a tendency for patients with BDD to utilize local (detail-oriented) rather than global (holistic) processing (Feusner et al., 2007). Specifically, patients with BDD demonstrated increased activation in the inferior frontal gyrus and lateral temporal parietal regions compared to controls, as well as abnormal amygdala activity (right greater than left; Feusner et al., 2007). When viewing their own faces, subjects with BDD showed hypoactivity in the primary and secondary visual processing regions (left occipital cortex) for LSF faces and hyperactivity in the frontostriatal system (left orbitofrontal cortex and bilateral head of the caudate) for HSF faces (Feusner, Moody, et al., 2010).

Psychopharmacologic treatment studies provide indirect support for the role of serotonin (5-HT) and dopamine dysfunction in BDD (Hadley et al., 2002; Vulink et al., 2016). Patients with BDD typically demonstrate a selective therapeutic response to high-dose serotonin reuptake inhibitors (SRIs; Hadley et al., 2002). Additional evidence for the role of the 5-HT system comes from exacerbation of BDD symptoms following depletion of tryptophan, a 5-HT precursor amino acid (Barr et al., 1992), and administration of *meta*-chlorophenylpiperazine (mCPP), a 5-HT agonist (Hollander & Wong, 1995). Dysregulation of 5-HT and dopamine systems may contribute to the dysregulated attention, inhibition, and mood states observed in these individuals (Feusner et al., 2008; Saxena & Feusner, 2006). Studies have also begun to examine the role of oxytocin in the pathophysiology of BDD, with a recent study showing that individuals with BDD displayed higher serum oxytocin levels, as compared to healthy controls, and that oxytocin levels correlated positively with BDD symptom severity (Fang et al., 2019). Because oxytocin is a hypothalamic neuropeptide that mediates a range of socioemotional and social cognitive processes, the data suggest possible disruptions in the oxytocin system in BDD, although it is still unclear whether increased production of endogenous oxytocin is a cause or a consequence of BDD.

Last, genetic factors may play a role in the etiology of BDD. BDD appears to have a strong heritable component. In family studies, between 5.8% and 8.0% of patients with BDD report BDD among first-degree relatives (Bienvenu et al., 2000; Phillips, Gunderson, et al., 1998; Phillips, Menard, Fay & Weisberg, 2005; Saxena & Feusner, 2006). In a twin study of adolescents and young adults, heritability of BDD was estimated to be up to 49% (Enander et al., 2018). Similarly, the presence of obsessive-compulsive disorder (OCD) in one's immediate family has also been associated with increased risk for the development of BDD, OCD, and other obsessive-compulsive spectrum disorders. In a sample of 1,074 twin pairs, 64% of the phenotypic correlation between OCD and BDD was explained by shared genetic factors (Monzani et al., 2014). In a genetic association study, Richter et al. (2004) found an association between the gamma-aminobutyric acid receptor subunit alpha-2 (*GABRA2*) gene and BDD, and comorbid BDD and OCD (but not OCD alone), and a trend was observed toward an association with the serotonin transporter promoter polymorphism (5-HTTPRL) short allele. Further investigation into the genetics of BDD are needed to inform our understanding of the neurophysiology of BDD and to determine potential linkage peaks.

Psychological Factors

PSYCHODYNAMIC THEORIES

Psychodynamic theories of BDD focus on unconscious sexual or emotional conflicts, feelings of inferiority, guilt, or poor self-image that are thought to have been displaced onto the body part(s) of concern. Deeply rooted problems are conceptualized as being displaced onto appearance, so as to make the underlying problem less threatening (Phillips, 2005). For example, in a case of a young woman with concerns about breast size, the hypothesized core issue was ambivalence about growing up (i.e., becoming a woman) and sexuality (Horowitz et al., 2002). In another case, a woman's "abnormal looking, ugly, and deformed" eyebrows were conceptualized as stemming from low self-esteem and a sense of hopelessness about heterosexual relationships (Bloch & Glue, 1988). Psychodynamic theorists suggest that problems are rooted in childhood experiences, and the body part onto which concerns are displaced (e.g., the nose, mouth) are frequently more palatable representations of other, more emotionally threatening body parts (e.g., the penis). From an object-relations theory perspective, some have linked the emergence of BDD to narcissistic injury from early mirroring (i.e., young child perceiving an unfavorable reflection of itself mirrored in the mother's facial expression; Lemma, 2009). The goal of dynamic psychotherapy is to aid the patient to resolve the unconscious conflicts, which in turn should be expected to resolve the BDD symptoms. While therapies driven by psychodynamic theories may be helpful in resolving general life difficulties, they are not adequate in explaining the etiology of BDD, nor has there been any empirical support for psychodynamic treatment of BDD (Phillips, 2005).

COGNITIVE-BEHAVIORAL THEORIES

Cognitive-behavioral theories of BDD maintain a diathesis-stress model, by which an individual biologically predisposed to BDD develops onset of symptoms subsequent to an environmental stressor. Because BDD typically develops around adolescence, the hormonal, psychological, and social changes that occur during puberty have been proposed as proximal stressors. Stressors may also include socioenvironmental factors, such as appearance-based reinforcement (teasing or praise). Subsequently, individuals can develop maladaptive beliefs about their appearance and the importance of appearance; for instance, believing that self-worth and social acceptance are based in appearance, and that in order to be loved or accepted, one must look perfect. Situations that trigger maladaptive beliefs induce feelings of shame, disgust, anxiety, and depression (Veale et al., 1996; Wilhelm et al., 2010).

Cognitive factors, including selective attention and negative interpretive biases, likely contribute to a vulnerability to, and maintenance of, this vicious cycle. In neuropsychological tests of verbal and nonverbal memory, patients with BDD tend to focus on the small details and features, rather than on the global framework (Deckersbach et al., 2000). This is consistent with clinical observations of patients with BDD selectively attending to certain details of their appearance while ignoring global physical appearance (Greenberg et al., 2014; Grocholewski et al., 2012). In addition to demonstrating selective attention to appearance-based stimuli relative to healthy controls, individuals with BDD tend to overestimate the physical attractiveness of others and underestimate their own physical attractiveness (Buhlmann et al., 2008). Thus, individuals with BDD focus only on self-perceived imperfections (i.e., aspects of their appearance with which they are dissatisfied). Experimental research and clinical observations also suggest that these individuals erroneously interpret everyday ambiguous social exchanges or facial expressions as negative or contemptuous and as a consequence of their flawed appearance (Buhlmann et al., 2011; Summers & Cougle, 2016).

Selective attention to perceived flaws and misinterpretation of social information contribute to an increase in distress, which prompts individuals to engage in compulsive or escape (avoidant) behavior designed to reduce distress or enhance appearance. Negative reinforcement occurs when these safety behaviors provide temporary relief from distress; however, such behaviors preclude learning of adaptive responses, and subsequently increase the frequency of, and distress associated with, intrusive appearance-related cognitions and behaviors over time. Indeed, experimental research has demonstrated that engagement in appearance-related safety behaviors (i.e., mirror-checking, excessive grooming, reassurance-seeking, comparing self to others, camouflaging) has a direct impact on severity of BDD symptoms, beliefs about the importance of appearance, and maladaptive interpretive styles of ambiguous information even in healthy individuals who do not present with significant appearance concerns (Summers & Cougle, 2016).

Socioenvironmental Factors

Contemporary Western culture has placed a remarkable emphasis on appearance and the importance of attaining the ideal appearance. Billions of industry dollars are spent each year advertising implicit and explicit messages about the importance of attractiveness and encouraging people of all ages to spend their disposable income on products, clothing, and services designed to reach this unattainable standard (Wilhelm, 2006). Social networking sites, such as Instagram, foster social comparisons and feelings of inadequacy (Holland & Tiggemann, 2016). Social media provide a platform for garnering validation through "likes," which individuals can misconstrue as a metric of their self-worth. There is no seeming end to the pursuit of ideal beauty—one's teeth can always be a little straighter or whiter, one's hair can always be smoother, and one's muscles can always be larger.

With this omnipresent pressure to look good, even perfect, it is not surprising that some individuals take the messages personally and to an extreme. The fact that many plastic surgeons provide multiple surgeries for the same patient, on the same body part, suggests that even the medical community may inadvertently collude with societal pressures. Thus, socioenvironmental factors likely contribute to the development and maintenance of BDD; however, BDD is not exclusively an American, or even Western, phenomenon. BDD has been reported across cultures, even in countries with minimal advertising and with different standards of beauty (Faravelli et al., 1997; Fontenelle et al., 2006; Hitzeroth et al., 2001; Suzuki et al., 2003; Tignol et al., 2007). While the most common areas of concern involve the face, nose, hair, and skin, the significance or meanings of these body areas may vary cross-culturally. Culture may influence the body part of concern (Marques et al., 2011), as well as patients' access to, and attitudes toward, mental health treatment. However, in a cross-cultural study of BDD, Bohne et al. (2002) found similar prevalence rates in nonclinical samples of American (4%, $N = 101$) and German (5.3%, $N = 133$) students. Thus, it is unlikely that socioenvironmental emphasis on appearance is a necessary or sufficient cause of BDD. However, it is important to note that the extant literature has focused on examining BDD in progressive, Western, and developed societies and there is still a gap in understanding how BDD can present across cultures.

Cognitive-Behavioral Model

The cognitive-behavioral model of BDD (Veale, Gournay, et al., 1996; Wilhelm et al., 2010) acknowledges the role of psychological, biological, and socioenvironmental factors in the etiology and maintenance of an individual's BDD. For instance, a trigger situation, such as seeing one's reflection in the mirror, may set off a cycle of BDD thoughts and behaviors. A cognitive bias (selective attention) may make individuals with BDD vulnerable to attend to minor appearance concerns. For example, individuals with BDD have a tendency to pay attention to only certain (perceived flawed) details in the reflected image, rather than experiencing the holistic image in the mirror (e.g., attending to a minor blemish or a small patch of hair rather than on the rest of one's face or overall appearance). Next, the individual experiences negative thoughts, based on his or her existing values and assumptions about appearance standards and the importance of physical appearance.

Patients with BDD tend to attach undue significance to appearance as a factor in their self-worth and social acceptance. For example, the individual may experience a thought like "My hair is limp," followed by the subsequent interpretation, "If my hair is limp, I look defective; no one will want to date me." Beliefs that "I have to be perfect to be loved" and "Appearance is the most important thing" are common in BDD. This type of negative thinking is typically followed by negative emotions, including anxiety, shame, disgust, guilt, and sadness. Anyone might see a mirror and think, "Oh, my hair looks limp today," but the level of importance placed on appearance in determining one's self-worth will determine how much of an impact it will have on one's emotional state. Thus, in BDD, any perceived imperfection becomes cause for severe distress, and patients with BDD are compelled to try to ameliorate their distress by engaging in rituals (e.g., excessive grooming or camouflaging, reassurance-seeking, mirror-checking, skin-picking) or avoidance (such as avoidance of bright lighting, mirrors, or social situations) in order to improve their perceived flaw or to prevent distress. Paradoxically, while BDD-related behaviors may provide some short-term relief, attending to appearance concerns via rituals and avoidance can worsen the perceived flaw (e.g., picking at perceived acne can cause reddening and infection of the skin) and increase preoccupation and distress over time.

Assessment

Classification

BDD is defined by a preoccupation with a perceived flaw in one's physical appearance, which causes clinically significant distress or impairment and is not better accounted for by another disorder (APA, 2013). BDD is further characterized by time-consuming and repetitive appearance-related behaviors or mental compulsions. In previous iterations of the *Diagnostic and Statistical Manual of Mental Disorders* (e.g., *DSM-IV*), BDD was classified as a somatoform disorder, given the "imagined" quality of the individual's perceived physical flaws. However, due to parallels in the symptom presentation between BDD and OCD (i.e., obsessions and compulsions anchored to appearance), BDD was reclassified in the *DSM-5* under the obsessive-compulsive and related disorders (OCRDs). Given that certain features of BDD overlap with other psychiatric illnesses (e.g., body dissatisfaction, compulsive rituals, social avoidance, body-focused repetitive behaviors, feelings of hopelessness, delusional beliefs), careful differential assessment via a structured clinical interview (e.g., SCID-5; First et al., 2015) is imperative when working with this population in order to help differentiate between—and rule out other—*DSM-5* diagnoses.

Assessment of BDD Symptoms

BDD is a disorder associated with secrecy and shame. Most people will not volunteer information about their symptoms, due to embarrassment or fear of being considered vain. Individuals may be afraid of drawing additional attention to their perceived imperfection by talking about it. Thus, when assessing BDD and related symptomatology, it is important to inquire about areas of concern, appearance-related thoughts, behaviors, distress, and impairment. As already noted, preoccupation with perceived appearance flaws manifests in time-consuming (e.g., more than one hour and often three to eight hours per day) thoughts and behaviors, including excessive mirror-checking, camouflaging to hide the flaw, grooming, reassurance-seeking, scrutinizing or comparing with others' appearance, changing clothes, touching or measuring body parts, dieting, and tanning (Phillips, Didie, et al., 2006; Phillips, Menard, Fay, & Weisberg, 2005). The behaviors are often compulsive; patients feel compelled to repeatedly check, hide, or improve the perceived imperfection in order to reduce or prevent distress.

Patients also avoid people and situations that might exacerbate their appearance concerns. It is important to ask about situations that patients may be avoiding, or that they endure under great duress and with the use of rituals or neutralizing behaviors. For example, patients may alternate between checking and avoiding mirrors and other reflective surfaces (e.g., storefront windows). They may avoid activities or situations they believe would accentuate their flaws (e.g., bright lighting) or that would require revealing areas of concern (e.g., intimate sexual encounters, going to a beach or pool). Patients avoid social engagements, such as parties or dating, that they feel would lead to rejection based on their appearance, and they may stop going to work or school altogether. A majority of individuals with BDD are either single or divorced, which suggests difficulty forming and maintaining intimate relationships (Phillips, Pagano, Menard, et al., 2006). In addition, insight is often very limited in BDD, and degree of insight can vary over the course of the disorder. For more information about BDD assessment, please refer to Chapter 13.

Treatment

Effective treatments are available for BDD. Cognitive-behavioral therapy (CBT) and pharmacotherapy with SRIs are considered the first-line treatments for BDD.

Although many patients seek cosmetic treatment, cosmetic procedures typically offer little relief and often worsen BDD symptoms (Crerand et al., 2005; Phillips, Grant, et al., 2001; Sarwer & Crerand, 2008). Of the minority of patients who experience an improvement in BDD symptoms after cosmetic procedures, benefits tend to be short term, and some patients become preoccupied by worries about how long the improvement will last (Crerand et al., 2005). More commonly, patients become increasingly distraught after surgery and may blame themselves for electing a procedure they feel caused them disfigurement. In addition to turning against the self, extreme dissatisfaction following cosmetic procedures has resulted in threats, lawsuits, and homicides against physicians who performed the procedures (Sarwer & Crerand, 2008).

CBT

CBT is the most studied and empirically supported psychosocial treatment for BDD. CBT is based on the cognitive-behavioral model of BDD and aims to improve functioning and quality of life by identifying and modifying maladaptive thought and behavior patterns. CBT for BDD also addresses current mood and life events as they influence BDD symptoms. Most studies have combined cognitive and behavioral methods, although CBT, cognitive therapy (CT; cognitive restructuring alone), and behavior therapy (BT; exposure and response prevention alone) have all been found to be effective for treating BDD in adults and adolescents and can be delivered successfully in group (Rosen et al., 1995; Wilhelm et al., 1999) and individual formats (Greenberg et al., 2016; Mataix-Cols et al., 2015; McKay, 1999; McKay et al., 1997; Neziroglu et al., 1996; Veale, Boocock, et al., 1996; Veale et al., 2014; Wilhelm et al., 2014, 2019). Comprehensive treatments generally include psychoeducation, self-monitoring, exposure with response prevention (E/RP), cognitive restructuring, and relapse prevention; treatment may also include mindfulness/attention retraining, habit reversal, and activity scheduling.

CBT for BDD was first studied systematically by Rosen and colleagues (1995), who developed a group CBT protocol. Compared to a no-treatment control group, 82% of the CBT group responded to treatment and reported a significant reduction in BDD symptoms, with treatment gains maintained in 77% of the CBT group at follow-up. Wilhelm and colleagues (1999) also reported significant reductions in mean scores on the Yale-Brown Obsessive-Compulsive Scale Modified for BDD (BDD-YBOCS) after a group treatment protocol: BDD-YBOCS scores decreased a mean of 9.6 points, from 29.9 to 20.3. The earliest randomized controlled trial (RCT) testing the efficacy of individual CBT as compared to a wait-list control group found significantly greater reductions in mean BDD-YBOCS scores for BDD patients who received CBT (Veale, Gournay, et al., 1996).

Later RCTs expanded this research by using larger samples to compare CBT for BDD to wait-list controls, and CBT for BDD to other forms of therapy (Veale et al., 2014; Wilhelm et al. 2014, 2019). Wilhelm et al. (2014) found that 50% of participants with primary BDD receiving CBT for BDD were treatment responders after 12 weeks of a 24-week program, and 81% were treatment responders by the end of the treatment program. Continuing this research, Wilhelm et al. (2019) tested CBT for BDD against supportive psychotherapy. Findings differed by site: CBT led to greater reductions in BDD severity and associated symptoms at one of the two research sites. The efficacy of CBT and supportive psychotherapy was found to be equivalent at the second site. Thus, while supportive psychotherapy can be beneficial for BDD, CBT is more consistently effective. Another study by Veale et al. (2014) compared 12 weeks of CBT to 12 weeks of anxiety management for BDD; of the two groups, participants who received CBT showed significantly greater symptom improvement. Literature has also found CBT to be effective for adolescents with BDD (Greenberg et al., 2010; Krebs et al., 2017; Mataix-Cols et al., 2015). In a study by Mataix-Cols and colleagues (2015), adolescents (12 to 18 years old) were randomly assigned to either CBT for BDD or a wait-list control group. Participants in the CBT group showed significant improvement in severity, insight, depression, and quality of life as compared to the wait-list control group.

Empirical research is still needed to determine the optimal length, frequency, and mechanisms of treatment. It has been suggested that between 16 and 24 sessions of CBT for BDD may be optimal (National Institute for Clinical Excellence, 2005). Spacing apart the final sessions and the use of booster sessions may help to reinforce a patient's independent use of skills (Wilhelm et al., 2010). In addition, modular psychological treatments are promising (Eifert et al., 1997; Wilhelm et al., 2011) and allow for a flexible, individualized approach to treatment. For example, a modular manual for BDD (Wilhelm et al., 2011) offers specific modules to address skin-picking, muscle dysmorphia (e.g., weight/shape concerns, excessive exercise, problematic substance/steroid use), and the desire to pursue cosmetic surgery. Therapists administer measures that assess specific symptomatology and subsequently use only the appropriate modules (Wilhelm et al., 2011). Recent evidence indicates that within-subject improvements in certain maladaptive behaviors (checking, grooming, and avoidance behaviors), as well as maladaptive beliefs, mediated improvements in BDD symptom severity during CBT over a 24-week period (Fang et al., 2020). These data are the first to examine mechanisms underlying CBT for BDD and are consistent with targeted mechanisms in cognitive-behavioral models of BDD.

ASSESSMENT AND PSYCHOEDUCATION

CBT begins with a careful assessment of BDD and related symptoms. Clinicians should inquire about BDD-related areas of concern, thoughts, behaviors, and impairment. An assessment of motivation is also helpful to determine potential barriers to treatment (e.g., resistance to a psychological treatment is common when insight is poor). The treatment rationale and CBT approach to BDD should be discussed, and patients should understand that the goal of CBT is to elicit and modify maladaptive beliefs and behaviors that serve to maintain their symptoms. Each session begins with a review of symptoms and homework completed since the previous session, and an agenda is set to determine which strategies to cover during the appointment; agendas are determined collaboratively between therapist and patient. Each session ends with a review and discussion of an assignment to be completed during the week (e.g., thought-tracking, planned exposure, ritual reduction). The importance of between-session homework should be stressed, as skills learned in session must be practiced frequently to engrain learning and reduce symptomatology. The session review allows for patient feedback and for the therapist to address any questions or concerns about the session or homework. The patient is asked to refrain from engaging in surgical or dermatological procedures during the course of CBT, as such procedures undermine the goals of therapy and can worsen body image issues. If the patient is ready to engage in treatment, it can be useful to set and sign a treatment contract agreeing to the treatment goals and plan.

Following a thorough assessment, the first phase of active treatment includes psychoeducation, in which the therapist provides information about BDD and the cognitive-behavioral model. The therapist and patient review factors that may have contributed to the development and maintenance of the patient's BDD. As already mentioned, the cognitive-behavioral model of BDD acknowledges the impact of biological and socioenvironmental factors, but it focuses treatment strategies on the specific beliefs and behavior patterns currently contributing to the maintenance of symptoms. The model highlights how patients' appearance-related distress is an understandable consequence of their beliefs, but that these beliefs are often the inaccurate and/or unhelpful result of a cognitive bias (e.g., selective attention and erroneous interpretive styles). Moreover, maladaptive thoughts are upsetting, and thus lead to drastic behaviors intended to alleviate distress. Patients learn that appearance-related ritualistic and avoidant behavior may provide short-term relief or accommodation, but paradoxically worsen BDD beliefs, maladaptive behavioral tendencies, and distress in the long run.

In the context of individualizing the model for each patient, details about the patient's BDD, including course, family history, daily routine, past treatments, and co-occurring disorders, should be discussed. More specifically, the clinician inquires about dissatisfaction with each part of the face or body, beliefs about appearance ("I need to look perfect to leave the house"), related maladaptive behaviors (excessive body-checking, grooming, makeup, camouflage, exercise, etc.), and avoided situations (e.g., social gatherings, work events, dating).

MOTIVATIONAL ENHANCEMENT

In addition to assessment of motivation, the first phase of treatment often includes motivational enhancement strategies (Miller & Rollnick, 2002). Many patients with BDD are ambivalent about receiving therapy for their disorder and may see a considerable downside to giving up maladaptive beliefs and behaviors. It is important for clinicians to maintain a nonjudgmental stance, to allow for a candid discussion of pros and cons of change and the impact BDD has had on a patient's life. The clinician must avoid the trap of trying to persuade the patient that the BDD concerns are irrational, or, worse still, trying to reassure the patient about any appearance issues. For instance, rather than arguing with the patient about pursuing another cosmetic surgery procedure, the therapist may use Socratic questioning regarding the pros and cons of further surgery. It is helpful to provide the patient with psychoeducation about the outcome for patients with BDD who have undergone cosmetic surgery and to have the patient integrate any personal data they may have from their own prior surgeries. Most patients can agree that appearance has had a severe impact on their life and functioning; thus, coming to a common goal of improving functioning and quality of life can be an effective approach.

Increased symptom severity and poor insight may require a slower pace of treatment. Moving quickly through treatment may be tempting with very ill patients; however, patients may still be ambivalent about engaging in CBT and thus overtly or covertly resist using CBT strategies. Assigning homework, such as symptom monitoring, from the beginning of treatment helps to socialize the patient to this central expectation of CBT for BDD and allows the therapist to help the patient problem-solve barriers to homework as needed.

COGNITIVE STRATEGIES

The second active phase of CBT for BDD involves cognitive evaluation and restructuring. Cognitive restructuring helps to increase insight into maladaptive beliefs about appearance concerns. It is helpful to review common cognitive distortions, errors in thinking that affect how we feel about certain situations, particularly as they relate to BDD. Typical cognitive distortions associated with BDD include jumping to conclusions ("If I go to the party, nobody will talk to me"); mind-reading ("That man didn't make eye contact; that must mean he thinks I look hideous and deformed"); and all-or-nothing thinking ("This pimple makes me disgusting"). Homework during this phase of treatment involves using thought records to monitor the frequency and impact of BDD-related thinking errors as they come up in daily life.

After the patient has learned to identify problematic BDD thoughts, he or she practices generating alternative ways of thinking by developing and evaluating rational responses to the distorted beliefs ("That man didn't make eye contact; maybe he was thinking about something else, or maybe he is shy"). Cognitive-restructuring exercises are guided by the use of thought record and restructuring forms. Homework involves having the patient fill out restructuring forms when they notice their anxiety or distress building, and/or before engaging in a maladaptive BDD behavior. Of note, although there is utility in orienting the patient to cognitive-restructuring skills, recent research suggests the value of limiting cognitive preparation in advance of exposure-based work, so as to maximize "expectancy violation" (i.e., the discrepancy between the patient's feared outcome/expectation and the actual outcome of an exposure; see Craske et al., 2014). Thus, when reviewing the outcome of behavioral experiments, one might instead place greater emphasis on the lesson learned (e.g., "How did the exposure go, and is this different from what you expected?"; "What is the take-away lesson from this experience?").

BEHAVIORAL STRATEGIES

Once a patient has gained a foundational understanding of the procedures for cognitive restructuring, behavioral strategies may be initiated. The initial functional assessment—demonstrating how distorted thought patterns lead to distress and subsequent behaviors meant to mitigate this distress—likely revealed maladaptive behaviors to be discussed and targeted for change. Reviewing the role of rituals and avoidance in the maintenance of the patient's BDD reinforces the rationale for E/RP: the patient's gradual exposure to anxiety-provoking situations without the use of rituals or safety behaviors. It is helpful to remind patients that while rituals and avoidance may provide short-term relief, these behaviors actually function to worsen distress and problematic beliefs in the long run as the individual comes to erroneously attribute their safety to the behavior (Summers & Cougle, 2018). The therapist will help the patient to develop a list of anxiety-provoking and avoided situations (hierarchy) that he or she is encouraged to gradually re-enter (exposure) without the use of rituals or safety behaviors (response prevention). Initial exposure tasks are mildly to moderately challenging and likely to produce a mastery experience for the patient; for example, going to the supermarket without styling one's hair, and without touching it or checking it in the store or in the car mirror. Over time, patients embark on more difficult tasks, such as meeting friends at a busy restaurant or bar without having styled their hair and refraining from touching or checking their hair during the outing. Increasing normal activities can sometimes function as an E/RP assignment (e.g., going through the day without the typical camouflage, such as loose clothing, hat, or sunglasses). Activities are repeated until the patient has had the opportunity to habituate to the anxiety, consolidate new knowledge about the most likely outcome (compared to the anticipated/feared outcome), and can perform the activity without the use of any safety or neutralizing behaviors. Avoidance of social activities, or activities that would require showing off one's body, is common. For example, patients may avoid shopping (i.e., changing and observing themselves in a dressing room), swimming, going to the beach, intimate sexual encounters, going to work or class, or accepting social invitations, for fear of appearance-based social rejection. In this case, situations aimed at broadening overall social experiences are included in the exposure hierarchy. For example, instead of avoiding friends on days when she thought her nose or hair looked really "awful," a patient is encouraged to go out twice per week with friends for lunch or dinner without engaging in excessive grooming or camouflaging rituals.

E/RP exercises are encouraged to be set up as behavioral experiments, with the goal of information-gathering to test a particular hypothesis: "If I don't wear that long-sleeved shirt, someone will comment on my hairy arms." In a behavioral experiment, patients are asked to record specific observable predictions about the outcome of designated tasks, and then to re-evaluate their beliefs based on the actual outcome. Finally, behavioral change tasks can be assigned with the purpose of behavioral activation and enhancing a holistic sense of self—for instance, encouraging a patient to hone a new skill or hobby in order to increase their mood, self-efficacy, and expand their vision of self-worth beyond appearance.

An attentional retraining task known as mirror retraining is a behavioral strategy unique to the treatment of BDD and other body image disorders (Delinsky & Wilson,

2006; Wilhelm, 2006; Wilhelm et al., 2013). Individuals with BDD often have a conflicted relationship with mirrors and other reflective surfaces. A patient may alternate between spending hours in front of the mirror inspecting, grooming, prodding, or picking, and extraordinary efforts to avoid catching any glimpse of their reflection. Attentional retraining in the mirror helps patients to see "the big picture" and to view themselves in a holistic way—rather than homing in on perceived "hot spots" and problem areas—by teaching the patient to observe and describe his or her body in objective, nonjudgmental terms. For example, patients learn to modify negative self-talk so that "frizzy, wiry, muddy" hair is described as "shoulder length, dark brown, wavy." As part of this exercise, patients typically stand in front of a full-length mirror and describe their whole body, starting with their hair and ending with their feet. Ideally, the patient should describe each body area as if going through a scanner; patients should be guided not to skip over certain features or to dedicate more time to areas of BDD-specific concern (i.e., perseverating/scrutinizing) compared to other, more neutral body areas. Patients are instructed to refrain from negative labeling and to avoid ritual and safety behaviors (e.g., touching or measuring flaws, closing eyes). It is helpful for the therapist to demonstrate the task first. Initially, mirror retraining can be a very challenging and emotionally charged task for patients, but after repeated trials, most patients report mirror retraining to be one of the most powerful experiences during CBT. Beyond changing the individual's relationship with their image in the mirror, attentional retraining and mindfulness strategies can also be helpful in teaching patients to be in the moment and to participate in the task at hand. This is particularly useful when it comes to being mindful of certain mental rituals, such as being self-critical and comparing themselves to others while engaged in social activities or work.

ADVANCED COGNITIVE STRATEGIES

After some cognitive and behavioral progress has been made, treatment targets the patient's core beliefs. Core beliefs are the deeply rooted beliefs individuals hold about themselves, the future, and the world. Whereas a healthy person might endorse the statement, "I'm a good enough person" or "I'm attractive enough," a person with BDD is more likely to hold core beliefs like "I'm inadequate," "I'm worthless," or "I'm unlovable" (Simmons & Phillips, 2017; Veale, Boocock, et al., 1996; Veale, Gournay, et al., 1996). These core beliefs filter a patient's experiences, are self-maintaining, and, if not addressed, are likely to impede CBT progress and long-term maintenance of gains. Often a patient's core beliefs will have manifested during the course of the therapy. However, the therapist can help to elicit core beliefs by using the downward arrow technique. Using this approach, the therapist acts as a broken record, continuing to ask a patient to elaborate on the worst consequences of their beliefs (e.g., "And if that were true, what would that mean?") until the patient reaches a core belief. Once the maladaptive core belief is elicited, distorted core beliefs can be tested through cognitive-restructuring records, behavioral experiments, and strategies like the cognitive continuum. Patients are encouraged to take a more objective approach by evaluating beliefs as if they were detectives or scientists, judging the accuracy and utility of beliefs based on evidence and pros and cons of holding the belief. For example, for a core belief of being unlovable, a patient could be asked to generate a continuum of "lovability" from 0 ("completely and universally hated") to 100 ("completely and universally loved"). The patient would first assign a rating on the scale, and then anchor the continuum by providing examples of behavior for each of the extremes (0 and 100) and for the middle of the scale (50). Patients should also be asked to consider situational factors that may impact one's score on the continuum. Once patients have acquired these data, they will re-rank themselves on the revised scale and generate a more neutral, adaptive belief based on the new evidence. Self-compassion strategies are also useful to incorporate in this module of treatment.

RELAPSE PREVENTION

Finally, a relapse prevention plan is essential to helping patients maintain treatment gains. Aspects of relapse prevention for BDD may include developing a formal list of strategies, encouraging self-therapy sessions, recognizing triggers for increased BDD concerns, and differentiating a lapse (short-term increase in symptoms) from a relapse (return of full disorder). If the patient holds maladaptive beliefs about ending therapy, these are elicited and evaluated before ending the treatment. Therapy sessions may be spaced out toward the end of treatment, so that the patient becomes more independent of the therapist and more accustomed to selecting and implementing strategies. (For a more detailed description of CBT for BDD, see Wilhelm et al., 2013. For a more detailed description of CBT for adolescent BDD, see Greenberg et al., 2010.)

Technological Advances in BDD Treatment

Though in-person CBT is efficacious for patients with BDD, patient care is limited by clinician availability and treatment access (Paganini et al., 2018; Wilhelm, Weingarden, Ladis, et al., 2020). These barriers to care have led researchers to harness technological advances to better disseminate CBT for BDD. Early research focused on the development of Internet-delivered CBT (iCBT), which is broadly defined as a CBT program delivered over an Internet-based platform. iCBT has been found to be effective in treating both subclinical and clinical samples for various disorders (e.g., insomnia, anxiety, and depression; Andrews et al., 2018; Carlbring et al., 2018). Enander and colleagues (2016) conducted an RCT in which they compared 12 weeks of iCBT for BDD (BDD-NET) to Internet-based supportive therapy. They found promising results, with a 54% treatment response rate in the BDD-NET group, compared to only 6% in the Internet-delivered supportive therapy group. Recently, in the first BDD treatment study with global inclusion criteria, it was also shown that BDD-NET can be safely delivered across international borders (Gentile et al., 2019).

Research emphasis has started to shift to smartphone-delivered CBT apps. Unlike iCBT, smartphone apps enable accessible on-demand treatment from any location, increasing the ability for patients to incorporate treatment into their daily environments (Wilhelm, Weingarden, Greenberg, et al., 2020). These modalities also offer the potential to bring effective treatments to populations typically unable to access them (e.g., underserved populations), those typically excluded from treatment trials. A pilot study testing a novel 12-week smartphone-delivered CBT protocol for BDD ($N = 10$) showed promising results across patient and clinician-rated measures of symptom severity, insight, and quality of life. Ninety percent of the sample were considered treatment responders, and gains were maintained at three-month follow-up (Wilhelm, Weingarden, Greenberg, et al., 2020).

Some studies have begun to examine the utility of computerized interpretation bias modification (IBM) for BDD as a means of altering maladaptive interpretive styles thought to maintain symptomatology. For instance, Summers and Cougle (2016) developed a multisession IBM program to train individuals with BDD to reject threat interpretations in favor of benign/healthier interpretations of ambiguous evaluation- and appearance-relevant situations (Summers & Cougle, 2016). Relative to a matched-activity placebo, four 25-minute sessions of IBM led to substantial reductions in threat biases and BDD symptoms on self-report and behavioral measures. Preliminary extensions of this work suggest that virtual reality is an effective tool for eliciting and assessing problematic interpretive biases in vivo (Summers, Schwartzberg, & Wilhelm, 2021); this may represent a promising avenue for continued treatment efforts in the area of IBM for BDD.

Pharmacological Treatment

Available data indicate appropriate pharmacotherapy improves BDD and associated symptoms, such as depression and functional disability (Phillips, 2010; Ipser et al., 2009). SRIs have been the most extensively studied pharmacotherapy for BDD and are considered the first-line medication treatment (Ipser et al., 2009; National Institute for Clinical Excellence, 2005). RCTs have demonstrated that BDD symptoms significantly improve with SRI treatment, with a response rate of 53% to 73% (intention-to-treat analyses; see Ipser et al., 2009).

The first controlled medication study for BDD compared clomipramine to desipramine in a double-blind cross-over design (Hollander et al., 1999). Subjects ($N = 29$) were randomized to eight weeks of each medication. Clomipramine was more effective than the non-SRI antidepressant desipramine in reducing BDD symptom severity (Hollander et al., 1999). Furthermore, the data underscore the importance of specifically treating BDD symptoms, and not just depression, in patients with BDD (Hollander et al., 1999; Phillips & Hollander, 2008).

In a double-blind placebo-controlled trial, subjects ($N = 67$) were randomized to 12 weeks of treatment with fluoxetine or placebo (Phillips et al., 2002). Fluoxetine was significantly more efficacious than placebo; more than half (53%) of subjects responded to fluoxetine, compared to 18% response to placebo. Moreover, a retrospective analysis of this cohort demonstrated a protective effect of fluoxetine against worsening of suicidal symptoms (Phillips & Kelly, 2009).

Another RCT examined the effects of escitalopram discontinuation on time to relapse in patients who initially responded to escitalopram (Phillips et al., 2016). Responders were randomized to either continued treatment with escitalopram or to switch to a placebo for six months. Time to relapse was longer in those who continued to receive the SRI, and fewer patients relapsed on SRI compared to placebo (18% vs. 40%, respectively; Phillips et al., 2016). These findings corroborated other RCTs showing that SRIs are more effective than placebos, and they further suggested that relapse is more likely when medication is discontinued.

Open-label studies have also been done with other SRIs. A 16-week open-label trial of fluvoxamine significantly reduced BDD severity in 63% of subjects ($N = 30$; Phillips, Dwight, et al., 1998). In a 10-week open trial of fluvoxamine, 10 of 15 subjects were much or very much improved on the CGI, and 10 of 12 who completed treatment were responders (Perugi et al., 1996). Open-label studies of citalopram ($N = 15$) and escitalopram ($N = 15$) were also promising, with improvements in BDD symptoms, functioning, and quality of life in about 73% of participants (Phillips, 2006; Phillips & Najjar, 2003).

SRIs are potentially efficacious for children and adolescents with BDD; however, data are limited (Albertini et al., 1996; Phillips et al., 1995). In a case series of 33 children and adolescents, 53% ($N = 19$) of subjects treated with an SRI demonstrated significant improvement in BDD symptoms (Albertini & Phillips, 1999). Of note, SRIs are already indicated for the treatment of similar disorders in pediatric populations, including OCD and depression.

It is recommended that SRIs be administered at their optimal dose (i.e., highest tolerated dose) and duration (e.g., at least 12–16 weeks) before other medications or augmentation strategies are tried. Phillips and colleagues (2006) examined the characteristics of pharmacotherapy (i.e., frequency, type, dose, and adequacy) received by 151 individuals with BDD (Phillips, Pagano, & Menard, 2006). While nearly three quarters (72.9%) of the sample had received pharmacotherapy (mean number of medications = 5, SD = 4.5)—most commonly SRIs—SRI trials were not adequate. Thus, most patients had not received medication at the dose or duration associated with BDD symptom improvement. When prescribed appropriately for BDD, most SRIs were effective. In a chart review of 90 patients, 63% ($N = 55$) of adequate SRI trials led to clinically significant improvement in BDD symptoms (Phillips, Albertini, et al., 2001).

Successful SRI treatment can reduce BDD symptoms, including preoccupation with appearance and related behaviors. Insight and depression may also improve over the course of treatment. Following successful pharmacotherapy, patients may report a change in the distress associated with appearance, although they may believe they look the same.

Conversely, some patients do report a belief that their appearance has improved over the course of SRI treatment. For patients who would like, or need, to discontinue medication, gradual tapering is recommended to mitigate the rate of relapse (Phillips et al., 2012). Combining SRI discontinuation with CBT may also help reduce the risk of relapse; however, this approach requires empirical investigation.

Non-SRI medications have not been well studied as monotherapy for BDD. Venlafaxine, a serotonin-norepinephrine reuptake inhibitor (SNRI), was found to be effective in improving BDD symptoms in a small open trial ($N = 11$; Allen et al., 2008). Until larger, controlled studies are completed, SRIs are the first-line medication.

In a chart review study, 43% of patients who did not respond to an initial SRI responded to at least one subsequent SRI trial (Phillips, Albertini, et al., 2001). Patients who respond initially to an SRI, but who need to switch (e.g., due to side effects, insurance coverage), fare even more favorably with subsequent SRI trials, with 92% of subsequent trials resulting in response (Phillips, Albertini, et al., 2001). Thus, if a patient has not responded to an adequate SRI trial (high dose, 12–16 weeks), another SRI may be tried.

Augmentation strategies may be warranted if patients do not respond to an adequate SRI trial (Phillips & Hollander, 2008). A small double-blind controlled trial examined pimozide versus placebo augmentation of fluoxetine ($N = 28$); pimozide was not more efficacious than placebo (Phillips, 2005). Buspirone augmentation has been shown to provide improvement in patients who had not responded, or only partially responded, to SRI treatment (Phillips, Albertini, et al., 2001).

Combining CBT with an SRI may be helpful for some patients; however, empirical research is needed to investigate the efficacy of combined approaches.

Treatment Selection

A meta-analysis comparing medications to CBT, BT, and CT found that all approaches led to improvements in BDD symptoms and depression (Williams et al., 2006). Large effect sizes were found both for case series and RCTs, with significantly larger effect sizes for CBT than for pharmacotherapy. No significant differences emerged between CBT and BT, or between BT and pharmacotherapy.

Although CBT and SRIs are effective monotherapies, no studies have examined their combined efficacy in treating BDD. Existing research in OCD (see Chapter 21) may be helpful in understanding the role for combined treatment in specific clinical BDD situations. For example, E/RP (Foa et al., 2005), CT (Wilhelm et al., 2005), and SRI (Koran et al., 2007) monotherapies have all been found to be effective in reducing OCD severity. In studies exploring combined treatment of OCD, both E/RP and combined therapies fare better than medication alone (Foa et al., 2005). However, combined treatment (SRI + E/RP) may be more effective for some patients, including patients with more severe symptoms, with comorbid depression (Cottraux et al., 1990; Hohagen et al., 1998), or with dominant obsessions (Hohagen et al., 1998).

In the absence of data on combined treatments in BDD, an adequate trial of SRI or CBT monotherapy may be administered before augmenting treatment in cases of mild to moderate BDD. However, patient factors, including symptom severity, delusionality, comorbidity, treatment adherence, and partial response to an adequate monotherapy, should be considered when determining the best combination or sequencing of therapies (for review, see Simpson & Liebowitz, 2005). For example, even after an adequate trial of SRI therapy, many patients continue to be symptomatic. CBT can be used to taper patients from medication or, when used concurrently, to continue to reduce symptom severity and improve both functioning and quality of life (Simpson et al., 2008). Conversely, if, after an adequate trial of CBT, a patient's BDD symptoms, BDD-related delusions, or clinically significant depression is unremitting, augmentation with an SRI may be considered.

Finally, the empirical literature should be taken together with patient's preference for treatment. In the absence of empirical support for combination therapy in BDD, it is important to consider the financial and psychological burden of adding unnecessary treatment. Making sure the patient is an active participant in his or her treatment can increase motivation and treatment compliance, both of which are positively associated with outcome. This is of particular importance in CBT, where the goal of treatment is to enhance accurate attributions and self-efficacy. When a patient simultaneously begins two treatments—for example, a psychological and a pharmacological intervention—the patient may be prone to attribute change to the medication rather than to active changes they have made to their thought and behavior patterns. Enhancing a patient's ability to make personal attributions regarding treatment gains is important to achieving and maximizing outcome in CBT.

Case Vignette

Julia, described at the beginning of this chapter, was 24 years old when she presented for treatment. Her decision to seek treatment was not due to her own body image concerns; it was a way to assuage her husband's concerns about her. The couple had already had numerous fights about surgeries and Julia's seemingly irrational concerns regarding her nose and hair. At intake, the strong conviction with which Julia held her beliefs about her perceived imperfections became apparent. During the assessment, the therapist asked about BDD and related symptoms. The therapist used a SCID-5 to assess other disorders, the BDD-Diagnostic Module to diagnose BDD, and the BDD-YBOCS and Body Dysmorphic Disorder Symptom Scale (BDD-SS) to further explore the details and severity of Julia's appearance-related concerns. Julia met diagnostic criteria for severe BDD (with poor but not delusional insight; BDD-YBOCS score = 35) and major depressive disorder. Julia described how her depression worsened and her withdrawal increased after her second rhinoplasty procedure a year earlier. She feared that "others would be scared off when they saw her disfigured nose."

For the few months preceding intake, Julia reported leaving the house only a handful of times, following time-intensive camouflaging and checking rituals. Her depression started subsequent to, and only in the context of, her BDD symptoms. Although Julia was resistant to psychiatric treatment, she felt strongly about improving the quality of her life and helping to ease the distress her concerns had caused her husband. Julia voiced her skepticism about improving without changing her appearance; however, after reviewing the evidence (i.e., her dissatisfaction following previous surgeries), she agreed it was worth trying something new. Julia was not amenable to pharmacotherapy. Had she been amenable, SRI monotherapy would have also been an appropriate consideration, given her poor insight and depressive symptoms. However, given Julia's preference, she and the therapist agreed to begin CBT for BDD; having Julia's husband sign on as part of the treatment team (i.e., offering help and support with homework assignments) facilitated the decision to pursue CBT.

Following the initial evaluation and assessment of symptoms, motivational issues around treatment were discussed. The therapist used Socratic questioning to elicit the pros and cons of Julia's current beliefs and behaviors. Julia was able to agree that some aspects of her beliefs and behaviors were maladaptive, insofar as they were time-consuming, expensive, and causing her and her husband to become upset. After Julia was on board with treatment, Julia and the therapist discussed the individual factors that contributed to the development and maintenance of Julia's BDD. For instance, as a first-generation American, Julia recalled the pressures she felt as a child to fit in. She remembered feeling that she "didn't fit in anywhere because [she] wasn't as White as [her] friends, or as Chinese as [her] parents or cousins." Having grown up in a mostly Caucasian, upper middle-class neighborhood, Julia reported that her friends would frequently play with, and comment on, her "stick-straight, silky hair" or petite nose. When Julia began experiencing physical and psychological changes during puberty, she remembered thinking, "There's something wrong with me" and "It's not okay for me to have a problem, I will disgrace my family," which caused her to keep her appearance concerns bottled up inside. Julia felt very ashamed about her appearance and ashamed that she worried so much about it. She never sought help from a mental health professional for her concerns.

During the initial stages of treatment, Julia was taught how to identify her current maladaptive thoughts and to evaluate them more objectively. For example, Julia was avoiding leaving the house because of feared negative social evaluation based on her nose. The therapist helped Julia to monitor her negative thoughts in trigger situations using thought records and to identify cognitive distortions (mind-reading, jumping to conclusions). One strategy involved using Socratic questioning ("Has anyone commented negatively on your nose?" "What have people said to you?") to evaluate her beliefs more objectively and to generate a more accurate belief. Another useful strategy was developing and modifying a self-esteem pie chart, in which various components of self-esteem were identified and targeted for development. For example, Julia was able to recognize that by basing her self-esteem solely on her appearance, she was neglecting many positive qualities that made her feel good about herself, including her intelligence, creativity, strong family relationships, and personality characteristics (e.g., being a kind, loyal, and compassionate wife, daughter, and friend).

As Julia became more adept at cognitive restructuring, a hierarchy was developed to address anxiety-provoking and avoided situations (phone calls, bright lighting, social activities). Items from the hierarchy were worked on, in and out of session, to gradually introduce Julia to anxiety-provoking situations without the use of rituals or safety behaviors. For example, the therapist first asked Julia to attend sessions with makeup but without her sunglasses, and over time worked up to more difficult assignments until Julia was able to tolerate each experience. Attentional (i.e., mirror) retraining was used to help Julia perceive the big picture. She learned how to use a mirror without focusing selectively on hot spots like her nose or hair. Julia was reminded that anyone who spends a significant time staring at their least favorite feature could be expected to become discouraged about their appearance. Finally, Julia's core beliefs (e.g., "I'm unacceptable") were addressed and modified using cognitive strategies, such as the cognitive continuum, so that she could develop more adaptive and accurate beliefs (e.g., "Nobody is perfect, but I'm good enough and have friends, family, and a husband who cares about me."), and they were considered via an exploration of Julia's beliefs in their cultural context. Julia and the therapist discussed how acculturation stress contributed to Julia's sense that she did not fit in; they discussed within-group intergenerational conflicts that Julia experienced in her own family as a first-generation Asian American, as well as the conflict Julia felt between fitting in at home versus in her peer group.

Julia's treatment lasted 22 sessions, with the two last sessions tapered over two-week periods. The final sessions were spent identifying and planning for future challenges (e.g., her brother's wedding, applying for jobs). By the end of treatment, Julia was reasonably independent in applying all of her skills and managing BDD triggering situations. Her BDD-YBOCS score had decreased from 35 (severe) to 10 (subclinical), and the prospect of further surgery was no longer appealing to Julia. Although Julia still experienced some negative beliefs about her appearance, they were less frequent, intense, and meaningful to her. As Julia's symptoms improved, she was able to take classes and work toward a career in graphic design. Julia no longer avoided phone calls or social invitations, and by the end of treatment, Julia was going out on a date night with her husband and having lunch with at least one friend on a weekly basis. (A more detailed description of the treatment strategies is found in Wilhelm et al., 2010.)

Troubleshooting: Clinical Considerations and Challenges

Several factors can complicate the treatment of individuals with BDD. As noted, persons with BDD often elude accurate diagnosis because they are not likely to seek treatment for BDD symptoms. Shame and embarrassment may preclude individuals from seeking treatment, and those who seek treatment often seek physical (i.e., medical and nonmedical cosmetic) treatment for psychological concerns.

Ambivalence and Motivation

Ambivalence about treatment is common and may stem in part from a patient's level of insight into the disorder. Of patients with BDD who present for psychiatric or psychological services, many have done so at the urging of loved ones (e.g., spouses or parents). In addition to ambivalence due to poor or wavering insight, patients may also report uneasiness about treatment. For example, patients may describe a negative association with being on a medication, or the difficulty associated with intentional exposure to previously avoided situations. Thus, motivation to change may be low and/or fluctuate during treatment. Moreover, many patients have poor insight into their symptoms and mistakenly believe that cosmetic procedures are their only hope, which can make them afraid to commit to a treatment focused on psychological rather than physical change. Motivational enhancement strategies (e.g., motivational interviewing; Miller & Rollnick, 2002) can be used to resolve ambivalence and to increase a patient's readiness to engage in treatment. Motivation can be assessed using the University of Rhode Island Change Assessment Questionnaire (URICA; DiClemente & Hughes, 1990), a 32-item self-report questionnaire that measures four stages of change: precontemplation, contemplation, action, and maintenance. Motivation will likely wax and wane over the course of treatment; thus, motivational enhancement strategies should be used throughout treatment as needed. In addition, a clear treatment rationale and a gradual, collaborative approach to treatment can help patients feel more comfortable, and thus more engaged in the treatment.

Insight in BDD

Level of insight may affect treatment, and considerations should be made when working with patients with fixed beliefs (absent insight). Patients who are convinced that their problems are physically based may be difficult to engage in a psychosocial treatment aimed at reducing psychological distress. In such cases, a more gradual approach is recommended, with a focus on evaluating the utility and associated distress of self-defeating beliefs, rather than refuting the accuracy of such beliefs (Wilhelm et al., 2010). Concurrent or sequential pharmacotherapy with CBT may also be indicated for patients with BDD who have low insight.

Depression and Suicidality

Depressive symptoms (e.g., lethargy, anhedonia, impaired concentration) can make it difficult for patients to participate effectively in treatment. Thoroughly assessing the nature of, and impairment caused by, depressive symptoms can help inform a decision about treatment focus and sequencing. For example, when depression seems primary or interferes with a patient's ability to engage in CBT, a decision may be made to target the depression directly through CBT (focused on depressive symptoms) or pharmacotherapy. Due to the markedly high rates of suicidality associated with BDD, depressive symptoms, including suicidality, should be monitored closely throughout treatment. Acute suicidality may warrant a higher level of care.

Skills Deficits and Quality of Life

Successful treatment involves increasing a patient's functioning and quality of life; usually this is achieved via symptom reduction. However, other quality-of-life factors may need to be addressed, including skills deficits and psychosocial stressors. Because of its early onset, BDD can interrupt typical skills acquisition, such as social and problem-solving skills, and the ability to tolerate and cope with distressing emotions. Areas for skills building should be identified throughout the course of treatment. Similarly, patients with BDD, particularly those with severe symptoms, may have limited financial, occupational, and social resources. In addition, many patients have spent so much time engaged in BDD-related thoughts and rituals that they have given up other daily activities or hobbies. Thus, a comprehensive treatment should focus on helping patients to rebuild activity across the various dimensions of their life, increasing social networks, hobbies, and occupational activity.

Special Populations

Adolescents

Adolescence is a period of substantial physical, psychological, emotional, and social changes combined with an increased value placed on body image (Levine & Smolak, 2002). Accordingly, it is no wonder that adolescents are so concerned with, and often dismayed by, their appearance. BDD typically has its onset during adolescence, when appearance concerns are common, and it is often normalized as something one ought to "tough out" or "grow out of." Compared to adults, adolescents with BDD tend to have higher lifetime suicide rates and to endorse more delusional beliefs about their appearance (Phillips, Didie, et al., 2006). Adolescents with BDD spend excessive periods of time (i.e., more than one hour, often three to eight hours) thinking about imagined or minor imperfections. The concern is so upsetting that teens with BDD often spend hours trying to fix or hide the perceived defect by checking their appearance repeatedly in the mirror, excessive grooming, camouflaging (e.g., with makeup, hair products, hats, tanning), and frequent reassurance seeking. Rituals can take the place of homework, classes, and social gatherings with peers. Due to appearance-related thoughts and behaviors, adolescents with BDD may fall behind in school, may refuse to go to classes, and may become socially isolated. Concurrently, during adolescence, teens are faced with a number of developmental challenges, including identity formation and increasing dependence on peer groups for identification and approval (Levine & Smolak, 2002). These developmental processes are interrupted by BDD, which can lead to deficits in social skills, emotion regulation, and developing a stable sense of self. Thus, treatment for adolescents, as well as for adults who developed symptoms during adolescence, should identify and modify skills deficits. For a description of the assessment of, and CBT for, adolescent BDD, see Greenberg and colleagues (2010).

Ethnic Minorities
Although general body dissatisfaction is more prevalent in Western cultures, where physical attractiveness is highly valued, the prevalence of clinically significant BDD seems relatively consistent across cultures (Borda et al., 2011; Cansever et al., 2003; Fontenelle et al., 2006). Culture and ethnic identity development may have an important influence on the body area of concern, as well as patients' access to, and attitudes toward, mental health treatment (Marques et al., 2011). Cross-cultural studies are still needed to examine clinical features in clinical samples. Research is also needed to explore the relationship between BDD and its cultural variants, including *taijin kyofusho*, a Japanese phobia in which individuals are afraid of offending others by their "deformed body" (Suzuki et al., 2003), and koro or *suo yang*, an Asian genital retraction syndrome in which males are preoccupied by penile (or females by labia, nipples, or breasts) shrinking or retraction into the body, resulting in death (Chowdhury, 1996). Clinicians should inquire about cultural considerations, including acculturation and ethnic identity development, as part of assessment, and they should address cultural factors as needed in treatment.

Conclusion

There is a growing clinical and research interest in BDD. However, BDD treatment outcome research is still scarce relative to other disorders, and individuals struggling with BDD remain reluctant to seek treatment.

While patients with BDD share common core features, such as preoccupation with an imagined or slight appearance flaw and compensatory (ritualistic and avoidant) behaviors, the heterogeneity of BDD symptomatology has not been fully elucidated. Small and biased samples make it difficult to draw meaningful conclusions about the impact of psychological (e.g., comorbidity, insight), epidemiological (e.g., age, gender, culture), and other patient factors (e.g., motivation for change). More controlled studies are needed in order to adequately determine the relative efficacy of existing treatments and strategies for optimizing augmentation techniques. Studies of combined and sequential pharmacotherapy and CBT are also necessary to help address patients who do not respond adequately to SRI or CBT monotherapy.

BDD is a severe disorder with substantial psychosocial impact. Shame and poor insight often preclude individuals from seeking treatment for BDD symptoms, or from disclosing appearance-related concerns unless specifically queried. Thus, while patients may seek treatment for comorbid disorders, such as anxiety or depression, their struggles with BDD frequently go undetected and untreated. Healthcare providers need to be aware of the disorder and of the need to specifically screen patients for BDD. Given the early onset of BDD, it is particularly important to screen for BDD in adolescents. Increased awareness of this disorder may help to promote early detection and treatment. Early diagnosis and treatment may help reduce the personal and public health sequelae typically associated with BDD, including functional impairment, reduced quality of life, hospitalization, and morbidity.

References

Albertini, R. S., & Phillips, K. A. (1999). Thirty-three cases of body dysmorphic disorder in children and adolescents. *Journal of the American Academy of Child and Adolescent Psychiatry*, *38*(4), 453–459.

Albertini, R. S., Phillips, K. A., & Guevremont, D. (1996). Body dysmorphic disorder. *Journal of the American Academy of Child and Adolescent Psychiatry*, *35*(11), 1425–1426.

Allen, A., Hadley, S. J., Kaplan, A., Simeon, D., Friedberg, J., Priday, L., Baker, B. R., Greenberg, J. L., & Hollander, E. (2008). An open-label trial of venlafaxine in body dysmorphic disorder. *CNS Spectrums*, *13*(2), 138–144.

American Psychiatric Association (APA). (2013). *Diagnostic and statistical manual of mental disorders* (5th ed.).

Andrews, G., Basu, A., Cuijpers, P., Craske, M. G., McEvoy, P., English, C. L., & Newby, J. M. (2018). Computer therapy for the anxiety and depression disorders is effective, acceptable and practical health care: An updated meta-analysis. *Journal of Anxiety Disorders*, *55*, 70–78.

Angelakis, I., Gooding, P. A., & Panagioti, M. (2016). Suicidality in body dysmorphic disorder (BDD): A systematic review with meta-analysis. *Clinical Psychology Review*, *49*, 55–66.

Barr, L. C., Goodman, W. K., & Price, L. H. (1992). Acute exacerbation of body dysmorphic disorder during tryptophan depletion. *The American Journal of Psychiatry*, *149*, 1406–1407.

Bienvenu, O. J., Samuels, J. F., Riddle, M. A., Hoehn-Saric, R., Liang, K.-Y., Cullen, B. A., Grados, M. A., & Nestadt, G. (2000). The relationship of obsessive-compulsive disorder to possible spectrum disorders: Results from a family study. *Biological Psychiatry*, *48*(4), 287–293.

Bjornsson, A. S., Didie, E. R., Grant, J. E., Menard, W., Stalker, E., & Phillips, K. A. (2013). Age at onset and clinical correlates in body dysmorphic disorder. *Comprehensive Psychiatry*, *54*(7), 893–903.

Blashill, A. J., Grunewald, W., Fang, A., Davidson, E., & Wilhelm, S. (2022). Conformity to masculine norms and symptom severity among men diagnosed with muscle dysmorphia vs. body dysmorphic disorder. *PLOS ONE*, *15*(8). https://doi.org/10.1371/journal.pone.0237651

Bloch, S., & Glue, P. (1988). Psychotherapy and dysmorphophobia: A case report. *The British Journal of Psychiatry*, *152*(2), 271–274.

Bohne, A., Keuthen, N. J., Wilhelm, S., Deckersbach, T., & Jenike, M. A. (2002). Prevalence of symptoms of body dysmorphic disorder and its correlates: A cross-cultural comparison. *Psychosomatics*, *43*(6), 486–490.

Borda, T., Neziroglu, F., Santos, N., Donnelly, K., & Rivera, R. P. (2011). Status of body dysmorphic disorder in Argentina. *Journal of Anxiety Disorders*, *25*(4), 507–512.

Buhlmann, U., Etcoff, N. L., & Wilhelm, S. (2008). Facial attractiveness ratings and perfectionism in body dysmorphic disorder and obsessive-compulsive disorder. *Journal of Anxiety Disorders*, *22*(3), 540–547.

Buhlmann, U., Glaesmer, H., Mewes, R., Fama, J. M., Wilhelm, S., Brähler, E., & Rief, W. (2010). Updates on the prevalence of body dysmorphic disorder: A population-based survey. *Psychiatry Research*, *178*(1), 171–175.

Buhlmann, U., Gleiß, M. J. L., Rupf, L., Zschenderlein, K., & Kathmann, N. (2011). Modifying emotion recognition deficits in body dysmorphic disorder: An experimental investigation. *Depression and Anxiety*, *28*(10), 924–931.

Cansever, A., Uzun, Ö., Dönmez, E., & Özşahin, A. (2003). The prevalence and clinical features of body dysmorphic disorder in college students: A study in a Turkish sample. *Comprehensive Psychiatry*, *44*(1), 60–64.

Carey, P., Seedat, S., Warwick, J., Heerden, B. van, & Stein, D. J. (2004). SPECT imaging of body dysmorphic disorder. *Journal of Neuropsychiatry and Clinical Neuroscience*, *16*(3), 357–359.

Carlbring, P., Andersson, G., Cuijpers, P., Riper, H., & Hedman-Lagerlöf, E. (2018). Internet-based vs. face-to-face cognitive behavior therapy for psychiatric and somatic disorders: An updated systematic review and meta-analysis. *Cognitive Behaviour Therapy*, *47*(1), 1–18.

Chowdhury, A. N. (1996). The definition and classification of koro. *Culture, Medicine and Psychiatry*, *20*(1), 41–65.

Cottraux, J., Mollard, E., Bouvard, M., Marks, I., Sluys, M., Nury, A. M., Douge, R., & Cialdella, P. (1990). A controlled study of fluvoxamine and exposure in obsessive-compulsive disorder. *International Clinical Psychopharmacology*, *5*(1), 17–30.

Craske, M. G., Treanor, M., Conway, C. C., Zbozinek, T., & Vervliet, B. (2014). Maximizing exposure therapy: An inhibitory learning approach. *Behaviour Research and Therapy*, *58*, 10–23.

Crerand, C. E., Phillips, K. A., Menard, W., & Fay, C. (2005). Nonpsychiatric medical treatment of body dysmorphic disorder. *Psychosomatics*, *46*(6), 549–555.

Deckersbach, T., Savage, C. R., Phillips, K. A., Wilhelm, S., Buhlmann, U., Rauch, S. L., Baer, L., & Jenike, M. A. (2000). Characteristics of memory dysfunction in body dysmorphic disorder. *Journal of the International Neuropsychological Society*, *6*(6), 673–681.

Delinsky, S. S., & Wilson, G. T. (2006). Mirror exposure for the treatment of body image disturbance. *International Journal of Eating Disorders*, *39*(2), 108–116.

DiClemente, C. C., & Hughes, S. O. (1990). Stages of change profiles in outpatient alcoholism treatment. *Journal of Substance Abuse*, *2*(2), 217–235.

Eifert, G. H., Schulte, D., Zvolensky, M. J., Lejuez, C. W., & Lau, A. W. (1997). Manualized behavior therapy: Merits and challenges. *Behavior Therapy*, *28*(4), 499–509.

Enander, J., Andersson, E., Mataix-Cols, D., Lichtenstein, L., Alström, K., Andersson, G., Ljótsson, B., & Rück, C. (2016). Therapist guided internet based cognitive behavioural therapy for body dysmorphic disorder: Single blind randomised controlled trial. *British Medical Journal*, *352*, 1–8.

Enander, J., Ivanov, V. Z., Mataix-Cols, D., Kuja-Halkola, R., Ljótsson, B., Lundström, S., Pérez-Vigil, A., Monzani, B., Lichtenstein, P., & Rück, C. (2018). Prevalence and heritability of body dysmorphic symptoms in adolescents and young adults: A population-based nationwide twin study. *Psychological Medicine*, *48*(16), 2740–2747.

Fang, A., Jacoby, R. J., Beatty, C., Germine, L., Plessow, F., Wilhelm, S., & Lawson, E. A. (2019). Serum oxytocin levels are elevated in body dysmorphic disorder and related to severity of psychopathology. *Psychoneuroendocrinology*, *113*, 104541.

Fang, A., Steketee, G., Keshaviah, A., Didie, E., Phillips, K. A., & Wilhelm, S. (2020). Mechanisms of change in cognitive behavioral therapy for body dysmorphic disorder. *Cognitive Therapy and Research*, *44*(3), 596–610.

Faravelli, C., Salvatori, S., Galassi, F., Aiazzi, L., Drei, C., & Cabras, P. (1997). Epidemiology of somatoform disorders: A community survey in Florence. *Social Psychiatry and Psychiatric Epidemiology*, *32*(1), 24–29.

Feusner, J. D., Moody, T., Hembacher, E., Townsend, J., McKinley, M., Moller, H., & Bookheimer, S. (2010). Abnormalities of visual processing and frontostriatal systems in body dysmorphic disorder. *Archives of General Psychiatry*, *67*(2), 197–205.

Feusner, J. D., Neziroglu, F., Wilhelm, S., Mancusi, L., & Bohon, C. (2010). What causes BDD: Research findings and a proposed model. *Psychiatric Annals*, *40*(7), 349–355.

Feusner, J. D., Townsend, J., Bystritsky, A., & Bookheimer, S. (2007). Visual information processing of faces in body dysmorphic disorder. *Archives of General Psychiatry*, *64*, 1417–1425.

Feusner, J. D., Yaryura-Tobias, J., & Saxena, S. (2008). The pathophysiology of body dysmorphic disorder. *Body Image*, *5*(1), 3–12.

First, M. B., Williams, J. B., Karg, R. S., & Spitzer, R. L. (2015). *User's guide to structured clinical interview for DSM-5 disorders (SCID-5-CV) clinical version*. American Psychiatric Publishing.

Foa, E. B., Liebowitz, M. R., Kozak, M. J., Davies, S., Campeas, R., Franklin, M. E., Huppert, J. D., Kjernisted, K., Rowan, V., & Schmidt, A. B. (2005). Randomized, placebo-controlled trial of exposure and ritual prevention, clomipramine, and their combination in the treatment of obsessive-compulsive disorder. *The American Journal of Psychiatry*, *162*(1), 151–161.

Fontenelle, L. F., Telles, L. L., Nazar, B. P., De Menezes, G. B., Do Nascimento, A. L., Mendlowicz, M. V., & Versiani, M. (2006). A sociodemographic, phenomenological, and long-term follow-up study of patients with body dysmorphic disorder in Brazil. *The International Journal of Psychiatry in Medicine*, *36*(2), 243–259.

Gabbay, V., Asnis, G. M., Bello, J. A., Alonso, C. M., Serras, S. J., & O'Dowd, M. A. (2003). New onset of body dysmorphic disorder following fronto-temporal lesion. *Neurology, 61*, 123–125.

Gabbay, V., O'Dowd, M. A., Weiss, A. J., & Asnis, G. M. (2002). Body dysmorphic disorder triggered by medical illness? *The American Journal of Psychiatry, 159*, 493.

Gentile, A. J., La Lima, C., Flygare, O., Enander, J., Wilhelm, S., Mataix-Cols, D., & Rück, C. (2019). Internet-based, therapist-guided, cognitive-behavioural therapy for body dysmorphic disorder with global eligibility for inclusion: An uncontrolled pilot study. *BMJ Open, 9*(3), e024693.

Grace, S. A., Buchanan, B. G., Maller, J. J., Toh, W. L., Castle, D. J., & Rossell, S. L. (2017). Reduced cortical thickness in body dysmorphic disorder. *Psychiatry Research: Neuroimaging, 259*, 25–28.

Grace, S. A., Labuschagne, I., Kaplan, R. A., & Rossell, S. L. (2017). The neurobiology of body dysmorphic disorder: A systematic review and theoretical model. *Neuroscience and Biobehavioral Reviews, 83*, 83–96.

Greenberg, J. L., Markowitz, S., Petronko, M. R., Taylor, C. E., Wilhelm, S., & Wilson, G. T. (2010). Cognitive-behavioral therapy for adolescent body dysmorphic disorder. *Cognitive and Behavioral Practice, 17*(3), 248–258.

Greenberg, J. L., Mothi, S. S., & Wilhelm, S. (2016). Cognitive-behavioral therapy for adolescent body dysmorphic disorder: A pilot study. *Behavior Therapy, 47*(2), 213–224.

Greenberg, J. L., Reuman, L., Hartmann, A. S., Kasarskis, I., & Wilhelm, S. (2014). Visual hot spots: An eye tracking study of attention bias in body dysmorphic disorder. *Journal of Psychiatric Research, 57*, 125–132.

Grocholewski, A., Kliem, S., & Heinrichs, N. (2012). Selective attention to imagined facial ugliness is specific to body dysmorphic disorder. *Body Image, 9*(2), 261–269.

Hadley, S. J., Newcorn, J. H., & Hollander, E. (2002). The neurobiology and psychopharmacology of body dysmorphic disorder. In D. J. Castle & K. A. Phillips (Eds.), *Disorders of body image* (pp. 139–155). Wrightson Biomedical Publishing.

Hitzeroth, V., Wessels, C., Zungu-Dirwayi, N., Oosthuizen, P., & Stein, D. J. (2001). Muscle dysmorphia: A South African sample. *Psychiatry and Clinical Neurosciences, 55*(5), 521–523.

Hohagen, F., Winkelmann, G., Rasche-Räuchle, H., Hand, I., König, A., Münchau, N., Hiss, H., Geiger-Kabisch, C., Käppler, C., & Schramm, P. (1998). Combination of behaviour therapy with fluvoxamine in comparison with behaviour therapy and placebo: Results of a multicentre study. *The British Journal of Psychiatry, 173*(S35), 71–78.

Holland, G., & Tiggemann, M. (2016). A systematic review of the impact of the use of social networking sites on body image and disordered eating outcomes. *Body Image, 17*, 100–110.

Hollander, E., Allen, A., Kwon, J., Aronowitz, B., Schmeidler, J., Wong, C., & Simeon, D. (1999). Clomipramine vs desipramine crossover trial in body dysmorphic disorder: Selective efficacy of a serotonin reuptake inhibitor in imagined ugliness. *Archives of General Psychiatry, 56*(11), 1033–1039.

Hollander, E., & Wong, C. M. (1995). Body dysmorphic disorder, pathological gambling, and sexual compulsions. *The Journal of Clinical Psychiatry, 56*(Suppl. 4), 7–12.

Horowitz, K., Gorfinkle, K., Lewis, O., & Phillips, K. A. (2002). Body dysmorphic disorder in an adolescent girl. *Journal of the American Academy of Child and Adolescent Psychiatry, 41*(12), 1503–1509.

Ipser, J. C., Sander, C., & Stein, D. J. (2009). Pharmacotherapy and psychotherapy for body dysmorphic disorder. *Cochrane Database of Systematic Reviews, 1*, CD005332.

Koran, L. M., Abujaoude, E., Large, M. D., & Serpe, R. T. (2008). The prevalence of body dysmorphic disorder in the United States adult population. *CNS Spectrums, 13*(4), 316–322.

Koran, L. M., Hanna, G. L., Hollander, E., Nestadt, G., & Simpson, H. B; American Psychiatric Association. (2007). Practice guideline for the treatment of patients with obsessive-compulsive disorder. *The American Journal of Psychiatry, 164*(7Suppl), 5–53.

Krebs, G., Fernández de la Cruz, L., Monzani, B., Bowyer, L., Anson, M., Cadman, J., Heyman, I., Turner, C., Veale, D., & Mataix-Cols, D. (2017). Long-term outcomes of cognitive-behavioral therapy for adolescent body dysmorphic disorder. *Behavior Therapy, 48*(4), 462–473.

Lemma, A. (2009). Being seen or being watched? A psychoanalytic perspective on body dysmorphia. *The International Journal of Psychoanalysis, 90*(4), 753–771.

Levine, M. P., & Smolak, L. (2002). Body image development in adolescence. In T. F. Cash & T. Pruzinsky (Eds.), *Body image: A handbook of theory, research, and clinical practice* (pp. 74–82). Guilford.

Marques, L., LeBlanc, N., Weingarden, H., Greenberg, J. L., Traeger, L. N., Keshaviah, A., & Wilhelm, S. (2011). Body dysmorphic symptoms: Phenomenology and ethnicity. *Body Image, 8*(2), 163–167.

Mataix-Cols, D., de la Cruz, L. F., Isomura, K., Anson, M., Turner, C., Monzani, B., Cadman, J., Bowyer, L., Heyman, I., & Veale, D. (2015). A pilot randomized controlled trial of cognitive-behavioral therapy for adolescents with body dysmorphic disorder. *Journal of the American Academy of Child and Adolescent Psychiatry*, *54*(11), 895–904.

Mathew, S. J. (2001). PANDAS variant and body dysmorphic disorder. *The American Journal of Psychiatry*, *158*(6), 963.

McKay, D. (1999). Two-year follow-up of behavioral treatment and maintenance for body dysmorphic disorder. *Behavior Modification*, *23*(4), 620–629.

McKay, D., Todaro, J., Neziroglu, F., Campisi, T., Moritz, E. K., & Yaryura-Tobias, J. A. (1997). Body dysmorphic disorder: A preliminary evaluation of treatment and maintenance using exposure with response prevention. *Behaviour Research and Therapy*, *35*(1), 67–70.

Miller, W. R., & Rollnick, S. (2002). Motivational interviewing: Preparing people for change [Book review]. *Journal of Studies on Alcohol*, *63*(6), 776–777.

Monzani, B., Rijsdijk, F., Harris, J., & Mataix-Cols, D. (2014). The structure of genetic and environmental risk factors for dimensional representations of DSM-5 obsessive-compulsive spectrum disorders. *JAMA Psychiatry*, *71*, 182-189.

Naga, A. A., Devinsky, O., & Barr, W. B. (2004). Somatoform disorders after temporal lobectomy. *Cognitive Behavioral Neurology*, *17*(2), 57–61.

National Institute for Clinical Excellence. (2005). *Obsessive-compulsive disorder: Core interventions in the treatment of obsessive-compulsive disorder and body dysmorphic disorder*. HMSO.

Neziroglu, F., McKay, D., Todaro, J., & Yaryura-Tobias, J. A. (1996). Effect of cognitive behavior therapy on persons with body dysmorphic disorder and comorbid Axis II diagnoses. *Behavior Therapy*, *27*(1), 67–77.

Otto, M. W., Wilhelm, S., Cohen, L. S., & Harlow, B. L. (2001). Prevalence of body dysmorphic disorder in a community sample of women. *American Journal of Psychiatry*, *158*(12), 2061–2063.

Paganini, S., Teigelkoetter, W., Buntrock, C., & Baumeister, H. (2018). Economic evaluations of Internet-and mobile-based interventions for the treatment and prevention of depression: A systematic review. *Journal of Affective Disorders*, *225*, 733–755.

Perugi, G., Giannotti, D., Di Vaio, S., Frare, F., Saettoni, M., & Cassano, G. B. (1996). Fluvoxamine in the treatment of body dysmorphic disorder (dysmorphophobia). *International Clinical Psychopharmacology*, *11*(4), 247–254.

Phillips, K. A. (2005). *The broken mirror: Understanding and treating body dysmorphic disorder* (revised and expanded edition). Oxford University Press.

Phillips, K. A. (2006). An open-label study of escitalopram in body dysmorphic disorder. *International Clinical Psychopharmacology*, *21*(3), 177-179.

Phillips K. A. (2010). Pharmacotherapy for body dysmorphic disorder. *Psychiatric Annals*, *40*(7), 325–332.

Phillips, K. A., Albertini, R. S., & Rasmussen, S. A. (2002). A randomized placebo-controlled trial of fluoxetine in body dysmorphic disorder. *Archives of General Psychiatry*, *59*(4), 381–388.

Phillips, K. A., Albertini, R. S., Siniscalchi, J. M., Khan, A., & Robinson, M. (2001). Effectiveness of pharmacotherapy for body dysmorphic disorder: A chart-review study. *The Journal of Clinical Psychiatry*, *62*(9), 721-727.

Phillips, K. A., Atala, K. D., & Albertini, R. S. (1995). Case study: Body dysmorphic disorder in adolescents. *Journal of the American Academy of Child &and Adolescent Psychiatry*, *34*(9), 1216–1220.

Phillips, K. A., Didie, E. R., Menard, W., Pagano, M. E., Fay, C., & Weisberg, R. B. (2006). Clinical features of body dysmorphic disorder in adolescents and adults. *Psychiatry Research*, *141*(3), 305–314.

Phillips, K. A., Dwight, M. M., & McElroy, S. L. (1998). Efficacy and safety of fluvoxamine in body dysmorphic disorder. *The Journal of Clinical Psychiatry*, *59*(4), 165–171.

Phillips, K. A., Grant, J., Siniscalchi, J., & Albertini, R. S. (2001). Surgical and nonpsychiatric medical treatment of patients with body dysmorphic disorder. *Psychosomatics*, *42*(6), 504–510.

Phillips, K. A., Gunderson, C. G., Mallya, G., McElroy, S. L., & Carter, W. (1998). A comparison study of body dysmorphic disorder and obsessive-compulsive disorder. *The Journal of Clinical Psychiatry*, *59*(11), 568–575.

Phillips, K. A., & Hollander, E. (2008). Treating body dysmorphic disorder with medication: Evidence, misconceptions, and a suggested approach. *Body Image*, *5*(1), 13–27.

Phillips, K. A., & Kelly, M. M. (2009). Suicidality in a placebo-controlled fluoxetine study of body dysmorphic disorder. *International Clinical Psychopharmacology*, *24*(1), 26–28.

Phillips, K. A., Keshaviah, A., Dougherty, D. D., Stout, R. L., Menard, W., & Wilhelm, S. (2016). Pharmacotherapy relapse prevention in body dysmorphic disorder: A double-blind, placebo-controlled trial. *The American Journal of Psychiatry, 173*(9), 887–895.

Phillips, K. A., McElroy, S. L., Keck, P. E., Pope, H. G., & Hudson, J. I. (1993). Body dysmorphic disorder: 30 cases of imagined ugliness. *The American Journal of Psychiatry, 150*, 302–308.

Phillips, K. A., Menard, W., & Fay, C. (2006). Gender similarities and differences in 200 individuals with body dysmorphic disorder. *Comprehensive Psychiatry, 47*(2), 77–87.

Phillips, K. A., Menard, W., Fay, C., & Pagano, M. E. (2005). Psychosocial functioning and quality of life in body dysmorphic disorder. *Comprehensive Psychiatry, 46*(4), 254–260.

Phillips, K. A., Menard, W., Fay, C., & Weisberg, R. (2005). Demographic characteristics, phenomenology, comorbidity, and family history in 200 individuals with body dysmorphic disorder. *Psychosomatics, 46*(4), 317–325.

Phillips, K. A., & Najjar, F. (2003). An open-label study of citalopram in body dysmorphic disorder. *The Journal of Clinical Psychiatry, 64*(6), 715–720.

Phillips, K. A., Pagano, M. E., & Menard, W. (2006). Pharmacotherapy for body dysmorphic disorder: Treatment received and illness severity. *Annals of Clinical Psychiatry, 18*(4), 251–257.

Phillips, K. A., Pagano, M. E., Menard, W., & Stout, R. L. (2006). A 12-month follow-up study of the course of body dysmorphic disorder. *The American Journal of Psychiatry, 163*(5), 907–912.

Phillips, K. A., Pinto, A., Hart, A. S., Coles, M. E., Eisen, J. L., Menard, W., & Rasmussen, S. A. (2012). A comparison of insight in body dysmorphic disorder and obsessive-compulsive disorder. *Journal of Psychiatric Research, 46*(10), 1293–1299.

Phillips, K. A., Quinn, G., & Stout, R. L. (2008). Functional impairment in body dysmorphic disorder: A prospective, follow-up study. *Journal of Psychiatric Research, 42*(9), 701–707.

Pope, C. G., Pope, H. G., Menard, W., Fay, C., Olivardia, R., & Phillips, K. A. (2005). Clinical features of muscle dysmorphia among males with body dysmorphic disorder. *Body Image, 2*(4), 395–400.

Rauch, S. L., Phillips, K. A., Segal, E., Makris, N., Shin, L. M., Whalen, P. J., Jenike, M. A., Caviness, V. S., Jr., & Kennedy, D. N. (2003). A preliminary morphometric magnetic resonance imaging study of regional brain volumes in body dysmorphic disorder. *Psychiatry Research, 122*(1), 13–19.

Richter, M. A., Tharmalingam, S., Burroughs, E., King, N. A., Menard, W. E., Kennedy, J. L., & Phillips, K. A. (2004, December). *A preliminary genetic investigation of the relationship between body dysmorphic disorder and OCD* [Paper presentation]. American College of Neuropsychopharmacology Annual Meeting, San Juan, Puerto Rico.

Rief, W., Buhlmann, U., Wilhelm, S., Borkenhagen, A. D. A., & Brähler, E. (2006). The prevalence of body dysmorphic disorder: A population-based survey. *Psychological Medicine, 36*(6), 877–885.

Rosen, J. C., Reiter, J., & Orosan, P. (1995). Cognitive-behavioral body image therapy for body dysmorphic disorder. *Journal of Consulting and Clinical Psychology, 63*(2), 263–269.

Salib, E. A. (1988). Subacute sclerosing panencephalitis (SSPE) presenting at the age of 21 as a schizophrenia-like state with bizarre dysmorphophobic features. *The British Journal of Psychiatry, 152*, 709–710.

Sarwer, D. B., & Crerand, C. E. (2008). Body dysmorphic disorder and appearance enhancing medical treatments. *Body Image, 5*(1), 50–58.

Saxena, S., & Feusner, J. D. (2006). Toward a neurobiology of body dysmorphic disorder. *Primary Psychiatry, 13*(7), 41–48.

Schieber, K., Kollei, I., de Zwaan, M., & Martin, A. (2015). Classification of body dysmorphic disorder—What is the advantage of the new DSM-5 criteria? *Journal of Psychosomatic Research, 78*(3), 223–227.

Simmons, R. A., & Phillips, K. A. (2017). Core clinical features of body dysmorphic disorder: Appearance preoccupations, negative emotions, core beliefs, and repetitive and avoidance behaviors. In K. A. Phillips (Ed.), *Body dysmorphic disorder: Advances in research and clinical practice* (pp. 61–80). Oxford University Press.

Simpson, H. B., Foa, E. B., Liebowitz, M. R., Ledley, D. R., Huppert, J. D., Cahill, S., Vermes, D., Schmidt, A. B., Hembree, E., & Franklin, M. (2008). A randomized, controlled trial of cognitive-behavioral therapy for augmenting pharmacotherapy in obsessive-compulsive disorder. *The American Journal of Psychiatry, 165*(5), 621–630.

Simpson H. B., & Liebowitz M. R. (2005). Combining pharmacotherapy and cognitive-behavioral therapy in the treatment of OCD. In J. S. Abramowitz & A. C. Houts (Eds.), *Concepts and controversies in obsessive-compulsive disorder* (pp. 359–376). Springer.

Sreshta, N., Pope, H. G., Hudson, J. I., & Kanayama, G. (2017). Muscle dysmorphia. In K. A. Phillips (Ed.), *Body dysmorphic disorder: Advances in research and clinical practice* (pp. 81–93). Oxford University Press.

Summers, B. J., & Cougle, J. R. (2016). Modifying interpretation biases in body dysmorphic disorder: Evaluation of a brief computerized treatment. *Behaviour Research and Therapy, 87*, 117–127.

Summers, B. J., & Cougle, J. R. (2018). An experimental test of the role of appearance-related safety behaviors in body dysmorphic disorder, social anxiety, and body dissatisfaction. *Journal of Abnormal Psychology, 127*(8), 770–780.

Summers, B. J., Schwartzberg, A. C., & Wilhelm, S. (2021). A virtual reality study of cognitive biases in body dysmorphic disorder. *Journal of Abnormal Psychology, 130*(1), 26–33.

Suzuki, K., Takei, N., Kawai, M., Minabe, Y., & Mori, N. (2003). Is taijin kyofusho a culture-bound syndrome? *The American Journal of Psychiatry, 160*(7), 1358.

Tasios, K., & Michopoulos, I. (2017). Body dysmorphic disorder: Latest neuroanatomical and neuropsychological findings. *Psychiatrike = Psychiatriki, 28*(3), 242–250.

Tignol, J., Biraben-Gotzamanis, L., Martin-Guehl, C., Grabot, D., & Aouizerate, B. (2007). Body dysmorphic disorder and cosmetic surgery: Evolution of 24 subjects with a minimal defect in appearance 5 years after their request for cosmetic surgery. *European Psychiatry, 22*(8), 520–524.

Veale, D., Anson, M., Miles, S., Pieta, M., Costa, A., & Ellison, N. (2014). Efficacy of cognitive behaviour therapy versus anxiety management for body dysmorphic disorder: A randomised controlled trial. *Psychotherapy and Psychosomatics, 83*(6), 341–353.

Veale, D., Boocock, A., Gournay, K., Dryden, W., Shah, F., Willson, R., & Walburn, J. (1996). Body dysmorphic disorder: A survey of fifty cases. *The British Journal of Psychiatry, 169*(2), 196–201.

Veale, D., Gournay, K., Dryden, W., Boocock, A., Shah, F., Willson, R., & Walburn, J. (1996). Body dysmorphic disorder: A cognitive behavioural model and pilot randomised controlled trial. *Behaviour Research and Therapy, 34*(9), 717–729.

Vulink, N. C., Planting, R. S., Figee, M., Booij, J., & Denys, D. (2016). Reduced striatal dopamine D2/3 receptor availability in body dysmorphic disorder. *European Neuropsychopharmacology, 26*(2), 350–356.

Wilhelm, S. (2006). *Feeling good about the way you look: A program for overcoming body image problems*. Guilford.

Wilhelm, S., Buhlmann, U., Hayward, L. C., Greenberg, J. L., & Dimaite, R. (2010). A cognitive-behavioral treatment approach for body dysmorphic disorder. *Cognitive and Behavioral Practice, 17*(3), 241–247.

Wilhelm, S., Otto, M. W., Lohr, B., & Deckersbach, T. (1999). Cognitive behavior group therapy for body dysmorphic disorder: A case series. *Behaviour Research and Therapy, 37*(1), 71–75.

Wilhelm, S., Phillips, K. A., Didie, E., Buhlmann, U., Greenberg, J. L., Fama, J. M., Keshaviah, A., & Steketee, G. (2014). Modular cognitive-behavioral therapy for body dysmorphic disorder: A randomized controlled trial. *Behavior Therapy, 45*(3), 314–327.

Wilhelm, S., Phillips, K. A., Fama, J. M., Greenberg, J. L., & Steketee, G. (2011). Modular cognitive-behavioral therapy for body dysmorphic disorder. *Behavior Therapy, 42*(4), 624–633.

Wilhelm, S., Phillips, K. A., Greenberg, J. L., O'Keefe, S. M., Hoeppner, S. S., Keshaviah, A., Sarvode-Mothi, S., & Schoenfeld, D. A. (2019). Efficacy and posttreatment effects of therapist-delivered cognitive behavioral therapy vs supportive psychotherapy for adults with body dysmorphic disorder: A randomized clinical trial. *JAMA Psychiatry, 76*(4), 363–373.

Wilhelm, S., Phillips, K. A., & Steketee, G. (2013). *Cognitive-behavioral therapy for body dysmorphic disorder: A treatment manual*. Guilford.

Wilhelm, S., Steketee, G., Reilly-Harrington, N. A., Deckersbach, T., Buhlmann, U., & Baer, L. (2005). Effectiveness of cognitive therapy for obsessive-compulsive disorder: An open trial. *Journal of Cognitive Psychotherapy, 19*(2), 173–179.

Wilhelm, S., Weingarden, H., Greenberg, J. L., McCoy, T. H., Ladis, I., Summers, B. J., Matic, A., & Harrison, O. (2020). Development and pilot testing of a cognitive-behavioral therapy digital service for body dysmorphic disorder. *Behavior Therapy, 51*(1), 15–26.

Wilhelm, S., Weingarden, H., Ladis, I., Braddick, V., Shin, J., & Jacobson, N. C. (2020). Cognitive-behavioral therapy in the digital age: Presidential address. *Behavior Therapy, 51*(1), 1–14.

Williams, J., Hadjistavropoulos, T., & Sharpe, D. (2006). A meta-analysis of psychological and pharmacological treatments for body dysmorphic disorder. *Behaviour Research and Therapy, 44*(1), 99–111.

CHAPTER 23
Treatment of Hoarding Disorder

Jessica R. Grisham, Melissa M. Norberg, *and* Keong Yap

Abstract

Hoarding disorder (HD) is a chronic and debilitating psychological disorder with wide ranging negative effects on individuals, their families, and the community. In this chapter we review the current evidence for the use of pharmacological and psychological interventions in HD. Our review showed that cognitive-behavioral interventions are efficacious. However, many gaps and issues exist. In particular, research has not evaluated the efficacy of pharmacological treatments in comparison to control treatments. Furthermore, psychological treatment outcomes are modest and treatment effectiveness is further reduced by high dropout rates. Recent studies evaluating modifications to cognitive-behavioral interventions such as incorporating cognitive rehabilitation and exposure/sorting therapy, contingency management, community services such as a local fire officer, and the inclusion of student-facilitated in-home sessions show that improvements to outcomes are possible and provide an impetus for large scale clinical trials. We conclude the chapter with a discussion of the challenges that affect treatment outcomes for HD and provide suggestions for future directions in research.

Key Words: hoarding disorder, cognitive-behavioral therapy, intervention, treatment, efficacy

Improving, evaluating, and disseminating effective treatment for hoarding disorder (HD) is an urgent public health priority. HD is a severe, chronic mental illness that worsens with age (Grisham et al., 2006; Tolin, Meunier, et al., 2010) and has an estimated prevalence of 2.5% (Postlethwaite et al., 2019). HD profoundly burdens patients and their family members, neighbors, and, in some cases, their entire community due to unsanitary, unsafe living conditions (Drury et al., 2014; Neave et al., 2017; Tolin et al., 2008) and an increased risk of fire-related death (Bratiotis, 2013; Kysow et al., 2020). Individuals with HD report poor quality of life and significant functional impairment (Ong et al., 2015; Tolin, Das, et al., 2019) and they have a four to elevenfold increase in risk of life-threatening medical conditions (e.g., respiratory diseases, diabetes, heart attack; Kessler et al., 2001; Tolin et al., 2008). Hoarding also negatively affects work engagement and workplace relationships (Mathes et al., 2019), such that HD sufferers report an average of 7.0 work impairment days per month, which is more than individuals with depression, posttraumatic stress disorder (PTSD), arthritis, asthma, and diabetes (Tolin et al., 2008).

Since 2000, the field of hoarding treatment research has grown rapidly as investigators have attempted to address the significant burden associated with this debilitating disorder. Psychological interventions for HD have shown some promise, but treatment outcomes remain modest and inadequate, underscoring the need for continued treatment innovation. This chapter summarizes existing treatment outcome research for HD and highlights opportunities for innovation. To provide a context for interpreting treatment outcomes in the subsequent sections, the discussion begins with a brief description of the Saving Inventory–Revised (Frost et al., 2004), the most commonly used self-report measure of hoarding symptoms and treatment outcome (for additional information regarding this measure and other self-report, interview, and behavioral measures of hoarding and related phenomena, see Chapter 14). The chapter then reviews the current state of the evidence for pharmacological and psychological treatments for HD. The chapter concludes by describing ongoing challenges in hoarding treatment and outlining future directions to address these challenges.

Saving Inventory–Revised

The Saving Inventory–Revised (SI-R) is a 23-item questionnaire with three subscales assessing excessive acquisition of purchased and free items, saving and discarding behaviors, and excessive clutter as a result of these behaviors. The SI-R has been shown to discriminate between individuals with hoarding problems and nonhoarding obsessive-compulsive disorder (OCD) cases and controls (Frost et al., 2004) and to correlate with additional indices of hoarding interference, such as self and observer ratings of clutter in the home (Frost et al., 2004; Tolin et al., 2007b). Research has demonstrated that the SI-R is sensitive to change during individual cognitive-behavioral therapy (CBT; Steketee et al., 2010; Tolin et al., 2007b) and treatment via support groups (Frost et al., 2011). Recent research across the life span has suggested an optimal clinical cutoff score of 39 (Kellman-McFarlane et al., 2019). The SI-R has been translated into at least four different languages, reflecting the applicability of the measure internationally, and it has been validated for older adults (Ayers et al., 2017).

Pharmacological Treatment Outcome Research

Pharmacological approaches to hoarding initially occurred in the context of treatment trials for OCD. In these OCD medication trials, the presence of hoarding symptoms was typically found to be a negative treatment predictor (Black et al., 1998; Bloch et al., 2014; Hazari et al., 2016; Mataix-Cols et al., 1999; Stein et al., 2007; Winsberg et al., 1999). In an open trial of paroxetine and CBT for nondepressed individuals with OCD, nonresponders had significantly higher baseline scores on the hoarding subscale of the Yale-Brown Obsessive-Compulsive Scale (Y-BOCS) Checklist than treatment responders

(Black et al., 1998). Moreover, only 18% of those who reported hoarding symptoms responded to treatment, whereas 67% of patients without prominent hoarding symptoms responded to treatment. Likewise, Mataix-Cols et al. (1999) found that hoarding was the only factor on the Y-BOCS to predict poor serotonin reuptake inhibitor (SRI) treatment outcome, after controlling for baseline symptom severity, across six placebo-controlled treatment trials.

In contrast to the above findings, Saxena et al. (2007) found that individuals with hoarding symptoms responded as well to SRIs as those without hoarding symptoms. Individuals with OCD (N = 79) were treated openly with the SRI paroxetine. Those with hoarding symptoms showed a reduction of 23% on the Y-BOCS score, while non-hoarding patients showed a 24% reduction in symptoms. Although this study provides some limited support for the use of serotonergic medications for hoarding symptoms, the treatment response of both groups was suboptimal. Moreover, individuals with hoarding symptoms were on paroxetine for a significantly greater number of days than were individuals without hoarding symptoms. Finally, it is impossible to determine whether the treatment targeted hoarding symptoms, given that a hoarding-specific outcome measure was not utilized. Overall, a meta-analysis by Bloch and colleagues (2014) concluded that hoarding symptoms that occur within the context of OCD are associated with poor pharmacological treatment outcome.

Few studies have investigated medication treatments specifically for HD since its establishment in the *DSM-5* as a distinct diagnosis, separate from OCD (Piacentino et al., 2019). The previously described trials were conducted on populations with OCD rather than specifically on patients with HD. Pharmacotherapy approaches for HD specifically have included only paroxetine, a selective serotonin reuptake inhibitor (SSRI; Saxena et al., 2007), venlafaxine, a serotonin-norepinephrine reuptake inhibitor (SNRI; Saxena & Sumner, 2014) and extended-release methylphenidate and atomoxetine (stimulants; Grassi et al., 2016; Rodriguez et al., 2013). Although SSRIs are still the most common pharmacotherapy utilized in patients with HD, they have never been studied for HD in a randomized, placebo-controlled trial (Piacentino et al., 2019).

In one of the few studies of pharmacotherapy for HD, Saxena et al. (2014) treated 24 patients with HD with extended-release venlafaxine (i.e., Effexor XR), an SNRI. In the 23 patients who completed treatment, hoarding symptoms improved significantly, with a mean 36% decrease in UCLA Hoarding Severity Scale (UHSS) scores and a mean 32% decrease in SI-R scores. Sixteen of the 23 completers (70%) were classified as responders. Unfortunately, age was negatively correlated with improvement in hoarding symptom severity, suggesting venlafaxine may be less effective in older adults with HD. It is also important to note that the evidence level provided by this study is low due to its nonblind, uncontrolled design and small sample.

Due to some evidence that inattention and impulsivity could represent core aspects of HD, two studies have investigated attention deficit/hyperactivity disorder (ADHD) medications for HD, such as methylphenidate (Rodriguez et al., 2013) and atomoxetine (Grassi et al., 2016). The first study was a case series of methylphenidate used in four patients with HD who were SSRI/SNRI-resistant; the patients reacted well to treatment and showed improvement on the Continuous Performance Test (Rodriguez et al., 2013). However, no randomized controlled trial (RCT) followed this case series, so the evidence again remains limited. In another trial by Grassi and colleagues (2016), eleven patients with HD completed an open trial with the ADHD medication atomoxetine at a flexible dose. Six patients were classified as full responders and three as partial responders on the UHSS. The improvement in hoarding symptoms corresponded with reduced patient disability and increased global functioning. As with previous medication and HD research, however, the Grassi et al. (2016) study was limited by its small sample and lack of a control condition.

In conclusion, because no RCTs have tested the efficacy of pharmacotherapy for HD, evidence regarding medication approaches to HD is limited and should be interpreted with caution (Kress et al., 2016). No medications are currently marketed to treat HD, although there is very preliminary evidence that hoarding symptoms might improve with the use of specific pharmacological interventions (Grassi et al., 2016; Saxena & Sumner, 2014). RCTs of these interventions with large HD samples are necessary before any conclusions may be drawn. Because of HD's high comorbidity rates with other mental health disorders, medication may be useful in treating co-occurring symptoms. However, compliance with medication may be especially challenging for individuals with HD because they are more prone to medication mismanagement given their cluttered living environments. Moreover, individuals with HD might be resistant to medication as a treatment approach. Rodriguez et al. (2016) surveyed 272 participants who self-reported hoarding behaviors regarding the acceptability of currently available treatments and services. The researchers found that SRI treatment was among the least acceptable, with only cleaning and removal services and court-appointed guardians having lower ratings.

Psychological Treatment Outcome Research

A handful of treatment outcome studies for OCD have found that hoarding symptoms are associated with treatment drop-out and poor treatment outcomes (Abramowitz et al., 2003; Mataix-Cols et al., 2002; Rufer et al., 2006). For example, Abramowitz et al. (2003) found that only 31% of individuals with hoarding symptoms evidenced clinically significant change after receiving exposure and response prevention (E/RP) as compared to post-E/RP clinically significant change in 46% to 76% of individuals who experienced other types of obsessions and compulsions. It has been suggested that poor treatment response among those with hoarding problems may be associated with treatment refusal and/or lack of motivation to engage due to poor insight (Christensen & Greist, 2001). However, findings from one study suggest that the poor treatment response exhibited in the early studies may have been due to failure to recognize and treat the very different beliefs associated with hoarding (e.g., saving newspapers because of a fear of missing out on an important opportunity vs. saving objects due to a fear of contamination). When Seaman et al. (2010) used Salkovskis's (1985) cognitive model of OCD to formulate the mechanisms underlying patients hoarding symptoms for the delivery of tailored CBT, treatment outcomes did not differ from those for individuals with other OCD subtypes.

Because of the poor response achieved in the early OCD studies, Steketee and Frost (2007, 2014) developed a specific CBT for HD. The treatment approach was derived from the cognitive-behavioral model, which conceptualizes hoarding as a multifaceted problem that results from information-processing deficits, problems with emotional attachment, rigid beliefs about possessions and saving, and behavioral avoidance (Frost & Hartl, 1996). In the discussion that follows, the key elements of the treatment are summarized: psychoeducation, motivational strategies, skills training, exposure, and cognitive restructuring. Taken together, these cognitive-behavioral strategies are thought to broadly increase self-efficacy, to target maladaptive beliefs, and to reduce behavioral avoidance. (For more detailed descriptions and examples, see the relevant treatment manuals, such as Steketee & Frost (2014), *Treatment for hoarding disorder: Therapist guide*, 2nd edition.)

CBT for Hoarding

The hypothetical case of Stella, a client with HD in her late sixties who currently lives alone, illustrates the main components of standard CBT for hoarding. Stella is a retired school administrator with two adult children. She describes herself as being "on her own" most of the time, and she has few people that she interacts with regularly. She is an avid reader and is also passionate about sewing and other craft projects. Stella has been a collector and self-described "sentimental saver" since adolescence, and she described her mother as exhibiting similar tendencies. Stella's symptoms reached a clinical level after her divorce at age 43. The clutter began to cause her difficulty in navigating her house, and several rooms are now unusable. Stella feels ashamed to have people over, which has contributed to her chronic feelings of loneliness.

Stella has amassed a very large number of books and newspapers, as well as many bits and pieces of miscellaneous craft materials that she has collected and saved over the years for potential projects. She also meets criteria for recurrent major depressive disorder and struggles with the accompanying fatigue. She reports concerns about missing out on items that could be used to create something beautiful, as well as environmental fears about discarding potentially useful items and having them end up in a landfill. Stella primarily acquires items from picking through her neighbors' trash, shopping at art supply and craft stores, buying items online, and visits to local thrift stores. She also has several newspaper and magazine subscriptions.

Psychoeducation and Case Formulation

Treatment begins with psychoeducation, in which clients are provided with information about the cognitive-behavioral model of HD. As part of the psychoeducation process, the therapist works collaboratively with the client to develop a hypothesis about what contributes to the hoarding behavior. A model is built that incorporates potential distal and proximal causes and consequences of the hoarding behavior to identify goals and points of intervention. For example, Stella shared her family history and discussed how her mother's beliefs about avoiding wastefulness and using possessions as repository of memories may have contributed to her own hoarding difficulties. To help identify environmental conditions that affect her behavior, a functional assessment was conducted.

Stella identified triggers for buying episodes by exploring recent events. She reported that she visited a thrift shop after an argument with her sister about her clutter. She identified that her triggering thoughts before buying a large artbook was "I can't let her tell me what to do," "My things are special, not just junk," and "I deserve to buy beautiful things." She also identified that she felt angry. The immediate consequences of finding the book and purchasing it were positive mood and excitement. After identifying the immediate consequences, Stella identified the long-term consequences of buying the book (e.g., adding to the clutter, feeling guilty), The therapist then summarized the model. Collectively, the functional assessment and model help the client to obtain a working knowledge of how their collecting and saving behaviors are maintained. The model and functional assessment may be more detailed in individual treatment, but group treatment for HD also includes clients' working to build a basic conceptual model of their hoarding (Muroff et al., 2014).

Motivation

As previously mentioned, individuals with hoarding problems often fail to see their behavior as problematic (Frost et al., 2010; Grisham et al., 2006), and many patients enter treatment in response to the demands of friends and family members (Chasson et al., 2014). Because individuals are unlikely to change their behavior unless they decide changes are necessary, CBT for HD utilizes the principles of motivational interviewing (MI; Miller & Rollnick, 2002). MI often is used at the beginning of treatment to develop a collaborative relationship and to resolve initial ambivalence and then later in therapy when motivation falters in response to discarding tasks.

MI strategies are used to increase patients' awareness of the consequences experienced and the risks faced as a result of hoarding, while helping patients to imagine a better future, so that they become more motivated to achieve a less cluttered life. The key principles of MI are to express empathy, to develop discrepancy, to roll with resistance, and to support self-efficacy (Miller & Rollnick, 2002). For Stella, the therapist highlighted the discrepancy between her desire to keep all her possessions, which required a great deal of time to organize and manage, and her desire to spend more of her available time working on her art projects (as well as her desire to live a less cluttered life and to spend more time with friends or family). These principles are applied using a variety of strategies, such as imagery, goal-setting, and the decisional balance exercise.

Stella's therapist conducted a clutter visualization task to better understand Stella's motivation for change. In the task, Stella would visualize a cluttered room in her house and determine how much discomfort she felt as a result of that clutter, as well as her associated thoughts (Steketee & Frost, 2014). To perform the clutter visualization task, the therapist asks the client to close her eyes and to imagine turning around in the middle of the chosen room. The client uses a scale from 0 (no discomfort) to 100 (the most discomfort imaginable) to describe her discomfort. This task can be followed by the unclutter visualization task, in which clients visualize the same room devoid of clutter. During a clutter visualization, Stella reported feelings of anxiety, guilt, and shame, mixed with some positive feelings when she envisioned a few of her favorite items, whereas she described feelings of lightness, relief, and freedom during the unclutter visualization. A review of the information presented during these tasks can lead to discussions of potential treatment barriers and goal-setting.

Goal-setting can be a useful tool for increasing patients' motivation when it is combined with an assessment of reasons for change. In the *Buried in Treasures* manual, Tolin, Frost, and Steketee (2007a, 2013) encouraged individuals with HD to write out their goals along with why the goals are important to them. Clients are asked to reflect why they want to work on their hoarding, what will happen if they are successful, and what will happen if they do not change. Stella reported a goal of inviting her adult children over for a dinner, and longer-term plans to travel. Individuals with HD are asked to remember their goals when treatment becomes difficult. Thus, goal-setting can serve as a motivator early in treatment and later on when patients are confronted with decisions to discard.

One way to expose the ambivalence that patients feel about working on clutter is by using the decisional balance exercise (Miller & Rollnick, 2002). A decisional balance is a metaphor for a scale that weighs the pros and cons of discarding. In this exercise, individuals are asked to list all of their motivators to discard on one side of the scale and all of their motivators for acquiring and saving on the other side of the scale. "Benefits of discarding" and "costs of acquiring and saving" make up "motivators to discard," while "benefits of acquiring and saving" and "costs of discarding" form "motivators to acquire and save." If ambivalence is demonstrated, clients can be asked to "tip the scale" in favor of discarding by increasing the number of items on the benefits of discarding side. They may choose to ask their friends, family, group members, and therapist for additional reasons to discard.

Another way to tip the scale is to decrease the weight of the motivators to acquire and save. To do so, clients write down a benefit of acquiring and saving (for Stella, this may be having interesting objects available for future craft projects) and then write a list of problems and costs associated with that benefit (Stella may describe that the clutter prevents her from relaxing on her couch or inviting anyone over). Next, clients write down a positive nonhoarding alternative, followed by a list of reasons why that positive alternative is better. These steps are repeated for each motivator to save and acquire. The decisional balance scale not only can increase motivation, but also can serve to increase insight and to improve problem-solving skills.

Skills Training

Individuals with hoarding problems often display skills deficits, such as difficulties with problem-solving, time-management, and categorization (Frost & Gross, 1993; Steketee et al., 2003; Wincze et al., 2007). Skills training is implemented to address clients' deficits in these areas (Frost & Gross, 1993; Steketee & Frost, 2003; Wincze et al., 2007).

When patients demonstrate difficulties generating solutions to problems, other than avoidance, they may need problem-solving training. This involves teaching patients to follow six simple steps: (1) identify the problem; (2) brainstorm solutions; (3) evaluate the pros and cons of each solution; (4) pick a solution based on the evaluation; (5) implement the solution; and (6) evaluate the outcome. Thus, problem-solving training involves teaching patients to follow simple steps to break down and address the challenges and obstacles related to their hoarding difficulties.

Time-management training may include encouraging patients to record their appointments and tasks in an electronic or paper calendar, prioritizing tasks, getting rid of distractions, and identifying and eliminating "time stealers." When Stella identified that she found it difficult to prioritize time to sort and discard, her therapist helped her to schedule time in her week, preferably when she was most energized and motivated. Organizational training may also involve Stella's preparing for sorting by obtaining storage containers and labels and researching where items will go in and outside of her homes, including recycling agencies, charitable organizations, and trash collection. Skills training for sorting also involves creating an organizational plan that lists categories of saved items (e.g., mail, photos, clothing), locations for storing the saved items, and rules for letting go. Usually, clients with HD are also advised to follow the rule of three and the "only handle it once" rule (OHIO). The rule of three requires them to discard an item if they have more than three of the same item, and OHIO specifies that items should not be sorted more than once.

A common obstacle observed in hoarding treatment is that patients are unable to complete their homework assignments (Steketee & Frost, 2007, 2014). Sometimes, clients report to the therapist that they forgot that they had a homework assignment, and other times they report not having enough time to complete it. If the former occurs, the therapist may suggest that the client use the problem-solving steps to generate solutions; however, if the latter occurs, the therapist may find it necessary to implement time-management training. Besides encouraging patients to record all of their appointments and tasks in an electronic calendar or a daily planner, therapists also may need to instruct patients to set aside a specific time of day to plan their activities and to record them into their planners. Other time-management training may include making lists, breaking complex tasks down into smaller, more manageable tasks, prioritizing tasks, getting rid of distractions, and identifying and eliminating time stealers.

Imaginal and In Vivo Exposure

Discarding exposures are aimed at reducing the avoidance associated with fears about making wrong decisions, losing information, having a poor memory, loss, and embarrassment. They are carried out as a way to overcome fear and discomfort via the process of habituation (Steketee & Frost, 2014). Imaginal exposures may be used when patients are too fearful to begin sorting and discarding. During imaginal exposures, clients are asked to close their eyes and imagine their feared situation with as many sensory and visual details as possible. Therapists inquire about the thoughts and feelings associated with the situation and encourage the client to think about the worst possible aspect of the situation.

Because exposures are aimed at reducing avoidance, therapists should review with their clients how avoidance serves to maintain their hoarding behaviors and explain how exposure works to lessen their fears through the process of habituation and hypothesis testing. Exposure assignments should be tailored to target the patients' specific avoidance behaviors. For example, Stella reported that she avoids noticing the clutter in her home so that she can maintain a positive mood; for her, a relevant exposure would be to go home and examine the clutter.

In discarding exposures, the number of outcomes should be limited to two: save or discard. Once a decision has been made, the item should be placed where it belongs according to the organizational plan that was developed. Therapists can assist in discarding exposures by asking challenging questions, such as "Do you really need it?"; "If you do not keep this, will you suffer financially or physically?"; "Do you have a specific plan for this item and will you use it within a reasonable time frame?"; and "Will getting rid of this help you solve your hoarding problem?" After a few exposures have been completed, clients are asked to identify which questions facilitated their decision-making and to write them down on a note card to be used when completing discarding exposures as homework. As therapy progresses, clients are encouraged to abandon the note card and to generate the questions from memory. An alternative, particularly for clients who react defensively to the challenging questions, is to ask them to simply list their thoughts out loud during the decision-making process. Thought listing may be helpful in reducing object attachment and the distress associated with discarding by creating psychological distance from hoarding-related beliefs (Frost et al. 2016).

In addition to increasing motivation (i.e., clutter and unclutter visualization tasks), imaginal exposures can be used when patients are too fearful to begin sorting and discarding. During imaginal exposures, clients describe the situation in the first person and provide sensory and visual details to make the image as clear as possible. Therapists should inquire about the thoughts and feelings associated with the situation and encourage the client to think about the worst possible aspect of the situation. Discomfort ratings can be taken every five to ten minutes until the client's peak discomfort has decreased by half. When this occurs, the imaginal exposure can be discontinued and then a plan to conduct an in vivo exposure can be made.

Nonacquiring exposures are included to address clients' urges to acquire. In a nonacquiring exposure, the client must identify places in which they have experienced difficulties resisting urges to acquire. Stella identified some of her favourite thrift stores and then completed "nonshopping" exposures, progressing from driving or walking by places where she typically acquires to browsing and picking up desirable items without acquiring them (Frost & Steketee, 1999). When possible, nonacquiring exposures that are expected to be extremely challenging for clients should be done in the presence of the therapist. In the early stages of the nonacquiring exposures, clients should leave their money at home; however, when patients gain experience, they should incorporate bringing money into the exposures.

Cognitive Strategies

Erroneous beliefs about control, responsibility, and memory are proposed to contribute to HD (Kyrios et al., 2018; Steketee et al., 2003). Thus, several strategies are used to identify and challenge maladaptive thoughts, including psychoeducation about problematic thoughts, thought records, and the downward arrow. Psychoeducation about thoughts involves reviewing a list of problematic thinking styles associated with compulsive hoarding, such as all-or-nothing thinking, overgeneralization, and jumping to conclusions. Stella reported her automatic thoughts as, "If I can't figure out the perfect place for this, I should just leave it here," "I will never find this if I move it," and "My sister only offered to help me clean up because she thinks I'm inadequate and plans to throw away everything I own."

Thought records help patients identify the connection between triggering events, automatic thoughts, emotions, and behavior. To create a thought record, four columns are drawn on a paper and are labeled Situation, Emotions, Automatic Thoughts, and Behavior. When a hoarding-relevant event occurs, patients use the thought record to write down the event, the thoughts they experienced in that situation, how they felt, and what they did. Once clients become adept at noticing their automatic thoughts and resultant emotions and behaviors, they can then challenge their thoughts by adding a fifth column, Alternative Beliefs. Alternative beliefs can be generated by asking a series of questions that cause patients to look at the evidence for and against an automatic thought.

Another way to train clients how to challenge their hoarding-related beliefs is by using the downward arrow technique. The downward arrow method uses Socratic questioning to explore catastrophic fears associated with hoarding. The purpose of the technique is to identify core beliefs that underlie hoarding behaviors. Typical questions asked during the technique include, "In thinking about getting rid of this item, what thoughts occur to you?" "If you got rid of this item, what do you think would happen?" "If this were true, why would it be so upsetting?" "If that were true, what's so bad about that?" "What's the worst part about that?" Finally, "What does that mean about you?" Once core beliefs are discovered, they can be examined and challenged.

The thinking styles of overgeneralization and emotional reasoning can strengthen the importance of possessions to such a point that it seems essential to save them. In order for patients to determine the true value of a possession, they must distinguish between what they truly need from what they simply want. The Needs versus Wants Scales can assist in making this decision. The form initially asks patients to rate their need and desire for a specific item. Patients are then asked a series of questions to reflect on the importance of, and need for, the item. Such questions include, "Would you die without the item?" and "Do you have to have this for your work?" Clients are then asked to rate their need for the item again. They are then asked a second series of questions that target want, such as "Are you keeping this item for sentimental reasons?" and "Is this the best way to remember?" Clients are asked for a final rating of their need for the item and then are instructed to reflect on what they learned from the exercise.

Finally, behavioral experiments can serve as a powerful strategy for testing the specific beliefs that support clients' hoarding. To conduct a behavioral experiment, clients write down the context of the situation, their specific hypothesis of what will happen with discarding, and their anticipatory discomfort. They then conduct the experiment and write down what actually happened and their actual discomfort. They then state whether their hypothesis was supported. For example, Stella kept her possessions in sight so that she did not forget about them; a relevant exposure was for her to put several items out of sight and then periodically to assess whether she still remembered them.

Relapse Prevention

Relapse prevention is designed to help individuals with HD to continue to make progress and to manage current and future stressors without reverting to hoarding behaviors. Relapse prevention begins with a review of the cognitive-behavioral model of hoarding, followed by a review of the various skills that have been enhanced throughout the course of treatment. Those skills that have been most helpful for a particular patient are emphasized. In order to foster self-efficacy, clients' accomplishments are highlighted. Taking "after" photos of the areas of the home in which patients have worked can facilitate this (Saxena & Maidment, 2004). If "before" pictures were taken during the assessment phase, patients can appreciate the improvement they have made and be reminded about the benefit of their hard work.

Finally, a review of the ups and downs of treatment can assist clients in developing realistic expectations of what the future might entail. This can lead to a discussion of their strengths and weaknesses. Clients can be asked to generate their own strategies to overcome any weaknesses by using the six problem-solving steps they learned during therapy. Therapists should also ask clients to reflect on the entire course of therapy and to describe what they have learned, what they still need to work on, and their new goals.

Psychological Treatment Outcomes

In 2007, Tolin et al. (2007b) published the first open trial exploring the utility of a hoarding-specific treatment (Steketee & Frost, 2007).[1] Fourteen participants were offered 26 individual treatment sessions, with 25% of the sessions to be conducted within the participant's home. Ten participants completed treatment, and they evidenced an average 28% reduction in their hoarding severity from before to after treatment. Sixty percent of participants were deemed to have met criteria for clinically significant change (Tolin et al., 2007b) based on Criterion B and the two-step procedure described by Jacobson and Truax (1991). This was defined as a posttreatment SI-R score that was within two standard deviations of the SI-R nonclinical mean (50 or less) and a change in SI-R scores that was greater than the reliable change index (a change of 14 points or more). A later RCT of the treatment also supported its use for HD (Steketee et al., 2010). When mid-treatment response was compared to 12-week wait-list data, participants who received individual CBT for HD evidenced a 15% reduction in their hoarding symptoms, whereas wait-list control participants evidenced a 2% reduction. A 27% reduction in hoarding symptoms was evidenced in pre- to posttreatment data for all participants (including wait-list control participants who received delayed treatment). Forty-one percent of treatment completers evidenced clinically significant change (Steketee et al., 2010), and gains were maintained at one-year follow-up (Muroff et al., 2014).

Muroff et al. (2009) examined whether treatment was effective when delivered in a group setting. Groups met once weekly for two hours for 16 ($N = 27$) or 20 ($N = 5$) weeks, and participants were offered two home sessions. At posttreatment evaluation, participants had reduced their hoarding severity by 14% on average, but their maladaptive beliefs about possessions had not improved. When examining data from the final group only, which was delivered in a more structured manner, Muroff et al. (2009) found a reduction in hoarding-related beliefs as well as a 22% reduction hoarding severity. Muroff et al. (2012) later compared the group treatment to bibliotherapy and found it was more effective at reducing hoarding symptoms, but not at improving daily functioning in the home.

Gilliam et al. (2011) tested whether group CBT for HD was effective. Treatment was carried out over 16 or 20 sessions and followed a structured approach that included stringent rules regarding attendance, punctuality, and homework compliance. Thirty of 45 participants completed treatment. Modified intent-to-treat analyses showed that participants experienced a 26% reduction in their hoarding severity and a 21% improvement in

---

[1] An early version of the treatment was trialed in a single-subject multiple-baseline study and in a pilot study with seven individuals, with promising results (Hartl & Frost, 1999; Steketee et al., 2000).

their ability to function in their homes. When Jacobson and Truax's Criterion C was used to establish whether a posttreatment SI-R score was clinically significant (i.e., functioning was closer to the mean of the nonclinical population than the clinical population; 42 or less) and a reliable change index of 14 points was applied, 31% of treatment completers met criteria for clinically significant change.

Three other groups of researchers have examined the effectiveness of group CBT for HD based on Steketee and Frost's (2007) manual. Mathews et al. (2016) delivered 16 sessions of group CBT for HD to 41 individuals who self-identified as having hoarding problems. The 31 individuals who provided posttreatment data demonstrated a 15% reduction in their hoarding severity, in conjunction with slight improvements in their maladaptive beliefs about possessions and their ability to function in their homes. Moulding et al. (2017) delivered 12 sessions of group CBT to 77 participants, 41 of whom completed posttreatment assessments. These individuals reduced their hoarding severity by 22% on average and experienced improvements in their maladaptive thoughts about possessions. Twenty-seven percent of participants evidenced clinically significant change.[2] Chandler et al. (2019) evaluated a 11- to 12-session group treatment, which included a visit from an official of the local Fire Office who discussed fire safety. Participants (N =25) decreased their hoarding severity by 34% on average and 35% met criteria for clinically significant change.[3]

Because HD is chronic and progressive and poses substantial risks for older individuals (e.g., falls), researchers have been interested in ensuring that treatment is effective for this population. Weiss et al. (2020) offered 15 sessions of CBT for HD coupled with in-home support to 29 older individuals (M_{age} = 67; SD = 8). Fifty-nine percent of participants dropped out of treatment. The ten remaining individuals evidenced an average 22% reduction in their hoarding severity after treatment. Having less self-control was moderately related to greater hoarding severity after treatment.

In their first trial, Ayers et al. (2011) delivered 26 sessions of individual CBT, following the manual developed by Steketee and Frost (2007), to 12 older adults (M_{age} = 73.77; SD = 6.54). The first 20 sessions were conducted twice weekly, and the final six were conducted weekly to allow for careful monitoring and assistance with homework compliance. Twenty-five percent of sessions occurred in participants' homes. At posttreatment evaluation, three patients (25%) achieved clinically significant change, defined as a 35% reduction on two hoarding severity outcome measures and a score of 3 (minimally improved) or better on the Clinical Global Impression-Improvement (CGI) scale. These three patients had received CBT for HD previously and were more compliant with homework assignments than participants who did not improve. However, all three appeared to relapse by the six-month follow-up. Therapists reported that participants exhibited

---

[2] Using Gilliam et al.'s (2011) two-step criteria for clinically significant change.
[3] Using Gilliam et al.'s (2011) two-step criteria for clinically significant change.

executive functioning problems that contributed to poor treatment compliance, whereas participants noted that cognitive strategies were too abstract and too difficult to follow. They instead appreciated the simplicity of exposure and its ability to teach them that they can tolerate discarding (Ayers et al., 2012).

As a result of these findings, Ayers, Saxena, et al. (2014) developed a novel intervention to compensate for executive dysfunction. The intervention, which integrates cognitive rehabilitation with behavior therapy, is called Cognitive Rehabilitation and Exposure/Sorting Therapy (CREST). CREST de-emphasizes the use of cognitive therapy techniques and places more emphasis on strengthening problem-solving, organizational skills, prospective memory, and cognitive flexibility than does Steketee and Frost's (2007) manual. Exposure activities are aimed at promoting habituation to distress caused by discarding and nonacquiring. In the first trial of the treatment, Ayers et al. (2014) found that eight of 11 participants (72%) met a somewhat more stringent clinically significant change criterion: a 35% reduction on two hoarding severity outcome measures and a score of 2 (much improved) or better on the CGI scale.

In a later RCT, Ayers, Dozier, Twamley, et al. (2018) found that participants who received CREST ($N = 31$) achieved better outcomes than individuals receiving case management ($N = 27$).[4] On average, CREST participants reduced their hoarding symptoms by 38% and improved their daily life functioning in the home by 32%, whereas case-management participants reduced their hoarding symptoms by 25% and improved their daily functioning by 13%. Compared to case-management participants, after treatment, CREST participants were more likely to achieve a score of 1 or 2 on the CGI scale (78% vs. 28%) and to score below 41 on the SI-R or below 4 on the Clutter Image Rating (CIR) scale (88% vs 50%). CREST participants also evidenced greater improvements in cognitive flexibility and task switching, skills required for making decisions about possessions, than did case-management participants (Ayers et al., 2020).

In a nonrandomized study, Ayers, Dozier, Taylor, et al. (2018) delivered CREST in a group format and compared it to exposure therapy alone; they found that CREST participants fared slightly better than exposure-only participants. With the same criteria for recovery as Ayers, Dozier, Twamley, et al. (2018) used, 32% of CREST participants were classified as treatment responders on the SI-R (vs. 26% of exposure participants), 68% were classified as treatment responders on the CIR scale (vs. 51% of exposure participants), and 44% were classified as treatment responders on the CGI scale (vs. 34% of exposure participants).

Like Ayers and colleagues, other researchers have invested in improving treatment outcomes by incorporating novel strategies. In the first instance, DiMauro et al. (2014) examined whether cognitive remediation could improve cognitive skills and hoarding

---

[4] Case managers were not allowed to assist with removal of clutter; thus, the version of case management used in this study may or may not reflect case management delivered outside a research trial.

severity in comparison to relaxation training. In both conditions, participants engaged in three 40-minute sessions per week for eight weeks. Individuals in the cognitive remediation condition completed drill-and-practice computerized cognitive exercises to improve aspects of attention, memory, and executive functioning, whereas those in the relaxation condition listened to and followed meditation, relaxation, and stress-reduction CDs and DVDs. Neither condition led to improvements in memory, executive functioning, or hoarding severity, but the cognitive remediation condition was associated with an improvement in attention.

In another trial, St-Pierre-Delorme and O'Connor (2016) examined the usefulness of virtual reality-enhanced inference-based treatment. Inference-based treatment aims to help individuals recognize obsessional doubt and its illusory and selective nature and to become tolerant of the void when safety behaviors are resisted. After receiving 24 sessions of group inference-based treatment, participants received five individual sessions of virtual reality treatment. In the experimental condition, participants created a virtual environment that resembled their homes and then sorted and discarded objects that were pictures of items from their actual homes. In the control condition, also in a virtual environment, participants sorted and discarded objects that did not belong to them. The experimental and control participants did not differ in hoarding severity at the end of the treatment, but both evidenced statistically significant reductions (6% to 13%) from before treatment.

O'Connor et al. (2018) trialed 20 weeks of group CBT for HD that additionally targeted self-identity. The new components aimed to increase participants' understanding of how identity motives are linked to hoarding and to empower participants' sense of self so that they would not rely on possessions to create an illusory self. Thirteen percent (2 of 16) of participants evidenced clinically significant change immediately after the intervention, and this increased to 32% at a six-month follow-up.[5]

To overcome low intrinsic motivation and treatment compliance among clients with HD, Worden et al. (2017) added contingency management to standard CBT for HD and tested its effects with 14 individuals. Participants received $30 for each 1-point reduction on the CIR scale and $10 for each 1-point reduction maintained from the previous rating; ratings were made by independent evaluators every four weeks for 16 weeks. Twenty-nine percent of participants dropped out of treatment. Average hoarding severity reduction was 32%. Using less stringent criteria (i.e., a reliable change index of 11.76 points), 67% of the nine individuals who completed the SI-R after treatment met criteria for clinically significant change.

Tolin, Wootton, et al. (2019) then reconfigured CBT for HD to also include contingency management, a virtual store for nonacquiring practice, and instruction in

---

[5] Using Gilliam et al.'s (2011) two-step criteria for clinically significant change.

mindfulness-based skills for acceptance and tolerance of negative emotions. They evaluated the 16-week protocol among 87 individuals, randomly assigning half of the individuals to a wait-list control condition. Thirty-three percent of individuals dropped out of treatment prematurely. Individuals who received the revamped CBT for HD reduced their hoarding severity by 30%, whereas the wait-list control group reduced it by 4%. Forty-two percent of the treatment group fell below a score of 43 on the SI-R after treatment, but the authors did not report how many of these individuals changed by a reliable amount from before treatment. Maladaptive beliefs about cognitions partially mediated treatment outcomes.

One other attempt has been made to target the emotional dysregulation associated with HD. Chou et al. (2020) developed a 16-session compassion-focused group treatment for HD that attempts to de-shame individuals, promote treatment goals that will lead to a better life, and increase emotional awareness and regulation. To achieve these aims, participants are taught that hoarding exists on a continuum and that no one is to blame, and participants engage in imagery, mindfulness, and compassion exercises, such as enacting different parts of the self through chair work. Individuals who had previously received group CBT were non-randomly assigned to receive either compassion-focused treatment or a second round of CBT for HD. Among treatment completers, 62% of those assigned to compassion-focused therapy achieved a 14-point or greater reduction on the SI-R, compared to 29% of those who received CBT for HD a second time. Participants in both groups evidenced improvements in decision-making and reductions in shame, but only participants assigned to compassion-focused treatment evidenced reductions in self-criticism and improved their ability to tolerate distress and to provide self-assurance when things go wrong.

Treatment Provided by Nonprofessionals
Steketee and Frost's (2007) therapist guide has also been adapted into a highly structured self-help book, *Buried in Treasures* (Tolin et al., 2007a; Tolin et al., 2014). Frost et al. (2011) examined whether nonprofessionals can use the book to facilitate support groups that reduce hoarding symptoms. In the first study, undergraduates who had read the self-help book and had taken a senior seminar focused on hoarding behavior facilitated the support groups. After 13 sessions, participants reported reductions in their hoarding severity (25% on average) and maladaptive beliefs about possessions, as well as improvement in their ability to carry out daily activities in the home. Frost et al. (2011) noted that 59% of participants met criteria for clinically significant change one month after treatment ceased, but they did not report the specific criteria used to derive this figure. These results were replicated in a second study and were confirmed by ratings from an independent observer. Next, Frost et al. (2012) compared the effectiveness of this approach to a wait-list control group. In this trial, the support group was led by a peer support coordinator who suffered from hoarding problems himself. Treatment completers evidenced statistically significant

changes in hoarding severity (31% on average), maladaptive thoughts, and activities of daily living, while the wait-list control did not. Thirty percent of treatment completers met criteria for clinically significant change.[6]

Mathews et al. have also been interested in exploring the utility of peer-facilitated support for HD. In the first trial, 20 individuals who self-identified with hoarding problems reported an average 28% reduction in their hoarding severity (Mathews et al., 2016). A later non-inferiority trial randomized 323 individuals to 15 weeks of peer support that was guided by *Buried in Treasures* (Tolin et al., 2007a) or to 16 weeks of psychologist-led group CBT for HD guided by Steketee and Frost's (2007) therapist guide (Mathews et al., 2018). The two treatment groups did not differ in their rates of clinically significant change (33% of CBT for HD participants and 29% of peer-support participants).[7] Improvements in functioning in the home (11%) and drop-out rates also did not differ between the two treatments (29%), but session attendance was higher for group CBT for HD than for peer-facilitated support (73% vs 58%). Some lessening in functional gains was found at the three-month and beyond follow-up for both groups, and only ongoing help from family and/or friends was associated with maintenance of gains. In a follow-up study, both treatments were found to improve visual memory, visual detection, decision-making, information-processing speed, visuospatial processing, and attention/working memory (Zakrzewski et al., 2020).

Adjunctive In-Home Support Provided by Nonprofessionals

Because home sessions are costly and require a substantial time commitment that many therapists are unable to provide, three small studies have examined the potential helpfulness of having students deliver home sessions to individuals receiving CBT for HD. Muroff et al. (2012) had undergraduates deliver four home sessions, Crone et al. (2020) had undergraduates deliver eight home sessions, and Linkovski et al. (2018) had graduates deliver 10 home sessions. Muroff et al. (2012) found 36% of participants evidenced clinically significant change, Linkovski et al. (2018) found 40% did, whereas Crone et al. (2020) found 67% met criteria for clinically significant change.[8] The greater rate of clinically significant change noted in the study by Crone et al. (2020) may have been due to training students how to engage in MI and by requiring them to engage in routine outcome monitoring at each session. Additionally, participants in the Crone et al. (2020) study reported that they were highly satisfied with how much control they felt over the decluttering process, the convenience of the program, and how accepted and motivated their Clutter Buddies made them feel.

---

[6] Using Gilliam et al.'s (2011) two-step criteria for clinically significant change.
[7] Using Gilliam et al.'s (2011) two-step criteria for clinically significant change.
[8] Using Gilliam et al.'s (2011) two-step criteria for clinically significant change.

Online Treatment

Researchers also have tested whether the Internet can be used to improve treatment access and response. Muroff et al. (2010) evaluated an online self-help support group for individuals with hoarding problems and OCD. This program required participants to post behavioral goals, action activities, or progress toward goals at least once per month or they would be removed from the group. Leaders and members provided support in understanding and applying the concepts covered in the Steketee and Frost (2007) manual. The 30 group members who engaged in assessments every three months for 15 months reported a 16% decrease in their hoarding severity. Because members enrolled and unenrolled in the program throughout the study period, it is unclear what proportion of the group completed the assessments (e.g., there were 62 members at Time 1 and 89 members at Time 5). Thus, the results may not be representative of all group members.

Fitzpatrick et al. (2018) examined the potential usefulness of an eight-week online program in providing ongoing, low-cost support to individuals who have received group CBT for HD. The program reinforced ideas presented during group treatment and additionally targeted relaxation, motivation, barriers to continued decluttering, and relapse prevention. Participants could send their e-therapist up to two emails per week. In a small nonrandomized trial, those who received the online program after group CBT reported greater reductions in clutter than those who received only group therapy; however, neither group reported being better able to discard their possessions or having more adaptive thoughts about their possessions. Thus, it is unclear what mechanism led to reduced clutter.

Ivanov et al. (2018) examined whether adding Internet-based clinician support between group CBT sessions might increase engagement and improve outcomes. Group CBT followed the Tolin et al. (2017) manual, whereas the online support system (COMMIT) included a copy of the treatment manual, participants' treatment goals, each week's homework assignment, and questionnaires to monitor treatment progress. Scores were visually depicted on a graph, and participants were encouraged to upload Before and After photos of each decluttering session. Participants were encouraged to email their therapist via COMMIT so that therapists could provide personalized feedback, motivational support, and practical guidance on decluttering. After 16 weeks of treatment, participants' hoarding severity decreased (27% on average), and their maladaptive thoughts about possessions improved, but their health-related quality of life did not. All 20 participants who started treatment completed it; however, one participant missed five consecutive sessions. Each week on average, participants accessed COMMIT for 70 minutes, sent two messages to their therapists, and partially completed their homework. Neither homework compliance nor time spent on COMMIT predicted change on outcome measures.

Special Populations

Kellett et al. (2015) delivered 12 sessions of CBT for HD to 14 adults with an intellectual disability who evidenced problems with clutter. The treatment was adjusted for the population, so that psychoeducation, hoarding formulations, and diary keeping were reduced in amount and complexity and individual sessions were extended from one to two hours. All sessions occurred in people's homes. Hoarding severity decreased by 37% from before to after treatment and by 50% at the six-month follow-up. Notably, pretreatment hoarding severity scores were substantially lower for participants in this sample than for participants in other CBT for HD studies.

Treatment for Family Members
Chasson et al. (2014) developed a 14-session training program that includes psychoeducation, harm-reduction techniques, MI training, and instruction on how to minimize family accommodation. Nine adult family members of a loved one with HD started the program; five of the individuals completed it. These individuals reported that the program helped them. Specifically, the program improved their knowledge of hoarding, their application of MI, and their hopefulness about their family members' hoarding, while reducing their use of unhelpful coping strategies.

Summary
Since Steketee and Frost released their first CBT for HD manual in 2007, several studies have been conducted to examine the treatment's effectiveness, whether it is delivered in an online, group, or individual setting. Researchers have also modified the treatment or developed alternatives in order to improve treatment outcomes. Slightly more promising outcomes have been reported with Ayers et al.'s CREST program, with involvement of a local fire officer, with contingency management, and with use of students to conduct home sessions, but these approaches require further evaluation and replication with larger samples, adequate follow-up periods, and adequate control conditions. Although treatment outcomes have improved, drop-out rates and reductions in hoarding severity as measured by the SI-R are variable, and outcomes overall remain inadequate. In the majority of HD treatment studies, drop-out is still high and only a third of individuals experience clinically significant change. However, it is important to note that cross-study comparisons are difficult because not all studies have reported on individual change and those that have, have often relied on different formulations. Although the most common approach has been to use Gilliam et al.'s (2011) two-step criteria for clinically significant change, Norberg et al. (2021) posit that these criteria are too liberal and suggest that future researchers utilize more stringent criteria for identifying clinically significant change (i.e., SI-R total scores must reduce by at least 20 points and the posttreatment score must be 38 or less).

Challenges and Future Directions

Clinical characteristics common to many patients with HD, including psychiatric comorbidities, interpersonal problems, emotion regulation difficulties, strong object attachment, impaired cognitive functioning, poor insight, lack of motivation for treatment, and health and safety concerns, contribute to the unique challenge of improving effective treatment for this population. Furthermore, individuals who complete research trials have been shown to differ from individuals who receive community support for HD, which calls into question the generalizability of current HD research (Woody et al., 2020).

Improving Treatment Outcomes
COMORBID PSYCHOPATHOLOGY

Individuals with HD report high rates of psychiatric comorbidity (Frost et al., 2011; Ivanov et al., 2020). Approximately 50% of patients with HD have a major depressive disorder diagnosis, and more than 20% have social anxiety and/or generalized anxiety disorder (Frost, Steketee, & Tolin, 2011; Hall et al., 2013). Relatively high rates of attention deficit/hyperactivity disorder, especially inattentive presentations (Tolin & Villavicencio, 2011), impulse control disorders (Frost, Steketee, & Tolin, 2011), and alcohol dependence (Raines et al., 2017; Samuels et al., 2002, 2008) have also been reported. Although HD is now recognized as a separate disorder from OCD, comorbid OCD is still reported in about 20% of patients with HD (Frost, Steketee, & Tolin, 2011). Several studies have also shown an association with a history of interpersonal trauma (Chou, Tsoh, Smith, et al., 2018; Kehoe & Egan, 2019; Landau et al., 2011), although the prevalence of comorbid PTSD is not higher in people with HD than in individuals with anxiety disorders and OCD (Frost, Steketee, & Tolin, 2011).

Interestingly, recent studies examining predictors of treatment response to CBT show that comorbid psychiatric conditions may not substantially impact treatment outcomes. Muroff et al. (2014) found that only comorbid social anxiety predicted treatment response, but not comorbid depression, OCD, or inattention. Likewise, in their meta-analysis, Tolin et al. (2015) found that depression was not a significant moderator of treatment outcomes. Ayers et al. (2019) showed only weak, nonsignificant associations between depression and anxiety severity with treatment response and attrition. It should be noted that not all comorbidities were evaluated in these studies due to either low prevalence (e.g., kleptomania) or exclusion criteria (e.g., substance abuse and psychosis) and further research is needed to examine how such patients respond to HD treatment.

Although patients with HD and comorbid conditions do benefit from CBT, comorbidities may still complicate the clinical picture and interfere with treatment. For example, a patient in one of our HD treatment groups reported severe, lifelong OCD symptoms related to contamination in addition to her collecting and saving behavior. When she participated in sorting and discarding tasks during therapy and as homework, her contamination concerns made her anxious about handling certain items. She had developed rituals related to these concerns, including wearing rubber gloves and performing a series of elaborate cleaning procedures before and after each sorting task. These OCD-related behaviors considerably impaired her ability to effectively reduce the clutter in her home.

Thus, depending on the specific factors involved, it may be advantageous for some individuals with hoarding difficulties to pursue treatment for comorbid conditions prior to participating in HD treatment. Research is needed to examine whether established treatments for comorbid conditions, such as SSRIs for depression, are effective in preparing patients for HD treatment. Alternatively, it may be beneficial to address the underlying cognitive and emotional mechanisms that underpin both HD and comorbid disorders.

COGNITIVE AND EMOTIONAL MECHANISMS

Disorder-specific and transdiagnostic processes may play a more important role in predicting hoarding severity and treatment outcomes than comorbidities. Higher levels of avoidant coping (Ayers et al., 2019) and perfectionism (Muroff et al., 2014) were the strongest predictors of treatment response. Maladaptive beliefs about possessions (but not perceived cognitive impairment) mediated treatment response to group CBT (Tolin, Wootton, et al., 2019). Other transdiagnostic factors affecting HD include distress intolerance (Grisham, Roberts, et al., 2018; Worden et al., 2019), intolerance of uncertainty (Burgess et al., 2018; Castriotta et al., 2019), emotion regulation difficulties (Taylor et al., 2018; Tolin et al., 2018; Worden et al., 2019), psychological inflexibility (Carbonella & Timpano, 2016; Krafft et al., 2019; Ong et al., 2018), behavioral avoidance (Ayers, Castriotta, et al., 2014; Wheaton et al., 2013), interpersonal processes (David et al., 2020; Grisham, Martyn, et al., 2018; Yap et al., 2020), insecure attachment (Mathes et al., 2020; Neave et al., 2016; Norberg et al., 2018; Yap & Grisham, 2019, 2020), self-ambivalence (Frost et al., 2007; Kings et al., 2017; Moulding et al., 2016), and self-criticism and shame (Chou, Tsoh, Vigil, et al., 2018; Chou et al., 2020). Modifications to current HD treatment to address these underlying mechanisms could lead to improvements in treatment outcomes. Consistent with this proposition, a recent naturalistic study of CBT for HD enhanced with a transdiagnostic emotion regulation module found a low rate of attrition and a high proportion of clients achieving clinically significant change (Grisham et al., 2022).

Given the efficacy of transdiagnostic interventions for other psychological disorders (Ferrari et al., 2019; Sakiris & Berle, 2019), it is possible that transdiagnostic interventions, such as compassion-focused therapy, dialectical behavior therapy, or acceptance and commitment therpy (Chou et al., 2020; Eppingstall et al., 2020; Hayes et al., 2012), could be used to target hoarding symptoms. However, to date, no RCTs using transdiagnostic interventions for HD, apart from the study by Chou et al. (2020), have been conducted. Given the unique challenges associated with hoarding symptoms, these interventions will need to be modified to directly address hoarding behaviors. However, it could be helpful to use these treatments in their current form to improve transdiagnostic processes that may help ready participants for hoarding-specific treatment. Alternatively, a staged approach could be investigated in which the treatments are provided only if an individual does not benefit from hoarding-specific treatment, such as was done by Chou et al. (2020). Addressing transdiagnostic processes presents an opportunity to improve current HD interventions. Further research is needed to examine which transdiagnostic approaches should be integrated into HD treatment.

ETIOLOGIC HETEROGENEITY

As with most psychological disorders, a wide range of etiologic factors have been reported in HD, including traumatic life events, attachment issues, emotional dysregulation, genetics, and neurocognitive factors (Dozier & Ayers, 2017; Hombali et al., 2019; Kyrios et al., 2018). The development of HD and HD-related beliefs probably requires a combination of etiologic factors, but it is also likely that there is heterogeneity in etiology such that different combinations of factors result in similar HD presentations, reflecting an equifinality with multiple developmental pathways (Cicchetti & Rogosch, 1996). One individual could develop HD due to a genetic predisposition, attentional deficits, and decision-making difficulties, while another individual could develop HD due to early interpersonal trauma, attachment issues, and emotion dysregulation. Thus, in addition to addressing disorder-specific and transdiagnostic processes, improving treatments may require a consideration of etiologic factors that are unique to the individual.

SUBTYPES AND RELATED CONDITIONS

There is also some heterogeneity in the presentation of hoarding symptoms but a lack of research into treatments for the less common symptom subtypes, such as animal hoarding (Dozier et al., 2019; Ung et al., 2016), hoarding with squalor (Luu et al., 2018), and hoarding-related conditions that result in significant functional impairment but do not fulfill HD criteria, such as excessive collecting (Nordsletten & Mataix-Cols, 2012) and hoarding without clutter (e.g., through the excessive use of storage facilities). The limited research into treatments for these symptom presentations may be due to low prevalence or poor insight, causing difficulties in study recruitment.

GENERALIZABILITY

Another pressing problem related to heterogeneity is the question of the generalizability of HD research findings. Woody et al. (2020) recently found significant differences between community clients and the typical HD research participant. Specifically, compared to the community clients, participants in HD research tended to be female, were younger, were more likely to be married, had higher socioeconomic status, had better insight, and had lower levels of clutter and squalor. Unfortunately, some factors also predict poor treatment outcomes, including male gender (Tolin et al. 2015; Muroff et al., 2014) and older age (Tolin et al., 2015). Ayer et al. (2019) also found that poor insight and clutter significantly affected attrition rates, although demographic characteristics did not significantly affect symptom improvement, possibly because their intervention was designed for older adults.

BEYOND RCTS

Due to issues of heterogeneity, improving treatment outcomes may require more than just the typical RCT that only evaluates the efficacy of treatment packages. Mediators and moderators of treatment outcomes (Ayers et al., 2019; Muroff et al., 2014; Tolin et al., 2019) and dismantling studies are needed to provide evidence of which processes need to be addressed in HD treatments. In line with a process-based approach (Hayes et al., 2019), more studies using single-case research designs are also needed to examine the effectiveness of interventions for some symptom subtypes and demographic groups that are harder to recruit for large-scale RCTs (Kazdin, 2019). Furthermore, single-case research designs allow for the testing of individualized treatment approaches and elucidating the role of underlying cognitive and emotional mechanisms and etiological factors (Bentley et al., 2019; Thompson et al., 2020).

ROUTINE OUTCOME MONITORING

Another potential future direction in hoarding assessment and treatment is routine outcome monitoring. Because many individuals do not adequately respond to treatment for HD, waiting until the end of treatment to evaluate outcomes prevents clients from benefiting from the assessment. Patient-focused research, on the other hand, involves regularly monitoring and tracking an individual's treatment response so that clinicians can use this information to shift treatment in a manner that may facilitate client improvement (Harmon et al., 2005). Effective feedback requires that the discrepancy between what is thought to be happening and what is truly happening be brought into awareness, so that it can stimulate corrective action (Macdonald & Mellor-Clark, 2015). A meta-analysis of the effects of routine outcome monitoring found that, in general, clients who engage in routine outcome monitoring have 2.6 to 3.5 times higher odds of experiencing reliable change, while having about half the odds of experiencing deterioration (Lambert & Shimokawa, 2011).

To date, two hoarding trials have utilized routine outcome monitoring. In Clutter-Buddies (Crone et al., 2020), undergraduate volunteers asked participants ($N = 6$) to complete the SI-R at the beginning of each home session. At the first session, participants viewed a graph that displayed the clinical cutoff score and the average nonclinical score of the SI-R, and then they set a goal score. At each session, participants' new SI-R scores were added to their graphs, which facilitated a discussion of participant progress. This pilot program was highly successful overall (67% of participants evidenced clinically significant change) and participants reported that the weekly tracking of their progress was one of the most useful elements. In the second trial, routine outcome monitoring was conducted through an online program (Ivanov et al., 2018). The online support system did not influence CBT group outcomes, which may suggest that routine outcome monitoring is more effective when provided in person. Until future research bears this out, researchers and clinicians may consider routine monitoring of individuals' treatment progress given the existing evidence for these interventions outside of the hoarding field.

Improving Treatment Engagement, Retention, and Access

The effectiveness of an efficacious treatment is limited by the extent to which a treatment is feasible, acceptable, and accessible. Challenges to the effective implementation of HD treatment include poor insight and motivation among patients with HD, health and safety concerns, and the lack of treatment dissemination and resources.

INSIGHT AND MOTIVATION

Many patients with HD have poor insight and may not appreciate the severity of their symptoms, or they may seem unaware of how much hoarding has negatively impacted their lives and that of significant others (DiMauro et al., 2013; Frost et al., 2010; Tolin, Fitch, et al., 2010). Further, hoarding behaviors tend to be ego-syntonic (Grisham et al., 2005). Individuals may have overvalued ideation and positive attitudes toward their possessions and hoarding behaviors. For example, they may feel morally obligated to save objects for environmental reasons (Frost et al., 2018) or hold on to possessions that are perceived as integral to their identity (Dozier et al., 2017; Moulding et al., 2021). Some individuals who present for treatment may have been pressured to do so by family members (Drury et al., 2014). Such patients may react with defensiveness, making them prone to skipping sessions, arriving late, and not doing homework. Not surprisingly, poor insight and motivation prevent individuals from accessing treatment and are associated with higher drop-out rates (Ayers et al., 2019). Given the significant role of insight and motivation in treatment outcomes, they should be routinely assessed in research trials to gain a better understanding of which interventions work best for clients with poor insight and motivation.

HEALTH AND SAFETY PROBLEMS

Clinicians who treat patients with HD often encounter specific ethical dilemmas related to the physical condition of the patient's home environment. The accumulation of clutter can lead to unhealthy and unsafe living environments (Bratiotis et al., 2011; Snowdon et al., 2007). For example, a staircase filled with objects creates a risk of falling, a heater surrounded by objects is a fire hazard, and an excessively unkempt house leads to exposure to dust pollen and bacteria, which can have deleterious health effects. In addition, the accumulation of urine and feces from animal hoarding poses risks for the animals themselves and can damage the structure of home, threatening the health and safety of the individual and those living nearby (Patronek & Nathanson, 2016).

When there are health and safety concerns, it is essential for therapists to discuss these issues with clients while still respecting their clients' autonomy. However, depending on the local laws, therapists may be required to intervene to protect the individual and those living nearby. Occasionally, older adults or children are involved, and issues of mandatory reporting of neglect arise. Such breaches of confidentially can potentially damage the therapeutic relationship, especially since only half of individuals with HD acknowledge the lack of sanitation in their homes (Tolin et al., 2008). Excessive clutter, and in particular squalor, that leads to violations of local health, housing, and sanitation laws can result in mandated interventions, such as forced cleanouts. These interventions can be highly distressing for clients. They are also likely to reinforce clients' beliefs that they are not in control of their possessions, thus reducing motivation to discard and impeding future cooperation.

Addressing health and safety problems, particularly for individuals with poor insight, may require a harm-reduction approach that focuses on reducing and managing harmful consequences of HD rather than on discarding and the cessation of hoarding behaviors (Tompkins, 2011). Harm minimization may also involve a case-management approach to coordinate resources and foster collaboration among diverse services and professions across community sectors, such as the fire department, veterinarians, housing, legal, and health services (Bratiotis et al., 2019; Kysow et al., 2020; Strong et al., 2019). Another possible approach to deal with health and safety issues is early intervention. Given the relatively early age of onset of HD (Grisham et al., 2006), it may be important to target hoarding behaviors prior to clinical levels of severity and the entrenchment of hoarding beliefs. Unfortunately, there is still very little research evaluating the efficacy of harm-reduction and early intervention approaches for HD.

Summary

There are many avenues for further research that could lead to improvements in treatment outcomes for HD, including examining staged approaches to reduce the impact of comorbidities and transdiagnostic processes, innovative approaches to enhancing motivation and engagement. More mediation and moderation research is needed, in addition to adequately powered RCTs and a standardized approach to evaluating outcomes. Issues of heterogeneity and generalizability may be addressed through the evaluation of individualized interventions using single-case designs. Finally, harm reduction, routine outcome monitoring, case management, and early intervention approaches that are effective for other serious psychiatric conditions need to be developed and evaluated for HD.

Although there has been a growth in HD research, it is evident that much more research is needed, and reviews have lamented the slow pace of HD research (Davidson et al., 2019; Mataix-Cols & Fernández de la Cruz, 2018). A search on PsycINFO with hoarding disorder as a subject term revealed only 53 peer-reviewed papers in 2019, compared to 571 for OCD and 156 for binge eating disorder, which was introduced into the *DSM-5* at the same time as hoarding disorder. More investment into HD research will lead to better treatment outcomes and provide a stronger basis for increased funding to support the dissemination and implementation of HD interventions in community settings.

References

Abramowitz, J. S., Franklin, M. E., Schwartz, S. A., & Furr, J. M. (2003). Symptom presentation and outcome of cognitive-behavioral therapy for obsessive-compulsive disorder. *Journal of Consulting and Clinical Psychology*, *71*(6), 1049–1057.

Ayers, C. R., Bratiotis, C., Saxena, S., & Wetherell, J. L. (2012). Therapist and patient perspectives on cognitive-behavioral therapy for older adults with hoarding disorder: A collective case study. *Aging & Mental Health*, *16*(7), 915–921.

Ayers, C. R., Castriotta, N., Dozier, M. E., Espejo, E. P., & Porter, B. (2014). Behavioral and experiential avoidance in patients with hoarding disorder. *Journal of Behavior Therapy and Experimental Psychiatry*, *45*(3), 408–414.

Ayers, C. R., Davidson, E. J., Dozier, M. E., & Twamley, E. W. (2020). Cognitive rehabilitation and exposure/sorting therapy for late-life hoarding: Effects on neuropsychological performance. *The Journals of Gerontology: Series B*, *75*(6), 1193–1198.

Ayers, C. R., Dozier, M. E., & Mayes, T. L. (2017). Psychometric evaluation of the Saving Inventory–Revised in older adults. *Clinical Gerontologist*, *40*(3), 191–196.

Ayers, C. R., Dozier, M. E., Taylor, C. T., Mayes, T. L., Pittman, J. O. E., & Twamley, E. W. (2018). Group cognitive rehabilitation and exposure/sorting therapy: A pilot program. *Cognitive Therapy and Research*, *42*(3), 315–327.

Ayers, C. R., Dozier, M. E., Twamley, E. W., Saxena, S., Granholm, E., Mayes, T., & Wetherell, J. L. (2018). Cognitive rehabilitation and exposure/sorting therapy (CREST) for hoarding disorder in older adults. *The Journal of Clinical Psychiatry*, *79*(2), 85–93.

Ayers, C. R., Pittman, J. O. E., Davidson, E. J., Dozier, M. E., Mayes, T. L., & Almklov, E. (2019). Predictors of treatment outcome and attrition in adults with hoarding disorder. *Journal of Obsessive-Compulsive and Related Disorders*, *23*, 100465.

Ayers, C. R., Saxena, S., Espejo, E., Twamley, E. W., Granholm, E., & Wetherell, J. L. (2014). Novel treatment for geriatric hoarding disorder: An open trial of cognitive rehabilitation paired with behavior therapy. *The American Journal of Geriatric Psychiatry*, *22*(3), 248–252.

Ayers, C. R., Wetherell, J. L., Golshan, S., & Saxena, S. (2011). Cognitive-behavioral therapy for geriatric compulsive hoarding. *Behaviour Research and Therapy*, *49*(10), 689–694.

Bentley, K. H., Kleiman, E. M., Elliott, G., Huffman, J. C., & Nock, M. K. (2019). Real-time monitoring technology in single-case experimental design research: Opportunities and challenges. *Behaviour Research and Therapy*, *117*, 87–96.

Black, D. W., Monahan, P., Gable, J., Blum, N., Clancy, G., & Baker, P. (1998). Hoarding and treatment response in 38 nondepressed subjects with obsessive-compulsive disorder. *The Journal of Clinical Psychiatry*, *59*(8), 420–425.

Bloch, M. H., Bartley, C. A., Zipperer, L., Jakubovski, E., Landeros-Weisenberger, A., Pittenger, C., & Leckman, J. F. (2014). Meta-analysis: Hoarding symptoms associated with poor treatment outcome in obsessive-compulsive disorder. *Molecular Psychiatry*, *19*(9), 1025–1030.

Bratiotis, C. (2013). Community hoarding task forces: A comparative case study of five task forces in the United States. *Health & Social Care in the Community*, *21*(3), 245–253.

Bratiotis, C., Schmalisch, C. S., Steketee, G., Dowal, S. L., Edsell-Vetter, J., Frost, R. O., Halfmann, P., & Patronek, G. (2011). *The hoarding handbook: A guide for human service professionals*. Oxford University Press.

Bratiotis, C., Woody, S., & Lauster, N. (2019). Coordinated community-based hoarding interventions: Evidence of case management practices. *Families in Society*, *100*(1), 93–105.

Burgess, A., Frost, R. O., Marani, C., & Gabrielson, I. (2018). Imperfection, indecision, and hoarding. *Current Psychology*, *37*(2), 445–453.

Carbonella, J. Y., & Timpano, K. R. (2016). Examining the link between hoarding symptoms and cognitive flexibility deficits. *Behavior Therapy*, *47*(2), 262–273.

Castriotta, N., Dozier, M. E., Taylor, C. T., Mayes, T., & Ayers, C. R. (2019). Intolerance of uncertainty in hoarding disorder. *Journal of Obsessive-Compulsive and Related Disorders*, *21*, 97–101.

Chandler, A., Fogg, R., & Smith, J. G. (2019). Effectiveness of group cognitive behavioral therapy for hoarding disorder: Evaluation of outcomes. *Journal of Obsessive-Compulsive and Related Disorders*, *21*, 144–150.

Chasson, G. S., Carpenter, A., Ewing, J., Gibby, B., & Lee, N. (2014). Empowering families to help a loved one with hoarding disorder: Pilot study of Family-As-Motivators training. *Behaviour Research and Therapy*, *63*, 9–16.

Chou, C.-Y., Tsoh, J., Vigil, O., Bain, D., Uhm, S. Y., Howell, G., Chan, J., Eckfield, M., Plumadore, J., Chan, E., Komaiko, K., Smith, L., Franklin, J., Vega, E., Delucchi, K., & Mathews, C. A. (2018). Contributions of self-criticism and shame to hoarding. *Psychiatry Research*, *262*, 488–493.

Chou, C. Y., Tsoh, J. Y., Shumway, M., Smith, L. C., Chan, J., Delucchi, K., Tirch, D., Gilbert, P., & Mathews, C. A. (2020). Treating hoarding disorder with compassion-focused therapy: A pilot study examining treatment feasibility, acceptability, and exploring treatment effects. *British Journal of Clinical Psychology*, *59*(1), 1–21.

Chou, C.-Y., Tsoh, J. Y., Smith, L. C., Bain, L. D., Botcheva, L., Chan, E., Chan, J., Eckfield, M., Howell, G., Komaiko, K., Plumadore, J., Salazar, M., Uhm, S. Y., Vega, E., Vigil, O., Delucchi, K., & Mathews, C. A. (2018). How is hoarding related to trauma? A detailed examination on different aspects of hoarding and age when hoarding started. *Journal of Obsessive-Compulsive and Related Disorders*, *16*, 81–87.

Christensen, D. D., & Greist, J. H. (2001). The challenge of obsessive-compulsive disorder hoarding. *Primary Psychiatry*, *8*, 79–86.

Cicchetti, D., & Rogosch, F. A. (1996). Equifinality and multifinality in developmental psychopathology. *Development and Psychopathology*, *8*(4), 597–600.

Crone, C., Angel, Z., Isemann, S., & Norberg, M. M. (2020). Clutter-Buddies: A volunteer program to assist clients undergoing group cognitive behavioural therapy. *Journal of Obsessive-Compulsive and Related Disorders*, *27*, 100559.

David, J., Aluh, D. O., Blonner, M., & Norberg, M. M. (2021). Excessive object attachment in hoarding disorder: Examining the role of interpersonal functioning. *Behavior Therapy*, *52*(5), 1226–1236. https://doi.org/10.1016/j.beth.2021.02.003

Davidson, E. J., Dozier, M. E., Pittman, J. O. E., Mayes, T. L., Blanco, B. H., Gault, J. D., Schwarz, L. J., & Ayers, C. R. (2019). Recent advances in research on hoarding. *Current Psychiatry Reports*, *21*(9), 91.

DiMauro, J., Genova, M., Tolin, D. F., & Kurtz, M. M. (2014). Cognitive remediation for neuropsychological impairment in hoarding disorder: A pilot study. *Journal of Obsessive-Compulsive and Related Disorders*, *3*(2), 132–138.

DiMauro, J., Tolin, D. F., Frost, R. O., & Steketee, G. (2013). Do people with hoarding disorder under-report their symptoms? *Journal of Obsessive-Compulsive and Related Disorders*, *2*(2), 130–136.

Dozier, M. E., & Ayers, C. R. (2017). The etiology of hoarding disorder: A review. *Psychopathology*, *50*(5), 291–296.

Dozier, M. E., Bratiotis, C., Broadnax, D., Le, J., & Ayers, C. R. (2019). A description of 17 animal hoarding case files from animal control and a humane society. *Psychiatry Research*, *272*, 365–368. https://doi.org/10.1016/j.psychres.2018.12.127

Dozier, M. E., Taylor, C. T., Castriotta, N., Mayes, T. L., & Ayers, C. R. (2017). A preliminary investigation of the measurement of object interconnectedness in hoarding disorder. *Cognitive Therapy and Research*, *0*(0), 1–7.

Drury, H., Ajmi, S., de la Cruz, L. F., Nordsletten, A. E., & Mataix-Cols, D. (2014). Caregiver burden, family accommodation, health, and well-being in relatives of individuals with hoarding disorder. *Journal of Affective Disorders*, *159*, 7–14.

Eppingstall, J., Xenos, S., & Yap, K. (2020). Acceptance and commitment therapy for hoarding disorder: A proposed treatment protocol for individuals. *Australian Psychologist*, *55*(3), 183–195.

Ferrari, M., Hunt, C., Harrysunker, A., Abbott, M. J., Beath, A. P., & Einstein, D. A. (2019). Self-compassion interventions and psychosocial outcomes: A meta-analysis of RCTs. *Mindfulness*, *10*, 1455–1473.

Fitzpatrick, M., Nedeljkovic, M., Abbott, J.-A., Kyrios, M., & Moulding, R. (2018). "Blended" therapy: The development and pilot evaluation of an Internet-facilitated cognitive behavioral intervention to supplement face-to-face therapy for hoarding disorder. *Internet Interventions*, *12*, 16–25.

Frost, R. O., Gabrielson, I., Deady, S., Dernbach, K. B., Guevara, G., Peebles-Dorin, M., Yap, K., & Grisham, J. R. (2018). Scrupulosity and hoarding. *Comprehensive Psychiatry*, *86*, 19–24.

Frost, R. O., & Gross, R. C. (1993). The hoarding of possessions. *Behaviour Research and Therapy*, *31*(4), 367–381.

Frost, R. O., & Hartl, T. L. (1996). A cognitive-behavioral model of compulsive hoarding. *Behaviour Research and Therapy*, *34*(4), 341–350.

Frost, R. O., Kyrios, M., McCarthy, K. D., & Matthews, Y. (2007). Self-ambivalence and attachment to possessions. *Journal of Cognitive Psychotherapy*, *21*(3), 232–242.

Frost, R. O., Ong, C., Steketee, G., & Tolin, D. F. (2016). Behavioral and emotional consequences of thought listing versus cognitive restructuring during discarding decisions in hoarding disorder. *Behaviour Research and Therapy*, *85*, 13–22.

Frost, R. O., Pekareva-Kochergina, A., & Maxner, S. (2011). The effectiveness of a biblio-based support group for hoarding disorder. *Behaviour Research and Therapy*, *49*(10), 628–634.

Frost, R. O., Ruby, D., & Shuer, L. J. (2012). The Buried in Treasures Workshop: Waitlist control trial of facilitated support groups for hoarding. *Behaviour Research and Therapy*, *50*(11), 661–667.

Frost, R. O., & Steketee, G. (1999). Issues in the treatment of compulsive hoarding. *Cognitive and Behavioral Practice*, *4*(6), 397–407.

Frost, R. O., Steketee, G., & Grisham, J. R. (2004). Measurement of compulsive hoarding: Saving Inventory Revised. *Behaviour Research and Therapy*, *42*, 1163–1182.

Frost, R. O., Steketee, G., & Tolin, D. F. (2011). Comorbidity in hoarding disorder. *Depression and Anxiety*, *28*(10), 876–884.

Frost, R. O., Tolin, D. F., & Maltby, N. (2010). Insight-related challenges in the treatment of hoarding. *Cognitive and Behavioral Practice*, *17*(4), 404–413.

Gilliam, C. M., Norberg, M. M., Villavicencio, A., Morrison, S., Hannan, S. E., & Tolin, D. F. (2011). Group cognitive-behavioral therapy for hoarding disorder: An open trial. *Behaviour Research and Therapy*, *49*(11), 802–807.

Grassi, G., Micheli, L., Di Cesare Mannelli, L., Compagno, E., Righi, L., Ghelardini, C., & Pallanti, S. (2016). Atomoxetine for hoarding disorder: A pre-clinical and clinical investigation. *Journal of Psychiatric Research*, *83*, 240–248.

Grisham, J. R., Brown, T. A., Liverant, G. I., & Campbell-Sills, L. (2005). The distinctiveness of compulsive hoarding from obsessive-compulsive disorder. *Journal of Anxiety Disorders*, *19*(7), 767–779.

Grisham, J. R., Frost, R. O., Steketee, G., Kim, H.-J., & Hood, S. (2006). Age of onset of compulsive hoarding. *Journal of Anxiety Disorders*, *20*(5), 675–686.

Grisham, J. R., Martyn, C., Kerin, F., Baldwin, P. A., & Norberg, M. M. (2018). Interpersonal functioning in hoarding disorder: An examination of attachment styles and emotion regulation in response to interpersonal stress. *Journal of Obsessive-Compulsive and Related Disorders*, *16*, 43–49.

Grisham, J. R., Roberts, L., Cerea, S., Isemann, S., Svehla, J., & Norberg, M. M. (2018). The role of distress tolerance, anxiety sensitivity, and intolerance of uncertainty in predicting hoarding symptoms in a clinical sample. *Psychiatry Research*, *267*, 94–101.

Grisham, J. R., Yap, K., Isemann, S., Svehla, J., Briggs, N., & Norberg, M. M. (2022). A naturalistic study of emotion regulation-enhanced cognitive-behavioral group therapy for hoarding disorder in a community setting. *Journal of Affective Disorders Reports*, *10*, 100450.

Hall, B. J., Tolin, D. F., Frost, R. O., & Steketee, G. (2013). An exploration of comorbid symptoms and clinical correlates of clinically significant hoarding symptoms. *Depression and Anxiety*, *30*(1), 67–76.

Harmon, C., Hawkins, E. J., Lambert, M. J., Slade, K., & Whipple, J. S. (2005). Improving outcomes for poorly responding clients: The use of clinical support tools and feedback to clients. *Journal of Clinical Psychology*, *61*(2), 175–185.

Hayes, S. C., Hofmann, S. G., Stanton, C. E., Carpenter, J. K., Sanford, B. T., Curtiss, J. E., & Ciarrochi, J. (2019). The role of the individual in the coming era of process-based therapy. *Behaviour Research and Therapy*, *117*, 40–53.

Hayes, S. C., Strosahl, K. D., & Wilson, K. G. (2012). *Acceptance and commitment therapy: The process and practice of mindful change* (2nd ed.). Guilford.

Hazari, N., Narayanaswamy, J. C., & Arumugham, S. S. (2016). Predictors of response to serotonin reuptake inhibitors in obsessive-compulsive disorder. *Expert Review of Neurotherapeutics*, *16*(10), 1175–1191.

Hombali, A., Sagayadevan, V., Tan, W. M., Chong, R., Yip, H. W., Vaingankar, J., Chong, S. A., & Subramaniam, M. (2019). A narrative synthesis of possible causes and risk factors of hoarding behaviours. *Asian Journal of Psychiatry*, *42*, 104–114.

Ivanov, V. Z., Enander, J., Mataix-Cols, D., Serlachius, E., Månsson, K. N. T., Andersson, G., Flygare, O., Tolin, D., & Rück, C. (2018). Enhancing group cognitive-behavioral therapy for hoarding disorder with between-session internet-based clinician support: A feasibility study. *Journal of Clinical Psychology*, *74*(7), 1092–1105.

Ivanov, V. Z., Mataix-Cols, D., Serlachius, E., Brander, G., Elmquist, A., Enander, J., & Rück, C. (2020). The developmental origins of hoarding disorder in adolescence: A longitudinal clinical interview study following an epidemiological survey. *European Child & Adolescent Psychiatry*, *30*(3), 415–425.

Jacobson, N. S., & Truax, P. (1991). Clinical significance: A statistical approach to defining meaningful change in psychotherapy research. *Journal of Consulting and Clinical Psychology*, *59*(1), 12–19.

Kazdin, A. E. (2019). Single-case experimental designs: Evaluating interventions in research and clinical practice. *Behaviour Research and Therapy, 117*, 3–17.

Kehoe, E., & Egan, J. (2019). Interpersonal attachment insecurity and emotional attachment to possessions partly mediate the relationship between childhood trauma and hoarding symptoms in a non-clinical sample. *Journal of Obsessive-Compulsive and Related Disorders, 21*, 37–45.

Kellett, S., Matuozzo, H., & Kotecha, C. (2015). Effectiveness of cognitive-behaviour therapy for hoarding disorder in people with mild intellectual disabilities. *Research in Developmental Disabilities, 47*, 385–392.

Kellman-McFarlane, K., Stewart, B., Woody, S. R., Ayers, C. R., Dozier, M. E., Frost, R. O., Grisham, J., Isemann, S., Steketee, G., Tolin, D. F., & Welsted, A. (2019). Saving Inventory–Revised: Psychometric performance across the lifespan. *Journal of Affective Disorders, 252*, 358–364.

Kessler, R. C., Mickelson, K. D., Barber, C. B., & Wang, P. S. (2001). The association between chronic medical conditions and work impairment. In A. S. Rossi (Ed.), *Caring and doing for others: Social responsibility in the domains of the family, work, and community* (pp. 403–426). University of Chicago Press.

Kings, C. A., Moulding, R., & Knight, T. (2017, 2017/07/01/). You are what you own: Reviewing the link between possessions, emotional attachment, and the self-concept in hoarding disorder. *Journal of Obsessive-Compulsive and Related Disorders, 14*, 51–58.

Krafft, J., Ong, C. W., Twohig, M. P., & Levin, M. E. (2019). Assessing psychological inflexibility in hoarding: The Acceptance and Action Questionnaire for Hoarding (AAQH). *Journal of Contextual Behavioral Science, 12*, 234–242.

Kress, V. E., Stargell, N. A., Zoldan, C. A., & Paylo, M. J. (2016). Hoarding disorder: Diagnosis, assessment, and treatment. *Journal of Counseling & Development, 94*(1), 83–90.

Kyrios, M., Mogan, C., Moulding, R., Frost, R. O., Yap, K., & Fassnacht, D. B. (2018). The cognitive-behavioural model of hoarding disorder: Evidence from clinical and non-clinical cohorts. *Clinical Psychology and Psychotherapy, 25*(2), 311–321.

Kysow, K., Bratiotis, C., Lauster, N., & Woody, S. R. (2020). How can cities tackle hoarding? Examining an intervention program bringing together Fire and Health authorities in Vancouver. *Health & Social Care in the Community, 28*(4), 1160–1169.

Lambert, M. J., & Shimokawa, K. (2011). Collecting client feedback. *Psychotherapy, 48*(1), 72–79.

Landau, D., Iervolino, A. C., Pertusa, A., Santo, S., Singh, S., & Mataix-Cols, D. (2011). Stressful life events and material deprivation in hoarding disorder. *Journal of Anxiety Disorders, 25*(2), 192–202.

Linkovski, O., Zwerling, J., Cordell, E., Sonnenfeld, D., Willis, H., La Lima, C. N., Baker, C., Ghazzaoui, R., Girson, R., Sanchez, C., Wright, B., Alford, M., Varias, A., Filippou-Frye, M., Shen, H., Jo, B., Shuer, L., Frost, R. O., & Rodriguez, C. I. (2018). Augmenting Buried in Treasures with in-home uncluttering practice: Pilot study in hoarding disorder. *Journal of Psychiatric Research, 107*, 145–150.

Luu, M., Lauster, N., Bratiotis, C., Edsell-Vetter, J., & Woody, S. R. (2018). Squalor in community-referred hoarded homes. *Journal of Obsessive-Compulsive and Related Disorders, 19*, 66–71.

Macdonald, J., & Mellor-Clark, J. (2015). Correcting psychotherapists' blindsidedness: Formal feedback as a means of overcoming the natural limitations of therapists. *Clinical Psychology & Psychotherapy, 22*(3), 249–257.

Mataix-Cols, D., & Fernández de la Cruz, L. (2018). Hoarding disorder has finally arrived, but many challenges lie ahead. *World Psychiatry, 17*(2), 224–225.

Mataix-Cols, D., Marks, I. M., Greist, J. H., Kobak, K. A., & Baer, L. (2002). Obsessive-compulsive symptom dimensions as predictors of compliance with and response to behaviour therapy: Results from a controlled trial. *Psychotherapy and Psychosomatics, 71*(5), 255–262.

Mataix-Cols, D., Rauch, S., Manzo, P., Jenike, M., & Baer, L. (1999). Use of factor-analyzed symptom dimensions to predict outcome with serotonin reuptake inhibitors and placebo in the treatment of obsessive-compulsive disorder. *The American Journal of Psychiatry, 156*, 1409–1416.

Mathes, B. M., Henry, A., Schmidt, N. B., & Norberg, M. M. (2019). Hoarding symptoms and workplace impairment. *British Journal of Clinical Psychology, 58*(3), 342–356.

Mathes, B. M., Timpano, K. R., Raines, A. M., & Schmidt, N. B. (2020). Attachment theory and hoarding disorder: A review and theoretical integration. *Behaviour Research and Therapy, 125*, 103549.

Mathews, C. A., Mackin, R. S., Chou, C.-Y., Uhm, S. Y., Bain, L. D., Stark, S. J., Gause, M., Vigil, O. R., Franklin, J., Salazar, M., Plumadore, J., Smith, L. C., Komaiko, K., Howell, G., Vega, E., Chan, J., Eckfield, M. B., Tsoh, J. Y., & Delucchi, K. (2018). Randomised clinical trial of community-based peer-led and psychologist-led group treatment for hoarding disorder. *The British Journal of Psychiatry Open, 4*(4), 285–293.

Mathews, C. A., Uhm, S., Chan, J., Gause, M., Franklin, J., Plumadore, J., Stark, S. J., Yu, W., Vigil, O., Salazar, M., Delucchi, K. L., & Vega, E. (2016). Treating hoarding disorder in a real-world setting: Results from the Mental Health Association of San Francisco. *Psychiatry Research*, *237*, 331–338.

Miller, W. R., & Rollnick, S. (2002). *Motivational interviewing: Preparing people for change* (2nd ed.). Guilford.

Moulding, R., Kings, C., & Knight, T. (2021). The things that make us: self and object attachment in hoarding and compulsive buying-shopping disorder. *Current Opinion in Psychology*, *39*, 100–104.

Moulding, R., Mancuso, S. G., Rehm, I., & Nedeljkovic, M. (2016). The self in the obsessive-compulsive-related disorders: Hoarding disorder, body dysmorphic disorder, and trichotillomania. In M. Kyrios, R. Moulding, G. Doron, S. S. Bhar, M. Nedeljkovic, & M. Mikulincer (Eds.), *The self in understanding and treating psychological disorders* (pp. 123–133). Cambridge University Press.

Moulding, R., Nedeljkovic, M., Kyrios, M., Osborne, D., & Mogan, C. (2017). Short-term cognitive-behavioural group treatment for hoarding disorder: A naturalistic treatment outcome study. *Clinical Psychology & Psychotherapy*, *24*(1), 235–244.

Muroff, J., Steketee, G., Bratiotis, C., & Ross, A. (2012). Group cognitive and behavioral therapy and bibliotherapy for hoarding: A pilot trial. *Depression and Anxiety*, *29*(7), 597–604.

Muroff, J., Steketee, G., Frost, R. O., & Tolin, D. F. (2014). Cognitive behavior therapy for hoarding disorder: Follow-up findings and predictors of outcome. *Depression and Anxiety*, *31*(12), 964–971.

Muroff, J., Steketee, G., Himle, J., & Frost, R. O. (2010). Delivery of Internet treatment for compulsive hoarding (D.I.T.C.H.). *Behaviour Research and Therapy*, *48*(1), 79–85.

Muroff, J., Steketee, G., Rasmussen, J., Gibson, A., Bratiotis, C., & Sorrentino, C. (2009). Group cognitive and behavioral treatment for compulsive hoarding: A preliminary trial. *Depression and Anxiety*, *26*(7), 634–640.

Neave, N., Caiazza, R., Hamilton, C., McInnes, L., Saxton, T. K., Deary, V., & Wood, M. (2017). The economic costs of hoarding behaviours in local authority/housing association tenants and private home owners in the north-east of England. *Public Health*, *148*, 137–139.

Neave, N., Tyson, H., McInnes, L., & Hamilton, C. (2016). The role of attachment style and anthropomorphism in predicting hoarding behaviours in a non-clinical sample. *Personality and Individual Differences*, *99*, 33–37.

Norberg, M. M., Chasson, G. S., & Tolin, D. F. (2021). A standardized approach to calculating clinically significant change in hoarding disorder using the Saving Inventory–Revised. *Journal of Obsessive Compulsive and Related Disorders*, *28*, 100609.

Norberg, M. M., Crone, C., Kwok, C., & Grisham, J. R. (2018). Anxious attachment and excessive acquisition: The mediating roles of anthropomorphism and distress intolerance. *Journal of Behavioral Addictions*, *7*(1), 171–180.

Nordsletten, A. E., & Mataix-Cols, D. (2012). Hoarding versus collecting: Where does pathology diverge from play? *Clinical Psychology Review*, *32*(3), 165–176.

O'Connor, K., Bodryzlova, Y., Audet, J. S., Koszegi, N., Bergeron, K., & Guitard, A. (2018). Group cognitive-behavioural treatment with long-term follow-up and targeting self-identity for hoarding disorder: An open trial. *Clinical Psychology & Psychotherapy*, *25*(5), 701–709.

Ong, C., Pang, S., Sagayadevan, V., Chong, S. A., & Subramaniam, M. (2015). Functioning and quality of life in hoarding: A systematic review. *Journal of Anxiety Disorders*, *32*, 17–30.

Ong, C. W., Krafft, J., Levin, M. E., & Twohig, M. P. (2018). An examination of the role of psychological inflexibility in hoarding using multiple mediator models. *Journal of Cognitive Psychotherapy*, *32*(2), 97–111.

Patronek, G., & Nathanson, J. N. (2016). Understanding animal neglect and hoarding. In L. Levitt, G. Patronek, & T. Grisso (Eds.), *Animal maltreatment: Forensic mental health issues and evaluations* (pp. 159–193). Oxford University Press.

Piacentino, D., Pasquini, M., Cappelletti, S., Chetoni, C., Sani, G., & Kotzalidis, G. D. (2019). Pharmacotherapy for hoarding disorder: How did the picture change since its excision from OCD? *Current Neuropharmacology*, *17*(8), 808–815.

Postlethwaite, A., Kellett, S., & Mataix-Cols, D. (2019). Prevalence of hoarding disorder: A systematic review and meta-analysis. *Journal of Affective Disorders*, *256*, 309–316.

Raines, A. M., Chavarria, J., Allan, N. P., Short, N. A., & Schmidt, N. B. (2017). Hoarding behaviors and alcohol use: The mediating role of emotion dysregulation. *Substance Use & Misuse*, *52*(13), 1684–1691.

Rodriguez, C. I., Bender, J., Jr., Morrison, S., Mehendru, R., Tolin, D., & Simpson, H. B. (2013). Does extended release methylphenidate help adults with hoarding disorder? A case series. *Journal of Clinical Psychopharmacology*, *33*(3), 444–447.

Rodriguez, C. I., Levinson, A., Patel, S. R., Rottier, K., Zwerling, J., Essock, S., Shuer, L., Frost, R. O., & Simpson, H. B. (2016). Acceptability of treatments and services for individuals with hoarding behaviors. *Journal of Obsessive-Compulsive and Related Disorders*, *11*, 1–8.

Rufer, M., Fricke, S., Moritz, S., Kloss, M., & Hand, I. (2006). Symptom dimensions in obsessive-compulsive disorder: Prediction of cognitive-behavior therapy outcome. *Acta Psychiatrica Scandinavica*, *113*(5), 440–446.

Sakiris, N., & Berle, D. (2019). A systematic review and meta-analysis of the Unified Protocol as a transdiagnostic emotion regulation based intervention. *Clinical Psychology Review*, *72*, 101751.

Salkovskis, P. M. (1985). Obsessional-compulsive problems: A cognitive-behavioural analysis. *Behaviour Research and Therapy*, *23*(5), 571–583.

Samuels, J. F., Bienvenu, O. J., Grados, M. A., Cullen, B., Riddle, M. A., Liang, K. Y., Eaton, W. W., & Nestadt, G. (2008). Prevalence and correlates of hoarding behavior in a community-based sample. *Behaviour Research and Therapy*, *46*(7), 836–844.

Samuels, J. F., Bienvenu, O. J., Riddle, M. A., Cullen, B. A. M., Grados, M. A., Liang, K. Y., Hoehn-Saric, R., & Nestadt, G. (2002). Hoarding in obsessive compulsive disorder: Results from a case-control study. *Behaviour Research and Therapy*, *40*(5), 517–528.

Saxena, S., Brody, A. L., Maidment, K. M., & Baxter, L. R., Jr. (2007). Paroxetine treatment of compulsive hoarding. *Journal of Psychiatric Research*, *41*(6), 481–487.

Saxena, S., & Maidment, K. M. (2004). Treatment of compulsive hoarding. *Journal of Clinical Psychology*, *60*(11), 1143–1154.

Saxena, S., & Sumner, J. (2014). Venlafaxine extended-release treatment of hoarding disorder. *International Clinical Psychopharmacology*, *29*(5), 266–273.

Seaman, C., Oldfield, V. B., Gordon, O., Forrester, E., & Salkovskis, P. M. (2010). The impact of symptomatic hoarding in OCD and its treatment. *Behavioural and Cognitive Psychotherapy*, *38*(2), 157–171.

Snowdon, J., Shah, A., & Halliday, G. (2007). Severe domestic squalor: A review. *International Psychogeriatrics*, *19*(1), 37–51.

St-Pierre-Delorme, M.-E., & O'Connor, K. (2016). Using virtual reality in the inference-based treatment of compulsive hoarding. *Frontiers in Public Health*, *4*, 149.

Stein, D. J., Andersen, E. W., & Overo, K. F. (2007). Response of symptom dimensions in obsessive-compulsive disorder to treatment with citalopram or placebo. *Brazilian Journal of Psychiatry*, *29*(4), 303–307.

Steketee, G., & Frost, R. O. (2003). Compulsive hoarding: Current status of the research. *Clinical Psychology Review*, *23*(7), 905–927.

Steketee, G., & Frost, R. O. (2007). *Compulsive hoarding and acquiring: Therapist guide*. Oxford University Press.

Steketee, G., & Frost, R. O. (2014). *Treatment for hoarding disorder: Workbook* (2nd ed.). Oxford University Press.

Steketee, G., Frost, R. O., & Kyrios, M. (2003). Cognitive aspects of compulsive hoarding. *Cognitive Therapy and Research*, *27*(4), 463–479.

Steketee, G., Frost, R. O., Tolin, D. F., Rasmussen, J., & Brown, T. A. (2010). Waitlist-controlled trial of cognitive behavior therapy for hoarding disorder. *Depression and Anxiety*, *27*(5), 476–484.

Steketee, G., Frost, R. O., Wincze, J., Greene, K. A., & Douglass, H. (2000). Group and individual treatment of compulsive hoarding: A pilot study. *Behavioural and Cognitive Psychotherapy*, *28*(3), 259–268.

Strong, S., Federico, J., Banks, R., & Williams, C. (2019). A collaborative model for managing animal hoarding cases. *Journal of Applied Animal Welfare Science*, *22*(3), 267–278.

Taylor, J. K., Moulding, R., & Nedeljkovic, M. (2018). Emotion regulation and hoarding symptoms. *Journal of Obsessive-Compulsive and Related Disorders*, *18*, 86–97.

Thompson, B. L., Twohig, M. P., & Luoma, J. B. (2020). Psychological flexibility as shared process of change in acceptance and commitment therapy and exposure and response prevention for obsessive-compulsive disorder: A single case design study. *Behavior Therapy*, *52*(2), 286–297.

Tolin, D. F., Das, A., Hallion, L. S., Levy, H. C., Wootton, B. M., & Stevens, M. C. (2019). Quality of life in patients with hoarding disorder. *Journal of Obsessive-Compulsive and Related Disorders*, *21*, 55–59.

Tolin, D. F., Fitch, K. E., Frost, R. O., & Steketee, G. (2010). Family informants' perceptions of insight in compulsive hoarding. *Cognitive Therapy and Research*, *34*(1), 69–81.

Tolin, D. F., Frost, R. O., & Steketee, G. (2007a). *Buried in treasures: Help for compulsive acquiring, saving, and hoarding.* Oxford University Press.

Tolin, D. F., Frost, R. O., & Steketee, G. (2007b). An open trial of cognitive-behavioral therapy for compulsive hoarding. *Behaviour Research and Therapy, 45*(7), 1461–1470.

Tolin, D., Frost, R. O., & Steketee, G. (2013). *Buried in treasures: Help for compulsive acquiring, saving, and hoarding.* Oxford University Press.

Tolin, D. F., Frost, R. O., & Steketee, G. (2014). *Buried in treasures: Help for compulsive acquiring, saving, and hoarding* (2nd ed.). Oxford University Press.

Tolin, D. F., Frost, R. O., Steketee, G., Gray, K. D., & Fitch, K. E. (2008). The economic and social burden of compulsive hoarding. *Psychiatry Research, 160*(2), 200–211.

Tolin, D. F., Frost, R. O., Steketee, G., & Muroff, J. (2015). Cognitive behavioral therapy for hoarding disorder: A meta-analysis. *Depression and Anxiety, 32*(3), 158–166.

Tolin, D. F., Levy, H. C., Wootton, B. M., Hallion, L. S., & Stevens, M. C. (2018). Hoarding disorder and difficulties in emotion regulation. *Journal of Obsessive-Compulsive and Related Disorders, 16*, 98–103.

Tolin, D. F., Meunier, S. A., Frost, R. O., & Steketee, G. (2010). Course of compulsive hoarding and its relationship to life events. *Depression and Anxiety, 27*(9), 829–838.

Tolin, D. F., & Villavicencio, A. (2011). Inattention, but not OCD, predicts the core features of hoarding disorder. *Behaviour Research and Therapy, 49*(2), 120–125.

Tolin, D. F., Wootton, B. M., Levy, H. C., Hallion, L. S., Worden, B. L., Diefenbach, G. J., Jaccard, J., & Stevens, M. C. (2019). Efficacy and mediators of a group cognitive–behavioral therapy for hoarding disorder: A randomized trial. *Journal of Consulting and Clinical Psychology, 87*(7), 590–602.

Tolin, D. F., Worden, B. L., Wootton, B. M., & Gilliam, C. M. (2017). *A cognitive-behavioral group treatment manual for hoarding disorder: Therapist manual.* Wiley-Blackwell.

Tompkins, M. A. (2011). Working with families of people who hoard: A harm reduction approach. *Journal of Clinical Psychology: In session, 67*(5), 497–506.

Ung, J. E., Dozier, M. E., Bratiotis, C., & Ayers, C. R. (2016). An exploratory investigation of animal hoarding symptoms in a sample of adults diagnosed with hoarding disorder. *Journal of Clinical Psychology, 73*(9), 1114–1125.

Weiss, E. R., Landers, A., Todman, M., & Roane, D. M. (2020). Treatment outcomes in older adults with hoarding disorder: The impact of self-control, boredom and social support. *Australasian Journal on Ageing, 39*(4), 375–380.

Wheaton, M. G., Fabricant, L. E., Berman, N. C., & Abramowitz, J. S. (2013). Experiential avoidance in individuals with hoarding disorder. *Cognitive Therapy and Research, 37*(4), 779–785. 2

Wincze, J. P., Steketee, G., & Frost, R. O. (2007). Categorization in compulsive hoarding. *Behaviour Research and Therapy, 45*(1), 63–72.

Winsberg, M. E., Cassic, K. S., & Koran, L. M. (1999). Hoarding in obsessive-compulsive disorder: A report of 20 cases. *The Journal of Clinical Psychiatry, 60*(9), 591–597.

Woody, S. R., Lenkic, P., Bratiotis, C., Kysow, K., Luu, M., Edsell-Vetter, J., Frost, R. O., Lauster, N., Steketee, G., & Tolin, D. F. (2020). How well do hoarding research samples represent cases that rise to community attention? *Behaviour Research and Therapy, 126*, 103555.

Worden, B., Levy, H. C., Das, A., Katz, B. W., Stevens, M., & Tolin, D. F. (2019). Perceived emotion regulation and emotional distress tolerance in patients with hoarding disorder. *Journal of Obsessive-Compulsive and Related Disorders, 22*, 100441.

Worden, B. L., Bowe, W. M., & Tolin, D. F. (2017). An open trial of cognitive behavioral therapy with contingency management for hoarding disorder. *Journal of Obsessive-Compulsive and Related Disorders, 12*, 78–86.

Yap, K., Eppingstall, J., Brennan, C., Le, B., & Grisham, J. (2020). Emotional attachment to objects mediates the relationship between loneliness and hoarding symptoms. *Journal of Obsessive-Compulsive and Related Disorders, 24*, 100487.

Yap, K., & Grisham, J. R. (2019). Unpacking the construct of emotional attachment to objects and its association with hoarding symptoms. *Journal of Behavioral Addictions, 8*(2), 249–258.

Yap, K., & Grisham, J. R. (2020). Object attachment and emotions in hoarding disorder. *Comprehensive Psychiatry, 100*, 152179.

Zakrzewski, J. J., Gillett, D. A., Vigil, O. R., Smith, L. C., Komaiko, K., Chou, C.-Y., Uhm, S. Y., Bain, L. D., Stark, S. J., Gause, M., Howell, G., Vega, E., Chan, J., Eckfield, M. B., Tsoh, J., Delucchi, K., Mackin, R. S., & Mathews, C. A. (2020). Visually mediated functioning improves following treatment of hoarding disorder. *Journal of Affective Disorders, 264*, 310–317.

CHAPTER 24

Treatment of Trichotillomania and Skin-Picking Disorder

Martin E. Franklin, Diana Antinoro, Emily J. Ricketts, *and* Douglas W. Woods

Abstract

Trichotillomania and skin-picking disorder are classified in the *DSM-5* under the broader category of OCD and related disorders, and each of these conditions share both topographical and functional similarities to one another. The treatment literatures for both conditions suggest a growing evidence base, grounded in randomized controlled trial methodology, that supports certain behavioral treatments, most notably habit reversal training and derivative treatments such as acceptance-enhanced behavior therapy. The extant pharmacotherapy and psychotherapy literatures for each are discussed, habit reversal is described, examples of a habit reversal training protocol are presented, and current efforts in treatment development and recommendations for future directions in research are provided.

Key Words: trichotillomania, skin-picking disorder, pharmacotherapy, cognitive-behavioral therapy, habit reversal training, acceptance-enhanced behavior therapy

Introduction

This chapter briefly begins with brief descriptions of trichotillomania (TTM) and skin-picking disorder (SPD; also called excoriation), then provides a review of the pharmacotherapy and psychosocial treatment outcome literature separately for each of the conditions. Notably, in contrast to anxiety or depression, the psychopathology literatures on TTM and SPD indicate that distorted or maladaptive cognitions do not play a central role in the etiology or maintenance of the conditions (Mansueto et al., 1999; Miguel et al., 1995). Accordingly, cognitive therapy techniques are not typically emphasized in the psychosocial treatments of TTM and SPD that have been studied thus far. The protocols are more accurately characterized as behavioral treatments, although some do include ancillary cognitive interventions (Franklin & Tolin, 2007; Woods & Twohig, 2008). Therefore, the section headings in the chapter are labeled as such. The literature review also reveals that the application of behavioral treatments, specifically habit reversal training (HRT), continues to hold the greatest promise for TTM and SPD. The application of HRT is described in detail, and the chapter concludes with a section on future directions in treatment research.

TTM

Phenomenology and Implications for Treatment

TTM has been defined as the recurrent pulling out of one's hair, resulting in hair loss; some patients note an increasing sense of tension before pulling, followed by a feeling of gratification or relief after the pulling episode, but these features are no longer required for diagnosis (American Psychiatric Association [APA], 2013). Pulling sites vary and include, from most to least common, the scalp, eyelashes, eyebrows, pubic region, face, and body (Franklin et al., 2008; Santhanam et al., 2008; Schlosser et al., 1994; Tolin et al., 2007; Woods et al., 2006). Many individuals with TTM engage in certain behaviors before hair-pulling, including hair touching, twirling, or stroking (Casati et al., 2000; du Toit et al., 2001), and postpulling rituals like rubbing hair strands across their lips; examining, biting, or chewing the root of the hair; and, occasionally, trichophagia (i.e., hair ingestion; Christenson et al., 1991; Woods et al., 2006). At least two distinct styles of hair-pulling have been noted, focused and automatic hair-pulling (see Chapter 5). Focused pulling usually involves a conscious effort to pull and includes using pulling to regulate emotion. Automatic pulling, in contrast, involves a lack of awareness of the pulling, and generally occurs during sedentary activities like watching television, reading, or driving. It is believed that those with TTM exhibit both styles, although they may have a greater tendency toward one or the other (Flessner et al., 2008). Clinically, it seems that HRT is ideally suited for the more automatic episodes, whereas other augmentative strategies to assist with affect management may be needed to address focused pulling.

Pharmacotherapy

Studies examining the efficacy of pharmacotherapy for TTM in adults focused initially on treatment with medications with established serotonergic properties, which reflected the previously prevailing view that TTM is a variant of obsessive-compulsive disorder (OCD) and thus ought to be responsive to the same medications proven efficacious for OCD. Swedo et al. (1989) found the tricyclic antidepressant clomipramine to be superior to desipramine at posttreatment assessment in a double-blind crossover study; long-term response to clomipramine varied widely, with an overall 40% reduction in symptoms maintained at four-year follow-up (Swedo et al., 1993). However, Christenson et al. (1991) failed to find an advantage for the selective serotonin reuptake inhibitor (SSRI) fluoxetine over placebo (PBO) in another double-blind crossover study, and Streichenwein and Thornby (1995) failed to detect an effect for fluoxetine compared to PBO despite having increased the maximum fluoxetine dose to 80 mg. Similarly, Ninan et al. (2000) found an advantage for cognitive-behavioral therapy (CBT) involving HRT over both CMI and PBO, which did not differ significantly from each other. A randomized controlled trial (RCT) found HRT superior to both fluoxetine and wait-listing but failed to find a significant effect for FLU compared to wait-listing (van Minnen et al., 2003). With respect to combined treatment approaches, Dougherty and colleagues (2006) found an advantage for behavior therapy plus the SSRI fluvoxamine over either treatment alone, suggesting the potentiating effects of combined treatment. A recent meta-analysis examined effects associated with SSRIs from six randomized, placebo-controlled studies, and found a moderate treatment effect relative to PBO and little variability in treatment response; moreover, no moderators of treatment response were identified (McGuire et al., 2014), thus leaving unanswered the question of which patients would be more likely to respond to SSRIs compared to other forms of intervention.

In light of the limitations evident for the efficacy of the SSRIs, other classes of medication have been considered and evaluated in the treatment of TTM. The atypical neuroleptic olanzapine has been found to be more efficacious than PBO in adults with TTM (Van Ameringen et al., 2010), but the unfavorable side-effect profile of this class of medications limits olanzapine's use as a first-line intervention. The most important development in pharmacotherapy for TTM involves the use of the glutamate modulator *N*-acetylcysteine (NAC), which was found superior to PBO in an RCT for adults with primary TTM (Grant et al., 2009). Treatment response rates for the NAC condition were clearly superior to the control condition and comparable to those observed in CBT trials with adults. Furthermore, the side-effect profile was quite favorable. This development in adult TTM, however, did not hold in pediatric TTM, in which an RCT in youth with TTM demonstrated that NAC failed to separate from PBO (Bloch et al., 2013). NAC is not an FDA-regulated product, so it is readily available in health-food stores. Notably, despite an underdeveloped empirical literature on NAC, in the authors' recent clinical experience running CBT trials and clinics, they have encountered many TTM patients who have tried or are currently receiving NAC.

As is evident from the above review, the TTM pharmacotherapy literature to date is both underdeveloped and equivocal. SSRIs and clomipramine have generally not been found highly efficacious in RCTs, and the encouraging news about NAC in adults was not replicated in youth. There is as yet no clear pharmacotherapy candidate for future study and direct comparison to alternative treatments (e.g., behavior therapy) in TTM. The absence of an empirically supported pharmacotherapy for pediatric TTM in particular restricts recommendations that can be made to parents whose children suffer from the disorder, although there is ample evidence for the efficacy of SSRIs for the frequent comorbid anxiety and depression in TTM (Franklin et al., 2008; Panza et al., 2013). Clinically, a wide array of pharmacotherapy options are still attempted for TTM, including serotonin reuptake inhibitors, psychostimulants, mood stabilizers, atypical neuroleptics, and naltrexone, yet the empirical literature on any of these interventions for pediatric TTM remains weak.

HRT

OVERVIEW

A wide array of behavioral and cognitive-behavioral treatments and treatment packages have been applied to TTM, involving components like self-monitoring, aversion, covert sensitization, negative practice, relaxation training, competing response training, cognitive restructuring, and overcorrection. Of all the options, the package that has received the most attention thus far for TTM and other habit/impulse control disorders is HRT (Azrin & Nunn, 1973), which, as applied to TTM, typically includes awareness training/self-monitoring procedures and instructions to reinforce urges to pull by engaging in a competing response that uses the same muscle groups and is incompatible with pulling (e.g., shelling peanuts, fist-clenching).

OUTCOME RESEARCH

Progress has been made in the last ten years in examining the efficacy of behavioral treatments for TTM, and meta-analytic reviews specifically support the efficacy of HRT or have included HRT elements (Lee et al., 2019; McGuire et al., 2014). In the first RCT examining behavior therapy for TTM (Azrin et al., 1980), HRT was superior to negative practice, with patients in the HRT group reporting a 99% reduction in number of hair-pulling episodes compared, to a 58% reduction among patients in the negative practice group. The HRT group maintained their gains at 22-month follow-up, with patients reporting 87% reduction in comparison to before treatment. However, the generalizability of the findings was limited by the absence of a formal treatment protocol, exclusive reliance on self-reports as the sole outcome measure, and limited patient participation in the follow-up phase.

Since then, several more RCTs have indicated that treatments involving HRT are efficacious. In a small trial, Ninan et al. (2000) found a CBT package emphasizing HRT superior to clomipramine and PBO at posttreatment evaluation; clomipramine and PBO failed to separate from one another. In their study, van Minnen et al. (2003) randomized 43 patients with TTM to receive either behavior therapy, fluoxetine, or wait-list for 12 weeks. Patients in the behavior therapy group experienced a greater reduction in their TTM symptoms than did patients in the FLU or wait-list groups. The study by Dougherty et al. (2006), reviewed above, suggested an additive effect for sertraline compared to HRT alone.

Several studies have incorporated HRT into protocols that have included other psychotherapy methods and generally have found empirical support for the more complex protocols in adults with TTM. Woods and colleagues (2006) compared acceptance-enhanced behavior therapy (AEBT) to a wait-list control in a randomized design of adults with TTM, and found evidence for the efficacy of AEBT in adults; a larger study comparing AEBT to psychoeducation/supportive counseling (PSC) is in preparation (see Neal-Barnett et al., 2019). Moritz and Rufer (2011) examined a procedure known as self-help decoupling, which included components included in HRT, and found benefit for treatment of both TTM and concomitant OCD symptoms. Further, Shareh and colleagues (2018) combined HRT with "meta-cognitive methods" and found that protocol superior to a wait-list control. Notably, although standard HRT was not used as a comparison condition in any of these randomized trials, none of the studies yielded outcomes that were markedly superior to what had been found previously with HRT alone. Moreover, across all of the trials it is evident that treatment response is neither universal nor complete, and thus treatment development work and examination of moderators should continue until behavioral interventions can be fine-tuned to be more efficacious, or until there are sufficiently large samples to support examination of variables that would indicate which patients are most and least likely to respond to these interventions.

With respect to treatments for TTM in youth, there are only two RCTs available in which HRT has been examined. Franklin and colleagues (Franklin, Edson, et al. 2011), following on from an encouraging open trial for children and adolescents ages 7 to 17 inclusive (Tolin et al., 2007), found HRT superior to a minimal attention-control condition in 24 youth with TTM; moreover, treatment gains were well maintained for six months after discontinuation, which provided further encouragement for the prospect of earlier intervention yielding both more robust and more durable outcomes. In that same trial, very young patients tended to fare better than older children and adolescents (Franklin et al., 2010), attesting again to the potential utility of early intervention. In a larger sample, Rahman et al. (2017) randomized 40 children and adolescents with TTM to receive either HRT or treatment as usual (TAU); HRT was found to be superior to TAU in both the percentage of treatment responders as well as on the continuous measures of symptom severity, and treatment gains were generally maintained at the two-month follow-up assessment. Approximately half of those assigned to TAU in fact received no treatment at all, which complicates interpretation of study findings. Findings from a larger study comparing HRT to PSC are currently being prepared (see Morris et al., 2016).

Randomized and open studies of behavior therapy or CBT that have included follow-up data suggest problems with relapse in adults. Lerner et al. (1998), Keuthen et al. (2001), Mouton and Stanley (1996), and Keijsers et al. (2006) indicated that relapse was common, whereas Azrin et al. (1980) reported maintenance of gains; an open study and an RCT of HRT for children and adolescents found better maintenance of gains over time than typically reported in adult studies (Franklin, Edson, et al., 2011; Tolin et al., 2007). Clinically, several TTM treatment experts (e.g., Christenson & Mackenzie, 1994; Vitulano et al., 1992) have observed that patients often experience a recurrence of hair-pulling after treatment, especially in response to external stressors. Mouton and Stanley (1996) suggested that additional attention might need to be given to extending awareness training and the use of competing responses to maximize long-term outcome. Keuthen and colleagues included elements of dialectical behavior therapy in their RCT of HRT and did find some protection against relapse after treatment discontinuation using that enhanced protocol (Keuthen et al., 2012).

Review of a Typical HRT Protocol
OVERVIEW

The HRT program typically delivered in the authors' clinic settings for both TTM and SPD first involves eight weekly sessions that are each an hour long, followed by a maintenance phase of four sessions conducted biweekly to promote maintenance of gains. Booster sessions can then be employed as needed to ensure continued use of techniques, management of emergent symptoms via techniques used in acute treatment, and provision of continuing support.

Session 1 begins with the therapist and patient trying to determine whether the patient is aware of the pulling or picking, whether the patient can identify early warning signs of the behaviors, and whether the pulling or picking occurs in many different settings or in only one or two (e.g., upstairs bathroom). The rationale for, and details of, self-monitoring are introduced during this session. If the patient cannot successfully monitor pulling or picking for developmental reasons, parents are enlisted to assist. Psychoeducation is also included in the first session, because patients and their families may have received misinformation or no information about TTM or SPD prior to contact with the clinic. The therapist uses clinical examples, epidemiological information, and analogies to more common nervous habits (such as nail-biting) to begin the process of destigmatizing patients. The therapist explains that TTM and SPD appear to be responsive to stress and are associated with internal and external cues, such as places where the behavior occurs, physical sensations, visual cues, sedentary activities like talking on the phone, and emotional states like boredom. The therapist shares with the patient typical patterns of pulling or picking, describes differences among individuals with respect to what they do with pulled hair or picked skin, and generally tries to convey knowledge and acceptance to the child or adolescent. The importance of improving awareness of urges is emphasized with age-appropriate metaphors and analogies (e.g., "It's hard to know how to outsmart TTM or SPD if we don't know when it's likely to come and bug you . . . "), as increased awareness is critical for successful implementation of stimulus control and habit reversal. The patient is sent home with instructions to begin monitoring pulling using self-monitoring forms available in the behavior therapy manual.

Session 2 introduces stimulus control (SC) techniques. Following review of self-monitoring data, the therapist explains the rationale for SC approaches. In SC interventions, patients are taught to interfere with pulling by wearing band-aids on fingers in high-risk situations, by not touching their face or scalp with bare hands, by looking into mirrors in well-lit areas like bathrooms, and by placing signs that have meaning to the patient in places associated with pulling or picking (e.g., near the telephone). The patient and the therapist consider SC methods that might be employed during the week; suggestions are tailored to the specifics of the patients' behaviors.

Session 3 involves the introduction of competing response/habit reversal procedures. The session begins with review of self-monitoring data, discussion of progress in identifying high-risk situations and in using SC methods to prevent pulling or picking behavior or to stop the behavior sooner than the patient has been able to do previously. Instruction in habit reversal begins by the therapist helping the patient identify how to interrupt the chain of pulling or picking movements, preferably with a physically competing response.

Competing responses that are often used include playing with clay, shelling peanuts, and making tight fists and holding them for several minutes. Patients are instructed to implement the competing response/habit reversal procedures at the first sign of urges. Therapists bring with them to the session several objects or "manipulatives" that can be used for competing response training in order to allow the patient to try out some of the possibilities. Arrangements are made for the patient either to borrow one of the objects from the therapist or to purchase one during the week.

Sessions 4 to 6 involve continuation of SC and HRT. These sessions begin with inspection of self-monitoring data and review of high-risk situations and use of treatment procedures during the previous week. Positive reinforcement of effort is emphasized, as is the analogy of "acting like a detective to outsmart your TTM or SPD." Therapists work with patients to identify times when the treatment procedures have proven easy to implement and useful, as well as times when they have not. Patient and therapist together troubleshoot for those times and places when treatment procedures have not been effective or have not been put in place. Involvement of family in treatment efforts during the previous week is also reviewed, with helpful efforts acknowledged and reinforced and less helpful efforts discussed.

Session 7 focuses on relapse prevention. In addition to reviewing self-monitoring data and use of treatment procedures as described above, therapists introduce the concept of relapse prevention for patients who have made at least some progress in treatment. Patients are taught to imagine coping effectively with stressful situations, instead of returning to pulling or picking as a means to cope. Discussion of relapse prevention begins early on in treatment, but it is emphasized particularly in sessions 7 and 8, as well as during the maintenance phase. Techniques include focusing on how to control setbacks and how to differentiate "lapses" from "relapses," and the patient is taught that occasional setbacks are a natural occurrence rather than an uncontrollable catastrophe. Typically, when a patient has experienced ups and downs during treatment, discussion focuses on how the patient got back on track during the active treatment phase when a lapse was encountered. Patients are also reminded that they are better equipped to deal with future lapses because of what they have learned in treatment. Patients and therapists also design a written list of procedures that the patient can use if they sense a return to previous functioning; calling the therapist for assistance is typically included on this list. Identified triggers and effective responses to the triggers are reviewed with family members to ensure that they are sufficiently aware of the patient's high-risk situations and affective states. Families are advised on how to help the patient cope with occasional setbacks, because strong negative responses to lapses can demoralize patients to the point that they choose not to intervene.

Sesssion 8 includes further discussion of relapse prevention and wrapping up of acute treatment. Self-monitoring data and use of techniques are reviewed, relapse prevention methods are discussed further, and the session focuses particularly on preparing for the reduction of session frequency. Patients are reminded that they have learned the core skills needed to "fight back" against TTM or SPD, and their efforts during the treatment are reviewed and praised. The patient is encouraged to discuss any concerns about ending the acute phase of treatment, and parent(s) are brought into the last half of the session to hear a summary of progress and future efforts from the patient's perspective. For younger patients, these sessions can be conducted as a "graduation ceremony," complete with a certificate of achievement and reminder lists of how to stay on track in the "battle against TTM or SPD."

The maintenance phase of treatment typically includes four in-person sessions conducted over an eight-week period to promote maintenance of gains. This approach is informed by the data on relapse discussed above. Therapists first ask patients whether they have experienced any increases in urges or in actual pulling or picking behavior in the time since the previous contact. In the event that the patient does report any of these changes, the therapist normalizes the increases, contextualizes them as challenges to be faced rather than as failures on the part of the patient or of the therapy, asks if there were any contributing factors that might have led to the increases (e.g., academic challenges, interpersonal stressors), and helps to develop an effective "battle plan" to deal with the behavior itself and to manage the precipitating events without relying on pulling or picking. For patients who report no change in their pulling or picking symptoms or urges, therapists pose hypothetical situations (e.g., "Let's say that it's the week before finals and your TTM/SPD is starting to bug you again at night—how would you deal with that?") and ask patients to elaborate on how they would manage the situations. All patients are encouraged to contact the therapist prior to the next scheduled appointment if a crisis develops.

SPD

Phenomenology and Implications for Treatment

SPD has been defined as recurrent skin-picking, resulting in skin lesions, despite repeated attempts to decrease or stop picking (APA, 2013). Subclinical skin-picking is rather common, so in order to for the patient to receive an SPD diagnosis, the behavior needs to cause significant distress or impairment in important areas of functioning and cannot be attributed to the physiological effects of a substance or other medical condition, such as psoriasis. The placement of SPD with TTM in the *DSM-5* category of obsessive-compulsive and related disorders reflects the theoretical and phenomenological overlap of the conditions; indeed, SPD and TTM have nearly identical *DSM-5* diagnostic criteria (Lochner et al., 2012).

As is the case with TTM, SPD involves multiple sites, with the face, scalp, arms, and legs being the most common (Tucker et al., 2011). Antecedents of skin-picking include blemishes on the skin, an unpleasant urge, and negative emotional states, such as anxiety, tension, or boredom (Keuthen et al., 2010; Tucker et al., 2011). Clinically, many patients with SPD are highly responsive to visual cues suggesting skin imperfections, and they report that picking may commence in an effort to "smooth out" an area that then gets worse with the picking behavior, which then kicks off a cycle of checking, picking, and rechecking. As in TTM, the behavior is thought to be negatively reinforced, because the urge and negative emotional states are usually reduced after picking (Selles et al., 2016; Tucker et al., 2011). Not surprisingly, skin-picking severity is positively correlated with distress and damage to skin (Neziroglu et al., 2008) as well as impulsivity and anxiety (Grant & Chamberlain, 2017). Physical and functional impairment has been found in those picking enough to warrant a formal diagnosis (Flessner & Woods, 2006).

The styles of skin-picking also overlap considerably with the hair-pulling styles identified in TTM. Automatic picking occurs outside one's awarenesss, whereas focused picking is more intentional and ritualistic (Walther et al., 2009). Several studies have examined the association between automatic and focused picking, emotion regulation capacities, and personality traits (Pozza et al., 2020; Schienle et al., 2018). Pozza et al. (2016) found that while difficulty engaging in goal-directed behavior was evident in both subtypes, a lack of strategies for regulating negative emotions was specifically related to focused picking. Accordingly, most behavioral protocols for SPD contain techniques designed to help manage negative affect. Schienle et al. (2018) found that impulse-control difficulties predicted focused skin-picking, but a lack of emotional clarity predicted automatic skin-picking. Each patient should receive a careful functional assessment of skin-picking that explicates antecedents, exact behaviors, and consequences, because the specific sequences of the behaviors may suggest different clinical intervention points for a given patient. As with any behavioral intervention, there is a tension between adherence to the protocol and flexibility to respond to the particular context for a given patient: this delicate dance between flexibility and fidelity has been described elsewhere (Franklin & Turk Karan, 2022; Kendall et al., 2018), and is applicable in the behavioral treatment of SPD as well.

Pharmacotherapy

Pharmacotherapy for SPD is an underdeveloped area of study, with only five published RCTs available to inform clinical decision-making. This is not at all surprising given SPD's relatively recent inclusion in the *DSM* and the lack of scientific data available until recently chronicling its pernicious effects on patients. Even before the formal recognition of SPD, small RCTs addressing "pathological skin-picking" had been conducted, and the agents pursued were also reflective of the overarching view that the condition was an offshoot of OCD. However, randomized studies examining the efficacy of SSRIs for skin-picking yielded mixed results at best for fluoxetine (Simeon et al., 1997) and citalopram (Arbabi et al., 2008); a single trial of lamotrigine demonstrated that active treatment failed to separate at all from PBO (Grant et al., 2010).

Increasing interest in the role of glutamate in the pathophysiology of body-focused repetitive behaviors resulted in efforts to test agents that affected this neurotransmitter in particular. Grant and colleagues (2016) initiated an RCT examining the efficacy of NAC, the same compound found efficacious for TTM in adults. In the largest pharmacotherapy trial ever conducted in SPD, Grant and colleagues randomized 66 patients to receive either NAC or a matched PBO. NAC was superior to PBO on the continuous measures of outcome as well as the percentages of completers classified as responders, with 47% and 19% responder rates, respectively. As was the case in the TTM study, NAC was well tolerated, and no serious adverse effects were observed. Of note, observed differences between the conditions seemed to be driven by reduction in urges, which suggests that NAC might be especially useful for patients who engage in focused rather than automatic picking, the latter of which is characterized by picking that is outside conscious awareness.

HRT

OVERVIEW

Not surprisingly, the same variety of behavioral techniques applied to the treatment of TTM have also been attempted for SPD, owing to a belief that "nervous habits" share similar origins and maintaining factors. Components of behavioral interventions, such as self-monitoring, aversion, covert sensitization, negative practice, relaxation training, competing response training, cognitive restructuring, and overcorrection, have been applied, and skin-picking was included among the conditions thought to be responsive to HRT (Azrin & Nunn, 1973). Improving awareness and breaking the association between urge and behavior by substituting a response, known as a competing response, was thought to be potentially helpful. By responding to urges to pick by engaging in a competing response that uses the same muscle groups and is incompatible with picking (e.g., shelling peanuts, fist-clenching), patients were believed to be mitigating the negative reinforcing effects of responding to urges by actually picking.

OUTCOME RESEARCH

In the first RCT of HRT for skin-picking, Teng and colleagues (2006) randomized 25 adult participants to three sessions of HRT or to a wait-list control group. Despite the relatively brief treatment duration, six participants dropped out prematurely; of those who completed the trial, participants assigned to HRT fared significantly better than the control group participants, both in terms of self-reported skin-picking and on blind rater assessments of damage to the skin at posttreatment evaluation and follow-up.

In a larger study that again paralleled the TTM literature, Moritz and colleagues (2012) tested self-guided decoupling, a variant of HRT, against HRT alone; both treatments were administered via self-help manuals. Seventy patients participated in the study, which found an advantage for HRT over decoupling in intent-to-treat analyses as well as completer analyses. The absence of follow-up data prevents examination of the durability of either form of treatment, and the flexible design of the interventions themselves makes it difficult to draw strong conclusions about what patients actually received and learned in treatment.

Capriotti and colleagues (2015) sought to examine the efficacy of AEBT for SPD, because there were concerns that affect-driven, intentional picking may not be as responsive to HRT unless techniques are included to help address negative emotion. This case series followed the treatment of four patients treated using a formal manual (Woods & Twohig, 2008); results indicated that three of four participants showed a substantial decrease in picking behavior after treatment. Future studies that follow on from this promising case series should include larger sample sizes, a control condition to account for nonspecific effects of attention and repeated assessment, and random assignment to condition.

AEBT for TTM and SPD

The typical course of treatment for TTM or SPD using HRT is presented above, and the outcome data that are available provide evidence for the efficacy of the procedures (for reviews, see Lee et al., 2019; McGuire et al., 2014). At the same time, the literature also points out that treatment response for HRT alone is neither universal nor complete, and the adult literature in particular highlights issues with relapse after treatment discontinuation. It is in this context that treatment development efforts have been made, and most of the newer interventions have focused on augmenting HRT with clinical procedures designed to help patients manage the affect that can serve as a prompt for urges to pull or pick (Keuthen et al., 2012). One such set of procedures is acceptance and commitment therapy (ACT), which has been used successfully as a treatment for OCD (Twohig et al., 2010), has been incorporated into treatment of tic disorders (Franklin, Best, et al., 2011), and has now been brought to bear to augment HRT for TTM (Woods et al., 2006) and SPD (Capriotti et al., 2015).

A detailed, coherent explication of relational frame theory is beyond the scope of this chapter, but this theory is thought to provide the conceptual foundation of ACT (see Twohig et al., 2006; Woods & Twohig, 2008). As described by Capriotti and colleagues and laid out in detail in Woods and Twohig (2008), AEBT is delivered in ten 60-minute sessions and includes the following procedures: psychoeducation and functional analysis (Session 1) and the introduction of HRT and SC (Session 2), followed in Sessions 3 to 7 by a series of ACT exercises aimed at: (a) values clarification; (b) enhancing willingness to accept aversive internal states, such as urges to pull or pick; and (c) commitment to living in accordance with one's values while experiencing aversive internal states. As the outcome literature develops and as novel statistical and methodological advances are used to examine individual participant data from these studies in an effort to identify moderators of outcome (see Kemp et al., 2020), it is hoped that greater clarity can be discovered regarding which patients will respond well to HRT alone versus those who need augmentation with procedures designed to help them manage aversive internal states, such as are provided in ACT. The field is very much in need of the development of this knowledge base to inform clinical decision-making.

HRT: What's in a Name?

Psychology's use of the term "habit reversal" originated in the 1970s during the height of behavioral psychology. Originally designed to treat nervous habits and tics (Azrin & Nunn, 1973), habit reversal has been shown to be effective with many other psychological and behavioral difficulties, such as stuttering, alcohol abuse, enuresis, and behavior problems (Azrin & Foxx, 1971; Azrin & Nunn, 1974; Azrin et al., 1980; Hunt & Azrin, 1973). Based on the colloquial understanding of the term "habit," one may assume that the target behavior could be treated simply. Unfortunately, this work is often difficult and the use of the word "habit" often prohibits the full understanding of the distress, impairment, and dysfunction associated with the disorders. Additionally, it may imply that the patient is to blame for "not stopping" the symptoms. Furthermore, it minimizes the need for a more formal, systematic approach. Although the HRT term is still used today, clinicians should be cautious about the other messages use of the term could send..

Future Directions

Pharmacotherapy Treatment Development

With the possible exception of NAC, pharmacotherapy research for TTM and SPD remains stagnant. This lack of progress plays out in the clinical realm with unfortunate consequences: despite a pharmacotherapy outcome literature that can only be described as discouraging, TTM and SPD continue to be treated medically mostly with SSRIs (Franklin et al., 2008; Woods et al., 2006). This may be an artifact of TTM's topographic similarity to OCD and a function of the lack of basic research in TTM to identify its specific neurobiological and neuroanatomical pathways, although interest in the role of glutamate in behavioral conditions continues to increase. Despite its similarity to OCD in the form of repetitive behavior, TTM's response to SSRIs is far less robust or consistent than the response in OCD (Christenson et al., 1991; Stanley et al., 1997; Streichenwein & Thornby, 1995), with multiple double-blind experiments yielding limited results. Discussions in the literature of TTM's addictive qualities (Grant et al., 2007) may promote further investigation of the use of compounds found efficacious for addictive disorders.

Pharmacotherapy development for TTM and SPD may be informed by an increasing focus on neurobiological variables and mechanisms, and the relationship between these factors and the development of novel interventions. Additional efforts have suggested that opioid blockers may be more appropriate for TTM, shifting focus to the dopamine system and the pleasure-seeking (positive reinforcement) found in TTM (Grant et al., 2007), as opposed to the negative reinforcement observed in OCD and likely in the maintenance of tics as well. In addition to discriminating between diagnoses, it is essential to identify which types of medication are most effective in treating the different subtypes of each disorder. Psychiatry will greatly benefit from further identification of these essential and unique aspects of the disorders that direct pharmaceutical intervention. In order to push past the treatment plateaus that appear to have been reached, a return to basic science may well be needed to stimulate new ideas. With regard to the available pharmacotherapies for both TTM and SPD, it is essential to improve knowledge about both the efficacy and safety of long-term use, maximum dose–response ratios, and clinical management of side effects. Ideally, public and government enthusiasm for the value of science can be restored, which in turn may encourage a return of research funding to previous levels (if not greater levels) to help alleviate human suffering, including that experienced by individuals with TTM and SPD.

DISSEMINATION

Across the randomized studies of psychosocial interventions for TTM and SPD reviewed in this chapter, data are convergent in suggesting the efficacy of HRT. What remains to be discovered is whether the treatments can be readily disseminated into the clinical and medical settings where most patients would be likely to access care. Given that establishment of a treatment's efficacy requires design elements that emphasize internal validity at the cost of external validity and that efficacy studies logically precede examination of treatment effectiveness (Franklin, 2005; Franklin et al., 2006), all of the RCTs discussed here were conducted in centers with a significant amount of technical and clinical expertise. In light of the data from Marcks et al. (2004) suggesting widespread misunderstanding of behavioral treatments, it is imperative to determine which treatments can be taught most easily to patients, their families, and clinicians, and to examine the effectiveness of these interventions when they are delivered in community clinical settings as opposed to the Ivory Tower of academic settings.

A number of dissemination models now warrant further testing, including one that was used with great success in pediatric OCD in recent years. The efficacy of CBT for pediatric OCD is now well established (Abramowitz et al., 2005; Barrett et al., 2008), and a recent study examined the effectiveness of a "supervision of supervisors" model wherein master's level clinicians in Norway provided manualized CBT to pediatric patients presenting for treatment of OCD (Valderhaug et al., 2007). The clinicians employed a manualized treatment (Piacentini et al., 1998) under the supervision of psychologists who were very familiar with CBT for OCD; the supervisors were provided regular access to the manual's creator, Dr. Piacentini, as part of the study. Findings from the open trial were extremely encouraging: the outcomes achieved both at end of acute treatment and at follow-up were comparable to what had been found in pediatric OCD RCTs and in open studies conducted in centers that developed the CBT protocol for pediatric OCD (Franklin et al., 1998). The NORDLOTS trial followed on from this work—in that trial, 269 pediatric patients with OCD received open treatment with CBT, followed by random assignment of partial and nonresponders to receive either additional CBT or augmentation with sertraline (Skarphedinsson et al., 2015; Torp et al., 2015). This same dissemination model should now be applied to the treatment of TTM and SPD to promote better access to empirically supported treatment for those families who do not live within commuting distance of subspecialty settings.

References

Abramowitz, J. S., Whiteside, S. P., & Deacon, R. J. (2005). The effectiveness of treatment for pediatric obsessive-compulsive disorder: A meta-analysis. *Behavior Therapy, 36*, 55–63.

American Psychiatric Association (APA). (2013). *Diagnostic and statistical manual of mental disorders* (5th ed.).

Arbabi, M., Farnia, V., & Balighi, K. (2008). Efficacy of citalopram in treatment of pathological skin picking. *Acta Medica Iranica, 46*(5), 367–372.

Azrin, N. H., & Foxx, R. (1971). A rapid method of toilet training the institutionalized retarded. *Journal of Applied Behavior Analysis, 2*, 323–334.

Azrin, N. H., & Nunn, R. G. (1973). Habit-reversal: A method of eliminating nervous habits and tics. *Behaviour Research and Therapy, 11*, 619–628.

Azrin, N. H., & Nunn, R. G. (1974). A rapid method of eliminating stuttering by a regulated breathing approach. *Behaviour Research and Therapy, 12*, 279–286.

Azrin, N. H., Nunn, R. G., & Frantz, S. E. (1980). Treatment of hair pulling (trichotillomania): A comparative study of habit reversal and negative practice training. *Journal of Behavior Therapy and Experimental Psychiatry, 11*, 13–20.

Barrett, P. M., Farrell, L., Pina, A. A., Peris, T. S., & Piacentini, J. (2008). Evidence-based psychosocial treatments for child and adolescent obsessive-compulsive disorder. *Journal of Clinical Child and Adolescent Psychology, 37*, 131–155.

Bloch, M. H., Panza, K. E., Grant, J. E., Pittenger, C., & Leckman, J. F. (2013). *N*-Acetylcysteine in the treatment of pediatric trichotillomania: A randomized, double-blind, placebo-controlled add-on trial. *Journal of the American Academy of Child and Adolescent Psychiatry, 52*(3), 231–240.

Capriotti, M. R., Ely, L. J., Snorrason, I., & Woods, D. W. (2015). Acceptance-enhanced behavior therapy for excoriation (skin-picking) disorder in adults: A clinical case series. *Cognitive and Behavioral Practice, 22*(2), 230–239.

Casati, J., Toner, B. B., & Yu, B. (2000). Psychosocial issues for women with trichotillomania. *Comprehensive Psychiatry, 41*, 344–351.

Christenson, G. A., Mackenzie, T. B., & Mitchell, J. E. (1991). Characteristics of 60 adult chronic hair pullers. *The American Journal of Psychiatry, 148*, 365–370.

Christenson, G. A., & Mackenzie, T. B. (1994). Trichotillomania. In M. Hersen & R. T. Ammerman (Eds.), *Handbook of prescriptive treatments for adults* (pp. 217–235). Plenum.

Dougherty, D. D., Loh, R., Jenike, M. A., & Keuthen, N. J. (2006). Single modality versus dual modality treatment for trichotillomania: Sertraline, behavioral therapy, or both? *The Journal of Clinical Psychiatry, 67*, 1086–1092.

du Toit, P. L., van Kradenburg, J., Niehaus, D. J. H., & Stein, D. J. (2001). Characteristics and phenomenology of hair pulling: An exploration of subtypes. *Comprehensive Psychiatry, 42*, 247–256.

Flessner, C. A., Conelea, C. A., Woods, D. W., Franklin, M. E., Keuthen, N. J., & Cashin, S. E. (2008). Styles of pulling in trichotillomania: Exploring differences in symptoms severity, phenomenology, and functional impact. *Behaviour Research and Therapy, 46*, 345–347.

Flessner, C. A., & Woods, D.W. (2006). Phenomenological characteristics, social problems, and the economic impact associated with chronic skin picking. *Behavior Modification, 30*, 944–963.

Franklin, M. E. (2005). Seeing the complexities: A comment on "Combined psychotherapy and pharmacotherapy for mood and anxiety disorders: Review and analysis." *Clinical Psychology: Science & Practice, 12*, 151–161.

Franklin, M. E., Best, S. H., Wilson, M. A., Loew, B., & Compton, S. N. (2011). Habit reversal training and acceptance and commitment therapy for Tourette syndrome: A pilot project. *Journal of Developmental and Physical Disabilities, 23*(1), 49–60.

Franklin, M. E., Cahill, S. P., & Compton, S. N. (2006). What is the question? A comment on "Investigating treatment mediators when simple random assignment to a control group is not possible." *Clinical Psychology: Science and Practice, 13*, 337–341.

Franklin, M. E., Edson, A. L., & Freeman, J. B. (2010). Behavior therapy for pediatric trichotillomania: Exploring the effects of age on treatment outcome. *Child and Adolescent Psychiatry and Mental Health, 4*, 6.

Franklin, M. E., Edson, A. L., Ledley, D. A., & Cahill, S. P. (2011). Behavior therapy for pediatric trichotillomania: A randomized controlled trial. *Journal of the American Academy of Child and Adolescent Psychiatry, 50*(8), 763–771.

Franklin, M. E., Flessner, C. A., Woods, D. W., Keuthen, N. J., Piacentini, J. C., Moore, P. S., et al. (2008). The Child and Adolescent Trichotillomania Impact Project (CA-TIP): Exploring descriptive psychopathology, functional impairment, comorbidity, and treatment utilization. *Journal of Developmental and Behavioral Pediatrics, 29*, 493–500.

Franklin, M. E., Kozak, M. J., Cashman, L. A., Coles, M. E., Rheingold, A. A., & Foa, E. B. (1998). Cognitive-behavioral treatment of pediatric obsessive-compulsive disorder: An open clinical trial. *Journal of the American Academy of Child & Adolescent Psychiatry, 37*(4), 412–419.

Franklin, M. E., & Tolin, D. F. (Eds.). (2007). *Treating trichotillomania: Cognitive behavioral therapy for hair pulling and related problems.* (pps. 76-94) Springer Science and Business Media.

Franklin, M. E., & Turk Karan, S. 2022). Empirically supported treatment for Obsessive-compulsive disorder: Core elements and adaptive applications. In P. C. Kendall (Ed.), *Flexibility within fidelity: Breathing life into a manual* (pp. 76–94). Oxford University Press.

Grant, J. E., & Chamberlain, S. R. (2017). Clinical correlates of symptom severity in skin picking disorder. *Comprehensive Psychiatry, 78*, 25–30.

Grant, J. E., Chamberlain, S. R., Redden, S. A., Leppink, E. W., Odlaug, B. L., & Kim, S. W. (2016). N-Acetylcysteine in the treatment of excoriation disorder: A randomized clinical trial. *JAMA Psychiatry, 73*(5), 490–496.

Grant, J. E., Odlaug, B. L., Chamberlain, S. R., & Kim, S. W. (2010). A double-blind, placebo-controlled trial of lamotrigine for pathological skin picking: Treatment efficacy and neurocognitive predictors of response. *Journal of Clinical Psychopharmacology, 30*(4), 396–403.

Grant, J. E., Odlaug, B. L., & Potenza, M. N. (2007). Addicted to hair pulling? How an alternate model of trichotillomania may improve outcome. *Harvard Review of Psychiatry, 15*, 80–85.

Hunt, G. M., & Azrin, N. H. (1973). A community-reinforcement approach to alcoholism. *Behaviour Research and Therapy, 11*, 91–104. https://doi.org/10.1016/0005-7967(73)90072-7

Keijsers, G. P., van Minnen, A., Hoogduin, C. A., Klaassen, B. N., Hendriks, M. J., & Tanis-Jacobs, J. (2006). Behavioural treatment of trichotillomania: Two-year followup results. *Behaviour Research and Therapy, 44*, 359–370.

Kemp, J., Barker, D., Benito, K., Herren, J., & Freeman, J. (2020). Moderators of psychosocial treatment for pediatric obsessive-compulsive disorder: Summary and recommendations for future directions. *Journal of Clinical Child and Adolescent Psychology, 50*(4), 478–485. http://dx.doi.org.proxy.library.upenn.edu/10.1080/15374416.2020.1790378

Kendall, P. C., & Frank, H. E. (2018). Implementing evidence-based treatment protocols: Flexibility within fidelity. *Clinical Psychology: Science and Practice, 25*(4), 12.

Keuthen, N. J., Fraim, C., Deckersbach, T., Dougherty, D. D., Baer, L., & Jenike, M. A. (2001). Longitudinal follow-up of naturalistic treatment outcome in patients with trichotillomania. *The Journal of Clinical Psychiatry, 62*, 101–107.

Keuthen, N. J., Koran, L. M., Aboujaoude, E., Large, M. D., & Serpe, R. T. (2010). The prevalence of pathologic skin picking in US adults. *Comprehensive Psychiatry, 51*(2), 183–186.

Keuthen, N. J., Rothbaum, B. O., Fama, J., Altenburger, E., Falkenstein, M. J., Sprich, S. E., Spric, S. E., Kearns, M., Meunier, S., Jenike, M. A., & Welch, S. S. (2012). DBT-enhanced cognitive-behavioral treatment for trichotillomania: A randomized controlled trial. *Journal of Behavioral Addictions, 1*(3), 106–114.

Lee, M. T., Mpvaenda, D. N., & Fineberg, N. A. (2019). Habit reversal therapy in obsessive compulsive related disorders: A systematic review of the evidence and CONSORT evaluation of randomized controlled trials. *Frontiers in Behavioral Neuroscience, 13*, 15.

Lerner, J., Franklin, M. E., Meadows, E. A., Hembree, E., & Foa, E. B. (1998). Effectiveness of a cognitive-behavioral treatment program for trichotillomania: An uncontrolled evaluation. *Behavior Therapy, 29*, 157–171.

Lochner, C., Grant, J. E., Odlaug, B. L., Woods, D. W., Keuthen, N. J., & Stein, D. J. (2012). DSM-5 field survey: Hair pulling disorder (Trichotillomania). *Depression and Anxiety, 29*, 1025–1031. https://doi.org/10.1002/da.22011

Mansueto, C. S., Golomb, R. G., Thomas, A. M., & Stemberger, R. M. (1999). A comprehensive model for behavioral treatment of trichotillomania. *Cognitive and Behavioral Practice, 6*, 23–43.

Marcks, B. A., Woods, D. W., & Ridosko, J. L. (2004). The effects of trichotillomania disclosure on peer perceptions and social acceptability. *Body Image, 2*, 299–306.

McGuire, J. F., Ung, D., Selles, R. R., Rahman, O., Lewin, A. B., Murphy, T. K., & Storch, E. A. (2014). Treating trichotillomania: A meta-analysis of treatment effects and moderators for behavior therapy and serotonin reuptake inhibitors. *Journal of Psychiatric Research, 58*, 76–83.

Miguel, E. C., Coffey, B. J., Baier, L., Savage, C. R., Rauch, S. L., & Jenike, M. A. (1995). Phenomenology of intentional repetitive behaviors in obsessive-compulsive disorder and Tourette's disorder. *The Journal of Clinical Psychiatry, 56*, 246–255.

Moritz, S., Fricke, S., Treszl, A., & Wittekind, C. E. (2012). Do it yourself! Evaluation of self-help habit reversal training versus decoupling in pathological skin picking: A pilot study. *Journal of Obsessive-Compulsive and Related Disorders, 1*(1), 41–47.

Morris, S. H., Kratz, H. E., Burke, D. A., Zickgraf, H. F., Coogan, C., Woods, D., & Franklin, M. E. (2016). Behavior therapy for pediatric trichotillomania: Rationale and methods for a randomized controlled trial. *Journal of Obsessive-Compulsive and Related Disorders, 9*, 116–124.

Mouton, S. G., & Stanley, M. A. (1996). Habit reversal training for trichotillomania: A group approach. *Cognitive and Behavioral Practice, 3*, 159–182.

Neal-Barnett, A., Woods, D. W., Espil, F. M., Davis, M., Alexander, J. R., Compton, S. N., Walther, M. R., Twohig, M. P., Saunders, S. M., Cahill, S. P., & Franklin, M. E. (2019). Acceptance-enhanced behavior therapy for trichotillomania: Randomized controlled trial rationale, method, and strategies for recruiting minority participants. *Bulletin of the Menninger Clinic, 83*(4), 399–431.

Neziroglu, F., Rabinowitz, D., Breytman, A., et al. (2008). Skin picking phenomenology and severity comparison. *The Journal of Clinical Psychiatry 10*: 306–312.

Ninan, P. T., Rothbaum, B. O., Marsteller, F. A., Knight, B. T., & Eccard, M. B. (2000). A placebo-controlled trial of cognitive-behavioral therapy and clomipramine in trichotillomania. *The Journal of Clinical Psychiatry 61*, 47–50.

Panza, K. E., Pittenger, C., & Bloch, M. H. (2013). Age and gender correlates of pulling in pediatric trichotillomania. *Journal of the American Academy of Child and Adolescent Psychiatry, 52*(3), 241–249.

Piacentini, J., Jacobs, C., Maidment, K., & Bergman, R. L. (1998). Individual CBT and family (ERP/family) treatment: A multicomponent treatment program for children and adolescents with obsessive-compulsive disorder. Unpublished manuscript, Los Angeles, CA.

Pozza, A., Albert, U., & Dèttore, D. (2020). Early maladaptive schemas as common and specific predictors of skin picking subtypes. *BMC Psychology, 8*(1). https://doi.org/10.1186/s40359-020-0392-y

Pozza, A., Giaquinta, N., & Dèttore, D. (2016). Borderline, avoidant, sadistic personality traits and emotion dysregulation predict different pathological skin picking subtypes in a community sample. *Neuropsychiatric Disease and Treatment, 12*, 1861–1867.

Rahman, O., McGuire, J., Storch, E. A., & Lewin, A. B. (2017). Preliminary randomized controlled trial of habit reversal training for treatment of hair pulling in youth. *Journal of Child and Adolescent Psychopharmacology, 27*(2), 132–139.

Santhanan, R., Fairley, M., & Rogers, M. (2008). Is it trichotillomania? Hair pulling in childhood: A developmental perspective. *Clinical Child Psychology and Psychiatry, 13*, 409–418.

Schienle, A., Zorjan, S., Übel, S., & Wabnegger, A. (2018). Prediction of automatic and focused skin picking based on trait disgust and emotion dysregulation. *Journal of Obsessive-Compulsive and Related Disorders, 16*, 1–5.

Schlosser, S., Black, D. W., Blum, N., & Goldstein, R. B. (1994). The demography, phenomenology, and family history of 22 persons with compulsive hair pulling. *Annals of Clinical Psychiatry, 6*, 147–152.

Selles, R. R., McGuire, J. F., Small, B. J., & Storch, E. A. (2016). A systematic review and meta-analysis of psychiatric treatments for excoriation (skin-picking) disorder. *General Hospital Psychiatry, 41*, 29–37.

Shareh, H. (2018). A preliminary investigation of metacognitive therapy and habit reversal as a treatment for trichotillomania. *Behavioural and Cognitive Psychotherapy, 46*(1), 1–20.

Simeon, D., Stein, D. J., Gross, S., Islam, N., Schmeidler, J., & Hollander, E. (1997). A double-blind trial of fluoxetine in pathologic skin picking. *The Journal of Clinical Psychiatry, 58*(8), 341–347.

Skarphedinsson, G., Weidle, B., Thomsen, P. H., Nissen, J. B., Melin, K. H., Hybel, K., Valderhaug, R., Wentzel-Larsen, T., Compton, S. N., & Ivarsson, T. (2015). Continued cognitive-behavior therapy versus sertraline for children and adolescents with obsessive-compulsive disorder that were non-responders to

Stanley, M. A., Breckenridge, J. K., & Swann, A. C. (1997). Fluvoxamine treatment of trichotillomania. *Journal of Clinical Psychopharmacology, 17*, 278–283.

Stewart, R. S., & Nejtek, V. A. (2003). An open-label, flexible-dose study of olanzapine in the treatment of trichotillomania. *The Journal of Clinical Psychiatry, 64*, 49–52.

Streichenwein, S. M., & Thornby J. I., (1995). A long-term, double-blind, placebo-controlled crossover trial of the efficacy of fluoxetine for trichotillomania. *The American Journal of Psychiatry, 152*, 1192–1196.

Swedo, S. E., Lenane, M. C., & Leonard, H. L. (1993). Long-term treatment of trichotillomania (hair pulling) [Letter to the editor]. *The New England Journal of Medicine, 329*, 141–142.

Swedo, S. E., Leonard, H. L., Rapoport, J. L., Lenane, M. C., Goldberger, E. L., & Cheslow, D. L. (1989). A double-blind comparison of clomipramine and desipramine in the treatment of trichotillomania (hair pulling). *The New England Journal of Medicine, 321*, 497–501.

Teng, E. J., Woods, D. W., & Twohig, M. P. (2006). Habit reversal as a treatment for chronic skin picking: A pilot investigation. *Behavior Modification, 30*(4), 411–422.

Tolin, D. F., Franklin, M. E., Diefenbach, G. J., Anderson, E., & Meunier, S. A. (2007). Pediatric trichotillomania: Descriptive psychopathology and an open trial of cognitive-behavioral therapy. *Cognitive Behaviour Therapy, 36*, 129–144.

Torp, N. C., Dahl, K., Skarphedinsson, G., Thomsen, P. H., Valderhaug, R., Weidle, B., Melin, K. H., Hybel, K., Nissen, J. B., Lenhard, F., Wentzel-Larsen, T., Franklin, M. E., & Ivarsson, T. (2015). Effectiveness of cognitive behavior treatment for pediatric obsessive-compulsive disorder: Acute outcomes from the Nordic Long-term OCD Treatment Study (NORDLOTS). *Behaviour Research and Therapy, 64*, 15–23.

Tucker, B. T., Woods, D. W., Flessner, C. A., Franklin, S. A., & Franklin, M. E. (2011). The Skin Picking Impact Project: Phenomenology, interference, and treatment utilization of pathological skin picking in a population-based sample. *Journal of Anxiety Disorders, 25*(1), 88–95.

Twohig, M. P., Hayes, S. C., & Masuda, A. (2006). Increasing willingness to experience obsessions: Acceptance and commitment therapy as a treatment for obsessive compulsive disorder. *Behavior Therapy, 37*, 3–13.

Twohig, M., Hayes, S. C., Plumb, J., Pruitt, L. D., Collins, A. B., Hazlett-Stevens, H., & Woidneck, M. R. (2010). A randomized controlled trial of acceptance and commitment therapy versus progressive relaxation training for obsessive compulsive disorder. *Journal of Consulting and Clinical Psychology, 78*, 705–716.

Valderhaug, R., Larsson, B., Götestam, K. G., & Piacentini, J. (2007). An open clinical trial of cognitive-behaviour therapy in children and adolescents with obsessive-compulsive disorder administered in regular outpatient clinics. *Behaviour Research and Therapy, 45*(3), 577–589. https://doi.org/10.1016/j.brat.2006.04.011

Van Ameringen, M., Mancini, C., Patterson, B., Bennett, M., & Oakman, J. (2010). A randomized, double-blind, placebo-controlled trial of olanzapine in the treatment of trichotillomania. *The Journal of Clinical Psychiatry, 71*(10), 1336–1343.

van Minnen, A., Hoogduin, K. A., Keijsers, G. P., Hellenbrand, I., & Hendriks, G. (2003). Treatment of trichotillomania with behavioral therapy or fluoxetine. *Archives of General Psychiatry, 60*, 517–522.

Vitulano, L. A., King, R. A., Scahill, L., & Cohen, D. J. (1992). Behavioral treatment of children and adolescents with trichotillomania. *Journal of the American Academy of Child and Adolescent Psychiatry, 31*, 139–146.

Walther, M. R., Flessner, C. A., Conelea, C. A., & Woods, D. W. (2009). The Milwaukee Inventory for the Dimensions of Adult Skin Picking (MIDAS): Initial development and psychometric properties. *Journal of Behavior Therapy and Experimental Psychiatry, 40*(1), 127–135.

Woods, D. W., Flessner, C. A., Franklin, M. E., Keuthen, N. J., Goodwin, R. D., Stein, D. J., et al. (2006). The Trichotillomania Impact Project (TIP): Exploring phenomenology, functional impairment, and treatment utilization. *The Journal of Clinical Psychiatry, 67*, 1877–1888.

Woods, D. W., & Twohig, M. P. (2008). *Trichotillomania: An ACT-enhanced behavior therapy approach therapist guide*. Oxford University Press.

PART V

Obsessive-Compulsive and Related Disorders in Special Populations

CHAPTER 25

Obsessive-Compulsive and Related Disorders in Older Adults

John E. Calamari, Cheryl N. Carmin, Amanda Messerlie, *and* Sibel Sarac

Abstract

While the population ages, the obsessive-compulsive and related disorders (OCRDs) remain understudied in older adults. Several OCRDs occur regularly in late life and are highly debilitating for older people. Other OCRDs have not been studied in older adults. This chapter summarizes the important emotional changes that are now known to characterize late life as a context for understanding older adults' mental health. The chapter reviews estimates of late-life OCRD prevalence and whether the symptoms experienced by older people differ from symptoms in other age groups. The chapter examines age at onset and life course as important factors for understanding how the conditions come to affect older people. Studies on the life course of hoarding disorder (HD) suggest that while the condition begins early in life, the disorder is both chronic and progressive. Older adults often experience HD in severe form. Emerging information on the developmental course of HD and its prevalence in older adults has precipitated increased research and refinements in treatment. In contrast, late-life obsessive-compulsive disorder (OCD) remains neglected, and controlled treatment outcome studies have not occurred with older people. While most patients' OCD begins early in life, evidence suggests that there is a subgroup who experience the disorder for the first time in late life. To better understand late-life OCRDs, new models test whether the important changes occurring in late life might interact with disorder risk factors to precipitate late-life obsessional disorders. The results of initial tests of these models are encouraging.

Key Words: obsessive-compulsive disorder, older adults, obsessive-compulsive and related disorders, aging

Introduction

The population is aging. This demographic shift has occurred in the United States and internationally as a result of multiple factors (Knight & McCallum, 2011). Life expectancies have increased for both men and women, who now can expect to live into their mid-seventies or eighties, and by the end of the decade older people will make up almost 20% of the population of the United States (U.S. Census Bureau, 2003). The aging of the population warrants increased research that aims to better understand and treat older adults' mental health problems, and this focus should be a public health priority.

While there have been advances in the treatment of the psychiatric illnesses experienced by older people (Hinrichsen, 2020; Knight & McCallum, 2011), the study and treatment of obsessive-compulsive disorder (OCD) has progressed more slowly (for reviews, see Calamari et al., 2017; Dozier & Ayers, 2017).

This chapter reviews what is currently known about the late-life occurrence of OCD as well as the four conditions now designated as related disorders. In the fifth edition of the *Diagnostic and Statistical Manual of Mental Disorders* (*DSM-5*; American Psychiatric Association [APA], 2013) a new classification category appeared, the obsessive-compulsive and related disorders (OCRDs). As described in the *DSM-5*, the OCRDs have important commonalities with OCD that include similar phenomenology, shared etiologic mechanisms, and similar positive treatment responses to specific classes of intervention. In addition to OCD, the OCRDs are body dysmorphic disorder (BDD), hoarding disorder (HD), trichotillomania (TTM), and skin-picking disorder (SPD). This chapter briefly overviews the significant changes in the classification of OCD in *DSM-5*; for a more in-depth review of the conceptualization and classification of OCD, see Chapter 2.

Important to understanding late-life psychopathology is awareness of the developmental context in which the problems occur. There have been significant advances in knowledge about late-life development and the important changes that take place. These changes include what has been referred to as the positivity effect (Charles & Robinette, 2015). Older people report experiencing fewer negative emotions, greater emotional stability throughout the day, and increased overall happiness (Charles et al., 2001; Mroczek & Kolarz, 1998). This chapter summarizes the new understandings of older adults' more positive emotional experiences, which might be understood as counterforces to the well-recognized stressors of late life (e.g., increasing health problems and cognitive decline).

For OCD and the other OCRDs, this chapter summarizes the current conceptualization and definition of each disorder as seen in *DSM-5*. The available information on each condition's phenomenology as it has been observed in older people is examined. The discussion includes whether older adults experience different symptoms. This issue has significant implications for the accurate diagnosis of OCRDs in older people (Dozier & Ayers, 2017) and for understanding late-life OCD and related disorders broadly (Calamari et al., 2017). The chapter also critically reviews studies of OCRD prevalence in older people and the implications disorder prevalence has for understanding late-life OCRDs. For example, while there have been consistent reports of lower prevalence rates of OCD in older adults (Bassil et al., 2011; Kessler et al., 2005), the investigations have had methodological limitations.

The age at which a disorder begins is important for understanding the psychopathology affecting older adults. For example, when OCD is identified in an older adult, is it because symptoms that began earlier in life have continued into late life? Could OCD occur for the first time in late life? Do the subclinical OCD symptoms experienced earlier in life become more severe and debilitating in late life for some people? Understanding when in life a condition begins has implications for understanding the disorder's pathogenesis. Additionally, the understanding of a disorder's age-at-onset will often determine the age groups which psychopathology researchers will most often turn their attention (cf. Calamari et al., 2002). That is, for conditions understood to begin in early adulthood, research is more likely to be completed with young adult or middle-aged samples than with people age 60 or older. The chapter examines the age-at-onset issue and, relatedly, reviews the available information about risk and protective factors for the OCRDs and whether these factors differ for older adults.

Last, the chapter provides an overview of the psychosocial treatment of late-life OCRDs.[1] The best evidence-based psychosocial interventions for each condition (as well as their effectiveness) are briefly described. Whether the effectiveness of the evidence-based intervention has been directly evaluated with older adults, its efficacy with older people, and whether modifications of the treatment were necessary for its effective use in older adults are all described.

Of course, the framework outlined here for review of late-life OCD and the other OCRDs is aspirational. The empirical information needed to answer many important questions is limited or absent at present. These limitations are pointed out in the discussion, along with areas for future study.

Late-Life Development

Calamari et al. (2017) summarized the changes that occur during late life that they considered most important for understanding the context in which older adults' obsessional disorders occur. They noted that contemporary gerontologists view late life as a period of important and dynamic changes (Woods, 2008), contrary to stereotypic ideas of old age as a time of stagnation followed by broad and rapid cognitive and physical decline. Nonetheless, late life is also a time of significant challenges that are attributable to multiple factors, including age-related increases in health problems (Garroway & Rybarczyk, 2015; Woods, 2008), the effects of cognitive aging (Salthouse, 2010), and the important interaction between the two processes. Some of the health problems regularly occurring in late life negatively affect cognitive functioning (Woods, 2008). The significant changes in physical and cognitive functioning have important implications for the structuring of psychological assessment and treatment broadly. These changes make the evaluation and treatment of late-life obsessional disorders particularly challenging (Calamari et al., 2017; Dozier & Ayers, 2017).

Important changes in health and cognitive functioning, as well as other significant stressors of late life (e.g., the death of one's spouse), affect the development of mental

---

[1] The review is limited to the psychosocial treatment of late-life OCRDs because Dr. Raymond Ownby, an expert on geriatric psychopharmacology and a co-author of the older adult chapter in the previous edition of this handbook, was not available for this update.

health problems directly. Dozier and Ayers (2017) noted that these life-stage issues may also interact in complex ways, or interact with other processes. For example, the authors suggested that older adults who carry a vulnerability for OCD might develop excessive concerns about their cognitive functioning. Such an older adult might become overly concerned about age-related changes in memory functioning and hypervigilant for signs of memory difficulties (e.g., forgetting the names of acquaintances). This obsessional focus could then lead to related compulsive behaviors (e.g., repetitive "self-tests" of one's ability to recall names of current or past acquaintances). Later in the chapter, models which evaluate how changes in late life might interact with other risk factors and lead to older adults' adjustment disorders are reviewed. Several initial empirical evaluations of these models are also reviewed.

Cognitive Aging, Cognitive Functioning, and Anxiety

There is a well-established association between aging and changes in cognitive functioning (Salthouse, 2010), although it is important to note that many older people do not develop cognitive impairment, such as dementia. Most older people cope effectively with cognitive aging and other late-life changes successfully, maintaining high levels of functionality (for a review, see Diehl & Wahl, 2020). Further, many of the age-related cognitive changes experienced by older adults involve a slow decline in specific cognitive abilities; a smaller number of cognitive abilities show a steeper decline, which most often occurs in the very old when it is not associated with the occurrence of neurologic disease (Woods, 2008). The most recent and sophisticated analyses of cognitive change and aging (Salthouse, 2019) indicate that normal aging involves a nearly linear decline in processing speed, starting in early adulthood. As people grow older, there are accelerating declines in memory functioning and reasoning abilities, while vocabulary knowledge typically increases with age until people are in their sixties (Salthouse, 2019).

Of importance to understanding late-life obsessional disorders is the well-established association between anxiety symptoms and cognitive functioning (Beaudreau & O'Hara, 2008; Woods, 2008). Calamari et al. (2017) noted that although this association is often evaluated from the perspective that chronic anxiety accelerates later declines in cognitive functioning, there have been very few longitudinal studies (Salthouse, 2012). That is, there is not clear evidence on which process causes the other or if there is a reciprocal relationship between anxiety and cognitive functioning.

Beaudreau and O'Hara (2009) evaluated the relationship between anxiety, depression, and cognitive functioning in a sample of community-living older adults; theirs is one of few studies that have examined both depression and anxiety together. Only anxiety was associated with lower scores on the study measures of processing speed, shifting attention, and inhibition. Based on the pattern of associations found, including the relationship between anxiety and inhibition deficits, Beaudreau and O'Hara hypothesized that focal inhibitory deficits might be importantly related to late-life anxiety. In a subsequent review of relevant late-life anxiety and cognitive functioning studies, Beaudreau et al. (2013) concluded that level of cognitive control was reliably associated with late-life anxiety, and that cognitive control might be an important mechanism for understanding the cognitive functioning–anxiety relationship. Cognitive control was operationalized as the ability to initiate goal-directed behavior successfully and was understood as being similar to the executive functioning construct. The investigators concluded that there was significant support for a reciprocal relationship between anxiety and cognitive control, and they suggested that both age and anxiety symptom levels were independently and inversely related to levels of cognitive control. Dysfunction in a component of the cognitive control system, response inhibition, has been importantly implicated in OCD and some other OCRDss (Fontenelle et al., 2020).

A recent study evaluated a model of how late-life cognitive changes might influence anxiety symptom development. Wilkes et al. (2013) investigated whether negative affect, a risk factor for mood or anxiety disorders, might interact with older adults' cognitive functioning to predict scoring on a measure of memory-function concerns. In this longitudinal analysis conducted with a community sample of older adults, memory-function concerns measured at the mid time point were hypothesized to mediate the relationship between the time 1 negative affect–cognitive functioning interaction to predict time 3 anxiety symptoms. That is, they posited that older adults with elevated negative affect and lower cognitive functioning would experience more concerns about memory, which would lead to more anxiety. Support was found for several of the investigators' predictions. Wilkes et al. suggested that vulnerability processes like elevated negative affect, possibly a long-standing personality characteristic carried into late life, could increase negative reactions to, and diminish effective coping with, the more difficult experiences of aging.

Older and Happier

Socioemotional selectivity theory (SST; Carstensen et al., 1999) has been an important catalyst for many studies of the emotional experiences of older adults. The theory posits that individuals' life motivations and goals change over the life span. Older adults' increasing recognition of their limited remaining years causes a shift to prioritizing present experiences and their emotional well-being as most important (Carstensen et al., 1999). This perspective stands in contrast to younger adults, with a greater future orientation and related longer-term objectives (e.g., education or career goals). An important tenet of SST is that emotional well-being may improve in later life, and a substantial number of studies provided support for the hypothesis. In an evaluation of the emotional experiences over the course of a day in older and younger adults, older people reported fewer negative emotions and more stability in their emotional experiences (Carstensen et al., 2000). Similarly, in an evaluation of changes in positive and negative affect in a large nationally representative sample, older people reported higher positive affect and lower negative affect, although associations with age were complex (e.g., nonlinear). Age-related decreases in negative affect appear to be the most reliable difference found in comparisons of older and younger adults, and this difference has been replicated in multiple studies (Ready & Robinson, 2008).

In summary, late life is a dynamic period often characterized by increased happiness, successful adaptation, and continuing personal growth for many older adults (Calamari et al., 2017). Nonetheless, age-related changes in health and cognition are fundamental challenges of late life, and older people confront these issues to varying degrees earlier or later in the aging process. The increased health problems or cognitive changes associated with aging are significant stressors, and these challenges alone may precipitate the mental health difficulties experienced by some older adults. An alternative risk model could involve more complex relationships between multiple factors, including the important functional changes that occur as people age, as well as specific disorder-related risk factors. Such models are being developed to explain the high prevalence of anxiety disorders in late life (Kessler et al., 2005) and to explain late-life OCD. In this chapter in the first edition of this handbook, evaluations of these types of models were characterized as tests of a developmental stage hypervigilance hypothesis (Carmin et al., 2012).

Late-Life OCD and OCRDs

Changes in the Classification of OCD

A major change in the classification of OCD occurred in the revision of the psychiatric disorder nosology in 2013. As mentioned, with the publication of the *DSM-5*, OCD was separated from the anxiety disorders and was placed in the OCRDs (APA, 2013). The OCRDs included OCD and several conditions understood to be importantly similar, and this new grouping resulted from long-standing work on the idea of OCD as a spectrum of disorders. (For an extended discussion of the OCD spectrum, see Chapter 2.) Disorders on the OCD spectrum are believed to be similar to OCD across multiple dimensions, including the brain systems affected, phenomenology commonalities, and shared etiologies.

As a result of commonalities in etiology, OCD spectrum disorders have been hypothesized to be frequently comorbid with OCD. The OCRD category in the *DSM-5* resulted from consensus about how broad the OCD spectrum should be and decisions about what factors were most important to consider (Hollander et al., 2009; Phillips et al., 2010). In *DSM-5*, the basis for the OCRD category is summarized as "increasing evidence of these disorders relatedness to one another in terms of a range of diagnostic validators as well as the clinical utility of grouping these disorders in the same chapter" (p. 235).

As mentioned in the Introduction, five disorders are included in the OCRDs: OCD and four conditions judged importantly related to OCD—BDD, HD, TTM, and SPD. Two of these disorders had been classified in earlier editions of the *DSM* in other diagnostic groupings, and two disorders, HD and SPD, were new in the *DSM-5* taxonomy. The following sections review how the OCRDs are defined in *DSM-5*, beginning with OCD, before reviewing how disorder symptoms appear in older adults.

OCD

Other than several wording changes, the definitions of obsessions and compulsions remain the same in *DSM-5*. Obsessions are defined as:

1. Recurrent and persistent thoughts, urges, or images that are experienced, at some time during the disturbance, as intrusive and unwanted, and that in most individuals cause marked anxiety or distress.
2. The individual attempts to ignore or suppress such thoughts, urges, or images, or to neutralize them with some other thought or action (i.e., by performing a compulsion; APA, 2013, p. 237).

Compulsions also continue to be defined by two core characteristics:

1. The individual feels driven to perform repetitive behaviors (e.g., handwashing, ordering, checking) or mental acts (e.g., praying, counting, repeating words silently) in response to an obsession or according to rules that must be applied rigidly.
2. The behaviors or mental acts are aimed at preventing or reducing anxiety or distress, or preventing some dreaded event or situation; however, these behaviors or mental acts are not connected in a realistic way with what they are designed to neutralize or prevent, or are clearly excessive (APA, 2013, p. 237).

As was the case in preceding *DSM* taxonomy (APA, 2000), the presence of either obsessions or compulsions is adequate to meet diagnostic criteria. The obsessions and compulsions must be time-consuming, which continues to be defined as taking more than one hour per day. The poor insight specifier for OCD is now structured to recognize the range of insight levels that might be seen in clinical presentation: *with good or fair insight*, *with poor insight*, and *with absent insight/delusional beliefs*. New to the *DSM-5* characterization of OCD is a tic-related specifier. The specifier is applied when the individual's OCD is comorbid with a tic disorder or if the individual has a history of a tic disorder.

As was done in earlier versions of the *DSM*, the possible influence of the individual's stage of development on symptom presentation is acknowledged, but the caveat remains limited to presentations in young children. No suggestions are made that older adults with OCD might present differently.

OLDER ADULTS' EXPERIENCE OF OCD

A challenge to identifying OCD symptom differences in older adults is the now well-recognized symptom heterogeneity of OCD (McKay et al., 2004). The specific obsessional concerns or compulsive behaviors seen in the clinical presentation in any age group can take many different forms. Despite this significant heterogeneity, four to five clusters of symptoms (e.g., contamination obsessions with washing compulsions) have been identified (McKay et al., 2004). Further, although there have been limited longitudinal studies, available information suggests that while an individual's specific symptoms may vary over the course of OCD, their obsessional concerns remain largely within a particular symptom cluster (Mataix-Cols et al., 2002). In their review of late-life OCD, Calamari et al. (2017) concluded that there was no evidence that the core phenomenology of OCD was different for older adults, although some information suggested that current life concerns sometimes affect older peoples' symptom presentations.

The relationship between late-life concerns and OCD symptoms is seen in multiple case reports of late-life OCD. The symptoms have focused on age-related health concerns (e.g., bowel functioning; Hatch, 1997; Ramchandani, 1990) or cognitive functioning and memory loss (Calamari et al., 2012; Grant et al., 2007; Jenike, 1991). In a study of OCD and its relationship to age, Cath et al. (2017) examined the large Netherlands Twins Register. The only age-related change found on measures of OCD symptoms was an increase in checking with age, which was attributable to differences found in the participants over age 60. In another study evaluating a large national sample of community-living older adults with OCD, investigators found that older adults experienced the full range of OCD symptoms typically seen in middle-aged samples (Grenier et al., 2009). The symptom types most frequently observed were contamination and washing (22.0%), ordering (22.0%), checking (17.1%), counting (14.6%), and repeating (12.2%).

LATE-LIFE OCD PREVALENCE

Although once considered a rare condition, OCD is now recognized as a frequently occurring psychiatric disorder. The lifetime prevalence estimates for OCD often fall in the 2% to 3% range (e.g., 2.3%; Ruscio et al., 2010), although prevalence estimates vary by age. In the National Comorbidity Survey Replication, lifetime prevalence was estimated at 2.3% for individuals in the 33 to 44 age range, but it was much lower in older adults age 60 and older (0.7%; Kessler et al., 2005). Cath et al. (2017) estimated the prevalence of OCD and its relationship to age. A provisional diagnosis of OCD was made based on psychometrically sound self-report measure scores and *DSM-5* criteria. The overall prevalence of provisional OCD was 5.7%. Although the highest rate of estimated OCD was found in the late-teen to young adult age group, an unanticipated second high prevalence estimate was found for people age 60 to 70. Nestadt et al. (1998) had earlier reported similar results in an analysis of epidemiologic data, identifying a subgroup, mostly women, with OCD onset occurring in their sixties.

Dozier and Ayers (2017) noted in their review that while the estimates of late-life OCD prevalence have been higher in some studies compared to the estimates reported in Kessler et al.'s (2005) epidemiologic study, the prevalence rates of OCD have consistently been low, and late-life OCD appears substantially less prevalent than late-life anxiety or mood disorders. Long-term longitudinal studies of the life course of OCD are needed to better understand the relationship between prevalence and age, and such studies should continue into late life to understand older adults' experience of the disorder.

An additional issue that might importantly affect prevalence estimates of late-life OCD is the setting in which the older adult resides and whether studies estimating OCD prevalence sample from this group. Epidemiologic studies of late-life OCD have included only older adults living independently in the community. When prevalence studies have included older people living in supported living settings, prevalence estimates have been consistently higher (Calamari et al., 2017; Carmin et al., 2012). For example, Bland et al. (1988) found a six-month prevalence of OCD in independently living older adults of 0.9% for men and 1.0% for women. For older adults living in supported settings, the prevalence estimates were 1.4% for men and 4.7% for women. In an evaluation of the large older adult sample contained in the Swedish Population Register, which includes persons living in supported living settings, the OCD one-month prevalence was 2.9% (Klenfeldt et al., 2014). Dozier and Ayers (2017) noted that because of the particularly debilitating effects of OCD in older people, individuals with the condition are more likely to reside in a supported living setting.

WHEN DID OLDER ADULTS' OCD BEGIN?

While contemporary studies of OCD identify variability in age at onset, results almost always indicate that significant symptoms begin for most affected people between later childhood and early adulthood. For example, in a quantitative meta-analysis of studies of OCD age at onset, Taylor (2011) identified two onset patterns, early onset (mean age 11) and late onset (mean age 23). Taylor validated the observed age-at-onset differences, identifying several associated neuropsychological test performance differences, but he did not find treatment response differences between the two onset patterns. To better understand the age of onset of OCD and its implications for older adults, the authors further examined the studies by Cath et al. (2017) and Dell'Osso et al. (2017) that evaluated relationships between OCD, age, or age at onset.

Using cross-sectional data, Cath et al. (2017) estimated the relationship between age and disorder prevalence for both OCD and HD. The investigators found higher estimated OCD prevalence in young adults, lower prevalence in middle age, and a significant increase in prevalence that occurred at approximately age 65 and older. These findings were very different from the prevalence–age relationship found for HD. HD prevalence showed a definitive linear increase over the life span, and HD was most prevalent in older adults. We note that Cath et al.'s data do not address when older adults with OCD first experienced the condition. In other investigations, one of the strongest predictors of late-life OCD has been chronic subclinical OCD symptoms (i.e., for more than 10 years) earlier in life (Frydman et al., 2014). This suggests that most older adults with OCD experienced symptoms earlier in life before their symptoms increased in severity in late life.

Dell'Osso et al. (2017) evaluated a large multinational clinical sample of individuals presenting for treatment. Participants had a primary OCD diagnosis, and the sample's mean age was 42.0 (*SD* = 12.6). The investigators evaluated the relationship between the participants' current age and the age of onset of their OCD. Age at onset was defined as when symptoms were first associated with significant life interference. The mean age at onset was approximately 19 years. Further, only 6% of the large, treatment-seeking clinical sample were 65 years old or older. Patients age 65 or older had a significantly later age at onset than younger patients (approximately age 29 versus age 19). No other reliable differences were found between the small older adult group and the rest of the sample, other than older adults being less likely to have been involved in cognitive-behavioral therapy (CBT) for OCD.

RISK AND PROTECTIVE FACTORS

Frydman et al. (2014) conducted one of the largest studies of risk factors for late-onset OCD, which they defined as onset at age 40 or later. Data from the Brazilian Research Consortium for OCD were analyzed. First occurrence of OCD after age 40 was found for only 8.6% of the sample. As already mentioned, results from their analyses indicated that late-onset OCD was most likely to occur in individuals with long histories of subclinical symptoms. Additionally, late-onset OCD was associated female sex, experiencing a major traumatic event at or after age 40, and a recent history of pregnancy (self or partner; Frydman et al., 2014).

As already mentioned, models have been developed to test whether the important changes and challenges of late life might interact with other risk processes to precipitate mental health difficulties in older adults (Calamari et al., 2002). These models were described as tests of a developmental stage hypervigilance hypothesis (Carmin et al., 2012). Two studies have tested this type of model's utility in explaining late-life OCD.

Teachman (2007) evaluated relationships between subjective cognitive concerns (e.g., perceptions of, or worry about, cognitive functioning), OCD-related dysfunctional beliefs, which are posited to be cognitive risk factors for OCD (Frost & Steketee, 2002), and OCD symptom severity. Study participants ranged from age 18 to over 70 years old. Teachman hypothesized that dysfunctional beliefs (e.g., overimportance of thoughts, need to control thoughts) would lead to hypervigilance focused on cognitive functioning, which would partially mediate the relationship between dysfunctional beliefs and OCD symptom severity. Results supported this mediational model. No differences were found in model fit in evaluations of older and younger participants.

Prouvost et al. (2016) tested a developmental stage hypervigilance model with longitudinal data. Participants were older adults age 65 or older from a community sample and who were cognitively intact. The investigators hypothesized that initial scores on measures of cognitive functioning would predict changes in older adults' OCD symptoms through a hypothesized risk factor for OCD, cognitive self-consciousness (CSC). CSC has been defined as excessive awareness of, and attention to, thought experiences (Cartwright-Hatton & Wells, 1997). CSC was identified as an important construct in the development of Wells and colleagues' Metacognitions Questionnaire (Cartwright-Hatton & Wells, 1997). CSC has been found to be related to OCD in several investigations with middle-age samples and has been hypothesized to be a cognitive risk factor for the development of OCD (Janeck et al., 2003).

Prouvost et al. (2016) found that scores on measures of cognitive functioning were related to changes in CSC levels, which were related to changes in OCD symptoms. Thus, CSC scores mediated the relationship between cognitive functioning and OCD symptoms, as predicted. Poorer initial cognitive functioning predicted increases in CSC over time, which in turn predicted increases in OCD symptoms over the 18 months of the study. The model was supported when general cognitive functioning was the predictor (i.e., age- and education-adjusted total score on the Dementia Rating Scale-2 [DRS-2]; Jurica et al., 2001). Furthermore, two DRS-2 subscale scores were tested as predictors in the model. Conceptualization scores at time 1 predicted score increases in CSC, which predicted increasing OCD symptoms. The mediational role of CSC was again supported. The model was not supported when Initiation/Perseveration subscale score was the predictor variable in the model. Prouvost et al. had hypothesized that scoring on both the Conceptualization and Initiation/Perseveration subscales would function as predictor variables in the model because of the measures' likely sensitivity to the cortical-striatal dysfunction associated with OCD.

PSYCHOSOCIAL TREATMENT OF LATE-LIFE OCD

Unfortunately, although significant gains have been made in interventions for late-life HD, there have not been equivalent advances in the treatment of older adults' OCD. In this chapter in the first edition of this handbook (Carmin et al., 2012), psychosocial treatment for late-life OCD was comprehensively reviewed, and the authors concluded that CBT was probably efficacious for treating older adults with OCD. However, the authors' significant caveat was that treatment studies had been very limited. Controlled clinical trials were lacking and any treatment outcome information was limited (i.e., based on a small uncontrolled treatment study or case reports). Carmin et al. (2012) summarized the treatment study by Carmin et al. (1998), an uncontrolled evaluation of treatment of 11 older and 11 younger adult inpatients with OCD. At that time, the study was the only evaluation of OCD treatment outcome other than case study reports. A similar conclusion has been reached about the importance of Carmin et al.'s (1998) study and the undeveloped state of late-life OCD treatment research in more recent reviews of late-life OCD (Calamari et al., 2017; Dozier & Ayers, 2017), and no new studies exist that allow a different conclusion now (cf. Jazi & Asghar-Ali, 2020). Therefore, the discussion next summarizes information on efficacious psychosocial treatments for OCD broadly, as well as the limited information on late-life OCD treatment.

The most frequently used psychosocial treatment for OCD is a form of behavior therapy, exposure and response prevention (E/RP), although this intervention is often generically referred to as CBT regardless of whether a cognitive therapy is added to it or not. Although pharmacotherapy is the most frequently used intervention to treat OCD, this is not as a result of the medication's being more effective (for a review, see Öst et al., 2015). In the largest controlled clinical trial conducted to date, E/RP was associated with the strongest treatment response, with 57% of the treatment group considered excellent responders (Foa et al., 2005).

Öst et al. (2015) conducted a quantitative meta-analysis of controlled clinical trials evaluating the effectiveness of E/RP, cognitive therapy, or their combination. Data from 37 studies met inclusion criteria for the review, thereby making the study the largest meta-analysis of randomized clinical trials for OCD treatment. Results indicated that the overall effect size associated with CBT treatment was 0.57, considered a medium effect size. A large effect size was found in treatment studies where CBT was compared to a wait-list control (1.31). Simply put, CBT is an effective treatment for OCD.

Again, much of the information on the treatment of older adults' OCD comes from case studies. These studies were reviewed in the first volume of this handbook (Carmin et al., 2012) and in two recent reviews of late-life OCD (Calamari et al., 2017; Dozier & Ayers, 2017). In a case report by Jones et al. (2012), E/RP was used to treat an 80-year-old man with a 65-year history of OCD. The client received 14 individual, 50-minute E/RP treatment sessions. Treatment outcome was a 65% symptom reduction from baseline to posttreatment follow-up at seven months. At follow-up, the patient's OCD severity score was no longer in the clinical range on the well-validated symptom severity measure used in the study.

The most extensive treatment study of late-life OCD was conducted by Carmin et al. (1998). They treated 11 older adults with OCD with E/RP and compared self-rated symptom reductions between older adults and 11 younger adults with OCD who were also treated with E/RP. The younger adult comparison group was matched on OCD severity and level of depression. Sixty percent of the older adults were treatment responders, which was defined as a 50% or greater reduction in symptoms. The two age groups' response to E/RP treatment did not differ.

HD in Older Adults

In the *DSM-5*, HD is described by three clusters of symptoms: (1) persistent difficulty discarding possessions, regardless of their actual value, that results from a perceived need to save the items, and because of distress associated with discarding them; (2) the excessive accumulation of possessions that congest and clutter living areas and substantially compromises the living areas' intended use (e.g., cannot cook in the kitchen); and (3) clinically significant distress and impairment (p. 247; APA, 2013). As with OCD, a specifier for level of insight is included, along with the same ordinal ratings of level. An additional specifier provided in the *DSM-5* for HD is whether symptoms currently include the excessive acquisition of additional items. There is some evidence that late-life HD is characterized by lower levels of acquisition (Dozier & Ayers, 2014).

HD has been an increasing focus of psychopathology researchers. Some of the most recent research and clinical attention focused on HD appears to result from both the condition's new status as a psychiatric disorder and from growing recognition that the disorder is both prevalent and debilitating. Concurrent with researchers' increased interest in HD has been the accelerating study of the condition in affected older people. There is evidence that HD might be substantially more prevalent among older adults (Samuels et al., 2008) and that older people with HD experience both more severe symptoms and greater disorder-related impairment (Ayers et al., 2010; Kim et al., 2001). There is evidence that HD is both chronic and progressive, such that symptoms increase in severity over the life span (Ayers et al., 2010), which may explain the high prevalence estimates and the severe symptoms seen in older people with HD.

HD appeared for the first time as a psychiatric disorder in *DSM-5*. Before then, the symptoms of HD were understood as one of several symptom subtypes of OCD, and empirical evaluations of symptom heterogeneity often identified HD symptoms as a specific dimension or subgroup (McKay et al., 2004). As research on HD progressed, the condition's symptoms became better understood, as did how the condition differs from OCD. These differences include HD's significantly diminished response to the effective treatments for OCD, E/RP (for a review, see Pertusa et al., 2010).

HD is now recognized as a distinct and complex psychiatric disorder with several associated characteristics. These include cognitive processing deficits that affect attention-focusing ability, deficits in organization and categorization skills, and perceived memory impairments, although many evaluations of objective memory functioning fail to find deficiencies (Moshier et al., 2016). While several types of dysfunctional beliefs have been consistently related to OCD (Frost & Steketee, 2002), the problematic beliefs seen in HD are phenomenologically different. Individuals with HD most often have exaggerated beliefs that focus on possessions, such as the meanings and emotional significance of the objects (Frost & Rasmussen, 2012; Kellett & Holden, 2014). For example, a patient with HD treated by the first author of this chapter described that discarding any newspaper that contained an article about friends or family would feel like a slight to them and would diminish the relationship she had with them. An additional distinction between HD and OCD is disorder-related insight. While people with OCD are now recognized as showing greater variability in insight than was earlier understood, most people with HD have poor insight and underappreciate the significant negative effects their symptoms have on their functionality and quality of life (Frost & Rasmussen, 2012). For example, the family members of people with HD frequently describe their affected relative as having vary poor insight about the condition's significant effects on their life and the extent of their disability (Tolin et al., 2010).

OLDER ADULTS' EXPERIENCE OF HD

The core symptoms of late-life HD appear very similar to the symptoms reported in middle-aged samples, other than the lower levels of acquisition. Dozier and Ayers (2014) found differences in older adults' reasons for saving, which they suggested might explain reduced acquisition. They found that age was negatively associated with usefulness as a reason for saving or acquiring objects. Although multiple categories of cognitive deficits have been associated with HD in adult samples (Dozier & Ayers, 2017), cognitive impairment appears to be more substantial and debilitating in older people with HD (Ayers et al., 2015). The importance of addressing older adults' cognitive functioning in treatment for HD is addressed in the section "Psychosocial Treatment of Late-Life HD."

HD PREVALENCE AND AGE

Although long-term longitudinal studies of HD are needed to better understand disorder prevalence and life course, available information indicates that HD is a common psychiatric disorder and that older adults are disproportionately affected. Samuels et al. (2008) analyzed data from a large epidemiologic study of psychiatric disorders. In their sample, the point prevalence for what the investigators defined as significant hoarding symptoms was 3.7%, with prevalence estimates increasing with age. Only 2.3% of the youngest age group experienced HD, while 6.2% of the older age group (55 to 94 years old) had the condition.

Cath et al. (2017) evaluated the relationship between age and HD symptom severity using the extensive Netherlands Twins Register, which included participants ranging in age from 15 to 97. Although self-reported symptoms were used for diagnosis, the *DSM-5* diagnostic criteria were employed. Cath et al. (2017) found that the overall prevalence of a provisional HD diagnosis was 2.12%. The likelihood of HD rose approximately 20% for every five years of age. For individuals over age 70, the prevalence of HD was more than 6%. No prevalence differences were found between men and women.

Last, Postlethwaite et al. (2019) conducted a quantitative meta-analysis of studies that evaluated HD prevalence. The point prevalence estimates were based on 10 studies and ranged from 0.8% to 6.03%. Lifetime prevalence estimates were obtained from only two studies and were 0.8% and 3.5%. Based on these data and using a random effects model, the pooled point prevalence estimate was 2.6% and the pooled lifetime prevalence estimate was 1.7%, which were not significantly different. No sex differences in prevalence were found. The investigators concluded that the relationship between prevalence and age could not be evaluated because few older adults were included in studies.

THE DEVELOPMENTAL PROGRESSION OF OLDER ADULTS' HD

In their review, Calamari et al. (2017) examined both HD age at onset and the disorder's developmental progression. Hoarding symptoms in at least mild form are consistently found to begin in childhood or adolescence (Frost & Rasmussen, 2012). By the late twenties or early thirties, HD appears to become more severe (Grisham et al., 2006). Dozier and Ayers (2017) also concluded in their review that most evidence indicates an early onset of HD in the majority of people with the condition. Long-term longitudinal studies are needed to fully understand the characteristics of early HD symptoms and how the symptoms progress. Unlike OCD, which has been characterized as showing a waxing and waning pattern of symptom severity (Skoog & Skoog, 1999) or even to remit (Fineberg et al., 2013), studies of HD consistently indicate that the course is chronic and unremitting (Frost & Rasmussen, 2012). Of importance to understanding late-life HD and its treatment, older adults with the condition will have most often experienced symptoms since an early age. The frequently seen negative effects of HD on social functioning and vocational success (Dozier & Ayers, 2017) will have been experienced, and the disorder-related cognitive impairments will have likely grown more substantial. The older adult with HD will be a challenging patient to treat.

In several studies of the developmental progression of HD, older adults with the condition have been guided through the recollection of symptom levels over their life. Dozier et al. (2016) evaluated 82 community-living older adults (M_{age}, 66.3; SD = 5.8) who met *DSM-5* criteria for HD. In the study, HD symptom onset was operationalized as the first decade in which the participant reported that symptoms had reached at least mild severity. Onset of a possible HD diagnosis was operationalized as the first decade in which the participant reported experiencing mildly severe symptoms in each disorder symptom category: excessive saving, difficulty discarding, and excessive clutter. The investigators found that the median age of onset of disorder symptoms was between 10 and 20 years. The median age of a possible HD diagnosis was between 20 and 30 years. Only 23% of study participants reported HD onset after age 40, and most of these individuals had prior subclinical HD symptoms. A small group reported first symptoms occurring after age 40. No participant reported HD onset after age 70. Furthermore, all participants reported increasing symptoms; no instances of remission or decreasing symptoms were reported. Additionally, the trajectory of different hoarding symptoms changed during the fifth and sixth decades of life. Clutter continued to increase in severity, while saving and discarding symptoms stabilized (Dozier et al., 2016).

Using a similar methodology, Ayers et al. (2010) found that older adults also recalled HD symptoms growing more severe each decade. Using different methods, Steketee et al. (2012) evaluated older adults and found 37 was the mean age of onset of HD.

Approximately 35% of their older adult sample reported onset before age 20, while almost 39% reported that their HD began after age 50.

RISK AND PROTECTIVE FACTORS

In their review of HD, Dozier and Ayers (2017) noted that there are few definitive risk factors for HD, including for the disorder's occurrence in late life. Risk factor information comes largely from studies evaluating the characteristics of individuals with the disorder.

In some studies, individuals with HD have reported traumatic experiences earlier in life (Ayers et al., 2010; Frost et al., 2011) although more research is needed to understand if the association is reliable and what processes might mediate the association. The cognitive deficits associated with HD are most often related to executive functioning (Dozier & Ayers, 2017), and the deficits appear more severe in older adults with HD (Calamari et al., 2017). Davidson et al. (2019) concluded in their review that HD not only is distinguished by a profile of cognitive functioning deficits, but also is characterized by heightened perceptions of cognitive impairment. For example, when compared to patients with OCD, patients with HD exhibited a greater discrepancy between their performance on objective tests of memory and their perceptions of memory impairment (Moshier et al., 2016).

PSYCHOSOCIAL TREATMENT OF LATE-LIFE HD

The most widely applied and tested psychosocial treatment for HD is a multicomponent form of CBT that has now been manualized for use by clinicians and to guide patients through treatment (Steketee & Frost, 2014a, 2014b). The treatment protocol includes motivational interviewing to address low insight and limited patient motivation, training in decision-making and categorization, and exposure therapy related to discarding and resisting urges to acquire. The protocol also includes cognitive restructuring to alter the dysfunctional beliefs characteristic of HD. The CBT protocol for HD is based on the cognitive-behavioral model of compulsive hoarding (Frost & Hartl, 1996; Steketee & Frost, 2003). Tolin et al. (2015) completed a quantitative meta-analysis of the effectiveness of CBT for HD with adults. The investigators concluded that treatment produced significant symptom reductions for several symptom classes and effect sizes were large. The effect of treatment on measures of functional impairment was smaller, and residual symptom levels remained closer to the clinical levels of the disorder. Tolin et al. concluded that CBT for HD was a promising treatment approach, although further refinements in intervention were needed.

Early evaluations of late-life HD treatment involved uncontrolled case series or smaller uncontrolled clinical trials. Turner et al. (2010) evaluated the Steketee and Frost (2014a, 2014b) CBT protocol with six older adults with HD. Treatment was associated with a small decrease in participants' HD symptoms. Ayers et al. (2011) evaluated CBT with cognitively unimpaired older adults (over age 65; $N = 12$) with HD. A statistically significant reduction in HD symptoms resulted, although the symptom reduction was small. Further evaluation of older adults' responses to CBT suggested that cognitive therapy procedures had limited value, that exposure exercises were well accepted by older adults, and that attempting to ameliorate poor executive functioning might improve outcome (Ayers et al., 2012). From this analysis, a treatment for late-life HD emerged.

The new treatment for late-life HD, Cognitive Rehabilitation and Exposure/Sorting Therapy (CREST), has several components. The CREST intervention includes cognitive training targeting prospective memory and executive functioning, an exposure therapy component, and relapse prevention (Ayers et al., 2014). In an initial open trial of CREST, Ayers et al. (2014) found that hoarding symptoms improved significantly, with all participants characterized as treatment responders or partial responders. HD symptom reductions were in the medium to large range. In the later controlled clinical trial (Ayers et al., 2018), HD symptoms decreased significantly in intent-to-treat analyses. Treatment gains were maintained at 12-month follow-up. Additionally, in further evaluation of the controlled clinical trial data, Ayers et al. (2020) found that the CREST treatment for late-life HD resulted in significant executive functioning changes, and improvements in cognitive flexibility and inhibition. Results from the study suggest that CREST treatment for older adults with HD both reduces HD symptoms and improves cognitive functioning, which might have more general positive effects.

Do Older Adults Experience BDD?

With the publication of the *DSM-5*, BDD shifted from its former classification as a somatoform disorder and became an OCRD. Corresponding with this change, the BDD diagnostic criteria were refined. Emphasis on both a preoccupation with physical defects that are not apparent to others, and the presence of repetitive behaviors or mental rituals associated with these appearance related concerns, are emphasized. The repetitive behaviors described as characteristic of BDD in the *DSM-5* now include mirror-checking, reassurance-seeking, and extensive, time-consuming grooming rituals; and mental rituals which may involve comparisons of appearance to others (APA, 2013, pp. 242–243). Additionally, when the clinical presentation involves a preoccupation with a relative lack of muscle mass, a *With muscle dysmorphia* specifier is applied (APA, 2013, p. 243). Lastly, a specifier for rating level of patient insight is provided that is very similar to the insight specifiers for OCD and HD.

Our careful review identified three case descriptions of older adults with BDD that were provided by Phillips (2005) in her book on the condition. The late-life cases described by Phillips are the basis of reports in BDD reviews that the condition has been observed in people as old as age 80 (Bjornsson et al., 2013). To the best of our knowledge, Phillips's report is the only published case descriptions of late-life BDD.

Phillips (2005) described an 80-year-old woman struggling with BDD since she was a child. She felt other people judged her as unattractive reporting that this feeling began early in life. She reported feeling shame now as an older adult because of her continued focus on her appearance. A second case described was a 70-year-old woman reporting that her symptoms began while she was a teenager. She reported that her appearance concerns currently resulted in approximately eight hours of mirror checking, adjusting makeup, selecting clothing, and obtaining reassurance from her husband. A third case involved a woman in her sixties who had concerns that focused on wrinkles around her eyes. She reported spending hours a day in a mirror examining these lines and was seeking cosmetic surgery.

The paucity of information about late-life BDD might be related to current understanding of disorder onset which is thought to typically occur in late childhood or adolescence (Bjornsson et al., 2013). The absence of information about older adults with BDD is not because the disorder is rare. BDD is relatively common, with a reported lifetime prevalence of 0.7% to 2.4% (Bjornsson et al., 2013). However, BDD may be significantly underreported (Schulte et al., 2020). A reason for this lack of reporting is the intense shame associated with the disorder, which patients have reported as a barrier to seeking treatment (Schulte et al., 2020). Based on Phillips's (2005) older adult case descriptions, shame or embarrassment might affect older adults' reporting of symptoms or seeking treatment.

Body-Focused Repetitive Behaviors

Included in the OCRD category are two body-focused repetitive behaviors. Trichotillomania involves three core symptoms: 1. "Recurrent pulling out of one's hair, resulting in hair loss"; 2. "Repeated attempts to decrease or stop hair pulling"; and 3. "The hair pulling causes significant distress or impairment in social, occupational, or other areas of functioning" (p. 251). Skin-picking disorder (i.e., excessive skin-picking; SPD; also known as excoriation) appeared in the psychiatric disorder nosology in the United States for the first time in *DSM-5*. The diagnostic criteria for SPD are very similar to TTM (p. 254). TTM is an understudied condition, and information relevant to late-life TTM is scarce. SPD is a newly defined psychiatric disorder that has been the subject of minimal attention especially in later life.

Do older adults experience TTM? We can report that they appear to, but can say little more. Bartley et al. (2017) reported a case involving a woman in her mid-seventies who developed TTM for the first time. Dermatologic causes for the significant hair loss were ruled out. The patient was responsive to habit reversal training.

Grant et al. (2020) evaluated a large United States community sample to estimate TTM prevalence. Current TTM prevalence was 1.7% and no gender differences were found. Current prevalence was 2.3% for young men (age 18 to 29) and 2.6% for young women. For older people (age 50 to 69), point prevalence was 0.5% for men and 0.9%

for women. The mean age of onset reported for TTM was 17.7 years for the people in the community sample with the condition, although the reported age range was large (range 1–61 years). Like BDD, TTM is thought to be an early onset condition often beginning during adolescence (Krooks et al., 2018). Without treatment, TTM symptoms appear to persist and follow a chronic course (Ankad et al., 2014; Schumer et al., 2015).

Concluding Comments

While the OCRDs are not the most frequent form of psychopathology experienced by older people, conservative estimates suggest that millions of older adults experience HD or OCD. Emerging information about the developmental progression of HD suggest that the condition is a chronic and unremitting disorder, which might be most prevalent in older people. Further, older adults with HD experience severe symptoms that are highly debilitating and which negatively impact their quality of life. The very limited information on late-life BDD or body focused repetitive disorders suggests that older adults experience these conditions, although no information is available on how often.

The OCRDs remain under studied in older adults, although important advances have occurred. HD has been an increasing focus of research including studies of the disorder's developmental progression. Recognition that the disorder is both prevalent and severely debilitating for affected older adults has resulted in development of age-adapted treatment. Cognitive Rehabilitation and Exposure/Sorting Therapy (CREST) developed by Ayers and colleagues addresses aspects of cognitive aging important to treatment response in an modified CBT protocol. Initial evaluations of the intervention demonstrated that this treatment produced both significant symptom reduction and improvement in older peoples' executive functioning. The CREST intervention could be a helpful prototype for addressing other OCRDs. The treatment of late-life OCD could be advanced with adaptations of this model.

References

American Psychiatric Association (APA). (2013). *Diagnostic and statistical manual of mental disorders* (5th ed.).
American Psychiatric Association. (2000). *Diagnostic and statistical manual of mental disorders* (4th ed., text rev.).
Ankad, B., Varna Naidu, M., Beergouder, S., & Sujana, L. (2014). Trichoscopy in trichotillomania: A useful diagnostic tool. *International Journal of Trichology*, 6(4), 160–163.
Ayers, C. R., Bratiotis, C., Saxena, S., & Wetherell, J. L. (2012). Therapist and patient perspectives on cognitive-behavioral therapy for older adults with hoarding disorder: A collective case study. *Aging and Mental Health*, 16, 915–921.
Ayers, C. R., Davidson, E. J., Dozier, M. E., & Twamley, E. W. (2020). Cognitive rehabilitation and exposure/sorting therapy for late-life hoarding: Effects on neuropsychological performance. *The Journals of Gerontology: Series B: Psychological Sciences and Social Sciences*, 75(6), 1193–1198. https://doi.org/10.1093/geronb/gbz062
Ayers, C. R., Dozier, M. E., Taylor, C. T., Mayes, T. L., Pittman, J. O. E., & Tawmley, E. W. (2018). Group cognitive rehabilitation and exposure/sorting therapy: A pilot program. *Cognitive Therapy and Research*, 42, 315–327. doi:10.1007/sl0608-017-9878-1
Ayers, C. R., & Najmi, S. (2014). Treatment of obsessive-compulsive spectrum disorders in late-life. In E. A. Storch & D. McKay (Eds.), *Obsessive-compulsive disorder and its spectrum: A life-span approach* (pp. 97–116). American Psychological Association.

Ayers, C. R., Najmi, S., Mayes, T. L., & Dozier, M. E. (2015). Hoarding disorder in older adulthood. *The American Journal of Geriatric Psychiatry, 23*(4), 416–422.

Ayers, C. R., Saxena, S., Golshan, S., & Wetherell, J. L. (2010). Age at onset and clinical features of late life compulsive hoarding. *International Journal of Geriatric Psychiatry, 25*, 142–149.

Ayers, C. R., Wetherell, J. L., Golshan, S., & Saxena, S. (2011). Cognitive-behavioral therapy for geriatric compulsive hoarding. *Behaviour Research and Therapy, 49*, 689–694.

Bartley, M. M, Lapid, M. I., & Grant, J. E. (2017). Pulling your hair out in geriatric psychiatry: A case report. *International Psychogeriatrics, 29*, 691–694.

Bassil, N., Ghandour, A., & Grossberg, G. (2011). How anxiety presents differently in older adults. *Current Psychiatry, 10*, 65–71.

Beaudreau, S. A., MacKay-Brandt, A., & Reynolds, J. (2013). Application of a cognitive neuroscience perspective of cognitive control to late-life anxiety. *Journal of Anxiety Disorders, 27*(6), 559–566.

Beaudreau, S. A., & O'Hara, R. (2008). Late-life anxiety and cognitive impairment: A review. *American Journal of Geriatric Psychiatry, 16*, 790–803.

Beaudreau, S. A., & O'Hara, R. (2009). The association of anxiety and depressive symptoms with cognitive performance in community-dwelling older adults. *Psychology and Aging, 24*(2), 507.

Bjornsson, A., Didie, E., Grant, J., Menard, W., Stalker, E., & Phillips, K. (2013). Age at onset and clinical correlates in body dysmorphic disorder. *Comprehensive Psychiatry, 54*(7), 893–903.

Bland, R. C, Newman, S. C., & Orn, H. (1988). Prevalence of psychiatric disorders in the elderly in Edmonton. *Acta Psychiatrica Scandinavica, 338*(Suppl.), 57–63.

Calamari, J., Janeck, A., & Deer, T. M. (2002). Cognitive processes and obsessive-compulsive disorder in older adults. In R. O. Frost & G. Steketee (Eds.), *Cognitive approaches to obsessions and compulsions: Theory, assessment & treatment* (pp. 315–336). Pergamon.

Calamari, J. E., Pontarelli, N. K., Armstrong, K. M., & Salstrom, S. A. (2012). Obsessive-compulsive disorder in late life. *Cognitive and Behavioral Practice, 19*, 136–150.

Calamari, J. E., Wilkes, C. M., & Prouvost C. (2017). The nature and management of obsessive compulsive disorder and the obsessive compulsive related disorders experienced by older adults. In J. Abramowitz, D. McKay, & E. Storch (Eds.), *The Wiley handbook of obsessive-compulsive related disorders* (pp. 1097–1118). Wiley.

Carmin, C., Calamari, J. E., & Ownby, R. (2012). OCD and spectrum conditions in older adults. In G. Steketee (Ed.), *Oxford handbook of obsessive compulsive and spectrum disorders* (pp. 453–468). Oxford University Press.

Carmin, C. N., Pollard, C. A, & Ownby, R. L. (1998). Cognitive behavioral treatment of older versus younger adults with OCD. *Clinical Gerontologist, 19*, 81–88.

Carstensen, L. L., Isaacowitz, D. M., & Charles, S. T. (1999). Taking time seriously: A theory of socioemotional selectivity. *American Psychologist, 54*(3), 165.

Carstensen, L. L., Pasupathi, M., Mayr, U., & Nesselroade, J. R. (2000). Emotional experience in everyday life across the adult life span. *Journal of Personality and Social Psychology, 79*(4), 644–655. https://doi.org/10.1037/0022-3514.79.4.644

Cartwright-Hatton, S., & Wells, A. (1997). Beliefs about worry and intrusions: The Meta-Cognitions Questionnaire and its correlates. *Journal of Anxiety Disorders, 11*(3), 279–296.

Cath, D. C., Nizar, K., Boomsma, D., & Mathews, C. A. (2017). Age-specific prevalence of hoarding and obsessive-compulsive disorder: A population-based study. *The American Journal of Geriatric Psychiatry, 25*(3), 245–255.

Charles, S. T., Reynolds, C. A., & Gatz, M. (2001). Age-related differences and change in positive and negative affect over 23 years. *Journal of Personality and Social Psychology, 80*, 136–151.

Charles, S. T., & Robinette, J. W. (2015). Emotion and emotion regulation. In P. A. Lichtenberg, B. T. Mast, B. D. Carpenter, & J. Loebach Wetherell (Eds.), *APA handbook of clinical geropsychology, Vol. 1. History and status of the field and perspectives on aging* (pp. 235–258). American Psychological Association. https://doi.org/10.1037/14458-011

Davidson, E. J., Dozier, M. E., Pittman, J. O., Mayes, T. L., Blanco, B. H., Gault, J. D., Schwarz, L. J., & Ayers, C. R. (2019). Recent advances in research on hoarding. *Current Psychiatry Reports, 21*(9), 91.

Dell'Osso, B., Benatti, B., Rodriguez, C. I., Arici, C., Palazzo, C., Altamura, A. C., Hollander, E., Fineberg, N., Stein, D. J., Nicolini, H., & Lanzagorta, N. (2017). Obsessive-compulsive disorder in the elderly: A report from the International College of Obsessive-Compulsive Spectrum Disorders (ICOCS). *European Psychiatry*, *45*, 36–40.

Diehl, M., & Wahl, H. W. (2020). Risks and potentials of adult development and aging: Understanding the challenges and opportunities of successful aging. In M. Diehl & H. W. Wahl (Eds.), *The psychology of later life: A contextual perspective* (pp. 153–180). American Psychological Association.

Dozier, M. E., & Ayers, C. R. (2014). The predictive value of different reasons for saving and acquiring on hoarding disorder symptoms. *Journal of Obsessive-Compulsive and Related Disorders*, *3*(3), 220–227.

Dozier, M. E., & Ayers, C. R. (2017). Description and prevalence of OCD in the elderly. In J. Abramowitz, D. McKay, & E. Storch (Eds.), *The Wiley handbook of obsessive-compulsive related disorders* (pp. 44–55). Wiley.

Dozier, M. E., Porter, B., & Ayers, C. R. (2016). Age of onset and progression of hoarding symptoms in older adults with hoarding disorder. *Aging & Mental Health*, *20*(7), 736–742.

Fineberg, N. A., Hengartner, M. P., Bergbaum, C., Gale, T., Rossler, W., & Angst, J. (2013). Remission of obsessive-compulsive disorders and syndromes: Evidence from a prospective community cohort study over 30 years. *International Journal of Psychiatry in Clinical Practice*, *17*(3), 179–197.

Foa, E. B., Liebowitz, M. R., Kozak, M. J., Davies, S., Campeas, R., Franklin, M. E., Huppert, J. D., Kjernisted, K., Rowan, V., Schmidt, A. B., & Simpson, H. B. (2005). Randomized, placebo-controlled trial of exposure and ritual prevention, clomipramine, and their combination in the treatment of obsessive-compulsive disorder. *The American Journal of Psychiatry*, *162*(1), 151–161.

Fontenelle, L. F., Oldenhof, E., Moreira-de-Oliveira, M. E., Abramowitz, J. S., Antony, M. M., Cath, D., Carter, A., Dougherty, D., Ferrão, Y. A., Figee, M., Harrison, B. J., Hoexter, M. Q., Soo Kwon, J., Küelz, A., Lazaro, L., Lochner, C., Marazziti, D., Mataix-Cols, D., McKay, D., . . . International OCRDs Neuroscience Consensus Group. (2020). A transdiagnostic perspective of constructs underlying obsessive-compulsive and related disorders: An international Delphi consensus study. *Australian and New Zealand Journal of Psychiatry*, *54*(7), 719–731.

Frost, R. O., & Hartl, T. L. (1996). A cognitive-behavioral model of compulsive hoarding. *Behaviour Research and Therapy*, *34*(4), 341–350.

Frost, R. O., & Rasmussen, J. L. (2012). Phenomenology of obsessive-compulsive disorder. In G. Steketee (Ed.), *Oxford handbook of obsessive-compulsive and spectrum disorders* (pp. 70–88). Oxford University Press.

Frost, R. O., & Steketee, G. (Eds.) (2002). *Cognitive approaches to obsessions and compulsions: Theory, assessment, and treatment*. Pergamon/Elsevier Science.

Frost, R. O., Steketee, G., & Tolin, D. F. (2011). Comorbidity in hoarding disorder. *Depression and Anxiety*, *28*, 876–884.

Frydman, I., do Brasil, P. E., Torres, A. R., Shavitt, R. G., Ferrao, Y. A., Rosario, M. C., Miguel, E. C., & Fontenelle, L. F. (2014). Late-onset obsessive-compulsive disorder: Risk factors and correlates. *Journal of Psychiatric Research*, *49*, 68–74.

Garroway, A. M., & Rybarczyk, B. (2015). Aging, chronic disease, and the biopsychosocial model. In P. A. Lichtenberg, B. T. Mast, B. D. Carpenter, & J. L. Wetherell (Eds.), *APA handbook of clinical geropsychology, Vol. 1: History and status of the field and perspectives on aging* (pp. 563–586). American Psychological Association.

Grant, J., Dougherty, D., & Chamberlain, S. (2020). Prevalence, gender correlates, and co-morbidity of trichotillomania. *Psychiatry Research*, *288*, 112948.

Grant, J. E., Mancebo, M. C., Pinto, A, Williams, K. A., Eisen, J. L., & Rasmussen, S. A. (2007). Late-onset obsessive compulsive disorder: Clinical characteristics and psychiatric comorbidity. *Psychiatry Research*, *152*(1), 21–27.

Grenier, S., Preville, M., Boyer, R., & O'Connor, K. (2009). Prevalence and correlates of obsessive-compulsive disorder among older adults living in the community. *Journal of Anxiety Disorders*, *23*, 858–865.

Grisham, J. R., Frost, R. O., Steketee, G., Kim, H., & Hood, S. (2006). Age of onset of compulsive hoarding. *Journal of Anxiety Disorders*, *20*(5), 675–686.

Hatch, M. L. (1997). Conceptualization and treatment of bowel obsessions: Two case reports. *Behaviour Research and Therapy*, *35*, 253–257.

Hinrichsen, G. A. (2020). Overview of treatment. In G. A. Hinrichsen (Ed.), *Assessment and treatment of older adults: A guide for mental health professionals* (pp. 79–97). American Psychological Association.

Hollander, E., Kim, S., Braun, A., Simeon, D., & Zohar, J. (2009). Cross-cutting issues and future directions for the OCD spectrum. *Psychiatry Research*, *170*(1), 3–6.

Janeck, A. S., Calamari, J. E., Riemann, B. C, & Heffelfinger, K. (2003). Too much thinking about thinking? Metacognitive differences in obsessive-compulsive disorder. *Journal of Anxiety Disorders*, *17*(2), 181–195.

Jazi, N., & Asghar-Ali, A. (2020). Obsessive-compulsive disorder in older adults: A comprehensive literature review. *Journal of Psychiatric Practice*, *26*(3), 175–184.

Jenike, M. A. (1991). Geriatric obsessive-compulsive disorder. *Journal of Geriatric Psychiatry and Neurology*, *4*(1), 34–39.

Jones, M. K., Wootton, B. M., & Vaccaro, L. D. (2012). The efficacy of danger ideation reduction therapy for an 86-year-old man with a 63-year history of obsessive-compulsive disorder: A case study. *International Journal of Psychological and Behavioral Sciences*, *6*(6), 1231–1237.

Jurica, P. J., Leitten, C. L., & Mattis, S. (2001). *Dementia rating Scale-2: DRS-2: Professional manual*. Psychological Assessment Resources.

Kellett, S., & Holden, K. (2014). Emotional attachment to objects in hoarding: A critical review of the evidence. In R. O. Frost & G. Steketee (Eds.). *Oxford handbook of hoarding and acquiring* (pp. 120–138). Oxford University Press.

Kessler, R. C., Berglund, P., Demler, O., Jin, R., Merikangas, K. R., & Walters, E. E. (2005). Lifetime prevalence and age of onset distributions of DSM-IV disorders in the National Comorbidity Survey Replication. *Archives of General Psychiatry*, *62*, 593–602.

Kim, H. J., Steketee, G., & Frost, R. O. (2001). Hoarding by elderly people. *Health & Social Work*, *26*, 176–184.

Klenfeldt, I. F., Karlsson, B., Sigstrom, R., Backman, K., Waern, M., Ostling, S., Gustafson, D., & Skoog, I. (2014). Prevalence of obsessive-compulsive disorder in relation to depression and cognition in an elderly population. *American Journal of Geriatric Psychiatry*, *22*, 301–308.

Knight, B. G., & McCallum, T. J. (2011). Older adults. In J. C. Norcross, G. R. VandenBos, & D. K. Freedheim (Eds.), *History of psychotherapy: Continuity and change* (pp. 458–466). American Psychological Association. https://doi.org/10.1037/12353-026

Krooks, J. A., Weatherall, A. G., & Holland, P. J. (2018). Review of epidemiology, clinical presentation, diagnosis, and treatment of common primary psychiatric causes of cutaneous disease. *Journal of Dermatological Treatment*, *29*(4), 418–427.

McKay, D., Abramowitz, J. S., Calamari, J. E., Kyrios, M., Radomsky, A., Sookman, D., Taylor, S., & Wilhelm, S. (2004). A critical evaluation of obsessive-compulsive disorder subtypes: Symptoms versus mechanisms. *Clinical Psychology Review*, *24*(3), 283–313.

Moshier, S. J., Wootton, B. M., Bragdon, L. B., Tolin, D. F., Davis, E., DiMauro, J., & Diefenbach, G. J. (2016). The relationship between self-reported and objective neuropsychological impairments in patients with hoarding disorder. *Journal of Obsessive-Compulsive and Related Disorders*, *9*, 9–15.

Mroczek, D. K., & Kolarz, C. M. (1998). The effect of age on positive and negative affect: A developmental perspective on happiness. *Journal of Personality and Social Psychology*, *75*(5), 1333–1349.

Nestadt, G., Bienvenu, O. J., Cai, G., Samuels, J., & Eaton, W. W. (1998). Incidence of obsessive-compulsive disorder in adults. *The Journal of Nervous and Mental Disease*, *186*, 401–406.

Öst, L. G., Havnen, A., Hansen, B., & Kvale, G. (2015). Cognitive behavioral treatments of obsessive-compulsive disorder. A systematic review and meta-analysis of studies published 1993–2014. *Clinical Psychology Review*, *40*, 156–169.

Pertusa, A., Frost, R. O., Fullana, M. A., Samuels, J., Steketee, G., Tolin, D., Saxena, S., Leckman, J. F., & Mataix-Cols, D. (2010). Refining the diagnostic boundaries of compulsive hoarding: A critical review. *Clinical Psychology Review*, *30*, 371–386.

Phillips, K. A. (2005). *The broken mirror: Understanding and treating body dysmorphic disorder* (Rev. & exp ed.). Oxford University Press.

Phillips, K. A., Stein, D. J., Rauch, S. L., Hollander, E., Fallon, B. A., Barsky, A., Fineberg, N., Mataix-Cols, D., Ferrao, Y. A., Saxena, S., & Wilhelm, S. (2010). Should an obsessive-compulsive spectrum grouping of disorders be included in DSM-V? *Depression and Anxiety*, *27*(6), 528–555.

Postlethwaite, A., Kellett, S., & Mataix-Cols, D. (2019). Prevalence of hoarding disorder: A systematic review and meta-analysis. *Journal of Affective Disorders*, *256*, 309–316.

Prouvost, C., Calamari, J. E., & Woodard, J. L. (2016). Does cognitive self-consciousness link older adults' cognitive functioning to obsessive-compulsive symptoms? *Behaviour Research and Therapy*, *85*, 23–32.

Ramchandani, D. (1990). Trazodone for bowel obsession. *The American Journal of Psychiatry*, *147*(1), 124.

Ready, R. E., & Robinson, M. D. (2008). Do older individuals adapt to their traits? Personality–emotion relations among younger and older adults. *Journal of Research in Personality*, *42*(4), 1020–1030.

Ruscio, A. M., Stein, D. J., Chiu, W. T., & Kessler, R. C. (2010). The epidemiology of obsessive-compulsive disorder in the National Comorbidity Survey Replication. *Molecular Psychiatry*, *15*, 53–63.

Salthouse, T. (2012). Consequences of age-related cognitive declines. *Annual Review of Psychology*, *63*, 201–226. https://doi.org/10.1146/annurev-psych-120710-100328

Salthouse, T. A. (2010). *Major issues in cognitive aging*. Oxford University Press.

Salthouse, T. A. (2019). Trajectories of normal cognitive aging. *Psychology and Aging*, *34*(1), 17.

Samuels, J. E., Bienvenu, O. J., Grados, M. A., Cullen, Be, Riddle, M. A., Liang, K, Eaton, W. W., & Nestadt, G. (2008). Prevalence and correlates of hoarding behavior in a community-based sample. *Behaviour Research and Therapy*, *46*(7), 836–844.

Schulte, J., Schulz, C., Wilhelm, S., & Buhlmann, U. (2020). Treatment utilization and treatment barriers in individuals with body dysmorphic disorder. *BMC Psychiatry*, 20, 69.

Schumer, M., Panza, K., Mulqueen, J., Jakubowski, E., & Bloch, M. (2015). Long-term outcome in pediatric trichotillomania. *Depression & Anxiety*, *32*, 737–743.

Skoog, G., & Skoog, I. (1999). A 40-year follow-up of patients with obsessive-compulsive disorder. *Archives of General Psychiatry*, *56*(2), 121–127.

Steketee, G., & Frost, R. (2003). Compulsive hoarding: Current status of the research. *Clinical Psychology Review*, *23*, 905–927.

Steketee, G., & Frost, R. O. (2014a). *Treatments that work. Treatment for hoarding disorder: Therapist guide* (2nd ed.). Oxford University Press.

Steketee, G., & Frost, R. O. (2014b). *Treatments that work. Treatment for hoarding disorder: Workbook* (2nd ed.). Oxford University Press.

Steketee, G., Sorrentino Schmalisch, C., Dierberger, A., DeNobel, D., & Frost, R. O. (2012). Symptoms and history of hoarding in older adults. *Journal of Obsessive-Compulsive and Related Disorders*, *1*, 1–7.

Taylor, S. (2011). Early versus late onset obsessive-compulsive disorder: Evidence for distinct subtypes. *Clinical Psychology Review*, *31*(7), 1083–1100.

Teachman, B. A. (2007). Linking obsessional beliefs to OCD symptoms in older and younger adults. *Behaviour Research and Therapy*, *45*(7), 1671–1681.

Tolin, D. F., Fitch, K. E., Frost, R. O., & Steketee, G. (2010). Family informants' perceptions of insight in compulsive hoarding. *Cognitive Therapy and Research*, *34*(1), 69–81.

Tolin, D. F., Frost, R. O., Steketee, G., & Muroff, J. (2015). Cognitive behavioral therapy for hoarding disorder: A meta-analysis. *Depression and Anxiety*, *32*(3), 158–166.

Turner, K., Steketee, G., & Nauth, L. (2010). Treating elders with compulsive hoarding: A pilot program. *Cognitive and Behavioral Practice*, *17*(4), 449–457.

U.S. Census Bureau. (2003). *Statistical abstract of the United States*.

Wilkes, C. M., Wilson, H. W., Woodard, J. L., & Calamari, J. E. (2013). Do negative affect characteristics and subjective memory concerns increase risk for late life anxiety? *Journal of Anxiety Disorders*, *27*, 608–618.

Woods, B. (2008). Normal and abnormal ageing. In K. Laidlaw & B. Knight (Eds.), *Handbook of emotional disorders in later life: Assessment and treatment* (pp. 33–58). Oxford University Press.

CHAPTER 26
Obsessive-Compulsive and Related Disorders in Children and Adolescents

Scott M. Lee, Gary Liu, Allison Meinert, Jamie Manis, Andrew G. Guzick, Sophie C. Schneider, Wayne K. Goodman, *and* Eric A. Storch

Abstract

This chapter discusses obsessive-compulsive and related disorders, including obsessive-compulsive disorder, body dysmorphic disorder, hoarding disorder, trichotillomania, and skin-picking disorder, among children and adolescents. For each disorder, the phenomenology, assessment, comorbidity, etiology, and extant treatment data are reviewed. While much of the knowledge is derived from literature and clinical expertise regarding obsessive-compulsive and related disorders in the adult population, it is hoped that that the synthesis of information presented will contribute to optimal care of pediatric patients with these disorders. Furthermore, it is hoped that this review will foster additional scholarship and understanding of the conditions towards improved care and new innovations in this population.

Key Words: obsessive-compulsive disorder, body dysmorphic disorder, hoarding disorder, trichotillomania, skin-picking disorder, children, adolescents, treatment, assessment

Introduction

The obsessive-compulsive and related disorders (OCRDs) include obsessive-compulsive disorder (OCD), body dysmorphic disorder (BDD), hoarding disorder (HD), trichotillomania (TTM), and skin-picking disorder (SPD, also called excoriation) as delineated in the fifth edition of the *Diagnostic and Statistical Manual of Mental Disorders* (*DSM-5*, American Psychiatric Association [APA], 2013). These disorders have been linked by a variety of shared phenomenological characteristics, including commonalities in presentation (e.g., repetitive behaviors), family history, comorbidity patterns, psychological and psychiatric treatment approaches, and, while data continue to emerge, in brain circuitry and neurotransmitter/peptide abnormalities (Storch, Abramowitz, & Goodman, 2008). While all five of the disorders are diagnostically classified under the OCRD umbrella per *DSM-5*, there is still open debate about whether TTM and SPD, which are often grouped in the body-focused repetitive behaviors (BFRBs), ought to be classified in the OCRD cluster (Abramowitz, 2018). Much of the debate centers on the phenotypic distinctions and genetic characteristics of BFRBs, which are discussed in greater detail in the TTM section of this chapter.

As is true for many psychiatric disorders, much of the available information on OCRDs has been extrapolated from adult studies and extended to children. Accordingly, there is relatively less data available on children with OCRDs. With this in mind, the purpose of the present chapter is to review the literature on OCRDs in children and adolescents. For each disorder, the phenomenology, assessment, comorbidity, etiology, and extant treatment data are reviewed, with the hope that the synthesis of information will foster additional scholarship and understanding of these conditions.

OCD

OCD is characterized by the presence of obsessions (persistent and distressing intrusive thoughts, ideas, impulses, or images) and/or compulsions (repetitive or ritualistic behaviors or mental acts that reduce or prevent distress in response to the obsessive thoughts), which are time-consuming and/or cause significant distress or impairment of day-to-day functioning (APA, 2013). OCD affects 1% to 3% of children and adolescents (Kessler et al., 2005; Zohar, 1999). For many of these children, functional impairments across a variety of domains are substantial, including academic, social, and familial difficulties (Lack, 2012; Piacentini et al., 2003; Sarvet, 2013). As many as 50% of individuals with OCD have symptom onset before age 18 years, and the average age of onset in the United States is 19.5 years (Nakatani et al., 2011; Ruscio et al., 2010). Research also suggests that children with prepubescent or "early-onset" OCD may represent a unique subtype that is associated with a stronger genetic component, tic disorder comorbidity, and male gender (Albert et al., 2015; Brakoulias et al., 2017; Dell'Osso et al., 2016). Childhood-onset OCD often remains chronic throughout the life span, with increases in functional impairment if it is left untreated (Bloch & Storch, 2015).

Symptom Phenomenology

Virtually all individuals with an OCD diagnosis have both obsessions and compulsions, although compulsions are typically easier to identify than obsessions in children due to the overt nature of many compulsions as well as children's variable ability to report on internal experiences (Hirschtritt et al., 2017). Obsessions and compulsions have a functional relationship, in that intrusive or involuntary obsessions evoke rituals and avoidance that serve to reduce distress; the negatively reinforcing distress reduction further motivates engagement in compulsions (Starcevic et al., 2011).

Assessment

The presentation of OCD symptoms in children shares many similarities to that seen in adults. Common obsessions include contamination fears, aggressive/sexual/religious obsessions, and symmetry concerns; common compulsions include cleaning rituals, checking, reassurance-seeking/confessing, ordering and repeating rituals, and hoarding behaviors (Gallant et al., 2008). Indeed, factor analytic studies of the Children's Yale-Brown Obsessive-Compulsive Scale Symptom Checklist (Scahill et al., 1997) produced similar results to the studies for adults, indicating a stability of broad symptom dimensions across ages (Mataix-Cols et al., 2008). While symptoms present similarly in adults and children, there are still distinct characteristics among the two populations. Symptoms in younger children may be less cognitively developed. Relative to adults and adolescents, children have poorer insight on average (Selles et al., 2014), although the majority demonstrate good to excellent symptom insight (Selles, Højgaard, et al., 2018). Studies have confirmed the variability in insight and have shown that those with greater insight have less severe symptoms (Selles, Højgaard, et al., 2018). Finally, as is true among adults with OCD, family accommodation is ubiquitous among youth (Caporino et al., 2012; Storch et al., 2007).

Comorbidity
Up to 76% of youth with an OCD diagnosis meet criteria for a comorbid disorder (Coskun et al., 2012; Geller et al., 2003; Sarvet, 2013; Storch, Merlo, et al., 2008). Recent studies of children and adolescents with OCD estimate rates of comorbidity with anxiety disorders to be 19% to 50%; with tic disorders, 11% to 19%; with disruptive behavior disorders, 7% to 10%; and with attention deficit/hyperactivity disorder (ADHD), 9% to 13% (Peris et al., 2017; Torp, Dahl, Skarphedinsson, Thomsen, et al., 2015). Depressive disorders have been estimated to occur in approximately a quarter of adolescents with OCD as well, although they are relatively less common in school-age children (Peris et al., 2017). Other studies of samples of youth with OCD have noted significant rates of comorbidity with bipolar disorder (15%; Joshi et al., 2010) and autism spectrum disorder (ASD; 3% to 7%; Meier et al., 2015; Torp, Dahl, Skarphedinsson, Thomsen, et al., 2015). Notably, the presence of a comorbid condition often interacts with the primary obsessive-compulsive symptoms and is typically associated with increased OCD symptom severity (Langley et al., 2010). Further, the presence of emotional and behavioral comorbidities may negatively affect response to both pharmacological and psychosocial treatments (Geller et al., 2003; Storch, Merlo, et al., 2008; Torp, Dahl, Skarphedinsson, Compton, et al., 2015), particularly in the case of disruptive behavior, ADHD, and major depression (Storch, Merlo, et al., 2008).

Etiology
Although a complete review of all potential etiologic factors associated with OCD is beyond the scope of this chapter, multiple factors, including biological and psychosocial factors, as well as interactions among these factors, likely contribute to the etiology and maintenance of OCD. Biologically, neurochemical models highlight the role of serotonergic, dopaminergic, and glutamate systems in symptom expression, as evidenced

by medication trials that target neurotransmission in these systems (Gassó et al., 2015; O'Neill et al., 2017; Sinopoli et al., 2017). In addition to neurotransmitter dysregulation, OCD is associated with neuroanatomical abnormalities (see also Chapter 7). For example, relative to healthy controls, both children and adults with symptoms of OCD had increased gray matter of the anterior cingulate gyrus (Cheng et al., 2016; Rotge et al., 2010), increased volume of the thalamus (Fitzgerald et al., 2011; Shaw et al., 2015), and decreased volume of the globus pallidus (Shaw et al., 2015). These findings support a fundamental dysfunction of frontal-striatal circuitry in OCD (Fitzgerald et al., 2011), such that feedback loops involving the orbitofrontal cortex, thalamus, and striatum (in the basal ganglia) are hypothesized to mediate intrusive thoughts and repetitive behaviors (Fitzgerald et al., 2011; Weber et al., 2014). Finally, established heritability studies (see also Chapter 6) have demonstrated that the risk for OCD is directly proportional to the degree of genetic relatedness, where first-degree relatives shared the greatest risk and second- and third-degree relatives had relatively less risk; although no specific susceptibility genes have been found at this time (Mataix-Cols et al., 2013).

In addition to biological factors, cognitive-behavioral theory sheds light on the psychosocial factors associated with OCD and provides an empirically based, well-established framework for understanding the acquisition and maintenance of obsessive-compulsive symptoms. From a behavioral perspective (see also Chapter 10), the repertoire of developed behaviors or rituals aims to reduce feelings of distress or anxiety. If these emotions are reduced, the individual effectively creates a negative reinforcement loop—such that the likelihood of engaging in the chosen repertoire of behaviors or rituals is increased during future periods of distress. Cognitive theorists (see also Chapter 11) highlight faulty beliefs or appraisals and cognitive errors (e.g., an exaggerated importance of the thoughts, inflated concern about the importance of being able to control the thoughts, inability to tolerate ambiguity) that children have regarding intrusive thoughts, images, and impulses (Riesel et al., 2015) rather than the actual occurrence of such thoughts. Integrating the cognitive and behavioral models provides a cyclical pattern of thoughts and behaviors whereby cognitive misattributions result in anxiety/distress. This leads to anxiety-reducing rituals that are helpful in the short term but impair function in the long term. However, because of the short-term relief that rituals/avoidance may bring, children are more likely to perform the rituals in response to intrusive thoughts (Turner, 2006). Notably, the cycle prevents adaptive learning from taking place, as the child performs routines and rituals rather than facing the possibility of feared consequences and learning that the likelihood of the fears' occurring and/or their associated consequences are not as catastrophic as they initially perceived (Hezel & Simpson, 2019).

Treatment
Both cognitive-behavioral therapy (CBT) with exposure and response prevention (E/RP) and selective serotonin reuptake inhibitors (SSRIs) have shown efficacy in

methodologically rigorous clinical trials, which are described in Chapters 17 and 19 of this volume. The American Academy of Child and Adolescent Psychiatry (AACAP) recommends CBT with E/RP as the first-line monotherapy for children with OCD of mild/moderate severity, but combined with an SSRI for those with severe symptoms (Geller & March, 2012; Schneider & Storch, 2017b). However, most affected adults and children initially receive pharmacotherapy or non-CBT psychotherapy (Mancuso et al., 2010), and duration between symptom onset and treatment is often extended (Marques et al., 2010). This highlights the need to increase patient access to evidence-based psychological care.

Pharmacological treatment for OCD is an effective, relatively safe, and readily available treatment modality. Modulation of serotonergic transmission is thought to improve OCD symptomology (Del Casale et al., 2019). Currently, there are four medications approved by the FDA for use in pediatric populations with OCD: clomipramine, a tricyclic antidepressant prescribed for children 10 years old and older (Mallinckrodt LLC, 2012), and three SSRIs: fluoxetine, for children seven years old and older (Dista Labs, 2009); fluvoxamine, for children eight years old and older (Teva Generics, 2008); and sertraline, for children six years old and older (Pfizer, 2016). The efficacy of clomipramine has been shown to rival that of (or even surpass) the efficacy of SSRIs (Soomro et al., 2008; Varigonda et al., 2016); however, this agent is not typically used as a first-line medication given the greater number of associated side effects and the necessity to monitor cardiovascular function and, rarely, complete blood counts and liver function tests (Hirsch, 2020). While the SSRIs are associated with some modest side effects among youth (Ivarsson et al., 2015; Varigonda et al., 2016), they are generally well tolerated and are considered safe (Geller & March, 2012; Schneider & Storch, 2017b). Increased risk of suicidality, or "activation syndrome," and other adverse side effects (e.g., irritability, restlessness, emotional lability) have been linked to SSRI initiation and/or dosage increases, particularly among young adults (Ivarsson et al., 2015). While clomipramine and the FDA-approved SSRIs have been shown to significantly reduce obsessive-compulsive symptoms in children (Ivarsson et al., 2015; Varigonda et al., 2016; Yamamuro et al., 2016), it should be noted that symptom remission is relatively rare (20%; Ivarsson et al., 2015; Varigonda et al., 2016). Some research among adults with OCD has shown that augmenting SSRI interventions with antipsychotics can improve treatment efficacy. Unfortunately, side effects, including substantial weight gain and metabolic syndrome, are common and may outweigh the potential benefits of using antipsychotics for treatment, and they have not been well studied in youth.

CBT with E/RP differs from traditional psychotherapy in its structured incorporation of core skills for symptom management. During CBT, a therapist provides psychoeducation that teaches the child and family what OCD is, how compulsions and avoidance maintain symptoms, and how to deal with symptomatology. Cognitive strategies (see also Chapter 20) include constructive self-talk and cultivating detachment in order to counter anxious thoughts, a process sometimes referred to as externalizing OCD (McGuire et al., 2015; Schneider & Storch, 2017b). In constructive self-talk, the child is taught how to identify problematic self-statements (e.g., "OCD will always be in control") and how to respond in a positive, accurate, and forceful manner (e.g., "OCD can't boss me around"). Therapists also guide children to cultivate detachment from obsessions. As opposed to suppressing intrusive thoughts, the child learns to regard them as "brain hiccups" that do not need attention.

As its name implies, the two elements of E/RP for youth with OCD are exposure (i.e., confronting situations that elicit obsessional anxiety) and response prevention (i.e., deterring the ritualistic or compulsive behaviors that serve to reduce or avoid anxiety in the short term). In E/RP, the patient is exposed to fear-producing stimuli and is challenged to limit rituals that might typically be used to alleviate anxiety. After extended exposures, the patient habituates to feelings of distress and has opportunities for corrective learning about obsessive fears (McGuire et al., 2015; Schneider & Storch, 2017b). Further, continued exposures to the feared stimulus without ritual engagement lead to progressively lower levels of distress and learning that the feared outcome does not occur (McGuire et al., 2015; Schneider & Storch, 2017b).

For the pediatric population in particular, E/RP also should address parental/caregiver accommodation of symptoms, a process in which parents facilitate compulsions (e.g., providing "special" items like food and hand sanitizer, or providing excessive reassurance) or avoidance (e.g., allowing children to miss social, school, or family events that could provoke OCD triggers) in order to reduce distress in the short term (Peris et al., 2017). Greater levels of accommodation are related to attenuated E/RP response in youth, while reductions in accommodation predict improvement in OCD symptoms (McGuire et al., 2015; Schneider & Storch, 2017b). Thus, in treatment, parents and caregivers are challenged to reduce accommodation while maintaining a warm, supportive relationship during the course of E/RP.

Among youth with OCD, CBT has been demonstrated to be superior to SSRI monotherapy, wait-list control conditions, and attention control conditions (McGuire et al., 2015; Schneider & Storch, 2017b). Overall, response and remission rates in controlled trials are quite high—particularly when patients received combination (i.e., CBT plus SSRI) therapy—with up to 85% of youth being classified as responders and 53% achieving clinical remission after treatment (McGuire et al., 2015; Öst et al., 2016).

BDD

BDD is characterized by intense preoccupation with perceived flaws in appearance that are minimal or not observable by others, with excessive compensatory behaviors to fix the flaws. With an estimated incidence of 1.7% in adolescents (Schneider et al., 2017), BDD is associated with substantial distress, impairment in everyday functioning, poor quality of life, and high rates of suicidality (Krebs et al., 2020; Phillips, 2000; Phillips et al., 2006).

Symptom Phenomenology

Although any body part may be the focus of concern, patients most often experience distress related to their facial features, hair, or skin (Phillips et al., 2005; Schneider et al., 2019). As a direct consequence of distress over appearance, patients often perform compensatory ritualistic behaviors, such as mirror-checking, hiding the defects, skin-picking, comparing themselves to others, and seeking reassurance that their appearance is acceptable to others (Mufaddel et al., 2013; Nicewicz & Boutrouille, 2020; Weingarden et al., 2018).

BDD often begins during adolescence, with a mean age of onset of 16 to 17 years (Bjornsson et al., 2013). One study of a large adolescent sample ($N = 3,149$) reported that 1.7% met *DSM-IV* criteria for BDD, which is similar to the prevalence reported in the adult population (Schneider et al., 2017). However, its prevalence among adolescent psychiatric inpatients is greater, ranging from 6.7% to 13.1% (Dyl et al., 2006; Grant et al., 2001).

Assessment

Presenting symptoms of BDD are similar in adolescents and adults (Albertini & Phillips, 1999; Phillips et al., 2006), with bodily concerns most frequently centered on the skin (68%), nose (64%), hair (64%), face (53%), and mouth (49%; Rautio et al., 2020). Similar to adults, pediatric patients also engage in compulsive compensatory behaviors, including camouflaging, comparing to others, mirror-checking, and seeking reassurance (Hadley et al., 2002). Most pediatric patients engage in more than one BDD-related compulsion (mean = 4.5; Albertini & Phillips, 1999) and over a quarter of patients carry out compulsive behaviors for more than eight hours a day (Dyl et al., 2006; Phillips et al., 2006). While the presentation may be similar across age groups, adolescents with BDD have more delusional beliefs and higher rates of suicide attempts than adults with BDD (Jafferany et al., 2019; Phillips et al., 2006).

To aid clinicians in diagnosis, commonly used assessments for BDD in adolescents include the BDD adaptation of the Yale-Brown Obsessive-Compulsive Scale–Adolescent Version (BDD-Y-BOCS-A; Krebs, Fernández de la Cruz, & Mataix-Cols, 2017; Wilhelm et al., 2016) and the Body Image Questionnaire–Child and Adolescents Version (Veale, 2009).

Etiology

Disease models of BDD often contain biological and psychosocial components and their interactions with each other. Biologically, at the synaptic level, dysregulation of the serotonergic system has been linked to BDD (Li et al., 2013). Neuroimaging studies have implicated various brain regions, including frontal-striatal circuit dysfunction, left hemispheric dominance, and hyperresponsiveness of the amygdala and insula (Feusner et al., 2008). At the cognitive-behavioral level, the defects in neurocircuitry are associated with both biased information-processing and dysfunctional behavioral strategies that are involved in the etiology and maintenance of BDD (Clerkin & Teachman, 2008; Prazeres et al., 2013). Patients with BDD tend to interpret ambiguous situations as threatening (Buhlmann et al., 2002). For example, compared to those without BDD they often interpret facial expressions as more negatively valenced (Buhlmann et al., 2004, 2006). Furthermore, other factors, such as cultural socialization, interpersonal experiences, physical characteristics, and personality attributes, have been proposed to both incite and perpetuate BDD (Cash & Pruzinsky, 2004; Neziroglu & Cash, 2008; Neziroglu et al., 2004; Veale, 2004; Veale et al., 1996). In the pediatric population in particular, bullying and teasing can perpetuate a child's preoccupations with personal flaws. This leads to the classic ritualistic behaviors in BDD (e.g., grooming, avoidance of social situations), which are similar in function to those described in OCD, in that they are negatively reinforced through the short-term relief they provide (Labuschagne et al., 2013). Finally, prevalence is higher among adolescent girls than among boys (Phillips et al., 2006). However, increasing attention is being given to muscle dysmorphia, which affects more males than females and is characterized by excessive concern about muscularity and physical appearance (Tod et al., 2016).

Comorbidity

Pediatric BDD is associated with considerable distress and significantly impaired psychosocial functioning, including poor grades, social withdrawal, and school attrition (Krebs, Fernández de la Cruz, & Mataix-Cols, 2017). School drop-out rates for pediatric BDD have been reported to be as high as 37%, with an additional 20% attending school only part-time due to their BDD (Mataix-Cols et al., 2015). Furthermore, adolescent BDD is highly linked to depression (81%), suicidal ideation (17%–77%), suicide attempts (3%–63%), social phobias (40%), OCD (27.8%), eating disorders, and substance use disorders (44.4%; Grant et al., 2005; Mufaddel et al., 2013; Phillips, 2007; Phillips et al., 2006; Ruffolo et al., 2006; Tassin et al., 2014).

The high rate of comorbid psychiatric conditions makes diagnosing and treating BDD challenging, because the comorbid disorders share similar phenomenological features. Furthermore, patients are often reluctant to share appearance concerns due to embarrassment or shame (Schneider & Storch, 2017a; Weingarden et al., 2017). As a result, BDD is largely underdiagnosed and merits greater attention (Phillips & Hollander, 2008). In addition to the BDD-Y-BOCS-A, appearance-specific questions are useful and essential for diagnosis if BDD is suspected (Varma & Rastogi, 2015).

Treatment

Treatment of BDD is focused on both pharmacotherapy and CBT (Hong et al., 2018; Krebs, Fernandez de la Cruz, & Mataix-Cols, 2017) . Placebo-controlled trials among adults with BDD have demonstrated the efficacy of various SSRIs, including clomipramine

(Hollander et al., 1999), fluvoxamine (Phillips et al., 1998), fluoxetine (Phillips et al., 2002), and citalopram (Phillips & Najjar, 2003)—all of which are discussed in greater detail in Chapter 22. Such trials have not been replicated in the pediatric population, although case reports have reported efficacy of tricyclic antidepressants (Hong et al., 2019; Sobanski & Schmidt, 2000).

CBT has been shown to be effective for treating BDD in various clinical trials (Krebs, Fernández de la Cruz, Monzani, et al., 2017; Rabiei et al., 2012). Investigations specific to treating adolescent BDD are promising, with initial studies demonstrating marked improvement of symptoms (up to 68%) following CBT (Greenberg et al., 2016; Krebs et al., 2013; Mataix-Cols et al., 2015), treatment durability, and efficacy relative to treatment with just psychoeducation and monitoring (Krebs, Fernández de la Cruz, Monzani, et al., 2017; Mataix-Cols et al., 2015).

Future studies aimed at identifying potential moderating variables in treatment response (e.g., age of onset, family constellation, insight, motivation for treatment, comorbid diagnoses) may lead to improved treatment outcomes. Furthermore, comprehensive examinations of treatment specifically tailored to pediatric BDD are still lacking beyond the preliminary, albeit promising, pediatric-focused CBT studies. Studies on pharmacotherapy and combination therapy (i.e., pharmacotherapy plus CBT) for BDD in this population have not been published and need further development in the future. As is true for any disorder, elucidating the underlying etiology and maintenance factors may allow for more targeted and effective treatments; therefore, future studies that empirically test existing models and propose new theories for understanding BDD are warranted.

HD

Hoarding had previously been considered a subtype of OCD, although HD was introduced as a separate diagnosis in the *DSM-5* due to differences in comorbidity patterns, insight, neurobiology, and treatment responses (Mataix-Cols et al., 2010). A large community pediatric study ($N = 16,718$) corroborated that children with HD had unique clinical correlates and comorbidities (i.e., greater correlation with ADHD and lesser correlation with anxiety) that were not seen in matched children with obsessive-compulsive symptoms. Specifically, the study found a relationship between HD and the inattentive components of ADHD and not the hyperactivity and impulsivity pieces (Burton et al., 2016). Another study analyzing phenotypic correlations between six obsessive-compulsive traits (i.e., cleaning/contamination, symmetry/ordering, superstition, rumination, counting/checking, and hoarding) found the hoarding trait to be the least correlated with the other five dimensions (Burton et al., 2018). These phenotypic analyses are consistent with the new *DSM-5* designation.

HD is characterized as a persistent difficulty in discarding or parting with possessions, regardless of their actual value, which is due to a perceived need to save items and distress associated with discarding them. The results are the accumulation of possessions that congest and clutter active living areas and substantially compromise their intended use (APA, 2013). Diagnosis can be further specified by excessive acquisition and level of patient insight (Morris et al., 2016).

HD often presents in childhood in a mild form or with associated clinical characteristics (e.g., collecting school paraphernalia, old clothing, garbage), and continues to worsen across the life span (Dozier et al., 2016; Storch et al., 2011). Although there is a clear pediatric component to the disorder, prevalence has been characterized in only a few studies. One twin study (N = 3,974) found prevalence between 2% and 3.7%, while another study found the rate to be 9.27% (Alvarenga et al., 2015; Ivanov et al., 2013). Further studies need to be done to more accurately determine hoarding prevalence, with sensitivity to developmental differences in hoarding symptoms, given that the accumulation of possessions that frequently causes impairment in HD often takes years or decades to progress. Thus, although age of symptom onset typically is around 10 to 20 years and the disorder persists throughout the lifetime, youth rarely present to clinical or research settings with concerns about difficulty discarding or excessive accumulation due to their parents' setting limits and the difficulty of accumulating possessions (Dozier et al., 2016; Tolin et al., 2010).

Symptom Phenomenology

Youth and adults with HD share the core deficit of difficulty discarding, although their clinical presentation is quite different (Soreni, 2020). While adults with HD present with highly unsafe home environments and disrupted social, family, and professional lives due to clutter, children do not have the time, space, financial independence, or control over their home for hoarding problems to impact their daily lives (Storch et al., 2011). Instead, hoarding symptoms in children present as an excessive emotional attachment to objects (Chen et al., 2017), which may stem from attachment anxiety due to earlier childhood traumas (Kehoe & Egan, 2019). A number of developmental disorders, such as Prader-Willi syndrome, ADHD, and ASD, are associated with the severity of hoarding (Hacker et al., 2016; La Buissonnière-Ariza et al., 2018). Because collecting items is a developmentally normal process in childhood, it is important to be able to distinguish between normal acquisition and pathologic hoarding behavior (Morris et al., 2016).

Comorbidity

HD is comorbid with other psychiatric and medical disorders, including OCD, ADHD, and ASD. Frequency of hoarding symptoms among pediatric patients with OCD has ranged between 6% and 48%, and this variability is likely due to inconsistent diagnostic criteria for clinically significantly hoarding versus normative behavior (Morris et al., 2016). Although hoarding was historically categorized as a subtype of OCD, HD has high rates of comorbidity with ADHD, with one study of 99 youth finding that 29% had ADHD and clinically significant symptoms of hoarding (Hacker et al., 2016). This, paired with research evaluating executive dysfunction and organization problems in adults with HD, has led experts to believe that ADHD may be more closely related to HD than to OCD (Sheppard et al., 2010). When considering youth with ADHD and potential HD, however, it is important to understand if excessive clutter is caused by disorganization rather than difficulty discarding items due to sentimental attachment or a belief that it will be needed in the future. Finally, among the few studies that have been done, elevated HD symptoms were reported in 25% of children with ASD (i.e., 10 of 40 patients; Dykens et al., 1996; Storch et al., 2016). Both disorders naturally predispose patients to collect/hoard, and these numbers represent patients who were found to have clinically significant symptoms that extended beyond the expected behavior.

Etiology
The etiology of HD is multifactorial, with a combination of environmental and genetic factors at play. In a twin study, hoarding was suggested to have a significant genetic element, more so in monozygotic twin boys than in dizygotic twin boys or in twin girls in general (Ivanov et al., 2013). Similar to what was reported for TTM, first-degree relatives are more likely to present with HD symptomology (e.g., saving, cluttering, and difficulty discarding) compared to the general population (Steketee et al., 2015). Interestingly, environmental factors may have a greater influence in HD among the pediatric population than among the adult population (Morris et al., 2016). Developmental disorders, including Prader-Willi syndrome and ASD, have been linked with youth hoarding (Dykens & Shah, 2003; Storch et al., 2016). Some information also suggests that early childhood experiences may motivate hoarding behaviors in youth. For example, hoarding has been documented among youth in foster care (Plimpton et al., 2009).

Treatment
Treatment modalities for pediatric patients with HD are modeled on CBT principles, which generally include psychoeducation, case formulation, motivational interviewing, skills training, exposure therapy, and cognitive therapy (see Chapter 23; Steketee et al., 2010; Tolin, Frost, & Steketee, 2007). Developmentally appropriate versions of the model have been used in the pediatric population, with particular focus on addressing the difficulty discarding and HD's effect on family functioning, although only case studies have been published to date (Park et al., 2014). Among youth with primary OCD and hoarding behaviors, presence of hoarding behaviors did not affect CBT outcome (Højgaard et al., 2019). No pharmacotherapy specifically targeting HD has been evaluated in the pediatric population (Piacentino et al., 2019). Treatment is an area highlighted for future research (Guzick et al., 2020).

TTM

TTM (i.e., hair-pulling disorder) is marked by pulling out of one's hair, noticeable hair loss, clinically significant distress and impairment in functioning, and repeated attempts to decrease or stop hair-pulling behavior (APA, 2013). As noted in the introduction, there is much debate about whether TTM and SPD, which are often classified in the BFRBs, are phenotypically and etiologically similar to the three OCRDs discussed so far. These distinctions are made throughout the discussion of TTM here.

The start of hair-pulling often, but not always, coincides with, or follows, the onset of puberty, with the average age of onset for TTM being in late childhood, from 10 to 13 years, or in adolescence, from age 15 to age 17 (Grant & Chamberlain, 2016; Grant et al., 2020). The prevalence of TTM is estimated to range from 0.6% to 3.5%, although studies have typically utilized small convenience samples with young adults (Grant et al., 2020). Clinical adult samples suggest that TTM has a strong female preponderance, with a female to male ratio of 4:1 (Grant et al., 2020), although community samples have found a more equal sex distribution of TTM in childhood (Panza et al., 2013). TTM typically runs a chronic course without treatment, with symptom severity waxing and waning across the life span (Christenson et al., 1991; Grant & Chamberlain, 2016).

Symptom Phenomenology

The nature of hair-pulling behavior varies widely among individuals with TTM (see further detail in Chapter 5). Although it is generally limited to one or two sites (Chamberlain et al., 2007), hair-pulling can occur at any site on the body, with common sites being the scalp, eyebrows, eyelashes, stomach, back, face, arms, legs, and pubic area (Duke et al., 2010). Duration of hair-pulling episodes varies, and the behavior may last for a few minutes or up to several hours (Grant & Chamberlain, 2016). Resulting hair loss can range from barely noticeable to complete baldness (Parakh & Srivastava, 2010).

Oral behaviors (e.g., chewing, biting, or swallowing the hair) can accompany hair-pulling and may lead to serious medical complications. Trichobezoars, masses of hair that are trapped in the intestinal tract (Thakur et al., 2007), have been documented in children as young as three years old (Singh et al., 2013). Pediatric TTM can also result in skin irritation, infection at the site where the hair is pulled, and repetitive motion injuries to the hands (Harrison & Franklin, 2012).

In addition to medical complications, TTM can lead to significant functional and emotional impairment. Children and adolescents with TTM frequently experience social isolation, shame, embarrassment, fear of negative peer evaluation, low self-esteem, social anxiety, and avoidance of social situations (Anwar & Jafferany, 2019; Grant et al., 2016; Harrison & Franklin, 2012; Odlaug et al., 2010; Tung et al., 2015). Furthermore, TTM can result in impairment in academic and social domains, including making friends, getting closer to friends, and the ability to function in school and complete schoolwork (Snorrason et al., 2015).

Assessment

Hair-pulling behavior has been conceptualized in two pulling styles: automatic and focused (Flessner et al., 2008). Unfocused (automatic) hair-pulling usually occurs without the individual's being fully aware of the behavior, whereas focused hair-pulling is more intentional and is often done to relieve stress or tension (Flessner et al., 2007) or when an individual sees or feels that a hair is "not right" (e.g., coarse, irregular, or out of place; Grant, 2019). Both of these subtypes of TTM are phenotypically distinct from the OCRDs discussed so far. Unfocused hair-pulling is in direct contrast to the very conscious effort to act on a compulsion to temporarily reduce anxiety. And focused hair-pulling is done to relieve tension, which Abramowitz (2018) argued is different from relieving anxiety, which is what helps to define an OCRD.

In a sample of youth with TTM who were 10 to 17 years old, most engaged in both styles of pulling, and those who tended to pull in a focused manner had more severe pulling symptoms (Flessner et al., 2007). A more recent factor analysis provided evidence for another framework for TTM subtype dimensions, revealing internally regulated pulling and awareness of pulling (Alexander et al., 2016). These factors refer to the degree to which pulling is done to regulate emotional discomfort and the degree to which a person is aware of pulling, respectively (Alexander et al., 2016). Understanding this hair-pulling conceptualization is important for clinicians if they suspect a diagnosis of pediatric TTM. Formal assessment methods (see Chapter 15), particularly the clinical interview, can help elucidate the nature of the hair-pulling behavior, its associated symptoms, and its severity. The Massachusetts General Hospital Hair-Pulling Scale (MGH-HPS), a modification of the Yale-Brown Obsessive-Compulsive Scale, is a validated assessment tool that is frequently used for TTM in the pediatric population (Nelson et al., 2014).

Comorbidity

In addition to OCD, anxiety, depression, and disruptive behaviors are common comorbidities in TTM. Among a pediatric sample, 40.9% of whom were diagnosed with at least one comorbid psychiatric disorder, the most frequent concomitant disorders were mood disorders (19.4%), anxiety disorders (28.5%), and ADHD (16.1%; Franklin et al., 2008). Corroborating a high pediatric comorbidity with depression, youth with TTM frequently endorse depressive symptoms (Lewin et al., 2009). Additionally, in a study of 10- to 14-year-old children with ASD, 3.9% met the three-month point prevalence criteria for TTM, which is a significantly higher rate than is found in the general population (Simonoff et al., 2008). A recent study of patients with TTM across the life span found significant association between TTM and OCD, along with impulse control disorders, including kleptomania, pyromania, SPD, and bulimia nervosa. Notably, there was no significant association of TTM with BDD, which is another OCRD (Gerstenblith et al., 2019).

Etiology

Little research has been done on the genetic and neurobiological mechanisms of TTM specifically in the pediatric population, so most data relate to studies on TTM in adults (see Chapter 5 for greater detail). Evidence suggests genetic vulnerability to TTM, with a recent case-control study reporting a significantly higher recurrence risk among first-degree relatives (Keuthen et al., 2014). Although further study is needed to determine specific genetic abnormalities related to the pathophysiology of TTM, multiple genes have been identified as associated with TTM symptoms in animals (Greer & Capecchi, 2002; Shmelkov et al., 2010; Welch et al., 2007). Rare variations in the *Sapap3* gene have been associated with pathological grooming and hair-pulling in humans (Bienvenu et al., 2009; Züchner et al., 2009). Adult twin studies have not yet identified a gene but have reported two distinct predominantly heritable factors. The first factor is shared by all five OCRDs covered in this chapter, particularly among OCD, BDD, and HD, while the second factor is shared only by the two BFRBs, TTM and SPD (Monzani et al., 2014). The two findings suggest that TTM and SPD are etiologically distinct from the other OCRDs and should inspire further consideration of whether these BFRBs should have a distinct classification (Stein et al., 2016).

Limited neurochemistry research, primarily on treatment response to medications, suggests that several neurotransmitter and neuropeptide systems play a role in TTM symptom expression (Johnson & El-Alfy, 2016). Consistent with research on OCD and BDD, serotonin-related genes are implicated in TTM. Treatment response to the tricyclic antidepressant clomipramine supports the involvement of the serotonergic system, while stereotypic behaviors, including hair-pulling, have been reduced in response to dopamine blockers (Van Ameringen et al., 2010). Evidence for dysfunction in cortico-striato-thalamo-cortical (CSTC) circuit activity and for excitatory/inhibitory signaling imbalance among children with TTM suggests that pediatric TTM may be marked by sensitivity to excitatory effects of glutamate (Peris et al., 2020), the excitatory neurotransmitter in CSTC circuits, which are central to dysfunction in OCD (Ahmari & Dougherty, 2015). While the literature, which predominantly focuses on adult TTM patients, can be informative about pediatric TTM, further research specifically focused on pediatric TTM is needed to better elucidate etiology and to evaluate potential developmental differences in pediatric populations.

Treatment

Although treatment for TTM in youth is less developed than treatment for TTM in the adult population, leading treatment modalities include habit reversal training (HRT) and behavioral therapy. Pharmacotherapy for pediatric TTM still merits further investigation. HRT is a behavioral therapy that is considered the first-line treatment for pediatric TTM (Franklin et al., 2011). The three components of HRT includes awareness training, stimulus control, and competing response practice (Rehm et al., 2015). Awareness training helps children to become aware of their hair-pulling as well as the situations and factors that often precede the hair-pulling episodes. Stimulus control focuses on avoiding or modifying external triggers for hair-pulling, and competing response practice focuses on performing an alternative act that is incompatible with hair-pulling (Morris et al., 2013). Support from caregivers during HRT is often helpful for children with TTM; caregivers can provide positive reinforcement for use of competing responses and gentle reminders when they notice hair-pulling. Meta-analyses have demonstrated the efficacy of HRT in the adult population (see Chapter 24). A study on the efficacy of HRT in pediatric patients with TTM ($N = 40$) has also revealed that HRT yields significant reductions in TTM severity. The improvements were maintained up to three months after HRT (Rahman et al., 2017).

Often, HRT is combined with other behavioral techniques, including components of CBT; acceptance and commitment therapy, in which individuals experience the urge to pull and accept it without acting on it (Lee et al., 2018; Woods et al., 2006); and dialectical behavior therapy, including mindfulness training, emotion-regulation skills, and building distress tolerance (Keuthen et al., 2012). These behavioral interventions have been shown to be efficacious and durable in early trials. The first randomized controlled trial (RCT) in pediatric patients with TTM ($N = 24$) found that an eight-week behavioral therapy protocol significantly reduced TTM symptomatology at the immediate conclusion of treatment and eight weeks following treatment (Franklin et al., 2011). A second RCT ($N = 40$) supported the initial findings, demonstrating significantly reduced MGH-HPS scores among children who received HRT compared to control groups (Rahman et al., 2017). Although HRT is considered first-line therapy, an open trial of individualized CBT ($N = 22$) has been promising, with 77% of participants achieving statistically significant reduction in TTM severity with CBT monotherapy alone (Tolin, Franklin, et al., 2007). Such findings are promising and merit further investigation with greater sample sizes in the pediatric population.

While the early results are certainly encouraging, the fact remains that studies of treatment for TTM in youth are, at present, less developed than in the adult population. This is particularly true in pharmacotherapy for pediatric TTM. Pharmacologic agents that are similar to those used in OCD, such as clomipramine, SSRIs, olanzapine, N-acetylcysteine, and naltrexone, have been proposed for TTM, and a few articles have begun to show their efficacy in the pediatric population (Farhat et al., 2020; Slikboer et al., 2017). For example, a case study reported success with olanzapine augmentation in treatment of an adolescent with TTM (Pathak et al., 2004). Similarly, a small, open-label pilot study found naltrexone was a potential treatment for pediatric TTM—8 of 14 children showed improvement (De Sousa, 2008). These studies are encouraging, although behavioral therapy is thought to be more efficacious (Bloch et al., 2007; McGuire et al., 2014). The field would benefit from studies of combined behavioral therapy and pharmacotherapy, studies about treating specific comorbid disorders, and studies that investigate the role of parents in treatment.

SPD

SPD (i.e., excoriation) is characterized by recurrent skin-picking that results in skin lesions, with repeated attempts to decrease or stop skin-picking and clinically significant distress or impairment in social, occupational, or other important areas of functioning (APA, 2013). As mentioned in the discussion of TTM, SPD is often classified together with TTM under the umbrella of BFRBs (Stein et al., 2016).

Widespread prevalence studies of SPD in the pediatric population have not been conducted, although the estimated prevalence in the general population is around 2% (Al Hawsawi & Pope, 2011). Studies of adults with pathological skin-picking have found that almost half report skin-picking before age 10 (Odlaug & Grant, 2007) and over 90% after age 30 (Ricketts et al., 2018). Women are more likely to be affected than men, although specific studies need to confirm this ratio in the pediatric population. (Wong et al., 2013).

Symptom Phenomenology

SPD presents as superficial skin lesions, sometimes associated with crusting, scarring, or hyperpigmentation. Often, skin-picking is associated with a sensation of relief, which explains its recurrence and progression to self-injury (Chiriac et al., 2015).

Assessment

Assessment tools have been developed specifically for SPD. Most notable is the Skin Picking Scale (SPS), which has been shown to be a valid and accurate method of self-evaluation in its original form and in subsequent updates and modifications (Keuthen et al., 2001; Schumer et al., 2016). In addition, a version of the Yale-Brown Obsessive-Compulsive Scale specifically modified for neurotic excoriation (NE-YBOCS) is commonly used for evaluation of SPD and for research (Blum et al., 2018).

Comorbidity

In adults, SPD is comorbid with OCD (26%) and other psychiatric disorders, including anxiety (64%), depression (53%), and TTM (13%; Grant & Chamberlain, 2020). In patients with BDD, excoriation may manifest as a compulsive ritual, although this has not been explicitly observed in the pediatric population (Grant et al., 2006). While systematic studies on youth with primary concerns of SPD have not been conducted, one survey found that 38% of youth with OCD or anxiety disorders endorsed some level of skin-picking, with 18% endorsing at least "moderate" skin-picking (Selles, La Buissonnière Ariza, et al., 2018).

Etiology

Like other diagnoses in the OCRD cluster, SPD has a multifactorial etiology, with both biological and psychosocial factors contributing. Much of the literature on the etiology of SPD relates to adults, and few pediatric-specific studies and reviews are available (see Chapter 5 for more detail on the adult-specific etiologies). Of note, as mentioned in the TTM section, adult studies have found that SPD shares a distinct highly heritable factor exclusively with TTM and not with other OCRDs (Monzani et al., 2014). In the pediatric population specifically, genetic susceptibility to increased emotional sensitivity can predispose patients to self-soothing behaviors like skin-picking, while psychosocial factors can reinforce these behaviors and perpetuate emotional impulsivity (Stargell et al., 2016).

Treatment

The mainstay of SPD treatment is HRT and pharmacotherapy, particularly SSRIs and lamotrigine (Schumer et al., 2016). This has been extrapolated from the adult literature (see Chapter 24), and few data specifically pertaining to the pediatric population have been published. One case study in a child with SPD and ASD was performed to assess HRT adaptation in the pediatric population, and although the results were promising, results need to be replicated with larger samples and with children without developmental disabilities (Cavalari et al., 2014). Treatment modalities in the pediatric population probably can mirror those implemented in the adult population (Woods & Houghton, 2016), although they would require an increased emphasis on parental involvement and reinforcement of competing responses.

Future Directions and Issues

The literature on pediatric OCD has made great strides in approaching the depth and breadth of the literature on adult OCD, revealing several factors that often distinguish children with OCD from adults with OCD, including insight, the role of parental accommodation, and a potential early-onset subtype characterized by a higher genetic component and comorbid tic disorder. Unfortunately, the pediatric OCRD literature is less mature, which is concerning because the OCRDs often manifest in childhood and adolescence. The literature gap leaves the pediatric patient population and their providers in the dark about the optimal developmentally sensitive assessment, management, and treatment approach for these functionally impairing disorders. Moreover, the existing literature often extrapolates its findings from the adult literature, which does not always take into account factors unique to youth, such as insight level, parental involvement, and comorbid disorders that are more often identified in childhood, such as neurodevelopmental disorders. As a result, providers may not recognize OCRDs (presuming they are developmentally appropriate), and they may not know how to integrate families into patient care, adapt the treatment modalities in a developmentally and cognitively appropriate way, address the numerous potential comorbidities, and confidently prescribe pharmacotherapy with special consideration of titration, pharmacodynamics, and side effects. In light of this, efforts to study OCRDs in pediatric populations is imperative to appropriately understand and support this vulnerable population.

References

Abramowitz, J. S. (2018). Presidential address: Are the obsessive-compulsive related disorders related to obsessive-compulsive disorder? A critical look at DSM-5's new category. *Behavior Therapy*, *49*(1), 1–11. https://www.sciencedirect.com/science/article/pii/S0005789417300655

Ahmari, S. E., & Dougherty, D. D. (2015). Dissecting OCD circuits: From animal models to targeted treatments. *Depression and Anxiety*, *32*(8), 550–562.

Al Hawsawi, K., & Pope, E. (2011). Pediatric psychocutaneous disorders: A review of primary psychiatric disorders with dermatologic manifestations. *American Journal of Clinical Dermatology*, *12*(4), 247–257.

Albert, U., Manchia, M., Tortorella, A., Volpe, U., Rosso, G., Carpiniello, B., & Maina, G. (2015). Admixture analysis of age at symptom onset and age at disorder onset in a large sample of patients with obsessive-compulsive disorder. *Journal of Affective Disorders*, *187*, 188–196.

Albertini, R. S., & Phillips, K. A. (1999). Thirty-three cases of body dysmorphic disorder in children and adolescents. *Journal of the American Academy of Child and Adolescent Psychiatry*, *38*(4), 453–459.

Alexander, J. R., Houghton, D. C., Twohig, M. P., Franklin, M. E., Saunders, S. M., Neal-Barnett, A. M., Compton, S. N., & Woods, D. W. (2016). Factor analysis of the Milwaukee Inventory for Subtypes of Trichotillomania–Adult Version. *Journal of Obsessive-Compulsive and Related Disorders*. https://epublications.marquette.edu/psych_fac/229

Alvarenga, P. G., Cesar, R. C., Leckman, J. F., Moriyama, T. S., Torres, A. R., Bloch, M. H., Coughlin, C. G., Hoexter, M. Q., Manfro, G. G., Polanczyk, G. V., Miguel, E. C., & do Rosario, M. C. (2015). Obsessive-compulsive symptom dimensions in a population-based, cross-sectional sample of school-aged children. *Journal of Psychiatric Research*, *62*, 108–114.

American Psychiatric Association (APA). (2013). *Diagnostic and statistical manual of mental disorders* (5th ed.). https://dsm.psychiatryonline.org/doi/pdf/10.1176/appi.books.9780890420249.dsm-iv-tr

Anwar, S., & Jafferany, M. (2019). Trichotillomania: A psychopathological perspective and the psychiatric comorbidity of hair pulling. *Acta Dermatovenerologica Alpina, Pannonica, et Adriatica*, *28*(1), 33–36.

Bienvenu, O. J., Wang, Y., Shugart, Y. Y., Welch, J. M., Grados, M. A., Fyer, A. J., Rauch, S. L., McCracken, J. T., Rasmussen, S. A., Murphy, D. L., Cullen, B., Valle, D., Hoehn-Saric, R., Greenberg, B. D., Pinto, A., Knowles, J. A., Piacentini, J., Pauls, D. L., Liang, K. Y., Willour, V. L., . . . Nestadt, G. (2009). Sapap3 and pathological grooming in humans: Results from the OCD collaborative genetics study. *American Journal of Medical Genetics. Part B, Neuropsychiatric Genetics*, *150B*(5), 710–720.

Bjornsson, A. S., Didie, E. R., Grant, J. E., Menard, W., Stalker, E., & Phillips, K. A. (2013). Age at onset and clinical correlates in body dysmorphic disorder. *Comprehensive Psychiatry*, *54*(7), 893–903.

Bloch, Landeros-Weisenberger, A., Dombrowski, P., Kelmendi, B., Wegner, R., Nudel, J., Pittenger, C., Leckman, J. F., & Coric, V. (2007). Systematic review: pharmacological and behavioral treatment for trichotillomania. *Biological Psychiatry*, *62*(8), 839–846.

Bloch, M. H., & Storch, E. A. (2015). Assessment and management of treatment-refractory obsessive-compulsive disorder in children. *Journal of the American Academy of Child and Adolescent Psychiatry*, *54*(4), 251–262.

Blum, A. W., Chamberlain, S. R., Harries, M. D., Odlaug, B. L., Redden, S. A., & Grant, J. E. (2018). Neuroanatomical correlates of impulsive action in excoriation (skin-picking) disorder. *The Journal of Neuropsychiatry and Clinical Neurosciences*, *30*(3), 236–241.

Brakoulias, V., Starcevic, V., Belloch, A., Brown, C., Ferrao, Y. A., Fontenelle, L. F., Lochner, C., Marazziti, D., Matsunaga, H., Miguel, E. C., Reddy, Y. C. J., do Rosario, M. C., Shavitt, R. G., Shyam Sundar, A., Stein, D. J., Torres, A. R., & Viswasam, K. (2017). Comorbidity, age of onset and suicidality in obsessive-compulsive disorder (OCD): An international collaboration. *Comprehensive Psychiatry*, *76*, 79–86.

Buhlmann, U., Etcoff, N. L., & Wilhelm, S. (2006). Emotion recognition bias for contempt and anger in body dysmorphic disorder. *Journal of Psychiatric Research*, *40*(2), 105–111.

Buhlmann, U., McNally, R. J., Etcoff, N. L., Tuschen-Caffier, B., & Wilhelm, S. (2004). Emotion recognition deficits in body dysmorphic disorder. *Journal of Psychiatric Research*, *38*(2), 201–206.

Buhlmann, U., McNally, R. J., Wilhelm, S., & Florin, I. (2002). Selective processing of emotional information in body dysmorphic disorder. *Journal of Anxiety Disorders*, *16*(3), 289–298.

Burton, C. L., Crosbie, J., Dupuis, A., Mathews, C. A., Soreni, N., Schachar, R., & Arnold, P. D. (2016). Clinical correlates of hoarding with and without comorbid obsessive-compulsive symptoms in a community pediatric sample. *Journal of the American Academy of Child and Adolescent Psychiatry*, *55*(2), 114–21.e2. https://tspace.library.utoronto.ca/handle/1807/77693

Burton, C. L., Park, L. S., Corfield, E. C., Forget-Dubois, N., Dupuis, A., Sinopoli, V. M., Shan, J., Goodale, T., Shaheen, S. M., Crosbie, J., Schachar, R. J., & Arnold, P. D. (2018). Heritability of obsessive-compulsive trait dimensions in youth from the general population. *Translational Psychiatry*, *8*(1), 191.

Caporino, N. E., Morgan, J., Beckstead, J., Phares, V., Murphy, T. K., & Storch, E. A. (2012). A structural equation analysis of family accommodation in pediatric obsessive-compulsive disorder. *Journal of Abnormal Child Psychology*, *40*(1), 133–143.

Cash, T. F., & Pruzinsky, T. (2004). *Body image: A handbook of theory, research, and clinical practice*. Guilford.

Cavalari, R. N. S., DuBard, M., & Luiselli, J. K. (2014). Simplified habit reversal and treatment fading for chronic skin picking in an adolescent with autism. *Clinical Case Studies*, *13*(2), 190–198.

Chen, D., Bienvenu, O. J., Krasnow, J., Wang, Y., Grados, M. A., Cullen, B., Goes, F. S., Maher, B., Greenberg, B. D., McLaughlin, N. C., Rasmussen, S. A., Fyer, A. J., Knowles, J. A., McCracken, J. T., Piacentini, J., Geller, D., Pauls, D. L., Stewart, S. E., Murphy, D. L., . . . Samuels, J. (2017). Parental bonding and hoarding in obsessive-compulsive disorder. *Comprehensive Psychiatry*, *73*, 43–52.

Cheng, B., Cai, W., Wang, X., Lei, D., Guo, Y., Yang, X., Wu, Q., Gong, J., Gong, Q., & Ning, G. (2016). Brain gray matter abnormalities in first-episode, treatment-naive children with obsessive-compulsive disorder. *Frontiers in Behavioral Neuroscience*, *10*, 141.

Chiriac, A., Brzezinski, P., Pinteala, T., Chiriac, A. E., & Foia, L. (2015). Common psychocutaneous disorders in children. *Neuropsychiatric Disease and Treatment*, *11*, 333–337.

Christenson, G., Mackenzie, T., & Mitchell, J. (1991). Characteristics of 60 adult chronic hair pullers. *The American Journal of Psychiatry*, *148*(3), 365–370.

Clerkin, E. M., & Teachman, B. A. (2008). Perceptual and cognitive biases in individuals with body dysmorphic disorder symptoms. *Cognition & Emotion*, *22*(7), 1327–1339.

Coskun, M., Zoroglu, S., & Ozturk, M. (2012). Phenomenology, psychiatric comorbidity and family history in referred preschool children with obsessive-compulsive disorder. *Child and Adolescent Psychiatry and Mental Health*, *6*(1), 36.

De Sousa, A. (2008). An open-label pilot study of naltrexone in childhood-onset trichotillomania. *Journal of Child and Adolescent Psychopharmacology*, *18*(1), 30–33.

Del Casale, A., Sorice, S., Padovano, A., Simmaco, M., Ferracuti, S., Lamis, D. A., Rapinesi, C., Sani, G., Girardi, P., Kotzalidis, G. D., & Pompili, M. (2019). Psychopharmacological treatment of obsessive-compulsive disorder (OCD). *Current Neuropharmacology*, *17*(8), 710–736.

Dell'Osso, B., Benatti, B., Hollander, E., Fineberg, N., Stein, D. J., Lochner, C., . . . Menchon, J. M. (2016). Childhood, adolescent and adult age at onset and related clinical correlates in obsessive-compulsive disorder: A report from the International College of Obsessive-Compulsive Spectrum Disorders (ICOCS). *International Journal of Psychiatry in Clinical Practice*, *20*(4), 210–217.

Dista Labs. (2009). *Prozac*. https://www.accessdata.fda.gov/drugsatfda_docs/label/2009/018936s075s077 lbl.pdf

Dozier, M. E., Porter, B., & Ayers, C. R. (2016). Age of onset and progression of hoarding symptoms in older adults with hoarding disorder. *Aging & Mental Health*, *20*(7), 736–742.

Duke, D. C., Keeley, M. L., Geffken, G. R., & Storch, E. A. (2010). Trichotillomania: A current review. *Clinical Psychology Review*, *30*(2), 181–193.

Dykens, E. M., Leckman, J. F., & Cassidy, S. B. (1996). Obsessions and compulsions in Prader-Willi syndrome. *Journal of Child Psychology and Psychiatry, and Allied Disciplines*, *37*(8), 995–1002.

Dykens, E. M., & Shah, B. (2003). Psychiatric disorders in Prader-Willi syndrome: Epidemiology and management. *CNS Drugs*, *17*(3), 167–178.

Dyl, J., Kittler, J., Phillips, K. A., & Hunt, J. I. (2006). Body dysmorphic disorder and other clinically significant body image concerns in adolescent psychiatric inpatients: Prevalence and clinical characteristics. *Child Psychiatry & Human Development*, *36*(4), 369–382.

Farhat, L. C., Olfson, E., Levine, J. L. S., Li, F., Franklin, M. E., Lee, H.-J., Lewin, A. B., McGuire, J. F., Rahman, O., Storch, E. A., Tolin, D. F., Zickgraf, H. F., & Bloch, M. H. (2020). Measuring treatment response in pediatric trichotillomania: A meta-analysis of clinical trials. *Journal of Child and Adolescent Psychopharmacology*, *30*(5), 306–315.

Feusner, J. D., Yaryura-Tobias, J., & Saxena, S. (2008). The pathophysiology of body dysmorphic disorder. *Body Image*, *5*(1), 3–12.

Fitzgerald, K. D., Welsh, R. C., Stern, E. R., Angstadt, M., Hanna, G. L., Abelson, J. L., & Taylor, S. F. (2011). Developmental alterations of frontal-striatal-thalamic connectivity in obsessive-compulsive disorder. *Journal of the American Academy of Child and Adolescent Psychiatry*, *50*(9), 938–948.

Flessner, C. A., Woods, D. W., Franklin, M. E., Keuthen, N. J., Piacentini, J., Cashin, S. E., & Moore, P. S. (2007). The Milwaukee Inventory for Styles of Trichotillomania-Child Version (MIST-C): Initial development and psychometric properties. *Behavior Modification*, *31*(6), 896–918.

Flessner, C. A., Woods, D. W., Franklin, M. E., Keuthen, N. J., Piacentini, J., & Trichotillomania Learning Center-Scientific Advisory Board (TLC-SAB). (2008). Styles of pulling in youths with trichotillomania: Exploring differences in symptom severity, phenomenology, and comorbid psychiatric symptoms. *Behaviour Research and Therapy*, *46*(9), 1055–1061.

Franklin, M. E., Edson, A. L., Ledley, D. A., & Cahill, S. P. (2011). Behavior therapy for pediatric trichotillomania: A randomized controlled trial. *Journal of the American Academy of Child and Adolescent Psychiatry*, *50*(8), 763–771.

Franklin, M. E., Flessner, C. A., Woods, D. W., Keuthen, N. J., Piacentini, J. C., Moore, P., Cohen, S. B., Wilson, M. A., & Trichotillomania Learning Center-Scientific Advisory Board. (2008). The Child and Adolescent Trichotillomania Impact Project: Descriptive psychopathology, comorbidity, functional impairment, and treatment utilization. *Journal of Developmental and Behavioral Pediatrics*, *29*(6), 493–500.

Gallant, J., Storch, E. A., Merlo, L. J., Ricketts, E. D., Geffken, G. R., Goodman, W. K., & Murphy, T. K. (2008). Convergent and discriminant validity of the Children's Yale-Brown Obsessive-Compulsive Scale–Symptom Checklist. *Journal of Anxiety Disorders*, *22*(8), 1369–1376.

Gassó, P., Ortiz, A. E., Mas, S., Morer, A., Calvo, A., Bargalló, N., Lafuente, A., & Lázaro, L. (2015). Association between genetic variants related to glutamatergic, dopaminergic and neurodevelopment pathways and white matter microstructure in child and adolescent patients with obsessive-compulsive disorder. *Journal of Affective Disorders*, *186*, 284–292.

Geller, D. A., Biederman, J., Stewart, S. E., Mullin, B., Farrell, C., Wagner, K. D., Emslie, G., & Carpenter, D. (2003). Impact of comorbidity on treatment response to paroxetine in pediatric obsessive-compulsive disorder: is the use of exclusion criteria empirically supported in randomized clinical trials? *Journal of Child and Adolescent Psychopharmacology*, *13*(Suppl. 1), S19–S29.

Geller, D. A., & March, J. (2012). Practice parameter for the assessment and treatment of children and adolescents with obsessive-compulsive disorder. *Journal of the American Academy of Child and Adolescent Psychiatry*, *51*(1), 98–113.

Gerstenblith, T. A., Jaramillo-Huff, A., Ruutiainen, T., Nestadt, P. S., Samuels, J. F., Grados, M. A., Cullen, B. A., Riddle, M. A., Liang, K. Y., Greenberg, B. D., Rasmussen, S. A., Rauch, S. L., McCracken, J. T., Piacentini, J., Knowles, J. A., Nestadt, G., & Joseph Bienvenu, O. (2019). Trichotillomania comorbidity in a sample enriched for familial obsessive-compulsive disorder. *Comprehensive Psychiatry*, *94*, 152123.

Grant, J. E. (2019). Trichotillomania (hair pulling disorder). *Indian Journal of Psychiatry*, *61*(7), 136.

Grant, J. E., & Chamberlain, S. R. (2016). Trichotillomania. *American Journal of Psychiatry*, *173*(9), 868–874.

Grant, J. E., & Chamberlain, S. R. (2020). Prevalence of skin picking (excoriation) disorder. *Journal of Psychiatric Research*, *130*, 57–60.

Grant, J. E., Dougherty, D. D., & Chamberlain, S. R. (2020). Prevalence, gender correlates, and co-morbidity of trichotillomania. *Psychiatry Research*, *288*, 112948.

Grant, J. E., Kim, S. W., & Crow, S. J. (2001). Prevalence and clinical features of body dysmorphic disorder in adolescent and adult psychiatric inpatients. *The Journal of Clinical Psychiatry*, *62*(7), 517–522.

Grant, J. E., Menard, W., Pagano, M. E., Fay, C., & Phillips, K. A. (2005). Substance use disorders in individuals with body dysmorphic disorder. *The Journal of Clinical Psychiatry*, *66*(3), 309–316.

Grant, J. E., Menard, W., & Phillips, K. A. (2006). Pathological skin picking in individuals with body dysmorphic disorder. *General Hospital Psychiatry*, *28*(6), 487–493.

Grant, J. E., Redden, S. A., Leppink, E. W., Chamberlain, S. R., Curley, E. E., Tung, E. S., & Keuthen, N. J. (2016). Sex differences in trichotillomania. *Annals of Clinical Psychiatry*, *28*(2), 118–124.

Greenberg, J. L., Mothi, S. S., & Wilhelm, S. (2016). Cognitive-behavioral therapy for adolescent body dysmorphic disorder: A pilot study. *Behavior Therapy*, *47*(2), 213–224.

Greer, J. M., & Capecchi, M. R. (2002). *Hoxb8* is required for normal grooming behavior in mice. *Neuron*, *33*(1), 23–34.

Guzick, A. G., Schneider, S. C., & Storch, E. A. (2020). Future research directions in children and hoarding. *Children Australia*, *45*(3), 175–181.

Hacker, L. E., Park, J. M., Timpano, K. R., Cavitt, M. A., Alvaro, J. L., Lewin, A. B., Murphy, T. K., & Storch, E. A. (2016). Hoarding in children with ADHD. *Journal of Attention Disorders*, *20*(7), 617–626.

Hadley, S. J., Greenberg, J., & Hollander, E. (2002). Diagnosis and treatment of body dysmorphic disorder in adolescents. *Current Psychiatry Reports*, *4*(2), 108–113.

Harrison, J. P., & Franklin, M. E. (2012). Pediatric trichotillomania. *Current Psychiatry Reports*, *14*(3), 188–196.

Hezel, D. M., & Simpson, H. B. (2019). Exposure and response prevention for obsessive-compulsive disorder: A review and new directions. *Indian Journal of Psychiatry*, *61*(Suppl. 1), S85–S92.

Hirsch, M. (2020). Tricyclic and tetracyclic drugs: Pharmacology, administration, and side effects. In P. P. Roy-Byrne & D. Solomon (Eds.), *UpToDate*. UpToDate.

Hirschtritt, M. E., Bloch, M. H., & Mathews, C. A. (2017). Obsessive-compulsive disorder: advances in diagnosis and treatment. *JAMA*, *317*(13), 1358–1367.

Højgaard, D. R. M. A., Skarphedinsson, G., Ivarsson, T., Weidle, B., Nissen, J. B., Hybel, K. A., Torp, N. C., Melin, K., & Thomsen, P. H. (2019). Hoarding in children and adolescents with obsessive-compulsive disorder: Prevalence, clinical correlates, and cognitive behavioral therapy outcome. *European Child & Adolescent Psychiatry*, *28*(8), 1097–1106.

Hollander, E., Allen, A., Kwon, J., Aronowitz, B., Schmeidler, J., Wong, C., & Simeon, D. (1999). Clomipramine vs desipramine crossover trial in body dysmorphic disorder: Selective efficacy of a serotonin reuptake inhibitor in imagined ugliness. *Archives of General Psychiatry*, *56*(11), 1033–1039.

Hong, K., Nezgovorova, V., & Hollander, E. (2018). New perspectives in the treatment of body dysmorphic disorder. *F1000Research*, *7*, 361.

Hong, K., Nezgovorova, V., Uzunova, G., Schlussel, D., & Hollander, E. (2019). Pharmacological treatment of body dysmorphic disorder. *Current Neuropharmacology*, *17*(8), 697–702.

Ivanov, V. Z., Mataix-Cols, D., Serlachius, E., Lichtenstein, P., Anckarsäter, H., Chang, Z., Gumpert, C. H., Lundström, S., Långström, N., & Rück, C. (2013). Prevalence, comorbidity and heritability of hoarding symptoms in adolescence: A population based twin study in 15-year olds. *PLOS ONE*, *8*(7), e69140.

Ivarsson, T., Skarphedinsson, G., Kornør, H., Axelsdottir, B., Biedilæ, S., Heyman, I., Asbahr, F., Thomsen, P. H., Fineberg, N., March, J., & Accreditation Task Force of The Canadian Institute for Obsessive Compulsive Disorders. (2015). The place of and evidence for serotonin reuptake inhibitors (SRIs) for obsessive compulsive disorder (OCD) in children and adolescents: Views based on a systematic review and meta-analysis. *Psychiatry Research*, *227*(1), 93–103.

Jafferany, M., Osuagwu, F. C., Khalid, Z., Oberbarnscheidt, T., & Roy, N. (2019). Prevalence and clinical characteristics of body dysmorphic disorder in adolescent inpatient psychiatric patients—A pilot study. *Nordic Journal of Psychiatry*, *73*(4–5), 244–247.

Johnson, J., & El-Alfy, A. T. (2016). Review of available studies of the neurobiology and pharmacotherapeutic management of trichotillomania. *Journal of Advertising Research*, *7*(2), 169–184.

Joshi, G., Wozniak, J., Petty, C., Vivas, F., Yorks, D., Biederman, J., & Geller, D. (2010). Clinical characteristics of comorbid obsessive-compulsive disorder and bipolar disorder in children and adolescents. *Bipolar Disorders*, *12*(2), 185–195.

Kehoe, E., & Egan, J. (2019). Interpersonal attachment insecurity and emotional attachment to possessions partly mediate the relationship between childhood trauma and hoarding symptoms in a non-clinical sample. *Journal of Obsessive-Compulsive and Related Disorders*, *21*, 37–45.

Kessler, R. C., Berglund, P., Demler, O., Jin, R., Merikangas, K. R., & Walters, E. E. (2005). Lifetime prevalence and age-of-onset distributions of DSM-IV disorders in the National Comorbidity Survey Replication. *Archives of General Psychiatry*, *62*(6), 593–602.

Keuthen, N. J., Altenburger, E. M., & Pauls, D. (2014). A family study of trichotillomania and chronic hair pulling. *American Journal of Medical Genetics. Part B, Neuropsychiatric Genetics*, *165B*(2), 167–174.

Keuthen, N. J., Rothbaum, B. O., Fama, J., Altenburger, E., Falkenstein, M. J., Sprich, S. E., Kearns, M., Meunier, S., Jenike, M. A., & Welch, S. S. (2012). DBT-enhanced cognitive-behavioral treatment for trichotillomania: A randomized controlled trial. *Journal of Behavioral Addictions*, *1*(3), 106–114.

Keuthen, N. J., Wilhelm, S., Deckersbach, T., Engelhard, I. M., Forker, A. E., Baer, L., & Jenike, M. A. (2001). The Skin Picking Scale: Scale construction and psychometric analyses. *Journal of Psychosomatic Research, 50*(6), 337–341.

Krebs, G., Bolhuis, K., Heyman, I., Mataix-Cols, D., Turner, C., & Stringaris, A. (2013). Temper outbursts in paediatric obsessive-compulsive disorder and their association with depressed mood and treatment outcome. *Journal of Child Psychology and Psychiatry, and Allied Disciplines, 54*(3), 313–322.

Krebs, G., Fernández de la Cruz, L., & Mataix-Cols, D. (2017). Recent advances in understanding and managing body dysmorphic disorder. *Evidence-Based Mental Health, 20*(3), 71–75.

Krebs, G., Fernández de la Cruz, L., Monzani, B., Bowyer, L., Anson, M., Cadman, J., Heyman, I., Turner, C., Veale, D., & Mataix-Cols, D. (2017). Long-term outcomes of cognitive-behavioral therapy for adolescent body dysmorphic disorder. *Behavior Therapy, 48*(4), 462–473.

Krebs, G., Fernández de la Cruz, L., Rijsdijk, F. V., Rautio, D., Enander, J., Rück, C., Lichtenstein, P., Lundström, S., Larsson, H., Eley, T. C., & Mataix-Cols, D. (2020). The association between body dysmorphic symptoms and suicidality among adolescents and young adults: A genetically informative study. *Psychological Medicine, 52*(7), 1268–1276.

La Buissonnière-Ariza, V., Wood, J. J., Kendall, P. C., McBride, N. M., Cepeda, S. L., Small, B. J., Lewin, A. B., Kerns, C., & Storch, E. A. (2018). Presentation and correlates of hoarding behaviors in children with autism spectrum disorders and comorbid anxiety or obsessive-compulsive symptoms. *Journal of Autism and Developmental Disorders, 48*(12), 4167–4178.

Labuschagne, I., Rossell, S. L., Dunai, J., Castle, D. J., & Kyrios, M. (2013). A comparison of executive function in body dysmorphic disorder (BDD) and obsessive-compulsive disorder (OCD). *Journal of Obsessive-Compulsive and Related Disorders, 2*(3), 257–262.

Lack, C. W. (2012). Obsessive-compulsive disorder: Evidence-based treatments and future directions for research. *World Journal of Psychiatry, 2*(6), 86–90.

Langley, A. K., Lewin, A. B., Bergman, R. L., Lee, J. C., & Piacentini, J. (2010). Correlates of comorbid anxiety and externalizing disorders in childhood obsessive compulsive disorder. *European Child & Adolescent Psychiatry, 19*(8), 637–645.

Lee, E. B., Haeger, J. A., Levin, M. E., Ong, C. W., & Twohig, M. P. (2018). Telepsychotherapy for trichotillomania: A randomized controlled trial of ACT enhanced behavior therapy. *Journal of Obsessive-Compulsive and Related Disorders, 18*, 106–115. doi:10.1016/j.jocrd.2018.04.003

Lewin, A. B., Piacentini, J., Flessner, C. A., Woods, D. W., Franklin, M. E., Keuthen, N. J., Moore, P., Khanna, M., March, J. S., Stein, D. J., & TLC-SAB. (2009). Depression, anxiety, and functional impairment in children with trichotillomania. *Depression and Anxiety, 26*(6), 521–527.

Li, W., Arienzo, D., & Feusner, J. D. (2013). Body dysmorphic disorder: Neurobiological features and an updated model. *Zeitschrift Fur Klinische Psychologie Und Psychotherapie, 42*(3), 184–191.

Mallinckrodt LLC. (2012). *Anafranil.* https://www.accessdata.fda.gov/drugsatfda_docs/label/2012/019906 s037lbl.pdf

Mancuso, E., Faro, A., Joshi, G., & Geller, D. A. (2010). Treatment of pediatric obsessive-compulsive disorder: A review. *Journal of Child and Adolescent Psychopharmacology, 20*(4), 299–308.

Marques, L., LeBlanc, N. J., Weingarden, H. M., Timpano, K. R., Jenike, M., & Wilhelm, S. (2010). Barriers to treatment and service utilization in an Internet sample of individuals with obsessive-compulsive symptoms. *Depression and Anxiety, 27*(5), 470–475.

Mataix-Cols, D., Boman, M., Monzani, B., Rück, C., Serlachius, E., Långström, N., & Lichtenstein, P. (2013). Population-based, multigenerational family clustering study of obsessive-compulsive disorder. *JAMA Psychiatry, 70*(7), 709–717.

Mataix-Cols, D., Fernández de la Cruz, L., Isomura, K., Anson, M., Turner, C., Monzani, B., Monzani, B., Cadman, J., Bowyer, L., Heyman, I., Veale, D., & Krebs, G. (2015). A pilot randomized controlled trial of cognitive-behavioral therapy for adolescents with body dysmorphic disorder. *Journal of the American Academy of Child and Adolescent Psychiatry, 54*(11), 895–904.

Mataix-Cols, D., Frost, R. O., Pertusa, A., Clark, L. A., Saxena, S., Leckman, J. F., Stein, D. J., Matsunaga, H., & Wilhelm, S. (2010). Hoarding disorder: A new diagnosis for DSM-V? *Depression and Anxiety, 27*(6), 556–572.

Mataix-Cols, D., Nakatani, E., Micali, N., & Heyman, I. (2008). Structure of obsessive-compulsive symptoms in pediatric OCD. *Journal of the American Academy of Child and Adolescent Psychiatry, 47*(7), 773–778.

McGuire, J. F., Piacentini, J., Lewin, A. B., Brennan, E. A., Murphy, T. K., & Storch, E. A. (2015). A meta-analysis of cognitive behavior therapy and medication for child obsessive-compulsive disorder: Moderators of treatment efficacy, response, and remission. *Depression and Anxiety, 32*(8), 580–593.

McGuire, J. F., Ung, D., Selles, R. R., Rahman, O., Lewin, A. B., Murphy, T. K., & Storch, E. A. (2014). Treating trichotillomania: A meta-analysis of treatment effects and moderators for behavior therapy and serotonin reuptake inhibitors. *Journal of Psychiatric Research, 58*, 76–83.

Meier, S. M., Petersen, L., Schendel, D. E., Mattheisen, M., Mortensen, P. B., & Mors, O. (2015). Obsessive-compulsive disorder and autism spectrum disorders: Longitudinal and offspring risk. *PLOS ONE, 10*(11), e0141703.

Monzani, B., Rijsdijk, F., Harris, J., & Mataix-Cols, D. (2014). The structure of genetic and environmental risk factors for dimensional representations of DSM-5 obsessive-compulsive spectrum disorders. *JAMA Psychiatry, 71*(2), 182–189.

Morris, S. H., Jaffee, S. R., Goodwin, G. P., & Franklin, M. E. (2016). Hoarding in children and adolescents: A review. *Child Psychiatry & Human Development, 47*(5), 740–750.

Morris, S. H., Zickgraf, H. F., Dingfelder, H. E., & Franklin, M. E. (2013). Habit reversal training in trichotillomania: Guide for the clinician. *Expert Review of Neurotherapeutics, 13*(9), 1069–1077.

Mufaddel, A., Osman, O. T., Almugaddam, F., & Jafferany, M. (2013). A review of body dysmorphic disorder and its presentation in different clinical settings. *The Primary Care Companion to CNS Disorders, 15*(4). doi:10.4088/PCC.12r01464

Nakatani, E., Krebs, G., Micali, N., Turner, C., Heyman, I., & Mataix-Cols, D. (2011). Children with very early onset obsessive-compulsive disorder: Clinical features and treatment outcome. *Journal of Child Psychology and Psychiatry, and Allied Disciplines, 52*(12), 1261–1268.

Nelson, S. O., Rogers, K., Rusch, N., McDonough, L., Malloy, E. J., Falkenstein, M. J., Banis, M., & Haaga, D. A. F. (2014). Validating indicators of treatment response: Application to trichotillomania. *Psychological Assessment, 26*(3), 857–864.

Neziroglu, F., & Cash, T. F. (2008). Body dysmorphic disorder: Causes, characteristics, and clinical treatments. *Body Image, 5*(1), 1–2.

Neziroglu, F., Roberts, M., & Yaryura-Tobias, J. A. (2004). A behavioral model for body dysmorphic disorder. *Psychiatric Annals, 34*(12), 915–920.

Nicewicz, H. R., & Boutrouille, J. F. (2020). Body dysmorphic disorder (BDD, dysmorphobia, dysmorphic syndrome). *StatPearls*.

Odlaug, B. L., & Grant, J. E. (2007). Childhood-onset pathologic skin picking: Clinical characteristics and psychiatric comorbidity. *Comprehensive Psychiatry, 48*(4), 388–393.

Odlaug, B. L., Kim, S. W., & Grant, J. E. (2010). Quality of life and clinical severity in pathological skin picking and trichotillomania. *Journal of Anxiety Disorders, 24*(8), 823–829.

O'Neill, J., Piacentini, J., Chang, S., Ly, R., Lai, T. M., Armstrong, C. C., Bergman, L., Rozenman, M., Peris, T., Vreeland, A., Mudgway, R., Levitt, J. G., Salamon, N., Posse, S., Hellemann, G. S., Alger, J. R., McCracken, J. T., & Nurmi, E. L. (2017). Glutamate in pediatric obsessive-compulsive disorder and response to cognitive-behavioral therapy: Randomized clinical trial. *Neuropsychopharmacology, 42*(12), 2414–2422.

Öst, L.-G., Riise, E. N., Wergeland, G. J., Hansen, B., & Kvale, G. (2016). Cognitive behavioral and pharmacological treatments of OCD in children: A systematic review and meta-analysis. *Journal of Anxiety Disorders, 43*, 58–69.

Panza, K. E., Pittenger, C., & Bloch, M. H. (2013). Age and gender correlates of pulling in pediatric trichotillomania. *Journal of the American Academy of Child and Adolescent Psychiatry, 52*(3), 241–249.

Parakh, P., & Srivastava, M. (2010). The many faces of trichotillomania. *International Journal of Trichology, 2*(1), 50–52.

Park, J. M., McGuire, J. F., & Storch, E. A. (2014). Compulsive hoarding in children. In R. Frost & Gail (Eds.), *The Oxford handbook of hoarding and acquiring* (pp. 330–340). Oxford University Press.

Pathak, S., Danielyan, A., & Kowatch, R. A. (2004). Successful treatment of trichotillomania with olanzapine augmentation in an adolescent. *Journal of Child and Adolescent Psychopharmacology, 14*(1), 153–154.

Peris, T. S., Piacentini, J., Vreeland, A., Salgari, G., Levitt, J. G., Alger, J. R., Posse, S., McCracken, J. T., & O'Neill, J. (2020). Neurochemical correlates of behavioral treatment of pediatric trichotillomania. *Journal of Affective Disorders, 273*, 552–561.

Peris, T. S., Rozenman, M., Bergman, R. L., Chang, S., O'Neill, J., & Piacentini, J. (2017). Developmental and clinical predictors of comorbidity for youth with obsessive compulsive disorder. *Journal of Psychiatric Research, 93*, 72–78.

Pfizer. (2016). *Zoloft.* https://www.accessdata.fda.gov/drugsatfda_docs/label/2016/019839S74S86S87_20990S35S44S45lbl.pdf

Phillips, K. A. (2000). Quality of life for patients with body dysmorphic disorder. *The Journal of Nervous and Mental Disease, 188*(3), 170–175.

Phillips, K. A. (2007). Suicidality in body dysmorphic disorder. *Primary Psychiatry, 14*(12), 58–66.

Phillips, K. A., Albertini, R. S., & Rasmussen, S. A. (2002). A randomized placebo-controlled trial of fluoxetine in body dysmorphic disorder. *Archives of General Psychiatry, 59*(4), 381–388.

Phillips, K. A., Didie, E. R., Menard, W., Pagano, M. E., Fay, C., & Weisberg, R. B. (2006). Clinical features of body dysmorphic disorder in adolescents and adults. *Psychiatry Research, 141*(3), 305–314.

Phillips, K. A., Dwight, M. M., & McElroy, S. L. (1998). Efficacy and safety of fluvoxamine in body dysmorphic disorder. *The Journal of Clinical Psychiatry, 59*(4), 165–171.

Phillips, K. A., & Hollander, E. (2008). Treating body dysmorphic disorder with medication: Evidence, misconceptions, and a suggested approach. *Body Image, 5*(1), 13–27.

Phillips, K. A., Menard, W., Fay, C., & Weisberg, R. (2005). Demographic characteristics, phenomenology, comorbidity, and family history in 200 individuals with body dysmorphic disorder. *Psychosomatics, 46*(4), 317–325.

Phillips, K. A., & Najjar, F. (2003). An open-label study of citalopram in body dysmorphic disorder. *The Journal of Clinical Psychiatry, 64*(6), 715–720. https://europepmc.org/article/med/12823088

Piacentini, J., Bergman, R. L., Keller, M., & McCracken, J. (2003). Functional impairment in children and adolescents with obsessive-compulsive disorder. *Journal of Child and Adolescent Psychopharmacology, 13*(Suppl. 1), S61–S69.

Piacentino, D., Pasquini, M., Cappelletti, S., Chetoni, C., Sani, G., & Kotzalidis, G. D. (2019). Pharmacotherapy for hoarding disorder: How did the picture change since its excision from OCD? *Current Neuropharmacology, 17*(8), 808–815.

Plimpton, E. H., Frost, R. O., Abbey, B. C., & Dorer, W. (2009). Compulsive hoarding in children: Six case studies. *International Journal of Cognitive Therapy, 2*(1), 88–104.

Prazeres, A. M., Nascimento, A. L., & Fontenelle, L. F. (2013). Cognitive-behavioral therapy for body dysmorphic disorder: A review of its efficacy. *Neuropsychiatric Disease and Treatment, 9*, 307–316.

Rabiei, M., Mulkens, S., Kalantari, M., Molavi, H., & Bahrami, F. (2012). Metacognitive therapy for body dysmorphic disorder patients in Iran: Acceptability and proof of concept. *Journal of Behavior Therapy and Experimental Psychiatry, 43*(2), 724–729.

Rahman, O., McGuire, J., Storch, E. A., & Lewin, A. B. (2017). Preliminary randomized controlled trial of habit reversal training for treatment of hair pulling in youth. *Journal of Child and Adolescent Psychopharmacology, 27*(2), 132–139.

Rautio, D., Jassi, A., Krebs, G., Andrén, P., Monzani, B., Gumpert, M., Lewis, A., Peile, L., Sevilla-Cermeño, L., Jansson-Fröjmark, M., Lundgren, T., Hillborg, M., Silverberg-Morse, M., Clark, B., Fernández de la Cruz, L., & Mataix-Cols, D. (2020). Clinical characteristics of 172 children and adolescents with body dysmorphic disorder. *European Child & Adolescent Psychiatry, 31*(1), 133–144. doi:10.1007/s00787-020-01677-3

Rehm, I., Moulding, R., & Nedeljkovic, M. (2015). Psychological treatments for trichotillomania: Update and future directions. *Australasian Psychiatry, 23*(4), 365–368.

Ricketts, E. J., Snorrason, Í., Kircanski, K., Alexander, J. R., Thamrin, H., Flessner, C. A., Franklin, M. E., Piacentini, J., & Woods, D. W. (2018). A latent profile analysis of age of onset in pathological skin picking. *Comprehensive Psychiatry, 87*, 46–52.

Riesel, A., Endrass, T., Auerbach, L. A., & Kathmann, N. (2015). Overactive performance monitoring as an endophenotype for obsessive-compulsive disorder: Evidence from a treatment study. *The American Journal of Psychiatry, 172*(7), 665–673.

Rotge, J.-Y., Langbour, N., Guehl, D., Bioulac, B., Jaafari, N., Allard, M., Aouizerate, B., & Burbaud, P. (2010). Gray matter alterations in obsessive-compulsive disorder: An anatomic likelihood estimation meta-analysis. *Neuropsychopharmacology, 35*(3), 686–691.

Ruffolo, J. S., Phillips, K. A., Menard, W., Fay, C., & Weisberg, R. B. (2006). Comorbidity of body dysmorphic disorder and eating disorders: Severity of psychopathology and body image disturbance. *The International Journal of Eating Disorders, 39*(1), 11–19.

Ruscio, A. M., Stein, D. J., Chiu, W. T., & Kessler, R. C. (2010). The epidemiology of obsessive-compulsive disorder in the National Comorbidity Survey Replication. *Molecular Psychiatry, 15*(1), 53–63.

Sarvet, B. (2013). Childhood obsessive-compulsive disorder. *Pediatrics in Review, 34*(1), 19–27.

Scahill, L., Riddle, M. A., McSwiggin-Hardin, M., Ort, S. I., King, R. A., Goodman, W. K., Cicchetti, D., & Leckman, J. F. (1997). Children's Yale-Brown Obsessive-Compulsive Scale: Reliability and validity. *Journal of the American Academy of Child and Adolescent Psychiatry, 36*(6), 844–852.

Schneider, S. C., Mond, J., Turner, C. M., & Hudson, J. L. (2019). Sex differences in the presentation of body dysmorphic disorder in a community sample of adolescents. *Journal of Clinical Child and Adolescent Psychology, 48*(3), 516–528.

Schneider, S. C., & Storch, E. A. (2017a). Improving the detection of body dysmorphic disorder in clinical practice. *Journal of Cognitive Psychotherapy, 31*(4), 230–241.

Schneider, S. C., & Storch, E. A. (2017b). Update on the treatment of pediatric obsessive-compulsive disorder. *Psychiatric Annals, 47*(11), 537–541.

Schneider, S. C., Turner, C. M., Mond, J., & Hudson, J. L. (2017). Prevalence and correlates of body dysmorphic disorder in a community sample of adolescents. *The Australian and New Zealand Journal of Psychiatry, 51*(6), 595–603.

Schumer, M. C., Bartley, C. A., & Bloch, M. H. (2016). Systematic review of pharmacological and behavioral treatments for skin picking disorder. *Journal of Clinical Psychopharmacology, 36*(2), 147–152.

Selles, R. R., Højgaard, D. R. M. A., Ivarsson, T., Thomsen, P. H., McBride, N., Storch, E. A., Geller, D., Wilhelm, S., Farrell, L. J., Waters, A. M., Mathieu, S., Lebowitz, E., Elgie, M., Soreni, N., & Stewart, S. E. (2018). Symptom insight in pediatric obsessive-compulsive disorder: Outcomes of an international aggregated cross-sectional sample. *Journal of the American Academy of Child and Adolescent Psychiatry, 57*(8), 615–619.

Selles, R. R., La Buissonnière Ariza, V., McBride, N. M., Dammann, J., Whiteside, S., & Storch, E. A. (2018). Initial psychometrics, outcomes, and correlates of the Repetitive Body Focused Behavior Scale: Examination in a sample of youth with anxiety and/or obsessive-compulsive disorder. *Comprehensive Psychiatry, 81*, 10–17.

Selles, R. R., Storch, E. A., & Lewin, A. B. (2014). Variations in symptom prevalence and clinical correlates in younger versus older youth with obsessive-compulsive disorder. *Child Psychiatry & Human Development, 45*(6), 666–674.

Shaw, P., Sharp, W., Sudre, G., Wharton, A., Greenstein, D., Raznahan, A., Evans, A., Chakravarty, M. M., Lerch, J. P., & Rapoport, J. (2015). Subcortical and cortical morphological anomalies as an endophenotype in obsessive-compulsive disorder. *Molecular Psychiatry, 20*(2), 224–231.

Sheppard, B., Chavira, D., Azzam, A., Grados, M. A., Umaña, P., Garrido, H., & Mathews, C. A. (2010). ADHD prevalence and association with hoarding behaviors in childhood-onset OCD. *Depression and Anxiety, 27*(7), 667–674.

Shmelkov, S. V., Hormigo, A., Jing, D., Proenca, C. C., Bath, K. G., Milde, T., Shmelkov, E., Kushner, J. S., Baljevic, M., Dincheva, I., Murphy, A. J., Valenzuela, D. M., Gale, N. W., Yancopoulos, G. D., Ninan, I., Lee, F. S., & Rafii, S. (2010). Slitrk5 deficiency impairs corticostriatal circuitry and leads to obsessive-compulsive-like behaviors in mice. *Nature Medicine, 16*(5), 598–602.

Simonoff, E., Pickles, A., Charman, T., Chandler, S., Loucas, T., & Baird, G. (2008). Psychiatric disorders in children with autism spectrum disorders: Prevalence, comorbidity, and associated factors in a population-derived sample. *Journal of the American Academy of Child and Adolescent Psychiatry, 47*(8), 921–929.

Singh, K., Singh, A., Vidyarthi, S. H., & Rangera, M. (2013). Trichobezoar in a toddler. *Indian Journal of Medical Specialities, 4*, 301–304.

Sinopoli, V. M., Burton, C. L., Kronenberg, S., & Arnold, P. D. (2017). A review of the role of serotonin system genes in obsessive-compulsive disorder. *Neuroscience and Biobehavioral Reviews, 80*, 372–381.

Slikboer, R., Nedeljkovic, M., Bowe, S. J., & Moulding, R. (2017). A systematic review and meta-analysis of behaviourally based psychological interventions and pharmacological interventions for trichotillomania: A meta-analysis. *The Clinical Psychologist, 21*(1), 20–32.

Snorrason, I., Berlin, G. S., & Lee, H.-J. (2015). Optimizing psychological interventions for trichotillomania (hair-pulling disorder): An update on current empirical status. *Psychology Research and Behavior Management, 8*, 105–113.

Sobanski, E., & Schmidt, M. H. (2000). "Everybody looks at my pubic bone"—A case report of an adolescent patient with body dysmorphic disorder. *Acta Psychiatrica Scandinavica, 101*(1), 80–82.

Soomro, G. M., Altman, D., Rajagopal, S., & Oakley-Browne, M. (2008). Selective serotonin re-uptake inhibitors (SSRIs) versus placebo for obsessive compulsive disorder (OCD). *Cochrane Database of Systematic Reviews, 1,* CD001765.

Soreni, N. (2020). Phenomenology of childhood hoarding. *Children Australia, 45*(3), 138–144.

Starcevic, V., Berle, D., Brakoulias, V., Sammut, P., Moses, K., Milicevic, D., & Hannan, A. (2011). Functions of compulsions in obsessive-compulsive disorder. *The Australian and New Zealand Journal of Psychiatry, 45*(6), 449–457.

Stargell, N. A., Kress, V. E., Paylo, M. J., & Zins, A. (2016). Excoriation disorder: Assessment, diagnosis and treatment. *The Professional Counselor, 6*(1), 50–60.

Stein, D. J., Kogan, C. S., Atmaca, M., Fineberg, N. A., Fontenelle, L. F., Grant, J. E., Matsunaga, H., Reddy, Y. C. J., Simpson, H. B., Thomsen, P. H., van den Heuvel, O. A., Veale, D., Woods, D. W., & Reed, G. M. (2016). The classification of obsessive-compulsive and related disorders in the ICD-11. *Journal of Affective Disorders, 190,* 663–674.

Steketee, G., Frost, R. O., Tolin, D. F., Rasmussen, J., & Brown, T. A. (2010). Waitlist-controlled trial of cognitive behavior therapy for hoarding disorder. *Depression and Anxiety, 27*(5), 476–484.

Steketee, G., Kelley, A. A., Wernick, J. A., Muroff, J., Frost, R. O., & Tolin, D. F. (2015). Familial patterns of hoarding symptoms. *Depression and Anxiety, 32*(10), 728–736.

Storch, E. A., Abramowitz, J., & Goodman, W. K. (2008). Where does obsessive-compulsive disorder belong in DSM-V? *Depression and Anxiety, 25*(4), 336–347.

Storch, E. A., Geffken, G. R., Merlo, L. J., Jacob, M. L., Murphy, T. K., Goodman, W. K., Larson, M. J., Fernandez, M., & Grabill, K. (2007). Family accommodation in pediatric obsessive-compulsive disorder. *Journal of Clinical Child and Adolescent Psychology, 36*(2), 207–216.

Storch, E. A., Merlo, L. J., Larson, M. J., Geffken, G. R., Lehmkuhl, H. D., Jacob, M. L., Murphy, T. K., & Goodman, W. K. (2008). Impact of comorbidity on cognitive-behavioral therapy response in pediatric obsessive-compulsive disorder. *Journal of the American Academy of Child and Adolescent Psychiatry, 47*(5), 583–592.

Storch, E. A., Nadeau, J. M., Johnco, C., Timpano, K., McBride, N., Jane Mutch, P., Lewin, A. B., & Murphy, T. K. (2016). Hoarding in youth with autism spectrum disorders and anxiety: Incidence, clinical correlates, and behavioral treatment response. *Journal of Autism and Developmental Disorders, 46*(5), 1602–1612.

Storch, E. A., Rahman, O., Park, J. M., Reid, J., Murphy, T. K., & Lewin, A. B. (2011). Compulsive hoarding in children. *Journal of Clinical Psychology, 67*(5), 507–516.

Tassin, C., Reynaert, C., Jacques, D., & Zdanowicz, N. (2014). Anxiety disorders in adolescence. *Psychiatria Danubina, 26*(Suppl. 1), 27–30.

Teva Generics. (2008). *Luvox.* https://www.accessdata.fda.gov/drugsatfda_docs/label/2008/022235lbl.pdf

Thakur, B., Prasai, A., Piya, U., & Pathak, R. (2007). Gastric trichobezoar presenting as gastric outlet obstruction—A case report. *Nepal Medical College Journal.* https://www.semanticscholar.org/paper/90e244c5589f496d185a31640d6365c182261cce

Tod, D., Edwards, C., & Cranswick, I. (2016). Muscle dysmorphia: Current insights. *Psychology Research and Behavior Management, 9,* 179–188.

Tolin, D. F., Franklin, M. E., Diefenbach, G. J., Anderson, E., & Meunier, S. A. (2007). Pediatric trichotillomania: Descriptive psychopathology and an open trial of cognitive behavioral therapy. *Cognitive Behaviour Therapy, 36*(3), 129–144.

Tolin, D. F., Frost, R. O., & Steketee, G. (2007). An open trial of cognitive-behavioral therapy for compulsive hoarding. *Behaviour Research and Therapy, 45*(7), 1461–1470.

Tolin, D. F., Meunier, S. A., Frost, R. O., & Steketee, G. (2010). Course of compulsive hoarding and its relationship to life events. *Depression and Anxiety, 27*(9), 829–838.

Torp, N. C., Dahl, K., Skarphedinsson, G., Compton, S., Thomsen, P. H., Weidle, B., Hybel, K., Valderhaug, R., Melin, K., Nissen, J. B., & Ivarsson, T. (2015). Predictors associated with improved cognitive-behavioral therapy outcome in pediatric obsessive-compulsive disorder. *Journal of the American Academy of Child and Adolescent Psychiatry, 54*(3), 200–207.e1.

Torp, N. C., Dahl, K., Skarphedinsson, G., Thomsen, P. H., Valderhaug, R., Weidle, B., Melin, K. H., Hybel, K., Nissen, J. B., Lenhard, F., Wentzel-Larsen, T., Franklin, M. E., & Ivarsson, T. (2015). Effectiveness of cognitive behavior treatment for pediatric obsessive-compulsive disorder: Acute outcomes from the Nordic Long-term OCD Treatment Study (NordLOTS). *Behaviour Research and Therapy, 64,* 15–23.

Tung, E. S., Flessner, C. A., Grant, J. E., & Keuthen, N. J. (2015). Predictors of life disability in trichotillomania. *Comprehensive Psychiatry, 56*, 239–244.

Turner, C. M. (2006). Cognitive-behavioural theory and therapy for obsessive-compulsive disorder in children and adolescents: Current status and future directions. *Clinical Psychology Review, 26*(7), 912–938.

Van Ameringen, M., Mancini, C., Patterson, B., Bennett, M., & Oakman, J. (2010). A randomized, double-blind, placebo-controlled trial of olanzapine in the treatment of trichotillomania. *The Journal of Clinical Psychiatry, 71*(10), 1336–1343.

Varigonda, A. L., Jakubovski, E., & Bloch, M. H. (2016). Systematic review and meta-analysis: Early treatment responses of selective serotonin reuptake inhibitors and clomipramine in pediatric obsessive-compulsive disorder. *Journal of the American Academy of Child and Adolescent Psychiatry, 55*(10), 851–859.

Varma, A., & Rastogi, R. (2015). Recognizing body dysmorphic disorder (dysmorphophobia). *Journal of Cutaneous and Aesthetic Surgery, 8*(3), 165–168.

Veale, D. (2004). Body dysmorphic disorder. *Postgraduate Medical Journal, 80*(940), 67–71.

Veale, D. (2009). Body dysmorphic disorder. In M. M. Antony & M. B. Stein (Eds.), *Oxford handbook of anxiety and related disorders* (pp. 541–550). Oxford University Press.

Veale, D., Boocock, A., Gournay, K., Dryden, W., Shah, F., Willson, R., & Walburn, J. (1996). Body dysmorphic disorder: A survey of fifty cases. *The British Journal of Psychiatry, 169*(2), 196–201.

Weber, A. M., Soreni, N., & Noseworthy, M. D. (2014). A preliminary study of functional connectivity of medication naïve children with obsessive-compulsive disorder. *Progress in Neuro-Psychopharmacology & Biological Psychiatry, 53*, 129–136.

Weingarden, H., Renshaw, K. D., Davidson, E., & Wilhelm, S. (2017). Relative relationships of general shame and body shame with body dysmorphic phenomenology and psychosocial outcomes. *Journal of Obsessive-Compulsive and Related Disorders, 14*, 1–6.

Weingarden, H., Shaw, A. M., Phillips, K. A., & Wilhelm, S. (2018). Shame and defectiveness beliefs in treatment seeking patients with body dysmorphic disorder. *The Journal of Nervous and Mental Disease, 206*(6), 417–422.

Welch, J. M., Lu, J., Rodriguiz, R. M., Trotta, N. C., Peca, J., Ding, J.-D., Feliciano, C., Chen, M., Adams, J. P., Luo, J., Dudek, S. M., Weinberg, R. J., Calakos, N., Wetsel, W. C., & Feng, G. (2007). Cortico-striatal synaptic defects and OCD-like behaviours in *Sapap3*-mutant mice. *Nature, 448*(7156), 894–900.

Wilhelm, S., Greenberg, J. L., Rosenfield, E., Kasarskis, I., & Blashill, A. J. (2016). The Body Dysmorphic Disorder Symptom Scale: Development and preliminary validation of a self-report scale of symptom specific dysfunction. *Body Image, 17*, 82–87.

Wong, J. W., Nguyen, T. V., & Koo, J. Y. (2013). Primary psychiatric conditions: Dermatitis artefacta, trichotillomania and neurotic excoriations. *Indian Journal of Dermatology, 58*(1), 44–48.

Woods, D. W., & Houghton, D. C. (2016). Evidence-based psychosocial treatments for pediatric body-focused repetitive behavior disorders. *Journal of Clinical Child and Adolescent Psychology, 45*(3), 227–240.

Woods, D. W., Wetterneck, C. T., & Flessner, C. A. (2006). A controlled evaluation of acceptance and commitment therapy plus habit reversal for trichotillomania. *Behaviour Research and Therapy, 44*(5), 639–656.

Yamamuro, K., Ota, T., Iida, J., Kishimoto, N., Nakanishi, Y., Matsuura, H., Uratani, M., Okazaki, K., & Kishimoto, T. (2016). A longitudinal event-related potential study of selective serotonin reuptake inhibitor therapy in treatment-naïve pediatric obsessive compulsive disorder patients. *Psychiatry Research, 245*, 217–223.

Zohar, A. H. (1999). The epidemiology of obsessive-compulsive disorder in children and adolescents. *Child and Adolescent Psychiatric Clinics of North America, 8*(3), 445–460.

Züchner, S., Wendland, J. R., Ashley-Koch, A. E., Collins, A. L., Tran-Viet, K. N., Quinn, K., Timpano, K. C., Cuccaro, M. L., Pericak-Vance, M. A., Steffens, D. C., Krishnan, K. R., Feng, G., & Murphy, D. L. (2009). Multiple rare *SAPAP3* missense variants in trichotillomania and OCD. *Molecular Psychiatry, 14*(1), 6–9.

CHAPTER 27

Obsessive-Compulsive Disorder and Cultural Issues

Yoon Hee Yang, Richard Moulding, Maja Nedeljkovic, Elham Foroughi, Guy Doron, and Michael Kyrios

Abstract

This chapter discusses the cross-cultural understanding of obsessive-compulsive disorder (OCD). Epidemiological studies suggest a reasonably consistent prevalence of OCD around the world. The role of culturally influenced factors (such as religiosity and beliefs) in the presentation of OCD is also considered, with religion being considered particularly important in the presentation of OCD, although not in its prevalence *per se*. The influence of cultural factors on help-seeking behaviors and its role in assessment (including misdiagnosis) is considered. The importance of culture for treatment is also discussed, including the role of religious factors, along with other issues relating to working with clients from minority cultures. Limitations of the literature base are discussed, particularly the lack of non-Western studies and the lack of comparative cross-cultural studies.

Key Words: cross-cultural psychology, cross-cultural treatment, epidemiology, obsessive-compulsive disorder, cognition, beliefs

Introduction

While the social and cultural context are often neglected in modern psychological formulations, they are clearly of great relevance to the individual psychological phenomena that are embedded within them. As defined by Betancourt and Lopez (1993), culture is the values, beliefs, and practices that pertain to a given ethnocultural group and that are transmitted across generations. Cultural factors greatly influence the way we think, how we behave, and the responses we receive about our behaviors, thus often determining, encouraging, or sanctioning specific behaviors. Therefore, researchers have emphasized the importance of understanding the way that culture shapes mental illness (Draguns, 1980; Kleinman, 1977; Marsella, 1980). For example, according to Tseng (1997), culture can influence the perceptions of psychopathology (i.e., what defines a disorder), its phenomenology (i.e., the specific symptom content), the development or prevention of psychopathology (e.g., supports, demands), and an individual's perception and description of the specific disorders, all of which could have significant implications for the etiology and treatment of psychological disorders.

The occurrence of obsessive-compulsive disorder (OCD) is not restricted to a specific culture or a particular era. Clinical and epidemiological data from a range of geographic and ethnic settings have shown consistency in the presence and main characteristics of OCD. Nevertheless, this does not mean that the disorder is immune to cultural influence. Variations in culture imply important differences in meaning construction between ethnocultural groups, therefore differences in self-perception, definitions of mental disorder and normality, and social interactions (Fabrega, 1989; Marsella & Yamada, 2000; Marsella et al., 2002). This may be particularly important in OCD because the construction of meaning and interpretations of common intrusive phenomena have been suggested to play a major role in the development and maintenance of specific obsessive and compulsive symptoms. Current cognitive-behavioral models of OCD suggest that obsessional and compulsive symptoms develop as a result of misinterpretation of, and reaction to, normal intrusive experiences. This is corroborated by numerous findings demonstrating that intrusive thoughts and experiences occur in the majority of the population (Rachman & de Silva, 1978; Salkovskis & Harrison, 1984; Pascual-Vera et al., 2019; cf. Rassin & Muris, 2007). Similarly, repetitive and ritualized behaviors are common in the nonclinical population (Muris et al., 1997) and are apparent in culturally prescribed religious practices. Thus, compulsions in and of themselves are not indicators of OCD, unless they are performed in ways inconsistent with shared cultural norms accepted by the individual.

Rachman (1997, 1998) brought attention to the importance of the intrusive thought content in the development of obsessions, suggesting that obsessions encompassing themes from the major moral systems (e.g., sex, aggression, blasphemy) are more likely to be misinterpreted as significant, personally revealing, or threatening. Because moral systems differ across cultures, logically it follows that the obsessions that are most egodystonic would also differ across cultures. Specifically, morality is closely influenced by religious concerns; therefore, many studies on cultural differences in OCD have examined the impact of religion. This also applies to other factors, such as self-beliefs, that are shaped within one's culture (Aardema et al., 2021; Moulding et al., 2021). Studies examining the impact of religious beliefs on contamination and scrupulosity concerns have provided probably the strongest support for the role of culture in shaping OCD symptoms. In addition, people in a particular culture at a particular time are likely to share a common history and specific social and environmental concerns, which would be reflected in the nature of their preoccupations. For example, HIV/AIDS and asbestos-related concerns have become increasingly prominent among contamination/cleaning symptoms, particularly in Western countries. Equally, obsessive concerns about COVID-19 (Aardema, 2020; French & Lyne, 2020) were clearly only possible after the emergence of COVID as a transnational concern.

In sum, culture could potentially influence the manifestation of symptoms as well as the course of a disorder and, therefore, its assessment and treatment. This chapter reviews the epidemiology and phenomenology of OCD across various geographical and cultural settings. It also examines the influence of culture-specific factors on assessment and treatment. Such an examination can give important insights into the mechanisms involved in the development and maintenance of disorders within a culture and better inform our approaches to assessment and treatment.

OCD Prevalence across Cultures

Increasing knowledge about OCD and the development of more objective, comprehensive, and reliable assessment methods have led to a growing interest in the epidemiology of the disorder worldwide. The first comprehensive epidemiological account of OCD came from the results of the National Epidemiological Catchment Area (ECA) Survey conducted across various regions in the United States in 1984 using the Diagnostic Interview Schedule (DIS; Robins et al., 1981). The results from the study placed OCD as the fourth most common psychiatric disorder, after phobias, substance use disorders and major depression, with a 6-month point prevalence of 1.6% and a lifetime prevalence of 2.5%. Six other international studies using similar methodology, conducted in Puerto Rico, Canada, Germany, Taiwan, New Zealand, and Korea, found annual prevalence rates ranging from 1.1% to 1.8% and lifetime prevalence rates between 1.9% and 2.5%. Several other international studies used the DIS in populations from Germany, Hong Kong, Iceland, and Hungary, finding lifetime prevalence rates ranging from 1.1% in Hong Kong to 2.7% in Hungary.

Epidemiological studies using other structured interview schedules have also been conducted and have shown similar results, with lifetime prevalence rates from 0.5% to 2%. The exception was Morocco, which had considerably higher overall prevalence (6.4%) than other countries. Morocco also had the greatest gender difference: the majority of individuals with OCD were women. The reasons for these differences were unclear in the absence of further data from the region. Taiwan was the other exception; it had a lower prevalence rate (one year prevalence rate of 0.065%, Huang et al., 2014), but also had lower rates of psychiatric disorders more generally. Using an alternative data set and adjusting for help-seeking behaviors, Huang et al. (2014) suggested that the adjusted prevalence of OCD in Taiwan would be between 0.23% and 0.7%, values that fit with prevalence rates reported for other countries (0.3% to 4%). It is unclear whether the difference in prevalence in Taiwan is due to differences in reporting of psychiatric diagnoses. It has been suggested that in Asian cultures there is a greater reluctance to disclose psychological problems and seek treatment, and a greater tendency to keep problems in the family (Cheung, 1991; Staley & Wand, 1995). Alternatively, the prevalence rates may reflect specific environmental and/or cultural factors that act as protective factors. Countries in the Far East recorded lower prevalence rates in other studies as well, supporting the need for further cross-cultural research in this region.

The most recent meta-analysis (Fawcett et al., 2020) of 34 studies from North America (26.5%), South America (2.9%), Africa (2.9%), Middle East (14.7%), Asia-Pacific (32.4%), and Europe (20.6%) had similar findings, with rates of 1.3%, 0.8%, and 1.1% for global lifetime, period, and current prevalence. However, the review reported no credible regional effects. The study is noteworthy because reviews of global prevalence rates are extremely rare; however, only one study was included from each of South America and Africa, and studies from Asia-Pacific included Australia and New Zealand, which are regionally Asia-Pacific countries, but culturally Western. Therefore, the cross-cultural findings of this analysis need to be interpreted with caution.

Help-Seeking Behaviors

While the prevalence rates seem similar across nations, it was noted that Taiwan had a lower rate, and prevalence rates from Asian countries may be underestimated given the lower rate of help-seeking behavior in those countries. The Asian trend in help-seeking behavior may be due to stigma around mental disorders and attribution of mental disorders to personal characteristics. For example, Nakane et al. (2005) reported that while Australians believed physiological explanations for psychiatric disorders, Japanese people were more likely to believe in "weakness of character" as a cause of psychiatric disorders, although both populations also believed in social and personal vulnerability causes. Such differences have also been observed between different cultural groups within nations. For example, compared to Caucasian British participants, Indian British participants were more likely to endorse supernatural causes for mental health issues (Jobanputra & Furnham, 2005), and consistent results were reported in a another study, where South Asian British participants endorsed supernatural causes as well as biological causes (Bhikha et al., 2015). In Singapore, Chinese Singaporeans were more likely than Malay Singaporeans to believe in personality-based causes (Pang et al., 2018).

Different beliefs about the causes of psychiatric disorders inevitably lead to differences in help-seeking behavior. For example, in a cross-cultural study of the United States and China, European and Chinese Americans were more likely to utilize mental health professionals than were Hong Kong and Mainland Chinese participants (Chen & Mak, 2008). In the previously mentioned study by Bhikha and colleagues (2015), the South Asian British participants were likely to use both medication and traditional healing, which is consistent with their beliefs in both biological and supernatural causes for psychiatric disorders. However, studies have shown that younger populations have better awareness of mental illness and mental health professionals (Picco et al., 2016; Subramaniam et al., 2016).

Another factor that may be linked to poorer help-seeking behavior, and therefore a lower apparent prevalence rate, is mental health literacy (MHL). MHL refers to one's knowledge of, and attitude toward, mental disorders, and it influences people's recognition of, and the prevention and management of, mental health issues (Jorm et al., 1997). MHL studies have shown that Asian participants had lower levels of MHL than did Western participants, and Asians were also less likely to seek professional help (Furnham & Chan, 2004; Furnham & Hamid, 2014; Loo et al., 2012). Jorm et al. (2005) found that, compared to Japanese participants, Australian participants reported higher levels of MHL and believed general practitioners to be helpful for mental disorders, while Japanese participants believed in self-management or seeking help from family. This result has been consistently supported by other studies.

Loo et al. (2012) conducted a cross-cultural study with participants from Hong Kong, Malaysia, and Britain to investigate their MHL about a range of disorders, including OCD, social phobia, depression, bipolar disorder, and pediatric attention-deficit/hyperactivity disorder (ADHD). British participants reported the highest MHL (seven out of nine disorders) and endorsed professional help the most, followed by participants from Hong Kong (two out of nine disorders) and Malaysia. In terms of OCD, 75% of British participants correctly labeled the disorder described in vignettes, which was more than twice as high as the correct response rate of Hong Kong (30%) and Malaysian (28%) participants. Description of people with OCD not only revealed misunderstandings of the disorder (e.g., labeling it as monophobia) but also revealed stigma applied to OCD in these countries (e.g., "clean freak"). In findings similar to previous findings in the literature, British participants were more likely to endorse professional help, while Hong Kong participants showed higher endorsement of self-help, and Malaysian participants were more likely to seek social help.

Lui et al. (2016) conducted a similar study in Hong Kong and found that OCD was best recognized compared to other disorders, including personality disorders. However, OCD was still only correctly identified by 40.1% of participants. The authors also reported a negative correlation between MHL and physical attributions and suggested that because somatization is more common in Asian countries, it may be one of the reasons for lower MHL, a finding that is supported by some previous studies (e.g., Kramer et al., 2002; Parker et al., 2001). The authors argued that people with lower MHL are likely to report higher physical attributions due to stigma and lower understanding of mental health issues. Similarly, in a cross-cultural study comparing MHL regarding depression and schizophrenia in Australia, South Korea, and Japan, Australian participants showed the highest MHL, followed by South Korean and then Japanese participants (Lee & Suh, 2010).

Another explanation for disparities in MHL between different countries is the cultural rules for display of emotion. Overt expressions of emotion are considered inappropriate for adults in South Korea, and this may have contributed to higher recognition of bipolar disorder in the sample (Jeon & Furnham, 2017). Similar to other Eastern countries, South Korea reported poor recognition of OCD, with many participants labeling the symptoms described in vignettes as "mysophobia." However, overall, professional help was preferred in this population, contrary to findings from other Asian countries. This may be due to the fact that South Korea has been Westernized, but the findings also suggest that while Koreans believe in professional help, this may not be reflected in their actual help-seeking behavior.

Social structural differences between countries may also contribute to differences in social awareness of mental disorders and help-seeking behavior. For example, the general practitioner (GP) is a starting point in the healthcare system and is easy to access in Britain and Australia, where it was the most recommended form of help. Because a GP is easier to access than a psychiatrist/psychologist, differences in healthcare systems may also be affecting this trend. However, in many other countries, there is a greater shortage of mental health professionals and higher costs of mental healthcare (Mubarak et al., 2003; Tsang et al., 2003, as cited in Loo et al., 2012). For example, Jeon and Furnham (2017) noted that stigma and accessibility of mental health services, coupled with a cultural focus on interdependence in the family, may be hindering actual help-seeking behavior in South Korea. GPs were rated as being less effective than parents and psychiatrists/psychologists. Interestingly, in their study, watching psychology-related TV programs was related to higher recognition of OCD. This indicates that poorer MHL may be also due to disorders not getting as much media attention, because South Koreans showed higher MHL for disorders that are more prevalent. Based on these findings, it can be argued that while the prevalence rates of OCD seem similar or lower in some Asian countries, the prevalence may be much more underreported than in some Western countries. The reasons would also go beyond social stigma and collectivistic beliefs, which are often used as explanations in the literature.

Help-seeking behaviors and the reliability of diagnosis of OCD differ not only across countries, but even with respect to minority cultures within Western countries. For example, Williams et al. (1998) cited more general research suggesting that in the United States, African Americans are less likely to seek treatment in psychiatric settings, preferring instead to see a minister or a physician, or to visit the emergency department in a crisis situation. Individuals may also present to alternative settings for treatment. For instance, Friedman et al. (1993) found that in a sample of African American dermatology patients, 15% met criteria for a diagnosis of OCD, a significantly higher rate than expected in a general medical population (2% to 3%).

With respect to help-seeking behavior, Goodwin et al. (2002) reported on U.S. participants who were screened in the 1996 National Anxiety Disorders Screening Day. On this day, participants presented for screening in response to advertisements in various media outlets. The participants viewed a video that dramatized the symptoms of several disorders, including OCD, before completing a questionnaire and seeing a mental health professional for final diagnosis. Goodwin et al. noted that of the 15,606 participants presenting for screening, about one fifth (3,069) met criteria for OCD. Participants with

OCD were likely to be younger, male, and White, and were less likely to be married. The researchers found that access to some form of mental health treatment for OCD was heavily influenced by age (older), gender (female), and race (Caucasian). Thus, "while readiness for treatment was a consistent and significant predictor of treatment, race and age are just as powerful determinants of access to care" (p. 148).

Even when presenting for treatment, individuals with OCD from minority groups may be misdiagnosed. Friedman et al. (2003) reported that, of 62 outpatients with OCD at an inner-city clinic in Brooklyn, 39% of African Americans versus 14% of Caucasian participants with OCD received an initial (mis)diagnosis of panic disorder. Hatch et al. (1996) suggest that, because African Americans with affective disorders are more often misdiagnosed with schizophrenia, those with OCD may be particularly susceptible to misdiagnosis due to the potentially bizarre OCD-related rituals in this population.

Gender Differences across Cultures

OCD is a heterogeneous disorder, and gender differences can be observed in many aspects, including the average onset age and the obsessional themes. A recent meta-analysis (Fawcett et al., 2020) reported that women are 1.6 times more likely to be diagnosed with OCD than men, but differences exist across samples. The authors suggested that hormonal influences, including perinatal experiences, may be the reason behind the sex differences, and they posited that perinatal experiences could also explain why women are more likely to experience contamination and cleaning symptoms. While there seems to be a slightly higher prevalence in women across studies, with the differences being statistically significant in three studies from Germany, New Zealand, and Iran, some inconsistencies are observed in gender ratio, with another German study recording slightly higher lifetime prevalence among men. The notable exception to the slightly higher ratio of women in samples is the substantially higher prevalence among women in Morocco. In contrast, a higher prevalence in men was reported in psychiatric samples in Egypt and India (Jaisoorya et al., 2008; Khanna et al., 1986; Okasha et al., 1994). These findings are likely to reflect sociocultural factors related to differential access to psychiatric services and different patterns of referrals for the two genders in these cultures. In general, there is a tendency for an earlier age of onset among men across the various regions, with the average age of onset ranging from mid/late twenties and early thirties across various sites (for review, see Matsunaga & Seedat, 2007; Staley & Wand, 1995).

Gender differences in presentation have also shown remarkable consistency across various cultures, with sexual, symmetry, and harm themes more common presentations among men and contamination/dirt obsessions and cleaning compulsions more common among women. These trends have been found across Brazil, India, Iran, Italy, Spain, Taiwan, Japan, and Turkey (Fontenelle et al., 2002; Ghassemzadeh et al., 2002; Jaisoorya et al., 2008; Juang & Liu, 2001; Karadağ et al., 2006; Labad et al., 2008; Lensi et al., 1996; Matsunaga et al., 2000; Tükel et al., 2004; Torresan et al., 2008). However, while the aforementioned meta-analysis by Fawcett et al. supported these gender differences, a quantitative review by Hunt (2020) reported that OCD presentations did not vary by gender other than the greater rate of sexual obsessions among men. Hunt (2020) suggested that the differences found in previous studies may be due to other factors that led to changes in the frequency of multiple OCD presentations.

In addition to epidemiological data, studies examining OCD in psychiatric populations have provided further support for the consistency in prevalence and core characteristics of OCD across various regions (for review, see Fawcett et al., 2020; Fontenelle et al., 2004; Staley & Wand, 1995). Although there are gender differences, themes of dirt/contamination, harm/aggression, symmetry, religion/morality/sex, and somatic concerns are present across various cultures, although there appears to be variation in the predominance of specific themes across different cultural and ethnic groups.

Limitations

Overall, irrespective of the assessment instruments or methods used, the available cross-cultural epidemiological research suggests only slight variability across various geographic regions in the world, with somewhat lower prevalence rates in the Far East. However, there are considerable limitations in terms of variability in methodology (assessment tools, interviewers, mode of assessment) and availability of reliable data from specific regions (Central Asia, Eastern Europe, Africa). The use of different methodologies across studies makes comparisons difficult. For example, the use of lay interviewers has been suggested to inflate prevalence data due to the interviewers' overestimation of distress and misinterpretation of concerns and worries as obsessions (Crino et al., 2005; Fontenelle et al., 2006). In a prevalence study using the CIDI administered by lay telephone interviewers, Stein and colleagues recorded the one-month prevalence of OCD at 3.1%, in contrast to a much lower figure of 0.6% found after face-to-face interviews with professionals. However, several studies employing the CIDI and lay interviewers have reported lower than general rates (e.g., Bijl et al., 1998; Grabe et al., 2001; Andrade et al., 2002), indicating that other factors may also play a role in influencing the prevalence estimations from such surveys.

In addition, most assessment measures have been developed in English-speaking Western countries (United States and United Kingdom) and may be culturally or linguistically inappropriate in other cultural contexts. For example, using the DIS and a design comparable to that of the ECA, a Puerto Rican study found a lifetime prevalence for OCD of 3%. However, this rate dropped to 1.1% in a subsequent study using a version of the DIS modified to account for cultural and linguistic factors and including a more detailed examination of the differences between OCD symptoms and obsessive personality (Canino et al., 1987). The role of the diagnostic criteria employed is particularly pertinent, with studies using *International Classification of Diseases* (ICD) criteria or specific hierarchical approaches (Research Diagnostic Criteria) arriving at lower estimates of prevalence.

Therefore, the establishment and use of specific standardized internationally valid assessment methods are necessary to improve the validity and reliability of cross-cultural data for OCD. The available data are predominantly Western-centric, with little data from Central and Southeast Asia, Eastern and Southern Europe, and Africa. In addition, most of the available data are from metropolitan areas, which are more likely to be subject to globalization, thus minimizing culture-specific influences. The very few studies that have included rural samples suggest lower prevalence in rural areas relative to urban areas (e.g., 0.3% in rural areas versus 0.9% in metropolitan areas in Taiwan; 2.2% versus 3.7% in Puerto Rico). Interestingly, the trend seems consistent across several geographic regions—possibly suggesting that urban versus rural factors may play a role in the prevalence of the disorders, or at least in the tendency to report them.

Similarly, only a few studies have examined differences between cultural groups within specific geographic regions. The ECA study reported slightly lower rates for OCD among Hispanics (1.8%) than among Caucasians (2.4%) or African-Americans (2.5%; Hollander et al., 1998). A study examining only the Los Angeles site indicated that the prevalence seemed to increase with length of stay in the United States, with U.S.-born Mexican Americans recording higher lifetime prevalence (2.4%) than Mexican immigrants (1.6%) but still lower prevalence than among Caucasians (3.2%), suggesting a possible influence of cultural and environmental factors on prevalence. While the differences were nonsignificant, this line of research is important because it provides a more fine-grained analysis of the role of specific cultural and environmental factors and their interaction in determining the prevalence of OCD.

Phenomenology across Cultures

While research on the prevalence of OCD across cultures shows some consistency, there are few data about the influence of cultural factors on the form and content of OCD symptoms across cultures (Greenberg & Witztum, 1994). As noted by de Silva (2006), the content of obsessions and compulsions may reflect common concerns in a culture. For example, religious obsessions are reported to be common in the Middle East (Mahgoub & Abdel-Hafeiz, 1991; Okasha et al., 1994) and aggressive obsessions in South America (Fontenelle et al., 2004), but findings have been inconclusive. In their review, Williams et al. (2016) suggested that sexual orientation obsessions may be culture-bound to Western countries.

According to a quantitative review (Hunt, 2020), OCD presentations were significantly different across cultural regions (United States/Europe, South America, South Africa, Asia, and the Middle East). In fact, symmetry obsessions and ordering compulsions were the only presentations not significantly varying across regions. However, once the total number of symptom categories were controlled for, OCD presentations were not as variable as previously reported across age, gender, and cultural regions. Albeit with small effect sizes, the significant cultural differences reported in Hunt's review are similar to those that have been generally found in the literature and the common cultural values in those areas with religious obsessions, contamination obsessions, and washing compulsions in Middle East (Okasha et al., 1994). Contamination and washing-related symptoms were also apparent in Asia, perhaps because the Indian population formed the majority of the Asian sample for Hunt's review: both Middle East and Indian culture stress the importance of purity (de Silva, 2006; Fernea & Fernea, 1994). However, other cultural differences from Hunt's review are not well explained in the literature, such as the greater levels of hoarding symptoms reported in Brazil and South Africa, or the differences are novel and inconsistent with related literature, such as the lower levels of somatic symptoms reported in Asia. Such findings reflect the limited knowledge about cultural differences in OCD presentations, and the differences warrant further exploration. For example, symmetry/ordering did not significantly vary across cultural regions but was linked to greater severity of OCD, which suggests a more traitlike vulnerability not greatly influenced by culture (Summerfeldt et al., 2015, as cited in Hunt, 2020).

Cultural differences were found not just among nations, but within nations as well. For example, in the United States, there seems to be a trend for African Americans to score higher on the symptom measures, especially concerning contamination/washing-related symptoms, although studies that compared symptoms between African and European Americans have been inconclusive, with some studies reporting no significant differences (Thomas et al., 2000; Williams et al., 2013; Wu & Wyman, 2016). Previously, it was found that African Americans reported high levels of disgust sensitivity (Haidt et al, 1994), which may be linked to contamination fears. This trend also may reflect historical factors, such as discrimination and segregation; for example, historical associations of African Americans with "dirtiness" may have led to symptoms related to contamination/washing (Williams et al., 2008, 2017).

Other studies have included different ethnoracial groups in the United States in their investigations. Washington et al. (2008) compared five U.S. ethnoracial groups (African, European, Hispanic, Southeast Asian, South Asian/East Indian) and found that the two Asian groups reported higher total symptom levels than did the other groups, with the Asian and Hispanic groups reporting higher contamination/washing symptoms than did the European group. No significant differences were reported between African and European American participants. Wheaton et al. (2013) extended these results in their study of four ethnoracial groups (Asian, African, Hispanic, European Americans) and reported that Asian Americans reported higher total obsessive belief scores than the others, and that Asian and African Americans, compared to the European Americans, showed more contamination symptoms. Perfectionism/certainty was a stronger predictor of contamination in the Asian group than in the European group and was a stronger predictor of unacceptable thoughts in the Asian group compared to the African American group.

Asian Americans also reported higher levels of beliefs related to the importance of, and need to control, thoughts, although they reported only elevated symptoms related to contamination. Woo et al. (2010) also reported that Korean university students reported higher levels of symptoms than were reported in European studies (as cited in Ching & Williams, 2019). Similar results were also reported by Wu and Wyman (2016). In their study, African Americans and Asian Americans reported more contamination-related symptoms than did European Americans. Asian Americans reported overall higher symptom levels than African Americans reported, which was not consistent with the findings of Wheaton et al. (2013). The authors argued that there may have been multiple cultural factors behind this inconsistency. In addition to aforementioned factors, such as less help-seeking among Asian populations, the Asian American category encapsulates many different backgrounds, different levels of acculturation, and family history of immigration, and therefore further research is needed to elucidate the OCD phenomena in this population. Like Wheaton et al. (2013), Wu and Wyman (2016) posited that higher levels of maladaptive perfectionism in the Asian population may be linked to the increased level of OCD symptoms in this population.

Another explanation for the cultural differences in OCD phenomena is ethnic identity. Previously, ethnic identity has been investigated as a protective factor for OCD in African American samples (Williams et al., 2012; Williams & Jahn, 2017) and in Asian samples (Brittian et al., 2013; Choi et al., 2017). However, certain ethnic identities have been associated with higher levels of OCD symptoms. For example, in a longitudinal study, Willis and Neblett (2018) investigated how the link between past experiences of racism and later OCD symptoms are affected by different types of ethnic identity: multiculturalist identity (which emphasizes similarity between African Americans and the mainstream group), humanist identity (which emphasizes similarity among all ethnoracial groups), and race-focused identity (which emphasizes the uniqueness of African Americans). The results showed that multiculturalist and humanist identity were protective against the impact of experiences of racism on later OCD symptoms, but race-focused identity increased the risks of OCD symptoms. A similar trend was observed in Asian American samples as well, although these studies were not specific to OCD (Hovey et al., 2006; Tummala-Narra et al., 2018). In the study by Ching and Williams (2019), Asian Americans with a higher sense of ethnic identity reported greater contamination-related symptoms. Consistent with Williams et al. (2012), the authors used a "stereotype compensation" hypothesis to explain their results, positing that Asian Americans may develop contamination symptoms to counteract racist stereotypes, such as those related to unsanitary food, and a stronger ethnic identity could therefore lead to greater symptoms. However, given the significant levels of contamination concerns even after ethnic identity was controlled for, it could also be that Asian Americans place culturally greater importance on cleanliness. The study also found that ethnic identity was the reason behind harm-related intrusions, checking compulsions, and neutralizing compulsions, perhaps due to a strong sense of attachment to an ethnoracial group. The sample also reported significant levels of symmetry/ordering mediated by ethnic identity. Previously, Confucian values of harmony and balance (Matsunaga et al., 2008) or perfectionism (Wu & Wyman, 2016) were used to explain this trend in Asian populations; however, Ching and Williams (2019) also suggested that higher levels of ethnic identity may reflect attitudinal emphasis on achieving certainty, and they suggested that future studies look into how high standards in academic and professional contexts related to racial stereotypes of Asian Americans may be linked to this symptom dimension.

Investigation of the interaction between culture and psychopathology may advance the understanding of the factors affecting nosological entities and their validity across cultures. In OCD in particular, cross-cultural research has focused on the interaction between religion and specific belief/value systems.

Religion

Many of the studies focusing on the link between OCD and culture have examined the role of religion (Greenberg, 1984; Steketee et al., 1991). While the core features of OCD (obsessions and compulsions) appear to be similar across cultures, the prevalence rate of religious obsessions varies widely in clinical populations across the world. This is not surprising, because religion is often pivotal in many cultures, and hence can influence important constructs relevant to mental health, such as moral systems and perception of normality. Religious OCD symptoms, often referred to as scrupulosity, are characterized by excessive concern about minor and trivial aspects of the religion, often to the exclusion of more important issues (Nelson et al., 2006). In older studies, 10% of the clinical population reported religion-related obsessions in the United States (Eisen et al., 1999), 5% in England (Dowson, 1977), 11% in India (Akhtar et al., 1975), and 7% in both Singapore (Chia, 1996) and Japan (Matsunaga et al., 2000). In contrast, a much higher rate of religion-related obsessions is reported in studies from Muslim and Jewish cultures; for example, 40% in Bahrain (Shooka et al., 1998), 50% in both Israel (Greenberg, 1984) and Saudi Arabia (Mahgoub & Abdel-Hafeiz, 1991), and up to 60% in individuals with OCD in Egypt (Okasha et al., 1994). Religious obsessions can take the form of fears and doubts about sin, punishment from God, and blasphemy, while religious compulsions include excessive religious behaviors, such as seeking assurance on religious issues and praying (Hepworth et al., 2010).

OCD symptoms more often take the form of rituals in religions emphasizing rituals, whereas in religions where purity of thought and the equality of thought and action are implied, OCD symptoms take a more cognitive form and revolve around intrusive blasphemous obsessions. For example, Jewish religious teachings and practices are markedly ritualistic in nature. Everyday life is governed by a large number of laws, as stipulated in the Jewish Code of Law, or Shulchan Aruch (Hermesh et al., 2003). Jewish religious law emphasizes cleanliness, personal hygiene, and exactness and allows for repetition, providing the individual with OCD with another potential arena for the expression of their symptoms (Greenberg & Witztum, 1994).

Islam is also a very ritualistic religion; contamination themes and cleaning rituals are also dominant in Islamic practice, where each prayer is preceded by a ritualistic cleansing process (El woodoo or ablution), which requires several parts of the body to be washed in a fixed order and for a specific number of times. Therefore, while the rituals revolve around contamination and cleaning themes, they are tangled with issues of religious contamination and purity, which usually manifest as a fear of spiritual impurity. Indeed, the Islamic religion is linked more closely to compulsive symptoms than to obsessive beliefs when compared to Christian groups (Inozu et al., 2012). Okasha et al. (1994) also noted that there were similarities between the contents of obsessions in Muslim and Jewish samples. Thus, the content of OCD symptoms may be influenced by the more salient aspects of the religious teachings (i.e., observance of rules, hygiene) emphasized in each religion, regardless of the patient's religious affiliation. For example, Greenberg and Witzum (1994) reported that, in their investigation of symptoms in 34 Israeli patients, 13 of the 19 ultra-orthodox patients exhibited symptoms related to religious practices, while such symptoms were reported in only one of the 15 non-ultra-orthodox subjects. The authors reported four main preoccupations of the religious symptoms: prayer, dietary practices, menstrual practices, and cleanliness before prayer.

Similar findings were reported in Egypt, where the highest rate of scrupulosity was reported. In Egypt, Okasha et al. (1994) found that both obsessions and compulsions showed the influence of Islamic culture. The authors reported that, in the 90 Egyptian patients studied, the most commonly occurring obsessions were religious and contamination obsessions (60%) and somatic obsessions (49%), and the most commonly occurring compulsions were repeating rituals (68%), cleaning and washing compulsions (63%), and checking compulsions (58%). The investigators compared the phenomenology of OCD in their Egyptian sample with the symptoms in 82 Indian, 45 English, and 10 Israeli patients with OCD. While the obsessions in the Egyptian and Israeli patients were predominantly concerned with religious matters related to cleanliness and hygiene, in the Indian and British samples, common themes were related to orderliness and aggression issues. Similarly, in Saudi Arabia, also considered to be a conservative Muslim country, obsessions also frequently relate to religious practices, supporting the link between religion and OCD (Mahgoub & Abdel-Hafeiz, 1991).

In later studies, different patterns were observed in other Islamic cultures, such as Iran and Turkey. Ghassemzadeh et al. (2002) examined the content of symptoms in a sample of 135 Iranian patients with OCD recruited from three treatment settings. Doubts and indecisiveness were found to be the most common obsessions, reported by 85% of patients, followed by obsessional slowness, reported by 69% of patients. The third and fourth most common obsessions in this sample were fear of impurity (62%) and fear of contamination (60%). Obsessions with self-impurity content were more common in women, whereas blasphemous thoughts and orderliness compulsions were found to be more common in men. The most common compulsions in the sample were washing (73%), which was almost twice as common in females as in their male counterparts (82% vs. 45%), and checking (78%). A similar pattern has been reported from Bahrain, another Middle Eastern country, where 43% of women, compared to 23% of men, had dirt and contamination obsessions and 46% of women, compared to 31% of men, had cleaning and washing compulsions (Shooka et al., 1998).

Turkey, a secular state, with its geographical location spanning Eastern Europe and the Middle East, has both a liberal Muslim population as well as a more conservative and traditional group. Studies conducted in Turkey have reported contradictory results. On the one hand, studies from western Turkey did not show strong influences of religion. For example, one study in western Turkey reported prevalence rates of religious themes similar to those found in Western studies (5%), despite the influence of Muslim culture (Egrilmez et al., 1997). Karadağ and colleagues (2006) also reported the presence of religious obsessions in only 20% of their sample of patients with OCD from Denizli in western Turkey. On the other hand, Tek and Ulug (2001) examined a sample of Turkish patients with OCD in the country's capital city, Ankara, and reported that 42% of the patients experienced religious obsessions. Although highly religious patients tended to report more religious obsessions, there were no significant differences in the overall symptom severity of the obsessions and compulsions across the groups of patients with and without religious obsessions. This is congruent with findings from an earlier study in Ankara, by Tek et al. (1998), who reported a high frequency of patients (48%) suffering from religious obsessions (cited in Tek & Ulug, 2001). Finally, in Eastern Turkey, 34% of participants reported religious obsessions—the second most common obsessive theme after dirt and contamination (Tezkan & Millet, 1997; cited in Tek & Ulug, 2001). It should also be noted that some dirt and contamination obsessions may reflect concerns related to issues of purity in Muslim culture. Karadağ et al. (2006) proposed that the discrepancy in the reported prevalence rates of religious obsessions in Turkish studies may be due to the influence of diverse sociocultural factors in the various sites of the studies, suggesting that the prevalence rate may increase as one travels eastward, reflecting the more conservative and religious society in eastern Turkey.

The links between religion and contamination/cleaning-related symptoms are observed in other religions as well. Hindu patients in clinical studies from India have reported a preponderance of OCD symptoms with contamination and cleaning themes; such findings are seen as being congruent with the emphasis that the Hindu religion places on issues of purity and cleanliness and the presence of a variety of purification rituals in that religion (Chaturvedi, 1993; Khanna & Channabasavanna, 1988). Similarly, in Nepal, a predominantly Hindu nation, obsessions are often related to religious practices (Sharma, 1968). In contrast, Chia (1996) examined a large clinical sample consisting of a

Chinese majority in Singapore and found that there was no association between religiosity and symptom severity or presentation in the individuals diagnosed with OCD.

Religion and Maladaptive Cognition

Religion has been also linked to maladaptive beliefs and appraisals relevant to OCD, as well as OCD symptom presentation (see Himle et al., 2011 for a review; Abramowitz et al., 2004; Nelson et al., 2006). According to Rachman (1997), "People who are taught, or learn, that all their value-laden thoughts are of significance will be more prone to obsessions—as in particular types of religious beliefs and instructions" (p. 798). Studies have suggested that, perhaps due to the differences in religious doctrines and teachings, the relationship between religiosity and OCD-related cognitions might differ among various religions or even across different religious denominations. For example, Protestant Christianity places more importance on the individual's beliefs, intentions, or motivations than on the observance of rituals. Therefore, it would be plausible to suggest that increased concern about the importance of thoughts, thought control, and morality-related thought–action fusion (the belief that bad thoughts are morally equivalent to bad actions), would play a greater role in the religious cognitive world of a Christian (Zohar et al., 2005). Indeed, Rassin and Koster (2003) found that Protestants showed a greater tendency to believe that their thoughts were morally equivalent to actions (i.e., moral thought–action fusion) compared to Catholics, atheists, and members of other religions. Moreover, this cognitive bias was more strongly related to OCD symptoms among Protestants than among other religious groups. Similarly, Siev and Cohen (2007) reported that religiosity was associated with thought–action fusion in their Christian sample. This association was not replicated in their Jewish sample, who showed lower levels of morality-related thought–action fusion than their Christian counterparts.

This result was supported by later studies. For example, Williams et al. (2013) conducted an experiment with Christian, Jewish, and atheist/agnostic participants to investigate the relationship between thought–action fusion and OCD symptoms. The authors found that thought–action fusion mediated the link between religiosity and symptoms, and Christianity moderated the link between religiosity and thought–action fusion. Christians also formulated a significant relationship between religiosity and guilt and responsibility mediated by thought–action fusion. In this study, Protestants showed higher levels of moral thought–action fusion compared to atheist/agnostic participants, and moral thought–action fusion was linked to religiosity only in Christian group. However, detailed findings on relationships between religiosity, thought–action fusion subscales, negative affect, and OCD symptoms vary. Inozu et al. (2014) reported that, in a Turkish sample, thought–action fusion and disgust sensitivity mediated the link between religiosity and OCD symptoms even after depression was controlled for. While the impact of thought–action fusion did not vary across symptoms, the effects of disgust sensitivity were only significant for washing, checking, and ordering symptom subtypes. Wheaton et al. (2013) also reported that both European and Latino Americans reported significant relationships between the importance of, and need to control, thoughts and the unacceptable thoughts symptom dimension, and this relationship was stronger for the Latino group. The authors suggested that this may be due to Latino Americans' being predominantly Roman Catholic. Partial support for this premise was also provided by Abramowitz et al. (2002), who developed an inventory of religious OCD symptoms (scrupulosity) and administered it to a sample of American college students. The researchers found that highly devout participants scored higher on the two scales of the inventory, fear of sin and fear of God's punishment. However, highly devout Christians obtained higher scores on both scales than did highly devout Jews, suggesting that the components of obsessive religiosity examined by the inventory may be culture-specific.

In addition, Sica et al. (2002a) found that Italian Catholics with a high or moderate degree of religiosity, compared to less religious Catholics, showed higher scores on measures of obsessionality and OCD-related cognitions, such as the over-importance of thoughts, control of thoughts, perfectionism, and responsibility. Measures of control of thoughts and the over-importance of thoughts were associated with OCD symptoms only in religious subjects. However, it has been noted that the mean OCD score in the highly religious group in this study was lower than normative data for nonclinical groups reported in other studies (Huppert et al., 2007). Therefore, overall, these studies indicate that both religious affiliations and strength of devotion are associated with the presentation of obsessive-compulsive symptoms, as well as with beliefs and assumptions presumed to underlie the development and maintenance of symptoms in cognitive models (e.g., thought–action fusion, importance of thoughts).

In a cross-cultural study, Yorulmaz and colleagues (2009) compared the relationship between religiosity and obsessive-compulsive symptoms and cognitions in Muslim and Christian student samples from Turkey and Canada. The results indicated that, overall, the Muslim participants obtained higher scores on obsessive-compulsive symptoms and more strongly endorsed beliefs about the importance of, and the need to control, intrusive thoughts. However, regardless of religious affiliation, highly religious participants evidenced more obsessional thoughts and checking, reported more concern about the importance of thoughts and the need to control them, and endorsed more thought–action fusion in the morality domain. The participants' degree of religiosity was found to contribute to a significant difference on morality-related thought–action fusion in the Christian sample only. As with previous findings, highly religious Christians were more likely to engage in moral thought–action fusion in comparison to less religious Christians. Based on these findings, the authors concluded that religiosity is a relevant issue for OCD in both Islam and Christianity, although the characteristics of the religion may mediate the nature of the association.

In another study from a Muslim country, Naziry et al. (2005) examined the association of nonadaptive religious beliefs (pertaining to cleansing and hygiene codes) with the severity of OCD symptoms in an Iranian sample of 43 patients with OCD and predominately washing compulsions. The authors reported a significant positive association between the nonadaptive religious beliefs and the severity of the OCD symptoms. In addition, the nonadaptive religious beliefs measure was a better predictor of the severity of OCD symptoms than were other variables such as OCD-related cognitions as measured by the Beliefs Inventory (BI) and guilt feelings. Furthermore, the researchers did not find any significant association between individuals' level of religious commitment (e.g., participation in religious ceremonies) and the severity of the OCD symptoms. The authors argued that individuals with OCD are influenced by their faulty or ill-informed preconceived ideas about religious hygiene and washing codes rather than their level of religious commitment. Naziry et al. (2005) strongly recommended the inclusion of religion as an important cultural factor in OCD research and suggested that the identification of the patient's dysfunctional beliefs about religion and its codes of conduct need to be incorporated in the formulation of treatment plans.

Although there is an emerging body of research that supports a link between religiosity and OCD, the need for data from a greater number of countries, along with the relatively small sample sizes in many of the studies as well as differences in the assessment tools and measures used, all make it difficult to draw unequivocal conclusions about the nature of the relationship between religiosity and OCD (Sica et al., 2002b). Generally, it is held that there is little support for the notion that religiosity increases rates of OCD per se, although converging evidence suggests that the presentation of OCD symptoms and OCD-related cognitions may be influenced by religion.

Beliefs

An implicit assumption underlying current cognitive models is that OCD is influenced by the same cognitions across different cultures, although most cognitive research has been undertaken in Western English-speaking cultures. If there is consistency across cultures in the relationship between cognitions and symptoms, there would be greater confidence in the applicability to non-English settings of cognitive-behavior therapy, which was developed in the West (Kyrios et al., 2001). However, it is to be expected that culture may differentially influence the form of the beliefs that are thought to be relevant to OCD (see Sica et al., 2002b). Even in Western cultures, obsessional beliefs are not always reported by all patients with OCD (Taylor et al., 2006), and the specific factor structures of obsessive beliefs vary in different samples. For example, in comparison to the original three-factor structure of the Obsessive Beliefs Questionnaire (OBQ), Moulding et al. (2011) found a four-factor solution fit best in nonclinical samples from Australia and Israel, although when a three-factor solution was forced, it resembled the original three-factor solution.

It has been speculated that some of the beliefs in the OCD model would vary in their importance in different cultural settings. In an early study using university student samples in Italy and Australia, Kyrios et al. (2001) examined the relationships among OCD symptoms and three cognition and affect-related measures assessing responsibility, perfectionism, and guilt. They found similar factor structures for the measures across the cultures. In findings supporting the cross-cultural generalizability of the OCD model, there were little differences in the pattern of relationships among symptoms and affect/cognitions (responsibility, perfectionism, guilt) across the cohorts. The few notable differences included the higher magnitude of associations between self-oriented perfectionism and symptoms in the Australian sample, and relatively stronger relationships between OCD urges/worries and affective/cognitive variables in the Australian sample. The authors suggested that self-oriented perfectionism may play a greater role in the more individualized Australian culture, while urges/impulses may be seen as less problematic in the Italian context due to greater levels of acceptance in, Italian culture.

Sica et al. (2006) examined the original 87-item version of the OBQ in 46 Greek students, 348 Italian students and 73 American students. While beliefs were correlated with symptoms in all three groups, there were differences in the patterns of association. In all three groups, the correlation between the OBQ scales and obsessionality (Padua Inventory [PI] impaired control scale) was large, while correlations between the OBQ scales and PI urges scale were medium. However, the relationship of beliefs to checking and contamination changed by sample, being unrelated in the Greek sample, moderately related in the Italian sample, and highly related in the U.S. sample. Although their conclusions were limited by the small sample size of Greek students, the authors interpreted the results as indicating some cultural specificity in the relationship between pathological beliefs and OCD symptoms. For example, they suggested that a high level of uncertainty avoidance (and associated powerlessness) characterized the Greek participants and may have attenuated the relationship between the beliefs and symptoms. They further suggested that, while results generally supported the cognitive model, some culture-specific modifications may be necessary.

In a clinical study in Italy, Sica et al. (2004) examined the original six-domain version of the OBQ in groups with OCD, generalized anxiety disorder (GAD), and nonclinical controls. They found that intolerance of uncertainty, control of thoughts, and perfectionism differentiated all three groups, whereas threat estimation did not differentiate the GAD and OCD groups, and importance of thoughts and perfectionism were not higher in the GAD group versus the student controls. They suggested that the cognitive construct of responsibility "appears to have less relevance in non-Anglo-Saxon or Anglo-Celtic cultures" (p. 305), while the importance of thoughts may be relevant only in a subgroup with particular features, such as religious obsessions (Sica et al., 2004).

Findings from studies investigating the relevance of the proposed belief systems in the Middle East have returned conflicting findings. In two studies investigating the factor structure and specificity of OBQ to patients with OCD, Shams et al. (2004, 2006) found support for the three subscales, although only the importance/control of thoughts subscale was specific to OCD, with no significant differences between OCD patients and anxiety controls on responsibility/threat estimation and perfectionism/intolerance of uncertainty. Naziry et al. (2005) reported a negative association between dysfunctional cognitive beliefs as measured by the BI and symptoms in their sample of patients with OCD and predominately cleaning and washing symptoms. Ghassemzadeh et al. (2005) found significant differences between patients with OCD and anxiety and healthy controls on the Responsibility Attitudes Scale (RAS) and Responsibility Interpretation Questionnaire (RIQ). The authors suggested that the findings indicated the need to consider the inclusion of responsibility in theoretical formulations of, and treatment programs for, OCD in Iran. Foroughi et al. (2007) examined the psychometric properties and cross-cultural utility of a thought–action fusion scale in Iranian OCD and nonclinical samples and found remarkable similarities between the factor structure and psychometric properties and those in previous research in Western samples. Pourfaraj et al. (2008) also reported a positive correlation between the thought–action fusion construct and obsessive-compulsive symptoms in a large sample of university students in Iran. However, other studies have suggested that there may be cross-cultural differences in the pattern of correlations between thought–action fusion factors and OCD symptoms, with cultural features like religious affiliation accounting for some of the differences (Yorulmaz et al., 2004, 2009).

Furthermore, studies have examined several different language versions of the OBQ. In China, Wang et al. (2015) used a confirmatory factor analysis and found support for a three-factor version in a student (N = 569) and OCD sample (N = 66), albeit some indicators fell short of ideal levels and no alternative models were tested; all subscales related to Yale-Brown Obsessive-Compulsive Scale (Y-BOCS) scores in both samples. In a clinical sample in Brazil (N = 104), Bortoncello et al. (2012) conducted an exploratory factor analysis with a three-factor solution, finding a factor structure similar to the original scale. In an exploratory factor analysis in 200 students in Kuwait, when forcing three factors, Rahat et al. (2012) found three factors that were largely but not completely consistent with the original three-factor solution. Julien et al. (2008) found a poor fit using a confirmatory factor analysis in a French-speaking sample consisting of students from Montreal (N = 465) and Lyon (N = 53) and clinical participants with OCD in Quebec (N = 205) and Lyon (N = 85), and anxious controls in Quebec (N = 21). However, while there were some variations in the particular items that loaded according to sample analyzed, an exploratory factor analysis largely replicated the three-factor solution. The scales correlated with symptoms and were higher in the OCD sample than in the control samples, although the correlations were higher when correlating with self-report versus clinician-rated measures of symptoms. Overall, then, there is evidence from a number of translations suggesting that beliefs are relevant cross-culturally. However, some limitations are apparent, in that many of the studies did not test alternative models of symptoms, and more particularly, they didn't examine the relative contribution of the scales to symptoms in different cultures in a single study, in order to directly examine cultural differences.

Studies have examined the cultural specificity of beliefs within a country. Wheaton et al. (2013) administered the OBQ to a large U.S. student sample, including 1,199 European Americans, 215 African Americans, 116 Asian Americans, and 72 Latino Americans. The researchers found a significant overall difference, with the Asian American group scoring higher than the other groups, as well as being generally elevated on the subscales, although not all comparisons reached significance. However, in terms of OCD symptoms, the Asian Americans were more elevated only on contamination scores, with the authors speculating that the other elevation in beliefs may relate to other symptoms, such as social anxiety, which were not examined in the study. In terms of explaining symptoms, the authors found that beliefs were relatively poorer in predicting OCD symptoms in the African American sample, and that group membership moderated the prediction of contamination and unacceptable thoughts by OBQ dimensions, but not responsibility for harm or the need for symmetry.

In terms of the underlying intrusions that are theorized to be linked to OCD symptoms, a working group has examined the relative prevalence of intrusions in university students (N = 777), across 15 sites in 13 countries, using a structured interview (Clark et al., 2014; Moulding et al., 2014; Radomsky et al., 2014). Overall, 94% of the sample reported at least one type of unwanted intrusive thought in the preceding three months (Radomsky et al., 2014). Across the sample, the most common type of intrusions related to doubt, and the least common types were related to sex, religion, and immorality. However, there were a number of differences by sites, with more contamination intrusions in Makeni, Sierra Leone; less harm in Firenze/Padova, Italy, and Thessaloniki, Greece; greater doubt in Fredricton, Canada, in Vanecia, Italy, and in Chapel Hill, North Carolina; more religious intrusions in Ankara, Turkey, Chapel Hill, and Makeni; and more immorality-related intrusions in Fredricton, in Hong Kong, and in Chapel Hill.

When considering appraisals and control strategies, it was found that there were few site differences in terms of the strength of the relationship with frequency, distress, importance, and persistence of the most distressing intrusions (Moulding et al., 2014). The authors suggested that this finding added credence to the cognitive model, suggesting that it was equally relevant to non-English speaking Western countries (e.g., Spain, France) and to less Westernized countries, such as Iran and Sierra Leone. However, they cautioned that the number of sites included may have precluded finding differences. Considering a reduced data set from the 11 countries that did the full questionnaire pack, Clark et al. (2014) found that the frequency of intrusions related to dirt/contamination, doubt, and miscellaneous themes was related to OCD-symptom levels, even after controlling for country differences, a finding supporting the overall OCD model. In a later study with participants from seven countries across Europe, the Middle East, and South America

(N = 1,473), Pascual-Vera et al. (2019) administered a self-report measure of unwanted mental intrusions related to OCD, BDD, illness anxiety, and eating disorders. They found some differences in prevalence—individuals from Iran and Turkey experienced more OCD-related intrusions, and Israel participants fewer, while Turkish participants endorsed greater BDD-related intrusions. There were also differences in illness anxiety and Eating Disorder (ED)-related intrusions. The authors suggested that Iran and Turkey share some similarities due to their shared Muslim values, which are linked to self-identity and everyday life, and the need to follow specific rules and to maintain purity. Overall, the authors suggested that the studies showed more similarities than differences in the experience of unwanted mental intrusions across disorders, suggesting that their occurrence is common regardless of context.

In sum, there has been only limited investigation of the differential importance of OCD beliefs across cultures. However, there is surprisingly strong evidence for a similar factor structure and for the relevance of the factors to symptoms. However, there is some suggestion that belief domains may have differential importance within different settings and with different patients, which requires greater direct investigation. Furthermore, it is plausible that some domains may be more influenced by cultural context than others, particularly domains that are more greatly related to social context (responsibility) and to religious perceptions (importance and control of thoughts). Just as cognitive therapists need to be sensitive to the variable importance of beliefs and responses in individuals, they should also be aware of cultural influences on the associations among such variables.

Treatment and Assessment Issues

Culture and Assessment

During assessment it is important to note that cultural differences can also influence the responses of patients to questionnaires. Kyrios et al. (1996) commented on the range of mean scores on the Padua Inventory (PI), a 60-item inventory of OCD (Sanavio, 1988), across Australian, American, Dutch, and Italian nonclinical cohorts. They argued that a range of cultural factors could influence responses on questionnaire measures of OCD, including response styles, the distress caused by obsessive-compulsive phenomena, and social perceptions of obsessive-compulsive symptoms. They also cautioned against the use of assessment inventories in cohorts where normative data are not available.

Indeed, the responses to self-report instruments may be influenced by minority status. Thomas et al. (2000) found that Black U.S. university students (N = 214) scored almost one standard deviation higher than did White students (N = 1,633) on the Maudsley Obsessional Compulsive Inventory (MOCI), a 30-item true/false self-report measure of OCD symptoms. However, while high scores on the measure were associated with more diagnoses of OCD in the White population (obtained by interview methods), this was not the case in the Black population. That is, while the Black population endorsed more MOCI items, their scores were not associated with more diagnoses of OCD.

In another study, responses of Black ($N = 105$) and White ($N = 582$) participants were compared on an online version of the PI (Williams et al., 2005), and there were no overall differences between the samples on mean responses, but the Black participants were more likely to endorse the contamination subscale. Specific item-level differences were also found, over and above mean scale differences. For example, Black participants were more likely to report that they feel dirty after touching an animal, that they return home to check doors/windows, that they check letters before posting, that they feel the need to read passages more than once, that they are late because they keep on doing things more often than necessary, and that unwanted obscene words come into their minds and are hard to dismiss. White participants over-endorsed feeling dirty after touching money and impulses to tear their clothes off in public.

The authors speculated that varying cultural norms may underlie such differences; for example, they suggested that Black individuals are less likely to own pets than are Whites (Williams et al., 2008). In addition, as noted earlier, differences may be due to a self-presentation bias, where Black individuals may over-endorse certain items to counter negative stereotypes. Studies have found that priming racial salience by administering a measure of identification with ethnic background increases the PI contamination scores of Black, but not White, participants (Williams et al., 2008).

In sum, overall endorsement of OCD symptom levels on screening instruments and questionnaires is likely to be affected by cultural factors. Furthermore, differential endorsement of particular items and subscales within such measures may also be influenced by cultural schemas and the accessibility of those schemas. Such differences are likely to be emphasized in situations where racial identity is an issue, such as when a majority-culture therapist assesses a minority-culture client. Therefore, attention must be paid to the cultural setting that the measure is being used in, and whether the measure has been validated in that culture (see Williams et al., 2016).

Religious Factors in Treatment

While the role of religion as a factor in the form or prevalence of OCD has not been fully ascertained, that religious beliefs can influence cognitive-behavioral treatment is beyond question. OCD is a disorder where repugnant or immoral thoughts are a salient issue, with the perceptions about immorality influenced by religious beliefs. Furthermore, religious issues may affect factors like the therapeutic relationship, what is and is not permissible for behavioral strategies in treatment, and judgments about responsibility for treatment outcome.

In treatment, it is important for the therapeutic relationship that, rather than blaming a client's religious beliefs for their OCD, the therapist be cognizant of how a client's religious beliefs influence the manifestation of OCD. Consistent with theories about the importance of sensitivity to particular intrusive phenomena on the basis of individual's beliefs and experiences (Doron & Kyrios, 2005; Doron et al., 2007, 2008), it is likely that

OCD manifests itself in the most important areas of an individual's life (Purdon, 2004; Huppert et al., 2007). That is, in many instances, religion defines an individual's construction of their experiences and their behavioral motivations. For instance, Orthodox Jews may particularly fear experiencing repugnant obsessions on Yom Kippur, because this may preclude their gaining atonement and therefore from entering the Book of Life for the coming year (Paradis et al., 1996).

Difficulties in treating highly religious patients with OCD lie in framing therapy so that the client does not feel they are being asked to commit a sin. For example, asking a patient with intrusive sexual thoughts to expose themselves to the thoughts may be taken as asking them to defy their religious principles. In such cases, it is important to work with the patient to understand the limits of religiously acceptable behavior—so as to "create situations that violate OCD law, but not religious law" (Huppert et al., 2007, p. 932). It is also important that the patient clearly understands the rationale for treatment, and that the therapist works to enhance motivation for undergoing exposure. It is not that the therapist is trying to eliminate religion—indeed, OCD can be framed as a barrier to the patient's having a positive spiritual life—however, patients may excessively rely on rituals and rules rather than trusting their knowledge and soul (Huppert et al., 2007). Involvement of the client's spiritual leader can be important in establishing the acceptable guidelines for religious practice, such as ascertaining the normal frequency of praying (de Silva, 2006; Purdon, 2004) and teaching the client and therapist the correct interpretation of religious laws related to rituals and to therapy (Paradis et al., 1996). The religious leader's involvement can also serve to prevent them from unintentionally becoming a source of (obsessive) reassurance for the patient (Huppert et al., 2007).

Purdon (2004) noted that the difference between religious observance and religious obsession lies in the sense of certainty; that suggest to note with the client that if one is uncertain that one has committed a sin, then one cannot be held responsible for that sin. In therapy, Purdon suggested prohibiting the client from posing questions on the basis of doubt—the intrusion "Maybe I have committed a sin" cannot be allowed to lead to the question "Am I certain I did not sin?" Conversely, rituals can be framed within the certainty spectrum—one is not asking the patient to sin, but to tolerate a *small possibility that they may* sin (Huppert et al., 2007). Thus, techniques that put the behavior in perspective may be useful. For instance, the patient should consider where the feared accidental violation would lie relative to deliberate violations of religious law (e.g., buying a bacon cheeseburger from a fast-food restaurant, for those religions that prohibit eating meat/bacon; Huppert et al., 2007).

Greenberg and Witztum (2001) note additional factors that may assist in the discrimination between religion and obsession. First, compulsive behavior exceeds, and may disregard, the requirement of religious law. Second, compulsive behavior usually concentrates on specific areas and does not reflect an overall concern for religious practice. Third, the choice of obsessional area reflects general symptom themes in OCD, such as cleaning and checking. Fourth, the patient may neglect other areas of life as they focus specifically on one area; for example, they might have to omit sections of prayers due to the time they spend washing. Finally, the patient repeats rituals because of doubt alone, whereas religious codes often prohibit or discourage the repetition of rituals.

Other Culture-Related Factors in Treatment

Discussion of issues in the treatment of non-White patients has been limited. With respect to the treatment of minority cultures, Williams et al. (1998) presented two cases of African American individuals who attended a behavioral treatment in Washington, D.C. While many issues were common to the White and Black clients, culture did affect treatment. For example, one client with washing obsessions also believed that if she touched a spot that had been touched by another individual, that person would gain the power to "put the root" (or cast a spell) on her. While such beliefs were common to the particular cultural group, they could potentially lead to misdiagnosis of psychosis when the therapist is from a different culture and not knowledgeable about the patient group.

In addition, the minority culture clients were more sensitive to judgments about having the disorder and experienced greater shame due to symptoms (Williams et al., 1998). Such reactions led to difficulties in treatment, as the clients were reluctant to undergo exposure in public, and even to reveal their problems. The patients also felt more isolated, being individuals with OCD and members of a minority culture. Hatch et al. (1996) reported similar increased reluctance among Black clients, compared to White clients, to attend treatment, with the Black patients taking much longer even to admit to OCD symptoms. Hatch et al. recommended using a structured interview during psychiatric intake to help overcome reticence by patients in reporting symptoms, although Williams et al. (2016) cast doubt on the validity of such interviews with African American clients.

Due to secrecy, Hatch et al. (1996) found that African American patients with OCD were extremely reluctant to involve their family in treatment, and their families were also less likely to be drawn into assisting patients with their compulsions. Hatch et al. suggested coaching the client on how to convey such information, as opposed to the therapists seeking family meetings. However, when the family is involved, they may be extremely tolerant of the patient's OCD activities. Hatch and colleagues suggested that the therapist should expect resistance when broaching family involvement, consider abandoning such ideas if the resistance is too strong, and perhaps involve a friend or neighbor instead of a family member so as to lower such resistance.

A further issue in therapy is patient–therapist matching in terms of ethnicity. For example, will ethnic minorities disclose symptoms to therapists from the majority ethnic background? Will different backgrounds lead to a poorer therapeutic alliance? Finally, will therapists misinterpret symptoms reported by clients from different backgrounds? Karlsson (2005) conducted a review of the more general literature on ethnic matching. He noted that while archival studies of hospital records suggested higher drop-out rates and shorter length of treatment when client and therapist were of dissimilar ethnicity, due to the nature of the studies, it was difficult to establish the reason for the findings. In contrast, actual studies of psychotherapy found no effect on outcome due to ethnic incongruity. Based on clinical experience, Hatch et al. (1996) suggested that the issue of culture or race may need to be discussed when therapists from the majority culture work with clients from minority cultures. They considered it to be the therapist's responsibility to raise the issue of cultural and ethnic incongruity in order to enhance the therapeutic alliance and to uncover any destructive beliefs that the client may hold about the relationship (e.g., "You can't understand what it's like to be on public assistance," p. 313).

Conclusion

This chapter reviews evidence relevant to the cross-cultural aspects of OCD. It discusses cross-national prevalence rates, as well as the difficulties pertaining to prevalence assessments, such as variability in methods of assessment and in diagnostic criteria across studies. Differences in phenomenology are discussed, as well as the importance of culturally specific constructs in the disorder, including the influence of religion on the presentation of OCD. The chapter examines the issue of whether beliefs theorized to be relevant to OCD are constant across cultures. The final part of the chapter discusses the relevance of cultural factors to treatment, with an emphasis on the treatment of minority cultures. The factors include the relationship between minority group membership and decreased help-seeking behavior, as well as increased misdiagnosis. The chapter emphasizes the importance of taking culture into account when utilizing assessment instruments and when treating highly religious clients or clients with religious obsessions. Broader issues, such as the importance of the therapist's being culturally knowledgeable, and the issue of therapist–client matching, are also discussed.

References

Aardema, F. (2020). COVID-19, obsessive-compulsive disorder and invisible life forms that threaten the self. *Journal of Obsessive-Compulsive and Related Disorders, 26*, 100558.

Aardema, F., Radomsky, A. S., Moulding, R., Wong, S. F., Bourguignon, L., & Giraldo-O'Meara, M. (2021). Development and validation of the multidimensional version of the Fear of Self Questionnaire: Corrupted, culpable and malformed feared possible selves in obsessive-compulsive and body-dysmorphic symptoms. *Clinical Psychology and Psychotherapy, 28*, 1160–1180.

Abramowitz, J., Huppert, J. D., Cohen, A. B., Tolin, D. F., & Cahill, S. P. (2002). Religious obsessions and compulsions in a non-clinical sample: The Penn Inventory of Scrupulosity (PIOS). *Behaviour Research and Therapy, 40*, 825–838.

Abramowitz, J. S., Deacon, B. J., Woods, C. M., & Tolin, D. F. (2004). Association between Protestant religiosity and obsessive-compulsive symptoms and cognitions. *Depression and Anxiety, 20*, 70–76.

Akhtar, S., Wig, N. N., Varma, V. K., Pershad, D., & Verma, S. K. (1975). A phenomenological analysis of symptoms in obsessive-compulsive neurosis. *The British Journal of Psychiatry, 127*, 342–348.

Andrade, L., Walters, E. E., Gentil, V., & Laurenti, R. (2002). Prevalence osf ICD-10 mental disorders in a catchment area in the city of São Paulo, Brazil. *Social Psychiatry and Psychiatric Epidemiology, 37*, 316–325.

Betancourt, H., & Lopez, S. R. (1993). The study of culture, ethnicity, and race in American psychology. *American Psychologist, 48*, 629–637.

Bhikha, A., Farooq, S., Chaudhry, N., Naeem, F., & Husain, N. (2015). Explanatory models of psychosis amongst British South Asians. *Asian Journal of Psychiatry*, *16*, 48–54.

Bijl, R. V., Ravelli, A., & van Zessen, G. (1998). Prevalence of psychiatric disorder in the general population: Results of The Netherlands Mental Health Survey and Incidence Study (NEMESIS). *Social Psychiatry and Psychiatric Epidemiology*, *33*, 587–595.

Bortoncello, C., Braga, D., Gomes, J., de Souza, F., & Cordioli, A. (2012). Psychometric properties of the Brazilian version of the Obsessive Beliefs Questionnaire (OBQ-44). *Journal of Anxiety Disorders*, *26*(3), 430–434.

Brittian, A., Umaña-Taylor, A., Lee, R., Zamboanga, B., Kim, S., & Weisskirch, R., Castillo, L. G., Whitbourne, S. K., Hurley, E. A., Huynh, Q. L., & Brown, E. J. (2013). The moderating role of centrality on associations between ethnic identity affirmation and ethnic minority college students' mental health. *Journal of American College Health*, *61*(3), 133–140.

Canino, G. J., Bird, H. R., Shrout, P. E., Rubio-Stipec, M., Bravo, M., Martinez, R., Sesman, M., & Guevara, L. M. (1987). The Prevalence of Specific Psychiatric Disorders in Puerto Rico. *Archives of General Psychiatry*, *44(8)*, 727-735. https://doi.org/10.1001/archpsyc.1987.01800200053008

Chaturvedi, S. K. (1993). Neurosis across cultures. *International Review of Psychiatry*, *5*, 179–191.

Chen, S., & Mak, W. (2008). Seeking professional help: Etiology beliefs about mental illness across cultures. *Journal of Counseling Psychology*, *55*(4), 442–450.

Cheung, P. (1991). Adult psychiatric epidemiology in China in the 80s. *Culture, Medicine and Psychiatry*, *15*, 479–496.

Chia, B. H. (1996). A Singapore study of obsessive-compulsive disorder. *Singapore Medical Journal*, *37*, 402–406.

Ching, T., & Williams, M. (2019). The role of ethnic identity in OC symptom dimensions among Asian Americans. *Journal of Obsessive-Compulsive and Related Disorders*, *21*, 112–120.

Choi, S., Lewis, J., Harwood, S., Mendenhall, R., & Browne Huntt, M. (2017). Is ethnic identity a buffer? Exploring the relations between racial microaggressions and depressive symptoms among Asian-American individuals. *Journal of Ethnic & Cultural Diversity in Social Work*, *26*(1–2), 18–29.

Clark, D. A., Abramowitz, J., Alcolado, G. M., Alonso, P., Belloch, A., Bouvard, M., Coles, M. E., Doron, G., Fernández-Álvarez, H., & Garcia-Soriano, G. (2014). Part 3. A question of perspective: The association between intrusive thoughts and obsessionality in 11 countries. *Journal of Obsessive-Compulsive and Related Disorders*, *3*(3), 292–299.

Crino, R., Slade, T., & Andrews, G. (2005). The changing prevalence and severity of obsessive-compulsive disorder criteria from DSM-III to DSM-IV. *The American Journal of Psychiatry*, *162*, 876–882.

de Silva, P. (2006). Culture and obsessive-compulsive disorder. *Psychiatry*, *5*, 402–405.

Doron, G., & Kyrios, M. (2005). Obsessive-compulsive disorder: A review of possible specific internal representations within a broader cognitive theory. *Clinical Psychology Review*, *25*, 415–432.

Doron, G., Kyrios, M., & Moulding, R. (2007). Sensitive domains of self-concept in obsessive-compulsive disorder: Further evidence for a multidimensional model of OCD. *Journal of Anxiety Disorders*, *21*, 433–444.

Doron, G., Moulding, R., Kyrios, M., & Nedeljkovic, M. (2008). Sensitivity of self-beliefs in obsessive-compulsive disorder (OCD). *Depression and Anxiety*, *25*, 874–884.

Dowson, J. H. (1977). The phenomenology of severe obsessive-compulsive neurosis. *The British Journal of Psychiatry*, *131*, 75–78.

Draguns, J. G. (1980). Psychological disorders of clinical severity. In H. C. Triandis & J. G. Draguns (Eds.), *Handbook of cross-cultural psychology, Vol. 6: Psychopathology* (pp. 99–174). Allyn & Bacon.

Egrilmez, A., Gulseren, L., Gulseren, S., & Kultur, S. (1997). Phenomenology of obsessions in a Turkish series of OCD patients. *Psychopathology*, *30*, 106–110.

Eisen, J. L., Goodman, W. K., Keller, M. B., Warshaw, M. G., DeMarco, L. M., Luce, D. D., & Rasmussen, S. A. (1999). Patterns of remission and relapse in obsessive-compulsive disorder: A 2-year prospective study. *The Journal of Clinical Psychiatry*, *60*, 346–351.

Fabrega, H. (1989). Cultural relativism and psychiatric illness. *The Journal of Nervous and Mental Disease*, *77*, 415–425.

Fawcett, E. J., Power, H., & Fawcett, J. M. (2020). Women are at greater risk of OCD than men: A meta-analytic review of OCD prevalence worldwide. *The Journal of Clinical Psychiatry*, *81*(4), 19r13085.

Fernea, E., & Fernea, R. (1994). Cleanliness and culture. In W. J Lonner, & R. S Malpass (Eds.), *Psychology and culture* (pp. 65–69). Allyn & Bacon.

Fontenelle, L. F., Mendlowicz, M. V., Marques, C., & Versiani, M. (2004). Trans-cultural aspects of obsessive-compulsive disorder: A description of a Brazilian sample and a systematic review of international clinical studies. *Journal of Psychiatric Research*, *38*, 403–411.

Fontenelle, L. F., Mendlowicz, M. V., & Versiani, M. (2002). The effect of gender on the clinical features and therapeutic response in obsessive-compulsive disorder. *Revista Brasileira de Psiquiatria*, *24*, 7–11.

Fontenelle, L. F., Mendlowicz, M. V., & Versiani, M. (2006). The descriptive epidemiology of obsessive-compulsive disorder. *Progress in Neuro-psychopharmacology and Biological Psychiatry*, *30*, 327–337.

Foroughi, E., Shams, G., & Kyrios, M. (2007). *Psychometric validation of the Thought-Action Fusion Scale in an Iranian sample* [Poster presentation].Fifth World Congress of Behavioural & Cognitive Therapies, Barcelona, Spain.

French, I., & Lyne, J. (2020). Acute exacerbation of OCD symptoms precipitated by media reports of COVID-19. *Irish Journal of Psychological Medicine*, *37*(4), 291–294.

Friedman, S., Hatch, M. L., Paradis, C., Popkin, M., & Shalita, A. R. (1993). Obsessive compulsive disorder in two Black ethnic groups: Incidence in an urban dermatology clinic. *Journal of Anxiety Disorders*, *7*, 343–348.

Friedman, S., Smith, L. C., Halpern, B., Levine, C., Paradis, C., Viswanathan, R., Trappler, B., & Ackerman, R. (2003). Obsessive-compulsive disorder in a multi-ethnic urban outpatient clinic: Initial presentation and treatment response with exposure and response prevention. *Behavior Therapy*, *34*, 397–410.

Furnham, A., & Chan, E. (2004). Lay theories of schizophrenia. *Social Psychiatry and Psychiatric Epidemiology*, *39*(7), 543–552.

Furnham, A., & Hamid, A. (2014). Mental health literacy in non-Western countries: A review of the recent literature. *Mental Health Review Journal*, *19*(2), 84–98.

Ghassemzadeh, H., Bolhari, J., Birashk, B., & Salavati, M. (2005). Responsibility attitude in a sample of Iranian obsessive-compulsive patients. *International Journal of Social Psychiatry*, *51*(1), 13–22.

Ghassemzadeh, H., Mojtabai, R., Khamseh, A., Ebrahimkhani, N., Issazadegan, A., & Saif-Nobakht, Z. (2002). Symptoms of obsessive-compulsive disorder in a sample of Iranian patients. *International Journal of Social Psychiatry*, *48*, 220–228.

Goodwin, R., Koenen, K. C., Hellman, F., Guardino, M., & Struening, E. (2002). Helpseeking and access to mental health treatment for obsessive-compulsive disorder. *Acta Psychiatrica Scandinavica*, *106*, 143–149.

Grabe, H. J., Meyer, C., Hapke, U., Rumpf, H.-J., Freyberger, H. J., Dilling, H., & John, U. (2001). Lifetime-comorbidity of obsessive-compulsive disorder and subclinical obsessive-compulsive disorder in northern Germany. *European Archives of Psychiatry and Clinical Neuroscience*, *251*, 130–135.

Greenberg, D. (1984). Are religious compulsions religious or compulsive: A phenomenological study. *American Journal of Psychotherapy*, *38*, 524–532.

Greenberg, D., & Witztum, E. (1994). Cultural aspects of obsessive-compulsive disorder. In E. Hollander, D. Zohar, D. Marazzati, & B. Olivier (Eds.), *Current insights in obsessive compulsive disorder* (pp. 11–21). Wiley.

Greenberg, D., & Witztum, E. (2001). Treatment of strictly religious patients. In M. T. Pato & J. Zohar (Eds.), *Current treatments of obsessive-compulsive disorder* (pp. 173–191). American Psychiatric Publishing.

Haidt, J., McCauley, C., & Rozin, P. (1994). Individual differences in sensitivity to disgust: A scale sampling seven domains of disgust elicitors. *Personality and Individual Differences*, *16*(5), 701–713.

Hatch, M. L., Friedman, S., & Paradis, C. M. (1996). Behavioral treatment of obsessive-compulsive disorder in African Americans. *Cognitive and Behavioral Practice*, *3*, 303–315.

Hepworth, M., Simonds, L. M., & Marsh., R. (2010). Catholic priests' conceptualisation of scrupulosity: A grounded theory analysis. *Mental Health, Religion & Culture*, *13*(1), 1–16.

Hermesh, H., Masser-Kavitzky, R., & Gross-Isseroff, R. (2003). Obsessive-compulsive disorder and Jewish religiosity. *The Journal of Nervous and Mental Disease*, *191*, 201–203.

Himle, J. A., Chatters, L. M., Taylor, R. J., & Nguyen, A. (2011). The relationship between obsessive-compulsive disorder and religious faith: Clinical characteristics and implications for treatment. *Psychology of Religion and Spirituality*, *3*(4), 241–258.

Hollander, E., Greenwald, S., Neville, D., Johnson, J., Hornig, C. D., & Weissman, M. M. (1998). Uncomplicated and comorbid obsessive-compulsive disorder in an epidemiologic sample. *CNS Spectrums*, *3*(S1), 10–18.

Hovey, J., Kim, S., & Seligman, L. (2006). The Influences of cultural values, ethnic identity, and language use on the mental health of Korean American college students. *The Journal of Psychology*, *140*(5), 499–511.

Huang, L., Tsai, K., Wang, H., Sung, P., Wu, M., Hung, K., & Lin, S. (2014). Prevalence, incidence, and comorbidity of clinically diagnosed obsessive-compulsive disorder in Taiwan: A national population-based study. *Psychiatry Research*, *220*(1–2), 335–341.

Hunt, C. (2020). Differences in OCD symptom presentations across age, culture, and gender: A quantitative review of studies using the Y-BOCS symptom checklist. *Journal of Obsessive-Compulsive and Related Disorders*, *26*, 100533.

Huppert, J. D., Siev, J., & Kushner, E. S. (2007). When religion and obsessive-compulsive disorder collide: Treating scrupulosity in ultra-orthodox Jews. *Journal of Clinical Psychology*, *63*, 925–941.

Inozu, M., Karanci, A., & Clark, D. (2012). Why are religious individuals more obsessional? The role of mental control beliefs and guilt in Muslims and Christians. *Journal of Behavior Therapy and Experimental Psychiatry*, *43*(3), 959–966.

Inozu, M., Ulukut, F., Ergun, G., & Alcolado, G. (2014). The mediating role of disgust sensitivity and thought–action fusion between religiosity and obsessive-compulsive symptoms. *International Journal of Psychology*, *49*(5), 334–341.

Jaisoorya, T. S., Reddy, Y. C. J., Srinath, S., & Thennarasu, K. (2008). Sex differences in Indian patients with obsessive-compulsive disorder. *Comprehensive Psychiatry*, *50*, 70–75.

Jeon, M., & Furnham, A. (2017). Mental health literacy in South Korea. *International Journal of Culture and Mental Health*, *10*(4), 353–366.

Jobanputra, R., & Furnham, A. (2005). British Gujarati Indian immigrants' and British Caucasians' beliefs about health and illness. *International Journal of Social Psychiatry*, *51*(4), 350–364.

Jorm, A. F., Korten, A. E., Jacomb, P. A., Christensen, H., Rodgers, B., & Pollitt, P. (1997). Public beliefs about causes and risk factors for depression and schizophrenia. *Social Psychiatric Epidemiology*, *32*(3), 143–148.

Jorm, A., Nakane, Y., Christensen, H., Yoshioka, K., Griffiths, K., & Wata, Y. (2005). Public beliefs about treatment and outcome of mental disorders: a comparison of Australia and Japan. *BMC Medicine*, *3*(1), 1–14.

Juang, Y.-Y., & Liu, C.-I. (2001). Phenomenology of obsessive-compulsive disorder in Taiwan. *Psychiatry and Clinical Neurosciences*, *55*, 623–627.

Julien, D., Careau, Y., O'Connor, K. P., Bouvard, M., Rheaume, J., Langlois, F., Freeston, M. H., Radomsky, A. S., & Cottraux, J. (2008). Specificity of belief domains in OCD: Validation of the French version of the Obsessive Beliefs Questionnaire and a comparison across samples. *Journal of Anxiety Disorders*, *22*, 1029–1041.

Karadağ, F., Oguzhanoglu, N. K., Ozdel, O., Ateşci, F. C., & Amuk, T. (2006). OCD symptoms in a sample of Turkish patients: A phenomenological picture. *Depression and Anxiety*, *23*, 145–152.

Karlsson, R. (2005). Ethnic matching between therapist and patient in psychotherapy: An overview of findings, together with methodological and conceptual issues. *Cultural Diversity and Ethnic Minority Psychology*, *11*, 113–129.

Khanna, S., & Channabasavanna, S. M (1988). Phenomenology of obsessions in obsessive-compulsive neurosis. *Psychopathology*, *20*, 23–28.

Khanna, S., Rejendra, P. N., & Channabasavanna, S. M. (1986). Socio-demographic variables in obsessive compulsive disorder in India. *International Journal of Social Psychiatry*, *32*, 47–54.

Kleinman, A. (1977). Depression, somatization and the new "cross-cultural psychiatry." *Social Science and Medicine*, *11*, 3–10.

Kramer, E. J., Kwong, K., Lee, E., & Chung, H. (2002). Cultural factors influencing the mental health of Asian Americans. *Western Journal of Medicine*, *176*(4), 227–231.

Kyrios, M., Bhar, S., & Wade, D. (1996). The assessment of obsessive-compulsive phenomena: Psychometric and normative data on the Padua Inventory from an Australian non-clinical sample. *Behaviour Research and Therapy*, *34*, 85–95.

Kyrios, M., Sanavio, E., Bhar, S., & Liguori, L. (2001). Associations between obsessive-compulsive phenomena, affect and beliefs: Cross-cultural comparisons of Australian and Italian data. *Behavioral and Cognitive Psychotherapy*, *29*, 409–422.

Labad, J., Menchon, J. M., Alonso, P., Segalas, C., Jimenez, S., Jaurrieta, N., Leckman, J. F., & Vallejo, J. (2008). Gender differences in obsessive-compulsive symptom dimensions. *Depression and Anxiety*, *25*, 832–838.

Lee, S., & Suh, J. (2010). Mental health literacy of the Korean public: A comparison between depression and schizophrenia. *Korean Journal of Social Welfare Studies*, *41*(2), 127–158. https://doi.org/10.16999/kasws.2010.41.2.127

Lensi, P., Cassano, G. B., Correddu, G., Ravagli, S., Kunovac, J. L., & Akisal, H. S. (1996). Obsessive-compulsive disorder: Familial-developmental history, symptomatology, comorbidity and course with special reference to gender-related differences. *The British Journal of Psychiatry, 169*, 101–107.

Loo, P., Wong, S., & Furnham, A. (2012). Mental health literacy: A cross-cultural study from Britain, Hong Kong and Malaysia. *Asia-Pacific Psychiatry, 4*(2), 113–125.

Lui, C., Wong, C., & Furnham, A. (2016). Mental health literacy in Hong Kong. *International Journal of Social Psychiatry, 62*(6), 505–511.

Mahgoub, O. M., & Abedel-Hafeiz, H. B. (1991). Patterns of obsessive-compulsive disorder in eastern Saudi Arabia. *The British Journal of Psychiatry, 158*, 840–842.

Marsella, A. J. (1980). Depressive experience and disorder across cultures. In H. Triandis & J. Draguns (Eds.), *Handbook of cross-cultural psychology, Vol. 6: Psychopathology* (pp. 237–289). Allyn & Bacon.

Marsella, A. J., Kaplan, A., & Suarez, E. (2002). Cultural considerations for understanding, assessing, and treating depressive experience and disorder. In M. Reinecke & M. Davison (Eds.), *Comparative treatments of depression* (pp. 47–78). Springer.

Marsella, A. J., & Yamada, A. (2000). Culture and mental health: An introduction and overview of foundations, concepts, and issues. In I. Cuellar & F. Paniagua (Eds.), *The handbook of multicultural mental health: Assessment and treatment of diverse populations* (pp. 3–24). Academic Press.

Matsunaga, H., Kiriike, N., Matsui, T., Miyata, A., Iwasaki, Y., Fujimoto, K., Kasai, S., & Kojima, M. (2000). Gender difference in social and interpersonal features and personality disorders among Japanese patients with obsessive-compulsive disorder. *Comprehensive Psychiatry, 41*, 266–272.

Matsunaga, H., Maebayashi, K., Hayashida, K., Okino, K., Matsui, T., & Iketani, T., Kiriike, N., & Stein, D. J. (2008). Symptom structure in Japanese patients with obsessive-compulsive disorder. *The American Journal of Psychiatry, 165*(2), 251–253.

Matsunaga, H., & Seedat, S. (2007). Obsessive-compulsive spectrum disorders: Cross-national and ethnic issues. *CNS Spectrums, 12*, 392–400.

Moulding, R., Anglim, J., Nedeljkovic, M., Doron, G., Kyrios, M., & Ayalon, A. (2011). The Obsessive Beliefs Questionnaire (OBQ): Examination in nonclinical samples and development of a short version. *Assessment, 18*(3), 357–374.

Moulding, R., Coles, M. E., Abramowitz, J. S., Alcolado, G. M., Alonso, P., Belloch, A., Bouvard, M., Clark, D. A., Doron, G., & Fernández-Álvarez, H. (2014). Part 2. They scare because we care: The relationship between obsessive intrusive thoughts and appraisals and control strategies across 15 cities. *Journal of Obsessive-Compulsive and Related Disorders, 3*(3), 280–291.

Mubarak, A., Baba, I., Heng Chin, L., & Soon Hoe, Q. (2003). Quality of life of community-based chronic schizophrenia patients in Penang, Malaysia. *Australian & New Zealand Journal of Psychiatry, 37*(5), 577–585.

Muris, P., Merckelbach, H., & Clavan, M. (1997). Abnormal and normal compulsions. *Behaviour Research and Therapy, 35*, 249–252.

Nakane, Y., Jorm, A., Yoshioka, K., Christensen, H., Nakane, H., & Griffiths, K. (2005). Public beliefs about causes and risk factors for mental disorders: a comparison of Japan and Australia. *BMC Psychiatry, 5*, 33

Naziry, G., Dadfar, M., & Karimi Keisami, I. (2005). The role of religious commitment, non-adaptive religious beliefs, guilt feelings and non-adaptive cognitive beliefs in the severity of obsessive-compulsive symptoms. *Iranian Journal of Psychiatry and Clinical Psychology (Andisheh Va Raftar), 11*(3), 283–289.

Nelson, E. A., Abramowitz, J. S., Whiteside, S. P., & Deacon, B. J. (2006). Scrupulosity in patients with obsessive-compulsive disorder: Relationship to clinical and cognitive phenomena. *Journal of Anxiety Disorders, 20*, 1071–1086.

Okasha, A., Saad, A., Khalil, A., El-Dawla, A., & Yehia, N. (1994). Phenomenology of obsessive-compulsive disorder: A transcultural study. *Comprehensive Psychiatry, 35*, 191–197.

Pang, S., Subramaniam, M., Lee, S., Lau, Y., Abdin, E., & Chua, B., Picco, J. A. Vaingankar, & Chong, S. A. (2018). The Singaporean public beliefs about the causes of mental illness: Results from a multi-ethnic population-based study. *Epidemiology and Psychiatric Sciences, 27*(4), 403–412.

Paradis, C. M., Friedman, S., Hatch, M. L., & Ackerman, R. (1996). Cognitive behavioral treatment of anxiety disorders in Orthodox Jews. *Cognitive and Behavioral Practice, 3*, 271–288.

Parker, G., Gladstone, G., & Chee, K. (2001). Depression in the planet's largest ethnic group: The Chinese. *The American Journal of Psychiatry, 158*(6), 857–864.

Pascual-Vera, B., Akin, B., Belloch, A., Bottesi, G., Clark, D. A., Doron, G., Fernandez-Alvarez, H., Ghisi, M., Gomez, B., Inozu, M., Jimenez-Ros, A., Moulding, R., Ruiz, M. A., Shams, G., & Sica, C. (2019). The cross-cultural and transdiagnostic nature of unwanted mental intrusions. *International Journal of Clinical and Health Psychology, 19*(2), 85–96.

Picco, L., Abdin, E., Chong, S., Pang, S., Shafie, S., & Chua, B., Vaingankar, J.A., Ong, L.P., Tay, J., & Subramaniam, M. (2016). Attitudes toward seeking professional psychological help: Factor structure and socio-demographic predictors. *Frontiers in Psychology, 7*, 547.

Pourfaraj, M., Mohammadi, N., & Taghavi, M. (2008). Psychometric properties of revised Thought-Action Fusion Questionnaire (TAF-R) in an Iranian population. *Journal of Behavior Therapy and Experimental Psychiatry, 39*, 600–609.

Purdon, C. (2004). Cognitive-behavioral treatment of repugnant obsessions. *Journal of Clinical Psychology: In Session, 60*, 1169–1180.

Rachman, S. (1997). A cognitive theory of obsessions. *Behaviour Research and Therapy, 35*, 793–802.

Rachman, S. (1998). A cognitive theory of obsessions: Elaborations. *Behaviour Research and Therapy, 36*, 385–401

Rachman, S., & de Silva, P. (1978). Abnormal and normal obsessions. *Behaviour Research and Therapy, 16*, 233–248.

Radomsky, A. S., Alcolado, G. M., Abramowitz, J. S., Alonso, P., Belloch, A., Bouvard, M., Clark, D. A., Coles, M. E., Doron, G., & Fernández-Álvarez, H. (2014). Part 1—You can run but you can't hide: Intrusive thoughts on six continents. *Journal of Obsessive-Compulsive and Related Disorders, 3*(3), 269–279.

Rahat, M., Rahimi, C., & Mohamadi, N. (2012). Psychometric properties of the Arabic version of the Obsessive Compulsive Beliefs Questionnaire-44 in a student population. *Iranian Journal of Psychiatry, 7*(4), 184–190.

Rassin, E., & Koster, E. (2003). The correlation between thought–action fusion and religiosity in a normal sample. *Behaviour Research and Therapy, 41*, 361–368.

Rassin, E., & Muris, P. (2007). Abnormal and normal obsessions: A reconsideration. *Behaviour Research and Therapy, 45*, 1065–1070.

Robins, L. N., Helzer, J. E., Croughan, J., & Ratcliff, K. S. (1981). National Institute of Mental Health Diagnostic Interview Schedule. *Archives of General Psychiatry, 38*, 381–390.

Salkovskis, P. M., & Harrison, J. (1984). Abnormal and normal obsessions: A replication. *Behaviour Research and Therapy, 22*, 549–552.

Sanavio, E. (1988). Obsessions and compulsions: The Padua Inventory. *Behaviour Research and Therapy, 26*, 169–177.

Shams, G., Karamghadiri, N., Esmaili Torkanbori, Y., & Ebrahimkhani, N. (2004). Validation and reliability assessment of Persian version of Obsessive Beliefs Questionnaire-44. *Advances in Cognitive Science, 6*, 23–37.

Shams, G., Shams, G., Karamghadiri, N., Esmaili Torkanbori, Y., Rahiminejad, F., & Ebrahimkhani, N. (2006). Obsessional beliefs in patients with obsessive-compulsive disorder and other anxiety disorders as compared to the control group. *Advances in Cognitive Science, 2*, 83–90.

Sharma, B. P. (1968). Obsessive compulsive neurosis in Nepal. *Transcultural Psychiatry Research Review, 5*, 38–41.

Shooka, A., Al-Haddad, M. K., & Raees, A. (1998). OCD in Bahrain: A phenomenological profile. *International Journal of Social Psychiatry, 44*, 147–154.

Sica, C., Coradeschi, D., Sanavio, E., Dorz, S., Manchisi, D., & Novara, C. (2004). A study of the psychometric properties of the Obsessive Beliefs Inventory and Interpretation of Intrusions Inventory on clinical Italian individuals. *Journal of Anxiety Disorders, 18*, 291–307.

Sica, C., Novara, C., & Sanavio, E. (2002a). Religiousness and obsessive compulsive cognitions and symptoms in an Italian population. *Behaviour Research and Therapy, 40*, 813–823.

Sica, C., Novara, C., Sanavio, E., Dorz, S., & Coradeschi, D. (2002b). Obsessive compulsive disorder cognition across cultures. In R. O. Frost & G. Steketee (Eds.), *Cognitive approaches to obsessions and compulsions: Theory, assessment and treatment* (pp. 372–384). Elsevier.

Sica, C., Taylor, S., Arrindell, W. A., & Sanavio, E. (2006). A cross-cultural test of the cognitive theory of obsessions and compulsions: A comparison of Greek, Italian and American Individuals—A preliminary study. *Cognitive Therapy and Research, 30*, 585–597.

Siev, J., & Cohen, A. B. (2007). Is thought-action fusion related to religiosity? Differences between Christians and Jews. *Behaviour Research and Therapy, 40*, 813–823.

Staley, D., & Wand, R. (1995). Obsessive compulsive disorder: A review of the cross-cultural epidemiological literature. *Transcultural Psychiatry, 32*, 103–136.

Steketee, G., Quay, S., & White, K. (1991). Religion and guilt in OCD patients. *Journal of Anxiety Disorders, 5,* 359–367.

Subramaniam, M., Abdin, E., Picco, L., Pang, S., Shafie, S., & Vaingankar, J., Kwok, K.W., Verma, K., & Chong, S. A. (2016). Stigma towards people with mental disorders and its components—A perspective from multi-ethnic Singapore. *Epidemiology and Psychiatric Sciences, 26*(4), 371–382.

Summerfeldt, L., Gilbert, S., & Reynolds, M. (2015). Incompleteness, aesthetic sensitivity, and the obsessive-compulsive need for symmetry. *Journal of Behavior Therapy and Experimental Psychiatry, 49,* 141–149.

Taylor, S., Abramowitz, J. S., McKay, D., Calamari, J. E., Sookman, D., Kyrios, M., Wilhelm, S., & Carmin, C. (2006). Do dysfunctional beliefs play a role in all types of obsessive-compulsive disorder? *Journal of Anxiety Disorders, 20,* 85–97.

Tek, C., & Ulug, B. (2001). Religiosity and religious obsessions in obsessive-compulsive disorder. *Psychiatry Research, 104,* 99–108.

Tezcan, E., & Millet, B. (1997). Phenomenology of obsessive-compulsive disorders: Forms and characteristics of obsessions and compulsions in East Turkey. *Encephale, 23,* 342–350.

Thomas, J., Turkheimer, E., & Oltmanns, T. F. (2000). Psychometric analyses of racial differences on the Maudsley Obsessional Compulsive Inventory. *Assessment, 7,* 247–258.

Torresan, R., de Abreu Ramos-Cerqueira, A., de Mathis, M., Diniz, J., Ferrão, Y., Miguel, E., & Torres, A. R. (2008). Sex differences in the phenotypic expression of obsessive-compulsive disorder: An exploratory study from Brazil. *Comprehensive Psychiatry, 50,* 63–69.

Tsang, H., Tam, P., Chan, F., & Chang, W. (2003). Sources of burdens on families of individuals with mental illness. *International Journal of Rehabilitation Research, 26*(2), 123–130.

Tseng, W. S. (1997). Overview: Culture and psychopathology. In W. S. Tseng & J. Streitzer (Eds.), *Culture and psychopathology: A guide to clinical assessment* (pp. 1–27). Psychology Press.

Tükel, R., Polat, A., Geng, A., Bozkurt, O., & Atla, H. (2004). Gender-related differences among Turkish patients with obsessive-compulsive disorder. *Comprehensive Psychiatry, 45,* 362–366.

Tummala-Narra, P., Li, Z., Chang, J., Yang, E. J., Jiang, J., Sagherian, M., Phan, J., & Alfonso, A. (2018). Developmental and contextual correlates of mental health and help-seeking among Asian American college students. *American Journal of Orthopsychiatry, 88*(6), 636–649.

Wang, J., Wei, Z., Wang, H., Jiang, Z., & Peng, Z. (2015). Psychometric properties of the Chinese version of the Obsessive Beliefs Questionnaire-44 (OBQ-44). *BMC Psychiatry 15,* 188

Washington, C., Norton, P., & Temple, S. (2008). Obsessive-compulsive symptoms and obsessive-compulsive disorder: A multiracial/ethnic analysis of a student population. *The Journal of Nervous and Mental Disease, 196*(6), 456–461.

Wheaton, M. G., Berman, N. C., Fabricant, L. E., & Abramowitz, J. S. (2013). Differences in obsessive-compulsive symptoms and obsessive beliefs: A comparison between African Americans, Asian Americans, Latino Americans, and European Americans. *Cognitive Behaviour Therapy, 42*(1), 9–20.

Williams, K. E., Chambless, D. L., & Steketee, G. (1998). Behavioral treatment of obsessive-compulsive disorder in African Americans: Clinical issues. *Journal of Behavior Therapy and Experimental Psychiatry, 29,* 163–170.

Williams, M., Chapman, L., Wong, J., & Turkheimer, E. (2012). The role of ethnic identity in symptoms of anxiety and depression in African Americans. *Psychiatry Research, 199*(1), 31–36.

Williams, M., Davis, D., Thibodeau, M., & Bach, N. (2013). Psychometric properties of the Obsessive-Compulsive Inventory Revised in African Americans with and without obsessive-compulsive disorder. *Journal of Obsessive-Compulsive and Related Disorders, 2*(4), 399–405.

Williams, M., Debreaux, M., & Jahn, M. (2016). African Americans with obsessive-compulsive disorder: An update. *Current Psychiatry Reviews, 12*(2), 109–114.

Williams, M. T., & Jahn, M. E. (2017). Obsessive-compulsive disorder in African American children and adolescents: Risks, resiliency, and barriers to treatment. *American Journal of Orthopsychiatry, 87*(3), 291–303.

Williams, M. T., Taylor, R. J., Mouzon, D. M., Oshin, L. A., Himle, J. A., & Chatters, L. M. (2017). Discrimination and symptoms of obsessive-compulsive disorder among African Americans. *American Journal of Orthopsychiatry, 87*(6), 636–645.

Williams, M. T., Turkheimer, E., Schmidt, K. M., & Oltmanns, T. F. (2005). Ethnic identification biases responses to the Padua Inventory for obsessive-compulsive disorder. *Assessment, 12,* 174–185.

Williams, M. T., Turkheimer, E., Magee, E., & Guterbock, T. (2008). The effects of race and racial priming on self-report of contamination anxiety. *Personality and Individual Differences, 44,* 746–757.

Willis, H., & Neblett, E. (2018). OC symptoms in African American young adults: The associations between racial discrimination, racial identity, and obsessive-compulsive symptoms. *Journal of Obsessive-Compulsive and Related Disorders, 19*, 105–115.

Woo, C., Kwon, S., Lim, Y., & Shin, M. (2010). The Obsessive-Compulsive Inventory-Revised (OCI-R): Psychometric properties of the Korean version and the order, gender, and cultural effects. *Journal of Behavior Therapy and Experimental Psychiatry, 41*(3), 220–227.

Wu, K., & Wyman, S. (2016). Examination of racial differences in assessment of OCD symptoms and obsessive beliefs. *Journal of Obsessive-Compulsive and Related Disorders, 10*, 10–18.

Yorulmaz, O., Gencöz, T., & Woody, S. (2009). OCD cognitions and symptoms in different religious contexts. *Journal of Anxiety Disorders, 23*, 401–406.

Yorulmaz, O., Yilmaz, E., & Gencöz, T. (2004). Psychometric properties of the Thought-Action Fusion Scale in a Turkish sample. *Behaviour Research and Therapy, 42*, 1203–1214.

Zohar, A. J., Goldman, E., Calamary, R., & Mashiah, M. (2005). Religiosity and obsessive-compulsive behavior in Israeli Jews. *Behaviour Research and Therapy, 43*, 857–868.

INDEX

For the benefit of digital users, indexed terms that span two pages (e.g., 52–53) may, on occasion, appear on only one of those pages.

Tables, figures, and boxes are indicated by *t*, *f*, and *b* following the page number

A

AACAP. *See* American Academy of Child and Adolescent Psychiatry (AACAP)
AAI. *See* Appearance Anxiety Inventory (AAI)
AAQH. *See* Acceptance and Action Questionnaire for Hoarding (AAQH)
ABM programs. *See* attentional bias modification (ABM) programs
Abramowitz, J.S., 22–23, 279, 498, 539, 618–19, 731–32
Acceptance and Action Questionnaire for Hoarding (AAQH), 357–64*t*, 378
acceptance and commitment therapy (ACT)
 for SPD, 657
 for TTM, 657
acceptance-enhanced behavior therapy (AEBT)
 for SPD, 657
 for TTM, 76, 657
accommodation
 family, 435–38
 in OCD assessment, 319–20
N-acetylcysteine (NAC)
 for OCD, 462–63
 for TTM, 649
acquisition
 in self-report measures in HD assessment, 357–64*t*, 371
ACT. *See* acceptance and commitment therapy (ACT)

"activation syndrome," 694
Activities of Daily Living–Hoarding (ADL–H), 357–64*t*, 373–74
ADHD. *See* attention-deficit hyperactivity disorder (ADHD)
ADIS-IV. *See* Anxiety Disorders Interview Schedule for DSM-IV (ADIS-IV)
ADIS-5. *See* Anxiety Disorders Interview Schedule for DSM-5 (ADIS-5)
ADL–H. *See* Activities of Daily Living–Hoarding (ADL–H)
adolescent(s)
 BDD in, 46, 53, 58, 336, 607–8, 695–98 (*see also* body dysmorphic disorder (BDD), in children and adolescents)
 HD among, 85–87
 HD in, 698–700 (*see also* hoarding disorder (HD), in children and adolescents)
 OCD in, 691–95 (*see also* obsessive-compulsive disorder (OCD), in children and adolescents)
 OCRDs in, 690 (*see also specific disorders and* obsessive-compulsive and related disorders (OCRDs), in children and adolescents)
 SPD in, 705–6 (*see also* skin-picking disorder (SPD), in children and adolescents)
 TTM in, 107–8, 109, 701–5 (*see also* trichotillomania

(TTM), in children and adolescents)
adult(s)
 older (*see* older adults)
AEBT. *See* acceptance-enhanced behavior therapy (AEBT)
African Americans
 contamination obsessions and OCD among, 29
 TTM among, 112–13
age of onset
 BDD, 53
 BFRBDs, 111
 HD, 85–87
 nail-biting, 111
 OCD, 30
 SPD, 110
 TTM, 107–8
aging
 cognitive
  in older adults, 670–71
 of population
  OCRDs and, 667 (*see also specific disorders and* older adults, OCRDs in)
Alcolado, G.M., 174
Alexander, J.R., 404–5
ALIC. *See* anterior limb of the internal capsule (ALIC)
Alighieri, D., 73
Alverenga, P.G., 14
ambivalence
 BDD treatment issues related to, 606
American Academy of Child and Adolescent Psychiatry (AACAP)
 on OCD in children and adolescents, 693–94

Anderson, R.A., 514, 516–18, 544
anger
　BDD–related, 52
animal(s)
　genetic studies of, 135–36
animal hoarding, 82–84
　gender ratio, 83–84
　object hoarding vs., 83
　prevalence of, 83–84
　types of, 84
anterior capsulotomy
　for OCD, 483–85
anterior cingulotomy
　for OCD, 482–83
anterior limb of the internal capsule (ALIC)
　stimulation along, 487
antidepressant(s)
　for OCD, 573
　tricyclic
　　for OCD, 452, 454t
Antinoro, D., 99, 647
anxiety. *See also* social anxiety disorder (SAD)
　in older adults, 670–71
anxiety disorders. *See also specific disorders, e.g.,* generalized anxiety disorder (GAD)
　BDD and, 51, 63–64, 339–40
　DSM-5 on, 24
　HD and, 89–90
　OCD and, 19, 26, 423–27
　　assessment of, 423–27
　　differential diagnosis of, 424
　　prevalence of, 423–24
　　treatment implications, 426–27
　OCRDs and
　　neuroimaging of, 160
　　relationship between, 24
Anxiety Disorders Interview Schedule for DSM-IV (ADIS-IV), 424
Anxiety Disorders Interview Schedule for DSM-5 (ADIS-5), 312
appearance
　beliefs about
　　in cognitive-behavioral assessment of BDD, 346f, 347–48
　preoccupation with perceived flaws in
　　BDD–related, 47–48
Appearance Anxiety Inventory (AAI), 195–96, 341t, 342

appraisal(s)
　in OCD assessment, 324–29
　　clinical interviewing, 326–28
　　self-report measures, 325–26
　　thought records, 328–29
Approach-Avoidance Task, 197–98, 201
aripiprazole
　for OCD, 576
assumption(s)
　appearance-related
　　in cognitive-behavioral assessment of BDD, 346f, 347–48
attachment
　hoarding-related
　　assessment of, 357–64t, 376–78
attachment problems
　HD and, 90–91
attention
　HD and, 183–84
　selective
　　BDD and, 191–93
　　SPD and, 201
　　TTM and, 176–77
attentional biases
　OCD and, 177–79, 181
　TTM and, 197–98
attentional bias modification (ABM) programs, 181
attention-deficit hyperactivity disorder (ADHD)
　HD and, 90
augmentation strategies
　for BDD, 602
automatic behaviors
　nail-biting as, 102–3
automatic hair-pulling, 648, 702
automatic nail-biting, 102–3
avoidance behaviors
　in cognitive-behavioral assessment of BDD, 346f, 350
　in OCD assessment, 318
Ayers, C.R., 627–29, 634, 636, 669–70, 675, 680, 681–82, 683

B
BABS. *See* Brown Assessment of Beliefs Scale (BABS)
BAH. *See* Beliefs About Hoarding Questionnaire (BAH)
Barrios-Anderson, A., 473

BATs. *See* behavioral avoidance tests (BATs)
Baxter, L.R., Jr., 558
BDCS. *See* bivariate dual change score (BDCS)
BDD. *See* body dysmorphic disorder (BDD)
BDDE. *See* Body Dysmorphic Disorder Examination (BDDE)
BDD-PSR. *See* Psychiatric Status Rating Scale for BDD (BDD-PSR)
BDDQ. *See* Body Dysmorphic Disorder Questionnaire (BDDQ)
BDD-SS. *See* Body Dysmorphic Disorder Symptom Scale (BDD-SS)
BDDSY. *See* Body Dysmorphic Disorder Scale for Youth (BDDSY)
BDDSY Severity Scale. *See* Body Dysmorphic Disorder Scale for Youth (BDDSY) Severity Scale
BDD-YBOCS. *See* Yale-Brown Obsessive-Compulsive Scale Modified for BDD (BDD-YBOCS)
BDD-Y-BOCS-A. *See* Yale-Brown Obsessive-Compulsive Scale Modified for BDD, adaptation of (BDD-Y-BOCS-A)
BDI-II. *See* Beck Depression Inventory-II (BDI-II)
Beard, G., 14
Beaudreau, S.A., 670–71
Beck Depression Inventory-II (BDI-II), 400
bed nucleus of the stria terminalis (BNST)
　stimulation along, 487
behavior(s)
　automatic
　　hair-pulling as, 648, 702
　　nail-biting as, 102–3
　avoidance
　　in cognitive-behavioral assessment of BDD, 346f, 350
　　in OCD assessment, 318
　body-focused repetitive behaviors (*see* skin-picking

disorder (SPD);
trichotillomania (TTM))
compulsive (*see* compulsive
behaviors)
help-seeking (*see also* help-
seeking behaviors)
hoarding
described, 432
nonsuicidal self-injurious
SPD vs., 105–6
oral
hair-pulling and, 701
safety, 49–51
safety-seeking
in cognitive-behavioral
assessment of BDD, 338*b*,
346*f*, 349
behavioral avoidance tests (BATs),
322–24
behavioral conceptualizations
OCRDs–related, 248 (*see
also specific disorders and*
obsessive-compulsive
and related disorders
(OCRDs), behavioral
conceptualizations of)
behavioral measures
in HD assessment, 379–82
categorization, 380–81
described, 379–80
examples, 381–82
interpretive bias tasks, 381
in OCD assessment, 321–24,
322*t*
direct observation in, 322–24
self-monitoring in, 321, 322*t*
behavioral therapy. *See specific
types and disorders*
behavior disorders
body-focused repetitive (*see*
body-focused repetitive
behavior disorders
(BFRBDs))
belief(s)
appearance-related
in cognitive-behavioral
assessment of BDD, 346*f*,
347–48
CT for OCD–related, 537–38
delusional
BDD–related, 48–49
hoarding-related, 357–64*t*,
376–78
OCD–related
across cultures, 733–37

assessment of, 324–29,
433–34
psychiatric disorders causes–
related, 720
Beliefs About Hoarding
Questionnaire (BAH),
357–64*t*, 376–77
Beliefs Inventory (BI), 733
Benton Facial Recognition Test
(BFRT), 191
Betancourt, H., 717–18
BFRBDs. *See* body-focused
repetitive behavior
disorders (BFRBDs)
BFRT. *See* Benton Facial
Recognition Test (BFRT)
Bhikha, A., 720
BI. *See* Beliefs Inventory (BI)
bias(es)
BDD and
interpretative, 193
visuoperceptual, 190–93 (*see
also* visuoperceptual biases,
BDD and)
HD and
interpretive tasks related
to, 381
OCD and
attentional biases, 177–79,
181
encoding biases, 179
memory biases, 180
visuoperceptual biases,
176–77
TTM and
attentional, 197–98
BIDQ. *See* Body Image
Disturbance
Questionnaire (BIDQ)
biological approaches
to OCD, 473 psychiatric
neurosurgery, for OCD)
(*see also specific procedures
and* neuromodulation,
for OCD
future directions in, 492
modern, 481–90 psychiatric
neurosurgery, for OCD)
(*see also specific procedures
and* neuromodulation, for
OCD
bipolar disorder(s)
OCD and, 26–27, 421
BIQLI. *See* Body Image Quality
of Life Inventory (BIQLI)

biting
cheek- (*see* cheek-biting)
nail- (*see* nail-biting)
bivariate dual change score
(BDCS), 551
Bland, R.C., 675
Bleier, M., 307
BNST. *See* bed nucleus of the
stria terminalis (BNST)
body dysmorphic disorder (BDD),
40, 292–94, 584
in adolescents (*see* body
dysmorphic disorder
(BDD), in children and
adolescents)
age of onset, 53
anxiety related to, 51, 63–64,
339–40, 343–50
assessment of, 334, 591–92
case examples, 338*b*, 346*f*
clinician-administered
measures in, 340, 341*t*
cognitive-behavioral, 338*b*,
343–50, 346*f* (*see also*
cognitive-behavioral
assessment, of BDD)
diagnostic criteria, 336–38,
337*t*, 338*b*
insight in, 342–43
introduction, 334
outcomes measures, 340, 341*t*
OVIs in, 342–43
process measures in, 342
screening in, 335–36
self-report measures in,
335–36
beliefs related to
delusional, 48–49, 63
biological factors in, 586–88
case examples, 42–43, 584,
603–5
causes of, 586–90
biological factors, 586–88
cognitive-behavioral
theories, 589
psychodynamic theories, 588
psychological factors, 588–89
socioenvironmental factors,
590
in children and adolescents, 46,
58, 607–8, 695–98
assessment of, 696
causes of, 696–97
comorbidity of, 697
prevalence of, 695

INDEX | 751

body dysmorphic disorder
(BDD) *(cont.)*
symptoms of, 696
treatment of, 697–98
classification of, 41–42, 591
clinical features of, 47–52
anger/hostility, 52
camouflaging, 50–51
compulsive behaviors, 49–51
compulsive skin-picking, 50
depression, 51–52
distraction techniques, 51
emotional features, 51–52
insight/delusionality of
BDD beliefs, 48–49
preoccupation with
perceived appearance
flaws, 47–48
safety behaviors, 49–51
cognitive-behavioral model of,
590–91
cognitive-behavioral theories
of, 589
cognitive model, 293
empirical support, 293–94
comorbidity of, 54–55
in cosmetic surgery settings,
44–45
course of, 54
criteria for, 40–41
defined, 40–41, 260, 591
demographics of, 46–47
in dermatology settings, 44, 45
described, 6, 24–25, 40–41, 189,
260, 334, 585–86
diagnosis of, 336–38, 337t, 338b
diagnostic features of, 260–64
empirical evidence, 263–64
symptom development, 261
symptom maintenance,
261–63
differential diagnosis of, 339–40
DSM-III on, 42
DSM-IV on, 42, 591
DSM-5 on, 24–25, 41, 42, 591,
683
eating disorders vs., 339
epidemiology of, 43–46
in ethnic minorities, 608
features of, 292–93, 431–32, 695
forms of, 52–53
functional impairment
associated with, 55–56
future directions in, 65
gender ratio, 46, 58–59

historical background of, 41–42
ICD-11 on, 41, 336–38
introduction, 334, 584–85
IP in, 189–96
attention, 191–93
FIE, 191
fMRI, 190
interpretative biases, 193
memory, 193–94
treatment effects, 195–96
visuoperceptual biases, 190–
93 *(see also* visuoperceptual
biases, BDD and)
marital status and, 47
in military and veteran
populations, 45–46
neuroimaging of
emotional paradigms, 157
functional studies, 157
key findings, 157–58
neurochemical studies, 157
resting state studies, 157
structural studies, 157
treatment studies, 157
nondelusional, 63
OCD and, 61–63, 339, 430–32
in older adults, 683–84
in outpatient mental health
settings, 45
PDs with
categories of, 228–29
comorbidity of, 228–29
in course and treatment,
229–30
personality features of
in course and treatment,
229–30
dimensions, 229
phenomenology of, 40–46
prevalence of, 43–46, 64, 335, 585
in psychiatric inpatient
settings, 45
psychodynamic theories in, 588
psychological factors in, 588–89
psychotic disorders and, 63
QoL related to, 55–56
SAD and, 63–64
SAD vs., 339–40
schizophrenia and, 63
social functioning in, 55–56
sociocultural factors in, 59–61
healthcare utilization, 59–61
socioeconomic status and, 47
socioenvironmental factors
in, 590

SPD vs., 105
in special populations, 607–8
suicidality and, 56–58, 606–7
symptoms of
assessment of, 592
treatment of, 592–608
ambivalence about, 606
augmentation strategies, 602
case example, 603–5
CBT, 593–99 *(see also*
cognitive-behavioral
therapy (CBT), for BDD)
challenges related to, 605–7
in children and adolescents,
695–98
depression issues, 51–52,
606–7
E/RP, 597
IBM, 600
insight-related issues, 606
introduction, 592–93
motivation-related issues,
606
pharmacological, 600–2
QoL issues, 607
selection of, 602–3
skills deficits, 607
suicidality issues in, 606–7
technological advances,
599–600
troubleshooting, 605–7
TTM vs., 105
types of, 52–53
body dysmorphic disorder
(BDD) by proxy, 53
Body Dysmorphic Disorder
Examination (BDDE),
195–96
Body Dysmorphic Disorder
Questionnaire (BDDQ),
44, 336, 337t
Body Dysmorphic Disorder
Scale for Youth
(BDDSY), 336
Body Dysmorphic Disorder
Scale for Youth (BDDSY)
Severity Scale, 341t
Body Dysmorphic Disorders
Diagnostic Module, 337t
Body Dysmorphic Disorder
Symptom Scale (BDD-
SS), 336, 341t
body dysphoric disorder (BDD)
described, 24–25
DSM-5 on, 24–25

body-focused repetitive behavior
  disorders (BFRBDs), 102–
  3. *See also specific disorders,
  e.g.,* skin-picking disorder
  (SPD)
 age of onset, 111
 comorbidity with, 116
 cross-cultural features, 114–15
 demographics of, 111–12
 epidemiologic research
  limitations, 107
 functional impairment related
  to, 111–12
 gender ratio, 111
 longitudinal course, 111
 nonclinical forms of, 104
 OCD vs., 102
 in older adults, 684–85
 prevalence of, 107
 psychotic conditions and, 116
 types of, 102–3
Body Image Disturbance
  Questionnaire (BIDQ),
  337*t*
Body Image Quality of Life
  Inventory (BIQLI), 341*t*,
  343
Body Image Questionnaire–Child
  and Adolescent Version,
  696
boredom
 nail-biting related to, 102–3
Boston University, 476–77
Braga, D.T., 546–47
brain
 neurocircuitry of
  OCD–related, 491–92
Brakoulias, V., 28
Brennan, B.P., 451
broad OCD spectrum model,
  21–22
Brown Assessment of Beliefs Scale
  (BABS), 48, 328, 342, 434
Burckhardt, G., 474–75
Buried in Treasures, 621, 630–31
Burton, R., 13
buspirone
 for OCD, 465

C

Calamari, J.E., 11, 667
camouflaging
 BDD–related, 50–51
canine compulsive behaviors
 genetic studies of, 135–36

cannabidiol
 for OCD, 576
Capriotti, M.R., 657
caregiver(s)
 overwhelmed
  as animal hoarders, 84
Carmin, C.N., 667, 677–78
CAS. *See* Compulsive Acquisition
  Scale (CAS)
Cassin, S.E., 248
categorization
 in HD assesment, 185–86
 in HD assessment, 380–81
Cath, D.C., 674, 675–76, 680
Caucasian(s)
 TTM among, 112
CDI. *See* Children's Depression
  Inventory (CDI)
certainty needs
 CT for OCD–related, 536–37
 perfectionism and, 537
CGI scale. *See* Clinical Global
  Impression-Improvement
  (CGI) scale
CGI-S scale. *See* Clinician's
  Global Impression-
  Severity (CGI-S) scale
Chambless, D.L., 436–37, 541
change
 readiness for
  in OCD assessment, 320–21
Chasson, G.S., 633
cheek-biting, 103
 prevalence of, 107
Chia, B.H., 730–31
Childhood Retrospective
  Perfectionism Questionnaire
  (CHIRP), 220–21
children
 BDD in, 46, 58, 607–8, 695–98
  (*see also* body dysmorphic
  disorder (BDD), in
  children and adolescents)
 hair-pulling by (*see* hair-
  pulling, by children and
  adolescents)
 HD in, 86, 698–700 (*see
  also* hoarding disorder
  (HD), in children and
  adolescents)
 nail-biting by, 111
 OCD in, 691–95 (*see also*
  obsessive-compulsive
  disorder (OCD), in
  children and adolescents)

OCRDs in, 690 (*see also specific
  disorders and* obsessive-
  compulsive and related
  disorders (OCRDs), in
  children and adolescents)
 SPD in, 705–6 (*see also* skin-
  picking disorder (SPD), in
  children and adolescents)
 TTM in, 107–8, 109, 701–5
  (*see also* trichotillomania
  (TTM), in children and
  adolescents)
Children's Depression Inventory
  (CDI), 406
Children's Obsessional
  Compulsive Inventory,
  370
Children's Saving Inventory,
  15–item version (CSI–15),
  357–64*t*, 370–71
Children's Saving Inventory
  (CSI), 357–64*t*, 370–71
Children's Yale-Brown Obsessive-
  Compulsive Scale (CY-
  BOCS), 560
Children's Yale-Brown Obsessive-
  Compulsive Scale (CY-
  BOCS) Compulsions
  score, 370–71
Children's Yale-Brown Obsessive-
  Compulsive Scale
  (CY-BOCS) Symptom
  Checklist, 370, 691–92
Ching, T., 727–28
CHIRP. *See* Childhood
  Retrospective
  Perfectionism
  Questionnaire (CHIRP)
Chosak, A., 584
Chou, C.-Y., 630, 635–36
chromosomal rearrangements,
  134–35
CIDI. *See* Composite
  International Diagnostic
  Interview (CIDI)
CIR scale. *See* Clutter Image
  Rating (CIR) scale
citalopram
 for BDD, 601
Clark, D.A., 736–37
Clark, D.M., 507–8
Clark, S.B., 392
Clinical Global Impression-
  Improvement (CGI) scale,
  627–28

INDEX | 753

clinical interviewing
    in OCD assessment
        appraisals-related, 326–28
        beliefs-related, 326–28
Clinician's Global Impression-
        Severity (CGI-S) scale,
        406
clomipramine
    for BDD, 600
    for OCD, 451–52, 453*t*–56*t*
        in children and adolescents,
        694
clonazepam
    for OCD, 464*t*, 464
Cloninger, C.R., 221–22
clorgyline
    for OCD, 464*t*, 464–65
cluster criterion
    in HD diagnosis, 75*t*, 79–80
Clutter-Buddies, 637
Clutter-Hoarding Scale, 357–64*t*,
        372
Clutter Image Rating (CIR) scale,
        357–64*t*, 372, 386, 628
CNVs. *See* copy number variants
        (CNVs)
cognition(s)
    hoarding impact on
        assessment of, 357–64*t*,
        376–78
    maladaptive
        religion and, 731–33
    saving, 291
cognitive aging
    in older adults, 670–71
cognitive-behavioral assessment
    of BDD, 338*b*, 343–50, 346*f*
        appearance-related beliefs/
        assumptions, 346*f*, 347–48
        assessing disliked features,
        345, 346*f*
        avoidance behaviors in, 346*f*,
        350
        case example, 338*b*, 346*f*
        comparing in, 346*f*, 348–49
        developing cognitive-
        behavioral formulation,
        338*b*, 344–50, 346*f*
        developmental history in,
        346*f*, 347
        general assessment points,
        343–44
        general observations, 344
        imagery in, 345–47, 346*f*
        motivation for, 344

    rumination in, 346*f*, 348–49
    safety-seeking behaviors in,
        338*b*, 346*f*, 349
    self-portrait of perceived
        defects in, 345–47, 346*f*
cognitive-behavioral model(s)
    of BDD, 590–91
    of hoarding, 92
    of OCRDs, 279 (*see also specific
        disorders and* obsessive-
        compulsive and related
        disorders (OCRDs),
        cognitive models of)
cognitive-behavioral theories
    for BDD, 589
cognitive-behavioral therapy
        (CBT). *See also* cognitive
        therapy (CT)
    for BDD, 593–99
        advanced cognitive
        strategies, 598–99
        assessment-related, 594–95
        behavioral strategies, 596–98
        in children and adolescents,
        697–98
        cognitive strategies, 596
        introduction, 593–99
        motivational enhancement,
        595–96
        psychoeducation, 594–95
        relapse prevention, 599
    for HD, 619–25
        in children and adolescents,
        700
        cognitive strategies, 624–25
        decisional balance exercise,
        621
        downward arrow technique,
        624–25
        imaginal exposure, 623–24
        MI, 620–21
        motivation, 620–22
        Needs *versus* Wants Scales, 625
        OHIO rule, 622
        psychoeducation/case
        formulation, 620
        skills training, 622–23
        Socratic questioning, 624–25
        thought records, 624
        time-management training,
        622
        in vivo exposure, 623–24
    for OCD
        in children and adolescents,
        693–95

    CT and, 542–45
    efficacy of, 557
    Internet-based, 516–18
    pharmacotherapy with, 557
    sequential treatment with
        SRIs, 567–70, 568*t*
    W-CBT, 516–18
cognitive content specificity
        hypothesis, 281
cognitive flexibility
    HD and, 188
    SPD and, 202
    TTM and, 198–99
cognitive functioning
    in older adults, 670–71
cognitive inflexibility
    OCD and, 421–22
cognitive models
    OCRDs–related, 279 (*see also
        specific disorders, and*
        obsessive-compulsive
        and related disorders
        (OCRDs), cognitive
        models of)
Cognitive Rehabilitation and
        Exposure/Sorting Therapy
        (CREST), 628n, 628,
        683, 685
cognitive remediation (CR)
    for HD, 189
cognitive therapy (CT). *See also*
        cognitive-behavioral
        therapy (CBT)
    for OCD, 527
        CBT and, 542–45
        certainty needs, 536–37
        concealment, 538–39
        control of thoughts in,
        532–34
        described, 531–32
        evolution of, 527–29
        future directions in, 552–53
        inflated responsibility, 534–
        36, 535*f*, 536*f*
        long-term follow-up, 545–48
        mechanisms of action,
        550–52
        overestimation of threat,
        534–36, 535*f*, 536*f*
        perfectionism, 536–37
        psychoeducation, 529–31, 531*f*
        relationship among values,
        beliefs, and intrusions,
        537–38
        RT, 544

TAF in, 532–33
treatment outcome/literature review, 539–45
treatment response prediction, 548–50
vs. wait-listing or E/RP, 539–42
Cohen, A.B., 731
Collyer residence, 74
ComB model. *See* Comprehensive Behavioral (ComB) model
COMMIT, 632
comparing
in cognitive-behavioral assessment of BDD, 346f, 348–49
Composite International Diagnostic Interview (CIDI)
of WHO, 84
Comprehensive Behavioral (ComB) model, 266–67
Comprehensive Meta-Analysis, 560–63
compulsion(s)
defined, 4–5, 19, 673
described, 3–5
DSM-I on, 3–5
mental
defined, 20
Compulsive Acquisition Scale (CAS), 357–64t, 371
compulsive behaviors
BDD–related, 49–51
canine, 135–36
types of, 49–50
compulsive neurosis, 2
concealment
CT for OCD–related, 538–39
confidence
memory, 184
contamination obsessions
among African Americans, 29
disgust in, 297
religion and, 728–31
Continuous Performance Test, 617–18
COPS. *See* Cosmetic Procedures Screening (COPS)
copy number variants (CNVs), 134, 135
Cordioli, A.V., 543, 546–47
Corkin, S., 476–77
cortico-striato-thalamo-cortical (CSTC) circuits, 703

Cosmetic Procedures Screening (COPS), 336, 337t
Cottraux, J., 540, 560
couple-based E/RP
for OCD, 518–19
Cowan, E., 214
CR. *See* cognitive remediation (CR)
CREST. *See* Cognitive Rehabilitation and Exposure/Sorting Therapy (CREST)
Crone, C., 631
cross-disorder relationships
GWASs of OCD–related, 132–33
CSI. *See* Children's Saving Inventory (CSI)
CSI-15. *See* Children's Saving Inventory, 15-item version (CSI-15)
CSTC circuits. *See* cortico-striato-thalamo-cortical (CSTC) circuits
CT. *See* cognitive therapy (CT)
cultural issues
OCD–related, 717 (*see also* culture(s))
assessment of, 317–18, 724–25, 737–38
beliefs, 733–37
contamination/cleaning–related symptoms, 730–31
ethnic identity–related, 727–28
gender differences, 723–24
help-seeking behaviors, 720–23
introduction, 717–19
maladaptive cognition, 731–33
MHL impact on, 720–22
within nations, 726
phenomenology, 28–29, 725–28
prevalence of, 719–20
religion, 728–31, 738–40
treatment of, 738–41
culture(s). *See also specific cultures and* cultural issues
assessment issues related to, 737–38
BFRBDs related to, 114–15
cognitive models of OCRDs–related, 298–99

defined, 717–18
Eastern
TTM, 113–14
HD related to, 88
impact of, 717–19
OCD impact on, 717 (*see also* cultural issues, OCD–related)
phenomenology across, 725–28
SPD related to, 114
TTM related to, 112–14
culture-related syndromes, 25–26
CY-BOCS. *See* Children's Yale-Brown Obsessive-Compulsive Scale (CY-BOCS)
D-cyclosporine (DCS)
for OCD, 571–75, 572t

D

Dams, G.M., 11
Danger Ideation Reduction Therapy (DIRT), 540
DAPI. *See* Dimensional Assessment of Personality Impairment (DAPI)
DASS. *See* Depression Anxiety Stress Scale (DASS)
Davidson, E.J., 682
DAWBA. *See* Development and Well-Being Assessment (DAWBA)
DBS. *See* deep brain stimulation (DBS)
DCQ. *See* Dysmorphic Concerns Questionnaire (DCQ)
DCS. *See* D-cyclosporine (DCS)
Dead Souls, 73
decisional balance exercise, 621
decision-making
HD impact on, 91, 186–87
deep brain stimulation (DBS)
for OCD, 473–74, 486–88
for Parkinson's disease, 487
deep sequencing
of genome, 134, 135
De Lange, I., 518
Delayed Recognition Span Test, 197, 198
Delis Kaplan Executive Function System (D-KEFS), 185–86
Dell'Osso, B., 676
delusion(s)
BDD–related, 48–49

INDEX | 755

Dementia Rating Scale-2 (DRS-2), 677
depression
  BDD–related, 51–52, 606–7
  cognitive inflexibility and, 421–22
  features of, 422
  HD–related, 89
  OCD–related, 26–27, 421–23
Depression Anxiety Stress Scale (DASS), 412, 422
de Silva, P., 725
development
  late-life
    OCRDs related to, 669–72
  OCRDs–related
    cognitive models of, 298–99
Development and Well-Being Assessment (DAWBA), 335
  questions related to, 335
  self-report measures for adults, 335–36
Diagnostic and Statistical Manual of Mental Disorders, ed. 1 (DSM-I)
  on obsessional disorders, 18
  on OCD, 3–5, 11–12
Diagnostic and Statistical Manual of Mental Disorders, ed. 2 (DSM-II)
  ICD-8 and, 18, 23
  on obsessional disorders, 18
Diagnostic and Statistical Manual of Mental Disorders, ed. 3, revised (DSM-III-R)
  on OCPD, 216
  PDQ-R for, 226
Diagnostic and Statistical Manual of Mental Disorders, ed. 3 (DSM-III)
  on BDD, 42
  on obsessional disorders, 19–20
  on OCD, 19
Diagnostic and Statistical Manual of Mental Disorders, ed. 4 (DSM-IV)
  on BDD, 42, 591
  on OCD, 20
  on OCPD, 216
Diagnostic and Statistical Manual of Mental Disorders, ed. 5 (DSM-5)
  on anxiety disorders, 24
  on BDD, 24–25, 41, 42, 336–38, 591, 683

on GAD, 424
on HD, 25, 73, 74–82, 75*t*, 678–79
on OCD, 11–12, 24, 672–78
on OCPD, 216
on OCRDs, 24–26, 144, 174–75, 249, 668, 672–78, 690–91
on SPD, 684
on TTM, 684
Diagnostic Interview for Anxiety, Mood and OCD and Related Neuropsychiatric Disorders (DIAMOND), 312, 336–38, 337*t*, 356–65, 357–64*t*, 393–96, 409–10, 414–15, 424
Diagnostic Interview Schedule (DIS), 719
DIAMOND. *See* Diagnostic Interview for Anxiety, Mood and OCD and Related Neuropsychiatric Disorders (DIAMOND)
Diefenbach, G.J., 399
difficulty discarding criterion
  in HD diagnosis, 74–75, 75*t*
digital photos
  in HD assessment, 382
Digit Span Test, 198
Digit Symbol, 196–97
DiMauro, J., 628–29
Dimensional Assessment of Personality Impairment (DAPI), 229
Dimensional Obsessive-Compulsive Scale (DOCS)
  in OCD assessment, 317
Dimensional Yale-Brown Obsessive Compulsive Scale (DY-BOCS), 131–32, 315–16
direct observation
  in OCD–related behavioral assessment, 322–24
DIRT. *See* Danger Ideation Reduction Therapy (DIRT)
DIS. *See* Diagnostic Interview Schedule (DIS)
disgust
  cognitive models of OCRDs–related, 296–97
  in contamination fear, 297

described, 296–97
dismantling studies
  described, 508
  of E/RP for OCD, 508–10
distraction techniques
  BDD–related, 51
D-KEFS. *See* Delis Kaplan Executive Function System (D-KEFS)
DOCS. *See* Dimensional Obsessive-Compulsive Scale (DOCS)
dog(s)
  compulsive behaviors in, 135–36
Dollard, J., 500–1
Doron, G., 717
Dougherty, D.D., 451, 648–49
downward arrow technique
  HD treatment–related, 624–25
Dozier, M.E., 669–70, 675, 680, 681, 682
DRS-2. *See* Dementia Rating Scale-2 (DRS-2)
DSM-I. *See Diagnostic and Statistical Manual of Mental Disorders,* ed. 1 (DSM-I)
DSM-II. *See Diagnostic and Statistical Manual of Mental Disorders,* ed. 2 (DSM-II)
DSM-III. *See Diagnostic and Statistical Manual of Mental Disorders,* ed. 3 (DSM-III)
DSM-IV. *See Diagnostic and Statistical Manual of Mental Disorders,* ed. 4 (DSM-IV)
DSM-5. *See Diagnostic and Statistical Manual of Mental Disorders,* ed. 5 (DSM-5)
duloxetine
  for OCD, 465
DY-BOCS. *See* Dimensional Yale-Brown Obsessive Compulsive Scale (DY-BOCS)
dysfunctional beliefs. *See also specific types*
  OCD–related
    cognitive theories of, 15–16
dysmorphia
  muscle (*see* muscle dysmorphia)

Dysmorphic Concerns Questionnaire (DCQ), 195, 337t, 432
dysmorphophobia. *See* body dysmorphic disorder (BDD)
dysphoria
  muscle, 52–53
dysthymia
  OCD with, 26–27

E

Eastern cultures
  TTM among, 113–14
eating disorders
  BDD vs., 339
  HD and, 90
ECCS. *See* Environmental Cleanliness and Clutter Scale (ECCS)
ECT. *See* electroconvulsive therapy (ECT)
EEG. *See* electroencephalography (EEG)
Eisen, J.L., 17–18
electroconvulsive therapy (ECT)
  for OCD, 490
electroencephalography (EEG)
  in neuroimaging of OCRDs, 146–47
Emmelkamp, P.M., 518
emotion(s)
  BDD-related, 51–52
  expressed, 436–37
  HD-related, 635–36
Emotional Attachment subscale of SCI, 76
emotional dysregulation
  HD and, 90–91
emotional-processing theory
  E/RP for OCD and, 505–6
Enander, J., 599
encoding biases
  OCD and, 179
endophenotype(s)
  defined, 133
Enhancing Neuro Imaging Genetics through Meta-Analysis (ENIGMA) Consortium OCD Working Group, 133–34, 148–49
Environmental Cleanliness and Clutter Scale (ECCS), 357–64t, 373

E/RP. *See* exposure and response prevention (E/RP)
escitalopram
  for BDD, 601
Esquirol, J.E.D., 2, 14
estradiol
  for OCD, 575–76
ethnic identity
  cultural differences in OCD, 727–28
ethnic minorities
  BDD in, 608
European Study of the Epidemiology of Mental Disorders, 84
EVA Survey. *See* National Epidemiological Catchment Area (EVA) Survey
Eviction Intervention Services (EIS) Housing Research Center, 89
excessive acquisition specifier
  in HD diagnosis, 75t, 81–82
excessive worries
  intrusive obsessional thoughts vs., 20
excoriation. *See also* skin-picking disorder (SPD)
  defined, 236, 264
excoriation disorder. *See also* skin-picking disorder (SPD)
  described, 6
executive function
  HD and, 91, 185–88
    categorization/organization, 185–86
    cognitive flexibility/set shifting, 188
    decision-making, 186–87
    impulsivity, 187–88
    inhibition, 187–88
  TTM and, 198–201
    cognitive flexibility, 198–99
    impulsivity, 199–201
    inhibition, 199–201
Exogenous Cuing Task, 197–98
expectation(s)
  negative
    violation of, 506–7
explicit memory
  OCD and, 179
exploiters
  as animal hoarders, 84
exposure and response prevention (E/RP), 280
  for BDD, 597

    contemporary implementation of, 503–5
    for OCD, 502–3
  described, 498–99
  mechanisms underlying effects of, 505–18
    decontextualizing inhibitory associations, 507–8
    emotional-processing theory, 505–6
    inhibitory learning theory, 506–8
    violating negative expectancies, 506–7
  for OCD, 498
    animal model, 501
    in children and adolescents, 519, 693–95
    contemporary E/RP, 502–3
    couple-based, 518–19
    vs. CT, 539–42
    differential effects of, 508–9
    dismantling studies, 508–10
    early laboratory research, 499–501
    efficacy of, 508–18, 511t, 512t, 529
    family members, 518–19
    group therapy, 514
    historical background of, 499–502
    home-based vs. office-based treatment, 514–15
    ICBT, 516–18
    imaginal exposure, 504, 509
    implementation of, 503–5
    limitations of, 528
    long-term effects of, 510–13
    mental rituals, 513–14
    meta-analytic findings, 510
    in older adults, 678
    patient characteristics, 520–21
    procedural variations, 520
    RCTs, 510–13, 511t
    relapse prevention, 515–16
    response predictors, 519–21
    response prevention, 504
    short-term effects of, 510–13
    situational exposure, 504, 509
    SRIs with, 521
    supportive factors, 521
    technology-assisted approaches, 516–18
    translational research, 501–2
    in vivo exposure, 504, 509
  "reprogramming" vs., 506

expressed emotion, 436–37
eyebrow(s)
  preoccupation with appearance of
    case example, 42–43

F

face inversion effect (FIE)
  in BDD, 191
FAI–H. *See* Family
  Accommodation Interview
  for Hoarding (FAI–H)
Fals-Stewart, W., 511
family(ies)
  E/RP for OCD and, 518–19
  HD impact on
    assessment of, 357–64t,
      374–76
    treatment of, 633
  OCD impact on, 219, 435–38
    accommodation, 435–38
    assessment of, 435–38
    prevalence of, 435
  OCPD impact on, 219
family accommodation, 435–38
  in OCD assessment, 319–20,
    435–38
Family Accommodation
  Interview for Hoarding
  (FAI–H), 357–64t, 375–76
Family Accommodation Scale for
  Obsessive-Compulsive
  Disorder (FAS for OCD),
  319–20, 375–76, 437
Family Impact Scale for Hoarding
  (FISH), 357–64t, 374–75
Family Response to Hoarding Scale
  (FRHS), 357–64t, 374
Fang, A., 584
FAS for OCD. *See* Family
  Accommodation Scale for
  Obsessive-Compulsive
  Disorder (FAS for OCD)
female(s)
  animal hoarding by, 83–84
  BDD in, 46
  HD in, 87
  SPD in, 110
  TTM in, 107–8
FFM. *See* Five-Factor Model
  (FFM)
FIE. *See* face inversion effect
  (FIE)
Fineberg, N.A., 544
FISH. *See* Family Impact Scale
  for Hoarding (FISH)

Fitzpatrick, M., 632
Five-Factor Model (FFM), 221,
  223–24
Five Minute Speech Sample, 437
Flessner, C.A., 392
flexibility
  cognitive (*see* cognitive
    flexibility)
Florida Obsessive-Compulsive
  Inventory (FOCI)
  in OCD assessment, 316, 317
fluoxetine
  for BDD, 600–1
fluvoxamine
  for BDD, 601
fMRI. *See* functional magnetic
  resonance imaging (fMRI)
Foa, E.B., 505–6, 508–9, 510, 513,
  557–58, 560, 564–67
FOCI. *See* Florida Obsessive-
  Compulsive Inventory
  (FOCI)
focused hair-pulling, 648
Foroughi, E., 717
Fournier, S., 248
Franklin, M.E., 99, 647
Freeman, 475–76
Freeston, M.H., 513–14, 532–33,
  542–43
Freud, S.
  on obsessional disorders, 15–16
  on OCPD, 216–17
  psychoanalytic theory of, 15–16
  "Rat Man" case of, 2, 16
FRHS. *See* Family Response to
  Hoarding Scale (FRHS)
Friborg, O., 27–28, 427
Friedman, S., 722, 723
Fromm, E., 74
Frost, R.O., 73, 619, 621, 627–28,
  630–31, 632, 682–83
frustration
  nail-biting related to, 102–3
Frydman, I., 676
Fulton, 475, 477, 482
functional magnetic resonance
  imaging (fMRI)
  of BDD, 190
  of OCRDs, 146–47
Furnham, A., 722

G

GAF scale. *See* Global Assessment
  of Functioning (GAF)
  scale

Gallinat, C., 411
gamma knife capsulotomy (GKC)
  for OCD, 483–84
gamma knife radiosurgery
  (GKRS)
  for OCD, 474
GCTA. *See* genome-wide
  complex trait analysis
  (GCTA)
gender
  animal hoarding by, 83–84
  BDD by, 46, 58–59
  BFRBDs by, 111
  HD by, 87
  nail-biting by, 111
  OCD by
    across cultures, 723–24
  SPD by, 110
  TTM by, 107–8
generalized anxiety disorder
  (GAD)
  DSM-5 on, 424
  OCD and, 423–27
    assessment of, 425–26
    differential diagnosis of, 424
    prevalence of, 423–24
    treatment implications,
      426–27
genetics. *See specific disorders,
  e.g.,* obsessive-compulsive
  disorder (OCD)
genome(s)
  deep sequencing of, 134, 135
genome-wide association studies
  (GWASs)
  of OCD, 129–37
    alternate phenotypes, 130–31
    clinical subtypes/dimensions,
      131–32
    cross-disorder relationships,
      132–33
    described, 129–30
    endophenotypes, 133–34
    pharmacogenetics, 134
    variants, 134–35
genome-wide complex trait
  analysis (GCTA), 130
Ghassemzadeh, H., 729–30,
  734–35
Gilliam, C.M., 626–27
Giraldo-O'Meara, M., 174
GKC. *See* gamma knife
  capsulotomy (GKC)
GKRS. *See* gamma knife
  radiosurgery (GKRS)

Global Assessment of Functioning (GAF) scale, 45
Gogol, N., 73
Go/No-Go task, 186, 187, 200–1
Goodman, W.K., 690
Goodwin, R., 722–23
Grant, J.E., 414, 655–56, 684–85
Greenberg, B.D., 473
Greenberg, D., 729, 739–40
Greenberg, J.L., 584
Greist, J.H., 452–55
Grisham, J.R., 615
group therapy
    E/RP in OCD–related, 514
Guzick, A.G., 690
GWASs. *See* genome-wide association studies (GWASs)

H

Habit Questionnaire
    in SPD assessment, 413
habit reversal training (HRT)
    conceptualization of, 658
    described, 658
    SC techniques in, 652–53
    for SPD, 656–57
        in children and adolescents, 706
        outcome research, 656–57
        overview, 656
        review of, 651–54
    for TTM, 649–54
        in children and adolescents, 703–4
        outcome research, 650–51
        overview, 649–50
        review of, 651–54
hair-pulling. *See also* trichotillomania (TTM)
    by children and adolescents
        duration of episodes, 701
        prevalence of, 106
    defined, 264
    described, 265–67
    focused, 648
    nonclinical forms of, 103–4
    oral behaviors with, 701
    puberty onset and, 701
    sites of, 701
    styles of, 648
        in TTM assessment, 394t, 403–5

unfocused, 648, 702
hair-pulling disorder. *See* trichotillomania (TTM)
Hair Pulling Reward Scale (HPRS), 394t, 403
Hamilton Rating Scale for Depression, 422
Hansen, B., 549
HAS. *See* Hoarding Assessment Scale (HAS)
Hatch, M.L., 723, 740–41
HD. *See* hoarding disorder (HD)
HD-D. *See* Hoarding Disorder-Dimensional Scale (HD-D)
HDE. *See* Humanitarian Device Exemption (HDE)
HEI. *See* Home Environmental Index (HEI)
help-seeking behaviors
    across cultures, 720–23
    MHL and, 720–22
Hiss, H., 552
hoarding
    of animals, 82–84 (*see also* animal hoarding)
    cognitive-behavioral assessment of, 92
    impact on home
        assessment of, 357–64t, 371–74
    impairments related to
        assessment of, 357–64t, 371–74
    intolerance of uncertainty related to, 259–60
    of objects
        vs. animals, 83
    parent report of child, 357–64t, 370–71
Hoarding Assessment Scale (HAS), 357–64t, 368
hoarding behavior(s)
    described, 432
Hoarding Disorder-Dimensional Scale (HD-D), 357–64t, 369
hoarding disorder (HD), 73, 290–92, 615
    ADHD and, 90
    in adolescents (*see* hoarding disorder (HD), in children and adolescents)
    age of onset, 85–87
    animal hoarding, 82–84

anxiety disorders and, 89–90
assessment of, 355
    attachment issues, 90–91, 357–64t, 376–78
    behavioral measures/tasks, 379–82 (*see also* behavioral measures, in HD assessment)
    beliefs, 357–64t, 376–78
    categorization, 185–86, 380–81
    clinical cutoffs, 385
    cognitive features, 357–64t, 376–78
    diagnostic-based, 357–64t, 356–67
    discussion, 383–87
    family impact of, 357–64t, 374–76
    hoarding-related impairment, 357–64t, 371–74
    home conditions, 357–64t, 371–74
    images in, 385–86
    innovations in, 386–87
    interpretive bias tasks, 381
    interview-based, 357–64t, 356–67
    introduction, 355–56
    photos in, 385–86
    self-report measures, 75t, 367–71
    SI-R in, 616
    subjectivity of, 384–85
case examples, 73–74, 619–20
challenges related to, 633–39
    comorbid psychopathology, 634–35
    emotional mechanisms, 635–36
    etiologic heterogeneity, 636
    generalizability, 636
    health problems, 638–39
    improving engagement, retention, and access, 638–39
    insight-related, 638
    motivation-related, 638
    RCTs, 637
    routine outcome monitoring, 637
    safety problems, 638–39
    subtypes-related, 636
    treatment outcomes–related, 634–37

hoarding disorder (HD) (cont.)
  in children and adolescents,
    85–92, 698–700
    causes of, 700
    comorbidity of, 699–700
    parent report, 357–64t,
      370–71
    prevalence of, 699–700
    symptoms of, 699
    treatment of, 700
  cognitive-behavioral model
    of, 92
  cognitive model of, 291–92
    empirical support, 292
  comorbidity of, 89–90
  course of, 87
  cultural impact on, 88
  decision-making impact of, 91,
    186–87
  defined, 25, 257
  demographics of, 88–89
  depression and, 89
  described, 6, 25, 182, 257, 432,
    615–16
  diagnosis of, 74–82, 75t
    cluster criterion, 75t, 79–80
    difficulty discarding
      criterion, 74–75, 75t
    DSM-5 on, 74–82, 75t
    impairment and interference
      criterion, 75t, 80–81
    insight specifier, 75t, 82
    medical condition exclusion,
      75t, 81
    mental disorder exclusion,
      75t, 81
    perceived need to save
      criterion, 75t, 75–79
  diagnostic features of, 257–60
    empirical evidence, 258–60
    symptom development, 257
    symptom maintenance, 258
  DSM-5 on, 25, 73, 678–79
  eating disorders and, 90
  emotional dysregulation and,
    90–91
  epidemiology of, 73
  executive function deficits and,
    91, 185–86
  features of, 90–92, 290–91,
    679–80, 698–99
  gender ratio, 87
  historical background of, 73–74
  intolerance of uncertainty
    associated with, 259–60

introduction, 73–74, 355–56,
  615–16
IP in, 182–89
  attention, 183–84
  cognitive flexibility, 188
  described, 182–83
  executive function, 91,
    185–88 (see also executive
    function, HD and)
  impulsivity, 187–88
  inhibition, 187–88
  memory, 184
  metamemory, 184–85
  organization/categorization,
    185–86
  perception, 183
  processing, 183
  treatment effects, 188–89
loneliness and, 88–89
marital status and, 88–89
neuroimaging of
  cognitive paradigms, 156
  emotional paradigms, 156
  functional studies, 156
  key findings, 155–56
  resting state studies, 156
  structural studies, 155–56
obesity and, 90
OCD and, 28, 90, 430–32
OCPD and, 231–33
in older adults, 88–89, 678–83 (see
  also older adults, HD in)
PDs in
  in course and treatment,
    230–34
  perfectionism and, 91–92
  personality features of, 230–34
    in course and treatment, 234
    dimensions, 233
    PD categories, 231–33, 234
  phenomenology of, 73
  prevalence of, 84–85, 615–16
    in children and adolescents,
      699–700
  PTSD and, 77–78, 90
  socioeconomic status and, 89
  subtypes of
    challenges related to, 636
    symptoms of, 678–80
    clusters, 25
  tax return filing and, 89
  treatment of
    CBT, 619–25 (see also
      cognitive-behavioral
      therapy (CBT), for HD)

  challenges related to, 633–39
    (see also hoarding disorder
    (HD), challenges related to)
  in children and adolescents,
    698–700
  cognitive strategies in,
    624–25
  CR in, 189
  future directions in, 633–39
  improving engagement,
    retention, and access,
    638–39
  improving outcomes, 634–37
  introduction, 616
  pharmacological treatment
    outcome research, 616–18
  psychological treatment
    outcome(s), 626–33
    (see also psychological
    treatment outcome(s),
    HD–related)
  psychological treatment
    outcome research, 618–19
  relapse prevention, 625–26
"hoarding orientation," 74
Hoarding Rating Scale (HRS), 85
Hoarding Rating Scale–Interview
  (HRS–I), 357–64t, 365–67
Hoarding Scale (HS), 357–64t,
  367
Hohagen, F., 564–67
holistic processing
  BDD and, 190–91
Hollander, E., 5–6, 20–22
Home Environmental Index
  (HEI), 357–64t, 373
HOMES Multidisciplinary Risk
  Assessment, 357–64t,
    372–73
Hopkins Epidemiological
  Personality Disorder
  Study, 84–85
hostility
  BDD–related, 52
Houghton, D.C., 407–8
HPRS. See Hair Pulling Reward
  Scale (HPRS)
HRS. See Hoarding Rating Scale
  (HRS)
HRS–I. See Hoarding Rating
  Scale–Interview (HRS–I)
HRT. See habit reversal training
  (HRT)
HS. See Hoarding Scale (HS)
Huang, L., 719–20

Humanitarian Device Exemption (HDE)
  in severely refractory OCD management, 474
Hunt, C., 723–24

I

IBM. *See* interpretation bias modification (IBM)
ICBT. *See* Internet-based cognitive-behavioral therapy (ICBT)
ICD-8. *See International Classification of Diseases,* ed. 8 (ICD-8)
ICD-10. *See International Classification of Diseases,* ed. 10 (ICD-10)
ICD-11. *See International Classification of Diseases,* ed. 11 (ICD-11)
IDED. *See* Intradimensional/Extradimensional Task (IDED)
identity(ies)
  ethnic
    cultural differences in OCD, 727–28
III. *See* Interpretation of Intrusions Inventory (III)
image(s)
  in HD assessment, 385–86
imagery
  in cognitive-behavioral assessment of BDD, 345–47, 346f
imaginal exposure
  HD treatment–related, 623–24
  OCD treatment–related, 504, 509
imperfection
  sense of
    in obsessive-compulsive syndrome, 17
Importance/Control of Thoughts subscale
  of OBQ-44, 326
impulsion(s)
  described, 431
impulsivity
  HD and, 187–88
  SPD and, 201–2
  TTM and, 199–201
Inclusion of Other in Self Scale (IOS), 378

incompleteness
  described, 17–18
  experience of feelings of, 17–18
Inferno, 73
inflated responsibility
  CT for OCD–related, 534–36, 535f, 536f
  pie-charting, 534–35, 535t
  transfers, 535–36, 536f
inflexibility
  cognitive
    OCD and, 421–22
information processing (IP). *See also specific indications and disorders, e.g.,* obsessive-compulsive disorder (OCD), IP in
  in BDD, 189–96
  cognitive models of OCRDs–related, 299
  in HD, 182–89
  in OCD, 175–82
  in OCRDs, 174 (*see also specific disorders and* obsessive-compulsive and related disorders (OCRDs), IP in)
  in SPD, 201–2
  in TTM, 196–202
inhibition
  HD and, 187–88
  motor/response
    SPD and, 201–2
    TTM and, 199–201
inhibitory associations
  decontextualizing, 507–8
inhibitory learning
  optimal, 507
inhibitory learning model, 255–56
inhibitory learning theory
  E/RP for OCD and, 506–8
insanity
  partial
    OCD as, 2
insight(s)
  BDD–related
    assessment, 342–43
    treatment, 606
  described, 433
  HD–related, 638
  measures of, 434
  OCD–related, 433–34
    assessment, 433–34
  poor, 434
insight specifier
  in HD diagnosis, 75t, 82

International Classification of Diseases, ed. 8 (ICD-8)
  DSM-II and, 18, 23
International Classification of Diseases, ed. 10 (ICD-10)
  on OCD, 21, 23
International Classification of Diseases, ed. 11 (ICD-11)
  on BDD, 41, 336–38
  on OCRDs, 144
International OCD Foundation Genetics Collaborative (IOCDF-GC) study, 129–30
Internet
  E/RP for OCD delivery via, 516–18
Internet-based cognitive-behavioral therapy (ICBT)
  for OCD, 516–18
interpretation bias modification (IBM)
  for BDD, 600
Interpretation of Illusions scale
  subscales of, 326
Interpretation of Intrusions Inventory (III), 426
interpretative biases
  BDD and, 193
interpretive bias tasks
  in HD assessment, 381
interviewing
  clinical
    in OCD assessment, 326–28
  motivational
    HD treatment–related, 620–21
Intradimensional/Extradimensional Task (IDED), 199
intrusion(s)
  CT for OCD–related, 537–38
intrusive obsessional thoughts
  excessive worries vs., 20
in vivo exposure
  HD treatment–related, 623–24
  OCD treatment–related, 504, 509
IOCDF-GC study. *See* International OCD Foundation Genetics Collaborative (IOCDF-GC) study
IOS. *See* Inclusion of Other in Self Scale (IOS)

INDEX | 761

IP. *See* information processing (IP)
Islamic cultures
    rituals associated with, 729–30
Ivanov, V.Z., 632

J

Jacobsen, 475
Jacobson, N.S., 626–27
Jacoby, R.J., 22
Janet, P., 2, 41
    impact on OCD research, 16–18
    on OCPD, 216–17
jealousy
    obsessional, 25–26
Jenike, M.A., 451
Jeon, M., 722
Jewish Code of Law, 728–29
jikoshu-kyofu, 25–26
Jones, M.K., 540, 678
Jorm, A., 720–21
Julien, D., 735–36

K

Karadag, F., 730
Karlsson, R., 740–41
K-DISP. *See* Keuthen Diagnostic Interview for Skin Picking (K-DISP)
Kellett, S., 632–33
Kelly, D., 483
Kelly, M.M., 40
Kempe, P.T., 549
ketamine
    for OCD, 463, 576
Keuthen Diagnostic Interview for Skin Picking (K-DISP), 409–10
Keuthen, N.J., 402, 404–5, 409–11
Koster, E., 731
Kozak, M.J., 505–6, 509, 510
Kraepelin, E., 41
Krause, S.C., 174
Kyrios, M., 717

L

Ladouceur, R., 550
Lahoud, A., 392
Laky, Z.E., 584
Lancashire Quality of Life Profile, 438–39
laser interstitial thermal therapy (LITT)
    MRI-guided, 485

learning
    inhibitory
        optimal, 507
LeBeau, R.T., 402–3
Lee, S.M., 690
Leksell, 483–84
Leonhart, M.W., 174
Les Obsessions et la Psychasthéne, 2, 17
Levy, H.C., 379–80
LIFE. *See* Longitudinal Interval Follow-up Evaluation (LIFE)
LIFE-RIFT. *See* Range of Impaired Functioning Tool (LIFE-RIFT)
Lima, 475
limbic leucotomy
    for OCD, 483
Lindsay, M., 511–12
Linkovski, O., 631
literacy
    mental health (*see* mental health literacy (MHL))
LITT. *See* laser interstitial thermal therapy (LITT)
Liu, G., 690
lobotomy
    historical background of, 476–77
loneliness
    HD related to, 88–89
Longitudinal Interval Follow-up Evaluation (LIFE), 54
Loo, P., 721
Lopez, S.R., 717–18
Lui, C., 721
Luyten, L., 487

M

magnetic resonance imaging (MRI)
    in neuroimaging of OCRDs, 146–47
magnetoencephalography (MEG)
    in neuroimaging of OCRDs, 146–47
Mahaffey, B., 22–23
maintenance hypothesis
    in attentional biases in OCD, 177–79
major depressive disorder
    BDD and, 54
maladaptive cognition
    religion and, 731–33
maladaptive perfectionism, 225

male(s)
    BDD among, 46
    OCD among, 30
    TTM in, 107–8
Manis, J., 690
Marcks, B.A., 659
marital status
    BDD and, 47
    HD and, 88–89
Massachusetts General Hospital Hairpulling Scale (MGH-HPS), 394*t*, 399, 400–1, 432, 702
Massachusetts Institute of Technology, 476–77
Mataix-Cols, D., 616–17
"material scrupulosity"
    defined, 78–79
Mathews, C.A., 627, 631
Math, S.B., 30, 31
Maudsley Obsessional Compulsive Inventory (MOCI), 737
Mayo Clinics Anxiety Coach, 517
McKay, D., 279, 498
McLaughlin, N.C.R., 473
McLean, P.D., 540–41, 547
MCMI-III. *See* Millon Clinical Multiaxial Inventory-III (MCMI-III)
MCMI-IV. *See* Millon Clinical Multiaxial Inventory–4th ed. (MCMI-IV)
McNally, R.J., 506
medical condition exclusion
    in HD diagnosis, 75*t*, 81
Medical Outcomes Survey 36-item Short-Form Health Survey, 438–39
MEG. *See* magnetoencephalography (MEG)
Meinert, A., 690
melancholy
    religious (*see* "religious melancholy")
memantine
    for OCD, 462–63
memory
    BDD and, 193–94
    HD and, 184
    OCD and, 179
        explicit memory, 179
        memory biases, 180
        metamemory, 179
    TTM and, 198

memory biases
    OCD and, 180
memory confidence, 184
mental compulsions
    defined, 20
mental disorder exclusion
    diagnosis of
        excessive acquisition
            specifier, 75t, 81–82
        in HD diagnosis, 75t, 81
mental health literacy (MHL)
    across cultures, 720–22
    help-seeking behaviors related
        to, 720–22
mental rituals
    E/RP for
        OCD–related, 513–14
Menzies, R.G., 540
Merritt, O.A., 420
Messerlie, A., 667
Metacognitions Questionnaire,
    677
metamemory
    HD and, 184–85
    OCD and, 179
methylene blue
    for OCD, 575
Meyer, V., 499, 501–2
MGH-HPS. *See* Massachusetts
    General Hospital
    Hairpulling Scale
    (MGH-HPS)
MHL. *See* mental health literacy
    (MHL)
MI. *See* motivational interviewing
    (MI)
MIDAS. *See* Milwaukee
    Inventory for Dimensions
    of Adult Skin Picking
    (MIDAS)
Milby, J., 508–9
military populations
    BDD in, 45–46
Miller, N.E., 500–1
Millet, N., 29–30
Millon Clinical Multiaxial
    Inventory, ed. 3 (MCMI-
    III), 233
Millon Clinical Multiaxial
    Inventory, ed. 4 (MCMI-
    IV), 428
Milwaukee Inventory for
    Dimensions of Adult Skin
    Picking (MIDAS), 397t,
    412–13

Milwaukee Inventory for
    Subtypes of TTM–Adult
    Version (MIST-A), 100,
    394t, 404–5
Milwaukee Inventory for
    Subtypes of TTM–Child
    Version (MIST-C), 394t,
    406–7
Minaya, C., 279
Minnesota Trichotillomania
    Assessment Interview
    (MTAI), 400
mirror avoiders, 261–62
mirror checkers, 261–62
mirror-checking, 261–63
Mirsky, A., 476–77
MIST-A. *See* Milwaukee Inventory
    for Subtypes of TTM–
    Adult Version (MIST-A)
MIST-C. *See* Milwaukee
    Inventory for Subtypes
    of TTM–Child Version
    (MIST-C)
MOCI. *See* Maudsley
    Obsessional Compulsive
    Inventory (MOCI)
Moniz, 475, 477
monomania, 14
    OCD as, 2
mood disorders. *See also specific
    types, e.g.,* depression
    OCD and, 26–27, 421–23
        assessment of, 421–23
        depression, 421–23
        minor bipolar disorders, 421
        prevalence of, 421
        variance in, 421
mood states
    nail-biting and, 102
Moore, John, Bishop, 1–2
Moral thought–action fusion
    (TAF), 532–33, 731
Moritz, S., 650–51, 656
Morselli, E., 41–42
morsicatio buccarum. *See*
    cheek-biting
motivation
    BDD treatment–related, 606
    HD treatment–related, 620–22
motivational enhancement
    CBT for BDD–related, 595–96
motivational interviewing (MI)
    HD treatment–related, 620–21
motivational theory
    of OCD, 23

motor/response inhibition
    SPD and, 201–2
Moulding, R., 717
Mouton, S.G., 651
Mowrer, O.H., 261, 280, 500
MRI. *See* magnetic resonance
    imaging (MRI)
MTAI. *See* Minnesota
    Trichotillomania Assessment
    Interview (MTAI)
Mullen, J.J., 13–14
Multidimensional Perfectionism
    Scale, 224–25
Muroff, J., 355, 626, 631, 632
muscle dysmorphia, 586
    BDD–related, 52–53, 59
    case example, 43
muscle dysphoria
    described, 52–53

N

NAC. *See N*-acetylcysteine (NAC)
nail-biting, 102–3
    age of onset, 111
    as automatic behavior, 102–3
    boredom/frustration and,
        102–3
    in children, 111
    functional impairment related
        to, 112
    gender ratio, 111
    longitudinal course, 111
    mood states and, 102
    nonclinical forms of, 104
    prevalence of, 107
    severity of, 102
    tension and, 102
Nakane, Y., 720
Nakatani, E., 513
National Anxiety Disorders
    Screening Day, 722–23
National Commission for the
    Protection of Human
    Subjects of Biomedical
    and Behavioral Research
    (NCPHS), 476–77
National Comorbidity Survey
    Replication (NCS-R),
    84, 674
National Epidemiological
    Catchment Area (EVA)
    Survey, 719
National Epidemiologic Survey
    on Alcohol and Related
    Conditions, 84–85

National Psychiatric Morbidity Survey of 2000, 27–28
National Study Group on Chronic Disorganization (NSGCD), 357–64t, 372
National Survey of American Life, 29–30
National Vietnam Veterans Readjustment Study, 252
Naziry, G., 733, 734–35
NCPHS. *See* National Commission for the Protection of Human Subjects of Biomedical and Behavioral Research (NCPHS)
NCS-R. *See* National Comorbidity Survey Replication (NCS-R)
Neblett, E., 727–28
Nedeljkovic, M., 717
Needs *versus* Wants Scales, 625
negative expectancies
violation of
E/RP in, 506–7
negative priming effect, 178
NEO-FFI. *See* NEO-Five-Factor Inventory (NEO-FFI)
NEO-Five-Factor Inventory (NEO-FFI), 229
NEO-PI-R. *See* Revised NEO Personality Inventory (NEO-PI-R)
Netherlands Twin Registry (NTR), 85, 130, 680
neurasthenia
symptoms of, 14
neuroablation
surgical
future of, 485
procedures, 474
neuroanatomy
of OCRDs, 143 (*see also specific disorders and* obsessive-compulsive and related disorders (OCRDs), neuroimaging of)
neuromodulation
historical background of, 474–77
for OCD
DBS, 486–88
ECT, 490
future directions in, 492
introduction, 473–74

nonsurgical forms, 474, 488–90
surgical approaches, 485–88
TMS, 452, 453t, 489–90
VNS, 488
neuroscience
cognitive models of
OCRDs–related, 299
improving transparency/replicability in neuroimaging-related, 162
improving treatments through, 162
neurosis(es)
compulsive, 2
obsessive-compulsive, 216–17
DSM-I on, 3
Soteric, 74
neurostimulation
adjustments for, 486
for OCD, 473–74
neurosurgery
for psychiatric disorders (*see* psychiatric neurosurgery)
stereotactic
historical background of, 476
NeuroTrax battery, 189
Newth, S., 538
NE-YBOCS. *See* Yale-Brown Obsessive-Compulsive Scale Modified for Neurotic Excoriation (NE-YBOCS)
Neziroglu, F., 261, 432, 434
NIMH-TIS. *See* NIMH-Trichotillomania Impairment Scale (NIMH-TIS)
NIMH-Trichotillomania Impairment Scale (NIMH-TIS), 394t, 399, 401, 432
NIMH-Trichotillomania Severity Scale (NIMH-TSS), 394t, 399, 400–1, 432
NIMH-TSS. *See* NIMH-Trichotillomania Severity Scale (NIMH-TSS)
Ninan, P.T., 76
NJREs. *See* not just right experiences (NJREs)
NMDA receptor antagonists
for OCD, 571
nonsuicidal self-injurious behavior
SPD vs., 105–6

Norberg, M.M., 615
Nordic Long-Term OCD study (NordLOTS), 567, 574, 659–60
not just right experiences (NJREs), 220
OCD–related, 251–52
OCRDs–related
cognitive models of, 296
NSGCD. *See* National Study Group on Chronic Disorganization (NSGCD)
NTR. *See* Netherlands Twin Registry (NTR)
Nuttin, B.J., 486

O

OAQ. *See* Object Attachment Questionnaire (OAQ)
OAT. *See* Object Alternation Task (OAT)
obesity
HD and, 90
Object Alternation Task (OAT), 198–99
Object Attachment Questionnaire (OAQ), 357–64t, 377–78
object hoarding
animal hoarding vs., 83
OBO-44. *See* Obsessional Beliefs Questionnaire (OBO-44)
OBQ. *See* Obsessive Beliefs Questionnaire (OBQ)
obsession(s). *See also specific types, e.g.,* saving obsession
contamination (*see* contamination obsessions)
defined, 4–5, 19, 673
described, 2, 3–5
DSM-I on, 3–5
religious, 728
ruminations vs., 421–22
saving
in HD diagnosis, 75t, 75–79
Obsessional Beliefs Questionnaire (OBO-44)
subscales of, 326
obsessional disorders
DSM-I on, 18
DSM-III on, 19–20
early conceptualizations of, 13–15

764 | INDEX

early theoretical accounts, 15–18
  Janet's contribution to
    understanding OCD, 16–18
  psychoanalytic theory, 15–16
  psychoanalytic theory of, 15–16
  symptoms of, 14–15
obsessional jealousy, 25–26
obsessional thoughts
  intrusive
    vs. excessive worries, 20
Obsessive Beliefs Questionnaire
  (OBQ), 433, 733, 734–36
obsessive-compulsive and related
  disorders (OCRDs). *See
  also specific disorders, e.g.,
  obsessive-compulsive
  disorder (OCD)*
  anxiety disorders and
    neuroimaging of, 160
    relationship between, 24
  assessment of, 430–32
  behavioral conceptualizations
    of, 248 (*see also specific
    disorders*)
    BDD, 260–64
    diagnostic features, 249–56
    HD, 257–60
    introduction, 248–49
    OCD, 249–56
    SPD, 264–69
    TTM, 264–69
  brain circuits involved in
    model of, 146f
  brief overview, 6
  in children and adolescents,
    690 (*see also specific
    disorders*)
    BDD, 695–98
    future directions in, 706–7
    HD, 698–700
    introduction, 690–91
    issues related to, 706–7
    OCD, 691–95
    SPD, 705–6
    TTM, 701–5
  cognitive approaches to
    understanding, 279 (*see
    also obsessive-compulsive
    and related disorders
    (OCRDs), cognitive
    models of*)
  cognitive models of, 279
    BDD, 292–94
    cultural considerations,
      298–99

developmental
  considerations, 298–99
disgust related to, 296–97
future directions in, 296–99
HD, 290–92
IP and, 299
neuroscience and, 299
NJREs related to, 296
OCD, 279–90
testing and integrating,
  297–98
described, 5–6, 24, 430–31
DSM-5 on, 24–26, 144, 174–75,
  249, 672–78, 690–91
genetic studies of, 127
ICD-11 on, 144
IP in, 174 (*see also specific
  disorders, e.g., obsessive-
  compulsive disorder
  (OCD), IP in*)
  BDD, 189–96
  future directions in, 203–4
  HD, 182–89
  importance of, 175
  introduction, 174–75
  OCD, 175–82
  SPD, 201–2
  TTM, 196–202
neuroanatomy of, 143 (*see
  also specific disorders and
  obsessive-compulsive
  and related disorders
  (OCRDs), neuroimaging
  of*)
  contemporary
    neuroanatomical models,
    145–46, 146f
  importance of, 144–46
  introduction, 143–44
neuroimaging of (*see also
  specific disorders, e.g.,
  hoarding disorder (HD),
  neuroimaging of*)
  approaches and methods in,
    146–48
  BDD, 157–58
  future directions in, 161–62
  HD, 155–56
  improving how and what we
    measure, 161–62
  improving transparency/
    replicability in
    neuroscience, 162
  improving treatments
    through neuroscience, 162

key findings, 148–62
  OCD, 148–62
  SPD, 158–60
  study design, 147–48
  TTM, 158–60
OCD and, 430–32
  commonalities among, 668
  diagnostic distinctions
    between, 431
  treatment implications, 432
OCD spectrum and, 5–6
in older adults, 667 (*see also
  specific disorders and older
  adults*)
  BDD, 683–84
  HD, 678–83
  introduction, 667–72
  OCD, 672–78
  TTM, 684–85
personality features of, 214 (*see
  also specific disorders, e.g.,
  hoarding disorder (HD),
  personality features of*)
  BDD, 229–30
  future directions in, 238–39
  HD, 230–34
  OCD, 214–28
  SPD, 236–37
  TTM, 234–35
phenomenology of, 24–26
sense of imperfection in, 17
symptoms of
  assessment of, 433
treatment of, 449–663 (*see
  also specific disorders and
  treatment methods*)
  OCD, 451–557
types of (*see specific disorders*)
unspecific, 25–26
Obsessive Compulsive
  Cognitions Working
  Group (OCCWG), 283,
  285–86, 325–26, 433
  on perfectionism, 224–25
obsessive-compulsive disorder
  (OCD), 11
  age of onset of, 30
  anxiety disorders with, 19, 26,
    423–27 (*see also anxiety
    disorders, OCD and*)
  assessment of, 307
    appraisals-related, 324–29
    avoidance in, 318
    behavioral assessment,
      321–24, 322t

INDEX | 765

obsessive-compulsive disorder
    (OCD) (cont.)
  beliefs-related, 324–29,
    433–34
  case examples, 307–11, 313,
    314–15, 318–19, 321, 322t,
    322–23, 327
  cultural issues related to,
    737–38
  family accommodation in,
    319–20, 435–38
  functional impairment
    impact on, 318–19
  initial evaluation, 310–11
  introduction, 307–10
  readiness for change in,
    320–21
  self-report measures in, 316–18
  Y-BOCS in, 314–16
BDD and, 61–63, 339, 430–32
behavioral models of, 2–3
beliefs related to
  assessment of, 324–29,
    433–34 (see also belief(s),
    OCD–related)
BFRBDs vs., 102
biological approaches to
  future directions in, 492
  nonpharmacologic, 473
    psychiatric neurosurgery,
      for OCD) (see also
      neuromodulation, for
      OCD
biological models of, 2–3
bipolar disorder with, 26–27, 421
brain neurocircuitry related to
  models of, 491–92
causes of
  different beliefs about, 720
CBT for
  efficacy of, 557
  sequential treatment with
    SRIs, 567–70, 568t
  in children and adolescents,
    691–95
  assessment of, 691–92
  causes of, 692–93
  comorbidity of, 692
  prevalence of, 691
  symptoms of, 691–92
  treatment of, 499–502,
    693–95
classification of
  changes in, 672–78
  DSM-5 on, 11–12

clinical presentations of
  insight levels, 673
cognitive approach to, 531–32
cognitive inflexibility with,
  421–22
cognitive models of, 2–3,
  279–90
  cognitive content specificity
    hypothesis, 281
  contemporary models,
    281–84
  empirical status, 285t,
    289–90
  extending, 283–84
  historical perspective, 280–81
  introduction, 279–80
  predictions derived from,
    285t, 289–90
  Salkovskis's cognitive model,
    281–83
comorbidity of, 26–28, 218–19
  anxiety disorders, 423–27
    (see also anxiety disorders,
    OCD and)
  assessment of, 420
  cognitive inflexibility, 421–22
  mood disorders, 421–23
    (see also mood disorders,
    OCD and)
  OCPD, 427–30 (see also
    obsessive-compulsive
    personality disorder
    (OCPD))
  OCRDs, 430–32 (see also
    obsessive-compulsive
    and related disorders
    (OCRDs))
  PDs, 27–28, 221, 427–30 (see
    also personality disorders
    (PDs), OCD and)
  prevalence of, 420
conceptual models of, 1–3
contamination obsessions and
  among African Americans,
    29
CT for, 527 (see also cognitive
  therapy (CT), for OCD)
cultural issues related to, 717
  (see also cultural issues,
  OCD–related)
defined, 11, 24
depression with, 26–27, 421–23
described, 1–3, 19, 175, 249
diagnosis of, 3–5
diagnostic entities, 217–18

diagnostic features of, 249–56
  empirical evidence, 252–56
  symptom development,
    249–50
  symptom maintenance,
    250–52
differential diagnosis of, 311–13
DSM-I on, 3–5, 11–12, 18–20
  (see also under obsessional
  disorders)
DSM-III on, 19
DSM-IV on, 20
DSM-5 on, 24, 672–78
dysfunctional beliefs associated
  with
  cognitive theories of, 15–16
  rationally derived domains
    of, 283, 284t
dysthymia with, 26–27
early conceptualizations of,
  13–15
epidemiology of, 29–32
E/RP for, 498 (see also exposure
  and response prevention
  (E/RP), for OCD)
exposure-based treatment for,
  498 (see also exposure and
  response prevention (E/
  RP), for OCD)
family impact of
  assessment of (see also
    family(ies), OCD impact
    on)
features of, 691
gender ratio
  across cultures, 723–24
genetic studies of, 127
  in animals, 135–36
  future directions in, 136–37
  GWASs in, 129–37 (see also
    genome-wide association
    studies (GWASs), of
    OCD)
  introduction, 127–29
  research phases, 127–29
HD and, 28, 90, 430–32
historical background of, 1
ICD-10 on, 21, 23
impairment related to, 31–32
insights related to
  assessment of, 433–34
introduction, 420
IP in, 175–82
  attentional biases, 177–79,
    181

encoding biases, 179
memory, 179
metamemory, 179
priming, 178–79
reduced access to internal
    states, 180
treatment effects, 180–82
visual perception biases,
    176–77
Janet's impact on, 16–18
life course of, 30–31
    among males, 30
as monomania, 2
mood disorders with, 26–27
motivational theory of, 23
neuroimaging of
    cognitive paradigms, 149–51
    emotional interference, 153
    emotional paradigms, 151–52,
        152f
    functional studies, 149–54
    habit formation, 153
    key findings, 148–55
    neurochemical studies,
        154–55
    resting state studies, 153–54
    structural studies, 148–49
    treatment studies, 154
NJREs with, 251–52
nonpharmacological
    approaches to
    current landscape for, 477–81
    procedures/practices, 478
    psychiatric neurosurgery,
        473–74, 478–85 (see also
        psychiatric neurosurgery,
        for OCD)
    scientific context, 477
nosology of, 13–29
obsessive-compulsive spectrum
    disorders vs., 11–12
OCPD and
    comorbidity of, 427–30
    co-occurrence, 218t,
        218–19
    familial association, 219
    relationship between, 218t,
        216–21
OCRDs and
    commonalities among, 668
    diagnostic distinctions
        between, 431
    treatment implications, 432
in older adults, 672–78 (see also
    older adults, OCD in)

as partial insanity, 2
PDs in (see personality disorders
    (PDs), OCD and)
personality dimensions of,
    221–24
personality features of, 214–28
    in course and treatment,
        225–28
    OCPD-related, 216–21,
        218t
    PD categories, 214–16 (see
        also obsessive-compulsive
        personality disorder
        (OCPD))
    perfectionism, 224–25
    schizotypal PD–related, 221
pharmacotherapy for, 451, 557
    alternative monotherapies,
        463–65, 464t
    antidepressants, 573
    CBT with, 557
    clomipramine, 451–52,
        453t–56t
    contemporary treatment,
        452, 453t
    first-line treatment, 452–58,
        454t, 456t
    introduction, 451–52
    new agents, 575–76
    new medication possibilities,
        570–76, 572t
    non-placebo-controlled
        trials, 456t
    placebo-controlled trials,
        454t
    psychological treatments
        with, 557, 561t, 563f–66f
    second-line treatment,
        458–65, 459t
    SRI augmentation, 458–65,
        459t
    SRIs, 452–65, 453t–59t
    SSRIs, 451–52
    TCAs, 452, 454t
phenomenology of, 13–29
    comorbidity, 26–28
    culture/individual
        differences, 28–29
    early conceptualizations, 13–15
    early theoretical accounts, 15–18
    future directions in, 32–33
    OCD spectrum, 20–23 (see
        also obsessive-compulsive
        disorder (OCD)
        spectrum)

OCRDs, 24–26
psychiatric disorder
    taxonomy, 18–20
symptom types, 28–29
prevalence of, 29–30, 499
    across cultures, 719–20
psychotic disorders with, 27
QoL with, 438–39
relationship effects of, 32
schizophrenia spectrum
    disorders with, 27
schizophrenia with, 27
schizotypal PD and
    relationship between, 221
social functioning effects of, 32
SPD and
    diagnostic distinction, 105–6
spectrum of, 20–23 (see also
    obsessive-compulsive
    disorder (OCD) spectrum)
SUDs with, 27
suicide related to, 32
symptoms of, 14–15, 279 (see
    also obsessive-compulsive
    disorder (OCD),
    assessment of)
    assessment of, 307
    as rituals in religion, 728–29
treatment of
    behavioral therapy, 451–52,
        453t
    biological approaches to, 473
    psychiatric neurosurgery,
        for OCD); (see also
        neuromodulation, for
        OCD
    in children and adolescents,
        693–95
    CT, 527 (see also cognitive
        therapy (CT), for OCD)
    E/RP, 498 (see also exposure
        and response prevention
        (E/RP), for OCD)
    introduction, 473–74
    neuroablation, 474
    neuromodulation, 473 (see
        also neuromodulation, for
        OCD)
    pharmacological, 451 (see
        also obsessive-compulsive
        disorder (OCD),
        pharmacotherapy for)
    psychiatric neurosurgery,
        473 (see also psychiatric
        neurosurgery, for OCD)

INDEX | 767

obsessive-compulsive disorder
(OCD) (cont.)
RCTs in, 510–13, 511t
religious factors in, 738–40
TMS, 452, 453t, 489–90
TTM and
diagnostic distinction, 105–6,
430–32
obsessive-compulsive disorder
(OCD) spectrum, 24–26
broad OCD spectrum model,
21–22
culture-related syndromes, 25–26
described, 11–12
disorders within, 5–6
OCD vs., 11–12
OCRDs and, 5–6
"other specified OCRD," 25–26
phenomenology of, 20–23
"unspecific OCRD," 25–26
Obsessive-Compulsive
Inventory–Child Version
(OCI–CV) Hoarding
factor, 370
Obsessive-Compulsive
Inventory–Revised (OCI-
R), 357–64t, 369–70
in OCD assessment, 316
obsessive-compulsive neurosis,
216–17
DSM-I on, 3
obsessive-compulsive personality
disorder (OCPD)
comorbidity of, 218–19
described, 214–15
diagnostic entities, 217–18
DSM-III-R on, 216
DSM-IV on, 216
DSM-5 on, 216
HD and, 231–33
OCD and
comorbidity of, 427–30
co-occurrence, 218t,
218–19
familial association, 219
relationship between, 218t,
216–21
personality features of, 214–28
BDD, 228–30
in course and treatment,
225–28
prevalence of, 216, 219
symptom presentations, 217
obsessive-compulsive reaction
described, 18

DSM-I on, 3
within psychoneurotic
disorders, 18
OCCWG. See Obsessive
Compulsive Cognitions
Working Group
(OCCWG)
OCD. See obsessive-compulsive
disorder (OCD)
OCD Collaborative Genetic
Association Study
(OCGAS), 130
OCGAS. See OCD Collaborative
Genetic Association Study
(OCGAS)
OCI–CV Hoarding factor. See
Obsessive-Compulsive
Inventory–Child Version
(OCI–CV) Hoarding factor
OCI-R. See Obsessive-
Compulsive Inventory–
Revised (OCI-R)
O'Connor, K., 543–44, 629
OCPD. See obsessive-compulsive
personality disorder
(OCPD)
OCRDs. See obsessive-
compulsive and related
disorders (OCRDs)
O'Flaherty, V.M., 13
O'Hara, R., 670–71
OHIO rule. See "only handle it
once" (OHIO) rule
Okasha, A., 729
olanzapine
for TTM, 649
Olatunji, B.O., 551
older adults
aging impact on, 667–69
BDD in, 683–84
BFRBDs in, 684–85
happiness of, 671–72
HD in, 88–89, 678–83
described, 678–80
developmental progression
of, 681–82
prevalence of, 680–81
protective factors, 682
psychosocial treatment for,
682–83
risk factors, 682
late-life development changes
in, 669–72
anxiety, 670–71
cognitive aging, 670–71

cognitive functioning,
670–71
happiness, 671–72
mental health problems in
causes of, 669–70
OCD in, 672–78
E/RP for, 678
onset of, 675–76
prevalence of, 674–75
protective factors, 676–77
psychosocial treatment for,
677–78
risk factors, 676–77
symptoms, 674
OCRDs in, 667 (see also specific
disorders, e.g., hoarding
disorder (HD))
DMS-5 on, 668
introduction, 667–69
late-life development
changes and, 669–72
SPD in, 684–85
TTM in, 684–85
online treatment
HD–related, 632
"only handle it once" (OHIO)
rule, 622
onychophagia, 102–3. See also
nail-biting
oral behaviors
hair-pulling and, 701
Orzack, M., 476–77
Öst, L.G., 527–28, 545, 549–50,
678
"other specified OCRD," 25–26
outpatient mental health settings
BDD in, 45
overvalued ideas (OVIs)
in BDD assessment, 342–43
Overvalued Ideas Scale (OVIS),
337t, 342, 434
Overvalued Ideation Scale, 328
OVIs. See overvalued ideas
(OVIs)
OVIS. See Overvalued Ideas Scale
(OVIS)
Ownby, R., 669n.1
oxytocin
for OCD, 575

P

Padua Inventory–Revised and
Washington State University
Revision (PI-WSUR)
in OCD assessment, 316–17

Papez, 475–76
Parent Report on Child's Anxiety Symptoms (PROCAS), 406
Parkinson's disease
  DBS in, 487
PASAT, 197
Pascual-Vera, B., 736–37
PDQ-R. *See* Personality Diagnostic Questionnaire (PDQ-R)
PDs. *See* personality disorders (PDs)
Pediatric OCD Treatment Study (POTS I), 564–67
Perceived Criticism Measure, 437
perceived defects
  self-portrait of
    in cognitive-behavioral assessment of BDD, 345–47, 346f
perceived need to save criterion
  in HD diagnosis, 75–79, 75t
perception
  HD and, 183
  TTM and, 196
Perceptual Categorization Task, 185–86
perfectionism
  described, 224–25
  HD and, 91–92
  maladaptive, 225
  need for certainty and, 537
  OCCWG on, 224–25
  OCD–related, 224–25
    CT for, 536–37
personality
  FFM of, 221, 223–24
  psychobiological model of, 221–22
  unified biosocial model of, 221–22
Personality Diagnostic Questionnaire (PDQ-R)
  for DSM-III-R, 226
personality disorders (PDs). *See also specific disorders, e.g.,* hoarding disorder (HD)
  HD and, 230–34
  OCD and, 27–28, 214–28, 427–30
    assessment of, 427–30
    categories of, 214–16
    course of, 225–28
    prevalence of, 427

symptom overlap, 427–28
treatment implications, 225–28, 428–30
schizotypal
  OCD and, 221
  SPD and, 229–30, 237
  TTM and, 234, 235
PET. *See* positron emission tomography (PET)
PFIT. *See* Positive Family Interaction Therapy (PFIT)
pharmacotherapy
  for BDD, 600–2
  in children and adolescents, 697–98
  CBT and
    for OCD, 557
  for OCD, 451 (*see also specific agents and* obsessive-compulsive disorder (OCD), pharmacotherapy for)
  for SPD, 655–56, 658–60
    in children and adolescents, 706
    development of, 658–60
  for TTM, 648–49, 658–60
    in children and adolescents, 704–5
    development of, 658–60
phenelzine
  for OCD, 464–65, 464t
Phillips, K.A., 40, 683–84
photo(s)
  digital
    in HD assessment, 382
  in HD assessment, 385–86
  in SPD assessment, 414
photographic instrument (PI)
  in SPD assessment, 413–14
PI. *See* photographic instrument (PI)
pie-charting
  inflated responsibility–related, 534–35, 535t
Pinto, A., 214, 427–28
PITS. *See* Psychiatric Institute Trichotillomania Scale (PITS)
PI-WSUR. *See* Padua Inventory–Revised and Washington State University Revision (PI-WSUR)
Plyushkin syndrome, 74

Pollard, C.A., 320–21
Pool, J.L., 486
Positive Family Interaction Therapy (PFIT), 437
positive priming effect, 178
positron emission tomography (PET)
  in neuroimaging of OCRDs, 146–47
"possible self," 76
Postlethwaite, A., 680–81
posttraumatic stress disorder (PTSD)
  HD and, 77–78, 90
POTS I. *See* Pediatric OCD Treatment Study (POTS I)
Pourfaraj, M., 734–35
Pozza, A., 655
Preston, S.D., 379
priming
  OCD and, 178–79
PROCAS. *See* Parent Report on Child's Anxiety Symptoms (PROCAS)
processing
  HD and, 183
processing speed
  TTM and, 196–97
Prouvost, C., 677
psychasthenia
  defined, 17
psychiatric disorder(s)
  causes of
    different beliefs about, 720
psychiatric disorder taxonomy
  OCD in, 18–20
Psychiatric Genetics Consortium
  OCD sample, 131
psychiatric inpatient setting
  BDD in, 45
Psychiatric Institute Trichotillomania Scale (PITS), 394t, 399–400
psychiatric neurosurgery
  for OCD, 473–74, 478–85
    anterior capsulotomy, 483–85
    anterior cingulotomy, 482–83
    future directions in, 485, 492
    introduction, 473–74
    lesion procedures, 481–85
    limbic leucotomy, 483
    patient selection for, 478–81
    subcaudate tractotomy, 481–82

INDEX | 769

Psychiatric Status Rating Scale for BDD (BDD-PSR), 340, 341*t*
psychoanalytic theory
  Freud's, 15–16
  of obsessional disorders, 15–16
psychoeducation
  CBT for BDD–related, 594–95
  CT–related, 529–31, 531*f*
  HD treatment–related, 620
psychological treatment outcome(s)
  HD–related, 618–19, 626–33
    adjunctive in-home support provided by nonprofessionals, 631
    in family members, 633
    online treatment, 632
    provided by nonprofessionals, 630–31
    in special populations, 632–33
Psychology Experiment Building Language Continuous Performance Test, 187
psychoneurotic disorders
  obsessive-compulsive reaction within, 18
psychosis(es)
  BDD and, 63
  BFRBDs and, 116
  TTM and, 116
psychosocial treatment
  in older adults
    for HD, 682–83
    for OCD, 677–78
psychosurgery. *See also* psychiatric neurosurgery
  term of, 475
Psychosurgery Advisory Board, 476–77
Psychosurgery Review Board, 476–77
psychotic disorders
  BDD and, 63
  OCD with, 27
PTSD. *See* posttraumatic stress disorder (PTSD)
puberty
  hair-pulling related to, 701
Purdon, C., 420, 739
Puusepp, L., 475

Q
QoL. *See* quality of life (QoL)
Quality of Life Enjoyment and Satisfaction Questionnaire, 438–39

quality of life (QoL)
  BDD–related, 55–56, 607
  OCD–related, 438–39
question(s)
  Socratic
    HD treatment–related, 624–25

R
Rachman, S., 15–16, 538, 548, 718, 731
Radomsky, A.S., 174, 431
Rahat, M., 735–36
Rahman, O., 651
randomized clinical trials (RCTs)
  in HD treatment, 637
  in OCD treatment, 510–13, 511*t*
  in TTM treatment, 704
Range of Impaired Functioning Tool (LIFE-RIFT), 438–39
Rapid Visual Information Processing Task, 196–97
RAS. *See* Responsibility Attitudes Scale (RAS)
Rasmussen, S.A., 17–18, 484
Rassin, E., 731
"Rat Man" case
  Freud's, 2, 16
Rauch, S.L., 451
RAVLT. *See* Rey's Auditory-Verbal Learning Test (RAVLT)
RBANS. *See* Repeatable Battery for the Assessment of Neuropsychological Status (RBANS)
RCFT. *See* Rey-Osterrieth Complex Figure Test (RCFT)
RCTs. *See* randomized clinical trials (RCTs)
readiness for change
  in OCD assessment, 320–21
Rector, N.A., 248, 544–45
Rees, C.S., 514, 544
Regey, R., 248
relationship(s)
  cross-disorder
    GWASs of OCD–related, 132–33
  OCD impact on, 32
Relationship between Self and Items (RSI) Scale, 357–64*t*, 378
relaxation therapy (RT)
  for OCD, 544

relief
  sensation of
    skin-picking and, 705
religion
  contamination obsessions and, 728–31
  maladaptive cognition and, 731–33
  OCD across cultures related to, 728–31
  treatment issues, 738–40
"religious melancholy"
  described, 13
  scrupulosity as, 1–2
religious obsessions, 728
remediation
  cognitive
    for HD, 189
Repeatable Battery for the Assessment of Neuropsychological Status (RBANS), 194
repetitive behavior disorders
  body focused (*see* body-focused repetitive behavior disorders (BFRBDs))
"reprogramming"
  E/RP vs., 506
rescuers
  as animal hoarders, 84
responsibility(ies)
  inflated (*see* inflated responsibility)
Responsibility Attitudes Scale (RAS), 734–35
Responsibility Interpretation Questionnaire (RIQ), 734–35
Responsibility subscale
  of SCI, 78
responsibility transfers
  inflated responsibility–related, 535–36
Ressler, K.J., 571
Revised NEO Personality Inventory (NEO-PI-R), 223
Revised SIDP for DSM-IV (SIDP-R), 215–16
Rey-Osterrieth Complex Figure Test (RCFT), 190, 193, 194
Rey's Auditory-Verbal Learning Test (RAVLT), 193
Rhéaume, J., 550
Ricketts, E.J., 99, 647

RIQ. *See* Responsibility
    Interpretation
    Questionnaire (RIQ)
ritual(s)
    Islamic cultures–related,
        729–30
    mental
        E/RP for, 513–14
    OCD across cultures related to,
        728–31
    OCD symptoms and, 728–29
Robichaud, M., 527
Rodriguez, C.I., 618
Rosen, J.C., 593
Rowa, K., 514–15
RSI Scale. *See* Relationship
    between Self and Items
    (RSI) Scale
RT. *See* relaxation therapy (RT)
Rück, C., 484
Rufer, M., 650–51
rumination(s)
    in cognitive-behavioral
        assessment of BDD, 346*f*,
        348–49
    obsessions vs., 421–22

S

SAD. *See* social anxiety disorder
    (SAD)
safety behaviors
    BDD–related, 49–51
safety issues
    HD–related, 638–39
safety-seeking behaviors
    in cognitive-behavioral
        assessment of BDD, 338*b*,
        346*f*, 349
Saint Alphonsus Liguori, 13
Salkovskis, P.M., 429–30, 534–35,
    618–19
    cognitive model of, 281–83
Samuels, J.E., 127, 680
Sarac, S., 667
SAS-SR. *See* Social Adjustment
    Scale–Self-Report
    (SAS-SR)
saving cognitions, 291
Saving Cognitions Inventory
    (SCI), 357–64*t*, 376
    Emotional Attachment
        subscale of, 76
    Responsibility subscale of, 78
Saving Inventory–Revised (SI–R),
    357–64*t*, 367–68, 432, 616

saving obsession
    in HD diagnosis, 75–79, 75*t*
Saxena, S., 617
Schedule for Nonadaptive and
    Adaptive Personality
    (SNAP), 428
Schienle, A., 101–2, 655
schizophrenia
    BDD and, 63
    OCD with, 27
schizophrenia spectrum disorders
    OCD with, 27
schizotypal PD
    OCD and, 221
Schneider, S.C., 690
Schulchan Aruch, 728–29
SCI. *See* Saving Cognitions
    Inventory (SCI)
SCID. *See* Structured Clinical
    Interview for DSM-IV
    (SCID)
SCID-5. *See* Structured Clinical
    Interview for DSM-5
    (SCID-5)
SCID-II. *See* Structured Clinical
    Interview for DSM-III-
    R Axis II Personality
    Disorders (SCID-II)
SCID-I/P. *See* Structured Clinical
    Interview for DSM-IV
    Axis I Disorders–Patient
    Edition (SCID-I/P)
SCID-5-PD. *See* Structured
    Clinical Interview for
    DSM-5 Personality
    Disorders (SCID-5-PD)
scrupulosity
    described, 1–2
    "material," 78–79
    symptoms of, 13–14
    treatment of, 13–14
SC techniques. *See* stimulus
    control (SC) techniques
SDS. *See* Sheehan Disability Scale
    (SDS)
Seaman, C., 618–19
selective attention
    BDD and, 191–93
selective serotonin reuptake
    inhibitors (SSRIs)
    for OCD, 451–52
        in children and adolescents,
            693–94, 695
self(ves)
    "possible," 76

self-monitoring
    in OCD–related behavioral
        assessment, 321, 322*t*
self-report measures
    in BDD assessment
        for adolescents, 336
        for adults, 335–36
        DSM-5 on, 336
        ICD-11 on, 336
    in HD assessment, 75*t*, 367–71
        acquisition, 357–64*t*, 371
        parent report of child
            hoarding, 357–64*t*, 370–71
    in OCD assessment, 316–18
        appraisals-related, 325–26
        beliefs-related, 325–26
        cross-cultural validity of,
            317–18
    in SPD assessment, 397*t*,
        410–13
    in TTM assessment, 394*t*,
        401–3
sensation of relief
    skin-picking and, 705
sense of imperfection
    in obsessive-compulsive
        syndromes, 17
serotonin-nonepinephrine
    reuptake inhibitors
    (SNRIs)
    for BDD, 602
    for OCD, 465
serotonin reuptake inhibitors
    (SRIs)
    for BDD, 601–2
    for OCD, 452–65, 453*t*–59*t*
        E/RP with, 521
        sequential treatment with
            CBT, 567–70, 568*t*
set shifting
    HD and, 188
Shams, G., 734–35
Shareh, H., 650–51
Sharma, E., 30, 31
Sheehan Disability Scale (SDS),
    412, 438–39
Sheth, S.A., 482
shubo-kyofu, 25–26
Sica, C., 732, 734
SIDP. *See* Structured Interview
    for the DSM-III
    Personality Disorders
    (SIDP)
SIDP-R. *See* Revised SIDP for
    DSM-IV (SIDP-R)

INDEX | 771

Siev, J., 731
SIHD. *See* Structured Interview for Hoarding Disorder (SIHD)
Simpson, H.B., 513, 560
single-photon emission computed tomography (SPECT)
  in neuroimaging of OCRDs, 146–47
SI–R. *See* Saving Inventory–Revised (SI–R)
situational exposure
  in OCD treatment, 504, 509
16-item Responsibility Threat Estimation subscale
  of OBQ-44, 326
skin-picking. *See also* skin-picking disorder (SPD)
  compulsive
    BDD–related, 50
  nonclinical forms of, 104
  sensation of relief associated with, 705
  sites of, 654–55
  styles of, 655
Skin Picking Disorder–Dimensional Scale (SPD–D), 397t, 411
skin-picking disorder (SPD), 99, 295, 647
  age of onset, 110
  assessment of, 397t, 408–15
    complementary strategies, 413–14
    diagnostic-related, 409–10
    future directions in, 414–15
    Habit Questionnaire in, 413
    introduction, 408–9
    photos in, 414
    physician evaluation, 409
    PI in, 413–14
    self-report measures, 397t, 410–13
  BDD vs., 105
  in children and adolescents, 705–6
    assessment of, 705
    causes of, 706
    comorbidity of, 705
    prevalence of, 705
    symptoms of, 705
    treatment of, 706
  cognitive model of, 295
    empirical support, 295
  comorbidity of, 115–16
  cross-cultural features, 114
  defined, 101, 264, 654
  demographics of, 110–11
  described, 6, 101–2, 201, 264–65, 392–93
  diagnostic criteria for, 25
  diagnostic features of, 101–2, 264–69
    empirical evidence, 267–69
    symptom development, 265
    symptom maintenance, 266–67
  DSM-5 on, 684
  epidemiologic research limitations, 107
  features of, 295, 705
  functional impairment related to, 110–11
  gender ratio, 110
  healthcare utilization, 111
  introduction, 647
  IP in
    attention, 201
    cognitive flexibility, 202
    impulsivity, 201–2
    motor/response inhibition, 201–2
    treatment effects, 202
  longitudinal course, 110
  neuroimaging of
    cognitive paradigms, 159
    emotional paradigms, 159
    functional studies, 159
    key findings, 158–60
    resting state studies, 159
    structural studies, 158–59
  nonsuicidal self-injurious behavior vs., 105–6
  OCD and, 430–32
    diagnostic distinction, 105–6
  in older adults, 684–85
  PDs in
    in course and treatment, 237
  personality features of, 236–37
    in course and treatment, 237
    dimensions, 236–37
    PD categories, 236
  phenomenology of, 654–55
  prevalence of, 107
  styles of, 101–2
  subtypes of, 236–37
  symptoms of, 684
  treatment of, 654–60
    ACT, 657
    AEBT, 657
    in children and adolescents, 706
    dissemination of, 659–60
    future directions in, 658–60
    HRT, 656–57, 706
    implications of, 654–55
    pharmacotherapy, 655–56, 658–60, 706
Skin Picking Impact Scale–Short (SPIS–S), 412
Skin Picking Impact Scale (SPIS), 397t, 412
Skin Picking Reward Scale (SPRS), 397t, 412
Skin Picking Scale–Revised (SPS–R), 432
Skin Picking Scale (SPS), 397t, 410–11, 705
Skin Picking Treatment Scale (SPTS), 409–10
smartphone application
  E/RP for OCD delivery via, 516–18
SMT. *See* stress management training (SMT)
SNAP. *See* Schedule for Nonadaptive and Adaptive Personality (SNAP)
Snorrason, I., 410–11, 412
SNRIs. *See* serotonin-nonepinephrine reuptake inhibitors (SNRIs)
Social Adjustment Scale–Self-Report (SAS-SR), 55–56
Social and Occupational Functioning Assessment Scale, 54
social anxiety
  BDD–related, 51
social anxiety disorder (SAD)
  BDD and, 63–64
  BDD vs., 339–40
  prevalence of, 64
socioeconomic status
  BDD and, 47
  HD and, 89
socioemotional selectivity theory (SST), 671–72
Socratic questioning
  HD treatment–related, 624–25
Solomon, R.L., 499–500
Soteric neurosis, 74
SPACE. *See* Supportive Parenting for Anxious Childhood Emotions (SPACE)

Spatola, G., 484
SPD. *See* skin-picking disorder (SPD)
SPD–D. *See* Skin Picking Disorder–Dimensional Scale (SPD–D)
SPECT. *See* single-photon emission computed tomography (SPECT)
Spiegel, 476
SPIS. *See* Skin Picking Impact Scale (SPIS)
SPIS–S. *See* Skin Picking Impact Scale–Short (SPIS–S)
SPRS. *See* Skin Picking Reward Scale (SPRS)
SPS. *See* Skin Picking Scale (SPS)
SPS–R. *See* Skin Picking Scale–Revised (SPS–R)
SPTS. *See* Skin Picking Treatment Scale (SPTS)
SRIs. *See* serotonin reuptake inhibitors (SRIs)
SSRIs. *See* selective serotonin reuptake inhibitors (SSRIs)
SST. *See* socioemotional selectivity theory (SST)
STAI-T. *See* State-Trait Anxiety Inventory (STAI-T)
Stanley, M.A., 651
State-Trait Anxiety Inventory (STAI-T), 400
Steketee, G., 77–78, 79, 426–27, 429, 432, 436–38, 508–9, 549–50, 619, 621, 627–28, 630–31, 632, 682–83
stereotactic neurosurgery
 historical background of, 476
Stevens, K.T., 557
Stiede, J.T., 99
stimulus control (SC) techniques
 in HRT protocol, 652–53
Stop-Signal Task, 199–200, 201–2
Storch, E.A., 690
St-Pierre-Delorme, M.-E., 629
stress management training (SMT), 542
Stroop Color Word Naming test, 187–88, 197
 in BDD, 191–92
Structured Clinical Interview for DSM-III-R Axis II Personality Disorders (SCID-II), 215

Structured Clinical Interview for DSM-IV Axis I Disorders–Patient Edition (SCID-I/P), 393–96
Structured Clinical Interview for DSM-IV (SCID), 424
Structured Clinical Interview for DSM-5 Personality Disorders (SCID-5-PD), 428
Structured Clinical Interview for DSM-5 (SCID-5), 312, 336–38, 337*t*
Structured Interview for DSM-III Personality Disorders (SIDP), 215
Structured Interview for Hoarding Disorder (SIHD), 356, 357–64*t*
subcaudate tractotomy
 for OCD, 481–82
substance use disorders (SUDs)
 BDD and, 54–55
 OCD and, 27
SUDs. *See* substance use disorders (SUDs)
suicidal ideation
 BDD-related, 56–58
suicidality
 BDD-related, 56–58
 BDD treatment issues related to, 606–7
suicide
 OCD and, 32
suicide attempts
 BDD-related, 56–58
Summerfeldt, L.J., 17–18, 23, 428
Summers, B.J., 584
Sündermann, O., 334
suo yang, 608
Supportive Parenting for Anxious Childhood Emotions (SPACE), 437
Sustained Attention to Response Task, 187
Swedish Twin Registry, 85

T

TAF. *See* thought–action fusion (TAF)
taijin kyofusho, 25–26, 608
TAQ. *See* Treatment Ambivalence Questionnaire (TAQ)
tax return filing
 HD and, 89

Taylor, S., 30, 279, 498, 675
TCAs. *See* tricyclic antidepressants (TCAs)
TCI. *See* Temperament and Character Inventory (TCI)
TDI. *See* Trichotillomania Diagnostic Interview (TDI)
Teachman, B.A., 676
Tek, C., 730
telehealth
 E/RP for OCD delivery via, 516–18
Temperament and Character Inventory (TCI), 222
Teng, E.J., 414, 656
tension
 nail-biting and, 102
Teuber, H-L, 476–77
Thapaliya, S., 16
The Anatomy of Melancholy, 13
The Trail Making Test–Part B, 187–88
Thomas, J., 737
Thorsen, A.L., 143
thought(s)
 control of
  CT for OCD–related, 532–34
 intrusive obsessional
  vs. excessive worries, 20
thought–action fusion (TAF), 15–16, 532–33
 Moral, 532–33, 731
thought records
 HD treatment–related, 624
 in OCD assessment
  appraisals-related, 328–29
  beliefs-related, 328–29
threat
 overestimation of
  CT for OCD–related, 534–36, 535*f*, 536*f*
time-management training
 HD treatment–related, 622
Titrating Mirror Tracing Task (TMTT), 382
TMS. *See* transcranial magnetic stimulation (TMS)
TMTT. *See* Titrating Mirror Tracing Task (TMTT)
Tolin, D.F., 1, 406, 557, 621, 626, 629–30, 634
TPQ. *See* Tridimensional Personality Questionnaire (TPQ)

INDEX | 773

Trail-making Test A, 197
Trail-making Test B, 197
Trails B Test, 196–97
transcranial magnetic stimulation (TMS)
  for OCD, 452, 453t, 489–90
transfer(s)
  CT for OCD–related, 535–36, 536f
  responsibility-related
    inflated responsibility–related, 535–36
Treatment Ambivalence Questionnaire (TAQ), 426
trichobezoars, 100, 701
Trichotillomania Diagnostic Interview (TDI), 393–96
Trichotillomania Dimensional Scale (TTM-D), 394t, 402–3
Trichotillomania Scale for Children (TSC), 394t, 405–6
trichotillomania (TTM), 99, 294–95, 647
  affective states associated with, 100
  among African Americans, 112–13
  age of onset, 107–8
  assessment of, 393–408, 414–15
    adult measures used with child populations, 407
    clinician measures, 394t, 399–401
    complementary strategies, 407–8
    diagnostic-related, 393–99
    future directions in, 414–15
    hair-pulling style, 394t, 403–5
    introduction, 392–93
    physician evaluation, 393
    self-report measures, 394t, 401–3
  BDD vs., 105–6
  among Caucasians, 112
  in children and adolescents, 107–8, 109, 701–5
    assessment of, 702
    causes of, 703
    comorbidity of, 394t, 405–7, 702
    complications from, 701
    prevalence of, 701
    symptoms of, 701
    treatment of, 703–5
  cognitive model of, 294–95
    empirical support, 295
  comorbidity of, 115
  cross-cultural features, 112–14
  defined, 99, 264, 648
  demographics of, 107–9
  described, 6, 99–101, 196, 264–65, 392–93
  diagnostic features of, 99–101, 264–69
    empirical evidence, 267–69
    symptom development, 265
    symptom maintenance, 266–67
  DSM-5 on, 684
  among Eastern cultures, 113–14
  epidemiologic research limitations, 106
  features of, 294, 701
  functional impairment related to, 108–9
  gender ratio, 107–8
  hair-pulling styles, 100, 648
  healthcare utilization, 109
  introduction, 647
  IP in, 196–202
    attention, 197–98
    cognitive flexibility, 198–99
    executive function, 198–201 (see also executive function, TTM and)
    impulsivity, 199–201
    inhibition, 199–201
    memory, 198
    perception, 196
    processing speed, 196–97
    treatment effects, 201
  longitudinal course, 108
  neuroimaging of
    cognitive paradigms, 159
    emotional paradigms, 159
    functional studies, 159
    key findings, 158–60
    neurochemical studies, 159–60
    resting state studies, 159
    structural studies, 158–59, 158f
  nonclinical forms of, 103–4
  OCD and, 430–32
    diagnostic distinction, 105–6
  in older adults, 684–85
  PDs in
    in course and treatment, 234, 235
    personality features of, 234–35
    in course and treatment, 235
    dimensions, 234–35
    PD categories, 234
  phenomenology of, 648
  postpulling rituals, 100
  prepulling behaviors, 100
  prevalence of, 106
  psychotic conditions and, 116
  subtypes of, 702
  symptoms of, 25, 684
  treatment of, 648–54
    ACT, 657
    AEBT, 650–51, 657
    in children and adolescents, 703–5
    dissemination of, 659–60
    future directions in, 658–60
    HRT, 649–54
    implications, 648
    pharmacotherapy, 648–49, 658–60, 704–5
    RCTs in, 704
tricyclic antidepressants (TCAs)
  for OCD, 452, 454t
Tridimensional Personality Questionnaire (TPQ), 222
Truax, P., 626–27
TSC. See Trichotillomania Scale for Children (TSC)
Tseng, W.S., 717–18
TTM. See trichotillomania (TTM)
TTM-D. See Trichotillomania Dimensional Scale (TTM-D)
Twitchell, T., 476–77
Twohig, M.P., 657

U

UCLA Hoarding Severity Scale (UHSS), 357–64t, 365, 617
UHSS. See UCLA Hoarding Severity Scale (UHSS)
U.K. Twin Registry, 85
Ulug, B., 730
uncertainty
  intolerance of
    HD–related, 259–60
unfocused hair-pulling, 648, 702
unified biosocial model of personality, 221–22
University of Rhode Island Change Assessment Questionnaire, 321
"unspecific OCRD," 25–26

V

vagus nerve stimulation (VNS)
  for OCD, 488
Vallejo-Nagera, J.A., 74
value(s)
  CT for OCD–related, 537–38
van Balkom, 512
Vancouver Obsessional Compulsive Inventory (VOCI)
  in OCD assessment, 317
van den Heuvel, O.A., 143
van Minnen, A., 76
Van Noppen, B., 437–38
van Oppen, P., 539–40, 546, 549
Veale, D., 293–94, 334, 433, 434, 593–94
venlafaxine
  for BDD, 602
  for OCD, 465
veteran(s)
  BDD in, 45–46
vigilance hypothesis
  in attentional biases in OCD, 177–79
Visual Search, 197
visuoperceptual biases
  BDD and, 190–93
    holistic processing, 190–91
    selective attention, 191–93
  OCD and, 176–77
VNS. See vagus nerve stimulation (VNS)
VOCI. See Vancouver Obsessional Compulsive Inventory (VOCI)
Vogel, P.A., 516–17, 518–19, 543, 549

W

WAIS-III. See Weschler Adult Intelligence Scale (WAIS-III)
WAIS-R Digit Span, 197
wait-listing
  CT for OCD vs., 539–42
Walker, D.L., 571
Wang, J., 735–36
Washington, C., 726–27
Watts, 475–76
W-CBT. See web-camera delivery of CBT (W-CBT)
WCST. See Wisconsin Card Sorting Task (WCST)
web-camera delivery of CBT (W-CBT), 516–18
Weiss, 627
Wells, A., 677
Weschler Adult Intelligence Scale (WAIS-III), 183–84
Weschler Memory Scale (WMS-R), 183–84, 194
WES studies. See whole exome sequencing (WES) studies
Wheaton, M.G., 726–27, 731–32, 736
Whittal, M.L., 527
WHO. See World Health Organization (WHO)
whole exome sequencing (WES) studies, 129, 137
WHOQOL-100. See World Health Organization Quality of Life Assessment (WHOQOL-100)
Wilhelm, S., 541–42, 551–52, 573, 584
Wilkes, C.M., 671
Williams, K.E., 722, 740
Williams, M., 725, 727–28, 731–32
Williams, T.I., 102–3
Willis, H., 727–28
Wilson, K.A., 541
Wisconsin Card Sorting Task (WCST), 187–88, 199
Witzum, E., 729, 739–40
WMS-R. See Weschler Memory Scale (WMS-R)
Woo, C., 726–27
Woods, D.W., 99, 647
Woody, S.R., 307, 551, 636
Woolley, M., 73
Wootton, B.M., 629–30
Worden, B.L., 629
Work and Social Adjustment Scale, 319
World Health Organization Quality of Life Assessment (WHOQOL-100), 438–39
World Health Organization (WHO)
  CIDI of, 84
worry(ies)
  excessive
    vs. intrusive obsessional thoughts, 20
Wu, K., 726–27
Wycis, 476
Wyman, S., 726–27

X

Xavier, A.C.M., 413–14

Y

Yale-Brown Obsessive-Compulsive Scale Modified for BDD (BDD-Y-BOCS), 195–96, 340, 341t, 593
  adaptation of (BDD-Y-BOCS-A), 696
Yale-Brown Obsessive-Compulsive Scale Modified for Neurotic Excoriation (NE-YBOCS), 409–10, 705
Yale-Brown Obsessive-Compulsive Scale (Y-BOCS), 309, 314–16, 401–2, 432, 434, 510–11, 511t, 527–28, 560, 616–17, 702, 735–36
Yale-Brown Obsessive-Compulsive Scale (Y-BOCS) Symptom Checklist, 309
  in OCD assessment, 314–16
Yang, Y.H., 717
Yap, K., 615
Y-BOCS. See Yale-Brown Obsessive Compulsive Scale (Y-BOCS)
yohimbine
  for OCD, 575
Yorulmaz, O., 732
Yule, M.A., 527

Z

Zwangsneurose, 2